FOURTH EDITION

ADVANCED ACCOUNTING

Joe Hoyle
CSX Professor of Management and Accounting
Robins School of Business
University of Richmond

IRWIN

Burr Ridge, Illinois
Boston, Massachusetts
Sydney, Australia

Material from Uniform CPA Examination, Questions and Unofficial Answers, © 1963, 1971, 1975, and 1978–1989 by the American Institute of Certified Public Accountants, Inc., is reprinted or adapted with permission.

Senior sponsoring editor: Diane M. Van Bakel
Development editor: Margaret Haywood
Marketing manager: Cindy Ledwith
Project editor: Jean Lou Hess
Production manager: Diane Palmer
Art coordinator: Heather Burbridge
Art studio: The Image Center
Cover designer: Randy Scott
Compositor: Bi-Comp, Incorporated
Typeface: 10/12 Times Roman
Printer: R. R. Donnelley & Sons Company

Library of Congress Cataloging-in-Publication Data

Hoyle, Joe Ben.
    Advanced accounting / Joe B. Hoyle. — 4th ed.
      p.   cm.
    Includes bibliographical references and index.
    ISBN 0-256-12407-8
    1. Accounting. I. Title.
  HF5635.H863 1993
  657'.046—dc20   93–13312

Printed in the United States of America
5 6 7 8 9 DOC 0 9 8 7 6

For my father
Jethro Hoyle

*The real purpose
of books is to trap
the mind into
doing its own
thinking.*
Christopher
Morley

PREFACE

This textbook represents the fourth edition of *Advanced Accounting* that I have created over the past 13 or so years. In each of these editions, I have worked to produce an efficient educational instrument, one that is comprehensive and interactive but also interesting to college students. From the day I first conceived of *Advanced Accounting* in 1980, I have sought to produce a book that is actually engaging to read, similar to a magazine or newspaper. I want this textbook to convey to students the reasons why I find financial accounting to be so mentally stimulating, challenging, and even exciting. Learning can only be maximized if the textbook is able to capture the attention of students so that they will read and think seriously about each topic.

In comparing this textbook to previous editions (as well as to competing books), professors should note that much change has occurred recently in the various subjects covered by *Advanced Accounting*. Hence, my first job in producing this new edition was to update the entire coverage to include the accounting rules and principles that have come into existence during the past few years. However, a review of *Advanced Accounting* should not be limited to its ability to present newly produced accounting pronouncements. The pedagogical methodology that is found herein also needs to be considered. The book's ability to involve students and assist them in understanding many extremely complex accounting issues is of paramount importance to the learning process.

Consequently, this preface will first describe the changes in financial accounting that are included in this edition of *Advanced Accounting* and then explain the textbook's educational structure. Techniques that were developed in prior editions will be recounted as well as the additions made in this newest volume.

The Changing Accounting Environment

Accounting is evolutionary in nature; its rules and procedures are modified over the years to mirror new developments in the business world as well as current views and theories of financial reporting. That change is sometimes slow but sometimes quite sudden. For the various topics covered in *Advanced Accounting*, perhaps no period in history has had more impact than the early part of the 1990s. The Financial Accounting Standards Board (FASB), the Governmental Accounting Standards Board (GASB), and the American Institute of Certified Public Accountants (AICPA) have each chosen to examine a number of the subjects traditionally covered within an advanced accounting course and are in the process of rethinking old rules and producing new ones.

Students of accounting need to be aware that accounting is not static; it is a discipline in constant motion. *Advanced Accounting* has been created to ensure that students do not merely memorize old procedures but actually become aware of the current state of accounting: its principles and controversies, its theories and alternatives. This textbook urges students to consider the issues that are currently at the very forefront of professional deliberation and debate such as the definition of control as it pertains to subsidiaries, the objectives of producing consolidated financial statements, the development of international accounting standards, financial reporting by companies in bankruptcy reorganization, the basis of accounting appropriate for governmental units, the financial statements applicable to the reporting of not-for-profit organizations, and the method by which donations should be reported.

Updating This Edition

To ensure that *Advanced Accounting* is completely up-to-date, many recent changes in accounting (both already passed and still under consideration) are described and discussed herein:

- Coverage of consolidation accounting has been expanded (in Chapters 2 through 7) to include the FASB's recent discussion of relevant policy and procedure issues. For example, problems that arise in attempting to define control are examined. In addition, an overview is included of three different perspectives of consolidated financial statements that were put forth by the FASB: the economic unit concept, the proportionate consolidation concept, and the parent company concept.
- Discussion of the use of push-down accounting by subsidiaries has been extended in Chapter 3 because of increased usage for internal reporting as well as current interest within the profession as to situations in which a new basis of accounting is warranted.
- Income tax reporting has been revised in both Chapters 1 and 7 to correspond with *Statement of Financial Accounting Standards No. 109,* "Accounting for Income Taxes."
- Chapter 10's presentation of the accounting principles found in many of the countries of the world has been expanded and updated. This chapter also discusses the ongoing attempt of the International Accounting Standards Committee to harmonize financial reporting worldwide. The possibility of creating international accounting standards is a topic that has garnered much recent interest in the accounting profession.

- Chapter 12 is now devoted entirely to bankruptcy accounting. The requirements of the AICPA's *Statement of Position 90-7*, "Financial Reporting by Entities in Reorganization Under the Bankruptcy Code" have been added to the coverage. This pronouncement established new standards for companies as they undergo bankruptcy reorganization as well as when they emerge. Its guidelines are of special significance because of the number of companies going through reorganization in recent years.

- The struggle of the GASB to establish a new basis for state and local government accounting is described in Chapters 15 and 16. The GASB's *Statement No. 11*, "Measurement Focus and Basis of Accounting—Governmental Fund Operating Statements," was issued with the intent of making governmental accounting more akin to that used by profit-oriented businesses. However, its effective date has now been delayed as a result of severe criticism and debate. Consequently, coverage of applicable reporting standards in this textbook includes both current procedures as well as the changes that will be mandated when this statement takes effect.

- The GASB has also revised the parameters of a government's reporting entity through *Statement No. 14*, "The Financial Reporting Entity." This pronouncement, which is examined in Chapter 16, provides guidance for delineating a primary government unit and its component units for the purpose of creating a comprehensive annual financial report.

- The AICPA's Auditing Standards Board created a GAAP Hierarchy in its *Statement on Auditing Standards 69*, "The Meaning of 'Presents Fairly in Conformity with Generally Accepted Accounting Principles' in the Independent Auditor's Report." This standard, described in Chapter 17, establishes a ranking system for nongovernmental entities as well as state and local governments to use in evaluating the applicability of generally accepted accounting principles.

- In Chapter 18, the AICPA's *Audits of Providers of Health Care Services* is presented. The issuance of this pronouncement has had a significant effect on the accounting and financial reporting of health care entities such as hospitals and nursing homes.

- Chapters 17 and 18 discuss the FASB's efforts to create a uniform set of financial statements for all private not-for-profit organizations through *Statement of Financial Accounting Standards No. 117*, "Financial Statements of Not-for-Profit Organizations." The FASB has also developed rules (*Statement of Financial Accounting Standards No. 116*, "Accounting for Contributions Received and Contributions Made") for the reporting of contributions received by these groups. The new guidelines cover pledges, donated materials, donated services, and the conveyance of art works and other historical treasures. Consequently, *Advanced Accounting* now presents not-for-profit accounting in two full chapters rather than one and a half as in the past.

- Coverage of the Securities and Exchange Commission has been expanded to a full chapter because of that group's importance in ensuring fair and complete financial disclosure. The SEC's work to develop an electronic data gathering, analysis, and retrieval system (known as "Edgar") has been added in Chapter 20.

Educational Approach

Many of the pedagogical elements of the three previous editions of *Advanced Accounting* have been retained, expanded, and refined. Each of these features is intended to get students involved in their own education, to encourage them to ask why a particular approach to reporting is considered appropriate rather than just how the numbers are calculated.

Introduction of Controversies. At many points throughout this textbook, the controversial side of accounting is introduced. The development of financial reporting is shown as the result of a history of considered debate that continues today and into the future. Dissents to official pronouncements are described as are comment letters to the FASB. Published articles are discussed, many of which criticize GAAP. Some of the issues that are raised include:

- The equity method records revenues without the receipt of an asset. Is this timing of revenue recognition appropriate?
- Many countries do not permit the consolidation of finance subsidiaries but the U.S. requires it. Which approach is the fairest presentation?
- The pooling of interests method of reporting a business combination has always been controversial. Is it an illegitimate method, as some accountants believe?
- The amortization of goodwill is required by U.S. GAAP. Is this accounting rule damaging to the country, and, if so, is that an acceptable reason for change?
- In 1981, the FASB moved from one method of translating the financial statements of foreign subsidiaries to a different approach. Has the change actually produced an improvement in financial reporting?
- Is the development of a universal set of accounting principles for all countries of the world possible and, if so, should that be a desired objective?
- Current bankruptcy laws are sometimes utilized by companies to avoid massive litigation or other obligations. Is that an appropriate use of these legal rules?
- The GASB is attempting to establish a new basis of accounting for state and local government units. Is a new basis of accounting really needed?
- Private not-for-profit organizations must apply the pronouncements of the FASB whereas public not-for-profit organizations are required to follow the GASB. Are two sets of accounting principles necessary?

- A not-for-profit organization mails out a request for funds that includes educational materials. Should the total cost incurred be reported as fund-raising or should some portion be recorded as an educational expenditure?

Writing Style. No aspect of *Advanced Accounting* is more important than the writing style. The first edition was described by a reviewer as having a "conversational style," and that same approach has been used in each of the subsequent editions. Over the years, reviewers have been virtually unanimous in praising the writing style. I want this book to be interesting, not dull. I want students to enjoy reading about consolidations, segment reporting, bankruptcy accounting, governmental reporting, partnerships, the SEC, and the like.

Real-World Examples. Wherever possible, I have attempted to include information from actual situations so that students can make a connection to today's business environment. Quotations from publications such as *Forbes, The Wall Street Journal,* and *Business Week* are sprinkled liberally throughout the chapters. Data is pulled from business and government financial statements as well as from letters, phone calls, comment letters, official pronouncements, and the like. *Advanced Accounting* is intended to present the real world. A textbook should serve as an interface with the business community to allow students to understand the actual role played by financial accounting.

Discussion Questions. Reviewers and adopters of the previous edition of *Advanced Accounting* responded very favorably to the addition of discussion questions within each of the chapters. These questions, most of which are similar to mini-cases, help to explain the issues at hand in practical terms. Many times these cases are designed to demonstrate to students why a problem is a problem and worth considering. Often accounting rules are relatively easy to read and learn mechanically but extremely difficult to apply in the business world. The discussion questions are used to draw attention to this practical side of accounting. Several new discussion questions have been created and others have been completely rewritten.

Library Assignments. Introduced in the third edition, the library assignments feature has been extremely well received. Questions or topics for student research purposes were posed for each chapter along with a list of articles and other potential sources of information. In this latest edition of *Advanced Accounting,* several new library assignments have been included while previous assignments have been updated with the most recent articles available.

End-of-Chapter Materials. Approximately 40 new questions and 250 new problems have been added to this edition to provide professors with a wide variety of assignment materials. I wrote virtually all of the end-of-chapter material myself and have tested much of it in my own classes. Many problems from the third edition have been rewritten to make them more interactive, seeking responses at every step in the process rather than just a final solution.

Other Features.   This textbook includes many additional features that are intended to enhance the students' educational experience. Each chapter begins with a list of Questions to Consider to stimulate interest and provide an introduction to the coverage to come. A Summary is included at the end of the text material in every chapter to enable students to view the entire structure of the chapter and the accounting issues and principles that have been described. Chapters conclude with one or more Comprehensive Illustrations and Solutions that are designed to tie the chapter elements together and provide a review of all materials.

Supplements to the Text

To complement the text as an effective teaching and learning tool, there are a number of supplements available to instructors and students.

For the Instructor

The following items are available to chapters of the text:

- *Instructor's Manual*   In addition to providing complete, detailed solutions to all discussion questions and end-of-chapter questions and problems, this guide contains outlines and learning objectives for each chapter in order to assist the instructor in the organization and preparation of class lectures.
- *Test Bank*   Prepared by Sue Atkinson of Tarleton State University, this entirely new test bank includes a variety of questions—multiple choice, short answer, and discussion—and problems for each chapter with the level of difficulty (easy, medium, or hard) indicated for each one. The solutions for the multiple choice and short answer questions contain a brief rationale for the answer given.
- *Computerized Testing Software*   This improved microcomputer version of the test bank allows editing of questions; provides up to 99 different versions of each test; and allows question selection based on type of question and level of difficulty.
- *Solutions Transparencies*   To help clarify and reinforce the processes involved in solving the more complex problems in the text, the answers to selected problems are replicated on acetates that can be used in classroom presentations.
- *Check Figures*   A list of check figures gives key amounts for the problems to assist students in working through homework problems. Check figures are available in bulk, free to adopters.

For the Student

Students may choose items in this support package to enhance their learning experiences:

- *Working Papers/Study Guide*   In the study guide portion of this supplement, written by David B. Pariser of West Virginia University and Wig DeMoville of the University of Texas—Pan American, the important points of each chapter are summarized in outline style and reinforced by appropriate study questions and problems with solutions. An additional learning tool, a section of blank worksheets, is included to help students expedite the consolidation process in the end-of-chapter problems in the text.

- *Spreadsheet Applications Template Software (SPATS)*   This software package, developed by Doris deLespinasse of Adrian College, is available in 3.5″ and 5.25″ disks. The software includes a Lotus® 1-2-3® tutorial and innovatively designed templates that may be used with Lotus® 1-2-3® to solve many of the complicated problems in Chapters 2 through 9. These problems are indicated by a logo in the margin like the one shown here. Upon adoption, master disks of this package are available to instructors for classroom or laboratory use.

Acknowledgments

The work of a great many people is necessary to produce a textbook of the scope of *Advanced Accounting*. I wish to thank the reviewers who took their valuable time to provide me with excellent constructive comments on the third edition as a means of improving this current volume. Some of these individuals reviewed the entire book while others did only specific chapters. Many thanks go to all of them:

Charles Carslaw, University of Nevada at Reno
Myrtle W. Clark, University of Kentucky
Wig B. DeMoville, University of Texas—Pan American
David J. Harr, George Mason University
Anna Lee Meador, Marshall University
David O'Bryan, Pittsburg State University
Robert W. Rouse, College of Charleston
Raymond Slager, Calvin College
Judith K. Welch, University of Central Florida

Over the years, a number of individuals have written or called me directly to discuss both accounting and educational issues raised in this textbook. I always enjoy and appreciate every suggestion and comment about *Advanced Accounting*. I hope readers of this fourth edition will contact me with their thoughts and ideas.

I would also like to pass on a word of thanks to all of the people at Richard D. Irwin, Inc., who have participated in the creation of this edition, especially Margaret Haywood and Jean Lou Hess. They have been extremely helpful and very patient. I must address very special appreciation to my editor, Diane Van Bakel. Without her ideas, support, and encouragement, I am sure that this edition would never have been completed. She has been an excellent editor and just a wonderful friend. The world needs more people like Diane.

Many folks here at the University of Richmond have been of enormous assistance to me. My dean, R. Clifton Poole, has been unwavering in his support. My department chair, Robert Sanborn, has always been willing to listen to my complaints and worries and has offered much needed guidance. In addition, he has helped me keep the entire project in proper perspective. Both of my secretaries, Donna Gilliam and Laura Jarvis, have been ready to help at all times without a complaint. They are a wonderful bunch of people.

I would like to thank most, though, my family: my wife, Sarah, and my sons, Jamin and Brendan. They have now lived through four editions of this book. Few people can understand what a strain this type of project puts on a family. Despite my bad moods and literally thousands of hours in front of a word processor, they have never complained. They have always been encouraging and supportive even when I did not deserve encouragement and support. I am sure that they must have often felt that I loved the FASB and consolidated financial statements more than I loved them. I want them to know that is not true. They are the best family that a person could have.

I dedicate this book to my father, Jethro Hoyle. Only in the last few years have I come to fully appreciate what a wonderful person my father is. I hope that I can be just like him when I grow up.

Joe Hoyle

BRIEF CONTENTS

CONTENTS

19   Accounting for Estates and Trusts   1080

20   Financial Reporting and the Securities and Exchange Commission   1123

1 THE EQUITY METHOD OF ACCOUNTING FOR INVESTMENTS

Questions to Consider

- One corporation buys equity shares of another company. What methods are available to account for this investment and the income it generates? When is each method appropriate?

- What accounting is utilized when an owner gains enough shares to exert significant influence over the operating and financial decisions of an investee company but does not maintain actual control?

- When significant influence over an investee company is achieved, should the owner recognize revenue at the time dividends are received or when income is earned by the investee?

- If significant influence over an investee has been acquired, how does the shareholder account for any portion of the purchase price that exceeds the underlying book value of the investee company?

- At what point should profits be recognized on inventory that is transferred between related parties?

- If an owner records equity income currently that will not be subject to taxation until a subsequent period, when should the related income tax expense be recognized?

A footnote to the financial statements of The Seagram Company Ltd. for the year ending January 31, 1991, informed readers that "the Company owns 164.2 million shares, or 24.5 percent at January 31, 1991, of the outstanding common stock of E. I. du Pont de Nemours and Company. The Company and Du Pont have entered into an agreement which provides that the Company will be entitled to representation on the Du Pont board of directors proportional to its stock ownership. . . . The Company accounts for its interest in Du Pont using the equity method whereby its proportional share of Du Pont earnings is included in income."

Such information is hardly unusual in the business world; corporate as well as individual investors frequently acquire ownership shares of both domestic and foreign businesses. These investments can range from the purchase of a few shares to the acquisition of 100 percent control. Although large purchases of corporate equity securities (such as the one made by Seagram) are not uncommon, they pose a considerable number of problems for the accountant because a close relationship has been established without the investor gaining actual control. These issues are currently addressed by the **equity method.** This chapter deals with the procedures utilized in accounting for stock investments that fall under the application of this method.

Reporting Investments in Corporate Equity Securities

At present, accounting standards recognize three different approaches to the financial reporting of investments in corporate equity securities:

The lower-of-cost-or-market-value method (LCM). *Less than 20%*
The equity method. *20% – 50%*
The consolidation of financial statements.[1] *More than 50%*

These three are not interchangeable; a specific method is required by any given situation. The reporting of a particular investment depends on the degree of influence that the investor (stockholder) has over the investee, a factor best indicated by the relative size of ownership.

Lower-of-Cost-or-Market-Value Method.   In many instances, an investor possesses only a small percentage of an investee company's outstanding stock, perhaps only a few shares. Because of the limited level of ownership, the investor cannot expect to have a significant impact on the investee's operations or decision making. These shares are bought in anticipation of cash dividends or in appreciation of stock market values. Such investments are accounted for by using LCM as established by the Financial Accounting Standards Board (FASB) in its *Statement of Financial Accounting Standards No. 12 (SFAS 12)*, "Accounting for Certain Marketable Securities," December 1975. (As of December 15, 1993, the FASB requires the use of market value for these investments rather than LCM-*SFAS 115*. This change has no impact on the application of the equity method.)

Since a full coverage of *SFAS 12* is presented in intermediate accounting textbooks, only two of its basic principles are noted here.

---

[1] More than three methods of accounting for stock investments are actually found in practice. Consolidations, for example, are reported by either the purchase or the pooling of interests method, depending on specific criteria. The lower-of-cost-or-market-value method is applied to short-term stock portfolios in one way, but a different approach is required for long-term portfolios. In addition, under certain circumstances stock investments may be reported based on current market values, cost, or some other specialized process. Thus, the three methods shown here represent only the broad categories generally encountered.

First, income recognition by the investor is limited to the cash dividends that are collected.

Second, both short-term and long-term stock portfolios are carried on the investor's balance sheet at the lower of aggregate cost or market value.

These two principles are consistent with the conservatism traditionally found in accounting: Income is not recorded until collected and the asset may be reduced to a value below cost but not above. However, as will be shown, both procedures are in diametric contrast to the accounting process used in applying the equity method.

Consolidation of Financial Statements. Although many investments involve only a small percentage of stock, an investor can acquire enough shares to gain actual control over an investee's operation. In financial accounting, such control is recognized whenever a stockholder accumulates more than 50 percent of an organization's outstanding voting stock. At that point, rather than simply influencing the decisions of the investee, the investor clearly can direct the entire decision-making process. A review of the financial statements of America's largest organizations indicates that legal control of one or more subsidiary companies is an almost universal practice. PepsiCo, Inc., as just one example, holds a majority interest in the voting stock of literally hundreds of corporations.

A level of ownership large enough to enable an investor to control an investee presents an economic situation not adequately addressed by *SFAS 12*. Normally, when a majority of voting stock is held, the investor-investee relationship has become so closely connected that the two corporations are viewed as a single entity for reporting purposes. Hence, an entirely different set of accounting procedures is applicable. According to *Accounting Research Bulletin No. 51 (ARB No. 51)*, "Consolidated Financial Statements," August 1959, control generally requires the consolidation of the accounting information produced by the individual companies. Thus, a single set of financial statements is created for external reporting purposes with all assets, liabilities, revenues, and expenses being brought together.[2] The various procedures applied within this consolidation process are examined in subsequent chapters of the textbook.

Equity Method. Finally, a third type of investment relationship is appropriately accounted for by means of the equity method. In Seagram's ownership of 24.5 percent of the voting stock of Du Pont, less than control of the voting stock is held. Seagram is not even close to the level that indicates the need for consolidation. Yet, despite the lack of voting control, Seagram does maintain a large interest in this investee company. Through its ownership, Seagram can undoubtedly have an impact on the decisions and operations of Du Pont.

---

[2] As is discussed in the next chapter, owning a majority of the voting shares of an investee does not always lead to consolidated financial statements. The FASB is also considering whether control can be established without majority ownership.

In today's business world, many corporations such as Seagram hold significant ownership interests in other companies without having actual control. Just a few examples include Dow Jones & Company's holding of 33 percent of Bear Island Paper Company and Teledyne, Inc.'s ownership of 28 percent of Litton Industries and 45 percent of Curtiss-Wright Corporation. Sears, Roebuck & Company alone holds between 20 percent and 50 percent ownership in 38 separate corporations. Many other large investments are created through joint ventures whereby two or more companies form a new enterprise to carry out a specified operating purpose. For example, on March 11, 1991, *The Wall Street Journal* announced that Coca-Cola Company and Nestle S.A. had signed agreements for a joint venture to develop ready-to-drink coffees and teas. Each company initially invested $50 million.

For each of these investments, the investors have failed to achieve absolute control because they hold less than a majority of the voting stock. Thus, the preparation of consolidated financial statements is inappropriate. However, the large percentage of ownership indicates that each investor possesses some ability to affect the decision-making process of the investee. This influence denotes a relationship between the two parties that is not reflected adequately by the lower-of-cost-or-market-value method established by *SFAS 12*.

Generally accepted accounting principles (GAAP) recognize that stock investments do exist where neither the consolidation of financial statements nor the lower-of-cost-or-market-value method is really applicable. To reflect this relationship, such investments are accounted for by the equity method as officially established by *Opinion 18*, "The Equity Method of Accounting for Investments in Common Stock," issued by the Accounting Principle Board (APB) in March of 1971.

Applying the Equity Method

An understanding of the equity method is best gained by initially examining the APB's treatment of two questions:

1. What parameters identify the area of ownership where the equity method is applicable?
2. How should the investor report this investment and the income generated by it to reflect the relationship between the two companies?

Criteria for Utilizing the Equity Method

In sanctioning application of the equity method, the APB reasoned that an investor begins to gain the ability to influence the decision-making process of an investee as the level of ownership rises. According to *APB Opinion 18* (par. 17), achieving this "ability to exercise significant influence over operating and financial policies of an investee even though the investor holds 50 percent or less of the voting stock'' is the sole criterion for requiring application of the equity method.

Clearly a term such as *the ability to exercise significant influence* is nebulous and subject to a variety of judgments and interpretations in practice. At what point does the acquisition of one additional share of stock give an owner the ability to exercise significant influence? This decision becomes even more difficult in that only the *ability* to exercise significant influence need be present: The pronouncement does not specify that any actual influence must have ever been applied.

APB Opinion 18 provides guidance to the accountant by listing several conditions that indicate the presence of this degree of influence:

- Investor representation on the board of directors of the investee.
- Investor participation in the policy-making process of the investee.
- Material intercompany transactions.
- Interchange of managerial personnel.
- Technological dependency.
- Extent of ownership by the investor in relation to the size and concentration of other ownership interests in the investee.

No single one of these guides should be used exclusively in assessing the applicability of the equity method. Instead, all are evaluated together to determine the presence or absence of the sole criterion: the ability to exercise significant influence over the investee.

These guidelines alone do not eliminate the leeway available to each investor when deciding whether use of the equity method is appropriate. To provide a degree of consistency in applying this standard, the APB established a general ownership test. *If an investor holds between 20 and 50 percent of the voting stock of the investee, significant influence is normally assumed and the equity method applied.*

> The Board recognizes that determining the ability of an investor to exercise such influence is not always clear and applying judgment is necessary to assess the status of each investment. In order to achieve a reasonable degree of uniformity in application, the Board concludes that an investment (direct or indirect) of 20 percent or more of the voting stock of an investee should lead to a presumption that in the absence of evidence to the contrary an investor has the ability to exercise significant influence over an investee. Conversely, an investment of less than 20 percent of the voting stock of an investee should lead to a presumption that an investor does not have the ability to exercise significant influence unless such ability can be demonstrated.[3]

At first, the 20 percent rule may appear to be an arbitrarily chosen boundary established merely to provide accountants with a consistent method of reporting all investments. However, the essential criterion is still the ability to significantly

---

[3] *APB Opinion 18*, par. 17.

influence the investee, rather than 20 percent ownership.[4] If the absence of this ability is proven, the equity method should not be applied regardless of the percentage of shares held. Conversely, whenever this ability can be demonstrated, the equity method is appropriate without concern for the degree of ownership.

As an example, in 1991 The Williams Companies, Inc. accounted for its investment in Northern Border Pipeline Company by the equity method despite holding only a 12.25 percent interest. In the annual report for that year, Williams explained the use of this method by stating: "Companies in which Williams and its subsidiaries own 20 percent to 50 percent of the voting common stock, *or otherwise exercise sufficient influence over operating and financial policies of the company,* are accounted for under the equity method." (emphasis added)

Further guidance on the precise applicability of the equity method was provided in May 1981 when the FASB issued its *Interpretation 35,* "Criteria for Applying the Equity Method of Accounting for Investments in Common Stock." This pronouncement dealt specifically with using the equity method for investments in which the owner holds more than 20 percent of the outstanding shares. It is important because companies had tended to apply the equity method to all investments in the 20 to 50 percent range with little regard for the degree of influence actually present.

According to *Interpretation 35* (par. 3), above the 20 percent level of ownership, "the presumption that the investor has the ability to exercise significant influence over the investee's operating and financial policies stands until overcome by predominant evidence to the contrary." However, the pronouncement then went on to offer clarification by listing examples of occurrences that would provide evidence to nullify this presumption. *Interpretation 35* specifically states that the equity method is not appropriate for investments that demonstrate any of the following characteristics regardless of the investor's degree of ownership:

- An agreement exists between investor and investee whereby the investor surrenders significant rights as a shareholder.
- A concentration of ownership operates the investee without regard for the views of the investor.
- The investor attempts but fails to obtain representation on the investee's board of directors.

To summarize, the following table indicates the method of accounting that is applicable to various stock investments:

---

[4] Not everyone agrees with the wisdom of this rule. Two members of the APB, George R. Catlett and Charles T. Horngren, voted for *Opinion 18* but argued in an attached statement that "they do not agree with the arbitrary criterion of 20 percent combined with a variable test of 'significant influence' in paragraph 17, because such an approach is not convincing in concept and will be very difficult to apply in practice."

Criterion	Normal Ownership Level	Applicable Accounting Method
Lack of ability to significantly influence	Less than 20%	Lower of aggregate cost or market value (*FASB SFAS 12*)*
Presence of ability to significantly influence	20%–50%	Equity method (*APB Opinion 18*)
Control	Over 50%	Consolidated financial statements† (*ARB No. 51* and *APB Opinion 16*)

* As of December 15, 1993, market value should be used *(SFAS 115)*.

† As discussed in subsequent chapters, voting control over another company does not always lead to the consolidation of financial statements; for example, when such control may be only temporary.

Accounting for an Investment—the Equity Method

Now that the criterion leading to the application of the equity method has been identified, a review of its reporting procedures is appropriate. Knowledge of this accounting process is especially important to users of the investor's financial statements because the equity method affects both the timing of income recognition as well as the carrying value of the investment account.

In applying the equity method, the accounting objective is to report the investor's investment balances (the asset account and annual income) so that the close relationship existing between the companies is reflected. Hence, after recording the cost of the acquisition, the investor uses two equity method entries periodically to report the investment's impact:

- Under the equity method, investment income is recognized by the investor in the same time period as it is earned by the investee. If an investee reports income of $100,000 in 1995, a 30 percent owner should immediately increase its own income by $30,000. This earnings accrual reflects the essence of the equity method by emphasizing the connection between the two companies; a parallel is created between the investment account of the investor and the operations of the investee. Although the acquisition is initially recorded by the investor at cost, upward adjustments in the asset balance are recorded as soon as the investee makes a profit. A reduction is necessary if a loss is reported.
- The investor's investment account is decreased whenever a dividend is collected. Since distribution of cash dividends reduces the book value of the investee company, the investor mirrors this change by recording the receipt as a decrease in the carrying value of the investment rather than as revenue. Once again, a parallel is established between the investment account and the underlying activities of the investee: the reduction in book value of the investee creates a decrease in the investment. Furthermore, since income is recognized immediately by the investor when it is

earned by the investee, double counting would occur if subsequent dividend collections were also recorded by the investor as revenue.

Application of Equity Method	
Investee Event	*Investor Accounting*
Income is earned.	Proportionate share of income is recognized.
Dividends are distributed.	Dividends received are recorded as a reduction in investment.

Application of the equity method causes the investment account on the investor's balance sheet to fluctuate in direct relation to changes occurring in the book value of the investee company. As an illustration, assume that an investor acquires a 40 percent interest in a business enterprise. If the investor has the ability to significantly influence the investee, the equity method must be utilized. If the investee subsequently reports net income of $50,000, the investor increases the investment account (and its own net income) by $20,000 in recognition of a 40 percent share of these earnings. Conversely, a $20,000 dividend collected from the investee necessitates a reduction of $8,000 in this same asset account (40 percent of the total payout).

In contrast, as described earlier, the lower-of-cost-or-market-value method maintains investments at cost unless the market value of the entire portfolio is less. Also, income is only recognized at the time that dividends are received. Consequently, the differences between LCM and the equity method are more than theoretical; the figures being reported by the investor vary widely, depending on the approach deemed appropriate.

To illustrate, assume that Big Company owns a 20 percent interest in Little Company. This investment was purchased on January 1, 1995, for $200,000. Assume further that Little reports net income of $200,000, $300,000, and $400,000 during the next three years while paying dividends of $50,000, $100,000, and $200,000. To avoid valuation problems, assume that the market value of the investment stays above $200,000 for the entire three-year period.

As can be seen from Exhibit 1–1, different results are obtained by Big from the application of these two accounting methods. The lower-of-cost-or-market-value method retains the original cost of $200,000 while recognizing total dividend income of $70,000 over these three years. In comparison, recording by the equity method is more complex. The carrying value of the investment is adjusted upward to $310,000 with $180,000 in income being reported during this same period. Under the equity approach, each earnings accrual represents a 20 percent share of Little's income. Hence, during these three years, the investor is recognizing $110,000 in income that has not yet been received in the form of dividends ($180,000 reported by the equity method minus $70,000 dividends collected).

In reality, since most companies routinely retain some amount of earnings for permanent growth purposes, the chances are highly unlikely that all of the

---

EXHIBIT 1-1   Comparison of Equity Method and Lower-of-Cost-or-Market-Value Method (LCM)

Year	Income of Little Company	Dividends Paid by Little Company	Accounting by Big Company when Influence Is Not Significant (LCM)		Accounting by Big Company when Influence Is Significant (equity method)	
			Dividend Income	Carrying Value of Investment	Equity in Investee Income	Carrying Value of Investment
1995	$200,000	$ 50,000	$10,000	$200,000	$ 40,000*	$230,000†
1996	300,000	100,000	20,000	200,000	60,000*	270,000†
1997	400,000	200,000	40,000	200,000	80,000*	310,000†
Total income recognized			$70,000		$180,000	

* Equity in investee income is 20 percent of the current year income reported by Little Company.

† The carrying value of an investment under the equity method is the original cost plus income recognized less dividends received. For 1995, as an example, the $230,000 reported balance is the $200,000 cost plus $40,000 equity income less $10,000 in dividends received.

$110,000 will ever reach Big as cash dividends. Despite the uncertain nature of this income, the APB believed that the equity method provided the most consistent application of accrual accounting when the ability to exert significant influence over an investee was present.

Not surprisingly, the recognition of income under the equity method has been a controversial subject in accounting. Although neither cash nor other assets need be received, income is immediately reported by the investor. In most cases, as in Exhibit 1-1, accrued income is greater than the dividends received. Since this "extra" income ($110,000 in the previous example) is not available to the investor for growth purposes or for payment of its own dividends, the question can be raised as to whether a legitimate basis for recognition actually exists. One discussant of the equity method concluded: "There's nothing equitable about equity accounting. It is grossly misleading."[5]

The primary objective of this textbook is to assist each reader in achieving a basic understanding of financial accounting. However, to appreciate fully the complex nature of the subject, students need to be aware that many accounting principles are still the focus of controversy or, at least, discussion. The wisdom of official accounting pronouncements is often debated in the world of business. Although the APB chose to sanction the equity method for the reporting of investments, arguments are frequently rekindled both for and against its use in practice.

A return to Exhibit 1-1 shows that the carrying value of the investment fluctuates each year under the equity method. This recording parallels the changes occurring in the net asset figures reported by the investee. If the book value of the investee rises through income, an increase is made in the investment account;

---

[5] Richard Greene, "Equity Accounting Isn't Equitable," *Forbes,* March 31, 1980, p. 104.

Discussion Question: Does the Equity Method Really Apply Here?

Abraham, Inc., a New Jersey corporation, operates 57 bakeries throughout the northeastern section of the United States. In the past, the company's outstanding common stock has been owned entirely by its founder, James Abraham. However, during the early part of 1994, the corporation suffered a severe cash flow problem brought on by rapid expansion. To avoid bankruptcy, Abraham sought additional investment capital from a friend, Dennis Bostitch, who owned Highland Laboratories. Subsequently, Highland paid $700,000 cash to Abraham, Inc., to acquire enough newly issued shares of common stock for a one-third ownership interest.

At the end of 1994, the accountants for Highland Laboratories are discussing the proper method of reporting this investment. One argues for maintaining the asset at its original cost: "This purchase is no more than a loan to bail out the bakeries. Mr. Abraham will continue to run the organization with little or no attention paid to us. After all, what does anyone in our company know about baking bread? I would not be surprised if these shares are not reacquired by Abraham as soon as the bakery business is profitable again."

One of the other accountants disagrees, stating that the equity method is appropriate. "I realize that our company is not capable of running a bakery. However, the official rules state that we must have only the *ability* to exert significant influence. With one-third of the common stock in our possession, we certainly have that ability. Whether we use it or not, this ability means that we are required to apply the equity method."

How should Highland Laboratories account for its investment in Abraham, Inc.?

---

decreases such as losses and dividends cause reductions to be recorded. Thus, the equity method conveys information that describes the relationship created by the investor's ability to significantly influence the investee.

Accounting Procedures Used in Applying the Equity Method

Once guidelines for the application of the equity method have been established, the mechanical process necessary for recording basic transactions is quite straightforward. The investor accrues its percentage of the earnings reported by the investee each period. Dividend declarations reduce the investment balance to reflect the decrease in the investee's book value.

Referring again to the information presented in Exhibit 1–1, Little Company reported a net income of $200,000 during 1995 and paid cash dividends of $50,000.

These figures indicate that Little's net assets have increased by $150,000 during the year. Therefore, in the financial records of Big Company, the following journal entries are made in applying the equity method:

Investment in Little Company	40,000	
Equity in Investee Income		40,000
To accrue earnings of a 20 percent owned investee ($200,000 × 20%).		
Cash	10,000	
Investment in Little Company		10,000
To record receipt of cash dividend from Little Company ($50,000 × 20%).		

In the first entry, Big accrues income based on the reported earnings of the investee even though this amount greatly exceeds the cash dividend. The second entry reflects the actual receipt of the dividend and the related reduction in Little's net assets. The $30,000 net increment recorded here in Big's investment account ($40,000 − $10,000) represents 20 percent of the $150,000 increase in Little's book value that occurred during the year.

Although these two entries illustrate the basic reporting process used in applying the equity method, several other issues must be explored for a full understanding of this approach. More specifically, special procedures are required in accounting for each of the following:

1. Reporting a change to the equity method.
2. Reporting investee income from sources other than continuing operations.
3. Reporting investee losses.
4. Reporting the sale of an equity investment.

Reporting a Change to the Equity Method

In many instances, an investor's ability to significantly influence an investee will not be gained through a single stock acquisition. The investor may possess only a minor ownership for some years before purchasing enough additional shares to require conversion to the equity method. Before the investor achieves significant influence, any investment should be reported by the lower-of-cost-or-market-value method. After the investment reaches the point at which the equity method becomes applicable, a technical question arises about the appropriate means of changing from one method to the other.[6]

APB Opinion 18 (par. 19) answers this concern by stating that "the investment, results of operations (current and prior periods presented), and retained

---

[6] A switch to the equity method also may be required if the investee purchases a portion of its own shares as treasury stock. This transaction can increase the investor's percentage of outstanding stock.

earnings of the investor should be adjusted retroactively.'' *Thus, all accounts are restated so that the investor's financial statements appear as if the equity method had been applied from the date of the first acquisition.* By mandating retroactive treatment, the APB is attempting to ensure comparability from year to year in the financial reporting of the investor company.[7]

To illustrate this restatement procedure, assume that Giant Company acquires a 10 percent ownership in Small Company on January 1, 1995. Officials of Giant do not believe that their company has gained the ability to exert significant influence over Small. Hence, the investment is properly recorded through the use of the lower-of-cost-or-market-value method. Subsequently, on January 1, 1997, Giant purchases an additional 30 percent of the outstanding voting stock of Small, thereby achieving the ability to significantly influence the investee's decision making. From 1995 through 1997, Small reports net income and pays cash dividends as follows:

Year	Net Income	Cash Dividends
1995	$ 70,000	$20,000
1996	110,000	40,000
1997	130,000	50,000

In Giant's 1995 and 1996 financial statements, *as originally reported*, dividend revenue of $2,000 and $4,000, respectively, would be recognized based on receiving 10 percent of these distributions. The investment account is maintained at its cost unless the stock portfolio's market value is less. However, after changing to the equity method on January 1, 1997, Giant must restate these prior years to present the investment as if this method had always been applied. Thereafter, the 1995 statements should indicate equity income of $7,000 with $11,000 being disclosed for 1996 based on a 10 percent accrual of Small's income for each of these years. The investment account shown on the investor's balance sheet is increased by this income but reduced by dividend distributions.

The actual restatement for these earlier years can be computed as follows:

Year	Equity in Investee Income (10 percent)	Dividend Income as Reported	Retroactive Adjustment
1995	$ 7,000	$2,000	$ 5,000
1996	11,000	4,000	7,000
Total adjustment			$12,000

---

[7] One member of the APB voted against issuance of *Opinion 18* based in part on this retroactive approach. In his dissent, Newman T. Halvorson contended that ''at the time an investment qualifies for use of the equity method, a new reporting entity is created, and the accounts of the investor for periods prior to that time should not be adjusted retroactively to reflect an entity that did not exist.''

Giant's reported earnings for 1995 will be increased by $5,000 with a $7,000 increment needed for 1996. To bring about this retroactive change to the equity method, Giant prepares the following journal entry on January 1, 1997:

Investment in Small Company 12,000
    Retained Earnings—Prior Period Adjustment—
        Equity in Investee Income 12,000
    To adjust 1995 and 1996 records so that investment is accounted for
using the equity method in a consistent manner.

Giant's $12,000 prior period adjustment increases the income recognized in the previous two years. Furthermore, this change in the investment account reflects the rise in Small's book value during this period. Small's total net income of $180,000 earned in 1995 and 1996, less $60,000 in dividend payments, created a net asset increase of $120,000. As a 10 percent owner during this time, an addition of $12,000 to Giant's investment account is appropriate when applying the equity method.

Continuing with this example, Giant will make two other journal entries at the end of 1997, but they relate solely to the operations and distributions of that period.

Investment in Small Company 52,000
    Equity in Investee Income 52,000
    To accrue 40 percent of the 1997 income reported by the Small
Company ($130,000 × 40%).

Cash 20,000
    Investment in Small Company 20,000
    To record receipt of 1997 cash dividend from Small Company
($50,000 × 40%).

Reporting Investee Income from Sources Other than Continuing Operations

Traditionally, certain elements of income are presented separately within a set of financial statements. Examples include extraordinary items (see *APB Opinion 30*, "Reporting the Results of Operations," June 1973) and prior period adjustments (see FASB *SFAS 16*, "Prior Period Adjustments," June 1977). A concern that arises in applying the equity method is whether items appearing separately in the investee's income statement require similar treatment by the investor.

To examine this issue, assume that Large Company owns 40 percent of the voting stock of Tiny Company and accounts for this investment by means of the equity method. In 1995, Tiny reports net income of $200,000, a figure composed of $250,000 in income from continuing operations and a $50,000 extraordinary loss. Large Company accrues earnings of $80,000 based on 40 percent of the $200,000 net figure. However, for proper disclosure, the extraordinary loss incurred by the investee must also be reported separately on the financial statements of the investor. This handling is intended, once again, to mirror the close relationship between the two companies.

Based on the level of ownership, Large recognizes $100,000 as a component of operating income (40 percent of Tiny Company's $250,000 income from continuing operations) along with a $20,000 extraordinary loss (40 percent of $50,000). The overall effect is still an $80,000 net increment in Large's earnings, but this amount has been appropriately allocated between income from continuing operations and extraordinary items.

The journal entry to record Large's equity interest in the income of Tiny would be as follows:

```
Investment in Tiny Company  . . . . . . . . . . . . . . . . . . . . . .   80,000
Extraordinary Loss of Investee  . . . . . . . . . . . . . . . . . . . .   20,000
     Equity in Investee Income. . . . . . . . . . . . . . . . . . . .              100,000
   To accrue operating income and extraordinary loss from equity
   investment.
```

One additional aspect of this accounting should be noted. Even though this loss has already been judged as extraordinary by the investee, Large does not report its $20,000 share as a separate item unless that figure is considered to be material with respect to the investor's own operations.

Reporting Investee Losses

Although most of the previous illustrations have been based on the recording of profits, accounting for losses incurred by the investee is handled by a similar manner. The appropriate percentage of each loss is recognized immediately by the investor with the carrying value of the investment account also being reduced. Even though these procedures are consistent with the concept of the equity method, they fail to take into account all possible loss situations.

Permanent Losses in Value.   *APB Opinion 18* recognizes that investments may suffer permanent losses in market value that are not properly reflected through the equity method. Such declines can be caused by the loss of major customers, changes in economic conditions, loss of a significant patent or other legal right, and damage to the company's reputation, and the like. Permanent reductions in market value resulting from such adverse events might not be immediately reported by the investor through the normal equity entries discussed previously. Thus, *APB Opinion 18* (par. 19) established the following guideline:

> A loss in value of an investment which is other than a temporary decline should be recognized the same as a loss in value of other long-term assets. Evidence of a loss in value might include, but would not necessarily be limited to, absence of an ability to recover the carrying amount of the investment or inability of the investee to sustain an earnings capacity which would justify the carrying amount of the investment.

Thus, when a permanent decline in an equity method investment's value occurs, the investor must reduce the asset to fair market value. However, *APB Opinion 18* stresses that this loss must be permanent before such recognition becomes necessary. Under the equity method, a temporary drop in the market value of an investment is simply ignored.

Investment Reduced to Zero. Through the recognition of reported losses as well as any permanent drops in market value, the investment account may eventually be reduced to a zero balance. This condition is most likely to occur if extreme losses have been suffered by the investee or if the original purchase was made at a low, bargain price. Regardless of the reason, the carrying value of the investment account could conceivably be eliminated in total.

At the point at which an investment account is reduced to zero, the investor should discontinue using the equity method, rather than establish a negative balance. The investment retains a zero balance until subsequent investee profits eliminate all unrealized losses. Once the original cost of the investment has been eliminated, no additional losses can accrue to the investor (since the entire cost has been written off) *unless* some further commitment has been made on behalf of the investee.

MAPCO Inc., for example, in its 1987 financial statements explains the continued use of the equity method in accounting for an investment in which the original cost had been entirely eliminated through the recognition of operating losses:

> MAPCO's recorded deficit in the Seminole project was $24,517,000 at December 31, 1987, and is classified in "Deferred Items—Other." MAPCO has continued to apply the equity method and reduce its recorded value below zero *due to MAPCO being contingently liable as a guarantor for its portion of the debt requirements of the Seminole project.* (emphasis added)

Reporting the Sale of an Equity Investment

At any time, the investor may choose to sell part or all of its holdings in the investee company. If a sale occurs, the equity method continues to be applied until the transaction date, thus establishing an appropriate carrying value for the investment. The investor then reduces this balance by the percentage of shares being sold.

As an example, assume that Top Company owns 40 percent of the 100,000 outstanding shares of Bottom Company, an investment accounted for by means of the equity method. Although these 40,000 shares were acquired some years ago for $200,000, application of the equity method has increased the asset balance to $320,000 as of January 1, 1995. On July 1, 1995, Top elects to sell 10,000 of these shares (one fourth of its investment) for $110,000 in cash, thereby reducing ownership in Bottom from 40 percent to 30 percent. Bottom Company reports income of $70,000 during the first six months of 1995 and distributes cash dividends of $30,000.

   Top, as the investor, initially makes the following journal entries on July 1, 1995, to accrue the proper income and establish the correct investment balance:

Investment in Bottom Company.	28,000	
Equity in Investee Income		28,000
To accrue equity income for first six months of 1995 ($70,000 × 40%).		
Cash	12,000	
Investment in Bottom Company.		12,000
To record receipt of cash dividends from January through June 1995 ($30,000 × 40%).		

   These two entries increase the carrying value of Top's investment by $16,000, creating a balance of $336,000 as of July 1, 1995. The sale of one fourth of these shares can then be recorded as follows:

Cash	110,000	
Investment in Bottom Company		84,000
Gain on Sale of Investment		26,000
To record sale of one fourth of investment in Bottom Company (¼ × $336,000 = $84,000).		

   After the sale has been consummated, Top continues to apply the equity method to this investment based on 30 percent ownership rather than 40 percent. However, if the sale had been of sufficient magnitude to cause Top to lose its ability to exercise significant influence over Bottom, the equity method ceases to be applicable. For example, if Top Company's holdings were reduced from 40 percent to 15 percent, the equity method might no longer be appropriate after the sale. The shares still being held are reported according to the lower-of-cost-or-market-value method with the remaining book value becoming the new *cost* figure for the investment rather than the amount originally paid.

   If an investor is required to change from the equity method to the lower-of-cost-or-market-value method, no retroactive adjustment is made. Although, as previously demonstrated, a change to the equity method mandates a restatement of prior periods, the treatment is not the same when the investor's change is to the lower-of-cost-or-market-value method.

   A similar situation is shown in the footnote to the 1990 financial statements of SPX Corporation. In this case, though, loss of significant influence did not come from a sale of shares.

   Prior to 1988, the Company's 49 percent ownership in the Brazilian affiliate was recorded on the equity basis. Upon concluding in 1988 that the Company could no longer exert a significant influence over the Brazilian affiliate's operations, the Company began accounting for this investment using the cost method (effective January 1, 1988).

Excess of Investment Cost Over Book Value Acquired

After the basic concepts and procedures of the equity method have been mastered, more complex accounting issues can be introduced. Surely one of the most common problems encountered in applying the equity method concerns investment costs that exceed the proportionate book value of the investee company.[8]

Unless the investor acquires its ownership at the time of the investee's conception, paying an amount equal to book value is rare. Wal-Mart Stores, Inc., as just one example, reported a book value of $4.70 per share on January 31, 1991, but on that same date, the company's common stock was selling for over $33 per share on the New York Stock Exchange. To obtain Wal-Mart shares as well as the stock of many other businesses, payment of a significant premium is required. In this particular example, market value was approximately seven times that of book value.

A number of possible reasons exist for such a marked difference in the book value of a company and the price of its stock. A company's value at any time is based on a multitude of factors such as company profitability, the introduction of a new product, the history of dividend payments, projected operating results, and general economic conditions. Furthermore, stock prices are based, at least partially, on the perceived worth of a company's net assets, amounts that often vary dramatically from underlying book values. Asset and liability accounts shown on a balance sheet tend to measure historical costs rather than current worth. In addition, these reported figures are affected by the specific accounting methods adopted by a company. Inventory costing methods such as LIFO and FIFO, for example, obviously lead to different book values as do each of the acceptable depreciation methods.

If an investment is acquired at a price in excess of book value, logical reasons should exist to explain the additional cost incurred by the investor. Why was $33.00 paid for each share when the book value was only $4.70? In applying the equity method, the cause of such an excess payment can be divided into two general categories:

1. Specific investee assets and liabilities may have market values that differ from their present book values. The excess payment can be identified directly with individual accounts such as inventory, equipment, or franchise rights.

2. The investor could be willing to pay an extra amount because future benefits are expected to accrue from the investment. Such benefits might be anticipated as the result of factors such as the estimated profitability

---

[8] Although encountered less frequently, investments can be purchased at a cost that is less than the underlying book value of the investee. Accounting for this possibility is explored in later chapters.

of the investee or the relationship being established between the two companies. In this case, the additional payment is attributed to an intangible future value generally referred to as *goodwill* rather than to any specific investee asset or liability. For example, Air Products and Chemicals, Inc., disclosed on its September 30, 1990, balance sheet that the reported value of equity investments included $38.5 million in goodwill.

As an illustration, assume that Big Company is negotiating the acquisition of 30 percent of the outstanding shares of Little Company. Little's balance sheet reports assets of $500,000 and liabilities of $300,000 for a net book value of $200,000. After investigation, Big determines that Little's equipment is undervalued in the company's financial records by $60,000. One of its patents is also undervalued, but only by $40,000. By adding these valuation adjustments to Little's book value, Big arrives at an estimated worth for the company's net assets of $300,000. Based on this computation, Big offers $90,000 for a 30 percent share of the investee's outstanding stock.

Book value of Little Company (assets minus liabilities [or stockholders' equity])	$200,000
Undervaluation of equipment	60,000
Undervaluation of patent	40,000
Value of net assets	$300,000
Portion being acquired	30%
Acquisition price	$ 90,000

Although Big's purchase price is in excess of the proportionate share of Little's book value, this additional amount can be attributed to two specific accounts: Equipment and Patents. No part of the extra payment is traceable to any other projected future benefit. Thus, the cost of Big's investment is allocated as follows:

Payment by investor		$90,000
Percentage of book value acquired ($200,000 × 30%)		60,000
Payment in excess of book value		30,000
Excess payment identified with specific assets:		
Equipment ($60,000 undervaluation × 30%)	$18,000	
Patent ($40,000 undervaluation × 30%)	12,000	30,000
Excess payment not identified with specific assets—goodwill		–0–

Of the $30,000 excess payment made by the investor, $18,000 is assigned to the equipment whereas $12,000 is traced to a patent and its undervaluation. No amount of the purchase price is allocated to goodwill.

To take this example one step further, assume that the owners of Little reject the $90,000 price proposed by Big. They believe that the value of the company as a going concern is greater than the market value of its net assets. Since the management of Big believes that an especially profitable business relationship can be created through this purchase, the bid price is raised to $125,000 and accepted. This new acquisition price is allocated as follows:

Payment by investor		$125,000
Percentage of book value acquired ($200,000 × 30%)		60,000
Payment in excess of book value		65,000
Excess payment identified with specific assets:		
Equipment ($60,000 undervaluation × 30%)	18,000	
Patent ($40,000 undervaluation × 30%)	12,000	30,000
Excess payment not identified with specific assets—goodwill		$ 35,000

As can be seen from this example, *any extra payment that cannot be attributed to a specific asset or liability is assigned to the intangible asset goodwill.* Although the actual purchase price can be computed by a number of different techniques or simply result from negotiations, goodwill is always the excess amount not allocated to identifiable asset or liability accounts.

Under the equity method, the investor enters total cost in a single investment account, regardless of the allocation of any excess purchase price. If Big's bid of $125,000 is accepted by all parties, the acquisition is initially recorded at that amount despite the internal assignments made to equipment, patents, and goodwill. The entire $125,000 was paid to acquire this investment, and it is recorded as such.

The Amortization Process

The preceding extra payments were made in connection with assets (equipment, patents, and goodwill) having limited useful lives. Even though the actual dollar amounts are recorded within the Investment account, a definite historical cost can be attributed to these assets. With a cost to the investor as well as a specified life, the payment relating to each asset should be amortized over an appropriate time period.

Assume, for illustration purposes, that the equipment has a 10-year remaining life, the patent a 5-year life, and the goodwill an estimated 40-year life.[9] If the straight-line method is used with no salvage value,[10] *the investor's cost* should be amortized initially as follows:

---

[9] According to *APB Opinion 17*, "Intangible Assets," August 1970, intangible assets must be amortized over a period not to exceed 40 years.

[10] Unless otherwise stated, all amortization computations are based on the straight-line method with no salvage value.

Account	Cost Assigned	Useful Life	Annual Amortization
Equipment	$18,000	10 years	$1,800
Patent	12,000	5 years	2,400
Goodwill	35,000	40 years	875
Annual expense (for five years until patent cost is completely amortized)			$5,075

In recording this annual expense, Big is reducing a portion of the investment balance in the same way it would amortize the cost of any other asset that had a limited life. Therefore, at the end of the first year, the investor records the following journal entry under the equity method:

Equity in Investee Income 5,075
    Investment in Little Company   5,075
    To record amortization of excess payment allocated to equipment, a
patent, and goodwill.

Because this amortization relates to assets held by the investee, the investor does not establish a specific expense account. Instead, as shown in the previous entry, the expense is recognized through a decrease in the equity income accruing from the investee company.

To illustrate this entire process, assume that Tall Company purchases 20 percent of Short Company for $200,000. Tall can exercise significant influence over the investee, thus, the equity method is appropriately applied. The acquisition is made on January 1, 1995, when Short holds net assets with a book value of $700,000. Tall believes that the investee's building (10-year life) is undervalued within the financial records by $80,000 and equipment with a 5-year life is undervalued by $120,000. Any goodwill established by this purchase would be amortized over the maximum allowable time period. During 1995, Short reports a net income of $150,000 and pays a cash dividend at year's end of $60,000.

Tall's three basic journal entries for 1995 pose little problem:

January 1, 1995

Investment in Short Company 200,000
    Cash   200,000
    To record acquisition of 20 percent of the outstanding shares of
Short Company.

December 31, 1995

Investment in Short Company 30,000
    Equity in Investee Income   30,000
    To accrue 20 percent of the 1995 reported earnings of investee
($150,000 × 20%).

Cash 12,000
    Investment in Short Company   12,000
    To record receipt of 1995 cash dividend ($60,000 × 20%).

An allocation must be made of Tall's $200,000 purchase price to determine if an additional adjusting entry is necessary to recognize annual amortization associated with the extra payment:

Payment by investor	$200,000
Percentage of 1/1/95 book value ($700,000 × 20%)	140,000
Payment in excess of book value.	60,000
Excess payment identified with specific assets:	
Building ($80,000 × 20%) $16,000	
Equipment ($120,000 × 20%) 24,000	40,000
Excess payment not identified with specific assets—	
goodwill	$ 20,000

As can be seen, $16,000 of the purchase price is assigned to a building, $24,000 to equipment, with the remaining $20,000 attributed to goodwill. Each of these assets has a limited useful life; therefore, periodic amortization is required.

Asset	Attributed Cost	Useful Life	Annual Amortization
Building	$16,000	10 years	$1,600
Equipment	24,000	5 years	4,800
Goodwill	20,000	40 years	500
Total for 1995			$6,900

At the end of 1995, Tall must also record the following adjustment in connection with these cost allocations:

Equity in Investee Income	6,900	
Investment in Short Company		6,900
To record 1995 amortization of extra cost of building		
($1,600), equipment ($4,800), and goodwill ($500).		

Although these entries are shown separately here for better explanation, Tall would probably net the income accrual for the year ($30,000) and the amortization ($6,900) to create a single entry increasing the investment and recognizing equity income of $23,100.

Elimination of Unrealized Gains in Inventory[11]

Many large stock acquisitions are made for one primary purpose: to establish ties between companies to facilitate the direct purchase and sale of inventory items.

---

[11] Unrealized gains may involve the sale of items other than inventory. The intercompany transfer of depreciable fixed assets and land are discussed in a later chapter.

Such intercompany transactions may occur either on a regular basis or only sporadically. For example, the Coca-Cola Company disclosed that syrup and concentrate sales of $602 million were made in 1990 to its 49 percent-owned investee Coca-Cola Enterprises Inc.

Regardless of their frequency, inventory sales between investor and investee necessitate the use of special accounting procedures to ensure proper timing of revenue recognition. An underlying principle of accounting is that "revenues are not recognized until earned . . . and revenues are considered to have been earned when the entity has substantially accomplished what it must do to be entitled to the benefits represented by the revenues."[12] In the sale of inventory to an unrelated party, recognition of revenue is normally not in question; substantial accomplishment is achieved when the exchange takes place unless special terms are included in the contract.

Unfortunately, the earning process is not so clearly delineated in sales made between related parties. *Because of the relationship between investor and investee, the seller of the goods is said to retain a partial stake in the inventory for as long as it is held by the buyer.* Thus, the earning process is not considered complete at the time of the original sale. For proper accounting, revenue recognition must be deferred until substantial accomplishment is proven. Consequently, when the investor applies the equity method, reporting of the related profit on intercompany transfers is delayed until the ultimate disposition of the goods by the buyer. When the inventory is eventually consumed within operations or resold to an unrelated party, the original sale is culminated and the gross profit is fully recognized.

In accounting, transactions between related companies are identified as either *downstream* or *upstream*. Downstream transfers refer to the sale of an item by the investor to the investee. Conversely, an upstream sale describes one made to the investor by the investee (see Exhibit 1–2). *Although this distinction is not significant for carrying out the procedures of the equity method, it has definite consequences in the consolidation of financial statements, as discussed in Chapter 5.* Therefore, these two types of intercompany sales are examined separately even at this introductory stage.

Downstream Sales of Inventory

Assume that Big Company owns a 40 percent share of Little Company and accounts for this investment through the equity method. In 1995, Big sells inventory to Little at a price of $50,000. This figure includes a markup of 30 percent, or $15,000. By the end of 1995, Little has sold $40,000 of these goods to outside parties while retaining $10,000 in inventory for sale during the subsequent year.

Downstream sales have been made by the investor to the investee. In applying the equity method, recognition of the related profit must be delayed until these

---

[12] FASB, *Statement of Financial Accounting Concepts No. 6,* "Recognition and Measurement in Financial Statements of Business Enterprises" (Stamford, Conn.: December 1984), par. 83.

EXHIBIT 1–2

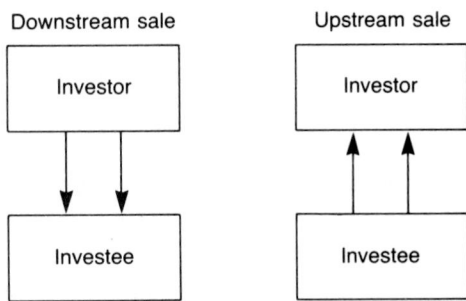

goods are disposed of by the buyer. Although total intercompany transfers amounted to $50,000 in 1995, $40,000 of this merchandise has already been resold, thereby justifying the normal reporting of profits. For the $10,000 still in the investee's inventory, the earning process has not yet been culminated. In computing equity income, this portion of the intercompany gain must be deferred until the goods are disposed of by Little.

The markup on the original sale was 30 percent of the transfer price; therefore, Big's profit associated with these remaining items is $3,000 ($10,000 × 30%). *However, because only 40 percent of the investee's stock is being held, just $1,200 ($3,000 × 40%) of this gain is actually relevant.* Big's ownership percentage reflects the intercompany portion of the gain. The total $3,000 gross profit within the ending inventory balance is not the amount deferred. Rather, 40 percent of that gain is viewed as the currently unrealized figure.

Remaining Ending Inventory	Gross Profit Percentage	Gain in Ending Inventory	Investor Ownership Percentage	Unrealized Intercompany Gain
$10,000	30%	$3,000	40%	$1,200

After calculating the appropriate deferral, the investor decreases current equity income by $1,200 to reflect the unrealized nature of the intercompany gain. This procedure temporarily removes this portion of the profit from the books of the investor in 1995 until the inventory is disposed of by the investee in 1996. Big accomplishes the actual deferral through the following year-end journal entry:

Deferral of Unrealized Gain

Equity in Investee Income 1,200
    Investment in Little Company 1,200
  To defer unrealized gain on sale of inventory to Little Company.

In the subsequent year, when this inventory is eventually consumed by Little or sold to unrelated parties, the deferral is no longer needed. The earning process has been completed and the $1,200 should be recognized by Big. By merely reversing the preceding deferral entry, the accountant succeeds in moving the investor's profit in the appropriate time period. Recognition has been shifted from the year of transfer to the year in which the earning process is substantially accomplished.

Subsequent Realization of Intercompany Gain

Investment in Little Company	1,200	
Equity in Investee Income		1,200

To recognize income on intercompany sale that has now been earned through sales to outsiders.

Upstream Sales of Inventory

Unlike consolidated financial statements (see Chapter 5), upstream sales of inventory are reported under the equity method in the same manner as downstream sales. Hence, any unrealized gain that remains in ending inventory must be deferred until such time as the items are used or sold to unrelated parties. To illustrate, assume that Big Company once again owns 40 percent of Little Company. During the current year, Little sells merchandise costing $40,000 to Big for $60,000. As of the end of the fiscal period, Big still retains $15,000 of these goods. Little reports net income of $120,000 for the year.

To reflect the basic accrual of the investee's earnings, Big records the following journal entry at the end of this year:

Income Accrual

Investment in Little Company	48,000	
Equity in Investee Income		48,000

To accrue income from 40 percent owned investee ($120,000 × 40%).

The amount of the gain remaining unrealized at year-end is computed using the markup of 33⅓ percent of the sales price ($20,000/$60,000):

Remaining Ending Inventory	Gross Profit Percentage	Gain in Ending Inventory	Investor Ownership Percentage	Unrealized Intercompany Gain
$15,000	33⅓%	$5,000	40%	$2,000

Based on this calculation, a second entry is required of the investor at year-end. Once again, a deferral of the unrealized gain created by the intercompany transfer is necessary for proper timing of income recognition. *Under the equity method, the direction of the sale has no influence on either the amount or the method of reporting.*

Discussion Question: Is This Really Only Significant Influence?

The Coca-Cola Company accounts for its ownership of Coca-Cola Enterprises (CCE) by use of the equity method as described here in Chapter 1. As of December 31, 1990, Coca-Cola held approximately 49 percent of the outstanding stock of CCE. According to the financial statements of CCE, "The Company and its subsidiaries are licensed bottlers of soft drink products of The Coca-Cola Company. . . . In the ordinary course of business, the Company purchases sweeteners, soft drink syrups and concentrate from The Coca-Cola Company. The Company paid The Coca-Cola Company approximately $919.6 million and $922.1 million for sweetener, syrup and concentrate purchases, during 1990 and 1989, respectively. . . . For 1990 and 1989, total direct marketing support provided to the Company by The Coca-Cola Company was approximately $186.3 million and $184.6 million, respectively."

If Coca-Cola acquires approximately 1 percent more of CCE, a majority of the stock will be held so that consolidation becomes a requirement. However, given the size of the present ownership and the dependence that CCE has on Coca-Cola for products and marketing, does Coca-Cola truly have no more than "the ability to exercise significant influence over the operating and financial policies" of CCE? Does the equity method fairly represent the relationship that exists? Or, does Coca-Cola actually control CCE despite the level of ownership, and should consolidation be required? In 1991, the FASB began to reexamine the boundary between the application of the equity method and consolidation. Should the rules be rewritten so that Coca-Cola must consolidate CCE rather than use the equity method? If so, at what level of ownership would the equity method no longer be appropriate?

Deferral of Unrealized Gain

Equity in Investee Income	2,000	
Investment in Little Company		2,000

   To defer recognition of intercompany unrealized gain
until inventory is used or sold to unrelated parties.

After the adjustment, Big, the investor, reports earnings from this equity investment of $46,000 ($48,000 − $2,000). The income accrual has been reduced because a portion of the intercompany gross profit is considered unrealized. When the $15,000 in merchandise is eventually consumed or sold by the investor, the preceding journal entry is reversed so that the effects of the gain are reported in the proper accounting period.

In an upstream sale, the investor's own Inventory account contains the unrealized gain. The previous entry, though, defers recognition of this profit by decreasing Big's investment account rather than the inventory balance. APB *Accounting Interpretation No. 1 of APB Opinion 18,* "Intercompany Profit Eliminations under Equity Method," November 1971, does permit the direct reduction of the investor's inventory balance as a means of accounting for this gain. Although this alternative is acceptable, decreasing the investment remains the traditional approach for deferring unrealized gains, even for upstream sales.

As a final note, whether upstream or downstream, the investor's sales and purchases are still reported as if the transactions were carried out with outside parties. Only the unrealized gain is deferred and that amount is adjusted solely through the equity income account. Furthermore, since the companies are not consolidated, the investee's reported balances are not altered at all to reflect the nature of these sales/purchases. Obviously, readers of the financial statements need to be made aware of the inclusion of these amounts in the income statement. Thus, the FASB issued *Statement No. 57,* "Related Party Disclosures," in March 1982; it required reporting companies to disclose certain information about related party transactions. These disclosures include the nature of the relationship, a description of the transactions, the dollar amounts of the transactions, and amounts due to or from any related parties at year-end.

Deferred Income Taxes[13]

The final issue that will be explored in this chapter concerns the deferral of income taxes. Although the equity method is appropriate for external reporting purposes, the Internal Revenue Code only taxes the amount of cash dividends actually collected. The dividend income reported to the tax authorities by the investor normally differs from the investment earnings recognized under the equity method.

To illustrate, assume that Giant owns 30 percent of Small and utilizes the equity method. If this investee reports a $100,000 profit for the current period, Giant immediately recognizes an income accrual of $30,000. However, if Small distributes a total dividend of $20,000 during the same year, Giant reports just the 30 percent received ($6,000) on its tax return.

Because these two methods vary, an important theoretical accounting question arises: Must Giant (the investor) report a liability for future taxes on the remainder of the income being recognized? Or, stated in a different fashion, should Giant's tax liability as reported in its financial statements be based on the $30,000 equity income accrual or the $6,000 that is currently taxable?

---

[13] The computation and reporting of deferred income taxes is an extremely complex topic that is normally examined in intermediate accounting textbooks. Coverage here is limited to a specific aspect of this issue relevant to the application of the equity method. Consequently, no other differences between taxable income and reported earnings are included in any of the illustrations.

Most companies routinely retain some portion of their earnings as a permanent basis for future growth. Therefore, an argument can be made that part of the $24,000 difference between the equity income being recognized by Giant ($30,000) and the current cash dividends ($6,000) collected from Small will never be distributed by the investee to the investor. If this portion of equity income is not conveyed, no tax effect will be created in the future. Thus, the assertion has been made that at least some portion of this difference produces no true liability for the investor.

This logic was rejected initially by the APB in *Opinion 24,* "Accounting for Income Taxes—Equity Method Investments," April 1972. A deferred income tax liability was required of the investor to reflect the *entire* amount of potential taxes incurred because of the current recognition of equity earnings. This conservative approach was said to best represent the matching principle: The tax expense is recognized in the same period as the related revenues. In addition, the argument that equity income in excess of current dividends ($24,000 in this example) would never become taxable was virtually impossible to prove. Either through future dividends or the ultimate sale of the investment, an eventual increase in the investor's taxable income seems inevitable.

The FASB reaffirmed this conclusion in *Statement of Financial Accounting Standards No. 109,* "Accounting for Income Taxes," which became effective December 15, 1992. This pronouncement again directs the investor to accrue a liability for future taxes on the excess $24,000 even though the amount is not subject to current taxation. This amount is identified by *Statement 109* (in its glossary) as a *taxable temporary difference,* "differences that result in taxable amounts in future years when the related asset or liability is recovered or settled, respectively."

Thus, utilization of the equity method normally creates a temporary taxable difference between the dividend income reported for tax purposes and the amount accrued by the investor for financial reporting.[14] *Statement 109* requires immediate recognition of a deferred tax effect. Because the income will be taxed in a subsequent period either through a dividend distribution or sale of the stock, the immediate recording of a debt on the $24,000 temporary difference is required.[15]

Under the present Internal Revenue Code of the United States, a corporation is allowed a reduction of 80 percent for any dividends collected from another domestic corporation if 20 percent or more of the outstanding stock is held.[16]

---

[14] Amortization expense relating to any amounts paid in excess of the investee's book value is not tax deductible. The writers of the tax laws apparently did not believe that an investment cost should be written off over time. Therefore, such amounts are not included in the computation of temporary differences.

[15] *SFAS 109* provides an exception: No deferred tax liability is required for a foreign corporate joint venture accounted for by means of the equity method if the difference is considered to be permanent in duration. As mentioned again in Chapter 7, the same rule applies to foreign subsidiaries.

[16] The corporate dividend received deduction is 70 percent if less than 20 percent of the investee's stock is owned. If 80 percent or more of the stock is held, intercompany dividends are not taxed.

Assuming a tax rate of 30 percent, the income tax to be paid by the investor (Giant) on the $6,000 received during the year from Small is only $360, computed as follows:

Taxes Currently Payable on $6,000 Dividend

Cash Dividends	80 Percent Deduction	Taxable Income	Tax Rate	Taxes Currently Payable
$6,000	$4,800	$1,200	30%	$360

Although only $360 in income taxes must be paid currently by the owner, *FASB Statement 109* dictates that an additional liability is created by the $24,000 temporary difference. However, computing the amount of this obligation can vary significantly, depending on a single assumption. If the stock is to be held by Giant for an indefinite period so that the investor anticipates the eventual receipt of these earnings as dividends, the 80 percent deduction is applicable to the current tax calculation. Conversely, if the investment is to be sold before these dividends are paid, the $24,000 is expected to be realized by the investor through a higher negotiated price. Thus, the dividend deduction is not relevant in determining the deferred liability.

Deferred Liability—Undistributed $24,000

Investor Anticipates Receiving Future Dividends

Undistributed Income within Investment	80 Percent Deduction	Income to Be Taxed	Tax Rate	Deferred Tax Liability
$24,000	$19,200	$4,800	30%	$1,440

Investor Anticipates Future Sale of Investment

Undistributed Income within Investment	Tax Rate	Deferred Tax Liability
$24,000	30%	$7,200

In the first case, the investor's total liability is $1,800 ($360 current and $1,440 future) because the income is to be realized as dividends. For the second possibility, a liability of $7,560 is required ($360 payable now with $7,200 assumed to be payable later when the stock is sold). Using either assumption, the investor's year-end adjusting entry includes a deferred income tax liability resulting from the undistributed earnings of the equity investee within the Investment in Small account.

Dividends to Be Received

Income Tax Expense–Current	360	
Income Tax Expense–Deferred	1,440	
Income Taxes Payable–Current		360
Deferred Income Taxes Payable		1,440

To record taxes on income accruing from equity investment.

Investment to Be Sold

Income Tax Expense–Current	360	
Income Tax Expense–Deferred	7,200	
Income Taxes Payable–Current		360
Deferred Income Taxes Payable		7,200

    To record taxes on income accruing from equity investment.

Summary

1. The equity method of accounting for an investment is designed to reflect the close relationship that can exist between an investor and an investee. More specifically, this approach is applied whenever the owner achieves the ability to apply significant influence to the investee's operating and financial decisions. Significant influence is presumed to exist at the 20 to 50 percent ownership level. However, the accountant must evaluate each situation, regardless of the percentage of ownership, to determine whether this ability is actually present.

2. To mirror the relationship between the companies, the equity method requires the investor to accrue income when earned by the investee. In recording this profit or loss, the investor separately reports items such as extraordinary gains and losses as well as prior period adjustments to highlight their nonrecurring nature. Dividend payments decrease the book value of the investee company; therefore, the investor reduces the book value of the investment account when collected.

3. When acquiring capital stock, an investor often pays an amount that exceeds the underlying book value of the investee company. For accounting purposes, such excess payments must be identified with either specific assets and liabilities (such as land or buildings) or allocated to an intangible asset referred to as goodwill. Each assigned cost (except for any amount attributed to land) is then amortized by the investor over the expected useful lives of the assets and liabilities. This amortization reduces the amount of equity income being reported.

4. If the entire investment or any portion is sold, the equity method is applied consistently until the date of disposal. A gain or loss is computed based on the adjusted book value at that time. Remaining shares are accounted for by means of either the equity method or the lower-of-cost-or-market-value method, depending on the investor's subsequent ability to significantly influence the investee.

5. Inventory (or other assets) may be transferred between investor and investee. Because of the relationship that exists between the two companies, the equity income accrual should be reduced to defer the intercompany portion of any markup included on these transfers until the items are either sold to outsiders or consumed. Thus, the amount of intercompany gain in ending inventory decreases the amount of equity income being recognized in the current period although this effect is subsequently reversed.

6. Income taxes are paid by the investor on the amount of dividends received from an investee (less a dividend deduction allowed by law). However, if the equity method is applied, the investor recognizes income for financial reporting purposes at the time it is earned by the investee. Because of this income accrual, the investment account determined for external reporting usually exceeds the asset's cost, the balance appropriate for tax purposes. This excess is viewed as a taxable temporary difference so that a deferred tax liability must be recognized by the investor.

Comprehensive Illustration

PROBLEM   (Estimated Time: 30 to 50 Minutes)

Every chapter in this textbook concludes with an illustration designed to assist students in tying together the essential elements of the material presented. After a careful reading of each chapter, attempt to work through the comprehensive problem. Then review the solution that follows the problem, noting the handling of each significant accounting issue.

Part A

On January 1, 1995, Big Company pays $70,000 for a 10 percent interest in Little Company. On that date, Little has a book value of $600,000, although equipment, which has a five-year life, is undervalued by $100,000 on its books.

On January 1, 1996, Big acquires an additional 30 percent of Little Company for $274,000. This second purchase provides Big with the ability to exert significant influence over Little. At the time of this transaction, Little's equipment with a four-year life was undervalued by only $80,000.

During these two years, Little reported the following operational results:

Year	Net Income	Cash Dividends Paid
1995	$210,000	$110,000
1996	250,000	100,000

Additional Information:

- The tax rate is 30 percent.
- Cash dividends are always paid on July 1 of each year.
- Any goodwill will be amortized over a 20-year period.
- Big plans to hold the investment indefinitely.

Required:

a. What income did Big originally report for 1995 in connection with this investment?

b. On comparative financial statements for 1995 and 1996, what figures should Big report in connection with this investment?

Part B *(This problem is a continuation of Part A)*

In 1997, Little Company reports $400,000 in income from continuing operations plus a $60,000 extraordinary gain. The company pays a $120,000 cash dividend. During this fiscal year, Big sells inventory costing $80,000 to Little for $100,000. Little continues to hold 30 percent of this merchandise at the end of 1997. Big maintains 40 percent ownership of Little throughout the period.

Required:

Ignoring income taxes, prepare all necessary journal entries for Big for the year of 1997.

SOLUTION

Part A

a. Big Company accounts for its investment in Little Company using the lower-of-cost-or-market-value method during 1995. Since only 10 percent of the outstanding shares were being held, significant influence was apparently not present. Thus, the $11,000 ($110,000 × 10%) received as dividends is recorded by the investor as income in the original financial reporting for that year.

b. To enhance comparability, a change to the equity method is recorded retroactively. Therefore, when the ability to exert significant influence over the operations of Little is established on January 1, 1996, both Big's 1995 and 1996 financial statements must be prepared by applying the equity method.

Big first evaluates the initial purchase of Little's stock to determine if either goodwill or incremental asset values need be reflected within the equity method procedures.

Purchase of 10 Percent of Voting Stock on January 1, 1995

Payment by investor.	$70,000
Percentage of book value acquired ($600,000 × 10%)	60,000
Payment in excess of book value	10,000
Excess payment identified with specific assets:	
Equipment ($100,000 × 10%).	10,000
Excess payment identified with specific assets—goodwill	–0–

As shown here, the $10,000 excess payment was made in recognition of the undervaluation of Little's equipment. This asset had a useful life at that time of five years; thus, the investor records amortization expense of $2,000 each year.

A similar calculation must be carried out for Big's second stock purchase:

Purchase of 30 Percent of Voting Stock on January 1, 1996

Payment by investor	$274,000
Percentage of book value* acquired ($700,000 × 30%)	210,000
Payment in excess of book value.	64,000
Excess payment identified with specific assets:	
Equipment ($80,000 × 30%).	24,000
Excess payment not identified with specific assets—goodwill	$ 40,000

---

* Little's book value on January 1, 1996, is computed by adding the 1995 net income of $210,000 less dividends paid of $110,000 to the previous book value of $600,000.

In this second acquisition, $24,000 of the payment is attributable to the undervalued equipment with $40,000 assigned to goodwill. Since the equipment now has only a four-year remaining life, annual amortization of $6,000 is appropriate ($24,000/4). The goodwill, which has an assumed life of 20 years, will be expensed at the rate of $2,000 per year ($40,000/20). Thus total amortization on this second purchase is initially $8,000 per year.

After the additional shares are acquired on January 1, 1996, Big's financial records for 1995 must be retroactively restated as if the equity method had been applied from the date of the initial investment.

Financial Reporting—1995

Equity in Investee Income (Income Statement)

Income reported by Little	$210,000
Big's ownership	10%
Accrual for 1995	$ 21,000
Less: equipment amortization (first purchase)	(2,000)
Equity in investee income–1995	$ 19,000

Investment in Little (Balance Sheet)

Cost of first acquisition	$ 70,000
1995 Equity in investee income (above).	19,000
Less: Dividends received ($110,000 × 10%)	(11,000)
Investment in Little–12/31/95	$ 78,000

The tax effects for 1995 should also be reconsidered. Big collected $11,000 in dividends from Little; thus, the investor's taxable income increased by $2,200 after subtracting the 80 percent deduction. Based on the 30 percent tax rate, Big paid $660 ($2,200 × 30%) in 1995 income taxes relating to this investment. However, *FASB Statement 109* also requires the recording of a liability on the taxable temporary difference that now exists because the equity accrual in the Investment in Little account exceeds the dividend distributed.

As shown, Big is accruing earnings of $21,000 (amortization is not deductible for tax purposes and has no impact on this computation), rather than $11,000. Because the investment increases by a net $10,000, recognition of a deferred tax liability on that amount is necessary. After subtracting the 80 percent dividend deduction (applicable because the stock will be held indefinitely), future taxable income is anticipated to increase by $2,000 rather than the entire $10,000. Thus, Big must also retroactively report deferred income taxes of $600 (30%) for 1995 to reflect the change being made to the equity method.

Financial Reporting—1996

Equity in Investee Income (Income Statement)

Income reported by Little	$250,000
Big's ownership	40%
Accrual for 1996	$100,000
Less amortization expense:	
Equipment (first purchase)	(2,000)
Equipment (second purchase)	(6,000)
Goodwill (second purchase)	(2,000)
Equity in investee income–1996	$ 90,000

Investment in Little (Balance Sheet)

Book value–12/31/95 (above)	$ 78,000
Cost of 1996 acquisition	274,000
Equity in investee income (above)	90,000
Less: Dividends received ($100,000 × 40%)	(40,000)
Investment in Little–12/31/96	$402,000

For current taxation purposes, Big reports $8,000 ($40,000 dividends collected less the 80 percent dividend exclusion). The 30 percent tax rate necessitates recognition of $2,400 as the current portion of Big's income tax liability for 1996. However, the reporting of a deferred tax liability is also required. Big's equity income accrual for this same period is $100,000 (40% × $250,000). The $60,000 rise in the investment account ($100,000 income less $40,000 in dividends—once again amortization is ignored) is another taxable temporary difference. According to *Statement 109,* a new deferred tax liability is created. Of this $60,000 difference, taxes would be assessed on only $12,000 after subtracting the 80 percent dividend reduction. At a 30 percent tax rate, Big records $3,600 as a deferred income tax for 1996.

Part B

On July 1, 1997, Big receives a $48,000 cash dividend from Little (40% × $120,000). According to the equity method, receipt of this dividend reduces the carrying value of the investment account:

Cash	48,000	
Investment in Little Company		48,000
To record receipt of 1997 dividend from investee.		

Big records no other journal entries in connection with this investment until the end of 1997. At that time, the annual accrual of income is made as well as the adjustment to record amortization (see Part A for computation of expense). The investee's continuing income is reported separately from the extraordinary item.

Investment in Little Company	184,000	
Equity in Investee Income		160,000
Extraordinary Gain of Investee		24,000

To recognize reported income of investee based on a 40 percent ownership level of $400,000 operating income and $60,000 extraordinary gain.

Equity in Investee Income	10,000	
Investment in Little Company		10,000

To record annual amortization on excess payment made in relation to equipment ($2,000 from first purchase and $6,000 from second) and goodwill ($2,000).

Big only needs to make one other equity entry during 1997. Intercompany sales have occurred and a portion of the inventory continues to be held by Little. Therefore, an unrealized gain exists that must be deferred. The markup on the sales price was 20 percent ($20,000/$100,000). Since $30,000 of this merchandise is still in the possession of the investee, the related gain is $6,000 ($30,000 × 20%). However, Big owns only 40 percent of the outstanding stock of Little; thus, the unrealized intercompany gain at year's end is $2,400 ($6,000 × 40%). That amount must be deferred until the inventory is consumed by Little or sold to unrelated parties in subsequent years.

Equity in Investee Company	2,400	
Investment in Little Company		2,400

To defer unrealized gain on intercompany sale.

Questions

1. A company acquires a rather large investment in another corporation. What criteria are used to determine whether the equity method of accounting should be applied by the investor to this investment?

2. What indicates an investor's ability to significantly influence the decision-making process of an investee?

3. The Jones Company possesses a 25 percent interest in the outstanding voting shares of the Sandridge Company. Under what circumstances might Jones decide that the equity method would not be appropriate to account for this investment?

4. Smith, Inc. has maintained an ownership interest in Watts Corporation for a number of years. This investment has been accounted for by means of the equity method. What transactions or events create changes in the Investment in Watts Corporation account being recorded by Smith?

5. Although the equity method is a generally accepted accounting principle (GAAP), recognition of equity income has been criticized. What theoretical problems can be brought up by opponents of the equity method?

6. Because of the acquisition of additional investee shares, an investor may be forced to change from the lower-of-cost-or-market-value method to the equity method. Which procedures are applied to effect this type of accounting change?

7. Riggins Company accounts for its investment in Bostic Company by means of the equity method. During the past fiscal year, Bostic reported an extraordinary gain on its income statement. How would this extraordinary item affect the financial records of the investor?

8. During the current year, the common stock of the Davis Company suffers a permanent drop in market value. In the past, Davis has made a significant portion of its sales to one customer. This buyer recently announced its decision to make no further purchases from the Davis Company, an action that led to the loss of market value. Hawkins, Inc. owns 35 percent of the outstanding shares of Davis, an investment that is recorded according to the equity method. How would the loss in value affect the financial reporting of this investor?

9. Wilson Company acquired 40 percent of Andrews Company at a bargain price because of losses that are expected to result from Andrews's failure in marketing several new products. The price paid by Wilson was only $100,000, although Andrews's corresponding book value was much higher. In the first year after acquisition, Andrews lost $300,000. In applying the equity method, how should Wilson account for this loss?

10. After purchasing shares of stock in an investee corporation, how is the investor's allocation to goodwill determined?

11. In a stock acquisition accounted for by the equity method, a portion of the purchase price is often attributed to goodwill or to specific assets or liabilities. How are these amounts reported at the time of acquisition? How are these amounts accounted for in subsequent periods?

12. Princeton Company holds a 40 percent interest in the outstanding voting stock of Yale Company. On June 19 of the current year, Princeton sells part of this investment. What accounting should Princeton make on June 19? What accounting will Princeton make for the remainder of the current year?

13. What is the difference between downstream and upstream sales? How does this difference impact application of the equity method?

14. How is the unrealized gain on intercompany sales calculated? What effect does an unrealized gain have on the recording of an investment if the equity method is applied?

15. How are intercompany transfers reported in the separate financial statements of an investee if the investor is using the equity method?

16. How is an investor taxed on the income that accrues from an equity investee?

17. How are deferred income taxes computed in connection with equity income?

Library Assignments

1. Read the following articles and any others available in the library on the equity method:

   "Equity Earnings," *Forbes,* March 31, 1980.
   "Equity Accounting Isn't Equitable," *Forbes,* March 31, 1980.

   Also read *APB Opinion No. 18,* "The Equity Method of Accounting for Investments in Common Stock" (including the dissent and qualifications that follow the pronouncement). Prepare a report to either justify the continued use of the equity method as a generally accepted accounting principle or suggest revisions or abolishment of this approach.

2. Obtain the latest financial statements of The Dow Chemical Company, American Cyanamid Company, or any other corporation holding stock investments reported by the equity method. For these investments, indicate the placement and amount of both the balance sheet and the income statement figures. What percentage of total assets do these investments constitute? Describe the information that is conveyed about these investments in the reporting company's notes to the financial statements.

3. Read "The Influence of Accounting Principles on Management Investment Decisions: An Illustration" in the June 1988 issue of *Accounting Horizons.* The authors state that "The results of this survey indicate that the equity-accounting standard does impact investment decisions by influencing the size of the investment position taken." Should accounting principles affect a company's operating and financing decisions? How can accounting principles be written that would only report a company's activities and have no impact on operating and financing decisions?

Problems

1. When an investor uses the equity method to account for investments in common stock, cash dividends received by the investor from the investee should be recorded as:
   a. A deduction from the investor's share of the investee's profits.
   b. Dividend income.

    c. A deduction from the stockholders' equity account, dividends to stock-
holders.

    d. A deduction from the investment account.

(AICPA adapted)

2. Which of the following is not an indication that an investor company has the ability to significantly influence an investee?

    a. Material intercompany transactions.

    b. The company owns 30 percent of the company but another owner holds the remaining 70 percent.

    c. Interchange of personnel.

    d. Technological dependency.

3. Sisk Company has owned 10 percent of Maust, Inc. for the past several years. This ownership did not allow Sisk to have significant influence over Maust. Recently, Sisk acquires an additional 30 percent of Maust and now does have this ability. How will this change be reported by the investor?

    a. A cumulative effect of an accounting change is shown in the current income statement.

    b. No change is recorded; the equity method is used from the date of the new acquisition.

    c. A retroactive adjustment is made to restate all prior years to the equity method.

    d. Sisk has the option of choosing the method to be used to show this change.

4. On January 1, 1995, Puckett Company paid $1.6 million for 50,000 shares of Harrison's voting common stock which represents a 40 percent investment. No allocation to goodwill or other specific account was made. Significant influence over Harrison is achieved by this acquisition. Harrison distributed a dividend of $2 per share during 1995 and reported net income of $560,000. What is the balance in the Investment in Harrison account found in the financial records of Puckett as of December 31, 1995?

    a. $1,724,000.

    b. $1,784,000.

    c. $1,844,000.

    d. $1,884,000.

5. In January 1995, Wilkinson Corporation acquired 20 percent of the outstanding common stock of Bremm, Inc., for $700,000. This investment gave Wilkinson the ability to exercise significant influence over Bremm. Bremm's assets on that date were recorded at $3,900,000 with liabilities of $900,000. Any excess of cost over book value of Wilkinson's investment was attributed to goodwill having a remaining useful life of 10 years.

    In 1995, Bremm reported net income of $170,000. In 1996, Bremm reported net income of $210,000. Dividends of $70,000 were paid in each of these two years. What is the reported balance of Wilkinson's Investment in Bremm at December 31, 1996?

a. $728,000.

b. $748,000.

c. $756,000.

d. $776,000.

6. Ace purchases 40 percent of Baskett Company on January 1, 1995, for $500,000. Although not used, this acquisition did give Ace the ability to apply significant influence to the operating and financing policies of Baskett. Baskett reports assets on that date of $1,400,000 with liabilities of $500,000. One building with a seven-year life is undervalued on Baskett's books by $140,000. Any goodwill is to be amortized over 10 years. During 1995, Baskett reports net income of $90,000 while paying dividends of $30,000. What is the Investment in Baskett balance in Ace's financial records as of December 31, 1995?

a. $504,000.

b. $507,600.

c. $513,900.

d. $516,000.

7. Simpson Company reports net income of $140,000 each year and pays an annual cash dividend of $50,000. The company holds net assets of $1,200,000 on January 1, 1995. On that date, Wallase purchases 10 percent of the outstanding stock for $150,000. Later, on January 1, 1997, Wallase buys an additional 20 percent of Simpson's stock for $300,000. This second purchase gives Wallase the ability to significantly influence Simpson. Good-will is to be amortized over its maximum life. On December 31, 1997, what is the Investment in Simpson balance in Wallase's financial records?

a. $477,200.

b. $484,550.

c. $487,900.

d. $492,150.

8. What is a downstream sale?

a. A sale from a large company to a small company.

b. A sale from an investor to its investee.

c. A sale from one manufacturer to another manufacturer.

d. A sale from a small company to a large company.

9. Panner, Inc., owns 30 percent of Watkins and applies the equity method. During the current year, Panner buys inventory costing $54,000 and then sells it to Watkins for $90,000. At the end of the year, only $20,000 merchandise is still being held by Watkins. What amount of unrealized gain must be deferred by Panner in reporting this investment on the equity method?

a. $2,400.

b. $4,800.

    c. $8,000.

    d. $10,800.

10. Camato, Inc., buys 40 percent of Swisher Company on January 1, 1995, for $530,000. The equity method of accounting is to be used. The net assets of Swisher on that date were $1.2 million. Any goodwill is to be written off over the maximum possible life. Swisher immediately begins supplying inventory to Camato as follows:

Year	Cost to Swisher	Transfer Price	Amount Held by Camato at Year End (at Transfer Price)
1995	$70,000	$100,000	$25,000
1996	96,000	150,000	45,000

Inventory held at the end of one year by Camato is sold at the beginning of the next.

    Swisher reports net income of $80,000 in 1995 and $110,000 in 1996 while paying $30,000 in dividends each year. What is the equity income in Swisher to be reported by Camato in 1996?

    a. $34,050.

    b. $39,270.

    c. $46,230.

    d. $51,450.

11. Eastwood, Inc., purchased 35 percent of Tanner Company on July 1, 1995, for $180,000. This purchase was for 60,000 shares of stock and gave Eastwood significant influence over Tanner. This investment is to be held indefinitely. Tanner earned income evenly throughout the year of $250,000. On November 10, 1995, Tanner declared and paid a $.40 per share dividend. Assuming Eastwood has a 40 percent tax rate, what is that company's current tax liability and deferred tax liability?

    a. $1,440 current and $16,060 deferred.

    b. $9,600 current and $7,900 deferred.

    c. $1,920 current and $1,580 deferred.

    d. $1,920 current and $3,950 deferred.

12. On January 3, 1995, Haskins Corporation acquired 40 percent of the outstanding common stock of Clem Company for $990,000. This acquisition gave Haskins the ability to exercise significant influence over the investee. The book value of the acquired shares was $790,000. Any excess cost over the underlying book value was assigned to a patent that was undervalued on Clem's balance sheet. This patent has a remaining useful life of 10 years. For the year ended December 31, 1995, Clem reported net income of $260,000 and paid cash dividends of $80,000. At December 31, 1995, what should Haskins report as its Investment in Clem?

13. On January 1, 1995, Alison, Inc., paid $60,000 for a 40 percent interest in Holister Corporation. This investee had assets with a book value of $200,000 and liabilities of $75,000. A patent held by Holister having a $5,000 book value was actually worth $20,000. This patent had a six-year remaining life. Any goodwill associated with this acquisition will be amortized over 20 years. During 1995, Holister earned income of $30,000 and paid dividends of $10,000 while in 1996, income was $50,000 and dividends $15,000.

    Assuming that Alison has the ability to significantly influence the operations of Holister, what balance should appear in the Investment in Holister account as of December 31, 1996?

14. On January 1, 1995, Ruark Corporation acquired a 40 percent interest in Batson, Inc. for $210,000. On that date, Batson's balance sheet disclosed net assets of $360,000. During 1995, Batson reported net income of $80,000 and paid cash dividends of $25,000. Goodwill is to be amortized over its maximum life. Ruark sold inventory costing $30,000 to Batson during 1995 for $40,000. Batson used all of this merchandise in its operations during 1995. Make all of Ruark's journal entries for 1995 to apply the equity method to this investment.

15. Waters, Inc., acquires 10 percent of Denton Corporation on January 1, 1995, for $210,000 although the book value of Denton on that date was $1,700,000. Denton held land that was undervalued on its accounting records by $100,000. During 1995, Denton earned a net income of $240,000 while paying cash dividends of $90,000. On January 1, 1996, Waters purchased an additional 30 percent of Denton for $600,000. Denton's land is still undervalued on that date but now by $120,000. The equity method will now be applied. Any goodwill is to be amortized by Waters over a 20-year period. During 1996, Denton reported income of $300,000 and distributed dividends of $110,000. Prepare all of the 1996 journal entries for Waters.

16. McKeon Inc., sold $150,000 in inventory to Schilling Company during 1995 for $225,000. Schilling resold $105,000 of this merchandise in 1995 with the remainder to be disposed of during 1996. Assuming McKeon owns 25 percent of Schilling and applies the equity method, what journal entry is recorded at the end of 1995 to defer the unrealized gain?

17. Hager holds 30 percent of the outstanding shares of Jenkins and appropriately applies the equity method of accounting. Goodwill amortization associated with this investment amounts to $9,000 per year. For 1995, Jenkins reports earnings of $80,000 and pays cash dividends of $30,000. During that year, Jenkins acquired inventory for $50,000, which was then sold to Hager for $80,000. At the end of 1995, Hager continues to hold merchandise with a transfer price of $40,000.

    a. What Equity in Investee Income should Hager report for 1995?

    b. How will the intercompany transfer affect Hager's reporting in 1996?

    c. If the inventory had been sold from Hager to Jenkins, how would the above answers have been changed?

18. On January 1, 1995, Monroe, Inc., purchased 10,000 shares of Brown Company for $250,000, giving Monroe 10 percent ownership of Brown. On January 1, 1996, Monroe purchased an additional 20,000 shares (20 percent) for $590,000. This latest purchase gave Monroe the ability to apply significant influence over Brown. Assume that no goodwill is involved in either acquisition.

    Brown reports net income and dividends as follows. These amounts are assumed to have occurred evenly throughout these years.

	Net Income	Cash Dividends
1995	$350,000	$100,000
1996	$480,000	$110,000
1997	$500,000	$120,000

    On July 1, 1997, Monroe sells 2,000 shares of this investment for $46 per share, thus, reducing its interest from 30 to 28 percent. However, the company retains the ability to significantly influence Brown. What amounts appear in Monroe's 1997 income statement?

19. On January 1, 1995, Wilder, Inc., purchased 100,000 shares of Marple Company for $320,000, giving Wilder 30 percent ownership and the ability to apply significant influence to the operating and financing decisions of Marple. Wilder anticipates holding this investment for an indefinite time. In making this acquisition, Wilder paid an amount equal to the book value for these shares. The fair market value of each asset and liability was the same as its book value. Dividends and income for Marple for 1995 were as follows:

Dividends	$.35 per share
Income	$330,000

    Assuming a 40 percent tax rate, prepare all journal entries for Wilder for 1995.

20. Slice, Inc., owns 40 percent of the outstanding shares of Wilson, an investment accounted for by the equity method. During 1995, Slice earns an operating income (not including any income accrued from its investment in Wilson) of $310,000. For this same period, Wilson reported earnings of $130,000 and paid cash dividends of $50,000. Slice has an effective tax rate of 35 percent and anticipates holding its investment in Wilson for an indefinite period.

    What income tax expense journal entry would Slice, Inc., record at the end of 1995?

    If Slice expects to sell its interest in Wilson in the near future, how does that decision change the 1995 income tax expense journal entry?

21. Collins, Inc., purchases 10 percent of Merton Corporation on January 1, 1995, for $345,000. Collins acquires an additional 15 percent of Merton on

January 1, 1996, for $580,000. The equity method of accounting has now become appropriate for this investment. No intercompany sales have occurred.

a. How does Collins initially determine the income to be reported in 1995 in connection with its ownership of Merton?

b. What factors should have influenced Collins in its decision to apply the equity method in 1996?

c. What factors might have prevented Collins from adopting the equity method after this second purchase?

d. What is the objective of the equity method of accounting?

e. What criticisms have been leveled at the equity method?

f. In comparative statements for 1995 and 1996, how would Collins determine the income to be reported in 1995 in connection with its ownership of Merton? Why is this accounting appropriate?

g. How is the allocation of Collins's payments made?

h. If Merton pays a cash dividend, what impact does it have on the financial records of Collins? Why is this accounting appropriate?

i. On financial statements for 1996, what amounts are included in Collins's Investment in Merton account? What amounts are included in Collins's Equity in Income of Merton account?

22. Parrot Corporation holds a 42 percent ownership of Sunrise, Inc. The equity method is being applied. No goodwill or other allocation occurred in the purchase of this investment. During 1995, intercompany inventory transfers were made between the two companies. A portion of this merchandise was not resold until 1996. During 1996, additional transfers were made.

a. What is the difference in upstream transfers and downstream transfers?

b. How does the direction of an intercompany transfer (upstream versus downstream) affect the application of the equity method?

c. How is the intercompany unrealized gain computed in applying the equity method?

d. How should Parrot compute the amount of equity income to be recognized in 1995? What entry is made to record this income?

e. How should Parrot compute the amount of equity income to be recognized in 1996?

f. If none of the transferred inventory had remained at the end of 1995, how would application of the equity method have been affected by these transfers?

g. How do these intercompany transfers affect the financial reporting of Sunrise?

23. Several years ago, Einstein, Inc., bought 40 percent of the outstanding voting stock of the Brooks Company. The equity method is appropriately applied. On August 1 of the current year, Einstein sold a portion of these shares.

    a. How does Einstein compute the book value of this investment on August 1 to determine its gain or loss on the sale?

    b. How should Einstein account for this investment after August 1?

    c. If Einstein retains only a 2 percent interest in Brooks so that virtually no influence is held, what figures appear in the investor's income statement for the current year?

    d. If Einstein retains only a 2 percent interest in Brooks so that virtually no influence is held, does the investor have to retroactively adjust any previously reported figures?

24. Palmer Corporation holds a 30 percent interest in Lynn, Inc. The equity method is being applied. No goodwill or other allocations were created by the original purchase.

    During 1995, Lynn reported a net income of $120,000 and paid a cash dividend of $50,000.

    a. Why do these events create a deferred income tax liability for Palmer?

    b. Will this tax ever be paid by Palmer?

    c. In what two ways can the amount of this liability be computed?

    d. If Palmer's tax rate is 28 percent and the company expects to hold this investment indefinitely, what is the year-end income tax entry?

25. Russell owns 30 percent of the outstanding stock of Thacker and has the ability to significantly influence the investee's operations and decision making. On January 1, 1995, the balance in the Investment in Thacker account is $335,000. Amortization associated with this acquisition is $9,000 per year. In 1995, Thacker earns an income of $90,000 and pays cash dividends of $30,000. Previously, in 1994, Thacker had sold inventory costing $24,000 to Russell for $40,000. All but 25 percent of this merchandise was consumed by Russell during 1994. The remainder was used during the first few weeks of 1995. Additional sales were made to Russell in 1995; inventory costing $28,000 was transferred at a price of $50,000. Of this total, 40 percent was not consumed until 1996.

Required:

    a. What amount of income would Russell recognize in 1995 from its ownership interest in Thacker?

    b. What is the balance in the Investment in Thacker account at the end of 1995?

26. Cates owns 40 percent of Zagner, an investment that is being accounted for by the equity method. Zagner follows a policy of paying dividends equal to 30 percent of its income each year. During the current year, Zagner reported earning $180,000 in net income. Cates has an effective tax rate of 38 percent.

    What journal entry would the company record at the end of the current year for income taxes relating to the investment in Zagner? Assume the investment is to be held for an indefinite time.

27. On January 1, 1995, Ace acquires 15 percent of Zip's outstanding common stock for $52,000. Zip earns a net income of $80,000 in 1995 and pays dividends totaling $30,000. On January 1, 1996, Ace buys an additional 10 percent of Zip for $45,000. This second purchase gives Ace the ability to significantly influence the decision making of Zip. During 1996, Zip earns $100,000 and pays $40,000 in dividends. Goodwill is to be amortized over a 10-year life. As of December 31, 1996, Zip reports a net book value of $390,000.

    a. On Ace's December 31, 1996, balance sheet, what balance is reported for the Investment in Zip account?

    b. What amount of equity income should Ace report for 1996?

28. Anderson acquires 10 percent of the outstanding voting shares of Barringer on January 1, 1995, for $92,000. An additional 20 percent of the stock is purchased on January 1, 1996, for $210,000, which gives Anderson the ability to significantly influence Barringer. Barringer has a book value of $800,000 at January 1, 1995, and records net income of $180,000 for the following year. Dividends of $80,000 were paid by Barringer during 1995. The book values of all Barringer's asset and liability accounts are considered as equal to fair market values. Any goodwill is to be amortized to maximize the reported profits each year.

    Barringer reports $210,000 in net income during 1996 and $230,000 in 1997. Dividends of $100,000 are paid in each of these years.

    a. On comparative income statements issued in 1997 by Anderson for 1995 and 1996, what amounts of income would be reported in connection with the company's investment in Barringer?

    b. If Anderson sells its entire investment in Barringer on January 1, 1998, for $400,000 cash, what is the impact on Anderson's income?

    c. Assume that Anderson sells inventory to Barringer during 1996 and 1997 as follows:

Year	Cost to Anderson	Price to Barringer	Year-End Balance (at Transfer Price)
1996	$35,000	$50,000	$20,000 (sold in following year)
1997	33,000	60,000	40,000 (sold in following year)

    What amount of equity income should be recognized by Anderson for the year of 1997?

29. Smith purchases 5 percent of Barker's outstanding stock on October 1, 1995, for $8,150. An additional 10 percent of Barker is acquired for $15,900 on July 1, 1996. A final 20 percent is purchased on December 31, 1997, for $36,200. With this final acquisition, Smith achieves the ability to significantly influence the decision-making process of Barker.

    Barker has a book value of $100,000 as of January 1, 1995. Information follows concerning the operations of this company for the 1995–97 period.

All income and dividends can be assumed as having occurred evenly throughout the years.

Year	Reported Income	Dividends
1995	$20,000	$ 8,000
1996	30,000	16,000
1997	24,000	9,000

On Barker's financial records, the book values of all assets and liabilities are the same as their fair market values. Any goodwill is to be amortized over a 20-year period. Amortization for a portion of a year should be based on months.

Required:

    a. On comparative income statements issued in 1998 for the years of 1995, 1996, and 1997, what would Smith report as its income derived from this investment in Barker?

    b. On a balance sheet as of December 31, 1997, what should Smith report as its Investment in Barker?

    c. What is the amount of goodwill remaining in the Investment in Barker account as of December 31, 1997?

    d. Assume Barker reports a net income in 1998 of $40,000 and pays a cash dividend of $10,000. If the corporate tax rate is 30 percent, what deferred income tax liability should Smith recognize for this year? Assume that the investment will be held for an indefinite period.

30. Hobson acquires 40 percent of the outstanding voting stock of the Stokes Company on January 1, 1995, for $210,000 in cash. The book value of Stokes's net assets on that date was $400,000, although one of the company's buildings, with a $60,000 carrying value, was actually worth $100,000. This building had a 10-year remaining life. Any goodwill is to be amortized by Hobson over a 20-year life.

Stokes sells inventory to Hobson during 1995 with an original cost of $60,000. This merchandise was sold to Hobson at a price of $90,000. Hobson still holds $15,000 (transfer price) of this amount in inventory as of December 31, 1995. These goods are to be sold to outside parties during 1996.

Stokes reports a loss of $60,000 for 1995, $40,000 from continuing operations and $20,000 from an extraordinary loss. The company still manages to pay a $10,000 cash dividend during the year.

During 1996, Stokes reports a $40,000 net income and distributes a cash dividend of $12,000. Additional inventory sales of $80,000 are made to Hobson during the period. The original cost of the merchandise was $50,000. All but 30 percent of this inventory has been resold to outside parties by the end of the 1996 fiscal year.

Prepare all journal entries for Hobson for 1995 and 1996 in connection with this investment. Assume that the equity method is applied. Ignore income tax effects.

31. Penston Company owns 40 percent (40,000 shares) of Scranton, Inc., which was purchased several years ago for $182,000. Since the date of acquisition, the equity method has been properly applied and the book value of the investment account as of January 1, 1995, is $248,000. Goodwill amortization of $12,000 is still being recognized each year. During 1995, Scranton reports net income of $200,000, $320,000 in operating income earned evenly throughout the year, and a $120,000 extraordinary loss incurred on October 1. No dividends were paid during the year. Penston sells 8,000 shares of Scranton on August 1, 1995, for $94,000 in cash. However, Penston does retain the ability to significantly influence the investee.

    During the last quarter of 1994, Penston sold $50,000 in inventory (which had originally cost Penston only $30,000) to Scranton. At the end of that fiscal year, Scranton's inventory retained $9,000 (at sales price) of this merchandise, which was subsequently sold in the first quarter of 1995.

    On Penston's financial statements for the year ended December 31, 1995, what income effects would be reported from its ownership in Scranton? Ignore income taxes.

32. On July 1, 1995, the Abernethy Company acquires 30,000 of the outstanding shares of the Chapman Company for $24 per share. This acquisition gave Abernethy a 25 percent ownership of Chapman and allowed Abernethy to significantly influence the decisions of the investee.

    As of July 1, 1995, the investee had assets with a book value of $2 million and liabilities of $400,000. At the time, Chapman held equipment appraised at $120,000 above book value. Company land was valued at $160,000 above book value. The equipment was considered to have an eight-year life with no salvage value. Goodwill is being amortized over 10 years. Depreciation and amortization are computed using the straight-line method.

    Chapman follows a policy of paying 50 cents per share as a cash dividend every April 1 and October 1. Chapman's income, earned evenly throughout each year, was 1995—$280,000; 1996—$360,000; and 1997—$380,000.

    In addition, Abernethy sold inventory costing $90,000 to Chapman for $150,000 during 1996. Chapman resold $90,000 of this inventory during 1996 and the remaining $60,000 during 1997.

Required:

  a. Prepare a schedule computing the equity income to be recognized by Abernethy during each of these years.

  b. Compute Abernethy's investment balance as of December 31, 1997.

    c. Assume that Abernethy has an effective tax rate of 32 percent and the investment would be held indefinitely. Prepare Abernethy's income tax journal entry for 1995.

33. On January 1, 1995, Plano Company acquired 8 percent (16,000 shares) of the outstanding voting shares of the Sumter Company for $192,000, an amount equal to the underlying book value of Sumter. Sumter pays a cash dividend to its stockholders each year of $100,000 on September 15. Sumter reports net income of $300,000 in 1995, $360,000 in 1996, $400,000 in 1997, and $380,000 in 1998. Each income figure can be assumed to have been earned evenly throughout its respective year. In addition, the market value of these 16,000 shares has remained more than $192,000 throughout 1995 and 1996.

    On January 1, 1997, Plano purchased an additional 32 percent (64,000 shares) of Sumter for $1,050,000 in cash. This price represented a $134,800 payment in excess of the book value of Sumter's underlying net assets. Plano was willing to make this extra payment to establish better ties with Sumter. All assets were considered appropriately valued on Sumter's books. Any goodwill established by this acquisition was considered permanent.

    On July 1, 1998, Plano sold 10 percent (20,000 shares) of the outstanding shares of Sumter for $425,000 in cash. Although this interest was sold, Plano maintained the ability to significantly influence the decision-making process of Sumter. Assume that a weighted average costing system is used by Plano.

Required:

    a. Prepare the journal entries for Plano for the years of 1995 through 1998. Ignore income taxes.

    b. Assuming an effective tax rate of 36 percent, compute the balance in the deferred income taxes payable account as of December 31, 1997.

34. On January 1, 1995, Lake Company acquired 40 percent of the outstanding voting shares of Slide Company for $600,000. On that date, Slide reports assets and liabilities with book values of $1.8 million and $600,000, respectively. A building owned by Slide had an appraised value of $250,000, although it had a book value of only $100,000. This building had a 12-year remaining life and no salvage value. It was being depreciated on the straight-line method. Any goodwill established by the acquisition of Slide is considered to have a 20-year life.

    Slide generated net income of $250,000 in 1995 and a loss of $100,000 in 1996. In each of these two years, Slide paid a cash dividend of $60,000 to its stockholders.

    During 1995, Slide sold inventory to Lake that had an original cost of $50,000. The merchandise was sold to Lake for $80,000. Of this balance,

$60,000 was resold to outsiders during 1995 and the remainder was sold during 1996. In 1996, Slide sold inventory to Lake for $150,000. This inventory had cost only $90,000. Lake resold $100,000 of the inventory during 1996 and the rest during 1997.

Required:

For 1995 and then for 1996, compute the equity income to be reported by Lake for external reporting purposes.

CONSOLIDATION OF FINANCIAL INFORMATION

Questions to Consider

- When one company gains control over another company, how should the relationship between the two parties be presented for external reporting purposes?
- When the relationship between two companies is being assessed, how should control be determined?
- The assets and liabilities of some subsidiary organizations are added directly to the records of the parent company. In other cases, the parent chooses to let the new subsidiary remain in operation as a separate legal entity. How is the accounting process affected by this decision?
- A business combination can be accounted for as either a purchase or a pooling of interests. Why are two methods available? When should each be used? How do they differ? What balances are reported at the date of acquisition for each method? What arguments are made against the pooling of interests method?
- Investment bankers and other financial advisors are paid millions of dollars for assisting one company in acquiring another. What accounting is made of these costs?
- Prior to 1987, many companies chose not to consolidate their finance subsidiaries. Why were these operations omitted from the consolidation process? Why has this practice been changed?

Financial statements, published and distributed to owners, creditors, and other interested parties, appear to report the operations and financial position of a single company. In reality, these statements frequently represent a number of separate organizations tied together through common control (a *business combination*). As an example, the financial statements published for the Unisys Corporation consist of information from more than 175 legally separate but related corporations.[1] Unisys's balance sheet, statement of earnings, and statement of cash flows report financial information gathered from this multitude of companies as if only a single enterprise existed. Whenever financial statements represent more than one corporation, they are said to be *consolidated*.

Consolidated financial statements are hardly unusual in today's business world. Most major organizations, and many smaller ones, hold control over an array of organizations. PepsiCo, Inc., as another example, annually consolidates data from more than 200 companies into a single set of financial statements. By gaining control over these companies (often known as *subsidiaries*), which include Pizza Hut, Kentucky Fried Chicken, Taco Bell, and Frito-Lay, a single business combination has been formed by PepsiCo (the *parent*) that should be viewed as a single reporting entity.

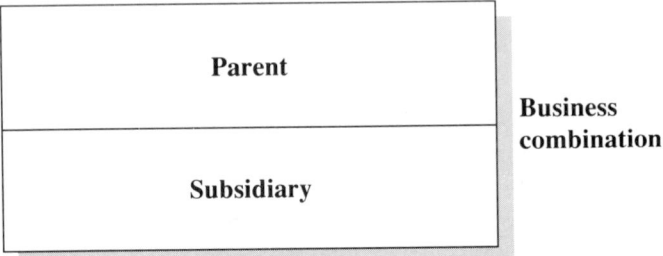

The consolidation of financial information as exemplified by Unisys and PepsiCo is one of the most complex procedures in all of accounting. To comprehend this process completely, the theoretical logic that underlies the creation of a business combination must be understood. Furthermore, a variety of mechanical steps have to be mastered to ensure that proper accounting is achieved for this single reporting entity. The following coverage is designed to introduce both of these aspects of the consolidation process.

Expansion through Corporate Takeovers

Every day, I buy companies for $100 million, $150 million, $200 million. Now, that's real gambling. Las Vegas doesn't entice me.[2]

Victor Posner

---

[1] *Moody's Industrial Manual* (New York: 1991).

[2] Michael Allen, "Victor Posner Battles a Variety of Financial and Legal Difficulties," *The Wall Street Journal*, July 14, 1987, p. 1.

EXHIBIT 2-1	Ten Largest Takeovers in History as of December 31, 1991, Involving U.S. Companies*		
Acquiring Company	Acquired Company	Cost (in billions)	Year
Kohlberg Kravis	RJR Nabisco	$30.6	1989
Time	Warner Communications	14.1	1990
Philip Morris	Kraft	13.4	1988
Chevron	Gulf Oil	13.3	1984
Bristol-Myers	Squibb	12.1	1989
Texaco	Getty Oil	10.1	1984
Du Pont	Conoco	8.0	1981
Beecham Group	SmithKline Beckman	7.9	1989
AT&T	NCR	7.9	1991
British Petroleum	Standard Oil	7.8	1987

* Compiled from "Mergers Boom Became a Bust, Experts Say," *The Wall Street Journal,* January 2, 1990, p. R–1; "Wall Street Dismantles Much of Its M&A Machinery," *The Wall Street Journal,* January 2, 1991, p. R–4; and "Merger Activity Fell for Third Year in a Row," *The Wall Street Journal,* January 2, 1992, p. R–4.

During recent years, the United States and the rest of the world have seen an enormous number of corporate takeovers, transactions in which one company gains control over another. As indicated by Exhibit 2–1, 9 of the 10 biggest combinations involving U.S. companies have occurred since 1984. Many varied reasons exist for a takeover. The parent company might believe that it has the expertise to earn a higher rate of return on the subsidiary's assets than the previous management achieved. Or, the parent may believe that a larger organization will be more cost efficient. The elimination of duplicate costs such as data processing and marketing can make a single entity more profitable than the separate parent and subsidiary had been in the past. Recent bank mergers have often been based on this efficiency assumption.

In many of the mergers of the 1980s, the investors believed that the market price of a specific company was significantly below the actual fair value of the underlying net assets. With that assessment, attempting to gain control becomes especially enticing. The potential risk of loss is reduced if portions of the subsidiary's assets can be sold to cover a major part of the acquisition cost. At one time, corporations in the oil industry proved to be particularly vulnerable to this strategy.

Takeovers also result because many businesses seek the continuous expansion of their organizations, especially into diversified areas. Acquiring control over a vast network of different businesses has been a strategy utilized by a number of companies (sometimes known as *conglomerates*) for decades. Entry into new industries is immediately available to the parent without having to construct facilities, develop products, train management, or create market recognition. Many corporations have successfully utilized this strategy to produce huge, highly profitable organizations. Unfortunately, others have discovered that the task of managing a widely diverse group of businesses can prove to be a costly learning experience.

Mergers and acquisitions have become so prevalent in recent years that an entire vocabulary has developed to describe the various parties, transactions, and strategies.

Horizontal Integration.   The growth of an organization through the acquisition of competitors. Chrysler's 1987 takeover of American Motors was an example of horizontal integration as was Chemical Bank's acquisition of Manufacturers Hanover.

Vertical Integration.   The acquisition by a company of either a supplier or customer. In vertical integration, the takeover is made in hopes of creating a more cost efficient organization. Du Pont's 1981 acquisition of Conoco was carried out, in part, so that Du Pont could have a ready supplier of oil for the various products that the company manufactures.

Target Company.   A business organization that is the object of a takeover attempt.

Tender Offer.   A legal proposal made to a target company's stockholders seeking to acquire all or a percentage of the outstanding shares. Tender offers may contain a provision whereby the transaction is rescinded unless a specified number of shares are obtained. Thus, if the potential owner is unable to gain control, the entire proposal can be revoked.

Leveraged Buyout.   A takeover financed almost entirely by borrowed money often derived from the selling of bonds. The rash of mergers in the 1980s was only possible because of the ability of investors to raise enormous sums of money through the creation of debt. Unfortunately, in some cases servicing this debt proved to be impossible, leading eventually to numerous bankruptcies.

Leveraged buyouts are usually the work of a small group of investors, often including the management of the target company. The buyers sometimes anticipate holding the company for a relatively short period followed by a public issuance of new stock that could lead to a huge profit.

Hostile Takeover Attempt.   A threatened or actual tender offer made by a company, group, or individual that is viewed as unfavorable by the target company's current management. This negative reaction sometimes results because the proposed price is considered to be too low. Frequently, though, the resistance is created because the employees fear the termination of their jobs following the takeover. Thus, an entrenched management may be acting primarily to protect its own self-interest, rather than serving the stockholders when takeover attempts are spurned.

Raider. A company, group, or individual attempting the hostile takeover of a business. Some raiders, such as Victor Posner (quoted earlier), have become well-known figures in the modern business world while accumulating vast amounts of wealth. Unfortunately, some of these individuals used inside information or other illegal actions in the process.

White Knight. A potential buyer that seeks to acquire a target company at the request of that organization's management. Often, the white knight's bid is sought after a raider has initiated a takeover attempt. Management may hope to extract a higher price from the white knight or improve the chances of retaining its own employment. Revlon, Inc., for example, unsuccessfully attempted to use Forstmann Little & Company as a white knight in 1985 after Pantry Pride Inc. made a hostile offer.

Recapitalization Plan. A change by a target company, usually in its debt-equity position, that makes the business unappealing to a raider. As an illustration, after a hostile tender offer was put forth for the stock of Harcourt Brace Jovanovich, Inc., the board of directors increased total debt from $837 million to $2.9 billion followed by a dividend to stockholders of more than $40 per share. The resulting debt-laden company immediately became a much less enticing acquisition. Unfortunately, the company was not able to service this enormous debt and eventually had to allow itself to be acquired by General Cinema to avoid bankruptcy.

The Consolidation Process

The consolidation of financial information into a single set of statements becomes necessary whenever a single economic entity is created by the business combination of two or more companies. As stated in *Accounting Research Bulletin No. 51* (abbreviated *ARB 51*), "Consolidated Financial Statements," August 1959 (par. 2): "There is a presumption that consolidated statements are more meaningful than separate statements and that they are usually necessary for a fair presentation when one of the companies in the group directly or indirectly has a controlling financial interest in the other companies."

This sentiment was reiterated nearly 30 years later in *Financial Accounting Standards Board Statement No. 94,* "Consolidation of All Majority-Owned Subsidiaries," October 1987 (par. 30): "Consolidated financial statements became common once it was recognized that boundaries between separate corporate entities must be ignored to report the business carried on by a group of affiliated corporations as the economic and financial whole that it actually is."

Thus, in producing financial statements for external distribution, the reporting entity transcends the boundaries of incorporation to encompass all companies where control is present. Even though the various companies may retain their legal identities as separate corporations, the resulting information is more meaningful to outside parties when consolidated into a single set of financial statements.

To understand the process of preparing consolidated financial statements for a business combination, three questions should be addressed:

- How is a business combination formed?
- What constitutes a controlling financial interest?
- How is the consolidation process carried out?

Business Combinations—Creating a Single Economic Entity

A business combination refers to any set of conditions in which two or more organizations are joined together through common control. *APB Statement 4* (chap. 5, par. 3) describes the entity that results from a business combination:

> Accounting information pertains to entities, which are circumscribed areas of interest. In financial accounting the entity is the specific business enterprise. The enterprise is identified in its financial statements. . . . The boundaries of the accounting entity may not be the same as those of the legal entity, for example, a parent corporation and its subsidiaries treated as a single business enterprise.

To illustrate, assume that Acme Company obtains a majority of the voting stock of Zero, Inc. Through this transaction, Acme achieves the ability to control both parties; all assets and liabilities are under its authority. For financial reporting purposes, these two companies now comprise a single economic unit. The companies are so closely connected that they should be viewed as one enterprise rather than two. Consequently, consolidation of their individual financial statements is appropriate.

Business combinations are formed by a wide variety of transactions with a number of different formats. For example, each of the following is identified as a business combination although differing widely in legal form. In every case, two or more enterprises are being united into a single economic entity so that consolidated financial statements are required.

1. One company obtains the assets, and possibly liabilities, of another company in exchange for cash, other assets, liabilities, stock, or a combination of these. The second organization normally ceases operations and dissolves itself as a legal corporation. Thus, only the acquiring company remains in existence, having absorbed the acquired net assets directly into its own operations. Any business combination in which only one of the original companies continues to exist is referred to in legal terms as a *statutory merger*.

2. One company obtains the capital stock of another in exchange for cash, other assets, liabilities, stock, or a combination of these. After gaining control, the acquiring company may decide to transfer all assets and liabilities to its own financial records with the second company being dissolved as a separate corporation.[3] The business combination is, once again, a statutory merger because

---

[3] Although the acquired company has been legally dissolved, it frequently continues to operate as a separate division within the surviving company's organization.

only one of the companies maintains legal existence. This statutory merger, however, is achieved by obtaining equity securities rather than by buying the target company's assets. Because stock is purchased, the acquiring company must gain 100 percent control of all shares before legally dissolving the subsidiary.

3. Two or more companies transfer either their assets or their capital stock to a newly formed corporation. The original companies are both dissolved, leaving only the new organization remaining in existence. A business combination effected in this manner is a *statutory consolidation.* The use here of the term *consolidation* should not be confused with the accounting meaning of that same word. In accounting, consolidation refers to the mechanical process of bringing together the financial records of two or more organizations to form a single set of statements. A statutory consolidation denotes a specific type of business combination in which two or more existing companies are united under the ownership of a newly created company.

The business combination of NCNB Corporation and C&S/Sovran Corporation illustrates the formation of a statutory consolidation. In 1991, the stockholders of these two organizations created a single entity by transferring their ownership interests to a newly established corporation known as Nations-Bank Corporation. Because only this new company remained in existence as a legal entity, the business combination had been formed through a statutory consolidation.

4. One company achieves legal control over another by the acquisition of a majority of voting stock. *Although control is present, no dissolution takes place; each company remains in existence as an incorporated operation.* The Miller Brewing Company, as an example, continued to retain its legal status as a corporation after being acquired by Philip Morris. Separate incorporation is frequently preferred in order to take full advantage of any intangible benefits accruing to the acquired company as a going concern. Better utilization of such factors as trade names, employee loyalty, and the company's reputation may be possible where the subsidiary maintains its own legal identity.

One important aspect of this final type of business combination should be noted. Because the asset and liability account balances are not physically combined as in statutory mergers and consolidations, each company continues to maintain an independent accounting system. To reflect the creation of the combination, the acquiring company enters the financial impact of the takeover transaction into its own records by establishing a single investment asset account. However, the newly acquired subsidiary omits any recording of this event; the stock being obtained by the parent comes from the subsidiary's shareholders. Thus, the financial records of the subsidiary are not directly affected by a takeover.

As can be seen, business combinations are created in many distinct forms. Since the specific format is a critical factor in the subsequent consolidation of financial information, Exhibit 2–2 provides an overview of the various combinations.

EXHIBIT 2–2   **Business Combinations**

Type of Combination	Action of Acquiring Company	Action of Acquired Company
Statutory merger through asset acquisition	Acquires assets and often liabilities	Dissolves and goes out of business
Statutory merger through capital stock acquisition	Acquires all stock and then transfers assets and liabilities to its own books	Dissolves as a separate corporation, often remaining as a division of the acquiring company
Statutory consolidation through capital stock or asset acquisition	Newly created to receive assets or capital stock of original companies	Original companies may dissolve while remaining as separate divisions of newly created company
Acquisition of more than 50 percent of the voting stock	Acquires stock that is recorded as an investment; controls decision making of acquired company	Remains in existence as legal corporation, although now a subsidiary of the acquiring company

Control—An Elusive Quality

ARB 51, as quoted previously, states that consolidated financial statements are usually necessary when one company has a controlling financial interest over another. However, nowhere in the official accounting pronouncements is a "controlling financial interest" actually defined. Traditionally, in the United States, control is considered to exist if one company holds more than 50 percent of another company's voting stock. Thus, control has been tied directly to ownership. However, in the decades since *ARB 51* was issued, the complexity of business combinations has grown significantly so that control is not always that easy to define.

The FASB has a comprehensive study underway of consolidation issues including the question of control. Chances seem likely that consolidation will eventually be required for less-than-majority-owned subsidiaries if the parent has rights, risks, and benefits equivalent to those that result from majority ownership.

The types of situations that led the FASB to study the issue of control include the following cases. In none of these instances is a majority of the voting stock held. Thus, historically in the United States, consolidation would probably not occur.[4] However, one company certainly does have the potential to exercise a degree of authority over the other. In looking at such cases, two interrelated questions must be addressed: Does one company actually have a controlling

---

[4] In contrast, Australia, Canada, New Zealand, the United Kingdom, and the European Community have all issued new standards over the past five years specifying control rather than ownership as the basis for consolidation. See "The Debate Over Consolidating Statements," *Financial Executive*, March/April 1992.

financial interest over the other? Has a business combination been created that necessitates the production of consolidated financial statements?

- Company A owns 48 percent of Company B. At the stockholders' meeting each year, only about 90 percent of the outstanding shares are voted so that Company A always casts a majority of the shares on every ballot.

- Company C owns 40 percent of Company D. Ms. Z is president of Company D and owns 11 percent of its stock. Ms. Z is a former vice president and friend of Company C and has always voted her shares in the same manner as Company C.

- Company E owns none of Company F. However, Company E holds convertible bonds issued by Company F. Company E has the option at any time to convert these bonds into 51 percent of the outstanding voting shares of Company F.

- As described in Chapter 1, The Coca-Cola Company holds 49 percent of Coca-Cola Enterprises. Furthermore, the investee is heavily dependent on the investor for products and marketing.

In studying these issues, the Board has described what is meant by control:

A parent company's ability to establish a subsidiary's operating and financing policies encompasses the ability to decide how the subsidiary's resources are obtained, used, and financed—the same decisions the parent makes for its own, directly held, resources. . . . control normally entails the ability to elect or remove a majority of a subsidiary's board of directors, to determine the composition of the board, or otherwise control a majority of the votes cast at a meeting of the board of directors. . . . control normally includes the ability of the controlling party to obtain stockholder approval of those decisions requiring that approval.[5]

Consolidation of Financial Information

Whenever one company gains control over another, a business combination is established. Financial data gathered from the individual companies must then be brought together to form a single set of consolidated statements. Although the steps in this process can be numerous, the objectives of a consolidation are rather limited. The asset, liability, equity, revenue, and expense accounts of the companies are simply combined. As a part of this process, reciprocal accounts and intercompany transactions must be adjusted or eliminated to ensure that all reported balances truly represent the single entity.

Applicable consolidation procedures vary significantly depending on the legal format employed in creating a business combination. *For a statutory merger or a statutory consolidation, where the acquired company (or companies) is legally dissolved, only one accounting consolidation ever occurs.* On the date of the

---

[5] FASB, "Discussion Memorandum—An Analysis of Issues Related to Consolidation Policy and Procedures," September 10, 1991, paragraphs 144–46.

combination, the surviving company simply records the various account balances from each of the dissolving companies. Because all accounts are permanently brought together in this manner, no further consolidation procedures are required. After all of the balances have been transferred to the survivor, the financial records of the acquired companies are closed out as part of the dissolution.

Conversely, in a combination where all companies retain incorporation, a different set of consolidation procedures is appropriate. Because the companies preserve their legal identities, each continues to maintain its own independent accounting records. *Thus, no permanent consolidation of the account balances is ever made. Rather, the consolidation process must be carried out anew each time that the reporting entity prepares financial statements for external reporting purposes.*

Where separate record-keeping is maintained, the accountant faces a unique problem: the financial information must be brought together periodically without disturbing the accounting systems of the individual companies. Since these consolidations are not produced within the financial records, worksheets have traditionally been used to expedite the process. Worksheets are not part of either companies' accounting records or of the resulting financial statements. Instead, they are an efficient structure for organizing and adjusting the information used in the preparation of consolidated statements.

Consequently, the legal characteristics of a business combination have a significant impact on the approach that is taken to the consolidation process:

What is to be consolidated:

- If dissolution takes place, all account balances are physically consolidated in the financial records of the surviving company.
- If separate incorporation is maintained, only the financial statement information is consolidated and not the actual records.

When does the consolidation take place?

- If dissolution takes place, a permanent consolidation occurs at the date of the combination.
- If separate incorporation is maintained, the consolidation process is carried out at regular intervals whenever financial statements are to be prepared.

How are the accounting records affected?

- If dissolution takes place, the surviving company's accounts are adjusted to include all balances of the dissolved company. The dissolved company's records are closed out.
- If separate incorporation is maintained, each company continues to retain its own records. Using worksheets facilitates the periodic consolidation process without disturbing the individual accounting systems.

Purchase versus Pooling of Interests

Although the choice made between separate incorporation and dissolution has a mechanical effect on the consolidation process, an additional, but even more significant, distinction must be made for accounting purposes. According to *Opinion 16,* "Business Combinations" (par. 42), the APB concluded that "some business combinations should be accounted for by the purchase method and other combinations should be accounted for by the pooling of interests method." Purchases and poolings of interest are the two accounting methods used to record business combinations. The APB's decision to permit both methods is important since widely differing reported balances result.

Not surprisingly, an understanding of both the purchase method and the pooling of interests method is essential in achieving a basic knowledge of the consolidation process. Several aspects of their application must be understood at the beginning of this discussion.

First, purchases and poolings of interests involve contrasting perspectives of the very nature of a business combination.

Second, differences are created in every area of the resulting consolidated financial statements (assets, liabilities, revenues, expenses, and equities), depending on the method in use.

Third, purchases and poolings of interests are not alternatives; each is applied to a specific type of business combination.

The Need for Two Different Consolidation Methods

Two separate accounting approaches to the consolidation process have evolved over the years because business combinations can differ so significantly. The type of exchange that establishes a combination varies from case to case as does the subsequent organization of the combined companies. Hence, during this century, the term *business combination* has come to encompass an extremely wide range of transactions. In *Opinion 16,* the APB reasoned that one consolidation method alone could not properly account for all possible combinations. Thus, both the purchase method and the pooling of interests method were designated as appropriate means of reporting business combinations.

In drawing a distinction between these two approaches, paragraph 11 of *Opinion 16* states that "the purchase method accounts for a business combination as *the acquisition of one company by another,*" (emphasis added) whereas paragraph 12 asserts that "the pooling of interests method accounts for a business combination as *the uniting of the ownership interests of two or more companies* by exchange of equity securities. No acquisition is recognized because the combination is accomplished without disbursing resources of the constituents." (emphasis added)

Because purchases and poolings of interests are designed to account for theoretically different types of combinations, the Board went on to specify that "the two methods are not alternatives in accounting for the same business combination'' (par. 43). In effect, this pronouncement has divided all business combinations into two distinct classifications. Specific consolidation procedures can then be applied to reflect more closely the essence of a particular combination. Consequently, knowledge of both methods should be based on an understanding of the nature of the business combination that each describes. After the identifying characteristics of these two approaches have been delineated, the mechanical procedures used to carry out a particular consolidation should be easier to comprehend.

The Purchase Method.   The purchase method assumes that one company buys the assets or equity securities of another company through a bargained exchange. This transaction establishes an acquisition price that is then used in the application of historical cost principles.

Thus, major characteristics associated with a purchase combination are (1) an acquiring company and (2) a cost figure derived from an exchange transaction. As shown in Exhibit 2–3, for example, Philip Morris paid $5.8 billion to obtain General Foods. This business combination was accounted for as a purchase since Philip Morris was clearly the acquiring company at this established price. Because the purchase method is based on recording the investment in the same manner as any other acquisition, it has always been considered an acceptable accounting treatment for producing consolidated statements. *The acquired assets and liabilities are recorded at their market values because they are being purchased. Only revenues and expenses generated by these assets and liabilities after the date of the takeover are attributed to the business combination.*

The Pooling of Interests Method.   As far back as the 1920s but especially during the 1940s, an awareness began to develop among accountants that some business combinations possessed characteristics markedly different from those identified

---

EXHIBIT 2–3   Business Combination—Purchase

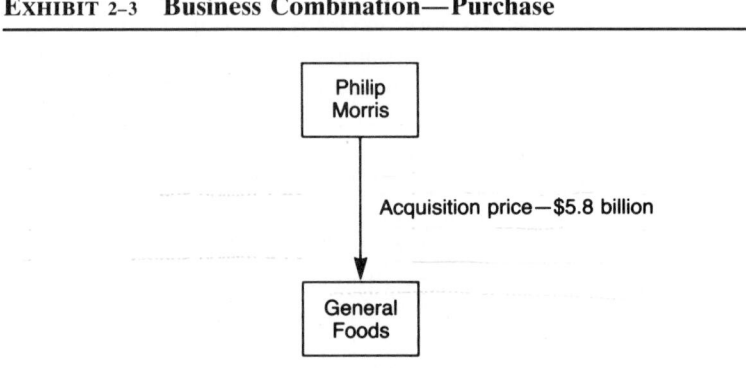

with the purchase method. These differences were most evident in combinations in which two companies of comparable size were united solely through an exchange of equity securities. In such cases, the distinction between acquiring company and acquired company was not always clear. The resulting combinations resembled brother-sister affiliations rather than the parent-subsidiary configurations associated with the purchase method. Furthermore, a precise acquisition price often proved difficult to determine since the combinations were created through the exchange of securities. As stated in *APB Opinion 16* (par. 23):

> The fair value of stock issued is not always objectively determinable. A market price may not be available for a newly issued security or for securities of a closely held corporation. Even an available quoted market price may not always be a reliable indicator of fair value of consideration received because the number of shares issued is relatively large, the market for the security is thin, the stock price is volatile, or other uncertainties influence the quoted price.

The assertion was also made that no bargained transaction actually transpired *between the companies* when securities alone were exchanged. According to *Opinion 16* (par. 16), "an exchange of stock to effect a business combination is in substance a transaction between the combining stockholder groups and does not involve the corporate entities."

Since the basic characteristics of a purchase consolidation did not always appear in every business combination, the idea soon spread that two distinct types of combinations existed. Gradually, alternative consolidation procedures began to emerge based on pooling of interests concepts. Over the decades, this method has been applied to a significant number of business combinations.

For example, the Goodyear Tire & Rubber Company exchanged nearly 25 million shares of its common stock for all of the outstanding common stock of Celeron Corporation to create a combination accounted for as a pooling of interests. As noted in Exhibit 2–4, Goodyear actually issued its stock in exchange for the shares held by the owners of Celeron. Consequently, the combined assets of these two companies were controlled by both the Goodyear shareholders and the previous Celeron owners (who now held Goodyear stock). Regardless of the

---

EXHIBIT 2-4 **Business Combination—Pooling of Interests***

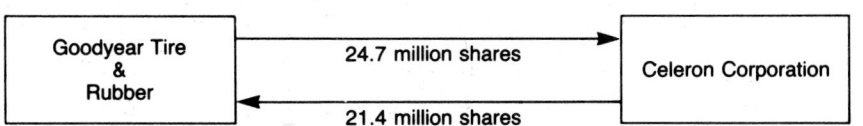

* This diagram is intended merely to represent the relationship created by a pooling of interests. The shares delivered by Celeron actually came from its owners who in turn received the 24.7 million shares of Goodyear Tire & Rubber directly from the company.

number of shares exchanged, this same joint control is always found in a pooling of interests.

Hence, a pooling of interests is characterized as a continuation of ownership where neither a parent nor subsidiary can be easily identified. The combination is created by an exchange of voting stock that is not viewed as a bargained transaction with a precise acquisition price. To reflect these qualities, two important steps are taken in accounting for a consolidation created as a pooling of interests:

1. The book values of the assets and liabilities of both companies become the book values reported by the combination.
2. The revenue and expense accounts are combined retroactively as well as prospectively.

As is discussed later in this chapter, the pooling of interests method is quite controversial because (1) the subsidiary's book values are retained and (2) application can have a positive effect on net income reported by the combination (immediately as well as in the future). The impact on earnings caused this method to become extremely popular during the 1960s, so popular that many groups called for its abolishment. However, the APB decided in 1970 in *Opinion 16* that both the pooling of interests method as well as the purchase method would be acceptable accounting procedures for business combinations.

To prevent wide-scale abuse of the pooling method, the Board did place tight restrictions on its usage by establishing 12 criteria as prerequisites for application. According to *Opinion 16*, each of these 12 criteria has to be present in a business combination to justify adoption of the pooling method. By setting strict guidelines, the Board hoped to ensure that only combinations clearly outside the essence of a purchase would fall under the pooling of interests classification. *Business combinations that fail to meet even 1 of these 12 criteria must be accounted for by the purchase method.*

These criteria, which are presented in the appendix at the end of this chapter, have two overriding objectives: First, they define a pooling of interests as a single transaction (or series of transactions occurring over a limited period of time) in which two independent companies are united solely through the exchange of voting common stock. To ensure the complete fusion of the two organizations, one company has to obtain substantially all (90 percent or more) of the voting stock of the other.

The second general objective of these criteria is to prevent purchase combinations from being disguised as poolings. Past experience had shown the APB that combination transactions were frequently manipulated so that they would qualify for pooling of interests treatment (usually to increase reported earnings). However, subsequent events, often involving cash being paid or received by the parties, revealed the true nature of the combination: one company was purchasing the other in a bargained exchange. A number of the APB's 12 criteria were designed to stop the possibility of this practice.

For example, to be considered a pooling of interests, no agreement can exist to reacquire any of the shares issued in creating the combination. This rule prevents the parties from eventually receiving cash or other assets as part of the transaction. For the same reason, significant assets of the combined companies cannot be sold for two years unless duplication exists. These restrictions help to ensure that only combinations meeting the essence of a pooling are given that treatment: a continuation of the companies and a continuation of the ownership.

The APB chose not to establish any guideline as to the relative size of the companies. Historically, comparable size had always been a theoretical requirement for a pooling of interests. In creating *Opinion 16,* the Board declined to set an arbitrary boundary for applying the pooling method, although relationships such as nine to one and three to one were discussed during the deliberations.

Discussion Question: Are Purchases and Poolings of Interests Truly Different?

James Atkinson is the sole owner of Acme Taxicab Company, a small organization with 15 vehicles. He wants to expand his operation and approaches Roy Wilbury, owner of Wilbury's Cabs. Wilbury's company operates eight taxicabs in the same city as Acme Taxicab Company.

Scenario One. Atkinson suggests to Wilbury that the two companies join together for their mutual benefit. "We can save money on advertisement, maintenance, and other overhead costs. Instead of two small companies, we will be co-owners of a larger organization operating 23 taxicabs throughout the city. The resulting enterprise will simply be more profitable. I currently own all 1,000 shares of my company's common stock. I will issue another 600 shares to you in exchange for all of the outstanding shares of Wilbury's Cabs."

Scenario Two. Atkinson offers to buy Wilbury's Cabs to expand the Acme Taxicab Company. "I will pay you a fair value in cash for your entire company. I'll buy your assets or buy your stock. You could retire or you can even work for me but I want to have 23 taxicabs operating throughout the city."

What characteristics of a pooling of interests are seen in the first scenario? What characteristics of a purchase are found in the second? In both cases, the two companies would ultimately form a single economic entity with 23 vehicles. Are these transactions sufficiently different to warrant the application of two distinct accounting methods producing widely varying financial results?

Procedures for Consolidating Financial Information

Legal as well as accounting distinctions divide business combinations into at least four separate categories. To facilitate the introduction of consolidation accounting, the various procedures utilized in this process are introduced according to the following sequence:

1. Purchase method where dissolution takes place.
2. Purchase method where separate incorporation is maintained.
3. Pooling of interests method where dissolution takes place.
4. Pooling of interests method where separate incorporation is maintained.

As a basis for this coverage, assume that Small Company owns one hotel and the land surrounding it. Although the hotel and its furniture have a book value of $400,000, they are worth $600,000. The land is on Small's books at its original cost of $300,000 although currently valued at $400,000. Small also has a mortgage note payable of $200,000 on this property. Because interest rates are currently low, this liability (incurred at a higher rate of interest) has a present value of $250,000.

Giant Company owns two hotels in the same geographic region as Small Company. Giant wants to expand its operations and hopes to acquire Small Company on December 31, 1995. The accounts reported by both Giant and Small on that date are listed in Exhibit 2–5. In addition, the estimated fair market value of Small's assets and liabilities is included.

EXHIBIT 2–5   Basic Consolidation Information

	Giant Company	Small Company	
	Book Value 12/31/95	*Book Value 12/31/95*	*Fair Market Value 12/31/95*
Current Assets	$ 400,000	$ 300,000	$ 300,000
Land	500,000	300,000	400,000
Buildings and furniture (net)	1,000,000	400,000	600,000
Mortgage note payable	(300,000)	(200,000)	(250,000)
Net assets	$1,600,000	$ 800,000	$1,050,000
Common stock—$10 par value	$ 600,000		
Common stock—$5 par value . . .		$ 200,000	
Additional paid-in capital	40,000	20,000	
Retained earnings, 1/1/95	870,000	470,000	
Dividends paid	110,000	10,000	
Revenues	1,000,000	500,000	
Expenses	800,000	380,000	
Retained earnings, 12/31/95	960,000*	580,000*	

* Retained earnings balance after closing out revenues, expenses, and dividends paid.

Small's net assets have a book value of $800,000 but a fair market value of $1,050,000. Only the assets and liabilities have been appraised here; the capital stock, retained earnings, dividend, revenue, and expense accounts represent historical measurements rather than any type of future values. Although these equity and income accounts may give some indication of the overall worth of the organization, none of these figures represents an item that is actually transferrable by the company.

Purchase Method Where Dissolution Takes Place

Since purchase prices can vary significantly from combination to combination, the consolidation procedures in this initial section are demonstrated using four examples, each with a different price.

Purchase Price Equals Fair Market Value.   Assume that, after negotiations with the owners of Small, Giant agrees to pay them $1,050,000 for all of Small's assets and liabilities: cash of $250,000 and 20,000 unissued shares of its $10 par value common stock that is currently selling for $40 per share. Small will then dissolve itself as a legal entity.

As with any acquisition, the price established here is based on the value of the consideration rendered:

Cash	$250,000
Common stock issued (20,000 shares at a $40 per share	
fair market value).	800,000
Purchase price	$1,050,000

Hence, Giant's cost is exactly equal to the $1,050,000 fair market value of the assets and liabilities being procured.

The purchase method is appropriate for consolidating the financial information of these two companies since all of the essential characteristics are present. A bargained exchange occurred between Giant, the acquiring company, and the owners of Small. This transaction indicates a $1,050,000 purchase price will be the basis used in arriving at consolidated figures for the financial statements of the resulting single economic entity. In addition, since some cash was paid rather than having a pure exchange of voting securities, at least 1 of the 12 criteria for a pooling of interests has not been met.

At the date of acquisition, the purchase method consolidates all subsidiary asset and liability accounts based on their fair market values. The acquired assets and liabilities are recorded as if the parent had simply obtained them by paying market value. Because the negotiated price here equals this total value, the parent records each of these accounts as though purchased individually. As is subsequently demonstrated, variations from this rule do exist if less than market value is paid by the parent.

Because Small Company is to be dissolved, a consolidation entry is made directly onto the financial records of Giant (the surviving company). As a purchase, Small's assets and liabilities are consolidated at market value; original book values are ignored. Revenue, expense, dividend, and equity accounts cannot be transferred to a parent and are omitted in recording the creation of this business combination as a purchase.

Purchase Method—Parent Pays Market Value—Subsidiary Dissolved

Giant Company's Financial Records—December 31, 1995

Current Assets	300,000	
Land	400,000	
Buildings and Furniture	600,000	
Mortgage Note Payable		250,000
--		
Cash (paid by Giant)		250,000
Common Stock (20,000 shares issued by Giant at $10 par value) . .		200,000
Additional Paid-In Capital (value of shares issued by Giant in		
excess of par value)		600,000

To record purchase of net assets of Small Company for $1,050,000. Subsidiary accounts are recorded at market value which total to the same $1,050,000. (Dashed line separates the accounts acquired from Small and the consideration paid by Giant. Included for clarification purposes only.)

Giant's financial records now show $900,000 in the Land account ($500,000 former balance + $400,000 acquired), $1,600,000 in Buildings and Furniture ($1,000,000 + $600,000), and so forth. These items have been added into Giant's balances (see Exhibit 2–5) at their fair market values. Conversely, Giant's revenue balance continues to report the company's own $1,000,000 with expenses remaining at $800,000 and dividends of $110,000. *In a purchase, only the subsidiary's revenues, expenses, dividends, and equity transactions incurred subsequent to the takeover affect the business combination.*[6]

Purchase Price Exceeds Fair Market Value.   The bargained price in this second illustration is assumed to be $1,140,000 in exchange for all of Small's assets and liabilities. The mode of payment by Giant will be $340,000 in cash plus 20,000 shares of common stock with a market value of $40 per share (or $800,000 in

---

[6] Chapter 4 describes an alternative method of reporting a purchase that occurs within the current year. All of the subsidiary's revenues and expenses for the entire year are included in the consolidated totals with the income earned prior to the purchase then being subtracted on the income statement as a single Preacquisition Income figure. Thus, consolidated net income is not affected by subsidiary operations occurring before the purchase but the reported revenue and expense balances are more comparable with future periods.

total). The resulting purchase price is $90,000 more than the $1,050,000 fair market value of Small's net assets. In purchase combinations, such excess payments are not unusual. As an example, when American Brands, Inc. acquired ACCO World Corporation in 1987, the purchase price of $608.2 million was $519.5 million in excess of the fair market value of this subsidiary's net assets.

The $1,050,000 market value of Small's net assets certainly has an influence on the size of any takeover offer. However, Giant's $1,140,000 acquisition price could have been affected by any number of other factors such as Small's history of profitability, the company's reputation, the quality of its personnel, or the economic condition of the industry in which it operates. If Small, for example, has demonstrated the ability to generate especially high profits, Giant would probably be willing to pay an extra amount for this company.

One additional factor frequently has an impact on an acquisition price: the presence of competitive buyers. If Giant is forced to outbid other companies to acquire Small, the purchase price may be no more than a representation of this bidding war. As an illustration, Du Pont initially offered $87.50 per share in its attempt to obtain Conoco. Subsequently, during a month-long takeover battle with both The Seagram Company and Mobil Oil Corporation, Du Pont was forced to raise this offer, first to $95 and then to $98 to acquire enough shares to gain control of Conoco.

Whenever the price paid in a purchase exceeds total fair market value, all of the subsidiary's assets and liabilities are consolidated at fair market value with the additional payment allocated to the intangible asset goodwill. This excess amount may actually reflect the profitability often inherent in a going concern, the creative ability of a research group, market conditions that surrounded the acquisition, or myriad other possible factors. Because the conditions that can influence a purchase price are virtually unlimited, any amount paid in excess of fair market value is simply assigned arbitrarily to goodwill.

Alternative account titles such as Unamortized Cost in Excess of Market Value or some variation have also been widely used in recent years to identify this general allocation of any excess purchase price. Allied-Signal Inc., for example, reported a $1.1 billion asset as a "cost in excess of net assets of acquired companies" on its December 31, 1990, balance sheet. Traditionally, the term *goodwill* has referred to a computationally derived excess payment based on the estimated future profits of a going concern. Since the extra amount paid in the purchase of another company may actually be a function of many other factors, a more descriptive label such as the one reported by Allied-Signal might be preferable. However, goodwill is specifically used in *APB Opinion 16* and is, therefore, incorporated throughout this textbook.

Returning to Giant's $1,140,000 purchase, $90,000 of this price was in excess of the fair market value of Small's net assets. Thus, goodwill of that amount is entered into Giant's accounting system along with the fair market value of each individual account. The actual journal entry made by Giant at the date of acquisition would be:

Purchase Method—Parent Pays More Than Market Value—Subsidiary Dissolved

Giant Company's Financial Records—December 31, 1995

Current Assets.	300,000	
Land .	400,000	
Buildings and Furniture.	600,000	
Goodwill	90,000	
Mortgage Note Payable.		250,000
Cash (paid by Giant) .		340,000
Common Stock (20,000 shares issued by Giant at $10 par value) .		200,000
Additional Paid-In Capital (value of shares issued by Giant in excess of par value) .		600,000

To record purchase of net assets of Small Company for $1,140,000. Subsidiary accounts are recorded at market value with $90,000 excess payment attributed to goodwill.

Once again, Giant's financial records show $900,000 in its Land account ($500,000 former balance + $400,000 acquired), $1,600,000 in Buildings and Furniture ($1,000,000 + $600,000), and so forth. As the only change, a Goodwill balance of $90,000 has been established to account for the excess purchase price paid by Giant.

Purchase Price Less Than Fair Market Value.   For this third example, the price paid to the owners of Small is assumed to be $900,000. Giant conveys $100,000 of this amount in cash and issues 20,000 shares of common stock having a $40 per share (or $800,000 total) fair market value. To add a new element to this illustration, Giant is forced to pay $30,000 in accountants' and lawyers' fees directly associated with the combination as well as $10,000 for registering and issuing the shares of common stock.

In this combination, the parent's cost comprises more than one component. According to *APB Opinion 16,* any direct costs of establishing a purchase combination should be included as part of the total acquisition price. Expenditures such as payments to lawyers and accountants as well as finders' fees are necessary to carry out a purchase and are thus capitalized. Such costs can be quite significant. In describing the takeover battle for RJR Nabisco, *Time* magazine estimated that the "hundreds of lawyers and investment bankers involved in the bidding stand to earn a total of as much as $1 billion for their expertise."[7]

---

[7] John Greenwald, "Where's the Limit?" *Time,* December 5, 1988, p. 67.

Based on *APB 16*, the accountants' and lawyers' fees of $30,000 are included by Giant in computing a purchase price of $930,000, the total cost of acquiring Small's assets and liabilities ($900,000 to the owners of Small and $30,000 for these direct costs). However, the remaining $10,000 was paid to register and issue the common stock. This amount is considered a cost associated with these securities rather than a cost of the purchase. As such, the $10,000 is assumed to be a reduction in the paid-in capital recorded for the newly issued shares.

Giant's total purchase price of $930,000 is $120,000 less than the fair market value of Small's net assets. Allocation of full market values to each asset and liability is simply not possible; some reduction must be made. A cost of $930,000 cannot be assigned to accounts having a fair market value of $1,050,000 without an adjustment. Addressing this problem, *APB Opinion 16* (par. 87) states that "the values otherwise assignable to noncurrent assets acquired (except long-term investments in marketable securities) should be reduced by a proportionate part of the excess to determine the assigned values." *Therefore, when a purchase price is less than total fair market value of the net assets, noncurrent accounts, such as land, buildings, and equipment, are consolidated at reduced balances. All remaining assets and liabilities continue to be recorded at their fair market values.*

Since Giant paid $120,000 less than fair market value ($1,050,000 − $930,000), the balances of any noncurrent assets being acquired (other than long-term investments in marketable securities) must be decreased by that amount. As indicated in Exhibit 2–5, the two applicable accounts in this example have a total fair market value of $1,000,000:

Noncurrent Asset Accounts	Fair Market Values	
Land	$ 400,000	40%
Buildings and Furniture	600,000	60
Totals.	$1,000,000	100%

Because of Giant's payment, these two accounts must be reduced in consolidation by a total of $120,000 (from $1 million to $880,000). The balance reported for land is lowered by $48,000 ($120,000 × 40%). The remaining $72,000 ($120,000 × 60%) is assigned as a decrease to the Buildings and Furniture account. Therefore, for consolidation purposes, Small's land is recorded by Giant at $352,000 ($48,000 less than its $400,000 fair market value). The Buildings and Furniture account is entered as $528,000 ($600,000 − $72,000). All other assets and liabilities are consolidated at their fair market values.

**Purchase Method—Parent Pays Less Than Market Value—
Subsidiary Dissolved**

Giant Company's Financial Records—December 31, 1995

Current Assets.	300,000

Land	352,000
Buildings and Furniture.	528,000

Mortgage Note Payable.	250,000

- -

Cash (paid by Giant to Small's owners).	100,000
Common Stock (20,000 shares issued by Giant at $10	
par value).	200,000
Additional Paid-In Capital (value of shares issued by Giant in	
excess of par value)	600,000
Cash (consolidation costs)	30,000

Additional Paid-In Capital (stock costs).	10,000	
Cash		10,000

To record purchase of net assets of Small Company. Payment includes
$30,000 direct consolidation costs and the $10,000 cost of registering and
issuing common stock. Total purchase price of $930,000 is $120,000 less than
market value of the net assets, an amount assigned to noncurrent assets
(other than long-term investments in marketable securities).

Purchase Price Less Than Fair Market Value—Deferred Credit. In this final
illustration, the exchange price for Small's net assets is assumed to be $40,000
with payment made entirely in cash. Obviously, expending this amount for net
assets valued at $1,050,000 is an extreme case that indicates an unusual circum-
stance such as imminent bankruptcy, large contingent liabilities, or an urgent need
by the present owners for immediate liquidation. A company, for example, that
has its entire business centered on marketing one patent might see the price of its
stock drop to nearly zero if the legality of that patent were seriously threatened.

With a purchase price of only $40,000, Small's assets and liabilities must be
consolidated at balances $1,010,000 less than their total fair market value of
$1,050,000. As was indicated in the previous example, this decrease is initially
made in the recording of noncurrent assets. However, these two assets (land and
buildings and furniture) have a total worth of only $1,000,000. Even decreasing
their balances to zero will not fully account for the $1,010,000 difference between
the purchase price and total fair market value. A further reduction of $10,000 has
to be assigned within the consolidation process.

*Whenever a purchase price is less than fair market value so that the acquired
noncurrent asset balances are eliminated entirely, any additional reduction is
recorded as a* deferred credit. All other assets and liabilities are still brought into
the combination at fair market value. This Deferred Credit account results from a
bargain purchase, but only comes into existence after the applicable noncurrent
assets are first decreased to zero. Thus, before recognition of a credit is neces-

sary, either the price has to be extremely low or the acquired noncurrent assets must be of a relatively small value.

For reporting purposes, the deferred credit is frequently labeled as an "excess of market value over cost of acquisition." The balance is presented within the liability section of the consolidated balance sheet and amortized over a period of up to 40 years.

Because the $40,000 price in this illustration is $1,010,000 less than fair market value, Giant's journal entry to record its purchase of Small's assets and liabilities would:

1. Recognize no balances for the two noncurrent asset accounts.
2. Allocate the remaining $10,000 reduction to a Deferred Credit account.
3. Report all remaining asset and liability accounts at fair market value.

Purchase Method—Parent Pays Less Than Market Value and Deferred Credit is Recognized—Subsidiary Dissolved

Giant Company's Financial Records—December 31, 1995

Current Assets 300,000	
Land . . . . –0–	
Buildings and Furniture . . . . –0–	
Mortgage Note Payable	250,000
Deferred Credit—Excess of Market Value over Cost of	
Acquisition	10,000
Cash (paid by Giant)	40,000

To record acquisition of Small's net assets for $40,000, an amount $1,010,000 below market value.

Summary of the Purchase Method. In a purchase, acquired assets and liabilities are normally consolidated at their fair market values. However, the relationship between purchase price and total market value can necessitate some alterations to this rule. An excess payment, for example, leads to the creation of a Goodwill account. A low purchase price forces a reduction in the recorded balance of noncurrent assets and possibly the recognition of a deferred credit. Exhibit 2–6 summarizes the possible allocation scenarios.

Purchase Method Where Separate Incorporation Is Maintained

When separate incorporation is retained by each company in a purchase combination, many aspects of the consolidation process are identical to those demonstrated in the previous section. Fair market value, as an example, still serves as the basis for initially consolidating the subsidiary's asset and liability accounts.

EXHIBIT 2–6   Consolidation Values—The Purchase Method

Purchase price equals the fair market value of net assets.	Acquired assets and liabilities are assigned their fair market values.
Purchase price is greater than the fair market value of the net assets.	Acquired assets and liabilities are assigned their fair market values. The excess payment is attributed to goodwill.
Purchase price is less than the fair market value of the net assets.	Current assets, liabilities, and long-term investments in marketable securities are assigned their fair market values. The values of other noncurrent assets are reduced proportionally. If necessary, a deferred credit is recognized.

Recognition of goodwill or a deferred credit may again be necessary, depending on the size of the purchase price.

Despite such similarities, several significant differences do exist in a purchase consolidation in which each company remains a legally incorporated entity. Most noticeably, the consolidation of the financial information is only simulated rather than having the acquiring company physically record the acquired assets and liabilities. Since dissolution does not occur, independent record-keeping continues to be maintained by each company. To facilitate the preparation of consolidated financial statements, a worksheet and consolidation entries are employed using the data gathered from these separate companies.

A worksheet provides the structure for generating information to be reported by the single economic entity. An integral part of this process is the inclusion of consolidation journal entries. *These adjustments and eliminations are entered on the worksheet and represent alterations that would be required if the financial records were to be physically united.* Since no actual union occurs, consolidation entries are never formally recorded in the journals of either company. Instead, they are produced solely for use on the worksheet to assist in deriving consolidated account balances of the two separate companies.

To illustrate using the previous information, assume that Giant acquires Small Company on December 31, 1995, by issuing 26,000 shares of $10 par value common stock valued at $40 per share (or $1,040,000 in total). Direct consolidation costs of $50,000 are also paid by Giant. Hence, the purchase price totals $1,090,000 ($1,040,000 + $50,000). Although only voting stock is being issued to the owners of Small, the assumption is made that at least 1 of the other 12 criteria for a pooling of interests has not been met. Perhaps, Small was a subsidiary of another company and, thus, not autonomous. Or, some agreement might have been made to reacquire the shares issued in this transaction. Consequently, the purchase method is appropriate.

For business reasons, Giant decides to allow Small to continue as a separate corporation. Therefore, whenever financial statements for this combination are to be prepared, a worksheet is utilized in simulating the consolidation of these two companies.

Although the assets and liabilities are not being transferred, Giant must still record the payment made to Small's owners. When the subsidiary remains separate, the parent establishes an Investment account that initially reflects the purchase price.

Purchase Method—Subsidiary is Not Dissolved

Giant Company's Financial Records—December 31, 1995

Investment in Small Company (purchase price)	1,090,000	
Cash (paid for direct consolidation costs)		50,000
Common Stock (26,000 shares issued by Giant at $10 par value) .		260,000
Additional Paid-In Capital (value of shares issued by Giant in		
excess of par value)		780,000

  To record purchase of Small Company, which will maintain its separate legal identity.

As demonstrated in Exhibit 2–7, a worksheet can be prepared on the date of acquisition to arrive at consolidated totals for this combination. The entire process consists of seven steps:

Step 1.   Whenever a worksheet is being constructed, a formal allocation of the purchase price should be made as was done for the equity method in Chapter 1.[8] Thus, the following schedule is appropriate for Giant's purchase of Small:

Purchase price paid by Giant		$1,090,000
Book value of Small (see Exhibit 2–5)		800,000
Excess of cost over book value		$ 290,000
Allocations made to specific accounts based on difference in fair market		
values and book values:		
Land ($400,000 − $300,000)	$100,000	
Buildings and furniture ($600,000 − $400,000)	200,000	
Mortgage note payable ($250,000 − $200,000)	(50,000)	250,000
Excess cost not identified with specific accounts—goodwill		$ 40,000

No part of the $290,000 excess payment is attributed to the current assets because the book value and market value are identical. The mortgage note payable shows a negative allocation: since this debt's present value is more than book value, the company's net assets are actually worth *less*.

---

[8] This allocation procedure is helpful but not critical if dissolution occurs. Unless the purchase price is less than total market value, the asset and liability accounts are simply added directly into the parent's books at their assessed worth with any excess assigned to goodwill.

EXHIBIT 2–7   Purchase Method—Date of Acquisition

GIANT COMPANY AND SMALL COMPANY
Consolidation Worksheet
For Period Ending December 31, 1995

			Consolidation Entries		
Accounts	*Giant Company*	*Small Company*	*Debits*	*Credits*	*Consolidated Totals*
Income Statement					
Revenues	(1,000,000)				(1,000,000)
Expenses	800,000				800,000
Net income	(200,000)				(200,000)
Statement of Retained Earnings					
Retained earnings, 1/1/95	(870,000)				(870,000)
Net income (above)	(200,000)				(200,000)
Dividends paid	110,000				110,000
Retained earnings, 12/31/95	(960,000)				(960,000)
Balance Sheet					
Current Assets	350,000 *	300,000			650,000
Investment in Small Company	1,090,000 *	–0–		(1) 800,000	–0–
				(2) 290,000	
Land	500,000	300,000	(2) 100,000		900,000
Buildings and furniture	1,000,000	400,000	(2) 200,000		1,600,000
Goodwill	–0–	–0–	(2) 40,000		40,000
Total assets	2,940,000	1,000,000			3,190,000
Mortgage note payable	(300,000)	(200,000)		(2) 50,000	(550,000)
Common stock	(860,000)*	(200,000)	(1) 200,000		(860,000)
Additional paid-in capital	(820,000)*	(20,000)	(1) 20,000		(820,000)
Retained earnings, 12/31/95 (above)	(960,000)	(580,000)	(1) 580,000		(960,000)
Total liabilities and equities	(2,940,000)	(1,000,000)			(3,190,000)

NOTE: Parentheses indicate a credit balance.

* Balances have been adjusted for issuance of stock and payment of consolidation costs.

Step 2. The financial figures from the separate companies as of the date of acquisition (see Exhibit 2–5) are recorded in the first two columns of the worksheet (see Exhibit 2–7). Giant's accounts have been adjusted for the investment entry recorded earlier. As another preliminary step, Small's revenue, expense, and dividend accounts have been closed into retained earnings. In a purchase, the operations of the subsidiary prior to the December 31, 1995, takeover have no direct bearing on the business combination. These activities occurred before Small was obtained; thus, the resulting data should not be reflected in the consolidated statements.

Step 3. In Entry 1 on the worksheet, the $800,000 component of the Investment in Small Company account that equates to the book value of the subsidiary's net assets is removed. For external reporting purposes, the combination should report each individual account rather than a single investment balance. In effect, this portion of the Investment in Small Company account is deleted so that it can be replaced by the specific assets and liabilities that it represents.

Step 4. Small's stockholders' equity accounts are also eliminated through the same consolidation entry (Entry 1). These balances (Common Stock, Additional Paid-In Capital, and Retained Earnings) are historical measurements referring to subsidiary transactions that took place before the creation of the combination. By removing these accounts, only Small's assets and liabilities remain to be combined with the parent company figures. By removing these accounts, only Small's assets and liabilities remain to be combined with the parent company figures. Since this equity total also represents the $800,000 book value of the subsidiary, Entry 1 always balances.

Step 5. In Entry 2, the $290,000 excess payment in the Investment in Small Company is removed and assigned to the specific accounts indicated by the purchase price allocation. Consequently, land is increased by $100,000 to agree with Small's market value; $200,000 is attributed to the buildings and furniture and $50,000 to the mortgage note payable. The unexplained excess of $40,000 is recorded as goodwill.

Step 6. All accounts are extended into the "Consolidated Totals" column. For accounts such as Current Assets, this process is no more than the addition of Small's book value to that of Giant. However, where applicable, this extension also includes any allocations to establish the fair market value of Small's asset and liability accounts. Land, as an example, is being increased by $100,000. By raising the subsidiary's book value to market value, the reported balances are the same as in the previous examples where dissolution occurred. The use of a worksheet does not alter the consolidated figures, only the method of deriving those numbers.

Step 7. Consolidated expenses are subtracted from revenues to arrive at a net income of $200,000. Totals (such as net income and ending retained earnings) are *not* directly consolidated on the worksheet. Rather, the components (such as revenues and expenses) are extended and then combined to derive the appropriate figure. Net income is then carried down on the worksheet to the Statement of Retained Earnings and used (along with beginning retained earnings and dividends paid) to compute this December 31, 1995, equity balance. In the same manner, ending retained earnings of $960,000 is entered into the balance sheet to arrive at total liabilities and equities of $3,190,000, a number which reconciles with the total of consolidated assets.

The balances in the final column of Exhibit 2–7 are used to prepare consolidated financial statements for the business combination of Giant Company and

Small Company. The worksheet entries have served as a catalyst for bringing together the two independent sets of financial information. Thus, the actual accounting records of both Giant and Small remain unaltered by this consolidation process.

A Pooling of Interests—Rationale for Different Accounting

As stated previously, the pooling of interests method has evolved over the years as an alternative for reporting business combinations that demonstrate specific characteristics. In theory, a pooling involves the union of two companies so that a continuity of ownership is maintained. The underlying concept is that nothing has been changed by the combination except the composition of the reporting entity. *Thus, the book values of the two companies are simply brought together to form consolidated financial statements.* This approach is in diametric contrast to a purchase where one company clearly acquires another and then utilizes the purchase price as a basis for valuing the subsidiary's assets and liabilities.

ARS 5 (p. 15) explains that

> The "pooling-of-interests accounting" treatment is generally supported by reasoning that no new basis of accountability is required since the two (or more) companies are continuing operations as one company in a manner similar to that which existed in the past. The presumption is that in effect there has been no purchase or sale of assets, but merely a fusion, merging, or pooling of two formerly separate economic entities into one new economic entity.

Since a fusion of the companies rather than a takeover occurs, no purchase price is computed in a pooling of interests. Without a cost figure, no basis exists for either revaluing acquired asset and liability accounts to fair market value or recognizing goodwill. Book values are simply retained. This absence of a purchase price creates many of the significant reporting differences between the pooling of interests method and the purchase method.

The approach to consolidating revenues and expenses is also altered in a pooling of interests. Because a union is occurring, the operations of each company are said to continue in a manner unaffected by the combination. In theory, nothing has changed for either company except the composition of the reporting entity. Since the two companies have merged into one, the financial results of all past operations continue to be relevant information. *Consequently, in a pooling of interests, revenues and expenses are combined on a retroactive basis.* This treatment differs markedly from a purchase where only the operations of the subsidiary after the date of acquisition are attributed to the consolidated entity.

The business combination of AT&T and NCR serves as an illustration of this retroactive treatment. Although this pooling of interests did not occur until September 19, 1991, the consolidated income statement for 1991 included all revenues and expenses for both companies for the entire year. In this manner, the operations of the two companies were being reported as one entity. Furthermore, the same restatement procedure was applied to all prior years. In 1990, for example, AT&T disclosed separate revenues of $55.9 billion, while NCR reported $6.3 billion. When the two companies were subsequently joined, the newly created company (AT&T and Subsidiaries) reported that total 1990 revenues had been $62.2 billion.

In contrast, if AT&T had acquired NCR in 1991 through a purchase, the operations of the subsidiary prior to September 19 would have had no effect on the business combination. The revenues reported by AT&T for 1990 would remain at $55.9 billion. However, because the combination was a pooling, the past operating figures for the two companies were brought together. Although the companies were separate entities in 1990, the subsequently consolidated statements do purport to show the financial results of the business combination for that year. By restating the prior years, the operations of the component companies (AT&T and NCR) are being reported even though their combination had not yet been formed at that particular time.

Pooling of Interests Where Dissolution Takes Place

To demonstrate the formation of a pooling of interests, assume that Giant Company and Small Company decide to join operations on December 31, 1995 (see Exhibit 2–5). This combination is created when Giant issues 19,000 new shares of its common stock, with a $10 par value and a $40 market value per share, to the owners of Small in exchange for all of the company's outstanding common shares. Small transfers its assets and liabilities to Giant and dissolves itself as a separate corporation. Stock registration fees of $5,000 are paid by Giant as well as $3,000 in other costs directly associated with the combination. In creating this business combination, the companies followed all 12 criteria established by *APB Opinion 16* for a pooling of interests (see the appendix at the end of the chapter).

As stated earlier, a pooling of interests consolidates all accounts at their historical book values. Therefore, the reported value of each of Small's accounts (assets, liabilities, revenues, expenses, and dividends paid) can simply be transferred into Giant's financial records through a journal entry. To ensure that adequate disclosure is provided, *APB Opinion 16* does require that the details of the separate operations be presented in a note to the consolidated statements.

In contrast to the purchase method, no part of the $8,000 in consolidation costs is capitalized; the entire amount is recorded here as an expense. According to *APB Opinion 16* (par. 58), "The pooling of interests method records neither the acquiring of assets nor the obtaining of capital. Therefore, costs incurred to effect a combination accounted for by that method and to integrate the continuing operations are expenses of the combined corporation rather than additions to assets or direct reductions of stockholders' equity." To maintain book value, the cost of uniting the organizations is not viewed as a change in either asset or contributed capital accounts; thus, an expense is recorded by the combined entity.

Entering the book values of Small's assets, liabilities, revenues, expenses, and dividends into the records of Giant poses little trouble.[9] Likewise, the $8,000 in direct consolidation costs is simply assigned directly to expense. However, the recording of the 19,000 shares of stock being issued by Giant should be noted. According to Exhibit 2–5, Small is reporting contributed capital (the Common Stock and Additional Paid-In Capital accounts) of $220,000 and retained earnings of $470,000.[10] Because poolings retain book value, Giant uses these same figures in recording the issuance of its own stock. In that way, Small's equity balances are included within the consolidated totals.

Regardless of the amounts reported by Small, Giant's Common Stock account must be increased by $190,000 to reflect the $10 par value of these 19,000 shares. To arrive at the $220,000 figure that corresponds with Small's total contributed capital, Giant also records $30,000 as additional paid-in capital. The entry is then completed with a $470,000 credit to retained earnings. Small's contributed capital total and retained earnings have both been added into the business combination at book value.

Pooling of Interests Method—Subsidiary Dissolved

Giant Company's Financial Records—December 31, 1995

Current Assets	300,000	
Land	300,000	
Buildings and Furniture	400,000	
Dividends Paid	10,000	
Expenses	380,000	
Mortgage Note Payable		200,000
Revenues		500,000
Common Stock (19,000 shares issued by Giant at $10 par value)		190,000
Additional Paid-In Capital (to equate contributed capital with $220,000 amount reported by Small)		30,000
Retained Earnings, 1/1/95 (to record amount equal to book value of Small)		470,000
Expenses (consolidation costs)	8,000	
Cash		8,000

To record book value of Small's account obtained through a pooling of interests. Direct consolidation costs are expensed.

After recording these accounts, Giant's financial records show $800,000 in land ($500,000 + $300,000), $1,400,000 in buildings and furniture ($1,000,000 +

---

[9] As is discussed in Chapter 3, dividends paid between the related companies after a combination is created are intercompany transfers that have to be eliminated. In a pooling of interests, though, any amounts distributed to previous owners before the combination was created continue to be reported as Dividends Paid.

[10] Although the date of the pooling was September 19, Small's Retained Earnings balance as of the first day of the year is recorded by the combination with the company's current revenues, expenses, and dividends being reported separately.

$400,000), and so on. The Revenues account now holds $1,500,000 ($1,000,000 + $500,000) while expenses are recorded at $1,188,000 ($800,000 + $380,000 + $8,000 in consolidation costs). *Since book values are retained, the various asset, liability, revenue, expense, and dividend balances are not affected by the number of shares issued by Giant.* If 1,900 shares or 190,000 shares had been exchanged rather than 19,000, the same consolidated figures would have still been appropriate for these accounts.

By comparing this consolidation to previous illustrations, several areas of distinct contrast can be seen between the purchase method and the pooling of interests method:

	Consolidation—Purchase Method	Consolidation—Pooling of Interests Method
Assets and liabilities of subsidiary	Recorded at fair value*	Recorded at book value
Goodwill	Excess of purchase price over fair value of subsidiary net assets	Not recognized
Revenues and expenses of subsidiary	Accrued only after date of acquisition	Recognized retroactively
Shares issued to create business combination	Recorded at fair value if any shares are issued	Based on book value of subsidiary's contributed capital and retained earnings at beginning of year
Consolidation costs	Included as part of purchase price unless incurred in connection with issuance of stock, a cost which reduces paid-in capital	Expensed immediately

* If purchase price is less than fair market value, noncurrent assets (except for any long-term investments in marketable securities) are recorded at reduced amounts. A deferred credit may also be required.

When recording a pooling of interests, one potential variation to the previous entry may be encountered. Although poolings are based on retaining book values, the recording of contributed capital can cause a problem. Because issued shares are always credited for par value, Giant's common stock had to be recorded as $190,000 although Small's balance for this same account was $200,000. As indicated, Giant increased its additional paid-in capital by $30,000 so that total contributed capital equaled Small's $220,000 balance (see Exhibit 2–8).

If Giant had originally issued only 18,000 shares, its Common Stock account would be credited for $180,000 with an accompanying $40,000 added to additional paid-in capital. Once again, the $220,000 total book value of Small's contributed capital is replicated by the entry. Conversely, as shown in Exhibit 2–8, if 23,000 shares with a par value of $230,000 were exchanged by Giant to create this pooling, a $10,000 *reduction* to additional paid-in capital is necessary to arrive at the

EXHIBIT 2-8　Recording of Shares Issued in a Pooling of Interests

	Small's Book Values (Exhibit 2-5)	Giant Company Issues			
		19,000 Shares	18,000 Shares	23,000 Shares	29,000 Shares
Common stock	$200,000	$190,000	$180,000	$230,000	$290,000
Additional paid-in capital	20,000	30,000	40,000	(10,000)	(40,000)*
Total contributed capital	220,000	220,000	220,000	220,000	250,000
Retained earnings, 1/1/95	470,000	470,000	470,000	470,000	440,000 †

* Giant's Additional Paid-In Capital account is reduced from $40,000 to zero.

† Since the contributed capital of issued shares is $30,000 greater than that reported by Small, retained earnings must be $30,000 lower.

appropriate $220,000 total. In each case, the book value of Small's total contributed capital is retained by the combination.

A slightly different problem arises in recording total contributed capital for a pooling when the number of issued shares is relatively large. Assume, as an example, that 29,000 shares of common stock are exchanged by Giant to establish this pooling of interests with Small. The $290,000 par value of the stock necessitates a $70,000 reduction in Giant's additional paid-in capital to equal the $220,000 contributed capital reported by Small.

However, Exhibit 2–5 indicates that Giant's Additional Paid-In Capital account only holds a $40,000 balance. Because a negative contributed capital balance is not possible, Giant's additional paid-in capital is first dropped to zero with the remaining $30,000 decrease being made in retained earnings. Exhibit 2–8 shows that only $440,000 in retained earnings (rather than Small's $470,000 balance) is recorded by the business combination when 29,000 shares are issued. *Thus, if Giant's issued shares have a total par value greater than Small's total contributed capital, a reduction must be made. Giant initially decreases its own Additional Paid-In Capital account. However, if that amount proves to be insufficient, the Retained Earnings balance must also be reduced.*

Discussion Question: How Does a Purchase Differ from a Pooling of Interests?

On December 31, 1995, Acme Taxicab Company agrees to form a business combination with Wilbury's Cabs. Acme will exchange 600 shares of its previously unissued, $20 par value stock with Roy Wilbury for all of the outstanding shares of Wilbury's Cabs. Acme's common stock has a fair market value on that date of $100 per share.

continued

The only assets owned by Wilbury's Cabs are eight used taxicabs having a fair market value of $5,000 each. Because of accelerated depreciation, the average book value of these assets is $2,000. Acme has 15 automobiles of its own with a total book value of $60,000 but a fair market value of $74,000.

During 1995, the two companies separately reported the following revenues and expenses:

	Acme	*Wilbury*
Revenues	$220,000	$95,000
Expenses	150,000	60,000

Based on the information presented here, no determination is possible as to whether a pooling of interests or a purchase has been created.

- On a consolidated balance sheet as of December 31, 1995, how will the reported asset balances differ, depending on the type of method that is appropriate?
- If a business combination is created as a purchase, one set of assets and liabilities is adjusted to fair market value whereas the other is left at book value. Why are both sets of assets and liabilities not revalued?
- On a consolidated income statement for 1995, how will the balances differ, depending on the method considered appropriate?
- Are external decision makers properly served by allowing such widely varying numbers to be reported depending on whether a purchase or a pooling of interests has taken place?
- Based on the facts presented in the case, which set of financial statements best mirrors the economic reality of the business combination that has occurred?

Pooling of Interests Where Separate Incorporation Is Maintained

The combination of Giant Company and Small Company is presented again to demonstrate a pooling of interests, one in which both companies retain their separate legal identities. For this illustration, the same exchange is used as in the purchase consolidation shown in Exhibit 2–7. Thus, Giant issues 26,000 shares of common stock on December 31, 1995, for all of Small's outstanding shares. In addition, direct consolidation costs of $50,000 are incurred. Small's accounts are not transferred to Giant's financial records; both companies continue as separate corporations and maintain independent accounting systems. However, the assumption is made here that the combination meets all 12 requirements for a pooling of interests.

Giant must first record the issuance of 26,000 shares of common stock to create this business combination. Because Small is not being dissolved, Giant establishes an investment balance rather than recording Small's individual accounts. Because the combination is a pooling, this figure is based on Small's $690,000 book value as of the beginning of the year. Using the January 1 total allows the current revenues, expenses, and dividends to be included as separate items in recording the business combination.

The issued shares are recorded by Giant at their par value of $260,000. The Additional Paid-in Capital account is reduced by $40,000 to arrive at total contributed capital of $220,000, the same book value as Small's contributed capital. Retained earnings at January 1, 1995, are also included in this entry since operating activities are retroactively consolidated in a pooling of interests. The direct consolidation costs are expensed immediately.

Pooling of Interests Method—Subsidiary Not Dissolved

Giant's Financial Records—December 31, 1995

Investment in Small Company (1/1/95 book value)	690,000	
Additional Paid-In Capital (to align contributed capital with that of Small)	40,000	
Common Stock (26,000 shares at $10 par value).		260,000
Retained Earnings, 1/1/95 (to record balance equal to book value of Small)		470,000
Expenses (direct consolidation costs)	50,000	
Cash		50,000

To record issuance of 26,000 shares of stock in exchange for all of the outstanding shares of Small in a combination accounted for as a pooling of interests. Direct consolidation costs are properly expensed.

When the common stock shares are exchanged, the combination is formed, and consolidated financial statements can be prepared using the worksheet produced in Exhibit 2–9. This pooling of interests is carried out through the following series of steps:

Step 1. Prior to creating this worksheet, Giant's balances are adjusted to show (1) the effect of its issuance of stock and (2) the direct consolidation costs. The updated accounts are then entered into the appropriate columns on the worksheet (see Exhibit 2–5 for original book values).

Step 2. The Investment in Small Company account is eliminated as part of the basic consolidation entry. In the same manner as the purchase method, the Investment account is not consolidated; rather, the specific accounts that it represents should be reported by the business combination. Therefore, the $690,000 investment is removed on the worksheet so that it can be replaced by the individual balances of Small Company.

EXHIBIT 2-9   Pooling of Interests—Date of Acquisition

GIANT COMPANY AND SMALL COMPANY
Consolidation Worksheet
For Period Ending December 31, 1995

Accounts	Giant Company	Small Company	Consolidation Entries		Consolidated Totals
			Debits	Credits	
Income Statement					
Revenues	(1,000,000)	(500,000)			(1,500,000)
Expenses	850,000	380,000			(1,230,000)
Net income	(150,000)	(120,000)			(270,000)
Statement of Retained Earnings					
Retained earnings, 1/1/95	(1,340,000)*	(470,000)	(1) 470,000		(1,340,000)
Net income (above)	(150,000)	(120,000)			(270,000)
Dividends paid	110,000	10,000			120,000
Retained earnings, 12/31/95	(1,380,000)	(580,000)			(1,490,000)
Balance Sheet					
Current assets	350,000*	300,000			650,000
Investment in Small Company	690,000*	–0–		(1) 690,000	–0–
Land	500,000	300,000			800,000
Buildings and furniture (net)	1,000,000	400,000			1,400,000
Total assets	2,540,000	1,000,000			2,850,000
Mortgage note payable	(300,000)	(200,000)			(500,000)
Common stock	(860,000)*	(200,000)	(1) 200,000		(860,000)
Additional paid-in capital	–0–*	(20,000)	(1) 20,000		–0–
Retained earnings, 12/31/95 (above)	(1,380,000)	(580,000)			(1,490,000)
Total liabilities and equities	(2,540,000)	(1,000,000)			(2,850,000)

NOTE: Parentheses indicate a credit balance.
* Balances have been adjusted for issuance of stock and payment of consolidation costs.

Step 3.   Small's stockholders' equity balances are also eliminated by this same entry. In a purchase, these figures are removed because only assets and liabilities can actually be transferred to the parent. Conversely, for a pooling where a fusion of ownership interests is said to occur, the equity figures for both companies must be included. However, Small's equity accounts have already been brought into the consolidated totals through the recording of Giant's 26,000 shares of issued stock.

The initial investment entry has already added these equity balances to Giant's records prior to consolidating the financial statements. Thus, Small's common stock, additional paid-in capital, and retained earnings must be eliminated on the worksheet to prevent their inclusion in the final figures a second time. The beginning-of-year balance for Small's retained earnings is being removed to allow the 1995 revenues, expenses, and dividends to be reported by the business combination.

Step 4. For a pooling of interests, the actual consolidation process is carried out by adding together the book values of each account. For example, Giant's revenue of $1,000,000 and Small's revenue of $500,000 are extended for a consolidated total of $1,500,000. Where a consolidation entry affects an account (such as the elimination of Small's equity accounts), the impact of that adjustment must also be reflected in this extension process. However, since a purchase price is not determined in a pooling, no goodwill is recognized and no valuation adjustments are made to any asset or liability.

Step 5. For each of the financial statements on the worksheet, a total is calculated. The income statement ends with a net income balance, the statement of retained earnings computes ending retained earnings, and the balance sheet arrives at total assets as well as total liabilities and equities. As discussed previously, these final figures are not derived by consolidating the respective balances of the separate companies. Instead, the components in each statement are extended and then used to compute the ending balance.

On the income statement demonstrated here, revenues and expenses are added to produce totals of $1,500,000 and $1,230,000, respectively, indicating consolidated net income of $270,000. This figure is moved to the corresponding line within the statement of retained earnings. Each of the other elements constituting this second statement are extended to produce ending retained earnings of $1,490,000. This total is then included within the stockholders' equity section of the consolidated balance sheet enabling it to properly balance.

Step 6. After all accounts have been consolidated, the final balances on the worksheet are used to prepare financial statements for the business combination of Giant Company and Small Company. Exhibit 2–10 provides a comparison of the figures developed for the purchase consolidation shown previously in Exhibit 2–7 and the pooling of interests in Exhibit 2–9.

Pooling of Interests—The Controversy

Since the basic characteristics of a pooling of interests have now been presented, the long history of controversy that has surrounded this method can be better understood. Over the years, the legitimacy of the pooling of interests method has frequently been questioned. One major theoretical problem associated with the pooling method is that it ignores cost figures indicated by the transaction that created the combination. The number of shares exchanged has no impact on consolidated asset and liability balances. What is normally a significant event for

---

EXHIBIT 2–10 **Comparison of Purchase Method and Pooling of Interests Method**

General Information: 26,000 shares of Giant Company (par value of $10 per share but a market value of $40 per share) issued for all oustanding shares of Small Company on December 31, 1995. Cash of $50,000 paid for direct consolidation costs.

	Purchase Method (Exhibit 2–7)	Pooling of Interests Method (Exhibit 2–9)
Revenues	$1,000,000	$1,500,000
Expenses	(800,000)	(1,230,000)
Net income	$ 200,000	$ 270,000
Retained earnings, 1/1/95	$ 870,000	$1,340,000
Net income (above)	200,000	270,000
Dividends paid	(110,000)	(120,000)
Retained earnings, 12/31/95	$ 960,000	$1,490,000
Current assets	$ 650,000	$ 650,000
Land	900,000	800,000
Buildings and furniture (net)	1,600,000	1,400,000
Goodwill	40,000	–0–
Total assets	$3,190,000	$2,850,000
Mortgage note payable	$ 550,000	$ 500,000
Common stock	860,000	860,000
Additional paid-in capital	820,000	–0–
Retained earnings, 12/31/95 (above)	960,000	1,490,000
Total liabilities and equities	$3,190,000	$2,850,000

---

both companies is simply omitted from any accounting consideration. *All book values are retained as if nothing has happened. APB Opinion 16 (par. 39) itself admits*

> The most serious defect attributed to pooling of interests accounting by those who oppose it is that it does not accurately reflect the economic substance of the business combination transaction. They believe that the method ignores the bargaining which results in the combination by accounting only for the amounts previously shown in accounts of the combining companies.

As a further argument put forth against pooling of interests consolidations, many accountants believe that only one accounting approach should be applicable for all business combinations. They hold that all combinations are essentially the same. Even though a variety of formats do exist, critics contend that a parent and an acquisition price can be determined in virtually every case. In addition, conveying freely traded stock is held to be the same as conveying cash. According to this argument, the availability of two radically different accounting methods is simply not warranted. Interestingly, the pooling of interests method is primarily found in the United States. "Of all the major industrialized countries, only Great Britain allows anything resembling pooling, and its rule makers are modifying the rules to prevent most poolings."[11]

The depth of controversy sparked by the pooling of interests method is clearly demonstrated in *Accounting Research Study No. 5 (ARS 5)* where Arthur Wyatt stated that "no basis exists in principle for a continuation of what is presently known as 'pooling-of-interests' accounting *if* the business combination involves an exchange of assets and/or equities between independent parties."[12]

Additionally, in a dissent to *APB Opinion 16*, Sidney Davidson, Charles Horngren, and J. S. Seidman asserted that

> The real abuse is pooling itself. On that, the only answer is to eliminate pooling. . . . Elimination of pooling will remove the confusion that comes from the coexistence of pooling and purchase accounting. Above all, the elimination of pooling would remove an aberration in historical cost accounting that permits an acquisition to be accounted for on the basis of the seller's cost rather than the buyer's cost of the assets obtained in a bargained exchange.

As another concern, objective criteria for differentiating between a purchase and a pooling have always been difficult to identify. Despite the vast accounting differences between the two methods, establishing clear-cut boundaries to separate a pooling of interests from a purchase is not really possible. The conditions indicating a pooling lie in very subjective areas such as the intention of the owners and the relationship of the companies. These distinctions are so nebulous that even subtle differences can be crucial in ascertaining whether a true pooling of interests has occurred.[13]

The acceptability of the pooling of interests method might, indeed, have been eliminated years ago except for its popularity in the business world. Preference for the pooling method is based largely on the desirable impact that it usually produces on reported net income. The most obvious effect is the inclusion of the subsidiary's net income as if that company had always been part of the consolidated entity. This retroactive treatment can lead to immediate improvement in the profitability picture being reported.

As an illustration, assume that near the end of 1995, the management of Ace Company realizes that net income for that year will amount to only $400,000 compared to $500,000 for 1994. If 100,000 shares of Ace's common stock are outstanding, these income figures represent earnings per share of $4 for 1995, down from $5 in 1994. Assume further that just prior to the end of 1995, Ace issues 40,000 shares of its own common stock in exchange for all of the outstanding common stock of Short Company in a combination meeting all 12 criteria for a

[11] Michael Davis, "APB 16: Time to Reconsider," *Journal of Accountancy*, October 1991, p. 99.

[12] Arthur Wyatt, "A Critical Study of Accounting for Business Combinations," *Accounting Research Study No. 5* (New York: AICPA, 1963), p. 105.

[13] For example, see "Is Now the Time to Revisit Accounting for Business Combinations?" by Richard Dieter in the July 1989 issue of *The CPA Journal* beginning on page 44.

pooling of interests. Short had generated a net income of $300,000 for 1995 after suffering a loss of $80,000 in 1994.

To account for this pooling of interests, Ace must retroactively combine the income figures of both companies, thus reporting $700,000 ($400,000 + $300,000) in earnings for 1995 against only $420,000 ($500,000 − $80,000) for 1994. The corresponding earnings per share figures are now $5 for 1995 ($700,000/140,000 shares) versus $3 for 1994 ($420,000/140,000 shares).

Without a single change in operations, Ace has turned a declining profit year into one that appears to indicate a dramatic increase in earnings.[14] Disclosure requirements do dictate that the notes to the consolidated financial statements clearly outline the effect of Short's operations on reported income figures. Many critics, however, feel that such notes are overshadowed by the figures presented on the face of the statements.

Another income effect helps to further account for the popularity enjoyed by the pooling of interests method. In a purchase combination, the subsidiary's assets and liabilities are adjusted to fair market value with goodwill often recognized. Such allocations are viewed as cost figures of the business combination, costs that have only limited useful lives (except when relating to land). Thus, these amounts (which can be extremely large) must be amortized over future accounting periods. The resulting expense, encountered only in the purchase method, serves to reduce consolidated net income year after year.

Conversely, a pooling of interests consolidates all accounts at their book values so that no additional amortization expense is ever recognized. Therefore, in most business combinations, the income reported for each succeeding year is higher using the pooling method than would have been the case if consolidated by the purchase method.[15]

Given these reporting advantages, the desire by businesses to create combinations that qualify as poolings is not surprising. Historically, the accounting profession has attempted to define the characteristics of a pooling of interests in such a way as to restrict its use to combinations that were clearly fusions of two independent companies. Over the years, however, the identification of attributes considered to be essential to a pooling of interests has proven to be a difficult task.

Guidance was provided in this area in 1950 when the Committee on Accounting Procedure of the AICPA issued *ARB 40*. This pronouncement suggested that accountants review several factors in judging whether a particular business combination qualified as a true pooling of interests. These factors were (1) continuity of ownership, (2) relative size of the companies, (3) continuity of management,

---

[14] A real-life illustration of using poolings of interests to improve reported earnings can be found in "Muddying the Waters" by Abraham J. Briloff in the October 8, 1990, edition of *Barron's* beginning on page 14.

[15] For example, see "Time, Warner Alter Merger-Pact Terms after Accounting Challenge by the SEC," *The Wall Street Journal*, April 14, 1989, p. B3.

and (4) activities of a similar or complementary nature. *ARB 40* failed, however, to specify the relative importance of each of these four or the means of ascertaining their existence in a particular combination.

With this latitude available, many companies attempted to stretch the pooling criteria to include a wide variety of business combinations. Subsequently, the accounting profession tried to clarify the definition of a pooling in *ARB 48*, "Business Combinations," January 1957 (par. 6), by stating "where one of the constituent corporations is clearly dominant (for example, where the stockholders of one of the constituent corporations obtain 90 percent or 95 percent or more of the voting interest in the combined enterprise), there is a presumption that the transaction is a purchase rather than a pooling of interests."

Despite the efforts to give structure to consolidation accounting, these official pronouncements failed to delineate clearly the boundary separating a purchase from a pooling combination. Thus, during the 1950s and 1960s, many combinations were accounted for as poolings of interests despite having only the barest semblance to the pooling concept. Finally, in 1970 after pressure was applied by the SEC, the Accounting Principles Board issued *Opinion 16* to provide restrictive guidelines for establishing a pooling of interests.

As indicated previously, the APB stated that if any 1 of 12 specified criteria was absent in a combination, the purchase method had to be applied (see appendix at the end of the chapter). Today, this pronouncement continues to limit the pooling approach to combinations that are the complete fusion of two independent companies formed through the exchange of voting common stock. No alteration of assets or liabilities can result (except for consolidation costs) and the owners of the two companies must be the owners of the combined organization.

If *Opinion 16* was designed to limit the use of the pooling of interests method, it has apparently been successful. *Accounting Trends & Techniques*, in an annual survey of 600 companies, found 144 poolings of interests in 1967 and 184 in 1968. After *APB Opinion 16,* that number had fallen to 31 in 1975 and 43 in 1976. By 1990, only 10 of the companies reported poolings of interests during the current fiscal period. Despite the drop in frequency, this method continues to be important because some of the larger combinations are carried out in this manner. The merger of NCNB Corporation and C&S/Sovran Corporation to form Nations-Bank, for example, was a pooling of interests as was the combination of AT&T and NCR.

Unconsolidated Subsidiaries

Over the years, accountants have attempted to identify situations in which consolidation of financial information might not be appropriate for every subsidiary. The FASB addressed this issue in 1987 when it released *Statement No. 94*. This pronouncement required that all companies more than 50 percent owned must be consolidated with the exception of two cases:

1. <u>An investment where control is only temporary.</u> If the parent company anticipates surrendering control over a subsidiary in the near future through disposition of part or all of its ownership, consolidation would no longer be considered appropriate. As an illustration, a footnote to the 1988 annual report of Fuqua Industries, Inc. informed readers that a wholly owned subsidiary, Georgia Federal Bank, was omitted from consolidation because a contract had been signed to sell the operation. The temporary nature of the relationship nullifies any potential informational benefit derived from presenting consolidated financial statements.

2. <u>An investment where control does not actually rest with the majority owners.</u> Without control, the concept of a single economic entity is not applicable. In legal reorganizations and bankruptcies, for example, operational authority over the subsidiary is held by parties other than the parent company. Severe restrictions imposed by foreign governments also limit or remove the power held by the owners. For example, the 1990 financial statements of Unocal Corporation state "the consolidated financial statements of the company include the accounts of subsidiaries more than 50 percent owned, except for certain Brazilian subsidiaries which are accounted for by the cost method due to currency restrictions imposed by the Brazilian government."

Both of these exceptions to the consolidation principle are predicated on the tentative quality of the control held by the parent. The relationship does not indicate the existence of a single economic entity.

Prior to the issuance of *Statement 94,* another important exception to consolidation was allowed. At that time, business combinations were permitted to omit subsidiaries from consolidation because of nonhomogeneity. *ARB 51* had suggested that a subsidiary should remain unconsolidated if the nature of its operations differed so significantly from that of the parent that the combined companies could not be viewed as a single entity. Despite ownership of a majority of voting stock, these companies had to be reported by use of the equity method so that only an investment asset and an equity income balance appeared in the consolidated statements.

Because of the complex nature of the activities in most modern businesses, application of the nonhomogeneity rule was subject to individual judgment. Traditionally, companies gave a broad interpretation to the concept of a single economic entity, so that virtually all subsidiaries were consolidated despite apparent differences in the nature of their operations. However, one important exception to this general rule did exist. *ARB 51* stated, as an example, that "separate statements . . . may be preferable for a finance company where the parent and the other subsidiaries are engaged in manufacturing operations." Following the Board's suggestion, many business combinations segregated finance subsidiaries from their consolidated statements, reporting them on the equity basis. Thus, in 1987, for example, General Motors did not consolidate its finance subsidiary, General Motors Acceptance Corporation (GMAC).

The practice of omitting such subsidiaries from consolidation was criticized vigorously over the years as an excuse for removing large amounts of debt from the entity's balance sheet. Since the individual accounts of an unconsolidated subsidiary are not included in consolidated statements, finance operations could incur significant obligations that would not appear as liabilities of the business combination. One study found, for example, that the debt-to-equity ratio of Borg-Warner in 1985 was .70 without consolidation of a finance subsidiary but 3.06 with it included.[16]

Consequently, the FASB voted to eliminate this practice. <u>*Statement 94* removed nonhomogeneity as a justification for omitting a subsidiary from consolidation.</u> Thus, finance subsidiaries must now be included in consolidated statements. The topic, though, continues to be debated not only in the United States but also throughout the world. A recent study "reports that financial subsidiaries generally are not consolidated with nonfinancial companies other than in the United States. However, in just the seven months since that survey took place a number of countries, including Canada, New Zealand, and the United Kingdom, have revised their standards to eliminate or minimize diversity of operations as justification for nonconsolidation."[17]

Not surprisingly, *SFAS 94* has not been completely popular with the management of the companies affected.[18] These officials did not relish placing such heavy debt onto their balance sheet. Speaking for the typical corporate accountant, *Industry Week* (from an article by John S. McClenahen, "FASB Faulted," *Industry Week*, November 7, 1988, p. 17) argued

> *FASB Statement 94,* as the standard is formally known, will make such a mess of balance sheets as to render them "meaningless" complains the corporate CFO. Companies with substantial finance subsidiaries—including General Motors, General Electric, and Westinghouse—will be forced to throw a layer of short-time liability "snow" over the performance of their basic "operating" business he contends . . . "Why anybody would think it's better disclosure to cover up all the really important elements of how they are running their operating business . . . absolutely baffles my mind," he states.[19]

Obviously, when setting standards for financial reporting, the FASB is rarely able to please all of the people.

---

[16] Joseph C. Rue and David E. Tosh, "Should We Consolidate Finance Subsidiaries?" *Management Accounting,* April 1987, p. 46.

[17] FASB, "Consolidation Policy and Procedures," paragraph 38.

[18] Accounting principles can sometimes have a considerable impact on the operations of an entity. As an example, one report found that 30 of 157 surveyed companies chose to sell an unconsolidated subsidiary or drop their ownership level below 50 percent at approximately the time that SFAS 94 took effect. This report suggested that many of these companies had decided to dispose of some or all of their interest rather than consolidate the extra debt. See "SFAS 94: Did It Produce Its Intended Effect?" *The CPA Journal*, April 1992, p. 56.

[19] As is discussed in a subsequent chapter, segment disclosure alleviates some of the possible problems of consolidation by providing financial information about the various components of a business. Chrysler Corporation has addressed this same issue in a different manner by publishing two sets of financial statements side by side. One set properly includes Chrysler Financial Services and the company's car rental operation in the consolidated figures. The other supplemental statements have reported these operations using the equity method.

Summary

1. Consolidation of financial information is required for external reporting purposes whenever one organization gains control of another, thus forming a single economic entity. In many combinations, all but one of the companies is dissolved as a separate legal corporation. Therefore, the consolidation process is carried out only at the date of acquisition to bring together all accounts into a single set of financial records. In other combinations, the companies retain their identities as separate enterprises and continue to maintain their own individual accounting systems. For these cases, consolidation is a periodic process necessary whenever financial statements are to be produced. This periodic procedure is frequently accomplished through the use of a worksheet and consolidation entries.

2. Every business combination must be accounted for as either a purchase or a pooling of interests. To differentiate the applicable use of these methods, 12 criteria were established by the APB. If all 12 are satisfied, the combination must be viewed as a pooling of interests. Otherwise, the purchase method is appropriate. The two methods are not interchangeable; a specific approach is required based on these criteria.

3. A purchase is said to have been created when one entity acquires control over another. An acquisition price is determined based on the exchange transaction and includes all direct consolidation costs unless expended in the issuance of stock. The assets and liabilities of the acquired company are consolidated based on their fair market values at the date of purchase. If the price paid exceeds the total fair market value of the net assets, the residual amount is recorded in the consolidated financial statements as goodwill, an intangible asset.

4. For a purchase, if the acquisition price is less than total fair market value, a reduction in the consolidated balances is necessary. The acquired company's assets and liabilities are recorded at fair market value, except for noncurrent assets (other than long-term investments in marketable securities). Because of the bargain purchase, these noncurrent assets are consolidated at amounts less than their fair values. The reduction is the difference between the parent's purchase price and the total fair market value of the subsidiary's assets and liabilities. This figure is prorated based on the fair market values of the various noncurrent assets. A deferred credit account is also created if the reduction exceeds the total value of the applicable noncurrent assets.

5. A pooling of interests is formed by uniting the ownership of two companies through the exchange of securities. This method accounts for the new combination by consolidating all accounts at book value. Neither goodwill nor any other account valuation adjustment is recognized because no acquisition price is established. Without a purchase price, direct consolidation costs cannot be capitalized; they must be expensed immediately. For a pooling of interests, all revenues, expenses, and other operational accounts are consolidated on a retroactive basis.

6. The pooling of interests method has often been criticized because it relies on book values only and, therefore, ignores the exchange transaction that formed the economic entity. Poolings have also been questioned because of the retroactive treatment of operating results. Consequently, a company can increase reported earnings by pooling with another company rather than by improving operating efficiency.

7. Subsidiaries can be left unconsolidated if control is only temporary or if it is not actually held by the majority owners. However, nonhomogeneity can no longer be used as a reason for omitting finance subsidiaries from consolidation.

Comprehensive Illustration

PROBLEM   (Estimated Time: 45 to 65 Minutes)

Following are the account balances of the Marston Company and the Richmond Company as of December 31, 1995. The appraised values of the Richmond Company assets and liabilities have also been included.

	Marston Company Book Value 12/31/95	Richmond Company Book Value 12/31/95	Richmond Company Appraised Value 12/31/95
Cash	$ 600,000	$ 200,000	$ 200,000
Receivables	900,000	300,000	290,000
Inventory	1,100,000	600,000	720,000
Buildings (net).	3,000,000	800,000	1,000,000
Equipment (net)	6,000,000	500,000	600,000
Accounts payable	(400,000)	(200,000)	(200,000)
Notes payable	(3,400,000)	(1,100,000)	(1,100,000)
Totals	$ 7,800,000	$ 1,100,000	$ 1,510,000
Common stock—$20 par value	$(2,000,000)		
Common stock—$5 par value		$ (720,000)	
Additional paid-in capital	(900,000)	(100,000)	
Retained earnings, 1/1/95	(2,300,000)	(130,000)	
Revenues	(6,000,000)	(900,000)	
Expenses	3,400,000	750,000	

NOTE: Parentheses indicate a credit balance.

Additional Information (not recorded in the preceding figures):

- On December 31, 1995, Marston issues 50,000 shares of its $20 par value common stock for all of the outstanding shares of Richmond Company.
- In creating this combination, Marston pays $10,000 in stock issuance costs and $20,000 in other direct combination costs.

Required:

a. Assume that Marston's stock has a fair market value of $32.00 per share and that this combination does not meet all 12 criteria for a pooling of interests.

Prepare the necessary journal entries if Richmond is to dissolve itself as a separate legal entity.

b. Repeat requirement *a.* but with the assumption that this transaction meets all 12 criteria for a pooling of interests.

c. Assume that Marston's stock has a fair market value of $28.52 per share and that this combination does not meet all 12 criteria for a pooling of interests. Richmond will retain separate legal incorporation and maintain its own accounting systems. Prepare a worksheet to consolidate the accounts of the two companies.

d. Repeat requirement *c.* but assume that this transaction meets all 12 criteria for a pooling of interests.

SOLUTION

a. For a purchase, the accountant should first determine the parent company's acquisition price. Since Marston's stock is valued at $32.00 per share, the 50,000 issued shares are worth $1,600,000 in total. The $10,000 stock issuance cost is reported as a reduction to additional paid-in capital. The other $20,000 direct combination costs must be added to the value of the issued shares to arrive at a purchase price of $1,620,000. This total is compared to the $1,510,000 market value of Richmond's assets and liabilities. Since Marston has paid $110,000 over fair market value ($1,620,000 − $1,510,000), that figure would be recognized as goodwill.

Because dissolution is to occur, Richmond's asset and liability accounts are transferred to Marston and entered at fair market value with the excess recorded as goodwill. The payment of the stock issuance costs is journalized separately to avoid confusion.

Marston Company's Financial Records—December 31, 1995

Cash	200,000	
Receivables	290,000	
Inventory	720,000	
Buildings	1,000,000	
Equipment	600,000	
Goodwill	110,000	
Accounts Payable		200,000
Notes Payable		1,100,000
Common Stock (Marston) (par value)		1,000,000
Additional Paid-In Capital (market value in excess of par value)		600,000
Cash (paid for consolidation costs)		20,000
To record purchase of Richmond Company.		
Additional Paid-In Capital	10,000	
Cash (stock issuance costs)		10,000
To record payment of stock issuance costs.		

b. As a pooling of interests, Richmond's account balances (including revenues and expenses) are transferred at their book values. The biggest concern in this process is the recording of contributed capital. Richmond's accounts indicate total contributed capital of $820,000: common stock of $720,000 and additional paid-in capital of $100,000. However, the par value of the 50,000 shares issued by Marston is $1,000,000 (at $20 per share). To arrive at the same $820,000 figure reported by Richmond, Marston's Additional Paid-In Capital account must be reduced by $180,000 in recording these new shares.

Marston's recording of this combination follows. As this combination is a pooling of interests, all $30,000 of the consolidation costs are recorded as expenses.

Marston Company's Financial Records—December 31, 1995

Cash	200,000	
Receivables	300,000	
Inventory	600,000	
Buildings (net).	800,000	
Equipment (net)	500,000	
Expenses	750,000	
Additional Paid-In Capital (Marston) (to align contributed capital		
totals).	180,000	
Accounts Payable		200,000
Notes Payable.		1,100,000
Common Stock (Marston) (par value)		1,000,000
Retained Earnings, 1/1/95		130,000
Revenues		900,000
To establish a pooling of interests with Richmond Company.		
Expenses	30,000	
Cash		30,000
To record payment of consolidation costs.		

c. In this third illustration, a purchase combination is once again created. Since a different value is attributed to the issued shares, a new purchase price must be calculated:

50,000 shares of stock at $28.52 each.	$1,426,000
Other direct combination costs	20,000
Purchase price.	$1,446,000

As the subsidiary is maintaining separate incorporation, Marston has to establish an investment account to reflect the $1,446,000 purchase price:

Marston's Financial Records—December 31, 1995

Investment in Richmond Company.	1,446,000	
Common Stock (Marston) (par value).		1,000,000
Additional Paid-In Capital (market value in excess of par value).		426,000
Cash (paid for combination costs)		20,000
To record purchase of Richmond Company.		
Additional Paid-In Capital.	10,000	
Cash (paid for stock issuance costs)		10,000
To record payment of stock issuance costs.		

Separate incorporation is being maintained; thus, a worksheet must be developed for consolidation purposes. The parent needs to analyze the purchase price to determine the allocations required to the individual accounts:

Purchase price paid by Marston.		$1,446,000
Book value of Richmond		1,100,000
Excess of cost over book value		$ 346,000
Allocations made to specific accounts based on difference in fair market		
values and book values:		
Receivables ($290,000 − $300,000).	$ (10,000)	
Inventory ($720,000 − $600,000)	120,000	
Buildings ($1,000,000 − $800,000)	200,000	
Equipment ($600,000 − $500,000)	100,000	410,000
Bargain purchase		$ (64,000)

Marston's $1,446,000 purchase price is $64,000 less than the $1,510,000 fair market value of Richmond's individual accounts. This reduction must be assigned to the subsidiary's noncurrent assets (other than long-term investments in marketable securities) based on their fair market values:

	Fair Market Value	Percentage of Fair Market Value	Reduction	Percentage of Reduction
Buildings	$1,000,000	62.5%	$64,000	$40,000
Equipment	600,000	37.5	64,000	24,000
Totals	$1,600,000	100.0%		$64,000

Thus, within the consolidation worksheet, the subsidiary's buildings are assigned a reduced value of $960,000 ($1,000,000 − $40,000). The Equipment account is adjusted to $576,000 ($600,000 − $24,000).

Exhibit 2–11 can now be developed using the following steps to arrive at totals for the consolidated financial statements:

- Marston's balances have been updated on this worksheet to include the effect of both the newly issued shares of stock and the combination costs.
- Richmond's revenue and expense accounts have been closed out to retained earnings since this combination is a purchase.
- Entry 1 on the worksheet eliminates the $1,100,000 book value component of the Investment in Richmond Company account along with the subsidiary's stockholders' equity accounts.
- Entry 2 adjusts all of Richmond's assets and liabilities to fair market value based on the allocations determined earlier. However, the values attributed to the Buildings account and the Equipment account have been reduced by a total of $64,000 to reflect the bargain purchase made.

EXHIBIT 2–11   Comprehensive Illustration—Solution—Purchase Method

MARSTON COMPANY AND RICHMOND COMPANY
Consolidation Worksheet
For Period Ending December 31, 1995

Accounts	Marston Company	Richmond Company	Consolidation Entries Debit	Consolidation Entries Credit	Consolidated Totals
Income Statement					
Revenues	(6,000,000)				(6,000,000)
Expenses	3,400,000				3,400,000
Net income	(2,600,000)				(2,600,000)
Statement of Retained Earnings					
Retained earnings, 1/1/95	(2,300,000)				(2,300,000)
Net income (above)	(2,600,000)				(2,600,000)
Retained earnings, 12/31/95	(4,900,000)				(4,900,000)
Balance Sheet					
Cash	570,000*	200,000			770,000
Receivables	900,000	300,000		(2) 10,000	1,190,000
Inventory	1,100,000	600,000	(2) 120,000		1,820,000
Investment in Richmond Company	1,446,000*	–0–		(1) 1,100,000	–0–
				(2) 346,000	
Buildings (net)	3,000,000	800,000	(2) 160,000		3,960,000
Equipment (net)	6,000,000	500,000	(2) 76,000		6,576,000
Total assets	13,016,000	2,400,000			14,316,000
Accounts payable	(400,000)	(200,000)			(600,000)
Notes payable	(3,400,000)	(1,100,000)			(4,500,000)
Common stock	(3,000,000)*	(720,000)	(1) 720,000		(3,000,000)
Additional paid-in capital	(1,316,000)*	(100,000)	(1) 100,000		(1,316,000)
Retained earnings, 12/31/95 (above)	(4,900,000)	(280,000)†	(1) 280,000		(4,900,000)
Total liabilities and equities	(13,016,000)	(2,400,000)			(14,316,000)

NOTE: Parentheses indicate a credit balance.

* Balances have been adjusted for combination transaction and payment of consolidation costs.

† Beginning retained earnings plus revenues minus expenses.

d. This final example returns to the pooling of interests concept. As such, the change in value of Marston's common stock (to $28.52 per share) has no impact on consolidated totals; poolings are always based on book values.

Since separate accounting systems are maintained, Marston records the issuance of its 50,000 shares as an investment. As a pooling, the total is set equal to Richmond's $950,000 book value at January 1, 1995, a figure derived from the company's three stockholders' equity accounts. As in part *b.*, Marston must reduce its own additional paid-in capital so that total contributed capital of $820,000 is recorded, the same figure reported by the subsidiary. The par value of the shares issued by Giant ($1 million) less a reduction here of $180,000 gives this identical balance. Retained earnings as of January 1 of $130,000 is also recorded since poolings are reported on a retroactive basis.

EXHIBIT 2–12   Comprehensive Illustration—Solution—Pooling of Interests Method

MARSTON COMPANY AND RICHMOND COMPANY
Consolidation Worksheet
For Period Ending December 31, 1995

Accounts	Marston Company	Richmond Company	Consolidation Entries Debit	Consolidation Entries Credit	Consolidated Totals
Income Statement					
Revenues	(6,000,000)	(900,000)			(6,900,000)
Expenses	3,430,000 *	750,000			4,180,000
Net income	(2,570,000)	(150,000)			(2,720,000)
Statement of Retained Earnings					
Retained earnings, 1/1/95	(2,430,000)*	(130,000)	(1) 130,000		(2,430,000)
Net income (above)	(2,570,000)	(150,000)			(2,720,000)
Retained earnings, 12/31/95	(5,000,000)	(280,000)			(5,150,000)
Balance Sheet					
Cash	570,000 *	200,000			770,000
Receivables	900,000	300,000			1,200,000
Inventory	1,100,000	600,000			1,700,000
Investment in Richmond Company	950,000 *	–0–		(1) 950,000	–0–
Buildings (net)	3,000,000	800,000			3,800,000
Equipment (net)	6,000,000	500,000			6,500,000
Total assets	12,520,000	2,400,000			13,970,000
Accounts payable	(400,000)	(200,000)			(600,000)
Notes payable	(3,400,000)	(1,100,000)			(4,500,000)
Common stock	(3,000,000)*	(720,000)	(1) 720,000		(3,000,000)
Additional paid-in capital	(720,000)*	(100,000)	(1) 100,000		(720,000)
Retained earnings, 12/31/95 (above)	(5,000,000)	(280,000)			(5,150,000)
Total liabilities and equities	(12,520,000)	(2,400,000)			(13,970,000)

NOTE: Parentheses indicate a credit balance.
* Balances have been adjusted for combination transactions and payment of consolidation costs.

Marston's Financial Records—December 31, 1995

Investment in Richmond Company.	950,000	
Additional Paid-In Capital (to align contributed capital totals).	180,000	
Common Stock (Marston) (par value)		1,000,000
Retained Earnings, 1/1/95.		130,000

To record the issuance of 50,000 shares to create a pooling of interests with Richmond Company.

Expenses	30,000	
Cash		30,000

To record payment of combination costs, which are viewed as expenses in a pooling of interests.

After Marston's entries have been recorded, the consolidation worksheet found in Exhibit 2–12 can be produced. The investment account is eliminated on this worksheet so that the book value of Richmond's individual accounts can be consolidated (assets, liabilities, revenues, and expenses). Richmond's stockholders' equity accounts are also removed on this worksheet since they have already been added to Marston's records through the first journal entry.

APPENDIX
TWELVE CRITERIA FOR A POOLING OF INTERESTS[20]

1. Attributes of combining companies.
   a. Each of the combining companies is autonomous and has not been a subsidiary or division of another corporation within two years before the plan of combination is initiated.
   b. Each of the combining companies is independent of the other combining companies.
2. Characteristics of the combination.
   a. The combination is effected in a single transaction or is completed in accordance with a specific plan within one year after the plan is initiated.
   b. A corporation offers and issues only common stock with rights identical to those of the majority of its outstanding voting common stock in exchange for substantially all of the voting common stock interest of another company at the date the plan of combination is consummated. Substantially all of the voting common stock means 90 percent or more for this condition.
   c. None of the combining companies changes the equity interest of the voting common stock in contemplation of effecting the combination either within

---

[20] Established by *APB Opinion 16*.

two years before the plan of combination is initiated or between the dates the combination is initiated and consummated; changes in contemplation of effecting the combination may include distributions to stockholders and additional issuances, exchanges, and retirements of securities.

   d. Each of the combining companies reacquires shares of voting common stock only for purposes other than business combinations, and no company reacquires more than a normal number of shares between the dates the plan of combination is initiated and consummated.

   e. The ratio of the interest of an individual common stockholder to those of other common stockholders in a combining company remains the same as a result of the exchange of stock to effect the combination.

   f. The voting rights to which the common stock ownership interests in the resulting combined corporation are entitled are exercisable by the stockholders; the stockholders are neither deprived of nor restricted in exercising those rights for a period.

   g. The combination is resolved at the date the plan is consummated and no provisions of the plan relating to the issue of securities or other consideration are pending.

3. Absence of planned transaction.

   a. The combined corporation does not agree directly or indirectly to retire or reacquire all or part of the common stock issued to effect the combination.

   b. The combined corporation does not enter into other financial arrangements for the benefit of the former stockholders of a combining company, such as a guaranty of loans secured by stock issued in the combination, which in effect negates the exchange of equity securities.

   c. The combined corporation does not intend or plan to dispose of a significant part of the assets of the combining companies within two years after the combination other than disposals in the ordinary course of business of the formerly separate companies and to eliminate duplicate facilities or excess capacity.

Questions

1. What is a business combination?
2. Describe the different types of legal arrangements that can take place to create a business combination.
3. What is meant by consolidated financial statements?
4. Within the consolidation process, what is the purpose of a worksheet?
5. What characteristics are associated with a business combination accounted for as a purchase? What characteristics are associated with a business combination accounted for as a pooling of interests?

6. Jones Company obtains all of the common stock of Hudson, Inc. by issuing 50,000 shares of its own stock. Under these circumstances, why might the determination of an acquisition price be difficult?

7. What is the accounting basis for consolidating assets and liabilities in a business combination recorded as a purchase? What is the accounting basis for consolidating assets and liabilities in a business combination recorded as a pooling of interests?

8. How are a subsidiary's revenues and expenses consolidated in a purchase? How are a subsidiary's revenues and expenses consolidated in a pooling of interests?

9. Richmond Company acquires control over Schmidt Company. How will the determination be made as to whether this combination is to be accounted for as a purchase or as a pooling of interests?

10. Morgan Company purchases all of the outstanding shares of Jennings, Inc. for cash. Morgan pays more than the fair market value of the company's net assets. How should the payment in excess of fair market value be accounted for in the consolidation process?

11. Catron Corporation is having liquidity problems, and as a result, all of its outstanding shares are sold to Lambert, Inc. for cash. Because of Catron's problems, Lambert is able to acquire this stock at less than the fair market value of the company's net assets. How is this reduction in price accounted for within the consolidation process?

12. How is a deferred credit created in a consolidation?

13. Sloane, Inc. issues 25,000 shares of its own common stock in exchange for all of the outstanding shares of Benjamin Company. Benjamin will remain a separately incorporated operation. How does Sloane record the issuance of these shares if this combination is a purchase? How does Sloane record the issuance of these shares if this combination is a pooling of interests?

14. To obtain all of the stock of Molly, Inc., Harrison Corporation issued its own common stock. Harrison had to pay $98,000 to lawyers, accountants, and a stock brokerage firm in connection with services rendered during the creation of this business combination. In addition, Harrison paid $56,000 in costs associated with the stock issuance. If this combination is to be accounted for as a purchase, how will these two costs be recorded? If this combination is to be accounted for as a pooling of interests, how will these two costs be recorded?

15. Two companies that have been in business for a number of years join together to create a new business combination. If this arrangement is appropriately recorded as a pooling of interests, how will the prior operations of the two companies be reported? If this arrangement is appropriately recorded as a purchase, how will the prior operations of the two companies be reported?

16. Under what conditions will a parent company omit a subsidiary from consolidation despite owning over 50 percent of the outstanding voting stock?

Library Assignments

1. Read "What's off, What's on?" in the February 20, 1989, issue of *Forbes* as well as "Consolidations: An Overview of the FASB DM," in the April 1992 issue of the *Journal of Accountancy* and "The Debate Over Consolidating Statements," in the March/April 1992 issue of *Financial Executive*. As indicated, Masco Corporation does not consolidate Masco Industries because less than 50 percent of the voting stock is held. Write a short report discussing whether the FASB should set criteria for control (and consolidation) other than majority ownership.

2. Read the following as well as any other published information on the consolidation of finance subsidiaries:

   "Should We Consolidate Finance Subsidiaries?" *Management Accounting,* April 1987.

   "Unconsolidated Finance Subsidiaries: Characteristics and Debt/Equity Effects," *Accounting Horizons,* March 1988.

   "Mishmash Accounting," *Forbes,* November 27, 1989.

   "FASB Faulted," *Industry Week,* November 7, 1988.

   "SFAS 94: The Prodigal Son Becomes Part of the Family Picture," *The CPA Journal,* February 1989.

   "Consolidation of All Majority-Owned Subsidiaries," *FASB Statement No. 94* (including the dissent at the end of the pronouncement and both appendices).

   Write a report to either justify the FASB's decision to consolidate finance subsidiaries or offer a preferred alternative.

3. Locate *The Wall Street Journal General Index* for the most recent year. Under the heading "Mergers and Acquisitions," find one or more articles describing a recent corporate takeover. After reading these stories, answer the following questions:

   - Was the acquisition a purchase or a pooling of interests?
   - What was exchanged to create the combination?
   - Was the takeover hostile or negotiated?
   - If hostile, did the company being acquired take any actions in hopes of preventing the takeover?
   - If this transaction was a purchase, does the article specify the amount, if any, of goodwill to be recognized?
   - Does the article speculate as to the impact of the acquisition on the acquiring company's future profits?
   - What other information is provided?

4. Read the following as well as any other published information concerning the pooling of interests method:

   "APB 16: Time to Reconsider," *Journal of Accountancy,* October 1991.

   "Merger Mania—Should Pooling Be Abolished?" *The National Public Accountant,* June 1990.

"A History of Pooling of Interests Accounting for Business Combinations
in the United States," *Accounting Historians Journal*, December 1991.
"Does Pooling Present Fairly?" *The CPA Journal*, December 1974.
"Is Now the Time to Revisit Accounting for Business Combinations?"
The CPA Journal, July 1989.
"Muddying the Waters," *Barron's*, October 8, 1990.
"Pooling vs. Purchase and Goodwill: A Long-standing Controversy
Abates," *Mergers & Acquisitions*, Fall 1980.

Write a report discussing whether the pooling of interests method should be
abolished as a generally accepted accounting principle.

5. Read the following as well as any other published information describing the
accountant's role in the takeover process:

"Allocating Purchase Price in an Acquisition: A Practical Guide," *Journal
of Accountancy*, November 1987.
"1 + 1 = 3," *Management Accountant*, April 1987.

Write a report discussing the accountant's role in the acquisition of a subsidiary company.

Problems

1. Which of the following is the best theoretical justification for consolidated
financial statements?
   a. In form the companies are one entity; in substance they are separate.
   b. In form the companies are separate; in substance they are one entity.
   c. In form and substance the companies are one entity.
   d. In form and substance the companies are separate.
   (AICPA)

2. What is a statutory merger?
   a. A merger approved of by the Securities and Exchange Commission.
   b. An acquisition involving both the purchase of stock as well as assets.
   c. A takeover completed within one year of the initial tender offer.
   d. A business combination in which only one company continues to exist
   as a legal entity.

3. Which of the following characteristics is not associated with a purchase?
   a. One company acquires either the stock or assets of another company.
   b. A clearly identified cost figure is evident for the transaction.
   c. The distinction as to which organization is the acquiring company and
   which is the acquired is not always clear.
   d. Cash or debt or stocks can be used as payment for the acquired
   company.

4. Williams Company obtains all of the outstanding stock of Jaminson, Inc.,
in a purchase transaction. In a consolidation prepared immediately after
the takeover, at what value will the inventory owned by Jaminson be
consolidated?

   a. Jaminson's historical cost.

   b. A percentage of the acquisition cost paid by Williams.

   c. The inventory will be omitted in the consolidation.

   d. At the fair market value on the date of the purchase.

5. When is the recognition of a deferred credit required in consolidating financial information?

   a. When any bargain purchase is created.

   b. In a pooling of interests that is created in the middle of a fiscal year.

   c. In a purchase, when the value of all assets and liabilities cannot be determined.

   d. When the amount of a bargain purchase is greater than the value of the noncurrent assets (other than marketable securities) held by the acquired company.

6. Haynes, Inc., obtains all of the outstanding common stock of Tallent Company on October 1, 1995. Tallent earns net income of $10,000 per month. A consolidated income statement is to be prepared for the year ended December 31, 1995. What is the impact on net income of including Tallent in the consolidated statements?

   a. Increased by $120,000 in a purchase; increased by $120,000 in a pooling of interests.

   b. Increased by $120,000 in a purchase; increased by $30,000 in a pooling of interests.

   c. Increased by $30,000 in a purchase; increased by $120,000 in a pooling of interests.

   d. Increased by $30,000 in a purchase; increased by $30,000 in a pooling of interests.

7. A business combination is accounted for properly as a pooling of interests. Which of the following costs related to effecting the business combination should enter into the determination of the net income of a combined corporation for the period in which the expenses are incurred?

	Fees of Finders and Consultants	Registration Fees
a.	No	Yes
b.	No	No
c.	Yes	No
d.	Yes	Yes

(AICPA adapted)

8. Which of the following transactions related to a business combination would require that the combination be accounted for as a purchase?

   a. The combination is to be completed within 12 months from the date the plan was initiated.

   b. Ninety-two percent of one company's common stock is exchanged for only common stock in the other company.

c. The combined company is to retire a portion of the common stock exchanged to effect the combination within 12 months of the combination.

d. The combined company will dispose of numerous fixed assets representing duplicate facilities subsequent to the combination.

(AICPA)

9. How should equipment obtained in a business combination be shown under each of the following methods?

	Pooling of Interests	*Purchase*
a.	Recorded value	Recorded value
b.	Recorded value	Fair value
c.	Fair value	Fair value
d.	Fair value	Recorded value

(AICPA adapted)

10. Starten Company has common stock of $300,000 and retained earnings of $400,000. Premtick, Inc. has common stock of $600,000 and retained earnings of $800,000. On January 1, 1995, Premtick issues 31,000 shares of common stock with a $10 par value and a $30 fair market value for all of Starten's outstanding common stock. A pooling of interests has been created. Immediately after the combination is created, what is the balance in consolidated retained earnings?

a. $800,000.

b. $1,200,000.

c. $1,190,000.

d. $1,420,000.

11. Which of the following is not an appropriate reason for leaving a subsidiary unconsolidated?

a. The subsidiary is in bankruptcy.

b. The subsidiary is to be sold in the near future.

c. A foreign government threatens to take over the assets of the subsidiary.

d. The subsidiary is in an industry that is significantly different than that of the parent.

Problems 12 and 13 are based on the following information: Prior to being united in a business combination, Atkins, Inc. and Waterson Corporation had the following stockholders' equity figures:

	Atkins	Waterson
Common stock ($1 par value) . . .	$180,000	$ 45,000
Additional paid-in capital	90,000	20,000
Retained earnings	300,000	110,000

Atkins issues 51,000 new shares of its common stock valued at $3 per share for all of the outstanding stock of Waterson.

12. Assume that Atkins is acquiring Waterson through a purchase. Immediately afterwards, what are consolidated additional paid-in capital and retained earnings, respectively?
 a. $104,000 and $300,000.
 b. $110,000 and $410,000.
 c. $192,000 and $300,000.
 d. $212,000 and $410,000.

13. Assume that Atkins and Waterson are being joined in a pooling of interests. Immediately afterwards, what are consolidated additional paid-in capital and retained earnings, respectively?
 a. $104,000 and $300,000.
 b. $104,000 and $410,000.
 c. $110,000 and $300,000.
 d. $110,000 and $410,000.

Problems 14 and 15 are based on the following information: Hampstead, Inc. has only three assets:

	Book Value	Fair Market Value
Inventory . . .	$110,000	$150,000
Land	700,000	600,000
Buildings . . .	700,000	900,000

Miller Corporation purchases Hampstead by issuing 100,000 shares of its $10 par value common stock.

14. If Miller's stock is worth $20 per share, at what value will the inventory, land, and buildings be consolidated, respectively?
 a. $110,000, $600,000, $900,000.
 b. $110,000, $700,000, $700,000.
 c. $150,000, $600,000, $900,000.
 d. $150,000, $700,000, $900,000.

15. If Miller's stock is worth $15 per share, at what value will the inventory, land, and buildings be consolidated, respectively?
 a. $110,000, $695,000, $695,000.
 b. $150,000, $525,000, $825,000.
 c. $150,000, $540,000, $810,000.
 d. $136,363, $545,455, $818,182.

Problems 16 through 23 are based on the following information: Allen, Inc. obtains control over Tucker, Inc. on July 1, 1995. The book value and fair market value of Tucker's accounts on that date (prior to creating the combination) follow, along with the book value of Allen's accounts:

	Allen Book Value	Tucker Book Value	Tucker Market Value
Revenues	$250,000	$130,000	
Expenses	170,000	80,000	
Retained earnings, 1/1/95	130,000	150,000	
Cash and receivables	140,000	60,000	$ 60,000
Inventory	190,000	145,000	175,000
Land	230,000	180,000	200,000
Buildings (net)	400,000	200,000	225,000
Equipment (net)	100,000	75,000	75,000
Liabilities	540,000	360,000	350,000
Common stock	300,000	70,000	
Additional paid-in capital	10,000	30,000	

16. Assume that Allen issues 10,000 shares of common stock with a $5 par value and a $40 fair market value to obtain all of Tucker's outstanding stock. If this transaction is a purchase, how much goodwill should be recognized?
    a. –0–.
    b. $15,000.
    c. $35,000.
    d. $100,000.

17. Assume that Allen issues 10,000 shares of common stock with a $5 par value and a $40 fair market value for all of the outstanding stock of Tucker. What is the consolidated land balance if this transaction is a pooling of interests?
    a. $380,000.
    b. $410,000.
    c. $420,000.
    d. $430,000.

18. For the fiscal year ending December 31, 1995, how will consolidated net income of this business combination be determined if Allen acquires all of Tucker's stock in a pooling of interests?
    a. Allen's income for the past year plus Tucker's income for the past six months.
    b. Allen's income for the past year plus Tucker's income for the past year.
    c. Allen's income for the past six months plus Tucker's income for the past six months.
    d. Allen's income for the past six months plus Tucker's income for the past year.

19. For the fiscal year ending December 31, 1995, how will consolidated net income of this business combination be determined if Allen acquires all of Tucker's stock in a purchase?
    a. Allen's income for the past year plus Tucker's income for the past six months.

    b. Allen's income for the past year plus Tucker's income for the past year.

    c. Allen's income for the past six months plus Tucker's income for the past six months.

    d. Allen's income for the past six months plus Tucker's income for the past year.

20. Assume that Allen issues 16,000 shares of common stock with a $5 per share par value and a $40 fair market value in exchange for all of the outstanding shares of Tucker. What will be the consolidated Additional Paid-In Capital and Retained Earnings (January 1, 1995, balance) if this combination is recorded as a pooling of interests?

    a. $10,000 and $130,000.

    b. $30,000 and $280,000.

    c. $30,000 and $130,000.

    d. $40,000 and $280,000.

21. Assume that Allen issues 16,000 shares of common stock with a $10 per share par value and a $40 fair market value in exchange for all of the outstanding shares of Tucker. What will be the consolidated Additional Paid-In Capital and Retained Earnings (January 1, 1995, balance) if this combination is recorded as a pooling of interests?

    a. $10,000 and $130,000.

    b. –0– and $230,000.

    c. –0– and $80,000.

    d. $40,000 and $280,000.

22. Assume that Allen issues preferred stock with a par value of $200,000 and a fair market value of $335,000 for all shares of Tucker in a combination accounted for as a purchase. What will be the balance in the consolidated Inventory, Land, and beginning Retained Earnings accounts?

    a. $365,000, $410,000, and $130,000.

    b. $365,000, $430,000, and $130,000.

    c. $352,500, $417,500, and $280,000.

    d. $335,000, $430,000, and $280,000.

23. Assume that Allen pays a total of $370,000 in cash for all of the shares of Tucker. In addition, Allen pays $30,000 to a group of attorneys for their work in arranging the acquisition. What will be the balance in consolidated goodwill and retained earnings?

    a. –0– and $90,000.

    b. –0– and $280,000.

    c. $15,000 and $280,000.

    d. $15,000 and $130,000.

24. Two methods are used to account for business combinations: purchase and pooling of interests.

Required:

a. A business combination is being accounted for as a purchase.

    (1) What is the theoretical rationale behind this method?

(2) How should the amount of goodwill be determined at the date of acquisition?

b. A business combination is being accounted for as a pooling of interests.

   (1) What is the theoretical rationale behind this method?

   (2) How should the various stockholders' equity accounts be reported?

(AICPA adapted)

25. Spellman Company will soon acquire Moore, Inc. Spellman will issue shares of its stock for all of the outstanding stock of Moore. Therefore, this combination might be accounted for as either a purchase or a pooling of interests. The fair market value of the shares being issued will exceed the value of Moore's net assets.

Required:

a. How does the method of accounting for a business combination affect the recognition of goodwill?

b. If goodwill is to be reported by this business combination, how is the amount determined?

c. Why should consolidated financial statements be prepared?

d. What condition must first exist before the consolidation of financial statements is necessary?

e. Does the method of accounting for a business combination affect the decision to prepare consolidated financial statements?

(AICPA adapted)

26. Flaherty Company entered into a business combination with Steeley Company during 1995. The combination was accounted for as a pooling of interests.

    Flaherty Company also acquired all of the voting common stock of Rubin Company during 1995. This combination was accounted for as a purchase and resulted in goodwill.

    Registration fees were incurred in issuing common stock in both of these combinations. Other costs, such as legal and accounting fees, were also paid.

Required:

a. In the business combination accounted for as a pooling of interests, how should the assets and liabilities of the two companies be included within consolidated statements? What is the rationale for accounting for a business combination as a pooling of interests?

b. In the business combination accounted for as a pooling of interests, how should the registration fees and the other direct costs be recorded?

c. In the business combination accounted for as a pooling of interests, how should the results of the operations for 1995 be reported?

d. In the business combination accounted for as a purchase, how should the assets and liabilities of the two companies be included within consolidated statements? What is the rationale for accounting for a business combination as a purchase?

e. In the business combination accounted for as purchase, how should the registration fees and the other direct costs be recorded?

f. In the business combination accounted for as a purchase, how should the results of the operations for 1995 be reported?

(AICPA adapted)

27. Bakel Corporation has the following account balances:

Receivables	$ 80,000
Inventory	200,000 *280,000*
Land	600,000 *400,000*
Building	500,000 *600,000*
Liabilities	400,000 *330,000*
Common stock	100,000
Additional paid-in capital . . .	100,000
Retained earnings, 1/1/95 . . .	700,000
Revenues	300,000
Expenses	220,000

Several of Bakel's accounts have market values that differ from book value: land—$400,000; building—$600,000; inventory—$280,000; and liabilities—$330,000. Homewood, Inc., obtains all of the outstanding shares of Bakel by issuing 20,000 shares of common stock having a $5 par value but a $55 fair market value. Stock issuance costs amount to $10,000. The transaction is to be accounted for as a purchase.

a. What is the purchase price in this combination?

b. What is the book value of Bakel's net assets on the date of the takeover?

c. How are the stock issuance costs handled? *Debit PIC*

d. How does the issuance of these shares affect the stockholders' equity accounts of Homewood, the parent?

e. What allocations are made of Homewood's purchase price to specific accounts and to goodwill?

f. How do Bakel's revenues and expenses affect consolidated totals? Why?

g. How do Bakel's common stock and additional paid-in capital balances affect consolidated totals?

h. In financial statements prepared immediately following the takeover, what impact will this acquisition have on the various consolidated totals?

i. If Homewood's stock had been worth only $40 per share rather than $55, how would the consolidation of Bakel's assets and liabilities have been affected? *Credit Differential*

28. Harcourt Company has the following account balances:

Receivables	$ 90,000
Inventory	500,000
Land	700,000
Buildings	200,000
Liabilities	800,000
Common stock	100,000
Additional paid-in capital . . .	90,000
Retained earnings, 1/1/95 . . .	440,000
Revenues	400,000
Expenses	340,000

(handwritten annotations: 470,000; 900,000; 400,000; 840,000)

Several of Harcourt's accounts have market values that differ from book value: land—$900,000; building—$400,000; inventory—$470,000; and liabilities—$840,000. Lee Corporation obtains all of the outstanding shares of Harcourt by issuing 20,000 shares of common stock having a $10 par value but a $62 fair market value. Stock issuance costs amount to $10,000. The transaction is to be accounted for as a pooling of interests. Before recording the issuance of these new shares, Lee has a Common Stock account of $2 million and Additional Paid-In Capital of $1.3 million.

a. What is the book value of Harcourt's net assets on the date of the take-over?

b. How are the stock issuance costs handled?

c. Assume that both companies will retain their identities as separate corporations. What journal entry would Lee record for the issuance of its stock?

d. How would the answer to part c. have changed if Lee's stock had a $1 per share par value rather than $10 per share?

e. How would the answer to part c. have changed if Lee's stock had a $10 per share par value but Lee issued 30,000 shares rather than 20,000?

f. How do Harcourt's revenues and expenses affect consolidated totals? Why?

g. In financial statements prepared immediately following the takeover, what impact would Harcourt's accounts have on the various consolidated totals?

h. Give 3 of the 12 requirements that must be met for a combination to be accounted for as a pooling of interests.

29. Winston has the following account balances as of February 1, 1995:

Inventory	$ 600,000
Land.	500,000
Buildings (net) (valued at $1,000,000) . . .	900,000
Common stock ($10 par value)	800,000
Retained earnings (January 1, 1995)	1,100,000
Revenues.	600,000
Expenses.	500,000

Arlington pays $1.4 million cash and issues 10,000 shares of its $30 par value common stock (valued at $80 per share) for all of Winston's outstanding stock. Stock issuance costs amount to $30,000. Prior to recording these newly issued shares, Arlington reports a Common Stock account of $900,000 and Additional Paid-In Capital of $500,000.

Required:

For each of the following accounts, determine what balance would be included in a February 1, 1995, consolidation.
   a. Goodwill.
   b. Expenses.
   c. Retained Earnings, 1/1/95.
   d. Buildings.

30. Use the same information as presented in problem 29 but assume that Arlington pays cash of $2.3 million. No stock is issued. An additional $40,000 is paid in direct combination costs.

Required:

For each of the following accounts, determine what balance would be included in a February 1, 1995, consolidation.
   a. Goodwill.
   b. Expenses.
   c. Retained Earnings, 1/1/95.
   d. Buildings.

31. Use the same information as presented in problem 29 but assume that Arlington pays $2,020,000 in cash. An additional $20,000 is paid in direct combination costs.

Required:

For each of the following accounts, determine what balance will be included in a February 1, 1995, consolidation.
   a. Inventory.
   b. Goodwill.
   c. Expenses.
   d. Buildings.
   e. Land.

32. Use the same information as presented in problem 29 but assume that Arlington issues 30,000 shares of common stock ($30 par value but a fair market value of $80 per share) for all of Winston's outstanding stock in a transaction that qualifies as a pooling of interests. Stock issuance costs of $35,000 are paid along with $24,000 of other direct combination costs.

Required:

For each of the following accounts, determine what balance will be included in a February 1, 1995, consolidation.

    a. Buildings.
    b. Goodwill.
    c. Expenses.
    d. Retained Earnings, 1/1/95.

33. On December 31, 1995, Bingham Company and Laredo Company have the following account balances:

	Bingham	Laredo
Revenues	$100,000	$ 80,000
Expenses	60,000	50,000
Net income	40,000	30,000
Retained earnings, 1/1/95	$210,000	$ 70,000
Net income	40,000	30,000
Dividends	30,000	–0–
Retained earnings, 12/31/95	220,000	100,000
Cash	$ 80,000	$ 20,000
Receivables	60,000	60,000
Inventory	100,000	70,000
Buildings and equipment (net)	200,000	100,000
Total assets	440,000	250,000
Current liabilities	$ 20,000	$ 10,000
Long-term liabilities	70,000	50,000
Common stock	110,000	90,000
Additional paid-in capital	20,000	–0–
Retained earnings, 12/31/95	220,000	100,000
Total liabilities and equities	440,000	250,000

After these figures were prepared, Bingham issued 10,000 shares of its $10 par value stock for all of the outstanding shares of Laredo. Bingham's stock had a $25 per share fair market value. Bingham also paid $10,000 in direct combination costs and $20,000 in stock issuance costs. Laredo holds a building that is worth $40,000 more than its current book value.

Required:

a. Assume that this combination is a pooling of interests. Determine consolidated balances for this combination as of December 31, 1995.

b. Assume that this combination is a purchase. Determine consolidated balances for this combination as of December 31, 1995.

34. Following are the financial balances for the Parrot Company and the Sun Company as of December 31, 1995. Also included are fair market values for the Sun Company accounts.

	Parrot Company *Book Value* *12/31/95*	Sun Company *Book Value* *12/31/95*	*Market Value* *12/31/95*
Cash	$ 290,000	$ 120,000	$ 120,000
Receivables	220,000	300,000	300,000
Inventory	410,000	210,000	260,000
Land	600,000	130,000	110,000
Buildings (net).	600,000	270,000	330,000
Equipment (net)	220,000	190,000	220,000
Accounts payable	(190,000)	(120,000)	(120,000)
Accrued expenses	(90,000)	(30,000)	(30,000)
Long-term liabilities	(900,000)	(510,000)	(510,000)
Common stock—$20 par value . . .	(660,000)		
Common Stock—$5 par value. . . .		(210,000)	
Additional paid-in capital	(70,000)	(90,000)	
Retained earnings, 1/1/95	(390,000)	(240,000)	
Revenues	(960,000)	(330,000)	
Expenses	920,000	310,000	

NOTE: Parentheses indicate a credit balance.

Required:

In the following situations, determine the value that would be shown in consolidated financial statements for each of the accounts listed below. Each problem should be viewed as an independent occurrence. These transactions all take place on December 31, 1995.

Accounts	
Inventory	Revenues
Land	Additional Paid-In Capital
Buildings	Expenses
Goodwill	Retained Earnings, 1/1/95

a. Parrot acquires the outstanding stock of Sun by issuing $760,000 in long-term liabilities.

    b. Parrot acquires the outstanding stock of Sun by paying $160,000 in cash and issuing 10,000 shares of its own common stock with a value of $40 per share. Direct combination costs of $20,000 are paid by Parrot as well as $5,000 in stock issuance costs.

    c. Parrot obtains the outstanding stock of Sun by issuing 12,000 shares of common stock with a value of $40 per share. This transaction meets all 12 requirements for a pooling of interests.

    d. Parrot obtains the outstanding stock of Sun by issuing 16,000 shares of common stock with a value of $40 per share. This transaction meets all 12 requirements for a pooling of interests. Stock issuance costs of $8,000 are paid.

    e. Parrot obtains the outstanding stock of Sun by issuing 19,000 shares of its common stock with a value of $40 per share. This transaction meets all 12 requirements for a pooling of interests. Direct combination costs of $9,000 are paid by Parrot.

35. The financial statements for Hope, Inc., and Kaisley Corporation for the year ending December 31, 1995, follow. Kaisley's buildings are undervalued on its financial records by $50,000.

	Hope	Kaisley
Revenues.	$ 400,000	$ 400,000
Expenses.	240,000	240,000
Net income.	$ 160,000	$ 160,000
Retained earnings, 1/1/95.	$ 600,000	$ 400,000
Net income.	160,000	160,000
Dividends paid	90,000	90,000
Retained earnings, 12/31/95.	$ 670,000	$ 470,000
Cash.	$ 130,000	$ 100,000
Receivables and inventory	200,000	200,000
Buildings (net)	600,000	300,000
Equipment (net).	600,000	500,000
Total assets.	$1,530,000	$1,100,000
Liabilities.	$ 200,000	$ 200,000
Common stock	630,000	360,000
Additional paid-in capital.	30,000	70,000
Retained earnings	670,000	470,000
Total liabilities and equities.	$1,530,000	$1,100,000

On December 31, 1995, Hope issues 45,000 new shares of its $10 par value stock to the owners of Kaisley in exchange for all of the outstanding shares of that company. Hope's shares had a fair market value on that date of $30 per share. Hope paid $30,000 to a bank for assisting in the arrangements. Hope also paid $20,000 in stock issuance costs.

This combination meets all 12 requirements of a pooling of interests. What are the appropriate consolidated balances?

36. The financial statements for Willeslye, Inc., and Barrett Company for the year ending December 31, 1995, follow:

	Willeslye	Barrett
Revenues	$ 900,000	$ 300,000
Expenses	660,000	200,000
Net income	$ 240,000	$ 100,000
Retained earnings, 1/1/95	$ 800,000	$ 200,000
Net income	240,000	100,000
Dividends paid	90,000	–0–
Retained earnings, 12/31/95	$ 950,000	$ 300,000
Cash	$ 80,000	$ 110,000
Receivables and inventory	400,000	170,000
Buildings (net)	900,000	300,000
Equipment (net)	700,000	600,000
Total assets	$2,080,000	$1,180,000
Liabilities	$ 500,000	$ 410,000
Common stock	360,000	200,000
Additional paid-in capital	270,000	270,000
Retained earnings	950,000	300,000
Total liabilities and equities	$2,080,000	$1,180,000

On December 31, 1995, Willeslye issues $300,000 in debt and 15,000 new shares of its $10 par value stock to the owners of Barrett to purchase all of the outstanding shares of that company. Willeslye shares had a fair market value of $40 per share.

Willeslye also paid $30,000 to a broker for arranging the transaction. In addition, Willeslye paid $40,000 in stock issuance costs. Barrett's equipment was actually worth $700,000 but its buildings were only valued at $280,000.

What are the consolidated balances for the following accounts?

- Net Income
- Retained Earnings, 1/1/95
- Equipment
- Goodwill
- Liabilities
- Common Stock
- Additional Paid-In Capital

37. Merrill acquires 100 percent of the outstanding voting shares of Harriss Company on January 1, 1995. To obtain these shares, Merrill pays $200,000

in cash and issues 10,000 shares of its own $10 par value common stock. On this date, Merrill's stock has a fair market value of $18 per share. Merrill also pays $10,000 to a local investment company for arranging the acquisition. An additional $6,000 was paid by Merrill in stock issuance costs.

The book values for both Merrill and Harriss as of December 31, 1994, follow. The fair market value of each of Harriss's accounts is also included. In addition, Harriss holds a fully amortized patent that still retains a $30,000 value.

	Merrill, Inc. *Book Value*	Harriss Company	
		Book Value	*Fair Market Value*
Cash.	$300,000	$ 40,000	$ 40,000
Receivables	160,000	90,000	80,000
Inventory	220,000	130,000	130,000
Land	100,000	60,000	60,000
Buildings (net)	400,000	110,000	140,000
Equipment (net)	120,000	50,000	50,000
Accounts Payable	160,000	30,000	30,000
Long-Term Liabilities . . .	380,000	170,000	150,000
Common Stock	400,000	40,000	
Retained Earnings.	360,000	240,000	

Required:

a. Assume that this combination is a statutory merger so that Harriss's accounts are to be transferred to the records of Merrill with Harriss subsequently being dissolved as a legal corporation. Prepare the journal entries for Merrill that are required to record this merger.

b. Assume that no dissolution is to take place in connection with this combination. Rather, both companies retain their separate legal identities. Prepare a worksheet to consolidate the two companies as of January 1, 1995.

38. The following are preliminary financial statements for Green Company and Gold Company for the year ending December 31, 1995.

	Green Company	Gold Company
Sales	$300,000	$190,000
Expenses	(200,000)	(110,000)
Net income	$100,000	$ 80,000
Retained earnings, 1/1/95	$400,000	$210,000
Net income—above.	100,000	80,000
Dividends paid	(30,000)	–0–
Retained earnings, 12/31/95	$470,000	$290,000
Current assets	$300,000	$100,000
Land	100,000	90,000
Buildings (net)	400,000	280,000
Total assets	$800,000	$470,000
Liabilities	$ 90,000	$110,000
Common stock	160,000	60,000
Additional paid-in capital	80,000	10,000
Retained earnings, 12/31/95	470,000	290,000
Total liabilities and equities	$800,000	$470,000

(handwritten in margin: 170,000)

On December 31, 1995 (subsequent to the preceding statements), Green exchanges 8,000 shares of its $10 par value common stock for all of the outstanding shares of Gold. This transaction meets all 12 criteria for a pooling of interests. Green's stock on that date has a fair market value of $55 per share. Green was willing to issue 8,000 shares of stock because Gold's land was appraised at $170,000. Green also paid $12,000 to several attorneys and accountants who assisted in creating this combination.

Required:

a. Assuming that these two companies retain their separate legal identities, prepare a consolidation worksheet as of December 31, 1995.

b. Assuming that Gold's accounts are transferred to the records of Green, prepare the necessary journal entries within Green's accounting system as of December 31, 1995.

39. On January 1, 1995, the Lee Company purchased 100 percent of the outstanding common stock of Grant Company. To acquire these shares, Lee issued $200,000 in long-term liabilities and 20,000 shares of common stock having a par value of $1 per share but a fair market value of $10 per share. Lee paid $30,000 to accountants, lawyers, and brokers for assistance in bringing about this purchase. Another $12,000 was paid in connection with stock issuance costs.

Prior to these transactions, the balance sheets for the two companies were as follows:

	Lee Company Book Value	Grant Company Book Value
Cash	$ 60,000	$ 20,000
Receivables	270,000	90,000
Inventory	360,000	140,000
Land	200,000	180,000
Buildings (net).	420,000	220,000
Equipment (net)	160,000	50,000
Accounts payable	(150,000)	(40,000)
Long-term liabilities	(430,000)	(200,000)
Common stock—$1 par value	(110,000)	
Common stock—$20 par value		(120,000)
Additional paid-in capital	(360,000)	–0–
Retained earnings, 1/1/95	(420,000)	(340,000)

NOTE: Parentheses indicate a credit balance.

In Lee's appraisal of Grant, three accounts were deemed to be undervalued on the subsidiary's books: inventory by $5,000, land by $20,000, and buildings by $30,000.

Required:

a. Determine the consolidated balance for each of these accounts.

b. To verify the answers found in part a., prepare a worksheet to consolidate the balance sheets of these two companies as of January 1, 1995.

40. The Landover Corporation purchased all of the outstanding shares of Smithers, Inc. on January 1, 1995, for $295,000 cash. Several of Smithers' accounts have market values that differ from their book values on this date:

	Book Value	Fair Market Value
Land	$20,000	$70,000
Buildings	60,000	80,000
Equipment	40,000	30,000
Notes Payable	50,000	55,000

Prepare a consolidation worksheet at the date of acquisition based on the following information:

	Landover	Smithers
Cash	$ 36,000	$ 16,000
Receivables	116,000	52,000
Inventory	144,000	90,000
Investment in Smithers	295,000	–0–
Land	210,000	20,000
Buildings (net)	640,000	60,000
Equipment (net)	308,000	40,000
Total assets	$1,749,000	$278,000
Accounts payable	$ 88,000	$ 8,000
Notes payable	510,000	50,000
Common stock	380,000	80,000
Retained earnings	771,000	140,000
Total liabilities and equities . . .	$1,749,000	$278,000

41. The Lincoln Company obtains all of the outstanding shares of Swathmore, Inc. on December 31, 1995, in exchange for 7,000 shares of common stock. All 12 criteria of a pooling of interests have been met in this combination. Each of Lincoln's shares has a $10 par value and a $40 fair market value. Several of Swathmore's accounts have market values that differ from their book values on this date:

	Book Value	Fair Market Value
Inventory	$70,000	$100,000
Land	30,000	30,000
Equipment	50,000	60,000
Notes payable . . .	50,000	45,000

Financial statements for 1995 for the two companies are as follows:

	Lincoln	Swathmore
Revenues	$ 990,000	$540,000
Expenses	(640,000)	(330,000)
Net income	$ 350,000	$210,000
Retained earnings, 1/1/95	$ 830,000	$110,000
Net income	350,000	210,000
Dividends paid	(220,000)	(130,000)
Retained earnings, 12/31/95	$ 960,000	$190,000
Cash	$ 60,000	$ 29,000
Receivables	150,000	65,000
Inventory	190,000	120,000
Land	310,000	30,000
Buildings (net)	840,000	60,000
Equipment (net)	320,000	50,000
Totals	$1,870,000	$354,000
Accounts payable	$ 110,000	$ 34,000
Notes payable	370,000	50,000
Common stock	400,000	50,000
Additional paid-in capital	30,000	30,000
Retained earnings	960,000	190,000
Totals	$1,870,000	$354,000

Required:

a. Determine the consolidated balance for each of these accounts.

b. To verify the answers found in part a., prepare a worksheet to consolidate the financial statements of these two companies.

42. On December 31, 1995, the Sherman Company exchanges 17,000 shares of its common stock with a market value of $57 per share for 100 percent of the outstanding shares of the Atlanta Company. This transaction meets all 12 of the criteria for a pooling of interest. Prior to the exchange, the trial balances of both companies for the year of 1995 are as follows:

	Sherman Company Book Value	Atlanta Company Book Value
Debits		
Cash.	$110,000	$ 20,000
Receivables (net)	300,000	290,000
Inventory.	440,000	260,000
Land.	280,000	80,000
Buildings (net)	270,000	290,000
Equipment (net).	810,000	320,000
Expenses.	540,000	210,000
Dividends	30,000	–0–
Credits		
Accounts payable	120,000	60,000
Long-term liabilities	960,000	330,000
Common stock—$20 par value . . .	520,000	
Common stock—$25 par value . . .		300,000
Additional paid-in capital.	110,000	100,000
Retained earnings, 1/1/95	470,000	200,000
Revenues.	600,000	480,000

Additional Information:

- After the preparation of these trial balances, Sherman pays $20,000 in cash for costs incurred relating to this exchange. These expenditures covered the fees charged by lawyers and accountants involved with creating the business combination.
- Atlanta possesses land that has greatly appreciated in value since it was acquired. The book value of this land is estimated to be $60,000 less than fair market value.

Required:

a. Prepare a worksheet to consolidate the financial information of these two companies for the year ending December 31, 1995.

b. Prepare a worksheet to consolidate the financial information of these two companies for the year ending December 31, 1995, assuming that this combination was actually a purchase.

3

CONSOLIDATIONS— SUBSEQUENT TO THE DATE OF ACQUISITION

Questions to Consider

- How does a parent company account for a subsidiary organization in the years that follow the creation of a business combination? *Cost Method or Equity Method*
- What impact does the parent's method of accounting for a subsidiary have on each subsequent consolidation?
- Why do intercompany balances exist within the financial records of the separate companies? How are these reciprocals eliminated on a consolidation worksheet?
- How is the amortization of goodwill and other purchase price allocations recognized within consolidated financial statements?
- If the exact purchase price of a subsidiary is based on a future event, what effect does this contingency have on the consolidation process?
- Should a subsidiary company report on its own financial statements, the goodwill, other allocations, and subsequent amortization that can result from the purchase price paid by the parent?

In April of 1963, the H. J. Heinz Company acquired Star-Kist Foods, Inc., by exchanging .27 shares of convertible preferred stock for each share of Star-Kist common stock. Although this transaction involved two well-known companies, it was not unique; mergers and acquisitions have long been common in the business world. More than 1,300 mergers and acquisitions involved U.S. companies in 1963, a number that rose to 3,479 transactions in 1988 but then fell to 2,098 in 1991 (with a monetary value of $97.9 billion).[1]

---

[1] "Shades of the Past, Hopes for the Future," *Mergers & Acquisitions,* March-April 1992, p. 57. Of the total transactions in 1991, 1,695 involved U.S. companies acquiring other U.S. companies, whereas 217 represented foreign companies taking over U.S. companies. U.S. companies acquired 186 foreign companies during the period.

The current financial statements of the H. J. Heinz Company indicate that Star-Kist is still a component of this economic entity. However, Star-Kist continues to be a separately incorporated concern three decades after its purchase. As discussed in Chapter 2, a parent often chooses to let a subsidiary retain its identity as a legal corporation to better utilize the value inherent in a going concern.

For external reporting purposes, maintenance of incorporation creates an ongoing challenge for the accountant. In each subsequent period, consolidation must be simulated anew through the use of a worksheet and consolidation entries. Thus, for more than 30 years, the financial data for Heinz and Star-Kist have been brought together periodically to provide figures for the financial statements that represent this business combination.

Consolidation—The Effects Created by the Passage of Time

In the previous chapter, consolidation accounting was analyzed but only at the date that a combination was created. The present chapter carries this process one step further by examining the consolidation procedures that must be followed in subsequent periods whenever separate incorporation of the subsidiary is maintained.

Despite complexities created by the passage of time, the basic objective of all consolidations remains the same: to combine asset, liability, revenue, expense, and equity accounts based on the concepts of either the purchase method or the pooling of interests method. From a mechanical perspective, a worksheet and consolidation entries continue to be utilized to provide a structure for the production of a single set of financial statements for the entire business combination.

When a time factor is introduced into the consolidation process, additional complications are encountered. For internal record-keeping purposes, the parent must select and apply an accounting method to monitor the relationship between the two companies. The investment balance recorded by the parent varies over time as a result of the method chosen as does the income subsequently recognized. These differences affect the periodic consolidation process but not the figures to be reported by the combination. Regardless of the amount, the parent's Investment account is eliminated on the worksheet so that the subsidiary's actual assets and liabilities can be consolidated. Likewise, the income figure accrued by the parent is removed each period so that the subsidiary's revenues and expenses can be included when creating an income statement for the business combination.

Investment Accounting by the Acquiring Company

For external reporting, consolidation of a subsidiary becomes necessary whenever control exists. For internal record-keeping, though, the parent has the choice of three alternatives for monitoring the activities of its subsidiaries: the cost method, the equity method, or the partial equity method. *Since both the resulting investment balance as well as the related income is eliminated as part of every recurring consolidation, the selection of a particular method does not affect the totals ultimately reported for the combined companies.* Rather, this decision dictates the specific procedures subsequently utilized in consolidating the financial information of the separate organizations.

The actual choice of a method is often based on the internal reporting philosophy of the acquiring company. The *cost method* might be selected because it is easy to apply. The investment balance remains permanently on the parent's balance sheet at original cost. Only the dividends subsequently received from the subsidiary are recognized as income. No other adjustments are recorded. Thus, this method requires little effort while providing an accurate measure of the cash flows between the two companies.

In contrast, under *the equity method* the acquiring company accrues income when earned by the subsidiary. The impact of any amortization expense stemming from the original acquisition is recognized through periodic adjusting entries. Unrealized gains on intercompany transactions are deferred; dividends paid by the subsidiary serve to reduce the investment balance. As discussed in Chapter 1, the equity method is designed to create a parallel between the parent's investment accounts and the underlying operations of the acquired company.[2]

By utilizing this approach, the parent's accounts will present an accurate portrayal of the financial results of the entire business combination. Consequently, the equity method is often referred to in accounting as a single-line consolidation. The equity method is especially popular in companies where management wants to get a picture of overall profitability by looking at the periodic (such as monthly) figures developed by the parent.

However, application of the equity method does have a disadvantage: it requires more time and effort than does the cost method. Since the choice being made here is for internal reporting purposes only, the parent company must decide whether the additional information generated by the equity method is worth the effort. In recent years, the ever-increasing use of computers has made application of the equity method easier and, thus, more tempting.

A third method available to the acquiring company is *a partial application of the equity method*. Under this approach, income accruing from the subsidiary is recognized immediately by the parent. Dividends that are collected reduce the investment balance. However, no other equity adjustments (amortization or deferral of unrealized gains) are recorded. Thus, in many cases, earnings figures on the parent's books approximate consolidated totals but without the effort associated with a full application of the equity method.

---

[2] In Chapter 1, the equity method was introduced in connection with the external reporting of investments in which the owner held the ability to apply significant influence over the investee (usually by possessing 20 to 50 percent of the company's voting stock). Here, the equity method is utilized for the *internal* reporting of the parent for investments in which control is maintained. Although the accounting procedures are identical, the reason for using the equity method is different.

EXHIBIT 3-1 Internal Reporting of Investment Accounts by Acquiring Company

Method	Investment Account	Income Account	Advantages
Equity	Continually adjusted to reflect ownership of acquired company	Income is accrued as earned; amortization and other adjustments are recognized	Acquiring company totals give a true representation of consolidation figures
Cost	Remains at initially recorded cost	Cash received is recorded as Dividend Income	Easy to apply; measures cash flows
Partial equity	Adjusted only for accrued income and dividends received from acquired company	Income is accrued as earned; no other adjustments are recognized	Usually gives balances approximating consolidation figures, but is easier to apply than equity method

---

Each acquiring company must decide for itself the appropriate approach to utilize in recording the operations of its subsidiaries. For example, CSX Corporation applies the equity method. According to Gregory R. Weber, vice president and controller of CSX, "we maintain the parent holding company books on an equity basis, adjusted for monthly results. With 13 reporting subsidiaries, this approach provides the best method of controlling input into our system. As part of the consolidation process, intercompany transactions are eliminated where applicable."[3]

In contrast, Reynolds Metals Corporation has chosen to utilize the partial equity method approach. Allen Earehart, director of corporate accounting for Reynolds, states "we do adjust the carrying value of our investments annually to reflect the earnings of each subsidiary. We want to be able to evaluate the parent company on a stand-alone basis and a regular equity accrual is, therefore, necessary. However, we do separate certain adjustments such as the elimination of intercompany gains and losses and record them solely within the development of consolidated financial statements."[4]

Exhibit 3–1 provides a summary of these three reporting techniques. The method adopted only affects the acquiring company's separate financial records. No changes are created in either the subsidiary's accounts or the consolidated totals.

Since specific worksheet procedures differ based on the investment method being utilized by the parent, the consolidation process subsequent to the date of combination will be introduced twice. Initially, consolidations in which the acquiring company uses the equity method are reviewed. All procedures are then redeveloped where the investment is recorded by one of the alternative methods.

---

[3] Letter from Gregory R. Weber, February 27, 1992.
[4] Telephone conversation with Allen Earehart, August 9, 1988.

Subsequent Consolidation—Investment Recorded by the Equity Method

Acquisition Made during the Current Year

As a basis for this illustration, assume that Parrot Company obtains all of the outstanding common stock of Sun Company on January 1, 1995. Parrot acquires this stock for $760,000 in cash but pays an additional $40,000 in direct consolidation costs. Since cash is being paid, the purchase method is applicable; a pooling of interests requires that the business combination be created only through the exchange of voting common stock.

The book values as well as the appraised values of Sun's accounts are as follows:

	Book Value 1/1/95	Fair Market Value 1/1/95	Difference
Current assets	$ 320,000	$ 320,000	–0–
Land	200,000	250,000	+ 50,000
Buildings (10-year life)	320,000	400,000	+ 80,000
Equipment (5-year life)	180,000	150,000	(30,000)
Liabilities	(420,000)	(420,000)	–0–
Net book value.	$ 600,000	$ 700,000	$100,000
Common stock—$40 par value.	$(200,000)		
Additional paid-in capital	(20,000)		
Retained earnings, 1/1/95	(380,000)		

For this combination, the assumption is being made that any amortization relating to purchase price allocations is calculated using the straight-line method with no estimated salvage value.[5] Goodwill is to be amortized over a 20-year period.

With the inclusion of the $40,000 direct consolidation costs, a total of $800,000 has been paid by Parrot in this purchase of Sun Company. As shown in Exhibit 3–2, individual allocations can be determined to adjust Sun's accounts from their book values on January 1, 1995, to fair market values. Since the total value of these assets and liabilities was only $700,000, goodwill of $100,000 must be recognized for consolidation purposes.

---

[5] Unless otherwise stated, all amortization expense computations in this textbook are based on the straight-line method with no salvage value.

EXHIBIT 3–2

PARROT COMPANY
Allocation of Purchase Price
January 1, 1995

Purchase price by Parrot Company	$ 800,000
Book value of Sun Company	(600,000)
Excess of cost over book value	200,000
Allocation to specific accounts based on fair market values:	
Land . . . . $ 50,000	
Buildings 80,000	
Equipment (overvalued) . . . . (30,000)	100,000
Excess cost not identified with specific accounts—goodwill	$ 100,000

EXHIBIT 3–3 **Annual Amortization**

PARROT COMPANY
Amortization Schedule—Allocation of Purchase Price

Account	Allocation	Useful Life	Annual Amortization
Land	$ 50,000	Permanent	–0–
Buildings	80,000	10 years	$8,000
Equipment	(30,000)	5 years	(6,000)
Goodwill	100,000	20 years	5,000
1995 amortization			$7,000*

* Amortization will be $7,000 annually for five years until the equipment allocation is fully removed. At the end of each asset's life, future amortization will change.

Each of these allocated amounts (other than the $50,000 attributed to land) represents a cost incurred by Parrot that is associated with an account having a limited useful life. As discussed in Chapter 1, Parrot must amortize each of these cost figures over their expected lives. The expense recognition necessitated by this purchase price allocation is calculated in Exhibit 3–3.

One aspect of this amortization schedule warrants explanation. The fair market value of Sun's Equipment account was $30,000 *less* than book value. Therefore, instead of attributing an additional cost to this asset, the $30,000 allocation actually reflects a cost reduction. As such, the amortization shown in Exhibit 3–3 relating to Equipment is not an additional expense but rather an expense reduction.

> ## Discussion Question: Is the Amortization of Goodwill Bad for the Country?
>
> Interestingly, the recognition of amortization expense in connection with goodwill has a significant impact on global economics. In some countries, amortization of goodwill is not required to be recognized as a reduction in net income. Thus, purchase takeovers appear to be more profitable so that foreign companies are in a position to make offers that exceed the amount a U.S. company might be willing to bid. Foreign investors, therefore, have an apparent advantage over U.S. companies.
>
> For example, in an article entitled "Ill Will," Laura Jereski complained "Unencumbered by U.S. accounting rules (foreign companies), need not amortize goodwill, or, if they must, they can deduct it from their taxes. At the original price of $60 per share, as Grand Metropolitan initially offered for Pillsbury, goodwill would have caused a $100 million annual hit to operating earnings for a U.S. company. Why could Grand Met afford it? Because British accounting conventions deduct goodwill straight from equity, without requiring amortization; it affects the balance sheet but not the income statement." (*Forbes,* January 23, 1989, p. 41.)
>
> Consequently, in today's world of international competition, the amortization of goodwill required of U.S. companies appears to put them at a disadvantage in acquiring either foreign or domestic organizations. Should American accounting rules be influenced by such practical issues or should they be limited to purely theoretical arguments?

Having determined the allocation of the purchase price in the previous example as well as the associated amortization, the parent's separate record-keeping for 1995 can be constructed as shown on next page. Assume that Sun earns income of $100,000 during the year and pays a $40,000 cash dividend on August 1, 1995.

In this initial illustration, Parrot has adopted the equity method. Apparently, this company believes that the information derived from using the equity method outweighs the effort required in applying this approach.

Parrot's application of the equity method, as shown in this series of entries, causes the Investment in Sun Company account balance to rise from $800,000 to $853,000 ($800,000 − $40,000 + $100,000 − $7,000). During the same period, a $93,000 equity income figure (the $100,000 earnings accrual less the $7,000 amortization expense) is recognized by the parent.

The consolidation procedures for Parrot and Sun one year after the date of acquisition can next be illustrated. For this purpose, Exhibit 3–4 presents the separate 1995 financial statements for these two companies. Both investment

Application of the Equity Method

Parrot's Financial Records

1/1/95 Investment in Sun Company 800,000
            Cash   800,000
        To record purchase of Sun Company including direct
        consolidation costs.

8/1/95 Cash 40,000
            Investment in Sun Company   40,000
        To record receipt of cash dividend from subsidiary, an
        investment that is being accounted for by means of the
        equity method.

12/31/95 Investment in Sun Company 100,000
              Equity in subsidiary earnings   100,000
          To accrue income earned by 100 percent owned
          subsidiary.

12/31/95 Equity in subsidiary earnings 7,000
              Investment in Sun Company   7,000
          To recognize amortization on allocations made in
          purchase of subsidiary (see Exhibit 3–3).

accounts (the $853,000 asset balance and the $93,000 income accrual) have been recorded by Parrot based on applying the equity method.

Determining Consolidated Totals

Before becoming immersed in the mechanical aspects of a consolidation, the objective of this process should be understood. As indicated in Chapter 2, the revenue, expense, asset, and liability accounts of the subsidiary are to be added to the parent company balances. Within this procedure, several important guidelines must be followed:

- Sun's assets and liabilities are adjusted to reflect any allocations originating from the purchase price.
- Because of the passage of time, amortization of these allocations must also be recorded within the consolidation process.
- Any reciprocal or intercompany accounts have to be offset. If, for example, one of the companies owes money to the other, the receivable and the payable balances have no connection with an outside party. Both should be eliminated for external reporting purposes. When the companies are viewed as a single entity, the receivable and the payable are intercompany balances to be removed.

A consolidation of the two sets of financial information in Exhibit 3–4 is a relatively uncomplicated task and can even be carried out without the use of a

EXHIBIT 3-4   Separate Records—Equity Method Applied

PARROT COMPANY AND SUN COMPANY
Financial Statements
For Year Ending December 31, 1995

	Parrot Company	Sun Company
Income Statement		
Revenues.	$(1,500,000) *(1,900,000)*	$ (400,000)
Expenses. . . . . *inc 7,000 amort.*	900,000 *1,207,000*	300,000
Equity in subsidiary earnings	(93,000) *0*	–0–
Net income	$ (693,000) *(693,000)*	$ (100,000)
Statement of Retained Earnings		
Retained earnings, 1/1/95	$ (840,000)	$ (380,000)
Net income (above)	(693,000)	(100,000)
Dividends paid	120,000	40,000
Retained earnings, 12/31/95	$(1,413,000)	$ (440,000)
Balance Sheet		*Fmv*
Current assets.	$ 1,040,000 *1,440,000*	$ 400,000
Investment in Sun Company (at equity)	853,000 *0*	–0–
Land.	600,000 *850,000*	200,000 *250,000*
Buildings (net)	370,000	288,000
Equipment (net)	250,000	220,000
Total assets.	$ 3,113,000	$ 1,108,000
Liabilities.	$ (980,000)	$ (448,000)
Common stock	(600,000)	(200,000)
Additional paid-in capital.	(120,000)	(20,000)
Retained earnings, 12/31/95 (above)	(1,413,000)	(440,000)
Total liabilities and equities.	$(3,113,000)	$(1,108,000)

NOTE: Parentheses indicate a credit balance.

worksheet. Understanding the origin of each reported figure is the first step in gaining a knowledge of this process.

Revenues = $1,900,000. The revenues of the parent and the subsidiary are added together.

Expenses = $1,207,000. The expenses of the parent and the subsidiary are added together along with the $7,000 amortization expense for the year indicated in Exhibit 3–3.

Equity in subsidiary earnings = –0–. The investment income recorded by the parent is eliminated so that the subsidiary's revenues and expenses can be included in the consolidated totals.

Net income = $693,000. Consolidated revenues less consolidated expenses.

Retained earnings, 1/1/95 = $840,000. The parent figure only because the subsidiary was not owned prior to that date.

Dividends paid = $120,000. The parent company balance only because the subsidiary's dividends were paid intercompany to the parent and not to an outside party.

Retained earnings, 12/31/95 = $1,413,000. Consolidated retained earnings as of the beginning of the year plus consolidated net income less consolidated dividends paid.

Current assets = $1,440,000. The parent's book value plus the subsidiary's book value.

Investment in Sun Company = –0–. The asset recorded by the parent is eliminated so that the subsidiary's assets and liabilities can be included in the consolidated totals.

Land = $850,000. The parent's book value plus the subsidiary's book value plus the $50,000 allocation within the purchase price.

Buildings = $730,000. The parent's book value plus the subsidiary's book value plus the $80,000 allocation within the purchase price less 1995 amortization of $8,000.

Equipment = $446,000. The parent's book value plus the subsidiary's book value *less* the $30,000 cost reduction allocation plus the 1995 expense reduction of $6,000.

Goodwill = $95,000. The residual allocation shown in Exhibit 3–2 less $5,000 amortization expense for 1995.

Total assets = $3,561,000. Summation of consolidated assets.

Liabilities = $1,428,000. The parent's book value plus the subsidiary's book value.

Common stock = $600,000. The parent's book value since this combination was a purchase.

Additional paid-in capital = $120,000. The parent's book value since this combination was a purchase.

Retained earnings, 12/31/95 = $1,413,000. Computed above.

Total Liabilities and Equities = $3,561,000. Summation of consolidated liabilities and equities.

Consolidation Worksheet

Although the consolidated figures to be reported can be computed as just shown, accountants normally prefer to use a worksheet. A worksheet provides an organized structure for this process, a benefit that becomes especially important in consolidating complex combinations.

For Parrot and Sun, only five consolidation entries are needed to arrive at the same figures previously derived for this business combination. As discussed in Chapter 2, *worksheet entries are the catalyst for developing totals to be reported by the entity but are not physically recorded in the individual account balances of either company.*

Consolidation Entry S

Common Stock (Sun Company)	200,000	
Additional Paid-In Capital (Sun Company)	20,000	
Retained Earnings, 1/1/95 (Sun Company).	380,000	
Investment in Sun Company		600,000

As shown in Exhibit 3–2, Parrot can break its $800,000 purchase price into two components: (1) a $600,000 amount equal to Sun's book value and (2) a $200,000 figure attributed to the difference, at January 1, 1995, between the book value and market value of Sun's assets and liabilities (with a residual allocation made to goodwill). Entry S removes the $600,000 component of the Investment in Sun Company account so that the *book value* of each subsidiary asset and liability can be included in the consolidated figures. A second worksheet entry (Entry A) eliminates the remaining $200,000 portion of the purchase price, allowing the specific allocations to be recorded along with any goodwill.

Entry S also removes Sun's stockholders' equity accounts as of the beginning of the year. As a purchase, subsidiary equity balances generated prior to the acquisition are not relevant to the business combination and should be deleted. The elimination is made through this entry because the equity accounts and the $600,000 component of the Investment account represent reciprocal balances: both provide a measure of Sun's book value as of January 1, 1995.

Before moving to the next consolidation entry, a clarification point should be made. In actual practice, worksheet entries are usually identified numerically. However, the label "Entry S" is used in this example as a reference to the elimination being made of Sun's beginning Stockholders' equity. As a reminder of the purpose being served, all worksheet entries are identified in a similar fashion. Thus, throughout this textbook, "Entry S" always refers to the removal of the subsidiary's beginning stockholders' equity balances for the year against the book value portion of the Investment account.

Consolidation Entry A

Land	50,000	
Buildings	80,000	
Goodwill	100,000	
Equipment.		30,000
Investment in Sun Company		200,000

As indicated previously, the second worksheet entry removes the $200,000 component of the purchase price, replacing it with the specific allocations from the original purchase price (see Exhibit 3–2). In this manner, the individual assets and liabilities of the consolidated entity now reflect the extra cost incurred by Parrot in making this purchase. Sun's accounts are adjusted based on the $200,000 paid at the time of acquisition that was in excess of Sun's book value. No basis exists for continually revaluing the accounts to newly determined market values at the date of each subsequent consolidation.

This entry is labeled "Entry A" to indicate that it represents the **A**llocations made in connection with the parent's purchase price.

Consolidation Entry I

Equity in subsidiary earnings	93,000	
Investment in Sun Company		93,000

"Entry I" (for **I**ncome) removes the subsidiary income recognized by Parrot during the year so that the underlying revenue and expense accounts of Sun (and the current amortization expense) can be brought into the consolidated totals. The $93,000 figure eliminated here represents the $100,000 income accrual recognized by Parrot, reduced by the $7,000 in amortization. For consolidation purposes, the one-line amount appearing in the parent's records is not appropriate and is removed so that the individual balances can be included. The entry originally recorded by the parent is simply reversed on the worksheet to remove its impact.

Consolidation Entry D

Investment in Sun Company	40,000	
Dividends Paid		40,000

The dividends distributed by the subsidiary during 1995 must also be eliminated from the consolidated totals. The entire $40,000 payment was made to the parent so that, from the viewpoint of the consolidated entity, it is simply an intercompany transfer of cash. The distribution did not affect any outside party. Therefore, "Entry D" (for **D**ividends) is designed to offset the impact of this transaction by removing the subsidiary's Dividends Paid account. Because the equity method has been applied, receipt of this money by Parrot was recorded originally as a decrease in the Investment in Sun Company account. To eliminate the impact of this reduction, the Investment account is increased here.

Consolidation Entry E

Expenses	7,000	
Equipment	6,000	
Buildings		8,000
Goodwill		5,000

This final worksheet entry records the current year amortization expense relating to Parrot's purchase price. Since the equity method amortization was eliminated within Entry I, ''Entry E'' (for **E**xpense) now records the 1995 expense attributed to each of the specific account allocations (see Exhibit 3–3).

Thus, the worksheet entries necessary for consolidation when the parent has applied the equity method are as follows:

> ***Entry S***—Eliminates the subsidiary's stockholders' equity accounts as of the beginning of the current year along with the equivalent book value component within the parent's purchase price in the Investment account.
>
> ***Entry A***—Recognizes the unamortized allocations as of the beginning of the current year, costs that were associated with the original purchase price.
>
> ***Entry I***—Eliminates the impact of intercompany income accrued by parent.
>
> ***Entry D***—Eliminates the impact of intercompany dividend payments made by the subsidiary.
>
> ***Entry E***—Recognizes amortization expense for the current period on the allocations within the original purchase price.

Exhibit 3–5 provides a complete presentation of the December 31, 1995, consolidation worksheet developed for Parrot Company and Sun Company. The series of entries just described successfully brings together the separate financial statements of these two organizations. Note that the consolidated totals are the same as those computed for this combination previously in this chapter.

One aspect of this worksheet should be explained. Parrot is separately reporting net income of $693,000 as well as ending retained earnings of $1,413,000, figures that are identical to the totals generated for the consolidated entity. However, in a purchase combination, subsidiary income earned after the date of acquisition is to be *added* to that of the parent. Thus, a question arises in this example as to why the parent company figures alone equal the consolidated balances of both operations.

In reality, Sun's income for this period is contained in both Parrot's reported balances as well as in the consolidated totals. Through the application of the equity method, the 1995 earnings of the subsidiary have already been accrued by Parrot along with the appropriate amortization expense. *The parent's Equity in Subsidiary Earnings account is, therefore, an accurate representation of Sun's effect on consolidated net income.* If the equity method is employed properly, the worksheet process simply replaces this single $93,000 balance with the specific revenue and expense accounts that it represents. Consequently, the parent's net income and retained earnings mirror consolidated totals.

Consolidation Subsequent to Year of Acquisition—Equity Method

In many ways, every consolidation of Parrot and Sun prepared after the date of acquisition incorporates the same basic procedures outlined in the previous section. Unfortunately, the continual financial evolution undergone by the companies

EXHIBIT 3–5

Consolidation: Purchase Method
Investment: Equity Method

PARROT COMPANY AND SUN COMPANY
Consolidation Worksheet
For Year Ending December 31, 1995

Accounts	Parrot Company	Sun Company	Consolidation Entries		Consolidated Totals
			Debit	Credit	
Income Statement					
Revenues	(1,500,000)	(400,000)			(1,900,000)
Expenses	900,000	300,000	(E) 7,000		1,207,000
Equity in subsidiary earnings	(93,000)	–0–	(I) 93,000		–0–
Net income	(693,000)	(100,000)			(693,000)
Statement of Retained Earnings					
Retained earnings, 1/1/95	(840,000)	(380,000)	(S) 380,000		(840,000)
Net income (above)	(693,000)	(100,000)			(693,000)
Dividends paid	120,000	40,000		(D) 40,000	120,000
Retained earnings, 12/31/95	(1,413,000)	(440,000)			(1,413,000)
Balance Sheet					
Current assets	1,040,000	400,000			1,440,000
Investment in Sun Company	853,000	–0–	(D) 40,000	(S) 600,000	–0–
				(A) 200,000	
				(I) 93,000	
Land	600,000	200,000	(A) 50,000		850,000
Buildings (net)	370,000	288,000	(A) 80,000	(E) 8,000	730,000
Equipment (net)	250,000	220,000	(E) 6,000	(A) 30,000	446,000
Goodwill	–0–	–0–	(A) 100,000	(E) 5,000	95,000
Total assets	3,113,000	1,108,000			3,561,000
Liabilities	(980,000)	(448,000)			(1,428,000)
Common stock	(600,000)	(200,000)	(S) 200,000		(600,000)
Additional paid-in capital	(120,000)	(20,000)	(S) 20,000		(120,000)
Retained earnings, 12/31/95 (above)	(1,413,000)	(440,000)			(1,413,000)
Total liabilities and equities	(3,113,000)	(1,108,000)			(3,561,000)

NOTE: Parentheses indicate a credit balance.
Consolidation entries:
  (S) Elimination of Sun's stockholders' equity accounts as of January 1, 1995, and book value portion of purchase price.
  (A) Allocation of Parrot's cost in excess of Sun's book value.
  (I) Elimination of intercompany equity income.
  (D) Elimination of intercompany dividends.
  (E) Recognition of amortization expense on purchase price allocations.

prohibits an exact repetition of the consolidation entries demonstrated in Exhibit 3–5.

As a basis for analyzing the procedural changes necessitated by the passage of time, assume that Parrot Company continues to hold its ownership of Sun Company as of December 31, 1998. This date was selected at random; any date subsequent to 1995 would serve equally well to illustrate this process. As an additional factor, assume that Sun now has a $40,000 liability that is payable to Parrot.

For this consolidation, assume that the January 1, 1998, retained earnings balance of Sun Company has risen to $600,000. Since that account had a reported total of only $380,000 on January 1, 1995, Sun's book value apparently has increased by $220,000 during the 1995–97 period. Although knowledge of individual operating figures in the past is not required, Sun's reported totals help to clarify the consolidation procedures.

Year	Sun Company Net Income	Dividends Paid	Increase in Book Value	Ending Retained Earnings
1995	$100,000	$ 40,000	$ 60,000	$440,000
1996	140,000	50,000	90,000	530,000
1997	90,000	20,000	70,000	600,000
	$330,000	$110,000	$220,000	

For 1998, the current year, the assumption will be made that Sun reports net income of $160,000 and pays cash dividends of $70,000. Because it applies the equity method, earnings of $160,000 are recognized by Parrot. Furthermore, as shown in Exhibit 3–3, amortization expense of $7,000 is applicable to 1998 and must also be recorded by the parent. Consequently, Parrot reports an Equity in Subsidiary Earnings balance for the year of $153,000 ($160,000 − $7,000).

Although this income figure can be reconstructed with little difficulty, the current balance in the Investment in Sun Company account is more complicated. Over the years, the initial $800,000 purchase price has been subjected to adjustments for:

1. The annual accrual of Sun's income.
2. The receipt of dividends from Sun.
3. The recognition of annual amortization expense.

However, by analyzing these changes, Exhibit 3–6 can be developed to show the components of the balance in the Investment in Sun Company account as of December 31, 1998.

Following the construction of the Investment in Sun Company account, the consolidation worksheet developed in Exhibit 3–7 should be easier to understand. Current figures for both companies are presented in the first two columns. The

EXHIBIT 3–6

PARROT COMPANY
Investment in Sun Company Account
As of December 31, 1998
Equity Method Applied

Purchase price		$ 800,000
Entries recorded in prior years:		
Accrual of Sun Company's income		
1995	$100,000	
1996	140,000	
1997	90,000	330,000
Sun Company—Dividends paid		
1995	$ 40,000	
1996	50,000	
1997	20,000	(110,000)
Amortization expense		
1995	$ 7,000	
1996	7,000	
1997	7,000	(21,000)
Entries recorded in current year—1998:		
Accrual of Sun Company's income	$160,000	
Sun Company—Dividends paid	(70,000)	
Amortization expense	(7,000)	83,000
Investment in Sun Company, 12/31/98		$1,082,000

parent's investment balance and equity income accrual as well as Sun's income and stockholders' equity accounts correspond to the information given previously. Worksheet entries (lettered to agree with the previous illustration) are then utilized to consolidate all balances.

Several steps are necessary to arrive at these reported totals. The subsidiary's assets, liabilities, revenues, and expenses are added to those same accounts of the parent. The unamortized portion of the original purchase price allocations are included along with current amortization expense. The investment and equity income balances are both eliminated as is the subsidiary's stockholders' equity accounts. Intercompany dividends are removed with the same treatment required for the debt existing between the two companies.

Consolidation Entry S. Once again, this first consolidation entry offsets reciprocal amounts representing the subsidiary's book value as of the *beginning* of the current year. Sun's January 1, 1998, stockholders' equity accounts are eliminated against the book value portion of the parent's Investment account. Here, though, the amount eliminated is $820,000 rather than the $600,000 shown in Exhibit 3–5 for 1995. Both balances have changed during the 1995–97 period. Sun's operations caused a $220,000 increase in retained earnings. Parrot's application of the equity

EXHIBIT 3–7

Consolidation: Purchase Method
Investment: Equity Method

PARROT COMPANY AND SUN COMPANY
Consolidation Worksheet
For Year Ending December 31, 1998

Accounts	Parrot Company	Sun Company	Consolidation Entries Debit	Consolidation Entries Credit	Consolidated Totals
Income Statement					
Revenues	(2,100,000)	(600,000)			(2,700,000)
Expenses	1,300,000	440,000	(E) 7,000		1,747,000
Equity in subsidiary earnings	(153,000)	–0–	(I) 153,000		–0–
Net income	(953,000)	(160,000)			(953,000)
Statement of Retained Earnings					
Retained earnings, 1/1/98	(2,044,000)	(600,000)	(S) 600,000		(2,044,000)
Net income (above)	(953,000)	(160,000)			(953,000)
Dividends paid	420,000	70,000		(D) 70,000	420,000
Retained earnings, 12/31/98	(2,577,000)	(690,000)			(2,577,000)
Balance Sheet					
Current assets	1,705,000	500,000		(P) 40,000	2,165,000
Investment in Sun Company	1,082,000	–0–	(D) 70,000	(S) 820,000	–0–
				(A) 179,000	
				(I) 153,000	
Land	600,000	240,000	(A) 50,000		890,000
Buildings (net)	540,000	420,000	(A) 56,000	(E) 8,000	1,008,000
Equipment (net)	420,000	210,000	(E) 6,000	(A) 12,000	624,000
Goodwill	–0–	–0–	(A) 85,000	(E) 5,000	80,000
Total assets	4,347,000	1,370,000			4,767,000
Liabilities	(1,050,000)	(460,000)	(P) 40,000		(1,470,000)
Common stock	(600,000)	(200,000)	(S) 200,000		(600,000)
Additional paid-in capital	(120,000)	(20,000)	(S) 20,000		(120,000)
Retained earnings, 12/31/98 (above)	(2,577,000)	(690,000)			(2,577,000)
Total liabilities and equities	(4,347,000)	(1,370,000)			(4,767,000)

NOTE: Parentheses indicate a credit balance.
Consolidation entries:
  (S) Elimination of Sun's stockholders' equity accounts as of January 1, 1998, and book value portion of Investment account.
  (A) Allocation of Parrot's cost in excess of Sun's book value, unamortized values as of January 1, 1998.
  (I) Elimination of intercompany income.
  (D) Elimination of intercompany dividends.
  (E) Recognition of amortization expense on purchase price allocations.
  (P) Elimination of intercompany receivable/payable balances.

EXHIBIT 3-8   Amortization Relating to Individual Accounts as of January 1, 1998

Accounts	Original Allocation	Annual Amortization			Balance 1/1/98
		1995	*1996*	*1997*	
Land	$ 50,000	–0–	–0–	–0–	$ 50,000
Buildings	80,000	$ 8,000	$8,000	$8,000	56,000
Equipment	(30,000)	(6,000)	(6,000)	(6,000)	(12,000)
Goodwill	100,000	5,000	5,000	5,000	85,000
	$200,000	$7,000	$7,000	$7,000	$179,000
			$21,000		

method created a parallel effect on its Investment in Sun Company account (the income accrual of $330,000 less dividends collected of $110,000).

Although Sun's retained earnings balance is removed in this entry, the income earned by this company since the date of purchase is still included in the consolidated figures. Parrot accrues these profits annually through application of the equity method. Thus, elimination of the subsidiary's entire retained earnings is necessary; a portion was earned prior to the purchase and the remainder has already been recorded by the parent.

Entry S removes these balances as of the first day of 1998 rather than at the end of the year. The consolidation process is made a bit simpler by segregating the effect of preceding operations from the transactions of the current year. *Thus, all worksheet entries relate specifically to either the previous years (S and A) or the current period (I, D, E, and P).*

Consolidation Entry A.   In the initial consolidation (1995), cost allocations amounting to $200,000 were recorded but these balances have now undergone three years of amortization. As computed in Exhibit 3–8, expenses for these prior years totaled $21,000, leaving a balance of $179,000. Allocation of this amount to the individual accounts is also determined in Exhibit 3–8 and reflected in worksheet Entry A. As with Entry S, these balances are calculated as of January 1, 1998, so that the current year expenses may be recorded separately (in Entry E).

Consolidation Entry I.   As before, this entry eliminates the current equity income recorded currently by Parrot ($153,000) in connection with its ownership of Sun. The subsidiary's revenue and expense accounts are left intact so they can be included in the consolidated figures.

Consolidation Entry D.   This worksheet entry offsets the $70,000 intercompany dividend payment made by Sun to Parrot during the current period.

Consolidation Entry E. Amortization expense figures relating to Parrot's purchase price are individually recorded for 1998.

Before progressing to the final worksheet entry, note the close similarity of these entries with the five incorporated in the 1995 consolidation (Exhibit 3–5). Except for the numerical changes created by the passage of time, the entries are identical.

Consolidation Entry P. This last entry (labeled ''Entry P'' because it eliminates an intercompany **P**ayable) introduces a new element to the consolidation process. As noted earlier, intercompany debt transactions do not relate to outside parties. Therefore, Sun's $40,000 payable and Parrot's $40,000 receivable are reciprocals that must be removed on the worksheet because the companies are being reported as a single entity.

In reviewing Exhibit 3–7, note several aspects of the consolidation process:

- The stockholders' equity accounts of the subsidiary are removed.
- The Investment in Sun Company and the Equity in Subsidiary Earnings are both removed.
- The parent's retained earnings balance is not adjusted. Since the equity method has been applied, this account should be correct.
- The original allocations created by the purchase price are recognized but only after adjustment for annual amortization.
- Intercompany transactions such as dividend payments and the receivable/payable are offset.

Subsequent Consolidations—Investment Recorded on Other than the Equity Method

Acquisition Made during the Current Year

As discussed at the beginning of this chapter, the parent company may opt to use the cost method or the partial equity method for internal record-keeping rather than the equity method. Application of either alternative changes the balances recorded by the parent over time and, thus, the procedures followed in creating consolidations. However, *choosing one of these other approaches produces no alteration in any of the consolidated figures to be reported.*

Where the equity method is utilized, all reciprocal accounts are eliminated, unamortized cost allocations are assigned to specific accounts, and amortization expense is recorded for the current year. Application of either the cost method or the partial equity method has no effect on this basic process. For this reason, a number of the consolidation entries remain the same regardless of the accounting method being applied by the parent.

In reality, just three of the parent's accounts actually vary because of the method applied:

- The investment account.
- The income recognized from the subsidiary.
- The parent's retained earnings (in periods after the initial year of the combination).

Only the differences that are found in these balances affect the consolidation process when another method is applied. Thus, any time after the date of purchase, accounting for these three accounts is of special importance.

To illustrate the modifications required by the adoption of an alternative accounting method, the consolidation of Parrot and Sun as of December 31, 1995, is reconstructed. Only one differing factor is introduced: the method by which Parrot accounts for its investment. Exhibit 3–9 presents the 1995 consolidation based on Parrot's use of the cost method. Exhibit 3–10 demonstrates this same process assuming that the partial equity method was applied by the parent. Each entry on these worksheets is labeled to correspond with the 1995 consolidation in which the parent used the equity method (Exhibit 3–5). Furthermore, differences with the equity method (both on the parent company records and with the consolidation entries) are highlighted on each of the worksheets.

Cost Method Applied—1995 Consolidation. Although the cost method is theoretically in distinct contrast to the equity method, just a narrow range of reporting differences actually result. In the year of acquisition, Parrot's income and investment accounts relating to the subsidiary are the only accounts altered.

Under the cost method, income recognition in 1995 is limited to the $40,000 dividend received by the parent; no equity income accrual is made. At the same time, the Investment account retains its $800,000 cost. Unlike the equity method, no adjustments are recorded within this asset in connection with the current year operations, the dividends paid by the subsidiary, or amortization of any purchase price allocations.

After the composition of these two accounts has been established, worksheet entries can be used to produce the consolidated figures found in Exhibit 3–9 as of December 31, 1995.

Consolidation Entry S. As with the previous Entry S in Exhibit 3–5, the $600,000 component of the Investment account is eliminated against the beginning stockholders' equity of the subsidiary. Both are equivalent to Sun's net assets at January 1, 1995, and are, therefore, reciprocal balances that must be offset. This entry is not affected by the accounting method in use.

Consolidation Entry A. Parrot's $200,000 excess payment is allocated to Sun's assets and liabilities based on the fair market values at the date of acquisition. The $100,000 residual is attributed to goodwill. This procedure is also identical to the corresponding entry in Exhibit 2–5 where the equity method was applied.

EXHIBIT 3–9

Consolidation: Purchase Method
Investment: Cost Method

PARROT COMPANY AND SUN COMPANY
Consolidation Worksheet
For Year Ending December 31, 1995

Accounts	Parrot Company	Sun Company	Consolidation Entries Debit	Consolidation Entries Credit	Consolidated Totals
Income Statement					
Revenues	(1,500,000)	(400,000)			(1,900,000)
Expenses	900,000	300,000	(E) 7,000		1,207,000
Dividend income	(40,000) *	–0–	(I) 40,000 *		–0–
Net income	(640,000)	(100,000)			(693,000)
Statement of Retained Earnings					
Retained earnings, 1/1/95	(840,000)	(380,000)	(S) 380,000		(840,000)
Net income (above)	(640,000)	(100,000)			(693,000)
Dividends paid	120,000	40,000		(I) 40,000 *	120,000
Retained earnings, 12/31/95	(1,360,000)	(440,000)			(1,413,000)
Balance Sheet					
Current assets	1,040,000	400,000			1,440,000
Investment in Sun Company	800,000 *	–0–		(S) 600,000	–0–
				(A) 200,000	
Land	600,000	200,000	(A) 50,000		850,000
Buildings (net)	370,000	288,000	(A) 80,000	(E) 8,000	730,000
Equipment (net)	250,000	220,000	(E) 6,000	(A) 30,000	446,000
Goodwill	–0–	–0–	(A) 100,000	(E) 5,000	95,000
Total assets	3,060,000	1,108,000			3,561,000
Liabilities	(980,000)	(448,000)			(1,428,000)
Common stock	(600,000)	(200,000)	(S) 200,000		(600,000)
Additional paid-in capital	(120,000)	(20,000)	(S) 20,000		(120,000)
Retained earnings, 12/31/95 (above)	(1,360,000)	(440,000)			(1,413,000)
Total liabilities and equities	(3,060,000)	(1,108,000)			(3,561,000)

NOTE: Parentheses indicate a credit balance.
* Boxed items highlight differences with consolidation in Exhibit 3–5.
Consolidation entries:
   (S) Elimination of Sun's Stockholders' Equity Accounts as of January 1, 1995, and book value portion of purchase price.
   (A) Allocation of Parrot cost in excess of Sun's book value.
   (I) Elimination of intercompany dividends recognized by parent as income.

   (D) Entry is not needed when cost method is applied because Entry I eliminates intercompany dividends.

   (E) Recognition of amortization expense on purchase price allocations.

EXHIBIT 3–10

Consolidation: Purchase Method
Investment: Partial Equity Method

PARROT COMPANY AND SUN COMPANY
Consolidation Worksheet
For Year Ending December 31, 1995

Accounts	Parrot Company	Sun Company	Consolidation Entries		Consolidated Totals
			Debit	Credit	
Income Statement					
Revenues	(1,500,000)	(400,000)			(1,900,000)
Expenses	900,000	300,000	(E) 7,000		1,207,000
Equity in subsidiary earnings	(100,000) *	–0–	(I) 100,000 *		–0–
Net income	(700,000)	(100,000)			(693,000)
Statement of Retained Earnings					
Retained earnings, 1/1/95	(840,000)	(380,000)	(S) 380,000		(840,000)
Net income (above)	(700,000)	(100,000)			(693,000)
Dividends paid	120,000	40,000		(D) 40,000	120,000
Retained earnings, 12/31/95	(1,420,000)	(440,000)			(1,413,000)
Balance Sheet					
Current assets	1,040,000	400,000			1,440,000
Investment in Sun Company	860,000 *	–0–	(D) 40,000	(S) 600,000	–0–
				(A) 200,000	
				(I) 100,000 *	
Land	600,000	200,000	(A) 50,000		850,000
Buildings (net)	370,000	288,000	(A) 80,000	(E) 8,000	730,000
Equipment (net)	250,000	220,000	(E) 6,000	(A) 30,000	446,000
Goodwill	–0–	–0–	(A) 100,000	(E) 5,000	95,000
Total assets	3,120,000	1,108,000			3,561,000
Liabilities	(980,000)	(448,000)			(1,428,000)
Common stock	(600,000)	(200,000)	(S) 200,000		(600,000)
Additional paid-in capital	(120,000)	(20,000)	(S) 20,000		(120,000)
Retained earnings, 12/31/95 (above)	(1,420,000)	(440,000)			(1,413,000)
Total liabilities and equities	(3,120,000)	(1,108,000)			(3,561,000)

Note: Parentheses indicate a credit balance.
* Boxed items highlight differences with consolidation in Exhibit 3–5.
Consolidation entries:
  (S) Elimination of Sun's Stockholders' Equity Accounts as of January 1, 1995, and book value portion of purchase price.
  (A) Allocation of Parrot cost in excess of Sun's book value.
  (I) Elimination of parent's equity income accrual.
  (D) Elimination of intercompany dividend payment.
  (E) Recognition of amortization expense on purchase price allocations.

Consolidation Entry I. Under the cost method, the parent records dividend collections as income. Entry I removes this Dividend Income account along with Sun's Dividends Paid. From a consolidated perspective, these two $40,000 balances represent an intercompany transfer of cash that had no financial impact outside of the entity. In contrast to the equity method, subsidiary income has not been accrued by Parrot nor has amortization been recorded; thus, no further income elimination is needed.

Dividend Income	40,000	
Dividend Paid		40,000
To eliminate intercompany income.		

Consolidation Entry D. When the cost method is applied, intercompany dividends are recorded by the parent as income. Since these distributions were already removed from the consolidated totals by Entry I, no separate Entry D is required.

Consolidation Entry E. Regardless of the parent's method of accounting, the reporting entity must recognize amortization for the current year in connection with the original purchase price allocations. Thus, Entry E serves to bring the 1995 expense into the consolidated financial statements.

Consequently, using the cost method rather than the equity method changes only Entries I and D in the year of acquisition. Despite the change in methods, reported figures are still derived by (1) eliminating all reciprocals, (2) allocating the excess portion of the purchase price, and (3) recording amortization on these allocations. As indicated previously, the consolidated totals appearing in Exhibit 3–9 are identical to the figures produced previously in Exhibit 3–5. Although the income and the investment accounts on the parent company's separate statements vary, the consolidated balances are not affected.

One significant difference between the cost method and equity method does exist: the parent's separate statements do not reflect consolidated income totals when the cost method is used. Since equity adjustments (such as amortization) are ignored, neither Parrot's reported net income of $640,000 nor its retained earnings of $1,360,000 provides an accurate portrayal of consolidated figures.

Partial Equity Method Applied—1995 Consolidation. Exhibit 3–10 presents a worksheet to consolidate these two companies for 1995 (the year of acquisition) based on the assumption that Parrot applied the partial equity method. Again, the only changes from previous examples are found in (1) the parent's separate records for this investment and its related income and (2) worksheet Entries I and D.

As discussed earlier, under the partial equity approach the parent's record-keeping is limited to two periodic journal entries: the annual accrual of subsidiary income and the receipt of dividends. Hence, within the parent's records, only a few differences exist when the partial equity method is applied rather than the cost method. The entries recorded by Parrot in connection with Sun's 1995 operations illustrate both of these approaches.

	Parrot Company *Cost Method* *1995*			*Parrot Company* *Partial Equity Method* *1995*	
Cash	40,000		Cash	40,000	
Dividend Income . .		40,000	Investment in Sun		
Dividends collected			Company		40,000
from subsidiary.			Dividends collected		
			from subsidiary.		
			Investment in Sun		
			Company	100,000	
			Equity in Subsidiary		
			Earnings		100,000
			Accrual of subsidiary		
			income.		

Therefore, by applying the partial equity method, the Investment account on the parent's balance sheet rises to $860,000 by the end of 1995. This total is comprised of the original $800,000 purchase price adjusted for the $100,000 income recognition and the $40,000 cash dividend payment. The same $100,000 equity income figure also appears within the parent's income statement. These two balances are appropriately found in Parrot's records in Exhibit 3–10.

Because of the handling of income recognition and dividend payments, Entries I and D again differ on the worksheet. For the partial equity method, the $100,000 equity income is eliminated (Entry I) by reversing the parent's entry. Removing this accrual allows the individual revenue and expense accounts of the subsidiary to be reported without double-counting. The $40,000 intercompany dividend payment must also be removed (Entry D). The Dividend Paid account is simply deleted. However, elimination of the dividend from the Investment in Sun Company actually causes an increase because receipt was recorded by Parrot as a reduction in that account. All other consolidation entries (Entries S, A, and E) are the same for all three methods.

Consolidation Subsequent to Year of Acquisition—Other than the Equity Method

By again incorporating the December 31, 1998, financial data for Parrot and Sun (presented in Exhibit 3–7), consolidation procedures for the cost method and the partial equity method can be examined for years subsequent to the date of acquisition. *In both cases, establishment of an appropriate beginning retained earnings figure becomes a significant goal of the consolidation.*

This concern was not faced previously when the equity method was adopted. Under that approach, the parent's retained earnings balance mirrors the consolidated total so that no adjustment is necessary. In the earlier illustration, the

$330,000 income accrual for the 1995–97 period as well as the $21,000 amortization expense were recognized by the parent based on employment of the equity method (see Exhibit 3–6). Having been recorded in this manner, these two balances form a permanent part of Parrot's retained earnings and are included automatically in the consolidated total. Consequently, if the equity method is applied, the process is simplified; no worksheet entries are needed to adjust the parent's retained earnings to record subsidiary operations or amortization for past years.

Conversely, if a method other than the equity method is used, a worksheet change must be made to the parent's beginning retained earnings (in every subsequent year) to equate this balance with the consolidated total. To quantify this adjustment, the parent's recognized income for these past three years under each method is first determined (Exhibit 3–11). For consolidation purposes, beginning retained earnings must then be increased or decreased to create the same effect as the equity method.

Cost Method Applied—Subsequent Consolidation.   As shown in Exhibit 3–11, if the cost method is applied by Parrot during the 1995–97 period, $199,000 less income is recognized than under the equity method ($309,000 − $110,000). This difference has two causes. First, the $220,000 increase in the subsidiary's book value in the period prior to the current year has not been accrued by Parrot. Although the $110,000 in dividends were recorded as income, the remainder of the $330,000 earned by the subsidiary was never recognized by the parent.[6] Second, no accounting has been made of the $21,000 amortization expense. Thus, the parent's beginning retained earnings are $199,000 ($220,000 − $21,000) below the appropriate consolidated total and must be adjusted.[7]

To simulate the equity method so that the parent's beginning retained earnings agree with that of the combination, this $199,000 increase is recorded through a worksheet entry. The cost method figures reported by the parent are effectively being converted into equity method balances.

---

[6] Two different methods are indicated here for determining the $220,000 in nonrecorded income for prior years: (1) subsidiary income less dividends paid and (2) the change in the subsidiary's book value as of the first day of the current year. The second method only works if the subsidiary has had no other equity transactions such as the issuance of new stock or the purchase of treasury shares. Unless otherwise stated, the assumption is made that no such transactions have occurred.

[7] Since neither the income in excess of dividends nor amortization is recorded by the parent under the cost method, its beginning retained earnings are $199,000 less than the $2,044,000 reported under the equity method (Exhibit 3–7). Thus, a $1,845,000 balance is shown in Exhibit 3–12 ($2,044,000 − this $199,000). Conversely if the partial equity method had been applied, Parrot's failure to record amortization would cause retained earnings to be $21,000 higher than the figure derived by the equity method. For this reason, Exhibit 3–13 shows the parent with beginning retained earnings of $2,065,000 rather than $2,044,000.

EXHIBIT 3–11

PARROT'S INCOME RECOGNITION
Previous Years—1995–97

	Equity Method	Cost Method	Partial Equity Method
Equity accrual	$330,000	–0–	$330,000
Dividend income	–0–	$110,000	–0–
Amortization expense	(21,000)	–0–	–0–
Increase in parent's retained earnings	$309,000	$110,000	$330,000

Consolidation Entry *C

```
Investment in Sun Company . . . . . . . . . . . . . . . . . . .  199,000
    Retained Earnings, 1/1/98 (Parrot Company) . . . . . . . . . .        199,000
    To convert parent's beginning retained earnings from cost method
    to equity method.
```

This adjustment has been labeled Entry *C. The *C* refers to the conversion being made to equity method totals. The asterisk indicates that this equity simulation relates solely to transactions of prior periods. Thus, *Entry *C should be recorded before the other worksheet entries to align the beginning balances for the year.*

Exhibit 3–12 provides a complete presentation of the consolidation of Parrot and Sun as of December 31, 1998, based on the parent's application of the cost method. After Entry *C has been recorded on the worksheet, the remainder of this consolidation follows the same pattern as previous examples. Sun's stockholders' equity accounts are eliminated (Entry S) while the allocations stemming from the $800,000 purchase price are recorded (Entry A) at their unamortized balances as of January 1, 1998 (see Exhibit 3–8). Intercompany dividend income is removed (Entry I) and current year amortization expense is recognized (Entry E). To complete this process, the intercompany debt of $40,000 is offset (Entry P).

In retrospect, the only new element introduced here is the adjustment of the parent's beginning retained earnings. For a consolidation produced after the initial year of acquisition, an Entry *C is required if the equity method has not been applied by the parent.

Partial Equity Method Applied—Subsequent Consolidation. Exhibit 3–13 demonstrates the worksheet consolidation of Parrot and Sun as of December 31, 1998, where the investment accounts have been recorded by the parent using the partial

EXHIBIT 3–12

*Consolidation: Purchase
Method
Investment: Cost Method*

PARROT COMPANY AND SUN COMPANY
Consolidation Worksheet
For Year Ending December 31, 1998

Accounts	Parrot Company	Sun Company	Consolidation Entries Debit	Consolidation Entries Credit	Consolidated Totals
Income Statement					
Revenues	(2,100,000)	(600,000)			(2,700,000)
Expenses	1,300,000	440,000	(E) 7,000		1,747,000
Dividend income	(70,000) *	–0–	(I) 70,000 *		–0–
Net income	(870,000)	(160,000)			(953,000)
Statement of Retained Earnings					
Retained earnings, 1/1/98:					
Parrot Company	(1,845,000)† *			(*C) 199,000 *	(2,044,000)
Sun Company		(600,000)	(S) 600,000		–0–
Net income (above)	(870,000)	(160,000)			(953,000)
Dividends paid	420,000	70,000		(I) 70,000 *	420,000
Retained earnings, 12/31/98	(2,295,000)	(690,000)			(2,577,000)
Balance Sheet					
Current assets	1,705,000	500,000		(P) 40,000	2,165,000
Investment in Sun Company	800,000 *	–0–	(*C) 199,000 *	(S) 820,000	–0–
				(A) 179,000	
Land	600,000	240,000	(A) 50,000		890,000
Buildings (net)	540,000	420,000	(A) 56,000	(E) 8,000	1,008,000
Equipment (net)	420,000	210,000	(E) 6,000	(A) 12,000	624,000
Goodwill	–0–	–0–	(A) 85,000	(E) 5,000	80,000
Total assets	4,065,000	1,370,000			4,767,000
Liabilities	(1,050,000)	(460,000)	(P) 40,000		(1,470,000)
Common stock	(600,000)	(200,000)	(S) 200,000		(600,000)
Additional paid-in capital	(120,000)	(20,000)	(S) 20,000		(120,000)
Retained earnings, 12/31/98 (above)	(2,295,000)	(690,000)			(2,577,000)
Total liabilities and equities	(4,065,000)	(1,370,000)			(4,767,000)

NOTE: Parentheses indicate a credit balance.
* Boxed items highlight differences with consolidation in Exhibit 3–7.
† See footnote 7.
Consolidation entries:

(*C) To recognize additional earnings and amortization relating to ownership of subsidiary for years prior to 1998.

(S) Elimination of Sun's Stockholders' Equity accounts as of January 1, 1998, and book value portion of Investment account.
(A) Allocation of Parrot's cost in excess of Sun's book value, unamortized values as of January 1, 1998.
(I) Elimination of intercompany dividends recognized by parent as income.

(D) Entry is not needed when cost method is applied because Entry I eliminates intercompany dividend income.

(E) Recognition of amortization expense on purchase price allocations.
(P) Elimination of intercompany receivable/payable balances.

equity method. This approach accrues subsidiary income each year but records no other equity adjustments. Therefore, as of December 31, 1998, Parrot's Investment in Sun Company account has a balance of $1,110,000:

Purchase price		$ 800,000
Sun Company's 1995–97 increase in book value:		
Accrual of Sun Company's Income	$330,000	
Collection of Sun Company's Dividends	(110,000)	220,000
Sun Company's 1998 operations:		
Accrual of Sun Company's income	$160,000	
Collection of Sun Company's dividends	(70,000)	90,000
Investment in Sun Company, 12/31/98 (Partial equity method)		$1,110,000

As indicated here and in Exhibit 3–11, the yearly equity income accrual has been properly recognized by Parrot but amortization has not. Consequently, if the partial equity method is in use, the parent's beginning retained earnings must be adjusted to include this expense. The $21,000 amortization is recorded through Entry *C to simulate the equity method and, hence, consolidated totals.

Consolidation Entry *C

Retained Earnings, 1/1/98 (Parrot Company).	21,000	
Investment in Sun Company.		21,000
To convert parent's beginning retained earnings from partial equity method to equity method by including amortization.		

By recording Entry *C on the worksheet, all of the subsidiary's operational results for the 1995–97 period are included in the consolidation. As shown in Exhibit 3–13, the remainder of the worksheet entries follow the same basic pattern as that illustrated previously for the year of acquisition (Exhibit 3–10).

Summary of Investment Methods. Having three investment methods available to the parent means that three sets of entries must be understood to arrive at reported figures appropriate for a business combination. The process may initially seem like a confusing overlap of procedures. However, at this point in the coverage, only three worksheet entries are actually affected by the choice of either the equity method, partial equity method, or cost method: Entries *C, I, and D. Furthermore, accountants should never get so involved with a worksheet and its entries that they lose sight of the balances that this process is designed to calculate. These figures are never impacted by the parent's choice of an accounting method.

EXHIBIT 3–13

Consolidation: Purchase Method
Investment: Partial Equity Method

PARROT COMPANY AND SUN COMPANY
Consolidation Worksheet
For Year Ending December 31, 1998

Accounts	Parrot Company	Sun Company	Consolidation Entries Debit	Consolidation Entries Credit	Consolidated Totals
Income Statement					
Revenues	(2,100,000)	(600,000)			(2,700,000)
Expenses	1,300,000	440,000	(E) 7,000		1,747,000
Equity in subsidiary earnings	(160,000) *	–0–	(I) 160,000 *		–0–
Net income	(960,000)	(160,000)			(953,000)
Statement of Retained Earnings					
Retained earnings, 1/1/98:					
Parrot Company	(2,065,000)† *		(*C) 21,000 *		(2,044,000)
Sun Company		(600,000)	(S) 600,000		–0–
Net income (above)	(960,000)	(160,000)			(953,000)
Dividends paid	420,000	70,000		(D) 70,000	420,000
Retained earnings, 12/31/98	(2,605,000)	(690,000)			(2,577,000)
Balance Sheet					
Current assets	1,705,000	500,000		(P) 40,000	2,165,000
Investment in Sun Company	1,110,000 *	–0–	(D) 70,000	(*C) 21,000 *	–0–
				(S) 820,000	
				(A) 179,000	
				(I) 160,000 *	
Land	600,000	240,000	(A) 50,000		890,000
Buildings (net)	540,000	420,000	(A) 56,000	(E) 8,000	1,008,000
Equipment (net)	420,000	210,000	(E) 6,000	(A) 12,000	624,000
Goodwill	–0–	–0–	(A) 85,000	(E) 5,000	80,000
Total assets	4,375,000	1,370,000			4,767,000
Liabilities	(1,050,000)	(460,000)	(P) 40,000		(1,470,000)
Common stock	(600,000)	(200,000)	(S) 200,000		(600,000)
Additional paid-in capital	(120,000)	(20,000)	(S) 20,000		(120,000)
Retained earnings, 12/31/98 (above)	(2,605,000)	(690,000)			(2,577,000)
Total liabilities and equities	(4,375,000)	(1,370,000)			(4,767,000)

Note: Parentheses indicate a credit balance.
* Boxed items highlight differences with consolidation in Exhibit 3–7.
† See footnote 7.
Consolidation entries:

(*C) To record amortization of acquisition price allocations for years prior to 1998.

(S) Elimination of Sun's Stockholders' Equity accounts as of January 1, 1998, and book value portion of Investment account.
(A) Allocation of Parrot's cost in excess of Sun's book value, unamortized values as of January 1, 1998.
(I) Elimination of parent's equity income accrual.
(D) Elimination of intercompany dividend payment.
(E) Recognition of amortization expense on purchase price allocations.
(P) Elimination of intercompany receivable/payable balances.

Consolidated Totals Subsequent to Acquisition—Purchase Method*

Current revenues	Parent revenues are included Subsidiary revenues are included but only for the period since the acquisition
Current expenses	Parent expenses are included Subsidiary expenses are included but only for the period since the acquisition Amortization expense on the purchase price allocations is included by recognition on the worksheet
Investment (or dividend) income	Income recognized by parent is eliminated on the worksheet so that the balance is not included in consolidated figures
Retained earnings, beginning balance	Parent balance is included Subsidiary balance since the acquisition is included either as a regular accrual by the parent or through a worksheet entry to increase parent balance Past amortization expense on the purchase price allocations is included either as a part of parent balance or through a worksheet entry
Assets and liabilities	Parent balances are included Subsidiary balances are included Remaining unamortized purchase price allocations are included Intercompany receivable/payable balances are eliminated
Goodwill	Remaining unamortized purchase price allocation is included
Investment in subsidiary	Asset account recorded by parent is eliminated on the worksheet so that the balance is not included in consolidated figures
Capital stock and additional paid-in capital	Parent balances only are included although they will have been adjusted at date of purchase if stock was issued

* In the next few chapters, the necessity of altering some of these balances for consolidation purposes is discussed. Thus, the table shown here is not definitive but only included to provide a basic overview of the consolidation process as it has been described to this point.

Once the appropriate balance for each account is understood, worksheet entries can be used to assist the accountant in deriving these figures. To help clarify the consolidation process required under each of the three accounting methods, Exhibit 3–14 describes the purpose of each worksheet entry: first during the year of acquisition and second for any period following the year of acquisition.

Discussion Question: How Does a Company Really Decide Which Investment Method to Apply?

During the early stages of 1995, Pilgrim Products, Inc., buys a controlling interest in the common stock of Crestwood Corporation. This transaction fails to meet all of the 12 criteria of a pooling of interests and will, therefore,

continued

be recorded as a purchase. Shortly after the acquisition, a meeting of Pilgrim's accounting department is convened to discuss the internal reporting procedures required by the ownership of this subsidiary. Each member of the staff has a definite opinion as to whether the equity method, cost method, or partial equity method should be adopted. To resolve this issue, Pilgrim's chief financial officer outlines several of her concerns about the decision.

"I already understand how each methods works. I know the general advantages and disadvantages of all three. I realize, for example, that the equity method provides more detailed information whereas the cost method is much easier to apply. What I need to know are the factors specific to our situation that should be considered in deciding which method to adopt. I must make a recommendation to the president on this matter, and he will want firm reasons for my favoring a particular approach. I don't want us to select a method and then find out in six months that the information is not adequate for our needs or that the cost of adapting our system to monitor Crestwood outweighs the benefits derived from the data."

What are the factors that Pilgrim's officials should evaluate when making this decision?

Purchase Price—Contingent Consideration

A footnote to the 1990 financial statements of Hunt Manufacturing Company discloses the following contingency.

> On May 4, 1990, the Company acquired from Bunzi plc all of the outstanding stock of Seal Products, Incorporated and Ademco Limited and the business and certain specified assets and liabilities of Coated Specialties Limited . . . . The purchase price for the stock and assets consisted of cash consideration of approximately $37 million plus closing costs. The Company may also be required to pay a single contingent cash payment of up to 4.75 million British pounds sterling (approximately $9.2 million at December 2, 1990) based upon the cumulative net sales of (this group) and certain related products during the three-year period January 1, 1990, through December 31, 1992.

A business combination has been formed here but, as this footnote describes, a portion of the purchase price being paid by the parent will not be finalized until several years after the date of acquisition.

Where a subsequent payment, such as that described by Hunt's statements, is based solely on future earnings, the contingency has no initial impact on the purchase price or the consolidated figures. The potential disbursement should

EXHIBIT 3–14   Consolidation Worksheet Entries—Purchase Method

	Equity Method Applied	Cost Method Applied	Partial Equity Method Applied
Any time during year of acquisition:			
Entry S	Beginning stockholders' equity of subsidiary is eliminated against book value portion of investment account	Same as equity method	Same as equity method
Entry A	Excess purchase price is allocated to assets and liabilities based on difference in book values and fair market values; residual is assigned to goodwill	Same as equity method	Same as equity method
Entry I	Equity income accrual (including amortization expense) is eliminated	Dividend income is eliminated	Equity income accrual is eliminated
Entry D	Intercompany dividends paid by subsidiary are eliminated	No entry—intercompany dividends are eliminated in Entry I	Same as equity method
Entry E	Current year amortization expense of cost allocations is recorded	Same as equity method	Same as equity method
Entry P	Intercompany payable/receivable balances are offset	Same as equity method	Same as equity method
Any time following year of acquisition:			
Entry *C	No entry—equity income for prior years has already been recognized along with amortization expense	Increase in subsidiary's book value during prior years as well as amortization expense are recognized (conversion is made to equity method)	Amortization expense for prior years is recognized (conversion is made to equity method)
Entry S	Same as initial year	Same as initial year	Same as initial year
Entry A	Unamortized cost at beginning of year is allocated to specific accounts and to goodwill	Same as equity method	Same as equity method
Entry I	Same as initial year	Same as initial year	Same as initial year
Entry D	Same as initial year	Same as initial year	Same as initial year
Entry E	Same as initial year	Same as initial year	Same as initial year
Entry P	Same as initial year	Same as initial year	Same as initial year

only be disclosed in a note to the financial statements similar to the one just presented. When the contingency is ultimately resolved, any further payment made by the parent is simply added to the purchase price.

Thus, if goodwill was recognized at the date of acquisition, any later disbursement is assigned to this same intangible asset. Should another $100,000 be paid, for example, reported goodwill is increased by this amount. Conversely, if the original price was below fair market value so that the balances assigned to noncurrent assets were reduced (and possibly a deferred credit established), a subsequent payment serves to decrease the amount of these reductions. In either case, an increase in the initial purchase price resulting from a contingency of this type is not accounted for in a retroactive manner. Any resulting amortization expense is only recorded over the *remaining* life of the appropriate account.

A contingency can also result from the acquisition of a subsidiary if the price is based on the future value of the stock issued. Such arrangements are designed to ensure that the previous owners receive compensation that retains a minimum value for a specified period. For example, in discussing an earlier acquisition, the 1987 financial statements of Munsingwear, Inc. state that "the Company is obligated to issue additional shares of common stock at August 29, 1988 . . . in the event of a decline in the market value of the common stock." From an accounting perspective, this second type of extra payment is not viewed as an increase in the parent's purchase price. Rather, the possible distribution is a guarantee of the value of the consideration conveyed in the original transaction. Thus, no change is made in goodwill or any other allocations.

If additional shares of the parent's stock must be issued because of a subsequent drop in price, the parent records the new shares at fair market value. At the same time, the total attributed to the shares originally issued at the date of purchase is reduced by a corresponding amount to reflect the decrease in value. The net effect is that the parent's stock account is increased by the par value of the new shares issued with additional paid-in capital reduced by the same amount. The purchase price does not change.

To illustrate, assume that Large issues 10,000 shares of its $10 par value stock to acquire Small. This stock had a value on that date of $25 per share ($250,000 in total). In recording this transaction, Large increases:

- Its Common Stock account by the $100,000 par value of these shares.
- Additional Paid-In Capital by $150,000 to reflect the value in excess of par ($25 − $10).

Subsequently, the market value of this stock drops to $20 per share. Assume that the purchase agreement specified that the market value of the shares issued could not be reduced for a given period. To maintain the total value at $250,000, 2,500 more shares are issued to Small's previous owners. At $20 per share, the new total of 12,500 shares has the appropriate value of $250,000. The new shares are recorded at par value ($25,000 or 2,500 shares at $10 per share) with an accompanying reduction in additional paid-in capital. Therefore, total contributed capital from this purchase remains at $250,000.

Large's Financial Records—Subsequent Issuance of Shares

Additional Paid-In Capital 25,000
    Common Stock (par value) 25,000
To record issuance of 2,500 new shares of stock in connection
with previous acquisition of Small. Additional shares were
required because of drop in market value of shares originally
issued.

Discussion Question: Is This Income?

Artilio Corporation pays $1 million for all of the outstanding stock of Zepthan, Inc. Because of an urgent need for cash, the owners of Zepthan are forced to accept this price although the company's net assets have a value of $1.6 million.

Based on the guidelines for a bargain purchase previously demonstrated in Chapter 2, the $600,000 reduction is assigned to the subsidiary's noncurrent assets (other than long-term investments in marketable securities). Consequently, assume that the consolidated value of Zepthan's land is reduced by $50,000 with its buildings and equipment decreased by a total of $550,000. If the buildings and equipment have a life of 10 years, these negative allocations reduce amortization expense by $55,000 per year and, hence, increase income by that amount. Consolidated net income for the combination is projected to be approximately $250,000 per year for the foreseeable future. Thus, 22 percent is attributable to the bargain purchase ($55,000/$250,000). Despite the positive impact on income, amortization of bargain purchase figures is required.

Because of the annual decrease from amortization, a bargain purchase creates a consolidated entity that reports more income than the sum of the two component companies. As in the case of Artilio and Zepthan, the amount can be very significant. Should earnings be *increased* through an acquisition? Harvey Kapnick, former managing partner of Arthur Andersen & Company, casts doubts on this practice: "The real gimmick today is purchase accounting. . . . When you get negative goodwill,[1] it tends to inflate earnings unrealistically and therefore it misleads the investor."[2]

Should a business combination be allowed to increase reported earnings based on paying a bargain price to acquire a new subsidiary? Does this practice distort earnings? Does a reasonable alternative exist?

---

[1] *Negative goodwill* is a traditional accounting term referring here to the total fair market value in excess of the acquisition price.

[2] "Gimmick for All Seasons," *Forbes,* October 1, 1975, p. 62.

Push-Down Accounting

External Reporting

In the analysis of business combinations to this point, discussion has focused on (1) the recording by the parent company and (2) required consolidation procedures. Unfortunately, official accounting pronouncements give virtually no guidance as to the impact of a purchase on the separate financial statements of the subsidiary.

This issue has become especially significant in recent years because of a rash of management led buy-outs as well as corporate reorganizations. An organization, for example, might acquire a company and subsequently offer the shares back to the public in hopes of making a large profit. What should be reported in the subsidiary's financial statements being distributed with this offering? Such deals have reheated a long-standing debate over the merits of *push-down accounting,* the direct recording by a subsidiary of purchase price allocations and subsequent amortization.

For this reason, the FASB has been exploring the various possible methods of reporting by a company that has been acquired or reorganized. To illustrate, assume that Yarrow Company owns one asset: a building with a book value of $200,000 but a fair market value of $900,000. Mannen Corporation pays exactly $900,000 in cash to acquire Yarrow. Consolidation offers no real problem here: the building will be reported by the business combination at $900,000.

However, if Yarrow continues to issue separate financial statements (for example, to its creditors or potential stockholders), should the building be reported at $200,000 or $900,000? If adjusted, should the $700,000 increase be reported as a gain by the subsidiary or as an addition to contributed capital? Should depreciation be based on $200,000 or $900,000? If the subsidiary is to be viewed as a new entity with a new basis for its assets and liabilities, should retained earnings be returned to zero? If the parent acquires only 51 percent of Yarrow, does that change the answers to the previous questions? These questions represent just a few of the difficult issues currently being explored.

Proponents of push-down accounting provide justification founded on the contention that a change in ownership creates a new basis for subsidiary assets and liabilities. An unadjusted balance ($200,000 in the preceding illustration) is a cost figure applicable to previous stockholders. That total is no longer relevant information. Rather, according to this argument, it is the historical cost *paid by the current owner* that is important, a figure that is best reflected by the expenditure made in acquiring the subsidiary. Balance sheet accounts should be reported at the cost incurred by the present stockholders ($900,000 in the illustration) rather than the cost incurred by the company.

Currently, primary guidance concerning push-down accounting for external reporting purposes is provided by the Securities and Exchange Commission (SEC). Through Staff Accounting Bulletin No. 54 (*Application of "Push Down"*

Basis of Accounting in Financial Statements of Subsidiaries Acquired by Purchase) and Staff Accounting Bulletin No. 73 (*"Push Down" Basis of Accounting for Parent Company Debt Related to Subsidiary Acquisitions*), the SEC has indicated that

> push down accounting should be used in the separate financial statements of a "substantially wholly owned" subsidiary. . . . That view is based on the notion that when the form of ownership is within the control of the parent company, the accounting basis should be the same whether the entity continues to exist or is merged into the parent's operations. If a purchase of a "substantially wholly owned" subsidiary is financed by debt of the parent, that debt generally must be pushed down to the subsidiary. . . . As a general rule, the SEC requires push down accounting when the ownership change is greater than 95 percent and objects to push down accounting when the ownership change is less than 80 percent. However, if the acquired subsidiary has outstanding public debt or preferred stock, push down accounting is encouraged by the SEC but not required.[8]

Thus, the SEC requires the use of push-down accounting for the separate financial statements of any subsidiary where no substantial outside ownership exists of the company's common stock, preferred stock, and publicly held debt. Apparently, the SEC believes that a change in ownership of that degree justifies a new basis of reporting for the subsidiary's assets and liabilities. Until the FASB takes action, though, application is only required when the subsidiary desires to issue securities (stock or debt) to the public as regulated by the SEC.

Push-Down Accounting—Internal Reporting

Although the use of push-down accounting for external reporting is limited, this approach has gained significant popularity in recent years for internal reporting purposes.

> Subsidiaries owned by the Chesapeake Corporation are recorded using push-down accounting. Under this theory, the subsidiary adjusts its assets and liabilities to current value at the time of the acquisition while also recording the necessary goodwill. The subsidiary's net assets, as adjusted, would equal the amount recorded by the parent as the investment in subsidiary.[9]

> At the time of acquisition of each subsidiary, purchase method accounting is applied by James River Corporation on a push-down basis. The parent's investment equals the net book value of the subsidiary through an allocation of the purchase price to the net assets of the subsidiary on a fair market value basis.[10]

---

[8] FASB Discussion Memorandum, *An Analysis of Issues Related to New Basis Accounting,* December 18, 1991, p. 54.

[9] Letter from Timothy M. Harhan, senior corporate accountant with Chesapeake Corporation, dated February 17, 1992.

[10] Letter from Catherine M. Freeman, manager—financial projects with James River Corporation, dated February 6, 1992.

Push-down accounting has several advantages for internal reporting. For example, it simplifies the consolidation process. Because the allocations and amortization are already entered into the records of the subsidiary, worksheet Entries A (to recognize the allocations originating from the purchase price) and E (amortization expense) are not needed. Therefore, except for eliminating the effects of intercompany transactions, the assets, liabilities, revenues, and expenses of the subsidiary can be added directly to those of the parent to derive consolidated totals.

More importantly, push-down accounting provides better information for internal evaluation. Since the subsidiary's separate figures include amortization expense, the net income reported by the company is a good representation of the impact that the acquisition has on the earnings of the business combination. As an example, assume that Ace Corporation owns 100 percent of Waxworth, Inc. Waxworth uses push-down accounting and reports net income of $500,000: $600,000 from operations less $100,000 in amortization expense resulting from purchase price allocations. Thus, officials of Ace Corporation know that this acquisition has added $500,000 to the consolidated net income of the business combination. They can then evaluate whether these earnings provide a sufficient return for the parent's investment.

However, the recording of amortization expense by the subsidiary can lead to dissension. Members of the subsidiary's management may argue that they are being forced to record a large expense over which they have no control or responsibility. This amortization comes directly from the purchase price paid by the parent and is not a result of any action taken by the subsidiary. Chesapeake Corporation has considered this problem and resolved it in the following manner: "For internal reporting of income statement activity, earnings from operations are identified separately from amortization. This allows management to analyze the subsidiary's results without the effect of amortization."[11]

Subsequent Consolidations—Pooling of Interests

For consolidations prepared after the date of combination, a pooling of interests requires a slightly less complex set of procedures than does the purchase method. By reflecting on the fundamental concepts of a pooling, the essential differences between the subsequent consolidation entries employed by these two methods can be understood.

In Chapter 2 the purchase method is identified as applicable to combinations involving a takeover with the pooling of interests method appropriate when the combination is formed by a union of companies. Since a takeover does not occur, no acquisition price is ever calculated for a pooling. All assets and liabilities are simply consolidated at their book values. No allocations based on fair market value are computed nor is any goodwill recognized. Hence, amortization that

---

[11] Letter from Timothy H. Harhan.

would be associated with such cost factors is not encountered in a pooling of interests.

In mechanical terms, the absence of a purchase price means that worksheet entries relating to cost allocations (Entry A) and subsequent amortization expense (Entry E) are never found in a pooling. Obviously, as with push-down accounting, alleviating the necessity of working with these entries simplifies the entire consolidation process.

The company that issues its stock to consummate a pooling of interests must record these shares along with the resulting investment. This company must then adopt a method to account for this investment. One possibility is to apply the equity method to accrue income as it is earned by the other company and to adjust for intercompany transactions (as discussed in Chapter 5). The partial equity method might also be selected so that recording is limited to the periodic accrual of income.

However, any reference to a cost method would be a misnomer since, in a pooling of interests, no acquisition cost is ever established. Thus, for internal reporting purposes, the cost method is replaced by a *book value method* that has the same essential characteristics: the investment account permanently retains its initial balance (the book value of the other company) with any dividends received being recognized as income.

To illustrate the consolidation techniques employed in a pooling of interests, assume that Brother Company obtains 100 percent of the outstanding voting shares of Sister Company on January 1, 1995. To create this combination, Brother issues 10,000 shares of its own common stock in an exchange that meets all 12 requirements for a pooling of interests. On that date, Sister reports a total book value of $700,000 although market value is $950,000. For reporting purposes, the additional $250,000 is unimportant; only book value is relevant in accounting for a pooling of interests. Consequently, $700,000 is recorded by Brother as an investment. The book value method is applied by Brother; thus, this balance remains unchanged over the years.

For this example, consolidated financial statements are prepared as of December 31, 1998. Sister's book value has risen by $610,000 to $1,310,000 as of the first day of 1998. Assume also that Sister owes $90,000 to Brother at the end of this year. Exhibit 3–15 presents the worksheet for the 1998 consolidation of these two companies under the pooling of interests concept. Once again, the entries have been labeled to parallel the earlier consolidation examples, although neither Entry A nor Entry E is applicable to a pooling.

Because Brother applies the book value method, no recognition has been made of the increase in Sister's book value since the date of combination. Consequently, Brother's retained earnings at January 1, 1998, do not reflect a consolidated total; the $610,000 increment is not included. An Entry *C must be recorded on the worksheet to accrue this income that has been earned by Sister in excess of dividends distributed (the increase in net book value). After Brother's beginnings retained earnings have been properly adjusted in this manner, the remaining consolidation entries eliminate Sister's stockholders' equity (Entry S), the intercompany dividend income (Entry I), and the intercompany debt (Entry P).

EXHIBIT 3–15

Consolidation: Pooling of Interests Method
Investment: Book Value Method

BROTHER COMPANY AND SISTER COMPANY
Consolidation Worksheet
For Year Ending December 31, 1998

Accounts	Brother Company	Sister Company	Consolidation Entries		Consolidated Totals
			Debit	Credit	
Income Statement					
Revenues	(1,600,000)	(550,000)			(2,150,000)
Expenses	1,220,000	440,000			1,660,000
Dividend income	(40,000)	–0–	(I) 40,000		–0–
Net income	(420,000)	(110,000)			(490,000)
Statement of Retained Earnings					
Retained earnings, 1/1/98	(2,260,000)	(910,000)	(S) 910,000	(*C) 610,000	(2,870,000)
Net income (above)	(420,000)	(110,000)			(490,000)
Dividends paid	60,000	40,000		(I) 40,000	60,000
Retained earnings, 12/31/98	(2,620,000)	(980,000)			(3,300,000)
Balance Sheet					
Cash and receivables	590,000	140,000		(P) 90,000	640,000
Inventory	940,000	480,000			1,420,000
Investment in Sister Company	700,000	–0–	(*C) 610,000	(S) 1,310,000	–0–
Land	600,000	340,000			940,000
Buildings (net)	970,000	270,000			1,240,000
Equipment (net)	730,000	520,000			1,250,000
Total assets	4,530,000	1,750,000			5,490,000
Liabilities	(810,000)	(370,000)	(P) 90,000		(1,090,000)
Common stock	(800,000)	(300,000)	(S) 300,000		(800,000)
Additional paid-in capital	(300,000)	(100,000)	(S) 100,000		(300,000)
Retained earnings, 12/31/98 (above)	(2,620,000)	(980,000)			(3,300,000)
Total liabilities and equities	(4,530,000)	(1,750,000)			(5,490,000)

NOTE: Parentheses indicate a credit balance.
Consolidation entries:
  (*C) To recognize increase in book value of affiliated company during years prior to 1998.
  (S) Elimination of Sister's Stockholders' Equity accounts as of January 1, 1998, and book value portion of Investment account.
  (I) Elimination of intercompany dividends recognized by Brother as income.
  (P) Elimination of intercompany receivable/payable balances.

Summary

1. The procedures used to consolidate financial information generated by the separate companies in a business combination are affected by both the passage of time and the method applied by the parent in accounting for the subsidiary. Thus, no single consolidation process can be described that is applicable to all business combinations.

2. The parent might elect to utilize the equity method to account for a subsidiary. As discussed in Chapter 1, income is accrued by the parent when earned by the subsidiary and dividend receipts are recorded as reductions in the Investment account. The effects of amortization or any intercompany transactions are also reflected within the parent's financial records. The equity method provides the parent with accurate information concerning the subsidiary's impact on consolidated totals; however, it is usually somewhat complicated to apply.

3. The cost method and the partial equity method are two alternatives to the equity method. The cost method recognizes only the subsidiary's dividends as income while the asset balance remains at cost. This approach is simple and provides a measure of cash flows between the two companies. Under the partial equity method, the parent accrues the subsidiary's income as earned but does not record adjustments that might be required by amortization or intercompany transfers. The partial equity method is easier to apply than the equity method but, in many cases, the parent's income is a reasonable approximation of the consolidated total.

4. For a consolidation in any subsequent period, all reciprocal balances have to be eliminated. Thus, the subsidiary's equity accounts, the parent's investment balance, and intercompany income, dividends, and liabilities are removed. In addition, the remaining unamortized portions of the purchase price allocations are recognized along with amortization expense for the period. If the equity method has not been applied, the beginning retained earnings of the parent must also be adjusted for any previous income or amortization that has not yet been recorded.

5. The purchase price of a subsidiary can be based, at least in part, on future income levels or stock prices. If a subsequent payment is made because a specified amount of income is earned, consolidated goodwill is increased. However, if additional shares are issued because of a drop in the price of the parent's stock, the Common Stock and Additional Paid-In Capital accounts are realigned to agree with the new price.

6. Push-down accounting is the adjustment of the subsidiary's account balances to recognize allocations and goodwill stemming from the parent's purchase price. Subsequent amortization of these cost figures is also recorded by the subsidiary as an expense. At this time, push-down accounting is required by the SEC for the separate statements of the subsidiary only when no substantial outside ownership exists. The FASB is currently studying push-down accounting and may issue more specific rules on its application. However, for internal reporting purposes, push-down accounting is gaining popularity because it aids company officials in evaluating the impact that the subsidiary has on the business combination.

Comprehensive Illustration

PROBLEM

(Estimated Time: 40 to 65 Minutes)

On January 1, 1995, Top Company acquired all of the outstanding common stock of Bottom Company for $800,000 in cash. As of that date, one of Bottom's buildings with a five-year remaining life was undervalued on its financial records by $30,000. Equipment with a 10-year life was also undervalued but only by $10,000. The book values of all of Bottom's other assets and liabilities were equal to their fair market values at that time. Any goodwill indicated by this purchase is assumed to have the maximum life allowed for amortization purposes.

During 1995, Bottom reported net income of $100,000 and paid $30,000 in dividends. Earnings were $120,000 in 1996 with $20,000 in dividends distributed by the subsidiary. As of December 31, 1997, the companies reported the following selected balances:

	Top Company December 31, 1997		Bottom Company December 31, 1997	
	Debit	Credit	Debit	Credit
Buildings	$1,540,000		$460,000	
Cash and receivables	50,000		90,000	
Common stock.		$ 900,000		$400,000
Dividends paid.	70,000		10,000	
Equipment.	280,000		200,000	
Expenses	600,000		180,000	
Inventory	280,000		260,000	
Land	330,000		250,000	
Liabilities		480,000		260,000
Retained earnings, 1/1/97		1,360,000		490,000
Revenues		900,000		300,000

Required:

a. If the equity method is applied by Top, what are its investment account balances as of December 31, 1997?

b. If the cost method is applied by Top, what are its investment account balances as of December 31, 1997?

c. Regardless of the accounting method in use by Top, what are the consolidated totals as of December 31, 1997, for each of the following accounts:

Buildings	Revenues
Equipment	Net Income
Land	Investment in Bottom
Expenses	Dividends Paid

d. If this combination had met the 12 criteria for a pooling of interests, what would be the consolidated totals as of December 31, 1997, for the accounts listed in requirement *c*.

e. Prepare the worksheet entries required on December 31, 1997, to consolidate the financial records of these two companies. Assume that Top applied the equity method to its investment accounts and that the combination is a purchase.

f. How would the worksheet entries in requirement *e*. be altered if Top has used the cost method?

SOLUTION

a. To determine the investment balances under the equity method, four items must be known: the original cost, the income accrual, dividend payments, and amortization expense. Although the first three are indicated in the problem, amortization must be calculated separately. However, the book value of Bottom Company as of the date of acquisition is not given, and that figure is needed to determine the presence of goodwill.

Bottom's book value at January 1, 1997, totaled $890,000 (common stock of $400,000 plus retained earnings of $490,000). During the 1995–96 period, the subsidiary earned income of $220,000 ($100,000 in 1995 and $120,000 in 1996) while paying $50,000 in dividends ($30,000 in 1995 and $20,000 in 1996). These figures indicate a $170,000 net increase; thus, Bottom had a book value of $720,000 when acquired on January 1, 1995 ($890,000 − $170,000).

Following this computation, an allocation of Top's purchase price can be determined as well as the related amortization expense.

		Life (years)	Annual Amortization
Purchase price paid by Top Company	$ 800,000		
Book value of Sun Company, 1/1/95	(720,000)		
Excess cost over book value	80,000		
Excess cost allocated to specific accounts based on fair market values:			
Buildings	30,000	5	$6,000
Equipment	10,000	10	1,000
Excess cost not identified with specific accounts—goodwill	$ 40,000	40	1,000
Total annual expense			$8,000

Thus, if Top adopts the equity method to account for this subsidiary, the Investment in Bottom account holds a December 31, 1997, balance of $1,056,000, computed as follows:

Purchase price		$ 800,000
Bottom Company's 1995–96 increase in book value (income less		
dividends)		170,000
Amortization for 1995–96 ($8,000		
per year for two years)		(16,000)
Current year recognition (1997):		
Equity income accrual (Bottom's revenues		
less its expenses)	$120,000	
Amortization expense	(8,000)	
Dividend from Bottom.	(10,000)	102,000
Investment in Bottom Company, 12/31/97		$1,056,000

The $120,000 income accrual for 1997 and the $8,000 amortization expense indicate that an Equity in Subsidiary Earnings balance of $112,000 appears in Top's income statement for the current period.

b. If Top Company applies the cost method, the Investment in Bottom Company account permanently retains its original $800,000 balance and only the intercompany dividend of $10,000 is recognized by the parent as income in 1997.

c.

- The consolidated Buildings account as of December 31, 1997, holds a balance of $2,012,000. Although the two book value figures total to only $2 million, a $30,000 purchase price allocation was made to this account based on fair market value at date of acquisition. Since this amount is being amortized at the rate of $6,000 per year, the original allocation will have been reduced by $18,000 by the end of 1997, leaving only a $12,000 increase.
- On December 31, 1997, the consolidated Equipment account amounts to $487,000. The book values found in the financial records of Top and Bottom provide a total of $480,000. Once again, the allocation ($10,000) established by the purchase price must be included in the consolidated balance after being adjusted for three years of amortization ($1,000 × 3 years or $3,000).
- Land has a consolidated total of $580,000. Since the book value and fair market value of Bottom's land were in agreement at the date of acquisition, no allocation of the purchase price was made to this account. Thus, the book values are simply added together to derive a consolidated figure.
- Consolidated expenses of $788,000 are recognized for 1997. The figures reported by the two companies are added and then increased by $8,000 in amortization expense for the year, a balance that results from the purchase price allocations.
- The Revenues account appears as $1.2 million in the consolidated income statement. None of the worksheet entries in this example affects the indi-

vidual balances of either company. Consolidation results merely from the addition of the two book values.

- Net income for this business combination is $412,000: consolidated expenses of $788,000 subtracted from revenues of $1.2 million.
- The parent's Investment in Bottom account is removed entirely on the worksheet so that no balance is reported. For consolidation purposes, this account is always eliminated so that the individual assets and liabilities of the subsidiary can be included.
- Dividends paid by the combination should be reported as $70,000, the amount distributed by Top. Because Bottom's dividend payments are entirely intercompany, they are deleted in arriving at consolidated figures.

d. The consolidation of companies under the pooling of interests method is based primarily on the addition of book values. Therefore, consolidated totals for the first five accounts in this question can be determined merely by summing the separate balances:

- Buildings = $2,000,000 ($1,540,000 + $460,000)
- Equipment = $480,000 ($280,000 + $200,000)
- Land = $580,000 ($330,000 + $250,000)
- Expenses = $780,000 ($600,000 + $180,000)
- Revenues = $1,200,000 ($900,000 + $300,000)

- Consolidated net income is calculated by subtracting the $780,000 in expenses (just computed) from revenues of $1.2 million for a reported total of $420,000.
- As in a purchase, the Investment in Bottom account is eliminated so that the subsidiary's individual balances can be included.
- Only the parent's dividend ($70,000) is reported in the consolidated statements since Bottom's payment is an intercompany cash transfer.

e. Consolidation Entries Assuming Equity Method Used by Parent

Entry S

Common Stock (Bottom Company)	400,000	
Retained Earnings, 1/1/97		
(Bottom Company)	490,000	
Investment in Bottom Company		890,000

Elimination of subsidiary's beginning stockholders' equity accounts against book value portion of investment account.

Entry A

Buildings	18,000	
Equipment	8,000	
Goodwill	38,000	
Investment in Bottom Company		64,000

To recognize allocation of parent's unamortized cost in excess of subsidiary's book value. Balances represent original allocations less two years of amortization for the 1995–96 period.

Entry I

Equity in Subsidiary Earnings	112,000	
Investment in Bottom Company		112,000

To eliminate parent's equity income accrual, balance is computed
in requirement *a*.

Entry D

Investment in Bottom.	10,000	
Dividends Paid		10,000

To eliminate intercompany dividend payment made by subsidiary
to the parent (and recorded as a reduction in the investment
account since the equity method is in use).

Entry E

Expenses	8,000	
Buildings		6,000
Equipment.		1,000
Goodwill		1,000

To recognize amortization expense for 1997.

f. If the cost method rather that the equity method had been utilized by Top, three changes would have been required in the development of consolidation entries:

(1) An Entry *C is required to update the beginning retained earnings of the parent as if the equity method had been applied. Both an income accrual as well as amortization for the prior two years must be recognized since these balances were not recorded by the parent.

Entry *C

Investment in Bottom Company	154,000	
Retained Earnings, 1/1/97 (Top Company)		154,000

To convert cost figures to the equity method by accruing the net
effect of the subsidiary's operations (income less dividends) for the
prior two years ($170,000) along with amortization expense
($16,000) for this same period.

(2) An alteration is needed in Entry I since, under the cost method, only dividend payments are recorded by the parent as income.

Entry I

Dividend Income	10,000	
Dividends Paid		10,000

To eliminate intercompany dividend payments recorded by parent
as income.

(3) Finally, because the intercompany dividends have been eliminated in Entry I, no separate Entry D is needed.

Questions

1. Bell Corporation acquires a controlling interest in Dawkins, Inc. in a purchase transaction. Bell may utilize any one of three methods to account for this investment. Describe each of these methods, indicating their advantages and disadvantages.

2. Simpson Company obtains 100 percent control over Williams Company. Several years after the takeover, consolidated financial statements are being produced. For each of the following accounts, indicate the values that should be included in consolidated totals. Assume that Simpson acquired Williams in a transaction that must be viewed as a purchase.
   a. Equipment.
   b. Investment in Williams Company.
   c. Dividends paid.
   d. Goodwill.
   e. Revenues.
   f. Expenses.
   g. Common stock.
   h. Net income.

3. Using the information presented in question 2, determine each of the consolidated totals if the combination is to be accounted for as a pooling of interests.

4. When a parent company uses the equity method to account for an investment in a subsidiary, why do both the parent's net income and retained earnings balances agree with the consolidated totals?

5. When a parent company uses the equity method to account for a purchased investment, the amortization expense entry recorded during the year is eliminated on a consolidation worksheet as a component of Entry I. What is the necessity of removing this amortization?

6. When a parent company is applying the cost method or the partial equity method to an investment, an adjustment must be made to the parent's beginning retained earnings (Entry *C) in every period after the year of acquisition. What is the necessity for this entry? Why is no similar entry found when the equity method is utilized by the parent?

7. Several years ago, Jenkins Company acquired a controlling interest in Lambert Company. Lambert recently borrowed $100,000 from Jenkins. In consolidating the financial records of these two companies, how will this debt be handled?

8. Benns Company acquires Waters Company in a combination accounted for as a purchase. Benns adopts the equity method. At the end of six years, Benns reports an investment in Waters of $920,000. What figures constitute this balance?

9. One company is acquired by another in a purchase transaction in which $100,000 of the acquisition price is assigned to goodwill. Several years later a worksheet is being produced to consolidate these two companies. How is the reported value of the goodwill determined at this date?

10. Remo Company purchases Albane Corporation on January 1, 1995. As part of the purchase agreement, the parent states that an additional $100,000 payment to the former owners of Albane may be required in 1998 depending on the outcome of specified conditions. If this payment is subsequently made, how will Remo account for the extra cost?

11. When is the use of push-down accounting required and what is the rationale for its application?

12. How are the individual financial records of both the parent and the subsidiary affected in cases where push-down accounting is being applied?

13. Why has push-down accounting gained popularity for internal reporting purposes?

14. The consolidation process applicable to a pooling of interests is often viewed as easier than that used for a purchase. What creates this perception?

Library Assignments

1. Read the following as well as any other published information concerning goodwill:

   "Accounting Rules Favor Foreign Bidders," *The Wall Street Journal,* March 24, 1988, p. 30.

   "Ill Will," *Forbes,* January 23, 1989.

   "Goodwill—An Eternal Controversy," *The CPA Journal,* April 1993.

   "The Evolution of APB Opinion No. 17, 'Accounting for Intangible Assets': A Study of the U.S. Position on Accounting for Goodwill," *Accounting Historians Journal,* Spring 1981.

   "Goodwill Is Making a Lot of People Angry," *Business Week,* July 31, 1989.

   "Accounting for Goodwill," *Accounting Horizons,* March 1988.

   "A Peculiar Beauty Contest," *Forbes,* July 10, 1989.

   "An Edge to Foreign Buyers?" *Mergers & Acquisitions,* March–April 1988.

   Write a report to either justify the current treatment required for the recognition and amortization of goodwill or recommend an alternative method of accounting.

2. Read the following as well as any other published information concerning push-down accounting:

"Push-Down Accounting: FAS 200?" *Management Accounting,* November 1988.

"Business Combinations: Goodwill and Push-Down Accounting," *The CPA Journal,* August 1988.

"The Push-Down Accounting Controversy," *Management Accounting,* January 1987.

"Push Down Accounting: A Descriptive Assessment," *Accounting Horizons,* September 1988.

"Push-Down Accounting: Pros and Cons," *Journal of Accountancy,* June 1984

Write a report suggesting actions that the FASB should take in connection with the future application of push-down accounting.

Problems

1. A company acquires a subsidiary on January 1, 1995, and will prepare consolidated financial statements for the year ending December 31, 1995. For internal reporting purposes, the company has decided to apply the cost method. Why might the company have made this decision?

   a. It is a relatively easy method to apply.

   b. Operating results appearing on the parent's financial records reflect consolidated totals.

   c. The FASB now requires the use of this particular method for internal reporting purposes.

   d. Consolidation is not required when the cost method is used by the parent.

2. A company acquires a subsidiary on January 1, 1995, and will prepare consolidated financial statements for the year ending December 31, 1995. For internal reporting purposes, the company has decided to apply the equity method during 1995. Why might the company have made this decision?

   a. It is a relatively easy method to apply.

   b. Operating results appearing on the parent's financial records reflect consolidated totals.

   c. The FASB now requires the use of this particular method for internal reporting purposes.

   d. Consolidation is not required when the equity method is used by the parent.

3. Hansen, Inc. buys all of the outstanding stock of Shawnee Company on January 1, 1995, for $214,000. Annual amortization of $16,000 results from this purchase. Hansen reported net income of $60,000 in 1995 and $40,000 in 1996 and paid $18,000 in dividends each year. Shawnee reported net income of $33,000 in 1995 and $39,000 in 1996 and paid $8,000 in dividends

each year. What is the Investment in Shawnee balance on Hansen's books as of December 31, 1996, if the equity method has been applied?
  a. $238,000.
  b. $246,000.
  c. $278,000.
  d. $286,000.

4. Barrett Corporation buys 100 percent of Smith, Inc. on January 1, 1995, at a price in excess of the subsidiary's fair market value. On that date, Barrett's equipment (10-year life) has a book value of $300,000 but a fair market value of $400,000. Smith has equipment (10-year life) with a book value of $200,000 but a fair market value of $300,000. Barrett uses the partial equity method to record its investment in Smith. On December 31, 1997, Barrett has equipment with a book value of $210,000 but a fair market value of $330,000. Smith has equipment with a book value of $140,000 but a fair market value of $270,000. What is the consolidated balance for the Equipment account as of December 31, 1997?
  a. $600,000.
  b. $490,000.
  c. $480,000.
  d. $420,000.

5. How would the answer to question 4 have been affected if the parent had applied the cost method rather than the partial equity method?
  a. No effect: the method used by the parent is for internal reporting purposes only and has no impact on consolidated totals.
  b. The consolidated Equipment account would have a higher reported balance.
  c. The consolidated Equipment account would have a lower reported balance.
  d. The balance in the consolidated Equipment account cannot be determined for the cost method using the information given.

6. Brocklin, Incorporated buys all of the outstanding shares of New England Corporation on January 1, 1995, for $700,000 in cash. This price resulted in a $35,000 allocation to equipment and goodwill of $88,000. Because the subsidiary subsequently earned especially high profits, Brocklin was required to pay the previous owners of New England an additional $110,000 on January 1, 1997. How should this extra amount be reported?
  a. The additional $110,000 payment is a reduction in consolidated retained earnings.
  b. A retroactive adjustment is made to record the $110,000 as an additional expense for the year ending December 31, 1995.
  c. Consolidated goodwill as of January 1, 1997, is increased by $110,000.
  d. The $110,000 is recorded as an expense in 1997.

7. Cantalupe Corporation purchases Simon, Inc., on January 1, 1995, by issuing 13,000 shares of common stock with a $10 per share par value and a

$23 fair market value. This transaction results in the recording of $62,000 of goodwill. Subsequently, on January 1, 1997, Cantalupe is required to issue an additional 3,000 shares of stock to Simon's previous owners because of a drop in the market value of the initial 13,000 shares. How is this additional issuance of stock recorded?

a. The fair market value of the newly issued shares increases the Goodwill account balance.

b. The Investment balance is not affected but the parent's Additional Paid-In Capital is reduced by the par value of the newly issued shares.

c. All of the subsidiary's asset and liability accounts must be revalued for consolidation purposes based on their fair market values as of January 1, 1997.

d. The additional shares are assumed to have been issued on January 1, 1995, so that a retroactive adjustment is required.

8. What is push-down accounting?

a. A requirement that a subsidiary must use the same accounting principles as a parent company.

b. Inventory transfers made from a parent company to a subsidiary.

c. Recording by a subsidiary of the market value allocations found within the purchase price paid by a parent as well as subsequent amortization.

d. The adjustments required for consolidation when a parent has applied the cost method of accounting for internal reporting purposes.

9. Treadway Corporation purchases Hooker, Inc. on January 1, 1995. The parent pays more than the fair market value of the subsidiary's net assets. On that date, Treadway has equipment with a book value of $420,000 and a fair market value of $530,000. Hooker has equipment with a book value of $330,000 and a fair market value of $390,000. Hooker is going to use push-down accounting. Immediately after the acquisition, what Equipment account appears on Hooker's separate balance sheet and on the consolidated balance sheet?

a. $330,000 and $750,000.

b. $330,000 and $860,000.

c. $390,000 and $810,000.

d. $390,000 and $920,000.

Problems 10 through 12 are based on the following information:

Hans, Inc., purchases all of the oustanding stock of Sysk, Corporation, on January 1, 1995, for $310,000. Equipment with a 10-year life was undervalued on Sysk's financial records by $38,000. Goodwill resulting from this combination is $56,000 and will be amortized over its maximum life.

Sysk earned a reported net income of $150,000 in 1995 and $180,000 in 1996. Dividends of $60,000 were paid in each of these two years.

Selected account balances as of December 31, 1997, for the two companies are shown on the next page.

	Hans	*Sysk*
Revenues	$900,000	$700,000
Expenses	400,000	500,000
Investment Income	not given	—
Retained Earnings, 1/1/97	700,000	500,000
Dividends Paid	110,000	60,000

10. If the partial equity method has been applied, what is the consolidated net income?
    a. $700,000.
    b. $694,800.
    c. $690,600.
    d. $687,400.

11. If the equity method has been applied, what is the Investment in Sysk account balance within the records of Hans at the end of 1997?
    a. $644,400.
    b. $509,600.
    c. $520,000.
    d. $660,000.

12. If the cost method has been applied, what is the consolidated retained earnings balance as of January 1, 1997?
    a. $700,000.
    b. $910,000.
    c. $899,600.
    d. $1,019,600.

13. Herbert, Inc., buys all of the outstanding stock of Rambis Company on January 1, 1995. Annual amortization of $12,000 results from this purchase transaction. On the date of the takeover, Herbert reported retained earnings of $400,000 while Rambis reported a $200,000 balance. Herbert reported income of $40,000 in 1995 and $50,000 in 1996 and paid $10,000 in dividends each year. Rambis reported net income of $20,000 in 1995 and $30,000 in 1996 and paid $5,000 in dividends each year.

Required:

a. Assume that Herbert's reported income does not include any income derived from the subsidiary.
   • If the parent uses the equity method, what are the consolidated retained earnings on December 31, 1996?
   • If the parent uses the partial equity method, what are the consolidated retained earnings on December 31, 1996?
   • If the parent uses the cost method, what are the consolidated retained earnings on December 31, 1996?

b. Assume that Herbert's reported income does include income derived from the subsidiary.

- If the parent uses the equity method, what are the consolidated retained earnings on December 31, 1996?
- If the parent uses the partial equity method, what are the consolidated retained earnings on December 31, 1996?
- If the parent uses the cost method, what are the consolidated retained earnings on December 31, 1996?

c. Under each of the following situations, what is Entry *C on a 1996 consolidation worksheet?
- The parent uses the equity method.
- The parent uses the partial equity method.
- The parent uses the cost method.

14. Haynes, Inc., obtains 100 percent of Turner Company's common stock on January 1, 1995, by issuing 9,000 shares of $10 par value common stock. Haynes's shares had a $15 per share fair market value. On that date, Turner reported a net book value of $100,000. However, its equipment (with a five-year remaining life) was undervalued by $5,000 in the company's accounting records. Any goodwill would be amortized over 10 years.

The following figures come from the individual accounting records of these two companies as of December 31, 1995:

	Haynes	Turner
Revenues	$600,000	$230,000
Expenses	440,000	120,000
Investment Income	not given	—
Dividends Paid	80,000	50,000

The following figures come from the individual accounting records of these two companies as of December 31, 1996:

	Haynes	Turner
Revenues	$700,000	$280,000
Expenses	460,000	150,000
Investment Income	not given	—
Dividends Paid	90,000	40,000
Equipment	500,000	300,000
Retained Earnings, 12/31/96 Balance	800,000	180,000

Required:

a. If this combination is viewed as a purchase, what balance does Haynes' Investment in Turner account show on December 31, 1996, when the equity method is applied?

b. If this combination is viewed as a purchase, what is the consolidated net income for the year ending December 31, 1996?

c. If this combination is viewed as a purchase, what are the consolidated equipment and consolidated goodwill as of December 31, 1996? How would this answer be affected by the investment method applied by the parent?

d. If this combination is viewed as a purchase and Haynes has applied the equity method to account for its investment, what are consolidated retained earnings as of December 31, 1996? How would this answer be changed if Haynes had used the partial equity approach?

e. If this combination is viewed as a pooling of interests, what is the consolidated net income for the year ending December 31, 1996?

f. If this combination is viewed as a pooling of interests, what are the consolidated equipment and consolidated goodwill as of December 31, 1996?

g. If this combination is viewed as a purchase and Haynes has applied the cost method to account for its investment, what adjustment is needed to beginning retained earnings on a December 31, 1996, consolidation worksheet? How would this answer change if the partial equity method had been in use? How would this answer change if the equity method had been in use?

15. On January 1, 1995, Pure, Inc., issues 58 shares of previously unissued common stock for all of the outstanding shares of Simple Company. Pure's stock has a par value of $1 per share but a fair market value of $10 per share.

   Just prior to the creation of this combination, the following information is known about these two companies:

	Pure, Inc. Book Value	Simple Company Book Value	Simple Company Fair Market Value
Current assets.	$150	$ 60	$ 60
Equipment (10-year life)	600	200	260
Buildings (20-year life)	900	300	340
Liabilities.	450	160	160
Common stock	500	100	
Additional paid-in capital	100	50	
Retained earnings	600	250	

Any goodwill is to be amortized over a 40-year period.

   During 1995, Pure reported $100 in net income (excluding any investment or dividend income) and distributed $30 in dividends; Simple had $80 in net income and $20 in dividends. At the end of 1996, the following figures were reported by the two separate companies. Once again, Pure's figures do not include any investment or dividend income.

	Pure, Inc.	Simple Company
Revenues	$400	$250
Expenses	280	160
Dividends paid	40	30
Equipment	700	220
Buildings	800	280

Required:

a. If this business combination is accounted for as a purchase, what would be the consolidated revenues, expenses, and net income for the year ending December 31, 1996?

b. If this business combination is accounted for as a pooling of interests, what would be the consolidated revenues, expenses, and net income for the year ending December 31, 1996?

c. If this business combination is accounted for as a purchase, what would be the consolidated balance of the Investment in Simple Company account and the Investment Income account as of December 31, 1996?

d. If this business combination is accounted for as a purchase, what would be the consolidated balance of the Buildings account on December 31, 1996?

e. If this business combination is accounted for as a pooling of interests, what would be the consolidated balance of the Buildings account on December 31, 1996?

f. If this business combination is accounted for as a purchase, what would be the consolidated balance of retained earnings at December 31, 1996? What are the consolidated retained earnings if this combination meets all of the criteria for a pooling of interests?

16. Texas, Inc. obtains all of the outstanding stock of Chainsaw Corporation on January 1, 1995. At that date, Chainsaw owned only three assets and had no liabilities:

	Book Value	Fair Market Value
Inventory	$ 30,000	$ 40,000
Equipment (5-year life)	70,000	50,000
Building (10-year life).	100,000	150,000

Required:

a. If Texas pays $250,000 in cash for Chainsaw, what allocation should be assigned to the subsidiary's Building account and its Equipment account in a December 31, 1997, consolidation?

b. If Texas pays $220,000 in cash for Chainsaw, what allocation should be assigned to the subsidiary's Building account and its Equipment account in a December 31, 1997, consolidation?

c. If Texas pays $180,000 in cash for Chainsaw, what allocation should be assigned to the subsidiary's Building account and its Equipment account in a December 31, 1997, consolidation?

d. If Texas issues common stock valued at $180,000 (rather than paying cash) for Chainsaw in a pooling of interests, what allocation should be assigned to the subsidiary's Building account and its Equipment account in a December 31, 1997, consolidation?

Problems 17 through 21 are based on the following data:

Chapman Company obtains 100 percent of the stock of Abernethy Company on January 1, 1995. As of that date, Abernethy has the following trial balance:

	Debit	Credit
Accounts Payable		$ 50,000
Accounts Receivable	$ 40,000	
Additional Paid-In Capital		50,000
Buildings (net) (20-year life)	120,000	
Cash and Short-Term Investments	60,000	
Common Stock		250,000
Equipment (net) (5-year life)	200,000	
Inventory	90,000	
Land	80,000	
Long-Term Liabilities (mature 12/31/98)		150,000
Retained Earnings, 1/1/95		100,000
Supplies	10,000	
Totals	$600,000	$600,000

Any goodwill will be considered to have a 10-year life.

During 1995, Abernethy reported income of $80,000 while paying dividends of $10,000. During 1996, Abernethy reported income of $110,000 while paying dividends of $30,000.

The following five problems should be viewed as independent situations.

17. Assume that Chapman Company acquired the common stock of Abernethy for $490,000 in cash. As of January 1, 1995, Abernethy's land had a fair market value of $90,000, its buildings were valued at $160,000, and its equipment was appraised at $180,000. Chapman uses the equity method for this investment. Prepare consolidation worksheet entries for December 31, 1995, and December 31, 1996.

18. Assume that Chapman Company acquired the common stock of Abernethy for $500,000 in cash. Assume that the equipment and long-term liabilities

had fair market values of $220,000 and $120,000, respectively, on that date. Chapman uses the cost method to account for its investment. Prepare consolidation worksheet entries for December 31, 1995, and December 31, 1996.

19. Assume that Chapman Company acquired the common stock of Abernethy by issuing 10,000 shares of its $30 par value common stock. The stock had a fair market value of $42 per share on January 1, 1995. This transaction meets all 12 requirements for a pooling of interests. Assume that Abernethy's land on that date had a fair market value of $110,000, while the inventory was valued at $120,000. Chapman uses the book value method to account for this investment. Prepare consolidation worksheet entries for December 31, 1995, and December 31, 1996.

20. Assume that Chapman Company acquires the common stock of Abernethy by issuing 10,000 shares of its $30 par value common stock. The stock has a $42 per share fair market value on January 1, 1995. This transaction does not meet all 12 criteria for a pooling of interests. On January 1, 1995, Abernethy's inventory had a fair market value of $150,000. All of this inventory is assumed to have been sold during 1995. Chapman applies the equity method to account for this investment. Prepare the consolidation worksheet entries for December 31, 1995, and December 31, 1996.

21. Assume that Chapman Company acquired the common stock of Abernethy by paying $520,000 in cash. All accounts of Abernethy are estimated to have a value approximately equal to present book values. Chapman uses the partial equity method to account for its investment. Prepare the consolidation worksheet entries for December 31, 1995, and December 31, 1996.

22. Jefferson, Inc., purchases Hamilton Corporation on January 1, 1995. Immediately after the acquisition, the two companies have the following account balances. Hamilton's equipment (with a five-year life) is actually worth $450,000. Any goodwill will be amortized over the maximum allowable time period.

	Jefferson	Hamilton
Current Assets	$300,000	$210,000
Investment in Hamilton	510,000	
Equipment	600,000	400,000
Liabilities	200,000	160,000
Common Stock	350,000	150,000
Retained Earnings	860,000	300,000

In 1995, Hamilton earns a net income of $55,000 and pays a $5,000 cash dividend. At the end of 1996, selected account balances for the two companies are as follows:

	Jefferson	*Hamilton*
Revenues	$400,000	$240,000
Expenses	290,000	180,000
Investment Income	not given	
Retained Earnings, 1/1/96	990,000	350,000
Current Assets	360,000	140,000
Investment in Hamilton	not given	
Equipment	520,000	420,000
Liabilities	170,000	190,000

Required:

a. What will be the December 31, 1996, balance in the Investment Income account and the Investment in Hamilton account under each of the three methods described in this chapter?

b. How is the consolidated Expense account affected by the accounting method used by the parent to record ownership of this subsidiary?

c. How is the consolidated Equipment account affected by the accounting method used by the parent to record ownership of this subsidiary?

d. What is the consolidated Retained Earnings balance as of January 1, 1996, under each of the three methods described in this chapter?

e. What is Entry *C on a consolidation worksheet for 1996 under each of the three methods described in this chapter?

f. What is Entry S on a consolidation worksheet for 1996 under each of the three methods described in this chapter?

g. What is consolidated net income for 1996?

23. Following below are selected account balances from the Profitt Company and Simon Corporation as of December 31, 1995:

	Profitt	*Simon*
Revenues	$700,000	$ 400,000
Expenses	400,000	300,000
Investment Income	not given	
Dividends Paid	80,000	60,000
Retained Earnings, 1/1/95	600,000	200,000
Current Assets	400,000	500,000
Buildings (net)	900,000	400,000
Equipment (net)	600,000	1,000,000
Investment in Simon	not given	
Liabilities	500,000	1,380,000
Common Stock	600,000 ($20 par)	200,000 ($10 par)
Additional Paid-In Capital	150,000	80,000

On January 1, 1995, Profitt purchased all of the outstanding stock of Simon for $660,000 in cash and common stock. Profitt also pays $20,000 in lawyers' fees and other combination costs as well as $10,000 in stock issuance costs. At the date of acquisition, Simon's buildings (with a six-year remaining life) have a $440,000 book value but a fair market value of $560,000. Goodwill is assumed to have a 40-year life.

Required:

a. As of December 31, 1995, what is the consolidated Buildings balance?

b. As of December 31, 1995, what is the consolidated Retained Earnings balance?

c. For the year ending December 31, 1995, what is consolidated net income?

d. As of December 31, 1995, what is the consolidated balance to be reported for goodwill?

24. Foxx Corporation purchases all of the outstanding stock of Greenburg Company on January 1, 1995, for $600,000. Greenburg had net assets on that date of $470,000 although equipment with a 10-year life was undervalued on the records by $90,000. Any recognized goodwill will be amortized over its maximum possible life.

    Greenburg reports net income in 1995 of $90,000 and $100,000 in 1996. Dividends of $20,000 are paid by the subsidiary in each of these two years.

    Financial figures for the year ending December 31, 1997, follow:

	Foxx	Greenburg
Revenues	$ 800,000	$ 600,000
Expenses	(400,000)	(500,000)
Investment income	20,000	
Net Income	$ 420,000	$ 100,000
Retained earnings, 1/1/97	$1,100,000	$ 320,000
Net income	420,000	100,000
Dividends paid	(120,000)	(20,000)
Retained earnings, 12/31/97	$1,400,000	$ 400,000
Current assets	$ 300,000	$ 100,000
Investment in subsidiary	600,000	–0–
Equipment (net)	900,000	600,000
Buildings (net)	800,000	400,000
Land	600,000	100,000
Total assets	$3,200,000	$1,200,000
Liabilities	$ 900,000	$ 500,000
Common stock	900,000	300,000
Retained earnings	1,400,000	400,000
Total liabilities and equities	$3,200,000	$1,200,000

Required:

a. Determine the consolidated balance for each of the following accounts:

Expenses	Buildings
Dividends Paid	Goodwill
Revenues	Common Stock
Equipment	

b. How does the parent's choice of an accounting method for its investment affect the balances computed in requirement *a*?

c. Which method of accounting for this subsidiary is the parent actually using for internal reporting purposes?

d. If a different method of accounting for this investment had been used by the parent company, how could that method have been identified?

e. What would be the consolidated balance for retained earnings as of January 1, 1997, if each of the following methods had been in use?

Cost Method
Partial Equity Method
Equity Method

25. Big Corporation purchased Little Company on January 1, 1995, for $400,000 in cash. Little reported net assets at that time of $320,000. However, several of Little's accounts had fair market values that differed from book values:

	Book Value	Fair Market Value
Land	$ 60,000	$ 50,000
Buildings (10-year life)	100,000	120,000
Equipment (6-year life)	60,000	90,000

Goodwill is amortized over a 40-year period.

Following are financial statements for these two companies for the year ending December 31, 1995. Credit balances are indicated by parentheses.

	Big	Little
Revenues	$ (600,000)	$(300,000)
Expenses	400,000	180,000
Income of Little	(112,000)	–0–
Net income	$ (312,000)	$(120,000)
Retained earnings, 1/1/95	$ (700,000)	$(220,000)
Net income (above)	(312,000)	(120,000)
Dividends paid	142,000	80,000
Retained earnings, 12/31/95	$ (870,000)	$(260,000)
Cash	$ 176,000	$ 80,000
Receivables	210,000	90,000
Inventory	190,000	130,000
Investment in Little	432,000	–0–
Land	350,000	60,000
Buildings (net)	343,000	90,000
Equipment (net)	190,000	50,000
Goodwill	–0–	–0–
Total assets	$ 1,891,000	$ 500,000
Liabilities	$ (621,000)	$(140,000)
Common stock	(400,000)	(100,000)
Retained earnings (above)	(870,000)	(260,000)
Total liabilities and equity	$(1,891,000)	$(500,000)

a. How was the $112,000 "Income of Little" balance computed?

b. Without preparing a worksheet or consolidation entries, determine the totals to be reported for this business combination for the year ending December 31, 1995.

c. Verify the totals determined in part *b.* by producing a consolidation worksheet for Big and Little for the year ending December 31, 1995.

26. Following are separate financial statements for Mitchell Company and Andrews Company as of December 31, 1995. Mitchell acquired all of the outstanding stock of Andrews on January 1, 1991, by issuing 9,000 shares of its own common stock. This stock was valued at $50 per share while having a par value of $30 per share. In addition, Mitchell paid $20,000 to lawyers, accountants, and other parties for costs incurred in creating the combination. Although the transaction was carried out by the exchange of common stock, it did not meet all 12 criteria for a pooling of interests.

On the date of purchase, Andrews reported a book value of $360,000, although its buildings and equipment were undervalued by $60,000. This property was assumed to have a six-year life with no salvage value. Additionally, any goodwill recognized in this consolidation was viewed as having a 10-year life.

	Mitchell Company 12/31/95	Andrews Company 12/31/95
Revenues	$ 610,000	$ 370,000
Expenses	380,000	220,000
Net income	$ 230,000	$ 150,000
Retained earnings, 1/1/95	$ 880,000	$ 490,000
Net income (above).	230,000	150,000
Dividends paid	90,000	–0–
Retained earnings, 12/31/95	$1,020,000	$ 640,000
Cash	$ 110,000	$ 20,000
Receivables	380,000	220,000
Inventory	560,000	280,000
Investment in Andrews Company	470,000	–0–
Land	460,000	340,000
Buildings and equipment (net)	920,000	380,000
Total assets	$2,900,000	$1,240,000
Liabilities	$ 780,000	$ 470,000
Preferred stock.	300,000	–0–
Common stock.	500,000	100,000
Additional paid-in capital	300,000	30,000
Retained earnings, 12/31/95	1,020,000	640,000
Total liabilities and equities	$2,900,000	$1,240,000

a. Using the preceding information, prepare a consolidation worksheet for these two companies as of December 31, 1995.

b. Assuming that Mitchell applied the equity method to this investment, what account balances would be altered on the parent's individual financial statements?

c. Assuming that Mitchell applied the equity method to this investment, what changes would be necessary in the consolidation entries found on a December 31, 1995, worksheet?

d. Assuming that Mitchell applied the equity method to this investment, what changes would be created in the consolidated figures to be reported by this combination?

27. Tucson Company has reported the following income and dividend figures during the past few years:

	Net Income	*Dividends Paid*
1994	$80,000	$30,000
1993	70,000	30,000
1992	40,000	20,000
1991	50,000	20,000

Account balances for Arizona, Inc., and Tucson Company as of December 31, 1995 follow. Some of Arizona's accounts have been omitted from this list.

	Arizona	Tucson
Revenues	$600,000	$400,000
Expenses	400,000	250,000
Investment Income	not given	
Retained Earnings, 1/1/95	900,000	800,000
Dividends Paid	130,000	40,000
Current Assets	200,000	690,000
Land	300,000	290,000
Buildings (net)	500,000	230,000
Equipment (net)	200,000	250,000
Liabilities	400,000	350,000
Common Stock	300,000	40,000
Additional Paid in Capital	50,000	160,000

On January 1, 1991, Arizona acquired all of Tucson's stock by paying $1 million cash. Tucson's equipment (10-year life) was overvalued at that time by $30,000 but its buildings were undervalued by $50,000. These buildings had a five-year life; goodwill was to be amortized over 20 years.

Required:

a. Assuming that Arizona has applied the cost method, prepare consolidation entries as of December 31, 1995. What is the purpose of Entry *C?

b. Determine the consolidated totals for the following accounts; assume that the parent applies the partial equity method:

> Net Income
> Equipment (net)
> Buildings (net)
> Retained Earnings, 1/1/95

c. Determine the consolidated totals for the following accounts; assume that the parent applies the equity method:

> Net Income
> Equipment (net)
> Buildings (net)
> Retained Earnings, 1/1/95

 28. Following are the trial balances for the High Company and the Low Company as of December 31, 1995:

	High Company Trial Balance 12/31/95		Low Company Trial Balance 12/31/95	
	Debit	Credit	Debit	Credit
Accounts Payable		$ 170,000		$ 200,000
Accounts Receivable	$ 440,000		$ 80,000	
Buildings (net).	1,510,000		660,000	
Cash	60,000		10,000	
Common Stock		700,000		400,000
Dividends Paid	100,000		20,000	
Expenses	440,000		195,000	
Inventory	640,000		610,000	
Investment in Low Company . . .	1,260,000		–0–	
Investment Income.		50,000		–0–
Long-Term Liabilities		690,000		500,000
Machinery (net)	660,000		460,000	
Retained Earnings, 1/1/95		2,630,000		690,000
Revenues		870,000		245,000
Totals	$5,110,000	$5,110,000	$2,035,000	$2,035,000

High Company acquired all of the outstanding common stock of Low Company on January 1, 1992, for $940,000 in cash. On that date, Low's buildings (20-year life) were undervalued in the company's records by $100,000 while its machinery (10-year life) was overvalued by $20,000. Low's book value on the date of acquisition was $800,000. Any goodwill recognized in the consolidation is amortized over a 20-year life. High uses the partial equity method to account for this investment.

As of December 31, 1995, Low owes $20,000 to High.

Required:

Determine the consolidated figures that will be reported by the business combination of High Company and Low Company as of December 31, 1995.

29. Giant purchased all of the common stock of Small on January 1, 1995. Over the next few years, Giant applied the equity method to the recording of this investment. At the date of the original purchase, $90,000 of the price was attributed to undervalued land, while $50,000 was assigned to equipment having a 10-year life. The remaining $60,000 unallocated portion of the purchase price was viewed as goodwill to be amortized over a 30-year period.

Following are individual financial statements for the year ending December 31, 1999. On that date, Small owes Giant $10,000. Credits are indicated by parentheses.

	Giant	Small
Revenues	$(1,175,000)	$ (360,000)
Expenses	722,000	220,000
Equity in income of Small	(133,000)	–0–
Net income	$ (586,000)	$ (140,000)
Retained earnings, 1/1/99	$(1,409,000)	$ (620,000)
Net income (above)	(586,000)	(140,000)
Dividends paid	310,000	110,000
Retained earnings, 12/31/99	$(1,685,000)	$ (650,000)
Current assets	$ 398,000	$ 318,000
Investment in Small	985,000	–0–
Land	440,000	165,000
Buildings (net)	304,000	419,000
Equipment (net)	648,000	286,000
Goodwill	–0–	–0–
Total assets	$ 2,775,000	$1,188,000
Liabilities	$ (840,000)	$ (368,000)
Common stock	(250,000)	(170,000)
Retained earnings (above)	(1,685,000)	(650,000)
Total liabilities and equity	$(2,775,000)	$(1,188,000)

a. How was the $133,000 "Equity in Income of Small" balance computed?

b. Without preparing a worksheet or consolidation entries, determine the totals to be reported by this business combination for the year ending December 31, 1999.

c. Verify the figures determined in part *b.* by producing a consolidation worksheet for Giant and Small for the year ending December 31, 1999.

d. If Small had adopted the push-down method of accounting, how would the preceding accounts of the subsidiary have been affected? How would the worksheet process be changed? What impact does the application of push-down accounting have on consolidated financial statements?

30. Following are selected accounts for Mergaronite Company and Hill, Inc., as of December 31, 1995. Several of Mergaronite's accounts have been omitted.

	Mergaronite	*Hill*
Revenues.	$600,000	$250,000
Expenses.	400,000	150,000
Investment Income	not given	
Retained Earnings, 1/1/95.	900,000	600,000
Dividends Paid	130,000	40,000
Current Assets	200,000	690,000
Land.	300,000	90,000
Buildings (net)	500,000	140,000
Equipment (net).	200,000	250,000
Liabilities.	400,000	310,000
Common Stock	300,000	40,000
Additional Paid in Capital	50,000	160,000

Assume that Mergaronite took over Hill on January 1, 1991, in a purchase by issuing 7,000 shares of common stock having a par value of $10 per share but a fair market value of $100 each. On January 1, 1991, Hill's land was undervalued by $20,000, its buildings were overvalued by $30,000, and equipment was undervalued by $60,000. The buildings had a 10-year life; the equipment had a 5-year life. Goodwill of $100,000 resulted from this purchase and was to be written off over a 20-year period.

Required:

a. What are the December 31, 1995, consolidated totals for the following accounts:

> Revenues
> Expenses
> Buildings
> Equipment
> Goodwill
> Common Stock
> Additional Paid in Capital

b. In requirement *a.*, why can the consolidated totals be determined without knowing which method the parent has used to account for the subsidiary?

c. If the equity method is used by the parent, what consolidation entries would be used on a 1995 worksheet?

31. Alton Company acquired Zeidner, Inc. on January 1, 1991, in a business combination properly accounted for as a purchase. On that date, Zeidner held assets and liabilities with book values of $700,000 and $200,000, respectively. Alton paid a total of $670,000 to acquire all of the outstanding stock of Zeidner. At the date of this purchase, Zeidner possessed equipment (with a five-year life) that had a value $50,000 in excess of its book value. In addition, Zeidner had buildings worth $80,000 more than their book value. These buildings had a remaining life expectancy of 20 years.

Any goodwill that results from the acquisition will be amortized over the maximum 40-year period.

Following are the individual financial statements for these two companies for the year ending December 31, 2000. Alton owes Zeidner $30,000 at this point in time. Without preparing consolidation entries or setting up a worksheet, determine the consolidated totals for Alton Company and Zeidner, Inc.

	Alton Company	Zeidner, Inc.
Income Statement		
Revenues.	$ 600,000	$ 500,000
Expenses.	(300,000)	(300,000)
Investment income from Zeidner Company	200,000	–0–
Net income.	$ 500,000	$ 200,000
Statement of Retained Earnings		
Retained earnings, 1/1/00.	$1,500,000	$ 650,000
Net income (above)	500,000	200,000
Dividends paid	(200,000)	(50,000)
Retained earnings, 12/31/00.	$1,800,000	$ 800,000
Balance Sheet		
Current assets	$ 230,000	$ 300,000
Investment in Zeidner Company	1,270,000	–0–
Land.	100,000	200,000
Buildings.	300,000	400,000
Equipment	600,000	300,000
Goodwill	–0–	–0–
Total assets.	$2,500,000	$1,200,000
Liabilities	$ 300,000	$ 100,000
Common stock	400,000	300,000
Retained earnings, 12/31/00.	1,800,000	800,000
Total liabilities and equities.	$2,500,000	$1,200,000

32. On January 1, 1995, Romeo, Incorporated, exchanged 10,000 shares of previously unissued common stock for all of the outstanding shares of Juliet Company. This combination met all 12 criteria for a pooling of interests. Romeo's common stock had a $20 par value but a fair market value of $48 per share. On the date of the exchange, Juliet reported $370,000 in stockholders' equity:

Common Stock	$200,000
Additional Paid-In Capital	50,000
Retained Earnings	120,000

Romeo originally offered only 8,000 shares for Juliet's stock but raised that bid based on favorable earnings projections. In addition, equipment held by the subsidiary (with a 10-year remaining life) was estimated to be undervalued on the accounting records by $70,000. Goodwill is always amortized by these companies over a 20-year period.

During 1995, Juliet reported net income of $80,000 and paid cash dividends of $60,000. In accounting for this investment, Romeo utilized the equity method.

Following are the December 31, 1996, trial balances for these two companies. Determine the consolidated balances that would be reported by this combination.

	Romeo Incorporated	Juliet Company
Debits		
Accounts Receivable	$ 140,000	$ 40,000
Buildings	620,000	260,000
Cash	60,000	10,000
Dividends Paid	130,000	60,000
Equipment	490,000	330,000
Expenses	390,000	110,000
Inventory	190,000	110,000
Investment in Juliet Company	420,000	–0–
Land	300,000	200,000
Total Debits	$2,740,000	$1,120,000
Credits		
Additional Paid-In Capital	$ 190,000	$ 50,000
Common Stock	600,000	200,000
Investment Income from Juliet Company	90,000	–0–
Liabilities	580,000	530,000
Retained Earnings, 1/1/96	680,000	140,000
Revenues	600,000	200,000
Total Credits	$2,740,000	$1,120,000

33. Broome paid $430,000 cash for all of the outstanding common stock of Charlotte, Inc. on January 1, 1995. The subsidiary had a book value of $340,000 on that date (common stock of $200,000 and retained earnings of $140,000), although equipment recorded at $40,000 (with a five-year remaining life) was assessed as having an actual worth of $70,000. Any goodwill is to be amortized over 20 years.

During the subsequent three years, Charlotte reported the following balances:

	Net Income	Dividends Paid
1995	$65,000	$25,000
1996	75,000	35,000
1997	80,000	40,000

On January 1, 1997, Broome paid an additional $20,000 to the previous owners of Charlotte, an amount that was due because the subsidiary's earnings for the first two years had exceeded $120,000.

a. Prepare consolidation worksheet entries as of December 31, 1997, assuming that Broome has applied the cost method.
b. Prepare consolidation worksheet entries as of December 31, 1997, assuming that Broome has applied the partial equity method.

34. Palm Company acquired 100 percent of the voting stock of Storm Company on January 1, 1991, by issuing 10,000 shares of its $10 par value common stock (having a fair market value of $13 per share). Palm also paid $10,000 in consolidation costs to lawyers and investment analysts. As of that date, Storm had stockholders' equity totaling $105,000. Land shown on Storm's accounting records was undervalued by $10,000. Equipment (with a five-year life) was undervalued by $5,000. Goodwill amortization was to be over a 40-year period.

Following are the separate financial statements for the two companies for the year ending December 31, 1995. Assume that the 12 criteria for a pooling of interests have not been met.

	Palm Company	Storm Company
Revenues	$ 485,000	$190,000
Expenses	(290,000)	(122,000)
Equity in subsidiary earnings.	66,500	–0–
Net income	$ 261,500	$ 68,000
Retained earnings, 1/1/95	$ 661,000	$ 98,000
Net income (above)	261,500	68,000
Dividends paid	(175,500)	(40,000)
Retained earnings, 12/31/95	$ 747,000	$126,000
Current assets	$ 268,000	$ 75,000
Investment in Storm Company	218,500	–0–
Land	427,500	58,000
Buildings and equipment (net)	713,000	161,000
Total assets	$1,627,000	$294,000
Current liabilities	$ 110,000	$ 19,000
Long-term liabilities	80,000	84,000
Common stock	600,000	60,000
Additional paid-in capital	90,000	5,000
Retained earnings, 12/31/95	747,000	126,000
Total liabilities and equities	$1,627,000	$294,000

a. How was the $66,500 balance in the Equity in Subsidiary Earnings account derived?

b. Prepare a worksheet to consolidate the financial information for these two companies.

c. How would Storm's individual financial records differ if the push-down method of accounting had been applied?

35. The Tyler Company acquired all of the outstanding stock of Jasmine Company on January 1, 1995, for $206,000 in cash. Jasmine had a book value of only $140,000 on that date. However, equipment (having an eight-year life) was undervalued by $40,000 on Jasmine's financial records. A building with a 20-year life was overvalued by $10,000. Tyler amortizes all goodwill over the maximum allowable life. Subsequent to the acquisition, Jasmine reported the following:

	Net Income	Dividends Paid
1995	$50,000	$10,000
1996	60,000	40,000
1997	30,000	20,000

In accounting for this investment, Tyler has used the equity method. Selected accounts taken from the financial records of these two companies as of December 31, 1997, are as follows:

	Tyler Company	Jasmine Company
Revenues—Operating	$310,000	$104,000
Expenses	198,000	74,000
Equipment (net)	320,000	50,000
Buildings (net)	220,000	68,000
Common Stock	290,000	50,000
Retained Earnings, 12/31/97 Balance	410,000	160,000

Required:

Determine the following account balances as of December 31, 1997:

a. Investment in Jasmine Company (on Tyler's individual financial records).

b. Equity in subsidiary earnings (on Tyler's individual financial records).

c. Consolidated net income.

d. Consolidated equipment (net).

e. Consolidated buildings (net).

f. Consolidated goodwill (net).

g. Consolidated common stock.

h. Consolidated retained earnings, 12/31/97.

36. During 1995, Abbott Corporation issued shares of its common stock for all of the outstanding stock of Drexel, Inc., in a transaction meeting all of the qualifications for a pooling of interests. Drexel's book value was only $120,000 at the time, but Abbott issued 10,000 shares valued at $18 per share. Abbott was willing to convey these shares because it felt that buildings (10-year life) were undervalued on Drexel's records by $40,000 while equipment (5-year life) was undervalued by $20,000. Goodwill is amortized by this business combination over a 30-year period.

Following are the individual financial records for these two companies for the year ending December 31, 1998.

	Abbott	Drexel
Revenues	$ 310,000	$ 90,000
Expenses	(220,000)	(60,000)
Equity in subsidiary earnings	30,000	–0–
Net income	$ 120,000	$ 30,000
Retained earnings, 1/1/98	$ 640,000	$ 85,000
Net income	120,000	30,000
Less: Dividends paid	(70,000)	(20,000)
Retained earnings, 12/31/98	$ 690,000	$ 95,000
Current assets	$ 159,000	$ 57,000
Investment in Drexel	155,000	–0–
Buildings (net)	472,000	71,000
Equipment (net)	404,000	107,000
Total assets	$1,190,000	$235,000
Liabilities	$ 160,000	$ 80,000
Common stock	300,000	60,000
Additional paid-in capital	40,000	–0–
Retained earnings, 12/31/98 (above)	690,000	95,000
Total liabilities and equities	$1,190,000	$235,000

a. Without making consolidation entries or setting up a worksheet, determine the consolidated totals for this business combination.

b. Verify the balances determined in part *a.* by preparing a worksheet as of December 31, 1998.

4

CONSOLIDATED FINANCIAL STATEMENTS AND OUTSIDE OWNERSHIP

Questions to Consider

- Total ownership is not a necessary requirement for consolidation; a parent need only gain control of another company to create a business combination. If less than 100 percent of a subsidiary's voting stock is obtained, how is the presence of the other remaining owners reflected in consolidated financial statements? What accounting is appropriate for this noncontrolling interest? How are these figures computed and where are they reported on the consolidated statements?

- If a parent holds less than complete ownership, are the subsidiary's assets and liabilities consolidated at 100 percent of their fair market values or should the reported figures be affected by the degree of the parent's ownership?

- If a parent acquires several blocks of a subsidiary's stock over a period of time prior to gaining control, how are the various purchases consolidated?

- How are a subsidiary's revenues and expenses reported on a consolidated income statement when the parent gains control within the current year?

- When a portion, or all, of a subsidiary's stock is sold, how is the resulting gain or loss calculated? By what accounting method are any shares that remain reported?

A note to the 1989 financial statements of Fuqua Industries, Inc., contains the following information:

> On March 29, 1988, Fuqua combined its photofinishing operation with the domestic photofinishing operations of Eastman Kodak Company. The combined entity, Qualex Inc., engages in wholesale photofinishing in the United States . . . In accordance with the shareholders' agreement, Fuqua received 51 percent of the voting stock of Qualex. . . . Kodak received 49 percent of the voting stock of Qualex. . . . Fuqua has consoli-

dated the accounts of Qualex as Fuqua has a controlling interest in the new company. Kodak's portion of ownership and equity in the income of Qualex are reflected in Fuqua's consolidated financial statements as a minority interest.

Fuqua includes *all of the financial figures* generated by Qualex within consolidated financial statements. How does Fuqua account for the 49 percent interest in this subsidiary owned by Eastman Kodak?

A number of reasons exist for one company to hold less than 100 percent ownership of a subsidiary. The parent may not have had sufficient resources available to obtain all of the outstanding stock. As a second possibility, a few stockholders of the subsidiary could have elected to retain their ownership, perhaps in hopes of getting a better price at a later date. In the preceding case of Fuqua and Eastman Kodak, the level of ownership of the newly created company was simply negotiated between the two stockholders.

Lack of total ownership is most frequently encountered with foreign subsidiaries. The laws of some countries prohibit outsiders from maintaining complete control of domestic business enterprises. In other areas of the world, a parent may seek to establish better relations with a subsidiary's employees, customers, and local government by maintaining some percentage of native ownership.

Regardless of the reason for owning less than 100 percent, the parent consolidates the financial data of every subsidiary where control is present. As discussed in Chapter 2, *complete ownership is not a prerequisite for consolidation.* A single economic entity is formed whenever one company is able to control the decision-making process of another.

Although most parent companies do possess 100 percent ownership of their subsidiaries, a significant number, such as Fuqua, establish control with a lesser amount of stock. The remaining outside owners (Eastman Kodak, in this illustration) are collectively referred to as a *noncontrolling interest* or by the more traditional term *minority interest.* The presence of these other stockholders poses a number of reporting questions for the accountant. Whenever less than 100 percent of a subsidiary's voting stock is held, how should the subsidiary's accounts be valued within consolidated financial statements? How should the presence of these additional owners be acknowledged?

Discussion Question: How Do We Report This Other Owner?

The Hartstone Company was created approximately 15 years ago and presently owns several large retail clothing stores in and around Lakeland, Minnesota. Hartstone's capital stock is held equally by its four founders: Scott Arnold, Janine Bostio, Garrison Cantleberry, and Ingrid Jorgesson.

Until recently, Thomas Warwick was the sole owner of a competing business in the nearby city of Kalshburg. Because Warwick was nearing

continued

retirement age, he opted to sell 90 percent of his company (which encompassed only one store) to Hartstone. Since the business had been in Warwick's family for several generations, he wanted to retain 10 percent ownership. Hartstone paid cash for this acquisition. Based on past profitability, the negotiated price for the shares was set to indicate a total value of $2 million, although the current book value of the store was only $1.4 million.

At the end of the current year, the owners of Hartstone must produce consolidated financial statements for the first time. Consequently, they are having a discussion with their accountant concerning the appropriate method of reporting Thomas Warwick's 10 percent interest in the Kalshburg store.

Scott Arnold: These statements are designed to represent the Hartstone Company and our assets, liabilities, revenues, and expenses. Warwick owns none of our stock. I see no reason to include any figure at all for him. Readers would naturally assume that he controls a portion of Hartstone; we would be misleading them. He has nothing to do with our company.

Janine Bostio: I think you are wrong. Warwick owns 10 percent of one of our stores. He is a partial owner of this asset, and since we are consolidating the entire Kalshburg store, we have to recognize that he has an equity interest. The price indicates a $2,000,000 value; so his ownership should be recognized at $200,000.

Garrison Cantleberry: I agree with Scott; the statements are designed to represent Hartstone Company, and Warwick is certainly not a stockholder of Hartstone. However, we do have a legal obligation to him. If we ever liquidate the Kalshburg store, he would be entitled to a portion of the residual. Even now, when the store pays a dividend, he must be paid 10 percent of each distribution. We have an obligation to him that can only be properly disclosed as a liability.

Ingrid Jorgesson: I have trouble with recording a liability. I understand that we eventually might have a debt to Warwick, but at this point in time we are under no obligation to him. To me, a possible future claim should not be recorded as an actual liability. However, Warwick has retained a $140,000 investment in one of our assets. That is his cost. Since this amount doesn't seem to be either debt or equity, why don't we record it separately between our liabilities and the stockholders' equity? Anyone reading the statements can add this figure to either balance if desired or simply ignore it entirely.

As the accountant, what recommendation would you make to your clients and why? Should Warwick's interest be recognized? If so, where should the figure be reported and what amount should be disclosed?

Consolidations Involving a Noncontrolling Interest[1]

In any combination in which a noncontrolling interest remains, an intriguing theoretical controversy is created as to (1) the appropriate consolidation values that should be assigned to the subsidiary's accounts and (2) the method of disclosing the presence of the other owners. This debate involves more than a problem of reporting; it ultimately concerns the fundamental objectives of consolidated financial statements.

As an illustration, had Fuqua Industries held all of the stock of Qualex, only one method of valuation would have been available. When total ownership exists, the subsidiary's assets and liabilities are always consolidated based on their fair market values at the date of acquisition with any excess cost assigned to goodwill.[2] Since no other owners would exist, disclosure of a noncontrolling interest is not relevant.

In contrast, whenever less than 100 percent of a subsidiary is acquired, the parent has the option of adopting any one of several different theoretical methods to calculate the consolidated values of the acquired accounts. Each of these approaches uses a different technique for reporting the presence of the noncontrolling interest. One author has gone so far as to label the availability of these alternatives as "multiple choice accounting."[3]

As a basis for examining these alternative valuation theories, assume that Small Company possesses net assets as follows:

Book value	$110,000
Fair market value . . .	130,000

In the current year, Big Company purchases 70 percent of the outstanding voting stock of Small for $140,000. Big's willingness to pay this price can be construed as an indication that Small, taken as a whole, has an implied value of $200,000 ($140,000/70 percent). *The accounting controversy centers on whether the parent's $140,000 cost or the $200,000 implied value of the subsidiary should serve as the valuation basis for subsequently consolidated figures.*[4]

---

[1] The term *minority interest* has been used almost universally over the decades to identify the presence of other outside owners. However, in the FASB's September 10, 1991, discussion memorandum, *An Analysis of Issues Related to Consolidation Policy and Procedures,* the term *noncontrolling interest* was applied. Since this newer term is more descriptive, it is used throughout this textbook.

[2] To avoid unnecessary complexities in analyzing this issue, bargain purchases are not illustrated. In addition, this controversy does not relate to a pooling of interests where accounts are always consolidated at their book values.

[3] Ronald Mano, "Consolidated Financial Statements: More Multiple Choice Accounting?" *Mergers & Acquisitions,* Winter 1979.

[4] In a 100 percent purchase, the implied value of the subsidiary is the parent's purchase price. Thus, only one valuation basis is present and, at least from a mechanical perspective, no problem exists.

Incorporating the cost figure suggests that consolidated statements are primarily intended as a report of the parent company and the results of its $140,000 investment. Conversely, by utilizing the $200,000 implied value, the emphasis is focused on accounting for Big and Small as two individual components forming a single economic entity.

Unfortunately, virtually nothing in official accounting pronouncements has ever addressed the issue of valuation theory in combinations involving less than 100 percent ownership. Thus, the positions adopted at present are based on traditional approaches that have evolved over the years. However, this issue was recently opened up for examination by the FASB. This examination might possibly lead to the issuance of an official standard that requires one theory to be used. However, until that time, companies are free to apply any one of several approaches in reporting the accounts of a subsidiary. The following section presents three of the theories outlined by the FASB.

The Economic Unit Concept[5]

If the accounting emphasis in preparing consolidated statements is placed on the business combination being formed (rather than on the parent's investment), an approach referred to as the *economic unit concept* (also known as the *entity theory*) is generally endorsed. This concept is founded on the proposition that the subsidiary and especially the subsidiary's individual accounts cannot be divided along ownership lines. A controlled company must always be consolidated as a whole regardless of the level of ownership.

Proponents argue that this concept provides the most consistent perspective of the consolidation process. It also gives the best view of the assets and liabilities that have come under the control of the parent company. If, in the previous illustration, Small owns land with a book value of $8,000 but a fair market value of $10,000, the economic unit concept requires the $10,000 figure to be reported within consolidated statements whether the parent acquires 70 percent, 100 percent, or any other level of control. The owners of Big control all of the resources of both Big and Small despite holding only 70 percent of the subsidiary's voting stock.

Therefore, in accounting for Big's acquisition of Small, the economic unit concept would base consolidated totals on the $200,000 implied value of the subsidiary taken as a whole. All of the subsidiary's assets and liabilities are included at their fair market values with any excess assigned to goodwill. Because the individual market values total only $130,000 but the implied value of the company as a whole equals $200,000, the excess $70,000 is assigned to goodwill.

Since the total value of every asset and liability is attributed to the consolidated entity, the partial ownership held by outside parties must also be acknowledged. *Including 100 percent of the value of a subsidiary's accounts when only 70 percent of the stock is owned creates an imbalance that can only be rectified by*

---

[5] Variations do exist of each approach that is presented here. To avoid unnecessary complication, only three of the basic theories are described.

the recognition of a 30 percent noncontrolling interest. Hence, $60,000 (30 percent of the total implied value being included in the consolidation) is attributed to the other owners of Small.

Economic Unit Concept

Implied value of Small ($140,000/70%)	$200,000
Fair market value assigned to Small's accounts	130,000
Fair market value not assigned to identifiable accounts—goodwill	$ 70,000
Noncontrolling interest (30% of the $200,000 implied value included in consolidated totals).	$ 60,000

Although Small's outside owners do not possess an equity interest in the parent company, the $60,000 balance is presented within consolidated stockholders' equity section when the economic unit concept is in use. This placement is based on the assertion that the two companies should be viewed together as a single entity. The outside parties do own a component part of the resulting business combination; thus, their interest is viewed as an equity (or ownership) balance to be reported within the consolidated balance sheet.

After the balance sheet valuations have been established for the economic unit concept, a logical extension can be made to the construction of a consolidated income statement. Once again this approach recognizes 100 percent of the subsidiary's balances. Its entire income is included. By consolidating every account in total, the fundamental objective of reporting the subsidiary as an indivisible unit within the consolidated entity is being fulfilled. Furthermore, this approach effectively reports the income that is generated by the net assets under the control of the parent company.

Consequently, for Big's acquisition of Small, 100 percent of the subsidiary's revenues and expenses should be included in the consolidated figures. Because only 70 percent of Small is actually owned, a 30 percent claim to the subsidiary's earnings must be separately deducted in recognition of the noncontrolling interest. This portion of consolidated net income is viewed as an allocation to these other owners. The share of total income attributed to them often appears as a separate decrease within the statement of retained earnings.

In computing the part of consolidated income to be assigned to the noncontrolling interest, a theoretical question arises as to the impact of any amortization incurred in connection with the price paid by the parent. As shown in Chapter 3, recognition of an expense is necessitated by the allocations made to specific accounts as well as to goodwill. Within the business combination, is this expense attributed to the parent or to the subsidiary?

A logical extension of the economic unit concept is that each purchase price allocation is perceived as a revaluation of a subsidiary asset or liability to fair market value. Subsequent amortization of these costs would be assumed, therefore, to relate to this company rather than to its parent. Since the expense is viewed as an adjustment to the subsidiary's net income, computation of the noncontrolling interest's share of these earnings is directly affected.

For example, what is the noncontrolling interest in the subsidiary's income in the following situation?

Portion of subsidiary owned by parent	90 percent
Subsidiary's reported net income	$300,000
Amortization expense on purchase price alloca- tions	$ 40,000

The economic unit concept presumes that the expense is that of the subsidiary. Thus, the allocation of consolidated income made to the noncontrolling interest is $26,000 (or 10 percent of earnings less amortization expense).

Under the economic unit theory, all consolidated totals (except for noncontrolling interest figures) are identical regardless of the degree of parent ownership. The parent controls the entire decision-making process of the subsidiary whenever control exists. Therefore, the economic unit concept views the subsidiary as an indivisible unit within the business combination. As such, fair market value serves as the basis for consolidating each asset and liability, even though the parent's interest may be significantly below 100 percent control. Any contrived division of the subsidiary accounts is, thus, avoided.

The Proportionate Consolidation Concept

The *proportionate consolidation concept* (also known as the *proprietary theory*) presumes that the ultimate objective of consolidated financial statements is to serve as a report to the stockholders of the parent company. These owners are perceived as being primarily interested in an accounting of parent company resources. Returning to the previous illustration, the entire accounting emphasis is placed on Big's $140,000 investment to acquire a 70 percent interest in Small.

Under proportionate consolidation, the values utilized for consolidation purposes represent the amount of the parent's payment attributed to each asset and liability. Big is paying for these assets and not for the company. Because 70 percent ownership has been acquired, that percentage of every account's fair market value at the date of purchase forms the basis for consolidated figures. If, for example, Small owns land with a book value of $8,000 but a fair market value of $10,000, a $7,000 component of the price (70 percent of fair market value) is said to have been Big's cost incurred in connection with this asset.

Under proportionate consolidation, goodwill of $49,000 is recognized: the amount of the purchase price in excess of the appropriate portion of the net assets' fair market value.

Proportionate Consolidation Concept

Purchase price	$140,000
Fair market value assigned to Small's accounts ($130,000 × 70%)	91,000
Cost in excess of fair market value—goodwill	$ 49,000
Noncontrolling interest	–0–

Although goodwill is computed here as a residual cost element, a more consistent view of proportionate consolidation is that this figure represents 70 percent of the subsidiary's total goodwill. As shown in the previous section, a goodwill figure of $70,000 is appropriate for the subsidiary as a whole (the $200,000 implied value of the company less the $130,000 market value of its net assets). Thus, the portion of this goodwill that is applicable to Big's investment is $49,000 ($70,000 × 70%).

Probably the most unique feature of the proportionate consolidation concept is the reporting of the noncontrolling interest; these outside owners are totally ignored in consolidated statements. Proponents of this theory hold that the presence of a noncontrolling interest is irrelevant to the stockholders of the parent company. An outside owner of a subsidiary has no capital invested in the parent company; furthermore, the parent has no legal obligation to this group. Thus, including any type of balance within consolidated financial statements to reflect a noncontrolling interest is viewed as serving no purpose. As one proponent argues: "It has some appealing characteristics. The most attractive is that financial statements using proportional consolidation don't present amounts for minority interest and therefore report only attributes of the reporting entities."[6]

Before leaving this discussion of proportionate consolidation, a quick extension of this concept can be made to income statement reporting. Not surprisingly, Big Company includes 70 percent of each of the subsidiary's revenue and expense accounts in the consolidated balances while showing no amount of the income total as associated with the noncontrolling interest. Within the framework of proportionate consolidation, this presentation is consistent. The parent's ownership entitles it to accrue only 70 percent of the subsidiary's income; the remaining 30 percent is applicable to outside owners. Any recording of this 30 percent share of Small's net income has no apparent relevance to the owners of Big Company.

In actual practice, little evidence exists to indicate significant usage of proportionate consolidation. Although omitting any mention of outside stockholders may be appealing, the division of each subsidiary account based on the ownership percentage is hard to justify. The parent has achieved control over all assets and liabilities, not just a 70 percent interest of each. However, this concept has recently gained some support for use in cases where control is present without majority ownership. As discussed in Chapter 2, a parent may effectively control a subsidiary although holding only 50 percent or even less of the outstanding voting stock. Proponents argue that proportionate consolidation would be a better reflection of the relationship between the two companies than the equity method that is currently required.

The Parent Company Concept

The *parent company concept* is sometimes viewed as a hybrid method because it incorporates a mixture of the assumptions found in the economic unit concept and

---

[6] Paul Rosenfield and Steven Rubin, "Minority Interest: Opposing Views," *Journal of Accountancy*, March 1986, p. 88.

proportionate consolidation. Two fundamental assertions provide the basis underlying this approach to consolidation valuation:

1. Holding control of a subsidiary provides the parent with an indivisible interest in that company. This statement is clearly derived from the economic unit concept.
2. Consolidated financial statements are produced primarily for the benefit of parent company stockholders. This idea is, of course, the basic argument used to substantiate proportionate consolidation.

Both of the assertions attributed to the parent company concept appear to have merit. However, as shown in the previous sections, they lead to radically differing sets of consolidated financial statements: one based on the implied value of the entire subsidiary and the other on the cost incurred in a partial acquisition. To arrive at consolidated statements that successfully merge these two approaches, the parent company concept adopts a compromise perspective. The subsidiary's book value and the purchase price paid by the parent are viewed as separate elements that can be accounted for individually within the consolidation process.

The book value of each subsidiary asset and liability is presumed to be indivisible and, therefore, not subject to an artificial allocation because of the specific level of ownership. Conversely, differences between the market value and underlying book value of these same accounts are only recognized because of the purchase price paid by the parent. Thus, if the parent acquires less than 100 percent of the subsidiary's voting stock, allocations attributed to individual accounts at the date of purchase should be based on the resulting ownership percentage. *The subsidiary's book value is consolidated in total along the lines of the economic unit concept whereas any cost in excess of book value is assumed to be a parent company expenditure appropriately allocated as indicated by the proportionate consolidation.*

Returning to Big's acquisition of Small, the appropriate consolidation values to be assigned under the parent company concept are computed as follows:

Parent Company Concept

Purchase price		$140,000
Book value of Small (100%)	$110,000	
Less: Recognition of noncontrolling interest (30%)	(33,000)	(77,000)
Cost in excess of underlying book value		63,000
Allocation based on fair market value in excess of book value ($130,000 − $110,000) × 70%		(14,000)
Goodwill		$ 49,000

The parent company concept includes the entire book value of each of Small's accounts within the consolidated statements but only 70 percent of the difference between fair market value and book value. Proponents justify this approach by pointing out that the subsidiary's cost figures are not affected by the parent's purchase and, therefore, should be consolidated in total. Conversely, the various allocations result solely from the price paid by the parent in a transaction negotiated to acquire 70 percent ownership. Thus, the investment is assumed to reflect only 70 percent of the change in the value of individual accounts.

As a practical example, Small's land, with an $8,000 cost but a fair market value of $10,000, is consolidated at a $9,400 balance: the entire $8,000 book value plus 70 percent of the $2,000 increase in its worth ($10,000 − $8,000). The subsidiary originally expended $8,000 for this land and the parent has now paid an additional $1,400 within the purchase price as a reflection of this change in value. Thus, to the business combination, the land's cost totals $9,400.

In the valuation schedule presented earlier, a noncontrolling interest of $33,000 is computed on the basis of Small's $110,000 book value rather than on either the fair market value of the net assets or the implied worth of the company taken as a whole. Under the parent company concept, only the book value of the subsidiary's accounts is consolidated in total. Although Big holds just 70 percent ownership, 100 percent of each book value is brought into the consolidation. Consequently, the presence of a noncontrolling interest equivalent to 30 percent of that particular total must also be recognized. The payment made by Big in excess of book value has no impact on the remaining outside owners and is not included in this calculation.

Some amount of disagreement exists among the users of the parent company concept as to the appropriate placement of the noncontrolling interest figure within the consolidated balance sheet. Arguments can be made for showing the balance as either a liability or an equity. However, proponents of this theory are most likely to isolate the noncontrolling interest between liabilities and stockholders' equity.

> The parent company concept views the consolidated financial statements as those of the parent—with the assets, liabilities, revenues, and expenses of the subsidiary merely substituting for the parent's investment on the balance sheet. . . . From that perspective, the noncontrolling (minority) interest is not a liability because the parent does not have a present obligation to pay cash or other assets. Nor does it appear to be owners' equity from a parent company perspective because the noncontrolling investors in a subsidiary do not have an ownership interest in the subsidiary's parent. . . . Thus, the parent company concept generally reports noncontrolling interest below liabilities but above stockholders' equity in consolidated statements.[7]

Currently, in practice, the appropriate placement of a noncontrolling interest balance remains an unresolved question. *Statement of Financial Accounting Concepts No. 6 (SFAC 6)*, "Elements of Financial Statements," issued in December of 1985 by the FASB recommends inclusion within equity (par. 254):

> Minority interests in net assets of consolidated subsidiaries do not represent present obligations of the enterprise to pay cash or distribute other assets to minority stock-

---

[7] FASB Discussion Memorandum, *An Analysis of Issues Related to Consolidation Policy and Procedures,* September 10, 1991, paragraphs 69 and 70.

holders. *Rather, those stockholders have ownership or residual interests in components of a consolidated enterprise.* The definitions in this Statement do not, of course, preclude showing minority interests separately from majority interests or preclude emphasizing the interests of majority stockholders for whom consolidated statements are primarily provided. Stock purchase warrants are also sometimes called liabilities but entirely lack the characteristics of liabilities. They also are part of equity. (emphasis added)

SFAC 6 pointedly avoids advocating any specific valuation theory, even though it clearly endorses disclosure of a noncontrolling interest within the stockholders' equity section of the consolidated balance sheet.

Interestingly, *International Accounting Standard No. 27,* "Consolidated Financial Statements and Accounting for Investments in Subsidiaries," 1989 (par. 33), addresses this same issue as follows: "Minority interests should be presented in the consolidated balance sheet separately from liabilities and parent shareholders' equity." In contrast to *SFAC 6,* this statement rejects the classification of a noncontrolling interest as an equity figure. Placement between the liability and equity sections is recommended in the same manner as used by the parent company concept.

Obviously, disagreement continues to exist as to the appropriate location of this balance sheet item. Today, the placement of a noncontrolling interest continues to vary with the reporting entity. Many companies disclose this figure as a single balance appearing directly after noncurrent liabilities. No accumulated total is provided for liabilities or equities, so that the reader is forced to decide whether the noncontrolling interest should be included in either classification or viewed as an item separate from both. Although this placement is often encountered in practice, no consensus currently exists as to the appropriate classification of this balance. However, if the FASB eventually takes action on consolidation policies and procedures, a specific location for the noncontrolling interest may well be required in the future.

In constructing a consolidated income statement, the parent company theory again demonstrates characteristics applicable to both the economic unit concept and proportionate consolidation. As with the economic unit concept, the book values of the various subsidiary accounts are included in total. Since these revenues and expenses are consolidated at 100 percent of their recorded balances, a 30 percent share of the subsidiary's net income is identified with the noncontrolling interest.

However, similar to proportionate consolidation, amortization is associated solely with the parent's investment because the allocations that create the expense result from the original payment. Consequently, amortization is not considered to have an impact on the calculation of noncontrolling interest. The additional cost is presumed to be that of the parent company and, thus, the expense is not directly related to the subsidiary's operations. For reporting purposes, the subsidiary's income is simply multiplied times the outside ownership percentage.

Under the parent company concept, the resulting noncontrolling interest figure has traditionally appeared as a reduction in arriving at consolidated net income. For example, following is the bottom portion of a typical income statement as reported by United Technologies:

UNITED TECHNOLOGIES CORPORATION
Year Ended December 31, 1990
(in millions)

Income before minority interests	$812.1
Less—Minority interests in subsidiaries' earnings	61.5
Net income	$750.6

Discussion Question: What Decision Should the FASB Make?

Whenever the FASB is studying an accounting issue, the board always seems to get plenty of advice. In response to its discussion memorandum, "An Analysis of Issues Related to Consolidation Policy and Procedures," the FASB received more than 70 letters. A sampling of these letters includes the following recommendations:

M. R. Schools, Jr., Virginia Power: Virginia Power believes that accounting information prepared under the proportionate consolidation approach provides the most relevant accounting information because it includes the interests of only the parent company shareholders.

David K. Owens, Edison Electric Institute: We generally support the "Parent Company Concept" because it emphasizes the interests of the parent shareholders and is most consistent with current practice.

Richard G. Rademacher, Sara Lee Corporation: By purchasing a controlling interest in an entity, management obtains the control of 100 percent of all assets and liabilities. It does not control only a proportionate share of each asset (i. e., 70% of a building) and the value of an asset recorded in consolidation does not vary dependent upon the percentage of ownership obtained. Therefore, we strongly oppose the parent company and proportionate share concepts of consolidation.

J. Michael Kelly, GTE Corporation: GTE has consistently responded in support of the parent company concept. The thrust of our support stems from this concept's emphasis on the interests of the parent's shareholders.

P. J. Lynch, Texaco Inc.: It is Texaco's view that neither the economic unit nor the parent company concept can be applied exclusively to all the issues raised in the DM. Accordingly, any future promulgation concerning consolidation policy should be a hybrid of the two concepts.

Joseph J. Martin, IBM: While we take a parent's view of deciding when to consolidate, we generally favor an economic unit theory approach on the mechanics of consolidation and financial statement presentation.

---

continued

John J. Mesloh, Pfizer Inc.: You may note that we favor the Parent Company view (which is consistent with our view of current written GAAP) of consolidation, as identified by the FASB. In short, we do not have too many issues with the current state of consolidation accounting.

What should the FASB decide to do?

As mentioned earlier, the FASB is currently studying valuation theories with the possibility that one concept may be mandated. Until that time, companies are free to select any approach and are not even required to disclose their choice. Although evidence is not readily available, the parent company concept is generally considered to be most commonly used in current practice. Therefore, except where noted, that concept is used throughout the remainder of this textbook. Knowledge of the alternatives is important, though; companies do apply these other approaches and their use may be promoted or required by the FASB in the future.

Valuation Theories—Overview

To provide a complete illustration of these three concepts, assume that Anderson Company acquires 60 percent of the voting stock of Zebulon Company on January 1, 1995. Anderson purchases this interest for $360,000 in cash at a time when Zebulon's assets and liabilities have the following values:

	Book Value 1/1/95	Fair Market Value 1/1/95
Current assets less liabilities.	$160,000	$160,000
Buildings and equipment (10-year life)	240,000	360,000
	$400,000	$520,000

Since Anderson's $360,000 payment was made to acquire 60 percent interest, Zebulon is apparently worth $600,000 when taken as a whole ($360,000/60 percent). In comparison to the $520,000 appraised value of the net assets, this implied value signifies *total* goodwill associated with Zebulon of $80,000. Any goodwill recognized by this business combination is assumed to be amortized over a life of 20 years.

Exhibit 4–1 presents alternative values that can be attributed to Zebulon's accounts on consolidated statements produced as of the date of acquisition. Quite

EXHIBIT 4–1   **Valuation Theories in Practice—Balance Sheet**

ANDERSON COMPANY AND ZEBULON COMPANY
Subsidiary Consolidation Figures
Balance Sheet
January 1, 1995

	Economic Unit Concept	Proportionate Consolidation Concept	Parent Company Concept
Current assets and liabilities:			
Book value.	$160,000 (100%)	$ 96,000 (60%)	$160,000 (100%)
Allocation based on fair market value.	–0–	–0–	–0–
Consolidated value	$160,000	$ 96,000	$160,000
Buildings and equipment:			
Book value.	$240,000 (100%)	$144,000 (60%)	$240,000 (100%)
Allocation based on fair market value	120,000 (100%)	72,000 (60%)	72,000 (60%)
Consolidated value	$360,000	$216,000	$312,000
Goodwill*	$ 80,000 (100%)	$ 48,000 (60%)	$ 48,000 (60%)
Noncontrolling interest, 1/1/95	$240,000 (40% of implied value)*	–0–	$160,000 (40% of book value)
Annual amortization of allocations:			
Buildings and equipment (10-year life).	$ 12,000	$ 7,200	$ 7,200
Goodwill (20-year life).	4,000	2,400	2,400
Annual expense	$ 16,000	$ 9,600	$ 9,600

* Implied value of company is $600,000 ($360,000/60%) with the value of net assets only $520,000. Total goodwill is $80,000 ($600,000 − $520,000).

obviously, differing figures are derived from each of the three valuation theories. The economic unit concept makes no division of any balance, whereas proportionate consolidation includes only 60 percent of subsidiary accounts because that portion represents the parent's ownership. The parent company concept adopts a compromise position: the book values of the subsidiary's assets and liabilities remain intact while all cost allocations (based on the difference in book values and fair market values) are computed using the parent's ownership percentage.

To carry this illustration to a natural conclusion, assume that Zebulon reports the following condensed income statement for the year of 1995:

Revenues.	$400,000
Expenses.	300,000
Net income	$100,000

These balances permit an examination of the totals to be included in the 1995 consolidated income statement. Exhibit 4–2 presents these figures, once again computed under each of the three theories described in this chapter. The eco-

EXHIBIT 4–2 **Valuation Theory in Practice—Income Statement**

ANDERSON COMPANY AND ZEBULON COMPANY
Subsidiary Consolidation Figures
Income Statement
For Year Ending December 31, 1995

	Economic Unit Concept	Proportionate Consolidation Concept	Parent Company Concept
Revenues	$400,000 (100%)	$240,000 (60%)	$400,000 (100%)
Expenses	300,000 (100%)	180,000 (60%)	300,000 (100%)
Amortization expense (see Exhibit 4–1)	16,000	9,600	9,600
Noncontrolling interest in subsidiary's net income	_____	_____	40,000 (40% of subsidiary income amortization not included)
Net effect on consolidated income	$ 84,000	$ 50,400	$ 50,400
Allocation of income:			
To controlling interest (60%)	$ 50,400		
To noncontrolling interest (40%).	$ 33,600		

nomic unit concept consolidates all accounts and assumes that amortization expense relates to the subsidiary. Proportionate consolidation includes only 60 percent of each revenue and expense and discloses no balance for the noncontrolling interest. The parent company concept recognizes all of the subsidiary's income statement accounts but attributes amortization to the parent so that the noncontrolling interest is not affected.

Consolidations Involving a Noncontrolling Interest—Subsequent to Acquisition

Having reviewed the basic philosophies of each of these three theories, this textbook now concentrates on the mechanical aspects of the consolidation process when an outside ownership is present. More specifically, consolidations for time periods subsequent to the date of acquisition are examined to analyze the full range of accounting complexities created by a noncontrolling interest. As indicated previously, this discussion centers on the parent company concept since it appears to be the most prevalent method in practice.

Computation of Noncontrolling Interest Balances

The presence of a noncontrolling interest does not dramatically alter the consolidation procedures demonstrated in Chapter 3. The unamortized balance of each purchase price allocation (as well as any goodwill or deferred credit) must still be computed and included within the consolidated totals. Amortization is recognized each year on these allocations. Reciprocal balances are eliminated.

Beyond these basic steps, the valuation and recognition of four noncontrolling interest balances do add a new dimension to the process of consolidating financial information. The accountant must determine and then enter each of these figures when constructing a worksheet:

- Noncontrolling interest in the subsidiary as of the beginning of the current year.
- Noncontrolling interest in the subsidiary's current year income.
- Noncontrolling interest in the subsidiary's dividend payments.
- Noncontrolling interest as of the end of the year (found by combining the three balances above).

To illustrate the appropriate consolidation procedures, assume that King Company acquires 80 percent of the outstanding stock of Pawn Company on January 1, 1995, for $960,000 in cash. The combination is to be accounted for as a purchase. King makes an additional $20,000 payment to lawyers, accountants, and appraisers to cover the direct costs associated with this acquisition. Exhibit 4–3 presents the book value of Pawn's accounts as well as the fair market value of each asset and liability on the date of purchase.

After inclusion of the direct consolidation costs, King's payment totals $980,000. From the information that has been presented, the purchase price can be attributed to Pawn's accounts as shown in Exhibit 4–4. Annual amortization relating to these allocations is also included in this schedule. Although expense figures are only computed for the initial years, some amount of amortization is

---

EXHIBIT 4–3   Subsidiary Accounts—Date of Acquisition

PAWN COMPANY
Account Balances
January 1, 1995

	Book Value	Fair Market Value	Differences
Current Assets.	$ 440,000	$ 440,000	–0–
Land	260,000	320,000	+$ 60,000
Buildings (20-year life)	480,000	600,000	+ 120,000
Equipment (10-year life)	110,000	100,000	(10,000)
Long-Term Liabilities (8-year maturity).	(550,000)	(510,000)	+ 40,000
Net Assets	$ 740,000	$ 950,000	+$210,000
Common Stock	$(230,000)		
Retained Earnings, 1/1/95.	(510,000)		

NOTE: Parentheses indicate a credit balance.

EXHIBIT 4–4

KING COMPANY AND PAWN COMPANY
Purchase Price Allocation and Amortization
January 1, 1995

	Allocation	Estimated Life (years)	Annual Amortization
Purchase price paid by King Company	$980,000		
80% of subsidiary book value ($740,000)			
(King Company's ownership)*	592,000		
Cost in excess of book value.	388,000		
Allocation to specific accounts based on difference			
between fair market value and book value:			
Land ($60,000 × 80%).	48,000		
Buildings ($120,000 × 80%)	96,000	20	4,800
Equipment ([$10,000] × 80%)	(8,000)	10	(800)
Long-term liabilities ($40,000 × 80%)	32,000	8	4,000
Goodwill.	$220,000	40	5,500
Annual amortization (initial years)			$13,500

* The parent company concept consolidates 100 percent of all asset and liability book values but also records an offsetting noncontrolling interest of 20 percent. The net effect is equal to 80 percent of the subsidiary's book value.

recognized in each of the 40 years following the acquisition (since that life is assumed for the goodwill).

Assume that consolidated financial statements are to be produced for the year ending December 31, 1996. This date was chosen arbitrarily. Any time period subsequent to 1995 could have served to demonstrate the applicable consolidation procedures. Having already calculated the purchase price allocations and related amortization, the consolidation of these two companies can be constructed along the lines demonstrated in Chapter 3. Only the presence of the 20 percent noncontrolling interest alters the previously explained process.

To complete the information needed for this combination, assume that Pawn Company has reported the following change in book value since King's acquisition:

Current year (1996)	
Net income.	$ 90,000
Less: Dividends paid	(50,000)
Increase in book value	$ 40,000
Prior years (only 1995 in this illustration):	
Increase in book value	$ 70,000

Assuming that King Company has applied the equity method, the composition of the Investment in Pawn Company account as of December 31, 1996, can be constructed as shown in Exhibit 4–5.

Exhibit 4–6 presents the separate financial statements for these two companies as of December 31, 1996, and the year then ended based on the information that has been provided.

Consolidated Totals.   Although the inclusion of a 20 percent outside ownership does complicate the consolidation process, the 1996 totals to be reported by this business combination can still be determined without the use of a worksheet:

Revenues = $1,340,000. The revenues of the parent and the subsidiary are added together. Under the parent company concept, the subsidiary's book value is included in total although only 80 percent of the stock is owned by King.

Expenses = $933,500. The expenses of the parent and the subsidiary are added together along with the $13,500 amortization expense for the year indicated in Exhibit 4–4.

Equity in subsidiary earnings = –0–. The investment income recorded by the parent is eliminated so that the subsidiary's revenues and expenses can be included in the consolidated totals.

Noncontrolling interest in subsidiary's income = $18,000. The outside owners are assigned 20 percent of Pawn's reported income of $90,000. According to the parent company concept, that amount is shown as a reduction within the consolidated income statement.

EXHIBIT 4–5

KING COMPANY
Investment in Pawn Company
Equity Method
December 31, 1996

Purchase price		$ 980,000
Prior year (1995);		
Increase in book value (80% × $70,000)	$ 56,000	
Amortization expense (Exhibit 4–4).	(13,500)	42,500
Current year (1996):		
Income accrual (80% × $90,000)	72,000	
Amortization expense (Exhibit 4–4).	(13,500)	
Equity in subsidiary earnings.	58,500*	
Dividends received (80% × $50,000)	(40,000)	18,500
Balance, 12/31/96		$1,041,000

---

* This figure appears in King's 1996 income statement.

EXHIBIT 4–6

KING COMPANY AND PAWN COMPANY
Separate Financial Statements
For December 31, 1996 and the Year Then Ended

	King	Pawn
Revenues	$ 910,000	$ 430,000
Expenses	(580,000)	(340,000)
Equity in subsidiary earnings (see Exhibit 4–5)	58,500	–0–
Net income	$ 388,500	$ 90,000
Retained earnings, 1/1/96	$ 876,100	$ 580,000
Net income (above)	388,500	90,000
Dividends paid	(60,000)	(50,000)
Retained earnings, 12/31/96	$1,204,600	$ 620,000
Current assets	$ 626,000	$ 445,000
Land	298,000	295,000
Buildings (net)	880,000	540,000
Equipment (net)	290,000	160,000
Investment in Pawn Company (see Exhibit 4–5)	1,041,000	–0–
Total assets	$3,135,000	$1,440,000
Long-term liabilities	$1,080,400	$ 590,000
Common stock	850,000	230,000
Retained earnings, 12/31/96	1,204,600	620,000
Total liabilities and equities	$3,135,000	$1,440,000

Net income = $388,500. Both consolidated expenses and the amount allocated to the noncontrolling interest are subtracted from consolidated revenues.

Retained earnings, 1/1/96 = $876,100. The parent company figure equals the consolidated total since the equity method was applied. If the cost method or the partial equity method had been used, the parent's balance would require adjustment to include any omitted figures.

Dividends paid = $60,000. The parent company balance only is reported. Part of the subsidiary's payments (80 percent) were intercompany to the parent and are eliminated. The remaining distribution was made to the outside owners and serves to reduce the balance attributed to them.

Retained earnings, 12/31/96 = $1,204,600. Balance is found by adding consolidated net income to the beginning retained earnings balance and then subtracting the consolidated dividends paid. Since the equity method was utilized, the parent company figure reflects the total for the business combination.

Current assets = $1,071,000. The parent's book value is added to the subsidiary's book value.

Land = $641,000. The parent's book value is added to the subsidiary's book value plus the $48,000 allocation within the purchase price (see Exhibit 4–4).

Buildings = $1,506,400. The parent's book value is added to the subsidiary's book value plus the $96,000 allocation within the purchase price less 1995 and 1996 amortization of $4,800 per year (see Exhibit 4–4).

Equipment = $443,600. The parent's book value is added to the subsidiary's book value *less* the $8,000 cost reduction allocation plus the 1995 and 1996 expense reduction of $800 per year (see Exhibit 4–4).

Investment in Pawn Company = –0–. The balance reported by the parent is eliminated so that the subsidiary's assets and liabilities can be included in the consolidated totals.

Goodwill = $209,000. The residual allocation shown in Exhibit 4–4 is reported after subtracting 1995 and 1996 amortization of $5,500 per year.

Total assets = $3,871,000. This balance is a summation of the consolidated assets.

Long-term liabilities = $1,646,400. The parent's book value is added to the subsidiary's book value less the $32,000 allocation within the purchase price plus 1995 and 1996 amortization of $4,000 per year (see Exhibit 4–4).

Noncontrolling interest in subsidiary = $170,000. The outside ownership is 20 percent of the subsidiary's year-end book value (common stock plus ending retained earnings) of $850,000. This $170,000 total can also be calculated as follows:

Noncontrolling interest at 1/1/96 (20 percent of $810,000 beginning book value—common stock plus 1/1/96 retained earnings)	$162,000
Noncontrolling interest in subsidiary's income (computed above)	18,000
Dividends paid to noncontrolling interest (20 percent of $50,000 total)	(10,000)
Noncontrolling interest at 12/31/96	$170,000

Common stock = $850,000. Only the parent's book value is reported since this combination is a purchase.

Retained earnings, 12/31/96 = $1,204,600. Computed above.

Total liabilities and equities = $3,871,000. This total is a summation of consolidated liabilities, noncontrolling interest, and equities.

Worksheet Process.   The consolidated totals for King and Pawn can also be determined by means of a worksheet as shown in Exhibit 4–7. A comparison of the worksheet entries made in this example with the entries incorporated in Chapter 3 (Exhibit 3–7) indicates that the presence of a noncontrolling interest does not create a significant number of changes in the consolidation procedures.

The worksheet still includes elimination of the subsidiary's stockholders' equity accounts (Entry S) although, as explained next, this entry is expanded to record the beginning noncontrolling interest for the year. The second worksheet entry recognizes the purchase price allocations at January 1 after one year of amortization (Entry A). Intercompany income as well as dividend payments are also removed (Entries I and D), while current year amortization expense is recorded (Entry E). The differences that can be cited with illustrations in the previous chapter relate exclusively to the recognition of four noncontrolling interest balances. In addition, *a separate Noncontrolling Interest column is added to the worksheet to accumulate the components that form the year-end figure to be reported on the consolidated balance sheet.*

Noncontrolling Interest—Beginning of Year. As discussed previously, Pawn's stockholders' equity accounts (common stock and beginning retained earnings) indicate a January 1, 1996, book value of $810,000. Thus, the 20 percent outside ownership is valued at $162,000 ($810,000 × 20 percent) as of the first day of the current year. This balance is recorded on the worksheet by means of Entry S:

Consolidation Entry S

Common Stock (Pawn)	230,000	
Retained Earnings, 1/1/96 (Pawn)	580,000	
Investment in Pawn Company (80%)		648,000
Noncontrolling Interest in Subsidiary, 1/1/96 (20%)		162,000

    To eliminate beginning stockholders' equity accounts of subsidiary along with book value portion of investment (equal to 80 percent ownership). Noncontrolling interest of 20 percent is also recognized.

The $162,000 balance assigned here to the outside owners at the beginning of the year is extended on the worksheet into the Noncontrolling Interest column (see Exhibit 4–7).

Noncontrolling Interest—Current Year Income. Exhibit 4–2 indicates that the parent company concept calculates the noncontrolling interest's share of current year earnings based on the subsidiary's income without regard for amortization. Thus, Pawn's 1996 earnings of $90,000 necessitate an assignment of $18,000 (20 percent) to the outside owners. This figure is shown as a reduction in arriving at consolidated net income. In effect, 100 percent of each subsidiary revenue and expense account is consolidated with an accompanying 20 percent decrease to reflect the presence of the noncontrolling interest. The 80 percent net effect corresponds to King's ownership.

    Since this $18,000 portion of consolidated income is viewed as accruing to the noncontrolling interest, an increase is necessary in the $162,000 beginning balance assigned (in Entry S) to these outside owners. The amount being attributed to the noncontrolling interest is raised because the subsidiary generated a profit during the period.

    Although this allocation could be recorded on the worksheet through an additional entry, the $18,000 is usually shown, as in Exhibit 4–7, by means of a columnar adjustment. The current year accrual is simultaneously entered in the

EXHIBIT 4–7 Noncontrolling Interest Illustrated

Consolidation: Purchase Method
Investment: Equity Method

KING COMPANY AND PAWN COMPANY
Consolidation Worksheet
For Year Ending December 31, 1996

Ownership: 80%

Accounts	King* Company	Pawn* Company	Consolidation Entries Debit	Consolidation Entries Credit	Noncontrolling Interest	Consolidated Totals
Income Statement						
Revenues	(910,000)	(430,000)				(1,340,000)
Expenses	580,000	340,000	(E) 13,500			933,500
Equity in subsidiary earnings	(58,500)	–0–	(I) 58,500			–0–
Noncontrolling interest in Pawn Company's income	–0–	–0–			(18,000)	18,000
Net income	(388,500)	(90,000)				(388,500)
Statement of Retained Earnings						
Retained earnings, 1/1/96:						
King Company	(876,100)					(876,100)
Pawn Company		(580,000)	(S) 580,000			–0–
Net income (above)	(388,500)	(90,000)				(388,500)
Dividends paid	60,000	50,000		(D) 40,000	10,000	60,000
Retained earnings, 12/31/96	(1,204,600)	(620,000)				(1,204,600)

Balance Sheet

Account			Debit	Credit	Noncontrolling Interest	Consolidated Totals
Current assets	626,000	445,000				1,071,000
Land	298,000	295,000	(A) 48,000			641,000
Buildings (net)	880,000	540,000	(A) 91,200	(E) 4,800		1,506,400
Equipment (net)	290,000	160,000	(E) 800	(A) 7,200		443,600
Investment in Pawn Company	1,041,000	-0-	(D) 40,000	(S) 648,000 (A) 374,500 (I) 58,500		-0-
Goodwill	-0-	-0-	(A) 214,500	(E) 5,500		209,000
Total assets	3,135,000	1,440,000				3,871,000
Long-term liabilities	(1,080,400)	(590,000)	(A) 28,000	(E) 4,000		(1,646,400)
Noncontrolling interest in Pawn Company, 1/1/96	-0-	-0-		(S) 162,000	(162,000)	
Noncontrolling interest in Pawn Company, 12/31/96	-0-	-0-			(170,000)	(170,000)
Common stock	(850,000)	(230,000)	(S) 230,000			(850,000)
Retained earnings, 12/31/96 (above)	(1,204,600)	(620,000)				(1,204,600)
Total liabilities and equities	(3,135,000)	(1,440,000)				(3,871,000)

* See Exhibit 4–6.

NOTE: Parentheses indicate a credit balance.

Consolidation entries:

(S) Elimination of subsidiary's stockholders' equity accounts along with recognition of January 1, 1996, noncontrolling interest.

(A) Allocation of parent's cost in excess of subsidiary's book value, unamortized balances as of January 1, 1996.

(I) Elimination of intercompany income (equity accrual less amortization expense).

(D) Elimination of intercompany dividend payments.

(E) Recognition of amortization expense on purchase price allocations.

consolidated Income Statement column as a *reduction* and in the Noncontrolling Interest column as an *increase*. This procedure indicates that a portion of the earnings included in the consolidated figures must be assigned to the outside owners rather than to the business combination.

Noncontrolling Interest—Dividend Payments.   The $40,000 dividend that went to the parent company is eliminated routinely through Entry D, but the remainder of Pawn's dividend was paid to noncontrolling interest. The impact of the dividend (20 percent of the subsidiary's total payment) distributed to the other owners must be acknowledged. As shown in Exhibit 4–7, this remaining $10,000 is extended directly into the Noncontrolling Interest column on the worksheet as a reduction. It represents the drop in the underlying book value of the outside ownership that resulted from the subsidiary's asset distribution.

Noncontrolling Interest—End of Year.   The ending assignment for these other owners is calculated by a summation of

1. The beginning balance for the year ($162,000).
2. Plus the appropriate share of the subsidiary's current income ($18,000).
3. Less the dividends paid to the outside owners ($10,000).

The Noncontrolling Interest column on the worksheet in Exhibit 4–7 serves to accumulate these figures. The $170,000 total is then transferred to the balance sheet where it appears in the consolidated statements.

Consolidated Financial Statements.   Having successfully consolidated the information for King and Pawn, the resulting financial statements for these two companies is produced in Exhibit 4–8. These figures can be computed directly or can be taken from the consolidation worksheet.

Effects Created by Alternative Investment Methods

One final aspect of the accounting for a noncontrolling interest needs to be explored. In the King and Pawn illustration, the equity method was utilized by the parent, with all worksheet entries based on that approach. As discussed in Chapter 3, had King incorporated either the cost method or the partial equity method, a few specific changes in the consolidation process would be required although the reported figures are not affected.

Cost Method.   As in Chapter 3, two balances are omitted by the parent if the cost method is applied. First, dividend income is recognized rather than an equity income accrual. Thus, the parent fails to accrue the percentage of the subsidiary's income earned in past years in excess of dividends (the increase in book value). Second, amortization expense is not recorded under the cost method and must also be included in the consolidation process if proper totals are to be achieved. Since neither of these figures is recognized in applying the cost method, an Entry

---

EXHIBIT 4-8   Consolidated Statements with Noncontrolling Interest

---

KING COMPANY AND CONSOLIDATED SUBSIDIARY
Income Statement
For Year Ending December 31, 1996

Revenues	$1,340,000
Expenses	(933,500)
Noncontrolling interest in subsidiary's income	(18,000)
Consolidated net income.	$ 388,500

KING COMPANY AND CONSOLIDATED SUBSIDIARY
Statement of Retained Earnings
For Year Ending December 31, 1996

Retained earnings, January 1, 1996	$ 876,100
Consolidated net income.	388,500
Less: Dividends paid	(60,000)
Retained earnings, December 31, 1996	$1,204,600

KING COMPANY AND CONSOLIDATED SUBSIDIARY
Balance Sheet
December 31, 1996

Assets

Current assets	$1,071,000
Land	641,000
Buildings (net)	1,506,400
Equipment (net)	443,600
Goodwill.	209,000
Total assets	$3,871,000

Liabilities and Equities

Long-term liabilities.	$1,646,400
Noncontrolling interest in subsidiary	170,000
Common stock—King Company	850,000
Retained earnings (above)	1,204,600
Total liabilities and equities	$3,871,000

---

*C is added to the worksheet to convert the previously recorded balances to the equity method. The parent's beginning retained earnings is affected by this adjustment as well as the Investment in Subsidiary account. The exact amount is computed as follows.

Conversion to Equity Method from Cost Method (Entry *C).   Combine:

1. The increase during past years since acquisition in the subsidiary's book value (income less dividends) times the parent's ownership percentage.
2. Total amortization expense for these same past years.

One other procedural change is required when the cost method is in use. Since no equity income accrual is recognized, only dividends received from the subsidiary are recorded by the parent as income. Entry I is used on the worksheet to remove this intercompany income. Because the dividends are eliminated in this manner, no Entry D is required.

Partial Equity Method. Again, an Entry *C is needed to convert the parent's retained earnings as of January 1, 1996, to the equity method. In this case, however, only the amortization expense for the prior years must be included. Under the partial equity method, the income accrual is appropriately recognized each period by the parent company so that no further adjustment is necessary.

Step Acquisitions

A note to the 1990 financial statements of Pennzoil Company describes the creation of a business combination through a series of separate purchases:

> The results of operations of Proven Properties Inc., a wholly owned subsidiary of Pennzoil, have been consolidated with Pennzoil's results subsequent to Pennzoil's acquisition from the outside investors of the 51.3 percent equity interest in PPI not already owned by Pennzoil in February 1990.

In all previous consolidation illustrations, control over a subsidiary was assumed to have been achieved through a single transaction. Obviously, Pennzoil's takeover of Proven Properties shows that a combination may also be the result of a series of stock purchases. These step acquisitions further complicate the consolidation process. The financial information of the separate companies must still be brought together, but no single purchase price exists. How do the initial acquisitions affect this process?

> If a parent-subsidiary relationship is established in a step acquisition, a problem arises that does not exist if the parent-subsidiary relationship is established in a single transaction. *That problem is how to include in consolidated financial statements the portion of the parent's interest in the subsidiary that was purchased prior to the date the parent-subsidiary relationship is established.* (emphasis added)[8]

For example, in consolidating the accounts of Proven Properties, the values to be reported could vary significantly depending on Pennzoil's handling of the 48.7 percent ownership that it held prior to gaining control.

Step Acquisitions—Parent Company Concept

Under the parent company concept, each investment is viewed as an individual purchase (sometimes referred to as a *layer*) with its own cost allocations and

---

[8] FASB, *An Analysis of Issues Related to Consolidation Policy and Procedures*, paragraph 289.

related amortization. To illustrate, assume that Art Company purchases 30 percent of Zip Company on January 1, 1995, for $164,000 in cash. As of the date of this acquisition, Zip is reporting a net book value of $400,000.

Assuming that Art has gained the ability to significantly influence the decision-making process of Zip, this investment, for external reporting purposes, is accounted for by means of the equity method as discussed in Chapter 1. Thus, Art must determine any allocations and amortization associated with its purchase price (see Exhibit 4–9). Goodwill is assumed here to represent all excess payments and to have the maximum possible life.

As discussed previously, application of the equity method requires the immediate accrual of investee income by the parent while any dividends received are recorded as a decrease in the Investment account. Art must also reduce both the income and asset balances in recognition of the annual $1,100 amortization indicated in Exhibit 4–9. If, over the next two years, Zip reports a total of $140,000 in net income and pays dividends of $40,000, the subsidiary's book value rises from $400,000 to $500,000. At the same time, the parent's investment account grows to $191,800:

Purchase Price—1/1/95.	$164,000
Accrual of 1995–96 Equity Income ($140,000 × 30 percent) . . .	42,000
Dividends Received 1995–96 ($40,000 × 30%)	(12,000)
Amortization ($1,100 per year for 2 years)	(2,200)
Investment in Zip, 12/31/96.	$191,800

On January 1, 1997, Art's ownership is raised to 80 percent by the purchase of another 50 percent of the outstanding common stock of Zip Company for $350,000. Although the equity method can still be utilized for internal reporting, this second purchase necessitates the preparation of consolidated financial statements beginning in 1997. Art now controls Zip; the two companies should be viewed as a single economic entity for external reporting purposes.

EXHIBIT 4–9 **Allocation of First Purchase**

ART COMPANY AND ZIP COMPANY
Purchase Price Allocation and Amortization
January 1, 1995

Purchase price.	$ 164,000
Book value equivalent of Art's ownership ($400,000 × 30%)	(120,000)
Goodwill	$ 44,000
Maximum life	40 years
Annual amortization expense	$ 1,100

EXHIBIT 4–10   Allocation of Second Purchase

ART COMPANY AND ZIP COMPANY
Purchase Price Allocation and Amortization
January 1, 1997

Purchase price	$ 350,000
Book value equivalent of Art's ownership ($500,000 × 50%)	(250,000)
Goodwill	$ 100,000
Maximum life	40 years
Annual amortization expense	$ 2,500

Before computing any consolidated balances, Art must make a separate cost allocation for this second purchase (Exhibit 4–10). This schedule does not supersede the allocation made in Exhibit 4–9 but merely supplements it for the price paid in acquiring the 50 percent block of Zip's stock.

Worksheet Consolidation for a Step Acquisition

To complete this example, assume that the subsidiary earns $100,000 in net income during 1997 and distributes $20,000 as a cash dividend. If the parent company continues applying the equity method to this investment, Art reports an Equity in Subsidiary Earnings balance of $76,400 for 1997 and an Investment in Zip Company of $602,200:

Investment in Zip, 12/31/96 (computed above)		$191,800
January 1, 1997—Second Acquisition.		350,000
Dividends Received—1997 ($20,000 × 80%).		(16,000)
Equity Income Accrual—1997 ($100,000 × 80%).	$80,000	
1997 Amortization: First Purchase (Exhibit 4–9)	(1,100)	
Second Purchase (Exhibit 4–10)	(2,500)	76,400
Investment in Zip, 12/31/97		$602,200

Once both investment balances have been determined, the worksheet shown in Exhibit 4–11 can be developed. Although this step acquisition might appear to be more complex than a single purchase, the actual consolidation process is the same as in previous examples.

- No conversion to the equity method (Entry *C) is required since that method has been applied by the parent. If a different approach were used, amortization expense for prior years would have to be recognized along with, possibly, the proportionate increase in the subsidiary's book value for this same period.

- The stockholders' equity accounts of Zip are removed through Entry S. This worksheet entry also establishes the $100,000 beginning balance for the 20 percent noncontrolling interest that still remains (20 percent multiplied by the $500,000 stockholders' equity as of January 1, 1997).

- The unamortized purchase price allocations are brought into the consolidation through Entry A. To avoid confusion, two figures are entered on the worksheet for goodwill. The $44,000 balance resulting from the first transaction has already undergone two years of amortization. Thus, only a cost of $41,800 remains at the beginning of the current period. Since the second allocation ($100,000) was made on January 1 of the current year, no expense has been recorded in prior years.

- Entry I on the worksheet eliminates the $76,400 equity income accrual calculated above.

- Entry D removes the $16,000 intercompany dividend paid to the parent in 1997. The remaining 20 percent ($4,000) was paid to the outside owners. Thus, that amount is extended to the Noncontrolling Interest column on the worksheet as a reduction.

- The final consolidation entry (Entry E) recognizes amortization for the current period. Again, two amounts are shown here for clarification since two separate purchases were made.

- The noncontrolling interest balances to be reported on the income statement and balance sheet must be computed before the worksheet can be completed. Since Art now holds 80 percent of Zip, the outside owner's share of the subsidiary's income is 20 percent of the $100,000 reported earnings (or $20,000). Once again, this assignment is recorded on the worksheet through a columnar entry: the Noncontrolling Interest column is increased by that amount with a parallel decrease to consolidated net income.

  For the balance sheet, the ending amount applicable to these outside owners is determined within the Noncontrolling Interest column: assigned income of $20,000 is added to the $100,000 beginning balance with dividends of $4,000 being subtracted. The $116,000 total is then reported on the balance sheet between the liabilities and stockholders' equity.

Retroactive Treatment Created by Step Acquisition

Because the initial 30 percent acquisition gave Art the ability to maintain significant influence over Zip, the investment balances in 1995 and 1996 were recorded using the equity method. For external reporting, the subsidiary's operations as well as related amortization were accounted for in those years in a manner that parallels the consolidation process. Thus, financial statements prepared and distributed by Art in 1995 and 1996 are considered comparable with the consolidated statements produced for 1997. Consequently, no retroactive adjustment of the earlier figures is required by Art's change in the method of reporting its investment in Zip.

EXHIBIT 4-11 Step Acquisition Illustrated

ART COMPANY AND ZIP COMPANY
Consolidation Worksheet
For Year Ending December 31, 1997

Consolidation: Purchase
Method
Investment: Equity Method

Accounts	Art Company	Zip Company	Consolidation Entries Debit	Consolidation Entries Credit	Noncontrolling Interest	Consolidated Totals
Income Statement						
Revenues	(600,000)	(260,000)				(860,000)
Expenses	425,000	160,000	(E) 3,600			588,600
Equity in subsidiary earnings	(76,400)	–0–	(I) 76,400			–0–
Noncontrolling interest in Zip Company's income	–0–	–0–			(20,000)	20,000
Net income	(251,400)	(100,000)				(251,400)
Statement of Retained Earnings						
Retained earnings, 1/1/97:						
Art Company	(760,000)					(760,000)
Zip Company		(230,000)	(S) 230,000			
Net income (above)	(251,400)	(100,000)				(251,400)
Dividends paid	126,400	20,000		(D) 16,000	4,000	126,400
Retained earnings, 12/31/97	(885,000)	(310,000)				(885,000)

Balance Sheet

	Company	Zip	Debits	Credits	Noncontrolling Interest	Consolidated Totals
Current assets	505,800	280,000				785,800
Land	205,000	90,000				295,000
Buildings (net)	646,000	310,000				956,000
Investment in Zip Company	602,200	–0–	(D) 16,000	(A) 141,800 (S) 400,000 (I) 76,400 (E) 1,100 (E) 2,500		–0–
Goodwill	–0–	–0–	(A) 41,800 (A) 100,000			138,200
Total assets	1,959,000	680,000				2,175,000
Liabilities	(459,000)	(100,000)				(559,000)
Noncontrolling interest in Zip Company, 1/1/97	–0–	–0–		(S) 100,000	(100,000)	
Noncontrolling interest in Zip Company, 12/31/97					(116,000)	(116,000)
Common stock	(355,000)	(200,000)	(S) 200,000			(355,000)
Additional paid-in capital	(260,000)	(70,000)	(S) 70,000			(260,000)
Retained earnings, 12/31/97 (above)	(885,000)	(310,000)				(885,000)
Total liabilities and equities	(1,959,000)	(680,000)				(2,175,000)

NOTE: Parentheses indicate a credit balance.

Consolidation entries:

(S) Elimination of subsidiary's stockholders' equity accounts along with recognition of January 1, 1997, noncontrolling interest.

(A) Allocation of parent's cost in excess of subsidiary's book value, unamortized balances as of January 1, 1997, two separate allocations are shown because two purchases were made.

(I) Elimination of intercompany income (equity accrual less amortization expense).

(D) Elimination of intercompany dividend payments.

(E) Recognition of amortization expense on goodwill resulting from purchase price.

Conversely, if Art had originally secured only a small percentage of Zip's shares (achieving less than significant influence), the lower-of-cost-or-market-value method would have been applied during 1995 and 1996. Under this approach, except for amounts received in the form of dividends, subsidiary income is ignored by the owner as is the recording of any amortization. However, gaining control of Zip in 1997 necessitates a transformation to consolidated statements, a change that strains the comparability of the results reported in the earlier years. Thus, to establish a proper degree of consistency, both the investment and income accounts are restated by the parent as if the equity method had been utilized from the date of the first acquisition.

ARB 51 (par. 9) does allow one exception to this restatement policy by indicating that "if small purchases are made over a period of time and then a purchase is made which results in control, the date of the latest purchase, as a matter of convenience, may be considered as the date of acquisition." Therefore, retroactive adjustment is not required when initial acquisition levels are relatively small. The ARB apparently felt that the difficulties encountered in restating such minor amounts outweighed the benefits derived from establishing comparability.

Step Acquisitions—Economic Unit Concept

Although this textbook is using the parent company concept for illustration purposes, comparison with the economic unit concept demonstrates significant differences. Because the FASB is studying the issue of consolidation policies, one method or the other might eventually be mandated or an entirely new approach could be required.

In the previous example, Art purchased 30 percent of Zip for $164,000. By applying the equity method, this investment had increased on the parent's books to $191,800 by January 1, 1997. At that point in time, Art paid an additional $350,000 for another 50 percent ownership although the subsidiary's book value amounted to only $500,000.

The economic unit concept bases consolidated figures on the total value of the subsidiary regardless of the parent's level of ownership. Since $350,000 was paid for half the stock, the implied value of the company was $700,000 ($350,000/50%). Based on that total, the original 30 percent ownership should be worth $210,000. Since Art's book value at that date was only $191,800, the economic unit concept would require the parent to recognize an immediate gain of $18,200 ($210,000 implied value less $191,800 book value). This increase in the Investment in Zip account to $560,000 ($191,800 book value + $18,200 gain + $350,000 second acquisition) gives a balance that is in line with the $700,000 implied value of the subsidiary as a whole ($700,000 × 80% = $560,000).

Critics of the economic unit concept argue that the parent might be willing to pay an exorbitant price for the final few shares needed to gain control of a subsidiary to create a large implied value and a greater reported gain. Proponents counter by asserting that the purchase price should not be used to value the subsidiary as a whole if a more accurate method can be found. In either case, controversy continues to surround the consolidation of financial statements, a debate that will probably last even if one method is eventually mandated by the FASB.

Preacquisition Income

In virtually all of the previous examples in this textbook, the parent has gained control of the subsidiary on the first day of the fiscal year. How is the consolidation process affected if a purchase is made on April 1 or August 19 or some other day within the year?[9]

If control is gained at a different time, a few obvious changes occur. The subsidiary's book value as of that date has to be computed so that an appropriate comparison with the purchase price can be made to determine allocations and goodwill. Amortization expense as well as any equity accrual and dividend collections are recognized for a period shorter than a year. The real issue to be resolved, though, is in consolidating the subsidiary's revenues and expenses. Obviously, these balances can be included just for the months after the takeover. However, this approach gives totals that may not be comparable to the figures reported in the future when ownership is for a full year.

Paragraph 10 of *ARB 51* addresses this issue by stating

> When a subsidiary is purchased during the year, there are alternative ways of dealing with the results of its operations in the consolidated income statement. One method, which usually is preferable, especially where there are several dates of acquisition of blocks of shares, is to include the subsidiary in the consolidation as though it had been acquired at the beginning of the year, and to deduct at the bottom of the consolidated income statement the preacquisition earnings applicable to each block of stock. This method presents results which are more indicative of the current status of the group, and facilitates future comparison with subsequent years.

Thus, when a purchase combination is created during the current year, this pronouncement recommends that the reporting emphasis be placed on promoting the statement user's ability to compare current and future periods. *To achieve this objective, the income statement accounts should be consolidated as if the parent had possessed its interest for the entire year.* Consequently, revenues and expenses are included in total within the consolidated figures. However, a single-line reduction (often referred to as *preacquisition income*) appears at the bottom of the income statement to remove the portion of these earnings that apply to the previous owners.

For example, the 1987 income statement of Nucorp, Inc. reports a reduction for preacquisition earnings of $307,000. A note to the financial statements indicates that the company held 49 percent of Pin Oak Petroleum until April of that year and 100 percent thereafter. According to the note, the income statement

---

[9] In a pooling of interests, operating results are consolidated retroactively as if the companies had always been together. Therefore, the specific date on which a pooling is formed has no impact on the resulting income statement.

included "the accounts of Pin Oak as though Pin Oak had been wholly owned at the beginning of the year and presented earnings accruing to the 51 percent ownership in Pin Oak prior to acquisition as preacquisition earnings."

Inclusion of this balance is a means of accounting for the prior group of stockholders in a manner similar to that accorded to any noncontrolling interest that remains. The only difference is that these previous owners ceased during the current year to be associated with the subsidiary. Thus, although an income allocation is reported for the period of their ownership, no end-of-year balance is recognized. Any dividends paid to the previous owners are likewise omitted from consolidation consideration.

To illustrate, assume that Berkeley Company purchases 90 percent of Waltins Company on October 1, 1995. The 1995 operations of this new subsidiary would impact the consolidated income statement as follows:

Impact on Consolidated Income Statement—1995
Berkeley owns 90 percent of Waltins for last three months

Revenues	100% of subsidiary's revenues are included
Expenses	100% of subsidiary's expenses are included plus amortization expense for three months
Noncontrolling interest . . .	Reduction is 10% of subsidiary's income for the entire year
Preacquisition income . . .	Reduction is 90% of subsidiary's income for the first nine months of the year
Net impact on consolidated net income.	Increased by 90% of subsidiary's income for the last three months of the year reduced by any amortization expense for this same period

---

The establishment of a Preacquisition Income account permits comparability between the figures reported for current and future years. The reader of the financial statements is able to measure the full impact of creating this combination through the inclusion of 100 percent of each subsidiary revenue and expense account. By reporting reductions for the noncontrolling interest (10 percent) and the previous owners (90 percent for nine months), consolidated net income successfully mirrors the parent's 90 percent ownership for the last three months of the year. Thus, the *ARB*'s suggested handling of this matter has no effect on the amount of consolidated net income. Rather, the pronouncement simply constructs the income statement in a manner that provides the desired comparability with future periods.

Before leaving this illustration, one further comment should be made. The term *preacquisition income* has been incorporated here since it appears to be most prevalent in practice. As can be observed in much of accounting, financial statement terminology is not always particularly descriptive. This allocation could also be reported as: *current year income accruing to previous owners prior to the date subsidiary was acquired.* This title is significantly more wordy but less subject to misinterpretation by the users of the financial data. Most companies, however, elect to stay with traditional terms such as *preacquisition income* when preparing statements for external reporting purposes.

Sales of Subsidiary Stock

Although this textbook has concentrated on the acquisition and ownership of large blocks of corporate securities, the eventual sale of these stocks is also encountered in the business world. For example, a note to the 1987 financial statements of McKesson Corporation states:

> In November 1986, the Company sold 2,000,000 common shares of its PCS, Inc. subsidiary to the public reducing the Company's ownership interest to 86.2 percent. The net proceeds from the sale of $24.5 million, resulted in a $23.1 million pretax gain.

Under the parent company concept, accounting for the disposition of such shares parallels the sale of any corporate asset: the investment is adjusted to the appropriate book value as of the date of sale and then removed from the records of the parent company.[10] Any difference in the recorded balance and the consideration being received is recognized as a gain or loss.

Establishment of Investment Book Value

Any needed adjustment of the investment account is dependent on the accounting method used by the parent for internal reporting purposes. If the equity method has been applied, little problem should exist in recording the transaction. The investment is correctly reported by the parent as of the beginning of the year so that only the normal equity method adjustments are needed to reflect operations and amortization for the current period.

However, if either the cost or the partial equity method has been utilized, the adjustment process is more complicated. As indicated previously, both of these alternatives offer a convenient means by which to monitor a subsidiary. Unfortunately, neither produces the accurate book value necessary for recording a sales transaction. Therefore, when either of these other methods has been applied, the parent's Investment in Subsidiary account must be updated as if the equity method had been applied since the date of acquisition.

To illustrate, assume that Giant Company owns 80 percent of Tiny Company. Initially, a 50 percent interest was acquired in 1987 for $600,000 with the additional 30 percent being purchased in 1990 for $440,000. If Giant elects to account for this subsidiary using the equity method, the Investment in Tiny account contains a $1,245,000 balance as of January 1, 1995, based on the following assumed figures:

---

[10] Unless control is surrendered, the economic unit concept views the sale of a subsidiary's stock as a treasury stock transaction so that no gain or loss is recognized.

	Cost	Income Accrual Since Acquisition	Dividends	Amortization	Investment Balance 1/1/95
1987 purchase	$ 600,000	$200,000	$(15,000)	$(40,000)	$ 745,000
1990 purchase	440,000	100,000	(6,000)	(34,000)	500,000
Totals	$1,040,000	$300,000	$(21,000)	$(74,000)	$1,245,000

Sale Made at Beginning of Year. Appropriate application of the equity method signifies that the $1,245,000 is a correctly recorded balance. Assuming that Giant sells this entire interest on January 1, 1995, for $1,400,000, the transaction is recorded as follows:[11]

Giant's Financial Records—January 1, 1995

Cash (or other assets)	1,400,000	
Investment in Tiny Company		1,245,000
Gain on Sale of Investment		155,000
To record January 1, 1995, sale of subsidiary.		

Since the sale is made on the first day of the year, no adjustment is required to recognize the 1995 operations of the subsidiary.

In contrast, if one of the alternative methods has been utilized by Giant, a preliminary entry is needed to establish the appropriate $1,245,000 balance.

> *Application of the cost method.* The $1,040,000 total of the two original payments continues to be reported by the parent for this investment so that a $205,000 increase is necessary (income in excess of dividends and amortization).
>
> *Application of the partial equity method.* A book value of $1,319,000 (income and dividends are recognized by the parent but not the $74,000 amortization) is found. An adjustment must be made to record the amortization.

Hence, depending on the method in use, one of the following entries is required of the parent prior to recording the sales transaction:

Giant's Financial Records—January 1, 1995
Cost Method Has Been Applied

Investment in Tiny Company	205,000	
Retained Earnings, 1/1/95 (Giant)		205,000
To establish correct equity balance by recognizing income accrual (in excess of dividends) for previous years as well as amortization.		

---

[11] Under the guidelines of *APB Opinion 30*, Giant may have to report this sale as the disposal of a segment. Because this issue is covered in most intermediate accounting textbooks, it will not be explored here.

Partial Equity Method Has Been Applied

Retained Earnings, 1/1/95 (Giant) 74,000

    Investment in Tiny Company 74,000

  To establish correct equity balance by recognizing amortization
relating to previous years.

These adjustments are equivalent to the Entry *C used in past consolidations to update the investment account when either the cost or partial equity methods has been applied. However, for a sale, this entry must be recorded directly into the parent's books rather than as a part of the worksheet process. Following the adjustment to $1,245,000, the parent records the sales transaction using the same journal entry presented in connection with the equity method.

Sale Made During the Year.   If this sale had transpired *within* the fiscal year, Giant still adjusts the investment to $1,245,000 (if necessary) but then extends application of the equity method over the period that the stock is held during 1995. The resulting book value must be correct as of the date of sale. The income accruing to Giant during this portion of the year is reported as a single-line item in the 1995 income statement. In this manner, subsidiary earnings continue to be recognized throughout the period of ownership even though consolidation is no longer applicable.

Cost-Flow Assumptions

If less than an entire investment is sold, the parent must select an appropriate cost-flow assumption whenever more than one purchase has been made. In the sale of securities, the use of specific identification based on serial numbers is acceptable, although averaging or FIFO assumptions are often applied. Use of the averaging method is especially appealing in that all shares are truly identical, creating little justification for identifying different cost figures with individual shares.

Returning to Giant's ownership of Tiny Company, assume that the parent sold only a 20 percent portion of the subsidiary on January 1, 1995 (thereby reducing its holdings from 80 to 60 percent). Averaging dictates the removal of $311,250 (20 percent/80 percent × $1,245,000) from the investment account. Conversely, adoption of FIFO requires that $298,000 be written off based on the currently reported value of the initial 1987 acquisition (20 percent/50 percent × $745,000).

Accounting for Shares that Remain

If only a portion of Giant's investment is sold, a determination must also be made as to the proper method of accounting for the shares that remain. Three possible scenarios can be envisioned:

1. Giant's interest may have been so drastically reduced that the parent no longer controls the subsidiary or even has the ability to significantly influence its decision making. For example, assume that Giant's ownership drops from 80 to 5 percent. In the current period prior to the sale, the 80 percent investment is reported by means of the equity method with the lower-of-cost-or-market-value method used for the 5 percent that remains thereafter. Consolidated financial statements are no longer applicable.

2. Giant may still be able to apply significant influence over the operations of Tiny, although control is no longer maintained. A drop in the level of ownership from 80 to 30 percent would normally meet this condition. In this case, the equity method is utilized by the parent for the entire year. Application is based on 80 percent until the time of sale and then on 30 percent for the remainder of the year. Again, consolidated statements cease to be appropriate since control has been lost.

3. The decrease in ownership may be relatively small so that the parent continues to maintain control over the subsidiary even after the sale. Giant's reduction of its ownership in Tiny from 80 to 60 percent is an example of this situation. After the disposal, consolidated financial statements are still required but the process is based on the *end-of-year ownership percentage*. As with step acquisitions, the accounting emphasis is placed here on maintaining comparability with future years. However, since only the retained shares (60 percent in this case) are consolidated, separate recognition must be made of any current year income accruing to the parent from its terminated interest. Thus, earnings on this portion of the investment (a 20 percent interest in Tiny for the time during the year that it is held) are shown in the consolidated income statement as a single-line item computed by means of the equity method.

Summary

1. A parent company need not acquire 100 percent of a subsidiary's stock to form a business combination. Only control over the decision-making process is necessary, a level that has historically been achieved by obtaining a majority of the voting shares. Ownership of any subsidiary stock that is retained by outside, unrelated parties is collectively referred to as a noncontrolling interest.

2. A purchase consolidation takes on an added degree of complexity when a noncontrolling interest is present. A decision must be made as to the theoretical approach by which subsidiary assets and liabilities are to be valued within the financial statements of the business combination. One alternative, the economic unit concept, presumes that the combination is composed of two identifiable companies and should be accounted for as such. Allocations associated with the subsidiary's assets and liabilities are determined using their total fair market value regardless of the degree of parent ownership. The calculation of any noncontrolling interest is based on this total and reported by the business combination as a component of stockholders' equity.

3. The proportionate consolidation concept focuses on the parent company by stressing the cost of buying a portion of the subsidiary. Under this approach, allocations are computed using the ownership percentage of each account's fair market value. No recognition of noncontrolling interest is reported in either the consolidated balance sheet or income statement.

4. In practice, the parent company concept appears to be most popular. According to this method, the book value of each subsidiary asset and liability is included in the total whereas the difference between fair market value and book value is consolidated based on the parent's ownership percentage. Any noncontrolling interest is measured using only the subsidiary's book value and reported between the liabilities and stockholders' equity.

5. Four noncontrolling interest figures actually appear in the annual consolidation process. Calculation of each is derived by multiplying the percentage of outside ownership by the subsidiary's book value. A balance as of the beginning of the year is brought into the worksheet first (through Entry S) followed by the noncontrolling interest's share of the subsidiary's income for the period (recorded by a columnar entry) . A decrease is recognized because of any dividends paid to these unrelated owners (with the amount appearing on the worksheet as the subsidiary's dividends that were not eliminated as intercompany). The final balance for the year is found as a summation of the Noncontrolling Interest column and is presented on the consolidated balance sheet, usually between the Liability and Stockholders' Equity sections. The income figure appears as a reduction within the income statement.

6. A parent may obtain control of a subsidiary by means of several separate purchases occurring over time, a process often referred to as a *step acquisition*. In such cases, each purchase is viewed as an individual investment with separate allocations and amortization.

7. When a purchase is made within a year, operating figures should be reported that are comparable with those of future years. Thus, revenues and expenses can be consolidated as if the acquisition had taken place on the first day of the year. A *preacquisition income* figure is then subtracted within the consolidated income statement to remove the effects of the subsidiary's operations relating to the time prior to the takeover.

8. A parent company may also sell all, or a portion, of a subsidiary. The appropriate book value for the investment must be established within the parent's separate records so that the gain or loss can be computed accurately. If the equity method has not been applied, the parent's investment balance should be restated to recognize any income and amortization previously omitted. The resulting balance is then compared to the amount received for the stock to arrive at the gain or loss. Any shares still being held will subsequently be reported by either consolidation, the equity method, or the lower-of-cost-or-market-value method, depending on the influence retained by the parent.

Comprehensive Illustration

PROBLEM   (Estimated Time: 60 to 75 Minutes)

On January 1, 1991, Father Company purchased an 80 percent interest in Sun Company for $410,000. As of that date, Sun reported total stockholders' equity of $400,000: $100,000 in common stock and $300,000 in retained earnings. In setting the acquisition price, Father had appraised three accounts as having values different from the balances reported within Sun's financial records.

Buildings (eight-year life)	Undervalued by $20,000
Land	Undervalued by $50,000
Equipment (five-year life)	Undervalued by $12,500

Any goodwill recognized within this combination was to be amortized over a 30-year period.

As of December 31, 1995, the trial balances of these two companies are as follows:

	Father Company	Sun Company
Debits		
Current assets.	$ 620,000	$ 280,000
Investment in Sun Company	410,000	–0–
Land.	200,000	300,000
Buildings (net)	640,000	290,000
Equipment (net).	380,000	160,000
Expenses.	550,000	190,000
Dividends	90,000	20,000
Total debits.	$2,890,000	$1,240,000
Credits		
Liabilities.	$ 910,000	$ 300,000
Common stock	480,000	100,000
Retained earnings, 1/1/95	704,000	480,000
Revenues.	780,000	360,000
Dividend income	16,000	–0–
Total credits	$2,890,000	$1,240,000

Within these figures, Sun has a $20,000 debt to the parent company.

Required:

a. Determine consolidated totals for Father Company and Sun Company for the year of 1995. Assume that the parent company concept is to be applied.

b. Prepare worksheet entries to consolidate the trial balances of Father Company and Sun Company for the year of 1995.

c. Assume that Father acquires an additional 5 percent of the outstanding shares of Sun Company on December 31, 1995. Discuss the effects of this transaction on the consolidated figures computed in requirement *a*.

d. Assume that Father uses the economic unit concept rather than the parent company concept. Discuss the effects of this change on the consolidated figures computed in requirement *a*.

SOLUTION

a. The consolidation of Father Company and Sun Company should begin with the allocation of the purchase price as shown in Exhibit 4–12. This process is based on the parent company concept and the parent's $410,000 expenditure. Since this consolidation is taking place after several years, the unamortized balances for the various allocations at the start of the current year should also be determined (see Exhibit 4–13).

EXHIBIT 4–12

FATHER COMPANY AND SUN COMPANY
Purchase Price Allocation and Amortization
January 1, 1991

	Allocation	Estimated Life (years)	Annual Amortization
Purchase price paid by Father Company	$ 410,000		
80% of subsidiary $400,000 book value (Father Company's ownership)	(320,000)		
Cost in excess of book value	90,000		
Allocation to specific accounts based on fair market value:			
Buildings ($20,000 × 80%)	16,000	8	$ 2,000
Land ($50,000 × 80%)	40,000		
Equipment ($12,500 × 80%)	10,000	5	2,000
Goodwill	$ 24,000	30	800
Annual amortization expense			$ 4,800
1991–94 amortization expense ($4,800 × 4)			$19,200

EXHIBIT 4–13

FATHER COMPANY AND SUN COMPANY
Unamortized Cost Allocation
January 1, 1995, Balances

Account	Original Allocation	Amortization 1991–94	Unamortized Balance 1/1/95
Buildings	$16,000	$8,000	$ 8,000
Land	40,000	–0–	40,000
Equipment.	10,000	8,000	2,000
Goodwill	24,000	3,200	20,800
Total			$70,800

Next, the parent's method of accounting for its subsidiary should be ascertained. The continuing presence in the investment account of the original $410,000 acquisition price indicates that Father is applying the cost method. This same determination can be made from the Dividend Income account that equals 80 percent of the subsidiary's dividends. Thus, the increase in Sun's book value as well as the amortization expense for the prior periods of ownership have been ignored in Father's accounting records. These amounts have to be added to the parent's January 1, 1995, retained earnings to arrive at a properly consolidated balance.

During the 1991–94 period of ownership, Sun's Retained Earnings account rose by $180,000 ($480,000 − $300,000). Father's 80 percent interest necessitates an accrual of $144,000 ($180,000 × 80 percent) for these years. In addition, the purchase price allocations require the recognition of $19,200 in amortization expense for this same period ($4,800 × 4 years). Thus, a net increase of $124,800 ($144,000 − $19,200) is needed to correct the parent's beginning retained earnings balance for the year.

Once the adjustment from the cost method to the equity method has been determined, the consolidated figures for 1995 can be calculated:

Current assets = $880,000. The parent's book value is added to the subsidiary's book value. The $20,000 intercompany balance is eliminated.

Investment in Sun Company = –0–. The intercompany ownership is eliminated so that the subsidiary's specific assets and liabilities can be consolidated.

Land = $540,000. The parent's book value is added to the subsidiary's book value plus the purchase price allocation (see Exhibit 4–12).

Buildings (net) = $936,000. The parent's book value is added to the subsidiary's book value plus the related purchase price allocation (see Exhibit

4–13) after taking into account five years of amortization (1991 through 1995).

Equipment (net) = $540,000. The parent's book value is added to the subsidiary's book value. The purchase price allocation has been completely amortized after five years.

Expenses = $744,800. The parent's book value is added to the subsidiary's book value plus amortization expense on the purchase price allocations for the year (see Exhibit 4–12).

Dividends Paid = $90,000. The parent company dividends only are consolidated. The subsidiary's dividends that were paid to the parent are eliminated; the remainder serve as a reduction in the Noncontrolling Interest balance.

Goodwill = $20,000. The original residual allocation from the purchase price is recognized after taking into account five years of amortization (see Exhibit 4–13).

Noncontrolling Interest in Subsidiary's Income = $34,000. The outside owners are assigned a 20 percent share of the subsidiary's income (revenues of $360,000 less expenses of $190,000 or $170,000).

Total of Consolidated Debit Balances = $3,784,800. This figure is a summation of the preceding balances.

Liabilities = $1,190,000. The parent's book value is added to the subsidiary's book value. The $20,000 intercompany balance is eliminated.

Common Stock = $480,000. The parent company balance only is reported.

Retained Earnings, 1/1/95 = $828,800. The parent company balance only is reported after a $124,800 increase is made as explained earlier to convert the parent's use of the cost method to the equity method.

Revenues = $1,140,000. The parent's book value is added to the subsidiary's book value.

Dividend Income = –0–. The intercompany dividend receipts are eliminated.

Noncontrolling Interest in Subsidiary, 12/31/95 = $146,000. The beginning balance is $116,000, 20 percent of the subsidiary's 1/1/95 book value ($580,000 as shown by the stockholders' equity accounts). This figure is increased by the noncontrolling interest's share of net income ($34,000 as computed above). The dividends paid to the outside owners (20 percent of $20,000 or $4,000) serve to decrease in the balance. The consolidated total is then derived from these three balances.

Total of Consolidated Credit Balances = $3,784,800. This figure is a summation of the preceding balances.

b. *Six* worksheet entries are necessary to produce a consolidation worksheet for Father Company and Sun Company.

ENTRY *C

Investment in Sun Company.	124,800	
Retained Earnings, 1/1/95 (parent)		124,800

As discussed earlier, this increment is required to adjust the parent's retained earnings from the cost method to the equity method. The amount is $144,000 (80 percent of the $180,000 increase in the subsidiary's book value during previous years) less $19,200 in amortization over this same four-year period ($4,800 × 4 years).

ENTRY S

Common Stock (subsidiary)	100,000	
Retained Earnings, 1/1/95 (subsidiary).	480,000	
Investment in Sun Company (80 percent)		464,000
Noncontrolling Interest in Sun Company (20 percent).		116,000

To eliminate beginning stockholders' equity accounts of the subsidiary and recognize the beginning balance attributed to the outside owners (20 percent).

ENTRY A

Buildings	8,000	
Land	40,000	
Equipment.	2,000	
Goodwill	20,800	
Investment in Sun Company.		70,800

To recognize unamortized purchase price allocations as of the first day of the current year (see Exhibit 4–13).

ENTRY I

Dividend Income.	16,000	
Dividends Paid		16,000

To eliminate intercompany dividend payments recorded by parent (using the cost method) as income.

ENTRY E

Amortization Expense	4,800	
Buildings		2,000
Equipment.		2,000
Goodwill		800

To record amortization expense for the current year (see Exhibit 4–12).

    c. This question asks about the impact created by Father's purchase of an additional 5 percent of Sun on December 31, 1995. Three direct effects can be listed:

    1. All of the noncontrolling interest balances will be calculated as if only 15 percent of the subsidiary's shares had been held by outside parties during the entire year. This handling allows for production of financial statements that will be comparable with the results reported in future years.

    2. A Preacquisition Income account is established to reflect the portion of Sun's 1995 income (5 percent) accruing to the previous owners. This balance reduces consolidated net income for the current year. In addition, any dividends paid to former stockholders must be eliminated since this group no longer holds an equity interest in Sun.

3. Any cost in excess of book value paid by Father in this latest purchase must be allocated to specific accounts and then recognized within the consolidated balance sheet. Because the acquisition occurs at the end of the fiscal year, no additional amortization expense is necessary for 1995.

   d. When the economic unit concept is being used, the implied value of the subsidiary taken as a whole becomes of paramount importance. In *a.* the parent paid $410,000 for 80 percent of the subsidiary. Therefore, Sun's implied value was $512,500 ($410,000/80 percent). Because the company's book value was only $400,000, goodwill of $112,500 is appropriate ($512,500 − $400,000). In addition, the allocations made to buildings, land, and equipment are 100 percent of the difference between fair value and book value rather than only 80 percent. Since these allocations and goodwill are higher, subsequent amortization would also be higher each year.

   The noncontrolling interest's share of the subsidiary's net income is not reported on the consolidated income statement but rather as a separate allocation. This amount is based on the subsidiary's net income after deducting amortization expense which is attributed to the company's asset and liability accounts.

Questions

1. What is meant by the term *noncontrolling interest*?

2. Atwater Company acquires 80 percent of the outstanding voting stock of Belwood Company. On that date, Belwood possesses a building with a $160,000 book value but a fair market value of $220,000. Assuming that a bargain purchase has not been made, at what value would this building be consolidated under each of the following?

   a. Economic unit concept.

   b. Proportionate consolidation concept.

   c. Parent company concept.

3. Giant Company acquired 70 percent of Small Company at the beginning of 1995. Subsequently, Giant reports net income for 1995 of $60,000 (without regard for the investment in Small). For the same period, this subsidiary reports earnings of $30,000. In acquiring this interest, Giant paid a total of $224,000, although Small's book value was only $200,000 at the time. A building with a 10-year life was undervalued on Small's accounting records by $10,000. Any other excess amount was attributed to goodwill with a life of 40 years. Under each of the following, what is the consolidated net income for 1995 after reduction is made for the noncontrolling interest's claims?

   a. Economic unit concept.

   b. Proportionate consolidation concept.

   c. Parent company theory.

4. How does the parent company concept merge the ideas put forth under the economic unit concept and proportionate consolidation?

5. Where should the noncontrolling interest's claims be reported in a consolidated set of financial statements.

6. How is the noncontrolling interest in a subsidiary company calculated as of the end of the current year?

7. Consolidated financial statements are being prepared by Sandridge Company and its consolidated subsidiary. Preacquisition income of $55,000 is presented within these statements. What does this Preacquisition Income account represent? How was the amount computed?

8. Tree, Inc., has held a 10 percent interest in the stock of Limb Company for several years. Because of the level of ownership, this investment has been accounted for by means of the lower-of-cost-or-market-value method. At the beginning of the current year, Tree acquires an additional 70 percent interest which provides the company with control over Limb. In preparing consolidated financial statements for this business combination, how is the previous 10 percent ownership interest accounted for by Tree?

9. Duke Corporation owns a 70 percent equity interest in UNCCH, a subsidiary corporation. During the current year, a portion of this stock is sold to an outside party. Before recording this transaction, Duke adjusts the book value of its investment account. What is the purpose of this adjustment?

10. In Question 9, how would the parent record the sales transaction?

11. In Question 9, how would the parent record the sales transaction if the economic unit concept is being used and control is retained?

12. In Question 9, how would Duke account for the remainder of its investment subsequent to the sale of this partial interest?

Library Assignments

1. Read the following articles and any others that might be available discussing the method of accounting for a noncontrolling interest:

    "Consolidations: An Overview of the FASB DM," *Journal of Accountancy,* April 1992.

    "Revising GAAP for Consolidations: Join the Debate," *The CPA Journal,* July 1992.

    "A Closer Look at Consolidated Financial Statement Theory," *CA Magazine,* January and February 1975.

    "Consolidated Financial Statements—Understanding Their Theories," *The Woman CPA,* April 1984.

    "Proportionate Consolidation and Financial Analysis," *Accounting Horizons,* December 1992.

"Minority Interest: Opposing Views," *Journal of Accountancy*, March 1986.

Prepare a report to justify the selection of one particular concept of consolidated values where a noncontrolling interest is present as well as a preferred placement for the balances reported for the noncontrolling interest.

2. Obtain the latest financial statements for the Atlantic Richfield Corporation, Sara Lee Corporation, or any other company reporting a noncontrolling interest. Indicate the placement of both the balance sheet and the income statement figures. Describe the information conveyed about the noncontrolling interest within the reporting company's notes to its financial statements.

Problems

Note: Unless otherwise stated, assume that the parent company concept is being used.

1. Bailey, Inc. buys 60 percent of the outstanding stock of Luebs, Inc. in a purchase that resulted in the recognition of goodwill. Luebs owns a piece of land that cost $200,000 but was worth $500,000 at the date of purchase. For each of the three concepts described in this chapter, what value would be attributed to this land in a consolidated balance sheet at the date of takeover?

	Economic Unit Concept	Proportionate Consolidation	Parent Company Concept
a.	$500,000	$300,000	$500,000
b.	$200,000	$120,000	$500,000
c.	$200,000	$120,000	$380,000
d.	$500,000	$300,000	$380,000

2. Jordan, Inc. holds 75 percent of the outstanding stock of Paxson Corporation. Paxson currently owes Jordan $400,000 for inventory acquired over the past few months. In preparing consolidated financial statements, what amount of this debt should be eliminated?
   a. $0.
   b. $100,000.
   c. $300,000.
   d. $400,000.

3. On January 1, 1995, Brendan, Inc., reports net assets of $760,000 although equipment (with a four-year life) having a book value of $440,000 is worth $500,000. Hope Corporation pays $692,000 on that date for an 80 percent ownership in Brendan. If goodwill is to be written off over a 10-year period, what is the consolidated goodwill balance on December 31, 1996?
   a. $20,800.
   b. $28,800.
   c. $34,200.
   d. $67,200.

4. On January 1, 1995, Turner Inc., reports net assets of $480,000 although a building (with a 10-year life) having a book value of $260,000 is now worth $310,000. Plaster Corporation pays $400,000 on that date for a 70 percent ownership in Turner. On December 31, 1997, Turner reports a Building account of $245,000 while Plaster reports a Building account of $510,000. What is the consolidated balance of the Building account?
   a. $779,500.
   b. $783,500.
   c. $790,000.
   d. $805.000.

5. On January 1, 1995, Hygille, Inc., reports net assets of $880,000 although a building (with a 20-year life) having a book value of $330,000 is now worth $400,000. Nuyt Corporation pays $840,000 on that date for an 80 percent ownership in Hygille. Goodwill is to be written off over its maximum life. On December 31, 1997, Hygille reports total expenses of $621,000 while Nuyt reports expenses of $714,000. What is the consolidated expense balance?
   a. $1,336,000.
   b. $1,338,000.
   c. $1,338,500.
   d. $1,339,800.

6. On January 1, 1995, Neville Inc., reports net assets of $540,000 although equipment (with a five-year life) having a book value of $90,000 is worth $130,000. Chamberlain Corporation pays $388,000 on that date for a 60 percent ownership in Neville. Goodwill is to be written off over a 10-year period. On December 31, 1997, Neville reports revenues of $400,000 and expenses of $300,000 while Chamberlain reports revenues of $700,000 and expenses of $400,000. The parent figures contain no income from the subsidiary. What is consolidated net income?
   a. $349,600.
   b. $351,200.
   c. $360,000.
   d. $391,200.

7. What is a basic premise of the economic unit concept?
   a. Consolidated financial statements should be primarily for the benefit of the stockholders of the parent company.
   b. Consolidated financial statements should only be produced if both the parent and the subsidiary are in the same basic industry.
   c. A subsidiary is an indivisible part of a business combination and should be included in whole regardless of the degree of ownership.
   d. Consolidated financial statements should not report a noncontrolling interest balance since these outside owners do not hold stock in the parent company.

8. A preacquisition income account.
   a. Is an adjustment to retained earnings when a pooling of interests is created.
   b. Is a reduction in consolidated net income that allows a subsidiary's revenues and expenses to be reported for the entire year even though acquisition took place during the current year.
   c. Is an income figure that requires the parent to pay an additional amount to create a business combination.
   d. Is the balance in a subsidiary's retained earnings account on the date that a business combination is created.

9. Ames, Inc., has a book value of $400,000 on January 1, 1995, and $550,000 on January 1, 1997. On both dates, the book value of the company's assets and liabilities were the same as fair market value. Hitchcock Corporation acquires 30 percent of Ames on January 1, 1995, for $160,000 in cash. Hitchcock purchases an additional 40 percent of Ames on January 1, 1997, for $240,000. Goodwill is being amortized over its maximum life. On a consolidated balance sheet as of December 31, 1997, what amount of goodwill is reported?
   a. $60,000.
   b. $57,000.
   c. $56,500.
   d. $55,500.

10. A parent buys 32 percent of a subsidiary in 1994 and then buys an additional 40 percent in 1996. In a step acquisition of this type, how does the economic unit concept differ from the parent company concept?
    a. In using the economic unit concept, all subsequent purchases are valued based on the implied value at the time of the first acquisition.
    b. In using the economic unit concept, the two purchases are recorded as separate acquisitions with their own allocations and goodwill.
    c. In using the economic unit concept, the first purchase is adjusted to its implied value based on the acquisition price of the second transaction with a resulting gain or loss being recorded.
    d. The economic unit concept views each company as a whole and, thus, cannot be applied unless 100 percent of the subsidiary's stock is held.

11. On April 1, 1995, Guns, Inc., purchases 70 percent of the outstanding stock of Roses Corporation for $430,000. The subsidiary's book value on that date was $500,000. Any resulting goodwill will be amortized over 40 years. During 1995, Roses generates revenues of $600,000 and expenses of $360,000. Both figures occur evenly throughout the year. On a consolidated income statement for the year ending December 31, 1995, what should be reported as the noncontrolling interest in the subsidiary's net income and as preacquisition income?
    a. $72,000 and $42,000.
    b. $70,500 and $60,000.

c. $70,500 and $40,500.

d. $72,000 and $41,650.

Problems 12 through 14 relate to the following information: David Company acquired 60 percent of Mark Company for $300,000 when Mark's book value was $400,000. On that date, Mark had equipment (with a 10-year life) that was undervalued in the financial records by $60,000. Any goodwill is amortized over 40 years. Two years later, the following figures are reported by these two companies (stockholders' equity accounts have been omitted).

	David Company Book Value	Mark Company Book Value	Mark Company Fair Market Value
Current assets	$ 620,000	$ 300,000	$ 320,000
Equipment.	260,000	200,000	280,000
Buildings	410,000	150,000	150,000
Liabilities	(390,000)	(120,000)	(120,000)
Revenues	(900,000)	(400,000)	
Expenses	500,000	300,000	
Investment income	Not Given		

12. What is consolidated net income prior to the reduction for the noncontrolling interest's share of the subsidiary's income?

    a. $455,800.

    b. $460,000.

    c. $494,000.

    d. $495,800.

13. What is the noncontrolling interest's share of the subsidiary's income and what is the ending balance of the noncontrolling interest in the subsidiary?

    a. $42,000 and $196,000.

    b. $40,000 and $212,000.

    c. $38,320 and $217,400.

    d. $37,600 and $224,000.

14. What is the consolidated balance of the Equipment account?

    a. $488,800.

    b. $498,400.

    c. $500,800.

    d. $508,000.

Problems 15 through 19 relate to the following information: On January 1, 1995, Polk Corporation and Strass Corporation had condensed balance sheets as follows:

	Polk	*Strass*
Current assets	$ 70,000	$20,000
Noncurrent assets.	90,000	40,000
Total assets	$160,000	$60,000
Current liabilities	$ 30,000	$10,000
Long-term debt	50,000	—
Stockholders' equity	80,000	50,000
Total liabilities and equities	$160,000	$60,000

On January 2, 1995, Polk borrowed $60,000 and used the proceeds to purchase 90 percent of the outstanding common shares of Strass. This debt is payable in 10 equal annual principal payments, plus interest, beginning December 31, 1995. The excess cost of the investment over the underlying book value of the acquired net assets is allocated to inventory (60 percent) and to goodwill (40 percent). On a consolidated balance sheet as of January 2, 1995,

15. Current assets should be:
    a. $99,000.
    b. $96,000.
    c. $90,000.
    d. $79,000.

16. Noncurrent assets should be:
    a. $130,000.
    b. $134,000.
    c. $136,000.
    d. $140,000.

17. Current liabilities should be:
    a. $50,000.
    b. $46,000.
    c. $40,000.
    d. $30,000.

18. Noncurrent liabilities, including noncontrolling interest, should be:
    a. $115,000.
    b. $109,000.
    c. $104,000.
    d. $55,000.

19. Stockholders' equity should be:
    a. $80,000.
    b. $85,000.
    c. $90,000.
    d. $130,000.
    (AICPA adapted)

20. On January 1, 1995, Harrison, Inc., purchased 90 percent of Starr Company. Annual amortization of $8,000 resulted from this transaction. Starr Company reported a Common Stock account of $100,000 and Retained Earnings of $200,000 at that date. The subsidiary earned $70,000 in 1995 and $90,000 in 1996 with dividend payments of $30,000 each year. Without regard for this investment, Harrison had income of $220,000 in 1995 and $260,000 in 1996.

  a. What is consolidated net income in each of these two years?

  b. What is the ending noncontrolling interest balance as of December 31, 1996?

21. Pistol, Inc., purchases 70 percent of Bytvl Company for $400,000. On that date, Bytvl had the following accounts:

	Book Value	Fair Market Value
Current assets	$210,000	$210,000
Land	170,000	180,000
Buildings	300,000	330,000
Liabilities	280,000	280,000

The buildings have a 10-year life and any resulting goodwill will be amortized over 20 years. In addition, Bytvl holds a patent worth $20,000 that has a five-year life but is not recorded on its financial records.

  a. Assume that the purchase took place on January 1, 1995. At the end of 1995, the two companies report the following balances:

	Pistol	Bytvl
Revenues	$900,000	$600,000
Expenses	600,000	400,000

  What figures would appear in a consolidated income statement for this year?

  b. Assume that the purchase took place on April 1, 1995. At the end of 1995, the two companies report the following balances:

	Pistol	Bytvl
Revenues	$760,000	$590,000
Expenses	540,000	380,000

  What figures would appear in a consolidated income statement for this year?

22. On January 1, 1995, Alva Company has one asset, an invention with a cost of $10,000. The asset has an estimated life of 10 years and a fair market value of $50,000. Menlo, Inc. buys 60 percent of the outstanding stock of Alva on that date for $40,000.

    During 1995, Alva generates revenues of $50,000 and expenses of $20,000. Any goodwill is to be amortized over its maximum possible life.

Required:

For each of the following, determine the amounts included in the 1995 consolidated financial statements for Alva's revenues, expenses (plus amortization, if applicable), noncontrolling interest in the subsidiary's income, goodwill, and the invention:

    a. Economic unit concept.

    b. Proportionate consolidation.

    c. Parent company concept.

23. Mabry, Inc. purchases 60 percent of Thompson Corporation on August 1, 1995, and an additional 30 percent on October 1, 1996. Annual amortization of $6,000 relates to the first acquisition and $10,000 to the second. Thompson reports the following figures for 1996:

Revenues.	$600,000
Expenses.	420,000
Retained earnings, 1/1/96.	540,000
Dividends paid	70,000
Common stock	310,000

    Without regard for this investment, Mabry earns $360,000 in net income during 1996.

    a. What is consolidated net income for 1996?

    b. What is the noncontrolling interest as of December 31, 1996?

24. Clark Corporation acquired 50 percent of Lamp, Inc. several years ago and an additional 30 percent on April 1 of the current year. Goodwill of $60,000 was computed in connection with the first acquisition, and that amount is being amortized over its maximum life. The following figures are reported by these two companies for the current year. Investment income is not included within the balances for Clark shown here. Income is assumed to have been earned evenly throughout the year, and no dividends were paid.

	Clark Corporation	Lamp, Inc.
Revenues	$600,000	$500,000
Expenses	380,000	300,000

     a. What is the noncontrolling interest's share of the subsidiary's net income?

     b. What is the amount of preacquisition income?

     c. What is the consolidated net income for these two companies?

25. Wilson Company acquired 7,000 of the 10,000 outstanding shares of Green Company on January 1, 1991, for $800,000. The subsidiary's book value on that date was $1,000,000. Any cost of this purchase in excess of Green's book value was assigned to goodwill with a 10-year life. On January 1, 1995, Wilson reported a $1,085,000 balance in the Investment in Green Company account based on application of the partial equity method. On October 1, 1995, Wilson sells 1,000 shares of the investment for $191,000. During 1995, Green reported net income of $120,000 and paid dividends of $40,000. These amounts are assumed to have been incurred evenly throughout the year.

     a. How are the 1,000 shares reported for the period from January 1, 1995, until October 1, 1995?

     b. What is the effect on net income of this sale of 1,000 shares?

     c. What accounting is now made of the 6,000 shares that Wilson continues to hold?

26. Robert Palmer and Anita Blackwood are the sole owners of Quinn Corporation. Palmer holds 70 percent of the stock while Blackwood owns the remaining 30 percent. On January 1, 1995, Quinn reports $10,000 in common stock and $90,000 in retained earnings. During each month of 1995, the company earns $15,000 in net income. Dividends of $5,000 are paid every month. At the end of the year, Quinn's net income is $180,000 (revenues of $400,000 less $220,000 in expenses), while $60,000 in dividends have been paid.

     The book value of Quinn Corporation on December 1, 1995, is $210,000 ($100,000 beginning balance plus $10,000 growth for 11 months). On that date, Brown, Inc., buys all of Palmer's interest. Blackwood retains her 30 percent share of the company's stock. Brown pays exactly book value for these shares ($147,000 or 70 percent of $210,000). The individual fair market values of Quinn's assets and liabilities are equal to their book values.

     Brown, Inc., is currently preparing consolidated financial statements for the year ending December 31, 1995.

     a. What amount of Quinn's revenues would be included in the consolidated income statement?

     b. What balance should be reported as the noncontrolling interest in Quinn's net income? Who is the noncontrolling interest?

     c. For consolidation purposes, what happens to the $3,500 per month in dividends that Palmer received for the first 11 months of the year?

     d. What amount of preacquisition income should be reported for consolidation purposes? Where is this figure disclosed? To whom does this income accrue?

27. Narcissus acquired 80 percent of the outstanding stock of Goldmund for $156,000. Just prior to this purchase, the following information is gathered from the two companies:

	Narcissus Book Value	Goldmund Book Value	Goldmund Fair Market Value
Current assets	$500,000	$150,000	$150,000
Land	100,000	30,000	40,000
Buildings and equipment (net)	600,000	160,000	180,000
Liabilities	300,000	200,000	200,000
Common stock	400,000	40,000	
Retained earnings.	500,000	100,000	

The buildings and equipment have a 10-year remaining life; any goodwill will be amortized over a 40-year period.

Subsequently, on December 31, 1995, the two companies are reporting the following account balances. Fair market values are presented where applicable.

	Narcissus Book Value	Goldmund Book Value	Goldmund Fair Market Value
Current assets	$300,000	$ 90,000	$ 90,000
Investment in Goldmund	156,000	–0–	–0–
Land.	150,000	60,000	74,000
Buildings and equipment (net)	570,000	180,000	216,000
Liabilities	246,000	185,000	185,000
Common stock	400,000	40,000	
Retained earnings, January 1, 1995	470,000	95,000	
Revenues.	300,000	100,000	
Expenses.	200,000	90,000	
Dividends paid	40,000	–0–	

Required:

a. On consolidated financial statements as of the date of acquisition, what balances are reported for the Buildings and Equipment account and the Goodwill account?

b. Assume that the purchase was made on January 1, 1991. What would be the consolidated Buildings and Equipment balance and the consolidated Goodwill balance on December 31, 1995?

c. Assume that the purchase was made during 1993. What is the consolidated net income for 1995 before subtracting the noncontrolling interest's share of the subsidiary's income?

d. Assume that the purchase was made during 1993. What is the noncontrolling interest's share of the subsidiary's income for the year ending December 31, 1995?

e. Assume that the purchase was made on July 1, 1995. Prepare a consolidated income statement for the year ending December 31, 1995.

f. Assume that the purchase was made on January 1, 1994. On October 1, 1995, Narcissus sells one-fourth of these shares for $82,000 in cash. What income effects appear on the consolidated income statement for 1995?

28. On January 1, 1993, Thacker acquires 70 percent of Barker in a purchase transaction. The new subsidiary reported common stock on that date of $300,000 with retained earnings of $180,000. A building was undervalued in the company's financial records by $20,000. This building had a 10-year remaining life. Goodwill of $60,000 is being amortized over its maximum life.

    Barker earns income and pays cash dividends as follows:

	Net Income	Dividends Paid
1993	$ 75,000	$39,000
1994	96,000	44,000
1995	110,000	60,000

    On December 31, 1995, Thacker owes $22,000 to Barker.

    a. If the equity method has been applied by Thacker, what are the consolidation entries needed as of December 31, 1995?

    b. If the cost method has been applied by Thacker, what Entry *C is needed for a 1995 consolidation?

    c. If the partial equity method has been applied by Thacker, what Entry *C is needed for a 1995 consolidation?

    d. What noncontrolling interest balances will appear in consolidated financial statements for 1995?

29. The Hearts Company acquired an 80 percent interest in Dylan Company as of January 1, 1994. Hearts paid $620,000 to the owners of Dylan to purchase these shares. In addition, Hearts paid several lawyers and merger analysts $44,000 for assisting in the acquisition.

    On January 1, 1994, Dylan reported a book value of $600,000 (common stock—$300,000; additional paid-in capital—$90,000; retained earnings—$210,000). Several of Dylan's buildings were undervalued by a total of $80,000. These buildings had a remaining life of 20 years. Any goodwill resulting from the takeover was assumed to have a 30-year life.

    During the 1994–96 time period, Dylan reported the following figures:

Year	Net Income	Dividends Paid
1994. . .	$ 70,000	$10,000
1995. . .	90,000	15,000
1996. . .	100,000	20,000

Required:

Determine the appropriate answers for each of the following questions:

a. What amount of amortization expense would be recognized in the consolidated financial statements for the initial years following this purchase?

b. If a consolidated balance sheet is prepared as of January 1, 1994, what amount of goodwill would be recognized?

c. If a consolidation worksheet is prepared as of January 1, 1994, what Entry S should be included?

d. On the separate financial records of the parent company, what amount of investment income would be reported for 1994 under each of the following accounting methods:

(1) The equity method.

(2) The partial equity method.

(3) The cost method.

e. On the separate financial records of the parent company, what would be the December 31, 1996, balance for the Investment in Dylan Company account under each of the following accounting methods:

(1) The equity method.

(2) The partial equity method.

(3) The cost method.

f. As of December 31, 1995, Hearts has a Buildings account on its separate records with a balance of $800,000 while Dylan has a similar account with a $300,000 balance. What would be the consolidated balance for the Buildings account? What would be the balance if the economic unit concept is used?

g. What would be the balance of consolidated goodwill as of December 31, 1996?

h. Assume that the parent company has been applying the equity method to this investment. On December 31, 1996, the separate financial statements for the two companies present the following information:

	Hearts Company	Dylan Company
Common stock	$500,000	$300,000
Additional paid-in capital	280,000	90,000
Retained earnings, 12/31/96 . . .	620,000	425,000

What will be the consolidated balance of each of these accounts?

i. Answer the same question as in requirement *h.*, but assume that the parent has been applying the partial equity method.

30. Following are several of the account balances taken from the records of Bigston and Lytle as of December 31, 1995. A few asset accounts have been omitted here. All revenues, expenses, and dividends occurred evenly throughout the year. Any goodwill is to be amortized over 30 years.

	Bigston	*Lytle*
Sales.	$ 800,000	$500,000
Cost of goods sold.	400,000	280,000
Expenses.	200,000	100,000
Investment income	not given	–0–
Retained earnings, 1/1/95.	1,400,000	700,000
Dividends	80,000	20,000
Land.	600,000	200,000
Buildings (net).	700,000	300,000
Equipment (net).	400,000	400,000
Liabilities	500,000	200,000
Common stock ($10 par value)	400,000	100,000
Additional paid-in capital.	500,000	600,000

On July 1, 1995, Bigston purchased 80 percent of Lytle for $1,300,000 in cash. In addition, Big paid $30,000 in direct consolidation costs. At that time, Lytle's buildings (with a 10-year life) were undervalued on its books by $100,000. On a consolidation prepared at the end of 1995, what balances would be reported for the following:

Preacquisition Income	Net Income
Sales	Retained Earnings, 1/1/95
Expenses	Buildings (Net)
Noncontrolling Interest in	Land
Subsidiary's Net Income	Goodwill

31. Monroe, Inc., acquires 60 percent of Sunrise Corporation for $414,000 cash on January 1, 1995. On that date, Sunrise had the following accounts:

	Book Value	*Fair Market Value*
Current Assets	$150,000	$150,000
Land	200,000	200,000
Buildings (net) (6-year life).	300,000	360,000
Equipment (net) (4-year life)	300,000	280,000
Liabilities	400,000	400,000

The companies' financial statements for the year ending December 31, 1998, follow. Determine all consolidated balances. Goodwill has a 10-year life.

	Monroe	Sunrise
Revenues.	$ 600,000	$ 300,000
Expenses.	410,000	210,000
Investment income.	42,000	
Net income	$ 232,000	$ 90,000
Retained earnings, 1/1/98	$ 700,000	$ 300,000
Net income	232,000	90,000
Dividends paid	92,000	70,000
Retained earnings, 12/31/98	$ 840,000	$ 320,000
Current assets.	$ 330,000	$ 100,000
Land	220,000	200,000
Buildings (net).	700,000	200,000
Equipment (net)	400,000	500,000
Investment in Sunrise	414,000	–0–
Total assets.	$2,064,000	$1,000,000
Liabilities.	$ 500,000	$ 200,000
Common stock	724,000	480,000
Retained earning, 12/31/98	840,000	320,000
Total liabilities and equities.	$2,064,000	$1,000,000

Answer the following questions:
a. How can the accountant determine that the cost method has been applied by the parent?
b. What is the annual amortization initially recognized in connection with this purchase?
c. If the partial equity method had been applied, what Investment Income would have been recorded by the parent in 1998? What if the equity method had been applied?
d. What is the consolidated balance for retained earnings as of January 1, 1998?
e. What is the noncontrolling interest in the subsidiary's 1998 income?
f. What is consolidated net income for 1998?
g. Within consolidated statements at January 1, 1995, what balance is included for the subsidiary's Buildings account?
h. What is the consolidated Buildings account as of December 31, 1998?

32. Father, Inc., buys 80 percent of the outstanding common stock of Sam Corporation on January 1, 1995, for $680,000 cash. Total book value of Sam on that date was only $600,000. However, Sam possessed several accounts that had fair market values differing from their book values:

	Book Value	Fair Market Value
Land	$160,000	$225,000
Buildings and equipment (10-year remaining life)	275,000	250,000
Notes payable (due in 8 years).	130,000	120,000

Any goodwill indicated by the purchase price is to be amortized over the maximum possible life. For internal reporting purposes, Father Inc. employs the equity method to account for this investment.

The following account balances are for the year ending December 31, 1995, for both companies. Determine consolidated balances for this business combination (either through individual computations or the use of a worksheet).

	Father	Sam
Revenues	$(1,360,000)	$(540,000)
Expenses	1,004,000	405,000
Equity in income of Sam	(105,000)	–0–
Net income	$ (461,000)	$(135,000)
Retained earnings, 1/1/95	$(1,265,000)	$(440,000)
Net income (above)	(461,000)	(135,000)
Dividends paid	260,000	65,000
Retained earnings, 12/31/95	$(1,466,000)	$(510,000)
Current assets.	$ 965,000	$ 528,000
Investment in Sam.	733,000	–0–
Land.	292,000	160,000
Buildings and equipment (net).	877,000	260,000
Total assets	$ 2,867,000	$ 948,000
Accounts payable	$ (191,000)	$(148,000)
Notes payable.	(460,000)	(130,000)
Common stock	(300,000)	(100,000)
Additional paid-in capital	(450,000)	(60,000)
Retained earnings (above)	(1,466,000)	(510,000)
Total liabilities and equities	$(2,867,000)	$(948,000)

NOTE: Credits are indicated by parenthesis.

33. Answer problem 32 again, this time use the economic unit concept.

34. Burke Corporation purchased 90 percent of the outstanding voting shares of Drexel, Inc., on December 31, 1993. Burke paid a total of $602,000 in cash for these shares. As of that date, Drexel had the following account balances:

	Book Value	Fair Market Value
Current assets	$160,000	$160,000
Land	120,000	150,000
Building (10-year life).	220,000	200,000
Equipment (5-year life)	160,000	200,000
Patents (10-year life)	–0–	50,000
Liabilities (5-year life)	200,000	180,000
Common stock.	180,000	
Retained earnings, 12/31/93	280,000	

The following adjusted trial balances are for these two companies on December 31, 1995:

	Burke Corporation	Drexel, Inc.
Debits		
Current Assets	$ 611,000	$ 250,000
Land	380,000	150,000
Buildings.	490,000	250,000
Equipment	873,000	150,000
Investment in Drexel, Inc.	701,000	–0–
Expenses.	620,000	160,000
Dividends Paid	110,000	70,000
Total Debits	$3,785,000	$1,030,000
Credits		
Liabilities	$ 860,000	$ 230,000
Common Stock	510,000	180,000
Retained Earnings, 1/1/95	1,367,000	340,000
Revenues	940,000	280,000
Investment Income	108,000	–0–
Total Credits	$3,785,000	$1,030,000

Required:

a. Without using a worksheet or consolidation entries, determine the balances to be reported as of December 31, 1995, for this business combination. Any goodwill will be amortized over the maximum possible life.

b. To verify the figures determined in requirement a., prepare a consolidation worksheet for Burke Corporation and Drexel, Inc., as of December 31, 1995.

35. Using the information presented in problem 34, produce a worksheet to consolidate the financial statements of Burke and Drexel incorporating the economic unit concept rather than the parent company concept.

36. Following are the individual financial statements for Up and Down for the year ending December 31, 1995:

	Up	Down
Sales	$ 600,000	$ 300,000
Cost of goods sold	300,000	140,000
Operating expenses	174,000	60,000
Dividend income	24,000	–0–
Net income	$ 150,000	$ 100,000
Retained earnings, 1/1/95	$ 700,000	$ 400,000
Net income	150,000	100,000
Dividends paid	80,000	40,000
Retained earnings, 12/31/95	$ 770,000	$ 460,000
Cash and receivables	$ 250,000	$ 100,000
Inventory	500,000	190,000
Investment in Down	526,000	–0–
Buildings (net)	524,000	600,000
Equipment (net)	400,000	400,000
Total assets	$2,200,000	$1,290,000
Liabilities	800,000	490,000
Common stock	630,000	340,000
Retained earnings, 12/31/95	770,000	460,000
Totals liabilities and stockholders' equity	$2,200,000	$1,290,000

Up acquired 60 percent of Down on April 1, 1995, for $526,000. On that date, equipment (with a six-year life) was overvalued by $30,000. Goodwill is to be amortized over five years. Income is earned by Down evenly during the year but the dividend was paid entirely on November 1, 1995.

Required:

a. Prepare a consolidated income statement for the year ending December 31, 1995.

b. Determine the consolidated balance for each of the following accounts as of December 31, 1995:

    Goodwill   Buildings (net)

    Equipment (net)   Dividends Paid

    Common Stock

37. Bon Air, Inc., acquired 70 percent (2,800 shares) of the outstanding voting stock of Creedmoor Corporation on January 1, 1992, for $250,000 cash. Creedmoor's net assets on that date totaled $230,000, but this balance included three accounts having actual values that differed from their book values:

	Book Value	Fair Market Value
Land	$30,000	$40,000
Equipment (20-year life)	50,000	30,000
Liabilities (10-year life)	70,000	50,000

Any goodwill created by this combination will be amortized over a 20-year life.

As of December 31, 1995, the two companies report the following balances:

	Bon Air	Creedmoor
Revenues.	$ 694,800	$250,000
Expenses.	(630,000)	(180,000)
Investment income	44,200	–0–
Net income.	$ 109,000	$ 70,000
Retained earnings, January 1, 1995	$ 760,000	$260,000
Net income.	109,000	70,000
Dividends paid	(68,000)	(10,000)
Retained earnings, December 31, 1995.	$ 801,000	$320,000
Current assets	$ 72,000	$120,000
Investment in Creedmoor Corp..	321,800	–0–
Land.	241,000	50,000
Buildings (net)	289,000	200,000
Equipment (net).	165,200	40,000
Total assets.	$1,089,000	$410,000
Liabilities	$ 180,000	$ 50,000
Common stock	50,000	40,000
Additional paid-in capital.	58,000	–0–
Retained earnings, December 31, 1995.	801,000	320,000
Total liabilities and equities.	$1,089,000	$410,000

Required:

(Each of the following are independent questions.)

a. Consolidated financial statements are being prepared on December 31, 1995. What balance should be reported for each of the following figures?

Expenses

Noncontrolling interest in Creedmore's net income

Revenues

Retained earnings, January 1, 1995

Net income

Dividends paid

Land

Equipment

Liabilities

Common stock

Retained earnings, December 31, 1995

Noncontrolling interest in Creedmore, December 31, 1995

b. If Bon Air sells 400 shares of this stock on December 31, 1995, for $60,000 cash, what journal entry is recorded?

38. The Seals Corporation purchased 80 percent of the outstanding stock of Croft, Inc. for $384,000. An appraisal of Croft made on that date determined that all book values appropriately reflected the actual worth of the underlying accounts except that a building with a 10-year life was undervalued by $20,000.

    Following are the separate financial statements for the year ending December 31, 1995. Croft's income is assumed to have been earned evenly throughout the year. In addition, the subsidiary's dividend payments have been made as four equal quarterly payments. Seals has inappropriately included the receipt of dividends in its Sales account rather than a separate Dividend Income account.

	Seals Corporation	Croft, Inc.
Sales	$ 600,000	$210,000
Cost of goods sold	(200,000)	(80,000)
Operating expenses.	(246,000)	(70,000)
Dividend income	–0–	–0–
Net income	$ 154,000	$ 60,000
Retained earnings, 1/1/95	$ 700,000	$280,000
Net income (above)	154,000	60,000
Dividends paid.	(70,000)	(20,000)
Retained earnings, 12/31/95	$ 784,000	$320,000
Current assets	$ 400,000	$220,000
Investment in Croft, Inc.	384,000	–0–
Buildings (net)	320,000	180,000
Equipment (net)	360,000	210,000
Total assets	$1,464,000	$610,000
Liabilities	$ 470,000	$190,000
Common stock.	210,000	100,000
Retained earnings, 12/31/95 (above)	784,000	320,000
Total liabilities and equities	$1,464,000	$610,000

Any goodwill indicated by this consolidation will be amortized over the maximum possible life.

Required:
  a. *Prepare* a worksheet to consolidate these two companies on the assumption that the purchase was made on January 1, 1995.
  b. *Without* using a worksheet determine consolidated totals for these two companies on the assumption that the purchase was made on October 1, 1995.

 39. Watson, Inc. acquires 60 percent of Houston, Inc. on January 1, 1992, for $400,000 in cash. On that date, assets and liabilities of the subsidiary had the following values:

	Book Values	Fair Market Values
Current assets	$320,000	$320,000
Equipment (net)(10-year life)	410,000	380,000
Buildings (net)(20-year life)	300,000	360,000
Current liabilities.	190,000	190,000
Bonds payable (due in 10 years)	370,000	350,000

Goodwill will be amortized over a 40-year period.

On December 31, 1995, these two companies report the following figures:

	Watson	Houston
Revenues.	$ 640,000	$ 280,000
Expenses.	(480,000)	(210,000)
Equity in subsidiary earnings	38,600	–0–
Net income.	$ 198,600	$ 70,000
Retained earnings, 1/1/95	$ 690,000	$ 380,000
Net income.	198,600	70,000
Dividends paid	(60,200)	(40,000)
Retained earnings, 12/31/95	$ 828,400	$ 410,000
Current assets	$ 215,000	$ 260,000
Investment in Houston.	500,400	–0–
Equipment (net).	500,000	420,000
Buildings (net)	413,000	520,000
Total assets.	$1,628,400	$1,200,000
Current liabilities	$ 390,000	$ 170,000
Bonds payable	100,000	370,000
Common stock	310,000	250,000
Retained earnings, 12/31/95	828,400	410,000
Total liabilities and equities.	$1,628,400	$1,200,000

Answer each of the following questions:
a. The parent is recognizing a $38,600 balance as its "equity in subsidiary earnings." How was this balance calculated?
b. Is an adjustment needed to the parent's retained earnings as of January 1, 1995? Why or why not?
c. How much amortization expense should be recognized for consolidation purposes in 1995?
d. What is the noncontrolling interest in the subsidiary's net income?
e. Prepare a consolidated income statement.
f. What allocations were made as a result of the purchase price? What amount of each allocation remains at the end of 1995?
g. What is the December 31, 1995, noncontrolling interest in the subsidiary? What three components make up this total?
h. Prepare a consolidated balance sheet.

40. Good Corporation acquired 80 percent of the outstanding stock of Morning, Inc., on January 1, 1992, for $1,400,000 in cash, debt, and stock. One of Morning's buildings, with a 10-year remaining life, was undervalued on the company's accounting records by $80,000. Any goodwill resulting from this transaction was also to be amortized over a 10-year period.

During subsequent years, Morning reports the following:

	Net Income	Dividends Paid
1992	$180,000	$100,000
1993	200,000	100,000
1994	300,000	100,000
1995	400,000	120,000

The following trial balances are for these two companies as of December 31, 1995. Morning owes Good $100,000 as of this date.

	Good	Morning
Debits		
Cash	$ 300,000	$ 200,000
Receivables	700,000	400,000
Inventory	400,000	500,000
Investment in Morning	1,400,000	–0–
Land	700,000	600,000
Buildings (net)	300,000	700,000
Expenses	400,000	100,000
Dividends paid	380,000	120,000
Total debits	$4,580,000	$2,620,000
Credits		
Liabilities	$ 200,000	$ 620,000
Common stock	1,000,000	460,000
Additional paid-in capital	600,000	40,000
Retained earnings, 1/1/95	1,800,000	1,000,000
Revenues	884,000	500,000
Dividend income	96,000	–0–
Total credits	$4,580,000	$2,620,000

Prepare consolidated financial statements for this business combination.

41. On January 1, 1995, Turner Company bought a 30 percent interest in Atlanta Company. The acquisition price was $257,000 and was negotiated under the assumption that all of Atlanta's accounts were fairly valued within the company's accounting records. During 1995, Atlanta reported net income of $90,000 and paid cash dividends of $60,000. Turner felt that the ability to significantly influence the operations of Atlanta had been achieved and, therefore, accounted for this investment by means of the equity method.

On April 1, 1996, Turner acquired an additional 30 percent interest in Atlanta for $309,000 in cash. As of this date, the parent believed that a patent developed by Atlanta was worth $100,000, even though it was not recorded within the financial records of the subsidiary. This patent is anticipated to have a remaining life of 15 years. Although the financial statements now have to be consolidated, Turner elects to continue applying the equity method to this investment for internal reporting purposes.

The following financial information is for these two companies for 1996. Assume that any goodwill will be amortized over a 10-year life. In addition, all of the subsidiary's operations as well as dividend payments are considered to have occurred evenly throughout the year.

	Turner Company	Atlanta Company
Revenues.	$ 660,000	$ 400,000
Expenses.	(398,000)	(280,000)
Income of subsidiary	57,250	
Net income.	$ 319,250	$ 120,000
Retained earnings, beginning balance	$ 821,000	$ 500,000
Net income (above)	319,250	120,000
Cash dividends paid to stockholders.	(148,000)	(80,000)
Retained earnings, ending balance.	$ 992,250	$ 540,000
Current assets	$ 481,000	$ 410,000
Investment in subsidiary	588,250	
Land.	388,000	200,000
Buildings.	700,900	630,000
Total assets.	$2,158,150	$1,240,000
Liabilities	$ 660,900	$ 380,000
Common stock	95,000	300,000
Additional paid-in capital.	410,000	20,000
Retained earnings, ending balance.	992,250	540,000
Total liabilities and equities.	$2,158,150	$1,240,000

Answer the following questions:

a. What allocation would Turner have made of the initial $257,000 acquisition price?

b. What is the book value of the Investment in Atlanta account at the end of 1995?

c. What allocation would Turner have made of the second $309,000 acquisition price?

d. On Turner's separate income statement for 1996, the Income of Subsidiary account has a balance of $57,250. How was this amount derived?

e. On Turner's separate balance sheet as of December 31, 1996, the Investment of Subsidiary account reports a balance of $588,250. How was this balance derived?

f. What is the consolidated retained earnings balance as of January 1, 1996? How is this amount determined?

g. Prepare a worksheet to consolidate the financial statements of these two companies as of December 31, 1996.

42. On January 1, 1995, Ace, Incorporated acquired 60 percent of the outstanding shares of Holt Company for $566,000 in cash. At the time of this purchase, Holt held a building (10 year remaining life) that was undervalued in the accounting records by $100,000. During 1995, Holt reported net income of $150,000 and paid cash dividends of $80,000. On May 1, 1996, Ace bought an additional 30 percent interest in Holt for $366,000. Ace reappraised Holt's assets and liabilities on this date and estimated that the company's buildings were currently undervalued by $180,000. At the time of this second purchase, these buildings had a nine-year remaining life. Any goodwill was to be amortized over 40 years.

The following financial information is for these two companies for 1996. Holt issued no additional capital stock during either 1995 or 1996. Income and dividends can be assumed as having been earned and paid evenly throughout each of the years.

	Ace, Incorporated	Holt Company
Revenues	$ 400,000	$ 300,000
Expenses	(200,000)	(120,000)
Investment income (partial equity method)	144,000	
Net income	$ 344,000	$ 180,000
Retained earnings, 1/1/96	$ 800,000	$ 500,000
Net income (above)	344,000	180,000
Dividends paid	(144,000)	(60,000)
Retained earnings, 12/31/96	$1,000,000	$ 620,000
Current assets	$ 200,000	$ 190,000
Investment in Holt Company	1,070,000	
Land	100,000	600,000
Buildings (net)	210,000	300,000
Equipment (net)	380,000	110,000
Total assets	$1,960,000	$1,200,000
Liabilities	$ 500,000	$ 200,000
Common stock	400,000	300,000
Additional paid-in capital	60,000	80,000
Retained earnings, 12/31/96	1,000,000	620,000
Total liabilities and equities	$1,960,000	$1,200,000

Required:

Determine the appropriate balances for consolidated financial statements for Ace, Incorporated, and Holt Company for December 31, 1996, and the year then ended. Show supporting computations in good form.

43. On January 1, 1991, Wilbourne Company acquired 6,000 of the 10,000 outstanding shares of Hampton Corporation. The purchase price included an allocation of $120,000 for goodwill. All of the assets and liabilities of Hampton had fair market values equal to their book values. The goodwill was to be amortized over the maximum life of 40 years.

On January 1, 1994, Wilbourne bought an additional 2,000 shares of Hampton increasing ownership to an 80 percent interest. In making this second acquisition, Wilbourne assigned $40,000 of the purchase price to a patent (life of 10 years) held by Hampton. An additional $40,000 was attributed to goodwill.

In need of raising cash, Wilbourne sold 1,000 shares of its investment in Hampton on April 1, 1995, for $140,000 in cash. A problem arose in connection with the recording of this sale. Wilbourne's accountants could not agree on the appropriate gain or loss to be recognized so they simply debited cash for $140,000 and credited the Investment account for the same amount. Because of the confusion, Wilbourne prepared no other entries for the investment for the year of 1995, although the equity method had been properly applied prior to this time.

The following individual financial records are for these two companies for 1995. Prepare a consolidation worksheet and the resulting financial statements. Assume that an averaging system is used to determine the appropriate book value of the shares that were sold.

	Wilbourne Company	Hampton Corporation
Revenues	$ 920,000	$ 600,000
Expenses	(650,000)	(440,000)
Equity income of Hampton Corporation	–0–	–0–
Net income	$ 270,000	$ 160,000
Retained earnings, 1/1/95	$1,430,000	$ 750,000
Net income (above)	270,000	160,000
Dividends paid	(150,000)	–0–
Retained earnings, 12/31/95	$1,550,000	$ 910,000
Cash	$ 60,000	$ 98,000
Receivables	430,000	210,000
Inventories	677,000	620,000
Investment in Hampton Corporation	883,000	–0–
Buildings and equipment (net)	620,000	514,000
Patents (net)	40,000	90,000
Total assets	$2,710,000	$1,532,000
Liabilities	$ 690,000	$ 322,000
Common stock	470,000	300,000
Retained earnings, 12/31/95	1,550,000	910,000
Total liabilities and equities	$2,710,000	$1,532,000

5

CONSOLIDATED FINANCIAL STATEMENTS— INTERCOMPANY ASSET TRANSACTIONS

Questions to Consider

- How does the intercompany transfer of inventory or other assets between parent and subsidiary affect the consolidation process?

- Gains on intercompany transactions are considered unrealized until the assets are resold to outsiders or consumed. Prior to the realization of these gains, what adjustments are required in producing consolidated financial statements?

- How does the presence of intercompany transactions affect the balances reported for any noncontrolling interest? What impact does the direction of these transfers (upstream versus downstream) have on the reporting of a noncontrolling interest?

- The intercompany sale of land and depreciable assets can also occur between the members of a business combination. What impact does the specific type of property being conveyed have on the consolidation process?

- Why does the transfer of a depreciable asset frequently result in the recording of excess depreciation in subsequent years?

In Chapter 1, the elimination of gains created by the transfer of inventory between two affiliated companies was analyzed in connection with equity method accounting. The central theme of that discussion was that intercompany profits are not considered to be realized until the earning process is culminated by a sale to an unrelated party. This same accounting logic applies to transactions between companies within a business combination. Since a single economic entity has been formed, such sales can create no profits. In reference to this issue, *ARB 51* (par. 7) states:

> As consolidated statements are based on the assumption that they represent the financial position and operating results of a single business enterprise, such statements should not include gain or loss on transactions among the companies in the group. Accordingly, any intercompany profit or loss on assets remaining within the group should be eliminated; the concept usually applied for this purpose is gross profit or loss.

The elimination of the accounting effects created by intercompany transactions is one of the most significant problems encountered in the consolidation process. The mere volume of transfers occurring within most large enterprises can be staggering. The 1991 annual report for the General Motors Corporation indicated the elimination of intersegment sales amounting to over *$3.6 billion!*

Such transactions are especially common in companies that have been constructed as a vertically integrated chain of organizations. These entities seek to reduce their costs by developing affiliations where one operation furnishes products to another. For example, in reporting on Du Pont's 1981 purchase of Conoco, *Time* magazine stated that "Du Pont's interest in Conoco is understandable. Petroleum is the raw material for some 80 percent of its products. Like all chemical makers, Du Pont has been badly hurt by the surge in oil prices since 1973. Now Du Pont will have its own private supply of crude."[1] Not surprisingly, Du Pont's intersegment sales jumped from less than $500 million in 1980 to more than $4.4 billion in 1983.

Intercompany asset transactions take several forms. As the preceding examples illustrate, inventory transfers are especially prevalent. However, the sale of land as well as depreciable assets can also occur between the parties within a combination. This chapter examines the consolidation procedures necessitated by each of these different types of intercompany asset transfers.

Intercompany Inventory Transactions

As discussed in previous chapters, the companies that make up a business combination frequently retain their legal identities as separate operating centers and maintain their own record-keeping. Thus, any sale of inventory made between these companies triggers the independent accounting systems of both parties. Revenue is duly recorded by the seller, while the purchase is simultaneously entered into the accounts of the buyer. For internal reporting purposes, recording an inventory transfer as a sale/purchase provides vital data to help measure the operational efficiency of each enterprise.[2]

---

[1] Charles Alexander, "History's Biggest Merger," *Time*, July 20, 1981, p. 49.

[2] For all intercompany transactions, the two parties involved view the events from different perspectives. Thus, the transfer is both a sale and a purchase, often creating both a receivable and a payable. To indicate the dual nature of such transactions, these accounts are indicated within this text as sales/purchases, receivables/payables, and so on.

Despite the informational benefits of accounting for the transaction in this manner, from a consolidated perspective neither a sale nor a purchase has occurred. *An intercompany transfer is merely the internal movement of inventory, an event that creates no net change in the financial position of the business combination taken as a whole.* Thus, in producing consolidated financial statements, the recorded effects of these transfers are eliminated so that only transactions with outside parties are reflected. Entries are included on the worksheet for this purpose; they adapt the financial information reported by the separate companies to the perspective of the consolidated enterprise. The entire impact of the intercompany transactions must be identified and then removed. The deleting of the actual transfer is described here first.

The Sales and Purchases Accounts

To account for related companies as a single economic entity, all intercompany sales/purchases accounts are eliminated. For example, if Arlington Company makes an $80,000 inventory sale to Zirkin Company, an affiliated party within a business combination, both parties record the transfer as a normal sale/purchase. The following worksheet entry is then necessary to remove the resulting balances from the consolidated figures. Cost of Goods Sold is reduced here under the assumption that the Purchases account is usually closed out prior to the consolidation process.

Consolidation Entry TI

Sales	80,000	
Cost of Goods Sold (purchases component)		80,000
To eliminate effects of intercompany transfer of inventory.		
(Labeled "TI" in reference to the transferred inventory.)		

In the preparation of consolidated financial statements, the preceding elimination must be made for all intercompany inventory transfers. The total recorded sales figure is deleted regardless of whether the transaction was downstream (from parent to subsidiary) or upstream (from subsidiary to parent).[3] Furthermore, the elimination is unaffected by any markup included in the transfer price. Since the entire amount of the transfer was between related parties, the total effect must be removed from the consolidated statements.[4]

---

[3] Downstream and upstream transactions were introduced in Chapter 1. Although the direction of the transfer did not influence the equity method of accounting (for external reporting), the distinction is significant in the preparation of consolidated statements.

[4] As is shown in the appendix to this chapter, the FASB's discussion memorandum, *An Analysis of Issues Related to Consolidation Policy and Procedures,* does identify alternative theoretical approaches to consolidation that advocate removing only the parent's portion of intercompany sales/purchases when a noncontrolling interest is present. In current practice, elimination of all intercompany sales/purchases (as shown here) appears to predominate. This approach is also followed by many of the concepts discussed by the FASB.

Unrealized Gains—Year of Transfer (Year One)

Removal of the sale/purchase is often just the first in a series of consolidation entries necessitated by inventory transfers. Despite the previous elimination, unrealized gains created by such sales may still exist in the accounting records at year's end. These gains initially result when the merchandise is priced at more than historical cost. Actual transfer prices are established in several ways, including the normal sales price of the inventory, sales price less a specified discount, or at a predetermined markup above cost. In a footnote to its 1991 financial statements, Ford Motor Company explains that

> Intercompany sales among geographic areas consist primarily of vehicles, parts, and components manufactured by consolidated subsidiaries and sold to other consolidated subsidiaries. Transfer prices between these companies are established through negotiations between the affected parties.

Regardless of the method used for this pricing decision, intercompany gains that remain unrealized at year end must be removed in arriving at consolidated figures.

All Inventory Remains at Year End.   In the preceding illustration, assume that Arlington acquired or produced this inventory at a cost of $50,000 and then sold it to Zirkin, an affiliated party, at the indicated price of $80,000. From a consolidated perspective, the inventory still has an historical cost of only $50,000. However, it is now reported in Zirkin's ledger as an asset at the $80,000 transfer price. In addition, because of the markup, Arlington has recorded a $30,000 gross profit as a result of this intercompany sale. Since the transaction did not occur with an outside party, recognition of this profit is not appropriate for the combination as a whole.

Thus, although the sale/purchase figures have been eliminated by consolidation entry TI shown earlier, the $30,000 inflation created by the transfer price still exists in two areas of the individual statements:

- Ending inventory remains overstated by $30,000.
- Gross profit has been artificially increased by this same amount.

Correction of the ending inventory only requires a reduction in the asset. However, before decreasing gross profit, the actual accounts affected by the unrealized gain must be identified. The ending inventory total serves as a negative component within the Cost of Goods Sold computation; it represents the portion of acquired inventory that was not sold. Thus, the $30,000 overstatement of the inventory that is still held incorrectly lowers this expense (the inventory that was sold). *Despite Entry TI, the inflated ending inventory figure causes cost of goods sold to be too low and, thus, profits to be too high by $30,000.* For consolidation purposes, the expense must be raised by this amount, an entry that properly removes the unrealized gain from consolidated net income.

Consequently, if all of the transferred inventory is retained by the business combination at the end of the year, the following worksheet entry also has to be included to eliminate the effects of the gain that remains unrealized within ending inventory.

Consolidation Entry G—Year of Transfer (Year One)
All Inventory Remains

Cost of Goods Sold (ending inventory component).	30,000	
Inventory (balance sheet account)		30,000
To remove unrealized gain created by intercompany sale.		

This entry (labeled *G* for gain) succeeds in reducing the consolidated Inventory account to its original $50,000 historical cost. Furthermore, increasing cost of goods sold by $30,000 effectively removes the unrealized gain from gross profit. Thus, both reporting problems created by the transfer price markup have been resolved by the impact of this worksheet entry.

Only a Portion of Inventory Remains. Obviously, a company does not buy inventory and then hold it for an indefinite time. The acquired items are used within the company's operations or resold to unrelated, outside parties. Intercompany gains are ultimately realized by the subsequent consumption or reselling of these goods. Therefore, only the transferred inventory still held at year's end continues to be recorded in the separate statements at a value more than the historical cost. For this reason, *the elimination of unrealized gains (Entry G) is not based on total intercompany sales but only on the amount of merchandise retained within the business at the end of the year.*

To illustrate, assume that Arlington transferred inventory costing $50,000 to Zirkin, a related company, for $80,000, thus recording a gross profit of $30,000. Assume further that by year's end Zirkin has resold $60,000 of these goods to unrelated parties but retains the other $20,000 (for resale in the following year). From the viewpoint of the consolidated company, the gain on the $60,000 portion of the intercompany sale has now been earned so that no adjustment is required for consolidation purposes.

Conversely, any gain recorded in connection with the $20,000 in merchandise that remains is still a component within Zirkin's Inventory account. Because the markup was 37½ percent ($30,000 gross profit/$80,000 transfer price), this retained inventory is stated at a value $7,500 more than the original cost ($20,000 × 37½%). The required reduction (Entry G) is not the entire $30,000 as shown previously but only the $7,500 unrealized gain that remains in ending inventory.

Consolidation Entry G—Year of Transfer (Year One)
40% of Inventory Remains (replaces previous entry)

Cost of Goods Sold (ending inventory component).	7,500	
Inventory		7,500
To remove portion of intercompany gain which is unrealized in year of transfer.		

Unrealized Gains—Year Following Transfer (Year Two)

Whenever an unrealized intercompany gain is present in ending Inventory, one further consolidation entry is eventually required. Although Entry G removes the gain from the *consolidated* inventory balances in the year of transfer, the $7,500 overstatement remains within the separate financial records of the buyer and seller. The effects of this gain are then carried into their beginning balances in the subsequent year. Hence, another worksheet elimination is necessary, but it is made in the period following the transfer. For consolidation purposes, the unrealized portion of the intercompany gain must be adjusted in two successive years (from ending inventory in the year of transfer and from beginning inventory of the next period).

Referring again to Arlington's sale of inventory to Zirkin, the $7,500 unrealized gain is still present in Zirkin's Inventory account at the start of the subsequent year. Once again, the overstatement is removed within the consolidation process but this time from the beginning inventory balance (which appears in the financial statements only as a positive component of cost of goods sold). This elimination is termed *Entry *G*. The asterisk indicates that the intercompany gain was created by a transfer made in a previous year.

Consolidation Entry *G—Year Following Transfer (Year Two)

Retained Earnings (beginning balance of seller)	7,500	
Cost of Goods Sold (beginning inventory component)		7,500

To remove unrealized gain from beginning figures so that it can be recognized currently in the period in which the earning process is completed.

By reducing cost of goods sold (beginning inventory) through this worksheet entry, the gross profit reported for this second year is increased. For consolidation purposes, the gain on the transfer is now recognized in the period in which the items are actually sold to outside parties. As shown by the following diagram, Entry G initially deferred the $7,500 gain because this amount was unrealized in the year of transfer. Entry *G now increases consolidated net income (by decreasing cost of goods sold) to reflect the earning process in the latter year.

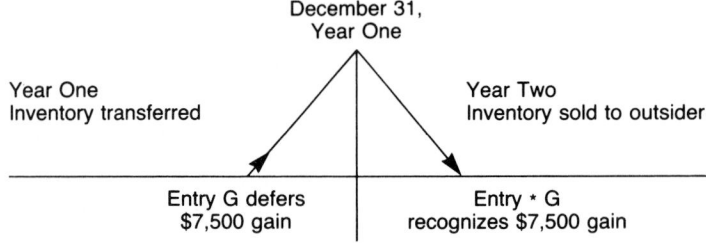

In Entry *G, removal of the $7,500 from beginning inventory (within cost of goods sold) appropriately increases current income and should not pose a significant conceptual problem. However, the rationale for decreasing the seller's beginning retained earnings deserves further explanation. This reduction removes the unrealized gain (recognized by the seller in the year of transfer) so that the profit can now be reported when actually earned. Despite the consolidation entries in Year One, the $7,500 gain remained on this company's separate books and was closed to retained earnings at the end of the period. Therefore, from a consolidated view, the buyer's inventory and the seller's retained earnings as of the beginning of Year Two contain the unrealized profit and must both be reduced in Entry *G.

The worksheet elimination of the sales/purchases balances (Entry TI) as well as the entry to remove the unrealized gain from ending inventory in Year One (Entry G) are both standard, regardless of the circumstances of the consolidation. Conversely, in one specific situation, the procedure used to eliminate the intercompany gain from Year Two's beginning accounts differs from the Entry *G just presented. If (1) the original transfer is downstream (made by the parent) and (2) the equity method has been applied for internal accounting purposes, the Investment in Subsidiary account replaces beginning retained earnings in Entry *G.

When using the equity method, the parent maintains appropriate income balances within its own individual financial records. Thus, any unrealized gain is removed by the parent at the end of Year One through an equity method adjustment that also decreases the Investment in Subsidiary account. With the gain eliminated, the retained earnings of the parent/seller at the beginning of the following year is correctly stated.[5] The account does not contain the unrealized gain and needs no adjustment. For consolidation purposes, cost of goods sold is still decreased in Entry *G but the Investment in Subsidiary account is increased (to offset the equity method reduction).

*Consolidation Entry *G—Year Following Transfer (Year Two)*
*(replaces previous Entry *G when transfers have been downstream and the equity method is in use)*

Investment in Subsidiary	7,500	
Cost of Goods Sold (beginning inventory component)		7,500

To remove impact of previously deferred unrealized gain to allow for recognition in the current period. The Investment account replaces retained earnings here because the equity method has been applied and the transfers were downstream. The retained earnings of the parent (the seller) have already been corrected by an equity adjustment.

Unrealized Gains—Effect on Noncontrolling Interest Valuation

The effects that intercompany inventory transfers have on a business combination are appropriately accounted for by the worksheet entries just described. However, one question remains: What impact do these procedures have on the

---

[5] If intercompany transfers are upstream, the subsidiary is the seller. Since application of the equity method only affects the records of the parent, the actual unrealized gain is not eliminated and must be removed from the retained earnings of the subsidiary/seller through Entry *G.

valuation of a noncontrolling interest? In regard to this issue, paragraph 13 of *ARB 51* states:

> The amount of intercompany profit or loss to be eliminated in accordance with paragraph 7 is not affected by the existence of a minority interest. The complete elimination of the intercompany profit or loss is consistent with the underlying assumption that consolidated statements represent the financial position and operating results of a single business enterprise. The elimination of the intercompany profit or loss *may be allocated proportionately* between the majority and minority interests. (Emphasis added)

The last sentence indicates that alternative approaches are available in computing the noncontrolling interest's share of a subsidiary's net income. According to this pronouncement, recognition of outside ownership *may or may not be* affected by unrealized gains resulting from intercompany transfers. Since consolidated net income is reduced by the amount attributed to a noncontrolling interest, the handling of this issue can have a significant impact on the reported profitability of a business combination.

To illustrate, assume that Large Company owns 70 percent of the voting stock of Small Company. To avoid any extraneous complications at this stage of the discussion, assume that no amortization expense resulted from this purchase. Assume further that Large reports current net income (from separate operations) of $500,000, while Small has earned $100,000. During the current period, intercompany transfers of $200,000 occurred with a total markup of $90,000. At the end of the year, an unrealized intercompany gain of $40,000 remains within the inventory accounts.

Clearly, the consolidated net income prior to the reduction for the 30 percent noncontrolling interest is $560,000, the two income balances less the unrealized gain. The problem facing the accountant is the computation of the noncontrolling interest's share of Small's income. Because of the flexibility allowed by *ARB 51*, this figure may be reported as either $30,000 (30 percent of the $100,000 earnings of the subsidiary) or $18,000 (30 percent of reported income after that figure is reduced by the $40,000 unrealized gain).

To determine an appropriate valuation for this noncontrolling interest allocation, an analysis must be made of the relationship between an intercompany transaction and the outside owners. If a transfer is downstream (the parent sells inventory to the subsidiary), a logical view would seem to be that the unrealized gain is that of the parent company. The parent made the original sale, therefore, the gross profit is included in its financial records. Since the subsidiary's income is unaffected, little justification exists for adjusting the noncontrolling interest to reflect the deferral of the unrealized gain. Consequently, in the example of Large and Small, if the transfers were downstream, the 30 percent noncontrolling interest would be $30,000 based on Small's reported income of $100,000.

In contrast, if inventory is sold by the subsidiary to the parent (an upstream transfer), the gross profit would be recognized in the subsidiary's financial records, even though part of this income remains unrealized from a consolidation perspective. Since the outside owners possess their interest in the subsidiary, a reasonable conclusion would be that valuation of the noncontrolling interest is calculated on the income actually earned by this company.

Thus, in this textbook, the noncontrolling interest's share of consolidated net income is computed based on *the reported income of the subsidiary after adjustment for any unrealized upstream gains*. Returning to the case of Large Company and Small Company, if the $40,000 unrealized gain was the result of an upstream sale from subsidiary to parent, only $60,000 of Small's $100,000 reported income has actually been earned by the end of the year. The allocation to the noncontrolling interest is, therefore, reported as $18,000, or 30 percent of this realized income figure.

Alternative Concepts of a Noncontrolling Interest. Although the noncontrolling interest figure is based here on the subsidiary's reported income adjusted for the effects of upstream intercompany transfers, *ARB 51*, as quoted earlier, does not require this treatment. Giving effect to upstream transfers in this calculation but not to downstream transfers is no more than an attempt to select the most logical approach from among acceptable alternatives. In fact, the FASB has put forth a number of possible methods of consolidating the results of intercompany transfers. Several of these alternatives are shown in the appendix at the end of this chapter.

Intercompany Inventory Transfers Summarized

To assist in overcoming the complications created by intercompany transfers, the consolidation process is demonstrated in three different ways:

- Before proceeding to a numerical example, the impact of intercompany transfers on consolidated figures is reviewed. Ultimately, the accountant must understand how the balances to be reported by a business combination are derived when unrealized gains result from either upstream or downstream sales.
- Next, two different consolidation worksheets are produced: one for downstream transfers and the other for upstream. The various consolidation procedures used in these worksheets are explained and analyzed.
- Finally, several of the worksheet entries used in developing a consolidation worksheet are shown side by side so that the differences created by the direction of the transfers can be better understood.

The Development of Consolidated Totals. The following summary discusses only the accounts impacted by intercompany transactions:

Revenues. The parent's book value is added to the subsidiary's book value but all intercompany transfers are then removed.

Cost of Goods Sold. This expense is one of the most difficult figures computed within the consolidation process. The parent's book value is added to the subsidiary's book value but all intercompany transfers are removed. The resulting balance is then decreased by any beginning unrealized gain (thus, raising net income) and increased by any ending unrealized gain (to reduce net income).

Expenses. The parent's book value is added to the subsidiary's book value plus any amortization expense for the year recognized on the purchase price allocations and goodwill.[6]

Noncontrolling Interest in Subsidiary's Net Income. The subsidiary's reported net income is adjusted for the effects of unrealized gains on upstream transfers (but not downstream transfers) and then multiplied by the percentage of outside ownership.

Retained Earnings at the Beginning of the Year. As in previous chapters, if the equity method has been applied, the parent's balance mirrors the consolidated total. When any other method is used, the parent's beginning retained earnings must be converted to the equity method by Entry *C. Accruals for this purpose are based on the income actually earned by the subsidiary in previous years (reported income adjusted for any unrealized upstream gains).

Inventory. The parent's book value is added to the subsidiary's book value. Any unrealized gain remaining at the end of the current year is removed to lower the reported balance to historical cost.

Land, Buildings, and Equipment. The parent's book value is added to the subsidiary's book value. This total is adjusted for any purchase price allocations and subsequent amortization.[7]

Noncontrolling Interest in Subsidiary at End of Year. The final total begins with the noncontrolling interest at the beginning of the year. This figure is based on the subsidiary's book value on that date after removing any unrealized gains on upstream sales. The beginning balance is then updated by adding the portion of the subsidiary's income assigned to these outside owners (computed above) and subtracting the noncontrolling interest's share of the subsidiary's dividend payments.

Intercompany Inventory Transfers Illustrated

To examine the various consolidation procedures relative to intercompany inventory transfers, assume that Top Company purchases 80 percent of the voting stock

---

[6] As discussed later in this chapter, consolidated expenses also have to be reduced to remove excess depreciation recognized whenever a depreciable asset is transferred between the companies within a business combination at a price more than the book value.

[7] As discussed later in this chapter, if land, buildings, or equipment have been transferred between parent and subsidiary, the separately reported balances must be returned to historical cost figures in deriving consolidated totals.

of Bottom Company on January 1, 1995. The parent pays a total of $400,000, a price that includes all directly related consolidation costs. Goodwill of $40,000 results from this purchase, a figure amortized at the rate of $1,000 per year for 40 years.

The subsidiary reports net income of $30,000 in 1995 and $70,000 in 1996, the current year. Dividend payments are $20,000 in the first year and $50,000 in the second. Top applies the cost method so that dividend income of $16,000 ($20,000 × 80 percent) and $40,000 ($50,000 × 80 percent) is recorded by the parent during these two years. Using the cost method in this initial example avoids the problem of computing the parent's investment account balances. However, this illustration is extended to demonstrate the changes necessary if the parent applies the equity method.

After the takeover, intercompany inventory sales occurred between the two companies as shown in Exhibit 5–1. A $10,000 intercompany debt also exists as of December 31, 1996.

The 1996 consolidation of Top and Bottom is presented twice. First, the transfers are assumed to be downstream from parent to subsidiary. Second, consolidated figures are recomputed with the transfers being viewed as upstream. This distinction is only significant because of the presence of a noncontrolling interest.

Downstream Sales.   In the first example, all inventory transfers are assumed to have been *downstream* from Top to Bottom. Based on that perspective, the worksheet to consolidate these two companies for the year ending December 31, 1996, has been constructed in Exhibit 5–2.

Most of the worksheet entries found in Exhibit 5–2 have been described and analyzed in previous chapters of this textbook. Thus, only four of these entries are examined in detail along with the computation of the noncontrolling interests in the subsidiary's income.

Entry *G.   Entry *G removes the unrealized gains carried over from the previous period. As $16,000 in transferred merchandise was retained by Bottom at the first of the current year, any related gain is unearned and must be deferred. The 1995 markup on these items was 25 percent ($20,000 gross profit/$80,000 transfer price)

EXHIBIT 5–1   Intercompany Transfers

	1995	1996
Transfer prices	$80,000	$100,000
Historical cost	60,000	70,000
Gross profit	$20,000	$ 30,000
Inventory remaining at year's end (at transfer price)	$16,000	$ 20,000

EXHIBIT 5–2   Downstream Inventory Transfers

TOP COMPANY AND BOTTOM COMPANY
Consolidation Worksheet
For Year Ending December 31, 1996

Consolidation: Purchase Method
Investment: Cost Method

Ownership: 80%

Accounts	Top Company	Bottom Company	Consolidation Entries Debit	Consolidation Entries Credit	Noncontrolling Interest	Consolidated Totals
Income Statement						
Sales	(600,000)	(300,000)	(TI) 100,000			(800,000)
Cost of goods sold	320,000	180,000	(G) 6,000	(*G) 4,000 (TI) 100,000		402,000
Expenses	170,000	50,000	(E) 1,000			221,000
Dividend income	(40,000)	–0–	(I) 40,000			–0–
Noncontrolling interest in Bottom Company's income					(14,000) ‡	14,000
Net income	(150,000)	(70,000)				(163,000)
Statement of Retained Earnings						
Retained earnings, 1/1/96:						
Top Company	(650,000)		(*G) 4,000 (S) 310,000 †			(653,000)
Bottom Company		(310,000)				–0–
Net income (above)	(150,000)	(70,000)				(163,000)
Dividends paid	70,000	50,000		(*C) 7,000 (I) 40,000	10,000	70,000
Retained earnings, 12/31/96	(730,000)	(330,000)				(746,000)
Balance Sheet						
Cash and receivables	280,000	120,000		(P) 10,000		390,000
Inventory	220,000	160,000		(G) 6,000		374,000

Account	Top Company	Bottom Company	Debits	Credits	Noncontrolling Interest	Consolidated Totals
Investment in Bottom Company	400,000	-0-	(*C) 7,000	(S) 368,000 (A) 39,000		-0-
Land	410,000	200,000				610,000
Plant assets (net)	190,000	170,000				360,000
Goodwill	-0-	-0-	(A) 39,000	(E) 1,000		38,000
Total assets	1,500,000	650,000				1,772,000
Liabilities	(340,000)	(170,000)	(P) 10,000			(500,000)
Noncontrolling interest in Bottom Company, 1/1/96	-0-	-0-		(S) 92,000	(92,000)	
Noncontrolling interest in Bottom Company, 12/31/96					(96,000)	(96,000)
Common stock	(430,000)	(150,000)	(S) 150,000			(430,000)
Retained earnings, 12/31/96 (above)	(730,000)	(330,000)				(746,000)
Total liabilities and equities	(1,500,000)	(650,000)				(1,772,000)

NOTE: Parentheses indicate a credit balance.

† Boxed items highlight differences with upstream transfers examined in Exhibit 5–3.

‡ Since intercompany sales are made downstream (by the parent), the subsidiary's earned income is the $70,000 reported figure with the 20% noncontrolling interest being allocated $14,000.

Consolidation entries:

(*G) Removal of unrealized gain from beginning figures so that it can be recognized in current period. Downstream sales attributed to parent.

(*C) Recognition of increase in book value and amortization relating to ownership of subsidiary for year prior to 1996.

(S) Elimination of subsidiary's stockholders' equity accounts along with recognition of January 1, 1996, noncontrolling interest.

(A) Allocation of parent's cost in excess of subsidiary's book value, unamortized balance as of January 1, 1996.

(I) Elimination of intercompany dividends recorded by parent as income.

(E) Recognition of amortization expense for current year on goodwill.

(P) Elimination of intercompany receivable/payable balances.

(TI) Elimination of intercompany sales/purchases balances.

(G) Removal of unrealized gain from ending figures so that it can be recognized in subsequent period.

indicating an unrealized gain of $4,000 (25 percent of the remaining $16,000 in inventory). Thus, Entry *G reduces cost of goods sold (or the beginning inventory component of that expense) by that amount as well as the January 1, 1996, Retained Earnings of Top (the seller of the goods).

Two effects are created by Entry *G: First, last year's profits, as reflected by the seller's beginning retained earnings, are reduced because the $4,000 gain was not earned at that time. Second, through the reduction in cost of goods sold, an increase in current year income is created. From a consolidation perspective, the gain is being correctly recognized in 1996 when the inventory is sold to an outside party.

Entry *C. Entry *C was introduced in Chapter 3 as an initial consolidation adjustment required whenever the equity method is not applied by the parent company. Entry *C converts the parent's beginning retained earnings to a consolidated total. In the current illustration, Top did not accrue its portion of the 1995 increase in Bottom's book value [($30,000 income less $20,000 paid in dividends) × 80% or $8,000] or record the $1,000 amortization expense for this same period. Since neither number has been recognized within the parent's individual records, both must be brought into the consolidation process through a $7,000 adjustment (Entry *C). The intercompany transfers did not affect this entry because they were downstream; the gains had no impact on the income recognized in connection with the subsidiary.

Entry TI. The intercompany sales/purchases for 1996 are eliminated by Entry TI. The entire $100,000 transfer recorded by the two parties during the current period is removed to arrive at consolidated figures for the business combination.

Entry G. Entry G defers the unrealized gain remaining at the end of 1996. The $20,000 in transferred merchandise retained by Bottom has a markup of 30 percent ($30,000 gross profit/$100,000 transfer price); thus, the unrealized gain amounts to $6,000. On the worksheet, Entry G eliminates this inflation in the Inventory asset balance as well as the ending inventory (negative) component of cost of goods sold. Because the gain remains unrealized, the increase in this expense account has the appropriate effect of lowering consolidated income.

Noncontrolling Interest's Share of the Subsidiary's Income. In this first illustration, the intercompany transfers were downstream. Thus, the unrealized gains are considered to relate solely to the parent company, creating no effect on the subsidiary or the outside ownership. For this reason, the noncontrolling interest's share of consolidated income is recorded as a columnar entry of $14,000, 20 percent of the $70,000 net income reported by Bottom.

By including these entries along with the other routine worksheet eliminations and adjustments, the accounting information generated by Top and Bottom can be brought together into a single set of consolidated financial statements. However, this process does more than simply delete intercompany transactions; reported income has been affected. A $4,000 gain is being removed on the worksheet from 1995 figures so that it can be recognized in 1996 (Entry *G). A $6,000 gain is deferred in a similar fashion from 1996 into 1997 (Entry G). However, these changes do not affect the noncontrolling interest since the transfers were downstream.

Upstream Sales.   A different set of consolidation procedures is necessary if the intercompany transfers were upstream from Bottom to Top. As previously discussed, upstream gains are attributed to the subsidiary rather than to the parent company. Therefore, had these transfers been upstream, the $4,000 gain moved from 1995 into the current year (Entry *G) as well as the $6,000 unrealized gain deferred from 1996 into the future (Entry G) are both considered adjustments to Bottom's reported totals.

Tying upstream gains to Bottom's income may be a logical perspective, but such treatment does complicate the consolidation process in several ways:

- Deferring the $4,000 gain from 1995 into 1996 dictates that the beginning retained earnings balance of the subsidiary (as the seller of the goods) should be adjusted to $306,000 rather than $310,000 found in the company's separate records on the worksheet.
- Because $4,000 of the income reported for 1995 was unearned at that time, Bottom's book value did not increase by $10,000 during the previous period (income less dividends as stated in the introduction) but only by an earned amount of $6,000.
- Bottom's earned income for the year of 1996 is $68,000 rather than the $70,000 found within the company's separate financial statements. This $68,000 figure is based on adjusting the timing of the reported income to reflect the deferral and recognition of the intercompany gains.

Earned Income of Subsidiary—Upstream Transfers

Income Reported by Bottom Company, 1996	Add: Gain from Previous Period Realized in 1996	Less: Gain Reported in 1996 to Be Realized in Later Period	1996 Income of Bottom Company from Consolidated Perspective
$70,000	$4,000	$(6,000)	$68,000

Determining Bottom's beginning retained earnings (realized) to be $306,000 and its 1996 income as $68,000 are preliminary calculations made in anticipation of the consolidation process. These newly computed totals are significant because they serve as the basis for several of the worksheet entries. However, the financial records of the subsidiary remain unaffected. In addition, because the cost method has been applied, no change is required in any of the parent's accounts on the worksheet.

To illustrate the effects of upstream inventory transfers, Exhibit 5–3 has been produced to consolidate the financial statements of Top and Bottom once again. *The individual records of the two companies have been left unchanged from Exhibit 5–2: the only difference in this second worksheet is that the intercompany transfers are assumed to have been made upstream from Bottom to Top.* This single change creates several important differences between Exhibits 5–2 and 5–3:

1. Since the intercompany sales were made upstream, the $4,000 deferral of the beginning unrealized gain (Entry *G) is no longer viewed as a reduction in the retained earnings of the parent company. Bottom was the seller of the merchandise; thus, the elimination made in Exhibit 5–3 reduces that company's January 1, 1996, equity balance. Following this entry, Bottom's beginning retained earnings on the worksheet is $306,000 which is, as discussed earlier, the appropriate total from a consolidated perspective.

2. Because $4,000 of Bottom's 1995 income is being deferred into 1996, the increase in the subsidiary's book value in the previous year is only $6,000 rather than $10,000 as reported. Consequently, conversion to the equity method (Entry *C) requires an increase of just $3,800:

$6,000 earned increase in subsidiary's book value during 1995 × 80%. . . .	$4,800
1995 amortization expense	(1,000)
Increase in parent's beginning retained earnings (Entry *C).	$3,800

3. Within Entry S, the valuation of the initial noncontrolling interest as well as the portion of the parent's investment account to be eliminated differ from the previous example. This worksheet entry removes the stockholders' equity accounts of the subsidiary as of the beginning of the current year. Thus, the $4,000 reduction made to Bottom's retained earnings to remove the 1995 unrealized gain must be taken into account in developing Entry S. After posting Entry *G, only $456,000 remains as the subsidiary's January 1, 1996, book value (the total of common stock and beginning retained earnings after adjustment for Entry *G). This figure then forms the basis for the 20 percent noncontrolling interest ($91,200) and elimination of the 80 percent parent company investment ($364,800).

4. Finally, to complete the consolidation, the noncontrolling interest's share of the subsidiary's net income is recorded on the worksheet as $13,600. This balance represents a 20 percent allocation of the $68,000 earned income figure attributed to Bottom. Upstream transfers have affected this computation although the downstream sales in the previous example did not. Thus, the noncontrolling interest balance reported previously in the income statement in Exhibit 5–2 differs from the allocation shown in Exhibit 5–3.

Consolidations—Downstream versus Upstream Transfers.   To help clarify the effect of downstream and upstream transfers, the worksheet entries that differ can be examined in greater detail.

<table>
<tr><td>

Downstream Transfers
(Exhibit 5–2)

</td><td>

Upstream Transfers
(Exhibit 5–3)

</td></tr>
<tr><td>

*Entry *G*

Retained earnings,
   1/1/96—Top 4,000
     Cost of goods sold 4,000
To remove 1995 unrealized gain from beginning balances of the seller.

</td><td>

*Entry *G*

Retained earnings,
   1/1/96—Bottom 4,000
     Cost of goods sold 4,000
To remove 1995 unrealized gain from beginning balances of the seller.

</td></tr>
<tr><td>

*Entry *C*

Investment in Bottom . . 7,000
   Retained earnings,
     1/1/96—Top 7,000
To convert 1/1/96 cost figures to the equity method. Income accrual is 80% of reported income of $10,000 less $1,000 amortization.

</td><td>

*Entry *C*

Investment in Bottom . . 3,800
   Retained earnings,
     1/1/96—Top 3,800
To convert 1/1/96 cost figures to the equity method. Income accrual is 80% of earned income of $6,000 (after removal of unrealized gain) less $1,000 amortization.

</td></tr>
<tr><td>

Entry S

Common
   stock—Bottom . . . 150,000
Retained earnings,
   1/1/96—Bottom . . . 310,000

   Investment in
     Bottom (80%) 368,000
   Noncontrolling
     interest—1/1/96
     (20%) 92,000
To remove subsidiary's stockholders' equity accounts and portion of investment balance. Book value at beginning of year is appropriate.

</td><td>

Entry S

Common
   stock—Bottom . . . 150,000
Retained earnings,
   1/1/96—Bottom (as
   adjusted) 306,000
   Investment in
     Bottom (80%) 364,800
   Noncontrolling
     interest—1/1/96
     (20%) 91,200
To remove subsidiary's stockholders' equity accounts (as adjusted in Entry *G) and portion of investment balance. Adjusted book value at beginning of year is appropriate.

</td></tr>
<tr><td>

Noncontrolling Interest in Subsidiary's Income = $14,000. 20 percent of Bottom's reported income.

</td><td>

Noncontrolling Interest in Subsidiary's Income = $13,600. 20 percent of Bottom's earned income (reported income after adjustment for unrealized gains).

</td></tr>
</table>

Effects on Consolidation of Alternative Investment Methods

In Exhibits 5–2 and 5–3, the cost method was utilized. However, when either the equity method or the partial equity method is applied, consolidation procedures normally continue to follow the same patterns analyzed in the previous chapters

EXHIBIT 5–3 Upstream Inventory Transfers

TOP COMPANY AND BOTTOM COMPANY
Consolidation Worksheet
For Year Ending December 31, 1996

Consolidation: Purchase Method
Investment: Cost Method

Ownership: 80%

Accounts	Top Company	Bottom Company	Consolidation Entries Debit	Consolidation Entries Credit	Noncontrolling Interest	Consolidated Totals
Income Statement						
Sales	(600,000)	(300,000)	(TI) 100,000			(800,000)
Cost of goods sold	320,000	180,000	(G) 6,000	(*G) 4,000 / (TI) 100,000		402,000
Expenses	170,000	50,000	(E) 1,000			221,000
Dividend income	(40,000)	–0–	(I) 40,000			–0–
Noncontrolling interest in Bottom Company's income					(13,600) ‡	13,600
Net income	(150,000)	(70,000)				(163,400)
Statement of Retained Earnings						
Retained earnings, 1/1/96:						
Top Company	(650,000)		(*G) 4,000 † / (S) 306,000			(653,800)
Bottom Company		(310,000)		(*C) 3,800		–0–
Net income (above)	(150,000)	(70,000)				(163,400)
Dividends paid	70,000	50,000		(I) 40,000	10,000	70,000
Retained earnings, 12/31/96	(730,000)	(330,000)				(747,200)
Balance Sheet						
Cash and receivables	280,000	120,000				390,000
Inventory	220,000	160,000		(G) 6,000		374,000
Investment in Bottom Company	400,000	–0–	(*C) 3,800	(S) 364,800 / (A) 39,000		–0–

Land	410,000	200,000				610,000
Plant assets (net)	190,000	170,000	(A) 39,000			360,000
Goodwill	-0-	-0-	(E) 1,000			38,000
Total assets	1,500,000	650,000				1,772,000
Liabilities	(340,000)	(170,000)				(500,000)
Noncontrolling interest in Bottom Company, 1/1/96	-0-	-0-		(S) 91,200	(91,200)	
Noncontrolling interest in Bottom Company, 12/31/96					(94,800)	(94,800)
Common stock	(430,000)	(150,000)	(S) 150,000			(430,000)
Retained earnings, 12/31/96 (above)	(730,000)	(330,000)	(P) 10,000			(747,200)
Total liabilities and equities	(1,500,000)	(650,000)				(1,772,000)

NOTE: Parentheses indicate a credit balance.

† Boxed items highlight differences with downstream transfers examined in Exhibit 5–2.

‡ Since intercompany sales are made upstream (by the subsidiary), the subsidiary's realized income is $68,000 ($70,000 reported balance plus $4,000 gain deferred from previous year less $6,000 deferred into next year) with the 20% noncontrolling interest being allocated $13,600.

Consolidation entries:

(*G) Removal of unrealized gain from beginning figures so that it can be recognized in current period. Upstream sales attributed to subsidiary.

(*C) Recognition of earned increase in book value and amortization relating to ownership of subsidiary for year prior to 1996.

(S) Elimination of adjusted stockholders' equity accounts along with recognition of January 1, 1996, noncontrolling interest.

(A) Allocation of parent's cost in excess of subsidiary's book value, unamortized balance as of January 1, 1996.

(I) Elimination of intercompany dividends recorded by parent as income.

(E) Recognition of amortization expense for current year on goodwill.

(P) Elimination of intercompany receivable/payable balances.

(TI) Elimination of intercompany sales/purchases balances.

(G) Removal of unrealized gain from ending figures so that it can be recognized in subsequent period.

of this textbook. As described earlier, though, a variation in Entry *G is required when the equity method is applied and downstream transfers have occurred. The investment account is increased rather than recording a reduction in the beginning retained earnings of the parent/seller. Otherwise, the specific accounting method in use creates no unique impact on the consolidation process for intercompany transactions.

The major complication encountered in connection with the parent's usage of the equity method is not always related to a consolidation procedure. Frequently, the composition of the investment balances appearing on the parent's separate financial records proves to be the most complex element of the entire process. Under the equity method, the investment accounts are subjected to (1) income accrual, (2) amortization, (3) dividends, and (4) adjustments required by unrealized intercompany gains. Thus, if Top Company applies the equity method and the transfers are downstream, the Investment in Bottom Company account would grow from $400,000 to $416,000 by the end of 1996. For that year, the Equity Income—Bottom Company account registers a $53,000 balance. Both of these totals result from the accounting shown in Exhibit 5–4.

If transfers are upstream, the individual investment accounts reported by the parent can be determined in the same manner as in Exhibit 5–4. Because of the change in direction, the gains are now attributed to the subsidiary. Thus, both

---

EXHIBIT 5–4   Investment Balances—Equity Method (downstream sales)

Investment in Bottom Company, 12/31/96

Cost		$400,000
Increase in Bottom Company book value:		
12/31/96 book value	$ 480,000	
1/1/95 book value	(450,000)	
Increase	30,000	
Top Company ownership	80%	24,000
Deferral of Top's 12/31/96 unrealized gain		
(downstream sale)		(6,000)
Amortization of goodwill, 1995–96		(2,000)
Investment in Bottom Company, 12/31/96		$416,000

Equity in Income of Bottom Company, 1996

1996—income accrual by Top Company:		
Reported income of Bottom Company	$ 70,000	
Top Company's ownership	80%	$ 56,000
Recognition of gain deferred		
from 1995 into 1996		4,000
Deferral of Top's 1996 unrealized gain into 1997		(6,000)
Amortization, 1996		(1,000)
Equity in Income of Bottom Company, 1996		$ 53,000

EXHIBIT 5–5 **Investment Balances—Equity Method (upstream sales)**

Investment in Bottom Company, 12/31/96

Cost		$400,000
Increase in Bottom Company book value:		
12/31/96 book value.	$ 480,000	
1/1/95 book value.	(450,000)	
Increase.	30,000	
Deferral of Bottom's 12/31/96 unrealized gain		
(upstream sale)	(6,000)	
Earned increase	$24,000	
Top Company's ownership	80%	19,200
Amortization of goodwill, 1995–96		(2,000)
Investment in Bottom Company, 12/31/96		$417,200

Equity in Income of Bottom Company, 1996

1996—income accrual by Top Company:		
Reported income of Bottom Company	$ 70,000	
Recognition of Bottom's gain deferred		
from 1995 into 1996	4,000	
Deferral of Bottom's 1996 unrealized		
gain into 1997	(6,000)	
Realized income	68,000	
Top Company's ownership	80%	$ 54,400
Amortization, 1996		(1,000)
Equity in Income of Bottom Company, 1996		$ 53,400

---

investment accounts hold balances that vary from the totals computed earlier. The Investment in Bottom Company balance becomes $417,200, whereas the Equity Income—Bottom Company account for the year is $53,400. The differences are the result of having upstream rather than downstream transactions. The components of these accounts are identified in Exhibit 5–5.

Discussion Question: What Price Should We Charge Ourselves?

Slagle Corporation is a large manufacturing organization. Over the past several years, Slagle has obtained an important component used in its production process exclusively from Harrison, Inc., a relatively small company in Topeka, Kansas. Harrison charges $90 per unit for this part:

continued

Variable cost per unit	$40.00
Fixed cost assigned per unit	30.00
Markup	20.00
Total price	$90.00

In hopes of reducing manufacturing costs, Slagle purchases all of the outstanding common stock of Harrison. This new subsidiary continues to sell merchandise to a number of outside customers as well as to Slagle. Thus, for internal reporting purposes, Harrison is being viewed as a separate profit center.

A controversy has now arisen among company officials about the amount that Harrison should charge Slagle for each component. The administrator in charge of the subsidiary wants to continue with a price of $90.00 as in the past. He believes this figure best reflects the profitability of the division: "If we are to be judged by our profits, why should we be punished for selling to our own parent company? If that occurs, my figures will look better if I forget Slagle as a customer and try to market my goods solely to outsiders."

In contrast, the vice president in charge of Slagle's production wants the price set at variable cost, total cost, or some derivative of these numbers. "We bought Harrison to bring our costs down. It only makes sense to reduce the transfer price, otherwise the benefits of acquiring this subsidiary are not apparent. I pushed the company to buy Harrison; if our operating results are not improved, I will get the blame."

Will the decision about the transfer price affect consolidated net income?

Which method would be easiest for the company's accountant to administer?

As the company's accountant, what advice would you give to these officials?

Intercompany Land Transfers

Although not as prevalent as inventory transactions, the intercompany sale of other assets does occasionally occur. For example, in 1981 Pillsbury transferred 24 of its Le Chateau restaurants (acquired in a merger with the Green Giant Company) to a wholly owned subsidiary, the Steak and Ale Restaurants of America, Inc. This particular transaction involved the intercompany transfer of land and buildings as well as equipment.

The final two sections of this chapter examine the worksheet procedures necessitated by noninventory transfers. Land transactions are analyzed first followed by a discussion of the effects created by the intercompany sale of depreciable assets such as buildings and equipment.

Accounting for Land Transactions

The consolidation procedures necessitated by intercompany land transfers partially parallel the process demonstrated in connection with inventory transactions. As with inventory, the sale of land creates a series of effects on the individual records of the two companies. The worksheet process must then restate the account balances to present all transactions from the perspective of a single economic entity.

By reviewing the sequence of events occurring in an intercompany land sale, the similarities to inventory transfers can be ascertained as well as the unique features of this transaction.

1. A gain (losses are rare in intercompany asset transfers) is reported by the original seller of the land, even though the transaction occurred between related parties. At the same time, the acquiring company capitalizes the inflated transfer price rather than the land's historical cost to the business combination.

2. The unrealized gain recorded by the seller is closed into retained earnings at the end of the year. From a consolidated perspective, this account has been artificially increased. Thus, both the Land account of the buyer and the Retained Earnings of the seller continue to contain the unrealized profit.

3. Only when the land is subsequently disposed of to an outside party is the gain on the original transfer actually earned. Therefore, appropriate consolidation techniques must be designed to eliminate the intercompany gain each period until the time of resale.

Clearly, two characteristics encountered in inventory transfers are also present in intercompany land transactions: inflated book values and unrealized gains subsequently culminated through sales to outside parties. Despite these similarities, significant differences do exist. Because of the nature of the transaction, no sales/purchases balances are recorded by the individual companies when land is transferred. Instead, a separate gain account is established by the seller. Since this gain is unearned, the balance has to be eliminated when preparing consolidated statements.

In addition, the subsequent resale of land to an outside party does not always occur in the year immediately following the transfer. Although inventory is normally disposed of within a relatively short period of time, land will often be held by the buyer for years if not permanently. Thus, the overvalued Land account can remain on the books of the acquiring company indefinitely. As long as the land is retained, elimination of the effects of the unrealized gain (the equivalent of Entry *G in inventory transfers) must be made for each subsequent consolidation. By repeating this worksheet entry every year, both the Land and the Retained Earnings accounts are properly stated in the consolidated financial statements.

Eliminating Unrealized Gains—Land Transfers

To illustrate these worksheet procedures, assume that Hastings Company and Patrick Company are related parties. On July 1, 1995, land that originally cost $60,000 is sold by Hastings to Patrick at a $100,000 transfer price. The seller reports a $40,000 gain; the buyer records the land at the $100,000 acquisition price. At the end of this fiscal period, the intercompany effect of this transaction must be eliminated for consolidation purposes:

Consolidation Entry TL (year of transfer)

Gain on Sale of Land.	40,000	
Land		40,000

To eliminate effects of intercompany transfer of land.
(Labeled "TL" in reference to the transferred land.)

This worksheet entry does eliminate the unrealized gain from the consolidated statements of 1995. However, as with the transfer of inventory, the effects created by the original transaction remain in the financial records of the individual companies for as long as the property is held. The gain recorded by Hastings carries through to retained earnings while Patrick's Land account retains the inflated transfer price. *Therefore, for every subsequent consolidation until the land is eventually sold, the elimination process must be repeated.* By including the following entry on each subsequent worksheet, the unrealized gain is removed from the asset and from the earnings reported by the combination.

Consolidation Entry *GL (every year following transfer)

Retained Earnings (beginning balance of seller)	40,000	
Land		40,000

To eliminate effects of intercompany transfer of land made in a previous year. (Labeled as "*GL" in reference to the gain on a land transfer occurring in a prior year.)

As in the handling of inventory transfers, the reduction in retained earnings is changed to an increase in the Investment account whenever the original sale is downstream and the equity method has been applied by the parent. In that specific situation, equity method adjustments have already corrected the timing of the parent's unrealized gain. Removing the gain has created a reduction in the Investment account that must be eliminated on the worksheet. Conversely, if sales were upstream, the retained earnings of the seller (the subsidiary) continues to be overstated even if the parent applies the equity method.

One final consolidation concern exists in accounting for intercompany transfers of land. If the property is ever sold to an outside party, the company making the sale records a gain or loss based on its recorded book value. However, this cost figure is actually the internal transfer price. The gain or loss being recognized is incorrect for consolidation purposes; it has not been computed by comparison to the land's historical cost. Once again, the separate financial records fail to reflect the transaction from the perspective of the single economic entity.

Therefore, if the land is eventually sold, the gain deferred at the time of the original transfer must be recognized. This profit has finally been earned by the sale of the property to outsiders. On the worksheet, the gain is removed one last time from beginning retained earnings (or the Investment account, if applicable). In this instance, though, the entry is completed by reclassifying the amount as a realized gain. The timing of income recognition has been switched from the year of transfer into the fiscal period in which the land is sold to the unrelated party.

Returning to the previous illustration, land was acquired by Hastings for $60,000 and sold to Patrick, a related party, for $100,000. Consequently, the $40,000 unrealized gain was eliminated on the consolidation worksheet in the year of transfer as well as in each succeeding period. However, if this land is subsequently sold to an outside party for $115,000, Patrick would recognize only a $15,000 gain. From the viewpoint of the business combination, the land (having been bought for $60,000) was actually sold at a $55,000 gain. To correct the reporting, the following consolidation entry must be made in the year that the property is sold to the unrelated party. This adjustment increases the $15,000 gain recorded by Patrick to the consolidated balance of $55,000.

Consolidation Entry *GL (year of sale to outside party)

Retained Earnings (Hastings)	40,000	
Gain on Sale of Land.		40,000

To remove intercompany gain from year of transfer so that total profit can be recognized in the current period when land is sold to an outside party.

As in the accounting for inventory transfers, the entire consolidation process demonstrated here accomplishes two major objectives:

1. Historical cost is reported for the transferred land for as long as it remains within the business combination.
2. Income recognition is deferred until the land is sold to outside parties.

Effect on Noncontrolling Interest Valuation—Land Transfers

The preceding discussion of intercompany land transfers has ignored the possible presence of a noncontrolling interest. In constructing financial statements for an economic entity that includes outside ownership, the guidelines already established for inventory transfers remain applicable.

If the original sale was a *downstream* transaction, neither the annual deferral nor the eventual recognition of the unrealized gain has any effect on the noncontrolling interest. The rationale for this treatment, as previously indicated, is that profits from downstream transfers relate solely to the parent company.

Conversely, if the transfer is made *upstream*, deferral and recognition of gains are attributed to the subsidiary and, hence, to the valuation of the noncontrolling interest. As with inventory, all noncontrolling interest balances are to be computed on the reported earnings of the subsidiary after adjustment for any upstream transfers.

To reiterate the accounting consequences stemming from land transfers, the following specific effects can be ascertained:

1. In the year of transfer, any unrealized gain is deferred and the land account is reduced to historical cost. When the gain is created by an upstream sale, the amount is also excluded in calculating the noncontrolling interest's share of the subsidiary's net income for that year.

2. Each year thereafter, the unrealized gain will be removed from the beginning retained earnings of the seller. If the transfer was upstream, eliminating this earlier gain directly affects the balances recorded within both Entry *C (if conversion to the equity method is required) and Entry S. The additional equity accrual (Entry *C, if needed) as well as the elimination of beginning stockholders' equity (Entry S) must be based on the newly adjusted balance in the subsidiary's retained earnings. This deferral process also has an impact on the noncontrolling interest's share of the subsidiary's income but only in the year of transfer and the eventual year of sale.

3. In the event that the land is ever sold to an outside party, the original gain is earned and must be reported by the consolidated entity.

Intercompany Transfer of Depreciable Assets

Just as land can be transferred between related parties, the intercompany sale of a host of other assets is possible. Equipment, patents, franchises, buildings, as well as other long-lived assets may be involved. Accounting for these transactions resembles that demonstrated for land sales. However, the subsequent calculation of depreciation or amortization does provide an added challenge in the development of consolidated statements.[8]

The Deferral of Unrealized Gains

When faced with intercompany sales of depreciable assets, the accountant's basic objective remains unchanged: *the deferral of unrealized gains to establish both*

---

[8] To avoid redundancy within this analysis, all further references are made to depreciation expense alone, although this discussion is equally applicable to the amortization of intangible assets or the depletion of wasting assets.

historical cost balances and appropriate income recognition within the consolidated statements. More specifically, gains created by these transfers are deferred until such time as the subsequent use or resale of the asset consummates the original transaction. For inventory sales, the culminating disposal normally occurs currently or in the year following the transfer. In contrast, transferred land is quite often never resold, thus permanently deferring the recognition of the intercompany profit.

For depreciable asset transfers, the ultimate realization of the gain normally occurs in a different manner; the property's use within the buyer's operations is reflected through depreciation. Recognition of this expense reduces the asset's book value every year and, hence, the overvaluation within that balance.

The depreciation systematically eliminates the unrealized gain not only from the asset account but also from retained earnings. For the buyer, excess expense results each year because the computation is based on the inflated transfer cost. This depreciation is then closed annually into retained earnings. *From a consolidated perspective, the extra expense gradually offsets the unrealized gain within this equity account. In fact, over the life of the asset, the depreciation process eliminates all effects of the transfer from both the asset balance as well as the Retained Earnings account.*

Depreciable Asset Transfers Illustrated

To examine the consolidation procedures required by the intercompany transfer of a depreciable asset, assume that Able Company sells equipment to Baker Company, a related party, at the current market value of $90,000. The equipment had originally been acquired by Able for $100,000 several years ago; since that time, $40,000 in accumulated depreciation has been recorded. The transfer is made on January 1, 1995, when the equipment has a 10-year remaining life.

Year of Transfer. The 1995 effects on the separate financial accounts of the two companies can be quickly enumerated:

1. Baker, as the buyer, enters the equipment into its records at the $90,000 transfer price. However, from a consolidated view, the $60,000 book value ($100,000 cost less $40,000 accumulated depreciation) is still appropriate.
2. Able, as the seller, reports a profit of $30,000, although nothing has yet been earned by the combination. This gain is then closed into the company's Retained Earnings account at the end of 1995.
3. Assuming application of the straight-line method of depreciation with no salvage value, Baker records expense of $9,000 at the end of 1995 ($90,000 transfer price/10 years). The buyer recognizes this amount rather than the $6,000 depreciation figure applicable to the consolidated entity ($60,000 book value/10 years).

To report these events as seen by the business combination, both the $30,000 unrealized gain and the $3,000 inflation in depreciation expense must be eliminated on the worksheet. For clarification purposes, two separate consolidation entries are shown here for 1995. However, they can be combined into a single adjustment.

Consolidation Entry TA: (year of transfer)

Gain on Sale of Equipment	30,000	
Equipment	10,000	
Accumulated Depreciation		40,000

To remove unrealized gain and return equipment accounts to balances based on original historical cost. (Labeled "TA" in reference to transferred asset.)

Consolidation Entry ED: (year of transfer)

Accumulated Depreciation	3,000	
Depreciation Expense		3,000

To eliminate overstatement of depreciation expense caused by inflated transfer price. (Labeled "ED" in reference to excess depreciation.)
Entry must be repeated for all 10 years of the equipment's life.

From the viewpoint of a single entity, these entries accomplish several objectives.

- The asset's historical cost of $100,000 is reinstated.
- By recording accumulated depreciation of $40,000, the January 1, 1995, book value is returned to the appropriate $60,000 figure.
- The $30,000 unrealized gain recorded by Able is eliminated so that this intercompany profit does not appear in the consolidated income statement.
- Depreciation for the year is reduced from $9,000 to $6,000, the appropriate expense based on historical cost.

Years Following Transfer.   Once again, the preceding worksheet entries do not actually remove the effects of the intercompany transfer from the individual records of these two organizations. Both the unrealized gain and the excess depreciation expense remain on the separate books and are closed into the retained earnings of the respective companies at year's end. Similarly, the Equipment account along with the related accumulated depreciation continue to hold balances based on the transfer price and not historical cost. *Thus, for every subsequent period, the separately reported figures must be adjusted on the worksheet to present the consolidated totals from the perspective of a single entity.*

To derive worksheet entries at any future point, the balances in the accounts of the individual companies must be ascertained and compared to the figures appropriate for the business combination. As an illustration, the separate records of Able and Baker two years after the transfer (December 31, 1996) follow. Consolidated totals are then calculated based on the original historical cost of $100,000 and accumulated depreciation of $40,000.

Individual Records, 12/31/96

Equipment—transfer price		$ 90,000
Accumulated depreciation (2 years)		$ 18,000)
Retained earnings, 1/1/96		
Unrealized gain	$(30,000)	
Depreciation expense (1995).	9,000	$(21,000)

Consolidated Perspective, 12/31/96

			Difference with Individual Records
Equipment—cost		$100,000	$ 10,000
Accumulated depreciation:			
Originally reported.	$(40,000)		
For 1995–96	(12,000)	$ (52,000)	$(34,000)
Retained earnings, 1/1/96			
Depreciation expense (1995)		$ 6,000	$ 27,000

NOTE: Parentheses indicate a credit.

Because effects of the transfer continue to exist in the separate financial records, the various accounts have to be corrected in each succeeding consolidation. However, the amounts involved must be updated every period because of the continual impact that depreciation has on these balances. As an example, to adjust the individual figures to the consolidated totals derived earlier, the 1996 worksheet must include the following entry. The two entries shown for 1995 have been combined in this second illustration.

Consolidation Entry *TA (year following transfer)

Retained Earnings, 1/1/96—Able		
(as original seller of asset)	27,000	
Equipment	10,000	
Depreciation Expense		3,000
Accumulated Depreciation		34,000

To eliminate remaining effects of 1995 transfer so that consolidated accounts are based on the original historical cost figures. See previous computations.

Although adjustments of the asset and depreciation expense remain constant, the change in beginning retained earnings and accumulated depreciation vary with each succeeding consolidation. At December 31, 1995, the individual companies closed out both the unrealized gain of $30,000 and the initial $3,000 overstatement of depreciation expense. Therefore, as reflected in Entry *TA, the beginning retained earnings account for 1996 is overvalued by a net amount of only $27,000 rather than $30,000. *Over the life of the asset, the unrealized gain in retained earnings will be systematically reduced to zero as excess depreciation expense ($3,000) is closed out each year.* Hence, on subsequent consolidation worksheets, the beginning retained earnings account is decreased by $27,000 in 1996, by $24,000 in 1997, and $21,000 in the following period. This reduction continues until the effect of the unrealized gain no longer exists at the end of 10 years.

If this equipment is ever resold to an outside party, the remaining portion of the gain would be consummated. As in the previous discussion of land, the intercompany profit that exists at that date must be recognized on the consolidated income statement to arrive at the appropriate amount of gain or loss on the sale.

Effect on Noncontrolling Interest Valuation—Depreciable Asset Transfers

Because of the lack of official guidance, no easy answer exists about the assignment of any income effects created within the consolidation process. Consistent with the previous sections of this chapter, all income is assigned here to the original seller. In Entry *TA, for example, the beginning retained earnings account of Able (the seller) is reduced. Both the unrealized gain on the transfer and the excess depreciation expense subsequently recognized are assigned to that party.

Thus, once again, downstream sales are assumed to have no effect on any noncontrolling interest values. The parent made the sale rather than the subsidiary. Conversely, the impact on income created by upstream sales must be taken into account in computing the balances attributed to these outside owners. Currently, this approach is one of many acceptable alternatives. However, in its future deliberations on consolidation policies and procedures, the FASB may possibly mandate a specific allocation pattern.

Summary

1. The transfer of assets, especially inventory, between the members of a business combination is a common practice. In producing consolidated financial statements, any effects on the separate accounting records created by such transfers must be removed because the transactions did not occur with an outside, unrelated party.

2. Inventory transfers are the most prevalent form of intercompany asset transaction. Despite being only a transfer, one company records a sale while the other reports a purchase. These balances are reciprocals that have to be offset on the worksheet in the process of producing consolidated figures.

3. Additional accounting problems result if inventory is transferred at a markup. Any portion of the merchandise still held at year-end would be valued at more than historical cost because of the inflation in price. Furthermore, the gross profit reported by the seller on these goods is unrealized from a consolidation perspective. Thus, this gain must be removed from ending inventory, a figure that appears as an asset on the balance sheet and as a negative component within cost of goods sold.

4. Unrealized inventory gains also create a consolidation problem in the year following the transfer. Within the separate accounting systems, the seller closes the gross profit to retained earnings. The buyer's ending inventory becomes the beginning balance (within cost of goods sold) of the next period. Therefore, the inflation must be removed again but this time in the subsequent year. Beginning retained earnings of the seller is decreased to eliminate the unrealized gain while cost of goods sold is reduced to remove the overstatement from the beginning inventory component. Through this process, the intercompany profit is deferred from the year of transfer so that recognition can be made at the point of disposal or consumption.

5. The deferral and subsequent realization of intercompany gains raises a question concerning the valuation of noncontrolling interest balances: Does the change in the period of recognition alter these calculations? Although the issue is being studied by the FASB, no formal answer to this question is yet found in official accounting pronouncements. In this textbook, the deferral of gains from upstream transfers (from subsidiary to parent) is assumed to affect the noncontrolling interest whereas downstream transactions (from parent to subsidiary) do not. When upstream transfers are involved, noncontrolling interest values are based on the earned figures remaining after adjustment for any unrealized gains.

6. Inventory is not the only asset that can be sold between the members of a business combination. For example, transfers of land sometimes occur. Once again, if the price exceeds original cost, the asset is stated on the buyer's records at an inflated value while an unrealized gain is recognized by the seller. As with inventory, the consolidation process must return the asset's recorded balance to cost while deferring the gain. Repetition of this procedure is necessary in every consolidation for as long as the land remains within the business combination.

7. The consolidation process required by the intercompany transfer of depreciable assets differs somewhat from that demonstrated for inventory and land. Unrealized gain created by the transaction must still be eliminated along with the overstatement of the asset. However, because of subsequent depreciation, these adjustments systematically change from period to period. Following the transfer, depreciation is computed by the buyer based on the new inflated transfer price. Thus, expense is recorded that reduces the carrying value of the asset at a rate in excess of appropriate depreciation; the book value moves closer to the historical cost figure each time that depreciation is recorded. Additionally, since the excess depreciation is closed annually to retained earnings, the overstatement of the equity account resulting from the unrealized gain is constantly reduced. To produce consolidated figures at any point in time, the remaining inflation in these figures (as well as in the current depreciation expense) must be determined and removed.

Comprehensive Illustration

PROBLEM   (Estimated Time: 45 to 65 Minutes)

On January 1, 1990, Daisy Company purchased 80 percent of Rose Company for $594,000 in cash. The total book value of Rose on that date was $610,000. The newly acquired subsidiary possessed equipment (10-year remaining life) that was undervalued by $75,000 in the company's accounting records and land that was undervalued by $15,000. Any goodwill associated with this purchase will be amortized over 10 years.

Daisy decided to acquire Rose so that the subsidiary could furnish component parts for the parent's production process. During the ensuing years, Rose did sell inventory to Daisy as follows:

Year	Cost to Rose Company	Transfer Price	Markup on Transfer Price	Transferred Inventory Being Held at End of Year (at transfer price)
1990	$ 60,000	$ 90,000	33.3%	$10,000
1991	80,000	100,000	20.0	15,000
1992	90,000	120,000	25.0	10,000
1993	100,000	140,000	28.6	20,000
1994	100,000	150,000	33.3	30,000
1995	96,000	160,000	40.0	40,000

Any transferred merchandise retained by Daisy at the end of a year was always put into production during the following period.

On January 1, 1993, Daisy sold several pieces of equipment to Rose. These assets had a 10-year remaining life and were being depreciated on the straight-line method with no salvage value. This equipment was transferred at an $80,000 price, although it had an original cost to Daisy of $100,000 and a book value at the date of exchange of $44,000.

On January 1, 1995, Daisy sold land to Rose for $60,000, the fair market value at that date. The original cost had been only $40,000. By the end of 1995, no payment had yet been made by Rose.

The following separate financial statements are for Daisy and Rose as of December 31, 1995. Daisy has applied the equity method to account for this investment.

	Daisy Company	Rose Company
Sales.	$ 900,000	$ 500,000
Cost of goods sold.	(600,000)	(300,000)
Operating expenses	(210,000)	(80,000)
Gain on sale of land	20,000	–0–
Income of Rose Company	65,400	–0–
Net income.	$ 175,400	$ 120,000
Retained earnings, 1/1/95	$ 620,000	$ 430,000
Net income.	175,400	120,000
Dividends paid	(55,400)	(50,000)
Retained earnings, 12/31/95	$ 740,000	$ 500,000
Cash and accounts receivable.	$ 380,000	$ 410,000
Inventory.	421,600	190,000
Investment in Rose Company.	711,600	–0–
Land.	452,800	280,000
Equipment	270,000	190,000
Accumulated depreciation	(180,000)	(50,000)
Total assets.	$2,056,000	$1,020,000
Liabilities	716,000	120,000
Common stock	600,000	400,000
Retained earnings, 12/31/95	740,000	500,000
Total liabilities and equities.	$2,056,000	$1,020,000

Required:

Answer the following questions:

a. By how much did Rose's book value increase during the period from January 1, 1990, through December 31, 1994?

b. During the initial years after the takeover, what annual amortization expense was recognized in connection with the parent's purchase price?

c. What amount of unrealized gain exists within the parent's inventory figures at the beginning and at the end of 1995?

d. Equipment has been transferred between the companies. What amount of excess depreciation is recognized in 1995 because of this transfer?

e. The parent reports Income of Rose Company for 1995 of $65,400. How was this figure calculated?

f. Without using a worksheet, determine consolidated totals.

g. Prepare the worksheet entries required at December 31, 1995, by the transfer of inventory, land, and equipment.

SOLUTION

a. The subsidiary's book value on the date of purchase was given as $610,000. At the beginning of 1995, the company's common stock and retained earnings total to $830,000 ($400,000 and $430,000, respectively). In the previous years, Rose's book value has apparently grown by $220,000 ($830,000 − $610,000).

b. To determine amortization, an allocation of the purchase price must first be made. The following allocations to equipment ($60,000) and goodwill ($34,000) lead to an annual expense of $9,400 for the initial years of the combination. The $12,000 assigned to land is not subject to amortization.

		Life (years)	Annual Amortization	Amortization 1990–95	Unamortized Value, 12/31/95
Purchase price . .	$ 594,000				
Book value of Rose Company ($610,000 × 80%)	(488,000)				
Excess cost over book value . . .	106,000				
Equipment undervaluation ($75,000 × 80%)	60,000	10	$6,000	$36,000	$24,000
Land undervaluation ($15,000 × 80%)	12,000				
Goodwill	$ 34,000	10	3,400	20,400	13,600
			$9,400		

c. Of the inventory transferred to Daisy during 1994, $30,000 is still held at the beginning of 1995. This merchandise contains an unrealized gain of $10,000 ($30,000 × 33.3% [rounded] markup for that year). At year's end, $16,000 ($40,000 remaining inventory × 40% markup) is viewed as an unrealized gain.

d. Excess depreciation for 1995 is $3,600. Equipment with a book value of $44,000 was transferred at a price of $80,000. The addition of $36,000 to this asset's account balance would be written off over 10 years for an extra $3,600 per year.

e. According to the separate statements given, the subsidiary reports net income of $120,000. However, in determining the income allocation between the parent and the noncontrolling interest, this reported figure must be adjusted for the effects of any *upstream* transfers. Since the inventory was sold upstream from Rose to Daisy, the $10,000 gain deferred in requirement c. from 1994 into the current period is attributed to the subsidiary (as the seller). Likewise, the $16,000 unrealized gain at year's end is viewed as a reduction in Rose's income.

    All other transfers are downstream and not considered to have an effect on the subsidiary. Therefore, the Income of Rose Company balance can be verified as follows:

Rose Company's reported income—1995	$120,000
Recognition of 1994 unrealized gain	+10,000
Deferral of 1995 unrealized gain	(16,000)
Earned income of subsidiary from consolidated perspective	114,000
Parent's ownership percentage	80%
Equity income accrual	$ 91,200
Adjustments attributed to parent's ownership:	
Amortization expense—1995 (see requirement *b.*)	(9,400)
Deferral of unrealized gain—land	(20,000)
Removal of excess depreciation (see requirement *d.*)	+3,600
Income of Rose Company—1995	$ 65,400

f. Each of the 1995 consolidated totals for this business combination can be determined as follows:

> *Sales* = $1,240,000. The parent book value is added to the subsidiary's book value less the $160,000 in intercompany transfers for the period.
>
> *Cost of Goods Sold* = $746,000. The computation begins by adding the parent book value to the subsidiary's book value less the $160,000 in intercompany transfers for the period. The $10,000 unrealized gain from the previous year is then deducted to enable this income to be recognized currently. Next, the $16,000 ending unrealized gain is added to cost of goods sold to defer the income until a later year when the goods are sold to an outside party.
>
> *Operating Expenses* = $295,800. The parent's book value is first added to the subsidiary's book value. Annual amortization of $9,400 on the purchase price allocations (see requirement *b.*) must also be included. Excess depreciation of $3,600 resulting from the transfer of equipment (see requirement *e.*) is removed.
>
> *Gain on Sale of Land* = –0–. This amount is eliminated for consolidation purposes because the transaction was intercompany.
>
> *Income of Rose Company* = –0–. The equity income figure is removed so that the actual revenues and expenses of the subsidiary can be included in the financial statements without double-counting.
>
> *Noncontrolling Interest in Subsidiary's Income* = $22,800. In requirement *d.*, the earned income of the subsidiary was computed as $114,000 after adjustments were made for unrealized upstream gains. Since outsiders hold 20 percent of the subsidiary, an allocation of $22,800 ($114,000 × 20%) is necessary.
>
> *Net Income* = $175,400. This total is derived from the previous consolidated balances. Since the equity method has been applied, consolidated net income is also equal to the balance reported by the parent.

Retained Earnings, 1/1/95 = $620,000. The equity method has been applied; therefore, the parent's balance is equal to the consolidated total.

Dividends Paid = $55,400. Only the amount the parent paid is shown in the consolidated statements. Distributions made by the subsidiary to the parent are eliminated as intercompany transfers. Any payment to the noncontrolling interest is viewed as a reduction in the ending balance attributed to these outside owners.

Cash and Accounts Receivable = $730,000. The two book values are added after removal of the $60,000 intercompany receivable created by the transfer of land.

Inventory = $595,600. The two book values are added after removal of the $16,000 ending unrealized gain (see requirement *c*.).

Investment in Rose Company = –0–. The investment balance is eliminated so that the actual assets and liabilities of the subsidiary can be included.

Land = $724,800. The two book values are added. The $20,000 unrealized gain created by the transfer is removed. The $12,000 allocation from the purchase price is added.

Equipment = $540,000. The two book values are added. Because of the intercompany transfer, $20,000 must also be included to adjust the $80,000 transfer price to the original $100,000 cost of the asset. A $60,000 allocation within the purchase price must also be recognized.

Accumulated Depreciation = $311,200. The book values are added together along with the $36,000 that has been written off in connection with the purchase price allocation to equipment ($6,000 per year for six years). The $56,000 in accumulated depreciation on the equipment (before its transfer) must also be reinstated. A reduction of $10,800 is then made to remove the excess depreciation subsequently recorded on this same equipment ($3,600 per year for three years).

Goodwill = $13,600. The $34,000 allocation is recognized less six years of amortization ($20,400 or $3,400 per year for six years).

Total Assets = $2,292,800. This figure is a summation of the preceding consolidated assets.

Liabilities = $776,000. The two book values are added after removal of the $60,000 intercompany payable created by the transfer of land.

Noncontrolling Interest in Subsidiary, 12/31/96 = $176,800. This figure is composed of several different balances:

Book value of subsidiary, 1/1/95 (common stock and beginning retained earnings). . .	$830,000
Unrealized gain on upstream transfer as of beginning of year	(10,000)
Earned book value of subsidiary, 1/1/95	$820,000
Noncontrolling interest	20%
Noncontrolling interest, 1/1/95.	$164,000
Noncontrolling interest in subsidiary's income (see above)	22,800
Less: Dividends paid to noncontrolling interest ($50,000 × 20%)	(10,000)
Noncontrolling interest, 12/31/95.	$176,800

Common Stock = $600,000. The parent company balance only is reported within the consolidated statements.

Retained Earnings, 12/31/95 = $740,000. Retained earnings are found by adding consolidated net income to the beginning retained earnings balance and then subtracting the dividends paid. All of these figures have been computed previously.

Total Liabilities and Equities = $2,292,800. This figure is the summation of all consolidated liabilities and equities.

g.
CONSOLIDATION WORKSHEET ENTRIES— INTERCOMPANY TRANSACTIONS
December 31, 1995

Inventory

*Entry *G*

Retained Earnings, 1/1/95—Subsidiary	10,000	
Cost of Goods Sold		10,000

To remove 1994 unrealized gain from beginning balances of the current year. Since transfers were upstream, retained earnings of the subsidiary (as the original seller) is being reduced. Balance is computed in requirement *c*.

Entry TI

Sales	160,000	
Cost of Goods Sold		160,000

To eliminate current year intercompany transfer of inventory.

Entry G

Cost of Goods Sold	16,000	
Inventory		16,000

To remove 1995 unrealized gain from ending accounts of the current year. Balance is computed in requirement *c*.

Land

Entry TL

Gain on Sale of Land	20,000	
Land		20,000

To eliminate gain created on first day of current year by an intercompany transfer of land.

Equipment

*Entry *TA*

Equipment	20,000	
Investment in Rose Company	28,800	
Accumulated Depreciation		48,800

    To remove unrealized gain (as of January 1, 1995) created by
intercompany transfer of equipment and to adjust equipment and
accumulated depreciation to historical cost figures.

        Equipment is increased from the $80,000 transfer price to
$100,000 cost.

        Accumulated depreciation of $56,000 was eliminated at time of
transfer. Excess depreciation of $3,600 per year has been recorded for
the two prior years ($7,200); thus, the accumulated depreciation is
now only $48,800 less than cost based figure.

        The unrealized gain on the transfer was $36,000 ($80,000 less
$44,000). That figure has now been reduced by two years of excess
depreciation ($7,200). Because the parent used the equity method and
this transfer was downstream, the adjustment here is to the
investment account rather than the parent's beginning retained
earnings.

Entry ED

Accumulated Depreciation	3,600	
Operating Expenses (depreciation)		3,600

    To eliminate the current year overstatement of depreciation created
by inflated transfer price.

Appendix: Transfers— Alternative Approaches

In this chapter, one method is used in consolidating the effects of intercompany transfers and unrealized gains when a noncontrolling interest is present. This approach was chosen because it is consistent with the guidelines put forth in *ARB 51*. Over the years, several other possibilities have been devised and considered. The FASB's discussion memorandum, *An Analysis of Issues Related to Consolidation Policy and Procedures,* describes eight methods of consolidating intercompany transactions (three for downstream transfers and five for upstream). The following table is designed to indicate the range of potential effects on consolidated totals by demonstrating six of these approaches (two for downstream and four for upstream). All methods except for proportionate consolidation have been included.

    The figures used in this illustration are the same as in the Large Company and Small Company example in the first section of this chapter.

- Large owns 70 percent of the outstanding stock of Small.
- Intercompany inventory transfers during the year amount to $200,000.
- The remaining unrealized gain at the end of the year is $40,000.
- Subsidiary reported income is $100,000.

Downstream Transfers (from parent to subsidiary)

	ARB 51* *Economic Unit Concept* *One Variation of Parent* *Company Concept* *(method used in this textbook)*	*Another* *Variation of* *Parent Company* *Concept*
Sales	Eliminate all $200,000 transfers	Eliminate $140,000 (70%) of the transfers
Purchases	Eliminate all $200,000 transfers	Eliminate $140,000 (70%) of the transfers
Unrealized gain	Eliminate all $40,000	Eliminate $28,000 (70%)
Income assigned to noncontrolling interests	30% of $100,000 reported income or $30,000	30% of $100,000 reported income or $30,000

Upstream Transfers (from subsidiary to parent)

	ARB 51 *Economic Unit Concept* *(method used in this* *textbook)*	*One Variation* *of Parent Company* *Concept*	*Another* *Approach Based On* *ARB 51*	*Another Variation* *of Parent Company* *Concept*
Sales	Eliminate all $200,000 transfers	Eliminate $140,000 (70%) of the transfers	Eliminate all $200,000 transfers	Eliminate all $200,000 transfers
Purchases	Eliminate all $200,000 transfers	Eliminate $140,000 (70%) of the transfers	Eliminate all $200,000 transfers	Eliminate all $200,000 transfers
Unrealized gain	Eliminate all $40,000	Eliminate $28,000 (70%)	Eliminate all $40,000	Eliminate $28,000 (70%)
Income assigned to noncontrolling interests	30% of $60,000 realized income after removing $40,000 unrealized gain or $18,000	30% of $100,000 reported income or $30,000	30% of $100,000 reported income or $30,000	30% of $100,000 reported income or $30,000

* Titles indicate authority for each approach.

Questions

1. Intercompany transfers between the component companies of a business combination are quite common. Why do these intercompany transactions occur so frequently?

2. Barker Company owns 80 percent of the outstanding voting stock of Walden Company. During the current year, intercompany sales amount to $100,000. These transactions were made with a markup equal to 40 percent of the transfer price. In consolidating the two companies, what amount of these sales would be eliminated?

3. How are unrealized inventory gains created, and what consolidation entries are necessitated by the presence of these gains?

4. James, Inc. sells inventory to Matthews Company, a related party. The inventory was sold at James's standard markup. At the end of the current fiscal year, some portion of this inventory is still being held by Matthews.

If consolidated financial statements are to be prepared, why are worksheet entries required in two different fiscal periods?

5. When intercompany gains are present in any year, how are the noncontrolling interest calculations affected?

6. A worksheet is being developed to consolidate Williams, Incorporated and Simpson Company. Considerable intercompany transactions have been made between these two organizations. How would the consolidation process be affected if these transfers were downstream? How would the consolidation process be affected if these transfers were upstream?

7. King Company owns a 90 percent interest in the outstanding voting shares of Pawn Company. Pawn reports a net income of $110,000 for the current year. Intercompany sales are made at regular intervals between the two companies. Unrealized gains of $30,000 were present in the beginning inventory balances, whereas $60,000 in similar gains were recorded at the end of the year. What is the noncontrolling interest's share of the subsidiary's net income?

8. The consolidation process that is applicable when intercompany land transfers have occurred is somewhat different from that used for intercompany inventory sales. What differences should be noted?

9. A subsidiary sells land to the parent company at a significant gain. The parent holds the land for two years and then sells it to an outside party, also for a gain. How are these events accounted for by the business combination?

10. Why does an intercompany sale of a depreciable asset (such as equipment or a building) require subsequent adjustments to depreciation expense within the consolidation process?

11. If an intercompany sale of a depreciable asset has been made at a price above book value, the beginning retained earnings of the seller are reduced when preparing each subsequent consolidation. Why does the amount of the adjustment change from year to year?

Library Assignments

1. Read Chapter 6, "Intercompany Transactions," of the FASB discussion memorandum *An Analysis of Issues Related to Consolidation Policy and Procedures*. Select an approach that should be used in preparing consolidated financial statements where intercompany transfers occur and then justify its adoption.

2. Read the following as well as any other published materials that might be available concerning transfer pricing:

"The Transfer Pricing Dilemma—And A Dual Pricing Solution," *Journal of Accountancy* (Focus on Industry section), September 1987.

"Does Your Transfer Price Make Cents?" *Management Accounting*, December 1987.

"Resolving Conflicts in Intracompany Transfer Pricing," *Accountancy*, November 1986.

"Transfer Pricing in the 1990s," *Management Accounting*, February 1992.

"Transfer Pricing in a Dynamic Market," *Management Accounting*, February 1988.

Write a report outlining several methods of setting transfer prices on intercompany transfers. Select one approach as preferable and justify its application.

Problems

1. What is the impact on consolidated financial statements of upstream and downstream transfers?
   a. No difference exists in consolidated financial statements between upstream and downstream transfers.
   b. Downstream transfers affect the computation of the noncontrolling interest's share of the subsidiary's income but upstream transfers do not.
   c. Upstream transfers affect the computation of the noncontrolling interest's share of the subsidiary's income but downstream transfers do not.
   d. Downstream transfers may be ignored since they are made by the parent company.

2. King Corporation owns 80 percent of Lee Corporation's common stock. During October 1995, Lee sold merchandise to King for $100,000. At December 31, 1995, 50 percent of this merchandise remains in King's inventory. For 1995, gross profit percentages were 30 percent for King and 40 percent for Lee. The amount of unrealized intercompany profit in ending inventory at December 31, 1995, that should be eliminated in the consolidation process is:
   a. $40,000.
   b. $20,000.
   c. $16,000.
   d. $15,000.

   (AICPA adapted)

3. When intercompany transfers occur, how is the noncontrolling interest's share of the subsidiary's income computed?
   a. The subsidiary's reported income is adjusted for the impact of upstream transfers prior to computing the noncontrolling interest's allocation.

    b. The subsidiary's reported income is adjusted for the impact of all transfers prior to computing the noncontrolling interest's allocation.

    c. The subsidiary's reported income is not adjusted for the impact of transfers prior to computing the noncontrolling interest's allocation.

    d. The subsidiary's reported income is adjusted for the impact of downstream transfers prior to computing the noncontrolling interest's allocation.

4. Bellgrade, Inc., acquired a 60 percent interest in the Hansen Company several years ago. During 1994, Hansen sold inventory costing $75,000 to Bellgrade for $100,000. A total of 16 percent of this inventory was not sold to outsiders until 1995. During 1995, Hansen sold inventory costing $96,000 to Bellgrade for $120,000. A total of 35 percent of this inventory was not sold to outsiders until 1996. In 1995, Bellgrade reported cost of goods sold of $380,000 while Hansen reported $210,000. What is consolidated cost of goods sold?

    a. $465,600.

    b. $473,440.

    c. $474,400.

    d. $522,400.

5. Top Company holds 90 percent of the common stock of Bottom Company. In 1995, Top reports sales of $800,000 and cost of goods sold of $600,000. For this same period, Bottom has sales of $300,000 and cost of goods sold of $180,000. During 1995, Top sold merchandise to Bottom for $100,000. The subsidiary still possesses 40 percent of this inventory at the end of 1995. Top had established the transfer price based on its normal markup. What are consolidated sales and cost of goods sold?

    a. $1,000,000 and $690,000.

    b. $1,000,000 and $705,000.

    c. $1,000,000 and $740,000.

    d. $970,000 and $696,000.

6. Use the same information as in problem 5 except assume that the transfers were from Bottom Company to Top Company. What are the consolidated sales and cost of goods sold for 1995?

    a. $1,000,000 and $720,000.

    b. $1,000,000 and $755,000.

    c. $1,000,000 and $696,000.

    d. $970,000 and $712,000.

7. Hardwood Inc., holds a 90 percent interest in Pittstoni Company. During 1994, Pittstoni sold inventory costing $77,000 to Hardwood for $110,000. A total of $40,000 of this inventory was not sold to outsiders until 1995. During 1995, Pittstoni sold inventory costing $72,000 to Hardwood for $120,000. A total of $50,000 of this inventory was not sold to outsiders until 1996. In 1995, Hardwood reported net income of $150,000 while Pitt-

stoni reported $90,000. What is the noncontrolling interest in the income of the subsidiary?

a. $8,000.

b. $8,200.

c. $9,000.

d. $9,800.

8. Dunn Corporation owns 100 percent of Grey Corporation's common stock. On January 2, 1995, Dunn sold to Grey, for $40,000, machinery with a carrying amount of $30,000. Grey is depreciating the acquired machinery over a five-year life by the straight-line method. The net adjustments to compute 1995 and 1996 consolidated net income would be an increase (decrease) of

	1995	1996
a.	($ 8,000)	$2,000
b.	($ 8,000)	–0–
c.	($10,000)	$2,000
d.	($10,000)	–0–

(AICPA adapted)

9. Wallton Corporation owns 70 percent of the outstanding stock of Hastings, Incorporated. On January 1, 1993, Wallton acquired a building with a 10-year life for $300,000. No salvage value was anticipated and the building was to be depreciated on the straight-line method. On January 1, 1995, Wallton sold this building to Hastings for $280,000. At that time, the building had a remaining life of eight years but still no expected salvage value. In preparing financial statements for 1995, how does this transfer affect the computation of consolidated net income?

a. Income must be reduced by $32,000.

b. Income must be reduced by $35,000.

c. Income must be reduced by $36,000.

d. Income must be reduced by $40,000.

Questions 10–15 are based on the following data:

On January 1, 1995, Jarel buys 80 percent of the outstanding voting stock of Suarez for $260,000. Of this payment, $20,000 was allocated to equipment (with a five-year life) that had been undervalued on Suarez's books by $25,000. Any goodwill would be amortized over its maximum life.

As of December 31, 1995, the financial statements appeared as follows:

	Jarel	Suarez
Revenues	$ 300,000	$200,000
Cost of goods sold	140,000	80,000
Expenses	20,000	10,000
Net income	$ 140,000	$110,000
Retained earnings, 1/1/95	$ 300,000	$150,000
Net income	140,000	110,000
Dividends paid	–0–	–0–
Retained earnings, 12/31/95	$ 440,000	$260,000
Cash and receivables	$ 210,000	$ 90,000
Inventory	150,000	110,000
Investment in Jarel	260,000	–0–
Equipment (net)	440,000	300,000
Total assets	$1,060,000	$500,000
Liabilities	$ 420,000	$140,000
Common stock	200,000	100,000
Retained earnings, 12/31/95	440,000	260,000
Total liabilities and equities	$1,060,000	$500,000

During 1995, Jarel bought inventory for $80,000 and sold it to Suarez for $100,000. Only half of this purchase has been paid for by Suarez by the end of the year. Sixty percent of these goods are still in the company's possession on December 31.

10. What is the total of consolidated revenues?
    a. $500,000.
    b. $460,000.
    c. $420,000.
    d. $400,000.

11. What is the total of consolidated expenses?
    a. $30,000.
    b. $35,000.
    c. $34,000.
    d. $38,000.

12. What is the total of consolidated cost of goods sold?
    a. $140,000.
    b. $152,000.
    c. $132,000.
    d. $145,000.

13. What is the consolidated total of noncontrolling interest appearing on the balance sheet?
    a. $72,000.
    b. $69,600.
    c. $67,000.
    d. $70,600.

14. What is the consolidated total for equipment (net) at December 31?
    a. $680,000.
    b. $756,000.
    c. $764,000.
    d. $848,000.

15. What is the consolidated total for inventory at December 31?
    a. $240,000.
    b. $248,000.
    c. $250,000.
    d. $260,000.

16. Following are several figures reported for Pop and Sam as of December 31, 1995:

	Pop	*Sam*
Inventory	$300,000	$100,000
Sales	700,000	500,000
Investment income . . .	not given	
Cost of goods sold . . .	300,000	200,000
Expenses	200,000	200,000

   Pop acquired 80 percent of Sam on January 1, 1988. Goodwill of $180,000 resulting from that transaction is being amortized over its maximum life. During 1995, Sam sells inventory costing $100,000 to Pop for $150,000. Of this inventory, 10 percent remains at year's end. On a 1995 consolidation, what totals would be reported for the following accounts:

   Inventory.
   Sales.
   Cost of Goods Sold.
   Expenses.
   Noncontrolling Interest in the Subsidiary's Net Income.

17. Smith Corporation acquired 80 percent of the outstanding voting stock of Huss, Inc. on January 1, 1988, when Huss had a net book value of $400,000. Goodwill established by this acquisition is being amortized at a rate of $5,000 per year.

Smith reports net income for 1995 of $300,000 while Huss reports $110,000. Smith distributed $100,000 in dividends during this period; Huss paid $40,000. At the end of the year, selected figures from the two companies' balance sheets were as follows:

	Smith Corporation	Huss, Inc.
Inventory	$140,000	$ 90,000
Land	600,000	200,000
Equipment (net)	400,000	300,000
Common stock	400,000	200,000
Retained earnings, 12/31/95	600,000	400,000

During 1994, intercompany sales of $90,000 (original cost of $54,000) were made. Only 20 percent of this inventory was still being held at the end of 1994. In 1995, $120,000 in intercompany sales were made with an original cost of $66,000. Of this merchandise, 30 percent had not been resold to outside parties by the end of the year.

Each of the following questions should be considered as an independent situation.

a. If the intercompany sales were upstream, what would be the noncontrolling interest's share of the subsidiary's 1995 net income?

b. What is the consolidated balance in the ending Inventory account?

c. If the intercompany sales were downstream, what would be the noncontrolling interest's share of the subsidiary's 1995 net income?

d. If the intercompany sales were downstream, what would be the consolidated net income prior to the reduction for the noncontrolling interest's share of the subsidiary's income? Assume that Smith uses the cost method to account for this investment.

e. If the intercompany sales were downstream, what would be the consolidated balance for retained earnings as of the end of 1995? Assume that Smith uses the partial equity method to account for this investment.

f. If the intercompany sales were upstream, what would be the consolidated balance for retained earnings as of the end of 1995? Assume that Smith uses the partial equity method to account for this investment.

g. Assume that no intercompany inventory sales occurred between Smith and Huss. Instead, in 1992, Huss sold land costing $30,000 to Smith for $50,000. On the 1995 consolidated balance sheet, what value should be reported for land?

h. Assume that no intercompany inventory or land sales occurred between Smith and Huss. Instead, on January 1, 1994, Huss sold equipment (that originally cost $100,000 but had a $60,000 book value on that date) to Smith for $80,000. At the time of sale, the equipment had a remaining useful life of five years. What worksheet entries are made for a December 31, 1995, consolidation of these two companies to eliminate the impact of the intercompany transfer? For 1995, what is the noncontrolling interest's share of Huss's net income?

18. Rockney owns 60 percent of the outstanding stock of Dabney. Dabney reports net income for 1995 of $120,000. Since being acquired, the subsidiary has regularly supplied inventory to Rockney at 20 percent more than cost. Sales to Rockney amounted to $252,000 in 1994 and $288,000 in 1995. Approximately one tenth of the inventory purchased during any one year is not used until the following period.

Required:

a. What is the noncontrolling interest's share of the Dabney's income in 1995?
b. Prepare the 1995 and 1996 consolidation entries that would be required by the preceding intercompany inventory transfers.

19. Several years ago Penguin, Inc., purchased an 80 percent interest in Snow Company. The book values of Snow's asset and liability accounts at that time were considered to be equal to their fair market values. Penguin paid an amount corresponding to the underlying book value of Snow so that no allocations or goodwill resulted from the purchase price.

   The following selected account balances are from the individual financial records of these two companies as of December 31, 1995:

	Penguin	Snow
Sales	$640,000	$360,000
Cost of goods sold	290,000	197,000
Operating expenses	150,000	105,000
Retained earnings, 1/1/95.	740,000	180,000
Inventory	346,000	110,000
Buildings (net)	358,000	157,000
Investment income	not given	

   Each of the following problems is an independent situation.

a. Assume that Penguin sells inventory to Snow at a markup equal to 40 percent of cost. Intercompany transfers were $90,000 in 1994 and $110,000 in 1995. Of this inventory, $28,000 of the 1994 transfers were retained and then sold by Snow in 1995 while $42,000 of the 1995 transfers were held until 1996.

   On consolidated financial statements for 1995, what balances would appear for the following accounts:

   Cost of Goods Sold.
   Inventory.
   Noncontrolling Interest in Subsidiary's Net Income.

b. Assume that Snow sells inventory to Penguin at a markup equal to 40 percent of cost. Intercompany transfers were $50,000 in 1994 and $80,000 in 1995. Of this inventory, $21,000 of the 1994 transfers were retained and then sold by Penguin in 1995, whereas $35,000 of the 1995 transfers were held until 1996.

On consolidated financial statements for 1995, what balances would appear for the following accounts:

Cost of Goods Sold.

Inventory.

Noncontrolling Interest in Subsidiary's Net Income.

c. Penguin sells a building to Snow on January 1, 1994, for $80,000, although the book value of this asset was only $50,000 on this date. The building had a five-year remaining life and was to be depreciated using the straight-line method with no salvage value.

On consolidated financial statements for 1995, what balances would appear for the following accounts:

Buildings (net).

Expenses.

Noncontrolling Interest in Subsidiary's Net Income.

20. Allen, Inc. owns all of the outstanding stock of Bowen Corporation. Amortization expense of $9,000 per year resulted from the original purchase. For 1995, the companies had the following account balances:

	Allen	Bowen
Sales	$900,000	$500,000
Cost of goods sold	400,000	300,000
Operating expenses . . .	300,000	120,000
Investment income . . .	not given	–0–
Dividends paid	60,000	40,000

Intercompany sales of $200,000 occurred during 1994 and again in 1995. This merchandise cost $140,000 each year. Of the total transfers, $60,000 was still held on December 31, 1994, with $45,000 unsold on December 31, 1995.

Required:

a. For consolidation purposes, does the direction of the transfers (upstream or downstream) affect the balances to be reported here.

b. Prepare a consolidated income statement for the year ending December 31, 1995.

21. Plimpton holds 100 percent of the outstanding shares of Stanger. On January 1, 1993, Plimpton transferred equipment to Stanger for $70,000. The equipment had cost $110,000 originally but had a $40,000 book value and

five-year remaining life at the date of transfer. Depreciation expense is computed according to the straight-line method with no salvage value.

Consolidated financial statements for 1995 are currently being prepared. What worksheet entries are needed in connection with the consolidation of this asset? Assume that the parent applies the partial equity method.

22. On January 1, 1995, Slaughter sold equipment to Bennett (a wholly owned subsidiary) for $120,000 in cash. The equipment had originally cost $100,000 but had a book value of only $70,000 when transferred. On that date, the equipment had a five-year remaining life. Depreciation expense is computed using the straight-line method.

    Slaughter earned $220,000 in net income in 1995 (not including any investment income) while Bennett reported $90,000.

Required:

a. What is the consolidated net income for 1995?

b. What is the consolidated net income for 1995 if Slaughter owns only 90 percent of Bennett?

c. What is the consolidated net income for 1995 if Slaughter owns only 90 percent of Bennett and the equipment transfer had been upstream?

d. What is the consolidated net income for 1996 if Slaughter reports $240,000 (does not include investment income) and Bennett $100,000 in income? Assume that Bennett is a wholly owned subsidiary and the equipment transfer was downstream.

23. Anchovy purchased 90 percent of Yelton on January 1, 1993. Of the original price paid by the parent, $60,000 was allocated to undervalued equipment (with a 10-year life) and $80,000 was attributed to goodwill (to be written off over a 20-year period).

    Since the takeover, Yelton has transferred inventory to its parent as follows:

Year	Cost	Transfer Price	Remaining at Year End
1993	$20,000	$ 50,000	$20,000 (at transfer price)
1994	49,000	70,000	30,000 (at transfer price)
1995	50,000	100,000	40,000 (at transfer price)

On January 1, 1994, Anchovy sold a building to Yelton for $50,000. The building had originally cost $70,000 but had a book value at the date of transfer of only $30,000. The building is estimated to have a five-year remaining life (straight-line depreciation is used with no salvage value).

Selected figures from the December 31, 1995, trial balances of these two companies are as follows:

	Anchovy	*Yelton*
Sales	$600,000	$500,000
Cost of goods sold	400,000	260,000
Operating expenses	120,000	80,000
Investment income.	not given	
Inventory	220,000	80,000
Equipment (net)	140,000	110,000
Buildings (net).	350,000	190,000

Determine consolidated totals for each of these account balances.

24. On January 1, 1995, Sledge has common stock of $120,000 and retained earnings of $260,000. During that year, Sledge reported sales of $130,000, cost of goods sold of $70,000, and operating expenses of $40,000.

On January 1, 1990, 80 percent of Sledge's outstanding voting stock was acquired by Percy, Inc. At that date, $60,000 of the purchase price was assigned to goodwill (with a 40-year life) and $20,000 to an undervalued building (with a 10-year life).

In 1994, Sledge sold inventory costing $9,000 to Percy for $15,000. Of this merchandise, Percy continued to hold $5,000 at the end of that period. During 1995, inventory costing $11,000 was transferred to Percy for $20,000. Half of these items are still being held at year's end.

On January 1, 1994, Percy sold equipment to Sledge for $12,000. This asset originally cost $16,000 but had a January 1, 1994, book value of $9,000. At the time of transfer, the equipment's remaining life was estimated to be five years.

Percy has properly applied the equity method to the investment in Sledge.

Required:

a. Prepare worksheet entries to consolidate these two companies as of December 31, 1995.

b. Compute the noncontrolling interest in the subsidiary's income for 1995.

25. Big purchased 90 percent of the outstanding shares of Little on January 1, 1993, for $345,000 in cash. The subsidiary's stockholders' equity accounts totaled $330,000 on that day. However, a building held by Little (with a nine-year remaining life) was undervalued in the accounting records by $20,000. Any goodwill resulting from the purchase price is to be amortized over a 10-year period.

Little reported net income of $60,000 in 1993 and $80,000 in 1994. The company followed a policy of paying dividends each year equal to 30 percent of income.

Little sells inventory to Big as follows:

Year	Cost to Little	Transfer Price to Big	Inventory Remaining at Year's End (at transfer price)
1993	$69,000	$115,000	$25,000
1994	81,000	135,000	37,500
1995	92,800	160,000	50,000

At December 31, 1995, Big owes Little $16,000 for inventory acquired during the current period.

The following separate account balances are for these two companies for December 31, 1995, and the year then ended. Credits are indicated by parentheses.

	Big	Little
Sales revenues	$ (862,000)	$(366,000)
Cost of goods sold	515,000	209,000
Expenses	186,600	67,000
Investment income—Little	(70,600)	—
Net income	$ (231,000)	$ (90,000)
Retained earnings, 1/1/95	$ (488,000)	$(278,000)
Net income (above)	(231,000)	(90,000)
Dividends paid	136,000	27,000
Retained earnings, 12/31/95	$ (583,000)	$(341,000)
Cash and receivables	$ 146,000	$ 98,000
Inventory	255,000	136,000
Investment in Little	456,000	—
Land, buildings, and equipment (net)	959,000	328,000
Total assets	$ 1,816,000	$ 562,000
Liabilities	$ (718,000)	$ (71,000)
Common stock	(515,000)	(150,000)
Retained earnings, 12/31/95	(583,000)	(341,000)
Total liabilities and equities	$(1,816,000)	$(562,000)

Answer each of the following questions:
a. How much did the book value of the subsidiary increase during the previous two years of ownership (1993 and 1994)?
b. What was the annual amortization resulting from the purchase price allocations?
c. Were the intercompany transfers upstream or downstream?

d. What unrealized gain existed as of January 1, 1995?

e. What was the subsidiary's realized retained earnings as of January 1, 1995?

f. What unrealized gain existed as of December 31, 1995?

g. What was the subsidiary's realized net income for 1995?

h. What amounts make up the $70,600 Investment Income—Little account balance for 1995?

i. What was the noncontrolling interest's share of the subsidiary's net income for 1995?

j. What amounts make up the $456,000 Investment in Little account balance as of December 31, 1995?

k. What Entry S is required in producing a 1995 consolidation worksheet?

l. Without preparing a worksheet or consolidation entries, determine the consolidation balances for these two companies.

26. Asphalt acquired 70 percent of Broadway on June 11, 1984. Based on the purchase price, goodwill of $300,000 was recognized which is being amortized at the rate of $10,000 per year. The 1995 financial statements are as follows:

	Asphalt	*Broadway*
Sales	$ 800,000	$ 600,000
Cost of goods sold	(535,000)	(400,000)
Operating expenses	(100,000)	(100,000)
Dividend income	35,000	–0–
Net income	$ 200,000	$ 100,000
Retained earnings, 1/1/95	$1,300,000	$ 850,000
Net income	200,000	100,000
Dividends paid	(100,000)	(50,000)
Retained earnings, 12/31/95	$1,400,000	$ 900,000
Cash and receivables	$ 400,000	$ 300,000
Inventory	298,000	700,000
Investment in Broadway	902,000	–0–
Fixed assets	1,000,000	600,000
Accumulated depreciation	(300,000)	(200,000)
Totals	$2,300,000	$1,400,000
Liabilities	$ 600,000	$ 400,000
Common stock	300,000	100,000
Retained earnings	1,400,000	900,000
Totals	$2,300,000	$1,400,000

Asphalt sells inventory costing $72,000 to Broadway during 1994 for $120,000. At year's end, 30 percent is left. Asphalt sells inventory costing $200,000 to Broadway during 1995 for $250,000. At year's end, 20 percent is left. Under these circumstances, what are the consolidated balances for the following accounts:

Sales.

Cost of Goods Sold.

Operating Expenses.

Dividend Income.

Noncontrolling Interest in Consolidated Income.

Inventory.

Noncontrolling Interest in Subsidiary, 12/31/95.

27. Compute the balances in problem 26 again assuming that the intercompany transfers were all made from Broadway to Asphalt.

28. Following are financial statements for Topper Company and Kirby Company for 1995:

	Topper	*Kirby*
Sales and other income	$ 800,000	$ 600,000
Cost of goods sold	500,000	400,000
Operating and interest expense	100,000	160,000
Net income	$ 200,000	$ 40,000
Retained earnings, 1/1/95	$ 990,000	$ 500,000
Net income	200,000	40,000
Dividends paid	130,000	–0–
Retained earnings, 12/31/95	$1,060,000	$ 540,000
Cash and receivables	$ 220,000	$ 170,000
Inventory	224,000	160,000
Investment in Kirby	654,000	–0–
Equipment (net)	600,000	400,000
Buildings	1,000,000	800,000
Accumulated depreciation—buildings	(100,000)	(200,000)
Other assets	200,000	100,000
Total assets	$2,798,000	$1,430,000
Liabilities	$1,138,000	$ 590,000
Common stock	600,000	300,000
Retained earnings, 12/31/95	1,060,000	540,000
Total liabilities and equity	$2,798,000	$1,430,000

• Topper purchased 90 percent of Kirby on January 1, 1984, for $654,000 in cash. On the date of acquisition, Kirby held equipment (5-year life) which was undervalued on the financial records by $50,000 and liabilities (20-year life) that were overvalued $30,000. Any goodwill is being amortized over its maximum life.

• Between January 1, 1984, and December 31, 1994, Kirby earned a net income of $600,000 and paid dividends of $340,000.

• Kirby sells inventory each year to Topper with a markup equal to 20 percent of the transfer price. Intercompany sales were $145,000 in 1994 and $160,000 in 1995. On January 1, 1995, 30 percent of the 1994 transfers were still on hand and, on December 31, 1995, 40 percent of the 1995 transfers remained in inventory. Topper still owes $20,000 on the final shipment.

• Topper sold a building to Kirby on January 1, 1994. It had cost Topper $100,000 but had $90,000 in accumulated depreciation at the time of this transfer. The price was $25,000 in cash. At that time, the building had a five-year remaining life.

Required:

Determine all consolidated balances either computationally or by the use of a worksheet.

29. Atkins, Inc., and Smith, Inc., formed a business combination on January 1, 1989, when Atkins acquired a 60 percent interest in the common stock of Smith for $372,000. The book value of Smith on that day was $350,000. Patents held by the subsidiary (with a 12-year remaining life) were undervalued within the company's accounting records by $120,000. Any goodwill indicated by the acquisition price is to be amortized over 10 years.

Intercompany inventory sales between the two companies have been made as follows:

Year	Cost to Atkins	Transfer Price to Smith	Ending Balance (at transfer price)
1989	$ 60,000	$ 72,000	$15,000
1990	70,000	84,000	25,000
1991	80,000	100,000	20,000
1992	100,000	125,000	40,000
1993	90,000	120,000	30,000
1994	120,000	150,000	50,000
1995	112,000	160,000	40,000

Smith sold a building to Atkins on January 1, 1993, for $80,000. The building had a net book value of $30,000 on that date and a five-year life. No salvage value was expected for this asset which was being depreciated by the straight-line method.

The individual financial statements for these two companies as of December 31, 1995, and the year then ended follow:

	Atkins, Inc.	Smith, Inc.
Sales	$ 700,000	$ 300,000
Cost of goods sold	(460,000)	(205,000)
Operating expenses	(170,000)	(70,000)
Income of Smith	15,000	–0–
Net income	$ 85,000	$ 25,000
Retained earnings, January 1, 1995. . . .	$ 690,000	$ 400,000
Net income (above)	85,000	25,000
Dividends paid	(45,000)	(5,000)
Retained earnings, December 31, 1995 . .	$ 730,000	$ 420,000
Cash and receivables	$ 185,000	$ 142,000
Inventory	233,000	229,000
Investment in Smith	474,000	–0–
Buildings (net)	308,000	202,000
Equipment (net)	220,000	86,000
Patents (net)	–0–	20,000
Total assets	$1,420,000	$ 679,000
Liabilities	$ 390,000	$ 159,000
Common stock	300,000	100,000
Retained earnings, December 31, 1995 . .	730,000	420,000
Total liabilities and equities	$1,420,000	$ 679,000

For each of the following accounts, determine the 1995 consolidated balance:

a. Cost of Goods Sold.

b. Operating Expenses.

c. Net Income.

d. Retained Earnings, January 1, 1995.

e. Inventory.

f. Buildings (net).

g. Patents (net).

h. Common Stock.

i. Noncontrolling Interest in Smith, December 31, 1995.

 30. Tall Company purchased 60 percent of the outstanding stock of Short, Inc., on January 1, 1993. A $70,000 portion of the purchase price was allocated to equipment with a 10-year remaining life while $40,000 was attributed to a building having a 20-year life. Goodwill of $60,000 was also recognized and has been amortized over a 30-year period.

Short sells inventory to Tall at a markup equal to 25 percent of the transfer price. Sales have been as follows:

Year	Transfer Price to Tall	Inventory Remaining at Year's End (at transfer price)
1993	$ 90,000	$30,000
1994	120,000	20,000
1995	140,000	40,000

Tall still owes $30,000 to Short for the last inventory shipment.

Following are the account balances at December 31, 1995, for both companies. Credit balances are indicated with parentheses.

	Tall	Short
Revenues	$ (984,000)	$(438,000)
Cost of goods sold	551,000	286,000
Operating expenses	198,000	112,000
Equity earnings of Short	(10,000)	–0–
Net income	$ (245,000)	$ (40,000)
Retained earnings, 1/1/95	$ (871,000)	$(350,000)
Net income (above)	(245,000)	(40,000)
Dividends paid	110,000	25,000
Retained earnings, 12/31/95	$(1,006,000)	$(365,000)
Cash and receivables	$ 239,000	$ 57,000
Inventory	454,000	95,000
Investment in Short	440,000	–0–
Land and buildings (net)	722,000	394,000
Equipment (net)	328,000	257,000
Total assets	$ 2,183,000	$ 803,000
Liabilities	$ (686,000)	$(288,000)
Common stock	(320,000)	(90,000)
Additional paid-in capital	(171,000)	(60,000)
Retained earnings	(1,006,000)	(365,000)
Total liabilities and stockholders' equity	$(2,183,000)	$(803,000)

Required:

a. The parent applies the equity method. How was the $10,000 balance in the Equity Earnings of Short account determined?

b. Construct a worksheet to arrive at consolidated figures to be used for external reporting purposes.

31. On December 31, 1992, the Silvey Company acquired 70 percent of the outstanding common stock of the Young Company for $665,000. The stockholders' equity accounts reported by Young on that date were as follows:

Common stock—$10 par value.	$300,000
Additional paid-in capital	90,000
Retained earnings.	410,000

In establishing the purchase price, Silvey appraised the assets of Young and ascertained that a building (with a five-year life) was undervalued within the accounting records by $50,000. Any goodwill recognized in this acquisition was to be amortized over 10 years.

During the subsequent years, Young sold inventory to Silvey at a 30 percent markup on the transfer price. Silvey consistently resold this merchandise in the year of acquisition or in the period immediately following. Transfers for the three years after this business combination was created amounted to:

Year	Transfer Price	Remaining Inventory— Year-End (at transfer price)
1993	$60,000	$10,000
1994	80,000	12,000
1995	90,000	18,000

In addition, Silvey sold several pieces of fully depreciated equipment to Young on January 1, 1994, for $20,000. The equipment had originally cost Silvey $50,000. Young plans to depreciate the cost of these assets over a five-year period.

In 1995, Young earns a net income of $160,000 while distributing $50,000 in cash dividends. These figures increase the subsidiary's retained earnings to a $740,000 balance at the end of 1995. During this same year, Silvey reported dividend income of $35,000 and an investment account containing the original cost balance of $665,000.

Required:

Prepare the 1995 consolidation worksheet entries for Silvey and Young. In addition, compute the noncontrolling interest's share of the subsidiary's net income for 1995.

32. Assume the same basic information as presented in problem 31 except that Silvey has employed the equity method of accounting. Hence, investment income is being reported for 1995 as $100,740 with an investment account balance of $838,220. Under these circumstances, prepare the worksheet entries required for the consolidation of Silvey Company and Young Company.

33. The individual financial statements for Bumpus Company and Keller Company for the year ending December 31, 1995, follow. Bumpus acquired a 60 percent interest in Keller on January 1, 1990. Goodwill of $100,000 was recognized within the original purchase price. This intangible asset is being amortized over 20 years.

Bumpus sold land with a book value of $60,000 to Keller on January 1, 1992, for $100,000. Keller still holds this land at the end of the current year.

Keller annually transfers inventory to Bumpus. In 1994, inventory costing $100,000 was shipped to Bumpus at a price of $150,000. During 1995, intercompany shipments totaled $200,000, although the original cost to Keller was only $140,000. In each of these years, 20 percent of the merchandise was not resold to outside parties until the period following the transfer. Bumpus owes Keller $40,000 at the end of 1995.

	Bumpus Company	Keller Company
Sales	$ 800,000	$ 500,000
Cost of goods sold	(500,000)	(300,000)
Operating expenses	(100,000)	(60,000)
Income of Keller Company	84,000	–0–
Net income	$ 284,000	$ 140,000
Retained earnings, 1/1/95	$1,116,000	$ 620,000
Net income (above)	284,000	140,000
Dividends paid	(115,000)	(60,000)
Retained earnings, 12/31/95	$1,285,000	$ 700,000
Cash	$ 177,000	$ 90,000
Accounts receivable	316,000	410,000
Inventory	440,000	320,000
Investment in Keller Company	766,000	–0–
Land	180,000	390,000
Buildings and equipment (net)	496,000	300,000
Total assets	$2,375,000	$1,510,000
Liabilities	$ 480,000	$ 400,000
Common stock	610,000	320,000
Additional paid-in capital	–0–	90,000
Retained earnings, 12/31/95	1,285,000	700,000
Total liabilities and equities	$2,375,000	$1,510,000

Required:

a. Prepare a worksheet to consolidate the separate 1995 financial statements produced by Bumpus and Keller.

b. How would the consolidation entries in requirement a. have differed if Bumpus had sold a building with a $60,000 book value (cost of $140,000) to Keller for

$100,000 instead of land as the problem reports? Assume that the building had a ten-year remaining life at the date of transfer.

34. Greene, Inc., obtained 100 percent of Meadow Corporation on January 1, 1991, in an exchange that did not meet all requirements for a pooling of interests. Meadow reported total stockholders' equity on this date of $300,000 although the stock issued by Greene in the transaction had a $170,000 par value but a fair market value of $450,000. On January 1, 1991, Meadow held land that was undervalued in the company's accounting records by $30,000. Any goodwill indicated by this takeover is to be amortized over the maximum possible life.

Inventory has been regularly transferred by Meadow to Greene. In 1994, merchandise costing $60,000 was sold to Greene for $100,000. Of this total, 30 percent was not resold to unrelated parties until the following year. In 1995, $75,000 in inventory was shipped to Greene for $150,000 with $20,000 (transfer price) still held at the end of the period.

On June 19, 1995, Greene sold land costing $12,000 to Meadow for $17,000. This money has not yet been paid.

The following account balances are for both companies as of December 31, 1995, and the year then ended. The parent has used the equity method to record this investment. Produce a worksheet to arrive at consolidated financial statements for this business combination. Credit balances are indicated by parentheses.

	Greene	Meadow
Revenues	$ (477,000)	$(358,000)
Cost of goods sold	289,000	195,000
General and administrative expenses	170,000	75,000
Gain on sale of land	(5,000)	–0–
Investment income	(82,000)	–0–
Net income	$ (105,000)	$ (88,000)
Retained earnings, 1/1/95	$ (365,000)	$(292,000)
Net income	(105,000)	(88,000)
Dividends distributed	70,000	20,000
Retained earnings, 12/31/95	$ (400,000)	$(360,000)
Cash and receivables	$ 169,000	$ 210,000
Inventory	281,000	232,000
Investment in Meadow	630,000	–0–
Land, buildings, and equipment (net)	487,000	284,000
Total assets	$ 1,567,000	$ 726,000
Liabilities	$ (466,000)	$(216,000)
Common stock	(410,000)	(120,000)
Additional paid-in capital	(291,000)	(30,000)
Retained earnings, 12/31/95	(400,000)	(360,000)
Total liabilities and stockholders' equity	$(1,567,000)	$(726,000)

6

INTERCOMPANY DEBT AND OTHER CONSOLIDATION ISSUES

Questions to Consider

- When an affiliate's debt instrument is bought from an outside party, the reciprocal balances (investment and debt, interest revenue and expense, etc.) usually do not agree. How is the consolidation process carried out in the year of acquisition as well as in each succeeding period?

- Some preferred stocks are viewed as equity interests but others, because of the rights conveyed, are considered to be equivalent to debts. How is this distinction drawn, and what impact does the nature of a subsidiary's preferred stock have on the consolidation process?

- What effect does the inclusion of a subsidiary have on the preparation of a consolidated statement of cash flows?

- If a subsidiary has debt or preferred stock or other items outstanding that can be exchanged for common stock, how are primary and fully diluted earnings per share computed for the business combination?

- Why would a subsidiary buy or sell more shares of its own stock after coming under the control of a parent company? What effect do such transactions have on consolidated financial statements?

The consolidation of financial information can be a highly complex process often encompassing a number of practical challenges. This chapter examines the procedures required by several additional issues:

- Intercompany debt.
- Subsidiary preferred stock.
- The consolidated statement of cash flows.
- Computation of consolidated earnings per share.
- Subsidiary stock transactions.

Each of these can create potential difficulties for an accountant attempting to produce fairly presented financial statements for a business combination.

Intercompany Debt Transactions

The previous chapter explored the consolidation procedures required by the intercompany transfer of inventory, land, and depreciable assets. In consolidating these transactions, all resulting gains were deferred until earned through either the usage of the asset or its resale to outside parties. Deferral was necessary because these gains, although legitimately recognized by the individual companies, were unearned from the perspective of the consolidated entity. The separate financial information of each company was adjusted on the worksheet to be consistent with the view that the related companies actually composed a single economic concern.

This same objective takes precedence in consolidating all intercompany transactions: the financial statements being produced must represent the business combination as one enterprise rather than as a group of independent organizations. Consequently, in designing consolidation procedures for intercompany transactions, the effects recorded by the individual companies must first be isolated. After the impact of each action has been analyzed, the worksheet entries necessary to recast these events from the vantage point of the business combination can be developed. Although this process involves a number of nuances and complexities, the desire for reporting financial information solely from the perspective of the consolidated entity remains constant.

The intercompany sale of inventory, land, and depreciable assets was introduced together (in Chapter 5) because these transfers result in similar consolidation procedures. In each case, one of the affiliated companies recognizes a gain prior to its actually being earned by the consolidated entity. The worksheet entries required by these transactions simply realign the separate financial information to agree with the viewpoint of the business combination. The gain is removed and the inflated asset value is reduced to historical cost.

The first section of this chapter examines the intercompany acquisition of bonds and notes. Although accounting for the related companies as a single economic entity continues to be the central goal, the consolidation procedures applied to intercompany debt transactions are in diametric contrast to the process utilized in Chapter 5 for asset transfers.

Before delving into this topic, note that *direct* loans used to transfer funds between affiliated companies create no unique consolidation problems. Regardless of whether such amounts are generated by bonds or notes, the resulting receivable/payable balances are necessarily identical. Because no money is owed to or from an outside party, these reciprocal accounts must be eliminated in each subsequent consolidation. A worksheet entry simply offsets the two corresponding balances. Furthermore, the interest revenue/expense accounts associated with direct loans also agree and are removed in the same fashion.

Acquisition of Affiliate's Debt from an Outside Party

The difficulties encountered in consolidating intercompany liabilities relate to a specific type of transaction: the purchase from an outside third party of an affiliate's debt instrument. A parent company, for example, might acquire a bond previously issued by a subsidiary on the open market. Despite the intercompany nature of this transaction, the debt remains an outstanding obligation of the original issuer while simultaneously being recorded as an investment by the acquiring company. Thereafter, even though related parties are involved, interest payments pass periodically between the two organizations.

Although both the debt and the investment are still reported by the individual companies, from a consolidation viewpoint this liability has been retired as of the date of acquisition. From that time forward, the debt is no longer owed to a party outside of the business combination. Subsequent interest payments are simply intercompany cash transfers. For the purpose of creating consolidated statements, worksheet entries must be developed that adjust the various balances to report the effective retirement of the debt.

Even acquiring an affiliate's bond or note from an unrelated party poses no significant consolidation problems if the purchase price equals the corresponding book value of the liability. Reciprocal balances existing within the individual records would always be identical in value and easily offset in each subsequent consolidation.

Realistically though, such reciprocity is rarely established when a debt is purchased from a third party. A variety of economic factors almost mandates that a difference exists between the price paid for the investment and the carrying amount of the obligation. The debt is originally sold under existing market conditions at a particular time. Any premium or discount associated with this issuance is then amortized over the life of the bond creating a continuous adjustment to book value. The acquisition of this instrument at a later date is made at a price influenced by current economic conditions, prevailing interest rates, and myriad other financial and market factors.

Therefore, the cost paid to purchase the debt might be either more or less than the book value of the liability currently found within the financial records of the issuing company. *To the business combination, this difference is a gain or loss because the acquisition effectively retires the bond; the debt is no longer owed to an outside party.* For external reporting purposes, this gain or loss must be recognized immediately by the consolidated entity as required by *APB Opinion 26*, "Early Extinguishment of Debt," October 1972.

Accounting for Intercompany Debt Transactions—Individual Financial Records

The accounting problems encountered in consolidating intercompany debt transactions are really fourfold:

1. Both the investment and debt accounts have to be eliminated now and for each future consolidation despite containing differing balances.

2. Subsequent interest revenue/expense (as well as any interest receivable/payable accounts) must be removed although these balances also fail to agree in amount.

3. Changes in all of the preceding accounts are constantly occurring because of the amortization process.

4. The gain or loss on retirement of the debt must be recognized by the business combination, even though this balance does not appear within the financial records of either company.

To illustrate, assume that Alpha Company possesses an 80 percent interest in the outstanding voting stock of Omega Company. On January 1, 1993, Omega issues $1 million in 10-year term bonds paying cash interest annually of 15 percent. Because of market conditions prevailing on that date, the debt is sold for $951,680 to yield an effective interest rate of 16 percent per year. Shortly thereafter, the prime interest rate begins to fall, and by January 1, 1995, the decision is made to retire this debt prematurely and refinance it at the currently lower rates. To carry out this plan, Alpha purchases all of these bonds in the open market on January 1, 1995, for $1,149,027. This price was based on an effective yield of 12 percent, which is assumed to be in line with the interest rates at the time.

Many reasons could exist for having Alpha, rather than Omega, reacquire this debt. For example, company cash levels at that date might necessitate Alpha's role as the purchasing agent. Also, contractual limitations may prohibit Omega from repurchasing its own bonds.

In accounting for this business combination, an early extinguishment of the debt has occurred. Thus, the difference between the $1,149,027 payment and the January 1, 1995, book value of the liability must be recognized in the consolidated statements as a gain or loss. The exact account balance reported for the debt on that date is dependent on the amortization process. Although the issue was recorded initially at the $951,680 exchange price, after two years the carrying value has increased to $956,581, calculated as follows:[1]

Bonds Payable—Book Value—January 1, 1995

Year	Book Value	Effective Interest (16 percent rate)	Cash Interest	Amortization	Year-End Book Value
1993	$951,680	$152,269	$150,000	$2,269	$953,949
1994	953,949	152,632	150,000	2,632	956,581

Since Alpha paid $192,446 in excess of the recorded liability ($1,149,027 − $956,581), a loss of this amount must be recognized by the consolidated concern.

---

[1] The effective rate method of amortization is demonstrated here because this approach is theoretically preferable. However, the straight-line method can be applied if the resulting balances are not materially different than the figures computed using the effective rate method.

If material, the $192,446 is highlighted as an extraordinary item. After the loss has been acknowledged, the bond is considered to be retired and no further reporting would be necessary by the *business combination* after January 1, 1995.

Despite the simplicity of this approach, neither company accounts for the event in this manner. Omega retains the $1 million debt balance within its separate financial records while amortizing the remaining discount each year. Annual cash interest payments of $150,000 (15 percent) continue to be made. At the same time, the investment is recorded by Alpha at the historical cost of $1,149,027, an amount that also requires periodic amortization. Furthermore, as the owner of these bonds, Alpha receives the $150,000 interest payments made by Omega.

To organize the accountant's approach to this consolidation, a complete analysis of the subsequent financial recording made by each of these companies should be produced. Only two journal entries would be recorded by Omega during 1995 if the assumption is made that interest is paid each December 31.

Omega Company's Financial Records

12/31/95	Interest Expense	150,000	
	Cash		150,000

To record payment of annual cash interest on $1 million, 15 percent bonds payable.

12/31/95	Interest Expense	3,053	
	Bonds Payable (or Discount on		
	Bonds Payable)		3,053

To adjust interest expense to effective rate based on original yield rate of 16 percent ($956,581 book value for 1995 × 16% = $153,053). Book value increases to $959,634.

Concurrently, Alpha journalizes entries to record its ownership of this investment:

Alpha Company's Financial Record

1/1/95	Investment in Omega Company Bonds	1,149,027	
	Cash.		1,149,027

To record acquisition of $1,000,000 in Omega Company bonds paying 15 percent cash interest, acquired to yield an effective rate of 12 percent.

12/31/95	Cash.	150,000	
	Interest Income.		150,000

To record receipt of cash interest from Omega Company bonds ($1,000,000 × 15%).

12/31/95	Interest Income.	12,117	
	Investment in Omega Company Bonds		12,117

To reduce $150,000 interest income to effective rate based on original yield rate of 12 percent ($1,149,027 book value for 1995 × 12% = $137,883). Book value decreases to $1,136,910.

Even a brief review of these entries indicates that the reciprocal accounts to be eliminated within the consolidation process do not agree in amount. To afford a better visualization, the dollar amounts appearing in each set of financial records are shown in Exhibit 6–1. Despite the presence of these recorded balances, none of the four intercompany accounts (the liability, investment, interest expense, and interest revenue) appear in the consolidated financial statements. *The only figure to be reported by the business combination is the $192,446 loss created by the extinguishment of this debt.*

Effects on Consolidation Process

As indicated in previous discussions, consolidation procedures serve to convert information generated by the individual accounting systems to the perspective of a single economic entity. A worksheet entry is, therefore, required on December 31, 1995, to eliminate the intercompany balances shown in Exhibit 6–1 and to recognize the loss resulting from the repurchase. Mechanically, the differences in the liability and investment balances as well as the interest expense and interest income accounts stem from the $192,446 deviation between the purchase price of the investment and the book value of the liability. Recognition of this loss, in effect, bridges the gap between the divergent figures.

Consolidation Entry B (December 31, 1995)

Bonds Payable	959,634	
Interest Income	137,883	
Extraordinary Loss on Retirement of Bond	192,446	
Investment in Omega Company Bonds		1,136,910
Interest Expense		153,053

To remove intercompany bonds and related interest accounts and record loss on the early extinguishment of this debt. (Labeled "B" in reference to bonds.)

EXHIBIT 6–1

ALPHA COMPANY AND OMEGA COMPANY
Effects of Intercompany Debt Transaction
1995

	Omega Company Reported Debt	Alpha Company Investment
1995 interest expense*	$ 153,053	$ –0–
1995 interest income†	–0–	137,883
Bonds payable*	(959,634)	–0–
Investment in bonds, 12/31/95†	–0–	1,136,910
Loss on retirement	–0–	–0–

NOTE: Parentheses indicate credit balances.

* Company total is adjusted for 1995 amortization of $3,053 (see journal entry).

† Adjusted for 1995 amortization of $12,117 (see journal entry).

The preceding entry successfully transforms the separate financial reporting of Alpha and Omega to that appropriate for the business combination. The objective of the consolidation process has been met: the statements present the bonds as having been retired on January 1, 1995. The debt as well as the corresponding investment are eliminated along with both interest accounts. Only the loss now appears on the worksheet to be reported within the consolidated financial statements.

Assignment of Retirement Gain or Loss

Perhaps the most intriguing issue to be addressed in accounting for intercompany debt transactions concerns the assignment of any gains and losses created by the retirement. Should the $192,446 loss just reported be attributed to Alpha or to Omega? From a practical perspective, this assignment is only important in the calculation and reporting of noncontrolling interest figures. However, the FASB's discussion memorandum, *An Analysis of Issues Related to Consolidation Policy and Procedures,* identifies four possible allocations (paragraph 384), each of which demonstrate theoretical merit.

First, a strong argument can be made that the liability being extinguished is that of the issuing company and, thus, any resulting income relates solely to that party. This approach assumes that only the debtor is actually affected by the retirement of any obligation. Proponents of this position hold that the acquiring company is merely serving as a purchasing agent for the original issuer of the bonds. Accordingly, in the previous illustration, the benefits derived from paying off the liability should accrue to Omega because that company's interest rate has been reduced through refinancing. The loss was incurred solely to obtain these lower rates. Therefore, under this assumption, the entire $192,446 is assigned to Omega, the issuer of the debt. This assignment is usually considered to be consistent with the economic unit concept.

Second, other accountants argue that the loss should be assigned solely to the investor (Alpha). According to proponents of this approach, the income effect is created by the acquisition of the bonds and the price negotiated by the buyer.

A third hypothesis is that the resulting gain or loss should be split in some manner between the two companies. This approach is consistent with both the parent company concept and proportionate consolidation. Since both parties are involved with the debt, this proposition contends that assigning income to only one company is arbitrary and misleading. Normally, such a division is based on the original face value of the debt. Hence, $149,027 of the loss would be allocated to Alpha with the remaining $43,419 assigned to Omega:

Alpha		Omega	
Purchase price	$1,149,027	Book value	$ 956,581
Face value	1,000,000	Face value	1,000,000
Loss—Alpha	$ 149,027	Loss—Omega	$ 43,419

Allocating the loss in this manner is an enticing solution; the subsequent accounting process creates an identical division within the individual financial records. Because both Alpha's premium and Omega's discount must be amortized, the loss figures eventually affect the reported earnings of the respective companies. Over the life of the bond, the $149,027 is recorded by Alpha as an interest income reduction while Omega increases its own interest expense by $43,419 because of the amortization of the discount.

A fourth perspective takes a more practical view of intercompany debt transactions: all repurchases are ultimately orchestrated by the parent company. As the controlling party in a business combination, the ultimate responsibility for retiring any obligation lies with the parent. The gain or loss resulting from the decision should, thus, be assigned solely to the parent regardless of the specific identity of the debt issuer or the acquiring company. In the current example, Alpha maintains control over Omega. Therefore, according to this theory, the financial consequences of reacquiring these bonds rest with Alpha so that the entire $192,446 loss must be attributed to that party.

Each of these arguments does have conceptual merit, and if the FASB eventually sets an official standard, any one approach (or possibly a hybrid) might be required. Unless otherwise stated, however, all income effects in this textbook relating to intercompany debt transactions are assigned solely to the parent company, as discussed in the final approach. Consequently, the results of extinguishing debt are always attributed to the party most likely to have been responsible for the action.

Discussion Question: Who Lost This $300,000?

Several years ago, the Penston Company purchased 90 percent of the outstanding shares of Swansan Corporation. The acquisition was made because Swansan produced a vital component used in Penston's manufacturing process. Penston wanted to ensure an adequate supply of this item at a reasonable price. The remaining 10 percent of Swansan's stock was retained by the former owner, James Swansan, who agreed to continue managing this organization. He was given responsibility over the subsidiary's daily manufacturing operations but not any of the financial decisions.

The takeover of Swansan has proven to be a successful undertaking for Penston. The subsidiary has managed to supply all of the parent's inventory needs as well as distribute a variety of items to outside customers.

At a recent meeting, the president of Penston and the company's chief financial officer began discussing Swansan's debt position. The subsidiary had a debt to equity ratio that seemed unreasonably high considering the significant amount of cash flows being generated by both companies. Payment of the interest expense, especially on the subsidiary's outstanding bonds, was a major cost, one that the corporate officials hoped to reduce.

continued

However, the bond indenture specified that Swansan could only retire this debt prior to maturity by paying 107 percent of face value.

This premium was considered prohibitive. Thus, to avoid contractual problems, Penston acquired a large portion of Swansan's liability on the open market for 101 percent of face value. Penston's purchase created an effective loss on the debt of $300,000: the excess of the price over the book value of the debt as reported on Swansan's books.

Company accountants are currently computing the noncontrolling interest's share of consolidated net income to be reported for the current year. They are unsure about the impact of this $300,000 loss. The subsidiary's debt was retired but the decision was made by officials of the parent company. Who lost this $300,000?

Intercompany Debt Transactions—Subsequent to Year of Acquisition

Even though the preceding Entry B has correctly eliminated Omega's bonds in the year of retirement, the debt remains within the financial accounts of both companies until maturity. Therefore, in each succeeding time period, all balances must again be consolidated so that the liability is always reported as having been extinguished on January 1, 1995. Unfortunately, a simple repetition of Entry B is not possible. Developing the appropriate worksheet entry is complicated by the amor-

---

EXHIBIT 6–2

ALPHA COMPANY AND OMEGA COMPANY
Effects of Intercompany Debt Transactions
1996

	Omega Company Reported Debt	Alpha Company Investment
1996 interest expense*	$ 153,541	–0–
1996 interest income†	–0–	$(136,429)
Bonds payable*	(963,175)	–0–
Investment in bonds, 12/31/96†	–0–	1,123,339
Income effect within retained earnings, 1/1/96‡	153,053	(137,883)

NOTE: Parentheses indicate credit balance.

* Company total is adjusted for 1996 amortization of $3,541 (see journal entry).

† Adjusted for 1996 amortization of $13,571 (see journal entry).

‡ The balance shown for the Retained Earnings accounts of the individual companies represents the 1995 reported interest figures.

tization process that produces continual change in the various account balances. Thus, as a preliminary step in each subsequent consolidation, current book values, as reported by the two parties, must be identified.

To illustrate, the 1996 journal entries for Alpha and Omega follow. Exhibit 6–2 shows the resulting account balances as of the end of that year.

Omega Company's Financial Records—December 31, 1996

Interest Expense.	150,000	
Cash		150,000

To record payment of annual cash interest on $1 million, 15 percent bonds payable.

Interest Expense.	3,541	
Bonds Payable (or Discount on Bonds Payable)		3,541

To adjust interest expense to effective rate based on an original yield rate of 16 percent ($959,634 book value for 1996 × 16% = $153,541). Book value increases to $963,175.

- -

Alpha Company's Financial Records—December 31, 1996

Cash	150,000	
Interest Income		150,000

To record receipt of cash interest from Omega Company bonds.

Interest Income	13,571	
Investment in Omega Company Bonds		13,571

To reduce $150,000 interest income to effective rate based on an original yield rate of 12 percent ($1,136,910 book value for 1996 × 12% = $136,429). Book value decreases to $1,123,339.

After the information in Exhibit 6–2 has been assembled, the necessary consolidation entry as of December 31, 1996, can be produced. This entry removes the balances reported at that date for the intercompany bonds, along with both of the interest accounts, to reflect the extinguishment of the debt on January 1, 1995. Since retirement took place in a prior period, the adjustment on the worksheet must also create a $192,446 reduction in retained earnings to represent the original loss.

*Consolidation Entry *B (December 31, 1996)*

Bonds Payable.	963,175	
Interest Income	136,429	
Retained Earnings, 1/1/96 (Alpha)	177,276	
Investment in Omega Company Bonds		1,123,339
Interest Expense		153,541

To eliminate intercompany bond and related interest accounts and to adjust retained earnings from $15,170 (currently recorded net balance) to $192,446. (Labeled as "*B" in reference to prior year bond transaction.)

In analyzing this latest consolidation entry, several important factors should be emphasized:

1. The balances found in each of the individual accounts have changed during the present fiscal period so that the current consolidation entry differs from Entry B. These alterations are a result of the amortization process. To ensure the accuracy of the worksheet entry, the adjusted balances have been isolated in Exhibit 6–2.

2. As indicated previously, all income effects arising from intercompany debt transactions are being assigned to the parent company. For this reason, the adjustment to beginning retained earnings in Entry *B is attributed to Alpha as is the $17,112 increase in current income ($153,541 interest expense elimination less the $136,429 interest revenue elimination).[2] Consequently, the noncontrolling interest balances are not altered by Entry *B.

3. The 1966 reduction made to beginning retained earnings in Entry *B ($177,276) does not agree with the original $192,446 retirement loss. A net deficit balance of $15,170 (the amount by which previous interest expense exceeds interest revenue) has already been recorded by the individual companies at the start of 1996. To achieve the proper consolidated total, an adjustment of only $177,276 is required ($192,446 − $15,170).

Retained earnings balance—consolidation perspective (loss on retirement of debt)		$192,446
Individual retained earnings balances, 1/1/96:		
Omega Company (interest expense—1995)	$153,053	
Alpha Company (interest income—1995)	(137,883)	15,170
Adjustment to consolidated retained earnings, 1/1/96		$177,276

Parentheses indicate a credit balance.

The periodic amortization of both the bond payable discount and the premium on the investment impacts the interest expense and revenue recorded by the two companies. As shown in this schedule, these two interest accounts do not offset exactly; a $15,170 net residual amount remains in retained earnings after the first year. Since this balance con-

---

[2] Had the effects of the retirement been attributed solely to the original issuer of the bonds, the $17,112 reduction in current income would have been assigned to Omega (the subsidiary), thus creating a change in the noncontrolling interest computations. As another alternative, the income effect could have been allocated between the two parties. Under that approach, $3,541 of the interest expense elimination is attributed to Omega. This figure represents the subsidiary's premium amortization ($153,541 − $150,000), the amount of expense recorded for the year in excess of the cash interest payment. The remainder of the adjustment is assigned to Alpha. Once again, since Omega's earnings are altered under this approach, a change would be required in the balances reported for the noncontrolling interest.

tinues to grow each year, the subsequent consolidation adjustments to record the loss decrease to $177,276 in 1996 and constantly get smaller thereafter. *Over the life of the bond, the amortization process gradually brings the totals in the individual Retained Earnings accounts into agreement with the consolidated balance.*

4. Entry *B as shown is appropriate for consolidations in which the parent has applied either the cost or the partial equity method. However, a deviation is required if the parent uses the equity method for internal reporting purposes. As discussed in Chapter 5, proper application of the equity method ensures that the parent's income and, hence, its retained earnings are correctly stated prior to consolidation. Alpha would have already recognized the loss in accounting for this investment. Consequently, no adjustment to retained earnings is needed. In this one case, the $177,276 debit in Entry *B is made to the Investment in Omega Company because the loss has become a component of that account.

Subsidiary Preferred Stock

On March 24, 1987, Kohlberg Kravis Roberts & Company purchased the outstanding common stock of Owens-Illinois Inc. for $60.50 per share. In addition, KKR acquired all of the preferred stock of Owens-Illinois for $363 per share or a total of $25.8 million. Although preferred shares are routinely issued by both small and large corporations, their presence within the equity structure of a subsidiary adds a new dimension to the consolidation process. What accounting should be made of a subsidiary's preferred stock and the parent's payments, such as this $25.8 million, that are made to acquire these shares?

The consolidation measures that are required in reporting the preferred stock of a subsidiary depend on the specific nature of the shares. Controversy has long existed as to whether such issues are more akin to equity or debt, a distinction that depends on the specified rights granted to the holders. The characteristics of many preferred shares resemble those attributed to long-term liabilities rather than to equity securities. For example, a stock with a call value and no rights except for a set, cumulative dividend is in substance almost identical to a bond payable. Conversely, preferred shares that offer voting and/or participation rights clearly demonstrate essential characteristics associated with an ownership interest.

Unfortunately, not all preferred stocks lend themselves to easy classification: the legal rights given to shareholders often vary significantly from issue to issue. For example, according to *Moody's Public Utility Manual—1991*, GTE Corporation had 21 different types of preferred stock outstanding, each with specific rights as to dividends, convertibility to common stock, and redemption prices. Such attributes can make the distinction between debt and equity quite nebulous. Because of this identification problem, the FASB has plans to study the issue within its financial instruments project. However, until a guideline is established, as is utilized in earnings per share computations, determining the true nature of many types of preferred stock still requires considerable individual judgment.

In consolidating subsidiary preferred stock, the accountant must first evaluate whether the shares are more similar to debt or to equity. If the stock resembles a debt, any shares acquired by the parent are recorded as if retired. Conversely, if a preferred stock is truly an equity instrument, the combination accounts for the purchased shares in the same manner as common stock: allocations are made to specific assets and liabilities with any residual payment assigned to goodwill.

Preferred Stock Viewed as a Debt Instrument

If a subsidiary's preferred stock has characteristics that primarily resemble a liability, consolidation techniques should parallel the process previously demonstrated for intercompany debt. To illustrate, assume that on January 1, 1995, High Corporation acquires control over Low Company by purchasing 80 percent of its outstanding common stock as well as 60 percent of its nonvoting, cumulative, preferred stock. Low owns land that is undervalued in its records by $100,000.

The purchase price paid by High was $1 million for the common shares and $62,400 for the preferred. On the date of acquisition, Low reported the following stockholders' equity balances. Note that the 1,000 shares of preferred stock outstanding have a $100 par value but can be called (retired) by Low for $110 per share.

Common stock, $20 par value (20,000 shares outstanding).	$ 400,000
Preferred stock, 6% cumulative with a par value of $100 and a $110 call value	
(1,000 shares outstanding) .	100,000
Additional paid-in capital .	200,000
Retained earnings.	516,400
Total stockholders' equity (book value) .	$1,216,400

Low's preferred stock carries no rights other than its cumulative dividend; thus, this issue is considered a debt instrument in nature. The $62,400 price paid by High is handled in a manner consistent with that of an intercompany bond. The payment made for these shares has no influence on the valuation of specific subsidiary accounts (such as the undervalued land) or the recognition of goodwill. Instead, the preferred stock acquired by the parent is eliminated on each subsequent worksheet as if the shares had been retired.

Although this handling parallels that of a long-term liability, one important distinction must be drawn. Preferred stock is legally an equity; thus, its retirement cannot result in the reporting of a gain or loss to the consolidated entity. Instead, the difference between the stock's par value and the acquisition price paid by the parent must be recorded as an adjustment to Additional Paid-In Capital (or to

Retained Earnings if a reduction is required and the Additional Paid-In Capital account is not of sufficient size).

The consolidation entry to account for this preferred stock acquisition follows. *Since the stock is viewed as the equivalent of debt, these shares (60 percent of the 1,000 outstanding) are simply eliminated as if retired.*

Preferred Stock (the 60 percent owned by High).	60,000	
Additional Paid-In Capital.	2,400	
Investment in Low Company's Preferred Stock		62,400

To eliminate preferred stock of Low Company acquired by the parent company.

This entry assumes that no part of the cumulative dividend is in arrears at the date of purchase. If a dividend had been owed on the preferred stock, a reduction in the subsidiary's retained earnings equal to that amount would have been included here rather than assigning the entire $2,400 difference to additional paid-in capital. This alteration presumes that a portion of the purchase price is paid to reimburse the former owners for the missed dividends.

Although the preceding worksheet entry removes the effects of High's acquisition, it ignores the residual 40 percent noncontrolling interest in the preferred stock. In recording an allocation to these outside owners, the appropriate amount to be recognized must be determined. When preferred stock is viewed as a debt, the call value (if present) is considered to be more relevant to the consolidated entity than par value. Thus, the outside owners are assigned a balance equal to the call value of the securities (plus any dividends in arrears). In the current illustration, the $110 figure reflects the cost required to retire each of the remaining 400 shares (40% of 1,000). Thus, the worksheet entry to recognize this noncontrolling interest is as follows:

Preferred Stock (40% owned by outsiders)	40,000	
Additional Paid-In Capital.	4,000	
Noncontrolling Interest in Low Company (call value)		44,000

To recognize the outside ownership of 40 percent of Low Company's preferred stock.

These entries have been presented separately to clarify the difference in consolidating parent-owned and outside-owned shares. In practice, these figures are combined to eliminate all of the subsidiary's preferred stock. Thus, a single consolidation entry should actually be incorporated in this illustration:

Consolidation Entry PS

Preferred Stock.	100,000	
Additional Paid-In Capital	6,400	
Investment in Low Company's Preferred Stock		62,400
Noncontrolling Interest in Low Company		44,000

To eliminate preferred stock of subsidiary (viewed as a debt) and record noncontrolling interest. (Labeled as "PS" in reference to preferred stock.)

Having accounted for Low's preferred stock, the elimination of the company's remaining stockholders' equity accounts can now be made. As with any purchase combination, a preliminary allocation of the purchase price paid for the common stock is essential. Because of the amounts attributed to preferred stock, only $1,110,000 of Low's total book value is assigned to the common stock at the date of acquisition:

Total book value of Low Company, 1/1/95.		$1,216,400
Allocated to preferred stock ownership:		
Acquisition price of High Company's interest	$62,400	
Call value of noncontrolling interest	44,000	(106,400)
Book value allocated to common stock		$1,110,000

Based on this book value, the $1 million paid by High for 80 percent of Low's common stock is allocated as shown in Exhibit 6–3. As indicated previously, land owned by Low is assumed here to be undervalued on the subsidiary's records by $100,000.

By utilizing the information from Exhibit 6–3, basic worksheet entries can be constructed as of January 1, 1995 (the date of purchase). After Entry PS removes the preferred shares and recognizes the noncontrolling interest in that stock, the remainder of Low's stockholders' equity accounts are eliminated by Entry S. In addition, a 20 percent noncontrolling interest in Low's common stock is established as $222,000 (20 percent of the $1,110,000 book value). The allocations made to the undervalued land and to goodwill are then recognized in Entry A. No other consolidation entries are needed as no time has passed since the acquisition took place.

Consolidation Entry S

Common Stock (Low Company).	400,000	
Additional Paid-In Capital (Low Company)	193,600	
Retained Earnings (Low Company)	516,400	
Investment in Low Company's Common Stock (80%)		888,000
Noncontrolling Interest in Low Company (20%)		222,000

To eliminate remaining stockholders' equity accounts after removal of preferred stock and to recognize noncontrolling interest in common stock.

Consolidation Entry A

Land	80,000	
Goodwill	32,000	
Investment in Low Company's Common Stock		112,000

To allocate excess cost paid for Low's common stock to specific account based on fair market value and to goodwill (see Exhibit 6–3).

In working with this illustration, note the structure that is followed in consolidating a subsidiary's preferred stock. First, a determination is made of the nature of the stock. Identifying Low Company's issue as a debt-type instrument signifi-

---

EXHIBIT 6–3

HIGH COMPANY AND LOW COMPANY
Allocation of Common Stock Purchase Price
January 1, 1995

Purchase price paid for common stock	$1,000,000
Common stock book value equivalent to High's ownership ($1,110,000 × 80%)	(888,000)
Cost in excess of book value	112,000
Allocation to specific accounts based on fair market value:	
Land ($100,000 × 80%)	80,000
Excess cost not identified with specific accounts—goodwill.	$ 32,000

---

cantly influenced the development of the consolidation process. Second, the subsidiary's book value is divided between the preferred and common stock interests. Assigning $106,400 of Low's book value to the preferred stock (the price of the purchased shares plus the call value of remainder) and the residual $1,110,000 to common stock led directly to the valuations and eliminations incorporated in this consolidation. As is subsequently demonstrated, this allocation of book value can vary considerably depending on the specific rights granted to the preferred shareholders.

Allocation of Subsidiary Income.   The final factor influencing a consolidation that includes subsidiary preferred shares is the allocation of the company's income between the two types of stock. A division must be made for every period subsequent to the takeover (1) in order to compute the noncontrolling interest's share and (2) for the parent's own recognition purposes. For a cumulative, nonparticipating preferred stock such as the one presently being examined, only the specified annual dividend is attributed to the preferred stock with all remaining income assigned to common stock. Consequently, if the assumption is made that Low reports earnings of $100,000 in 1995 while paying the annual $6,000 dividend on its preferred stock, income is allocated for consolidation purposes as follows:

	Income
Subsidiary total	$100,000
Preferred stock (6% dividend × $100,000 par value of the stock)	$ 6,000
Common stock (residual amount)	94,000

During 1995, High Company, as the parent, would be entitled to $3,600 in dividends from Low's preferred stock because of its 60 percent ownership. In addition, High holds 80 percent of Low's common stock so that another $75,200 of the income ($94,000 × 80 percent) is attributed to the parent. The noncontrolling interest in the subsidiary's income can be calculated in a similar fashion:

		Percent Outside Ownership	Noncontrolling Interest
Preferred stock dividend.	$ 6,000	40%	$ 2,400
Income attributed to common stock	94,000	20	18,800
Noncontrolling interests in subsidiary's income . . .			$21,200

Preferred Stock Viewed as an Equity Interest

Having established basic principles for a consolidation that includes subsidiary preferred stock that resembles debt, a second example can be utilized in which the stock is considered an equity. Continuing to employ High's acquisition of Low, assume now that the dividends of the subsidiary's preferred stock are fully participating as well as cumulative. Furthermore, the stock is not callable. Because the preferred shares convey additional rights in this case, the relative values of the two classes of stock differ from that of the previous example. Therefore, High is assumed to have paid only $894,496 for an 80 percent interest in Low's common stock but $149,968 for 60 percent of the preferred.

The ability to participate in the earnings of Low Company provides the preferred shareholders with an ownership interest that is akin to that of common stock. Thus, altering the rights of this issue has changed its essential nature to that of an equity interest rather than a debt. When subsidiary preferred stock is viewed as an equity, the consolidation process differs significantly from that examined in the previous illustration. *The preferred stock is handled in the same manner as common stock: any purchase price in excess of underlying book value is allocated to specific accounts as well as to goodwill. Income is accrued by the owners based on subsidiary earnings rather than on dividends.*

The cumulative participation rights entitle the holders of Low's preferred shares to a portion of the subsidiary's earnings each year. The specific division of income would be stipulated on the preferred stock certificate. That percentage is often based on the ratio of the total par values of the two classes of equity. Thus, 20 percent ($100,000 par value of the preferred stock divided by $500,000 total par value) of Low's annual income is assigned to the preferred shares. Additionally, because of the cumulative right, 20 percent of the subsidiary's retained earnings should also be attributed to the preferred stock (assuming that both classes of stock were originally issued on the same date). With these particular rights in force, allocation of the January 1, 1995, book value of Low Company is as follows:

Total book value of Low Company, 1/1/95		$1,216,400
Allocated to preferred stock ownership:		
Par value of preferred stock (no call value)	$100,000	
20% of total retained earnings ($516,400) based on cumulative, participation rights	103,280	(203,280)
Book value allocated to common stock (residual)		$1,013,120

Once the division of the subsidiary's book value has been established, High must allocate each of the acquisition payments. In this manner, the preferred stock is being accounted for as a true equity interest. Exhibit 6–4 analyzes both purchases: the $149,968 price paid for the preferred stock is shown first followed by the $894,496 amount invested in common stock. To complete this allocation, one theoretical question must be addressed: How is the undervaluation of the subsidiary's land to be treated? Since both stocks are considered equity interests, the $100,000 undervaluation is assumed to be reflected in each purchase price. Because of the participation feature of the preferred shares, the logical approach is to divide this $100,000 unrealized gain between the two stocks according to the par value ratio (20 : 80) or $20,000 to preferred stock and $80,000 to common.

From the information produced in Exhibit 6–4, the following consolidation entries for January 1, 1995 (the date of purchase) can be developed. Note that

EXHIBIT 6–4

HIGH COMPANY AND LOW COMPANY
Allocation of Preferred and Common Stock Purchase Prices
January 1, 1995

Preferred Stock	
Purchase price paid for preferred stock	$ 149,968
Preferred stock book value equivalent to High's ownership ($203,280 × 60%)	(121,968)
Cost in excess of book value.	$ 28,000
Allocation to specific accounts:	
Land ($20,000 × 60%).	12,000
Excess cost not identified with specific accounts—goodwill	$ 16,000
Common Stock	
Purchase price paid for common stock	$ 894,496
Common stock book value equivalent to High's ownership ($1,013,120 × 80%)	(810,496)
Cost in excess of book value.	$ 84,000
Allocation to specific accounts:	
Land ($80,000 × 80%).	64,000
Excess cost not identified with specific accounts—goodwill	$ 20,000

Entry A has been split into "A1" and "A2" to identify the allocations resulting from the preferred stock and common stock, respectively. This segregation is made merely to clarify the process; these two worksheet entries could easily be combined.

Consolidation Entry PS

Preferred Stock (Low Company)	100,000	
Retained Earnings (Low Company) (20%)	103,280	
Investment in Low Company Preferred Stock		
(60% ownership).		121,968
Noncontrolling Interest in Low Company (40%)		81,312

To eliminate subsidiary's preferred stockholders' equity accounts ($203,280) and recognize noncontrolling interest in preferred stock. Retained earnings is based on par value assignment.

Consolidation Entry S

Common Stock (Low Company)	400,000	
Additional Paid-In Capital (Low Company).	200,000	
Retained Earnings (Low Company) (80%)	413,120	
Investment in Low Company Common Stock		
(80% ownership).		810,496
Noncontrolling Interest in Low Company (20%)		202,624

To eliminate subsidiary's remaining stockholders' equity accounts ($1,013,120) and recognize noncontrolling interest in common stock. Retained earnings reflects Entry PS.

Consolidation Entry A1

Land	12,000	
Goodwill	16,000	
Investment in Low Company Preferred Stock		28,000

To allocate cost paid for preferred stock in excess of book value. (See Exhibit 6–4.)

Consolidation Entry A2

Land	64,000	
Goodwill	20,000	
Investment in Low Company Common Stock.		84,000

To allocate cost paid for common stock in excess of book value. (See Exhibit 6–4.)

Allocation of Subsidiary Income. The specific rights granted to the owners of the preferred stock also affect the subsequent allocation of the subsidiary's income each year. If the assumption is again made that Low reports net income for 1995 of $100,000, this amount must be divided between the two ownership interests based on the cumulative, participating rights of the preferred stock. These shares constitute 20 percent of the subsidiary's total par value with the remaining 80 percent coming from the holders of the common stock. Thus, net income is prorated according to this same ratio.

	Income
Subsidiary totals	$100,000
Preferred stock—possesses rights to 20% of total (based on relative par values).	$ 20,000
Common stock—residual 80% interest	80,000

Based on this allocation of the subsidiary's income for 1995, the noncontrolling interest's share of consolidated income can be determined:

		Percent Outside Ownership	Noncontrolling Interest
Income attributed to preferred stock	$20,000	40%	$ 8,000
Income attributed to common stock	80,000	20	16,000
Noncontrolling interests in subsidiary's income			$24,000

Consolidated Statement of Cash Flows

In November of 1987, the Financial Accounting Standards Board issued its *Statement No. 95*, "Statement of Cash Flows," mandating that companies include a statement of cash flows within a set of financial statements. Because of this pronouncement, details of an organization's cash flows must be reported for each period in which an income statement is presented. Prior to this time, a statement of changes in financial position had been required but *Statement No. 95* replaced it with the cash flows statement.

To this point in the coverage of consolidated financial statements, no mention has been made of cash flows for two reasons:

First, production of the statement of cash flows is a topic covered in detail in intermediate accounting textbooks.

Second, this consolidated statement is not prepared from the individual cash flows of the separate companies. Instead, the income statements and balance sheets are first brought together on the worksheet. The cash flows statement is then based on the resulting consolidated figures. *Thus, this statement is not actually produced by consolidation but rather it is created from numbers generated by that process.*

Although not directly created by the consolidation process, preparing a statement of cash flows for a business combination does introduce several accounting issues. In preparing this statement, noncontrolling interest balances, amortization, and intercompany transactions must all be properly handled.

Noncontrolling Interest.   On the consolidated income statement, the outside ownership of a noncontrolling interest is reflected as a decrease in net income. This reduction represents the earnings accrual assigned to these other owners. However, the only cash actually distributed to the noncontrolling interest is the portion of dividends paid to them by the subsidiary. Although the income statement presents the accrual rather than the dividend, the opposite is true of the cash flow statement: only cash transactions are included. *Thus, for this statement, two adjustments are made. First, the noncontrolling interest's share of the subsidiary's net income must be eliminated; second, the dividends paid to the outside owners are included.*

The noncontrolling interest's income accrual can be removed from the statement of cash flows in either of two ways. If the business combination is using the direct approach to disclose cash generated by operations, the specific cash inflows and outflows are identified. For example, the cash collected from customers is disclosed along with the cash paid for inventory and expenses. Since the noncontrolling interest's share of consolidated income is a noncash item, this balance is simply omitted from the statement.

The business combination could also, instead, determine the cash from operations by applying the indirect approach. Under this alternative, noncash as well as nonoperational items are removed from net income, which leaves a residual figure representing the increase or decrease in cash resulting from operations. If the indirect approach is used, the noncontrolling interest's share of consolidated income must be eliminated from net income since this reduction in earnings is a noncash account. The noncontrolling interest balance does not represent an actual cash payment or collection. Because the earnings assigned to these outside owners is a decrease (or negative) within consolidated income, the amount is eliminated by adding the number to net income.

Regardless of which approach is used, the noncontrolling interest income accrual is removed in computing the cash derived from operations. However, any dividend paid to the other owners during the period is an actual cash outflow incurred by the combination and must be included on the statement. Since this distribution is made to an owner, the amount is listed separately under the "Cash Flows from Financing Activities" section of the statement of cash flows.

Amortization.   The amortization of allocations made to specific accounts as well as to goodwill is recorded in the consolidation process by means of a worksheet adjustment (Entry E). This expense does not appear on either set of individual records but is still included in the income statement of the business combination. As a noncash decrease in income, this expense impacts the statement of cash flows in the same manner as the noncontrolling interest's share of consolidated income. If the direct approach is used by the business combination, the balance is omitted because this expense does not affect the amount of cash. In contrast, if the indirect approach is applied, the amortization expense is removed by adding the balance to net income.

Intercompany Transactions. As discussed previously in this text, a significant volume of transfers often occur between the related companies composing a business combination. The resulting effects of this intercompany activity must be eliminated on the worksheet so that the consolidated income statement and balance sheet reflect only transactions with outside parties. Likewise, the consolidated statement of cash flows should not include the impact of these transfers. Although the cash flows may be large, intercompany sales and purchases do not change the amount of cash being held by the business combination when viewed as a whole.

Since the statement of cash flows is derived from the consolidated balance sheet and income statement, the impact of all transfers has been removed prior to producing this last statement. Therefore, no special adjustments are needed to arrive at a proper presentation of cash flows. The elimination entries made on the worksheet have the added effect of providing correct data for the consolidated statement of cash flows.

Illustration. A complete illustration of the production of a consolidated statement of cash flows is presented in the second comprehensive illustration at the end of the chapter. This example examines the effect on this statement created by the presence of a noncontrolling interest, amortization expense, and intercompany transactions.

Consolidated Earnings per Share

One other intermediate accounting topic, the computation of earnings per share (EPS), is affected by the consolidation process. As required by *APB Opinion No. 15,* "Earnings Per Share," publicly held companies must disclose EPS each period. Armstrong World Industries, Inc., for example, reported earnings per share in 1991 of $.77 while Chrysler Corporation lost $3.28 per share during the same period.

Such figures are calculated through the following steps:

- Simple earnings per share is determined by dividing net income (after reduction for preferred stock dividends) by the weighted average number of common stock shares outstanding for the period. If the reporting entity has no dilutive warrants or other convertible items, simple EPS is presented on the face of the income statement. However, primary and fully diluted earnings per share, rather than simple EPS, are required if any dilutive convertibles are present.
- Primary earnings per share is computed by combining the effects of *any dilutive common stock equivalents* with simple earnings per share. Stock

warrants and options are always viewed as common stock equivalents but this term may also encompass certain convertible debt and convertible preferred stock.

- Fully diluted earnings per share is derived by combining the effects of *all dilutive convertibles* with simple earnings per share. Common stock equivalents are included in the computation of both primary and fully diluted earnings per share. However, any convertible debt or convertible preferred stock that is not considered a common stock equivalent is only a factor in arriving at fully diluted earnings per share.[3]

In most instances, the computation of earnings per share for a business combination follows this same general pattern. Consolidated net income along with the number of outstanding parent shares provides the basis for this calculation. If convertibles or warrants for the parent's stock exist that can possibly dilute the reported figure, they must be included as described earlier in determining primary and fully diluted EPS.

However, a problem arises if warrants or convertibles are outstanding that can dilute the subsidiary's earnings. Although the parent company is not directly affected, the potential impact of these items on consolidated net income must be given weight in computing earnings per share for the business combination as a whole. Because of possible conversion, the subsidiary earnings figure included in consolidated net income is not necessarily applicable to the earnings per share computation. *Thus, the accountant must make a separate determination of the amount of subsidiary income that should be used in deriving the earnings per share for the business combination.*

Earnings per Share Illustration.   Assume that Big Corporation has 100,000 shares of its common stock outstanding during the current year. The company has also issued 20,000 shares of nonvoting preferred stock paying an annual cumulative dividend of $5 per share ($100,000 total). Each of these preferred shares is convertible into two shares of Big's common stock. This preferred stock is not considered a common stock equivalent because the effective dividend rate was relatively high in comparison to the average Aa corporate bond yield rate at the date of issuance.

Assume further that Big owns 90 percent of Little's common stock and 60 percent of its preferred stock (which pays $12,000 in dividends per year). Annual

---

[3] Complete coverage of the earnings per share computation can be found in virtually any intermediate accounting textbook. To achieve an adequate understanding of this process, a number of complex procedures must be mastered including:

- Calculation of the weighted average number of common shares outstanding.
- Determination of whether convertible debt and preferred stock are common stock equivalents.
- Understanding of the method of including stock rights, convertible debt, and convertible preferred stock within the computation of primary and fully diluted earnings per share.
- Determination of whether a convertible is antidilutive.

amortization is $24,000. EPS computations are currently being made for 1995. During the year, Big reported separate income of $600,000 while Little earned $100,000. A simplified consolidation of the figures for the year indicates net income for the business combination of $662,400:

Big's separate income for 1995		$600,000
Amortization expense resulting from original purchase price		(24,000)
Little's separate income for 1995	100,000	
Noncontrolling interest in Little—common stock (10% of income after $12,000 in preferred stock dividends)	(8,800)	
Noncontrolling interest in Little—preferred stock (40% of dividends)	(4,800)	86,400
Consolidated net income		$662,400

Little has 20,000 shares of common stock and 4,000 shares of preferred stock outstanding. The preferred shares pay a $3 per year dividend and each can be converted into 2 shares of common stock (or 8,000 shares in total). Since Big owns only 60 percent of Little's preferred stock, a $4,800 dividend is distributed each year to the outside owners (40 percent of $12,000 total payment). Little's preferred stock is viewed as a common stock equivalent.

Assume finally that the subsidiary also has $200,000 in convertible bonds outstanding that were originally issued at face value. This debt has a cash and an effective interest rate of 10 percent ($20,000 per year) and can be converted by the owners into 9,000 shares of Little's common stock. These bonds are not common stock equivalents and none are owned by Big. The tax rate applicable to Little is 30 percent.

To better visualize these factors, the convertible items can be scheduled as follows:

Company	Item	Interest or Dividend	Conversion	Common Stock Equivalent	Big Owns
Big	Preferred stock	$100,000/year	40,000 shares	No	Not applicable
Little	Preferred stock	12,000/year	8,000 shares	Yes	60%
Little	Bonds	14,000/year*	9,000 shares	No	–0–

* Interest on the bonds is shown net of the 30% tax effect ($20,000 interest less $6,000 tax savings). No tax is computed for the preferred shares since distributed dividends do not create a tax impact.

Because the subsidiary has convertible items that may reduce the company's net income, Little's primary and fully diluted earnings per share must be derived *before* consolidated figures can be determined. Since Little's preferred stock is a common stock equivalent, the effect of any potential conversion must be included in its own primary earnings per share computation. The bonds are not common stock equivalents; thus, this debt is only a factor in the fully diluted calculation.

As shown in Exhibit 6–5, Little reports primary earnings of $3.57 per share and fully diluted earnings per share of $3.08. Two aspects of this schedule should be noted:

- The individual impact of the convertibles ($1.50 for the preferred stock and $1.56 for the bonds) did not raise the earnings per share figures. Thus, neither the preferred stock nor the bonds are antidilutive and both are properly included in these computations.
- Determining the earnings per share of the subsidiary is only necessary because of the possible dilutive impact. Without the subsidiary's convertible bonds and preferred stock, consolidated net income would form the basis for computing EPS for the business combination.

According to Exhibit 6–5, Little's income is viewed as $100,000 in the primary earnings per share calculation whereas the total is $114,000 for fully diluted EPS. The real issue here for the accountant is how much of these amounts should be included in computing consolidated earnings per share. This allocation is based on the percentage of shares controlled by the parent in each of the separate calculations. In deriving the subsidiary's primary EPS, 28,000 shares was the total used. Thus, the parent's 81 percent portion of these shares (22,800/28,000) is applied to the $100,000 income to determine the amount to be assigned to Big. Likewise, 37,000 shares was appropriate for fully diluted EPS. Big's 62 percent

---

EXHIBIT 6–5   **Subsidiary's Earnings Per Share**

LITTLE COMPANY
Primary and Fully Diluted Earnings per Common Share
For Year Ending December 31, 1995

	Earnings		Shares	
As reported	$100,000		20,000	
Preferred stock dividends	(12,000)			
Simple EPS	$ 88,000		20,000	$4.40
Effect of possible preferred stock conversion:				
Dividends saved	12,000	New Shares	8,000	$1.50 Impact (12,000/8,000)
Primary EPS.	$100,000		28,000	$3.57 (rounded)
Effect of possible bond conversion:				
Interest saved (net of taxes)	14,000		9,000	$1.56 Impact (14,000/9,000)
Fully diluted EPS	$114,000		37,000	$3.08 (rounded)

EXHIBIT 6–6

BIG COMPANY AND CONSOLIDATED SUBSIDIARY
Consolidated Primary Earnings per Common Share
For Year Ending December 31, 1995

	Earnings		Shares	
Computed below	$657,000*			
As reported			100,000	(Big's shares outstanding)
Preferred stock dividends (Big)	(100,000)		———	
Primary EPS (no common stock equivalents)	$557,000		100,000	$5.57

* Net income computation:

Big's separate income for 1995	$600,000	
Amortization expense resulting from original purchase price	(24,000)	
Portion of Little's income assigned to primary earnings per share calculation	81,000	(computed previously)
Earnings of the business combination applicable to primary earnings per share	$657,000	

BIG COMPANY AND CONSOLIDATED SUBSIDIARY
Consolidated Fully Diluted Earnings per Common Share
For Year Ending December 31, 1995

	Earnings		Shares	
Computed below	$646,680*			
As reported			100,000	(Big's shares outstanding)
Preferred stock dividends (Big)	(100,000)		———	
Simple EPS	$546,680		100,000	$5.47 (rounded)
Effect of possible preferred stock (Big) conversion:				
Dividends saved	100,000	New shares	40,000	$2.50 impact (100,000/40,000)
Fully diluted EPS	$646,680		140,000	$4.62 (rounded)

* Net income computation:

Big's separate income for 1995	$600,000	
Amortization expense resulting from original purchase price	(24,000)	
Portion of Little's income assigned to fully diluted earnings per share calculation	70,680	(computed previously)
Earnings of the business combination applicable to fully diluted earnings per share	$646,680	

ownership (22,800/37,000) is the basis for allocating the subsidiary's $114,000 income to the parent in this second computation.

Primary Earnings per Share

	Little Company Shares	*Big's Percentage*	*Big's Ownership*
Common stock	20,000	90%	18,000
Possible new shares—preferred			
stock	8,000	60	4,800
Total	28,000		22,800

Big's ownership (diluted): 22,800/28,000 = 81% (rounded)
Income assigned to Big (primary earnings per share computation):
  $100,000 × 81% = $81,000

Fully Diluted Earnings per Share

	Little Company Shares	*Big's Percentage*	*Big's Ownership*
Common stock	20,000	90%	18,000
Possible new shares—preferred			
stock	8,000	60	4,800
Possible new shares—bonds	9,000	–0–	–0–
Total	37,000		22,800

Big's ownership (diluted): 22,800/37,000 = 62% (rounded)
Income assigned to Big (fully diluted earnings per share computation):
  $114,000 × 62% = $70,680

Consolidated earnings per share can now be determined. Subsidiary income of $81,000 is included in arriving at primary earnings per share but only $70,680 is appropriate for the fully diluted EPS computation. Since two different income figures are utilized, primary and fully diluted calculations must be made separately as shown in Exhibit 6–6. Consequently, as determined in these schedules, this business combination should report primary earnings per share of $5.57 with fully diluted earnings per share of $4.62.

Subsidiary Stock Transactions

A footnote to the financial statements of the Gerber Products Company disclosed a transaction that had been carried out by one of the organization's subsidiaries: "The Company's wholly owned Mexican subsidiary sold previously unissued shares of common stock to Grupo Coral, S.A., a Mexican food company, at a price in excess of the shares' net book value." The footnote went on to state that Gerber had increased consolidated additional paid-in capital by $432,000 as a result of this stock sale.

As shown by this illustration, the level of parent ownership can be altered by subsidiary stock transactions. A subsidiary, for example, may decide to sell previously unissued stock to raise needed capital. Although a portion or even all of these new shares could be acquired by the parent company, such issues are frequently marketed entirely to outsiders. A subsidiary might also be legally forced to sell additional shares of its stock. As an example, companies holding control over foreign subsidiaries occasionally encounter this problem because of laws found in the individual localities. Issuance of new shares may be mandated if regulations require a certain percentage of local ownership as a prerequisite for operating within a country. Of course, changes in the level of parent ownership do not result solely from stock sales: a subsidiary can also repurchase its own stock. The acquisition, and possible retirement, of such treasury shares serves as a means of reducing the percentage of outside ownership.

Changes in Subsidiary Book Value—Stock Transactions

When a subsidiary subsequently buys or sells its own stock, a nonoperational increase or decrease occurs in the company's book value. Because the transaction need not involve the parent, the effect of this change is not automatically reflected in the parent's investment account. *Thus, a separate adjustment must be recorded to maintain reciprocity between the subsidiary's stockholders' equity accounts and the parent's investment balance.* The accountant measures the impact that the stock transaction has on the parent to ensure that this effect is appropriately recorded within the consolidation process.

An example can be constructed to demonstrate the mechanics of this issue. Assume that on January 1, 1995, Small Company has a book value of $700,000 as seen in the stockholders' equity section of the balance sheet on that day:

Common stock ($1.00 par value with 70,000 shares issued and outstanding)	$ 70,000
Retained earnings	630,000
Total stockholders' equity	$700,000

Based on the 70,000 outstanding shares, Small's book value at this time is $10 per common share ($700,000/70,000 shares).

On this same date, Giant Company acquired in the open market an 80 percent interest in Small Company (or 56,000 of the outstanding shares). To avoid unnecessary complications, the price of this stock is assumed to be $560,000, or $10 per share, exactly equivalent to the book value of the shares being purchased. The assumption is also made that no goodwill or other revaluations are indicated by this acquisition.

Under these conditions, the consolidation process would be rather uncomplicated. As of the date of purchase, only a single worksheet entry is required. The investment account is eliminated and the 20 percent noncontrolling interest recognized through the following routine entry:

Consolidation Entry S (January 1, 1995)

Common Stock (Small Company)	70,000	
Retained Earnings (Small Company).	630,000	
Investment in Small Company (80%).		560,000
Noncontrolling Interest in Small Company (20%)		140,000
To eliminate subsidiary's stockholders' equity accounts and		
record noncontrolling interest balance on this date.		

A subsidiary stock transaction is now introduced to demonstrate the effect created on the consolidation process. Assume that on January 2, 1995, Small sells 10,000 previously unissued shares of its common stock to outside parties for $16 per share.[4] Because of this transaction, Giant no longer possesses an 80 percent interest in a subsidiary having a $700,000 net book value. Instead, the parent now holds 70 percent (56,000 shares out of a total of 80,000) of a company with a book value of $860,000 ($700,000 previous book value plus $160,000 capital generated by the sale of additional shares). *Independently of any action by the parent company, the book value equivalency of this investment has risen from $560,000 to $602,000 (70% of $860,000).* This increase has been created by Small's ability to sell shares of stock at $6.00 more than the book value.

Small's new stock issuance has increased the underlying book value component of Giant's investment by $42,000 ($602,000 − $560,000). Thus, even with the rise in outside ownership, the business combination has grown in size by this amount, a change that must be reflected within the consolidated financial figures. As indicated by the Gerber example, this adjustment is frequently recorded to additional paid-in capital. Since the subsidiary's stockholders' equity is eliminated on the worksheet, any equity increase accruing to the business combination must be recognized by the parent. Therefore, the $42,000 increment is entered into Giant's financial records as an adjustment in both the investment account (since the underlying book value of the subsidiary has increased) as well as additional paid-in capital.

Giant Company's Financial Records—January 2, 1995

Investment in Small Company	42,000	
Additional Paid-in Capital (Giant Company)		42,000
To recognize change in equity of business combination created by		
issuance of 10,000 additional shares of common stock by Small		
Company, the subsidiary, at above book value.		

------

[4] This example has been created solely for demonstration purposes. Obviously, having the parent acquire stock at book value on one day with an outsider paying $6 per share more than book value on the following day is an unlikely situation. Normally, the prices would be similar or a greater length of time would transpire between the two acquisitions. In either case, the consolidation process is fundamentally unchanged.

Once the change in the parent's records has been made, the consolidation process can be carried out in a normal fashion. If, for example, the financial statements are to be brought together immediately following the sale of these additional shares, the following worksheet Entry S can be constructed. *Although the investment and subsidiary equity accounts are removed here, the change recorded earlier in Giant's additional paid-in capital remains within the consolidated figures.* Thus, the subsidiary's issuance of stock at more than the book value has increased the reported equity of the business combination.

Consolidation Entry S—January 2, 1995—after subsidiary's stock issuance

Common Stock (Small Company)	80,000	
Additional Paid-In Capital (Small Company)	150,000	
Retained Earnings (Small Company).	630,000	
Investment in Small Company (70%).		602,000
Noncontrolling Interest in Small Company (30%)		258,000

To eliminate subsidiary's stockholders' equity accounts and record noncontrolling interest balance on this date. Small's capital accounts have been updated to reflect the issuance of 10,000 shares of $1 par value common stock at $16 per share. The investment balance has also been adjusted for the $42,000 increment recorded earlier by the parent.

In 1983, because of a lack of formal guidance, the staff of the SEC decided that an adjustment necessitated by subsidiary stock transactions could be made to either additional paid-in capital or to a gain or loss account. For example, in 1987 Atlantic Richfield Company disclosed that a previously wholly owned subsidiary had "completed an initial public offering of 19,550,000 shares of its common stock, thereby decreasing ARCO's percentage ownership to 80.4 percent. The Company recognized an after-tax gain of $185 million from this transaction." The FASB is currently reviewing the appropriate method of reporting such transactions. The two sides of the issue are as follows:

> Those who would recognize a gain or loss in consolidation contend that the substantive result of a subsidiary's issuing additional shares is identical to a parent's selling a portion of its holding in the subsidiary. . . . A parent should not be able to choose alternative accounting treatments (gain or loss recognition versus capital transaction) simply by designating the subsidiary instead of itself to be the party to the transaction. (paragraph 266 of FASB discussion memorandum, "An Analysis of Issues Related to Consolidation Policy and Procedures").

> Those who contend that the subsidiary's issuance of additional stock is a capital transaction and should be accounted for as an adjustment to paid-in capital in consolidation, not as a gain or loss, see significant economic differences between a subsidiary's stock issuance and a parent's selling some of its shares of the subsidiary's stock. . . . The earning process for the parent is not culminated when a subsidiary issues additional stock to outsiders, but it is when a parent sells its shares of stock in the subsidiary. (paragraph 267)

Subsidiary Stock Transactions—Illustrated

No single example can demonstrate the many possible variations that could be created by different types of subsidiary stock transactions. To provide a working knowledge of this process, several additional cases are analyzed briefly. The original balances presented for Small (the 80 percent-owned subsidiary) and Giant (the parent) as of January 1, 1995, serve as the basis for these illustrations:

Small Company (subsidiary):	
Shares outstanding	70,000
Book value of company	$700,000
Book value per share	$10.00
Giant Company (parent):	
Shares owned of Small Company	56,000
Book value of investment	$560,000 (80%)

Each of the following cases should be viewed as an independent situation. In addition, all adjustments are made here to additional paid-in capital although, as discussed, recognition of a gain or loss might be an acceptable alternative.

Case 1. Assume that Small Company sells 10,000 shares of previously unissued common stock to outside parties for $8 per share.

Small is issuing its stock here at a price that is below the company's current book value of $10 per share. Selling shares to outsiders at a discount necessitates a drop in the recorded value of consolidated additional paid-in capital. The parent's ownership interest is being diluted, thus creating a decrease in the underlying book value of the parent's investment. This reduction can be measured as follows:

Adjusted book value of subsidiary ($700,000 + $80,000)	$780,000
Current parent ownership (56,000 shares/80,000 shares).	70%
Book value equivalency of ownership.	546,000
Current book value of investment account	560,000
Required *reduction*	$ 14,000

In the original illustration, new shares were sold by the subsidiary at $6 more than book value, thus increasing consolidated equity. Here, the opposite transpires; the shares are issued at a price less than book value, creating a decrease.

Giant Company's Financial Records

Additional Paid-In Capital (or Retained Earnings)		
(Giant Company)	14,000	
Investment in Small Company		14,000
To recognize change in equity of business combination created by issuance of 10,000 additional shares of Small's common stock at less than book value.		

Case 2. Assume that Small issues 10,000 new shares of common stock for $16 per share. Of this total, Giant acquires 8,000 shares to maintain its 80 percent level of ownership. Giant pays a total of $128,000 (8,000 × $16) for this additional stock. The remaining shares are bought by outside parties.

Under these circumstances, both the parent's investment account and the book value of the subsidiary are altered by the stock transaction. Thus, both figures must be updated prior to determining the necessity of an equity revaluation:

Adjusted book value of subsidiary ($700,000 + $160,000)	$860,000
Current parent ownership (64,000 shares/80,000 shares).	80%
Book value equivalency of ownership.	688,000
Current book value of investment (after including additional $128,000 acquisition)	688,000
Required change	$ –0–

No adjustment is required in this case because Giant's underlying interest remains properly aligned with the subsidiary's book value. Any time that new stock is sold to the parent in the same ratio as previous ownership, consolidated additional paid-in capital is unaffected. No proportionate increase or decrease is created by the transaction.

Case 3. Assume that Small issues 10,000 additional shares of common stock solely to Giant for $16 per share.

A different type of situation is faced here. As shown in the following computational schedule, this issuance causes the parent's investment account to again be in excess of the subsidiary's underlying book value (as in Case 1). However, in this latest example, the $10,500 difference is created by a parent company purchase rather than by the subsidiary's sale of common stock to outside parties. Thus, the reporting of this impact has to be altered to reflect Giant's acquisition of these new shares.

Adjusted book value of subsidiary ($700,000 + $160,000)	$860,000
Current parent ownership (66,000 shares/80,000 shares).	82.5%
Book value equivalency of ownership.	709,500
Current book value of investment (after including additional $160,000 acquisition)	720,000
Differences in subsidiary book value and investment book value after second purchase	$ 10,500

The $14,000 reduction in Case 1 was caused by the subsidiary's sale of stock to outsiders at a price less than book value, a transaction that mathematically diluted the value of the parent's investment. Since this action realigned the owner-ship interests to the apparent detriment of the business combination, additional paid-in capital was reduced. This result was achieved for consolidation purposes through a decrease in the parent's equity account as well as in the Investment in Small Company.

Conversely, in Case 3, the $10,500 difference has been created solely by an expenditure made by the parent. Since the price paid was more than the corre-sponding book value of the subsidiary, the excess is attributed to goodwill (unless the amount can be traced to specific asset or liability accounts). As in any pur-chase combination, Giant records the entire $160,000 payment as an investment and then utilizes Entry A on the consolidation worksheet to report the allocation. Because the parent made the acquisition, the transaction is handled differently than a subsidiary's sale of stock to outsiders at less than book value.

Case 4. Assume that instead of issuing new stock, Small reacquires 10,000 shares from outside owners. The price paid for this treasury stock is $16 per share.

This illustration is designed to present another type of subsidiary stock trans-action: the acquisition of treasury stock. Although the subsidiary's actions have changed, the basic accounting procedures are unaffected.

Adjusted book value of subsidiary ($700,000 − $160,000)	$540,000
Current parent ownership (56,000 shares/60,000 shares).	93⅓%
Book value equivalency of ownership.	504,000
Current book value of investment	560,000
Required *reduction*	$ 56,000

The subsidiary paid an amount in excess of the treasury stock's $10 per share book value. Consequently, the parent's interest is once again being diluted. This effect is created by a transaction between the subsidiary and the noncontrolling interest; the reduction is not the result of a purchase made by the parent. As in Case 1, the change must be reported as an adjustment in the parent's additional paid-in capital accompanied by a corresponding decrease in the investment ac-count (to $504,000 in this case). Again, for reporting purposes, this transaction results in lowering consolidated additional paid-in capital.

Giant Company's Financial Records

Additional Paid-In Capital (Giant Company)	56,000	
Investment in Small Company		56,000

To recognize change in equity of business combination created by
acquisition of 10,000 treasury shares by Small at above book value.

This fourth illustration represents a different subsidiary stock transaction, the purchase of treasury stock. Therefore, display of consolidation Entry S should also be presented. This entry demonstrates the worksheet elimination required when the subsidiary holds treasury shares.

Consolidation Entry S

Common Stock (Small Company)	70,000	
Retained Earnings (Small Company).	630,000	
Treasury Stock (Small Company) (at cost)		160,000
Investment in Small Company (93⅓%—		
subsequent to adjustment)		504,000
Noncontrolling Interest (6⅔% of net book value)		36,000

To eliminate equity accounts of Small Company and recognize
appropriate noncontrolling interest. Book value of Small is now
$540,000.

Case 5. Assume that Small issues a 10 percent stock dividend (7,000 new shares) to its owners at a time when the fair market value of the stock is $16 per share.

This final case illustrates that not all subsidiary stock transactions produce discernible effects upon the consolidation process. A stock dividend, whether large or small, serves to capitalize a portion of the issuing company's retained earnings and, thus, does not alter book value. Shareholders recognize the receipt of a stock dividend only as a change in the recorded cost of each share rather than as any type of adjustment in the investment balance. Since no net effect is perceived by either party, the consolidation process proceeds in a routine fashion. Therefore, a subsidiary stock dividend requires no special treatment prior to development of a worksheet.

Book value of subsidiary (no adjustment required)	$700,000
Current parent ownership (adjusted for 10% stock	
dividend—61,600 shares/77,000 shares)	80%
Book value equivalency of ownership.	560,000
Current book value of investment	560,000
Adjustment required by stock dividend	$ –0–

The consolidation Entry S that would be made just after the issuance of this stock dividend follows. The $560,000 component of the investment account continues to be offset against the stockholders' equity of the subsidiary. Although the parent's investment was not affected by the dividend, the equity accounts of the subsidiary have been realigned in recognition of the $112,000 stock dividend (7,000 shares of $1 par value stock valued at $16 per share).

Consolidation Entry S

Common Stock (Small Company)	77,000	
Additional Paid-In Capital (Small Company)	105,000	
Retained Earnings (Small Company).	518,000	
Investment in Small Company (80%).		560,000
Noncontrolling Interest (20%).		140,000

To eliminate stockholders' equity accounts of subsidiary and
recognize noncontrolling interest following issuance of stock dividend.

Summary

1. If one member of a business combination acquires an affiliate's debt instrument (a bond or note, for example) from an outside party, the purchase price usually differs from the book value of the liability. Thus, a gain or loss has been incurred from the perspective of the business combination. However, both the debt and investment remain in the individual financial accounts of the two companies while the gain or loss goes unrecorded. In the consolidation process, all balances must be adjusted to reflect the effective retirement of the debt.

2. Following the acquisition of one company's debt by a related party, interest income and expense are recognized. Since these accounts result from intercompany transactions, they must also be removed in every subsequent consolidation along with the debt and investment figures. Retained earnings also requires adjustment in each year after the purchase to record the impact of the gain or loss.

3. Amortization of intercompany debt/investment balances is often necessary because of discounts and/or premiums. Consequently, the interest income and interest expense figures reported by the two parties will not agree. The closing of these two accounts into retained earnings each year gradually reduces the consolidation adjustment that must be made to this equity account.

4. When acquired, many subsidiaries have preferred stock outstanding as well as common stock. The method of handling any subsidiary preferred shares within the consolidation process is dependent on the nature of the stock. Preferred issues that have a call value, no voting rights, and a set cumulative dividend are not easily distinguished from a debt. Conversely, preferred shares with a voting or participation right are clearly an ownership interest resembling common stock.

5. If a subsidiary's preferred stock is viewed as a debt-type instrument, any shares acquired by the parent are eliminated on the worksheet as if the stock had been retired. Since a gain or loss cannot be recognized in connection with a company's own stock transactions, the difference between par value and the parent's cost is adjusted through additional paid-in capital or retained earnings. Any shares still held by outside parties are reported as a noncontrolling interest, based on the call value of the stock.

6. A subsidiary preferred stock that is perceived as an equity interest is accounted for in the same manner as a common stock purchase. Any excess acquisition price paid for the preferred stock is assigned to specific accounts based on fair market value with any residual reported as goodwill. As a prerequisite to this process, the book value of the subsidiary must be divided between the two equity interests. This calculation is based on the rights specified for the preferred shareholders.

7. A statement of cash flows is required of every business combination. This statement is not created by consolidating the individual cash flows of the separate companies. Instead, both a consolidated income statement and balance sheet are produced and the cash flows statement is then developed from these figures. Within this statement, the noncontrolling interest's share of the subsidiary's income is not included because no cash flows result. However, the dividends paid to these outside owners must be listed as a financing activity.

8. For most business combinations, the determination of consolidated earnings per share follows the normal pattern presented in intermediate accounting textbooks. However, if the subsidiary has potentially dilutive items outstanding (stock warrants, convertible preferred stock, convertible bonds, etc.), a different process must be followed. The subsidiary's own primary and fully diluted earnings per share are computed as a preliminary procedure. The earnings used in each of these calculations are then allocated between the parent and the outside owners based on the ownership levels of the subsidiary's shares and the dilutive items. The portion of income assigned to the parent is included in determining the two earnings per share figures to be reported for the business combination.

9. A subsidiary may enter into stock transactions after the combination is created such as the issuance of additional shares or the acquisition of treasury stock. Such actions normally create a proportional increase or decrease in the subsidiary's equity when compared with the parent's investment. The change is measured and then reflected in the consolidated statements through the Additional Paid-In Capital account. Recognition of a gain or loss is also a possibility. To achieve the appropriate accounting, the parent adjusts the Investment in Subsidiary account as well as its own additional paid-in capital. Since this equity balance is not eliminated on the worksheet, the required increase or decrease is created in the consolidated figures.

Comprehensive Illustration

Because several topics have been covered in this chapter, two comprehensive illustrations are presented.

PROBLEM ONE: Intercompany Bonds, Preferred Stock, and Stock Transactions

(Estimated Time: 50 to 65 Minutes)

The individual financial statements for Big Company and Little Corporation for the year ending December 31, 1995, follow:

	Big Company	Little Corporation
Revenues	$ 900,000	$ 389,026
Expenses	(702,000)	(200,000)
Interest income	–0–	10,974
Dividend income—Little Corporation preferred stock	2,400	–0–
Income of subsidiary—Little Corporation common stock	116,400	–0–
Net income	$ 316,800	$ 200,000

	Big Company	Little Corporation
Retained earnings, 1/1/95	$1,300,000	$ 700,000
Net income (above).	316,800	200,000
Dividends—preferred stock	–0–	(6,000)
Dividends—common stock	(136,800)	(24,000)
Retained earnings, 12/31/95	$1,480,000	$ 870,000
Current assets	$ 484,525	$ 850,000
Investment in Big Company bonds	–0–	108,711
Investment in Little Corporation preferred stock	26,800	–0–
Investment in Little Corporation common stock	958,000	–0–
Land, buildings, and equipment (net)	600,000	750,000
Total assets	$2,069,325	$1,708,711
Current liabilities	$ 202,000	$ 138,711
Bonds payable ($200,000 face value)	177,325	–0–
Preferred stock—$60 par value; 1,000 shares outstanding	–0–	60,000
Common stock—$4 par value; 50,000 shares outstanding	200,000	
Common stock—$10 par value; 24,000 shares outstanding		240,000
Additional paid-in capital	10,000	400,000
Retained earnings (above)	1,480,000	870,000
Total liabilities and equities	$2,069,325	$1,708,711

NOTE: Parentheses indicate a reduction.

Additional Information:

On January 1, 1990, Big Company purchased 14,400 shares of Little's common stock (80 percent of the 18,000 shares outstanding at that date). Big also bought 40 percent of the company's outstanding preferred stock (400 shares). A total of $530,800 was paid by Big for these two investments: $504,000 for the common stock and $26,800 for the preferred. At the date of acquisition, Big believed that no significant difference existed between the book value of Little's assets and liabilities and their fair market values. Little Corporation reported the following stockholders' equity accounts on January 1, 1990:

Preferred stock—$60 par value, 10% cumulative dividend, nonparticipating, nonvoting; call value of $72 per share; 1,000 shares outstanding	$ 60,000
Common stock—$10 par value; 18,000 shares outstanding	180,000
Additional paid-in capital	100,000
Retained earnings	260,000
Total stockholders' equity.	$600,000

On January 1, 1994, Little acquired on the open market half of the $200,000 outstanding bonds payable of Big Company. The bonds pay 12 percent cash interest each December 31 but were originally issued at a price yielding an effective rate of 15 percent. On the date of Little's purchase, Big was reporting a total book value for this debt of $173,100. Because of a recent decline in the prime interest rate, Little had to pay $110,670 for these bonds. This price was calculated to produce a 10 percent yield. Each company uses the effective interest rate method of amortization.

To raise new capital for expansion, Little Corporation issued an additional 6,000 shares of common stock to outsiders on January 1, 1995. Because of the company's profitability, the stock was sold for $60 per share. Because none of these shares were acquired by Big, the parent did not record the transaction.

Big has applied the partial equity method to the investment in Little's common stock while using the cost method for preferred shares. From 1990 through 1994, Little's retained earnings went up $440,000. Since preferred stock dividends were paid in full each year, the entire increase was directly attributable to the common shares (80 percent owned by Big).

Because of Little's sale of additional shares at the beginning of 1995, Big now holds only 60 percent of the common stock (14,400/24,000). Thus, the parent recognized equity income of $116,400 in 1995 in connection with its ownership of the subsidiary's common stock, 60 percent of the $194,000 income applicable to common stock (the $200,000 reported total less the $6,000 preferred stock dividend). The year-end investment in the common stock balance is made up of the following components:

Purchase price—common stock	$504,000
Increase in book value during prior years ($440,000 × 80%)	352,000
Equity accrual for current year	116,400
Dividends paid on common stock during current year ($24,000 × 60%)	(14,400)
Investment in Little Corporation common stock—12/31/95	$958,000

Any goodwill will be amortized over a 40-year period.

Required:
Prepare consolidated balances for Big and Little for 1995 financial statements.

SOLUTION (ONE)

Specifying a single definitive approach to consolidating a complex business combination is not realistically possible. Clearly, though, certain aspects of the process should be handled first. Allocation of the purchase price has routinely been an initial step in previous examples. In this illustration, the allocation is complicated by the presence of Little's preferred stock. The nature of these shares must be identified as a prerequisite for the valuation of the common stock acquisition.

As the preferred stock is listed as nonvoting and nonparticipating, it possesses the basic characteristics of a debt issue and is handled in a corresponding manner. Thus, the price paid for the preferred shares does not directly affect the calculation of goodwill. Instead, 40 percent of the subsidiary's preferred stock is viewed as having been retired by Big's acquisition. Under this assumption, $70,000 of the January 1, 1990, book value is allocated to this stock.

Acquisition price paid by Big Company—400 shares of preferred stock (40% ownership)	$26,800
Call value of remaining 600 shares—$72 per share (noncontrolling interest)	43,200
Book value attributable to preferred stock	$70,000

Having allotted $70,000 to the preferred stock interest, the remaining $530,000 of Little's January 1, 1990, book value is applicable to the common shares. Based on this residual value, Exhibit 6–7 can be constructed to allocate the $504,000 purchase price paid by Big to acquire 80 percent ownership in Little's common stock. No similar schedule is necessary for the preferred shares since that stock is viewed, in this case, as a debt-type instrument.

A second concern to be addressed at the start of this consolidation revolves around the subsidiary stock transaction. Since Big (as stated in the problem) made no entry to reflect the change on the business combination, an adjustment must be recorded. Big originally acquired 80 percent of Little's outstanding common stock (14,400 shares out of a total of 18,000). However, the issuance of 6,000 new shares to outsiders reduces the parent's level of ownership to 60 percent (14,400/24,000 shares). Selling this stock for $60 per share has also increased Little's book value by $360,000. The impact of the subsidiary stock transaction can be measured as follows:

Little Corporation's 1/1/95 book value prior to stock sale ($600,000 book value at acquisition plus the $440,000 increment for the 1990–94 period)	$1,040,000
Little Corporation's 1/1/95 book value subsequent to stock issuance ($1,040,000 + $360,000)	$1,400,000
Little Corporation's book value applicable to preferred stock (see above)	(70,000)
Residual book value applicable to common stock	1,330,000
Current ownership by Big	60%
Book value equivalency of Big's common stock ownership	798,000
Unadjusted book value of Big's common stock investment [($1,040,000 previous book value − $70,000) × 80%]	776,000
Required increase in investment account created by subsidiary stock issuance	$ 22,000

EXHIBIT 6–7

BIG COMPANY AND LITTLE CORPORATION
Common Stock Purchase Price Allocation
January 1, 1990

Purchase price of common stock	$ 504,000
Common stock book value equivalent to Big's ownership ($530,000 × 80%)	(424,000)
Cost in excess of book value—all allocated to goodwill	$ 80,000
Assumed life of goodwill.	40 years
Annual amortization.	$ 2,000

The issuance of these new shares has created a $22,000 increase in the underlying equity of Little Corporation that is held by the parent. This transaction creates a change in the additional paid-in capital reported by the business combination. Although the increase could have been recorded by the parent at the time of sale, no entry was made. Consequently, an adjustment of $22,000 must be made to Big's additional paid-in capital.

After accounting for the previous computations, an analysis should be made of the intercompany bond transaction. Little's payment of $110,670 to retire a liability with a book value on Big's records of only $86,550 (half of the $173,100 total) produced an immediate loss of $24,120 on January 1, 1994. However, since the companies are being accounted for as two separate entities, neither the retirement nor the loss were recognized by either party. Both the debtor and creditor continue to account for these bonds as if they were still outstanding. Interest payments are made periodically as required while each company amortizes the difference between the book value of the bonds and their face value.

The bond and interest accounts found in Big's December 31, 1995, accounting records have been calculated in the following schedule. This presentation determines these balances for only one half of the bonds payable since only that amount is currently held within the business combination.

Big Company's Financial Records—Bonds Payable

Year	Beginning Book Value	Effective Interest (15 percent rate)	Cash Interest (12 percent rate)	Amortization	Year-End Book Value
1994	$86,550	$12,983	$12,000	$ 983	$87,533
1995	87,533	13,130	12,000	1,130	88,663

During this time, Little would have accounted for the investment in these same bonds as follows:

Little Corporation's Financial Records—Investment in Bonds

Year	Beginning Book Value	Effective Interest (10 percent rate)	Cash Interest (12 percent rate)	Amortization	Year-End Book Value
1994	$110,670	$11,067	$12,000	$ 933	$109,737
1995	109,737	10,974	12,000	1,026	108,711

After the financial figures relative to the intercompany bonds have been isolated, an appropriate elimination can be produced. Consolidated balances must report these bonds as having been retired on the date they were acquired by the subsidiary. Thus, the current $88,663 book value of the liability is removed as well as the $108,711 investment balance. At the same time, both the $13,130 interest expense reported by Big for the current period and the $10,974 interest income recognized by Little are eliminated.

To complete the handling of this bond, a $22,204 reduction is made to the parent's beginning retained earnings. Although the loss was actually $24,120, the previous $983 amortization of the bond payable discount in 1994 and the $933 amortization of the investment premium have already reduced the 1995 beginning retained earnings by a total of $1,916. A decrease of only $22,204 is needed to reflect the loss on retirement.

As the final step in establishing appropriate 1995 balances, Big's beginning retained earnings must be restated to be in conformity with application of the equity method for this investment. The $22,204 adjustment necessitated by the bond retirement was just explained. In addition, a $10,000 reduction is needed to recognize $2,000 of goodwill amortization (as computed in Exhibit 6–7) for each of the five years from 1990 through 1994.

Having analyzed this information, consolidated balances for the business combination of Big and Little for December 31, 1995, and the year then ended can be developed:

Revenues = $1,289,026. Since no intercompany inventory transfers took place between Big and Little, the two account balances are simply added together.

Expenses = $890,870. Amortization expense of $2,000 must be added to the book values while $13,130 in interest expense on the intercompany bond is removed.

Interest income = –0–. The amount reported by Little is an intercompany figure produced by the investment in Big's bonds. For consolidation purposes, this figure is removed entirely.

Dividend income—Little preferred stock = –0–. This intercompany cash transfer is eliminated.

Equity income—Little common stock = –0–. The accrual recorded by the parent is eliminated so that the specific revenues and expenses of the subsidiary can be included in the consolidated figures.

Noncontrolling interest in income attributed to Little's preferred stock = $3,600. This figure is 60 percent of the amount of dividends paid since the parent owns only 40 percent.

Noncontrolling interest in income attributed to Little's common stock = $77,600. This figure is 40 percent of the income earned by the subsidiary after payment of the preferred stock dividend ($200,000 − $6,000 or $194,000). Although Big originally purchased 80 percent of Little, the subsequent issuance of additional shares has reduced the parent's ownership to 60 percent.

Net income = $316,956. Consolidated expenses and the amounts attributed to the outside owners are subtracted from consolidated revenues.

Retained earnings, 1/1/95 = $1,267,796. Because the parent is applying the partial equity method, the amortization expense for the five previous years must be recognized ($2,000 for five years or $10,000) as well as the $22,204 reduction in connection with the loss on bond retirement (computation made above).

Dividends paid on preferred stock = –0–. The dividends paid by the subsidiary are eliminated as intercompany (40 percent) or attributed to the noncontrolling interest (60 percent).

Dividends paid on common stock = $136,800. This balance represents the amount distributed by the parent. The subsidiary's dividends are eliminated as intercompany or are attributed to the noncontrolling interest.

Retained earnings, 12/31/95 = $1,447,952. The consolidated beginning retained earnings balance plus net income for the year less the dividends paid.

Current assets = $1,334,525. The book values are added together.

Investment in Big Company bonds = –0–. The balance is eliminated as an intercompany account.

Investment in Little Corporation preferred stock = –0–. The balance is eliminated as an intercompany account.

Investment in Little Corporation common stock = –0–. The balance is eliminated so that the individual assets and liabilities of the subsidiary can be included in the consolidated figures.

Land, buildings, and equipment = $1,350,000. The two book values are added.

Goodwill = $68,000. The original allocation to goodwill was $80,000, an amount which has now been reduced by six years of amortization at $2,000 per year.

Total assets = $2,752,525. This figure is a summation of the consolidated asset balances.

Current liabilities = $340,711. The book values are added.

Bonds payable = $88,662. Half of the reported bonds are eliminated as an intercompany investment.

Noncontrolling interest in Little's preferred stock = $43,200. This figure is the call value of the shares held by outsiders (600 shares at $72 per share).

Noncontrolling interest in Little's common stock = $600,000. This balance is computed as follows:

40% of subsidiary's common stock book value at 1/1/95 ($1,330,000—based on stockholders' equity accounts at beginning of year after subtracting $70,000 applicable to preferred shares)	$532,000
Noncontrolling interest in Little's net income— common stock (computed above)	77,600
Noncontrolling interest in Little's dividends— common stock ($24,000 × 40%)	(9,600)
Year-end balance	$600,000

Preferred stock = –0–. Only parent figure is reported for contributed capital and Big has no preferred stock.

Common stock = $200,000. Parent company balance only is presented.

Additional paid-in capital = $32,000. Parent company balance is reported after the $22,000 adjustment is made because of the subsidiary's sale of additional shares of stock.

Retained earnings, 12/31/95 = $1,447,952. Amount is computed above.

Total liabilities and stockholders' equity = $2,752,525. Summation of the consolidated liabilities and equity accounts.

Comprehensive Illustration

PROBLEM TWO:
Consolidated
Statement of Cash
Flows and Earnings
Per Share

(Estimated Time: 35 to 45 Minutes)

Pop, Inc., acquires 90 percent of the 20,000 shares of Son Company's outstanding common stock on December 31, 1994. Of the purchase price, $80,000 was allocated to goodwill, a figure amortized at the rate of $2,000 per year. Immediately following the purchase, a consolidated balance sheet was constructed:

Cash	$ 130,000
Accounts receivable	220,000
Inventory	278,000
Land, buildings, and equipment (net)	1,120,000
Goodwill	80,000
Total assets	$1,828,000

Accounts payable. . . . . $ 296,000
Long-term liabilities 550,000
Noncontrolling interest 34,000
Preferred stock (2,000 shares outstanding). 100,000
Common stock (26,000 shares outstanding) 520,000
Retained earnings, 12/31/94 328,000
Total liabilities and stockholders' equity $1,828,000

During 1995, Pop transferred inventory costing $60,000 to Son for $100,000. By year's end, all but 10 percent of this merchandise had been sold to outside parties.

On January 17, 1995, Pop borrowed $100,000 from a local bank. Several months later, the parent acquired equipment for $60,000 cash. On November 10, 1995, Son sold a building with a $40,000 book value, receiving cash of $50,000. These transactions were all with outside parties.

Pop pays a $10,000 dividend each year to the holders of the company's preferred stock. Each share of this stock can be converted into three shares of common. Son's long-term debt is also convertible. Interest expense in 1995 (net of taxes) was $16,000. The debt can be exchanged for 10,000 shares of the subsidiary's common stock. Pop owns none of this debt.

Presented in Exhibit 6–8 is the 1995 consolidation worksheet for Pop and Son. Pop applies the equity method to account for the investment in Son. The $48,000 equity income figure reported by the parent is derived from the $54,000 annual accrual (90 percent of the $60,000 reported income of the subsidiary) less the $2,000 amortization and the $4,000 unrealized gain (10 percent of the original intercompany gross profit). The noncontrolling interest in Son's income is 10 percent of the subsidiary's reported income for 1995.

Required:

a. Prepare a consolidated statement of cash flows for Pop, Inc. and Son Company for the year ending December 31, 1995. Use the indirect approach for determining the amount of cash generated by normal operations.[5]

b. Compute primary earnings per share and fully diluted earnings per share for this business combination. Assume that neither of the convertible items (Pop's preferred stock nor Son's long-term debt) are common stock equivalents.

SOLUTION (TWO)

a. Consolidated Statement of Cash Flows
The problem specifies that the indirect approach should be used in preparing the consolidated statement of cash flows. Therefore, all items that do not represent

---

[5] Prior to attempting this problem, a review of an intermediate accounting textbook might be useful to obtain a complete overview of the production of a statement of cash flows.

EXHIBIT 6–8

Consolidation: Purchase Method
Investment: Equity Method

POP, INC. AND SON COMPANY
Consolidation Worksheet
Year Ending December 31, 1995

	Pop, Inc.	Son Company	Consolidation Entries Debit	Consolidation Entries Credit	Noncontrolling Interest	Consolidated Totals
Revenues	600,000	300,000	(TI) 100,000	(TI) 100,000		800,000
Cost of goods sold	(400,000)	(180,000)	(G) 4,000			(484,000)
Depreciation and amortization	(20,000)	(30,000)	(E) 2,000			(52,000)
Other expenses	(56,000)	(40,000)				(96,000)
Gain on sale of building	–0–	10,000				10,000
Equity in Son's income	48,000	–0–	(I) 48,000			–0–
Noncontrolling interest in Son's income	–0–	–0–			6,000	(6,000)
Net income	172,000	60,000				172,000
Retained earnings, 1/1/95	328,000	140,000	(S) 140,000			328,000
Net income	172,000	60,000				172,000
Dividends paid	(50,000)	(20,000)		(D) 18,000	(2,000)	(50,000)
Retained earnings, 12/31/95	450,000	180,000				450,000
Cash	180,000	30,000				210,000
Accounts receivable	260,000	90,000		(G) 4,000		350,000
Inventory	254,000	70,000		(S) 306,000		320,000
Investment in Son	416,000	–0–	(D) 18,000	(A) 80,000		–0–
				(I) 48,000		

			Consolidation Entries		Noncontrolling Interest	Consolidated Totals
	Parent	Son	Debit	Credit		
Land, buildings, and equipment (net)	640,000	450,000	(A) 80,000			1,090,000
Goodwill	-0-	-0-				78,000
Total assets	1,750,000	640,000				2,048,000
Accounts payable	210,000	80,000				290,000
Long-term liabilities	470,000	180,000				650,000
Noncontrolling interest in Son, 1/1/95	-0-	-0-		(E) 2,000 (S) 34,000	34,000	
Noncontrolling interest in Son, 12/31/95	-0-	-0-			38,000	38,000
Preferred stock	100,000	-0-				100,000
Common stock	520,000	200,000	(S) 200,000			520,000
Retained earnings (above)	450,000	180,000				450,000
Total liabilities and stockholders' equity	1,750,000	640,000				2,048,000

NOTE: Parentheses indicate a reduction.

Consolidation entries:

(S) Elimination of subsidiary's stockholders' equity accounts along with recognition of January 1, 1995, noncontrolling interest.

(A) Allocation of parent's cost in excess of subsidiary's book value.

(I) Elimination of intercompany income.

(D) Elimination of intercompany dividends.

(E) Recognition of amortization expense for 1995.

(TI) Elimination of intercompany sales/purchases balances.

(G) Deferral of unrealized gain so that it can be recognized in 1996.

cash flows from operations must be removed from the $172,000 consolidated net income. For example, the depreciation and amortization are both eliminated (noncash items) as well as the gain on the sale of the building (a nonoperational item). As discussed in the chapter, the noncontrolling interest's share of Son's net income is another noncash reduction that is also removed. In addition, the changes in consolidated accounts receivable, inventory, and accounts payable each produce a noncash impact on net income. The increase in accounts receivable, for example, indicates that the sales figure for the period was larger than the amount of cash collected so that adjustment is required in producing this statement.

From the information given, only five nonoperational changes in cash can be determined: the bank loan, the acquisition of equipment, the sale of a building, the dividend paid by Son to the minority interest, and the dividend paid by the parent. These transactions are each included in the consolidated statement of cash flows shown in Exhibit 6–9 that explains the $80,000 increase in cash experienced by the entity during 1995.

b. Consolidated Earnings per Share

The subsidiary has convertible debt outstanding that has a potentially dilutive effect on earnings per share. Therefore, primary and fully diluted EPS cannot be determined for the business combination directly from consolidated net income. First, both of these EPS figures must be calculated for the subsidiary. This information is then used in the computations made by the consolidated entity. Since Son has neither preferred stock nor any type of common stock equivalents outstanding, primary earnings per share is $3.00, a figure that is determined by dividing reported net income of $60,000 by the 20,000 outstanding shares of common stock.

Fully diluted earnings per share of $2.53 for the subsidiary can then be determined as follows:

Son Company—Fully Diluted Earnings per Share

	Earnings		Shares	
Primary EPS	$60,000		20,000	$3.00
Effect of possible debt conversion:				
Interest saved (net of taxes)	16,000	New shares	10,000	$1.60 impact (16,000/10,000)
Fully diluted EPS	$76,000		30,000	$2.53 (rounded)

Since Pop possesses 90 percent of the 20,000 shares used in Son's primary EPS calculation, $54,000 of these earnings ($60,000 × 90 percent) are assigned to

---

EXHIBIT 6–9

POP, INC. AND SON COMPANY
Consolidated Statement of Cash Flows
Year Ending December 31, 1995

Cash flows from operating activities

Net income		$ 172,000
Adjustments to reconcile net income to net cash provided by operating activities:		
Depreciation and amortization	$ 52,000	
Gain on sale of building	(10,000)	
Noncontrolling interest in Son's income	6,000	
Increase in accounts receivable	(130,000)	
Increase in inventory	(42,000)	
Decrease in accounts payable	(6,000)	(130,000)
Net cash provided by operations		$ 42,000

Cash flows from investing activities

Purchase of equipment	$ (60,000)	
Sale of building	50,000	
Net cash used in investing activities		(10,000)

Cash flows from financing activities

Payment of cash dividend—Pop	$ (50,000)	
Payment of cash dividend to noncontrolling owners of Son	(2,000)	
Borrowed from bank	100,000	
Net cash provided by financing activities		48,000
Net increase in cash		$ 80,000
Cash, January 1, 1995		130,000
Cash, December 31, 1995		$ 210,000

---

the consolidated computation of primary EPS. However, the parent owns none of the convertible debt included in computing fully diluted earnings per share. Pop holds only 18,000 (90 percent of the outstanding common stock) of the 30,000 shares used in this second EPS calculation. Consequently, in determining fully diluted EPS for the entire business combination, just $45,600 of the subsidiary's income is applicable:

$$\$76,000 \times 18,000/30,000 = \$45,600$$

Exhibit 6–10 can now be constructed to determine primary earnings per share of $6.23 for this business computation with fully diluted EPS of $5.11. Since the subsidiary's earnings figure is included separately in this computation, the individual income of the parent must be identified in the same manner. Thus, the effect of the equity income, intercompany (downstream) transactions, and amortization are taken into account in arriving at the parent's earnings alone.

EXHIBIT 6–10

POP, INC., AND SON COMPANY
Consolidated Earnings per Share
Year Ending December 31, 1995

	Earnings		Shares	
Primary Earnings per Share				
Pop's reported income	$172,000			
Remove equity income	(48,000)			
Remove unrealized gain	(4,000)			
Recognize amortization expense	(2,000)			
Preferred stock dividend	(10,000)			
Common shares outstanding (Pop, Inc.)			26,000	
Common stock income—Pop (for EPS computations)	$108,000		26,000	
Income of Son (computed above—for primary EPS)	54,000			
Primary EPS	$162,000		26,000	$6.23 (rounded)
Fully Diluted Earnings per Share				
Common stock income—Pop (computed above—for EPS computations)	$108,000		26,000	
Income of Son (above—for fully diluted EPS)	45,600			
	$153,600		26,000	$5.91 (rounded)
Effect of possible preferred stock conversion: Dividends saved	10,000	New shares	6,000	$1.67 impact (10,000/6,000)
Fully diluted EPS	$163,600		32,000	$5.11

Questions

1. A parent company acquires from a third party bonds that had been issued originally by one of its subsidiaries. What accounting problems are created by this purchase?

2. In question 1, why is the consolidation process simpler if the bonds had been acquired directly from the subsidiary rather than from a third party?

3. When one company's debt instruments are acquired by an affiliated company from a third party, how is the gain or loss on extinguishment of the debt calculated? When should this balance be recognized?

4. Several years ago, Bennett, Inc. bought a portion of the outstanding bonds of Smith Corporation, a subsidiary organization. The acquisition was made from an outside party. In the current year, how should these intercompany bonds be accounted for within the consolidation process?

5. One company purchases the outstanding debt instruments of an affiliated company on the open market. This transaction creates a gain that is appropriately recognized in the consolidated financial statements of that year. Thereafter, a worksheet adjustment is required to correct the beginning balance of the consolidated retained earnings. Why is the amount of this adjustment reduced from year to year?

6. A parent acquires the outstanding bonds of a subsidiary company directly from an outside third party. For consolidation purposes, this transaction creates a gain of $45,000. Should this gain be allocated to the parent or the subsidiary? Why?

7. Some preferred stocks possess characteristics that resemble an equity or ownership interest. Others, however, demonstrate traits similar to a debt instrument. How is the distinction drawn as to whether the preferred stock is actually an equity or a debt?

8. Perkins Company acquires 90 percent of the outstanding common stock of the Butterfly Corporation as well as 55 percent of its preferred stock. Because of the rights being conveyed, the preferred stock is considered to be a debt-type instrument. How should these preferred shares be accounted for within the consolidation process? How should the book value of Butterfly be allocated between the common and the preferred stock?

9. Assume the same information as in question 8 except that the preferred stock is viewed as an equity interest. How is the preferred stock now accounted for within the consolidation process? How should the book value of Butterfly be allocated between the common and the preferred stock?

10. A consolidated statement of cash flows is not produced using a worksheet as are the income statement and the balance sheet. What process is followed in preparing a consolidated statement of cash flows?

11. How do noncontrolling interest balances affect the consolidated statement of cash flows?

12. In many cases, consolidated earnings per share is computed based on consolidated net income and parent company shares and convertibles. However, a different process must be used for some business combinations. When is this alternative approach required?

13. A subsidiary has (1) a convertible preferred stock that is a common stock equivalent and (2) a convertible bond that is not a common stock equivalent. How are these items factored into the computation of earnings per share for the business combination?

14. Why might a subsidiary decide to issue new shares of common stock to parties outside of the business combination?

15. Washburn Company owns 75 percent of the outstanding common stock of Metcalf Company. During the current year, Metcalf issues additional shares to outside parties at a price more than book value. How does this transaction affect the business combination? How is this impact recorded within the consolidated statements?

16. Assume the same information as in question 15 except that the new shares are issued primarily to Washburn. How does this transaction affect the business combination?

17. Assume the same information as in question 15 except that Metcalf issues a 10 percent stock dividend instead of selling new shares of stock. How does this transaction affect the business combination?

18. If a parent must increase its investment because a subsidiary issues additional shares of stock, in what two ways can the adjustment be recorded?

Library Assignments

1. Read the following as well as any other published materials that might be available concerning the characteristics of preferred stocks:

    "Reporting Preferred Stock: Debt or Equity?" *Mergers & Acquisitions,* Spring 1980.

    "Accounting for Certain Recent Equity Financing Arrangements," *Review of Business,* Fall 1987.

    "A CPA's Field Guide to New Financial Instruments," *Journal of Accountancy* (Professional Notes section), October 1985.

    "Accounting for Redeemable Preferred Stock: Unresolved Issues," *Accounting Horizons,* June 1990.

    "Financial Instruments: A Report on the Liability-Equity Comment Letters and Public Hearings." (Status Report published by FASB), *Financial Accounting Series No. 103,* May 31, 1991.

    Write a report outlining an approach that can be taken to determine whether a preferred stock issue should be considered a debt instrument or an equity interest.

2. Read paragraphs 380–84 of the FASB's discussion memorandum, "An Analysis of Issues Related to Consolidation Policy and Procedures." Write a short report justifying one method of allocating any gains and losses that result from an intercompany bond transaction.

Problems

1. A subsidiary has a debt outstanding that was originally issued at a discount. At the beginning of the current year, the debt was acquired at a slight premium from outside parties by the parent company. Which of the following statements are true?

  a. Whether the balances agree or not, both the subsequent interest income and interest expense should be reported in a consolidated income statement.

  b. The interest income and interest expense will agree in amount and should be offset for consolidation purposes.

  c. In computing any noncontrolling interest allocation, the interest income should be included but not the interest expense.

  d. Although subsequent interest income and interest expense will not agree in amount, both balances should be eliminated for consolidation purposes.

2. A subsidiary issues a bond directly to its parent at a discount. Which of the following statements is true?

  a. Elimination is not necessary for consolidation purposes since the bond was acquired directly from the subsidiary.

  b. Because of the discount, the various interest accounts on the two sets of financial records will not agree.

  c. Since the bond was issued by the subsidiary, the amount attributed to a noncontrolling interest is always affected.

  d. All interest balances exactly offset for consolidation purposes.

3. A bond that had been issued by a parent company at a discount was acquired several years ago by its subsidiary from an outside party at a premium. Which of the following statements is true?

  a. The bond has no impact on a current consolidation because the acquisition was made in the past.

  b. The original loss would be reported in the current year's consolidated income statement.

  c. For consolidation purposes, retained earnings must be reduced at the beginning of the current year but by an amount smaller than the original loss.

  d. The various interest balances exactly offset so that no adjustment to retained earnings or to income is necessary.

4. A parent company acquires all of a subsidiary's common stock but only 70 percent of its preferred shares. This preferred stock is callable and pays a 7 percent annual cumulative dividend. No dividends are in arrears at the current time. How is the noncontrolling interest's share of the subsidiary's income computed?

  a. As 30 percent of the subsidiary's preferred dividend.

  b. No allocation is made since the dividends have been paid.

  c. As 30 percent of the subsidiary's income after all dividends have been subtracted.

  d. Income is assigned to the preferred stock based on total par value and 30 percent of that amount is allocated to the noncontrolling interest.

5. Aceton Corporation owns 80 percent of the outstanding stock of Voctax, Inc. During the current year, Voctax made $140,000 in sales to Aceton. How does this transfer affect the consolidated statement of cash flows?

a. The transaction should be included if payment has been made.

b. Only 80 percent of the transfers should be included because the sales were made by the subsidiary.

c. Because the transfers were from a subsidiary organization, the cash flows are reported as investing activities.

d. Because of the intercompany nature of the transfers, the amount is not reported in the consolidated cash flow statement.

6. Warrenton, Inc., owns 80 percent of Aminable Corporation. On a consolidated income statement, the Noncontrolling Interest in the Subsidiary's Income is reported as $37,000. Aminable paid a total cash dividend of $100,000 for the year. How is the consolidated statement of cash flows impacted?

a. The dividends paid to the outside owners is reported as a financing activity but the noncontrolling interest figure is not viewed as a cash flow.

b. The noncontrolling interest figure is reported as an investing activity but the dividends paid to the outside owners is omitted entirely.

c. Neither figure is reported on the statement of cash flow.

d. Both dividends paid and the noncontrolling interest are viewed as financing activities.

7. Thuoy Corporation is computing consolidated earnings per share. One of its subsidiaries has stock warrants outstanding. How do these convertible items affect the consolidated earnings per share computation?

a. No effect is created since the stock warrants were for the shares of the subsidiary company.

b. The stock warrants are not included in the computation unless they are antidilutive.

c. The effect of the stock warrants must be computed in deriving the amount of subsidiary income that is to be included in making the consolidated earnings per share calculation.

d. The stock warrants are only included in primary earnings per share but never in fully diluted earnings per share.

8. A parent company owns a controlling interest in a subsidiary whose stock has a book value of $31 per share. At the end of the current year, the subsidiary issues new shares entirely to outside parties at $45 per share. The parent still holds control over this subsidiary. Which of the following statements is true?

a. Since the shares were all sold to outside parties, the parent's Investment account is not affected.

b. Since the parent now owns a smaller percentage of the subsidiary, the parent's Investment account must be reduced.

c. Since the shares were sold for more than book value, the parent's Investment account must be increased.

d. Since the sale was made at the end of the year, the parent's Investment account is not affected.

9. Rodgers, Inc., owns Ferdinal Corporation. For 1995, Rodgers reports net income (without consideration of its investment in Ferdinal) of $200,000 while the subsidiary reports $80,000. The parent had a bond payable outstanding on January 1, 1995, with a book value of $212,000. The subsidiary acquired the bond on that date for $199,000. During 1995, Rodgers reported interest income of $22,000 while Ferdinal reported interest expense of $21,000. What is consolidated net income?
   a. $266,000.
   b. $268,000.
   c. $292,000.
   d. $294,000.

10. Thompkins, Inc., owns Pastimer Company. The subsidiary had a bond payable outstanding on January 1, 1994, with a book value of $189,000. The parent acquired the bond on that date for $206,000. Subsequently, Pastimer reported interest income of $18,000 in 1994 while Thompkins reported interest expense of $21,000. Consolidated financial statements are being prepared for 1995. What adjustment is needed for the retained earnings balance as of January 1, 1995?
   a. Reduction of $20,000.
   b. Reduction of $14,000.
   c. Reduction of $3,000.
   d. Reduction of $22,000.

11. Ace Company reports current earnings of $400,000 while paying $40,000 in cash dividends. Byrd Company earns $100,000 in net income and distributes $10,000 in dividends. Ace has held a 70 percent interest in Byrd for several years, an investment that it originally purchased at a price equal to the book value of the underlying net assets. Ace uses the cost method to account for these shares.

    On January 1, of the current year, Byrd acquired in the open market $50,000 of Ace's 8 percent bonds. The bonds had originally been issued several years ago for 92, reflecting a 10 percent effective interest rate. On the date of purchase, the book value of the bonds payable was $48,300. Byrd paid $46,600 based on a 12 percent effective interest rate over the remaining life of the bonds.

    What is consolidated net income for this year prior to reduction for the noncontrolling interest's share of the subsidiary's net income?
   a. $492,160.
   b. $493,938.
   c. $499,160.
   d. $500,258.

12. Using the same information presented in problem 11, what is the noncontrolling interest's share of the subsidiary's net income?
   a. $27,000.
   b. $28,290.
   c. $28,620.
   d. $30,000.

13. Able Company possesses 80 percent of the outstanding voting stock of Baker Company. Able uses the partial equity method to account for this investment. On January 1, 1992, Able sold 9 percent bonds payable with a $10 million face value (maturing in 20 years) on the open market at a premium of $600,000. On January 1, 1995, Baker acquired 40 percent of these same bonds from an outside party at 96.6 of face value. Both companies use the straight-line method of amortization. For a 1996 consolidation, what adjustment should be made to Able's beginning retained earnings as a result of this bond acquisition?

    a. $320,000 increase.

    b. $326,000 increase.

    c. $331,000 increase.

    d. $340,000 increase.

14. A company has common stock with a total par value of $400,000 and preferred stock with a total par value of $100,000. The book value of the company is $890,000. The preferred stock pays an 8 percent annual dividend whereas the common stock normally distributes a dividend each year that is equal to 10 percent of its par value. If this company is acquired by another, what portion of the book value should be assigned to the preferred stock? The preferred stock is considered an equity. (Round to the nearest dollar)

    a. $100,000.

    b. $395,555.

    c. $148,333.

    d. $178,000.

15. Top Company spent a total of $4,384,000 to acquire control over Bottom Company. This price was based on paying $424,000 for 20 percent of Bottom's preferred stock and $3,960,000 for 90 percent of its outstanding common stock. As of the date of purchase, Bottom's stockholders' equity accounts were as follows:

Preferred stock—9%, $100 par value, cumulative and participating; 10,000 shares outstanding	$1,000,000
Common stock—$50 par value; 40,000 shares outstanding	2,000,000
Retained earnings	3,000,000
Total stockholders' equity	$6,000,000

The owners of the preferred stock vote on any issues considered by the owners of the common stock.

Top believes that all of Bottom's accounts are correctly valued within the company's financial statements. What amount of consolidated goodwill should be recognized?

    a. $300,000.

    b. $316,000.

    c. $364,000.

    d. $384,000.

16. On January 1, 1995, Mitchell Company has a net book value of $1,500,000 as follows:

1,000 shares of preferred stock; par value $100 per share; cumulative, nonparticipating, nonvoting; call value $108 per share	$ 100,000
20,000 shares of common stock; par value $40 per share	800,000
Retained earnings	600,000
Total	$1,500,000

    Andrews Company acquires all of the outstanding preferred shares for $106,000 and 60 percent of the common stock for $916,400. Andrews believed that one of Mitchell's buildings, with a 12-year life, was undervalued on the company's financial records by $50,000.

    What amount of consolidated goodwill would be recognized from this purchase?

    a. $50,000.

    b. $51,200.

    c. $52,400.

    d. $56,000.

17. Aedion Company owns control over Breedlove, Inc. Aedion reports sales of $300,000 during 1995 while Breedlove reports $200,000. Inventory costing $20,000 was transferred from Breedlove to Aedion (upstream) during the year for $40,000. Of this amount, 25 percent is still in ending inventory at year's end. Total receivables on the consolidated balance sheet were $80,000 at the first of the year and $110,000 at year-end. No intercompany debt existed at the beginning or ending of the year. Using the direct approach, what is the consolidated amount of cash collected by the business combination from its customers?

    a. $430,000.

    b. $460,000.

    c. $490,000.

    d. $510,000.

18. Ames owns 100 percent of Nestlum, Inc. Although the Investment in Nestlum account has a balance of $596,000, the subsidiary's 12,000 shares have an underlying book value of only $40 per share. On January 1, 1995, Nestlum issues 3,000 new shares to the public for $50 per share. How does this transaction affect the Investment in Nestlum account?

    a. It is not affected since the shares were sold to outside parties.

    b. It should be increased by $24,000.

    c. It should be decreased by $119,200.

    d. It should be increased by $30,000.

Problems 19 through 21 are based on the following information:

Chapman Company purchases 80 percent of the common stock of Russell Company on January 1, 1989, when Russell has the following stockholders' equity accounts:

Common stock—40,000 shares outstanding	$100,000
Additional paid-in capital	75,000
Retained earnings.	340,000
Total stockholders' equity	$515,000

To acquire this interest in Russell, Chapman pays a total of $487,000 with any excess cost being allocated to goodwill.

On January 1, 1995, Russell reports a net book value of $795,000. Chapman has accrued the increase in Russell's book value through application of the equity method.

The following problems should be viewed as independent situations.

19. On January 1, 1995, Russell issues 10,000 additional shares of common stock for $25 per share. Chapman acquires 8,000 of these shares. How will this transaction affect the additional paid-in capital of the parent company?

    a. –0–.
    b. Increase it by $20,500.
    c. Increase it by $36,400.
    d. Increase it by $82,300.

20. On January 1, 1995, Russell issues 10,000 additional shares of common stock for $15 per share. Chapman does not acquire any of this newly issued stock. How would this transaction affect the additional paid-in capital of the parent company?

    a. –0–.
    b. Increase it by $16,600.
    c. Decrease it by $31,200.
    d. Decrease it by $48,750.

21. On January 1, 1991, Russell reacquires 8,000 of the outstanding shares of its own common stock for $24 per share. None of these shares belonged to Chapman. How would this transaction affect the additional paid-in capital of the parent company?

    a. –0–.
    b. Decrease it by $22,000.
    c. Decrease it by $30,500.
    d. Decrease it by $33,000.

22. Darges owns 51 percent of the voting stock of Walrus, Inc. The parent's interest was acquired several years ago on the date that the subsidiary was formed. Consequently, no goodwill or other allocation was recorded in connection with the purchase price.

On January 1, 1993, Walrus sold $1,000,000 in 10-year bonds to the public for 105. The bonds had a cash interest rate of 9 percent payable every December 31. Darges acquired 40 percent of these bonds on January 1, 1995, for 96 percent of face value. Both companies utilize the straight-line method of amortization.

Required:

a. What consolidation entry would be recorded in connection with these intercompany bonds on December 31, 1995?

b. What consolidation entry would be recorded in connection with these intercompany bonds on December 31, 1996?

c. What consolidation entry would be recorded in connection with these intercompany bonds on December 31, 1997?

23. Highlight, Inc., owns all of the outstanding stock of Kiort Corporation. The two companies report the following balances for the year ending December 31, 1995:

	Highlight	Kiort
Revenues and interest income	$670,000	$390,000
Operating and interest expense	(540,000)	(221,000)
Other gains and losses	120,000	32,000
Net income	$250,000	$201,000

On January 1, 1995, Highlight acquired bonds on the open market for $108,000 originally issued by Kiort. This investment had an effective rate of 8 percent. The bonds had a face value of $100,000 and a cash interest rate of 9 percent. At the date of acquisition, these bonds were shown as liabilities by Kiort with a book value of $84,000 (based on an effective rate of 11 percent). Determine the balances that should appear on a consolidated income statement for 1995.

24. Several years ago Absalom, Inc., sold $800,000 in bonds to the public. Annual cash interest of 8 percent ($64,000) was to be paid on this debt. The bonds were issued at a discount to yield 10 percent. At the beginning of 1995, McDowell Corporation (a wholly owned subsidiary of Absalom) purchased $100,000 of these bonds on the open market for $121,655, a price that was based on an effective interest rate of 6 percent. The bond liability had a book value on that date of $668,778.

Required:

a. What consolidation entry would be required for these bonds on December 31, 1995?

b. What consolidation entry would be required for these bonds on December 31, 1997?

25. Opus, Incorporated, owns 90 percent of Bloom Company. On December 31, 1995, Opus acquires half of Bloom's $500,000 in outstanding bonds.

These bonds had been sold on the open market on January 1, 1993, at a 12 percent effective rate. The bonds pay a cash interest rate of 10 percent every December 31 and are scheduled to come due on December 31, 2003. Bloom issued this debt originally for $435,763. Opus paid $283,550 for this investment indicating an 8 percent effective yield.

Required:

a. Assuming that both parties use the effective rate method, what gain or loss should be reported on the consolidated income statement for 1995 from the retirement of this debt?

b. Assuming that both parties use the effective rate method, what balances should appear in the Investment in Bloom Bonds account on Opus's records and the Bonds Payable account of Bloom as of December 31, 1996?

c. Assuming that both parties use the straight-line method, what consolidation entry would be required on December 31, 1996, because of these bonds? Assume that the parent is not applying the equity method.

26. Hapinst Corporation has the following stockholders' equity accounts:

Preferred stock (6% cumulative dividend)	$500,000
Common stock	750,000
Additional paid-in capital	300,000
Retained earnings	950,000

The preferred stock is participating and, therefore, is considered an equity instrument. Westyln Corporation buys 90 percent of this common stock for $1,600,000 and 70 percent of the preferred stock for $800,000. All of the subsidiary's assets and liabilities are viewed as having market values equal to their book values. What amount is attributed to goodwill on the date of acquisition?

27. Mace, Inc., acquires 90 percent of the outstanding common stock of Blade Company from the company's president for $2,520,000 and 40 percent of the preferred stock for $250,000. On the date of purchase, Blade had the following stockholders' equity accounts:

Common stock	$ 800,000
Preferred stock	200,000
Retained earnings	2,000,000
Total	$3,000,000

Required:

a. Assume that the preferred stock is both cumulative and fully participating and is, therefore, considered an equity interest. What is the total amount of goodwill to be recognized within consolidated financial statements?

b. Assume that the preferred stock is callable at 120 percent of par value and is, therefore, considered a debt instrument. What is the total amount of goodwill to be recognized within consolidated financial statements?

c. Assume that the preferred stock is callable at 120 percent of par value and is, therefore, considered a debt instrument. What is the total value assigned to the noncontrolling interests on the date of acquisition?

28. Smith, Inc., has the following stockholders' equity accounts as of January 1, 1995:

Preferred stock—$100 par, nonvoting and nonparticipating, 8 percent cumulative dividend	$ 2,000,000
Common stock—$20 par value	4,000,000
Retained earnings	10,000,000

Haried Company purchases all of the common stock of Smith on January 1, 1995, for $14,040,000. The preferred stock (which is callable at 108) remains in the hands of outside parties. Any goodwill indicated by this acquisition is to be amortized over the maximum possible period of time.

During 1995, Smith reports earning $450,000 in net income and pays $360,000 in cash dividends. Haried applies the equity method to this investment.

Required:

a. What is the noncontrolling interest's share of consolidated net income for this period?

b. What is the balance in the Investment in Smith account as of December 31, 1995?

c. What consolidation entries would be needed for 1995?

29. Through the payment of $10,468,000 in cash, Drexel Company acquires voting control over Young Company. This price was paid for 60 percent of the subsidiary's 100,000 outstanding common shares ($40 par value) as well as all 10,000 shares of 8 percent, cumulative, $100 par value preferred stock. Of the total payment, $3.1 million was attributed to the fully participating and fully voting preferred stock with the remainder paid for the common. This purchase is carried out on January 1, 1995, when Young reports retained earnings of $10 million and a total book value of $15 million. On this same date, a building owned by Young (with a 5-year remaining life) is undervalued in the financial records by $200,000, while equipment with a 10-year life is overvalued by $100,000. Goodwill is assumed to have a 20-year life.

During 1995, Young reports net income of $900,000 while paying $400,000 in cash dividends. Drexel has used the cost method to account for both of these investments.

Required:

Prepare consolidation entries that would be appropriate for the year of 1995.

30. The following information has been taken from the consolidation worksheet of Peak and its 90-percent-owned subsidiary, Valley:

- Peak reports a $12,000 gain on the sale of a building. The building had a book value of $32,000 but was sold for $44,000 cash.
- The noncontrolling interest in Valley's Income is reported as $23,000.
- Intercompany inventory transfers of $129,000 occurred during the current period.
- A $30,000 dividend was paid by Valley during the year with $27,000 of this amount going to Peak.
- Amortization of the goodwill created by Peak's purchase was $16,000 for the current period.
- Consolidated accounts payable decreased by $11,000 during the year.

Required:

Indicate how each of these events is reflected on a consolidated statement of cash flows.

31. Ames Company and its 80 percent owned subsidiary, Wallace, have the following income statements for 1995:

	Ames	Wallace
Revenues.	$ 500,000	$ 230,000
Cost of goods sold.	(300,000)	(140,000)
Depreciation and amortization	(40,000)	(10,000)
Other expenses	(20,000)	(20,000)
Gain on sale of equipment	30,000	–0–
Equity in earnings of Wallace.	48,000	–0–
Net income.	$ 218,000	$ 60,000

Additional Information:

- Intercompany transfers during 1995 amounted to $90,000 and were downstream from Ames to Wallace.
- Unrealized inventory gains at January 1, 1995, were $6,000, but at December 31, 1995, unrealized gains are $9,000.
- Annual amortization expense resulting from the purchase price is $11,000.
- Wallace paid dividends totaling $20,000.
- The noncontrolling interest's share of the subsidiary's income is $12,000.
- During 1995, consolidated inventory rose by $11,000 while accounts receivable and accounts payable declined by $8,000 and $6,000, respectively.

Required:

Using either the direct or the indirect approach, determine the amount of cash generated from operations during the period by this business combination.

32. Parent Corporation owns all 30,000 shares of the common stock of Subsid, Inc. Parent has 60,000 shares of its own common stock outstanding. In 1995, Parent earns income (without any consideration of its investment in Subsid) of $150,000 while Subsid reports $130,000. Annual amortization of $10,000 is recognized each year on the consolidation worksheet based on allocations within the original purchase price. Both companies have convertible bonds outstanding. The bond issued by Parent is a common stock equivalent whereas that of Subsid is not. During 1995, interest expense (net of taxes) is $32,000 for Parent and $24,000 for Subsid. Parent's bonds can be converted into 10,000 shares of common stock; Subsid's bonds can be converted into 12,000 shares. Parent owns 20 percent of Subsid's bonds. For consolidation purposes, what are primary and fully diluted earnings per share for this business combination?

33. Primus, Inc., owns all of the outstanding stock of Sonston, Inc. For 1995, Primus reports income (exclusive of any investment income) of $600,000. Primus has 100,000 shares of common stock outstanding. Sonston reports net income of $200,000 for the period with 40,000 shares of common stock outstanding. Sonston also has 10,000 stock warrants outstanding that allow the holder to acquire shares at $10 per share. The value of this stock was $20 per share throughout the year. Primus owns 2,000 of these warrants. What is the consolidated primary earnings per share?

34. Garfun, Inc., owns all of the stock of Simon, Inc. For 1995, Garfun reports income (exclusive of any investment income) of $480,000. Garfun has 80,000 shares of common stock outstanding. Garfun also has 5,000 shares of preferred stock outstanding that pay a dividend of $15,000 per year. Simon reports net income of $290,000 for the period with 80,000 shares of common stock outstanding. Simon also has a liability for 10,000 $100 bonds that pay annual interest of $8 per bond. Each of these bonds can be converted into three shares of common stock. Garfun owns none of these bonds. Assume a tax rate of 30 percent. What is the consolidated primary earnings per share? The bonds are common stock equivalents.

35. The following separate income statements are for Mason and its 80 percent owned subsidiary, Dixon:

	Mason	Dixon
Revenues.	$ 400,000	$ 300,000
Expenses.	(290,000)	(225,000)
Gain on sale of equipment	–0–	15,000
Equity earnings of subsidiary	72,000	–0–
Net income.	$ 182,000	$ 90,000
Outstanding common shares	50,000	30,000

Additional Information:

- Amortization expense resulting from the purchase price paid by Mason is $20,000 per year.
- Mason has convertible preferred stock outstanding that is not a common stock equivalent. Each of these 5,000 shares is paid a dividend of $4.00 per year. Each share can be converted into four shares of common stock.
- Stock warrants to buy 10,000 shares of Dixon are also outstanding. For $20, each warrant can be converted into a share of Dixon's common stock. The fair market value of this stock is $25 throughout the year. Mason owns none of these warrants.
- Dixon has convertible bonds payable that paid interest of $30,000 (after taxes) during the year. These bonds can be exchanged for 20,000 shares of common stock. Mason holds 15 percent of these bonds. The bonds are not common stock equivalents.

Required:

Compute primary and fully diluted earnings per share for this business combination.

36. Alice, Inc., owns 100 percent of Rughty, Inc. On Alice's books, the Investment in Rughty account is currently shown as $731,000 although the subsidiary's 40,000 shares have an underlying book value of only $12 per share.

   Rughty issues 10,000 new shares to the public for $15.75 per share. How does this transaction affect the Investment in Rughty account that appears on Alice's financial records?

37. Davis, Incorporated, acquired 16,000 shares of Maxwell Company several years ago. At the present time, Maxwell is reporting $800,000 as total stockholders' equity which is broken down as follows:

Common stock ($10 par value).	$200,000
Additional paid-in capital	230,000
Retained earnings	370,000
Total	$800,000

The following cases should be viewed as independent situations:

a. Maxwell issues 5,000 shares of previously unissued common stock to the public for $50 per share. None of this stock is purchased by Davis. What journal entry should Davis make to recognize the impact of this stock transaction?

b. Maxwell issues 4,000 shares of previously unissued common stock to the public for $25 per share. None of this stock is purchased by Davis. What journal entry should Davis make to recognize the impact of this stock transaction?

c. Maxwell issues 5,000 shares of previously unissued common stock for $42 per share. All of these shares are purchased by Davis. How would this transaction affect a consolidation prepared immediately thereafter?

38. On January 1, 1993, Abraham Company purchased 90 percent of the outstanding shares of Sparks Company. Sparks had a net book value on that date of $480,000: common stock ($10 par value) of $200,000 and retained earnings of $280,000. Sparks also possessed a tract of land that was undervalued by $80,000 on its financial statements.

    Abraham paid $584,000 for this investment. Goodwill created by the acquisition price was to be amortized over a 20-year period. Subsequent to the purchase, Abraham applied the cost method to its investment accounts.

    In the 1993–94 period, the subsidiary's book value rose by $100,000. During 1995, Sparks earned income of $80,000 while paying $20,000 in dividends. Also, at the beginning of the year, Sparks issued 4,000 new shares of common stock for $36 per share to finance the expansion of its corporate facilities. None of these additional shares were sold to Abraham and, hence, no entry was recorded by the parent company.

Required:

a. Prepare the consolidation entries that would be appropriate for these two companies for the year of 1995.

b. Assume that Sparks actually issued 5,000 new shares of stock (rather than 4,000 shares) at the beginning of 1995 for $25 per share. Abraham purchased 4,500 of these shares and recorded the acquisition at cost. Under these altered circumstances, prepare consolidation entries for 1995.

39. Giant purchases all of the outstanding shares of Little on January 1, 1992, for $460,000 in cash. Of this price, $30,000 was attributed to equipment with a 10-year remaining life. Goodwill of $40,000 has also been identified and will be expensed over a 20-year period. Giant applies the partial equity method so that income is accrued each period based solely on the earnings reported by the subsidiary.

    On January 1, 1995, Giant reports $200,000 in bonds outstanding with a book value of $188,000. Little purchases half of these bonds on the open market for $97,000.

    During 1995, Giant begins to sell merchandise to Little. During that year, inventory costing $80,000 was transferred at a price of $100,000. All but $10,000 (at sales price) of these goods were resold to outside parties by year's end. Little still owes $36,000 for inventory shipped from Giant during December.

    The following financial figures are for the two companies for the year ending December 31, 1995. Prepare a worksheet to produce consolidated balances. (Credits are indicated by parentheses.)

	Giant	Little
Revenues	$ (639,000)	$(466,000)
Cost of goods sold	345,000	198,000
Expenses	134,000	161,000
Interest expense—bonds.	24,000	–0–
Interest income—bond investment	–0–	(11,000)
Equity in income of Little	(118,000)	–0–
Net income.	$ (254,000)	$(118,000)
Retained earnings, 1/1/95.	$ (345,000)	
Retained earnings, 1/1/95.		$(361,000)
Net income (above)	(254,000)	(118,000)
Dividends paid	155,000	61,000
Retained earnings, 12/31/95.	$ (444,000)	$(418,000)
Cash and receivables	$ 133,000	$ 78,000
Inventory	171,000	87,000
Investment in Little	608,000	–0–
Investment in Giant bonds	–0–	98,000
Land, buildings, and equipment (net)	249,000	541,000
Total assets	$ 1,161,000	$ 804,000
Accounts payable	$ (225,000)	$(166,000)
Bonds payable	(200,000)	(100,000)
Discount on bonds	8,000	–0–
Common stock	(300,000)	(120,000)
Retained earnings (above)	(444,000)	(418,000)
Total liabilities and stockholders' equity	$(1,161,000)	$(804,000)

40. Fred, Inc., and Bub Corporation formed a business combination on January 1, 1991, when Fred purchased a 60 percent interest in the common stock of Bub for $310,000 in cash. The book value of Bub's assets and liabilities on that day totaled $300,000. Patents being held by Bub (with a 12-year remaining life) were undervalued by $100,000 within the company's financial records. Any goodwill indicated by this acquisition is to be amortized over a 10-year period.

Intercompany inventory transfers have been made between the two companies on a regular basis. Merchandise that is carried over from one year to the next is always sold in the subsequent period.

Year	Original Cost to Bub	Transfer Price to Fred	Ending Balance at Transfer Price
1991	$ 60,000	$ 72,000	$15,000
1992	70,000	84,000	25,000
1993	80,000	100,000	20,000
1994	100,000	125,000	40,000
1995	90,000	120,000	30,000

Half of the 1995 inventory transfers have not been paid for by Fred by the end of the year.

On January 1, 1992, Fred sold $15,000 in land to Bub for $22,000. Bub is still holding this land.

On January 1, 1995, Bub acquired $20,000 (face value) of Fred's bonds on the open market. These bonds had an 8 percent cash interest rate. On the date of repurchase, the liability was shown within Fred's records at $21,386, indicating an effective yield of 6 percent. Bub's acquisition price was $18,732 based on an effective interest rate of 10 percent.

Bub indicated earning a net income of $15,000 within its 1995 financial statements. The subsidiary also reported a beginning retained earnings balance of $300,000, dividends paid of $5,000, and common stock of $100,000. Bub has not issued any additional common stock since its takeover. Parent company has applied the equity method to record its investment in Bub.

Required:

a. Prepare consolidation entries for 1995.
b. Calculate the 1995 balance for the noncontrolling interest's share of consolidated net income. In addition, determine the ending 1995 balance for noncontrolling interest in the consolidated balance sheet.
c. Determine the consolidation entry needed in 1996 in connection with the intercompany bonds.

41. On January 1, 1995, Mona, Inc., purchased 80 percent of Lisa Company's common stock as well as 60 percent of its preferred shares. Mona paid $65,000 in cash for the preferred stock which is considered a debt-type instrument (because no voting rights were granted and the stock has a call value of 110 percent of the $50 per share par value). Mona also paid $552,800 for the common stock, a price that indicated goodwill of $40,000. This intangible asset is being amortized over a 40-year period. Lisa pays all preferred stock dividends (a total of $8,000 per year) on an annual basis. During 1995, Lisa's book value increased by $50,000.

On January 2, 1995, Mona acquired one half of Lisa's outstanding bonds payable to reduce the debt position of the business combination. Lisa's bonds had a face value of $100,000 and paid cash interest of 10 percent per year. These bonds had been issued to the public to yield 14 percent. Interest is paid each December 31. On January 2, 1995, these bonds payable had a total book value of $88,350. Mona paid $53,310, an amount indicating an effective interest rate of 8 percent.

On January 3, 1995, Mona sold fixed assets to Lisa. These assets had originally cost $100,000 but had accumulated depreciation of $60,000 when transferred. The transfer was made at a price of $120,000. These assets were estimated to have a remaining useful life of 10 years.

The individual financial statements for these two companies for the year ending December 31, 1996, are as follows:

	Mona, Inc.	Lisa Company
Sales and other revenues	$ 500,000	$ 200,000
Expenses	(220,000)	(120,000)
Dividend income—Lisa common stock	8,000	–0–
Dividend income—Lisa preferred stock	4,800	–0–
Net income	$ 292,800	$ 80,000
Retained earnings, 1/1/96	$ 700,000	$ 500,000
Net income (above)	292,800	80,000
Dividends paid—common stock	(92,800)	(10,000)
Dividends paid—preferred stock	–0–	(8,000)
Retained earnings, 12/31/96	$ 900,000	$ 562,000
Current assets	$ 130,419	$ 500,000
Investment in Lisa—common stock	552,800	–0–
Investment in Lisa—preferred stock	65,000	–0–
Investment in Lisa—bonds	51,781	–0–
Fixed assets	1,100,000	800,000
Accumulated depreciation	(300,000)	(200,000)
Total assets	$1,600,000	$1,100,000
Accounts payable	$ 400,000	$ 144,580
Bonds payable	–0–	100,000
Discount on bonds payable	–0–	(6,580)
Common stock	300,000	200,000
Preferred stock	–0–	100,000
Retained earnings, 12/31/96	900,000	562,000
Total liabilities and equities	$1,600,000	$1,100,000

Required:

a. What consolidation entry (or entries) would have been required as of January 1, 1995, to eliminate the subsidiary's common and preferred stocks?

b. What consolidation entry (or entries) would have been required as of December 31, 1995, to account for Mona's purchase of Lisa's bonds?

c. What consolidation entry (or entries) would have been required as of December 31, 1995, to account for the intercompany sale of fixed assets?

d. Assume that consolidated financial statements are being prepared for the year ending December 31, 1996. Calculate the consolidated balance for each of the following accounts:

   Goodwill.

   Fixed Assets.

   Accumulated Depreciation.

   Expenses.

   Noncontrolling Interest in Lisa's Net Income.

   Net Income.

42. Rogers Company holds 80 percent of the common stock of Andrews, Inc., and 40 percent of this subsidiary's convertible bonds. The following consolidated financial statements are for 1995 and 1996:

Rogers Company and Consolidated Subsidiary

	1995	1996
Revenues	$ 760,000	$ 880,000
Cost of goods sold	(510,000)	(540,000)
Depreciation and amortization	(90,000)	(100,000)
Gain on sale of building	–0–	20,000
Interest expense	(30,000)	(30,000)
Noncontrolling interest	(9,000)	(11,000)
Net income	$ 121,000	$ 219,000
Retained earnings, 1/1	300,000	$ 371,000
Net income	121,000	219,000
Dividends paid	(50,000)	(100,000)
Retained earnings, 12/31	$ 371,000	$ 490,000
Cash	$ 80,000	$ 140,000
Accounts receivable	150,000	140,000
Inventory	200,000	340,000
Buildings and equipment (net)	640,000	690,000
Goodwill	150,000	145,000
Total assets	$1,220,000	$1,455,000
Accounts payable	140,000	100,000
Bonds payable	400,000	500,000
Noncontrolling interest in Andrews	32,000	41,000
Common stock	100,000	120,000
Additional paid-in capital	177,000	204,000
Retained earnings	371,000	490,000
Total liabilities and equities	$1,220,000	$1,455,000

Additional Information:
- Bonds were issued during 1996 by the parent for cash.
- Amortization of goodwill amounts to $5,000 per year.
- A building with a cost of $60,000 but a $30,000 book value was sold by the parent for cash on May 11, 1996.
- Equipment was purchased by the subsidiary on July 23, 1996, using cash.
- Late in November of 1996, the parent issued stock for cash.
- During 1996, the subsidiary paid dividends of $10,000.

Required:

Prepare a consolidated statement of cash flows for this business combination for the year ending December 31, 1996. Either the direct or the indirect approach may be used.

43. Following are separate income statements for Alexander, Inc., and Raleigh Corporation as well as a consolidated statement for the business combination as a whole.

	Alexander	Raleigh	Consolidated
Revenues	$700,000	$500,000	$1,000,000
Cost of goods sold	(400,000)	(300,000)	(495,000)
Operating expenses.	(100,000)	(70,000)	(190,000)
Equity in earnings of Raleigh	104,000	–0–	–0–
Noncontrolling interest in Raleigh's income	–0–	–0–	(26,000)
Net income	$304,000	$130,000	$ 289,000

Additional Information:

- Intercompany inventory transfers are all downstream.
- The parent applies the partial equity method to this investment.
- Alexander has 50,000 shares of common stock and 10,000 shares of preferred stock outstanding. Owners of the preferred are paid an annual dividend of $40,000, and each share can be exchanged for two shares of common stock. This convertible has a high dividend rate and is not considered to be a common stock equivalent.
- Raleigh has 30,000 shares of common stock outstanding. The company also has 5,000 stock warrants outstanding. For $10, each warrant can be converted into a share of Raleigh's common stock. Alexander holds half of these warrants. The price of Raleigh's common stock was $20 per share throughout the year.
- Raleigh also has convertible bonds, none of which is owned by Alexander. During the current year, total interest expense (net of taxes) was $22,000. Although these bonds are not common stock equivalents, they can be exchanged for 10,000 shares of the subsidiary's common stock.

Required:

Determine primary and fully diluted earnings per share for this business combination.

44. On January 1, 1995, Paisley, Inc., paid $560,000 for all of the outstanding stock of Skyler Corporation. This cash payment was based on a price of $180 per share for Skyler's $100 par value preferred stock and $38 per share for the company's $20 par value common stock. The preferred shares are voting, cumulative, and fully participating; they have no set call value. At the date of purchase, the book values of Skyler's accounts equaled their market values. Any goodwill will be amortized over a 10-year period.

During 1995, Skyler sold inventory costing $60,000 to Paisley for $90,000. All but $18,000 (measured at transfer price) of this merchandise has been resold to outsiders by the end of the year. At the end of 1995,

Paisley continues to owe Skyler for the last shipment of inventory priced at $28,000.

Also, on January 2, 1995, Paisley sold equipment to Skyler for $20,000 although it had a book value of only $12,000 (original cost of $30,000). Both companies depreciate such property according to the straight-line method with no salvage value. The remaining life at this date was four years.

The following financial statements are for each company for the year ending December 31, 1995. Determine consolidated financial totals for this business combination.

	Paisley, Inc.	Skyler Corporation
Sales	$ (800,000)	$(400,000)
Costs of goods sold	528,000	260,000
Expenses	180,000	130,000
Gain on sale of equipment	(8,000)	–0–
Net income	$ (100,000)	$ (10,000)
Retained earnings, 1/1/95	$ (400,000)	$(150,000)
Net income	(100,000)	(10,000)
Dividends paid	60,000	–0–
Retained earnings, 12/31/95	$ (440,000)	$(160,000)
Cash	$ 30,000	$ 40,000
Accounts receivable	300,000	100,000
Inventory	260,000	180,000
Investment in Skyler Corporation	560,000	–0–
Land, buildings, and equipment	680,000	500,000
Accumulated depreciation	(180,000)	(90,000)
Total assets	$ 1,650,000	$ 730,000
Accounts payable	$ (140,000)	$ (90,000)
Long-term liabilities	(240,000)	(180,000)
Preferred stock	–0–	(100,000)
Common stock	(620,000)	(200,000)
Additional paid-in capital	(210,000)	–0–
Retained earnings, 12/31/95	(440,000)	(160,000)
Total equities	$(1,650,000)	$(730,000)

Parentheses indicate a credit balance.

7

OWNERSHIP PATTERNS AND INCOME TAXES

Consolidated Financial Statements

Questions to Consider

- A parent holds control over a subsidiary which, in turn, owns a majority of the voting stock of another company. Hence, the parent indirectly controls both of these subsidiaries. How does this type of ownership pattern affect the consolidation process for a business combination?
- If a subsidiary possesses stock of its parent company, what impact does the mutual ownership have on consolidated financial statements?
- How does a business combination qualify to file a consolidated income tax return? What advantages are gained by filing in this manner?
- Why does the filing of separate tax returns by the members of a business combination frequently create the need to recognize deferred income taxes?

Coverage of the accounting for business combinations is concluded here in Chapter 7 by analyzing two additional aspects of consolidated financial statements. First, the various patterns of ownership that can exist within a combination are presented. Indirect control of a subsidiary, connecting affiliations, and mutual ownership are all examined along with the consolidation procedures applicable to each of these organizational structures. The chapter then presents an overview of the income tax considerations relevant to the members of a business combination. Income tax accounting for both consolidated and separate corporate returns is discussed in light of current laws.

Indirect Subsidiary Control

Throughout previous chapters, only one type of relationship has been presented for every business combination. Specifically, a parent has always held a direct financial interest in a single subsidiary. This ownership pattern has been assumed to expedite the explanation of consolidation theories and techniques. In actual practice, though, much more elaborate corporate structures commonly exist. PepsiCo, Inc., as an example, controls literally scores of subsidiaries. However, PepsiCo owns voting stock in only a small percentage of these companies. Control is actually maintained through indirect ownership; PepsiCo's subsidiaries hold the stock of most of the companies within this business combination.

Although the presentation of PepsiCo's entire corporate structure would be a tedious task, a very small portion of this organization can be identified to illustrate indirect relationships. PepsiCo, the parent company, owns the voting stock of Recot, Inc., which, in turn, has total ownership of Frito-Lay, Inc. Frito-Lay holds the outstanding shares of QSR, Inc. This particular chain of ownership continues since QSR owns Quick Service Restaurants, Inc., a Delaware company that holds all of the stock of Kentucky Fried Chicken Corporation.

Because of the endless variety of ownership patterns that could be established, a graphic display is often produced to help prevent confusion. Thus, the line of ownership described in connection with PepsiCo follows. Upon visual examination, the relationship of these companies appears to be rather straightforward. PepsiCo owns only one of these subsidiaries directly but clearly holds indirect control over the remainder. This type of corporate configuration is often referred to as a father-son-grandson relationship (or sometimes as a pyramid) because of the pattern created by the descending tiers.

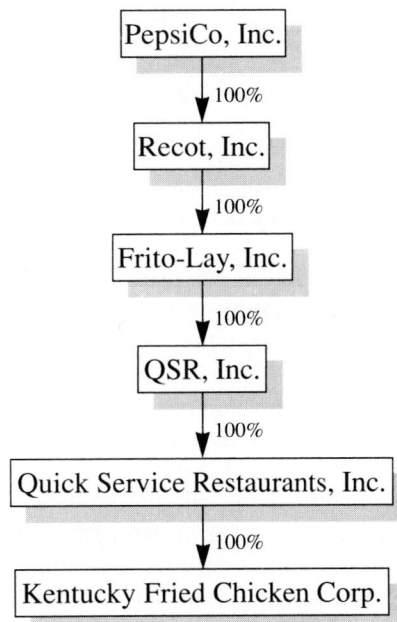

Forming a business combination as a series of indirect ownerships is not an unusual practice. Many businesses organize their operations in this manner to group individual companies along product lines, geographic districts, or some other logical criteria. The philosophy behind this structuring is that clearer lines of communication and responsibility reporting can be developed by placing direct control in proximity to each subsidiary. However, other indirect ownership patterns are simply the result of years of acquisition and growth. As an example, in purchasing General Foods, Philip Morris Companies, Inc., actually gained control over a number of corporations (including Oscar Mayer Foods Corporation, Maxwell House Coffee Company, and Birds Eye, Inc.). This control was not achieved directly by Philip Morris but rather indirectly through the acquisition of their parent company.

The Consolidation Process When Indirect Control Is Present

Regardless of a company's reason for establishing indirect control over a subsidiary, a new accounting problem is encountered: the financial information generated by several connecting corporations must be consolidated into a single set of financial statements. Fortunately, indirect ownership does not introduce any new conceptual issues but only affects the mechanical elements of this process. For example, a purchase price allocation, as well as an annual amortization expense figure, must be computed and recognized for every investment. In addition, all of the worksheet entries that have been demonstrated previously continue to apply. For business combinations involving indirect control, the entire consolidation process is basically repeated for each separate acquisition.

Calculation of Realized Income.   Although most consolidation procedures are unchanged by the presence of an indirect ownership, the isolation of each subsidiary's realized income does pose an added degree of difficulty. Appropriate determination of this figure is essential since it serves as the basis for calculating (1) equity income accruals and (2) the noncontrolling interest's share of consolidated income.

In previous chapters, the subsidiary's realized income has been determined by adjusting reported earnings for the effects of any upstream intercompany transfers. *However, where indirect control is involved, at least one company within the business combination (and possibly many) holds both a parent and a subsidiary position.* Any company in that position must first give proper recognition to the equity income accruing from its subsidiaries before computing its own realized income total. This guideline is not a theoretical doctrine but merely a necessary arrangement for calculating income totals in a predetermined order. The process begins with the grandson, then moves to the son, and finishes with the father. Only by following this systematic approach can the correct amount of realized income be determined for each individual company.

Realized Income Computation Illustrated.   To serve as an example of this procedure, assume that three companies form a business combination: Top Company owns 70 percent of Midway Company which, in turn, possesses 60 percent of Bottom Company. As can be seen from the following display, both subsidiaries are under the control of Top, although the parent's relationship with Bottom is only of an indirect nature.

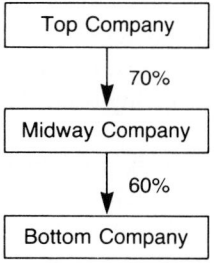

For illustration purposes, assume that the following information has been elicited from the 1995 individual financial records of the three companies making up this combination:

	Top Company	Midway Company	Bottom Company
Operating income	$600,000	$300,000	$100,000
Dividend income from investment in subsidiary (based on cost method)	80,000	50,000	
Reported net income	$680,000	$350,000	$100,000
Additional information:			
Net unrealized intercompany gains within current year income	$110,000	$ 80,000	$ 20,000
Amortization expense relating to purchase price of investment	20,000	15,000	–0–

Beginning, as specified, with the grandson of the organization, a calculation is made of each company's 1995 realized income. For example, from the perspective of the business combination, Bottom's income for the period would be only $80,000 after removing the $20,000 effect of the company's unrealized intercompany gains. Thus, $80,000 is the basis for the equity accrual by its parent as well as any noncontrolling interest recognition.

Once the grandson's income has been derived, this figure can then be used in computing the realized earnings of the son, Midway:

Operating income—Midway Company	$300,000
Equity income accruing from Bottom Company—60% of *realized* income of $80,000	48,000
Recognition of amortization expense relating to purchase of Bottom Company (above)	(15,000)
Removal of Midway's unrealized intercompany gain (above)	(80,000)
Realized income of Midway Company	$253,000

The $253,000 realized income figure determined for Midway varies significantly from the company's reported profit of $350,000. This difference is not unusual and is merely the result of establishing an appropriate consolidation perspective in viewing both the investment in its subsidiary and the effects of intercompany transfers. The recognition of all transactions is being brought into line with the company's vantage point within this business combination.

Continuing with this systematic calculation of each company's earnings, Top's realized income can now be determined. Only after the appropriate figure is computed for the son can the father's earnings within the business combination be derived.

Operating income—Top Company	$ 600,000
Equity income accruing from Midway Company—70% of	
realized income of $253,000	177,100
Recognition of amortization expense relating to	
purchase of Midway Company (above)	(20,000)
Removal of Top's unrealized intercompany gain (above)	(110,000)
Realized income of Top	$ 647,100

Having established realized income figures for each of these three companies, several aspects of this data should be noted:

1. Within the 1995 income statement reported for Top Company and its consolidated subsidiaries, a $107,900 balance would be disclosed as the "noncontrolling interests' share of subsidiary income." This total is based on the realized income figures of the two subsidiaries and is computed as follows:

	Realized Income	Outside Ownership	Noncontrolling Interests in Income
Bottom Company	$ 80,000	40%	$ 32,000
Midway Company.	253,000	30	75,900
Total.			$107,900

2. Although the cost method was applied to both of the investments in this illustration, the parents' individual accounting is not a factor in determining realized income totals. The cost figures were omitted and replaced with equity accruals in preparation for consolidation. The selection of a particular method is only relevant for internal reporting purposes; computation of realized earnings, as shown here, is based entirely on the equity income accruing from each subsidiary.

3. As demonstrated previously, if appropriate equity accruals are recognized, the parent's realized income can serve as a "proof figure" for the consolidated total. Parent earnings calculated in this manner equal the net income for the entire business combination. Thus, if the consolidation process is carried out correctly, the earnings to be reported by this entire organization should equal $647,100 as indicated previously for Top.

4. Whenever indirect control is established, a discrepancy exists between the percentage of stock being held and the income contributed to the business combination by a subsidiary. In this illustration, Midway possesses 60 percent of Bottom's voting stock but, mathematically, only 42 percent of Bottom's income is attributed to Top's controlling interest (70 percent direct ownership of Midway × 60 percent indirect ownership of Bottom). The remaining income earned by this subsidiary is assigned to the owners outside of the combination.

The validity of this 42 percent accrual is one aspect of the consolidation that is not readily apparent. Therefore, an elementary example can be constructed to demonstrate the mathematical accuracy of this percentage. Assume that neither Top nor Midway reports any earnings during the year but that Bottom has $100 in realized income. If Bottom declares a $100 cash dividend, $60 goes to Midway with the remaining $40 distributed to Bottom's noncontrolling interest. Assuming then that Midway uses this $60 to pay its own dividend, $42 (70 percent) is transferred to Top with $18 going to the outside owners of Midway.

Thus, 58 percent of Bottom's income should be attributed to parties outside of the business combination. An initial 40 percent belongs to Bottom's own noncontrolling interest while an additional 18 percent is eventually accrued by the other shareholders of Midway. Consequently, only 42 percent of Bottom's original income is considered as having been earned by the combination. Consolidated financial statements reflect this allocation by including 100 percent of the subsidiary's revenues and expenses while simultaneously recognizing a reduction for the 58 percent noncontrolling interests' in the subsidiary's net income.

Consolidation Process—Indirect Control

Having analyzed the calculation of realized income within a father-son-grandson configuration, a full-scale consolidation can now be produced. As is demonstrated, the worksheet process is not significantly altered by this type of ownership pattern. In reality, most worksheet entries are simply made twice; first for the son's investment in the grandson and then for the father's ownership of the son. Although this sudden doubling of entries may initially seem overwhelming, close examination reveals that the individual procedures remain unaffected.

As an illustration, assume that on January 1, 1993, Big purchases 80 percent of the outstanding common stock of Middle for $640,000. On that date, Middle has a book value (total stockholders' equity) of $700,000, which indicates the parent paid $80,000 in excess of the subsidiary's underlying $560,000 book value ($700,000 × 80 percent). This $80,000 is assigned to goodwill and amortized at the rate of $2,000 per year.

Following the acquisition, Middle's book value rises to $1,080,000 by the end of 1995, denoting a $380,000 increment during this three-year period ($1,080,000 − $700,000). Big applies the partial equity method; therefore, a $304,000 ($380,000 × 80%) increase in the investment account (to $944,000) is accrued by the parent over this same time span.

On January 1, 1994, Middle acquires 70 percent of Little for $461,000. Little's stockholders' equity accounts total $630,000, indicating that Middle has paid $20,000 more than the applicable book value of $441,000 ($630,000 × 70%). This entire $20,000 is allocated to goodwill so that, over a 40-year assumed life, amortization expense of $500 is recognized each year by the business combination. During 1994–95, Little's book value increases by $150,000 to a $780,000 total. Since Middle is also applying the partial equity method, $105,000 ($150,000 × 70%) has been added to the investment account to arrive at a $566,000 balance ($461,000 + $105,000).

To complete the introductory information for this illustration, assume that a number of intercompany upstream transfers have occurred over the past two years. The dollar volume of these transactions is chronicled here as well as the unrealized gain in each year's ending inventory.

	Little Company Transfers to Middle Company		Middle Company Transfers to Big Company	
Year	Transfer Price	Year-End Unrealized Gain	Transfer Price	Year-End Unrealized Gain
1994	$ 75,000	$20,000	$200,000	$30,000
1995	120,000	25,000	250,000	40,000

The worksheet to consolidate these three companies for the year ending December 31, 1995, is presented in Exhibit 7–1. The first three columns represent the individual statements for each of the organizations. This information is followed by the entries required to consolidate the various balances. To help identify the separate procedures, entries concerning the relationship between Big (father) and Middle (son) are marked with a "B," whereas an "L" denotes Middle's ownership of Little (grandson). The duplication of entries in this exhibit is done primarily to facilitate a clearer understanding of this consolidation. A number of these dual entries can be combined once a familiarity with the entire process is achieved.

To arrive at consolidated figures, Exhibit 7–1 incorporates the worksheet entries described next. By analyzing each of these adjustments and eliminations, the consolidation procedures necessitated by a father-son-grandson ownership pattern can be identified. Despite the presence of indirect control over Little, financial statements can be created for the business combination as a whole utilizing the process described in previous chapters.

Consolidation Entry *G.   Entry *G defers the unrealized intercompany gains contained in the beginning financial figures. Within their separate accounting systems, two of the companies prematurely recorded income ($20,000 by Little and $30,000 by Middle) in 1994 at the time of transfer. For consolidation purposes, a worksheet entry must be included in 1995 to eliminate these unrealized gains from both beginning retained earnings as well as cost of goods sold (the present location of the beginning inventory). Consequently, this gross profit is being appropriately recognized on the consolidated income statement of the current period.

Consolidation Entry *C. Neither Big nor Middle has applied the full equity method to their investments; therefore, the figures recognized during the years prior to the current period (1995) must now be updated on the worksheet. This process begins with the son's ownership of the grandson. Hence, Middle must reduce its 1994 income (now closed into retained earnings) by $500 to reflect the amortization applicable to that year. This expense would not have been recorded by Middle in applying the partial equity method.

In addition, since $20,000 of Little's previously reported earnings have just been deferred (in preceding Entry *G), the effect of this reduction on Middle's ownership must also be recognized. The parent's original equity accrual for 1994 was based on reported rather than realized profit; thus, too much income was recorded. Little's deferral necessitates a parallel $14,000 decrease ($20,000 × 70%) by Middle. Consequently, Middle's retained earnings balance as of January 1, 1995, as well as the Investment in Little account are reduced on the worksheet by a total of $14,500:

Reduction in Middle's Beginning Retained Earnings

1994 amortization expense	$ 500
Income effect created by Little's deferral of 1994 unrealized gain (reduction of previous accrual) ($20,000 × 70%)	14,000
Required reduction to Middle's beginning retained earnings (Entry L*C)	$14,500

A similar equity adjustment must also be made in connection with Big's ownership of Middle. The calculation of the specific amount to be recorded follows the same procedural path identified earlier for Middle's investment in Little. Once again, amortization expense for all prior years (1993 and 1994, in this case) has to be brought into the consolidation as well as the income reduction created by the deferral of Middle's $30,000 unrealized gain (Entry *G). *However, recognition must also be given to the effects associated with the $14,500 decrease in Middle's pre–1995 earnings described in the previous paragraph.* Although only recorded on the worksheet, this adjustment is a change in Middle's originally reported income. To reflect Big's ownership of Middle, the effect of this reduction must be included in arriving at the income balances actually accruing to the parent company. Thus, a decrease of $39,600 is needed in Big's beginning retained earnings to establish the proper accounting for its subsidiaries.

EXHIBIT 7-1

Consolidation: Purchase Method
Investment: Partial Equity Method

BIG COMPANY AND CONSOLIDATED SUBSIDIARIES
Consolidation Worksheet
For Year Ending December 31, 1995

Accounts	Big Company	Middle Company	Little Company	Consolidation Entries Debit	Consolidation Entries Credit	Noncontrolling Interest	Consolidated Totals
Income Statement							
Sales	(800,000)	(500,000)	(300,000)	(LTI) 120,000 (BTI) 250,000			(1,230,000)
Cost of goods sold	300,000	220,000	140,000	(LG) 25,000	(L*G) 20,000 (LTI) 120,000 (B*G) 30,000 (BTI) 250,000		305,000
Expenses	200,000	80,000	60,000	(BG) 40,000 (LE) 500 (BE) 2,000 (LI) 70,000 (BI) 216,000			342,500
Income of Little Company	–0–	(70,000)	–0–				–0–
Income of Middle Company	(216,000)	–0–	–0–				–0–
Noncontrolling interest in Little Company's net income	–0–	–0–	–0–			(28,500)	28,500
Noncontrolling interest in Middle Company's net income	–0–	–0–	–0–			(51,200)	51,200
Net income	(516,000)	(270,000)	(100,000)				(502,800)
Statement of Retained Earnings							
Retained earnings, 1/1/95:							
Big Company	(900,000)	–0–		(B*C) 39,600 (B*G) 30,000 (L*C) 14,500 (BS) 755,500			(860,400)
Middle Company	–0–	(800,000)		(L*G) 20,000 (LS) 580,000			–0–
Little Company	–0–	–0–	(600,000)				–0–
Net income (from above)	(516,000)	(270,000)	(100,000)				(502,800)
Dividends paid:							
Big Company	120,000	–0–	–0–				120,000
Middle Company	–0–	90,000	–0–		(BD) 72,000	18,000	–0–
Little Company	–0–	–0–	50,000		(LD) 35,000	15,000	–0–
Retained earnings, 12/31/95	(1,296,000)	(980,000)	(650,000)				(1,243,200)

Balance Sheet

	Big Company	Middle Company	Little Company	Consolidation Entries — Debit	Consolidation Entries — Credit	Consolidated Totals
Cash and receivables	600,000	300,000	280,000			1,180,000
Investment in Middle Company	944,000	-0-	-0-	(BD) 72,000	(B*C) 39,600; (BS) 684,400; (BI) 216,000; (BA) 76,000	-0-
Investment in Little Company	-0-	566,000	-0-	(LD) 35,000	(L*C) 14,500; (LS) 497,000; (LI) 70,000; (LA) 19,500	-0-
Inventory	300,000	260,000	290,000		(LG) 25,000; (BG) 40,000	785,000
Land, building, equipment	192,000	154,000	510,000	(LA) 19,500; (BA) 76,000		856,000
Goodwill	-0-	-0-	-0-		(LE) 500; (BE) 2,000	93,000
Total assets	2,036,000	1,280,000	1,080,000			2,914,000
Liabilities	(340,000)	(200,000)	(300,000)			(840,000)
Noncontrolling interest in Little Company, 1/1/95	-0-	-0-	-0-		(LS) 213,000	(213,000)
Noncontrolling interest in Middle Company, 1/1/95	-0-	-0-	-0-		(BS) 171,100	(171,100)
Total noncontrolling interest, 12/31/95	-0-	-0-	-0-		(430,800)	(430,800)
Common stock:						
Big Company	(400,000)	-0-	-0-			(400,000)
Middle Company	-0-	(100,000)	-0-	(BS) 100,000		-0-
Little Company	-0-	-0-	(130,000)	(LS) 130,000		-0-
Retained earnings (above)	(1,296,000)	(980,000)	(650,000)			(1,243,200)
Total liabilities and equities	(2,036,000)	(1,280,000)	(1,080,000)			(2,914,000)

NOTE: Parentheses indicate credit balance.

Consolidation Entries: Entries labeled with a "B" refer to the investment relationship between Big and Middle. Entries with an "L" refer to Middle's ownership of Little.

(*G) Removal of unrealized gain from beginning inventory figures so that it can be recognized in current period.

(*C) Conversion of partial equity method to equity method. Amortization for prior years is recognized along with effects of beginning unrealized upstream gains.

(S) Elimination of subsidiaries' stockholders' equity accounts along with recognition of January 1, 1995, noncontrolling interests.

(A) Allocation to goodwill, unamortized balance being recognized as of January 1, 1995.

(I) Elimination of intercompany income accrued during the period.

(D) Elimination of intercompany dividends.

(E) Recognition of amortization expense for the current period.

(TI) Elimination of intercompany sales/purchases balances created by the transfer of inventory.

(G) Removal of unrealized inventory gain from ending figures so that it can be recognized in subsequent period.

Reduction in Big's Beginning Retained Earnings

Amortization expense relating to acquisition of Middle Company—1993–1994 ($2,000 per year)	$ (4,000)
Income effect created by Middle Company's deferral of unrealized gain ($30,000 × 80%)	(24,000)
Income effect created by Middle Company's adjustment to its prior year's investment income ($14,500 × 80%) (above)	(11,600)
Required reduction to Big's beginning retained earnings (Entry B*C)	$(39,600)

Consolidation Entry S. The beginning stockholders' equity accounts of each subsidiary are eliminated here and noncontrolling interest balances as of the beginning of the year are recognized. As in previous chapters, the amounts involved in this entry have been directly affected by the preliminary adjustments described earlier. Because Entry *G removed a $20,000 beginning unrealized gain, Little's January 1, 1995, book value on the worksheet is $710,000 and not $730,000. This realized total serves as the basis for recording a $213,000 beginning noncontrolling interest (30 percent) as well as the $497,000 elimination (70 percent) from the parent's investment account.

In a similar vein, Middle's book value has already been decreased by $44,500 through Entries *G ($30,000) and *C ($14,500). Thus, the beginning stockholders' equity accounts for this company have now been adjusted to a total of $855,500 ($900,000 − $44,500). This balance leads to a $171,100 initial noncontrolling interest valuation (20 percent) and a $684,400 (80 percent) offset against Big's Investment in Middle account.

Consolidation Entry A. The unamortized goodwill balances remaining as of January 1, 1995, are removed from the two investment accounts so that this intangible asset can be separately identified on the consolidated balance sheet. Since amortization expense for the previous periods has already been recognized in Entry *C, only beginning totals for the year of $19,500 ($20,000 − $500) and $76,000 ($80,000 − $4,000) still remain from the original amounts paid.

Consolidation Entry I. This entry eliminates the current intercompany income figures accrued by each of the parents through their application of the partial equity method.

Consolidation Entry D. Intercompany dividends distributed during the year are removed here from the consolidated financial totals.

Consolidation Entry E. The annual amortization expense relating to each of the goodwill balances is recorded.

Consolidation Entry TI. The intercompany sales/purchases figures created by the transfer of inventory during 1995 are eliminated on the worksheet.

Consolidation Entry G. This final consolidation entry defers the intercompany inventory gains that remain unrealized as of December 31, 1995. The profit on these transfers·is removed until the merchandise is subsequently sold to unrelated parties.

Noncontrolling Interests' Share of Consolidated Income. To complete the steps that constitute this consolidation worksheet, recognition must be given to the 1995 income accruing to owners outside of the business combination. This allocation is based on the realized earnings of the two subsidiaries which, as previously discussed, is calculated beginning with the grandson (Little) followed by the son (Middle).

Little Company's Realized Income and Noncontrolling Interest

Reported operating income (from Exhibit 7–1)	$100,000
Realization of gains previously deferred from 1994	
(Entry L*G)	20,000
Deferral of gains unrealized as of 12/31/95 (Entry LG)	(25,000)
Little Company's realized income, 1995	95,000
Outside ownership	30%
Noncontrolling interest in Little Company's income	$ 28,500

Middle Company's Realized Income and Noncontrolling Interest

Reported operating income (from Exhibit 7–1 after removing	
income of Little Company)	$200,000
Amortization expense relating to acquisition of Little	
Company, current year	(500)
Realization of gains previously deferred from 1994	
(Entry B*G)	30,000
Deferral of gains unrealized as of 12/31/95 (Entry BG)	(40,000)
Equity income accruing from Little Company	
(70% of $95,000 realized income [above])	66,500
Middle Company's realized income, 1995	256,000
Outside ownership	20%
Noncontrolling interest in Middle Company's income	$ 51,200

Although computation of Big's realized earnings is not required here, as previously noted, this figure does provide a means of verifying the accuracy of the income total reported for the consolidated entity.

Big Company's Realized Income

Reported operating income (from Exhibit 7–1 after removing income of Middle Company)	$300,000
Amortization expense relating to acquisition of Middle Company, current year	(2,000)
Equity income accruing from Middle Company (80% of $256,000 realized income [above]).	204,800
Big Company's realized income, 1995.	$502,800

This $502,800 figure represents the income derived by the parent from its own operations plus the earnings accrued from the company's two subsidiaries (one directly owned and the other indirectly controlled). If calculated correctly, this balance equals the consolidated income of the business combination. As shown in Exhibit 7–1, the income reported by Big Company and consolidated subsidiaries does, indeed, net to this same total: $502,800. Although not completely conclusive, the agreement of these balances serves as strong evidence of the validity of the final figures found on the consolidation worksheet.

Indirect Subsidiary Control—Connecting Affiliation

The father-son-grandson organization is hardly the only corporate ownership pattern that can be encountered. The number of possible configurations found in the modern world of business is almost limitless. To assist in illustrating the consolidation procedures necessitated by these alternative patterns, a second basic ownership structure referred to as a *connecting affiliation* is discussed briefly.

A connecting affiliation exists whenever two or more companies within a business combination own an interest in another member of that organization. The simplest form of this configuration is frequently drawn as a triangle:

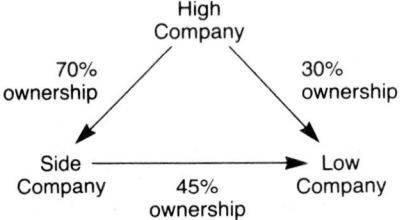

In this example, both High Company and Side Company maintain an ownership interest in Low Company, thus creating a connecting affiliation. Although neither of these individual companies possesses enough voting stock to establish direct control over Low's operations, a total of 75 percent of the outstanding shares is held by members of the combination. Consequently, control lies within the boundaries of the single economic entity, and the inclusion of Low's financial information as a part of consolidated statements is necessary.

Despite the potential for numerous variations in this basic ownership pattern, the process for consolidating a connecting affiliation is essentially unchanged from that demonstrated for a father-son-grandson organization. Perhaps, the most noticeable alteration is that more than two investments are always going to be present. In this triangular business combination, High possesses an ownership interest in both Side and Low while Side also maintains an investment in Low. Thus, unless combined in some manner, three separate sets of consolidation entries would appear on the worksheet. Although the added quantity of entries certainly provides a degree of mechanical complication, the basic concepts involved in the consolidation process remain the same regardless of the number of investments involved.

As with the father-son-grandson structure, one key aspect of the consolidation process warrants additional illustration: the determination of realized income figures for the individual companies. Therefore, assume that High, Side, and Low have separate operating incomes (without inclusion of any earnings from their subsidiaries) of $300,000, $200,000, and $100,000, respectively. Each company also retains a $30,000 net unrealized gain in their current year income figures. Assume further that annual amortization expense of $10,000 has been identified within the purchase price paid for each of the three investments.

In the same manner as a father-son-grandson organization, determination of realized earnings should begin with any companies that are solely in a subsidiary position (Low, in this case). Next, realized income is computed for companies that are both parents as well as subsidiaries (Side). Finally, this same calculation should be made for the one company (High) that has ultimate control over the entire combination. Realized income figures for the three companies in this combination would be derived as follows:

Low Company's Realized Income and Noncontrolling Interest

Reported operating income	$ 100,000
Deferral of Low Company's net unrealized gain	(30,000)
Low Company's realized income	70,000
Outside ownership	25%
Noncontrolling interest in Low Company's income	$ 17,500

Side Company's Realized Income and Noncontrolling Interest

Reported operating income	$200,000
Deferral of Side Company's net unrealized gain	(30,000)
Equity income accruing from Low Company (45% of $70,000 realized income)	31,500
Amortization expense relating to Side Company's acquisition of Low Company	(10,000)
Side Company's realized income	191,500
Outside ownership	30%
Noncontrolling interest in Side Company's income	$ 57,450

High Company's Realized Income

Reported operating income	$300,000
Deferral of High Company's net unrealized gain	(30,000)
Equity income accruing from Side Company (70% of $191,500 realized income)	134,050
Amortization expense relating to High Company's acquisition of Side Company	(10,000)
Equity income accruing from Low Company—direct ownership (30% of $70,000 realized income)	21,000
Amortization expense relating to High Company's acquisition of Low Company	(10,000)
High Company's realized income (and consolidated net income)	$405,050

Even though a connecting affiliation exists in this illustration, the basic tenets of the consolidation process remain the same:

- All effects from intercompany transfers are removed.
- The parents' beginning retained earnings figures are adjusted to recognize the equity income resulting from ownership of the subsidiaries in prior years. The determination of realized earnings for this period is necessary to properly align the balances with the perspective of a single economic entity.
- The beginning stockholders' equity accounts of each subsidiary are eliminated and the noncontrolling interests' figures as of the first day of the year are recognized.
- All unamortized allocation balances created by the original purchase prices are entered onto the worksheet.

- Amortization expense for the current year is recorded.
- Intercompany income and dividends are removed.
- The noncontrolling interests' share of the subsidiaries net income is computed (as just shown) and included in the financial statements of the business combination.

Mutual Ownership

One specific corporate structure that does require further analysis is a mutual ownership. This type of configuration exists whenever two companies within a business combination hold an equity interest in each other. This ownership pattern was sometimes created as a result of the financial battles that occurred during many of the takeover attempts prevalent during the 1980s. A defensive strategy (often referred to as the *Pac-Man Defense*) was occasionally adopted whereby the target company would attempt to avoid takeover by reversing roles and acquiring shares of its investor. Consequently the two parties came to hold shares of each other with one usually gaining control.

Two typical mutual ownership patterns follow. In A, the parent and the subsidiary possess a percentage of each other's voting shares; whereas in B, the mutual ownership exists between two subsidiary companies.

In accounting for a mutual ownership, unique conceptual issues are raised. These concerns center on the handling of any parent company stock owned by a subsidiary. *ARB 51* (par. 12) states that "shares of the parent held by a subsidiary should not be treated as outstanding stock in the consolidated balance sheet." This guidance is theoretically appropriate since the shares are not owned by parties outside of the business combination. Unfortunately, the actual reporting of such internally held stock can vary significantly, depending on the perspective taken as to the substance of the subsidiary's purchase.

Discussion Question: Mutual Ownership: What Do Those Shares Represent?

During 1995, Pierpont Corporation began a plan to acquire control over Sandstone, Inc., a competing company of similar size. An offer of $27 per share (to be paid in a combination of cash and stock) was initially made for Sandstone's common stock. In an attempt to maintain its independence, Sandstone began a counterattack by purchasing the outstanding common stock of Pierpont on the open market. Pierpont increased its offer to $31 and, finally, to $38 per share before successfully winning control over Sandstone. Eventually, 80 percent of Sandstone's shares were obtained. However, during the takeover struggle, Sandstone managed to acquire 30 percent of Pierpont's stock (75,000 shares) at a total cost of $8 million.

Following the purchase, Sandstone remained a relatively autonomous organization. The president and administrative officers retained their positions with the company, and Sandstone's principal stockholder before the takeover is now on the board of directors of Pierpont.

Within Sandstone's separate accounting records, the investment in Pierpont's stock is reported using the equity method. Thus, at the end of 1996, the asset's balance has risen to $8.7 million. Accounting officials of Pierpont, who are currently preparing consolidated financial statements, are attempting to determine the proper accounting for these 75,000 shares. According to the controller, "these shares are our own stock and they are being held within the business combination. The acquisition is no more than the intercompany purchase of treasury shares. Reporting should be simple; we show $8 million as the cost of treasury stock and eliminate all other related figures."

The assistant vice president for finance does not agree. "If we just remove all the balances, we will be using an income for Sandstone that has not been correctly calculated. Sandstone owns this investment and it generates a profit; that profit must be assigned to Sandstone in some manner or we are understating the income that this subsidiary's assets are producing."

The controller is not convinced: "Sandstone has no earnings from this investment. The dividends that we pay them are just intercompany cash transfers and they should not even be recognizing equity income accruals. We control them; Sandstone certainly does not have significant influence over us."

In computing the noncontrolling interest in Sandstone's income, how should the ownership of these 75,000 shares affect the determination of the subsidiary's realized income?

Treasury Stock Approach

Interestingly, when parent shares are obtained by a subsidiary, both of the prevalent methods of accounting take the same perspective: financial reporting should not vary based on the specific identity of the purchasing agent. For consolidation purposes, no legitimate accounting distinction can be drawn between an acquisition by the parent and the same transaction if it is made by a subsidiary. However, these two methods do disagree as to the underlying nature of a subsidiary's purchase of the parent's stock: should the shares be viewed as treasury stock or as an investment?

The *treasury stock approach* assumes that both parties should account for this transaction as the parent would record a purchase of its own stock. Conversely, according to the *conventional approach,* both the parent and the subsidiary must record all intercompany investments in the same manner. Since the parent recognizes income based on its ownership of the subsidiary, the subsidiary should recognize income from an investment in the parent. Although the distinction between these two approaches may seem subtle, the resulting financial figures can vary appreciably.

The treasury stock approach to mutual ownership focuses on the parent's control over the subsidiary. Even though the companies maintain separate legal incorporation, only a single economic entity actually exists, and it is under the dominance of the parent. Hence, according to proponents, stock or other items can be purchased by either company but all reporting for the business combination has to be from the parent's perspective. Although the subsidiary may serve as the purchasing agent, the acquisition of parent shares is still viewed as treasury stock in the consolidated statements. This perspective is firmly grounded in the parent company concept (discussed in Chapter 4), which accounts for all transactions from the vantage point of the parent's stockholders.

In present accounting practice, the treasury stock approach appears to predominate, although this popularity is undoubtedly based as much on the ease of application as on theoretical merit. *The cost of parent shares held by the subsidiary is merely reclassified on the worksheet into a treasury stock account.* Any dividend payments on this stock are considered intercompany cash transfers that must be eliminated. This reporting technique is simple and the shares are, indeed, no longer accounted for as if they were outstanding.

Conventional Approach

The conventional approach does provide a different view of a subsidiary's ownership of parent shares. This alternative theory presumes that the acquisition of parent stock is no more than another equity purchase made in one of the affiliated companies within a business combination. Thus, the consolidation of a mutual ownership should parallel the process that has already been demonstrated for a connecting affiliation: two investments are present rather than one. *In effect, this argument contends that accounting for the parent's investment and a subsidiary's investment by totally different methods is inconsistent.*

Proponents of the conventional approach feel that introducing a unique process, such as the treasury stock approach, simply because of the subsidiary's location within the corporate structure is not justified. To rectify this situation, the internally held shares of the parent company are consolidated in the same manner as an investment in a subsidiary. The conventional approach is aligned with the economic unit concept which contends that each company should be accounted for as an individual component within the business combination.

Probably the most distinctive aspect of the conventional approach is the determination of realized income figures. Because of the mutual ownership, each company occupies both a parent and a subsidiary position within the combination. Immediately, a paradox is created by this relationship. The income of neither company can be computed first; each is partially dependent on the final balance of the other. Unlike the previous indirect ownership examples, no systematic calculation of earnings is possible. Rather, mutual income accruals can be derived only by solving two simultaneous equations.

Clearly, these two approaches represent alternative perceptions of the same event: the subsidiary's purchase of parent stock. However, the underlying question here concerns the theoretical concept that should provide the basis for consolidated statements. What is the purpose of a consolidation and for whom are the financial statements prepared? After these central issues have been resolved, the handling of mutual ownerships (as well as other theoretical concerns) should follow as logical extensions of the selected concept.

Mutual Ownership Illustrated

To illustrate both the treasury stock and the conventional approaches, assume that on January 1, 1995, Sun Company purchases 10 percent of Pop Company. Sun pays $120,000 for these shares, an amount that exactly equals the proportionate book value of Pop. Many possible reasons could exist for this transaction. The acquisition may be simply an investment or possibly an attempt by Sun to forestall a takeover move by Pop. Regardless, Sun subsequently accounts for these shares according to the lower-of-cost-or-market-value method as required by *FASB SFAS 12*. To alleviate the necessity of dealing with extraneous accounting complexities, the assumption is made here that the shares constantly maintain a market value in excess of their original cost.

On January 1, 1996, Pop manages to gain control over Sun by acquiring a 70 percent ownership interest, thus creating a business combination. Details of Pop's purchase are as follows:

Purchase price of 70% interest, 1/1/96	$500,000
Sun Company's reported book value, 1/1/96	600,000
Excess cost over book value—assumed to be goodwill.	40-year life
Investment is being accounted for internally by means of the cost method.	

During the ensuing years, these two companies report the following balances and transactions:

	Sun Company			Pop Company		
Year	*Reported Operating Income*	*Dividend Income (10 percent ownership)*	*Dividends Paid*	*Reported Operating Income*	*Dividend Income (70 percent ownership)*	*Dividends Paid*
1995	$20,000	$3,000	$ 8,000	$ 90,000	–0–	$30,000
1996	30,000	5,000	10,000	130,000	$ 7,000	50,000
1997	40,000	7,000	15,000	160,000	10,500	70,000

Treasury Stock Approach Illustrated. One possible consolidation of Pop and Sun for the year of 1997 is presented in Exhibit 7–2. This worksheet has been developed under the treasury stock approach to mutual ownerships so that Pop's investment in Sun is consolidated along routine lines. This process begins with the determination of goodwill and the computation of annual amortization:

Purchase price	$ 500,000
Proportionate interest in Sun's book value ($600,000 × 70%)	(420,000)
Goodwill, January 1, 1996	$ 80,000
Annual amortization—40-year life	$ 2,000
Unamortized balance, January 1, 1997	$ 78,000

Following the calculation of goodwill and amortization, regular worksheet entries can be developed for Pop's investment. Since the cost method has been applied, the $7,000 dividend income recognized in the prior years of ownership (only 1996, in this case) is converted to an equity accrual in Entry *C. The parent should recognize 70 percent of the subsidiary's $35,000 income for 1996, or $24,500.[1] However, inclusion of the $2,000 amortization expense (computed above) dictates that $22,500 is the appropriate equity accrual. Because $7,000 in

---

[1] Although an intercompany transfer, the $5,000 dividend received from Pop is included here in measuring the subsidiary's previous income. Sun's book value was increased by this cash distribution; thus, some accounting must be made within the consolidation process. In addition, at the time of payment, the parent reduced its retained earnings. Hence, the intercompany portion of this dividend has to be reinstated or consolidated retained earnings will be too low.

dividend income has already been recognized by the parent, Entry *C records the necessary increase as $15,500 ($22,500 − $7,000).[2]

The remaining entries relating to Pop's investment are standard: the stock-holders' equity accounts of the subsidiary are eliminated (Entry S), the goodwill allocation is recognized (Entry A), and so on. Only two facets of Exhibit 7–2 have actually been affected by the existence of the mutual ownership. First, the $120,000 payment made by Sun for the parent's shares is reclassified into a Trea-sury Stock account (through Entry TS). Second, the $7,000 intercompany divi-dend flowing from Pop to Sun during the current year of 1997 is eliminated within Entry I (Entry I is used because the collection was recorded as income). The simplicity of applying the treasury stock approach should be apparent from this one example.

Before leaving the treasury stock approach, a final comment needs to be made in connection with the computation of the noncontrolling interest's share of Sun's income. In Exhibit 7–2, this balance is recorded as $14,100, or 30 percent of the subsidiary's $47,000 net income figure. A question can be raised as to the validity of including the $7,000 dividend within this income total since that payment is eliminated within the consolidation.

These dividends, although intercompany in nature, do increase the book value of the subsidiary company (see footnote 1). Therefore, the increment must be reflected in some manner to indicate the change in the amount attributed to the outsider owners. For example, the increase could have been recognized through a direct adjustment of $2,100 (30 percent of $7,000) in the noncontrolling interest balance being reported. More often, as shown here, such cash transfers are con-sidered to be income *when viewed from the perspective of these other unrelated parties.*

Conventional Approach Illustrated.   Exhibit 7–3 presents the consolidation of this same business combination based on the conventional method of reporting mutual holdings. Although many aspects of the worksheet are also routine, sev-eral entries involve procedures that are unique to the conventional approach. These distinctive elements concern the investment income accruals recorded for both Pop and Sun. According to the conventional approach, these figures must be calculated by identical methods to avoid any inconsistency.

---

[2] The necessary adjustment to beginning retained earnings can also be computed as follows:

Income of subsidiary—1996	$ 35,000
Dividends paid	(10,000)
Increase in book value	$ 25,000
Ownership percentage	70%
Income accrual	$ 17,500
Amortization—1996	(2,000)
Increase in beginning retained earnings	$ 15,500

EXHIBIT 7-2

Investment: Cost Method
Mutual Ownership: Treasury
Stock Approach

POP AND CONSOLIDATED SUBSIDIARY
Consolidation Worksheet
For Year Ending December 31, 1997

Accounts	Pop Company	Sun Company	Consolidation Entries Debit	Consolidation Entries Credit	Noncontrolling Interest	Consolidated Totals
Income Statement						
Revenues	(900,000)	(400,000)				(1,300,000)
Expenses	740,000	360,000	(E) 2,000			1,102,000
Dividend income	(10,500)	(7,000)	(I) 17,500			–0–
Noncontrolling interest in Sun Company's income ($47,000 × 30%)	–0–	–0–			(14,100)	14,100
Net income	(170,500)	(47,000)				(183,900)
Statement of Retained Earnings						
Retained earnings, 1/1/97:						
Pop Company	(747,000)	–0–		(*C) 15,500		(762,500)
Sun Company	–0–	(425,000)	(S) 425,000			–0–
Net income (above)	(170,500)	(47,000)				(183,900)
Dividends paid:						
Pop Company	70,000	–0–		(I) 7,000		63,000
Sun Company	–0–	15,000		(I) 10,500	4,500	–0–
Retained earnings, 12/31/97	(847,500)	(457,000)				(883,400)
Balance Sheet						
Current assets	855,500	331,000				1,186,500
Investment in Sun Company	500,000	–0–	(*C) 15,500	(S) 437,500 (A) 78,000		–0–
Investment in Pop Company	–0–	120,000		(TS) 120,000		–0–
Land, building, equipment (net)	642,000	516,000				1,158,000
Goodwill	–0–	–0–	(A) 78,000	(E) 2,000		76,000
Total assets	1,997,500	967,000				2,420,500
Liabilities	(550,000)	(310,000)				(860,000)
Noncontrolling interest in Sun Company, 1/1/97	–0–	–0–		(S) 187,500	(187,500)	
Noncontrolling interest in Sun Company, 12/31/97	–0–	–0–			(197,100)	(197,100)
Common stock	(600,000)	(200,000)	(S) 200,000			(600,000)
Retained earnings, 12/31/97 (above)	(847,500)	(457,000)				(883,400)
Treasury stock	–0–	–0–	(TS) 120,000			120,000
Total liabilities and equities	(1,997,500)	(967,000)				(2,420,500)

NOTE: Parentheses indicate a credit balance.

Consolidation entries:

(*C) Conversion of cost method to equity method. This entry recognizes 70 percent of the 1996 increase in Sun Company's book value ($25,000 × 70% = $17,500) less $2,000 amortization expense applicable to that year.

(S) Elimination of subsidiary's stockholders' equity accounts along with recognition of January 1, 1997, noncontrolling interest.

(TS) Reclassification of Sun Company's ownership in Pop Company into a Treasury Stock account.

(A) Allocation to goodwill, unamortized balance being recorded as of January 1, 1997.

(I) Elimination of intercompany dividend income for the period.

(E) Recognition of amortization expense for the current year.

EXHIBIT 7–3

POP AND CONSOLIDATED SUBSIDIARY
Consolidation Worksheet
For Year Ending December 31, 1997

Investment: Cost Method
Mutual Ownership:
Conventional Approach

Accounts	Pop Company	Sun Company	Consolidation Entries Debit	Consolidation Entries Credit	Noncontrolling Interest	Consolidated Totals
Income Statement						
Revenues	(900,000)	(400,000)				(1,300,000)
Expenses	740,000	360,000	(E) 1,895			1,101,895
Dividend income	(10,500)	(7,000)	(I) 17,500			–0–
Noncontrolling interest in Sun Company's income	–0–	–0–			(18,003)	18,003
Net income	(170,500)	(47,000)			(18,003)	(180,102)
Statement of Retained Earnings						
Retained earnings, 1/1/97:						
Pop Company	(747,000)	–0–	(SS) 77,033	(*C2) 23,328		(693,295)
Sun Company	–0–	(425,000)	(S) 442,033	(*C1) 17,033		–0–
Net income (above)	(170,500)	(47,000)			(180,102)	(180,102)
Dividends paid:						
Pop Company	70,000	–0–		(I) 7,000		63,000
Sun Company	–0–	15,000		(I) 10,500	4,500	–0–
Retained earnings, 12/31/93	(847,500)	(457,000)				(810,397)

Balance Sheet

	Pop	Sun	Debits	Credits	Noncontrolling Interest	Consolidated
Current assets	855,500	331,000				1,186,500
Investment in Sun Company	500,000	-0-	(*C2) 23,328	(S) 449,423 (A) 73,905		-0-
Investment in Pop Company	-0-	120,000	(*C1) 17,033	(SS) 137,033		-0-
Land, building, equipment (net)	642,000	516,000	(A) 73,905			1,158,000
Goodwill	-0-	-0-		(E) 1,895		72,010
Total assets	1,997,500	967,000				2,416,510
Liabilities	(550,000)	(310,000)				(860,000)
Noncontrolling interest in Sun Company, 1/1/97	-0-	-0-		(S) 192,610	(192,610)	
Noncontrolling interest in Sun Company, 12/31/97					(206,113)	(206,113)
Common stock:						
Pop Company	(600,000)		(SS) 60,000			(540,000)
Sun Company		(200,000)	(S) 200,000			-0-
Retained earnings, 12/31/97 (above)	(847,500)	(457,000)				(810,397)
Total liabilities and equities	(1,997,500)	(967,000)				(2,416,510)

NOTE: Parentheses indicate a credit balance.

Consolidation entries:

(*C1) Conversion of cost method to equity method for Sun's investment in Pop. This accrual for prior years (1995–1996) is computed by solving a set of simultaneous equations.

(*C2) Conversion of cost method to equity method for Pop's investment in Sun. This accrual for the prior year (1996) is computed by solving a set of simultaneous equations.

(S) Elimination of subsidiary's stockholders' equity accounts along with recognition of January 1, 1997, noncontrolling interest.

(SS) Elimination of 10 percent of Pop's stockholders' equity in recognition of intercompany holdings of Sun.

(A) Allocation to goodwill, unamortized balance being recorded as of January 1, 1997.

(I) Elimination of intercompany dividend income for the period.

(E) Recognition of amortization expense for the current year.

Since each of the stock purchases has been accounted for using the cost method, equity accruals (Entry *C) must be established to correct the recording of all pre-1997 investment earnings. This process should begin with the earliest acquisition: the purchase made by Sun. According to the schedule presented previously, Sun reported $23,000 in total earnings (operating income plus dividends) for 1995. However, based on the data given, Sun's *realized* income for that year was actually $29,000: its own $20,000 operating profit plus an accrual of 10 percent of Pop's earnings ($9,000 or 10 percent of $90,000). To record the appropriate investment income for this initial period, a $6,000 ($29,000 − $23,000) increase in Sun's beginning retained earnings must be included on the worksheet. No special difficulty is encountered in arriving at this first amount since the mutual ownership did not yet exist in 1995.

Before leaving this 1995 adjustment, an explanation is warranted concerning the validity of making an equity income accrual for a time period in which only 10 percent ownership was maintained. The business combination formed by these two companies did not come into existence until Pop's subsequent purchase on January 1, 1996. Thus, the lower-of-cost-or-market-value method was appropriately applied by Sun. If that method was proper at the time, should the income recognized for that period now be altered because of a takeover that occurred at a later date?

Despite the limited level of ownership at the time, a $6,000 equity accrual is still required for 1995 to report the subsequently created combination. As discussed in Chapter 1, retroactive adjustment to the equity method is mandated when such changes occur in the relationship between two companies. Only by applying this approach consistently can comparable financial statements be produced from year to year. Consequently, this $6,000 income accrual is recorded within the 1997 consolidation as an increase in the subsidiary's beginning retained earnings. The amount is included as a component of Entry *C1 found on the worksheet.

Computation of equity income accruals becomes significantly more involved in 1996 upon the creation of the mutual ownership. Since neither company's realized earnings can be determined first, they must be solved simultaneously. The following set of equations is utilized by the accountant to calculate the appropriate realized income figures earned by each company:

Sun's realized income
> = Sun's operating income + 10% of Pop's realized income

and

Pop's realized income
> = Pop's operating income + 70% of Sun's realized income

Only two of the balances needed in these equations are available for 1996: Sun's operating income for this year has already been reported as $30,000 while Pop's profits amounted to $128,105. The total for Pop comes from the $130,000 figure indicated previously for 1996 less $1,895 in amortization expense relating to its investment in Sun. This expense differs from the annual $2,000 charge previously derived in producing Exhibit 7–2. The change is necessary because the $6,000 accrual attributed above to Sun for 1995 alters the realized book value of the subsidiary on the date of the parent's purchase to $606,000. This adjustment, based on application of the conventional approach, was not made in the treasury stock approach.

Purchase price—70% of Sun Company		$ 500,000
Proportionate interest in Sun Company's book value:		
Reported book value, 1/1/96	$600,000	
Adjustment to book value—1995 equity income		
accrual relating to investment	6,000	
Adjusted book value, 1/1/96	606,000	
Ownership interest	70%	(424,200)
Goodwill		$ 75,800
Annual amortization—40-year life		$ 1,895

By inserting the two operating income figures, the simultaneous equations can be restated as follows. SRI and PRI are used here to indicate Sun's realized income and Pop's realized income, respectively.

$$SRI = \$30,000 + 10\% \text{ of PRI}$$

and

$$PRI = \$128,105 + 70\% \text{ of SRI}$$

To arrive at a single equation containing only one unknown, the equivalency of PRI formulated in the second equation can be used as a replacement within the first. In addition, to facilitate making the necessary mathematical computations, all percentages are restated in their decimal equivalents. Through these two alterations, the first equation can be solved to derive Sun's realized income for 1996:

$$SRI = \$30,000 + .10 \, (\$128,105 + .70 \, SRI)$$
$$SRI = \$30,000 + \$12,810.50 + .07 \, SRI$$
$$.93 \, SRI = \$42,810.50$$
$$SRI = \$46,033 \text{ (rounded)}$$

A quick comparison of Sun's 1996 realized income of $46,033 with the reported earnings of $35,000 (from operations and dividends) indicates a required increase in the subsidiary's retained earnings of $11,033. *This increment properly records the 1996 income of Sun derived from the investment in the parent company.* Thus, to consolidate the pre-1997 earnings of Sun, a total increase of $17,033 is recognized in Entry *C1 as of January 1, 1997, $6,000 in connection with 1995, and $11,033 for 1996.

Accrual of Sun's Equity Income for Years Prior to 1997

Year	Sun's Realized Income	Sun's Reported Income	Accrual
1995	$29,000	$23,000	$ 6,000
1996	46,033	35,000	11,033
Total increase in subsidiary's 1997 beginning retained earnings—Entry *C1			$17,033

A 1996 equity accrual for Pop's income is also required under the conventional approach because of the mutual ownership existing at that time. This adjustment must be determined in an identical manner. The second simultaneous equation is incorporated for this purpose along with the appropriate replacement from the first:

$$PRI = \$128,105 + .70\ (\$30,000 + .10\ PRI)$$
$$PRI = \$128,105 + \$21,000 + .07\ PRI$$
$$.93\ PRI = \$149,105$$
$$PRI = \$160,328 \text{ (rounded)}$$

Based on this calculated total of $160,328, Pop's originally reported income of $137,000 (operations plus dividends) must be updated on the worksheet by $23,328 (Entry *C2). Through this adjustment, the 1996 income earned from the investment in the subsidiary is correctly included in the consolidated retained earnings.

Having accounted for the pre-1997 operations of this business combination, the remaining consolidation entries utilized in Exhibit 7–3 are mostly routine. However, the elimination of Sun's Investment in Pop (Entry SS) merits further attention. The worksheet shows the parent with beginning stockholders' equity for 1997 of $1,370,328: common stock of $600,000 plus a January 1 retained earnings balance of $770,328 (after increasing the previously recorded income through Entry *C2). Since Sun's original purchase price was equal to Pop's proportionate book value, the newly adjusted investment balance of $137,033 necessarily equates to 10 percent of this same total. The investment was 10 percent of Pop's book value when acquired and Entry *C1 (based on the solution of the simultaneous equations) maintains this agreement.

Consequently, Sun's investment account can be eliminated on the worksheet (Entry SS) by a direct write-off against this portion of Pop's stockholders' equity; 10 percent of the company's common stock and 10 percent of its beginning retained earnings are eliminated. Although this process is more complicated than recording the cost of the intercompany purchase as treasury stock, the same goal is achieved: parent shares held by the subsidiary are not reported as outstanding on the consolidated statements. However, income is assigned to the subsidiary in the same manner that Pop used in recognizing income on its investment.

One final aspect of the consolidation process presented in Exhibit 7–3 should be analyzed: the 1997 computation of the noncontrolling interest in Sun's income (shown on the worksheet as $18,003). As in all previous illustrations, this allocation is based on the realized income of the subsidiary. However, under the conventional approach, the figure must be determined by solving two simultaneous equations. For this computation, Pop's operating income for the period ($160,000) has, once again, been reduced by $1,895 in amortization.

$$SRI = \$40,000 + 10\% \text{ of PRI}$$

and

$$PRI = \$158,105 + 70\% \text{ of SRI}$$

therefore

$$
\begin{aligned}
SRI &= \$40,000 + .10\,(\$158,105 + .70\ SRI) \\
SRI &= \$40,000 + \$15,810.50 + .07\ SRI \\
.93\ SRI &= \$55,810.50 \\
SRI &= \$60,011 \text{ (rounded)}
\end{aligned}
$$

The subsidiary's realized income is $60,011. Since the noncontrolling interest possesses 30 percent of Sun's voting stock, $18,003 ($60,011 × 30%) of the consolidated income is assigned to these outside owners. This balance varies significantly from the $14,100 allocation that was calculated under the treasury stock approach and recognized in Exhibit 7–2. Indeed, several of the consolidated totals (retained earnings, net income, etc.) will differ depending on the method adopted. Under the conventional approach, a portion of the parent's income is being assigned to the subsidiary. Consequently, a higher realized earnings figure is normally calculated for the subsidiary each year, an increase that produces an impact on the consolidated income balances.

Although the discussion here has focused exclusively on mutual ownerships between a parent and a subsidiary, similar relationships can exist between two subsidiaries within a business combination. The consolidation principles that are applicable in this circumstance are not altered substantially. The only major difference created by this type of configuration is that the treasury stock approach is no longer a viable option since parent shares are not being held. Rather, the conventional approach must be utilized based, once again, on determining realized income figures through the solution of two simultaneous equations.

Income Tax Accounting for a Business Combination

This textbook has not attempted to analyze the income tax implications involved in corporate mergers and acquisitions. Numerous complexities inherent in the tax laws in this area necessitate that only a comprehensive tax course can provide complete coverage. Furthermore, essential accounting issues may become overshadowed by intermingling an explanation of the financial reporting process with an in-depth study of related tax consequences.

Thus, coverage to this point of business combinations and consolidated financial statements has been designed solely to develop a basic understanding of the reporting that is required when one company gains control over another. The effort to isolate the examination of conceptual accounting matters is not intended to minimize the importance of the tax laws as they concern consolidated entities. In reality, one of the motives behind the creation of many business combinations is the reduction of tax liabilities.

Despite the desire to focus attention on basic accounting issues, income taxes can never be ignored. Certain elements of the tax laws have a direct impact on the financial reporting of any business combination. At a minimum, recognition of current income tax expense figures as well as deferred income taxes are required to present fairly the financial statements of the consolidated entity. Therefore, an introduction to the income taxation of a business combination is necessary for a complete understanding of the financial reporting process.

Affiliated Groups

A central issue in accounting for the income taxes of a business combination is the method by which the entity's tax returns are filed. For many combinations, only a single consolidated return is required whereas in other cases separate returns are prepared for some, or even all, of the component corporations. According to current tax laws, a business combination may elect to file a consolidated return encompassing all companies that comprise an *affiliated group* as defined by the Internal Revenue Code. All other corporations are automatically required to submit separate income tax returns. Consequently, a first step in working with the taxation process is the delineation of the boundaries of an affiliated group. Because of specific requirements outlined in the tax laws, this designation does not necessarily cover the same constituents as a business combination.

According to the Internal Revenue Code, the essential criterion for including a subsidiary within an affiliated group is the parent's ownership of at least 80 percent of the voting stock as well as at least 80 percent of each class of nonvoting stock. This ownership may be direct or indirect, although the parent must meet these requirements in connection with at least one directly owned subsidiary. As another condition, each company included in the affiliated group has to be a domestic (rather than a foreign) corporation. A company's options can be described as follows:

- Domestic subsidiary, 80 percent to 100 percent owned: may file as part of consolidated return or may file separately.
- Domestic subsidiary, less than 80 percent owned: must file separately.
- Foreign subsidiary: must file separately.

Clearly, a distinction can be drawn between business combinations (identified for financial reporting) and affiliated groups as defined for tax purposes. In Chapter 2, a business combination was described as containing all subsidiaries controlled by a parent company unless control was only temporary. Control is normally evidenced by the possession (either directly or indirectly) of a mere majority of voting stock. Conversely, the 80 percent rule established by the Internal Revenue Code creates a smaller circle of companies qualifying for inclusion in an affiliated group.

For the companies that compose an affiliated group, the filing of a consolidated tax return provides several distinct benefits:

- Intercompany profits are not taxed until realized, although in a similar manner, intercompany losses (which are rare) are not deducted until finally culminated.
- Intercompany dividends are nontaxable (this exclusion applies to all dividends between members of an affiliated group regardless of whether a consolidated return is filed).
- Losses incurred by one affiliated company can be used to reduce taxable income earned by other members of that group.

One of the most pervasive benefits that the Internal Revenue Code has to offer is the privilege of filing a consolidated tax return. If a group of corporations meets the standards for the "affiliated group" designation, consolidation permits the group to set off the profits of the prosperous components against the losses suffered by the units that have fallen on hard times."[3]

Deferred Income Taxes

Some of the deviations that exist between generally accepted accounting principles and income tax laws create *temporary differences* whereby (1) a variation exists between an asset or liability's recorded book value and its tax basis and (2) this difference results in taxable or deductible amounts in future years. Whenever a temporary difference is present, the recognition of a deferred tax asset or liability is required for financial reporting purposes. The specific amount of this income tax deferral depends somewhat on whether consolidated or separate returns are being filed. Thus, the tax consequences of several common transactions are analyzed here as a means of demonstrating the recording of income tax expense by a business combination.

Intercompany Dividends. For financial reporting, dividends between the members of a business combination are always eliminated; they represent intercompany transfers of cash. In tax accounting, dividends are also removed from income but only if at least 80 percent of the subsidiary's stock is held. Consequently, with this level of ownership, no difference exists between financial and tax reporting; all intercompany dividends are eliminated in both cases.

---

[3] Robert Willens, "Consolidated Returns and Affiliated Groups (with a nod to Wall Street)," *Journal of Accountancy,* February 1986, p. 60.

Income tax expense is not recorded. Deferred tax recognition is also ignored because no temporary difference has been created.

However, if less than 80 percent of subsidiary's stock is held, tax recognition becomes necessary. Any intercompany dividends are partially taxed because, at that level of ownership, 20 percent is taxable. The dividend received deduction on the tax return (the nontaxable portion) is only 80 percent.[4] Thus, an income tax liability is immediately created for the recipient. *In addition, deferred income taxes are required for any of the subsidiary's income not paid currently as a dividend.* A temporary difference has been created because tax payments will be necessary in future years when the earnings of this investment are eventually distributed to the parent. Hence, a current tax liability is recorded based on the dividends collected and a deferred tax liability is recorded for the taxable portion of any income not paid to the parent during the year.

Amortization of Goodwill. In a business combination, goodwill is amortized over an expected life of up to 40 years. Although recognized in financial accounting, this expense is never deductible for tax purposes.[5] Because two methods of accounting are being used, goodwill has a different reported book value and tax basis. However, since no future taxable or deductible amounts result, a temporary difference is not created. The amortization of goodwill does not lead to the recognition of a deferred income tax.[6]

Unrealized Intercompany Gains. Taxes on the unrealized gains that can result from transfers made between the related companies within a business combination create a special accounting problem. On consolidated financial statements, the impact of all such transactions is deferred. The same handling is true for a consolidated tax return; the gains are removed until realized. No temporary difference is created.

If separate returns are filed, though, tax laws require the profits to be reported in the period of transfer even though unearned by the business combination. Thus, the income is taxed immediately, prior to being earned from a financial reporting perspective. This ''prepayment'' of the tax creates a deferred income tax asset.[7]

---

[4] If less than 20 percent of a company's stock is owned, the dividend received deduction is only 70 percent. However, this level of ownership is not applicable to a subsidiary within a business combination.

[5] In some takeovers, the amortization of other allocations within the parent's purchase price (to accounts such as buildings and equipment) are also nondeductible for tax purposes. However, in certain specific cases, such amortization can be deducted. The tax laws in regard to business combinations are obviously quite complicated.

[6] A discussion of goodwill and its income tax implications can be found in ''Allocating the Purchase Price of a Business,'' *Management Accounting,* May 1988.

[7] In *SFAS 109,* the FASB required deferral of the amount of taxes paid on the unrealized gain by the seller. This approach was taken rather than computing the deferral based on the future tax effect caused by the difference between the buyer's book value and tax basis, a procedure which was consistent with the rest of the pronouncement. According to paragraph 124, this decision was made to help ''eliminate the need for complex cross-currency deferred tax computations'' when the parties are in separate tax jurisdictions.

Consolidated Tax Returns—Illustration

As an illustration of the accounting effects created by the filing of a consolidated tax return, assume that Great Company possesses 90 percent of Small Company's voting and nonvoting stocks. Assume also that Great originally paid $160,000 in excess of the subsidiary's proportionate book value, a cost assigned to goodwill and amortized at the rate of $4,000 per year. Subsequent to the acquisition, the two companies continued normal operations, which included significant intercompany transactions. Each company's operational and dividend incomes for the current time period follow as well as the effects of unrealized gains. No income tax accruals have been recognized within these totals.

	Great Company	Small Company (90% owned)
Operating income (excludes equity or dividend income from subsidiary as well as amortization)	$160,000	$40,000
Net unrealized gains in current year income (included in operating income above)	30,000	8,000
Dividend income (from Small)	9,000	–0–
Dividends paid	20,000	10,000

From the perspective of the single economic entity, Great's individual income for the period amounts to $126,000, $160,000 in operational earnings less $30,000 in unrealized gains and $4,000 amortization expense. Using this same approach, Small's income is calculated as $32,000 after removing the effects of the intercompany transfers ($40,000 operating income less $8,000 in unrealized gains). Thus, the income to be reported in consolidated financial statements before the reduction for noncontrolling interest is $158,000 ($126,000 + $32,000). For financial reporting, both intercompany dividends and unrealized gains have been omitted in arriving at this total. Income prior to the noncontrolling interest has been computed here since any allocation to these other owners is not deductible for tax purposes.

Because the parent owns more than 80 percent of Small's stock, the dividends collected from the subsidiary are tax free. Likewise, the intercompany gains are not taxable presently since a consolidated return is being filed. Hence, *financial and tax accounting are the same for both items;* neither of these figures produces a temporary difference so that recognition of a deferred income tax is ignored.

The amortization of goodwill also fails to create a temporary difference. This $4,000 is subtracted in computing the reported income for the business combination but can never be deducted on the tax return. No future taxable income or deduction is created by the amortization. Deferred income taxes are, again, not appropriate.

Since removing a $4,000 nondeductible expense would create an increase in taxable income, the affiliated group pays taxes on $162,000 rather than its reported income of $158,000. Assuming an effective rate of 30 percent, $48,600

($162,000 × 30%) must be conveyed to the government this year. Because no temporary differences are present, deferred income tax recognition is not applicable. Consequently, $48,600 is the only expense reported in connection with current income. This amount should be recorded as the income tax expense for the consolidated entity by means of a worksheet entry or through an individual accrual recorded by each company.

Assigning Income Tax Expense—Consolidated Return

Whenever a consolidated tax return is filed, an allocation of the total expense between the two parties must be determined. This figure is especially important to the subsidiary if it has to produce separate financial statements for a loan or a future issuance of equity. The subsidiary's expense is also needed as a basis for calculating the noncontrolling interest's share of consolidated income.

Several techniques exist to accomplish this proration. For example, the expense charged to the subsidiary is often based on the percentage of the total taxable income that comes from each company (the percentage allocation method) or on the taxable income figures that would be appropriate if separate returns were filed (the separate return method).[8]

To illustrate, the figures from Great and Small in the previous example are again utilized. Great owned 90 percent of Small's outstanding stock. Based on filing a consolidated return, total income tax expense of $48,600 was recognized. How should this figure be allocated between these two companies?

Percentage Allocation Method.   Total taxable income on this consolidated return was $162,000. Of this amount, $130,000 was applicable to the parent (operating income after deferral of unrealized gain) while $32,000 came from the subsidiary (computed in the same manner). Thus, 19.8 percent ($32,000/$162,000, rounded) of total expense should be assigned to the subsidiary, an amount that equals $9,622.80 (19.8 percent of $48,600).

Separate Return Method.   On separate returns, intercompany gains are taxable. Therefore, the separate returns of these two companies would appear as follows:

	Great	Small	Total
Operating income	$160,000	$40,000	
Assumed tax rate	30%	30%	
Income tax expense—separate returns	$ 48,000	$12,000	$60,000

---

[8] For other methods, see "How to Allocate a Consolidated Tax Liability among Members of the Affiliated Group," in the October 1986 issue of *The Practical Accountant;* or "Uncharted Territory: Subsidiary Financial Reporting," in the October 1989 issue of *Journal of Accountancy.*

By filing a consolidated return, an expense of only $48,600 is recorded for the business combination. Since 20 percent of taxable income on the separate returns ($12,000/$60,000) came from the subsidiary, $9,720 of the expense ($48,600 × 20%) should be assigned to Small.

Under this second approach, the noncontrolling interest's share of this subsidiary's income is then computed as follows:

Small Company—reported income	$ 40,000
Less: Unrealized intercompany gains	(8,000)
Less: Assigned income tax expense	(9,720)
Small Company—realized income	22,280
Outside ownership	10%
Noncontrolling interest in Small Company's income	$ 2,228

Filing Separate Tax Returns

Despite the advantages of filing as an affiliated group, a single consolidated return cannot always be used to encompass every member of a business combination. Separate returns are mandatory for foreign subsidiaries as well as for domestic corporations not meeting the 80 percent ownership rule. However, even if the conditions for inclusion within an affiliated group are met, a company may still elect to file separately. If all companies in an affiliated group are profitable and few intercompany transactions occur, separate returns may be preferred. By filing in this manner, the various companies have more flexibility in their choice of accounting methods as well as fiscal tax years.[9] Tax laws do require, though, that a company cannot switch back and forth between consolidated and separate returns. Once a company has elected to file a consolidated tax return each year as part of an affiliated group, obtaining permission from the Internal Revenue Service to file separately can be quite difficult.

The filing of a separate tax return by a member of a business combination often creates temporary differences because of (1) the immediate taxation of unrealized gains (and losses) and (2) the possible future tax effect of any subsidiary income in excess of dividend payments. Since temporary differences can result, recognition of a deferred tax asset or liability may be necessary. For example, as mentioned previously, intercompany gains and losses must be included on a separate return at the time of transfer rather than when the earning process is culminated. These gains and losses appear on both sets of records but, if unrealized at year's end, in different time periods. A temporary difference is

---

[9] At one time, the filing of separate returns was especially popular as a means of taking advantage of reduced tax rates on lower income levels. However, in the early part of the 1970s, Congress eliminated the availability of this tax saving.

produced between the transferred asset's book value and tax basis that affects future tax computations; thus, deferred taxes must be reported.

For dividend payments, deferred taxes are not required if 80 percent or more of the subsidiary's stock is owned. The transfer is nontaxable even on a separate return; no expense recognition is required.

If the amount distributed by a subsidiary that is less than 80 percent owned is equal to current earnings, 20 percent of the collection is taxed immediately but no temporary difference is created because no future tax effect is produced. Hence, again, deferred income tax recognition is not appropriate.

Conceptually, though, as discussed in Chapter 1, questions arise about the recognition of deferred taxes when a subsidiary less than 80 percent owned pays fewer dividends than its current income. If a subsidiary earns, for example, $100,000 but pays dividends of only $60,000, will the parent's share of the $40,000 remainder ever become taxable income? Do these undistributed earnings represent temporary differences? If so, immediate recognition of the associated tax effect is required even though payment of this $40,000 may not be anticipated for the foreseeable future.

In response to these concerns, *FASB Statement No. 109,* "Accounting for Income Taxes," February 1992 (par. 32) states that "a deferred tax liability shall be recognized for . . . an excess of the amount for financial reporting over the tax basis of an investment in a domestic subsidiary." Therefore, other than one exception noted later in this chapter, a temporary difference is created by any portion of the subsidiary's income not distributed in the form of dividends. These earnings would not be taxed until a later date; thus, a deferred tax liability is created. Since many companies retain a substantial portion of their income to finance growth, an expense is recognized here that might never be paid.

Deferred Tax on Undistributed Earnings—Illustrated.   Accounting for the income tax effect created by undistributed earnings is probably best demonstrated through a practical example. Assume that Parent Company owns 70 percent of Child Company. Because ownership is less than 80 percent, the filing of separate tax returns for the two companies is mandatory. In the current year, Parent's operational earnings (excluding taxes and any income from this investment) amount to $200,000 while Child reports a pretax net income of $100,000. During the period, the subsidiary paid a total of $20,000 in cash dividends, $14,000 (70 percent) to Parent, with the remainder going to the other owners. To avoid complications in this initial example, the assumption is made that no amortization expense or unrealized intercompany gains and losses are present.

The reporting of Child's income taxes does not provide a significant difficulty because no temporary differences are involved. Using an assumed tax rate of 30 percent, the subsidiary accrues income tax expense of $30,000 ($100,000 × 30%), leaving an after-tax profit of $70,000. *Since only $20,000 in dividends were paid, undistributed earnings for the period amount to $50,000.*

For Parent, Child's undistributed earnings represent a temporary tax difference. The following schedules have been developed to calculate Parent's current tax liability and deferred tax liability:

Income Tax Currently Payable—Parent Company

Reported operating income—Parent Company		$200,000
Dividends received	$ 14,000	
Less: Dividend deduction (80%)	(11,200)	2,800
Taxable income—current year		202,800
Tax rate		30%
Income tax payable—current period (Parent).		$ 60,840

Deferred Income Tax Payable—Parent Company

Undistributed earnings of Child Company	$ 50,000
Parent Company's ownership	70%
Undistributed earnings accruing to Parent	35,000
Dividend deduction upon eventual distribution (80%)	(28,000)
Income to be taxed—subsequent dividend payments.	7,000
Tax rate	30%
Deferred income tax payable	$ 2,100

These computations indicate a total income tax expense of $62,940: a current liability of $60,840 and a deferred liability of $2,100. The deferred balance results entirely from the undistributed earnings of Child. Although the subsidiary had an after-tax income of $70,000, only $20,000 was distributed in the form of dividends. According to *FASB Statement 109,* just quoted, the $50,000 being retained by Child represents a temporary tax difference to the stockholders. Thus, recognition of the deferred income tax associated with these undistributed earnings is required. Since the income is earned now, the liability must be recorded in the current period.

FASB Statement 109 is not completely inflexible on this matter; in connection with a subsidiary's undistributed income, one important exception to the recognition of deferred income taxes is provided. The pronouncement (par. 31) states that a deferred tax liability is not recognized for the excess of the amount for financial reporting over the tax basis of an investment in a *foreign* subsidiary unless the reversal of those temporary differences in the foreseeable future becomes apparent.

Thus, in the previous example, if the subsidiary is foreign and if the retention of these excess earnings seems to be permanent, the $2,100 deferred tax liability is omitted, reducing the total reported expense to $60,840.

Separate Tax Returns Illustrated. The full accounting impact created by the filing of separate tax returns can best be demonstrated by a complete example. As a basis for this illustration, assume that the following data has been reported by

Lion Corporation and its 60 percent owned subsidiary, Cub Company (a domestic corporation), for the year of 1995.

	Lion Corporation	Cub Company (60% owned by Lion)
Operating income	$500,000	$200,000
Unrealized intercompany inventory gains (included in operating income).	40,000	30,000
Dividend income from Cub Company	24,000	not applicable
Annual goodwill amortization expense— purchase of Cub Company	14,000	not applicable
Dividends paid	not applicable	40,000
Applicable tax rate	30%	30%

Subsidiary's Income Tax Expense. Since separate tax returns must be filed, the unrealized gains are not deferred but left within the operating incomes of both companies. Thus, Cub's taxable income for 1995 is $200,000, an amount that creates a current payable of $60,000 ($200,000 × 30%). The unrealized gain is a temporary difference for financial reporting purposes, creating a deferred income tax asset (payment of the tax comes before the income is actually earned) of $9,000 ($30,000 × 30%). Therefore, the appropriate expense to be recognized by the subsidiary for the period is only $51,000:

Income Tax Expense—Cub

Income currently taxable	$200,000	
Tax rate	30%	$60,000
Temporary difference (unrealized gain is taxed before being earned)	(30,000)	
Tax rate	30%	(9,000)
Income tax expense—Cub		$51,000

Consequently, Cub reports after-tax income of $119,000 ($200,000 operating income less $30,000 unrealized gain less $51,000 in income tax expense). This profit figure serves as the basis for recognizing $47,600 ($119,000 × 40% outside ownership) as the noncontrolling interest's share of consolidated income.

Parent's Income Tax Expense. On Lion's separate return, its own unrealized gains remain within income. The taxable portion of the dividends received from Cub must also be included. However, the amortization expense has no impact on this computation. Amortization of goodwill is never deductible. Since the $14,000 expense was not included in Lion's operating income, no adjustment is necessary for tax purposes. Hence, the parent's taxable earnings for 1995 would be $504,800, a balance that creates a $151,440 current tax liability for the company.

Income Tax Currently Payable—Lion

Operating income—Lion Corporation (includes $40,000 unrealized gains)		$500,000
Dividends received from Cub Company (60%)	$ 24,000	
Less: 80% dividend deduction	(19,200)	4,800
Taxable income		504,800
Tax rate		30%
Income tax payable—current (Lion)		$151,440

Although Lion's tax return information is presented here, the total tax expense to be reported for the period can only be determined by accounting for the impact of the two temporary differences: the parent's $40,000 in unrealized gains and the undistributed earnings of the subsidiary. The undistributed earnings amount to $47,400 computed as follows:

After-tax income of Cub (above)	$ 119,000
Dividends paid	(40,000)
Undistributed earnings	79,000
Lion's ownership	60%
Lion's portion of undistributed earnings	$ 47,400

The deferred income tax effects to be recorded by the parent can now be derived.

Deferred Income Taxes—Lion Company

Unrealized Gains	
Amount taxable now prior to being earned	$ 40,000
Tax rate	30%
Deferred income tax asset	$ 12,000
Undistributed Earnings of Subsidiary	
Undistributed earnings of Cub—to be taxed later (computed above)	$ 47,400
Dividend received deduction upon distribution (80%)	(37,920)
Income eventually taxable	$ 9,480
Tax rate	30%
Deferred income tax liability	$ 2,844

The two temporary differences exert opposite effects on Lion's reported income taxes. Because separate returns are filed, the unrealized gains are taxable in the current period despite not having actually been earned. From an accounting perspective, paying the tax on these gains now creates a deferred income tax asset of $12,000 ($40,000 × 30%). In contrast, the undistributed earnings are recognized currently by the parent (through consolidation of the investment). However, this portion of the subsidiary's income is not yet taxable to the parent. Since the tax payment is not required until the dividends are received, a deferred income tax liability of $2,844 is necessary ($9,480 × 30%).

The deferred tax asset is reported as a current asset since it relates to inventory whereas the deferred tax liability is long-term because it was created by ownership of the investment. Lion's reported income tax expense results from the creation of these three accounts:

Lion's Financial Records

Deferred Income Tax Asset—Current	12,000	
Income Tax Expense.	142,284	
Deferred Income Tax Liability—Long-Term		2,844
Income Tax Currently Payable		151,440
To record current and deferred taxes of parent company.		

Temporary Differences Generated by Business Combinations

Because of the nature of the transaction, some purchase combinations are deemed tax free (to the seller) by the tax laws whereas others are taxable. In most tax-free purchases and in a few taxable purchases, the resulting book values of the acquired company's assets and liabilities differ from their tax bases. Such differences result because the subsidiary's cost is retained for tax purposes (in tax-free exchanges) or because the allocations for tax purposes vary from those used for financial reporting (a situation found in some taxable transactions).

Thus, temporary differences may be created at the time that a business combination is first formed. Any deferred income tax assets and liabilities previously recorded by the subsidiary are not at issue; these accounts are consolidated in the same manner as other assets and liabilities. The question addressed here concerns differences in book value and tax basis that stem from the takeover.

As an illustration, assume that Son Company owns a single asset, a building. This property has a tax basis of $150,000 (cost less accumulated depreciation) but it presently has a fair market value of $210,000. Pop Corporation conveys a total value of $300,000 to acquire this company. The exchange is structured to be tax free. After this transaction, the building continues to have a tax basis of only $150,000. However, its consolidated book value is $210,000, an amount $60,000 more than the figure applicable for tax purposes. How does this $60,000 difference affect the consolidated statements?

In 1992, the FASB issued *Statement of Financial Accounting Standards No. 109,* "Accounting for Income Taxes," which established guidelines for the reporting of deferred income tax assets and liabilities created in a business combination. According to paragraph 127:

Values are assigned to identified assets and liabilities when a business combination is accounted for as a purchase. The assigned values frequently will be different from the tax bases of those assets and liabilities. The Board concluded that a liability or asset should be recognized for the deferred tax consequences of differences between the assigned values and the tax bases of the assets and liabilities (other than goodwill and leveraged leases) recognized in a purchase business combination.

Thus, according to this pronouncement, a deferred tax asset or liability is created by any temporary difference such as is found in Pop's purchase of Son. Because the tax basis of the asset is $150,000, but its recorded value within consolidated statements is $210,000, a temporary difference of $60,000 exists. Assuming that a 30 percent tax rate is appropriate, a deferred income tax liability of $18,000 ($60,000 × 30%) must be recognized by the newly formed business combination. Before *Statement 109,* this $18,000 would have been reported as a reduction in the consolidated value of the Buildings account. However, a liability is now recorded to reflect the future effect of recognizing lower depreciation for tax purposes (thus creating higher taxable income and additional payments). The FASB also apparently felt that this placement was more consistent with the asset and liability approach required by *Statement 109.*

Consequently, in a consolidated balance sheet prepared immediately after Pop obtains control over Son, the building would be recorded at fair market value of $210,000. In addition, the new deferred tax liability of $18,000 computed earlier is recognized. Since the net value of these two accounts is $192,000, goodwill of $108,000 is also recorded as the figure remaining from the $300,000 purchase price.

This $18,000 liability is then systematically reduced to zero over the life of the building. Depreciation for tax purposes must be computed on the $150,000 cost figure and would, therefore, be less each year than the expense shown for financial reporting purposes (based on $210,000). With less expense, taxable income would be more than book income for the remaining years of the asset's life. However, according to *Statement 109,* the extra payment that results is not charged to expense. Rather, the deferred tax liability (initially established at the date of purchase) is reduced by the additional amount.

To illustrate, assume that revenues of $40,000 per year are generated from this building. Assume also that it has a life of 10 years and that the straight-line method

	Financial Reporting	Income Tax Reporting
Revenues	$40,000	$40,000
Depreciation expense:		
10% of $210,000	21,000	
10% of $150,000		$15,000
Income	$19,000	$25,000
Tax rate	30%	30%
Tax effect	$ 5,700	$ 7,500

of depreciation is in use. (Amortization of the goodwill is ignored for this example since that expense is not tax deductible.)

Although $7,500 must be paid to the government, currently reported income would have caused only $5,700 of that amount. The other $1,800 ($6,000 reversal of temporary difference $\times$ 30%) resulted because of the use of the previous basis for tax purposes. Therefore, the following entry is made:

Income Tax Expense.	5,700	
Deferred Income Tax Liability (to remove part of balance created at		
date of purchase)	1,800	
Income Tax Currently Payable		7,500
To accrue current income taxes as well as impact of temporary		
difference in asset of subsidiary.		

Business Combinations and Operating Loss Carryforwards

Tax laws in the United States provide a measure of relief for companies incurring net operating losses (NOLs) when filing current tax returns. Such losses may be carried back for three years and applied as a reduction to taxable income figures previously reported. This procedure generates a cash refund of income taxes paid by the company during these earlier periods.

If a loss still exists after the carryback (or if the taxpayer elects not to carry the loss back), a carryforward for the subsequent 15 years is also allowed.[10] Carrying the loss forward reduces subsequent taxable income levels until the NOL is eliminated entirely or the time period expires. *Thus, NOL carryforwards can only benefit the company if taxable income can be generated in the future.* The immediate recognition of NOL carryforwards has always been controversial since it requires the company to anticipate making profits. In 1992, *Statement 109* of the Financial Accounting Standards Board established reporting rules for the appropriate recognition of such carryforwards.

Until recently, some business combinations were created, at least in part, to take advantage of tax carryforwards. If an acquired company had an unused NOL while the parent projected significant profitability, the carryforward was used on a consolidated return to reduce income taxes after the acquisition. However, U.S. laws have now been changed so that virtually all of a NOL carryforward can be used only by the company that reported the loss. Hence, the acquisition of companies with an NOL carryforward has ceased to be a popular business strategy. However, since the practice has not disappeared, reporting rules for a subsidiary's NOL carryforward are still needed.

Statement 109 requires the recording of a deferred income tax asset for any NOL carryforward. In addition, though, a valuation allowance must also be recognized

---

[10] If a taxpayer believes that tax rates will be higher in the future, choosing not to carry a loss back in favor of only a carryforward may be financially preferable.

if, based on the weight of available evidence, it is *more likely than not* (a likelihood of more than 50 percent) that some portion or all of the deferred tax assets will not be realized. The valuation allowance should be sufficient to reduce the deferred tax asset to the amount that is more likely than not to be realized. (par. 17e)

As an example, assume that a company has one asset (a building) worth $500,000. Because of recent losses, this company has an NOL carryforward of $200,000. The assumed tax rate is 30 percent so that a benefit of $60,000 ($200,000 × 30%) will be derived if future taxable profits are earned.

Assume that this company is purchased for $640,000. In accounting for the acquisition, the parent must anticipate the likelihood that some portion or all of the NOL carryforward will ever be utilized by the new subsidiary. If it is more likely than not that the benefit would be realized, goodwill of $80,000 results:

Purchase price		$640,000
Subsidiary assets:		
Building	$500,000	
Deferred income tax asset	60,000	560,000
Goodwill		$ 80,000

Conversely, if the chances that this subsidiary will use the NOL carryforward are only 50 percent or less, a valuation allowance must be recognized and consolidated goodwill is $140,000:

Purchase price			$640,000
Subsidiary assets:			
Building		$500,000	
Deferred income tax asset	$ 60,000		
Valuation allowance	(60,000)	–0–	500,000
Goodwill			$140,000

In this second case, a question arises if future taxes are successfully reduced by this carryforward: How should the valuation allowance be removed? *Statement 109* requires that these subsequent benefits first be recorded as a reduction to goodwill. Only if this asset is decreased to zero should income tax expense be reduced.

Summary

1. For consolidation purposes, a parent need not possess majority ownership of each of the component companies constituting a business combination. Often, control is of an indirect nature; a majority of one subsidiary's shares are held by another subsidiary. Although the parent might own stock in only one of these companies, control has been established over both. Such an arrangement is often referred to as a father-son-grandson or a pyramid configuration.

2. The consolidation of financial information for a father-son-grandson business combination does not differ conceptually from a consolidation involving only direct ownership. All intercompany, reciprocal balances are eliminated. Goodwill, other allocations, and amortization must usually be recognized if a purchase has taken place. Because more than one investment is involved, the quantity of worksheet entries increases, but that is more of a mechanical inconvenience than a conceptual concern.

3. One aspect of a father-son-grandson consolidation that does warrant attention is the determination of realized income figures for each of the subsidiaries. Any company within a business combination that holds both a parent and subsidiary position must first determine the income accruing from ownership of its subsidiary before computing its own realized earnings. This procedure is important because realized income is the basis for each parent's equity accruals as well as noncontrolling interest allocations.

4. If a subsidiary possesses shares of its parent, a mutual affiliation is said to exist. Although this investment is intercompany in nature and must be eliminated for consolidation purposes, the amount to be removed and the income allocated to the subsidiary can be computed in two different ways. The treasury stock approach simply reclassifies the cost of these shares as treasury stock with no equity accrual being recorded. In contrast, the conventional approach accounts for the shares as a regular investment in a related party. Under this second method, equity income accruals are attributed to the subsidiary in connection with ownership of the parent. Since the companies are both in parent and subsidiary positions, the amount of realized income cannot be directly derived by either party. These figures can be found only by solving two simultaneous equations.

5. Under present tax laws, a single consolidated income tax return can be filed by an affiliated group. Only domestic corporations are included and 80 percent of the voting stock as well as 80 percent of the nonvoting stock must be controlled (either directly or indirectly) by the parent. A consolidated return allows the companies to defer recognition of intercompany gains until realized. Furthermore, losses incurred by one member of the group reduce taxable income earned by the others. Intercompany dividends are also nontaxable on a consolidated return, although such distributions are never taxable when paid between companies within an affiliated group.

6. For some members of a business combination, separate tax returns are applicable. Foreign corporations, as an example, must report in this manner as well as any company not meeting the 80 percent ownership rule. In addition, a company might simply elect to file in this manner if no advantages are gained from a consolidated return. For financial reporting purposes, a separate return often necessitates recognition of deferred income taxes because temporary differences can result from unrealized transfer gains as well as intercompany dividends (if 80 percent ownership is not held).

7. When a purchase combination is created, the subsidiary's assets and liabilities sometimes have a tax basis that differs from their assigned values. In such cases, a deferred tax asset or liability must be recognized at the time of acquisition to reflect the tax impact of these differences.

Comprehensive Illustration

PROBLEM

(Estimated Time: 60 to 75 Minutes)

On January 1, 1995, Gold Company purchased 90 percent of Silver Company for $620,000. This price indicated goodwill of $80,000 based on the subsidiary's total book value of $600,000. The goodwill is expensed over a 40-year period at the rate of $2,000 per year.

Subsequently, on January 1, 1996, Silver acquired 10 percent of Gold for $150,000. This price equaled the appropriately adjusted book value of Gold's underlying net assets. Consequently, no allocation was made to either goodwill or any specific accounts.

On January 1, 1997, Gold and Silver each purchased 30 percent of the outstanding shares of Bronze for $100,000 apiece. Bronze had a book value on that date of $300,000 so that the underlying book value of each acquisition was $90,000 ($300,000 × 30%). Hence, goodwill of $10,000 was recognized as a component of each investment. Both goodwill balances are to be amortized over a 10-year period, necessitating an annual expense of $1,000 for Gold and Silver.

After the formation of this business combination, significant intercompany inventory sales were made from Silver to Gold. The volume of these transfers has been as follows:

Year	Transfer Price to Gold Company	Markup on Transfer Price	Inventory Retained At End of Year (at transfer price)
1995	$100,000	30%	$120,000
1996	160,000	25	90,000
1997	200,000	28	120,000

In addition, on July 1, 1997, Gold sold a tract of land to Bronze for $25,000. This property had originally cost $12,000 when acquired by the parent several years ago.

During the years of 1995 and 1996, Gold and Silver individually reported the following financial information. The cost method has been incorporated to account for all investments; thus, only dividend income has been recognized.

	Gold Company	*Silver Company*
1995:		
Operational income.	$180,000	$120,000
Dividend income—Silver Company (90%).	36,000	–0–
Dividends paid.	80,000	40,000
1996:		
Operational income.	240,000	150,000
Dividend income—Gold Company (10%)	–0–	9,000
Dividend income—Silver Company (90%).	27,000	–0–
Dividends paid.	90,000	30,000

The 1997 financial statements for each of the three companies composing this business combination are presented in Exhibit 7–4. Income tax effects have been ignored in deriving these figures.

EXHIBIT 7–4   Individual Financial Statements—1997

	Gold Company	*Silver Company*	*Bronze Company*
Sales	$ 800,000	$ 600,000	$ 300,000
Cost of goods sold	(380,000)	(300,000)	(120,000)
Operating expenses	(193,000)	(100,000)	(90,000)
Gain on sale of land	13,000	–0–	–0–
Dividend income from Gold Company	–0–	10,000	–0–
Dividend income from Silver Company.	36,000	–0–	–0–
Dividend income from Bronze Company	6,000	6,000	–0–
Net income	$ 282,000	$ 216,000	$ 90,000
Retained earnings, 1/1/97	$ 923,200	$ 609,000	$ 200,000
Net income (above)	282,000	216,000	90,000
Dividends paid	(100,000)	(40,000)	(20,000)
Retained earnings, 12/31/97	$1,105,200	$ 785,000	$ 270,000
Cash and receivables.	$ 250,000	$ 195,000	$ 130,000
Inventory	459,000	410,000	110,000
Investment in Silver Company	620,000	–0–	–0–
Investment in Gold Company	–0–	150,000	–0–
Investment in Bronze Company	100,000	100,000	–0–
Land, buildings, and equipment (net).	980,000	670,000	380,000
Total assets	$2,409,000	$1,525,000	$ 620,000
Liabilities	$ 603,800	$ 540,000	$ 250,000
Common stock	700,000	200,000	100,000
Retained earnings, 12/31/97	1,105,200	785,000	270,000
Total liabilities and equities	$2,409,000	$1,525,000	$ 620,000

Required:

a. Prepare worksheet entries to consolidate the 1997 financial statements for this combination. Assume that the mutual ownership between Gold and Silver is accounted for by means of the conventional approach. Compute the noncontrolling interests in Bronze's income and in Silver's income.

b. Assume that consolidated net income (before deducting any balance for the noncontrolling interests) amounts to $501,900. Assume further that the effective tax rate is 40 percent and that Gold and Silver file a consolidated tax return while Bronze files separately. Calculate the income tax expense to be recognized within the consolidated income statement for 1997.

SOLUTION

a. The 1997 consolidation entries for Gold, Silver, and Bronze follow.

Entry *G. The consolidation process begins with Entry *G that recognizes the intercompany gain (on transfers from Silver to Gold) created in the previous period. The unrealized gain within ending inventory is deferred from 1996 into the current period.

*Consolidation Entry *G*

Retained earnings, 1/1/97 (Silver Company)	22,500	
Cost of goods sold		22,500

To defer unrealized gains on intercompany sales made from Silver to Gold during the preceding year (25% markup × $90,000).

Entry *C1. Gold's ownership of Silver has been recorded using the cost method. This worksheet entry converts that number to a balance appropriate for the equity method. According to the information provided, Gold has recognized dividend income on its 90 percent investment in Silver of $36,000 (1995) and $27,000 (1996). However, Silver's total operational income for these prior years, after adjustment for intercompany transfers, amounted to $102,000 and $145,000, respectively:

1995 reported operational income—Silver	$120,000
Less: Unrealized gains (30% markup × $60,000)	(18,000)
1995 operational income—Silver	$102,000
1996 reported operational income—Silver	$150,000
Add: 1995 gains actually realized in 1996 (from above)	18,000
Less: 1996 unrealized gains (25% markup × $90,000)	(22,500)
1996 operational income—Silver	$145,500

As the mutual relationship between these two companies did not exist in 1995, the solving of simultaneous equations is not applicable for this initial period.

Gold's equity income can be computed directly: 90 percent of Silver's $102,000 in realized earnings ($91,800) less the $2,000 amortization expense associated with this acquisition. The resulting $89,800 balance indicates the need for an additional accrual of $53,800 on the worksheet to correct the $36,000 figure recognized by Gold.

In contrast, Gold's 1996 equity accrual should reflect the mutual relationship that has come into existence. As the conventional approach is to be applied, simultaneous equations will be incorporated. These equations include Silver's 1996 operational income of $145,500 (calculated above) and the $238,000 operational income of Gold (reported earnings for the year less the annual amortization expense).

Gold's 1996 realized income = $238,000 + 90% of Silver's realized income

and

Silver's 1996 realized income = $145,500 + 10% of Gold's realized income

therefore

$$GRI = \$238,000 + .9\,(\$145,500 + .1\,GRI)$$

$$GRI = \$238,000 + \$130,950 + .09\,GRI$$

$$.91\,GRI = \$368,950$$

Gold's realized income = $405,440 (rounded)

Gold recorded income in 1996 of only $267,000 ($240,000 from operations plus $27,000 in dividend income). Since its realized income is computed to be $405,440 here, an additional accrual of $138,440 ($405,440 − $267,000) is required to reflect ownership in Silver during this period. Combined with the $53,800 accrual calculated previously for 1995, a total worksheet adjustment of $192,240 must be made for Gold (Entry *C1) to recognize the appropriate equity income for these two prior years.

*Consolidation Entry *C1 (Gold)*

Investment in Silver Company	192,240	
Retained Earnings, 1/1/97 (Gold Company)		192,240

To convert Gold's investment income figures for the two preceding years to equity income accruals.

Entry *C2. At the beginning of 1996, Silver obtained a 10 percent interest in Gold, an investment that has also been recorded using the cost method. To apply the conventional approach, Silver must solve the same simultaneous equations as Gold to determine the correct equity accrual. Using these equations, a realized income figure for Silver of $186,044 can be calculated for 1996.

$$\text{SRI} = \$145,500 + 10\% \text{ of GRI}$$

and

$$\text{GRI} = \$238,000 + 90\% \text{ of SRI}$$

therefore

$$\text{SRI} = \$145,500 + .1 \ (\$238,000 + .9 \ \text{SRI})$$

$$\text{SRI} = \$145,500 + \$23,800 + .09 \ \text{SRI}$$

$$.91 \ \text{SRI} = \$169,300$$

Silver's 1996 realized income = $186,044 (rounded)

Consequently, total investment income of $40,544 ($186,044 realized earnings less $145,500 operating income) should be recognized by Silver for 1996. However, only the $9,000 received in the form of dividends was actually recorded during that period. Therefore, Entry *C2 is included on the worksheet to rectify the consolidated figures for this preceding year by recording $31,544 in additional earnings ($40,544 − $9,000).

*Consolidation Entry *C2 (Silver)*

Investment in Gold Company	31,544	
Retained Earnings, 1/1/97 (Silver Company)		31,544

To convert Silver's investment income figures for the prior year to equity income.

Remaining Consolidation Entries. After the three previous entries have been recorded, the remainder of the worksheet entries to consolidate these companies are relatively uncomplicated.

Consolidation Entry S1

Common Stock (Silver Company)	200,000	
Retained Earnings, 1/1/97 (Silver Company)		
(as adjusted above)	618,044	
Investment in Silver Company (90%)		736,240
Noncontrolling Interest in Silver Company, 1/1/97 (10%).		81,804

To eliminate the beginning stockholders' equity accounts of Silver and to recognize a 10 percent noncontrolling interest in the subsidiary. Retained earnings has been adjusted for Entry *G and Entry *C2.

Consolidation Entry S2

Common Stock (Gold Company) (10%)	70,000	
Retained Earnings (Gold Company) (10% of		
1/1/97 balance as adjusted above)	111,544	
Investment in Gold Company (as adjusted above).		181,544

To eliminate the January 1, 1997, equity of Gold Company's shares being held by Silver Company. Retained earnings has been adjusted for Entry *C1.

Consolidation Entry S3

Common Stock (Bronze Company)	100,000	
Retained Earnings, 1/1/97 (Bronze Company)	200,000	
Investment in Bronze Company (60%)		180,000
Noncontrolling Interest in Bronze Company, 1/1/97 (40%)		120,000

To eliminate beginning stockholders' equity accounts of Bronze and
to recognize outside ownership of the company's remaining shares.
The investments of both Gold and Silver are being accounted for
concurrently through this one entry.

Consolidation Entry A

Goodwill	96,000	
Investment in Silver Company		76,000
Investment in Bronze Company		20,000

To recognize January 1, 1997, goodwill balances. Although $80,000
was originally allocated to goodwill in the purchase of Silver, the
recognition of amortization for 1995 and 1996 has reduced that figure
by $4,000 ($2,000 per year). Conversely, as of the beginning of 1997,
no expense has yet been recorded on the $20,000 in goodwill
associated with the acquisitions of Bronze. Thus, a total allocation of
$96,000 is appropriate as of January 1, 1997.

Consolidation Entry I

Dividend Income from Gold Company	10,000	
Dividend Income from Silver Company	36,000	
Dividend Income from Bronze Company	12,000	
Dividends Paid (Gold Company)		10,000
Dividends Paid (Silver Company)		36,000
Dividends Paid (Bronze Company)		12,000

To eliminate dividend payments made between the companies and
recorded as income based on application of the cost method.

Consolidation Entry E

Amortization Expense	4,000	
Goodwill		4,000

To recognize the 1997 amortization expense for the various goodwill
balances. Amortization of $2,000 is recognized on the $80,000
allocation made in the acquisition of Silver while an additional $1,000
expense is associated with each of the two investments made in
Bronze.

Consolidation Entry TI

Sales	200,000	
Cost of Goods Sold		200,000

To eliminate the intercompany transfer of inventory made in 1997 by
Silver.

Consolidation Entry G

Cost of Goods Sold	33,600	
Inventory		33,600

To eliminate intercompany gains remaining in the December 31, 1997,
inventory of Gold. The unrealized gain is 28 percent (the markup for
1997) of the $120,000 ending inventory balance held by the parent.

Consolidation Entry GL

Gain on Sale of Land 13,000
   Land 13,000
     To eliminate gain on intercompany transfer of land made from Gold
     Company to Bronze during the year.

Noncontrolling Interest in Bronze Company's Income. As in all past examples, the noncontrolling interest's claim to a portion of consolidated income must be calculated based on the realized income of the subsidiary. In this illustration, the combination is a father-son-grandson configuration; therefore, computation of income must begin with Bronze. Since this subsidiary has neither unrealized intercompany gains nor amortization expense, the $90,000 income figure reported in Exhibit 7–4 is applicable. Thus, $36,000 ($90,000 × 40%) should be reported as the noncontrolling interest's share of Bronze's 1997 income.

Noncontrolling Interest in Silver Company's Income. Because of the mutual ownership with Gold, Silver's realized income for 1997 can only be determined by solving two simultaneous equations (since the conventional approach is being applied). Operational income figures for both parties are required as a prerequisite for this procedure.

Silver's Operational Income

Sales	$ 600,000
Cost of goods sold	(300,000)
Operating expenses	(100,000)
Amortization expense—purchase of Bronze	(1,000)
Equity in earnings of Bronze (30%)	27,000
1996 intercompany gains currently realized (Entry *G)	22,500
1997 intercompany unrealized gains being deferred (Entry G)	(33,600)
Operational income	$ 214,900

Gold's Operational Income

Sales	$ 800,000
Cost of goods sold	(380,000)
Operating expenses	(193,000)
Amortization expense—purchase of Silver	(2,000)
Amortization expense—purchase of Bronze	(1,000)
Equity in earnings of Bronze (30%)	27,000
Operational income	$ 251,000

Using these two income balances, the simultaneous equations can be constructed to determine Silver's realized income for the current year. This total serves as the basis for making the noncontrolling interest calculation.

$$SRI = \$214,900 + 10\% \text{ of } GRI$$

and

$$GRI = \$251,000 + 90\% \text{ of } SRI$$

therefore

$$SRI = \$214,900 + .1\,(\$251,000 + .9\,SRI)$$

$$SRI = \$214,900 + \$25,100 + .09\,SRI$$

$$.91\,SRI = \$240,000$$

Silver's realized income $= \$263,736$

Noncontrolling interest in Silver's income (10%) $= \$26,374$ (rounded)

b. For Bronze, no differences exist between book values and tax basis. No computation of deferred income taxes is required; thus this company's separate tax return is relatively straightforward. The $90,000 income figure being reported creates a current tax liability of $36,000 (based on the 40 percent tax rate).

In contrast, the consolidated tax return filed for Gold and Silver must include the following financial information. Where applicable, figures reported in Exhibit 7–4 have been combined for the two companies.

Tax Return Information—Consolidated Return

Sales	$1,400,000	
Less: Intercompany sales (1997)	(200,000)	$1,200,000
Cost of goods sold	680,000	
Less: 1997 intercompany purchases	(200,000)	
Less: 1996 intercompany gains recognized in 1997 (90,000 × 25%)	(22,500)	
Add: 1997 unrealized intercompany gains (120,000 × 28%)	33,600	491,100
Gross profit		708,900
Operating expenses (amortization is removed)		293,000
Operating income		$ 415,900
Other income (since Bronze is not part of affiliated group):		
Gain on sale of land		13,000
Dividend income—Bronze Company	$ 12,000	
Less: 80% deduction	(9,600)	2,400
Taxable income		$ 431,300
Tax rate		40%
Income tax payable by Gold Company and Silver Company for 1997		$ 172,520

A total of $208,520 must be paid to the government in 1997 by the members of this business combination ($36,000 by Bronze and $172,520 in connection with the consolidated return of Gold and Silver). However, according to *FASB Statement 109*, accounting for deferred income tax assets and/or liabilities is also necessitated by any temporary differences that originate or reverse during the year. *In this illustration, only the dividend payments from Bronze and the unrealized gain on the sale of land to Bronze actually create such differences.* Other items encountered do not lead to deferred income taxes:

- Because a consolidated return is being filed by Gold and Silver, the unrealized inventory gains are deferred for both tax purposes and financial reporting so that no difference is created.
- The dividends paid from Silver to Gold are not subject to taxation because these distributions were made between members of an affiliated group.
- Amortization expense on goodwill is never deductible so that, once again, no temporary difference results.

However, recognition of a deferred tax liability is required because Bronze's realized income ($54,000 after income tax expense of $36,000) is greater than its $20,000 dividend distribution. Gold and Silver own 60 percent of this subsidiary indicating that $32,400 ($54,000 × 60%) of its income is included on the consolidated income statement. Since this figure is $20,400 larger than the amount of dividends paid to Giant and Silver ($12,000 or 60% of $20,000), a deferred tax liability is required. The temporary difference is actually $4,080 (20% of $20,400) because of the 80 percent dividend deduction. The future tax effect on this difference is $1,632 based on the 40 percent tax rate being applied.

A deferred tax asset is also needed in connection with the intercompany sale of land from Gold to Bronze. Separate returns are being filed by these companies. Thus, the gain is taxed immediately, although this $13,000 will not be realized for reporting purposes until a future resale occurs. From an accounting perspective, the tax of $5,200 ($13,000 × 40%) is being prepaid in 1997.

Recognition of the current payable as well as the two deferrals leads to an income tax expense of $204,952:

Income Tax Expense	204,952	
Deferred Income Tax—Asset	5,200	
Income Taxes Payable—Current		208,520
Deferred Income Tax—Liability		1,632

Questions

1. What is meant by a father-son-grandson relationship?
2. When an indirect ownership is present, why is a specific ordering necessary for determining the realized incomes of the component corporations?

3. Able Company owns 70 percent of the outstanding voting stock of Baker Company which, in turn, holds 80 percent of Carter Company. Carter possesses 60 percent of the capital stock of Dexter Company. How much income actually accrues to the consolidated entity from each of these companies after giving consideration to the various noncontrolling interests?

4. How does the presence of an indirect ownership (such as a father-son-grandson relationship) affect the mechanical aspects of the consolidation process?

5. What is the difference between a connecting affiliation and a mutual ownership?

6. When a mutual ownership exists, two different views of this relationship can be adopted. What are these two views and how do they differ?

7. In accounting for mutual ownerships, why is the treasury stock approach more prevalent in practice than the conventional approach?

8. Alexander Company holds 80 percent of the outstanding common stock of Baxter Company. Baxter, in turn, owns 30 percent of the stock of Alexander. How is the realized income of these two companies computed if the conventional approach is being utilized?

9. For income tax purposes, how is an affiliated group defined?

10. What are the advantages to a business combination filing a consolidated tax return? Considering these advantages, why do some members of a business combination file separate tax returns?

11. Why is the allocation of the income tax expense figure between the members of a business combination important? By what methods can this allocation be made?

12. If separate income tax returns are filed by a parent and its subsidiary, why will the parent frequently have to recognize deferred income taxes? Why might the subsidiary have to recognize deferred income taxes?

13. In a recent acquisition, the consolidated value of a subsidiary's assets exceeded the basis appropriate for tax purposes. How does this difference affect the consolidated balance sheet?

14. Jones acquires Wilson, in part, because the new subsidiary has an unused net operating loss carryforward for tax purposes. How does this carryforward affect the consolidated figures at the date of acquisition?

15. A subsidiary is acquired that has a net operating loss carryforward. The related deferred income tax asset is $230,000. Because the parent feels that the chances are more likely that a portion of this carryforward will never be used, a valuation allowance of $150,000 is also recognized. At the end of the first year of ownership, the parent reassesses the situation and determines that the valuation allowance should be reduced to $110,000. What effect does this change have on the reporting of the business combination?

Library Assignment

1. Locate PepsiCo, Inc., or the Philip Morris Companies, Inc., in the most recent edition of *Moody's Industrial Manual*. Find at least three examples of father-son-grandson ownership patterns. By reading the history of the company in the manual, determine, if possible, the method by which the parents gained control over the three grandson organizations.

   Locate at least one other company in *Moody's Industrial Manual* with a considerable number of subsidiaries. Are most of these subsidiaries controlled directly by the parent or indirectly?

2. Read the following as well as any other published materials describing the various possible methods of allocating income tax expense among the members of a business combination:

   "How to Allocate a Consolidated Tax Liability among Members of the Affiliated Group," *The Practical Accountant*, October 1986.

   "Uncharted Territory: Subsidiary Financial Reporting," *Journal of Accountancy*, October 1989.

   Write a report explaining the various methods by which the income tax expense of a business combination can be assigned to its component companies.

Problems

1. In a father-son-grandson business combination, which of the following statements is true?
   a. The father company must always have its realized income computed first.
   b. The computation of a company's realized income has no effect on the realized income of other companies within a business combination.
   c. A father-son-grandson configuration does not require consolidation unless one company owns shares in all of the other companies.
   d. All companies that are solely in subsidiary positions must have their realized income computed first within the consolidation process.

2. A subsidiary owns shares of its parent company. Which of the following is true concerning the treasury stock approach?
   a. It is considered to be more difficult to apply than the conventional approach.
   b. The original cost of the subsidiary's investment is a reduction in consolidated stockholders' equity.
   c. The subsidiary accrues income on its investment by using the equity method.

d. The treasury stock approach eliminates these shares entirely within the consolidation process.

3. On January 1, 1995, a subsidiary buys 10 percent of the outstanding shares of its parent company. Although the total book value and fair market value of the parent's net assets were $4 million, the purchase price for these shares was $420,000. Goodwill is amortized in this business combination over a 40-year period. During 1995, the parent reported operational income (no investment income was included) of $510,000 while paying dividends of $140,000. How are these shares reported at December 31, 1995, if the treasury stock approach is used?

    a. The investment is recorded as $457,000 at the end of 1995 and then eliminated for consolidation purposes.

    b. Consolidated stockholders' equity is reduced by $457,000.

    c. The investment is recorded as $456,500 at the end of 1995 and then eliminated for consolidation purposes.

    d. Consolidated stockholders' equity is reduced by $420,000.

4. Which of the following is correct for two companies that want to file a consolidated tax return as an affiliated group?

    a. One company must hold at least 51 percent of the other company's voting stock.

    b. One company must hold at least 65 percent of the other company's voting stock.

    c. One company must hold at least 80 percent of the other company's voting stock.

    d. A consolidated tax return cannot be filed unless one company owns 100 percent of the voting stock of the other.

5. How does the amortization of goodwill affect the computation of income taxes on a consolidated tax return?

    a. It is a deductible expense but only if the parent owns 80 percent of the voting stock of the subsidiary.

    b. It is a temporary tax difference that creates a tax effect in subsequent years.

    c. It is never a deductible item.

    d. It is deductible for tax purposes but only if a consolidated tax return is being filed.

6. Which of the following is not a reason for two companies to file separate tax returns?

    a. The parent owns 68 percent of the subsidiary.

    b. They have no intercompany transactions.

    c. Intercompany dividends are only tax free on separate returns.

    d. Neither company has historically had an operating tax loss.

7. Bassett Company owns 80 percent of Crimson Corporation. Crimson Corporation owns 90 percent of Damson, Inc. Operational income totals for 1995 follow; these figures contain no investment income. Amortization

expense was not required by any of these purchases. Included in Damson's income is a $40,000 unrealized gain on intercompany transfers to Crimson.

	Bassett	Crimson	Damson
Operational income	$300,000	$200,000	$200,000

What is Bassett's realized income for the year?
a. $575,200.
b. $588,000.
c. $596,400.
d. $604,000.

8. Gardner Corporation holds 80 percent of Healthstone which, in turn, owns 80 percent of Icede. Operational income figures (without investment income) as well as unrealized upstream gains included in the income for the current year follow:

	Gardner	Healthstone	Icede
Operational income	$400,000	$300,000	$220,000
Unrealized gains	50,000	30,000	60,000

On a consolidated income statement for the year, what balance is reported for the noncontrolling interest in the subsidiaries' income?
a. $ 86,000.
b. $100,000.
c. $111,600.
d. $120,800.

9. Nesbitt Corporation owns 90 percent of Jones, Inc., while Jones owns 10 percent of the outstanding shares of Nesbitt. No goodwill or any other allocations were recognized in connection with either of these acquisitions. Nesbitt reports operational income of $190,000 for 1995 whereas Jones earned $70,000 during the same period. No investment income is included within either of these income totals. On a consolidated income statement, what is the noncontrolling interest in Jones's income if the conventional approach is being used?
a. $7,000.
b. $7,740.
c. $8,900.
d. $9,780.

10. Horton, Inc., owns 90 percent of the voting stock of Juvyn Corporation. The purchase price was in excess of book value and fair market value by

$80,000. Juvyn holds 20 percent of the voting stock of Horton. That purchase price was in excess of book value and fair market value by $20,000. All goodwill is to be amortized over a 20-year period.

During the current year, Horton reported operational income of $160,000 and dividend income from Juvyn of $27,000. At the same time, Juvyn reported operational income of $50,000 and dividend income from Horton of $14,000.

If the treasury stock approach is utilized, what will be reported as the Noncontrolling Interest in Juvyn's Net Income?

a. $5,000.
b. $5,400.
c. $6,300.
d. $6,400.

11. What would be the answer to problem 10 if the conventional approach were being used?

a. $9,781.
b. $9,964.
c. $10,414.
d. $11,864.

12. Cremmins, Inc., owns 60 percent of Anderson. During the current year, Anderson reported net income of $200,000 but paid a total cash dividend of only $40,000. What deferred income tax liability must be recognized in the consolidated balance sheet? Assume the tax rate is 30 percent.

a. $5,760.
b. $9,600.
c. $12,840.
d. $28,800.

13. Prybylos, Inc., owns 90 percent of Station Corporation. Both companies have been profitable for many years. During the current year, the parent sold merchandise costing $70,000 to the subsidiary for $100,000. At the end of the year, 20 percent of this merchandise was still being held. Assume that the tax rate is 25 percent and that separate tax returns are filed. What deferred income tax asset is created?

a. –0–.
b. $300.
c. $1,500.
d. $7,500.

14. What would be the answer to problem 13 if a consolidated tax return were filed?

a. –0–.
b. $300.
c. $1,500.
d. $7,500.

15. Hastoon Company purchases all of Zedner Company for $420,000 in cash. On that date, the subsidiary has net assets with a $400,000 fair market value but a $300,000 book value and tax basis. The tax rate is 30 percent. Neither company has reported any deferred income tax assets or liabilities. What amount of goodwill should be recognized on the date of the acquisition?

   a. $20,000.
   b. $36,000.
   c. $50,000.
   d. $120,000.

16. On January 1, 1995, Tree Company purchased 70 percent of Limb Company's outstanding voting stock for $250,000. Limb had a $300,000 reported book value on that date. Subsequently, on January 1, 1996, Limb Company acquired 70 percent of Leaf Company for $90,000 when Leaf had a $100,000 book value. All goodwill is assumed to have a maximum life.

   These companies report the following financial information. Investment income figures are not included.

	1995	1996	1997
Sales:			
Tree Company.	$400,000	$500,000	$650,000
Limb Company	200,000	280,000	400,000
Leaf Company.	Not available	160,000	210,000
Expenses:			
Tree Company.	$310,000	420,000	510,000
Limb Company	160,000	220,000	335,000
Leaf Company.	Not available	150,000	180,000
Dividends paid:			
Tree Company.	$ 20,000	40,000	50,000
Limb Company	10,000	20,000	20,000
Leaf Company.	Not available	2,000	10,000

Assume that the following questions are each independent:

a. If all companies use the equity method for internal reporting purposes, what is the December 31, 1996, balance in the Tree's Investment in Limb Company account?

b. If all companies use the cost method to account for their investments, what adjustments must Limb and Tree make to their beginning retained earnings balances on the 1997 consolidation worksheet?

c. What is the consolidated net income for this business combination for the year of 1997 prior to any reduction for the noncontrolling interests' share of the subsidiaries' net income?

d. What is the noncontrolling interests' share of the consolidated net income in 1997?

e. Assume that Limb made intercompany inventory transfers to Tree that result in the following unrealized gains at the end of each year:

Date	Amount
12/31/95	$10,000
12/31/96	16,000
12/31/97	25,000

What is the realized income of Limb in 1996 and 1997, respectively?

f. Assuming the same unrealized gains as presented in part *e.*, what worksheet adjustment must be made to the January 1, 1997, Retained Earnings account of Tree if that company has applied the cost method to its investment?

17. On January 1, 1995, Uncle Company purchased 80 percent of Nephew Company's capital stock for $500,000 in cash and other assets. Nephew had a book value of $600,000 on that date. Goodwill allocations are amortized over a 10-year period.

On January 1, 1997, Nephew acquired 30 percent of Uncle for $280,000. Uncle's appropriately adjusted book value as of that date was $900,000.

Operational income figures (includes no investment income) for these two companies follow. In addition, Uncle pays $20,000 in dividends to shareholders each year while Nephew distributes $5,000 annually.

Year	Uncle Company	Nephew Company
1995	$ 90,000	$30,000
1996	120,000	40,000
1997	140,000	50,000

The following questions should be viewed as independent problems:

a. Assume that the treasury stock approach is being utilized and that Uncle applies the equity method to account for this investment in Nephew. What is the Income of the Subsidiary being recognized by Uncle in 1997?

b. If the treasury stock approach is applied, what is the noncontrolling interest's share of the subsidiary's 1997 income?

c. Assume that the conventional approach is utilized and that Uncle applies the equity method to this investment in Nephew. What is the Income of the Subsidiary being recognized by Uncle in 1997?

d. If the conventional approach is being applied, what is the noncontrolling interest's share of the subsidiary's 1997 net income?

18. Gaddy, Inc., obtained 60 percent of Mabry Corporation on January 1, 1995. Annual amortization of $25,000 is to be recorded on the allocations made in connection with this purchase. On January 1, 1996, Mabry acquired 90 percent of Tucson Company's voting stock. Amortization on this second purchase amounted to $2,000 per year.

    For the year of 1998, these three companies reported the following information as accumulated by their separate accounting systems. Operating income figures do not include any investment or dividend income.

	Operating Income	Dividends Paid
Gaddy	$220,000	$120,000
Mabry	160,000	50,000
Tucson.	90,000	10,000

Required:

a. On consolidated financial statements for 1998, what is the noncontrolling interests' share of the subsidiaries' income?
b. What is consolidated net income for 1998?
c. If Mabry's operating income figures for 1998 include a net unrealized gain of $12,000, what is consolidated net income for that year?

19. Fonseca owns 80 percent of the voting stock of Carson. The purchase price exceeded the underlying book value of Carson's assets and liabilities by $60,000. At the same time, Carson holds a 30 percent interest in the outstanding shares of Fonseca. This stock was bought at a price $10,000 in excess of underlying book value. All goodwill is to be amortized over a useful life of 10 years.

    Both of these companies use the cost method to record their investments for internal reporting purposes. During the current year, the following information was reported:

	Operating Income	Dividend Income	Total Reported Income
Fonseca	$80,000	$16,000 (all from Carson)	$96,000
Carson	30,000	15,000 (all from Fonseca)	45,000

Required:

a. If the conventional approach is to be utilized, what reduction should be recorded in the consolidated income statement as the noncontrolling interest in Carson's net income?
b. If the treasury stock approach is applied, what reduction should be recorded in the consolidated income statement as the noncontrolling interest in Carson's net income?

20. Baxter, Inc., owns 90 percent of Wisconsin, Inc., and 20 percent of the Cleveland Company. Wisconsin, in turn, holds 60 percent of the outstanding stock of Cleveland. Total annual amortization of $17,000 resulted from the purchases made by Baxter. During the current year, Cleveland sold a variety of inventory items to Wisconsin for $40,000 although the original cost had been $30,000. Of this total, $12,000 in inventory (at transfer price) was still held by Wisconsin at year's end.

During this same period, Wisconsin sold merchandise to Baxter for $100,000 although the original cost had been only $70,000. At the end of the year, $40,000 these goods (at the transfer price) were still on hand.

The cost method is used to record each of these investments. No other investments are held by any of the companies.

Using the following separate income statements, determine the figures that would appear on a consolidated income statement.

	Baxter	Wisconsin	Cleveland
Sales.	$1,000,000	$ 450,000	$ 280,000
Cost of goods sold	(670,000)	(280,000)	(190,000)
Expenses.	(110,000)	(60,000)	(30,000)
Dividend income:			
Wisconsin	36,000	–0–	–0–
Cleveland	4,000	12,000	–0–
Net income.	$ 260,000	$ 122,000	$ 60,000

21. Alice Corporation bought 90 percent of the outstanding shares of Wonderland, Inc. several years ago for $610,000. Wonderland, in turn, acquired 10 percent of Alice for $111,000. Annual amortization expense of $12,000 resulted from Alice's purchase. The cost method is used to record each of these investments. No other investments are held by either company.

Required:

a. Based on the following separate income statements, produce the figures that would appear on a consolidated income statement. Assume that the treasury approach is being used.

	Alice	Wonderland
Sales	$1,300,000	$ 500,000
Cost of goods sold	(750,000)	(270,000)
Expenses	(220,000)	(120,000)
Dividend income	45,000	16,000
Net income	$ 375,000	$ 126,000

b. Assuming that the treasury stock approach is still in use, what are the consolidated totals for the following two accounts?

	Alice	Wonderland
Common stock	$880,000	$350,000
Treasury stock	–0–	–0–

22. The following figures are reported by Up and its 80 percent owned subsidiary (Down) for the year ending December 31, 1995. Down paid dividends of $30,000 during this period.

	Up	Down
Sales	$600,000	$300,000
Cost of goods sold	300,000	140,000
Operating expenses	174,000	60,000
Dividend income	24,000	–0–
Net income	$150,000	$100,000

Amortization expense relating to Up's takeover of Down is $30,000 per year. In 1994, unrealized gains of $30,000 on upstream transfers of $90,000 were deferred into 1995. In 1995, unrealized gains of $40,000 on upsteam transfers of $110,000 were deferred into 1996.

a. What figures appear in a consolidated income statement?

b. What income tax expense should be shown in the consolidated income statement if separate returns are filed? Assume that the tax rate is 30 percent.

23. Clarke has a controlling interest in the outstanding stock of Rogers. At the end of the current year, the following information has been accumulated for these two companies:

	Operating Income	Dividends Paid
Clarke	$500,000 (includes a $90,000 net unrealized gain on intercompany inven- tory transfers)	$90,000
Rogers	$240,000	$80,000

Amortization of goodwill in connection with Clarke's purchase of Rogers amounts to $25,000 per year.

Clarke uses the cost method to account for the investment in Rogers. Neither dividend nor other investment income is included in the operating income figures just presented. The effective tax rate for both companies is 40 percent.

Required:

a. Assume that Clarke owns 100 percent of the voting stock of Rogers and that a consolidated tax return is being filed. What amount of income taxes would this affiliated group pay in connection with the current period?

b. Assume that Clarke owns 92 percent of the voting stock of Rogers and that a consolidated tax return is being filed. What amount of income taxes would this affiliated group pay in connection with the current period?

c. Assume that Clarke owns 80 percent of the voting stock of Rogers but the companies have elected to file separate tax returns. What is the total amount of income taxes that these two companies pay for the current period?

d. Assume that Clarke owns 70 percent of the voting stock of Rogers so that separate tax returns are required. What is the total amount of income tax expense to be recognized in the consolidated income statement for the current period?

e. Assume that Clarke owns 70 percent of the voting stock of Rogers so that separate tax returns are required. What amount of income taxes does Clarke have to pay in connection with the current year?

24. On January 1, 1995, Piranto acquires 90 percent of the outstanding shares of Slinton. Goodwill of $60,000 is appropriately recognized as a component of the purchase price. This goodwill is amortized at the rate of $4,000 per year.

Financial information for these two companies for the years of 1995 and 1996 are as follows:

	1995	1996
Piranto Company:		
Sales.	$600,000	$800,000
Operational expenses	400,000	500,000
Unrealized gains as of end of year		
(included in above figures)	120,000	150,000
Dividend income—Slinton Company	18,000	36,000
Slinton Company:		
Sales.	200,000	250,000
Operational expenses	120,000	150,000
Dividends paid	20,000	40,000

Assume that a tax rate of 40 percent is applicable to both companies.

Required:

a. On consolidated financial statements for 1996, what would be the income tax expense and the income tax currently payable if Piranto and Slinton file a consolidated tax return as an affiliated group?

b. On consolidated financial statements for 1996, what would be the income tax expense and income tax currently payable for each company if they choose to file separate returns?

25. Lake acquired a controlling interest in Boxwood several years ago. Amortization of goodwill resulting from this purchase amounted to $38,000 per year. During the current fiscal period, these two companies have individually reported the following income figures (exclusive of any investment income):

Lake	$300,000
Boxwood	100,000

Lake paid a cash dividend of $90,000 during the current year while Boxwood distributed $10,000.

Boxwood sells inventory to Lake each period. Unrealized intercompany gains of $18,000 were present in Lake's beginning inventory for the current year while its ending inventory carried $32,000 in unrealized profits.

The following questions should be viewed as independent situations. The effective tax rate for both companies is 40 percent.

a. If Lake owns a 60 percent interest in Boxwood, what total income tax expense must be reported on a consolidated income statement for this period?

b. If Lake owns a 60 percent interest in Boxwood, what total amount of income taxes must be paid by these two companies for the current year?

c. If Lake owns a 90 percent interest in Boxwood and a consolidated tax return is being filed, what amount of income tax expense would be reported on a consolidated income statement for the year?

d. Assume that Lake owns a 90 percent interest in Boxwood while Boxwood possesses a 20 percent interest in Lake. No amortization expense is to be recognized in connection with Boxwood's acquisition of Lake. Using the conventional approach to mutual ownership, determine the noncontrolling interest in Boxwood's income for the year. Ignore income taxes.

26. Garrison holds a controlling interest in the outstanding stock of Robertson. For the current year, the following information has been gathered about these two companies:

	Garrison	Robertson
Operating income.	$300,000 (includes a $50,000 net unrealized gain on an intercompany transfer)	$200,000
Annual amortization expense—Investment in Robertson	30,000	–0–
Dividends paid	32,000	50,000
Tax rate	40%	40%

Garrison uses the cost method to account for the investment in Robertson. Dividend income for the current year is not included in Garrison's operating income figure.

Required:

a. Assume that Garrison owns 80 percent of the voting stock of Robertson. On a consolidated tax return, what amount of income taxes would be paid?

b. Assume that Garrison owns 80 percent of the voting stock of Robertson. On separate tax returns, what is the total amount of income taxes to be paid?

c. Assume that Garrison owns 70 percent of the voting stock of Robertson. What is the total amount of income tax expense to be recognized on a consolidated income statement?

d. Assume that Garrison holds 60 percent of the voting stock of Robertson. On a separate income tax return, what amount of income taxes would Garrison have to pay?

27. Leftwich recently purchased all of the stock of Kew Corporation and is now in the process of consolidating the financial data of this new subsidiary. Leftwich paid a total of $650,000 for the company, which has the following accounts:

	Fair Market Value	Tax Basis
Accounts receivable	$110,000	$110,000
Inventory	130,000	130,000
Land	100,000	100,000
Buildings.	180,000	140,000
Equipment	200,000	150,000
Liabilities	220,000	220,000

Assume that the effective tax rate is 30 percent. On a consolidated balance sheet prepared immediately after this takeover, what impact would the acquisition of Kew have on the individual asset and liability accounts reported by the business combination?

28. House Corporation was created in 1947 and has been operating profitably since that time. At the beginning of 1995, House purchased a 70 percent ownership in Room Company. Room's financial accounts as of that date were as follows:

	Book Value	Fair Market Value
Cash and receivables	$300,000	$300,000
Inventory	380,000	380,000
Buildings (20-year life)	200,000	260,000
Equipment (4-year life)	160,000	140,000
Land	260,000	260,000
Liabilities	510,000	510,000

House paid $701,000 in cash for this investment. Goodwill is to be amortized over the maximum allowable life.

During 1995 and 1996, Room earned net income totaling $160,000 while paying cash dividends of $50,000.

House has made regular acquisitions of inventory from Room at a markup of 25 percent more than cost. House's purchases during 1995 and 1996 as well as related ending inventory balances are as follows:

Year	Intercompany Purchases	Retained Intercompany Inventory— End of Year
1995	$120,000	$40,000
1996	150,000	60,000

On January 1, 1997, House and Room acted together as coacquirers of 80 percent of the outstanding common stock of Wall Company. The total price of these shares was $200,000, indicating that no goodwill or other specific valuation allocations were needed. Each company put up one half of this purchase price.

During 1997, House acquired additional inventory at a price of $200,000 from Room. Of this merchandise, 45 percent is still being held at year's end.

Room loaned Wall $40,000 on a 10 percent note on October 1, 1997. Although interest has been properly recorded, no part of this debt has been repaid as of December 31, 1997.

Wall's preferred stock is owned entirely by outside parties. This stock pays an 8 percent annual cumulative dividend. The stock is neither participating nor voting, although it does have a call value of 106 percent of par value. No dividends are currently in arrears on these shares.

Following are the financial records for these three companies for 1997. Prepare a consolidation worksheet. The partial equity method based on *operational earnings* has been applied to each investment.

	House Corporation	Room Company	Wall Company
Sales and other revenues	$ 900,000	$ 700,000	$ 300,000
Cost of goods sold	(551,120)	(300,000)	(140,000)
Operating expenses	(218,400)	(268,400)	(90,000)
Income of Room Company	92,120	–0–	–0–
Income of Wall Company	26,400	26,400	–0–
Net income	$ 249,000	$ 158,000	$ 70,000
Retained earnings, 1/1/97	$ 820,000	$ 590,000	$ 153,000
Net income (above)	249,000	158,000	70,000
Dividends paid	(100,000)	(96,000)	(50,000)
Retained earnings, 12/31/97	$ 969,000	$ 652,000	$ 173,000
Cash and receivables	$ 244,880	$ 354,000	$ 70,000
Inventory	390,200	320,000	103,000
Investment in Room Company	802,920	–0–	–0–
Investment in Wall Company	108,000	108,000	–0–
Buildings	385,000	320,000	144,000
Equipment	310,000	130,000	88,000
Land	180,000	300,000	16,000
Liabilities	632,000	570,000	98,000
Preferred stock	–0–	–0–	50,000
Common stock	820,000	310,000	100,000
Retained earnings, 12/31/97	969,000	652,000	173,000

29. Mighty Company purchased a 60 percent interest in Lowly Company on January 1, 1992, for $400,000 in cash. Lowly's book value at that date was reported as $500,000. Any goodwill resulting from this transaction was to be amortized over 20 years. Subsequently, on January 1, 1993, Lowly acquired a 20 percent interest in Mighty. The price of $240,000 was equivalent to 20 percent of Mighty's book value.

Neither company has paid dividends since these acquisitions occurred. On January 1, 1998, Lowly's book value was $800,000, a figure which rises to $840,000 (common stock of $300,000 and retained earnings of $540,000) by the end of the year. Mighty's book value was $1.7 million at the beginning of 1998 and $1.8 million (common stock of $1 million and retained earnings of $800,000) at December 31, 1998. No intercompany transactions have occurred and no additional stock has been sold. Each company applies the cost method in accounting for the individual investments.

Required:

a. What worksheet entries are required to consolidate these two companies for 1998? What is the noncontrolling interest in the subsidiary's net income for this year? Assume that the treasury stock approach is utilized.

b. Answer the same questions as in requirement *a.* but assume that the conventional approach is being applied to the mutual ownership.

c. How do the answers in requirement *b.* differ if, on January 1, 1996, Mighty sold equipment (costing $80,000) with a remaining life of 10 years and a $20,000 book value to Lowly for $50,000 in cash?

 30. On January 1, 1995, Travers Company purchased 90 percent of the outstanding stock of Yarrow Company. On the same date, Yarrow acquired an 80 percent interest in Stookey Company. Although both of these investments are to be accounted for by applying the cost method, no dividends are distributed by either Yarrow or Stookey during 1995 or 1996. Travers follows a policy of paying out cash dividends each year equal to 40 percent of operational earnings. Reported income totals for 1995 are as follows:

Travers Company	$300,000
Yarrow Company	160,000
Stookey Company	120,000

Goodwill is to be amortized over 20 years.

Following are the 1996 financial statements for these three companies. Stookey has made numerous transfers of inventory to Yarrow since the takeover: $80,000 (1995) and $100,000 (1996). These transactions include the same markup applicable to Stookey's outside sales. In each of these years, Yarrow has carried 20 percent of this inventory into the succeeding year before disposing of it.

An effective tax rate of 45 percent is applicable to all companies.

	Travers Company	Yarrow Company	Stookey Company
Sales	$ 900,000	$ 600,000	$ 500,000
Cost of goods sold	(480,000)	(320,000)	(260,000)
Operating expenses	(100,000)	(80,000)	(140,000)
Net income	$ 320,000	$ 200,000	$ 100,000

	Travers Company	Yarrow Company	Stookey Company
Retained earnings, 1/1/96.	$ 700,000	$ 600,000	$300,000
Net income (above)	320,000	200,000	100,000
Dividends paid	(128,000)	–0–	–0–
Retained earnings, 12/31/96.	$ 892,000	$ 800,000	$400,000
Current assets	$ 398,000	$ 360,000	$280,000
Investment in Yarrow Company	766,000	–0–	–0–
Investment in Stookey Company	–0–	364,000	–0–
Land, buildings, and equipment (net)	949,000	836,000	520,000
Total assets.	$2,113,000	$1,560,000	$800,000
Liabilities	$ 721,000	$ 460,000	$200,000
Common stock	500,000	300,000	200,000
Retained earnings, 12/31/96.	892,000	800,000	400,000
Total liabilities and equities.	$2,113,000	$1,560,000	$800,000

Required:

a. Prepare the 1996 consolidation worksheet for this business combination. Ignore income tax effects.

b. Determine the amount of income taxes to be paid by Travers and Yarrow on a consolidated tax return for the year of 1996.

c. Determine the amount of income taxes to be paid by Stookey on a separate tax return for the year of 1996.

d. Based on the answers to requirements *b.* and *c.*, what journal entry would be made by this combination to record 1996 income taxes?

31. Several years ago, Daniel Company purchased 90 percent of the outstanding voting stock of Murphy, Inc. At approximately the same time, Murphy acquired 10 percent of the common stock of Daniel. In both cases, the price paid was equal to the book value and fair market value of the underlying net assets. Therefore, no allocations were made to either goodwill or specific asset or liability accounts.

   Prior to the current year, the book value of Daniel has increased by $400,000 since the date of acquisition while Murphy's book value has risen by $150,000.

   Both companies use the cost method to account for their investments.

Required:

Using the following information for the year of 1995, prepare a consolidation worksheet based on the conventional approach to mutual holdings.

	Daniel	Murphy
Sales.	$ 600,000	$ 220,000
Expenses.	(400,000)	(126,000)
Dividend income	18,000	9,000
Net income.	$ 218,000	$ 103,000
Retained earnings, 1/1/95.	$ 850,000	$ 200,000
Net income.	218,000	103,000
Dividends paid	(90,000)	(20,000)
Retained earnings	$ 978,000	$ 283,000
Cash.	$ 20,000	$ 40,000
Receivables.	178,000	96,000
Inventory.	125,000	108,000
Investment in Murphy	189,000	–0–
Investment in Daniel.	–0–	50,000
Property, plant, and equipment (net)	651,000	361,000
Total assets.	$1,163,000	$ 655,000
Liabilities	$ 135,000	$ 212,000
Common stock	50,000	160,000
Retained earnings, 12/31/95.	978,000	283,000
Total liabilities and equities.	$1,163,000	$ 655,000

32. Politan Company acquired an 80 percent interest in Soludan several years ago. Any portion of the purchase price in excess of the corresponding book value of Soludan Company was assigned to goodwill. This intangible asset has subsequently undergone annual amortization based on a maximum possible life. In recent years, regular intercompany inventory sales have transpired between the two companies. No payment has yet been made on the latest transfer.

Following are the individual financial statements for the two companies as well as consolidated totals for the current year.

	Politan Company	Soludan Company	Consolidated Totals
Sales.	$ 800,000	$ 600,000	$1,280,000
Cost of goods sold.	(500,000)	(400,000)	(784,000)
Operating expenses	(100,000)	(100,000)	(202,000)
Income of Soludan	80,000	–0–	–0–
Noncontrolling interest in Soludan Company's income	–0–	–0–	(19,200)
Net income	$ 280,000	$ 100,000	$ 274,800

	Politan Company	Soludan Company	Consolidated Totals
Retained earnings, 1/1	$ 620,000	$290,000	$ 607,600
Net income (above)	280,000	100,000	274,800
Dividends paid	(70,000)	(20,000)	(70,000)
Retained earnings, 12/31	$ 830,000	$370,000	$ 812,400
Cash and receivables.	$ 240,000	$ 90,000	$ 310,000
Inventory.	190,000	160,000	338,000
Investment in Soludan Company	440,000	–0–	–0–
Land, buildings, and equipment	380,000	260,000	640,000
Goodwill	–0–	–0–	72,000
Total assets.	$1,250,000	$510,000	$1,360,000
Liabilities.	$ 270,000	$ 60,000	$ 310,000
Noncontrolling interest in Soludan Company	–0–	–0–	87,600
Common stock	120,000	80,000	120,000
Additional paid-in capital.	30,000	–0–	30,000
Retained earnings (above)	830,000	370,000	812,400
Total liabilities and equities.	$1,250,000	$510,000	$1,360,000

Required:

a. By what method is Politan accounting for its investment in Soludan?

b. What is the balance of the unrealized inventory gain being deferred at the end of the current period?

c. What figure was originally allocated to goodwill?

d. What was the amount of the current year intercompany inventory sales?

e. Were the intercompany inventory sales made upstream or downstream?

f. What was the balance of the intercompany liability at the end of the current year?

g. What unrealized gain was deferred into the current year from the preceding period?

h. The consolidated Retained Earnings account shows a balance of $607,600 rather than the $620,000 reported by the parent. What creates this difference?

i. How was the ending Noncontrolling interest in Soludan Company computed?

j. Assuming a tax rate of 40 percent, what income tax journal entry is recorded if these two companies prepare a consolidated tax return?

k. Assuming a tax rate of 40 percent, what income tax journal entry is recorded if these two companies prepare separate tax returns?

33. On January 1, 1995, Alpha acquired 80 percent of Delta. Of the total purchase price, $100,000 was allocated to goodwill. Subsequently, on January 1, 1996, Delta obtained 70 percent of the outstanding voting shares of Omega. In this second acquisition, $80,000 of the payment was assigned to goodwill. All goodwill balances are being amortized over a 20-year life.

Delta had a book value of $490,000 at January 1, 1995, whereas Omega reported a book value of $140,000 on January 1, 1996.

Delta has made numerous inventory transfers to Alpha since the business combination was formed. Unrealized gains of $15,000 were present in Alpha's inventory as of January 1, 2000. During the year, $200,000 in additional intercompany sales were made with $22,000 in gains remaining unrealized at the end of the period.

Both Alpha and Delta have utilized the partial equity method to account for their investment balances.

Required:

The following individual financial statements are for these three companies for the year 2000 along with consolidated totals. Develop the worksheet entries necessary to derive these reported balances.

	Alpha Company	Delta Company	Omega Company	Consolidated Totals
Sales	$ 900,000	$ 500,000	$200,000	$1,400,000
Cost of goods sold	(500,000)	(240,000)	(80,000)	(627,000)
Operating expenses	(294,000)	(129,000)	(50,000)	(482,000)
Income of subsidiary	144,000	49,000	–0–	–0–
Noncontrolling interest in income of Delta Company	–0–	–0–	–0–	(33,800)
Noncontrolling interest in income of Omega Company	–0–	–0–	–0–	(21,000)
Net income	$ 250,000	$ 180,000	$ 70,000	$ 236,200
Retained earnings, 1/1/00	$ 600,000	$ 400,000	$100,000	$ 550,200
Net income (above)	250,000	180,000	70,000	236,200
Dividends paid	(50,000)	(40,000)	(50,000)	(50,000)
Retained earnings, 12/31/00	$ 800,000	$ 540,000	$120,000	$ 736,400
Cash and receivables	$ 262,000	$ 210,000	$ 70,000	$ 522,000
Inventory	290,000	310,000	160,000	738,000
Investment in Delta Company	628,000	–0–	–0–	–0–
Investment in Omega Company	–0–	234,000	–0–	–0–
Property, plant, and equipment	420,000	316,000	270,000	1,006,000
Goodwill	–0–	–0–	–0–	130,000
Total assets	$1,600,000	$1,070,000	$500,000	$2,396,000
Liabilities	$ 600,000	$ 410,000	$280,000	$1,270,000
Common stock	200,000	120,000	100,000	200,000
Retained earnings, 12/31/00	800,000	540,000	120,000	736,400
Noncontrolling interest in Delta Company	–0–	–0–	–0–	123,600
Noncontrolling interest in Omega Company	–0–	–0–	–0–	66,000
Total liabilities and equities	$1,600,000	$1,070,000	$500,000	$2,396,000

BRANCH AND CONSIGNMENT ACCOUNTING

Questions to Consider

- How does the accounting for branch operations differ from consolidation accounting? What similarities can be found?
- What techniques do companies with numerous branch operations use to monitor the intracompany transfers and allocations that can continually occur?
- Why are intracompany inventory shipments frequently recorded at a transfer price in excess of cost? What impact do unrealized gains resulting from such prices have on the financial reporting of the company as a whole?
- What are the enticements to a company to distribute its inventory through a consignment marketing system?
- In consignment marketing, how does the reporting process of the consignor (the owner) differ from that of the consignee (the seller)?

Accounting for the operations of a business can become quite complicated whenever geographical separation is encountered between the various facets of the organization. Chapter 8 examines the special procedures necessary to record transactions occurring at significant distances from a central office. Branch accounting is analyzed first. This initial section of the chapter describes reporting systems designed to accumulate the financial data generated by operations in widely dispersed locations.

Following the coverage of branches, accounting for consignment sales is investigated. Companies use this marketing technique to place their inventory in retail outlets owned by other parties, an approach intended to achieve a wider distribution of merchandise than might otherwise be possible. Thus, both branch and consignment accounting systems must be capable of gathering information despite the great distances frequently involved.

Branch Accounting

> For many distributors, opening a branch is a key sign of success, fulfilling a long-time goal of expansion and giving them the satisfaction of literally seeing their business grow."[1]

Few aspects of the phenomenal expansion of American business during this century have been more evident than the development of branch operations. Many of today's largest enterprises achieved their present magnitude primarily by establishing individual branches throughout the country. As just one example, in 1991, the JCPenney Company, Inc., disclosed that it operated 1,312 retail stores, 487 drugstores, four catalog distribution centers, and two store distribution centers.

Previous chapters have analyzed the consolidation procedures used to produce financial statements when two or more incorporated enterprises form a business combination. As an extension of this coverage, the first section of Chapter 8 examines the accounting process utilized by companies subdivided into identifiable branch operations. Once again, a single economic entity is made up of a number of individual reporting units. In this case, though, the lines of distinction are internal rather than legal. Although titles such as *divisions, chain stores,* or *profit centers* are often applied to these separate operations, the term *branch* has traditionally been applied by accountants to indicate an unincorporated operation within a company that carries out a specific function.

Proliferation of Branch Operations

As is evident from the previous chapters, the production of consolidated financial statements can be a very complex process. Fortunately, the number of separately incorporated companies within most business combinations tends to be rather limited. Although hundreds of companies can be controlled by a common parent, that degree of legal dispersion is not particularly prevalent. For example, the Kellogg Company currently controls only 8 domestic subsidiaries and 34 foreign subsidiaries. In contrast, as indicated by the JCPenney organization, the number of separate branches existing within a single corporation can range into the thousands.

The extensive use of branch operations is especially common in modern retailing where companies attempt to attract customers by offering the convenience of numerous outlets. McDonald's Corporation, for example, had 11,803 separate operations on December 31, 1990 (8,576 in this country, with 3,227 outside of the United States). At that same time, the retail sales of Safeway Stores, Incorporated were being made through more than 1,100 supermarkets located in the United States and Canada. Development of branch operations for retailing purposes is not limited, though, to giant organizations such as

---

[1] Bill Kelley, "The Payoff in Branches," *Industrial Distribution*, October 1984, p. 33.

McDonald's and Safeway. Relatively small companies often attempt to expand their market base by establishing additional outlets in nearby communities.

This type of internal division is not even restricted to the retail function. Branch operations are commonly found in banking as well as in manufacturing and other industries. For example, at the end of 1990, E. I. du Pont de Nemours & Company was comprised of six separate industrial segments with production being carried out at more than 100 plants located throughout the United States and the rest of the world.

The Structuring of Branch Organizations

Although organizing and expanding a company through the development of separate units is widespread, no uniform model for a branch can be designed. The specific activities of a branch are dependent on its purpose as well as the nature of the company's operations. As an example, some branches merely collect cash and receive sales orders, thus acting primarily as agents for the company's home office. To record such routine functions, the accounting system need consist of little more than a cash receipts listing.

In contrast, many companies establish branches to execute a complete range of business activities, including inventory procurement or production, credit sales, advertising, and so forth. This second type of operation is likely to maintain extensive financial records utilizing all of the journals and ledgers normally found in an incorporated concern. Only the omission of stockholders' equity accounts would distinguish this reporting system from that of a corporation.

The development of branch accounting is also influenced by a company's philosophy toward its own internal structuring. For businesses that operate under a policy of decentralization authority, the creation of numerous, relatively independent branches is emphasized. Proponents of this organizational style assign a significant degree of responsibility to each unit and then monitor these operations accordingly, usually through periodically reported summaries.

Conversely, a corporation that stresses centralized management may still elect to establish a large quantity of branch operations but the primary authority for decision making tends to remain with the officials working in the home office. In such organizations, the company's accounting process should be designed to reflect this approach by making detailed operational data available to appropriate individuals. As always, the accountant must create a system that meets the informational needs of the enterprise.

In considering the procedures that a company should apply in accounting for individual branch operations, the sheer number of potential reporting units may appear to pose an overwhelming problem. Upon closer investigation, though, the accounting difficulties that might be associated with large-scale operations such as JCPenney or Safeway can be seen as primarily mechanical rather than conceptual. With the advent and nearly universal utilization of computer systems, most organizations have the capability of maintaining legitimate accounting control over hundreds, or even thousands, of branches located throughout the world.

Accounting for Intracompany Transactions

Although modern computers enable companies to isolate and record the operations of a multitude of separate branches, significant accounting problems still continue to exist. *Of special concern is the recording of the many interface events that can occur between the branch and the corporate home office.* Procedures must be in place to ensure that all intracompany transactions such as transfers and allocations are recorded in a consistent manner by both parties.

This problem is especially significant because the volume of such transactions can become quite large. Just to begin a branch's operations, cash and other assets are normally transferred from the company's home office. In addition, if the branch maintains a stock of inventory, a portion or even all of this merchandise may have to be shipped directly from a central corporate warehouse. Thereafter, should the branch prove to be profitable, excess cash balances might be transferred back to the home office on a regular, perhaps daily, basis.

Frequently, though, the accounting interaction transpiring between the branch and the home office goes beyond periodic asset transfers. Depending on the internal reporting philosophy of the organization, general expenses incurred by the home office may well be allocated, at least in part, to the separate branches. By assigning costs such as corporate accounting, data processing, and advertising to these units, their individual profitability can be measured more precisely. Thus, accurate comparisons are made available to corporate officials on a branch-by-branch or year-by-year basis.

Because of the volume as well as importance of intracompany transactions, the interface existing between the accounting systems of the home office and each branch operation must be monitored closely. To facilitate this process, all reporting units normally establish an intracompany account within their ledgers. Although these accounts are referred to by a variety of different titles, the terms *branch* and *home office* are common and are used in this textbook.

To be more precise, the financial records of the corporation's home office should include a separate Branch account for each of the individual units. These ledger accounts serve to record all intracompany transfers and allocations from the vantage of the home office. Therefore, the balance in a Branch account signifies the corporation's current equity investment in that particular operation. Simultaneously, a parallel Home Office account is maintained by each branch to record these same interface transactions but from the viewpoint of the branch. Hence, the accumulated total also represents the equity investment attributable to the home office.

Since these two accounts are used to record the same transfers and allocations, the Branch and Home Office balances should be equal and offsetting at all times. From a practical perspective, though, such reciprocity frequently does not exist. In many companies, the volume of intracompany transfers and allocations is significant, thus raising the possibility of human errors occurring within the recording process. Additionally, the physical separation that exists between the home office and the various branches can create timing differences in the entering of many intracompany transactions.

Discussion Question: How Do We Account for the Store in Greenville?

In 1987, several local investors opened a retail store in Spartanburg, South Carolina, to market fashionable clothes to both men and women. This operation proved to be quite successful; the break-even point in sales was reached in less than 2½ years. By 1994, the business had become well known throughout the region for both the price of its merchandise and the quality of its service. To capitalize on this reputation, the owners decided to open a second store in Greenville, approximately 25 miles away. Prior to beginning this new undertaking, the accounting department was asked to develop a plan that would extend the company's reporting system to encompass the new store. Two different approaches have been proposed, but the accounting department has not yet settled on a recommendation.

Plan One.　One member of the accounting department feels that very little formal record-keeping should be carried out at the new store. "Have the Greenville operation monitor its sales, purchases, and expenses. At the end of each day, they can send us the results by fax machine and we will post all transactions to our ledger accounts here in the home office. We can simply create additional accounts where necessary: 'Sales—Greenville,' 'Inventory—Greenville,' and so on. All the records will be here under our control, and we can produce comparable results by store whenever necessary. A lot of work would be duplicated if the company hires more accountants and sets up a separate system for this new operation."

Plan Two.　A second accountant argues that the Greenville branch should have an accounting department of its own. "First, you threaten to overload our system by adding all the transactions from this second store. In addition, keeping the multitude of transactions separated by store may prove to be quite difficult. I believe we should account for the home office here and let the company hire someone in Greenville to record the branch. The individual operations will be better monitored in this way, and we can consolidate the results periodically for external reporting purposes. Accounting is more efficient when carried out at the site of the business."

Both of these systems (as well as many variations) would work. Both are used by many companies. What factors should be weighed in deciding what system to adopt to account for the Greenville branch?

Therefore, periodic reconciliation of the Branch and Home Office accounts is a required procedure in most large organizations. Although this agreement of the Branch and Home Office accounts is necessary prior to financial reporting, reconciliation is usually carried out more often to facilitate the discovery of errors and other recording problems.

Branch Accounting Illustrated

To demonstrate the accounting procedures applicable to branch operations, assume that the Zimmerman Company opens a new retail outlet in Topeka, Kansas, during the early months of 1995. A small building is acquired by the corporation for $200,000 with an additional $50,000 being paid for equipment. Based on company policy, these fixed assets are to be maintained on the financial records of the home office. A cash balance of $10,000 is transferred to the branch to begin operations as well as $80,000 in inventory from Zimmerman's central warehouse.

The following entries should be recorded within the accounting systems of the two parties to reflect these initial transactions:

Home Office Records			*Branch Records*		
Building.	200,000		No entry because		
Equipment	50,000		of company policy.		
Cash		250,000			
Branch—Topeka. . . .	90,000		Cash	10,000	
Shipments to			Shipments from		
Branch		80,000	Warehouse	80,000	
Cash		10,000	Home Office. . . .		90,000

As can be seen even from this brief example, the Branch/Home Office accounts serve to connect the two accounting systems. Both balances now indicate that the home office has invested $90,000 in the operations of the branch. Since these figures are in agreement, they are directly offset in the preparation of financial statements for external reporting purposes.

The Shipments to Branch account found in the preceding entry is the equivalent of "Intracompany Sales" while Shipments from Warehouse is an "Intracompany Purchases" balance. These $80,000 figures are also reciprocals so that both are eliminated as a preliminary step whenever financial statements are being produced.

To provide a more complete illustration of branch operation accounting, assume that the following events subsequently transpire in 1995 in connection with the Topeka branch of the Zimmerman Company:

a. Cash sales of $75,000 are made.

b. A shipment of inventory is received from the home office with a transfer price of $50,000.

c. Salary expenses of $5,000 are paid.

d. Inventory costing $20,000 is acquired on account from outside vendors.

e. Invoices for utilities such as heat and light totaling $4,000 are paid.

f. Additional cash sales of $25,000 are made.

g. The home office pays $6,000 in property taxes assessed on the fixed assets located in Topeka. This cost is assigned to the branch.

h. Cash of $40,000 is transferred from the branch to home office's bank account.

i. The home office computes $10,000 as annual depreciation on the building and equipment located in Topeka. This expense is charged to the branch.

j. The home office assigns $6,000 of the current cost of a nationwide advertising campaign to its Topeka branch. Although this entry is recorded immediately by the home office, the information is not communicated to the Topeka branch until the first days of 1996.

k. The Topeka branch counts year-end inventory. Goods costing $90,000 are held on that date, indicating the cost of goods sold for the year of $60,000:

Initial shipment from home office	$ 80,000
Second shipment from home office	50,000
Purchase from outside vendors	20,000
Inventory available for sale	150,000
Ending inventory (per count)	(90,000)
Cost of goods sold	$ 60,000

l. The reciprocity of the Branch/Home Office intracompany accounts must be established by the company with any needed adjustments recorded.

m. After the reciprocal balances are brought into agreement, separate financial statements for the branch are prepared. These statements provide an indication of the operating success achieved by the branch as well as its current financial position.

n. The accounting information from both the home office and the branch are combined at the end of the period into a single set of financial statements to be distributed for external reporting purposes.

o. At the end of the fiscal year, all revenue and expense accounts of the branch operation are closed out. Because stockholders' equity accounts are not maintained by the branch, the resulting net income figure is closed into the company's Retained Earnings account located within the financial records of the home office.

The following journal entries are recorded by Zimmerman Company's home office and its Topeka branch to account for transactions *a* through *k*. Detailed explanations are then provided for the last four events: *l* through *o*.

Home Office Records			*Branch Records*		
a. No entry.			*a.* Cash	75,000	
			Sales		75,000
			Current branch sales.		
b. Branch—Topeka . . .	50,000		*b.* Shipments from		
Shipments to			Warehouse	50,000	
Branch		50,000	Home Office . . .		50,000
Inventory shipped			Inventory shipments		
to Topeka branch.			received from		
			central warehouse.		
c. No entry.			*c.* Salary Expense	5,000	
			Cash		5,000
			Payment of salary		
			expense.		
d. No entry.			*d.* Purchases.	20,000	
			Accounts Payable .		20,000
			Inventory acquired		
			from outside		
			vendors.		
e. No entry.			*e.* Utility Expense	4,000	
			Cash		4,000
			Payment of utility		
			expenses.		
f. No entry.			*f.* Cash	25,000	
			Sales		25,000
			Current branch		
			sales.		
g. Branch—Topeka . . .	6,000		*g.* Property Tax Expense .	6,000	
Cash		6,000	Home Office . . .		6,000
Paid property taxes			Property taxes paid		
for branch.			by home office.		
h. Cash	40,000		*h.* Home Office	40,000	
Branch—Topeka .		40,000	Cash		40,000
Received cash			Transferred cash to		
transfer from			home office.		
branch.					
i. Branch—Topeka . . .	10,000		*i.* Depreciation		
Accumulated			Expense	10,000	
Depreciation . .		10,000	Home Office . . .		10,000
Computed			Depreciation		
depreciation			allocated		
and assigned			from home office.		
balance to branch.					

	Home Office Records			*Branch Records*	

j. Branch—Topeka . . .   6,000
  Advertising
    Expense   6,000
  Portion of national
  advertising allocated
  to branch.

j. Not entered prior to
    year-end.

k. No entry.

k. Inventory (balance
    sheet)   90,000
      Inventory (income
        statement) . . .   90,000
    Recording of
    year-end
    inventory balance.

l. Reconciling Branch and Home Office Accounts.   At this point, the reciprocity of the Branch/Home Office accounts is verified prior to preparing financial statements. Because of the potential volume of intracompany transactions that can occur during a period of time, reconciliation frequently becomes a very extensive process. Problems often arise within the accounting systems that necessitate adjustments to establish the equality of these accounts.

Disagreements between the Branch/Home Office balances, for example, are created by timing differences: events recorded on one set of financial records have not, as of yet, been entered into the other. In-transit items such as inventory and cash often fall into this category as would any home office expense allocation that has not been communicated to the branch. The recording of the Advertising Expense in *j* is an example of this specific type of accounting problem.

Timing differences are especially prevalent in companies where the branch maintains a separate accounting system. The physical distance between the two parties frequently prohibits the simultaneous recording of all financial events. Such problems can usually be avoided in fully automated systems that utilize a centralized computer. The computer is simply programmed to reject changes to either the Home Office or the Branch account unless an offsetting entry is simultaneously made to the reciprocal account.

Even in such computerized systems, however, occasional human errors can arise within the recording process. Therefore, most companies review and reconcile the Branch/Home Office accounts on a weekly or monthly basis. To facilitate this procedure, especially in companies maintaining separate accounting systems, the branch operation is normally directed to file a periodic, perhaps daily, listing of all entries to the intracompany account. The accuracy of the balance can then be established by matching this list (on an individual item basis, if necessary) against the reciprocal figures on the home office's records.

Returning to the Zimmerman Company illustration, the two intracompany accounts hold the following balances as of the end of 1995:

	Branch Account (home office's records)	Home Office Account (branch's records)
Initial transfer of cash and inventory	$ 90,000	$ (90,000)
Subsequent inventory transfer	50,000	(50,000)
Property tax allocation.	6,000	(6,000)
Cash transferred to home office.	(40,000)	40,000
Depreciation expense allocation	10,000	(10,000)
Advertising expense allocation	6,000	–0–
End-of-period totals	$122,000	$(116,000)

Because this illustration has only a few transactions, the $6,000 timing difference created by the advertising expense allocation is immediately evident. In many cases, however, a detailed matching of the entries is necessary to isolate all of the deviations within the ending account balances. After the reconciling items have been ascertained, adjustments can be made directly to the financial records of the specific party. For example, the Topeka branch must record the following entry to correct the timing problem identified in the preceding reconciliation.

Home Office Records	*Branch Records*		
l. No adjustment needed since allocation has already been recorded.	*l.* Advertising Expense. .	6,000	
	Home Office . . .		6,000
	Advertising allocation from home office.		

m. Producing Financial Statements for the Branch.   After the reciprocity of the intracompany accounts is established, financial statements for the Topeka branch can be prepared as a basis for internal corporate analysis. These statements displayed in Exhibit 8–1 are based on the ledger balances that result from the previous series of journal entries. Since the $131,000 Home Office figure is the equivalent of an ownership interest, this account replaces the stockholders' equity section on the branch's balance sheet. Consequently, a separate statement disclosing the changes made in the Home Office account during the period is included as a substitute for a statement of retained earnings.

n. Producing Financial Statements for the Entire Company.   Once financial statements for the Topeka branch have been developed, the Zimmerman Company can proceed to create a single combined set of statements for its entire organization. To achieve this objective, the simulated union of the accounting records for Zimmerman Company's home office and the Topeka branch is presented in Exhibit 8–2.

EXHIBIT 8–1

TOPEKA BRANCH OF ZIMMERMAN COMPANY
Financial Statements

Income Statement
Year Ending December 31, 1995

Sales		$100,000
Cost of goods sold:		
Beginning inventory	–0–	
Shipments from warehouse	$130,000	
Purchases	20,000	
Goods available for sale	150,000	
Ending inventory	(90,000)	(60,000)
Gross profit		$ 40,000
Operating expenses:		
Salary expense	5,000	
Depreciation expense	10,000	
Utility expense	4,000	
Advertising expense	6,000	
Property tax expense	6,000	(31,000)
Net income of branch		$ 9,000

Home Office Account
Year Ending December 31, 1995

Account balance, January 1, 1995		–0–
Transfers from home office:		
Cash	$ 10,000	
Inventory	130,000	
Expense allocations:		
Property taxes	6,000	
Depreciation	10,000	
Advertising	6,000	$162,000
Transfers to home office:		
Cash		(40,000)
Net income (above)		9,000
Account balance, December 31, 1995		$131,000

Balance Sheet
December 31, 1995
Assets

Cash	$ 61,000
Inventory	90,000
Total assets	$151,000

Liabilities and Equity

Accounts payable	$ 20,000
Home office (above)	131,000
Total liabilities and equity	$151,000

EXHIBIT 8–2

ZIMMERMAN COMPANY
Worksheet to Combine Home Office and Topeka Branch
Year Ending December 31, 1995

Accounts	Home Office	Topeka Branch	Combination Entries Debit	Combination Entries Credit	Income Statement	Statement of Retained Earnings	Balance Sheet
Debits							
Cash	96,000	61,000					157,000
Accounts receivable	112,000	–0–					112,000
Inventory, 12/31/95	166,000	90,000					256,000
Buildings (net)	620,000	–0–					620,000
Equipment (net)	304,000	–0–					304,000
Branch—Topeka	122,000	–0–		(2) 122,000			
Dividends paid	30,000	–0–				30,000	
Inventory, 1/1/95	108,000	–0–			108,000		
Purchases	414,000	20,000			434,000		
Shipments from warehouse	–0–	130,000		(1) 130,000			
Salary expense	46,000	5,000			51,000		
Depreciation expense	34,000	10,000			44,000		
Utility expense	28,000	4,000			32,000		
Advertising expense	41,000	6,000			47,000		
Property tax expense	29,000	6,000			35,000		
Total debits	2,150,000	332,000					1,449,000
Credits							
Accounts payable	(86,000)	(20,000)					(106,000)
Long-term liabilities	(166,000)	–0–					(166,000)
Common stock	(303,000)	–0–					(303,000)
Additional paid-in capital	(83,000)	–0–					(83,000)
Retained earnings, 1/1/95	(544,000)	–0–				(544,000)	
Home office	–0–	(122,000)	(2) 122,000				
Sales	(672,000)	(100,000)			(772,000)		
Shipments to branch	(130,000)	–0–	(1) 130,000				
Inventory, 12/31/95	(166,000)	(90,000)			(256,000)		
Combined net income					(277,000)	(277,000)	
Combined retained earnings, 12/31/95						(791,000)	(791,000)
Total credits	(2,150,000)	(332,000)					(1,449,000)

NOTE: Parentheses indicate a credit balance.

On this worksheet, only one branch operation is included to avoid unnecessary mechanical complications. Although companies frequently maintain control over a multitude of branches, the individual combination procedures are merely repeated for each separate unit. Therefore, a better understanding of this process can be gained by focusing attention on a single operation. In this illustration, the data gathered from the Topeka branch provides a complete demonstration of the various procedures necessary for arriving at combined financial statements.

A quick perusal of the combination worksheet presented in Exhibit 8–2 indicates that it is considerably less complex than the consolidation examples previously presented in this text. Here, the entire process is limited to offsetting the intracompany accounts that exist within the individual financial records. In Entry 1, the $130,000 balances recorded by both parties in connection with the inventory shipments are eliminated. When viewed from an external perspective, these transactions have created no changes in the company's overall financial position; they were simply internal asset transfers. Similarly, the $122,000 equity balances found in the Home Office and Branch accounts at the end of the period are removed by Entry 2. As with consolidation, the individual account balances of the branch should be included in the financial statements of the single economic entity rather than the lump sum amount invested by the home office.

Since no other reciprocal balances exist in this particular example, the remaining accounts of both parties are merely extended to arrive at combined totals for the organization. Therefore, the figures found in the final three columns of the worksheet in Exhibit 8–2 represent the operations of Zimmerman Company for 1995 and its financial position at the end of that year. A trial balance worksheet is demonstrated here rather than the financial statement format used in previous chapters. This change is included simply to illustrate that worksheets may take different forms.

Before leaving Exhibit 8–2, one final comment should be made about the utilization of a worksheet in home office/branch combinations. Often, as in the Zimmerman illustration, the figures to be reported can be determined by a few relatively uncomplicated elimination entries. In such cases, the worksheet is frequently unnecessary; the combination process consists of little more than the addition of all nonreciprocal balances. Although a worksheet is presented here, its inclusion is mainly to afford a visual display of the procedures being employed. The use of a worksheet is always an optional technique which, in practice, can take various forms or even be omitted.

o. Recording Closing Entries for the Branch Operation.   The last requirement of the Zimmerman Company illustration can now be completed. The 1995 revenue and expense accounts of the Topeka branch must be closed out in anticipation of beginning a new fiscal year. Final balances are found on the worksheet in Exhibit 8–2. Because no equity accounts exist within the branch's own accounting system, the closing process is constructed to utilize the Retained Earnings account of the home office.[2]

Home Office Records			*Branch Records*		
o. Branch—Topeka . . .	9,000		*o.* Sales	100,000	
Retained Earnings .		9,000	Inventory (12/31/95) . .	90,000	
To record 1995			Shipments from		
income of Topeka			Warehouse . . .		130,000
branch.			Purchases.		20,000
			Salary Expense . .		5,000
			Depreciation		
			Expense		10,000
			Utility Expense . .		4,000
			Advertising		
			Expense		6,000
			Property Tax		
			Expense		6,000
			Home Office . . .		9,000
			To close out 1995		
			revenue and expense		
			accounts with net		
			income being		
			recorded on home		
			office books.		

These closing entries achieve two basic objectives: each of the branch's revenue and expense accounts is returned to a zero balance and the net income for the period is added to retained earnings. In a manner similar to that of other interface activities, the Home Office and Branch accounts serve here as the connecting agents between the two accounting systems.

Unrealized Gains Created by Intracompany Transfers

As can be seen from a review of the worksheet in Exhibit 8–2, the procedures used in the combination process run somewhat parallel to that of a consolidation. Fortunately, many of the complex consolidation issues analyzed in previous chapters are not present in branch accounting. For example, no allocation is made of a purchase price. Consequently, no related amortization expense has to be recognized.

As exemplified by Exhibit 8–2, the principal function of the combination process is the direct elimination of all reciprocal balances. *However, at least one major complication does carry over from the consolidation area: year-end inventory balances often contain unrealized gains as a result of intracompany transactions.*

---

[2] The individual revenue and expense accounts of the home office must also be closed out. Therefore, the Shipments to Branch balance is also reduced to zero at the end of this year.

Inventory transfers may be priced (as in the Zimmerman example) at historical cost; however, alternative possibilities do exist. As discussed in Chapter 5, a company can elect to record merchandise shipments at the normal sales price, at its variable cost, at cost plus a predetermined markup, or at some other established value. One survey found 11 different systems in use for setting transfer prices with the market price being the most popular (used by 25.1 percent of the respondents) followed by full production cost plus a markup (16.6 percent) and a negotiated price (16.6 percent).[3]

Although the actual transfer pricing decision should be based on the company's policy regarding internal profitability measurement, problems may be encountered with any specific approach. For example, charging the branch with only the cost of transferred goods leaves the home office reporting an unrealistically low income figure and allows the branch to show significant, perhaps undeserved, profit margins. Conversely, recording transfers at an amount more than cost might force the branch to set prices at artificially high levels to maintain a standard gross profit.

Clearly, the transfer pricing issue is an often discussed philosophical issue somewhat removed from financial accounting. However, the resulting management decision directly affects the subsequent combination process. If a profit markup is included by the home office, any transferred inventory held by the branch at year's end has a book value exceeding historical cost. For external reporting purposes, procedures must be applied within the combination process to eliminate these unrealized gains. Only in this manner can ending inventory be returned to its original cost while the intracompany profit is being deferred until the merchandise is eventually sold to outside parties.

Unrealized Gains Not Separately Recorded.   Several procedural techniques exist for dealing with unrealized inventory gains created by intracompany transactions. The exact process to be applied in a particular combination depends on the policy of the home office toward recording the gains at the time of transfer. Often, especially if profit margins are set at a standard percentage or amount, the home office makes no attempt to monitor the unrealized gains. Instead, the overvaluation is ignored until year-end and then eliminated from the inventory accounts based on the established markup. This approach is similar to that demonstrated previously in connection with the consolidation of incorporated subsidiaries.

To serve as an example, assume that inventory costing $200,000 is shipped by the home office to one of its branches. All such transfers are priced for internal reporting purposes based on a standard markup of 20 percent of historical cost but no separate recording is made of the transfer gain ($40,000 or 20 percent of $200,000). Under this policy, both parties simply record the intracompany shipments at $240,000. Subsequently, in producing financial statements at year's end, these two accounts are offset in the same manner as Entry 1 in Exhibit 8–2.

---

[3] Roger W. Tang, "Transfer Pricing in the 1990s," *Management Accounting*, February 1992, p. 24.

However, this elimination does not completely resolve the accounting problem created by the markup. The book value of any merchandise remaining with the branch is still overstated: the recorded account contains a portion of the unrealized gain. If the branch, for example, sells $180,000 of this transferred inventory (75 percent) but retains $60,000, the original cost of the ending balance would have been only $50,000 ($60,000/120%). For external reporting, the $10,000 inflation must be deferred on the combination worksheet through an additional entry.

Combination Entry (year of transfer)

Inventory (12/31/95) (income statement)
(or Cost of Goods Sold) 10,000
    Inventory (12/31/95) (balance sheet)   10,000
To remove unrealized intracompany gain from ending inventory
balances.

As in previous consolidation examples, this $10,000 unrealized gain reappears in the succeeding fiscal period as an element of the branch's beginning inventory balance. For this reason, the gain must be removed again, but this time in the year following the original transfer. Because of the intervening closing entries, the second elimination of the $10,000 intracompany profit is made as follows:

Combination Entry (year subsequent to transfer)

Retained earnings, 1/1/96 10,000
    Inventory (1/1/96) (income statement)
    (or Cost of Goods Sold)   10,000
To remove unrealized intracompany gain from beginning-of-year
balances.

Unrealized Gains Separately Recorded. Although the combination entries demonstrated earlier appropriately account for intracompany gains, this method of deferring unrealized profits is not applicable in all cases. A variation of this process is required if the home office chooses to keep an ongoing record of transfer gains. Separately accounting for markups at the time of shipment provides the company with a means of monitoring inventory balances, which may be especially important if a perpetual system is in use. Therefore, the $240,000 transfer could have been initially recorded by the two parties through the following journal entries:

Home Office Records			*Branch Records*		
Branch 240,000			Shipments from Home		
Shipments to			Office 240,000		
Branch	200,000		Home office . . .		240,000
Unrealized Gains .	40,000		To record shipments		
To record shipments			from home office at a		
to branch with gains			transfer price above		
separately			cost.		
monitored.					

Subsequently, if 75 percent of this inventory is sold to outside parties by the branch, the home office reclassifies the appropriate portion of the gain:

Home Office Records			*Branch Records*
Unrealized Gains (75%)	30,000		No entry recorded.
Realized Gains . .		30,000	
To reclassify			
inventory gains that			
have now been			
earned.			

This approach is adopted by some companies as a means of providing better control over inventory balances. By separating the original $40,000 gain, the home office is able to maintain inventory records at historical cost because the Shipments to Branch figure measures the cost of the transferred goods. However, a discrepancy has been introduced between the two reciprocal shipment accounts, one now reports $200,000 while the other shows $240,000. Consequently, in producing combination entries, the two gain accounts must be taken into consideration to establish agreement. They are both eliminated to remove the impact of the intracompany transaction.

Combination Entry (year of transfer)

Shipments to Branch.	200,000	
Unrealized Gains	10,000	
Realized Gains	30,000	
Shipments from Home Office		240,000
To eliminate the effects of intracompany inventory transfers.		

Despite the removal here of both home office gain accounts, the book value of any inventory retained by the branch is still inflated by the remaining portion of the intracompany profit. Thus, the $10,000 inventory reduction entry shown previously (to return the balance to cost) must be repeated. Indeed, this entry is necessary regardless of the method incorporated by the home office to monitor realized and unrealized gains.

Combination Entry (year of transfer)

Inventory (12/31/95) (income statement)		
(or Cost of Goods Sold)	10,000	
Inventory (12/31/95) (balance sheet)		10,000
To remove unrealized intracompany gain from ending inventory		
balances.		

When the practice of separately monitoring intracompany gains is applied by the home office, a slightly more complex accounting situation arises in the year *subsequent* to the transfer. The Unrealized Gain account on the home office records is not closed out at the end of the initial period; thus, the Retained Earnings account is correct rather than being $10,000 overstated (as in the previous illustration). For this reason, a different adjustment must be made to eliminate the intracompany profit from the subsequent figures. Assuming that the home office reclassifies the $10,000 to a Realized Gain account during 1996, this figure must be removed in preparing combined financial statements. The accompanying reduction to beginning inventory (within cost of goods sold) effectively increases gross profit in the period of actual realization.

Combination Entry (year subsequent to transfer)

Realized Gains 10,000
       Inventory (1/1/96) (income statement)
        (or Cost of Goods Sold) 10,000
   To remove previous intracompany gain from individual account balances.

Consignment Accounting

The establishment of branch operations is not the only technique available to a company attempting to achieve the wide-scale distribution of its product line. One alternative that has the potential for placing inventory items into thousands of outlets is consignment marketing. In its simplest form, a manufacturer or distributor (the *consignor*) gives possession of merchandise to a retailer (the *consignee*) while continuing to retain legal ownership. Although the inventory is then physically held by the consignee, title to the goods remains with the consignor.

The consignee serves in the capacity of a sales agent with ownership of the goods passing directly from the consignor to a third-party purchaser. Once the merchandise is sold, the consignor is entitled to any proceeds remaining from the revenue after the consignee has removed a predetermined sales commission and reimbursement for any specified expenses. Traditionally, the inventory is held by the consignee for a stated time with any unsold items then returned to the consignor.

Hanes Corporation, as one example, has achieved significant success in marketing L'eggs panty hose in this manner. The company "decided to distribute L'eggs on consignment. Hanes would own the display and the inventory. The store would provide only the sales space. Route sales representatives, mostly young women, would drive trucks to the stores, where they could refill empty racks on the spot. . . . It has paid off handsomely. L'eggs has captured over 15 percent of the U.S. hosiery market."[4]

Many of the advantages of consignment retailing are readily apparent from the illustration provided by the Hanes Corporation. A company can offer products at a great number of locations with a minimal cost while retaining control over merchandising and pricing. This strategy is especially appealing as a means of introducing a new product to retailers who might be hesitant about investing in an unproven item. The consignor is able to expand the product's market base while the consignee invests little and runs virtually no risk of incurring large losses if the merchandise fails to sell.

---

[4] Carol E. Curtis, "Nothing Beats a Great Pair of L'eggs," *Forbes*, September 29, 1980, p. 73.

Consignment marketing has become especially prevalent over the years in a number of widely varying industries. Antiques and art works, for example, are often sold in this manner as are plant seeds for home gardening. In a recent trend, a significant portion of medical supplies are placed in hospitals on consignment. This technique minimizes inventory losses as well as the amount of money tied up in supplies and, thus, may help reduce the high cost of health care.

Relationship between the Consignor and the Consignee

Prior to the initial transfer of inventory, the consignor and consignee should agree on a written contract clearly establishing the rights and responsibilities of both parties. Although contractual law is not the primary focus of this textbook, an accountant must be able to advise clients. Furthermore, a thorough knowledge of the various stipulations found in a consignment contract is needed as a basis for understanding and recording subsequent events.

A consignment agreement usually covers the following:

- The price charged to the consignee or the amount of commission to be paid.
- Responsibilities for expenses such as damaged merchandise, bad debts, and product warranties.
- The consignor's responsibility for reimbursing the consignee for costs such as advertising and delivery.
- The consignee's responsibility to store goods safely.
- Procedure for return of unsold goods.
- Invoicing procedures.
- Consignee's responsibility for periodic reporting to consignor.
- Rights upon termination of relationship.[5]

Consignment marketing provides both parties with rather unique accounting situations. The consignor must continue to report inventory that it no longer possesses while the consignee, despite physically holding the goods, has little or no cost to record. To reflect this arrangement, accounting procedures should be designed so that all inventory costs, especially those of the consignor, are correctly maintained. In addition, both reporting systems must ensure that no revenues are recognized until the point of actual sale.

To meet these objectives, companies have devised a wide variety of bookkeeping techniques to record consignment transactions. This textbook examines the general procedures most commonly encountered in practice. However, as long as all cost and revenue figures are properly stated, a degree of accounting flexibility is available in this area.

Because consignment transactions are viewed from two such differing perspectives, the accounting process employed by the consignor is in distinct con-

---

[5] Paul R. Kinny, "How To Protect Consigned Inventory," *Business Credit,* January 1991, p. 25.

trast to that of the consignee. In the following coverage, the procedures applicable to the consignor are examined first. This analysis is followed by a similar presentation of the recording techniques utilized by the consignee. Structuring the material in this manner avoids the confusion that can result from attempting to review both sides of the same transaction simultaneously.

Consignment Accounting—The Consignor

In organizing the accounting process, the consignor must first establish ledger accounts to monitor the various consignment transactions, especially the cost of its transferred inventory. Either of two approaches can be adopted for this purpose.

In many cases, a single holding account (usually referred to as a *Consignment-Out* account) is set up to record all consignment transactions initially: the original cost of the merchandise, sales revenue, commissions, and so on. *Every transaction is entered directly to this account and then appropriately reclassified for reporting purposes at the end of the fiscal period.* Although this method simplifies the day-to-day accounting process, a detailed analysis of the Consignment-Out balance has to be made on a regular basis. If many transactions have occurred, developing this periodic listing may be quite tedious and time consuming.

An alternative approach is available to the consignor for recording these same transactions. A Consignment Inventory account is established to monitor the merchandise costs with all other transactions being reported in a normal fashion. Under this approach, consignment revenues and expenses are recorded by the consignor as revenues and expenses. Thus, no extensive end-of-period analysis is required. However, the company's accounting system must be designed to ensure that all consignment transactions are properly classified within the financial records at the time of the event. Consequently, this method is most frequently used by companies with extensive consignment sales.

When reviewing these two methods of recording consignment transactions, a number of differences are noted. However, regardless of the specific procedures utilized in a company's bookkeeping system, all variations are purely mechanical. The resulting financial information is not dependent on the recording method being employed.

Consignment Accounting—Illustrated from the Consignor's Perspective

As a basis for demonstration, assume that Richmond Corporation enters into a consignment arrangement with Lee Company. At the beginning of each month, Richmond (the consignor) is to provide Lee with a stock of inventory having a cost of $50,000. Richmond is responsible for all transportation costs as well as advertising. The agreement also stipulates that Lee is to receive reimbursement for any expenses incurred in connection with a warranty given to customers specifying that defective merchandise will be fixed without charge.

In return, Lee offers the inventory for sale at a price 50 percent in excess of original cost. The contract further states that any credit sales are the responsibility of the consignee: Lee must, therefore, absorb losses resulting from bad debts. At the end of each month, Lee is to deduct all reimbursable expenses along with a 15 percent commission and forward the remainder of the sales revenue to Richmond.

As indicated earlier, the consignor's journal entries depend on the structure of that company's accounting system. To provide a better comparison of the alternative methods, Richmond's record-keeping is shown here in parallel. Thus, the initial shipment of consignment goods sent to Lee can be recorded by Richmond through either of the following two entries:

Consignor's Records *(Consignment-Out account is being used)*			*Consignor's Records* *(Consignment Inventory account is being used)*	
Consignment-Out	50,000		Consignment Inventory	50,000
Inventory		50,000	Inventory	50,000

The direct reduction to the Inventory account shown here is utilized by companies that maintain perpetual records. If the consignor accounts for inventory through a periodic system, the credit portion of this entry is more likely to be made to an account such as Consignments Shipped.

To continue with this illustration, assume that Richmond pays $900 in transportation costs to ship the inventory delivered to Lee. An additional $1,200 is then spent by the consignor for an advertising campaign to promote these products. Subsequently, at the end of the first month of this arrangement, Richmond receives the following statement from Lee in connection with this consignment merchandise:

Consignee's Report		
Consignment sales		$ 60,000
Less: Commissions (15%)	$9,000	
Repair expenses under warranty	2,000	(11,000)
Check enclosed		$ 49,000

Based on the information accumulated about this series of transactions, Richmond records the following three journal entries. Once again, the use of both Consignment-Out and Consignment Inventory accounts are illustrated here.

Consignor's Records *(Consignment-Out account)*			*Consignor's Records* *(Consignment Inventory account)*	
Consignment-Out.	900		Consignment Inventory	900
Cash		900	Cash	900
To record transportation cost for consignment inventory.			To record transportation cost for consignment inventory.	

Consignor's Records
(Consignment-Out account)

Consignment-Out.	1,200	
Cash		1,200

To record advertising made in connection with consignment inventory.

Cash	49,000	
Consignment-Out.		49,000

To record cash received from consignee.

Consignor's Records
(Consignment Inventory account)

Advertising Expense	1,200	
Cash		1,200

To record advertising made in connection with consignment inventory.

Cash	49,000	
Commission Expense	9,000	
Warranty Expense	2,000	
Consignment Sales		60,000

To record consignment sales and expenses as well as cash received from consignee.

Adjustment Process—Consignment-Out Approach. At the close of the month, assume that Richmond elects to review and adjust its consignment records immediately rather than wait until year's end. Periodic reclassification is especially important if numerous transactions are involved or if the consignor is producing interim financial statements.

Under the consignment-out approach, Richmond has a single consignment account with a balance of $3,100 at the end of this first month:

Consignment-Out Account

Inventory shipped	$ 50,000
Transportation.	900
Advertising	1,200
Sales revenue	(60,000)
Commissions	9,000
Warranty repairs.	2,000
Ending balance	$ 3,100

To achieve a proper accounting of Richmond's consignment transactions, each of these amounts must be reclassified. As stated, the Consignment-Out account merely holds the various transactions. Before an adjustment can be developed for this purpose, a cost of goods sold figure for the period must be calculated. Based on the standard 50 percent markup, the $60,000 revenue reported by the consignee indicates that the merchandise disposed of by the consignee had a base cost of $40,000 ($60,000/150%). Consequently, 80 percent of the original $50,000 shipment has now been sold ($40,000/$50,000). This percentage enables Richmond to compute its cost of goods sold as $40,720 with an ending inventory balance of $10,180:

Total inventory cost (historical cost plus $900 transportation).	$50,900
Cost of goods sold (80% sold).	$40,720
Ending consignment inventory (20% retained)	$10,180

Obviously, verifying the physical existence of this ending inventory is a control problem when consignment marketing is used. Many consignors have inventory at numerous retail locations. Under such conditions, periodic inspection is not always possible. Thus, the accuracy of the $10,180 figure being reported here may be entirely dependent on data provided by the consignee. Unfortunately, more than one consignor has learned that consignee record-keeping may not be as timely and correct as would be desired.

Having computed the cost of goods sold for the period, Richmond can produce the following reclassification entry to report its consignment transactions for the period. Although the appropriate $10,180 inventory balance is recorded here as a separate asset, the amount could also be left in the Consignment-Out account.

Consignor's Records
(Consignment-Out Approach)

Consignment Inventory	10,180	
Cost of Goods Sold	40,720	
Advertising Expense.	1,200	
Commission Expense	9,000	
Warranty Expense.	2,000	
Consignment Sales.		60,000
Consignment-Out		3,100

To reclassify consignment transactions occurring during the current
month to appropriate accounts.

One aspect of this reclassification should be specifically mentioned. Both the consignment sales figure and the related cost of goods sold are explicitly shown. Several alternatives exist for reporting this particular information. Richmond, for example, could net these two figures and record the resulting $19,280 gross profit as a single income item. This procedure is common in companies where consignment transactions make up only a small portion of total revenues.

As a second possibility, the components of the consignor's cost of goods sold can be presented individually: the beginning and ending inventory balances, shipments, freight, and so on. Although the cost of goods sold total would no longer be directly evident within the accounting records, additional information is made available by inclusion of each of these separate figures.

Adjustment Process—Consignment Inventory Approach. If Richmond had chosen to adopt the alternative method of recording these transactions, the Consignment Inventory account would hold an accumulated balance of $50,900 (cost plus transportation). The inventory costs alone are included in this total. Thus, a much less complicated end-of-period recording process is required. Although cost of goods sold has been omitted, sales and expense figures have already been properly classified during the month. Richmond needs to make only a single adjustment for reporting purposes: reclassification of the $40,720 (as just calculated) from an asset to an expense account.

Consignor's Records
(Consignment Inventory Approach)

Cost of Goods Sold	40,720	
Consignment Inventory		40,720

To record cost of goods that were sold on consignment during the month.

Although the entries vary, the consignment-out and consignment inventory approaches produce identical financial results for the consignor:

Consignment sales.			$ 60,000
Cost of goods sold:			
Beginning inventory		–0–	
Transfers.	$50,000		
Transportation	900	$ 50,900	
Goods available for sale		50,900	
Ending inventory (20%)		(10,180)	(40,720)
Gross profit.			$ 19,280
Less: Advertising and commissions			(10,200)
Warranty expense			(2,000)
Consignment net income			$ 7,080

Since reported financial information is not affected, a consignor may select either of these two methods for recording consignment transactions. The simplicity of the consignment-out approach is immediately appealing because so little attention is required. The holding account serves as a balancing figure for all consignment transactions made during the period. Unfortunately, the periodic reclassification process can be a rather pedestrian task, especially if large volumes of consignment shipments and sales are made on a regular basis.

In contrast, establishing a Consignment Inventory account requires more extensive analysis on a day-to-day basis but does not entail a rigorous review prior to preparing any type of financial report. For this reason, companies that engage in a significant amount of consignment transactions often design their accounting systems along the lines of the consignment inventory approach. Other enterprises that use consignment marketing less frequently are likely to rely on a Consignment-Out account rather than investing resources in the development of more extensive bookkeeping techniques.

Accounting Used by the Consignee

The coverage of consignment accounting switches at this point to the reporting procedures utilized by the consignee. Since this party has possession of the merchandise but not the title, an entirely different perspective of these transactions is assumed. The consignee never owns the inventory; thus, the cost of the asset and any associated obligation are simply ignored. Under normal conditions, the consignee does have to account for four events that occur in connection with consignment goods:

1. Expenditures made for reimbursable expenses.
2. Sales of the consignment merchandise.
3. Commissions earned on consignment sales.
4. Transfer of appropriate cash proceeds to the consignor.

To facilitate the recording process, a Consignment-In account is commonly maintained by the consignee. Because this account contains no inventory costs, only amounts due to and from the consignor are included. Thus, an ending debit balance represents a receivable from the consignor while a credit total indicates a liability.

Using the information in the previous example, Lee, as the consignee, would record four transactions in connection with the consignment inventory.

- Sale of goods for $60,000.
- Payment of $2,000 in reimbursable warranty costs.
- Recognition of 15 percent commission.
- Transfer to consignor of remaining $49,000 in cash: $60,000 revenues less $9,000 in commissions (15%) and warranty costs.

In reviewing the entries that follow, note that Lee makes only a memorandum entry to record the initial receipt of the consignment inventory. Since title to these items has not been conveyed, Lee bears none of the cost of these goods.

Consignee's Records

Memorandum entry: Received $50,000 in consignment inventory from Richmond Corporation.

Cash (or Accounts Receivable)	60,000	
Consignment-In		60,000

To record sale of merchandise being held on consignment.

Consignment-In	2,000	
Cash (or Accounts Payable)		2,000

To record expenditure for reimbursable repairs made in connection with product warranty on consigned goods.

Consignment-In	9,000	
Commissions Earned		9,000

To record 15 percent sales commission on consignment sales for the month.

Consignment-In	49,000	
Cash		49,000

To close out Consignment-In account by forwarding applicable balance to Richmond Corporation, the consignor.

Summary

1. Geographic separation places special demands on the gathering and reporting of financial information. In this chapter, accounting systems and procedures are examined that record transactions gathered from many, often distant, locations. The reporting process utilized by organizations that have created branch operations is explored first, followed by a similar coverage of consignment marketing.

2. Companies frequently establish individual operations, referred to as *branches*, throughout the country and even the world. Geographic dispersion is especially prevalent in both retailing and banking, which attempt to attract customers by offering merchandise and service at many convenient locations. The most significant accounting problem created by this type of organization is the recording of intracompany transactions and allocations. Normally, cash and inventory are transferred between the parties and common costs are assigned to the individual units. For accounting purposes, a Branch account is established on the home office's records for every branch. Likewise, a Home Office account is maintained by each individual branch operation to serve as the equivalent of an equity balance. Although these two accounts should be equal and offsetting at all times, periodic reconciliations are required to identify and correct any errors and timing differences.

3. Individual financial statements can be prepared for each branch on a regular basis. For external reporting purposes, though, combined statements encompassing all of the company's operations are necessary. Such statements can be produced through the use of a combination worksheet that utilizes simulated journal entries to eliminate all reciprocal balances. The Branch/Home Office accounts should be offset in this manner along with balances created by inventory transfers and any other intracompany transactions.

4. Intracompany inventory shipments may be made at a transfer price above historical cost. If any portion of this merchandise is not resold or used by the end of the fiscal period, the unrealized gain associated with these goods must be removed from the inventory balances. Both the asset account and the ending inventory figure (within cost of goods sold) are reduced. Some enterprises separately record these unrealized gains at the time of transfer. If this approach is followed, these additional account balances are eliminated within the combination process.

5. Wide-scale distribution of products can also be achieved through consignment marketing. A manufacturer or distributor (a *consignor*) transfers physical possession of merchandise to a retailer (a *consignee*) while continuing to maintain legal title. Since the consignee is not required to purchase the inventory, that party faces little risk of loss. The consignee normally holds the goods until sold and then forwards the receipts (less a commission and any reimbursable costs) to the consignor. If any of the inventory fails to sell, it is normally returned after a specified time.

6. As the owner, the consignor should account for the cost of consigned inventory until the time of sale. In addition, all related expenses as well as the resulting revenues must be properly monitored. Many consignors establish a Consignment-Out account in which all transactions are recorded initially. A detailed analysis is periodically required of the resulting balance so that the various components can be reclassified for reporting purposes. This approach is easy to apply, although accurate interim information is not always readily available.

7. A consignor can adopt an alternative accounting approach by using a Consignment Inventory account. Under this method, each consignment transaction is properly classified at the time of the event: sales are recorded as sales, expenses as expenses, and so on. More effort is required to record this data, but accurate information is constantly maintained. For reporting purposes, an adjusting entry to record ending inventory and cost of goods sold is still necessary.

8. Proper accounting procedures must also be established by the consignee. Since title to the goods is not being held, the consignee need not record inventory costs. Many companies do, however, set up a Consignment-In account for the recording of all sales, commissions, reimbursable costs, and the like. The components of this balance can then be analyzed and adjusted at any time that a report (or payment) is to be made to the consignor.

Comprehensive Illustration

PROBLEM

(Estimated Time: 35 to 50 Minutes)

The Rice Corporation is a distributor of widgets in Pueblo, Colorado. Historically, Rice has sold this product exclusively through a local department store on a consignment basis. In 1995, Rice also began to sell widgets in a branch outlet that the company opened in the nearby town of Chester. The trial balance for the Rice Corporation as of December 31, 1996, follows:

	Debits	Credits
Accounts payable		$ 39,000
Accounts receivable	$ 29,000	
Accumulated depreciation		18,000
Advertising expense	16,000	
Branch—Chester	145,000	
Buildings and equipment	66,000	
Cash	7,000	
Common stock		200,000
Consignment-out	120,000	
Depreciation expense	4,000	
Dividends paid	12,000	

	Debits	Credits
Inventory (income statement)	79,000	67,000
Inventory, 12/31/96	67,000	
Land	21,000	
Purchases	246,000	
Repair expense	13,000	
Retained earnings, 1/1/96		275,000
Salary expense	27,000	
Shipments to branch		88,000
Shipments to consignee		170,000
Utility expense	5,000	
Totals	$857,000	$857,000

For accounting purposes, Rice requires both the branch and the consignment dealer to file periodic operating reports. Following (on the left) are summaries of these transactional memos for the year of 1996 as well as the composition of Rice's own reciprocal accounts (on the right).

CHESTER BRANCH OF RICE CORPORATION
Home Office Account
1996

Beginning balance	$ (71,000)
Cash transfer	28,000
Inventory received	(36,000)
Allocation of advertising	(6,000)
Inventory received	(19,000)
Allocation of salary	(8,000)
Cash transfer	19,000
Inventory received	(22,000)
End-of-year balance	$(115,000)

RICE CORPORATION
Branch—Chester Account
1996

Beginning balance	$ 71,000
Inventory shipped—cost	36,000
Cash received	(28,000)
Inventory shipped—cost	16,000
Allocation of advertising expense	6,000
Allocation of salaries	8,000
Inventory shipped—cost	22,000
Inventory shipped—cost	14,000
End-of-year balance	$145,000

DEPARTMENT STORE— CONSIGNEE
Consignment Report
1996

Beginning balance	–0–
Reimbursable advertising	$ 3,000
Consignment sales	(128,000)
Partial consignment payment	94,000
Reimbursable insurance	2,000
Consignment sales	(162,000)
Consignment sales	(40,000)
Commissions earned (20%)	66,000
End-of-year balance	$(165,000)

NOTE: One third of last inventory shipment remains at end of year.

RICE CORPORATION
Consignment-Out Account
1996

Beginning balance (inventory)	$ 35,000
Inventory shipped	98,000
Packing of shipment	2,000
Freight for shipment	4,000
Payment received	(94,000)
Inventory shipped	72,000
Freight for shipment	2,000
Packing of shipment	1,000
End-of-year balance	$120,000

Required:

Prepare a worksheet to combine the accounting records of the Rice Corporation and its Chester branch so that financial statements can be produced. In creating this worksheet, assume that all parties are using FIFO inventory costing systems. Also assume that any omissions from the records just presented were caused by timing differences occurring at the end of the fiscal year. *Where unexplained discrepancies exist, assume that the account balances of the Rice Corporation's home office are correct.* Since the actual journals and ledgers are not available, any adjusting entries should be made directly on the worksheet. The final 1996 trial balance for the Chester branch follows:

	Debit	Credit
Accounts payable		$ 9,000
Accounts receivable	$ 44,000	
Accumulated depreciation		6,000
Advertising expense	6,000	
Buildings and equipment	54,000	
Cash	26,000	
Depreciation expense	4,000	
Home office		115,000
Insurance expense	4,000	
Inventory (income statement)	16,000	24,000
Inventory, 12/31/96	24,000	
Salary expense	17,000	
Sales		121,000
Shipments from home office	77,000	
Utility expense	3,000	
Totals	$275,000	$275,000

SOLUTION

As indicated within this chapter, monitoring the interaction between the various reporting systems is an essential activity of both branch and consignment accounting. Thus, as a preliminary step in preparing financial statements, Rice Corporation should reconcile the Home Office and Branch accounts. The Consignment-Out balance also needs to be brought into agreement with the information provided by the consignee. Once these interface accounts have been properly adjusted, the development of combined financial statements should be a rather uncomplicated process.

Branch Operations.   Although a number of different approaches are viable here, an analysis of the Home Office/Branch accounts provides a convenient starting point. As can be seen from the two individual trial balances, the home office is reporting a Branch balance of $145,000 whereas the reciprocal Home Office account (on the branch's books) holds a total of only $115,000. A comparison of the detailed listing of entries presented in the problem indicates that three recording errors have created this $30,000 difference:

- A cash transfer of $19,000 from the branch was not recorded by the home office prior to the end of the year.
- A $14,000 shipment of merchandise from the home office has not yet been acknowledged by the branch.
- An inventory transfer was entered by the branch as $19,000 rather than $16,000.

The first two of these problems are merely timing differences. In each case, one of the accounting systems failed to record information in the appropriate fiscal period. Corrections have been made on the combination worksheet (in Exhibit 8–3) through Entries 1 and 2. Since inventory (Entry 2) was in transit at year-end, an additional assumption is made that this merchandise was not included in the physical count, taken by the branch, an oversight rectified through Entry 3.

The final item is apparently a recording error made by the Chester branch (since the financial records of the home office are assumed to be correct). Thus, the $19,000 that was reported by the branch is reduced (in Entry 4) to the correct $16,000 balance. The combination of the home office and branch can then be consummated by the elimination of all reciprocals. Entry 5 offsets the intracompany inventory shipments, Entry 6 removes the adjusted $126,000 Home Office/Branch accounts.

Consignment Sales. Having now produced the entries necessary for combining the financial data of the home office and the branch, Rice's consignment transactions should be analyzed next. Since a Consignment-Out (or holding) account is utilized, a complete breakdown of its contents is a requisite for reclassifying the various balances.

As a basis for this procedure, the Consignment-Out account is compared with the report filed by the consignee. *However, no agreement is sought between the final balances since these accounts are not actually reciprocals.* Rather, reconciliation helps to identify any transactions that the consignor has not recorded properly. By comparing the details of these two accounts, Rice is able to determine

1. The cost of inventory still being held by the consignee.
2. The cost of consignment goods that were sold.
3. The revenue and expense figures for the period.
4. Any ending receivable balance due from the consignee.

To arrive at the amounts to be reported by the consignor, the following four schedules can be developed:

EXHIBIT 8-3

RICE CORPORATION
Combination Worksheet
For Year Ending December 31, 1996

Accounts	Home Office Debit	Home Office Credit	Chester Branch Debit	Chester Branch Credit	Combination Entries Debit	Combination Entries Credit	Income Statement	Statement of Retained Earnings	Balance Sheet
Accounts payable		39,000		9,000					(48,000)
Accounts receivable	29,000		44,000						73,000
Accumulated depreciation		18,000		6,000					(24,000)
Advertising expense	16,000		6,000		(7) 3,000		25,000		
Branch—Chester	145,000		-0-			(1) 19,000 (6) 126,000			-0-
Buildings and equipment	66,000		54,000						120,000
Cash	7,000		26,000						52,000
Commissions expense	-0-		-0-		(1) 19,000 (7) 66,000		66,000		
Common stock		200,000							(200,000)
Consignment inventory (balance sheet)	-0-		-0-		(7) 25,000				25,000
Consignment inventory (income statement)	-0-		-0-		(7) 35,000	(7) 25,000	(BI) 35,000 (EI) (25,000)		
Consignment-out	120,000	-0-	-0-			(7) 120,000			-0-
Consignment receivable	-0-		-0-		(7) 165,000				165,000
Consignment sales				-0-		(7) 330,000	(330,000)		
Depreciation expense	4,000		4,000				8,000		
Dividends paid	12,000		-0-					12,000	
Freight and packing	-0-		-0-		(7) 9,000 (4) 3,000 (6) 126,000		9,000		
Home office	-0-	-0-		115,000		(2) 14,000			-0-

Account	Trial Balance Dr	Trial Balance Cr	Adjustments Dr	Adjustments Cr	Combined Income Statement	Combined Retained Earnings	Combined Balance Sheet
Insurance expense	-0-		4,000	(7) 2,000	6,000		
Inventory (income statement)	79,000		16,000		(BI) 95,000		
Inventory, 12/31/96	67,000		24,000	(3) 14,000	(EI) (105,000)		105,000
Land	21,000						21,000
Purchases	246,000				246,000		
Repair expense	13,000				13,000		
Retained earnings, 1/1/96		275,000				(275,000)	
Salary expense	27,000		17,000		44,000		
Sales	-0-		121,000	(2) 14,000	(121,000)		
Shipments from home office		-0-	77,000		-0-		
Shipments on consignment	-0-			(4) 3,000			
Shipments to branch	-0-	88,000		(7) 170,000	170,000		
Shipments to consignee	-0-	170,000	3,000	(5) 88,000	-0-		
Utility expense	5,000		3,000		8,000		
Combined net income				(5) 88,000	(26,000)	(26,000)	
Combined retained earnings						(289,000)	(289,000)
Totals	857,000	857,000	275,000	275,000	(289,000)	(289,000)	-0-

NOTE: Parentheses indicate a credit balance.
"BI" represents beginning inventory; "EI" is ending inventory.
Worksheet entries are discussed in the text.

EXHIBIT 8-4   Financial Statements

RICE CORPORATION
Income Statement
for Year Ending December 31, 1996

	Home Office and Branch	Consignments	Totals
Sales	$121,000	$330,000	$451,000
Cost of sales:			
Beginning inventory.	$ 95,000	$ 35,000	$ 130,000
Purchases	246,000	–0–	246,000
Shipments on consignment.	(170,000)	170,000	–0–
Freight and packing.	–0–	9,000	9,000
Goods available	171,000	214,000	385,000
Ending inventory	(105,000)	(25,000)	(130,000)
Cost of goods sold	(66,000)	(189,000)	(255,000)
Gross profit	$ 55,000	$ 141,000	$ 196,000
Advertising expense			(25,000)
Commissions expense			(66,000)
Depreciation expense			(8,000)
Insurance expense			(6,000)
Repair expense			(13,000)
Salary expense			(44,000)
Utility expense			(8,000)
Net income			$ 26,000

Statement of Retained Earnings
for Year Ending December 31, 1996

Retained earnings, 1/1/96		$275,000
Net income (above)	$ 26,000	
Less: Dividends paid	(12,000)	14,000
Retained earnings, 12/31/96		$289,000

Balance Sheet
December 31, 1996

Assets

Cash		$ 52,000
Accounts receivable		73,000
Consignment receivable		165,000
Inventory		105,000
Consignment inventory		25,000
Land		21,000
Buildings and equipment	$120,000	
Less: Accumulated depreciation	(24,000)	96,000
Total assets		$537,000

Liabilities and Equities

Accounts payable		$ 48,000
Common stock	$200,000	
Retained earnings (above)	289,000	489,000
Total liabilities and equities		$537,000

NOTE: Although companies are required to report a statement of cash flows for every fiscal period in which an income statement is prepared, insufficient information is included in this illustration for that purpose. Thus, the statement of cash flows has been omitted.

Ending consignment inventory:

Total cost of last shipment (including freight and packing)	$ 75,000
Inventory remaining (as reported by consignee)	⅓
Cost of ending consignment inventory	$ 25,000

Cost of consignment goods sold:

Beginning inventory (per ledger account)	$ 35,000
Shipments to consignee.	170,000
Packing and freight.	9,000
Less: Ending inventory (above)	(25,000)
Cost of consignment goods sold	$ 189,000

Consignment revenue and expense balances:

Consignment sales (from consignee's report)	$ 330,000
Cost of goods sold (above)	(189,000)
Gross profit	141,000
Operating expenses (from consignee's report):	
Commissions	(66,000)
Advertising	(3,000)
Insurance	(2,000)
Consignment income	$ 70,000

Ending consignment receivable balance:

Consignment sales	$ 330,000
Less: Commissions—20%.	(66,000)
Less: Reimbursable expenses:	
Advertising	(3,000)
Insurance	(2,000)
Amount due from consignee	259,000
Partial payment received during year.	(94,000)
Consignment receivable—end of year	$ 165,000

Based on these computations, an extended worksheet entry can be produced by Rice to reclassify the various consignment figures. This entry recognizes consignment revenue, expense, and asset balances that should be reported by the company for the period.

Worksheet Entry 7

Consignment Receivable	165,000	
Commissions Expense	66,000	
Advertising Expense.	3,000	
Insurance Expense	2,000	
Shipments on Consignment	170,000	
Freight and Packing	9,000	
Consignment Inventory, 12/31/96 (balance sheet)	25,000	
Consignment Inventory (income statement).	35,000	25,000
Consignment Sales.		330,000
Consignment-Out		120,000

Exhibit 8–3 presents the completed worksheet for Rice Corporation and its various operations. The figures found in the last three columns can be utilized to produce financial statements for external reporting purposes. The seven entries just discussed have been used to combine the account balances of the company's home office and the Chester branch as well as report the consignment transactions for 1996.

When a company such as Rice relies on more than one method of distributing its products, a question arises as to the best approach to take for reporting the operational figures. Although no single format is applicable in all cases, one possible income statement is presented in the financial statements produced in Exhibit 8–4. Revenues, cost of goods sold, and gross profit are all disclosed for both branch and consignment transactions. Since no other allocation information has been given, the operating expenses are presented as common costs. In practice, many of these figures might also be divided between the two distributing functions of this company.

Questions

1. What is meant by the term *branch*?
2. Why is the development of branch operations so prevalent in retailing and banking?
3. When a corporation makes use of branch operations, accounting problems often arise in connection with intracompany transactions. What intracompany transactions are commonly encountered? What difficulties are presented?
4. In accounting for branch operations, many companies assign a portion of their general corporate expenses to the various branches. What is the rationale for such allocations?
5. Home Office and Branch accounts are frequently found in the accounting systems of companies that maintain branch operations. What is the purpose of these two accounts? Why should reciprocity be maintained between their balances?
6. How do the combination procedures applied in connection with branch operations resemble the consolidation process and in what ways are they different?
7. What is consignment marketing? What are the advantages to a company of selling on consignment?
8. What are the major objectives in accounting for consignment transactions?
9. A consignor can adopt either of two different approaches in the recording of consignments. Describe these approaches and indicate the advantages of each.
10. What is the purpose of a Consignment-In account?

Library Assignment

Read "I'll Gladly Pay You Tuesday" in the June 1986 issue of *Distribution*. Write a report describing the consignment marketing of products. Discuss the merits of this system and any potential drawbacks. Indicate the types of businesses that would most likely use this type of consignment approach.

Problems

1. Hayes, Inc., has a branch operation located in Duluth. On the home office financial records, Hayes reports a Duluth—Branch account with a $78,000 debit balance. At that same time, the branch operation is reporting a Home Office account with an $81,000 credit balance. Which of the following statements is true?
   a. Since two different sets of records are being kept, these two accounts are not designed to agree.
   b. The difference indicates that inventory may be in transit from the home office to the branch.
   c. The difference indicates that cash may be in transit from the branch to the home office.
   d. Cash may have been collected by the home office for the branch but not yet reported to the branch.

2. Lewis, Inc., operates a branch in Toledo, Ohio. On the home office financial records at the end of 1995, Lewis reports a Toledo—Branch account with an $167,000 debit balance. The branch operation is reporting on that same date a Home Office account with a $162,000 credit balance. Which of the following statements is true?
   a. Since two different sets of records are being kept, these two accounts are not designed to agree.
   b. The difference indicates that cash may be in transit from the branch to the home office.
   c. Cash may have been collected by the home office for the branch but not yet reported to the branch.
   d. The difference indicates that the home office might have assigned a $6,000 expense allocation to the branch that was incorrectly recorded by the branch as $11,000.

3. A company sells inventory from its home office and also from a branch operation in a nearby city. At the end of the fiscal year, what happens to the Branch account (on the home office's financial records) and the Home Office account (on the branch's financial records) when financial statements for the company as a whole are being produced?

    a. The Home Office account is eliminated but the Branch account balance is reported as an investment.

    b. The two accounts are reconciled and offset against each other.

    c. The Home Office account is reported as an equity account whereas the Branch account is shown as an investment.

    d. On these financial statements, the manner of reporting these two accounts depends on whether they have debit or credit balances.

4. A company has several branch operations that sell merchandise transferred from the home office. This inventory is transferred at as a price 20 percent more than cost. In producing financial statements for the company as a whole, what happens at the end of the year?

    a. The unrealized gain on any remaining inventory is eliminated for financial reporting purposes.

    b. The gain remains as reported since the amount would be immaterial.

    c. Any remaining gain is reported as a contra balance to the Purchases account.

    d. Any remaining gain is reported as a contra balance to the Branch account.

5. Consignment marketing is a popular means by which companies can get wide distribution of their products. Which of the following statements is true?

    a. The consignor has no risks.

    b. The consignor is guaranteed that all goods will be sold.

    c. The consignee might be willing to attempt to sell goods that it would otherwise not carry.

    d. The consignor has no costs to record as a result of this type of marketing.

6. What does the balance in a Consignment-Out account represent?

    a. The amount that a consignee owes to a consignor at any time.

    b. The consignor's cost of all consignment inventory being held by consignees.

    c. The amount of consignment sales made by the consignee during the current period.

    d. The net of all consignment costs incurred by a consignor less all receipts from the consignee.

7. Simpson Corporation starts a branch operation in a nearby town. Merchandise costing $80,000 is shipped to this branch along with equipment costing $50,000. During the initial year, the home office assigns $8,000 in expenses to the branch. The branch sells 70 percent of the inventory that it received for $80,000 and remits $40,000 in cash to the home office. What is the correct Home Office account balance on the records of the branch? Closing entries have not been made.

    a. $98,000.

    b. $104,000.

  c. $122,000.

  d. $178,000.

8. Lancaster, Inc., starts a branch operation to sell more of its merchandise. Inventory costing $60,000 is shipped to this branch at a transfer price of $90,000. During the initial year, the home office pays $17,000 in expenses for the branch. The branch sells 80 percent of the inventory that it received for $110,000 and remits $70,000 in cash to the home office. What is the correct Home Office account balance on the records of the branch? Closing entries have not been made.

  a. $7,000.

  b. $37,000.

  c. $75,000.

  d. $147,000.

9. Splicer starts a branch operation on January 1, 1995. Inventory costing $72,000 is shipped to this branch at a transfer price of $100,000. Freight is an additional $6,000. The branch sells 70 percent of this inventory for $110,000 and remits $70,000 in cash to the home office. On Splicer's financial statements for this period, what is the appropriate Cost of Goods Sold figure?

  a. $50,400.

  b. $54,600.

  c. $70,000.

  d. $74,200.

10. Storey Corporation operates a branch in Dallas, Texas. In October, the home office transferred $34,000 in inventory to this branch. Although the home office made the correct journal entry, the branch credited its Home Office account for $43,000. In November, the branch collected $1,000 on an account receivable for the home office. The home office was properly notified but debited its Branch account for $4,000. At the end of the year, the home office paid and recorded a $6,000 expense for the branch but the branch has not yet made the appropriate entry. Also, at year's end, the branch conveyed $25,000 in cash to the home office but the home office has not yet made the necessary entry. What corrections are needed?

  a. The home office needs to credit its Branch account for $24,000 and the branch needs to debit its Home Office account for $9,000.

  b. The home office needs to credit its Branch account for $30,000 and the branch needs to debit its Home Office account for $3,000.

  c. The home office needs to credit its Branch account for $22,000 and the branch needs to debit its Home Office account for $15,000.

  d. The home office needs to credit its Branch account for $28,000 and the branch needs to debit its Home Office account for $3,000.

11. A branch operation buys most of its inventory from outside parties. However, this year the home office transferred merchandise costing $50,000 to the branch for $80,000. At the end of the year, 20 percent of this merchan-

dise was still held by the branch. Although the inventory was correctly counted and reported, the branch did not tell the home office that this portion of the remaining goods came from transfers. Consequently, the home office assumed that all of the transferred merchandise had been sold to outside parties. What is the resulting impact on the net income reported for the company as a whole?

a. The net income figure would still be correctly calculated.

b. The net income figure would be $6,000 overstated.

c. The net income figure would be $30,000 overstated.

d. The net income figure would be $30,000 understated.

Problems 12 and 13 are based on the following information:

The Simon Company always ships merchandise to a branch outlet in Chicago at a 30 percent markup above cost. During 1995, this branch received $182,000 in such shipments while also acquiring goods from outside vendors at at cost of $96,000. Half of the branch's December 31, 1995, inventory of $57,200 came from home office acquisitions. At the beginning of 1995, the branch held merchandise with a transfer price of $49,400. All of this inventory had been purchased directly from the home office.

12. At the end of 1995, what is the adjusted balance in Simon's Unrealized Gain account?

a. $4,250.

b. $5,340.

c. $6,000.

d. $6,600.

13. For external reporting purposes, what cost of goods sold figure should be reported by the branch for this period?

a. $207,846.

b. $223,400.

c. $230,000.

d. $234,800.

14. Cochran, Incorporated, sends 1,000 units of inventory costing $80 each to a consignor to be sold at $120 per unit. Freight costs paid by Cochran total $2,000. The consignor also pays an additional $1,000 in advertising costs. The consignee sells 60 percent of this merchandise. The consignee is entitled to a commission equal to 10 percent of sales price. The consignee only remits $50,000 at this time. What profit has been earned by the consignor?

a. $13,800.

b. $14,000.

c. $14,600.

d. $15,000.

15. Crescent Corporation ships 2,000 units of inventory costing $30 each to a consignor to be sold at $70 per unit. Freight costs paid by Cochran amount to $8,000. Another $3,000 is paid by the consignor for advertising costs.

During the current period, the consignee sells 70 percent of this merchandise. The consignee is entitled to a commission equal to 20 percent of sales price. The consignee remits $78,400 at this time. What is the unadjusted balance in Crescent's Consignment-Out account?

a. $7,400 credit.

b. $22,400 credit.

c. $16,400 debit.

d. $31,400 debit.

16. Bears, Inc., owns a branch operation in Chicago. As of the end of the current year, the home office has a Chicago—Branch account with a $77,000 debit balance. At the same time, the branch is reporting a Home Office account with a $61,000 credit balance. An investigation uncovers the following:
   - During the year, the home office shipped merchandise costing $16,000 to the branch at a transfer price of $28,000. The branch accidently recorded the shipment as $38,000.
   - At year's end, the home office assigned $14,000 in expenses to the branch. The branch recorded this allocation as $19,000.
   - Also at year's end, the branch transferred $31,000 in cash to the home office. The home office has not yet recorded this money.

Required:

a. What is the reconciled balance of the Chicago—Branch and Home Office accounts?

b. What correcting entries are needed?

17. Wilson Company's home office has the following transactions with one of its branch operations located in Phoenix:

1995

Jan. 1   The beginning Branch account holds a debit balance of $86,000.

Jan. 2   The home office receives notice of a $32,000 cash transfer deposited on December 31, 1994, by the Phoenix branch. The home office had made no previous recording.

Jan. 6   The home office ships $30,000 in inventory to this branch at a $34,500 transfer price.

Jan. 10 The home office pays $1,000 monthly rent to the owner of the Phoenix branch's building. This cost is assigned to the operations of the branch (communication is made immediately).

Jan. 12 The home office allocates $3,000 of general corporate expenses to the branch (communication is made immediately).

Jan. 24 The home office ships $40,000 in inventory to the Phoenix branch at a transfer price of $46,000. The branch erroneously records the shipment as $64,000.

Jan. 31 The home office allocates $3,000 in transportation costs (that were incurred during January) to the branch. The assignment is not communicated to the branch until February 2, 1995.

Feb. 1 Notification of a $74,000 cash transfer is received by the home office. The deposit was made in Phoenix on January 31, 1995.

Required:

a. What is the unadjusted balance of the Branch—Phoenix account on the home office's books as of January 31, 1995?

b. What is the unadjusted balance of the Home Office account on the branch's financial records as of January 31, 1995?

c. What is the reconciled value for the Home Office/Branch accounts as of January 31, 1995?

d. Assume that a FIFO costing system is being used and that 25 percent of the final inventory shipment remains unsold at year-end. What is the amount of unrealized gain to be eliminated from the branch's ending inventory?

18. King Company sells its merchandise on consignment. This year the company began operations with $18,000 (8,000 units) of inventory out on consignment. During the year, inventory costing $66,000 (27,500 units) was shipped to the consignee. The related freight cost was $6,050. At the end of the period, King received the following statement from the consignee:

Sales (24,500 units at $6)	$147,000
Delivery cost of units sold	(4,900)
Advertising	(16,300)
Commissions	(29,400)
Check enclosed	$ 96,400

Required:

a. What is King's cost of goods sold if the company employs a FIFO system?

b. What is King's cost of goods sold if the company employs a LIFO system?

c. What is the adjusted book value of the Consignment-Out and Consignment-In accounts at the end of the year if both parties use a FIFO costing system?

19. The Lewis Corporation has a branch operation in Fairfax, Virginia. Because of the high volume of intracompany transactions, the company has encountered difficulty in reconciling its Home Office/Branch accounts. Following is a listing of the components of the Branch balance (from the home office's ledger) followed with the Home Office account as recorded by the branch.

BRANCH—FAIRFAX
Account Composition (on financial records of home office)

Jan.	1	Beginning balance	$ 62,000
Jan.	2	Cash received	(16,000)
Mar.	2	Inventory transferred	42,000
Apr.	1	Salary allocation	9,200
July	2	Inventory transferred	36,000
Sept.	5	Insurance expense allocation	1,000
Oct.	6	Cash received	(21,000)
Nov.	4	Inventory transferred	28,000
Dec.	31	Depreciation allocation	(3,000)
		End-of-year balance (debit)	$138,200

HOME OFFICE
Account Composition (on financial records of branch)

Jan.	1	Beginning balance	$(35,000)
Jan.	2	Inventory received	(11,000)
Mar.	5	Inventory received	(42,000)
Apr.	5	Salary allocation	(9,000)
Apr.	8	Cash transferred	45,000
July	6	Inventory received	(48,000)
Sept.	10	Insurance expense allocation	(1,000)
Oct.	4	Cash transferred	21,000
Nov.	8	Inventory received	(28,000)
Dec.	31	Cash transferred	15,000
		End-of-year balance (credit)	$(93,000)

Additional Information:

- A cash transfer received during the year was credited by the home office to Miscellaneous Income.
- The bookkeeper for the branch incorrectly recorded two amounts: a salary allocation and an inventory shipment.

Required:

a. Determine the correct balance for the Home Office/Branch accounts as of December 31.
b. Prepare adjusting entries for both parties as of December 31 to properly record these intracompany accounts.

20. The Columbia Company recently made the decision to open a branch of its business in Gaffney. Since that time, the following transactions have occurred in connection with this new operation:
 - The home office acquired $18,000 in equipment to be used (and recorded) by the branch.
 - The home office paid $3,000 to lease a building for the last six months of this year. This cost was charged to the branch.

- Inventory costing $80,000 was shipped to branch by the home office at a transfer price of $100,000. The home office separately records all of its unrealized gains.
- The branch paid $11,000 for various operating expenses.
- The branch sold 75 percent of the inventory received, collecting $105,000 in cash.
- The branch transferred $60,000 in cash to the home office.

Required:

a. Prepare journal entries for both the home office and the branch to record the previous transactions.
b. Prepare the worksheet entries that would bring about the combination of the home office and branch at the end of the period.
c. Produce entries to close out the operations of the branch at the end of the period.

21. During the first part of the current year, Nobula, Inc. begins a branch operation in Cherry Hill, New Jersey. Equipment costing $50,000 is immediately sent to this site. In addition, inventory costing $40,000 is transferred but at a price of $60,000. Cash of $10,000 is also conveyed to the branch.

    The following events occur thereafter:
    - The branch buys inventory from an outside party at a cost of $30,000. A periodic inventory system is in use.
    - The home office pays $10,000 rent on a building for the next eight months. The branch is notified of this payment.
    - Sales of $90,000 are made. Cash of $40,000 is collected immediately. The rest of the sales are made on account.
    - The branch pays $8,000 for advertising and another $5,000 for salaries.
    - The branch transfers $10,000 in cash to the home office. The money is received and recorded.
    - A $3,000 receivable is collected by the home office for the branch. The branch is notified of this collection.
    - The building rented by the branch is occupied for four months.

Required:

a. Prepare all necessary journal entries for both the branch and the home office.
b. Assume that one third of the transferred merchandise and one fourth of the inventory bought from outsiders remains at year's end. What is the net income of the branch operation?

22. In hopes of improving corporate profitability, Denmark, Inc., has opened a branch operation in the city of Norge. Merchandise is shipped to this branch at a transfer price 50 percent more than the home office's cost. At the end of 1995, Denmark allocated several expenses to the branch but the branch has not yet been notified about these amounts.

Advertising expense	$11,000 allocated to the Norge branch
Rent expense	7,000 allocated to the Norge branch
Miscellaneous expenses	6,000 allocated to the Norge branch

In addition, one $21,000 shipment of inventory has not yet been received or recorded by the Norge branch. A $9,000 cash transfer from the branch has not yet been received or recorded by the home office.

Following are the various account balances for the home office and the branch. Determine the total for each account to be presented in a set of financial statements prepared for the company as a whole.

	Home Office	Branch
Debits:		
Cash	$ 16,000	$ 11,000
Accounts receivable	81,000	37,000
Inventory, 12/31/95 (balance sheet)	97,000	60,000
Branch—Norge	177,000	–0–
Land, buildings, and equipment	361,000	99,000
Shipments from home office	–0–	159,000
Purchases	429,000	–0–
Depreciation expense	17,000	11,000
Advertising expense	29,000	18,000
Rent expense	14,000	9,000
Miscellaneous expenses	62,000	32,000
Inventory, 1/1/95	121,000	36,000
Total debits	$1,404,000	$472,000
Credits:		
Accumulated depreciation	$ 90,000	$ 18,000
Accounts payable	48,000	56,000
Notes payable	180,000	–0–
Home office	–0–	123,000
Common stock	60,000	–0–
Retained earnings, 1/1/95	260,000	–0–
Sales	489,000	215,000
Shipments to Norge branch	180,000	–0–
Inventory, 12/31/95 (income statement)	97,000	60,000
Total credits	$1,404,000	$472,000

23. The Jiminie Company began in 1995 to sell merchandise through a consignee. Prepare journal entries for Jiminie for the following transactions assuming that a Consignment-Out account is being used. In addition, prepare the year-end reclassification entry that would be needed.
    - 1,500 units of inventory costing $30 apiece are transferred to the consignee.

- Jiminie pays $4,500 in freight costs to have these units delivered to the consignee.
- Jiminie pays $3,000 to have the units insured enroute to the consignee.
- The consignee sells 1,000 units owned by Jiminie for $50 each. Consignee retains $5,000 as a commission and $2,000 to cover the cost of a local advertising campaign. The remaining $43,000 is forwarded to Jiminie.

24. During the current year, the Lang Corporation decided to begin selling its inventory on consignment. Hill, Inc., agrees to serve as a consignee. Hill receives a commission of 20 percent on every sale that is made. Lang transfers inventory to Hill having a cost of $55,000 but a sales value of $80,000. Lang pays an additional $4,000 in delivery costs.

    Hill sells 60 percent of this inventory for cash and remits the appropriate amount to Lang.

Required:

a. Prepare journal entries for both companies. Assume that Lang uses a Consignment Inventory account.
b. Compute the amount of profit earned by Lang from its consignment sales.
c. Determine the ending balance in the Consignment Inventory account on Lang's balance sheet.

25. Financial statement information follows for the Northern Company and its Millburn branch:

	Northern Company	Millburn Branch
Sales	$(300,000)	$(180,000)
Inventory, 1/1	40,000	10,000
Purchases	160,000	–0–
Intracompany shipments.	(90,000)	120,000
Inventory, 12/31	(25,000)	(20,000)
Unrealized gains	(30,000)	–0–
Operating expenses	140,000	28,000
Net income	$(105,000)	$ (42,000)
Retained earnings, home office, 1/1	$(620,000)	$ (90,000)
Net income (above)	(105,000)	(42,000)
Dividends (transfers)	70,000	20,000
Ending balance	$(655,000)	$(112,000)
Current assets	$ 225,000	$ 79,000
Millburn branch	122,000	–0–
Fixed assets (net).	586,000	93,000
Total assets	$ 933,000	$ 172,000
Liabilities	$(198,000)	$ (60,000)
Home office (above)	–0–	(112,000)
Common stock	(80,000)	–0–
Retained earnings (above)	(655,000)	–0–
Total liabilities and equities	$(933,000)	$(172,000)

At the end of the fiscal year, a $10,000 cash transfer from the branch was in transit.

Required:

Prepare a combination worksheet for the Northern Company and this branch operation.

26. Addams ships inventory with a cost of $98,000 to a consignee in hopes of generating additional revenues. Freight and transportation costs amounting to $7,000 were paid by Addams.

    The consignee subsequently sells 70 percent of this merchandise for $124,000, remitting $102,000 to Addams after subtracting a $20,000 commission and $2,000 in reimbursable selling costs.

    No adjusting or reclassification entries have, as of yet, been recorded by Addams.

Required:

a. What amount of net income should Addams recognize in connection with these consignment transactions?
b. If Addams uses a single Consignment-Out account, what is the current balance?
c. Assume that Addams uses a single Consignment-Out account. Prepare journal entries for Addams along with any needed adjusting or reclassification entries.
d. Assume that Addams uses a Consignment Inventory account. Prepare journal entries for Addams along with any needed adjusting or reclassification entries.
e. What is the current balance of the Consignment-In account found within the financial records of the consignee?

27. On January 1, 1995, Landon, Inc., opened a branch operation in the nearby community of Belwood. During the year that followed, the home office incurred the following transactions in connection with this newly formed branch:

    1995
    Jan. 1　Transferred several items to the Belwood branch:
    　　　　　Cash—$30,000
    　　　　　Inventory—$36,000 (cost)
    　　　　　Equipment—$122,000 (cost)
    June 2　Transferred inventory costing $18,000 to branch in Belwood.
    July 1　Paid 1995 property taxes of $5,000 assessed on assets held by the Belwood branch.
    Sept. 1　Transferred inventory costing $26,000 to the branch in Belwood.
    Dec. 31　Allocated a $6,000 portion of general corporate expenses to the Belwood branch.
    Dec. 31　Received cash transfer from Belwood branch.

During this same period, the Belwood branch recorded the following events:

1995

Jan. 10	Received initial transfers from home office.
Jan. 20	Paid $4,000 rent expense for the year.
Feb. 1	Sold half of inventory on hand for $27,000 cash.
Apr. 1	Sold remaining inventory for $33,000 cash.
May 1	Paid miscellaneous expenses of $7,000.
June 5	Received shipment of inventory.
July 6	Received communication concerning property tax payment.
Sept. 9	Received shipment of inventory.
Oct. 1	Sold the June 5 inventory for $26,000 in cash (a FIFO costing system is used).
Nov. 1	Paid miscellaneous expenses of $4,000.
Dec. 22	Transferred $63,000 cash to home office.
Dec. 31	Calculated and recorded depreciation expense of $4,000.
Dec. 31	Received communication from home office concerning expense allocation.

Required:

a. What amount of net income has been earned by the Belwood branch?

b. On December 31, 1995, prior to recording closing entries, what is the appropriate balance in the Home Office/Branch accounts?

c. Prepare journal entries for this period for the Belwood branch. Closing entries are not required. Assume that a perpetual inventory system is being used.

d. Prepare a balance sheet for the Belwood branch as of December 31, 1995.

e. Assume that all entries have been recorded properly by both parties. However, the home office has a policy of transferring inventory shipments at a price 20 percent above cost. What are the balances in the Branch and Home Office accounts on December 31, 1995, after all closing entries?

 28. Hopkins, Inc., sells a number of different items from its headquarters in Denver, Colorado. In recent years, in hopes of increasing sales volume, the company has opened two branches in nearby cities: Wilson and Simmons. Merchandise is shipped to these outlets periodically and recorded at a transfer price that includes a 50 percent markup over cost.

At the end of 1996, Hopkins assigns the following portions of several corporate expenses to these two branches. Although these allocations were recorded by the company headquarters, the branches did not receive this information prior to the end of the year.

Allocations	Wilson	Simmons
Advertising expense	$4,000	$5,000
Rent expense	3,000	4,000
Miscellaneous expenses	5,000	5,000

Required:

The following financial records are for the home office and these two branches as of December 31, 1996. Produce a worksheet to combine the accounts of these three operations so that a single set of financial statements can be prepared for Hopkins, Inc. Also prepare closing entries for each of the branches.

	Hopkins	Wilson	Simmons
Debits			
Cash	$ 25,000	$ 10,000	$ 30,000
Accounts receivable	94,000	20,000	38,000
Inventory, 12/31/96 (balance sheet)	214,000	35,000	40,000
Branch—Wilson	176,000	–0–	–0–
Branch—Simmons	232,000	–0–	–0–
Land, buildings, and equipment	330,000	120,000	90,000
Shipments from home office	–0–	90,000	170,000
Purchases	380,000	–0–	–0–
Depreciation expense	20,000	6,000	9,000
Advertising expense	30,000	10,000	10,000
Rent expense	10,000	5,000	15,000
Miscellaneous expenses	50,000	10,000	8,000
Inventory, 1/1/96	186,000	30,000	60,000
Total debits	$1,747,000	$336,000	$470,000
Credits			
Accumulated depreciation	$ 60,000	$ 12,000	$ 18,000
Accounts payable	20,000	5,000	24,000
Notes payable	240,000	–0–	10,000
Home office	–0–	164,000	218,000
Common stock	100,000	–0–	–0–
Retained earnings, 1/1/96	413,000	–0–	–0–
Sales	440,000	120,000	160,000
Shipments to branch	260,000	–0–	–0–
Inventory, 12/31/96 (income statement)	214,000	35,000	40,000
Total credits	$1,747,000	$336,000	$470,000

29. The Oregon Company has sold merchandise on consignment for a number of years. At the beginning of 1995, $85,000 of Oregon's consignment inventory is being held by Charlotte, Inc. Currently, Charlotte owes $36,000 to Oregon for consignment sales made during the previous year.

Following are the consignment transactions for Oregon that occurred during the first quarter of the new period:

1995

Jan. 9   Received $36,000 check from Charlotte.
Feb. 2   Received the following statement from Charlotte:

Sales	$110,000
Commissions	(27,500)
Advertising	(2,200)
Delivery	(1,600)
Amount due.	78,700
Current remittance.	(40,000)
Amount still due	$ 38,700

Feb. 20   Paid $1,000 insurance on consignment goods.
Feb. 27   Shipped inventory costing $68,000 to Charlotte.
Mar. 2   Paid $1,100 freight cost on the above shipment.
Mar. 6   Received $38,700 check from Charlotte.
Mar. 20   Received following statement from Charlotte:

Sales	$124,000
Commissions	(31,000)
Advertising	(2,500)
Delivery	(2,300)
Amount due.	88,200
Current remittance.	(50,000)
Amount still due	$ 38,200

Charlotte's latest statement also indicates that 30 percent of the inventory shipped on February 27 remains unsold. Oregon utilizes a FIFO inventory system.

Required:

a. Assume that Oregon uses a Consignment-Out (or holding) account to record its transactions. Prepare the journal entries for the first three months of 1995, including the reclassification entries needed at the end of the quarter.

b. Compute the net income derived by Oregon from these consignment transactions.

c. Assume that Oregon uses a Consignment Inventory account to record consignment transactions as they occur. Prepare the journal entries for the first three months of 1995, including the company's cost of goods sold entry.

d. Prepare journal entries for Charlotte for the first three months of 1995.

30. In hopes of increasing sales volume, the Heyman Company opened a branch outlet several years ago in the nearby city of Dover. Merchandise is shipped to this store periodically and recorded at a transfer price that includes a 40 percent markup over cost. At the end of 1996, Heyman assigns the following corporate expenses to this branch. Although the main office has properly recorded these allocations, no entry has yet been made by the branch.

	Expense	*Allocation to Dover*
Advertising		$9,000
Rent		6,000
Miscellaneous		2,000

The following trial balances are for the main office and the Dover branch as of December 31, 1996. One $14,000 inventory shipment has not been received or recorded by Dover.

Required:

Prepare a worksheet to combine the records of these two operations so that a single set of financial statements can be prepared for Heyman, Inc.

	Heyman	*Dover*
Debits		
Cash	$ 25,000	$ 18,000
Accounts receivable	108,000	25,000
Inventory, 12/31/96 (balance sheet)	209,000	42,000
Branch—Dover	207,000	—
Land, buildings, and equipment	340,000	112,000
Shipments from home office	—	96,000
Purchases	348,000	—
Depreciation expense	25,000	8,000
Advertising expense	36,000	15,000
Rent expense	12,000	5,000
Miscellaneous expenses	40,000	20,000
Inventory, 1/1/96	175,000	35,000
Total debits	$1,525,000	$376,000

	Heyman	Dover
Credits		
Accumulated depreciation.	$ 80,000	$ 16,000
Accounts payable	37,000	15,000
Notes payable	220,000	—
Home office	—	176,000
Common stock.	100,000	—
Retained earnings, 1/1/96	240,000	—
Sales	529,000	127,000
Shipments to branch	110,000	—
Inventory, 12/31/96 (income statement)	209,000	42,000
Total credits	$1,525,000	$376,000

31. The Brendan Company has always marketed a large percentage of its goods through a branch operation in the city of Davis, Florida. This year, the company also began to distribute some of its merchandise on consignment through Mark, Inc.

    Following are the December 31, 1995, trial balances for Brendan and for the Davis branch. From this information as well as the other data presented, construct a worksheet to combine these operations for external reporting purposes.

	Brendan Company	Davis Branch
Debits		
Cash	$ 6,000	$ 27,000
Receivables	29,000	42,000
Inventory	41,000	46,000
Consignment-out	56,000	–0–
Land	23,000	–0–
Buildings.	109,000	–0–
Equipment	43,000	127,000
Branch—Davis	111,000	–0–
Dividends paid	16,000	–0–
Inventory, 1/1/95	26,000	21,000
Purchases	275,000	64,000
Shipments from home office	–0–	153,000
Advertising expense.	14,000	17,000
Salary expense	31,000	16,000
Depreciation expense	9,000	12,000
Miscellaneous expense	20,000	4,000
Total debits	$809,000	$529,000

	Brendan Company	Davis Branch
Credits		
Accumulated depreciation	$ (36,000)	$ (27,000)
Accounts payable	(39,000)	(22,000)
Long-term liabilities	(164,000)	(12,000)
Common stock	(60,000)	–0–
Retained earnings, 1/1/95	(102,000)	–0–
Home office	–0–	(94,000)
Unrealized gains	(11,000)	–0–
Realized transfer gains	(45,000)	–0–
Sales	(115,000)	(328,000)
Shipments to branch	(110,000)	–0–
Shipments to consignee	(86,000)	–0–
Inventory, 12/31/95	(41,000)	(46,000)
Total credits	$(809,000)	$(529,000)

Additional Information:

- The Consignment-Out account measures inventory shipments made during the year. This balance has been reduced recently by a $30,000 payment received at the end of the year from Mark, Inc. accompanied by the following report:

Sold: 80% of consignment inventory		$125,000
Reductions:		
Commissions	$26,000	
Warranty expense	11,000	
Advertising expense	8,000	(45,000)
Check enclosed		(30,000)
Amount due		$ 50,000

- The branch's beginning inventory balance for the period contained $6,000 in unrealized intracompany gains whereas ending inventory is stated at an amount $11,000 in excess of cost.
- One intracompany shipment during the year was recorded incorrectly by the branch. The error amounted to $7,000.
- A $10,000 cash transfer was not recorded by the home office until the money was received on January 5, 1996.

32. Burt Corporation distributes merchandise through a consignment system. The company uses a standard cost accounting and records all inventory at a cost of $1,000 per unit. Following is the Consignment-Out account that Burt has maintained to record transactions with Hassle, Inc., a major consignee.

Date	Amount	Explanation
1/1	$97,000 debit	Beginning balance—89 units plus transportation cost
3/6	40,000 debit	Cost of inventory shipped to Hassle
3/19	6,000 debit	Freight cost on 3/6 shipment
4/8	9,000 debit	Local advertising incurred in connection with sale at Hassle
5/16	61,000 credit	Cash received from Hassle
6/1	20,000 debit	Loan to Hassle—10% annual interest
7/2	66,000 debit	Cost of inventory shipped to Hassle
7/11	6,500 debit	Freight cost on 7/2 shipment
8/3	1,000 credit	Item from last shipment is returned because of damage—loss is recorded
12/6	94,000 credit	Cash received from Hassle
12/31	$88,500 debit	Ending balance

When submitting cash to Burt during the year, Hassle filed the following two reports:

Date: May 10

Sales (at $2,000 per unit)		$104,000
Less: Commission	$20,000	
Delivery to customers	8,000	
Advertising	15,000	43,000
Amount remitted		$ 61,000

Date: December 1

Sales (at $2,000 per unit)		$164,000
Less: Commission	$40,000	
Delivery to customers	16,000	
Advertising	19,000	75,000
Amount currently due		$ 89,000
Loan repayment		5,000
Amount remitted		$ 94,000

Burt uses a FIFO system in recording inventory costs.

Required:

a. What cost of goods sold should be recognized by Burt in connection with the consignment sales made by Hassle?

b. What is the recorded cost of Burt's consignment inventory that is being held by Hassle as of December 31?

c. What income should be recognized by Burt in connection with the consignment sales made by Hassle?

d. What reclassification journal entry should Burt record at year's end?

e. What income would be recognized by Hassle in connection with its sales?

FOREIGN CURRENCY TRANSLATION AND REMEASUREMENT

Questions to Consider

- In preparing consolidated statements, how does a parent company that controls one or more foreign subsidiaries arrive at the account balances to be included for these operations?
- How does a company that has individual transactions denominated in a foreign currency determine the reported values of these balances for accounting purposes?
- What is a company's functional currency? How is this functional currency identified?
- Should a change in the relative value of a foreign currency balance held by a company create an income effect to be reported in its financial statements?
- When is remeasurement appropriate rather than translation of foreign currency balances?
- How does a remeasurement differ from a translation?
- What is a translation adjustment? How is it computed? Where should it be reported in a consolidated set of financial statements?
- What is a foreign currency hedge? What are the possible reasons for creating a foreign currency hedge? How should a hedge be reported?

As cross-border trade and investment flows reach new heights, big global companies are effectively making decisions with little regard to national boundaries. Though few companies are totally untethered from their home countries, the trend toward a form of "stateless" corporation is unmistakable. . . . In the past three years, Coke made more money in both Pacific and Western Europe than it did in the United States. Nearly 70 percent of General Motors Corporation's 1989 profits were from non-U.S. operations.[1]

---

[1] William J. Holstein, "The Stateless Corporation," *Business Week,* May 14, 1990, p. 98.

Today, a global economy is a reality. Even small businesses are involved in transactions occurring throughout the world. Merchandise is commonly bought and sold in markets from Chile to Australia and from Egypt to Japan. Large organizations rarely limit themselves to individual foreign transactions. They often choose to establish entire operations in a vast number of countries. Therefore, either through the development of export and import markets or the creation of foreign subsidiaries, modern-day business operations extend beyond national boundaries on an almost routine basis.

The Gillette Company, for example, currently controls subsidiaries in Argentina, Australia, Brazil, Chile, England, France, Germany, Hong Kong, Italy, Jamaica, Japan, Peru, Switzerland, and Turkey just to present a partial list. The Ford Motor Company and Eastman Kodak Company, generated $31.4 billion and $8.5 billion of their 1991 revenues, respectively, in markets outside of the United States. In both cases, foreign sales represented 44 percent of each company's consolidated total.

Thus, for any U.S. business, a portion of its transactions and accounts may be set (denominated) in a currency other than the dollar.

- The balances reported by a foreign subsidiary are probably recorded in the local currency of that country. An Italian subsidiary, for example, is likely to account for its transactions in lira.
- Even for a U.S. business, payments for raw materials, expenses, and other acquisitions or collections from sales may not always be made in dollars but rather in pesos, pounds, yen, and the like depending on the negotiated terms of the transaction.

Because of the magnitude of the amounts involved, accounting for balances denominated in a foreign currency has become an especially sensitive concern in recent years. Many companies must deal with a vast array of currencies. However, whenever financial statements are to be produced, only a single currency is reported. *Regardless of the currency in use, the balances included in these statements are not shown in pesos, liras, pounds, yen, and the like, but rather in their dollar equivalencies.* How is this process carried out?

In 1981, after much controversy, the Financial Accounting Standards Board issued *SFAS 52* ("Foreign Currency Translation") to guide the appropriate accounting of a balance denominated in a foreign currency.[2] Chapter 9 examines the requirements established by *SFAS 52* for determining and reporting these amounts, a process that seeks to ensure the fair presentation of the transactions and balances.

---

[2] As defined in *FASB SFAS 52,* foreign currency translation is the "process of expressing in the reporting currency of the enterprise those amounts that are denominated or measured in a different currency." Translation determines the value to be reported. This process should be differentiated from a conversion which denotes a physical "exchange of one currency for another." This chapter deals with translating (and remeasuring) balances for accounting purposes. The actual conversion of one currency into another is discussed only at the end of the chapter in describing hedging transactions.

Currency Exchange Rates—The Problems Caused by Fluctuations

For accounting purposes, the reporting of foreign currency figures is based on exchange rates. These rates measure the value by which one currency can physically be converted into another. One U.S. dollar, as an example, is worth a precise number of British pounds or French francs at any point in time.[3] Determining the relative value of an amount so that it can be reported by companies such as Gillette, Ford, and Eastman Kodak simply entails multiplying the foreign currency balances by an appropriate exchange rate. The rate is actually a ratio of the relative equal values of the two currencies which is stated, for convenience, as a fraction:

$$\frac{\text{Value of currency used for reporting purposes}}{\text{Relative value of currency in which amount is denominated}}$$

To illustrate this process, assume that the Hastings Corporation is preparing financial statements to be reported in U.S. dollars. A short-term debt of 50,000 francs is incurred by the company because of the acquisition of inventory. In addition, a long-term debt of 50,000 francs is incurred because of the acquisition of machinery. Although this information is to be presented in dollars, each transaction is actually denominated in a foreign currency. Assuming that the currency exchange rate stands at \$.25 = 1 franc (1F), each of the four accounts would be reported as \$12,500. On this date, the equivalent value of 50,000 francs is \$12,500.[4]

$$50,000F \times \$.25/1F = \$12,500$$

Considering the volume of business activity that transpires in foreign currencies, the intense interest in the reporting of balances such as these 50,000 franc liabilities and assets is understandable. The process by which foreign currency figures are measured and then recorded can have a dramatic impact on a company's financial statements. Although many accounting questions arise in connection with foreign currency balances, they all stem from a single cause: the effect created by fluctuations in exchange rates. *If the relative value of monetary currencies were to remain constant, translation problems would cease to exist; reported balances would all be calculated at the one applicable rate.* However, for many of the world's currencies, exchange rates change constantly (sometimes in a volatile manner) because of market conditions, government intervention, and myriad

---

[3] The exchange rates for many of the currencies can be found each day in *The Wall Street Journal.*

[4] The above exchange rate is referred to as a *direct quotation*; the U.S. dollar is stated in terms of one unit of the foreign currency. This same exchange rate could also be stated as an *indirect quotation*. In such cases, the number of francs that equals one unit of the U.S. currency is shown. The indirect quotation here would be four francs equals \$1.00. Stating the rate in this alternative manner has no effect on the account balances being reported:

$$50,000F \times \$1/4F = \$12,500$$

other factors. Thus, in determining equivalent values to be reported, a number of different currency rates are frequently available.

Whenever exchange rates fluctuate, two important theoretical questions must be addressed:

1. Is the exchange rate that was in effect at the time of the original transaction still applicable to an account balance or should the current rate now be used for reporting purposes?
2. Do changes that occur in the relative value of monetary currencies create a reportable effect (such as a gain or loss) on a company's financial position?

SFAS 52 (par. 59) recognized that satisfactory resolutions to these concerns would not be easily obtained:

> For enterprises conducting activities in more than a single currency, the practical necessities of financial reporting in a single currency require that the changing prices between two units of currency be accommodated in some fashion. People generally agree on this practical necessity but disagree on concepts and details of implementation. As a result, there is significant disagreement among informed observers regarding the basic nature, information content, and meaning of results produced by various methods of translating amounts from foreign currencies into the reporting currency. Each method has strong proponents and severe critics.

Discussion Question: How Do We Report This?

The Southwestern Corporation operates throughout Texas buying and selling widgets. In hopes of expanding into more profitable markets, the company recently decided to open a small subsidiary in the nearby country of Gualos. The currency in Gualos is the vilsek. For some time, the government of that country has held the exchange rate constant: 1 vilsek equals $.20 (or 5 vilseks equal $1.00).

Initially, Southwestern invested cash of $90,000 in this new operation. That money was converted into 450,000 vilseks ($90,000 × 5). One third of this money (150,000 vilseks or $30,000) was used to purchase land to be held for the possible construction of a plant, one third was invested in short-term marketable securities, and one third was spent in acquiring inventory for future resale.

Shortly thereafter, the Gualos government officially revalued the currency so that 1 vilsek is now worth $.23. Because of the strength of the local economy, the vilsek has gained buying power in relation to the U.S. dollar. The vilsek is now considered more valuable than in the past. The accoun-

continued

tants for Southwestern realize that a change has occurred; each of the assets is now worth more *in U.S. dollars* than the original $30,000 investment:

$$150,000 \text{ vilseks} \times \$.23/1 = \$34,500$$

Two of the company's top officers meet to determine the appropriate method for reporting this change in currency values.

Controller:

Nothing has changed. Our cost is still $30,000 for each item. That's what we spent. Accounting uses historical cost wherever possible. Thus, we should do nothing.

Finance Director:

Yes, but the old rates are meaningless now. We would be foolish to report figures based on a rate that no longer exists. The cost is still 150,000 vilseks for each item. You are right; the cost has not changed. However, the vilsek is now worth $.23 so our reported value must change.

Controller:

The new rate only affects us if we take money out of the country. We don't plan to do that for many years. The rate will probably change 20 more times before we remove money from Gualos. We've got to stick to our $30,000 historical cost. That's our cost and that's good, basic accounting.

Finance Director:

You mean that for the next 20 years we will be translating balances for external reporting purposes using an exchange rate that has not existed for years? That does not make sense. I have a real problem using an antiquated rate for the investments and inventory. They will be sold for cash when the new rate is in effect. These balances have no remaining relation to the original exchange rate.

Controller:

You misunderstand the impact of an exchange rate fluctuation. Within Gualos, no impact occurs. One vilsek is still one vilsek. The effect is only realized when an actual conversion takes place into U.S. dollars at a new rate. At that point, we will properly measure and report the gain or loss. That is when realization takes place. Until then our cost has not changed.

Finance Director:

I simply see no value at all in producing financial information that is based entirely on an exchange rate that does not exist. I don't care when realization takes place.

continued

Controller:
You've got to stick with historical cost, believe me. The exchange rate today isn't important unless we actually convert vilseks to dollars.

How should Southwestern report each of these three assets on its current balance sheet? Does the company have a gain because the value of the vilsek has increased relative to the U.S. dollar?

Possible Methods of Accounting for Currency Rate Changes

The Hastings Corporation example presented earlier can be used to demonstrate the quandary created by a fluctuation in relative currency values. Assume that immediately after purchasing the inventory and machinery and incurring both debts, the exchange rate changes to $.20 = 1F. Hastings must still pay 50,000 F to settle each of these two acquisitions; the contractual figure has not changed. However, this amount now has a different value in U.S. dollars. For accounting purposes, have any of the liability or asset balances been altered and, if so, how can the effect be measured and disclosed? Should the old value of the franc (the historical rate) or the new value of the franc (the current rate) be used to report the two liabilities, the inventory, and the machinery?

Over the years, four different theories have been proposed to resolve this dilemma:

Current/Noncurrent Method.   Because of their short-term nature, current assets and current liabilities are constantly updated according to this approach based on current exchange rates. All other accounts (including stockholders' equity balances and revenues and expenses) are measured at historical rates based on the date of the original transaction. For Hastings, the four account balances would be reported as follows:

Short-term debt (current rate)	50,000F × $.20/1F = $10,000
Inventory (current rate).	50,000F × $.20/1F = $10,000
Long-term debt (historical rate)	50,000F × $.25/1F = $12,500
Machinery (historical rate)	50,000F × $.25/1F = $12,500

The current/noncurrent approach was widely used until the 1960s. However, of the methods presented here, it has the least theoretical justification. The life of an asset or liability would seem to have little, if any, relation to whether a current exchange rate or a historical rate is applicable. Consequently, the current/noncurrent method is no longer viewed as appropriate.

Monetary/Nonmonetary Method.   Monetary assets and liabilities (usually cash, receivables, and payables) are balances that reflect a set future cash flow. An accounts receivable for $1,000 is fixed at that amount. An account payable for $3,000 represents that exchange of currency in the future. Since monetary accounts represent future cash flows of specified amounts, they are measured at current rates. All other accounts reflect past transactions and are reported at historical rates.

Short-term debt (current rate) . . . . 50,000F × \$.20/1F = \$10,000
Inventory (historical rate). . . . . 50,000F × \$.25/1F = \$12,500
Long-term debt (current rate) . . . . 50,000F × \$.20/1F = \$10,000
Machinery (historical rate) . . . . 50,000F × \$.25/1F = \$12,500

The monetary/nonmonetary approach was considered appropriate in the 1960s and the early 1970s. At that time, it was replaced by the temporal method that was quite similar but had certain refinements.

Temporal Method. The temporal method holds that all accounts have a money price and should be measured based on the exchange rate in effect at the date to which that money price pertains. Monetary assets and liabilities are viewed as having a future money price so that current rates are applicable. Most nonmonetary accounts have money prices representing past transactions; thus, historical rates are appropriate. However, according to this method, any nonmonetary assets and liabilities recorded at current prices or market value must use current rates. For example, long-term investments or inventory recorded at market values would be measured at current rather than historical rates. The original cost figure is no longer considered applicable. For the Hastings example, the four account balances would be presented as follows:

Short-term debt (current rate) . . . . 50,000F × \$.20/1F = \$10,000
Inventory (historical rate). . . . . 50,000F × \$.25/1F = \$12,500
Long-term debt (current rate) . . . . 50,000F × \$.20/1F = \$10,000
Machinery (historical rate) . . . . 50,000F × \$.25/1F = \$12,500

Note here that the balances reported for the temporal method are the same in this example as shown for the monetary/nonmonetary method. Unless nonmonetary accounts are present that are recorded at current prices, these methods produce the same results.

The temporal method was established as appropriate for all foreign currency balances by the FASB in 1975 in its *SFAS 8*, "Accounting for the Translation of Foreign Currency Transactions and Foreign Currency Financial Statements." As discussed in a later section of this chapter, *SFAS 8* was very unpopular with the business community because of the wide swings that it tended to cause in reported net income. It was subsequently replaced in 1981 by *SFAS 52* which limited, but did not abandon, the use of the temporal method. As discussed later, the temporal method is still applicable under *SFAS 52* for the remeasurement of individual foreign currency transactions. In addition, in two specific cases, the temporal method is used to remeasure the accounts of a foreign subsidiary.

Current Rate Method. The current rate approach measures all assets and liabilities at the current exchange rate. The current rate method assumes that all assets and liabilities are ultimately expected to impact future cash flows and, thus, should be based on the current exchange rate rather than any historical rate. For Hastings, the current rate method would lead to the following balances being reported:

Short-term debt (current rate) . . . . 50,000F × $.20/1F = $10,000

Inventory (current rate). . . . . 50,000F × $.20/1F = $10,000

Long-term debt (current rate) . . . . 50,000F × $.20/1F = $10,000

Machinery (current rate) . . . . 50,000F × $.20/1F = $10,000

SFAS 52 required the use of the current rate method but only in situations where the financial accounts of a foreign subsidiary are being translated. Although, as mentioned earlier, the temporal method may be applicable to some subsidiaries, the current rate method is used in a vast majority of cases.

Foreign Currency Balances and SFAS 52

In response to the numerous criticisms of *SFAS 8*, the FASB issued *SFAS 52*, "Foreign Currency Translation." Although *SFAS 52* has not been universally praised, it has avoided the intense criticism that haunted *Statement 8*.

One of the most important aspects of the new pronouncement was that the reporting of foreign currency balances was divided into two distinct processes: translation and remeasurement. As just indicated *translation is normally applicable whenever the financial statements of a foreign subsidiary are being prepared for consolidation. In contrast, remeasurement procedures are primarily (but not exclusively) utilized in reporting individual transactions denominated in a foreign currency.* Since these methods adopt different approaches in determining the account balances to be reported, two questions need to be answered:

- When is the use of each method appropriate?
- What are the various mechanical techniques involved with each method?

Translating the Accounts of a Foreign Subsidiary

A company that has a subsidiary in a foreign country must measure its accounts in the parent's currency as a prerequisite to consolidation. For example, all balances of a Swedish subsidiary of an American parent must be stated in U.S. dollars to allow for consolidation. Except as discussed later, this process is a translation. To be in accordance with U.S. generally accepted accounting principles (GAAP), the accounts reported for a foreign subsidiary are translated by four general procedures:

1. The financial accounts of each individual subsidiary (or branch) initially must be recorded in that entity's own *functional currency*. As defined by

SFAS 52 (Appendix E) the functional currency is the "currency of the primary economic environment in which the entity operates; normally, that is the currency of the environment in which an entity primarily generates and expends cash." For example, a subsidiary operating entirely in France probably assumes that the franc is its functional currency as that, in most instances, would be the currency in which most cash transactions are carried out. *If this subsidiary has any balances recorded that are denominated in a currency other than the franc, these amounts must be remeasured into the functional currency as a preliminary step in the translation process.*

2. Under the guidelines set by *SFAS 52*, the foreign statements are then adjusted to be in compliance with the generally accepted accounting principles of the United States. Many countries allow accounting techniques that have little resemblance to American standards. A consistency of principles within the consolidated statements is established by requiring that all component companies use GAAP.

3. The balance of each financial account must be translated from the subsidiary's functional currency into the *reporting currency* of the parent company. Although this textbook assumes U.S. dollars as the reporting currency, every parent must decide which currency is appropriate for financial statement presentation. As an example, an English parent corporation that chooses to apply the guidelines of *SFAS 52* would likely view the pound as its reporting currency.

    According to *SFAS 52*, the current rate method is normally appropriate for translating the subsidiary's functional currency into the parent's reporting currency.

    • *All of the subsidiary's assets and liabilities* are translated at the current exchange rate as of the balance sheet date.

    • For *revenues, expenses, gains, and losses,* translation is made at the historical rate in effect at the time of original accounting recognition. These events do not create future changes in net assets; they measure only past events. Rent expense, for example, that is recognized on May 9 should be translated using the May 9 rate. Since many income transactions are recorded on a regular, recurring basis throughout the year, *SFAS 52* does allow a weighted-average exchange rate to be used, where applicable, instead of specific rates. Consequently, sales and cost of goods sold—as just two examples—would probably be translated at an average rate for the year rather than using individual daily rates. However, if only a few sales occur, rates for those dates would be more appropriate.

    • Lastly, *all equity balances of the subsidiary* are translated at historical rates in a manner similar to that of income statement accounts. Although land, equipment, and the like are acquired in hopes of generating future increases in net assets, accounts such as common stock or additional paid-in capital are purely reflections of past exchanges.

· A problem arises in translating *retained earnings*. This figure is actually a composite of many previous transactions: all revenues, expenses, gains, losses, and declared dividends occurring over the life of the organization. To provide a precise translation, the timing and amount of each individual component would have to be identified separately with the appropriate historical rate then applied to every figure. Obviously, for any subsidiary in operation for a number of years, this process becomes virtually impossible. Rather than even making an attempt to translate retained earnings in this manner, a shortcut is usually incorporated for this computation. The figure reported at the end of each year becomes the beginning balance for the next. When *SFAS 52* was first applied, the final retained earnings balance computed under *SFAS 8* was simply carried over to start the following year.

4. An offsetting accounting effect is created every time that a subsidiary's assets and liabilities are updated to reflect current exchange rates. According to the now defunct *SFAS 8*, an increase in an asset's value or a decrease in a liability created a gain that increased net income. Conversely, a decrease in an asset or an increase in a liability was considered to represent a loss.

In a very significant change, *SFAS 52* nets the impact of increasing and decreasing the reported values of the subsidiary's assets and liabilities (based on the current rate). This figure is then disclosed as a single *translation adjustment,* an account that is included as *a separate component within the stockholders' equity section of the balance sheet.* Computation of this adjustment entails measuring the changes that occur during the year in the translated value of the subsidiary's assets and liabilities. As an accumulated figure, the ending balance is carried into the subsequent period.

To date, *SFAS 52* has avoided the extreme criticism showered upon *SFAS 8*. The most popular change was the removal from the consolidated income statement of gains and losses that resulted from the translation of foreign subsidiaries. The effect created by using current rates in translating the subsidiary's assets and liabilities from its functional currency into the parent's reporting currency is now accumulated each year within the equity section of the consolidated balance sheet. As is subsequently discussed, reportable gains and losses can still arise from foreign currency transactions and, in a few cases, because of foreign subsidiaries. However, *SFAS 52* has greatly limited the effect on consolidated net income that can result from exchange rate fluctuations.

Furthermore, *SFAS 52* mandated that the balance sheet exchange rate be consistently applied to all assets and liabilities. The current rate is now viewed by the FASB as the only one truly applicable to the present financial position of a foreign subsidiary. This approach is founded on an implicit assumption that the ultimate value of any asset or liability is dependent on its ability to affect future cash flows. Exchange rates existing at any previous point in time are no longer perceived as relevant to these translated balances. Income as well as equity accounts continue to be translated at historical rates since they do not generate future changes in net assets.

The Translation Process Illustrated

To provide a basis for demonstrating the translation procedures prescribed by *SFAS 52*, the income statement, statement of retained earnings, and balance sheet that follow are reported by the Danish subsidiary of an American corporation. All figures are denominated in kroner (Kr), the Danish currency.

DANISH SUBSIDIARY
Income Statement
For Year Ending December 31, 1995

Sales	400,000	Kr
Cost of goods sold	(208,000)	
Gross profit	192,000	Kr
Less:		
Salary expense	(56,000)	
Depreciation expense	(35,000)	
Miscellaneous expense	(42,000)	
Net income	59,000	Kr

Statement of Retained Earnings
For Year Ending December 31, 1995

Retained earnings, 1/1/95	–0–	
Net income (above)	59,000	Kr
Less: Dividends declared and paid, 5/1/91	(23,400)	
Retained earnings, 12/31/95	35,600	Kr

Balance Sheet
December 31, 1995

Assets

Cash	32,800	Kr
Receivables	41,820	
Inventory	101,680	
Land	77,080	
Building and equipment	308,320	
Less: Accumulated depreciation	(35,000)	
Total assets	526,700	Kr

Liabilities and Equities

Accounts payable	98,400	Kr
Long-term liabilities	302,400	
Common stock	90,300	
Retained earnings, 12/31/95	35,600	
Total liabilities and equities	526,700	Kr

Assume that this subsidiary began operations at the beginning of 1995, the current year. At that time, 70 percent of the common stock was issued with the remainder being sold on May 1, 1995. The building and equipment reported in the balance sheet were acquired at the first of the year, and land was purchased by the subsidiary on several occasions during 1995. The following exchange rates are assumed to be applicable:

January 1, 1995	$1.00 = 7.5 kroner
May 1, 1995	$1.00 = 7.8 kroner
December 31, 1995	$1.00 = 8.2 kroner
Weighted-average rate for 1995	$1.00 = 8.0 kroner

Step One—Identification of the Functional Currency.   As noted earlier, a preliminary step in the translation process is the determination of the functional currency applicable to the subsidiary's operations. What is the currency of the subsidiary's environment? If cash inflows and outflows consist of one specific currency such as pounds or francs, this monetary unit is very likely to be viewed as the entity's functional currency.

However, many foreign companies conduct their operations in more than a single currency. In such cases, *SFAS 52* (par. 8) states that "management's judgment will be required to determine the functional currency in which financial results and relationships are measured with the greatest degree of relevance and reliability." For example, if a subsidiary transacts business in both Italian lira and Austrian schillings, an evaluation has to be made of all pertinent facts before designating the most relevant functional currency. Although identification of the cash flow currency is the primary factor in this decision, Appendix A of *SFAS 52* recommends that other aspects of the foreign operation also be evaluated including:

- The location of primary sales markets.
- The source of expense items such as materials, labor, and other cost factors.
- The impact that any changes in exchange rates have on the subsidiary's sales prices.
- The source and denomination of financing.
- If one of the possible functional currencies is the parent's reporting currency, the volume of intercompany transactions is an important indicator.[5]

---

[5] One survey found that the denomination of a subsidiary's cash flows was considered to be the most important indicator of its functional currency followed by the location of its primary sales markets and the source of its expense items. See, *Determining the Functional Currency under Statement 52,* by Thomas G. Evans and Timothy S. Doupnik (Stamford, Conn.: FASB, 1986), p. 29.

Leaving the decision as to the identity of the functional currency up to management allows some leeway in this process. Different companies approach this selection in different ways:

> "For us it was intuitively obvious." versus "It was quite a process. We took the six criteria and developed a matrix. We then considered the dollar amount and the related percentages in developing a point scheme. Each of the separate criteria was given equal weight (in the analytical methods applied)."[6]

One alternative to the selection of a single functional currency is allowed by *SFAS 52*. A foreign subsidiary's activities may be reported as if several entities existed, each with its own functional currency. However, this option is only appropriate if each of these operations is "distinct and separable." A European subsidiary, for example, might be divided into a German operation with the deutsche mark as its functional currency and a French operation with the franc as its functional currency. One survey of 179 corporations indicated that 12.3 percent had opted to split at least one foreign subsidiary to report more than one functional currency.[7]

In the current illustration, since all of the account balances are *reported* in one currency, the Danish krone, it is used as the functional currency. However, the krone would not necessarily have to be the subsidiary's functional currency. The Belgian franc, as an example, could well be the functional currency if this entity's operations consist entirely of providing mechanical parts to a Belgian manufacturer who makes all payments in that currency. Similarly, if this subsidiary carries out significant transactions with its American parent, the U.S. dollar might be the primary cash flow currency. Some subsidiaries are simply operating as extensions of their parent company and have few cash flows in the local currency.

One other issue concerning the functional currency should be mentioned. If any of the accounts of the Danish subsidiary were denominated in a currency other than the krone, that balance would have to be *remeasured* into the functional currency prior to translation. For example, a payable of 10,000 Belgian francs would have to be remeasured into Danish krone before the translation process could commence. Translation requires that all of a subsidiary's balances must be stated in its functional currency. Because remeasurement differs from translation, a full review of this process is deferred until a later section of this chapter.

Step Two—Adjusting the Subsidiary Accounts to Be in Compliance with United States Generally Accepted Accounting Principles. Once the functional currency is identified and all balances have been remeasured into that currency, the subsidiary's accounts must be adjusted to be in compliance with the generally accepted accounting principles recognized in the United States. Financial statements can

---

[6] Jerry L. Arnold and William W. Holder, *Impact of Statement 52 on Decisions, Financial Reports and Attitudes* (Morristown, N.J.: Financial Executives Research Foundation, 1986), p. 89.

[7] Evans and Doupnik, *Determining the Functional Currency,* p. 25.

be truly informative only if the same set of principles has been applied throughout. Many countries permit accounting practices that are not allowed under GAAP: tax allocations are omitted, assets are recorded at market values above historical cost, excess depreciation is taken, and so on. If adherence to *SFAS 52* is required (or chosen), all variations must be eliminated by adjustment to GAAP. In this illustration, the assumption is made that the financial information is already stated according to U.S. GAAP so that no alterations are required.

Step Three—Translation of Financial Statements.   The actual translation process can now be carried out since all of the subsidiary's financial figures are recorded in the functional currency as well as being consistent with GAAP. Translating the Danish krone balances into the parent's reporting currency (U.S. dollars in this illustration) is based on exchange rates that are either current (for assets and liabilities) or historical (for all other accounts) as prescribed by *SFAS 52*.

DANISH SUBSIDIARY
Income Statement
For Year Ending December 31, 1995

Sales	400,000 Kr	×	1.00/8.0	=	$ 50,000
Cost of goods sold	(208,000)	×	1.00/8.0	=	(26,000)
Gross profit	192,000 Kr				24,000
Less:					
Salary expense	(56,000)	×	1.00/8.0	=	(7,000)
Depreciation expense	(35,000)	×	1.00/8.0	=	(4,375)
Miscellaneous expense	(42,000)	×	1.00/8.0	=	(5,250)
Net income	59,000 Kr				$ 7,375

Statement of Retained Earnings
for Year Ending December 31, 1995

Retained earnings, 1/1/95	–0–				–0–
Net income	59,000	Kr (above)			$ 7,375
Less: Dividends declared and paid, 5/1/95	(23,400)	×	1.00/7.8	=	(3,000)
Retained earnings, 12/31/95	35,600				$ 4,375

Balance Sheet
December 31, 1995

Assets

Cash	32,800 Kr	×	1.00/8.2	=	$ 4,000
Receivables	41,820	×	1.00/8.2	=	5,100
Inventory	101,680	×	1.00/8.2	=	12,400
Land	77,080	×	1.00/8.2	=	9,400
Building and equipment	308,320	×	1.00/8.2	=	37,600
Less: Accumulated depreciation	(35,000)	×	1.00/8.2	=	(4,268)
Total assets	526,700 Kr				$ 64,232

Liabilities and Equities

Accounts payable	98,400 Kr	×	1.00/8.2 =	$ 12,000
Long-term liabilities	302,400	×	1.00/8.2 =	36,878
Common stock.	90,300	(see schedule below)		11,901
Retained earnings	35,600	(above)		4,375
Equity adjustment from translation.	–0–	(explained below)		(922)
Total liabilities and equities	526,700 Kr			$ 64,232

Schedule—Translation of Common Stock Account

January 1, 1995, issuance (70%)	63,210 Kr	×	1.00/7.5 =	$ 8,428
May 1, 1995, issuance (30%).	27,090	×	1.00/7.8 =	3,473
Common stock account	90,300 Kr			$ 11,901

Several of the translation procedures demonstrated here do warrant further explanation:

1. Income statement balances are translated at the exchange rate in effect at the date of accounting recognition. The weighted-average rate for the period is utilized here since each revenue and expense in this illustration would have been recognized throughout the year. However, when an income account, such as a gain or loss, occurs at a specific point in time, the rate as of that date is applied. Depreciation expense is also translated at the average rate for the year; that was the time of recognition even though the journal entry may have been delayed until year-end for convenience.

2. Following the guidelines of *Statement 52*, all assets and liabilities are translated at the current exchange rate. (Because depreciation expense and accumulated depreciation are translated using different rates, they do not agree.)

3. The common stock balance is an equity account so that historical rates are considered appropriate. As this stock was issued on two occasions, separate translations are required to determine the $11,901 total being reported. The 23,400 Kr dividend payment is also an equity transaction; thus, translation is calculated at the specific rate in effect on May 1, the date of declaration.

4. Since the Danish subsidiary is newly organized, no beginning retained earnings balance exists. However, a January 1 figure is normally found in the financial records of any established business. For translation purposes, the components recorded within this account should be identified and individually translated. As previously indicated, though, most companies avoid this tedious procedure by carrying over the ending retained earnings total translated for the preceding year.

5. A translation adjustment is to be expected for virtually all foreign subsidiaries since current exchange rates serve as the basis for reporting assets and liabilities. For these accounts, every fluctuation in the currency rates produces a new reported value in the parent's currency. *Statement 52* requires the offsetting effect to be measured and disclosed within stockholders' equity rather than as a component of net income.

In rationalizing this placement, *SFAS 52* (pars. 113, 114) offered two contrasting positions on the conceptual nature of the translation adjustment. One view is that the "change in the dollar equivalent of the net investment is an unrealized enhancement or reduction, having no effect on the functional currency net cash flows generated by the foreign entity which may be currently reinvested or distributed to the parent." Philosophically, this position holds that gains and losses are created by changes in the exchange rate but they are unrealized in nature and should, therefore, not be included within net income.

The alternative perspective put forth by the FASB "regards the translation adjustment as merely a mechanical by-product of the translation process." This second contention argues that no meaningful effect is created by the fluctuation; the resulting translation adjustment merely serves to keep the balance sheet in equilibrium.

Interestingly enough, the FASB chose not to express a preference for either of these theoretical views. The Board felt no need to offer a hint of guidance as to the essential nature of the translation adjustment since both explanations point to its exclusion from the income statement. Thus, a balance sheet figure that can amount to millions is basically undefined.

6. Regardless of the placement or the perception of this adjustment, its calculation is a central element in the translation process. Because all assets and liabilities are to be reported at the current exchange rate, a company could conceivably compute a separate adjustment for each of these accounts. Every rate change would cause each translated value to either rise or fall so that a balancing figure (or an unrealized gain or loss) is required.

However, except for the subsidiary's net asset position (assets in excess of liabilities), all of these effects simply offset each other.[8] An increase in the translated value of a 50,000 mark asset caused by a currency rate fluctuation exactly counterbalances the impact of an increase in a 50,000 mark liability. In fact, if total assets are equal to liabilities throughout the year, these translation adjustments (although perhaps significant on an individual basis) net to a zero balance.

Thus, for calculation purposes, only the net asset position is exposed to the effects produced by changes in the exchange rate. Any impact on this net figure is not offset by a balancing effect on any other account. Consequently, computation of the annual translation adjustment is based solely on an analysis of the entity's net asset position during the period:

a. The net asset balance of the subsidiary at the beginning of the year is translated at the exchange rate in effect on that date.

b. Individual increases and decreases in the net asset balance during the year are also translated at the rates in effect at those times. Only a few events actually change net assets (for example: dividends, net income, stock issuances, and the acquisition of treasury stock). Transactions

---

[8] The procedures demonstrated here are equally applicable to a net liability position (liabilities are in excess of assets). Constant reference to net liabilities is avoided here, however, because that position is not as commonly encountered as a net asset position.

such as the acquisition of equipment or the payment of a liability have no effect on total net assets.

c. The translated beginning net asset balance (*a*) and the translated value of the individual changes (*b*) are then combined to arrive at the relative value of the net assets being held *prior* to the impact of any rate fluctuations.

d. The subsidiary's ending net asset balance is translated at the current balance sheet exchange rate to determine the reported value *after* all currency rate changes have occurred.

e. The translated value of the net assets prior to any rate changes (*c*) is compared with the ending translated value (*d*). The difference (which can be either an increase or a decrease) is the result of exchange rate fluctuations during the period. This translation adjustment is combined with any amount carried over from the preceding years and reported within consolidated stockholders' equity.

Step Four—Computation of Translation Adjustment.   Based on the process just described, determination of the translation adjustment to be reported by the Danish subsidiary in this example requires the following calculations:

	As Denominated		At Relative Value
Net asset balance, 1/1/95	–0–		–0–
Increases in net assets:			
Common stock issuance, 1/1/95	63,210	Kr × 1.00/7.5 =	$ 8,428
Common stock issuance, 5/1/95	27,090	× 1.00/7.8 =	3,473
Net income (from income statement).	59,000		7,375
Decreases in net assets:			
Dividends paid, 5/1/95	(23,400)	× 1.00/7.8 =	(3,000)
Net asset value prior to exchange rate fluctuations	125,900	Kr	$16,276
Net asset balance and relative value, 12/31/95.	125,900	Kr × 1.00/8.2 =	$15,354
Translation adjustment, 1995 (decrease in relative value of net assets)			$ (922)

Since this subsidiary began operations at the beginning of the current year, the $922 translation adjustment is the only amount applicable for reporting purposes. If a balance had already been created by translations in previous years, that earlier figure would have been combined with the $922 to arrive at an appropriate year-end total to be presented within stockholders' equity.

The Halliburton Company, as an example, disclosed a December 31, 1990, translation adjustment having a $19.0 million positive (or unrealized gain) balance.

This figure was composed of a $27.7 million positive translation effect relating directly to the year of 1990 and an $8.7 million negative effect (unrealized loss) recognized by the company in prior years. Each of these amounts resulted from changes in the reported values of a subsidiary's assets and liabilities, changes that were created by the use of current exchange rates in translating these accounts from the functional currency of the subsidiary into the U.S. dollar equivalency.

The Mobil Corporation went further in reporting that its $45 million positive translation adjustment at December 31, 1990, resulted from reporting the value of three account groups of its foreign subsidiaries. For this company, current exchange rates created the following effects:

- Properties, plants, and equipment—$542 million positive translation adjustment.
- Deferred income taxes—$495 million negative translation adjustment.
- Working capital, debt, and other items—$2 million negative translation adjustment.

Discussion Question: Was *SFAS 8* Really Wrong?

No accounting standard written by the Financial Accounting Standards Board has come in for more scorn or derision than FASB-8 on currency translation.[9]

Although many of the official accounting pronouncements produced over the past decades have generated discussion and controversy, few have created the disssension of the now-defunct *FASB SFAS 8*. This standard was released in 1975 to provide appropriate accounting standards for foreign currency balances but was then replaced in 1981 by *SFAS 52*. Thus, in 1975, the FASB believed that one method of accounting was preferrable but, a mere six years later, the Board adopted an entirely different approach to the foreign currency problem. Why the change, and is *SFAS 52* really better? Business executives appear, in general, to prefer *SFAS 52* but not all theoreticians agree that the newer pronouncement is an improvement.

SFAS 8 required the use of the temporal method for all foreign currency balances. Thus, the monetary assets and liabilities (and any accounts recorded at market value) of a foreign subsidiary were translated based on current rates. Historical rates were used for all other accounts including nonmonetary assets such as inventory and machinery. Any reporting changes that were made in the monetary balances because of fluctuations in the current exchange rate were reflected in net income. Movements in these rates could sometimes cause wild swings in reported income. IBM, for ex-

---

[9] Richard Greene, "Once More . . . with Feeling," *Forbes,* October 13, 1980, p. 192.

continued

ample, reported a $113 million exchange gain in 1978, a $52 million loss in 1979, and a $24 million gain in 1980.

Critics of this accounting standard strongly disputed the inclusion of these effects within operating income. They argued that the gains and losses remained unrealized until such time as the retranslated accounts were physically exchanged for U.S. dollars. Since conversion to dollars might not occur for years, if ever, the gains and losses were felt to be illusory in nature and misleading to the readers of financial statements. According to this argument, recognizing an income effect because of changes in the *dollar value* of a foreign balance presupposes an immediate relationship between the transaction and the U.S. currency. Furthermore, subsequent variations in currency rates would often eliminate or reverse the income effect without an actual conversion to dollars ever taking place.

Not surprisingly, many companies took drastic measures in response to *SFAS 8* to protect themselves from having to report large losses generated solely by erratic movements in exchange rates. Exposure to these changes in value could be eliminated by managing the account balances that were denominated in a foreign currency. For any specific currency, a company merely had to equate its cash, monetary assets, and market value assets with its total monetary liabilities. Exchange contracts to buy (a receivable) or sell (a payable) a foreign currency were often acquired for just that purpose. In this financial position, exchange losses occurring to one group of accounts would be exactly offset by gains recognized in the value of the other.

> Says Dow Chemical Treasurer Wilson Gay: "FASB-8 impelled us to the concept of zero balance-sheet exposure in 1977, after our first year of experience with *FASB-8* caused us a $60 million earnings swing from the previous year." Zero balance-sheet exposure means that the company limits its liabilities in any country to its monetary assets there.[10]

If the translated value of a foreign subsidiary's accounts receivable goes up, should the parent company recognize a gain (*SFAS 8*) or an increase in stockholders' equity (*SFAS 52*)? Should inventory that is held for resale by a foreign subsidiary be translated at the exchange rate in effect when acquired (*SFAS 8*) or at the current exchange rate (*SFAS 52*)? Should an accounting pronouncement affect a company's decision as to the amount of assets and liabilities that it would hold in any one currency?

---

[10] Howard Rudnitsky, "How Companies Cope," *Forbes,* January 23, 1978, p. 43.

Remeasurement of Foreign Currency Transactions

The translation of a subsidiary's accounts is only a single aspect, albeit a central one, in the reporting of foreign currency balances. A closely related procedure also sanctioned by *SFAS 52* is the remeasurement process. *Remeasurement is primarily encountered whenever either a parent or a foreign subsidiary has transactions denominated in a currency other than the entity's own functional currency.*

- For this reason, remeasurement is necessary if an English subsidiary, with the pound as its functional currency, acquires inventory and payment is to be made later in French francs. The foreign currency balances (inventory and accounts payable) have to be remeasured into pounds by the subsidiary as a preliminary step in the translation process.
- Remeasurement is also required if an American corporation sells merchandise in Japan and is to receive payment in yen. The figures for both accounts receivable and sales must be remeasured into U.S. dollars so that the financial effects can be properly reflected by the company.

Identifying the remeasurement of individual foreign currency transactions as a process separate from the translation of a foreign subsidiary's financial statements was an important decision made by the FASB since the two incorporate significantly different procedures. Translation utilizes current exchange rates for all assets and liabilities and presents the resulting translation adjustment in stockholders' equity.

- In contrast, remeasurement is virtually identical to the temporal method previously prescribed by *SFAS 8*. Only monetary assets and liabilities (as well as accounts recorded at market value) are remeasured at current exchange rates; historical rates are applicable to all other balances. Therefore, current rates would be utilized for the following accounts.
- Any gain or loss created by the remeasurement of these balances is recognized as a component of net income.

Partial Listing of Accounts to Be Remeasured at Current Exchange Rates

Assets	*Liabilities*
Cash on hand and demand and time deposits	Accounts and notes payable
Marketable securities carried at current market price	Accrued expenses payable
Accounts and notes receivable and any related unearned discount	Bonds payable
	Long-term debt
Allowance for doubtful accounts	Unamortized premium or discount on bonds or notes payable
Inventories carried at current selling price	
Inventories carried at net realizable value	Convertible bonds payable
Refundable deposits	Accrued pension obligations
Cash surrender value of life insurance	

The implicit justification for remeasurement is that foreign currency transactions create a direct relationship between monetary assets and liabilities denominated in another currency and the cash flows of the entity's own functional currency.[11] The English subsidiary, in the previous illustration, would probably convert pounds (its functional currency) into francs to pay the incurred liability. In the second example, the American corporation can be expected to physically exchange the Japanese yen that are received for U.S. dollars (its functional currency). Therefore, fluctuations in the relative value of a company's foreign currency *monetary assets and liabilities* are quite likely to be realized if the balances resulted from individual transactions.

For this reason, rate changes associated with these specific accounts are presumed to have a measurable effect on future cash flows of the functional currency and, thus, on reported income. An increase in the reported value of net monetary assets is a gain, whereas a decrease is a loss. In contrast, translation is a process designed solely to measure relative values for reporting purposes and is not intended to represent an anticipated impact on the entity's own functional currency cash flows. Therefore, the changes in value identified by the translation of a foreign subsidiary's assets and liabilities were not classified by *SFAS 52* as gains and losses.

Historical Rates—Remeasurement versus Translation

When accounts are either remeasured or translated, many are reported based on historical rates. In a remeasurement, all nonmonetary accounts are valued at historical rates; in a translation, all accounts other than assets and liabilities are valued at historical rates. However, *SFAS 52* requires that different historical rates be used in these two procedures. For remeasured accounts, the rate in effect on the date of the original transaction is appropriate. For translated accounts, the rate at the date of accounting recognition is used. In many cases, these two dates are the same. Two major exceptions, though, do exist: cost of goods sold and depreciation (and amortization) expense.

In remeasuring cost of goods sold and depreciation expense, the date of the original transaction is the day of acquisition. For example, to report a June 1, 1996, sale of inventory bought on November 1, 1995, the cost of goods sold should be based on the November 1, 1995, exchange rate to reflect the original purchase. To remeasure the 1996 depreciation of a building acquired on August 1, 1995, the expense is computed using the August 1, 1995, exchange rate because that was the day on which the asset was bought.

In translating cost of goods sold and depreciation expense, the date of accounting recognition is used. To translate the June 1, 1996, sale of inventory bought on November 1, 1995, cost of goods sold is determined using the June 1, 1996, exchange rate. On that day, the cost of goods sold was recognized. In

---

[11] Market value accounts are included in this category but, for convenience, are not separately identified at each mention.

recording the 1996 depreciation of a building acquired on August 1, 1995, the translated expense is based on the average rate for 1996, the rate in effect at the point of accounting recognition.

Comparison of Translation and Remeasurement

Under what conditions is each approach utilized?

Translation—Process is used in reporting a foreign subsidiary within a consolidated set of financial statements when the subsidiary's functional currency differs from the parent's reporting currency.

Remeasurement—Process is used in reporting individual transactions denominated in a currency other than the entity's own functional currency. As is discussed later in the chapter, remeasurement is also appropriate in consolidating foreign currency balances of a subsidiary that has the same functional currency as the parent or operates in a highly inflationary economy.

How are assets and liabilities reported?

Translation—All assets and liabilities are translated at the current exchange rate as of the balance sheet date.

Remeasurement—All monetary assets and liabilities as well as any accounts recorded at market value are reported based on the current exchange rate as of the balance sheet date. All other assets and liabilities are remeasured using the historical rates at the time of the original transactions.

How are revenues, expenses, dividends, and equity accounts reported?

Translation—Each of these accounts is translated at the historical rate as of the date of accounting recognition.

Remeasurement—Each of these accounts is remeasured at the historical rate as of the date of the original transaction.

If equipment is bought on January 1, 1989, how is depreciation expense for 1995 reported?

Translation—Depreciation expense for 1995 is translated using the average rate for 1995, the time of the accounting recognition.

Remeasurement—Depreciation expense for 1995 is remeasured using the historical rate as of January 1, 1989, the date of the original transaction.

When do translation and remeasurement procedures take place?

Translation—All balances are normally translated at the end of each period as a preliminary step in producing consolidated financial statements.

Remeasurement—Each individual transaction is recorded immediately at the exchange rate in effect on that date. Monetary assets and liabilities as well as market value accounts are remeasured at year's end based on the current exchange rate. If an entire set of statements is being remeasured, the process is carried out at the end of the fiscal period prior to consolidation.

How is the effect that is created by adjusting some reported values to current exchange rates calculated and disclosed?

Translation—A translation adjustment is computed on the changes in value of the net assets. The amount is accumulated each year and reported as a positive or negative balance within the stockholders' equity section of the consolidated balance sheet.

Remeasurement—A transaction gain or loss is computed on the changes in value of the net monetary assets and liabilities. The amount is reported each year within net income and is then closed out so that it does not accumulate.

The Remeasurement Process Illustrated—Single Time Period Involved

The remeasurement of individual foreign currency transactions can now be demonstrated. As a basis for this illustration, assume that on November 1, 1995, Myson, Inc., an American corporation (with the U.S. dollar as its functional currency), acquires inventory on account from a Japanese manufacturer for a negotiated price of 210,000 yen. On December 1, 1995, 210,000 yen are conveyed to the company by Myson to extinguish the debt.

All of the balances recorded by Myson in connection with this purchase were denominated in a currency other than its functional currency. Thus, before Myson can report these transactions, a remeasurement from yen into dollars must be calculated. Assume that the following exchange rates were in effect:

November 1, 1995	$1 = 210 yen
December 1, 1995	$1 = 200 yen

The relative value of the Japanese currency has increased during the month; fewer yen are now needed to equal a dollar. Since Myson was required to pay this obligation in a currency that had become more valuable, the company incurred a loss. To measure this change in value, remeasurement into dollar equivalencies is necessary.

November 1, 1995	210,000 yen × 1/210 = $1,000
December 1, 1995	210,000 yen × 1/200 = $1,050

After all balances have been remeasured into U.S. dollars, Myson is able to record the effects of both foreign currency transactions: the purchase and payment. *The liability is a monetary balance and is, thus, subject to the change in the relative value of the yen. Conversely, the inventory is nonmonetary so that no later adjustment is needed.* (All journal entries in this chapter are recorded in U.S. dollars.)

11/1/95	Inventory.	1,000	
	Accounts Payable		1,000
	Acquisition of inventory for 210,000 yen.		
12/1/95	Transaction Loss	50	
	Accounts Payable		50
	To recognize increase in relative value of monetary liability.		
	Accounts Payable	1,050	
	Cash		1,050
	Payment made of 210,000 yen.		

For convenience, the December 1 entries may be combined. They are shown separately here to emphasize the change in the value of the liability.

As can be seen from this single illustration, the remeasurement of a foreign currency transaction differs markedly from the translation process. The liability is remeasured at current rates whereas the inventory continues to be reported at the historical rate.. A $50 loss is created by the increase in the relative value of the yen occurring between the time the liability was incurred and the eventual payment. This loss would appear in Myson's 1995 income statement.

The Remeasurement Process Illustrated—Two Time Periods Involved

To provide a second example of the remeasurement process, assume that Myson buys a patent on December 1, 1995, for 308,800 English pounds payable in six months. The company's functional currency is still the U.S. dollar. The applicable exchange rates follow:

December 1, 1995	1.0 pound = $1.84
December 31, 1995	1.0 pound = $1.88
June 1, 1996	1.0 pound = $1.82

Although the balances resulting from this purchase and payment are denominated in pounds, Myson once again reports the financial effects in U.S. dollars. Since individual transactions are occurring outside of the functional currency, remeasurement is required. The equivalent dollar values as of identifiable reporting dates are calculated as follows:

December 1, 1995	308,800 pounds × 1.84/1.0 = $568,192
December 31, 1995	308,800 pounds × 1.88/1.0 = $580,544
June 1, 1996	308,800 pounds × 1.82/1.0 = $562,016

Myson henceforth reports the patent (a nonmonetary account) at $568,192 based on the December 1, 1995, exchange rate. In contrast, the liability (a monetary account) is continually subjected to remeasurement at the time of any change in the currency rates.

12/1/95	Patent.	568,192	
	Accounts Payable		
	(denominated in pounds)		568,192
	To record acquisition of patent for 308,800 pounds.		

Although an updated value for this debt could conceivably be determined on a daily basis, little benefit is derived by maintaining such precise accounting records. Often, as in the previous example, the effects of rate fluctuations are only recognized at the time of subsequent transactions. In the current illustration, however, this payable remains unsettled at the end of the year. To ensure proper financial reporting for each period, a remeasured balance must be calculated on that date.

According to the exchange rates, the value of the English pound as of December 31, 1995, has increased relative to the U.S. dollar (a pound now acquires a greater number of dollars). Since Myson's payment will be made in these more valuable pounds, the recorded liability must be increased from the $568,192 figure just shown to $580,544 with a corresponding $12,352 loss recognized in the company's income statement.

12/31/95	Transaction Loss.	12,352	
	Accounts Payable		12,352
	To remeasure monetary liability to a $580,544 value based on current exchange rate, recognizing the increase in the value of the debt as a loss.		

By June 1, 1996, the date of the actual payment, another swing in the currency exchange rate has reduced the relative value of the pound. The 308,800 pounds paid by Myson now has a lower value ($562,016) than the presently recorded liability ($580,544). Therefore, a transaction gain of $18,528 must be reported in this subsequent year because of the drop in value of the liability. Although the previously recorded loss of $12,352 was never realized, this figure is not adjusted in any retroactive manner. Instead, the loss is reported in the first year and the $18,528 gain is recognized in the second. Myson records the gain and its final payment through the following journal entries:

6/1/96	Accounts Payable	18,528	
	Transaction Gain		18,528
	To remeasure monetary liability to a $562,016 value based on current exchange rate, recognizing the decrease in the value of the debt as a gain (580,544 − 562,016).		
	Accounts Payable	562,016	
	Cash		562,016
	To record payment of 308,800 English pounds at the current exchange rate.		

Remeasuring a Subsidiary's Financial Statements

In certain circumstances, the remeasurement process can even extend to an entire set of subsidiary financial statements. As an illustration, assume that an American company starts a new business in England at the beginning of 1995. Although this subsidiary maintains accounting records in English pounds, a substantial portion of the operations are transacted directly with the American parent. Because of these cash flows, the decision is made to view the U.S. dollar as the subsidiary's functional currency. *Since the subsidiary's balances are not recorded in its func-*

tional currency, a remeasurement into dollars (rather than a translation) is required.

Using the parent's currency as the functional currency is a common practice. For example, a footnote to the 1991 financial statements of Zenith Electronics Corporation stated "the company uses the U.S. dollar as the functional currency for all foreign subsidiaries. Foreign exchange gains and losses are included in other operating income."

Remeasurement—Subsidiary and Parent Have Same Functional Currency

As a remeasurement, the English subsidiary applies the current exchange rate at December 31, 1995, to all monetary assets and liabilities (and market value accounts) while all other accounts retain historical rates. To demonstrate this procedure, assume that the American parent invested 50,000 pounds to start the English company on January 1, 1995. Selected transactions incurred by the subsidiary are as follows:

Equipment acquired 1/1/95	30,000 pounds
Inventory purchased throughout the year	100,000 pounds
Inventory sold throughout the year	70,000 pounds cost
	120,000 pounds sales price
Land acquired 7/1/95	15,000 pounds
Land sold 12/31/95	5,000 pounds cost
	8,000 pounds sales price
Advertising, rent, and salary—incurred throughout the year	Various amounts

During this period, the currency rates varied as follows:

January 1, 1995	1 pound = $1.50
July 1, 1995	1 pound = $1.55
Average, 1995	1 pound = $1.56
December 31, 1995	1 pound = $1.62

At year's end, the following trial balance is developed for this English subsidiary. Prior to consolidation, these accounts denominated in pounds are each remeasured into U.S. dollars (the subsidiary's functional currency) as shown. Because the figures are being remeasured, only the monetary and market value accounts are reported at the current exchange rate (1 pound = $1.62). All other balances are valued at the rates in effect on the date of their origination. Consequently, cost of goods sold and depreciation expense are remeasured at the historical rates when the inventory and equipment were purchased.

	Debit (pounds)	Credit (pounds)	Remeasurement Rate	Debit (dollars)	Credit (dollars)
Trial Balance					
Accounts payable		16,000	1.62/1.00		$ 25,920
Accounts receivable	25,000		1.62/1.00	$ 40,500	
Accumulated depreciation		3,000	1.50/1.00		4,500
Advertising expense	10,000		1.56/1.00	15,600	
Cash	18,000		1.62/1.00	29,160	
Common stock		50,000	1.50/1.00		75,000
Cost of goods sold	70,000		1.56/1.00	109,200	
Depreciation expense	3,000		1.50/1.00	4,500	
Equipment	30,000		1.50/1.00	45,000	
Gain on sale of land		3,000	(See explanation)		5,210
Inventory, 12/31/95	30,000		1.56/1.00	46,800	
Land	10,000		1.55/1.00	15,500	
Notes payable		20,000	1.62/1.00		32,400
Rent expense	9,000		1.56/1.00	14,040	
Retained earnings, 1/1/95		–0–			–0–
Salary expense	7,000		1.56/1.00	10,920	
Sales		120,000	1.56/1.00		187,200
Transaction gain	–0–	–0–	(See following schedule)		990
Totals	212,000	212,000		$331,220	$331,220

The gain of 3,000 pounds is one figure on this trial balance that cannot be remeasured directly. Cash of 8,000 pounds was collected on December 31, 1995, in a sale of land costing 5,000 pounds. As a monetary account, the cash being received is remeasured using the current exchange rate, whereas the land retains the historical rate as of the date of purchase (July 1, 1995). The gain is the difference in the remeasured value of these two figures:

Cash	8,000 pounds × 1.62/1.00 = $12,960
Land	5,000 pounds × 1.55/1.00 = $ 7,750
Gain on Sale (remeasured value received is greater than remeasured value given up)	$ 5,210

Since the subsidiary's monetary assets and liabilities are remeasured using constantly changing currency rates, a transaction gain or loss is also created. The $990 gain shown in this example is calculated based on the exposed total of these specific assets and liabilities. As seen in the following schedule, the beginning balance as well as each change made in the net monetary figure during the period is remeasured immediately to determine a value *prior* to any rate fluctuations ($10,350). The ending total for these same monetary accounts (7,000 pounds) is also remeasured to arrive at a relative value *after* all currency rate changes have occurred ($11,340). The $990 difference represents the effect on these accounts created by the movement in the rates. For a remeasurement, this amount is presented as a component of net income rather than within stockholders' equity.

In making this gain or loss calculation, more types of transactions can affect net monetary assets or liabilities than change net assets or liabilities (the exposed figure used in computing a translation adjustment). For example, neither the purchase of inventory nor the acquisition of equipment (or other nonmonetary asset) have any impact on a subsidiary's net assets but both transactions decrease net monetary assets.

Transaction Gain for 1995

	As Denominated in Pounds	Remeasurement Rate	Relative Value in Dollars
Beginning balance of monetary accounts	–0–		–0–
Increases in monetary accounts:			
Issued common stock, 1/1/95	50,000	1.50/1.00	$ 75,000
Sales, 1995	120,000	1.56/1.00	187,200
Sold land, 12/31/95	8,000	1.62/1.00	12,960
Decreases in monetary accounts:			
Acquired equipment, 1/1/95	(30,000)	1.50/1.00	(45,000)
Acquired inventory (evenly during the year)	(100,000)	1.56/1.00	(156,000)
Advertising, rent, and salary expenses, 1995	(26,000)	1.56/1.00	(40,560)
Acquired land, 7/1/95	(15,000)	1.55/1.00	(23,250)
Monetary accounts prior to exchange rate fluctuations	7,000*		$ 10,350
Monetary accounts and relative value, 12/31/95	7,000*	1.62/1.00	$ 11,340
Transaction gain, 1995 (increase in relative value)			$ 990

* The figure is equal to the net balance of accounts payable, accounts receivable, cash, and notes payable.

The decision made as to the functional currency of a foreign subsidiary can have a significant impact on a consolidated set of financial statements. If the U.S. dollar is viewed as the functional currency, remeasurement is required; only monetary accounts are reported at the current exchange rate and any fluctuations lead to changes in net income. Conversely, if the local currency is judged to be the functional currency, a translation is performed. The current exchange rate is utilized for all assets and liabilities with the resulting translation adjustment being accumulated within stockholders' equity. As discussed earlier in this chapter, *SFAS 52* provides guidance for determining the functional currency but the decision is made by the reporting company's management. Consequently, consistency is hard to obtain.

For comparison purposes, differences between translation and remeasurement can be seen by looking at the method used in reporting selected accounts.

	Remeasurement	*Translation*
Accounts receivable	Current balance sheet rate	Current balance sheet rate
Accumulated depreciation	Rate at the date of asset purchase	Current balance sheet rate
Cost of goods sold	Rate at the date inventory was acquired (may need separate remeasurement for beginning inventory, purchases, and ending inventory)	Rate at the date cost of goods sold was recorded
Depreciation expense	Rate at the date of asset purchase	Rate when recorded (usually average rate for current year)
Gain or loss on sale of land	Difference in remeasured value of asset and remeasured value of cash received	Rate at the date of sale (when recorded)
Equipment	Rate at the date equipment was purchased	Current balance sheet rate
Inventory	Rate at the date inventory was purchased	Current balance sheet rate

"Within rather broad parameters," says Peat, Marwick, Mitchell partner James Weir, choosing the functional currency "is basically a management call." So much so, in fact, that Texaco, Occidental, and Unocal settled on the dollar as the functional currency for most of their foreign operations, whereas competitors Exxon, Mobil, and Amoco chose primarily the local currencies as the functional currencies for their foreign businesses.[12]

Remeasurement in a Highly Inflationary Economy

The FASB in *Statement 52* mandates the use of the remeasurement process in one additional circumstance: the operation of a foreign subsidiary or branch in a highly inflationary economy. As stated in paragraph 107, "the Board nonetheless believes that a currency that has largely lost its utility as a store of value cannot be a functional measuring unit." Because of the uncertain value, the subsidiary's currency is not considered a reliable basis for conveying accounting information. Hence, in a highly inflationary environment, all of the financial balances of a foreign subsidiary must be *remeasured* directly into the parent's currency; translation does not occur.

As a guideline, the FASB defined a highly inflationary economy as one having a cumulative inflationary rate of approximately 100 percent or more over a three-year period. Unfortunately, during the 1989–91 time period, a number of countries achieved this dubious distinction including Afghanistan, Argentina, Brazil, the Dominican Republic, Poland, and Turkey.

---

[12] John Heins, "Plenty of Opportunity to Fool Around," *Forbes*, June 2, 1986, p. 139.

Hedging

Suddenly, in 1985, perhaps predictably but certainly through no fault of its own, Waterford Crystal of Kilbarry, Ireland, faced a potentially disastrous situation. The dollar began to sink against the Irish pound. . . . A Waterford wine decanter that sold in 1985 for $150 in the United States translated into 148 Irish pounds. By July 1986 $150 bought only 106 Irish pounds. . . . The crystalmaker seemed to face two unpleasant choices: raise its already high prices in the United States and almost certainly lose sales, or face a profit squeeze by holding dollar prices and accepting a lesser number of Irish pounds. But there was a third way out, and Waterford took it. It locked in a profitable exchange rate against a significant part of its anticipated U.S. receivables. Waterford bought forward contracts on the Irish pound.''[13]

All companies that deal in foreign currencies risk having to report adverse financial effects that can result from fluctuations in exchange rates.

- A transaction loss, arising from the remeasurement of monetary assets and liabilities at current rates, reduces reported net income.
- A negative adjustment may appear in the equity section of a consolidated balance sheet as a result of translating a foreign subsidiary's net assets at current exchange rates.

However, through a practice referred to as *hedging,* many organizations seek to protect themselves from the potentially negative impact of changes in foreign currency rates. A 1986 FASB research report found that 84 percent of the 162 companies surveyed hedged their foreign transaction exposure on a regular or selective basis.[14] A company can hedge its financial position at any time simply by entering into a transaction that eliminates exposure to the possible effects produced by future rate fluctuations. *This transaction is designed to create an equilibrium between asset and liability balances that are reported using current exchange rates.* The company's exposed position becomes zero; thus, subsequent increases or decreases in the relative value of these accounts exactly offset.

An American company, for example, that has an account receivable of 100,000 liras is in an exposed asset position. A decline in the value of the lira automatically produces a transaction loss since the liras being received are worth relatively less. Many strategies are available to hedge this exposed position and eliminate the risk involved. All are based on creating a counterbalancing 100,000 lira liability.

As one option, the company could borrow 100,000 liras and immediately convert these funds into dollars. At that point, the company has no further risk of

---

[13] Richard L. Stern, ''(Dangerous) Fun and Games in the Foreign Exchange Market,'' *Forbes,* August 22, 1988, p. 69.

[14] Scott R. Flicker and Dennis M. Bline, ''Managing Foreign Currency Exchange Risk,'' *Journal of Accountancy,* August 1990, p. 128.

loss from exchange rate fluctuations. Net exposure is zero: the foreign currency receivable balance (in liras) is the same as the newly created foreign currency liability (also in liras). *Any subsequent changes occurring in currency rates would then create identical gains and losses; net income would not be affected.*

Hedging through Forward Exchange Contracts

One of the most common hedging devices is the forward exchange contract. According to *SFAS 52* (Appendix E), a forward exchange contract is an "agreement to exchange at a specified future date currencies of different countries at a specified rate (forward rate)." Such contracts simply specify a future acquisition (a receivable) or sale (a liability) of a foreign currency for a predetermined amount.

Forward exchange contracts are marketed by currency brokers throughout the world. For example, a note to the 1990 financial statements of Deere & Company states that

> the company has entered into foreign exchange contracts and options to hedge the currency exposure. . . . At October 31, 1990, the company had foreign exchange contracts maturing in up to four months to exchange $126 million for 198 million deutsche marks to hedge foreign investments, 333 million Canadian dollars for $285 million to hedge foreign inventory and 144 million deutsche marks for $91 million to hedge short-term borrowings.

Eastman Kodak also reports heavy use of such contracts:

> To constantly adjust to market volatility, Kodak buys and sells $10 billion to $12 billion a year to protect its $1.5 billion exposure. . . . The most common form of hedging involves the forward market, where currencies are bought and sold for preset prices for delivery at a future date. In nearly all major currencies, big international banks will quote a price, or exchange rate, for the dollar up to a year in the future, sometimes longer.[15]

To illustrate the elements of a forward exchange contract, assume that on February 1, 1995, an American company agrees to buy 50,000 Swiss francs in 180 days. The current exchange rate (referred to as the *spot rate*) is $1.00 = 1.92 Swiss francs. However, the forward rate usually varies from that quotation depending on market perceptions of the future values of both currencies. For example, assuming that the 180-day forward rate is $1.00 = 1.84 Swiss francs, the value of the franc is expected to increase during this period relative to the U.S. dollar (fewer francs would be required to buy a dollar). Therefore, the forward exchange contract would state that $27,173.91 (50,000 × 1.00/1.84) will be paid in 180 days by the American company in exchange for 50,000 Swiss francs. Upon signing the contract, the company has a receivable denominated in Swiss francs and a liability payable in U.S. dollars.

---

[15] Michael R. Sesit, "By Trading Currencies, Kodak's Eric R. Nelson Saves the Firm Millions," *The Wall Street Journal*, March 5, 1985, p. 1.

The American company may have entered into this forward exchange agreement for any of several reasons. A liability or commitment could have been previously incurred in Swiss francs so that the company now needs a receivable as a hedge to prevent possible losses in the future. For example, if the company already has an obligation to pay 50,000 francs in exactly 180 days, exposure to any exchange rate fluctuations is eliminated by the newly acquired 50,000 franc receivable. Forward exchange contracts are also purchased for speculative reasons. Should the company believe that the relative value of one currency (the Swiss franc, in this case) will increase during the period, this agreement may not represent a hedge at all but rather an investment acquired in hopes of receiving a more valuable currency to generate a profit.

Sell Belg. francs forward

Forward Exchange Contracts Illustrated—Hedging an Actual Transaction. Although forward exchange contracts can be entered into for several reasons, the initial illustration here is of a contract established solely to act as a hedge to prevent rate fluctuations from affecting an actual transaction. For this purpose, assume that an American company sells inventory on December 1, 1995, to an enterprise for 100,000 Belgian francs with the amount to be paid in 90 days. Assuming that the spot rate on that date is $1.00 = 50 francs, the American company remeasures and records this foreign currency transaction as a $2,000 sale (100,000 × 1.00/50.0).

12/1/95	Accounts Receivable (to be collected in francs) 2,000	
	Sales	2,000

To ensure the value of this receivable, the company immediately signs a contract to sell 100,000 francs in 90 days. If the 90-day forward exchange rate is $1.00 = 52 francs, the company is agreeing to transfer 100,000 francs to the currency broker at that time for $1,923 (100,000 × 1.00/52.0). *Because fewer dollars will be collected than the $2,000 current value of the receivable, the company is accepting $77 as the cost of protection against future exchange rate fluctuations.*[16] To match this expense with the appropriate time periods, the $77 is initially recorded as a discount (or premium, if applicable) and then amortized over the life of the contract using the straight-line method.

The American company records the establishment of this forward exchange contract through the following journal entry:

12/1/95	Exchange Contract Receivable (dollars) 1,923	
	Discount on Exchange Contract. 77	
	Exchange Contract Payable (to be paid in francs)	2,000

---

[16] "Foreign currency hedging is not cheap. The average premium on an option, for example, runs from 1.5 percent to 4 percent but can be much more. So a hedge on $50 million into deutsche marks for one year might cost $2 million. As the expiration date of an option or future gets further out, its price goes higher. It gets more expensive, too, if the currency involved is more volatile or less frequently traded, like the Italian lira. If you do business abroad, you don't have much choice: You pay the man or risk disaster." Stern, "(Dangerous)," p. 71.

The $1,923 receivable portion of the contract is not a remeasured figure; the company actually collects this amount of U.S. dollars in 90 days. The liability, though, must be paid in francs and, as with all foreign currency monetary balances, is remeasured at the current exchange rate of $1.00 = 50 francs. A hedge has been successfully established; the amount to be received in francs (from the company's customer) equals the amount to be paid in francs (to the currency broker). A loss in value of one account is offset by a gain in the value of the other.

During the subsequent 90 days, the current exchange rate is used to remeasure both the account receivable created by the sale and the exchange contract payable, the two balances actually denominated in francs. A year-end adjustment is necessary, therefore, to establish appropriate figures for reporting purposes. If the December 31, 1995, spot rate is $1.00 = 55 francs, the remeasured value is no longer $2,000. The 100,000 francs receivable/payable would be reported at $1,818 (100,000 × 1.00/55.0), requiring $182 decreases ($1,818 − $2,000) in both foreign currency accounts:

12/31/95 Transaction Loss	182	
Accounts Receivable (to be collected in francs)		182
To record drop in relative value of 100,000 francs receivable from $2,000 to $1,818.		

12/31/95 Exchange Contract Payable (to be paid in francs)	182	
Transaction Gain		182
To record drop in relative value of 100,000 francs payable from $2,000 to $1,818.		

The gain and the loss are equal since the company has no net asset or liability exposure. The forward exchange contract is acting as a hedge to protect the company from the effects of exchange rate fluctuations.

As a separate accounting consideration, the cost applicable to the contract must be amortized to expense over the 90-day life of the agreement. Thus, an additional year-end adjustment is necessary to reclassify $27 of the discount balance in recognition of the 31 days that have passed during 1995 (31/90 × $77).

12/31/95 Currency Hedging Expense	27	
Discount on Exchange Contract		27
To record 31 days of amortization on discount relating to 90-day forward exchange contract.		

On March 1, 1996, both the trade receivable and the forward exchange contract come due. Assuming that the currency rate on that date is $1.00 = 51 francs, the 100,000 francs have a relative value of $1,961 (100,000 × 1.00/51.0). The receivable from the customer as well as the exchange contract payable to the currency broker have previously been adjusted to book values of $1,818. Thus, a second set of offsetting gains and losses is recognized at the settlement date ($1,961 − $1,818 or $143). To avoid confusion, both remeasurements are shown here first, followed by receipt of payment from the customer and then settlement of the forward exchange contract.

3/1/96   Accounts Receivable (to be collected in francs) 143

        Transaction Gain 143

Remeasurement (increase) is made in monetary account based on current exchange rate.

Transaction Loss 143

        Exchange Contract Payable (to be paid in francs) 143

Remeasurement (increase) is made in monetary account based on current exchange rate.

Cash (francs) 1,961

        Accounts Receivable. 1,961

To record collection of 100,000 francs from customer.

Exchange Contract Payable. 1,961

        Cash (francs) 1,961

Payment of 100,000 francs is made to settle forward exchange contract.

Cash (dollars) 1,923

        Exchange Contract Receivable 1,923

Receipt is made of $1,923 to settle forward exchange contract.

In addition, the remainder of the original $77 cost of the forward exchange contract is recognized as an expense attributed to this second time period.

3/1/96   Currency Hedging Expense. 50

        Discount on Exchange Contract. 50

To recognize remaining amortization of cost of forward exchange contract ($77 − $27).

Because of this hedging arrangement, the American company incurred only a $77 net expense despite the changes in the currency rates in both 1995 and 1996. This amount represents the predetermined cost of the forward exchange contract; all transaction gains and losses recognized thereafter offset each other exactly as did the inflows and outflows of francs. Therefore, the company received cash of $1,923, a figure that was legally fixed at the time the hedge was created.

Hedging a Future Commitment.   A currency hedge, such as the forward exchange contract just demonstrated, does not have to relate to a presently exposed monetary asset or liability. A company that has a future commitment (either to collect or pay a foreign currency) may elect to create a corresponding hedge to lock in the value of the anticipated transaction.

As an example, assume that on October 1, 1995, an American company agrees to pay 20,000 English pounds for inventory that will be delivered in six months on April 1, 1996. For accounting purposes, no liability has yet been incurred, only a purchase commitment. Despite the absence of a legal obligation, the company is clearly exposed to the effects of future currency rate changes. Should the relative value of the pound increase prior to April 1, 1996, the company will have to fulfill its commitment in a monetary unit that has become more valuable. For this reason, creating a hedge is often considered a wise financial strategy for commitments as well as for exposed asset and liability positions.

In this illustration, the assumption is made that the company immediately signs a forward exchange contract to buy 20,000 English pounds in six months as a means of eliminating the risk created by the purchase commitment. The company will pay a predetermined amount of U.S. dollars on April 1, 1996, to receive 20,000 pounds. Except for a single theoretical issue, accounting for the forward exchange contract appears rather uncomplicated. The foreign currency receivable (the 20,000 pounds) initially is recorded at the spot rate in effect on October 1, 1995, but will then be remeasured as of the December 31, 1995, year-end and then again at the date of settlement.

The problem that arises, however, concerns the disposition of the effects created by the remeasurement process. *Since a commitment rather than a legal liability has been incurred, no transaction gain or loss exists for the hedge to counterbalance.* The commitment is not formally journalized; thus, gains or losses in its value are not reflected by the company. Although the contract was acquired specifically to nullify the impact of rate fluctuations, those changes do not appear in the accounting records. Consequently, recognizing a gain or loss on the hedge alone would seem to betray the underlying reality of the economic events.

For this reason, *SFAS 52* provides that the effect of fluctuations in the relative value of an account designated as a hedge against a firm commitment should be deferred and then recorded as a cost element within the eventual foreign currency transaction. No gain or loss is recognized because only the hedging transaction is present within the accounting records.

To demonstrate this procedure, the following currency rates are considered applicable:

October 1, 1995 (six-month forward rate)	$1.00 = .42 pounds
October 1, 1995 (spot rate)	$1.00 = .46 pounds
December 31, 1995 (spot rate)	$1.00 = .45 pounds
April 1, 1996 (spot rate)	$1.00 = .50 pounds

As protection against rate changes that could affect the value of this purchase commitment, the American company has entered into a forward exchange contract specifying the acquisition of 20,000 English pounds in six months for $47,619 (20,000 × 1.00/.42). The company has agreed to this price even though 20,000 pounds are presently worth only $43,478 (20,000 × 1.00/.46). An extra $4,141 ($47,619 − $43,478) is being paid as insurance against the possibility of currency losses on this commitment. As in the previous example, this cost is deferred and then recognized as an expense over the life of the contract.

The signing of the forward exchange agreement would be journalized by the American company as follows. However, the commitment to acquire the inventory is not recorded at this time since no legal obligation exists.

10/1/95 Exchange Contract Receivable
(to be collected in pounds) 43,478
Discount on Exchange Contract. 4,141
    Exchange Contract Payable (dollars).   47,619
To record forward exchange contract: $47,619 to be paid for
20,000 English pounds.

By the end of this fiscal year, the exchange rate has changed; thus, remeasurement of the foreign currency balance (the receivable) is necessary. As the relative value of the English pound has increased, the 20,000 pounds to be collected from this contract are now worth more in U.S. dollars. At the current rate, the receivable should be reported as $44,444 (20,000 × 1.00/.45), a value that is $966 greater than the originally recorded balance of $43,478. Since no income effect is created by the hedge of a commitment, this gain is deferred until the actual inventory purchase is made. A Deferred Gain/Loss balance is maintained for this purpose so that all further changes, decreases as well as increases, can be recorded in this one account.

12/31/95 Exchange Contract Receivable
(to be collected in pounds) 966
    Deferred Transaction Gain/Loss*   966
To remeasure receivable balance at year-end exchange rate
with gain being deferred because hedge relates to a
commitment.

* In reference to this deferral process, *SFAS 52* (par. 21) does state that "losses shall not be deferred, however, if it is estimated that deferral would lead to recognizing losses in later periods."

Since three of the six months covered by this contract have now passed, half of the $4,141 cost incurred by the company should be expensed through an additional year-end adjustment.

12/31/95 Currency Hedging Expense 2,071
    Discount on Exchange Contract*.   2,071
To recognize three months of expense incurred in
connection with six-month forward exchange contract
($4,141 × 3/6).

* An alternative method of handling the discount is to defer all amortization until the time of the related foreign currency transaction.

To complete this illustration, assume that on April 1, 1996, the inventory is delivered as per the original purchase agreement. Since the forward exchange contract matures on this same date, the 20,000 pounds being received by the American company can be used to pay the newly incurred liability. However, concurrent with the recording of these transactions, another change in the exchange rate must be recognized. The relative value of the pounds to be collected from the forward exchange contract has now been reduced to $40,000 (20,000 × 1.00/.50). Once again, though, this adjustment (a $4,444 decline from the $44,444 book value as of December 31, 1995) does not affect income. Since a commitment is being hedged, a deferred loss is recorded in remeasuring the receivable.

4/1/96	Deferred Transaction Gain/Loss	4,444	
	Exchange Contract Receivable (pounds)		4,444
	To remeasure 20,000 pound receivable balance based on current exchange rate ($44,444 − $40,000).		
	Exchange Contract Payable	47,619	
	Cash (dollars)		47,619
	To record settlement of forward exchange contract through payment of $47,619.		
	Cash (pounds)	40,000	
	Exchange Contract Receivable		40,000
	To record settlement of forward exchange contract through collection of 20,000 English pounds.		

In recording the inventory acquisition, the two deferrals (a gain of $966 during the first three months and a loss of $4,444 for the last three) form a net loss balance of $3,478. This figure reflects the decline in value of the foreign currency receivable portion of the forward exchange contract from $43,478 as of October 1, 1995, to $40,000 on the date of settlement. Because a commitment was hedged, the deferral is not recognized as a loss but as a cost element of the purchased inventory. Therefore, although the American company pays pounds with a current exchange value of only $40,000 for this merchandise, the acquisition is recorded at a total cost of $43,478, *the predetermined amount established by the signing of the hedging arrangement.*

4/1/96	Purchases (or Inventory)	43,478	
	Cash (pounds)		40,000
	Deferred Transaction Gain/Loss		3,478
	To record purchase made with proceeds from six-month forward exchange contract.		

Finally, the company must also amortize the remaining cost originally agreed on in procuring this forward exchange contract:

4/1/96	Currency Hedging Expense	2,070	
	Discount on Exchange Contract		2,070
	To recognize final three months of amortization on cost incurred in connection with forward exchange contract.		

Although a commitment was incurred in this example rather than a liability, the currency hedge has still protected the company from the effects of variations in the exchange rate. A total of $47,619 was expended to acquire this inventory, but that amount was set by the forward exchange agreement and was not subject to change. The inventory actually cost only $43,478, the value of the commitment on October 1, 1995, the date the contract was signed. The remaining $4,141 was paid to secure the specified contract price. This fee was accepted by the company as the price necessary to eliminate exposure to rate fluctuations and is charged to expense rather than being considered a cost of the inventory.

Interestingly, the value of the pounds to be paid in this example declined after the forward exchange contract was acquired. Thus, the hedge actually prevented the American company from benefiting from an exchange gain rather than providing protection against a loss. This gamble is associated with all currency hedges, potential gains that might result from rate fluctuations are eliminated along with possible losses.

Hedging against a Subsidiary's Asset or Liability Position. In the preceding discussions, examples of forward exchange contracts have been analyzed under two different circumstances:

1. A hedge against rate changes affecting monetary asset and liability accounts resulting from individual foreign currency transactions. Any transaction gain or loss on this type contract is recognized immediately to counterbalance the corresponding income effect created by the exposed position.
2. A hedge against rate changes affecting a foreign currency commitment. Gains and losses are deferred until the eventual transaction date and then recorded as a net cost factor.

Currency hedges are also established in a third instance: a parent company can seek to protect a net asset or liability position (often referred to as a *net investment position*) maintained by a foreign subsidiary or branch. As previously discussed, the translation of foreign currency financial statements in anticipation of consolidation normally creates a translation adjustment. Even though this stockholders' equity item does not affect the calculation of net income, the parent may prefer to eliminate all potential reporting effects created by exchange rate fluctuations.

> More and more corporations are hedging their translation exposure—the recorded value of international assets such as plant, equipment and inventory—to prevent gyrations in their quarterly accounts. Though technically only paper gains or losses, translation adjustments can play havoc with balance-sheet ratios and can spook analysts and creditors alike.[17]

For this reason, a hedging transaction such as a forward exchange contract can be entered into by the parent to offset part or all of the subsidiary's exposed net investment position. Although forward exchange contracts are foreign currency transactions subject to remeasurement, gains and losses are not recognized as income when the net investment position of a subsidiary or branch is being hedged. *Since the arrangement is designed to counterbalance accounts that are being translated, any effect on the contract resulting from rate fluctuations is*

---

[17] Ida Picker, "Indecent Exposure," *Institutional Investor*, September 1991, p. 82.

classified as an offsetting translation adjustment rather than as a transaction gain or loss.

United Dominion Industries, for example, incurred a $12.8 million increase in its translation adjustment balance during the year ending December 31, 1990, because of the reporting of subsidiary operations. However, by means of hedging arrangements, the company managed to reduce the impact actually reported by $11.6 million so that the net change within stockholders' equity was only $1.2 million.

For a company such as United Dominion Industries that buys a forward exchange contract to hedge the net investment position of a foreign subsidiary, the initial recording is not affected. The foreign currency balance (either the payable or the receivable depending on the terms of the arrangement) is recorded at the spot rate. This figure is then remeasured periodically to reflect current exchange rates. However, no gain or loss is recognized because of any changes in the reported value but rather an increase or decrease is made in the Translation Adjustment account.

Forward Exchange Contract—Investment for Speculation

A forward exchange contract does not necessarily have to serve as a currency hedge. Companies also acquire such contracts as investments for speculation purposes. The buying and selling of currencies and contracts has reached phenomenal proportions in recent years. "People have been flocking to the currency markets. Average daily volume was $425 billion last year. . . . By contrast, on the New York Stock Exchange's biggest day, October 19, $21 billion worth of securities changed hands."[18]

If a fluctuation is anticipated in the value of a particular currency, a forward exchange contract can be negotiated in hopes of realizing a profit from the expected movement. However, since no hedge has been created by the purchase, all subsequent changes in the value of the contract are recognized immediately as transaction gains or losses.

To demonstrate the procedures used in accounting for a forward exchange contract that is acquired as an investment, assume that an American company agrees on December 2, 1995, to acquire 40,000 French francs from a broker in 90 days. The contract price is $6,557 based on a 90-day forward rate of $1.00 = 6.1 francs (40,000 × 1.00/6.1). The company is speculating that the relative value of this foreign currency will increase during the next 90 days and, thus, be worth more than $6,557 when collected. The signing of the contract is recorded as follows:

12/2/95	Exchange Contract Receivable (francs)	6,557	
	Exchange Contract Payable (dollars)		6,557
	To record acquisition of forward exchange contract held for investment.		

---

[18] Stern, "(Dangerous)," p. 70.

In this initial entry, the foreign currency receivable is recorded at the forward exchange rate rather than the December 2, 1995, spot rate that would have been applicable for a hedge. Because of the speculative nature of the purchase, the contract is viewed as an investment rather than a receivable. In many cases, the company does not anticipate holding the contract until maturity. Instead, it will be resold immediately whenever the company believes that the highest possible price has been achieved. Ownership of the contract, therefore, is providing the future benefit and not the eventual receipt of 40,000 francs. For this reason, remeasurement is based on the *market value of the contract* (the forward rate) rather than the current value of the francs (the spot rate).

At the end of the fiscal period, for example, the foreign currency balance (the receivable in this illustration) must be remeasured to account for changes occurring in the exchange rates. Because 30 days have now passed, the value of this investment is reflected by *the 60-day forward exchange rate* which indicates the current sales price of the contract. Assuming this rate to be $1.00 = 6.4 francs, the remeasured value has dropped to $6,250 (40,000 × 1.00/6.4). The $307 reduction in the reported balance from $6,557 to $6,250 would be recorded as a loss through the following adjusting entry:

12/31/95	Transaction Loss.	307	
	Exchange Contract Receivable.		307
	Value of 40,000 francs forward exchange contract is remeasured from $6,557 to $6,250.		

To conclude this illustration, assume that by January 31, 1996, the exchange rate of the franc has increased relative to the dollar so that the company is able to negotiate a sales price of $700 for the contract. The disposition is recorded as follows. The company has earned a $700 profit on this investment (without expending any money). Since a $307 loss was recorded in the first period, a $1,007 gain is reported in 1996 to arrive at the $700 profit actually earned.

1/31/96	Cash (dollars)	700	
	Exchange Contract Payable	6,557	
	Exchange Contract Receivable.		6,250
	Transaction Gain		1,007
	To record sale of forward exchange contract prior to its maturity.		

Summary

1. Because many companies have significant financial involvement in foreign countries, the process by which balances are reported in U.S. dollars is of special accounting importance. From 1975 through 1981, the temporal method—as prescribed by *Statement 8* of the Financial Accounting Standards Board—was used to arrive at the values shown for all figures denominated in a foreign currency.

During these years, this approach came under increasing attack from the business community (as well as from many accountants) and was eventually replaced by *Statement 52*.

2. *Statement 52* creates two separate procedures for reporting the value of foreign currency balances. Translation is usually applicable when the accounts of a foreign subsidiary are to be included within consolidated statements. However, remeasurement procedures are used if a company has individual transactions denominated in a currency other than that entity's functional currency. Remeasurement is also applied to an entire foreign subsidiary if the U.S. dollar is its functional currency or if the operation is in a country with a highly inflationary economy.

3. For translation purposes, *SFAS 52* requires that a foreign subsidiary's financial statements must be first remeasured into the entity's own functional currency. The statements are then adjusted to be in conformity with U.S. generally accepted accounting principles. All of the resulting asset and liability balances are translated into the parent's reporting currency at the current exchange rate (the spot rate) as of the balance sheet date. The subsidiary's other accounts (equities, revenues, expenses, etc.) are translated at the historical rate in effect at the time of accounting recognition. Changes in the reported values created by translating asset and liability accounts at current exchange rates are accumulated and reported as a separate component within consolidated stockholders' equity.

4. In applying the remeasurement process, only monetary assets and liabilities (as well as any accounts shown at market value) are reported at current exchange rates. All other accounts are remeasured using the historical rates in effect at the date of origination. Any increase or decrease in value resulting from the continual remeasurement of monetary accounts is reported within net income. If a foreign subsidiary is involved (rather than just an individual transaction), the amount of this gain or loss is determined by measuring the effect that rate fluctuations have on the exposed monetary asset or liability position of the company during the year.

5. The economic impact created by fluctuations in the value of foreign currencies has led many companies to develop strategies for limiting their risk of loss either on the income statement or within the stockholders' equity section of the balance sheet. These companies often hedge their financial position; they set exposed asset and liability balances (held in any foreign currency) at equal amounts. Subsequent swings in exchange rates create a counterbalancing effect: decreases in the reported value of one type of account exactly offset increases in the value of the other.

6. One popular means of hedging is the forward exchange contract, an agreement to exchange currencies in the future at a predetermined rate. In a forward exchange contract, either a receivable or payable (depending on the terms of the agreement) is created in a specified foreign currency. As a monetary account, this balance must be remeasured periodically based on current exchange rates. The resulting gain or loss serves to offset part (or all) of the income effect created by the company's other foreign currency transactions. However, if the exposed position of a foreign subsidiary is being hedged (rather than individual transactions), rate fluctuations affecting the contract result in a translation adjustment rather than gains and.losses. If a future commitment (either a purchase or sale) is being hedged, recognition of effects created by rate changes should be deferred until the actual transaction occurs. The deferral is then recorded as an adjustment to the reported value of the purchase or sale. Finally, a forward exchange contract can be acquired for investment purposes and not as a hedge. In this situation, remeasurement gains and losses are recognized immediately. However, remeasurement is carried out using the market rate of the contract rather than the spot rate for the receivable or payable.

Comprehensive Illustration

PROBLEM   (Estimated Time: 55 to 65 Minutes)

The Arlington Company is an American-based organization with numerous foreign subsidiaries. As a preliminary step in preparing consolidated financial statements for 1995, the financial information from each of these foreign operations must be translated into the parent's reporting currency, the U.S. dollar.

Arlington owns a subsidiary in Sweden, which has been in business for several years. On December 31, 1994, this entity's balance sheet was translated from Swedish kronor (its functional currency) into U.S. dollars as prescribed by *SFAS 52*. Equity accounts at that date were as follows (all credit balances):

Common stock	110,000 Kr	=	$21,000
Translation adjustment			$ 3,860
Retained earnings	194,800 Kr	=	$36,100

At the end of 1995, the Swedish subsidiary produces the trial balance that follows. These figures include all of the entity's transactions for the year except for the results of several sales made to a French corporation. A separate ledger has been maintained for these transactions since they were denominated in French francs. This ledger is presented after the company's trial balance.

Trial Balance—Subsidiary
December 31, 1995

	Debit	Credit
Accounts payable		39,000 Kr
Accounts receivable	126,000 Kr	
Accumulated depreciation		98,100
Bonds payable		125,000
Cash	41,000	
Common stock		110,000
Cost of goods sold	165,000	
Depreciation expense	10,900	
Discount on exchange contract	925	
Dividends paid, 7/1/95	25,000	
Exchange contract payable (to be collected in francs)		21,978
Exchange contract receivable	21,053	
Fixed assets.	228,000	
Inventory.	128,000	
Land	160,000	
Notes payable.		56,000
Other expenses	41,000	
Rent expense	12,000	
Retained earnings, 1/1/95		194,800
Salary expense	36,000	
Sales.		350,000
Totals	994,878 Kr	994,878 Kr

Ledger—Transactions in Francs
December 31, 1995

	Debit	Credit
Accounts receivable	28,000 F	
Accumulated depreciation		4,000 F
Cash	10,000	
Depreciation expense	4,000	
Fixed assets.	20,000	
Interest expense.	1,000	
Notes payable.		15,000
Sales.		44,000
Totals	63,000 F	63,000 F

Additional Information:

- The subsidiary began selling to the French company at the beginning of the current year. At that time, 20,000 francs were borrowed to acquire a truck for delivery purposes. A portion of that debt was paid before the end of the year. Sales were made evenly during the period.

- The currency exchange rates for the Swedish kronor are as follows:

January 1, 1995.	$1.00 = 5.0 kronor
Weighted-average rate for 1995.	$1.00 = 5.2 kronor
July 1, 1995	$1.00 = 5.3 kronor
December 31, 1995	$1.00 = 5.5 kronor

- The currency exchange rates applicable for the remeasurement of the foreign currency transactions are as follows:

January 1, 1995.	1.00 krona = .80 franc
Weighted-average rate for 1995.	1.00 krona = .86 franc
December 1, 1995.	1.00 krona = .91 franc
December 31, 1995	1.00 krona = .96 franc

- On December 1, 1995, the Swedish subsidiary decided to hedge the net monetary asset position denominated in French francs. Therefore, the company signed a three-month forward exchange contract whereby 21,053 Swedish kronor would be collected in exchange for the delivery of 20,000 francs. For recording purposes, the foreign currency liability (the 20,000 francs) was remeasured as 21,978 kronor based on the spot exchange rate on that date of 1 Kr = .91 F (20,000 × 1/.91). Since the value of the remeasured obligation (21,978 Kr) exceeded the receivable (21,053 Kr) by 925 kronor, this cost was recorded in a Discount account.
- The Swedish subsidiary expended 10,000 Kr during the year for research and development, a cost that has been capitalized within the Fixed Asset account. This expenditure had no effect on the depreciation recognized for the year.

Required:

Prepare financial statements for the year ending December 31, 1995, for this subsidiary. Translate these statements according to *SFAS 52* into U.S. dollars to facilitate the preparation of consolidated statements.

SOLUTION

Remeasurement of Foreign Currency Transactions. A portion of the Swedish subsidiary's operating results are presently stated in French francs. The liability created by the forward exchange contract is also denominated in this same currency. *These balances must be remeasured into the functional currency, Swedish kronor, before the translation process can begin.* In remeasuring these few accounts, the value of the monetary assets and liabilities are determined by using the current exchange rate (1 Kr = .96 F) whereas all other accounts utilize historical rates.

Remeasurement of Foreign Currency Transactions

Accounts receivable	28,000 F	×	1.0/.96	=	29,167 Kr
Accumulated depreciation.	4,000	×	1.0/.80	=	5,000
Cash	10,000	×	1.0/.96	=	10,416
Depreciation expense.	4,000	×	1.0/.80	=	5,000
Fixed assets	20,000	×	1.0/.80	=	25,000
Interest expense	1,000	×	1.0/.86	=	1,163
Notes payable	15,000	×	1.0/.96	=	15,625
Sales	44,000	×	1.0/.86	=	51,163
Exchange contract payable (hedge). . .	20,000	×	1.0/.96	=	20,833

Since the relative values of the receivable, cash, and two payables are computed based on current rates, each fluctuation in the exchange rates results in transaction gains and losses in the reporting of these accounts. This income effect can be calculated by monitoring changes in the net *monetary asset* position being exposed. As computed below, a transaction gain of 103 Kr is indicated by the remeasurement of these specific accounts from francs into kronor. Although the liability created by the forward exchange contract is actually reported within the

Transaction Gain for 1995

	As Denominated in Francs		Remeasurement Rate		Relative Value in Kronor
Net monetary asset balance, 1/1/95	–0–				–0–
Increases in net monetary assets and relative value at time of increase:* Operations (sales less interest expense)	43,000 F	×	1.0/.86	=	50,000 Kr
Decreases in net monetary assets and relative value at time of decrease:* Acquired truck, 1/1/95	(20,000)	×	1.0/.80	=	(25,000)
Acquired payable as a hedge, 12/1/95	(20,000)	×	1.0/.91	=	(21,978)
Net monetary asset value prior to exchange rate fluctuations	3,000† F				3,022 Kr
Net monetary asset balance and relative value, 12/31/95	3,000† F	×	1.0/.96	=	3,125 Kr
Transaction gain, 1995 (increase in relative value of net monetary assets).					103 Kr

* Changes between monetary accounts do not create a net increase or decrease. Thus, the borrowing of 20,000 francs as well as the subsequent payment on this note are not included.
† This balance represents the ending total of accounts receivable, cash, notes payable, and the exchange contract payable.

subsidiary's own trial balance, the monetary account is included in this same schedule since the balance is denominated in francs.

The remeasured figures from the French operation must be combined in some manner with the subsidiary's trial balance denominated in Swedish kronor. For example, the accounts may simply be added together on a worksheet. As an alternative, a year-end adjustment can be recorded in the accounting system of the Swedish subsidiary to add the remeasured balances for financial reporting purposes. In recording these figures, the foreign currency balance (the liability) of the forward exchange contract is also adjusted to the current rate.

12/31/95	Accounts Receivable	29,167 Kr	
	Cash	10,416	
	Depreciation Expense	5,000	
	Interest Expense	1,163	
	Fixed Assets	25,000	
	Exchange Contract Payable	1,145	
	Accumulated Depreciation		5,000 Kr
	Notes Payable		15,625
	Sales		51,163
	Transaction Gain		103

To record foreign currency transactions originally denominated in francs as well as to adjust the forward exchange contract payable from 21,978 kronor to 20,833.

Two other adjustments are necessary before the functional currency figures of the subsidiary are translated into the parent's reporting currency. First, periodic amortization must be recognized on the 925 Kr cost incurred in connection with the acquisition of the forward exchange contract. Second, the research and development costs incurred by the Swedish entity should be reclassified into an expense account as required by the FASB in *SFAS 2*, "Accounting for Research and Development Costs," December 1974. After this adjustment, the statements are aligned with U.S. generally accepted accounting principles.

12/31/95	Other Expenses	308 Kr	
	Discount on Exchange Contract		308 Kr

To recognize one-month amortization on cost of three-month forward exchange contract ($925 \times \frac{1}{3}$).

	Other Expenses	10,000 Kr	
	Fixed Assets		10,000 Kr

To adjust foreign statements to be in compliance with U.S. GAAP.

By combining all remeasured and adjusted balances with the Swedish subsidiary's trial balance, final figures can be derived. For example, total sales for the subsidiary are 401,163 Kr (350,000 + 51,163) while cash is 51,416 Kr (41,000 + 10,416), and so on. Having established all account balances in the functional currency (Swedish kronor), the subsidiary's statements should then be translated into U.S. dollars. The values to be reported for all assets and liabilities are based on the current exchange rate at the balance sheet date whereas all remaining accounts utilize the historical rate in effect at the date of accounting recognition.

Swedish Subsidiary
Income Statement
For Year Ending December 31, 1995

Sales.	401,163 Kr	×	1.00/5.2	=	$ 77,147
Cost of goods sold	(165,000)	×	1.00/5.2	=	(31,731)
Gross profit.	236,163 Kr				45,416
Less:					
Depreciation expense	(15,900)	×	1.00/5.2	=	(3,058)
Rent expense	(12,000)	×	1.00/5.2	=	(2,308)
Salary expense	(36,000)	×	1.00/5.2	=	(6,923)
Other expenses	(51,308)*	×	1.00/5.2	=	(9,867)
Other income and expense:					
Interest expense	(1,163)	×	1.00/5.2	=	(224)
Transaction gain	103	×	1.00/5.2	=	20
Net income.	119,895 Kr				$ 23,056

* The 308 Kr expense relating to the amortization of the forward exchange contract did not occur evenly throughout the entire year. Because of the immaterial size of this item, however, a separate translation at a specific rate is not being made.

Statement of Retained Earnings
For Year Ending December 31, 1995

Retained earnings, 1/1/95.	194,800 Kr	(carried over from previous year)			$ 36,100
Net income.	119,895	(above)			23,056
Less: Dividends paid	(25,000)	×	1.00/5.3	=	(4,717)
Retained earnings, 12/31/95.	289,695 Kr				$ 54,439

Balance Sheet
December 31, 1995

Cash.	51,416 Kr	×	1.00/5.5	=	$ 9,348
Accounts receivable	155,167	×	1.00/5.5	=	28,212
Exchange contract receivable.	21,053	×	1.00/5.5	=	3,828
Inventory	128,000	×	1.00/5.5	=	23,273
Land.	160,000	×	1.00/5.5	=	29,091
Fixed assets	243,000	×	1.00/5.5	=	44,182
Accumulated depreciation	(103,100)	×	1.00/5.5	=	(18,745)
Total assets.	655,536 Kr				$ 119,189
Accounts payable	39,000 Kr	×	1.00/5.5	=	$ 7,091
Notes payable	71,625	×	1.00/5.5	=	13,023
Bonds payable	125,000	×	1.00/5.5	=	22,727
Exchange contract payable.	20,833	×	1.00/5.5	=	3,788
Discount on exchange contract	(617)	×	1.00/5.5	=	(112)
Common stock	110,000	(carried over from previous year)			21,000
Retained earnings	289,695	(above)			54,439
Translation adjustment.		(see schedule below)			(2,767)
Total liabilities and equities	655,536 Kr				$ 119,189

Schedule—Computation of Translation Adjustment

Beginning net asset balance	304,800* Kr	×	1.00/5.0	=	$ 60,960
Increase in net assets: Net income.	119,895	(from income statement)			23,056
Decrease in net assets: Dividends paid	(25,000)	×	1.00/5.3	=	(4,717)
Ending net assets— value prior to rate changes	399,695† Kr				$ 79,299
Ending net assets— value after rate changes	399,695† Kr	×	1.00/5.5	=	$ 72,672
Translation adjustment for 1995 (decrease in relative value).					(6,627)
Beginning translation adjustment (indicated in problem)					3,860
Cumulative translation adjustment as of December 31, 1995					$ (2,767)

* Indicated by January 1, 1995, equity balances.
† Assets minus liabilities as found in balance sheet above.

Questions

1. What accounting problems underlie the debate over the appropriate method of determining the reported value for balances recorded in a foreign currency?
2. How was the temporal method applied in translating the financial statements of a foreign subsidiary into U.S. dollars under *SFAS 8* of the FASB?
3. Clarke Company has a subsidiary operating in a foreign country. In relation to this subsidiary, what is meant by the term *functional currency*? How is the functional currency determined?
4. Under *FASB SFAS 52*, how is the functional currency of a subsidiary translated into the reporting currency of the parent?
5. In translating the financial statements of a foreign subsidiary, why is the value assigned to retained earnings considered especially difficult to determine? How is this problem normally resolved?
6. A translation adjustment must be calculated and disclosed whenever financial statements of a foreign subsidiary are translated into the parent's reporting currency. How is this figure computed, and where is the amount reported in the financial statements?
7. What transactions or events affect a company's net asset position?

8. The FASB put forth two theories about the underlying nature of a "translation adjustment." What are these theories, and which one was considered to be correct by the FASB?

9. When is remeasurement rather than translation appropriate? How does remeasurement differ from translation?

10. What creates a transaction gain or loss, and where is this figure reported in a set of financial statements?

11. What transactions or events affect the net monetary asset position of a company?

12. What does the term *hedging* mean, and why do companies elect to follow this strategy?

13. What is a forward exchange contract?

14. Why would a company enter into a forward exchange contract?

15. A forward exchange contract creates both a payable and a receivable. Why is only one of these balances remeasured?

16. What is the appropriate method of accounting for a hedge?

17. What procedures are used in accounting for a hedge that is made against a firm commitment rather than against an actual asset or liability position?

18. How does the accounting for a forward exchange contract differ if the agreement is acquired for speculation rather than as a hedge?

Library Assignment

1. Read the following:
    "Plenty of Opportunity to Fool Around," *Forbes*, June 2, 1986.
    "Foreign Currency Translation," *Statement of Financial Accounting Standards No. 52*, FASB, paragraphs 5–10, 39–46, and 77–84.
  Write a short report addressing the following two questions: How could more guidance be given in the selection of a foreign subsidiary's functional currency? Should more official guidance be provided in connection with the selection of a foreign subsidiary's functional currency?

2. Read the following as well as any other published articles on hedging and hedge accounting:
    "Indecent Exposure," *Institutional Investor,* September 1991.
    "Foreign Exchange Exposure Management," *The CPA Journal* (Accounting for International Operations section), August 1988.
    "The Challenges of Hedge Accounting," *Journal of Accountancy,* November 1989.
    "(Dangerous) Fun and Games in the Foreign Exchange Market," *Forbes,* August 22, 1988.

"Foreign Exchange Rate Hedging and SFAS No. 52—Relatives or Strangers?" *Accounting Horizons*, December 1988.

Write a report describing the various reasons for creating hedges and the methods by which hedges can be established.

Problems

1. What is a subsidiary's functional currency?
   a. The parent's reporting currency.
   b. The currency in which transactions are denominated.
   c. The currency in which the entity primarily generates and expends cash.
   d. Always the currency of the country in which the company has its headquarters.

2. The translation process and the remeasurement process are being compared. Which of the following statements is true?
   a. The reported balance of inventory is normally the same under both methods.
   b. The reported balance of equipment is normally the same under both methods.
   c. The reported balance of sales is normally the same under both methods.
   d. The reported balance of depreciation expense is normally the same under both methods.

3. Which of the following statements is true for the translation process?
   a. A translation adjustment can affect consolidated net income.
   b. Equipment is translated at the historical exchange rate in effect at the date of its purchase.
   c. A translation adjustment is created by the change in the relative value of a subsidiary's net assets caused by currency rate fluctuations.
   d. A translation adjustment is created by the change in the relative value of a subsidiary's monetary assets and monetary liabilities caused by currency rate fluctuations.

4. A subsidiary of Byner Corporation has one asset (inventory) and no liabilities. The functional currency for this subsidiary is the peso. The inventory was acquired for 100,000 pesos when the exchange rate was $.16 = 1 peso. Consolidated statements are to be produced and the current exchange rate is $.19 = 1 peso. Which of the following statements is true for the consolidated financial statements?
   a. A transaction gain must be reported.
   b. A credit translation adjustment must be reported.
   c. A debit translation adjustment must be reported.
   d. A transaction loss must be reported.

5. At what rates should the following balance sheet accounts in foreign statements be translated into U.S. dollars?

	Equipment	Accumulated Depreciation—Equipment
a.	Current	Current
b.	Current	Average for year
c.	Historical	Current
d.	Historical	Historical

(AICPA adapted)

6. Certain balance sheet accounts of a foreign subsidiary of the Rose Company have been stated in U.S. dollars as follows:

	Stated at	
	Current Rates	*Historical Rates*
Accounts receivable, current	$200,000	$220,000
Accounts receivable, long-term	100,000	110,000
Prepaid insurance	50,000	55,000
Goodwill	80,000	85,000
	$430,000	$470,000

A foreign currency is the functional currency of this subsidiary. What total should be included in Rose's balance sheet for the preceding items?
   a. $430,000.
   b. $435,000.
   c. $440,000.
   d. $450,000.

7. Certain balance sheet accounts of a foreign subsidiary of the Rose Company have been stated in U.S. dollars as follows:

	Stated at	
	Current Rates	*Historical Rates*
Accounts receivable, current	$200,000	$220,000
Accounts receivable, long-term	100,000	110,000
Prepaid insurance	50,000	55,000
Goodwill	80,000	85,000
	$430,000	$470,000

The U.S. dollar is the functional currency of this subsidiary. What total should be included in Rose's balance sheet for the above items?

a. $430,000.

b. $435,000.

c. $440,000.

d. $450,000.

(AICPA adapted)

Questions 8 and 9 are based on the following information: A subsidiary of Salisbury, Inc. is located in a foreign country. The functional currency of this subsidiary is the schweikart (SWK). The subsidiary acquires inventory on credit on November 1, 1995, for 100,000 SWK which is sold on January 17, 1996, for 130,000 SWK. The subsidiary pays for the inventory on January 31, 1996. Currency exchange rates between dollars and schweikarts are as follows:

November 1, 1995	$.16 = 1 SWK
December 31, 1995	$.17 = 1 SWK
January 17, 1996	$.18 = 1 SWK
January 31, 1996	$.19 = 1 SWK
Average for 1996	$.20 = 1 SWK

8. What figure is reported for this inventory on Salisbury's consolidated balance sheet at December 31, 1995?

    a. $16,000.

    b. $17,000.

    c. $18,000.

    d. $19,000.

9. What figure is reported for cost of goods sold on Salisbury's consolidated income statement for the year ending December 31, 1996?

    a. $16,000.

    b. $17,000.

    c. $18,000.

    d. $19,000.

    e. $20,000.

10. A subsidiary of Clarke Corporation buys equipment and inventory on April 1, 1995, for 100,000 pesos each. These items are both paid for on June 1, 1995, and are still on hand at year's end. Currency exchange rates are as follows:

January 1, 1995	$.15 = 1 peso
April 1, 1995	$.16 = 1 peso
June 1, 1995	$.17 = 1 peso
December 31, 1995	$.19 = 1 peso

Assume that the peso is the subsidiary's functional currency. On a consolidated balance sheet as of December 31, 1995, what balances are reported?

    a. Equipment = \$16,000 and Inventory = \$16,000.
    b. Equipment = \$16,000 and Inventory = \$17,000.
    c. Equipment = \$19,000 and Inventory = \$16,000.
    d. Equipment = \$19,000 and Inventory = \$19,000.

11. Post, Inc., had a credit translation adjustment of \$30,000 for the year ended December 31, 1995. The functional currency of Post's subsidiary is the currency of the country in which that operation is located. Additionally, Post had a receivable from a foreign customer that is payable in the local currency of the customer. On December 31, 1994, this receivable for 200,000 local currency units (LCU) was correctly included in Post's balance sheet at \$110,000. When the receivable was collected on February 15, 1995, the U.S. dollar equivalent was \$120,000. In Post's 1995 consolidated income statement, how much should be reported as a transaction gain?
    a. \$0.
    b. \$10,000.
    c. \$30,000.
    d. \$40,000.
    (AICPA adapted)

12. On July 1, 1995, Haywood Company borrowed 1,680,000 lira from a foreign lender, evidenced by an interest-bearing note due on July 1, 1996. The note is denominated in lira. The U.S. dollar equivalent of the note principal is as follows:

Date	Amount
July 1, 1995 (date borrowed)	\$210,000
December 31, 1995 (Haywood's year end)	240,000
July 1, 1996 (date repaid)	280,000

    In its 1996 income statement, what amount should Clark include as a transaction gain or loss?
    a. –0–.
    b. \$70,000 gain.
    c. \$70,000 loss.
    d. \$40,000 gain.
    e. \$40,000 loss.
    (AICPA adapted)

13. Ace Corporation starts a subsidiary in a foreign country; the subsidiary will have the peso as its functional currency. On January 1, 1995, Ace buys all of the subsidiary's common stock for 20,000 pesos. On April 1, 1995, the subsidiary purchases inventory for 20,000 pesos with payment made on May 1, 1995. This inventory is sold on August 1, 1995, for 30,000 pesos, which are collected on October 1, 1995. Currency exchange rates are as follows:

January 1, 1995.	$.15 = 1 peso
April 1, 1995	$.17 = 1 peso
May 1, 1995	$.18 = 1 peso
August 1, 1995	$.19 = 1 peso
October 1, 1995.	$.20 = 1 peso
December 31, 1995	$.21 = 1 peso

In preparing consolidated financial statements, what translation adjustment will be reported at the end of 1995?

a. $400 credit balance.

b. $600 credit balance.

c. $1,400 credit balance.

d. $1,800 credit balance.

14. Saunders, Inc., is a company located in the United States with the dollar as its functional currency. Inventory is acquired for 100,000 pesos from a foreign supplier on December 1, 1995, on credit. This inventory is sold on February 1, 1996, and payment of the original liability is immediately made. Currency exchange rates are as follows:

December 1, 1995.	$.16 = 1 peso
December 31, 1995	$.18 = 1 peso
February 1, 1996	$.19 = 1 peso

What is the effect on net income of the change in conversion rates?

a. No income effect is created.

b. $2,000 loss in 1995 and a $1,000 loss in 1996.

c. $1,500 loss in 1995 and a $1,500 loss in 1996.

d. No effect in 1995 and a $3,000 loss in 1996.

15. The Houston Corporation operates a branch operation in a foreign country. Although this branch deals in pesos, the U.S. dollar is viewed as its functional currency. Thus, a remeasurement is necessary to produce financial information for external reporting purposes. The branch begins the year with 100,000 pesos in cash and no other assets or liabilities. However, the branch immediately uses 60,000 pesos to acquire equipment. On May 1, inventory costing 30,000 pesos is also purchased for cash. This merchandise is sold on July 1 for 50,000 pesos cash. The branch transfers 10,000 pesos to the parent on October 1 and records depreciation on the equipment for the year of 6,000 pesos. Currency exchange rates are as follows:

January 1, 1995.	$.16 = 1 peso
May 1, 1995	$.18 = 1 peso
July 1, 1995	$.20 = 1 peso
October 1, 1995.	$.21 = 1 peso
December 31, 1995	$.22 = 1 peso
Average for 1995	$.19 = 1 peso

What is the transaction gain to be recognized in the consolidated income statement?

a. $2,100.

b. $2,400.

c. $2,700.

d. $3,000.

16. The Palmer Corporation operates as a U.S. corporation. Palmer recently acquired a forward exchange contract. The company promised to pay 200,000 ramda in six months in exchange for $31,000. This contract was purchased because the company has a firm commitment from a customer to buy merchandise in six months for 200,000 ramda. At the date of acquiring the contract, $.17 = 1 ramda. After two months, $.18 = 1 ramda. How does Palmer reflect the change in the value of the ramda?

    a. Recognizes a $2,000 transaction loss.

    b. Recognizes a $2,000 transaction gain.

    c. Recognizes a $2,000 deferred transaction gain.

    d. Recognizes a $2,000 deferred transaction loss.

17. Deveto Corporation acquired merchandise from a foreign supplier on November 12, 1995, for 60,000 LCU (local currency units). The debt was paid on January 19, 1996. The following currency rates are known:

November 12, 1995.	$1 = .29 LCU
December 31, 1995.	$1 = .33 LCU
January 19, 1996.	$1 = .28 LCU

    How is the 1995 income statement of Deveto affected by the fluctuations in currency values? How is the 1996 income statement of Deveto affected by the fluctuation in currency values?

18. At what exchange rate should each of the following accounts be translated:

    Rent Expense

    Dividends Paid

    Equipment

    Notes Payable

    Sales

    Depreciation Expense

    Cash

    Accumulated Depreciation

    Common Stock   *Historic*

19. On January 1, 1995, Dandu Corporation started a subsidiary in a foreign country. On April 1, 1995, the subsidiary purchased inventory at a cost of 120,000 local currency units (LCU). One fourth of this inventory remained

unsold at the end of 1995 while 40 percent of the liability from the purchase had not yet been paid. The exchange rates were

January 1, 1995	$1 = 2.5 LCU
April 1, 1995	$1 = 2.8 LCU
Average for 1995.	$1 = 2.7 LCU
December 31, 1995.	$1 = 3.0 LCU

What should be the December 31, 1995, inventory and accounts payable balances for this foreign subsidiary as translated into U.S. dollars?

20. On December 1, 1995, the Dresden Company (an American company located in Albany, New York) purchases inventory from a foreign supplier for 60,000 local currency units (LCU). Payment will be made in 90 days after Dresden has sold this merchandise. Sales are made rather quickly and Dresden pays this entire obligation on January 28, 1996. Currency exchange rates are as follows:

December 1, 1995	$.88 = 1 LCU
December 31, 1995.	$.82 = 1 LCU
January 28, 1996.	$.90 = 1 LCU
March 31, 1996	$.85 = 1 LCU

Required:

Prepare all journal entries for the Dresden Company in connection with the purchase and payment.

21. A company carries out a set of transactions in a foreign country during 1995. Prepare all journal entries in U.S. dollars (the company's functional currency) along with any December 31, 1995, adjusting entries.

Exchange rates:

June 1, 1995	$.52 = 1 ertu
August 1, 1995	$.55 = 1 ertu
October 1, 1995.	$.60 = 1 ertu
November 1, 1995.	$.64 = 1 ertu
December 31, 1995	$.65 = 1 ertu

1995

June 1   Bought inventory for 20,000 ertus on credit.
Aug. 1   Sold all inventory for 30,000 ertus on credit.
Oct. 1   Paid 10,000 ertus on 6/1 purchase.
Nov. 1   Collected 10,000 ertus from 8/1 sale.

22. The Acme Corporation (a United States company located in Sarasota, Florida) has the following import/export transactions in 1995:

1995
Mar. 1   Bought inventory costing 50,000 pesos on credit.
May 1   Sold 60 percent of the inventory for 45,000 pesos on credit.
Aug. 1   Collected 40,000 pesos from customers.
Sept. 1   Paid 30,000 pesos to creditors.

Currency exchange rates are as follows:

March 1, 1995	$.17 = 1 peso
May 1, 1995	$.18 = 1 peso
August 1, 1995	$.19 = 1 peso
September 1, 1995	$.20 = 1 peso
December 31, 1995	$.21 = 1 peso

For each of the following accounts, what will Acme report on its 1995 financial statements if a remeasurement is appropriate?

Inventory

Cost of Goods Sold

Sales

Accounts Receivable

Accounts Payable

Cash

Transaction Gain/Loss

23. The following series of accounts is denominated as of December 31, 1995, in pesos. For reporting purposes, these figures need to be stated in U.S. dollars. For each balance, indicate the fraction that would be used if a translation is made. Then, again for each account, provide the fraction that would be necessary if a remeasurement is being made. The company was started in 1980. The buildings were acquired in 1982 and the patents in 1983.

	Translation	Remeasurement
Accounts payable		
Accounts receivable		
Accumulated depreciation		
Advertising expense		
Amortization expense (patents)		
Buildings		
Cash		
Common stock		
Depreciation expense		
Dividends paid (10/1/95)		
Notes payable—due in 1999		
Patents (net)		
Salary expense		
Sales		

Monetary exchange rates are as follows:

1980	1 peso = $.28
1982	1 peso = $.26
1983	1 peso = $.25
January 1, 1995	1 peso = $.24
April 1, 1995.	1 peso = $.23
July 1, 1995	1 peso = $.22
October 1, 1995	1 peso = $.20
December 31, 1995	1 peso = $.16
Average for 1995	1 peso = $.19

24. On November 10, 1995, the Ace Company sells inventory to a customer located in a foreign country. Ace agrees to accept 80,000 matejkas (MJ) in full payment for this inventory. Payment is to be made on February 1, 1996. On December 1, 1995, Ace enters into a forward exchange contract wherein 80,000 matejkas will be delivered to a currency broker in two months. The two-month forward exchange rate on that date was 1 MJ = $0.25. The spot rates on various dates are as follows:

November 10, 1995.	1 MJ = $0.29
December 1, 1995	1 MJ = $0.27
December 31, 1995	1 MJ = $0.24
February 1, 1996	1 MJ = $0.26

Ace's functional currency is the U.S. dollar.

Required:

a. What is the 1995 income effect created by the company's dealings in this foreign currency?

b. What is the 1996 income effect created by the company's dealings in this foreign currency?

c. What would be the effect on net income in 1995 if the sale had originally occurred on December 1, 1995, the same date that the forward exchange contract was acquired?

d. Assume that the customer had made a firm commitment on December 1, 1995, to buy the inventory for 80,000 MJ when delivered on February 1, 1996. The forward exchange contract was acquired on that date to hedge this commitment. What would have been the effect on 1995 net income?

25. The Bartlett Company has its headquarters in Cincinnati, Ohio, and views the U.S. dollar as its functional currency. The company has occasional transactions with companies in foreign countries. Prepare journal entries for the following transactions in U.S. dollars. Also prepare any necessary adjusting entries caused by fluctuations in the value of the foreign currencies. Assume that December 31 is Bartlett's year-end and that the company uses a perpetual inventory system.

1995

Feb. 1   Bought equipment for 40,000 liras on credit.

Apr. 1   Paid for the above equipment.

June 1   Bought inventory for 30,000 liras on credit.

Aug. 1   Sold 70 percent of above inventory for 40,000 liras on credit.

Oct. 1   Collected 30,000 liras from the sales made on August 1, 1995.

Nov. 1   Paid 20,000 liras on the debts incurred on June 1, 1995.

1996

Feb. 1   Collected remaining 10,000 liras from August 1, 1995, sales.

Mar. 1   Paid remaining 10,000 liras on the debts incurred on June 1, 1995.

Currency exchange rates are as follows:

February 1, 1995	$.44 = 1 lira
April 1, 1995	$.45 = 1 lira
June 1, 1995	$.47 = 1 lira
August 1, 1995	$.48 = 1 lira
October 1, 1995	$.49 = 1 lira
November 1, 1995	$.50 = 1 lira
December 31, 1995	$.52 = 1 lira
February 1, 1996	$.54 = 1 lira
March 1, 1996	$.55 = 1 lira

26. A company starts a subsidiary operation on January 1, 1995, in a foreign country. This subsidiary has the following transactions during 1995. Compute the translation adjustment for the year. The subsidiary's functional currency is the nerf.

1995
Jan. 1   Sold common stock to the parent for 16,000 nerf.
Feb. 1   Bought inventory on account for 16,000 nerf.
Mar. 1   Sold all inventory on account for 21,000 nerf.
Apr. 1   Collected 21,000 nerf from customers.
May 1   Paid 16,000 nerf in connection with February 1 purchase.
July 1   Borrowed 20,000 nerf on long-term note paying 10 percent interest per year.
July 1   Bought building for 20,000 nerf cash. The building will last 20 years, and the company uses straight-line depreciation with no salvage value.
Sept. 1   Paid 4,000 nerf dividend to parent.

Applicable conversion rates are as follows:

January 1, 1995	1 nerf = $.35
February 1, 1995	1 nerf = $.38
March 1, 1995	1 nerf = $.36
April 1, 1995	1 nerf = $.37
May 1, 1995	1 nerf = $.39
July 1, 1995	1 nerf = $.40
September 1, 1995	1 nerf = $.38
December 31, 1995	1 nerf = $.42
Average for first 6 months of 1995	1 nerf = $.37
Average for last 6 months of 1995	1 nerf = $.41
Average for 1995	1 nerf = $.39

27. The Fenwicke Company began operating a subsidiary in a foreign country on January 1, 1995, by acquiring all of the common stock for 40,000 LCU. This subsidiary immediately borrowed 100,000 LCU on a five-year note with 10 percent interest payable annually beginning on January 1, 1996. A building was then purchased for 140,000 LCU. This property had a 10-year anticipated life and no salvage value and is to be depreciated using the straight-line method. The building is rented for three years to a group of local doctors for 5,000 LCU per month. By year-end, payments totaling 50,000 LCU had been made. On October 1, 4,000 LCU were paid for a repair made on that date. A cash dividend of 5,000 LCU is transferred back to Fenwicke on December 31, 1995. The functional currency for the subsidiary is the LCU.

Currency exchange rates are as follows:

January 1, 1995	$2.00 = 1 LCU
October 1, 1995	$1.85 = 1 LCU
Average for 1995.	$1.90 = 1 LCU
December 31, 1995.	$1.80 = 1 LCU

Required:

Prepare an income statement, statement of retained earnings, and balance sheet for this subsidiary in LCU and then translate these amounts into U.S. dollars.

28. The Watson Company has a subsidiary in the country of Alonza where the local currency unit is the Kamel (KM). On December 31, 1994, the subsidiary has the following balance sheet:

Cash.	16,000 KM	Notes payable (due 1998) . .	19,000 KM
Inventory	10,000	Common stock	20,000
Land	4,000	Retained earning	10,000
Building	40,000		
Accumulated depreciation . .	(21,000)		
	49,000 KM		49,000 KM

This inventory was acquired on August 1, 1994; the land and buildings were acquired in 1964. The common stock was issued in 1958. During 1995, the following transactions took place:

1995
Feb. 1   Paid 5,000 KM on the note payable.
May 1   Sold entire inventory for 15,000 KM on account.
June 1   Sold land for 5,000 KM cash.
Aug. 1   Collected all accounts receivable.
Sept. 1   Signed long-term note to receive 6,000 KM cash.
Oct. 1   Bought inventory for 12,000 KM cash.
Nov. 1   Bought land for 4,000 KM on account.
Dec. 1   Paid dividend to parent—3,000 KM cash.
Dec. 31   Recorded depreciation for the entire year of 2,000 KM.

The exchange rates are as follows:

1958	1 KM = $.24
1964	1 KM = $.21
August 1, 1994	1 KM = $.31
December 31, 1994	1 KM = $.32
February 1, 1995	1 KM = $.33
May 1, 1995	1 KM = $.34
June 1, 1995	1 KM = $.35
August 1, 1995	1 KM = $.37
September 1, 1995.	1 KM = $.38
October 1, 1995	1 KM = $.39
November 1, 1995.	1 KM = $.40
December 1, 1995	1 KM = $.41
December 31, 1995	1 KM = $.42
Average for 1995	1 KM = $.37

Required:

a. If this is a translation, what is the translation adjustment determined solely for 1995?

b. If this is a remeasurement, what is the transaction gain or loss determined solely for 1995?

29. On November 1, 1995, an American company buys inventory from a supplier in the country of Spagnola. The price of this inventory was 10,000 thads (the local currency of Spagnola—abbreviated TD) to be paid in three months on February 1, 1996.

    Currency values are as follows:

November 1, 1995.	1 TD = $.21
December 1, 1995.	1 TD = $.24
December 31, 1995	1 TD = $.28
February 1, 1996	1 TD = $.25

Required:

a. How is the American company's net income affected in 1995 by the changes in the relative value of the thad? How is the American company's net income affected in 1996?

b. Assume that on December 1, 1995, the American company enters into a two-month forward exchange contract whereby 10,000 thads will be received on February 1, 1996, in exchange for $2,600. How is the American company's net income affected in 1995 by the acquisition of the inventory and the forward exchange contract? How is the American company's net income affected in 1996?

30. On October 1, 1994, a forward exchange contract was acquired whereby the Hawkins Company will pay 100,000 LCU in four months (on February 1, 1995) and receive $65,000 in U.S. dollars. The spot rate for the LCU is as follows:

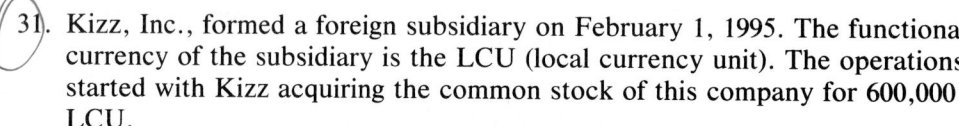

October 1, 1994.	1 LCU = $.69
December 31, 1994	1 LCU = $.71
February 1, 1995	1 LCU = $.72

   a. What journal entries are recorded for the forward exchange contract if it was entered into to hedge a 100,000 LCU receivable?

   b. What journal entries are recorded for the forward exchange contract if it was entered into to hedge a subsidiary with a 100,000 LCU exposed net asset position?

   c. What journal entries are recorded for the forward exchange contract if it was entered into to hedge a commitment that had been received for a 100,000 LCU cash sale for February 1, 1995. Include entries for the eventual sale.

31. Kizz, Inc., formed a foreign subsidiary on February 1, 1995. The functional currency of the subsidiary is the LCU (local currency unit). The operations started with Kizz acquiring the common stock of this company for 600,000 LCU.

   On December 31, 1995, the trial balance of the foreign subsidiary is translated into U.S. dollars so that Kizz, Inc. can prepare consolidated financial statements. The translated figures as of December 31, 1995, are as follows:

	Debit	Credit
Cash	$ 3,600	
Accounts receivable	20,250	
Inventory, 12/31/95	69,000	
Land, buildings, and equipment (acquired on 2/1/95).	120,000	
Accumulated depreciation		$ 12,000
Liabilities.		6,000
Common stock		120,000
Retained earnings, 2/1/95		–0–
Translation adjustment.		35,850
Sales.		106,000
Cost of goods sold.	40,000	
Depreciation expense	12,000	
Other expenses	15,000	
Totals	$279,850	$279,850

As of December 31, 1996, this foreign subsidiary has the following trial balance stated in LCU. A 145,000 LCU addition to the Land, Buildings, and Equipment account was made on July 1, 1996. Depreciation expense on all long-lived assets is recorded at 10 percent of ending cost per year, regardless of the date of purchase. Inventory is acquired and sold evenly throughout the year. A FIFO system is used.

	Debit	Credit
Cash	44,300 LCU	
Accounts receivable	82,000	
Inventory, 12/31/96	198,400	
Land, buildings, and equipment	625,000	
Accumulated depreciation		110,500 LCU
Liabilities		49,200
Common stock		600,000
Retained earnings, 1/1/96		179,400
Sales		473,000
Cost of goods sold	348,300	
Depreciation expense	62,500	
Other expenses	41,600	
Dividends paid	10,000	
Totals	1,412,100 LCU	1,412,100 LCU

Currency exchange rates for specific dates were as follows:

February 1, 1995	5.0 LCU = $1
Average for 1995	4.6 LCU = $1
December 31, 1995	4.0 LCU = $1
Average for 1996	4.3 LCU = $1
July 1, 1996	4.4 LCU = $1
December 31, 1996	4.1 LCU = $1

Answer each of the following questions:

a. What is the translated value of the subsidiary's Land, Buildings, and Equipment account as of December 31, 1996?

b. What is the translated value of the subsidiary's Retained Earnings account (January 1, 1996, balance) as of December 31, 1996?

c. What is the translated value of the subsidiary's Accumulated Depreciation account as of December 31, 1996?

d. What is the translated value of the subsidiary's Common Stock account as of December 31, 1996?

e. What translation adjustment should be presented by Kizz, Inc. in consolidated financial statements for the year ended December 31, 1996?

f. How much inventory was purchased by the subsidiary during 1996 in LCU?

g. What is the gross profit to be reported for this subsidiary for 1996 in U.S. dollars?

h. Assume that this subsidiary's functional currency is actually the U.S. dollar so that a remeasurement rather than a translation is required. What is the remeasured value of the subsidiary's accumulated depreciation and cost of goods sold?

32. On November 1, 1995, Tompson (a company with the U.S. dollar as its functional currency) enters into a four-month forward exchange contract whereby the company will receive 20,000 LCU (the currency of a foreign country) on March 1, 1996. In exchange, Tompson agrees to pay for these LCU at the rate of 1 LCU = $.68. The actual spot rate on November 1, 1995, is 1 LCU = $.62 but rises to 1 LCU = $.64 by December 31, 1995, and 1 LCU = $.69 on March 1, 1996. On December 31, 1996, a two-month forward exchange contract has a rate of 1 LCU = $.72.

Required:

a. Assume that Tompson entered into the four-month forward exchange contract to hedge the effects of a 20,000 LCU liability that was incurred on November 1, 1995, and will be paid on March 1, 1996. What amount of income should Tompson recognize in each of these two years?

b. Assume that Tompson entered into the four-month forward exchange contract to hedge the effects of a 20,000 LCU commitment that was made on November 1, 1995, to buy inventory on March 1, 1996. What amount of income would Tompson recognize in each of these two years? What journal entry would Tompson record for the purchase and payment of the inventory?

c. Assume that Tompson entered into the four-month forward exchange contract to hedge the effects of currency rate fluctuations on a foreign subsidiary which has the LCU as its functional currency. What amount of income should Tompson recognize in each of these two years?

d. Assume that Tompson entered into the four-month forward exchange contract for investment purposes and that the contract was sold on January 11, 1996, for $610 cash. What amount of income should Tompson recognize in each of these two years?

33. Aerkion Company starts the year of 1995 with two assets: cash of 22,000 LCU (local currency units) and land that originally cost 60,000 LCU when acquired on April 4, 1994. On May 1, 1995, the company rendered services to a customer for 30,000 LCU, an amount immediately paid in cash. On October 1, 1995, the company incurred an operating expense of 18,000 LCU which was immediately paid. No other transactions occurred during the year.

Currency exchange rates were as follows:

April 4, 1994	1 LCU = $.23
January 1, 1995	1 LCU = $.24
May 1, 1995.	1 LCU = $.25
October 1, 1995	1 LCU = $.26
Average for 1995.	1 LCU = $.27
December 31, 1995.	1 LCU = $.29

Required:

a. Assume that Aerkion is a foreign subsidiary of an American company that uses the U.S. dollar as its functional currency. Assume also that the LCU is the functional currency of the subsidiary. What is the translation adjustment for this subsidiary for the year of 1995?

b. Assume that Aerkion is a foreign subsidiary of an American company. Assume that the U.S. dollar is the functional currency of both the parent and the subsidiary so that a remeasurement is required. What is the transaction gain or loss for 1995?

c. Assume that Aerkion is a foreign subsidiary of an American company. On a December 31, 1995, balance sheet, what is the translated value of the Land account? On a December 31, 1995, balance sheet, what is the remeasured value of the Land account?

34. Benjamin, Inc., operates an export/import business. The company, located in Mobile, Alabama, has considerable dealings with companies in the country of Camerrand. All transactions with these companies are denominated in alaries (AL), the currency in use in Camerrand. During 1995, Benjamin acquires 20,000 widgets at a price of 8 AL per widget with payment to be made when the items are sold.

Currency exchange rates are as follows:

September 1, 1995	1 AL = $.46
December 1, 1995	1 AL = $.44
December 31, 1995.	1 AL = $.48
March 1, 1996	1 AL = $.45

Required:

a. Assume that Benjamin's acquisition took place on December 1, 1995, with payment being made on March 1, 1996. What is the effect of the rate fluctuations on reported income in 1995 and in 1996?

b. Assume that Benjamin's acquisition took place on September 1, 1995, with payment being made on December 1, 1995. What is the effect of the rate fluctuations on reported income in 1995?

c. Assume that Benjamin's acquisition took place on September 1, 1995, with payment being made on March 1, 1996. What is the effect of the rate fluctuations on reported income in 1995 and in 1996?

d. Assume that Benjamin's acquisition took place on December 1, 1995, with payment being made on March 1, 1996. Assume that on December 1, 1995, Benjamin entered into a three-month forward exchange contract to buy 160,000 AL at an exchange rate of 1 AL = $.47. Considering the acquisition of widgets, payment of the debt, and the forward exchange contract, what is the effect on income in 1995 and in 1996?

35. Lancer, Inc., starts a subsidiary in a foreign country on January 1, 1995. The following account balances are for the year ending December 31, 1998, and are stated in kanquo (KQ), the local currency.

Sales	200,000 KQ
Inventory (bought on 3/1/98)	100,000
Equipment (bought on 1/1/95)	80,000
Rent expense	10,000
Dividends (paid on 10/1/98)	20,000
Notes receivable (to be collected in 2001).	30,000
Accumulated depreciation—Equipment	24,000
Salary payable.	5,000
Depreciation expense	8,000

The following exchange rates are applicable:

January 1, 1995	$1 = 13 KQ
January 1, 1998	$1 = 18 KQ
March 1, 1998.	$1 = 19 KQ
October 1, 1998	$1 = 21 KQ
December 31, 1998	$1 = 22 KQ
Average for 1995	$1 = 14 KQ
Average for 1998	$1 = 20 KQ

Lancer is preparing account balances to produce consolidated financial statements. What fraction is needed for each of these accounts? Assume that the kanquo is the subsidiary's functional currency.

36. The Reed Company has a foreign subsidiary that began operations at the start of 1995 with assets of 132,000 toiks (the local currency unit) and liabilities of 54,000 toiks. During this initial year of operation, the subsidiary reported a profit of 26,000 toiks. Two dividends were distributed; each was for 5,000 toiks with one dividend paid on March 1 and the other on October 1.

Applicable exchange rates are as follows:

January 1, 1995 (start of business)	$0.80 = 1 toik
March 1, 1995	$0.77 = 1 toik
Weighted-average rate for 1995	$0.78 = 1 toik
October 1, 1995	$0.76 = 1 toik
December 31, 1995	$0.81 = 1 toik
February 1, 1996	$0.82 = 1 toik

Required:

a. Assume that the toik is the functional currency for this subsidiary. What translation adjustment would be calculated and reported by Reed for the year of 1995?

b. Assume that on October 1, 1995, Reed entered into a forward exchange contract to hedge the net investment in this subsidiary. On that date, Reed agreed to deliver 40,000 toiks in four months at a forward exchange rate of $0.82 = 1 toik. Prepare the journal entries required by this contract. In addition, compute the translation adjustment to be reported by Reed for the year of 1995 under this second set of circumstances.

37. Kingsfield starts a subsidiary operation in a foreign country on January 1, 1995. The currency in this country is the kumquat (KQ). To get this business started, Kingsfield invests 10,000 KQ. Of this amount, 3,000 KQ are expended immediately to acquire equipment. Later, on April 1, 1995, land is also purchased. All operational activities of the subsidiary transpire at an even rate throughout the year.

The currency exchange rates for this year are as follows:

January 1, 1995	1 KQ = $1.71
April 1, 1995	1 KQ = $1.59
June 1, 1995	1 KQ = $1.66
Weighted Average—1995	1 KQ = $1.64
December 31, 1995	1 KQ = $1.62

As of December 31, 1995, the subsidiary reports the following trial balance:

	Debits	Credits
Cash.	8,000 KQ	
Accounts receivable	9,000	
Equipment	3,000	
Accumulated depreciation		600 KQ
Land.	5,000	
Accounts payable		3,000
Notes payable (due 1999).		5,000
Common stock		10,000
Dividends paid (6/1/95).	4,000	
Sales.		25,000
Salary expense	5,000	
Depreciation expense	600	
Miscellaneous expenses	9,000	
Totals	43,600 KQ	43,600 KQ

Kingsfield is a corporation based in East Lansing, Michigan, and, therefore, views the U.S. dollar as its functional currency.

Required:

a. Assume that the functional currency of the subsidiary is the kumquat. Prepare a trial balance for the subsidiary in U.S. dollars so that consolidated financial statements can be prepared.

b. Assume that the subsidiary's functional currency is the U.S. dollar. Prepare a trial balance for consolidation purposes in U.S. dollars.

38. On November 1, 1995, the Derek Corporation of San Francisco acquires a six-month forward exchange contract. Under the terms of this agreement, Derek agrees to purchase 20,000 milazzos (MZ) at a forward rate of $1.00 = 2.4 MZ. The spot rate on that date is $1.00 = 2.1 MZ. Subsequent exchange rates are as follows:

December 31, 1995 (spot rate).	$1.00 = 2.25 milazzos
December 31, 1995 (four-month forward rate).	$1.00 = 2.50 milazzos
May 1, 1996 (spot rate).	$1.00 = 2.00 milazzos

Required:

a. Make all of the journal entries for Derek if the contract was acquired for investment purposes and was sold on February 23, 1996, for $410.

b. Make all of the journal entries for Derek if the company had incurred a commitment on November 1, 1995, to acquire equipment on May 1, 1996, for 20,000 milazzos.

c. Make all of the journal entries for Derek if the company acquired land on November 1, 1995, for 20,000 milazzos with payment to be made on May 1, 1996.

d. Make the journal entries for Derek if the company had a subsidiary with a net liability position in excess of 20,000 milazzos.

 39. Livingston Company is a wholly owned subsidiary of Rose Corporation. Livingston operates in a foreign country with financial statements recorded in goghs (GH), the company's functional currency. Financial statements for the year of 1995 are as follows:

Income Statement
For Year Ending December 31, 1995

Sales	270,000	GH
Cost of goods sold	(155,000)	
Gross profit	115,000	
Less: Operating expenses	(54,000)	
Gain on sale of equipment	10,000	
Net income	71,000	GH

Statement of Retained Earnings
For Year Ending December 31, 1995

Retained earnings, 1/1/95		216,000	GH
Net income	71,000 GH		
Less: Dividends paid	(26,000)	45,000	
Retained earnings, 12/31/95		261,000	GH

Balance Sheet
December 31, 1995

Assets

Cash	44,000	GH
Receivables	116,000	
Inventory	58,000	
Fixed assets (net)	339,000	
Total assets	557,000	GH

Liabilities and Equities

Liabilities	176,000	GH
Common stock	120,000	
Retained earnings, 12/31/95	261,000	
Total liabilities and equities	557,000	GH

Additional Information:

- The common stock was issued in 1989 when the exchange rate was $1.00 = .48 GH; fixed assets were acquired in 1990 when the rate was $1.00 = .50 GH.
- As of January 1, 1995, the retained earnings balance was translated as $395,000.
- The currency exchange rates for the current year are as follows:

January 1, 1995.	$1.00 = .60 goghs
April 1, 1995	$1.00 = .62 goghs
September 1, 1995	$1.00 = .58 goghs
December 31, 1995	$1.00 = .65 goghs
Weighted-average rate for 1995.	$1.00 = .63 goghs

- Inventory was acquired evenly throughout the year.
- A translation adjustment was reported on the December 31, 1994, balance sheet with a debit balance of $85,000.
- Dividends were paid on April 1, 1995, and a piece of equipment was sold on September 1, 1995.

Required:

Translate the foreign currency statements into the parent's reporting currency, the U.S. dollar.

40. The following account balances are for the Agee Company as of January 1, 1995, and again as of December 31, 1995. All figures are denominated in kroner (Kr).

	1/1/95	*12/31/95*
Accounts payable	(18,000)	(24,000)
Accounts receivable	35,000	79,000
Accumulated depreciation—buildings.	(20,000)	(25,000)
Accumulated depreciation—equipment	–0–	(5,000)
Bonds payable–due 2002	(50,000)	(50,000)
Buildings	118,000	97,000
Cash	35,000	8,000
Common stock.	(70,000)	(80,000)
Depreciation expense.	–0–	15,000
Dividends (10/1/95)	–0–	32,000
Equipment.	–0–	30,000
Gain on sale of building.	–0–	(6,000)
Rent expense	–0–	14,000
Retained earnings	(30,000)	(30,000)
Salary expense.	–0–	20,000
Sales	–0–	(80,000)
Utilities expense	–0–	5,000

Additional Information:

- More shares of common stock were issued during the year on April 1. Common stock was also sold at the start of operations in 1980.
- Buildings were bought in 1982. One building with a 16,000 Kr book value was sold on July 1 of the current year.
- Equipment was acquired on April 1, 1995.
- Retained earnings as of January 1, 1995, was reported as $62,319.

Currency exchange rates were as follows:

1980	$2.40 = 1 Kr
1982	$2.20 = 1 Kr
January 1, 1995	$2.50 = 1 Kr
April 1, 1995.	$2.60 = 1 Kr
July 1, 1995	$2.80 = 1 Kr
October 1, 1995	$2.90 = 1 Kr
December 31, 1995	$3.00 = 1 Kr
Average for 1995	$2.70 = 1 Kr

Required:

a. If a remeasurement is being carried out, what would be the transaction gain or loss for 1995?

b. If a translation is being carried out, what would be the translation adjustment for 1995?

41. The Sendelbach Corporation is an American-based organization with operations throughout the world. One of the company's subsidiaries is headquartered in Berlin. Although this wholly owned company operates primarily in Germany, transactions are also carried out in France. Therefore, the subsidiary maintains a ledger denominated in francs (F) as well as a general ledger in deutsche marks (DM).

  As of December 31, 1995, the German subsidiary is preparing financial statements in anticipation of consolidation with the American parent corporation. Both ledgers for the subsidiary are as follows:

Main Operation—Germany

	Debit	Credit
Accounts payable.		35,000 DM
Accumulated depreciation		27,000
Buildings and equipment	167,000 DM	
Cash	26,000	
Common stock		50,000
Cost of goods sold	203,000	
Depreciation expense	8,000	
Dividends paid, 4/1/95	28,000	
Gain on sale of equipment, 6/1/95		5,000
Inventory	96,000	
Notes payable—due in 1998		76,000
Receivables	68,000	
Retained earnings, 1/1/95		146,842
Salary expense	26,000	
Sales		312,000
Utility expense	9,000	
Branch operation	20,842	
Totals	651,842 DM	651,842 DM

Secondary Operation—France

	Debit	Credit
Accounts payable.		49,000 F
Accumulated depreciation		19,000
Building and equipment	40,000 F	
Cash	59,000	
Depreciation expense	2,000	
Inventory (beginning—income statement)	23,000	
Inventory (ending—income statement)		28,000
Inventory (ending—balance sheet)	28,000	
Purchases	68,000	
Receivables	21,000	
Salary expense	9,000	
Sales		124,000
Main office		30,000
Totals	250,000 F	250,000 F

Additional Information:

· The functional currency for the subsidiary is the deutsche mark while the
functional currency for Sendelbach is the U.S. dollar. The German and
French operations are not viewed as separate accounting entities.

· The building and equipment used in the French organization were acquired in 1983 when the currency exchange rate was 1 DM = 1.47 F.

- Inventory should be assumed as having been acquired evenly throughout the fiscal year.
- The Main Office account found on the French records should be considered an equity account. This balance was remeasured into 20,842 DM on December 31, 1994, and no further transactions have occurred.
- Currency exchange rates applicable to the French operation are as follows:

Weighted average, 1994	1 DM = 1.45 F
January 1, 1995.	1 DM = 1.50 F
Weighted-average rate for 1995.	1 DM = 1.48 F
December 31, 1995	1 DM = 1.54 F

- On the December 31, 1994, balance sheet, a translation adjustment was reported with a $7,268 credit balance.
- The subsidiary's common stock was issued in 1976 when the exchange rate was $1.00 = 2.72 DM.
- The December 31, 1994, balance of retained earnings for this subsidiary was 146,842 DM, a figure which has been translated into $59,933.
- The applicable currency exchange rates for translation purposes are as follows:

January 1, 1995.	$1.00 = 2.3 DM
April 1, 1995	$1.00 = 2.2 DM
June 1, 1995	$1.00 = 2.5 DM
Weighted-average for 1995.	$1.00 = 2.6 DM
December 31, 1995	$1.00 = 2.4 DM

Required:

a. Remeasure the French operational figures from francs into deutsche marks. (Hint: back into the beginning net monetary asset or liability position.)
b. Prepare financial statements for this subsidiary in its functional currency.
c. Translate the functional currency financial statements into U.S. dollars so that Sendelbach can prepare consolidated financial statements.
42. On January 1, 1995, the Wilbourne Corporation started a subsidiary operation in India. Wilbourne is an American company based in New York City and is the sole owner of this foreign entity, the Madvian Company. Following are the 1996 financial statements for the two operations. Wilbourne's information is stated in dollars while the Madvian statements are reported in rupees (R). Credit balances are presented in parentheses.

	Wilbourne Corporation	Madvian Company
Sales	$(200,000)	(800,000) R
Cost of goods sold	93,800	420,000
Salary expense	19,000	74,000
Rent expense	7,000	46,000
Other expenses	21,000	59,000
Dividend income—Madvian	(5,000)	–0–
Gain on sale of fixed asset, 10/1/96	–0–	(30,000)
Net income	$ (64,200)	(231,000) R
Retained earnings, 1/1/96	$(318,000)	(133,000) R
Net income	(64,200)	(231,000)
Dividends paid	24,000	50,400
Retained earnings, 12/31/96	$(358,200)	(313,600) R
Cash, receivables, and other current assets	$ 111,000	146,000 R
Inventory	96,000	296,300
Exchange contract receivable (dollars)	56,557	–0–
Exchange contract receivable (pesos)	40,000	–0–
Investment in Madvian (cost)	40,000	–0–
Fixed assets (net)	398,000	455,300
Total assets	$ 741,557	897,600 R
Accounts payable	$ (60,800)	(54,000) R
Notes payable—due in 1999	(100,000)	(140,000)
Exchange contract payable (rupees)	(55,000)	–0–
Premium on exchange contract	(1,557)	–0–
Exchange contract payable (dollars)	(40,000)	–0–
Common stock	(90,000)	(240,000)
Additional paid-in capital	(36,000)	(150,000)
Retained earnings, 12/31/96	(358,200)	(313,600)
Total liabilities and equities	$(741,557)	(897,600) R

Additional Information:

- During 1995, the first year of operation, Madvian reported income of 163,000 rupees earned evenly throughout the year. A dividend of 30,000 rupees was paid to Wilbourne on June 1 of that year. The 1996 dividend paid by Madvian was also made on June 1.

- On December 9, 1996, Madvian classified a 10,000 rupee expenditure as a rent expense, although this payment related entirely to charges for the first few months of 1997.

- On October 1, 1996, Wilbourne elected to hedge the net investment in this Indian subsidiary. Therefore, a six-month forward exchange contract was signed whereby Wilbourne agreed to pay 599,500 rupees at the end of that time in exchange for $56,557.

- On December 1, 1996, Wilbourne acquired another forward exchange contract based solely on the belief that the value of the Mexican peso would strengthen in the near future. This second agreement called for Wilbourne to pay $40,000 in three months in exchange for receiving 1.8 million pesos.

- The exchange rates for American dollars and Indian rupees is as follows:

January 1, 1995	$1.00 = 9.75 rupees
June 1, 1995	$1.00 = 9.88 rupees
Weighted-average rate for 1995	$1.00 = 9.92 rupees
December 31, 1995	$1.00 = 10.00 rupees
June 1, 1996	$1.00 = 10.08 rupees
October 1, 1996 (spot rate)	$1.00 = 10.90 rupees
October 1, 1996 (six-month forward rate)	$1.00 = 10.60 rupees
December 31, 1996 (spot rate)	$1.00 = 10.45 rupees
Weighted-average rate for 1996	$1.00 = 10.20 rupees

- The exchange rate for American dollars and Mexican pesos is as follows:

December 1, 1996 (spot rate)	$1.00 = 46.2 pesos
December 1, 1996 (three-month forward rate)	$1.00 = 45.0 pesos
December 31, 1996 (spot rate)	$1.00 = 45.3 pesos
December 31, 1996 (two-month forward rate)	$1.00 = 44.5 pesos

Required:

Prepare financial statements for the Wilbourne Corporation and its consolidated subsidiary. Assume that the U.S. dollar is the reporting currency of the parent company whereas the Indian rupee is the subsidiary's functional currency.

10

INTERNATIONAL ACCOUNTING STANDARDS/NATIONAL ACCOUNTING STANDARDS

Questions to Consider

- Why do accounting and reporting principles differ throughout the world?
- What benefits are to be gained by establishing acceptable international accounting standards? What obstacles stand in the way of international standards?
- What progress has the International Accounting Standards Committee (IASC) achieved in establishing uniform international standards?
- Who belongs to the IASC? How does this group enforce its standards?
- Why has the development of international accounting principles generated only limited interest until recent years?
- How do accounting principles differ between Japan, the United Kingdom, Germany, and other countries? What differences are found in the structure of the financial statements produced in these three countries? How has the accounting profession evolved throughout the world?
- By what different methods can assets be valued for financial reporting purposes?
- How do companies located in various countries prepare consolidated financial statements and what accounting is made of any purchased goodwill?

There are no distant points in the world any longer.
Wendell Willkie

In 1942, when this statement was first made during a radio broadcast, the world did appear to be a smaller place than previous generations had ever imagined.

Now, more than 50 years later, Wendell Willkie himself would have trouble believing the proximity of all nations. Satellite communications and supersonic travel allow constant contact to be maintained between even remote geographical areas. As a result, business expansion beyond national boundaries has become commonplace. In search of new markets, higher profits, and additional capital, companies look throughout the world for opportunities to grow and diversify. Money is raised by issuing debt and equity securities on exchanges in a number of different countries. The terms *global economy* and *multinational corporations* have become almost overused phrases in the business jargon of the 1990s.

Many American companies have managed to successfully penetrate the markets of different countries. For instance, products of the Coca-Cola Company can be found in a significant portion of the world as can the operations of McDonald's Corporation. Such organizations actually grow to be larger than some small countries. In 1991, five U.S. corporations alone generated aggregate foreign revenues of more than $230 billion![1]

	Foreign Revenue (billions)	Total Revenue (billions)	Foreign Revenue as Percentage of Total
Exxon	$78.1	$102.8	76%
IBM	40.1	64.8	62
General Motors	39.1	123.1	32
Mobil	38.8	56.9	68
Ford Motor	34.5	88.3	39

Economic growth throughout the world is not a purely American phenomenon. Many foreign investors have chosen to enter the United States by building manufacturing operations or establishing marketing outlets. Foreign automobile companies, for example, have constructed several new plants in the United States. Furthermore, an influx of investment capital has brought many U.S. companies under the control of organizations headquartered in other countries. For example, in just a two-year period, Sony managed to acquire both CBS Records and Columbia Pictures Entertainment.

> What could be more American than Good Humor ice cream? Or the 60-year-old fizz of Alka-Seltzer? Or the Thermos bottle? Well, these familiar trademarks now belong to someone else: the Dutch and the British, the West Germans and the Japanese, respectively. So do such U.S.-born corporate names as Smith Corona, Brooks Brothers and Pillsbury (all British); General Electric TV sets and home electronics (French); Wilson Sporting Goods (Finnish); and Carnation (Swiss). Last year foreign investors acquired nearly 400 U.S. businesses, worth a total of $60 billion.[2]

---

[1] "The 100 Largest U.S. Multinationals," *Forbes*, July 22, 1992, p. 298.
[2] William McWhirter, "I Came, I Saw, I Blundered," *Time*, October 9, 1989, p. 72.

Barring a financial catastrophe, the further development of a global economy seems inevitable. The increasing emergence of the Pacific Rim countries as well as significant consolidation within the European Economic Community should stimulate a continuing evolution. In addition, more American companies appear poised to expand into new areas of the world to increase profits and maintain a competitive position. As a result of such activities, companies as well as business leaders must be able to function in many countries where cultures and laws may be radically different. Success can be achieved only by coming to an understanding and appreciation of the traditions and characteristics that make each geographical region unique.

Just as cultures and laws vary, accounting principles are usually national in origin so that significant differences frequently exist from country to country. An American who is employed by a foreign organization must be aware that essential reporting standards may not always conform to U.S. generally accepted accounting principles. Likewise, an American company exporting merchandise to a foreign country or opening a subsidiary there must investigate the local rules and regulations to ensure complete compliance. *As organizations grow, a greater need is developed for all parties to understand the variety of accounting principles that exist throughout the world.*

This chapter provides an introduction into the accounting for multinational organizations. First, an examination is made of the international accounting standards that have been produced to date by the London-based International Accounting Standards Committee (IASC). Second, both the accounting principles and the accounting profession as they have developed in several major countries are described. Finally, reporting principles utilized around the world are analyzed in connection with specific accounting problems such as consolidation and the valuation of assets. This coverage provides a comparison of the similarities and differences between U.S. generally accepted accounting principles and the principles used in other areas of the world.

Discussion Question: Why Learn All Those Accounting Principles?

The Birmingham Corporation is headquartered in Brooklyn, New York, but has a number of production plants and distribution centers located throughout the United States. This organization produces specialty plastic components used in the manufacture of automobiles, radios, dishwashers, and a host of other products. A customer provides the specifications and Birmingham designs and produces the part.

Over the last decade, Birmingham has been extremely successful with both its revenues and profits growing at a fast rate. The company's stock is traded on the New York Stock Exchange at a price that has increased

continued

rapidly, especially during the most recent three years. Birmingham hopes to continue this success by branching into foreign markets. Tentative plans have been developed for building manufacturing plants in Canada, France, Germany, and possibly Japan. As a preliminary step in this expansion process, Birmingham's president has asked William Lederer, the chief financial officer, to investigate the accounting principles used in each of these four countries and report on any significant differences with U.S. GAAP. Lederer was not particularly excited about this assignment.

"Each plant will be headed by a team of our own people. The financial information will be gathered according to U.S. GAAP and will be translated into U.S. dollars for consolidation purposes. We can hire local tax attorneys to handle our tax planning and preparation but we will have no need for elaborate financial reporting in any of these countries. I think that you will find that U.S. GAAP is well understood in all highly developed countries such as Japan and France."

Is the CFO correct? Does an American company operating in a foreign country have a real need to understand local accounting principles?

International Accounting Standards

Companies normally produce financial statements according to the accounting principles of their home countries. Although many countries have sophisticated reporting guidelines, others do not. As a further complication, significant differences can be found even between countries having highly developed principles. For example, in Germany profits from long-term contracts are normally recognized at the point of completion, whereas in the United States the percentage of completion method is generally considered preferable.

Thus, two problems have created a recent push for international accounting principles.[3] First, inferior methods of accounting continue to exist today in many areas of the world, especially in developing countries. Second, the ability to make comparisons between companies is not always possible across geographic lines. It is this second problem that has received considerable attention as global equity

---

[3] Although many groups have called for the development of basic international accounting principles, the need for such guidelines is not universally accepted. "Full harmonization of international accounting standards is probably neither practical nor truly valuable. . . . It is not clear whether significant benefits would be derived in fact. A well-developed global capital market exists already. It has evolved without uniform accounting standards." (Richard Karl Goeltz, "International Accounting Harmonization: The Impossible (and Unnecessary?) Dream," *Accounting Horizons,* March 1991, pp. 85–86.

markets have expanded. "Comparability between a French and Japanese automobile manufacturer, for example, is destroyed when one company employs certain accounting principles which are opposite to the other company's accounting practice."[4]

The problems created by both inferior accounting principles as well as the lack of comparability are magnified at the time that a corporation attempts to raise funds through international capital markets. During the 1980s and 1990s, the sale of stocks, bonds, and other types of securities through such markets has become a predominant practice. By 1990, more than 500 companies throughout the world were listed on at least one stock exchange outside of their home countries. In 1989 alone, U.S. investors bought nearly $190 billion in debt and equity of foreign entities while foreign investors pumped approximately $490 billion into U.S. entities through similar acquisitions.[5]

Frequently, these investors must attempt to evaluate financial statements that utilize a wide variety of principles. In 1989, SmithKline Beckman reported total stockholders' equity of 3.5 billion British pounds in the United States while showing a negative balance of 300 million British pounds in the United Kingdom.[6] How do such differences affect investors? According to Ralph E. Walters, chairman of the steering committee of the International Accounting Standards Committee, "either international investors have to be extremely knowledgeable about multiple reporting methods or they have to be willing to take greater risks."[7]

Because of the wide diversity of accounting principles, companies attempting to raise capital in foreign countries may first have to restate their financial statements. In the United States, the Securities and Exchange Commission (SEC) requires foreign corporations to present financial statements that either comply with U.S. generally accepted accounting principles or disclose a reconciliation to U.S. GAAP. For example, the 1991 financial statements for Glaxo Holdings PLC (a British pharmaceutical company) provide the following information:

Profit before extraordinary items under U.K. GAAP	912 million pounds
U.S. GAAP adjustments:	
Goodwill amortization	(5)
Deferred taxation	(35)
Extraordinary items transferred to nonextraordinary	(31)
Net income under U.S. GAAP	841 million pounds

[4] John N. Slipkowsky, "An Appraisal of the International Accounting Standards Committee," *The CPA Journal,* May 1986, p. 84.

[5] Dennis E. Peavey and Stuart K. Webster, "Is GAAP the Gap to International Markets?" *Management Accounting,* August 1990, pp. 31–32.

[6] Shaun F. O'Malley, "Accounting Across Borders," *Financial Executive,* March-April 1992, p. 29.

[7] Stephen H. Collins, "The Move to Globalization," *Journal of Accountancy,* March 1989, p. 82.

Not all countries require this type of reconciliation. On the London and Netherlands stock exchanges, for example, companies can register their securities for trading purposes by presenting statements in conformity with international accounting standards. In this manner, the cost of preparing a multitude of different statements for each country is avoided. Although the policy of the SEC ensures the availability of adequate, understandable information, its refusal to accept any principles other than U.S. GAAP may have an adverse impact on the capital markets in this country. As of 1992, no German company (although Daimler-Benz will probably be listed on the New York Stock Exchange in 1993 or 1994) and few Japanese companies were authorized to sell securities in the United States. "In the U.S., BMW's motorcars are welcome. Its shares are not. That's because BMW, like most other major European companies, refuses to restate its German balance sheet in accordance with the rigorous Securities & Exchange Commission rules. So BMW, one of the world's most profitable car companies, is denied permission to list its securities on U.S. stock exchanges."[8]

Structure of the International Accounting Standards Committee

> International standards are here to stay and it seems most likely that the IASC will provide the text. After all, why reinvent the wheel?[9]

The idea of developing international accounting can be traced back to 1904 when the first international accounting conference was held in St. Louis. However, the concept has only received general interest during the past two decades. In hopes of eliminating the diversity of principles used throughout the world, the International Accounting Standards Committee (IASC) was formed in June 1973 by accountancy bodies in Australia, Canada, France, Germany, Japan, Mexico, the Netherlands, the United Kingdom and Ireland, and the United States. The IASC is a private organization based in London (in some ways similar to the FASB and GASB). Governments do not belong, only accounting organizations can be members. Since 1973, the initial group has grown to more than 100 accountancy bodies representing approximately 80 nations. From the United States, the American Institute of CPAs (AICPA) and the Instututute of Management Accountants (IMA) are members.

IASC accounting pronouncements are produced by a board consisting of representatives from 13 countries plus a representative from the International Association of Financial Analysts. In 1992, this board consisted of representatives from Australia, Canada, France, Germany, Italy, Japan, Jordan, Korea, the Netherlands, Norway/Scandinavia, South Africa, the United Kingdom, and the United States. The board normally meets three times a year for three or four days. The board also holds meetings twice a year with its consultative group made up of a

---

[8] Peter Fuhrman, "Esperanto for Accountants," *Forbes,* March 18, 1991, p. 72.

[9] Julia Irvine, "When the Navel Gazing Has to Stop," *Accountancy,* July 1991, p. 24.

wide range of parties including a member of the FASB. For any official pronouncement to be issued, at least 11 of the 14 board members must agree.

The goals of the IASC are detailed in the body's constitution:

> *a.* To formulate and publish in the public interest accounting standards to be observed in the presentation of financial statements and to promote their worldwide acceptance and observance.
>
> *b.* To work generally for the improvement and harmonization of regulations, accounting standards and procedures relating to the presentation of financial statements.[10]

Since its formation in 1973, the IASC has issued 31 International Accounting Standards (see Exhibit 10–1). These standards have addressed worldwide reporting concerns ranging from consolidated financial statements to accounting for income taxes and disclosure of related party transactions. *Because the IASC is a private body, these pronouncements cannot be enforced.* Instead, the IASC has attempted to gain acceptance in a number of ways. For example, countries that do not have extensive accounting principles are urged to adopt the IASC's guidelines, thus "guaranteeing a certain level of quality and compatibility for the particular standard."[11]

Conversely, countries that already have a developed system of accounting standards in place are asked to eliminate any material differences that exist with IASC pronouncements. "No enforcement mechanism exists to assure that the standards, once issued, are followed. Rather, the accounting professional body within each country has merely signed a pledge, representing that it will use its 'best efforts' to have the standard setters in their country move to accept the international standards."[12]

As a result of this best efforts pledge, the AICPA Board of Directors has formally stated that if significant variances exist between international standards and U.S. GAAP, "the AICPA will urge the FASB and/or GASB to give early consideration to such differences with a view to achieving harmonization of those areas in which a significant difference exists."[13]

One other method historically used by the IASC to gain support has been the acceptance of alternative accounting methods. Rarely has the board selected one approach to a problem in preference to all others. To get at least 11 of the 14 board members to support a new standard, usually at least two methods (and often more) have to be allowed. Although perhaps necessary from a political perspective, such compromise has brought the IASC under heavy criticism. As is discussed later in this chapter, the board is currently attempting to respond to these complaints by passing new standards to eliminate many alternative approaches.

---

[10] International Accounting Standards Committee Constitution, January 1983, para. 2.

[11] International Accounting Standards Committee, *Objectives and Procedures,* January 1983, para. 9.

[12] Arthur R. Wyatt, "Seeking Credibility in a Global Economy," *New Accountant,* September 1992, p. 6.

[13] AICPA, *International Accounting and Auditing Standards,* October 1, 1988, page 11,002.

EXHIBIT 10–1

INTERNATIONAL ACCOUNTING STANDARDS

	Title	*Issued*
IAS 1	Disclosure of Accounting Policies	1/75
IAS 2	Valuation and Presentation of Inventories in the Context of the Historical Cost System	10/75
IAS 3	(Superseded by *IAS 27* and *28*)	
IAS 4	Depreciation Accounting	10/76
IAS 5	Information to be Disclosed in Financial Statements	10/76
IAS 6	(Superseded by *IAS 15*)	
IAS 7	Cash Flow Statement (1993 revision of 1977 statement)	
IAS 8	Unusual and Prior Period Items and Changes in Accounting Policies	2/78
IAS 9	Accounting for Research and Development Activities	7/78
IAS 10	Contingencies and Events Occurring after the Balance Sheet Date	10/78
IAS 11	Accounting for Construction Contracts	3/79
IAS 12	Accounting for Taxes on Income	7/79
IAS 13	Presentation of Current Assets and Current Liabilities	11/79
IAS 14	Reporting Financial Information by Segment	8/81
IAS 15	Information Reflecting the Effects of Changing Prices	11/81
IAS 16	Accounting for Property, Plant, and Equipment	3/82
IAS 17	Accounting for Leases	9/82
IAS 18	Revenue Recognition	12/82
IAS 19	Accounting for Retirement Benefits in the Financial Statements of Employers	1/83
IAS 20	Accounting for Government Grants and Disclosure of Government Assistance	4/83
IAS 21	Accounting for the Effects of Changes in Foreign Exchange Rates	7/83
IAS 22	Accounting for Business Combinations	11/83
IAS 23	Capitalization of Borrowing Costs	3/84
IAS 24	Related Party Disclosures	7/84
IAS 25	Accounting for Investments	3/86
IAS 26	Accounting and Reporting by Retirement Benefit Plans	1/87
IAS 27	Consolidated Financial Statements and Accounting for Investments in Subsidiaries	4/89
IAS 28	Accounting for Investments in Associates	4/89
IAS 29	Financial Reporting in Hyperinflationary Economies	7/89
IAS 30	Disclosure in the Financial Statements of Banks and Similar Financial Institutions	8/90
IAS 31	Financial Reporting of Interests in Joint Ventures	12/90

Problems Faced by the IASC

The establishment of accounting principles that can be applied universally by businesses throughout the world is not an easy task. In many geographic areas, standards are accepted that have evolved gradually over a considerable period of time. Some of these principles have been created because of problems unique to the region. Resistance against any attempt to change (or even abolish) such traditional approaches should be expected. As stated by Dennis Beresford, chairman of the Financial Accounting Standards Board, ''high on almost everybody's list of obstacles is nationalism. Whether out of deep-seated tradition, indifference born of economic power, or resistance to intrusion of foreign influence, some say that national entities will not bow to any international body.''[14]

Unfortunately, nationalism is not the only problem confronting the IASC. Simply put, the countries throughout the world often have quite different characteristics. Capital marketing systems vary from place to place as do attitudes toward both the need for financial disclosure and the role of government oversight. Furthermore, the method by which accounting standards are set can have a great impact on the type of principles produced.

In the United States, for example, the private sector develops official accounting pronouncements through the work of the FASB and the GASB. However, in many areas of the world, the government is in charge of accounting rules which may, therefore, be set by official edict. In such countries, political pressures and economic goals sometimes outweigh accounting logic. Arriving at principles that satisfy all of the parties involved throughout the world seems an almost Herculean task for the IASC.

A better understanding of world accounting can be achieved by viewing accounting principles as having been developed under three different general models.[15] These models represent the variety of influences under which accounting principles are formed. Within each model, significant differences may still exist between specific countries. However, a similar heritage and environment is present as well as the overall objective of the financial reporting process.

British-American Model. (Includes countries such as Australia, Canada, Hong Kong, Israel, Mexico, the Netherlands, Panama, the United Kingdom, and the United States.) In these countries, the primary objective of accounting information is to enable decisions to be made by a large number of creditors and investors. Normally, the reporting entities (often multinational corporations) have access to large capital markets and depend on the sale of stocks and debt to raise significant amounts of funding. Investors tend to have a sophisticated level of knowledge and are able to utilize financial information effectively to make considered choices. Therefore, disclosure of adequate data to permit these decisions is often stressed.

Continental Model. (Includes countries such as Cameroon, Denmark, Egypt, France, Germany, Greece, Italy, Japan, Norway, Spain, Sweden, and Zaire.) Companies in this group are usually tied quite closely to banks that are the primary suppliers of financing. ''In many countries such as Germany and Japan, most of the capital is provided by a handful of banks. These banks can get the information they need directly from the company. As a result, there is no pressure

---

[14] Dennis R. Beresford, ''Accounting for International Operations,'' *The CPA Journal,* October 1988, pp. 79–80.

[15] Gerhard G. Mueller, Helen Gernon, Gary Meek, *Accounting—An International Perspective,* 2d ed. (Homewood, Ill.: Richard D. Irwin, 1991), pp. 15–18.

in Germany and Japan for open and full disclosure. Their standard setting is therefore less oriented to investors' needs."[16] For example, the Deutsche Bank holds nearly 30 percent of Daimler-Benz and controls several seats on the company's supervisory board.

Hence, in countries influenced by the Continental Model, little or no emphasis is placed on providing information to the investing public. Instead, reporting practice tends to emphasize proving compliance with government laws as well as the reduction of income taxes. Accounting tends to be quite conservative when open markets are not an influence on a reporting company; the need to demonstrate the ability to generate profits is significantly less important.

As an example of the conservative accounting in these countries, Telfonica de Espana (the Spanish telephone company) reported net income in 1987 of 53,247 million pesetas using Spanish accounting principles. However, in listing its stock on other exchanges, net income had to be adjusted to U.S. GAAP. This change increased the reported profit to 130,260 million pesetas, a jump of 145 percent.[17]

South American Model. (Includes countries such as Argentina, Bolivia, Brazil, Chile, Ecuador, and Peru.) These countries have been forced to develop accounting principles that deal with the ongoing impact of high levels of inflation. Price increases are such a pervasive phenomenon in these areas that unique accounting measures are required. In addition, financial reporting is often oriented toward income tax laws and the needs of government planners.

Consequently, to be successful, the IASC must produce accounting principles that meet the needs and objectives of each of these varying models. Despite the difficulty, the necessity for developing some form of universal accounting framework is becoming increasingly evident.

> The *Financial Times* recently warned international investors that the comparison of price earnings ratios is dogged not only by national discrepancies in accounting but also by entirely different philosophies of financial reporting. Whereas U.S. and U.K. financial statements are directed at current and potential investors, and thus tend to provide realistic estimates of earnings, German and Japanese accounts are still drawn up with the tax authorities in mind; thus, . . . they understate earnings."[18]

As an illustration of the effects of differing principles within just the members of the European Economic Community, the profits of one case study company were measured (in European Currency Units) using the accounting principles of various countries. The variations were almost startling:[19]

---

[16] Arthur R. Wyatt, "International Accounting Standards: Are They Coming to America?" *The CPA Journal,* October 1992, p. 16.

[17] Anthony Carey, "Harmonization: Europe Moves Forward," *Accountancy,* March 1990, p. 93.

[18] David Cairns, "Calling All National Standard Setters," *Accountancy,* February 1988, p. 13.

[19] Carey, "Harmonization," pp. 92–93.

Most Likely Profit—Case Study Company

Country	ECUs (millions)
Spain	131
Germany.	133
Belgium	135
Netherlands	140
France.	149
Italy.	174
United Kingdom	192

The Work of the IASC to Date

From 1973 until 1987, the IASC initially concentrated its efforts on developing accounting principles that would eliminate bad reporting practices around the world. In hopes of achieving a reasonable degree of worldwide acceptance, these standards tended to allow the continued use of numerous alternative approaches without expressing any preference. Furthermore, the inclusion of alternatives was often necessary to muster the 11 positive votes required for issuing a new standard.

As an example, *IAS 2* allowed inventory to be reported by using either FIFO, LIFO, weighted average, or the base stock method. For the same reason, both the U.S. treatment of expensing goodwill over a period of up to 40 years and the U.K. approach of writing off goodwill directly to stockholders' equity were allowed by the IASC.

Because of this flexibility, in many countries (such as the United States) with highly developed accounting systems, international accounting standards have been largely ignored in the past. The standards could not be enforced and did not appear to provide any significant improvement over the methods required by the home country. Gradually, however, interest in the work of the IASC has begun to increase. In the early part of the 1980s, for example, General Electric Company set an important precedent by indicating its adherence to international accounting standards. In its "Management Responsibility Report" as of December 31, 1990, the following disclosure is made:

> Accounting principles used in preparing the financial statements are those that are generally accepted in the United States. These principles are consistent in most important respects with standards issued by the International Accounting Standards Committee.

This statement by a major multinational company indicates an awareness of the importance of using accounting principles that can be understood throughout the world. Also, during the 1980s, the Toronto Stock Exchange asked Canadian companies to begin referring to the use of international accounting standards in their financial statements. Although this was only a request, more than 100 companies complied. Alcan Aluminum Ltd., for example, reported that its 1991 statements were "prepared in accordance with accounting principles generally accepted in Canada. . . . They conform in all material respects with accounting principles of the International Accounting Standards Committee."

As a further indication of the emerging recognition of the IASC, some European companies now present reconciliations of their reported income balances to amounts determined under international accounting standards. Metra Corporation, a Finnish enterprise specializing in construction and diesel engines, reported a net loss for the year ending February 28, 1991, of 73.3 million FIM. Because of the accounting rules of that country, this number was determined through extremely conservative methods. Thus, additional information was included by the company to indicate that a profit (rather than a loss) was earned amounting to 48 million FIM when calculated using the principles of the IASC.

The IASC—Limiting Alternative Methods of Accounting

Despite the increase in interest, a continuing problem plaguing the IASC has been the availability of optional accounting methods within its own standards. In many cases, only the very worst principles have been eliminated. Recently, though, the International Organization of Securities Commissions (IOSCO) has put pressure on the IASC to reduce the available options. The IOSCO has indicated the possibility of accepting international accounting standards for use in prospectuses of multinational companies. The IOSCO wants the IASC to reduce the number of acceptable methods. Once that goal is achieved, the IOSCO has stated that it will push the securities regulators in member countries to allow financial statements to be prepared in accordance with international accounting standards.

"Conformity with IASs could become the *only* additional requirement to compliance with the standards (including the law) of the home country in financial statements used in multinational offerings."[20] Clearly, acceptance by the IOSCO would provide international standards with an immediate and immense power. Companies would only be forced to follow two sets of guidelines: the rules of their home countries and the international accounting standards.

In the United States, the Securities and Exchange Commission (SEC) has made statements similar to those of the IOSCO. The chief accountant has indicated that if free choice among alternative treatments is restricted, the SEC may consider accepting international accounting standards in lieu of compliance with U.S. generally accepted accounting principles. Once again, a company would be faced with complying with fewer sets of rules when entering the international capital markets. "This could mean, for example, that if a French company had a simultaneous stock offering in the United States, Canada and Japan, financial statements prepared in accordance with international standards could be used in all three nations."[21]

---

[20] Cairns, "Calling All National Standards Setters," p. 13.

[21] Stephen H. Collins, "The SEC on Full and Fair Disclosure," *Journal of Accountancy*, January 1989, p. 84.

The IASC appears to have the opportunity to become an increasingly strong force in the world of accounting but only if it can eliminate the availability of optional methods. For this reason, a steering committee was formed in 1987 to examine the possibility of reducing the number of currently accepted alternatives. Subsequently, in January 1989, the IASC released an exposure draft of a standard entitled *Comparability of Financial Statements*. This proposal was designed to revise 12 of the board's previous statements to remove a significant portion of the alternative treatments.

Since that time, the IASC has studied the responses to *Comparability of Financial Statements* and has issued several new exposure drafts on specific issues addressed by that proposal (for example: inventories, research and development, revenue recognition, and business combinations). The IASC hopes to release final statements in a relatively short time for any (or all) of those areas on which agreement can be reached. Many view this project as the possible first act in making truly international accounting standards a reality. According to Art Wyatt, former IASC chairman, "We expect to eliminate 80 percent of the (current) alternatives by the end of 1993. We will have taken a major step to having a really useful standard."[22]

However, not everyone is necessarily pleased with the progress being made by the IASC. "Now that the London-based International Accounting Standards Committee is close to rolling out universal accounting standards, some American companies are getting cold feet. That's because, looking down the road, many U.S. companies fear that standards set in London may one day replace standards currently used in the U.S."[23] The IASC's proposals do not always agree with U.S. GAAP. For example, one exposure draft would expense all research costs but capitalize development costs in certain cases. Usage of pooling of interests accounting might be eliminated entirely or severely restricted. Goodwill would be amortized to expense but over an allowable period of only 5 years for most purchases. Initially, the IASC had indicated a desire to disallow the use of LIFO. After some strong lobbying, though, the board has decided to rethink that position.

If these exposure drafts can gain acceptance and become new international accounting standards, the IASC will have made an important stride in the task of harmonizing accounting principles throughout the world. Unfortunately, many questions remain unanswered. Will countries where the government controls the development costs of accounting principles have any interest in relinquishing part of that power to international accounting? Will countries with well-developed accounting principles, such as the United States, accept rules that differ from their own?

If the IASC, which meets a few times per year with virtually no staff, changes the handling of items such as development costs or goodwill amortization, will the

---

[22] Sharon Stangenes, "Global Accounting Rules Sought," *Chicago Tribune,* October 8, 1992, p. C–1.

[23] Roula Khalaf, "Esperanto for Accountants," *Forbes,* March 3, 1992, pp. 50–51.

full-time, well-staffed FASB make those same changes in U.S. GAAP just for conformity? Should the FASB make those changes? If not, how will the work of the IASC be affected? To date, such issues have not been faced. However, the FASB has given no indication in the past that it was willing to alter its principles simply to conform to international accounting standards.

A single, universal accounting language may well become an eventual reality but at this point no one can foresee what will actually happen. International accounting standards may be desirable or even necessary. However, whether acceptance can be won for any set of principles remains to be seen. Only time will tell whether the IASC is capable of establishing such principles.

Accounting Principles Around the World

Just like food dishes and native dress, accounting principles vary from country to country. To understand each unique set of reporting standards that have evolved, the structure and development of the accounting profession in these areas must be examined. An understanding of the techniques in use is then more easily achieved. Thus, the remainder of this chapter analyzes national accounting principles by presenting two types of information:

1. A discussion of the accounting profession as it is structured in a number of countries along with an introduction to the financial statements currently produced in these areas.
2. A study of several specific accounting problems and the method by which these issues have been resolved in different countries.

The Accounting Profession and Financial Statement Presentation

Japan

Japan is an increasingly dominant industrial and financial power; we will need to come to terms with that country's accounting policies. Japanese accounting in the 1990s is a product of a native medieval double entry bookkeeping system, a borrowing from German (and French) commercial legal codes in the late 19th century, and U.S.-inspired securities legislation of the postwar period.[24]

In Japan (like a number of other countries in the Continental Model), basic accounting principles are set primarily by the government. The Japanese Commercial Code requires annual audited financial statements of joint stock corporations (known as *Kabushiki Kaisha* or KK) that have stated capital of at least 500 million

---

[24] Christopher Nobes and Sadayoshi Maeda, "Japanese Accounts: Interpreters Needed," *Accountancy*, September 1990, p. 82.

yen or total liabilities of 20 billion yen or more. The Securities and Exchange Law imposes a similar reporting requirement on companies listed on Japanese stock exchanges as well as other companies issuing stocks and bonds in the amount of 100 million yen or more. Consequently, many Japanese companies must produce two sets of financial statements: one to fulfill the requirements of the Commercial Code and the other based on securities laws. The two sets of statements are very similar except that the securities laws require more disclosure and its requirements are more precisely defined.

The Commercial Code prescribes a few basic accounting principles (valuation of assets and liabilities, recording of deferred assets, and the like). These rules are supplemented by the *Financial Accounting Standards for Business Enterprises* developed by the Business Accounting Deliberation Council (BADC). The BADC is, therefore, the single most important source of accounting principles in Japan. The BADC is made up of individuals drawn from the government, business, education, and the accounting profession. Membership in this council is by appointment of the Ministry of Finance which, therefore, allows government control.

Financial reporting in Japan is also quite heavily influenced by tax laws. Companies usually follow the tax guidelines in producing their statements unless absolutely prohibited. Fortunately, the tax laws are written so that actual differences with official accounting pronouncements are few.

> The adjustment of book income to taxable income on the tax return is not allowed in principle. Therefore, the so-called two sets of books problem prevalent in the United States is rarely mentioned in Japan. When a discrepancy exists between the income tax code and other financial accounting regulations, the corporation inevitably follows the procedures endorsed by the income tax code.[25]

The Japanese Institute of Certified Public Accountants (JICPA) has not become a powerful force in the establishment of accounting principles. The Audit Committee of the JICPA, though, does issue papers describing preferable accounting practices.

To become a certified public accountant in Japan, three examinations must be passed: the first (from which college graduates are exempted) consists of mathematics, the Japanese language, and a thesis. The second is comprised of accounting, cost accounting, auditing, management, economics, and commercial law. Passing this second test qualifies one as a Junior CPA. Then, after three years of experience, a third examination is required to become a CPA. This final test is made up of accounting practice, auditing practice, and financial analysis.

Historically, accounting has not had the importance in Japan that is found in other developed nations.

> Not only do officials of Japanese companies generally ignore the stock market, they don't use complex financial information much themselves either. "Cost accounting

---

[25] Toshio Iino and Ryoji Inouye, "Financial Accounting and Reporting in Japan," *International Accounting* (New York: Harper & Row, 1984), p. 377.

doesn't exist," (says Daniel Maher, partner of Chuo/Coopers & Lybrand Consulting in Tokyo). "There are more accountants in Missouri than in all of Japan." In fact, there are only about 11,000 certified public accountants in Japan, compared with some 300,000 in the United States. Instead of corporate accounting departments or professional accountants, most Japanese companies have small accounting groups attached to projects and staffed by generalists who rotated through accounting between assignments to, say, personnel and sales.[26]

Financial statements required by the Japanese Commercial Code consist of the following:

- Balance sheet.
- Profit and loss statement.
- Proposal of appropriation of profit or disposition of loss.
- Business report.

The Japanese balance sheet is similar in appearance to that used in the United States. Assets usually are classified as either current (quick assets and inventories) or fixed (tangible assets such as buildings and equipment, intangibles, and long-term investments). Liabilities are divided between current and fixed (noncurrent). Retained earnings may show amounts that have been voluntarily reserved by corporate officials. Some items, such as bonuses to directors, that would be expensed in the United States may be charged directly to retained earnings in Japan.[27] In addition, stockholders' equity often reports legal reserves. For example, the equity section of the March 31, 1992, balance sheet of the Nippon Steel Corporation reported a legal reserve of more than 81 billion yen ($612 million) as a "revenue reserve." A footnote explained this balance as follows:

> Under the Commercial Code, the Company is required to appropriate a portion of earned surplus as a revenue reserve in amounts equal to at least 10 percent of cash dividends and directors' and statutory auditors' bonuses . . . and exactly 10 percent of interim cash dividends until such reserve equals 25 percent of the amount of capital stock account. This reserve is not available for dividends but may be used to reduce a deficit by resolution of shareholders' meeting or may be capitalized by resolution of the board of directors.

The profit and loss statement is divided into two sections: ordinary profit and loss and extraordinary (or special) items. The first part of this statement includes operating revenues and expenses as well as nonoperating items such as interest and dividend income. The extraordinary (or special) section includes gains and losses on the sale of investments and fixed assets and, in some cases, prior period adjustments. The unusual and infrequent criteria utilized in the United States is not applied. However, as in the United States, income taxes are subtracted at the

---

[26] Paula Doe, "What's Buried Inside Japanese Annual Reports?" *Electronic Business*, February 10, 1992, p. 28.

[27] KPMG Peat Marwick Minato, *The Accounting Profession in Japan* (New York: AICPA, 1988), p. 51.

bottom of the statement to arrive at net income. Comparative figures are not required. The income statement prepared for Nippon Steel in Exhibit 10–2 is a good example of this structure.

The United Kingdom. "The United Kingdom has the oldest accounting profession in the world today, and its reputation is second to none."[28] As this quotation indicates, no discussion of world accounting principles would be complete without a study of the United Kingdom, which has long been a world leader in commerce and accounting. Legal regulation of accounting is provided by the Companies Acts, a legislative series culminating in the Companies Act of 1989.

The Companies Acts are basic commercial legislation designed to provide legal rules for U.K. corporations concerning issues dealing with management, administration, and dissolution. However, these laws also cover the issuance and content of financial statements. The Act of 1985, for example, specifically refers to several fundamental accounting principles: going concern; consistency; accrual accounting; and the separation (not netting) of assets, liabilities, income, and expenditures.

In the United Kingdom, professional accounting organizations are quite important—membership now nears 200,000. A person may only be termed a *chartered accountant* through membership in the Institutes of Chartered Accountants in England and Wales, of Scotland, or in Ireland. Normally, a license to practice is available to members after two years of approved experience.

In total, six different professional groups exist with the largest being The Institute of Chartered Accountants in England and Wales. Until recently, these organizations collectively controlled the accounting standard setting process. Together, they formally created a Consultive Committee of Accountancy Bodies. It was a subcommittee of this group, the Accounting Standards Committee (ASC), that produced 24 statements of standard accounting practice (SSAPs) between 1971 and 1990 (as well as a number of Statements of Recommended Practice).

The ASC was originally created "to reduce and regularize the range of permissable accounting treatments applicable to comparable transactions and situations."[29] Over the years, the ASC gradually branched into a standard-setting role. However, the committee experienced difficulty because its pronouncements had to be accepted by each of the six professional organizations before being issued. Thus, the creation of accounting standards was agonizingly slow at times.

Consequently, the Accounting Standards Board (ASB) was formed on August 1, 1990, to replace the ASC as the standard-setting organization in the United Kingdom. The ASB is an independent body styled somewhat along the lines of the FASB. The ASB issues standards on its own authority. To date, the ASB has produced a few standards. For example, cash flow information is now required as a result of the ASB. In addition, the reporting of extraordinary items has been severely restricted.

---

[28] Geoffrey Alan Lee, "Accounting in the United Kingdom," *International Accounting* (New York: Harper & Row, 1984), p. 261.

[29] Emile Woolf, "The ASC at the Crossroads," *Accountancy*, September 1988, p. 72.

EXHIBIT 10–2   Japanese Income Statement

NIPPON STEEL CORPORATION
Nonconsolidated Statement of Income
Year Ended March 31, 1992

	Millions of yen
Operating income:	
Net sales	¥2,629,398
Operating expenses:	
Cost of sales.	2,142,866
Selling, general, and administrative expenses	322,357
	2,465,223
Operating profit	164,174
Nonoperating profit and loss:	
Nonoperating profit:	
Interest and dividend income	38,421
Profit on sale of marketable securities	8
Miscellaneous	21,243
	59,672
Nonoperating loss:	
Interest expenses.	86,762
Miscellaneous	36,878
	123,640
Ordinary profit.	100,206
Special profit:	
Profit on sale of land to a subsidiary	38,811
Profit on sale of investments in securities and	
investments in subsidiaries and affiliates	2,770
Reversal of reserve for estimated loss on planned	
disposal of tangible fixed assets	8,158
	49,739
Special loss:	
Loss on disposal of tangible fixed assets and other assets.	14,198
Loss on rationalization of steel production facilities	—
Write-down of investments in securities and	
investments in subsidiaries and affiliates	9,852
Loss on dissolution of subsidiaries, affiliates, and others	1,470
Past service cost under the retirement pension plan	20,168
	45,688
Income before income taxes	104,257
Income taxes:	
Currently payable	15,800
Accrued on translation gains	4,700
Net income	¥83,757
Per share:	
Net income	¥12.15
Cash dividends applicable to the year	¥6.00

A second body, the Review Panel, was created along with the ASB. The Review Panel monitors compliance with the accounting standards. This panel has the authority to seek a court order against companies producing financial statements that fail to provide a true and fair view.

Accounting principles and practice are also influenced by directives of the European Economic Community of which the United Kingdom is a partner. These directives seek to harmonize many of the commercial aspects of the group's membership. More specifically, the Fourth and Seventh Directives addressed accounting issues. However, since the Seventh Directive was adopted in 1983, no further move toward harmonization of accounting principles has been made and a number of alternatives continue to be acceptable in many areas of financial reporting.

Financial statements must be submitted to the shareholders at the annual meeting. A directors' report is included describing the directors' activities for the period, post balance sheet events, the business year in general, research and development activities, and a host of other information. The financial statements themselves are normally the balance sheet, the profit and loss account, and a cash flow statement. For the balance sheet and profit and loss account, several alternative formats are available (based on either a horizontal or a vertical presentation). After being selected, a particular format must be followed carefully and used consistently from year to year.

From the perspective of United States financial reporting, both the U.K. balance sheet and the profit and loss account have unique structures. The balance sheet begins with fixed assets. The current asset section is shown next with current liabilities being included to derive a net current asset figure. Long-term liabilities are then listed to arrive at net assets. The "capital and reserves" section can include adjustments that do not have an impact on the computation of net income such as the write-off of goodwill and asset revaluations.

As an illustration, the September 30, 1990, balance sheet of Lonrho PLC is presented in Exhibit 10–3. Because of terminology differences, parenthetical titles are included where appropriate for explanation.

In the United Kingdom, the profit and loss account is obviously the equivalent of an income statement. The statement begins with turnover (a net sales figure) followed by normal operating and financing expenses and then income taxes. Prior to inclusion of any extraordinary gains or losses (which have recently been restricted by the ASB), any minority interest in the consolidated net income is subtracted.[30] As in the United States, reported figures tend to be highly condensed with much of the information provided in the notes to the statements.

The consolidated profit and loss account of Glaxo Holdings PLC for the year ending June 30, 1991, provides an illustration of the statement often found in the United Kingdom. (See Exhibit 10–4.)

---

[30] Arthur Andersen & Company, *The Accounting Profession in the United Kingdom* (New York: AICPA, 1987), p. 64.

EXHIBIT 10–3   U.K. Balance Sheet

LONRHO PLC
Balance Sheet
September 30, 1990

	£m
Fixed assets	
Intangible assets	129
Tangible assets	1,794
Investments:	
Subsidiaries	—
Related companies	268
Other investments	61
	2,252
Current assets	
Stocks (inventory)	573
Debtors (receivables)	426
Investments	119
Cash at bank and in hand	355
	1,473
Creditors: Amounts falling due within one year (current liabilities)	(1,159)
Net current assets	314
Total assets less current liabilities	2,566
Creditors: Amounts falling due after more than one year	(946)
Provisions for liabilities and charges	(11)
	1,609
Capital and reserves	
Called up share capital	160
Share premium account	258
Revaluation reserve	916
Other reserves	(151)
Profit and loss account	201
Equity interests	1,384
Minority interests	225
	1,609

Germany.   Accounting principles in Germany are set by the government through acts of parliament. Currently, these mandatory principles are outlined in detail in the Third Book of the Commercial Code. Tax laws have had a significant influence on the reporting principles established by the code. Because of the legal nature of the accounting rules, interpretations are made by the country's courts in a manner somewhat similar to tax rulings in the United States. Actual changes in the accounting laws are rare since they must be passed by the legislative body. However, in December 1985, significant alterations were approved to bring the Ger-

---
EXHIBIT 10-4   U.K. Profit and Loss Account

GLAXO HOLDINGS PLC
Consolidated Profit and Loss Account
Year Ended June 30, 1991

	£m
Turnover	3,397
Operating costs less other income	2,293
Trading profit	1,104
Investment income less interest payable	179
Profit on ordinary activities before taxation	1,283
Taxation	359
Profit on ordinary activities after taxation	924
Minority interests	12
Profit before extraordinary items	912
Extraordinary items	31
Profit for the financial year	881
Dividends	420
Retained profit	461
Earnings per share	60.8p
Dividends per share	28.0p

---

man principles in line with the directives of the European Economic Community, pronouncements which had been designed to harmonize accounting within the member countries. The German Institute of Certified Public Accountants does issue some recommendations that serve as reporting guidelines.

German accounting laws vary according to company size. Three separate classifications are identified:[31]

Category	Balance Sheet Total (DM)	Sales (DM)	Employees
Large	15.5 million	32.0 million	250
Medium	3.9 million	8.0 million	50
Small	All others	All others	All others

NOTE: To qualify for a particular classification, two of the three criteria must be met for two consecutive years.

The financial information and disclosure required of the smaller companies is less extensive.

---

[31] The three criteria will be increased slightly to confirm with requirements of the European Community. Ernst & Young, *Doing Business in Germany* (New York, 1991), p. 75.

As in many countries where legislative accounting rules exist, German accounting is considered quite conservative. "It is greatly influenced by the German banks, because they provide the major investment and mandate the reporting requirements for many industries in Germany. . . . When individuals in other countries analyze the financial statements, they generally write up the figures because of the extreme conservatism of German policies and procedures."[32] Some evidence exists to indicate that German accounting may be in the process of change. "It is time, said the chief executive of Germany's largest bank at a recent press conference, for Germany to enter the civilized world. Hilmar Kopper, head of the Deutsche Bank, was referring to German companies accounting practices, and his remarks came shortly after Daimler-Benz had announced it would be moving from the teutonic version of accounting to the Anglo-American. . . . German accounting differs from Anglo-American in a number of important areas, not least that it makes no claim to provide a 'true and fair' view of economic reality." (David Waller, "Daimler-Benz Gears Up For a Drive On The Freeway," *The Financial Times,* April 29, 1993, page 18.)

The accounting profession in Germany is well established. The *Wirtschaftsprüfer* is the equivalent of a Certified Public Accountant. A person can use this designation only after passing a difficult examination. The exam is normally open only to college graduates with degrees in economics, law, or a related subject. The profession itself is a self-governing body known as the *Wirtschaftsprüferkammer*, which enforces strict rules on independence and ethics. "Because of the comprehensive requirements for entry into the profession, it is almost impossible to fulfill all of them before the age of 30, and most are 35 before they are admitted."[33]

In Germany, companies must produce a balance sheet each year as well as a profit and loss account (or income statement) and notes to the financial statements. A management report is also required to discuss issues such as current business position, significant subsequent events, future prospects, and research and development activities. Neither a statement of cash flows nor a statement of sources and uses of funds is mandatory.

The income statement must be produced according to one of two available formats. The *cost of sales* approach, which has grown in popularity in recent years with Germany's larger companies, is similar to the structure of the income statement typically found in the United States. In contrast, the *type-of-cost* statement is more traditional in Germany. This income statement presents inventory increases and decreases (along with the cost of self-constructed assets) as an adjustment to revenues. Net purchases are then subtracted as if they represented expenses. The statement of income for Daimler-Benz AG for the year ending December 31, 1990 (before its switch in accounting), is an example of the type-of-cost format often associated with German companies. (See Exhibit 10–5.)

---

[32] Roger K. Doost and Karen M. Ligon, "How U.S. and European Accounting Practices Differ," *Management Accounting*, October 1986, p. 40.

[33] Thomas G. Evans, Martin E. Taylor, and Oscar Holzmann, *International Accounting and Reporting* (New York: Macmillan, 1985), p. 39.

EXHIBIT 10-5   German Statement of Income

DAIMLER-BENZ AG
Consolidated Statement of Income
Year Ended December 31, 1990

DM millions

Sales revenue	85,500
Increase in inventories and other capitalized in-house output	2,840
Total output	88,340
Other operating income	3,598
Purchases of goods and services	(44,477)
Personnel expenses of which DM 1,347 million for old-age pensions	(26,890)
Amortization of intangible assets, depreciation of fixed assets and of leased equipment	(5,169)
Other operating expenses	(12,016)
Net income from affiliated, associated and related companies	4
Net interest income	989
Write-downs of financial assets and of marketable securities	(158)
Results from ordinary business activities	4,221
Income taxes	(1,814)
Other taxes	(612)
Net income	1,795
Profit carried forward from previous year	5
Transfer to retained earnings	(1,124)
Income applicable to minority shareholders	(145)
Loss applicable to minority shareholders	34
Unappropriated profit	565

This type-of-cost report is obviously quite unique when compared to a U.S. income statement.

Similar to the financial reporting in the United Kingdom, the German balance sheet begins with fixed assets followed by current assets. However, stockholders' equity is usually shown next before the reporting of any liabilities. *As with many foreign countries, reserve figures are common within stockholders' equity to record adjustments that are not viewed as impacting net income.* Unfortunately, German footnote disclosure does not always clarify the purpose of such balances. The December 31, 1991, balance sheet of the Volkswagen Group, for example, shows revenue reserves of nearly 8 billion deutsche marks. *Although this figure is approximately seven times larger than the company's net income for the period,* the footnote explanation is limited to "A total of DM 80 million was transferred from the net earnings of the parent company to 'Other revenue reserves' in accordance with section 58 subsection 2 of the German Corporation Act. The goodwill of DM 14 million deriving from acquisition of additional shares in three Group companies has been set off against 'Other revenue reserves'."

Although this footnote may not clearly explain the purpose of the company's revenue reserve, some investors believe the amounts have an important effect on net income.

> The U.S. strives for full disclosure; the Europeans, led by the Germans, tend to give companies ample latitude to conceal profits and liabilities. This in part helps explain why shares in European companies generally trade at higher price/earnings multiples than their U.S. counterparts: Investors assume that some portion of the European companies' profits lies tucked away in a hidden reserve, to be called upon to smooth out earnings in a down year.[34]

As shown in Exhibit 10–6, the German balance sheet ends with the reporting of the entity's liabilities and other credits. For the Volkswagen Group, only five general figures are actually presented in this section. The "undetermined liabilities" include estimated expenses such as pensions, warranties, and taxes.

Although the Liabilities figure found in Volkswagen's balance sheet is reasonably well explained through supplemental disclosure, the "Special items with an equity portion" provides another example of German footnotes. According to the information provided by the company, this balance is largely comprised of "depreciation of tax purposes" which is explained as:

> value adjustments in accordance with section 3 subsection 2 of the Border Area Promotion Act, section 4 of the Development Area Act, section 7d of the Income Tax Act, section 6b of the Income Tax Act, section 35 of the Income Tax Guidelines, section 14 of the Berlin Promotion Act, section 82d of the Income Tax Directive, section 82a of the Income Tax Directive, section 7c of the Income Tax Act and section 80 of the Income Tax Directive.

A footnote such as this helps to explain why many investors are becoming more interested in the development of international accounting standards.

The Accounting Profession Around the World.   Across the decades, the accounting profession has developed in different ways in different countries. As can be seen from the preceding coverage, the type of capital markets has a significant influence on the evolution of the profession. In addition, the method by which accounting standards are set (either by the government or by the private sector) has an impact on the accounting bodies formed and the powers they retain. Following is a brief overview of the accounting profession as it has developed in several countries of the world.

Argentina.   Professional accountancy can only be practiced by individuals with a degree from an Argentine university following five to seven years of study. The profession itself is governed by a variety of official bodies that are formed according to national laws. The most influential group is the Scientific and Technical Studies Center. This body along with several others has produced a number of technical accounting pronouncements that are mandatory.

---

[34] Fuhrman, "Esperanto," p. 72.

EXHIBIT 10–6   German Balance Sheet

VOLKSWAGEN GROUP
Balance Sheet
December 31, 1991

DM million

Assets

Fixed assets

Intangible assets	372
Tangible assets	21,126
Financial assets	2,655
Leasing and rental assets	6,293
	30,446

Current assets

Inventories	9,049
Receivables and other assets	18,675
Securities	2,329
Cash on hand, deposits at German Federal Bank and postal giro balances, cash in banks	9,255
	39,308

Prepaid and deferred charges	336
Balance-sheet total	70,090

Stockholders' equity and liabilities

Stockholders' equity

Subscribed capital of Volkswagen AG		1,656
Ordinary shares	1,350	
Nonvoting preferred shares	306	
Capital reserve		4,223
Revenue reserves		7,875
Net earnings available for distribution		373
Minority interest in consolidated subsidiaries		176
		14,303

Special items with an equity portion	3,823
Special item for investment subsidies	19
Undetermined liabilities	20,282
Liabilities	31,046
Deferred income	617
Balance-sheet total	70,090

Australia. The accounting profession in Australia is controlled by a mix of government and private regulation. Disclosure requirements are legally set within the Companies Code and Regulations. The Australian Accounting Research Foundation (AARF) actually produces specific auditing and accounting principles (known as Australian Accounting Standards). This foundation is sponsored by the two professional accounting groups that exist in this country: the Institute of Chartered Accountants in Australia (about 18,000 members) and the Australian Society of Accountants (about 57,000 members). Many of the pronouncements of the AARF must be approved legally by the Accounting Standards Review Board, a group established by the Ministerial Council of the government.

Canada.   The accounting profession is legally regulated separately by each province. To become a chartered accountant in Canada requires passing a uniform examination and completing a period of practical experience. The main organization for professional accountants is the Canadian Institute of Chartered Accountants (CICA). The *Handbook* of the CICA is the primary source of accounting principles in this country. The Accounting Standards Committee of the CICA prepares Recommendations for the *Handbook*. However, in Canada, those standards tend to be very broad so that the professional accountants are allowed to use their own judgment in specific cases.

France.   In France, accounting and auditing are viewed as two separate professions. The Ministry of Economy and Finance supervises the accountants, whereas the Ministry of Justice has authority over the auditors. Only in recent years have the accounting and auditing groups worked together in matters of common interest. To become a statutory auditor, a person must have a university degree, pass a qualifying test, and have two years of practical experience. Accounting principles are passed by the government and included within the Code of Commerce. Accounting opinions are produced by the Conseil National de la Comptabilité (the National Accounting Board). These opinions are in the form of proposed solutions to practical or theoretical problems. This body is composed of individuals representing a number of different interests: labor unions, banks, civil servents, industry, and practicing accountants.

Mexico.   Individuals who complete a required program of study of 4½ or 5 years in a Mexican university receive the title *contador público*. The title allows those individuals to place the initials C.P. before their names. They may practice public accounting if they are also registered with the Ministry of Education. The Mexican accounting profession is governed by the Mexican Institute of Public Accountants (the Instituto Mexicano de Contadores Públicos or IMCP), a group with approximately 12,000 members (of which about 5,000 are in public practice). The IMCP is an independent organization. Through its Accounting Principles Commission, accounting principles are formulated for the country. This commission is made up of professional accountants, financial executives, representatives of the stock exchanges, bankers, and the like. Historically, the principles that have been produced are quite similar to U.S. GAAP except for the handling of inflation and deferred taxes. A number of reporting areas have not yet been addressed by the commission.

Singapore.   The Companies Act sets forth the legal disclosure requirements for financial statements in Singapore; the Accountants Act regulates the profession. The main source of practical accounting standards are the pronouncements of the Institute of Certified Public Accountants of Singapore (Statements of Accounting

Standards or SASs). The standards of the International Accounting Standards Committee have had significant influence in Singapore and most are included within the SASs. The institute also issues statements of Recommended Accounting Practices (RAPs) that have less authority. The accounting principles in Singapore are not rigid rules; instead, professional judgment is emphasized. Although the country has approximately 6,000 accountants, only about 10 percent are in the practice of public accounting.

The Handling of Specific Accounting Problems Around the World

In the final section of this chapter, several specific financial reporting issues are examined from the perspective of individual countries as well as the current international accounting standards. No attempt is being made to describe the accounting principles of every nation. Instead, a cross-section of countries is presented in each case to indicate the range of possible treatments that have developed throughout the world.

Reported Value of Assets

United Kingdom. In the United Kingdom, companies are free to choose the method by which assets are valued. Although historical cost can serve as the basis, some (or all) accounts may be reported at a valuation basis. The method of valuation depends on the type of asset. Intangible assets, tangible fixed assets, inventory, and short-term investments can be stated at their current cost. Current cost is the lower of replacement cost or net realizable value. Market value is used for long-term investments and also serves as an allowed alternative for tangible fixed assets. If revaluation occurs, any accumulated depreciation is usually eliminated with the reported balance then being adjusted to the new basis. The change in the asset's value creates a "revaluation reserve," that is reported in the Capital and Reserves section of the balance sheet. Subsequent depreciation is based on the revalued figures.

Canada. Historical cost is capitalized and amortized over the useful life of the asset. Prior to 1990, Canadian companies were allowed to write assets up to an appraised value above cost. The procedure was rarely used and has now been eliminated.

Japan. The Japanese approach to reporting assets resembles the procedures used in the United States. Current assets are shown at cost unless market value is significantly less and recovery is not expected. The reporting of fixed assets is based on historical cost unless a permanent impairment of value has occurred.

France. Although historical cost is the basis for reporting, revaluing property, plant, and equipment as well as inventory to current value has been permitted in France since 1984. If revaluation occurs, it must apply to all applicable assets. To record the change, a separate reserve balance must be established within stock-holders' equity. Revaluation tends to be infrequent because increases in value are taxed (although the extra depreciation is subsequently allowed as a tax deduction). The revaluation of intangibles is not permitted. Occasional tax-free revaluations are allowed or required by the government when inflation rates are high. Such revaluations occurred in 1945, 1959, and 1976.

Brazil. Historical cost is used for reporting many assets. Because of the inflation rate, property, plant, and equipment and long-term investments are adjusted upward on each balance sheet date based on an inflation index produced by the government. Such adjustments are recorded in Brazil as income. The reported value of fixed assets may also be increased further, if necessary, to market value (current replacement cost) accompanied by an offsetting equity balance.

Korea. Historical cost is utilized in Korean companies. Revaluation to market value is allowed if the Bank of Korea wholesale price index has risen 25 percent or more since the date of an asset's acquisition or previous revaluation. Such adjustments are optional but can only be made on the first day of the business year. A revaluation is recorded through an increase in a capital reserve but a 3 percent tax is imposed on the company.

China. The reported value of assets is based on historical cost principles, and revaluations based on market value are not permitted. Chinese accounting is consistent in most respects with international accounting standards.

Germany. Historical cost is utilized unless the value has been impaired or losses are anticipated.

International Accounting Standards. Property, plant, and equipment should be reported at either historical cost or a revalued amount. If assets are revalued, an entire class must be adjusted or some systematic approach must be applied; assets cannot be revalued selectively. Any reduction in value is recorded as a decrease in net income, whereas an increase creates a "revaluation surplus" to be shown within the shareholders' equity section of the balance sheet. The IASC has recently proposed recognizing historical cost as the preferable approach with market value permitted only as an acceptable alternative and only if the values are kept up to date.

Business Combinations and Consolidation Accounting

United Kingdom. All subsidiaries are consolidated unless (1) control is only temporary, (2) restrictions hinder the parent's ability to exercise its rights, or (3) the subsidiary's activities are so dissimilar that consolidation would be misleading. Rules for a pooling of interests (a merger) are more lenient in the United Kingdom than in the United States. If a company makes an offer for all outstanding shares and obtains at least 90 percent, the use of pooling of interests accounting is permitted. Otherwise, the combination is viewed as a purchase (an acquisition).

Canada.   The pooling of interests method is very rarely used in Canada; it is only considered appropriate if the acquiring party cannot be identified. The purchase method is applied to all other business combinations. Consolidation is required unless control of a subsidiary is seriously impaired, control is temporary, or the activities of the subsidiary are considered to be dissimilar to that of the remainder of the combination.

Japan.   Acquisitions and mergers are rare in Japan so that consolidation accounting has not been well developed. As a result, until recently, parent company statements rather than consolidated statements were produced. Unconsolidated subsidiaries are sometimes used to hold (hide) badly performing assets. Mergers are accomplished through an exchange of stocks and are usually recorded by the pooling of interests method. However, if one company is clearly in a subsidiary position, purchase accounting is used. For a pooling, income statement figures are not combined retroactively as is the practice in the United States.

France.   Consolidation of financial statements has only been required since 1986, although voluntary preparation has been common for some time. Purchase accounting in France is similar to that used in the United States; however, control is assumed to exist if 40 percent or more of a company's voting stock is held (and no other stockholder owns more). The pooling of interests method is not considered acceptable. A subsidiary need not be consolidated if restrictions hinder the parent's control, the shares are held for resale, or the subsidiary's operations are so dissimilar to those of the parent that consolidated statements would be misleading. Joint ventures are consolidated proportionally.

Australia.   Purchase accounting is used and is similar to that found in the United States. The pooling of interests method is not allowed.

Korea.   Unaudited consolidated statements are generally attached to parent company statements to provide supplemental information. On the parent's own statements, all subsidiaries are recorded using the cost method. Recent attempts have been made in Korea to require more extensive reporting of consolidated figures. Rules have been produced but not yet enforced.

Germany.   Historically, large companies (defined by size of assets, sales, and employees) had to consolidate all domestic corporations but could omit foreign subsidiaries. Beginning in 1990, the size limit was reduced significantly for required consolidation. In addition, after that date, all foreign subsidiaries had to be included in the consolidated figures. The purchase method predominates but the pooling of interests method may be used if 90 percent of a subsidiary's voting stock is exchanged for new shares of the parent. However, as in Japan, operational figures are not consolidated retroactively when this method is applied.

Mexico.   All subsidiaries that are more than 50 percent controlled must be consolidated unless ownership is temporary, the subsidiary is bankrupt, or the activities of the subsidiary are significantly different than the remaining companies in the combination. Only the purchase method is appropriate.

International Accounting Standards.   All subsidiaries, both foreign and domestic, should be consolidated unless control is temporary, long-term restrictions impair control, or the activities are dissimilar. According to *IAS 22*, the purchase method should always be used except in rare cases where a uniting of interests occurs through an exchange of voting stock. In such combinations, the pooling of interests method is appropriate. The IASC is currently considering a change so that pooling of interests would only be allowed in the unusual case that an acquiring company could not be identified.

Accounting for Goodwill

United Kingdom.   Certainly one of the most controversial accounting rules in the United Kingdom is the handling of purchased goodwill. Although the amount is computed in the same manner as in the United States (the fair market value paid in excess of the fair market value of the net assets), goodwill traditionally has been written off immediately against an equity reserve. U.K. accounting rules allow the company to record goodwill as an asset and then amortize the cost over up to 40 years. However, this treatment does not appear to be widely used.

Canada.   The treatment of goodwill is similar to that used in the United States.

Japan.   Computation is similar to that found in the United States. The amount of goodwill may be charged directly to income if the amount is not considered significant. If capitalized, goodwill is amortized over a period of up to five years unless some other period of time can be justified.

Germany.   Goodwill is capitalized and amortized using the straight-line method over five years (including the year of acquisition). This period may be extended to 40 years if the longer period can be justified. In some cases, goodwill can be written off immediately to an equity account. For tax purposes, a life of 15 years is used.

Italy.   Flexible rules are available for the handling of goodwill. This cost may be written off immediately to stockholders' equity or to income. In addition, goodwill may be capitalized as an asset and then amortized as an expense over a 10-year period.

France.   Goodwill is capitalized and amortized as an expense over 5 to 20 years although no period of time is specified. In some unusual circumstances, goodwill can be written off directly to an equity account.

The Netherlands.   Goodwill can be (1) written off directly to income at the time of acquisition, (2) charged against a stockholders' equity account, or (3) amortized to expense over the anticipated period to be benefited (usually five years).

Singapore.   Goodwill is normally capitalized and then amortized to expense over its useful life. However, goodwill can also be charged against an equity account at the date of acquisition. A new proposal currently under study would eliminate this second option.

International Accounting Standards.   In an example of the availability of options found within international accounting standards, goodwill may be either capitalized and then written off to income or charged immediately against shareholders' equity. If capitalized, the cost should be amortized on a systematic method over an estimated useful life. The IASC is now proposing to limit such alternative treatments by requiring goodwill to be recorded as an asset which would be amortized as an expense over 5 years (although a period of up to 20 years could be used if justified).

Reporting Accounting Changes

United Kingdom.   Changes are permitted only if the new method can be justified as preferable. These changes are handled retroactively. Thus, no "cumulative effect of an accounting change" is included within the current year figures. Instead, past balances are adjusted to reflect the impact of the change in method.

Canada.   Accounting for a change in method is retroactive and, thus, similar to the approach used in the United Kingdom. Current recognition is appropriate, though, if necessary data cannot be gathered for restatement purposes. In contrast to the United Kingdom, a new method does not have to be preferable; changes are allowed as long as the method being adopted is a generally accepted accounting principle.

Korea.   Changes in accounting principles are only applied prospectively so that neither a retroactive restatement nor a cumulative effect adjustment is needed. Such changes can only be made if they make the statements more reliable or if mandated by a new accounting principle.

Japan.   In Japan, accounting changes are not made except for good reason and tend to be rare. If made, retroactive restatement is not allowed; the impact of the change on current year figures must be reported.

Denmark.   Changes are recorded prospectively (previous balances are not impacted) except when the changes is made because of a statutory requirement. In such cases, a prior period adjustment is used.

France. The effect of a change is recognized in current income with no restatement. As in Denmark, a change in accounting regulations is usually recorded retroactively.

Mexico. The accounting effect of a change is recognized in the current year. Because of legal requirements, no retroactive application is allowed.

Germany. Effect is recognized currently.

International Accounting Standards. In *IAS 8,* accounting changes were permitted but only if required by law or by a national accounting standards body or if the change would result in a more appropriate presentation of financial information. According to this pronouncement, the impact of the change on current and prior years should be quantified and disclosed. However, the IASC avoided prescribing a preferable method of presentation.

The Reporting of Inventory

United Kingdom. Inventory is carried at the lower of cost or net realizable value. LIFO is not permitted for tax purposes, and therefore, its application is rare.

Canada. Inventory is carried at lower of cost or market. Market value can be determined by any appropriate method. FIFO, LIFO, and averaging are all allowed by Canadian accounting standards. The reporting entity is supposed to select the method that provides the fairest matching of costs. As in the United Kingdom, LIFO is not accepted for tax purposes so that its use is limited.

New Zealand. Inventory is carried at lower of cost or net realizable value. Cost can be determined by FIFO or averaging but LIFO is not acceptable.

Sweden. Inventory is carried at lower of cost or real value. Real value is net realizable value or, in some cases, replacement cost. FIFO is required for tax purposes and, thus, is also the predominant method in Sweden for financial reporting purposes.

Spain. Inventory is carried at lower of cost or market value. Market value is replacement cost or net realizable value, if less. Specific identification is preferred for costing purposes. If specific identification of items is not possible, averaging should be applied. FIFO and LIFO are acceptable but only if the reporting entity considers them more appropriate. LIFO is not permitted for tax purposes.

Japan. Inventory is carried at lower of cost or market. Market value is usually the repurchase price. FIFO, LIFO, and averaging are all allowed as is specific identification.

Hong Kong.   Inventory is carried at lower of cost or net realizable value. FIFO, specific identification, and averaging are all frequently applied. LIFO is not normally used.

France.   Inventory is carried at lower of cost or either realizable value or replacement cost. FIFO and averaging are the only methods permitted for statutory reporting purposes. LIFO is allowed for consolidated financial statements.

Germany.   Inventory is carried at lower of cost or market. Market value is replacement cost or net realizable value. Specific identification is preferred. However, if not possible, the moving average method is recommended. FIFO and LIFO are permitted.

International Accounting Standards.   Inventory is carried at lower of cost or net realizable value. Currently, the IASC recognizes FIFO, specific identification, weighted average, LIFO, and the base stock method. A proposal has been made to require specific identification for specific projects and either FIFO or averaging for other inventory. However, recently, the IASC decided to reconsider the elimination of LIFO.

Foreign Currency Balances and Transactions

United Kingdom.   Individual transactions should be stated at the rate in effect at the date of the transaction. Subsequently, monetary assets and liabilities are restated at the current exchange rate with any change in these balances creating an increase or decrease in net income. For foreign subsidiaries, income statement accounts are normally translated at the average rate for the year. Balance sheet accounts are translated using the closing rate. Any effect created by the use of different rates is recorded as a reserve within the Capital and Reserve section of the balance sheet.

Nigeria.   Individual transactions are remeasured using the temporal method (see Chapter 9). However, any gains and losses on long-term monetary items with fixed lives (a bond, for example) must be deferred and amortized over the life of the item. Foreign subsidiaries are classified as either integrated or self-sustaining. The temporal method is applied to all integrated subsidiaries. The current rate method is considered appropriate for self-sustaining subsidiaries.

Canada.   Method is similar to that of Nigeria.

Spain.   In measuring individual transactions, tangible assets and investments are reported at historical rates. All other balance sheet accounts are shown at current rates. For income statement accounts, two separate groups are determined: the first for currencies fully convertible with the Spanish peseta and the second for all other currencies. For each group, an unrealized gain or loss is determined. Losses are then recognized as a reduction in income whereas gains are deferred. In reporting foreign subsidiaries, the current the rate method is applied. However, if the subsidiary is merely an extension of the parent, the temporal method is required.

Germany.   For foreign currency transactions, the historical exchange rate at the date of the transaction is applied. Subsequently, for receivables and payables, remeasurement may be required at current exchange rates. At year-end, receivables are reported based on the lower of the historical rate or the year-end rate.

Discussion Question: Which Accounting Method Really Is Appropriate?

In this era of rapidly changing technology, research and development expenditures are one of the most important factors in the future success of many companies. Organizations that spend too little on R & D risk being left behind by the competition. Conversely, companies that spend too much may waste money or not be able to make efficient use of the results.

In the United States, all research and development expenditures are expensed as incurred. This same treatment is used in Germany. However, expensing all research and development costs is not an approach used in much of the world. In the United Kingdom, development costs can be capitalized if a clearly defined project exists, the expenditure is separately identifiable, future revenues are expected to be greater than the capitalized cost, the company has the ability to complete the project, and the outcome has been assessed with reasonable certainty. In Spain, both research and development costs may be capitalized if the project is specifically identified, costs can be clearly defined, and good reason exists to believe that the project will be successful. Japanese accounting allows both research and development costs to be capitalized if the research is directed toward new goods or techniques, development of markets, or exploitation of resources. Korean businesses capitalize their research and development costs when they are incurred in relation to a specific product or technology, when costs can be separately identified, and when the recovery of costs is reasonably expected. A number of other methods are utilized throughout the world to record research and development costs.

Should any portion of research and development costs be capitalized? Is the expensing of all research and development expenditures the best method of reporting these vital costs? Is the American system necessarily the best approach? Which approach provides the best representation of the company's activities?

Conversely, payables are reported using the higher of the historical rate or the year-end rate. No requirements exist for translating foreign subsidiaries. Thus, changes may be recorded directly to net income or within stockholders' equity. For consistency purposes, the same method must be used each year.

Japan.   Foreign currency transactions are recorded initially at the rate in effect on the date of the transaction. Short-term monetary rights and obligations are remeasured subsequently using current exchange rates. Long-term monetary rights and obligations use the historical rate existing when acquired or incurred. However, if a significant change in the rate has occurred, the current rate must be used. Remeasurement of accounts to the current exchange rate affects net income. A similar method is used for translating foreign subsidiaries except that any translation adjustment account is presented as an asset or liability although reporting within net income or stockholders' equity is also encountered.

International Accounting Standards.   Individual foreign currency transactions should be initially recorded at the rate in effect on the date of the transaction. Monetary items are subsequently remeasured using current exchange rates with the impact affecting net income. However, a change in the reported value of a long-term monetary item may be deferred and recognized over its life. Foreign subsidiaries are separated into two classes: those that are an integral part of the parent's operations and those that are self-sustaining which accumulate cash, realize revenues, and incur expenses and costs normally with all transactions dominated in the local currency. For self-sustaining subsidiaries, the current rate should be used for all assets and liabilities. Income statement items are reported at historical rates (either actual or average for the period). In contrast, subsidiaries that are an integral part of the parent's operations should use the same method as the parent.

Summary

1. The world is rapidly developing a global economy with numerous multinational corporations. U.S. companies are expanding into other countries while foreign investors are acquiring many American businesses. Thus, a knowledge of the accounting principles applied throughout the world is necessary to be an efficient decision maker, especially when dealing with international capital markets. The wide diversity of these accounting principles can make the understanding of reported financial information as well as the comparison of companies a difficult task.

2. Because of the perceived need to eliminate inferior accounting principles and promote comparability across national boundaries, the International Accounting Standards Committee was formed in 1973. The IASC currently includes more than 100 member organizations from around the world and has produced 31 International Accounting Standards. As a private organization, the IASC cannot legally enforce these pronouncements. Instead, any country with a poor system of establishing accounting standards is urged to accept the work of the IASC. Other nations have been asked to harmonize standards with the pronouncements of this group. The IASC has also attempted to gain endorsement of its work by the regulators of the various capital markets throughout the world.

3. Unfortunately, nationalism as well as fundamental differences between countries and their economic systems have inhibited the acceptance of international standards. In hopes of achieving initial success, the IASC originally chose to allow numerous alternative procedures. However, the global markets have failed to endorse the work of the IASC in part because of the availability of so many options. Proposals are currently being put forth to eliminate many of these alternative treatments.

4. The accounting standards in Japan, Germany and several other countries are based on government regulation and are quite conservative. Financial institutions and government officials are considered the primary users of published financial data. In the United Kingdom, individual investors are the main users of statements (and accounting standards are set by the accounting profession). The financial statements of these countries exhibit a number of unique characteristics when viewed from the perspective of a U.S. company. For example, the profit and loss statement in Japan labels a wide variety of transactions as extraordinary (or special). In both Germany and the United Kingdom, the balance sheet begins with fixed assets.

5. The accounting principles in many foreign countries allow the presentation of reserves within stockholders' equity. These accounts are used to record many types of transactions so that net income is not affected. For example, such entries are made, in some countries, to adjust assets to their fair market values. Unfortunately, the purpose of reserve accounts are not always well explained in footnote disclosure.

6. Accounting principles throughout the world often differ from those applied in the United States. For example, although the recording of assets such as inventory, land, buildings, and equipment is based on historical cost in the United States, some countries allow companies to adjust these balances to higher values. This procedure is normally used to account for the impact of inflation. In addition, American companies produce consolidated financial statements based on either the purchase method or the pooling of interests method depending on 12 specific criteria. Some countries, though, apply the pooling of interests method to a variety of business combinations whereas in other areas this method is prohibited. In other countries (such as Korea), parent company statements alone are frequently produced with consolidation information included only as supplemental data. Goodwill resulting from a purchase may be charged to stockholders' equity (as in the United Kingdom) or written off over a period as short as 5 years (Germany) or as long as 40 years (the United States).

Comprehensive Illustration

PROBLEM   (Estimated Time: 15 to 20 minutes)

Part A

A company is preparing financial statements for the year ending December 31, 1995. To arrive at final figures, the company must account for goodwill of $1 million resulting from the acquisition of a subsidiary on January 1. The company wants to report the minimum amount of expense each year and can justify an almost unlimited life for the intangible benefits of the business combination from which the goodwill was derived.

What expense should be reported if the company is preparing statements under the accounting rules and principles of each of the following:

- United Kingdom.
- Canada.
- Japan.
- France.
- Germany.
- United States.
- Rules of the International Accounting Standards Committee.

Part B

A company plans to switch from one accounting principle to another at the beginning of 1995 and can justify this decision. Application of the new method would have increased net income in past years by $300,000 while raising net income in 1995 by $100,000.

What is the impact on current net income if the company is preparing statements under the accounting rules and principles of each of the following:

- United Kingdom.
- Canada.
- Mexico.
- Korea.
- United States.
- Rules of the International Accounting Standards Committee.

Part C

A company owns a piece of land that cost $400,000 when acquired in 1987. At the end of 1995, the land has a fair market value of $760,000.

What figure should be reported for this asset if the company is preparing statements under the accounting rules and principles of each of the following:

- United Kingdom.
- Canada.
- Japan.
- France.
- Korea.
- Brazil.
- Germany.
- United States.
- Rules of the International Accounting Standards Committee.

SOLUTION

Part A

United Kingdom.   Goodwill can be written off directly to stockholders' equity so that expense recognition is not necessary. This approach is popular because no expense is recorded. Thus, a maximum amount of net income is always reported.

Canada.   A period of up to 40 years can be used for amortization purposes so that the minimum expense for 1995 is $25,000.

Japan.   A five-year period is normally used for amortization purposes when this intangible asset is encountered. Thus, an expense of $200,000 is appropriate for 1995. A longer life may be used but only if that period of time can be justified.

France.   In France, a 5- to 20-year period is used as the life for goodwill. Since the minimum expense is desired, a 20-year period would be chosen to arrive at an expense of $50,000 each year.

Germany.   An amortization period of 5 years (including the year of acquisition) is normal but, if justified, the time period can be extended to 40 years. Consequently, under German accounting rules, the minimum amortization expense for 1995 is $25,000 if that longer period is considered appropriate.

United States.   As with Canada, a 40-year period is maximum. In this example, the expense to be recognized over that period is $25,000 per year.

International Accounting Standards.   The IASC currently recommends a five-year amortization period that can be extended to 20 years. However, as in the United Kingdom, a direct write-off to stockholders' equity is permitted. Thus, using this second option, no expense recognition is required. As discussed in the chapter, this alternative may soon be eliminated.

Part B

United Kingdom.   In reporting this change in accounting principle, the net income for past years would be increased by $300,000 while current income would rise by $100,000. Retroactive adjustment is utilized in the United Kingdom for accounting changes.

Canada.   As with the United Kingdom, the impact on past years would not affect the 1995 income. A $300,000 retroactive restatement is made to adjust all historical figures to the newly selected method. For 1995, only the $100,000 increase in net income is recognized.

Mexico.   The entire $400,000 impact is recorded within the current period. For legal reasons, a retroactive change in the reported figures for the past years is not allowed.

Korea.   The effect on the prior years would be left as is. Proper accounting would be limited to the effect on the current year; this change would increase net income by $100,000.

United States.   For most accounting changes, the affected income account (or accounts) is adjusted for the $100,000 so that no special treatment is required in the current operating figures. However, the $300,000 increase in past years' income is shown, net of taxes, at the bottom of the current income statement as a cumulative effect of an accounting change. A few changes (such as a switch from LIFO) are handled through retroactive restatement rather than by the calculation and reporting of a cumulative effect.

International Accounting Standards.   At present, accounting changes are allowed if required by official or legal accounting pronouncements or to achieve a more appropriate presentation. The effect on the current year ($100,000) and on past years ($300,000) must be calculated and disclosed. At present, the IASC has not identified a particular method for this reporting.

Part C

United Kingdom.   The reporting entity has the option of using either the $400,000 historical cost to report the land or can adjust this asset to its $760,000 market value.

Canada.   Historical cost figures ($400,000, in this case) are retained.

Japan.   In Japan, the historical cost of $400,000 would be utilized unless a permanent impairment of value had occurred.

France.   The $400,000 historical cost would be the basis for reporting. However, the company is allowed to adjust the value upward to $760,000 if all applicable assets are revalued. Since this increment is taxable, companies rarely avail themselves of the opportunity for such increases. At times when inflation is severe, the government may also allow (or mandate) a tax-free write-up to fair market value.

Korea. Historical cost is used unless the effects of inflation have been extreme. If the inflation rate since acquisition (as measured by the Bank of Korea wholesale price index) has been 25 percent or more, an adjustment to fair market value is allowed, although not required.

Brazil. Because of the high inflation rate, the historical cost of $400,000 is restated using a government inflation index. If this new figure does not approximate market value, a second adjustment to market value is allowed.

Germany. In the conservative German system, the $400,000 historical cost would be retained.

United States. The historical cost of $400,000 is appropriate for American companies. If permanent impairment of value has occurred, a downward adjustment is required.

International Accounting Standards. The IASC allows both historical cost and market value to be used. Decreases in value are recorded through a reduction in net income. Conversely, an increase in value is established by an increment in a surplus or reserve account reported within stockholders' equity.

Questions

1. Why would the knowledge of accounting principles used throughout the world be important to an American business person?
2. Since a multitude of accounting principles exist in the world, which specific principles are applicable to a particular company?
3. Why have international accounting standards been developed?
4. Why has the ability to make comparisons between companies of different countries become important in recent years?
5. What groups compose the membership of the International Accounting Standards Committee?
6. What are the goals of the IASC?
7. Why is the IASC not able to enforce the accounting principles that it issues?
8. Over the years, how has the IASC attempted to gain acceptance of the international standards that it has produced?

9. What problems has the IASC encountered in trying to gain acceptance for the international standards that have been issued?

10. What three different models have been identified to describe the development of accounting principles throughout the world? What is the major influence on each of these models?

11. What significant differences exist between the Continental Model and the British-American model?

12. Why have the standards issued by the IASC to date included many available alternatives? What changes in this approach have been proposed?

13. Why has interest in international accounting standards increased in recent years?

14. What impact would the acceptance of international accounting standards by the regulators of the global capital markets have?

15. What is the basis for the accounting principles used in Japan, the United Kingdom, and Germany?

16. How does an income statement produced by a Japanese company differ from that produced by an American corporation?

17. How does a balance sheet prepared for a U.K. company differ from the statement that would be produced by an American company?

18. Why is the net income figure computed by a German company often assumed to be understated?

19. What body now produces accounting standards in the United Kingdom? How does it differ from the group that was previously in charge of this process?

20. In the United States, historical cost is the basis for valuing assets, especially inventory, land, buildings, and equipment. What other valuation methods are utilized in countries around the world?

21. Why does a country such as Korea allow periodic increments in the reported value of assets?

22. How is the pooling of interests method applied in countries around the world?

23. How do companies in the United Kingdom usually account for goodwill? Why is this approach considered controversial?

24. How are accounting changes reported in countries around the world?

25. How are research and development costs recorded around the world?

Library Assignments

1. Read the following articles and any other published information concerning international accounting standards and the IASC:

   "International Accounting Standards: Are They Coming to America?" *The CPA Journal*, October 1992.

"An Appraisal of the International Accounting Standards Committee," *The CPA Journal*, May 1986.

"The Move to Globalization," *Journal of Accountancy*, March 1989.

"Calling All National Standards Setters," *Accountancy*, February 1988.

"The International Harmonization of Accounting: In Search of Influence,". *The International Journal of Accounting* 27, no. 3 (1992).

"Commentary—Internationalization of Accounting Standards," *Accounting Horizons,* March 1990.

"International Accounting Standards: A New Perspective," *Accounting Horizons,* September 1989.

"Is GAAP the Gap to International Markets?" *Management Accounting,* August 1990.

Write a report describing the activities of the International Accounting Standards Committee to date and discussing this group's chances of future success.

2. Obtain a set of financial statements for a foreign company such as Volkswagen, Sony, Toyota, Daimler-Benz, British Petroleum, or Nissan. List five major differences that can be identified between these statements and the statements that would be produced by a U.S. corporation.

Problems

1. Which of the following is not a reason for establishing international accounting principles?
   a. Some countries continue to use inferior accounting principles.
   b. Comparability is needed between companies operating in different areas of the world.
   c. Some of the accounting principles allowed in various countries report markedly different results for similar transactions.
   d. Demand in the United States is heavy for an alternative to U.S. generally accepted accounting principles.

2. The International Accounting Standards Committee (IASC) was formed by representatives of several different
   a. Government agencies.
   b. Accountancy bodies.
   c. Legislative organizations.
   d. Academic organizations.

3. The goal of the IASC is to
   a. Formulate and publish accounting standards as well as harmonize accounting standards.
   b. Establish a quality review process for all international financial statements.
   c. Promote adequate reporting disclosure so that unique accounting standards can continue to be employed around the world.

d. Require that all financial standards be consistent with the standards used in the United States because of its central role in the capital markets of the world.

4. Why does the IASC currently have only limited powers?
   a. The IASC is a private organization and, thus, cannot enforce the use of its official pronouncements.
   b. The IASC has always refused to mandate that its pronouncements must be followed.
   c. International capital markets establish and use their own accounting principles which must be followed in all cases.
   d. The IASC is a new organization that has not yet had time to exert significant influence in the world of accounting.

5. How does the Continental Model differ from the British-American Model?
   a. The Continental Model is primarily designed to meet the needs of the investing public.
   b. In the Continental Model, compliance with government regulations is of primary importance.
   c. The Continental Model was created primarily to deal with the problems of those financial reporting areas of the world burdened by high inflation rates.
   d. Accounting practices in the Continental Model tend to overstate reported earnings.

6. The IASC
   a. Held its first meeting in 1911.
   b. Is composed of representatives of various governmental accounting bodies.
   c. Began with 84 member organizations.
   d. Was formed in 1973.

7. Which of the following countries does not follow the British-American Model of accounting?
   a. Hong Kong.
   b. Spain.
   c. Australia.
   d. Canada.

8. According to critics, what is the major problem with the standards produced by the IASC?
   a. Too many popular methods have been eliminated.
   b. Too many optional methods have remained.
   c. The IASC has failed to examine and report on key accounting issues.
   d. The pronouncements tend to be too similar to U.S. GAAP.

9. Why would some German companies probably prefer to follow the accounting standards of the IASC?
   a. German accounting principles are extremely complicated so that appropriate financial statements can be difficult to produce.

  b. The Germans have tended to follow U.S. generally accepted accounting principles rather than develop their own accounting principles.

  c. German accounting principles are quite conservative so that net income usually appears to be low.

  d. The Germans have virtually no accounting principles so that comparison between companies within the country is virtually impossible.

10. Why have international accounting principles become a topic of special interest in recent times?

  a. The development of international capital markets and the continued consolidation of the European Community have created a need for comparable information from companies located around the world.

  b. The Financial Accounting Standards Board has recently asked the IASC to develop solutions to several specific accounting issues, including earnings per share.

  c. Most multinational companies have switched to international accounting standards rather than continue to use national standards.

  d. A number of IASC pronouncements have forced the FASB to change several significant American accounting principles.

11. What attempt is being made by the IASC to gain greater acceptance of international accounting standards?

  a. Rules are now being mandated for individual countries.

  b. An attempt is being made to provide more flexibility within the international standards.

  c. The IASC is developing a new system of accounting principles to be applied according to the size of the organization.

  d. Optional methods are being eliminated.

12. Japanese accounting principles are

  a. Promulgated by the Japanese Institute of Certified Public Accountants.

  b. Controlled by the government.

  c. Quite liberal in nature.

  d. Similar in most respects to international accounting standards.

13. In Japan, extraordinary items are

  a. Never reported.

  b. More limited than in the United States.

  c. Items not considered extraordinary in the United States.

  d. Unusual and infrequent.

14. In the United Kingdom, a balance sheet

  a. Begins with fixed assets and then reports current assets less current liabilities.

  b. Is not required except for companies of a specific size.

  c. Begins with stockholders' equity.

  d. Is similar to a balance sheet that would be produced by a U.S. company.

15. In the United Kingdom, Stocks and Debtors accounts are encountered. What do these balances represent?

	Stocks	*Debtors*
a.	Investments	Minority interest
b.	Treasury stock	Notes payable
c.	Capital stock	Notes receivable
d.	Inventory	Receivables

16. In the financial reporting utilized in the United Kingdom, to what does the term *turnover* refer?
    a. Net sales.
    b. Age of inventory.
    c. Length of time needed to collect accounts receivable.
    d. Profit as a percentage of net assets.

17. In German accounting, reserve account balances represent
    a. Assets invested for specified future use.
    b. Equity balances used to record adjustments not included in computing net income.
    c. Annual adjustments to net income caused by the effects of inflation.
    d. Contra asset accounts.

18. Accounting rules in Germany tend to vary according to what criterion?
    a. Age of a company.
    b. Number of shareholders.
    c. Size of a company.
    d. Type of business.

19. How do Japanese and United Kingdom accounting principles differ in the valuation of assets?
    a. In the United Kingdom, all assets are based on historical cost, while in Japan market value is always used.
    b. Both countries use a valuation basis for assets. In the United Kingdom, current cost is required, while in Japan market value is appropriate.
    c. In the United Kingdom, a valuation basis may be used but in Japan historical cost is appropriate unless a permanent impairment of value has occurred.
    d. In the United Kingdom, assets are always recorded at net present value, whereas in Japan current cost must be used.

20. Which of the following is a major influence on German financial reporting?
    a. The public that provides the financial capital.
    b. The Securities Transactions Committee.
    c. German banks because they provide a major portion of the financial capital.
    d. The International Accounting Standards Committee.

21. Which of the following is reported by a German company using a type-of-cost income statement format?
    a. All income items other than revenues from the sale of inventory are labeled as extraordinary gains and losses.
    b. Changes in inventory levels are reported as adjustments to sales.
    c. Cost of goods sold is shown prior to revenues.
    d. Income taxes are not viewed as expenses.

22. Why is the revaluation of assets rare in France?
    a. Inflation is low.
    b. Revaluation gains are taxed by the government.
    c. Revaluations can only be made with specific types of objective proof.
    d. Accounting principles are extremely conservative in France.

23. What basis is used for valuing assets in Korea?
    a. Lower of cost or market.
    b. Assessed value for taxation purposes.
    c. Current market value.
    d. Historical cost; however, if inflation is significant, revaluation is permitted.

24. In Korea, business combinations are usually reported through:
    a. Consolidated statements including only domestic companies.
    b. Parent company statements only.
    c. Consolidated statements including subsidiaries in which more than 80 percent of the voting stock is held.
    d. Use of the pooling of interests method only.

25. Goodwill
    a. Can be amortized over a 50-year period in Germany.
    b. Can be written off directly to stockholders' equity in the United Kingdom.
    c. Is accounted for in the same manner in Japan as in the United States.
    d. Is expensed immediately in Canada.

26. LIFO
    a. Is a preferred method according to international accounting standards.
    b. Is required in Japan.
    c. Is an allowed method in Canada.
    d. Is the predominant method used in the United Kingdom because of the rate of inflation.

27. In reporting research and development expenditures,
    a. Most countries follow the method used in the United States.
    b. Many countries capitalize some portion of research and development costs.
    c. Usually only one approach is found throughout the world.
    d. Most countries record all research and development costs as expenses when incurred.

28. Answer the following questions about international accounting:
    a. What factors have tended to prevent the acceptance of international accounting standards?
    b. What is the present composition of the International Accounting Standards Committee?
    c. What are the goals of the IASC?
    d. What problem has been associated with the pronouncements to date of the IASC? Why has this problem occurred and what is the IASC doing to resolve the concern?
    e. In what ways can the IASC become a stronger force in financial reporting throughout the world?

29. A multinational company is planning to raise a significant amount of capital funds by issuing stocks and bonds in the United States, the United Kingdom, Japan, and France. What impact would international accounting standards have on the reporting of this company?

30. A financial advisor is investigating two companies as possible investment recommendations. One of the companies is headquartered in Japan while the other operates in the United Kingdom. In comparing the financial statements of these two organizations, what aspects of the national accounting principles should the investor consider?

31. A German company reports a net income figure that is to be compared with that of a counterpart company located in the United States. What factors should be considered in making this evaluation?

32. Chapter 10 (as well as several previous chapters) has described a number of techniques used to account for goodwill. List the possible methods for reporting and amortizing this intangible asset. Which method actually provides the fairest presentation of the consolidated company's financial operations and position?

33. In what situations do the countries of the world allow some portion of research and development expenditures to be capitalized?

34. Compare and contrast a balance sheet produced by a German company with a balance sheet developed for a United Kingdom company.

35. Describe the various possible methods utilized throughout the world to account for:

    • Accounting changes.
    • Research and development expenditures.
    • Inventory costs.
    • Foreign currency balances.

SEGMENT REPORTING

Questions to Consider

- The consolidation process brings together the many, varied components of a business combination to form a single set of financial statements. How can a reader of such statements evaluate the results and prospects of the individual segments that make up the organization?
- How are the industry segments of a company identified, and how is the significance of each of these units determined?
- What guidance has the FASB provided to reporting entities concerning disclosure of foreign operations, export sales, and major customers?
- What information must a company disclose in its financial statements about its various segments?

An advertisement in *The Wall Street Journal* posed a question that is germane to the entire concept of reporting consolidated financial statements: "How do you get the whole picture when you're researching conglomerates?" Although this ad was designed to extol the analytical abilities of a well-known investment firm, the development of a legitimate answer to this inquiry has long been a concern of financial accounting.

In preparing statements for any business combination composed of diversified branches, divisions, or corporations, data must be blended together from many, varied activities. Because the resulting figures represent the entity as a single unit, the operations and financial position of individual components become indistinguishable. Such aggregated information can prove to be of limited value to decision makers, a problem that diminishes the potential utility of the financial statements.

Pfizer, Inc., as an illustration, reported consolidated net sales for 1991 of $6.95 billion. However, to a potential investor looking at the company, this revenue figure may be of limited importance; the source of this revenue is also information that is needed. Consequently, according to Pfizer's annual report, the company's revenue was generated from these different ventures: approximately $5.0 billion came from health care, $696 million from consumer products, $526 million from animal health care, and $730 million from specialty chemicals and minerals.

Additional information disclosed by Pfizer indicated that $3.8 billion of the 1991 consolidated sales were generated in the United States, $1.6 billion in Europe, $950 million in Asia, $432 million in Canada/Latin America, and $146 million in Africa and the Middle East. Such information, describing the various components of Pfizer's operations (both industry segments and geographic segments), can often be more useful to an analyst than the single sales figure reported in the consolidated income statement. "All investors like segment reporting—separate financials for each division—because it enables them to analyze how well each part of a corporation is doing."[1]

Disaggregated Information—Historical Perspective

To facilitate the analysis and evaluation of financial data, several groups began to push the accounting profession in the 1960s to require disclosure of disaggregated figures such as those reported by Pfizer. Not surprisingly, the timing of this movement corresponded with a period of significant corporate merger and acquisition activity. As business organizations expanded through ever-widening diversification, financial statement analysis became increasingly difficult.

> The broadening of an enterprise's activities into different industries or geographic areas complicates the analysis of conditions, trends, and ratios and, therefore, the ability to predict. The various industry segments or geographic areas of operations of an enterprise may have different rates of profitability, degrees and types of risk, and opportunities for growth.[2]

Because of the increasingly diverse activities of many organizations, disclosure of additional information was sought to help the readers of financial statements. The identity of the significant elements of an entity's operations was viewed as an important complement to consolidated totals. Thus, such organizations as the Financial Analysts Federation and the Financial Executives Institute provided support for the inclusion of data describing the major components (or segments) of an enterprise as a means of enhancing the informational content of corporate financial statements.

---

[1] Robert A. Parker, "How Do You Play the New Annual Report Game?" *Communication World*, September 1990, p. 26.

[2] *FASB SFAS 14*, "Financial Reporting for Segments of a Business Enterprise," December 1976, par. 59.

SFAS 14—Guidelines for Segment Reporting

As a result of the demand for disaggregated information, a number of official steps have been taken since the 1960s to encourage or mandate such presentation within financial statements. During this period, the Accounting Principles Board (APB) and the New York Stock Exchange both urged companies to present such data voluntarily. The Securities and Exchange Commission as well as the Federal Trade Commission required the reporting of certain line-of-business information within documents filed with those bodies.

However, because of the cost to generate this data and the fear that confidential information would be disclosed to competitors, not all reporting corporations agreed with these requirements. "Segment reporting came into being after a vicious battle waged between the Federal Trade Commission and big corporations in the mid-1970s. The corporations fought the FTC's demands for income statements and balance sheets on each of their different lines of business all the way to the Supreme Court, and they lost."[3]

The move toward dissemination of disaggregated information culminated in December 1976 with the release by the FASB of *SFAS 14*, "Financial Reporting for Segments of a Business Enterprise." This pronouncement established guidelines for the presentation within corporate financial statements of information to describe the various segments that constitute each reporting entity. Currently, though, as part of its broad project on consolidations and related matters, the FASB intends to look once again at the matter of disclosing disaggregated data to determine whether changes are needed in these requirements.

As an illustration of the current guidelines, a note to the 1990 financial statements of Timer Warner Inc. indicated that total consolidated revenues of nearly $12 billion were generated by the following separately identifiable industry segments (in millions):

Publishing	$2,926
Music	2,931
Filmed entertainment	2,904
Programming—HBO	1,266
Cable	1,751

The information reported by Time Warner went on to give the operating income, assets, depreciation and amortization, and the total amount of capital expenditures for each of these segments.

The disaggregated data reported by a company is not limited to an analysis of just industrial segments. The 1991 annual report of the Colgate-Palmolive Company, for example, disclosed the following information about its operations in several different geographical areas (in millions):

---

[3] Dana Wechsler and Katarzyna Wandycz, "An Innate Fear of Disclosure," *Forbes*, February 5, 1990.

	Net Sales	Operating Profit	Identifiable Assets
United States and Canada	$2,195.9	$ 98.8	$1,942.8
Europe.	1,968.7	25.8	1,243.6
Latin America	1,075.4	113.4	526.0
Asia and Africa	820.3	65.2	454.5

Data describing industry segments and geographical locations is not the only disaggregated information to be disclosed based on the standards set by *SFAS 14*. The financial statements of Caterpillar Inc. reported, as required by this same pronouncement, that $3.539 billion of its 1991 sales came from exporting products to customers outside of the United States (the largest amount was $1.011 billion to the Asia/Pacific area). Hasbro, Inc., was also complying with *Statement 14* by disclosing "sales to the Company's largest customer, Toys R Us, Inc., amounted to 17 percent of consolidated net revenues during 1991 and 14 percent in 1990 and 1989."

Segment Reporting Overview

As can be seen in these corporate illustrations, *SFAS 14* has had a significant impact on the financial reporting process. Presently, the disclosure of disaggregated (or segment) data is mandatory for all publicly held corporations.[4] In many cases, this information is made available within the financial statement notes. However, a company is also allowed to report segment data in the body of the statements or as a separate schedule attached to the financial statements.

Statement 14 requires specific financial information to be presented portraying as many as four distinct aspects of a company's operations. Although these disclosures will be analyzed in detail at later points in the chapter, the following overview is designed as an introduction to the major requirements established by the pronouncement.

1. *Industry segments.* A company must disclose for each reportable industry segment:
   a. Revenues.
   b. Operating profit or loss.
   c. Identifiable assets.

---

[4] *SFAS 14* originally mandated segment reporting of all companies. Because of the reporting burden that this rule placed on small, closely held companies (as well as a question as to the value of the information being conveyed in such cases), the necessity of including *SFAS 14* disclosures has been dropped for nonpublic enterprises. *FASB SFAS 21*, "Suspension of the Reporting of Earnings per Share and Segment Information by Nonpublic Enterprises," issued in April 1978, eliminated the requirement that such organizations report either segment information or earnings per share figures.

    d. Aggregate amount of depreciation, depletion, and amortization expense.

    e. Capital expenditures.

    f. Equity in the net income from an investment in the net assets of equity investees.

2. *Domestic and foreign operations.* A company must disclose for domestic operations as well as for operations in each significant foreign geographic area:

    a. Revenues.

    b. Operating profit or loss.

    c. Identifiable assets.

3. *Export sales.* A company must report for domestic operations:

    a. Amount of revenue derived from exporting products to unaffiliated customers in foreign countries.

4. *Major customers.* A company must disclose:

    a. Amount of revenue derived from sales to each major customer.

Usefulness of Disaggregated Financial Information

The reporting of segment information supposedly enhances the usefulness of a corporation's financial statements. Interestingly, in discussing disaggregation in *Statement 14*, the FASB warned that the resulting data would not enable comparisons to be made between the segments of different companies. Because companies can be organized in many ways, a segment identified by one enterprise cannot necessarily be equated to a segment found in any other company. The development of rigid, detailed disaggregation techniques that could be consistently applied by all companies was not considered an achievable goal. Thus, the FASB opted to provide guidance in several areas rather than prescribe strict rules that might lead to unrealistic comparisons being made between companies.

As one example, identification of the specific industry segments that compose a company is ultimately left to the judgment of the management. Thus, each entity may select a different approach for dividing the organization into segments. In addition, several methods exist for allocating common corporate expenses to the individual industry segments. Hence, *SFAS 14* (par. 76) includes the following disclaimer: "Information prepared in conformity with those standards may be of limited usefulness for comparing an industry segment of one enterprise with a similar industry segment of another enterprise."

This disavowal immediately raises a question as to the FASB's underlying reason for mandating disaggregation. According to *SFAS 14* (par. 76), "The purpose of the information required to be disclosed . . . is to assist financial statement users in analyzing and understanding the enterprise's financial statements by permitting better assessment of the enterprise's *past performance and future prospects.*" (emphasis added)

Thus, inclusion of data describes the various segments of an organization is justified because the reader of the financial statements is able to make a better year-to-year evaluation of the entity. The past and present operational success of each corporate component can be analyzed on an ongoing basis. General Cinema (now Harcourt General) Corporation, as an example, disclosed an overall increase of $25 million in its revenues between 1990 and 1991. However, during that time, two of its four industry segments (publishing and insurance) actually had a decline in revenues totaling more than $37 million. Although of significant interest to anyone evaluating the company, this information is not evident from the single revenue figure presented on the consolidated income statement.

Just as important, segment data can assist analysts in predicting the effects that will result from future changes in an organization's environment. For example, if a recession is anticipated for textile manufacturing, the degree of a company's involvement in that industry is vital information to a present or potential investor. Similarly, data describing operations in a particular area of the world is of immediate interest if political turbulence becomes prevalent in that vicinity.

Disaggregated Information—Industry Segments

The most commonly disclosed segment data found in corporate financial statements concerns the various industries in which a company does business. Because of diversification, a large percentage of the publicly held companies in the world today maintain operations in more than a single industry. For these companies, *SFAS 14* requires financial statement disclosure of disaggregated information to describe the operating results and financial position of each reportable segment. Thus, accountants must

- Identify the individual segments.
- Determine which of these segments are of significant size to warrant separate disclosure.

Identifying Industry Segments

In producing *Statement 14*, one of the principal issues faced by the FASB was the development of guidelines that could be applied in identifying the boundaries of a company's industry segments. To provide assistance in making this determination, *Statement 14* (par. 10[a]) defined an industry segment as a "component of an enterprise engaged in providing a product or service or a group of related products and services primarily to unaffiliated customers (i.e., customers outside the enterprise) for a profit."

Although this definition seems reasonable, problems are often encountered in actual application. An industry segment can be viewed as a very broad classification encompassing many, varied products and services that are only slightly related by nature. Conversely, a company may narrowly define its industry segments by including only closely related products or services within each segment. For example, a company producing baseball bats in one manufacturing plant and pool cues in a separate facility can properly view these operations as lying entirely within a single industry: production of sporting goods. Alternatively, this same enterprise may perceive these products as basically unrelated, therefore indicating the existence of two segments: the production of baseball bats and the production of pool cues.

According to the definition supplied by *SFAS 14*, the key distinction identifying the boundaries of an industry segment is the interrelationship of products and services, obviously a very subjective criterion. The pronouncement does offer additional guidance by listing three factors that should be weighed in determining the degree of relationship between specific products and services:

1. The nature of the products—their purposes and end uses.
2. The nature of the production process—the sharing, for example, of production or sales facilities or the use of similar raw materials.
3. Markets and marketing methods—the similarity of such factors as marketing areas, types of customers, and marketing methods.

Even with this assistance, the FASB has left the identification of a company's industry segments as a subjective process not controlled by absolute rules. Determination of an entity's segments must depend ultimately on decisions made by company officials. *SFAS 14* (par. 13) does proceed to suggest, however, that "an enterprise's existing profit centers—the smallest units of activity for which revenue and expense information is accumulated for internal planning and control purposes—represent a logical starting point for determining the enterprise's industry segments." As further guidance, the FASB recommends consulting an industry classification system. One such listing specifically mentioned is the Standard Industrial Classification system prepared by the Statistical Policy Division of the U.S. Office of Management and Budget.

Before leaving the issue of segment identification, one other problem should be described. According to the FASB, the division of a company's foreign operations into separate industry segments is not always practical, especially in worldwide organizations. In such cases, the reporting entity is directed to identify as many industry segments as possible. All remaining foreign operations are aggregated and accounted for as a single industry segment accompanied by appropriate disclosure.

Discussion Question: How Many Segments Do We Actually Have?

The Laurence Company was founded in 1939 to publish travel books. From its inception, the company was owned by J. T. Laurence and his family. In 1951, encouraged by the success of the book publishing business, Laurence started a monthly travel magazine that was soon followed by a series of

---

continued

atlases and maps describing major cities throughout the world. Based on the knowledge derived from their detailed study of world travel, the Laurence family created a travel agency in 1959 that has, since that time, opened numerous locations throughout the midwestern section of the United States.

In 1962, Laurence bought a failing restaurant in Charleston, South Carolina. His daughter-in-law became manager of this business and soon turned it into a quite profitable operation. Subsequently, Laurence acquired other restaurants in Orlando, Boston, San Francisco, St. Thomas, Phoenix, New Orleans, London, Tokyo, and Rome. Four of these restaurants were purchased along with hotels that were also brought into the Laurence Company. The Tokyo property included a large convention center and catering service.

Because the restaurants and hotels were located in exclusive areas, the Laurence family began to speculate in antiques and art work. These investments served as decorations until a buyer could be found. Thus, each facility was considered unique because of the displayed antiques and art work that were continually being changed.

Last year, for the first time, a portion of the common stock of the Laurence Company was issued to the public. Consequently, disclosure of segment information is now required. How many different industry segments does this company have?

Determining Significant Industry Segments

After a company has delineated its industry segments, a decision must be made as to which of these operations is of sufficient magnitude to warrant separate financial statement disclosure. In *SFAS 14*, the FASB designed three tests to be used in identifying industry segments for which disclosure is required:

- A revenue test.
- An operating profit or loss test.
- An identifiable assets test.

An industry segment need only to satisfy any one of these tests to be considered of significant size to necessitate disaggregation. Any segment that fails to meet even a single test is still included in the disclosure but is normally merged with a larger industry segment. As an alternative, all of these small segments can be grouped together in an "Other" or "Miscellaneous" category.

To apply these three tests, a segment's revenues, operating profit or loss, and identifiable assets must initially be computed. Because these three figures provide the basis for identifying significant segments, their calculations are reviewed here next. In establishing guidelines for deriving these balances, the FASB took an approach that differs somewhat from a consolidation perspective. The primary distinction concerns the handling of intersegment transactions. *Although removed entirely within the consolidation process, intersegment data is largely included in disaggregated disclosures.* Information describing these transactions is considered relevant in evaluating the contribution made to a company by each of its individual components. However, any transfers made between the companies within a single segment are omitted. They are neither disclosed in the financial statements nor included in this testing process.

Revenues Attributed to an Industry Segment. The calculation of an industry segment's revenues serves here as an introduction to the disaggregation techniques prescribed by *SFAS 14*. To provide complete information about a company's operations, the total of the revenues generated by sales to unaffiliated customers and the intersegment transfers are disclosed for each segment of significant size. Interest income is included within these revenue totals when derived from outside parties or intersegment trade receivables. However, any interest recognized on intersegment loans or advances is excluded unless earned by a segment that functions principally in a financial capacity. Furthermore, because of the operational nature of the disclosed segment figures, such income items as extraordinary gains and losses, the cumulative effect of a change in accounting principles, an allocation to a noncontrolling interest, equity income, and a gain or loss on a discontinued operation are omitted from the revenue totals.

To illustrate these various guidelines, assume that the York Corporation has a segment that manufactures plastic products. This segment reports the following revenue balances for the current year (in millions):

All Revenues—Plastics Segment

Sales to outsiders	$5.0
Interest earned from outsiders	.6
Intersegment sales	2.4
Intersegment interest income on trade receivables	.3
Intersegment interest income on loans	.5
Total revenues	$8.8

For *disaggregation purposes*, the York Corporation calculates revenues for this segment (and would separately disclose the amount if the segment is deemed significant in size) of $8.3 million, the summation of the first four of these figures. Since the operation is not principally of a financial nature, the interest income earned on intersegment loans is excluded from the total.

For disclosure purposes, this information could have been presented in any one of a number of ways such as the following:

Segment Disclosure

Plastics Segment

Revenues from unaffiliated parties.	$5.6 million
Intersegment revenues	2.7 million
Total.	$8.3 million

Only the $5.6 million figure would have been included in the consolidated income statement, the amount relating to transactions consummated with outside parties. Apparently, the FASB viewed the $8.3 million total as a better indicator by which to measure the contribution being made to this company by its plastics segment.

Calculation of Operating Profit and Loss.   Turning now to the operating profit or loss earned by an industry segment, a computational pattern is revealed that is similar to that utilized in determining segment revenues. In fact, the operating profit or loss is no more than the subtraction of a segment's operating expenses from the revenue figure derived in the first test.

Although most intersegment expenses are included in this calculation, several items must be omitted. The principal exclusions are interest expense and income taxes, neither of which is traditionally viewed as an operating expense.[5] General corporate expenses are also eliminated unless they relate to the operation of one or more industry segments of the business.

To demonstrate the calculation of a segment's operating profit or loss, assume that the plastics segment of the York Corporation introduced previously (with reportable revenues of $8.3 million) also has the following account balances (in millions):

All Expenses and Losses—Plastics Segment

Operating expenses—outside sales	$2.3
Operating expenses—intersegment sales	1.0
Interest expense	.4
Income taxes	1.4
Extraordinary loss	1.0
Total	$6.1

Both of the two operating expense figures (totaling $3.3 million) should be appropriately included in determining the disclosed information for this segment.

---

[5] Interest expense is included in determining the operating profit or loss of any industry segment that operates principally in a financial capacity.

Conversely, the interest expense, income taxes, and extraordinary loss are not viewed as operating figures and must be omitted.[6] Therefore, the operating profit applicable to this industry segment is $5 million ($8.3 million in revenues less $3.3 million of operating expenses).

Allocation of Common Costs. Although the determination of an industry segment's operating profit or loss appears to be rather mechanical, a choice of alternative procedures is available at one important juncture in this process. This option arises in connection with the handling of any operating costs that are not directly traceable to a single segment. Many expenses including rent, property taxes, insurance, and maintenance may be shared by two or more segments. In addition, costs incurred by the corporation as a whole (such as advertising and data processing) are often viewed as operating expenses to be assigned to the individual segments. According to *SFAS 14* (par. 10[a]), "those operating expenses incurred by an enterprise that are not directly traceable to an industry segment shall be *allocated on a reasonable basis* among those industry segments for whose benefit the expenses were incurred." (emphasis added)

A cost such as rent can logically be divided between the various segments based on the square footage of space being utilized while payroll accounting costs are often charged according to the number of employees working for each segment. However, other expenses do not always offer such obvious bases for allocation. The assignment of these common costs allows for some degree of management discretion. Such expenses as data processing or general accounting may even require rather sophisticated allocation procedures. Often, if no legitimate basis is readily apparent, a company may simply assign a cost to its segments in an arbitrary fashion, most commonly based on revenues or revenues less traceable costs.

As an illustration, assume that the Carter Company has three identifiable industry segments: furniture manufacturing, paper production, and lumber sales. Revenues and traceable costs relating to each of these segments follow. Traceable costs include all expenses that can be assigned directly to a segment without any need for allocation. (All figures are in millions.)

Industry Segments	Revenues	Traceable Costs	Revenues Less Traceable Costs
Furniture	$10.4	$5.0	$ 5.4
Paper	5.6	2.0	3.6
Lumber	4.0	1.0	3.0
Totals	$20.0	$8.0	$12.0

---

[6] The interest expense is excluded from this computation because the operations of this industry segment are not principally of a financial nature.

Assume further that the Carter Company has incurred an additional $6 million in expenses that cannot be attributed directly to any one of these three industry segments. An investigation of these costs indicates that $4 million of this total represents common expenses that resulted in connection with the operation of the segments. The remaining $2 million is identified as central administration expenses unrelated to the segments.

In calculating the operating profit or loss of each of Carter's segments, a reasonable allocation must be made of the $4 million in common costs, whereas the remaining $2 million is simply excluded. Expenses are not considered appropriate for disaggregation unless related to the operations of at least one of the segments.

Although specific bases for prorating some portion or even all of the $4 million may be evident, such expenses often require, as indicated earlier, some general method of assignment. To illustrate, two different allocations of the $4 million follow: the first is based on segment revenues; the second utilizes the company's revenue figures less traceable costs. As shown here, the amount of expense assigned to each of the three segments can vary significantly depending on the approach chosen.

Allocation Schedule 1
Common Costs Allocated According to Revenues
(in millions)

Furniture . . . . $10.4/$20 × $4 = $2.08
Paper . . . . $5.6/$20 × $4 = 1.12
Lumber . . . . $4.0/$20 × $4 = .80

Total $4.00

Allocation Schedule 2
Common Costs Allocated According to Revenues
Less Traceable Costs
(in millions)

Furniture . . . . $5.4/$12 × $4 = $1.80
Paper . . . . $3.6/$12 × $4 = 1.20
Lumber . . . . $3.0/$12 × $4 = 1.00

Total $4.00

Regardless of the technique used to assign the common costs, the operating expense figure attributed to a particular industry segment includes the allotted balance plus all directly traceable costs. In this example, if Carter chooses to divide the $4 million in common costs based solely on revenues (Allocation Schedule 1), the resulting operating profit disclosed for each segment is derived as follows (in millions):

Operating Profit—Common Costs Allocated on Revenues

Industry Segments	Revenues	Traceable Costs	Common Costs (allocated by revenues)	Operating Profit
Furniture	$10.40	$5.00	$2.08	$3.32
Paper	5.60	2.00	1.12	2.48
Lumber	4.00	1.00	.80	2.20

The Identifiable Assets of an Industry Segment. Having derived a revenue figure for an industry segment as well as its operating profit or loss, the next guidelines apply to the determination of an identifiable asset total. According to *SFAS 14* (par. 10[e]), "identifiable assets of an industry segment are those tangible and intangible enterprise assets that are used by the industry segment, including (i) assets that are used exclusively by that industry segment and (ii) an allocated portion of assets used jointly by two or more industry segments. Assets used jointly by two or more industry segments shall be allocated among the industry segments on a reasonable basis."

The guidance provided by the FASB to assist a company in determining the identifiable assets of its segments is consistent with that demonstrated for both revenues and operating profits and losses. Assets utilized in common by two or more segments must be allocated between the parties in some reasonable fashion. General corporate assets are excluded if not used in connection with the operation of a segment. Intersegment trade receivables are included in a segment's total because they relate to operations, but intersegment loans and advances are omitted (unless the segment holding the asset is principally a financial operation).

As an additional note, the portion of an intersegment investment account that represents the underlying net assets of a subsidiary must be excluded to avoid double-counting. Conversely, any of the investment's cost in excess of this book value figure (such as might be allocated to goodwill or specific asset and liability accounts) is considered an identifiable asset of the investor.

Determining Reportable Industry Segments

The computation of (1) revenues, (2) operating profits and losses, and (3) identifiable assets is merely a preliminary step in ascertaining an enterprise's reportable industry segments. These financial figures are incorporated in three separate tests designed to identify industry segments that possess a size significant enough to warrant separate disclosure. *The presentation of disaggregated information is required for every industry segment that meets even one of these three tests.*

1. *Revenue test.* An industry segment is considered significant if its revenues (as computed earlier) are 10 percent or more of the combined revenues of all industry segments.

2. *Operating profit or loss test.* An industry segment is considered significant if its operating profit or loss is 10 percent or more of the greater (in absolute numbers) of the combined operating profits of all profitable segments or the combined operating losses of all segments incurring a loss.

3. *Identifiable assets test.* An industry segment is considered significant if its identifiable assets are 10 percent or more of the combined identifiable assets of all industry segments.

Application of the revenue and identifiable assets tests would seem to pose few problems. In contrast, the operating profit or loss test is more complicated and warrants illustration. For this purpose, assume that the Durham Company has identified five separate industry segments within its operations. Based on the guidelines previously described, Durham has computed a current operating profit or loss figure for each of these segments:

Durham Company Segments—Operating Profits and Losses

Soft drinks	$1,700,000
Wine	(600,000)
Food products.	240,000
Paper packaging	880,000
Recreation parks	(130,000)
Net operating profit	$2,090,000

Three of these industry segments (soft drinks, food products, and paper packaging) report operating profits that total $2,820,000. The two remaining segments have losses for the year in the amount of $730,000.

Operating Profits		*Operating Losses*	
Soft drinks	$1,700,000	Wine	$600,000
Food products	240,000	Recreation parks	130,000
Paper packaging	880,000		
Total	$2,820,000	Total	$730,000

Consequently, $2,820,000 serves as the basis for the operating profit or loss test because that figure is greater in absolute terms than $730,000. Based on the 10 percent criterion, any segment with either an operating profit *or loss* of more than $282,000 (10% × $2,820,000) is considered significant and, thus, must be disclosed separately. According to this one test, the soft drink and paper packaging segments (with operating of $1.7 million and $880,000, respectively) are both judged to be reportable as is the wine segment, despite having a loss of $600,000.

Testing Procedures—Complete Illustration

To provide a comprehensive example of all three of these testing procedures, assume that the Jackson Company is a large business combination that comprises six industry segments: automotive, furniture, textbook, motion picture, appliance, and finance. Complete information about each of these segments appears in Exhibit 11–1 (see bottom of page 656).

The Revenue Test.   In applying the revenue test to the industry segments of the Jackson Company, only the interest on intersegment loans must be excluded. However, for the finance segment, that exception does not apply. Therefore, revenues for the various segments are calculated as follows (in millions):

	Automotive	Furniture	Textbook	Motion Picture	Appliance	Finance	
Sales to outsiders	$32.6	$6.9	$6.6	$22.2	$3.1	–0–	
Intersegment transfers	6.6	1.2	–0–	–0–	1.9	–0–	
Interest income—outsiders . . .	2.4	.9	.2	.6	.3	8.7	
Interest income— intersegment loans	not included	not included	not included	not included	not included	3.6	
							Total
Segment revenues	$41.6	$9.0	$6.8	$22.8	$5.3	$12.3	$97.8

Because these six segments have total revenues of $97.8 million, that figure is used in applying the revenue test. Based on the 10 percent significance level, any segment with revenues of more than $9.78 million qualifies for required disclosure. Accordingly, the automotive, the motion picture, and finance segments have all satisfied this particular criterion. Appropriate disaggregated information must, therefore, be presented within Jackson's financial statements for each of these three industry segments.

The Operating Profit or Loss Test.   Revenue figures for the six industry segments have already been determined. The accountant merely needs to subtract each segment's operating expenses to arrive at individual profit or loss totals. Income taxes are omitted from this calculation as are all interest expense balances (except for the finance segment). If common costs had been included in this illustration, an appropriate allocation of these expenses would have been necessary.

Industry Segments	Revenues	Operating Expenses	Operating Profit	Operating Loss
Automotive.	$41.6*	$21.9	$19.7	
Furniture.	9.0	4.6	4.4	
Textbook.	6.8	7.3		$ .5
Motion picture	22.8	24.0		1.2
Appliance	5.3	2.4	2.9	
Finance	12.3	9.2	3.1	
Totals	$97.8	$69.4	$30.1	$1.7

* All figures are in millions.

The $30.1 million total (the four operating profit figures) is greater in an absolute sense than the $1.7 million in operating losses. Therefore, this larger balance serves as the basis for the second industry segment test. Because the FASB has again established a 10 percent criterion, either an operating profit or loss of $3.01 million or more qualifies a segment for disaggregation. According to the income totals just calculated, the automotive, furniture, and finance segments of the Jackson Company are large enough to warrant separate disclosure.

EXHIBIT 11–1   Industry Segment Testing Illustrated

JACKSON COMPANY SEGMENTS

	Automotive	Furniture	Textbook	Motion Picture	Appliance	Finance
Revenues:						
Sales to outsiders	$32.6*	$6.9	$6.6	$22.2	$3.1	–0–
Intersegment transfers	6.6	1.2	–0–	–0–	1.9	–0–
Interest income—outsiders	2.4	.9	.2	.6	.3	$8.7
Interest income— intersegment loans	.5	.8	–0–	–0–	.2	3.6
Expenses:						
Operating expenses—outsiders . . .	17.1	3.6	7.3	24.0	1.6	2.3
Operating expenses— intersegment transfers.	4.8	1.0	–0–	–0–	.8	.8
Interest expense	2.1	1.0	2.2	4.6	–0–	6.1
Income taxes	6.6	1.4	(1.5)	(3.1)	.4	.1
Identifiable assets:						
Tangible	9.6	1.1	.8	10.9	.9	9.2
Intangible	1.8	.2	.7	3.6	.1	–0–
Intersegment loans	1.0	1.9	–0–	–0–	.5	5.4

* All figures in millions.

The Identifiable Assets Test.   The final test designed by the FASB is based on a segment's total identifiable assets. In applying this test, intersegment loans have been omitted, although, once again, the exclusion does not apply to Jackson's finance segment (in millions):

Automotive	$11.4
Furniture	1.3
Textbook	1.5
Motion picture	14.5
Appliance	1.0
Finance	14.6
Total identifiable assets	$44.3

Because 10 percent of the company's total equals $4.43 million, any segment holding at least that amount of identifiable assets is viewed as a reportable industry segment. Consequently, according to this final significance test, the automotive ($11.4 million), motion picture ($14.5 million), and finance ($14.6 million) segments are each considered of sufficient size to require disaggregation. The three remaining segments do not have enough identifiable assets to pass this particular test.

Analysis of Test Results.   A summary of all three industry segment tests as applied to the Jackson Company as follows:

Industry Segments	Revenue Test	Operating Profit or Loss Test	Identifiable Assets Test
Automotive	✔	✔	✔
Furniture		✔	
Textbook			
Motion picture	✔		✔
Appliance			
Finance	✔	✔	✔

For four of this company's industry segments (automotive, furniture, motion picture, and finance), specific data such as revenue figures and capital expenditures must now be disclosed. Since neither the appliance nor the textbook segments have met any of these three tests, disaggregated information describing their *individual* operations is not required. However, the financial data accumulated from these two nonsignificant segments still has to be presented. The figures might be combined and disclosed as aggregate amounts (perhaps in an ''Other segments'' category). As a second possibility, the company may decide to redefine its industry segments so that these two operations are included within one of the other industries.

Industry Segments—Additional Disclosure Requirements. Although a significant portion of the information to be disclosed for each reportable industry segment was outlined at the beginning of this chapter, *SFAS 14* also requires the inclusion of the following data:

- Types of products and services produced by each segment.
- Accounting policies relevant to the segment information if not otherwise disclosed in the financial statements.
- The amount of intersegment sales or transfers as a classification separate from sales made to unaffiliated parties.
- The basis of accounting utilized for intersegment transfers.
- A reconciliation of segment revenues, operating profits and losses, and identifiable assets with corresponding consolidation totals.
- An explanation of any unusual or infrequently occurring items included in operating profits and losses.
- Any change in the method of allocating common operating expenses among the industry segments.
- The effect on a segment's operating profit or loss created by a change in an accounting principle.

Dominant Industry Segments and Other Reporting Guidelines

After applying all three of these segment tests, a company may determine that a single industry encompasses virtually all operations. Concentration in one area of business is not unusual; organizations are sometimes able to grow to a significant size without substantial diversification. As an example, McDonald's Corporation, one of the largest corporations in the world, reported in its 1990 financial statements that the company operated primarily in only one industry. ''The Company operates exclusively in the food service industry. Substantially all revenues result from the sale of menu products at restaurants operated by the Company, its franchisees or affiliates.''

For a company with operations that exist almost exclusively within a single line of business, little differentiation would exist between segment information and the financial statements taken as a whole. Therefore, *SFAS 14* provides that a single segment which makes up more than 90 percent of a company's revenues, operating profit or loss, and identifiable assets is to be considered a ''dominant industry segment.'' In such cases, the extensive disclosure requirements previously outlined are not mandatory, although the identity of the dominant industry must be revealed. McDonald's Corporation met this requirement by denoting that food services was its only industry.[7]

Several other guidelines have been established by the FASB in connection with the disclosure of industry segment information. These rules are designed to ensure that the disaggregated data being presented is consistent from year to year and relevant to the needs of financial statement users. For example, any industry segment that has been reportable in the past and is expected to be reportable in the future should be disclosed separately in the current statements regardless of the outcome of the testing process. This degree of flexibility has been left within the rules to assure the ongoing usefulness of the disaggregated information, especially for comparison purposes.

In a similar manner, a segment that has qualified for disclosure in the current year may still be excluded from presentation if it was not significant in the past and is not expected to be reportable again in the future. Once again, the consistency of the presentation has been given high priority in setting the standards for disclosure.

One final issue raised by *SFAS 14* concerns the number of industry segments that should be disclosed. To enhance the value of the disaggregated information, a substantial portion of a company's operations should be presented individually. Thus, the FASB has stated that a sufficient number of segments is presumed to be included only if their combined sales to *unaffiliated customers* is at least 75 percent of the total company sales made to outsiders. If this lower limit is not achieved, additional segments must be separately disclosed despite their failure to satisfy even one of the three industry segment tests.

As an illustration, assume that the Brendan Corporation has identified seven industry segments that have generated revenues as follows (in millions):

Industry Segments	Sales to Unaffiliated Customers	Intersegment Transfers	Segment Revenues (and percent of total)
Housewares	$ 5.5	$ 1.6	$ 7.1 (9.3%)
Toys	6.2	–0–	6.2 (8.1%)
Pottery	3.4	7.9	11.3 (14.8%) ✔
Lumber	6.6	10.4	17.0 (22.3%) ✔
Lawn mowers	7.2	–0–	7.2 (9.4%)
Appliances.	2.1	6.2	8.3 (10.9%) ✔
Construction	19.2	–0–	19.2 (25.2%) ✔
Totals	$50.2	$26.1	$76.3 (100%)

---

[7] Despite the apparent diversity of American businesses, companies with dominant industry segments appear to be very common. In a survey of 600 companies, *Accounting Trends and Techniques* found that only 371 of these organizations reported industry segment revenues in 1990. The remainder must have viewed themselves as operating primarily in only one industry.

Based on the 10 percent revenue test, four of these segments are reportable (because each has total revenues of more than $7.63 million): pottery, lumber, appliances, and construction. Assuming that none of the other segments qualify as significant in either of the two remaining tests, disclosure of disaggregated data is only required for these four segments. However, the FASB's 75 percent rule has not been met; the reportable segments have generated just 62.4 percent of the company's total sales to unrelated parties (in millions):

Reportable Segments	*Sales to Unaffiliated Customers*
Pottery	$ 3.4
Lumber	6.6
Appliances	2.1
Construction	19.2
Total	$31.3

Information being disaggregated:
$31.3 million/$50.2 million = 62.4%.

To satisfy the 75 percent requirement, Brendan Corporation must also include the lawn mower segment within the disaggregated data being presented. With the addition of this nonsignificant segment, sales to outside parties of $38.5 ($31.3 + $7.2) million are now disclosed. This figure amounts to 76.7 percent of the company total ($38.5 million/$50.2 million). The two remaining segments—housewares and toys—could still be included separately within the disaggregated data; disclosure is not prohibited. However, information for these two segments would probably be reported as aggregate figures.

Discussion Question: Does IBM Really Have Only One Industry Segment?

Not all corporations have readily embraced segment reporting, especially of their industry segments. All disclosure has a cost; gathering and monitoring information for each segment may not be cheap. In addition, some companies fear that such data could be useful to their competitors. One solution is to define the company as having only one segment so that disaggregation is not required. With the very flexible guidelines established by the FASB for identifying segments, many companies are able to avoid presenting segment information in this manner (see footnote 7 in this chapter).

Consider IBM. As befits its size, the $63 billion (estimated 1989 sales) computer company is in several lines of business, including personal computers, main-

continued

frames, electronic mail systems and semiconductors (IBM's semiconductor facilities rank among the world's largest). How is each of these segments doing? That's hard to say. IBM reports figures for a grand total of one segment, called "information-processing systems, software, communications systems and other products and services." . . . Does anybody care? They should. Says Eugene Glazer, technology analyst at Dean Witter Reynolds: "Investors need to know how a company is doing in each major business. Maybe one business is so dominant and earning such huge profits that it's masking errors in other businesses."[8]

Should the FASB tighten up its rules on defining industry segments to ensure that all companies do present appropriately disaggregated information?

One final aspect of these reporting requirements should be mentioned. As discussed earlier, a company can identify industry segments according to narrow classifications, thus increasing the number of individual reporting units. If this approach is adopted, a company could possibly disclose so many segments that the disaggregated information would be of limited usefulness. *SFAS 14* (par. 19) does not prohibit this practice but does suggest that when the number of reported segments "increases above 10, the question of whether a practical limit has been reached comes increasingly into consideration, and combining the most closely related industry segments into broader reportable segments may be appropriate."

Disaggregated Information—Foreign and Domestic Operations

Although industry segment information may be the most prevalent type of disaggregated data, disclosure of foreign and domestic operations is also common. *Accounting Trends & Techniques* reported that 216 of the 600 companies surveyed in 1990 included revenue figures within their financial statements that were broken down according to geographic areas.[9] In establishing guidelines for this type of disclosure, the FASB encountered the same problems faced in connection with industry segment disaggregation:

How is a geographic segment to be delineated?

How is the significance of a segment to be ascertained?

What information should be disclosed for each segment?

---

[8] Dana Wechsler and Katazyna Wandycz, " 'An Innate Fear of Disclosure,' " *Forbes,* February 5, 1990, p. 126.

[9] A total of 131 of these 600 companies reported export sales and 151 listed sales to major customers.

Once again, the FASB (in *SFAS 14,* par. 85) opted not to establish specific rules for identifying the segments that make up a company, in this instance the geographic areas in which the company operates. As with industry segments, this decision has been left to the management's discretion. "The Board recognized . . . in this Statement that the variety of ways in which foreign operations are conducted made it impossible to define appropriate geographic areas for all enterprises. Therefore, only general guidelines for that determination are set forth."

Thus, a company is allowed to report operations separately on a country-by-country basis or, as an alternative, to combine a group of countries into a single geographic segment. The ultimate decision is left to company officials. In practical terms, larger corporations often disclose information by region (such as Latin America), by continent, or even by the grouping of two or more continents. The Unisys Corporation, for example, identifies only three separate geographic areas, but they are each of significant size: United States, Europe, and Americas/Pacific.

Other companies, especially smaller operations, are more likely to present disaggregated data for individual countries or small groups of countries. *SFAS 14* (par. 34) does provide guidance by indicating that operations in geographic areas should be combined based on such factors as "proximity, economic affinity, similarities in business environments, and the nature, scale, and degree of interrelationship of the enterprise's operations in the various countries."

Testing for Significant Geographic Segments

After a company determines its geographic segments, it must identify those of sufficient size to warrant separate financial statement disclosure. Two tests have been created for this purpose by the FASB. However, as with industry segments, a segment needs to meet only one for disaggregation to be necessary.

1. *Revenue test.* Disclosure is required for any geographic segment whenever its revenues (that were generated from unaffiliated customers) amount to 10 percent or more of consolidated revenues.
2. *Identifiable assets test.* Disclosure is required for any geographic segment whenever its identifiable assets are 10 percent or more of consolidated total assets.

Two aspects of these tests differ from the procedures designed for industry segments. First, both of these geographic tests are based on consolidated totals without inclusion of any intersegment transactions. Knowledge of the volume of shipments being made within the company between regions is not considered as useful in evaluating operations as is the amount of transfers carried on between industry segments. Second, no operating profit or loss test has been created here. This omission is necessary because of the difficulty that can be encountered in attempting to measure profits along purely geographic lines.

However, in a manner that does correspond to industry segment rules, disaggregated information must be presented for any geographic segment that meets either of the two tests. All remaining nonsignificant segments are then combined, with the resulting information presented in aggregate amounts. If no foreign segment proves to be individually reportable, the significance of a company's foreign operations as a whole must be evaluated. *Unless these aggregated figures meet at least one of the criteria, no foreign/domestic disclosure is required.* A company, for example, operating exclusively within the United States has no need to include geographic data.

Geographic Testing Procedures Illustrated

To provide an example of these guidelines, assume that the Wilkinson Company, a United States corporation, has divided its 1995 operations along the following geographic lines (in millions):

Geographic Segments	Sales to Unaffiliated Customers	Identifiable Assets
United States	$59.7 (72.3%)	$13.3 (73.1%)
Canada	6.5 (7.9%)	1.1 (6.0%)
Europe	3.9 (4.7%)	.8 (4.4%)
Latin America	7.1 (8.6%)	1.6 (8.8%)
Africa	5.4 (6.5%)	1.4 (7.7%)
Consolidated totals	$82.6 (100%)	$18.2 (100%)

For 1995, no single foreign segment is considered individually reportable. Not one of the four segments operating outside of the United States has either (1) generated at least 10 percent of total sales (made to unaffiliated customers) or (2) possesses 10 percent or more of total identifiable assets. However, disclosure of geographic data is still mandatory for this company because the foreign operations as a whole do meet both criteria (although satisfying only one is necessary). In total, the foreign segments provided 27.7 percent of the company's consolidated revenues and 26.9 percent of identifiable assets.

Under that circumstance, disaggregated information is only required for

- The company's domestic operations.
- The foreign operations in aggregate amounts.

Carrying this illustration one step further, assume that in 1996, Wilkinson Company's accounting records provide the following segment information (in millions):

Geographic Segments	Sales to Unaffiliated Customers	Identifiable Assets
United States	$66.7 (69.2%)	$16.7 (72.3%)
Canada.	10.2 (10.6%)	1.4 (6.0%)
Europe.	4.3 (4.5%)	1.1 (4.8%)
Latin America	7.6 (7.9%)	2.4 (10.4%)
Africa	7.5 (7.8%)	1.5 (6.5%)
Consolidated totals	$96.3 (100%)	$23.1 (100%)

In this second year, the Canadian segment now qualifies for disaggregation based on the revenue test while the operations in Latin America must also be disclosed because of the 10 percent identifiable assets test. Thus, in 1996, this company will present separate data for its domestic (U.S.) operations along with similar information for both the Canadian and Latin American segments. The results from Europe and Africa are still not viewed as material enough in size to require this same disclosure. Although disaggregation is permitted, financial information for these two areas would probably be aggregated and presented in the financial statements as having been generated by "Europe/Africa" or "Other geographic areas." No information describing the foreign operations as a whole is required since the individual geographic segments are disclosed.

Geographic Segments—Disclosure Requirements

The actual information to be reported for foreign and domestic operations is much less extensive than that required for industry segments. Companies with significant foreign operations must disclose:

- *Total revenues for each reportable geographic segment.* Both sales to unaffiliated customers as well as intersegment transfers are included in this disclosure; these totals, however, must be shown separately. Intersegment data is included here for informational purposes, even though the figures were not considered as a factor in performing the revenue test.

- *Profitability of each geographic segment.* The income to be reported may be the operating profit or loss derived for each region, although *SFAS 14* does permit a company to present total net income for the individual segments or some other profitability figure as an alternative. This flexibility is allowed because of the difficulties that can be encountered in gauging profits along purely geographic lines. Regardless of the specific method used in arriving at an income balance, the company must apply the same measure of profitability for all geographic segments.

- *Identifiable assets of each geographic segment.* This figure is derived in the same manner as previously defined within the discussion of industry segment reporting.
- *A reconciliation of segment revenues, profits, and identifiable assets with consolidated totals.*
- *The basis of accounting used for intersegment transfers.*

Disaggregated Information—Exports and Reliance on Major Customers

Export Sales. In describing disclosure requirements for domestic operations, *SFAS 14* specifies that the total amount of export sales made to unaffiliated companies in foreign countries must be separately disclosed, if material. More specifically, the volume of export sales is to be presented as disaggregated information if it constitutes 10 percent or more of the company's total sales to unaffiliated customers. The amount of export sales made to any specific geographic area should also be identified but only if that information is considered relevant.

As an example, the 1990 financial statements of Joslyn Corporation reported exports for that year as being more than $21 million (approximately 10.3 percent of consolidated sales). According to the information provided, these goods were sold in the following locations (in thousands):

Asia	$8,916
Europe	6,624
Western Hemisphere	4,686
Other	1,076

Major Customers. One final but important disclosure requirement was established by *SFAS 14*. A reporting entity must indicate its reliance on any major customer. *Presentation of this information is required whenever 10 percent or more of a company's revenues are derived from a single unaffiliated party.* The existence of all major customers must be disclosed along with the related amount of revenues. Interestingly enough, the financial statements need not reveal the identity of the customer, merely the presence.

For this reason, Note 3 to the 1990 financial statements of Briggs & Stratton Corporation indicated that significant sales had been made to two "major engine customers that exceeded 10 percent of total net sales. Sales to these customers were: 1990—customer A $168,421,000 (17%) and customer B $109,087,000 (11%)."

Several years after issuance, the FASB clarified *SFAS 14* in connection with the disclosure of major customers. The question was raised as to whether different agencies within a government should be considered as separate customers. In response, *Statement of Financial Accounting Standards No. 30,* "Disclosure of Information about Major Customers," was released in 1979. According to paragraph 6 of this pronouncement, "a group of entities under common control shall be regarded as a single customer, and the federal government, a state government, a local government (for example, a county or municipality), or a foreign government shall each be considered as a single customer."

Disaggregated Information—The Future

Now that *SFAS 14* has been in use for nearly two decades, the FASB has decided to reexamine the reporting of disaggregated information. In February 1993, a research report was released by the FASB (*Reporting Disaggregated Information* by Paul Pacter) as a preliminary step in this study. This report provides an overview of current standards and practices, segment reporting internationally, criticisms of the current standards, and recent research findings. The report concludes by raising a number of issues including the following:

1. Are the bases for disaggregation (industries, foreign operations, exports, and major customers) still appropriate?
2. Are the methods of grouping industries and foreign operations still appropriate?
3. Is the type and amount of disclosure that is required still appropriate?
4. Is a different method of presentation now needed?
5. Is disaggregated information useful in interim statements?
6. Should disaggregation only be required of publicly held companies?
7. Is disaggregated data harmful to competition?

If the FASB chooses to amend or replace *SFAS 14,* the answers to such questions will have a significant impact on the presentation of this important element of financial reporting.

Summary

1. The consolidation of information from many, varied companies into a set of consolidated financial statements tends to camouflage the characteristics of the individual components. Consequently, during the 1960s, several groups made a strong push to require that disaggregated information be included as an integral part of financial reporting to provide a more efficient means of analyzing business combinations.

2. The move toward dissemination of disaggregated information culminated in 1976 with the release by the FASB of *Statement 14,* "Financial Reporting for Segments of a Business Enterprise." This pronouncement established guidelines for the required presentation of information describing the various segments that make up a reporting entity. Data must now be disclosed by all publicly held companies to identify as many as four distinct aspects of their operations: industry segments, domestic and foreign operations, export sales, and sales to major customers.

3. The most commonly presented segment information found today in corporate financial statements describes the industries in which a company does business. The entity must first identify its separate industry segments. According to *SFAS 14,* this determination should be based on factors such as the nature of the company's products and manufacturing process as well as the marketing methods in use. However, the identification of specific segments is ultimately left to the discretion of company officials.

4. After the industry segments have been delineated, a company must determine which of these operations is of significant magnitude to warrant separate disclosure. *SFAS 14* created three tests to be applied to identify segments for which disclosure is required: a revenue test, an operating profit or loss test, and an identifiable assets test. A segment need only satisfy one of these to be considered of sufficient size to necessitate disclosure. Each test is based on identifying segments that meet a 10 percent minimum of an overall total as defined by the FASB. In the revenue test, as an example, intersegment transfers are included as is interest income except when earned on intersegment loans (unless the segment operates principally in a finance capacity). Conversely, such nonoperating items as equity income and extraordinary gains and losses should be omitted from this test.

5. The operating profit and loss test also has a 10 percent criterion based on the greater (in an absolute sense) of the total of all segments with profits or all segments with losses. To determine each operating profit or loss figure, expenses directly attributable to a segment are subtracted from revenues. Any common operating costs incurred by the company as a whole are allocated to the various segments on some logical basis while general expenses unrelated to the segments are not assigned. Income tax and interest expense are normally omitted.

6. The final significance test is based on total identifiable assets (both tangible and intangible) held by the segments. Once again, a 10 percent level is considered to be of a sufficient magnitude to warrant separate disclosure. Assets directly utilized by a segment are included in this test as well as a portion of any item jointly used by more than one segment. Intersegment trade receivables are also added to the computation because they relate to operations, but intersegment loans and advances are omitted unless the segment holding the asset is principally a financial operation.

7. *SFAS 14* does set parameters for the number of industry segments that should be reported by an enterprise. As a minimum, the separately disclosed units must generate at least 75 percent of the total sales made to unaffiliated parties. For an upper limit, the pronouncement suggests that the disclosure of more than 10 industry segments reduces the usefulness of the information. Finally, if one segment composes more than 90 percent of all three tests, it is viewed as a dominant industry segment so that the extensive disclosure requirements are not mandatory for the company.

8. Separate disclosure of foreign and domestic operations is also common. Procedures applied to a company's geographic segments parallel the process used in connection with industry segments: individual segments are identified and then judged for significance. The testing procedures, however, are comprised of only a revenue test (based on sales to outside customers) and an identifiable assets test. Again, 10 percent is the standard by which sufficient size for required disclosure is determined. If none of the foreign segments prove to be individually reportable, the significance of the foreign operations as a whole must be measured. Unless these aggregated figures meet at least one of the two geographical tests, no foreign/domestic disclosures are necessary.

9. Disclosure of two other types of disaggregated information is required by *SFAS 14*. The volume of an enterprise's export sales must be presented if this total constitutes 10 percent or more of sales made to outside parties. In addition, the reporting entity has to indicate reliance on major customers whenever 10 percent or more of consolidated revenues are derived from a single unaffiliated party.

Comprehensive Illustration

PROBLEM   (Estimated Time: 25 to 40 Minutes)

The Atwood Corporation, an enterprise located in the United States, manufactures several different products: cotton, leather, synthetic fibers, plastics, and wood. The company has developed a number of subsidiaries that carry on operations throughout the world.

At the end of 1995, the company reported the following revenues (in millions):

	United States	Canada and Mexico	Europe	Africa
Cotton				
Sales to customers	$1,739	$442	$506	$1,171
Transfers	–0–	–0–	–0–	146
Leather				
Sales to customers	330	84	49	66
Transfers	42	–0–	22	–0–

	United States	Canada and Mexico	Europe	Africa
Synthetic fibers				
Sales to customers	290	16	–0–	37
Transfers	7	–0–	–0–	10
Plastics				
Sales to customers	348	–0–	–0–	616
Transfers	21	–0–	–0–	74
Wood				
Sales to customers	116	–0–	–0–	–0–
Transfers	17	–0–	–0–	–0–

Additional Information:

- Atwood incurred expenses of $4,719 million during the current year. These expenses have been classified as follows (in millions):

Operating expenses—traceable	
Cotton	$1,950
Leather	771
Synthetic fibers	257
Plastics	336
Wood	87
Operating expenses—common	900
Central administration expenses	390
Interest expense	22
Loss on sale of equipment—plastics	6

- Tax rates vary within every country and area, but effective rates for each geographic segment are as follows:

United States	42%
Canada and Mexico	39
Europe	45
Africa	34

- Atwood has elected to allocate all common operating costs to the various segments based on total revenues.
- Atwood's operations had the following identifiable assets at the end of 1995 (in millions):

Industry Segments	United States	Canada and Mexico	Europe	Africa
Cotton	$906	$129	$86	$226
Leather.	416	74	91	81
Synthetic fibers	152	10	–0–	16
Plastics	283	–0–	–0–	94
Wood	77	–0–	–0–	–0–

Required:

a. Determine the industry segments that should be disaggregated in connection with the production of Atwood's 1995 financial statements.

b. Determine the geographic segments that should be disaggregated in connection with the production of Atwood's 1995 financial statements.

c. Determine the volume of export sales that would be required to necessitate disclosure.

d. Determine the volume of revenues that have to be generated from a single customer to necessitate disclosure.

SOLUTION

a. Identification of Atwood's reportable industry segments is dependent on the three significance tests described in this chapter. The revenue test can be performed directly from the information provided:

Revenue Test (in millions)

Industry Segments	Total Revenues (including transfers)
Cotton	$4,004 (65.1%)
Leather.	593 (9.6%)
Synthetic fibers	360 (5.8%)
Plastics	1,059 (17.3%)
Wood	133 (2.2%)
Total	$6,149 (100%)

Reportable segments (revenues equal 10 percent or more of total)—cotton and plastics.

The operating profit and loss test can be carried out next. However, this test cannot be applied directly. The $900 million in common operating expenses must first be assigned to the various segments. Central administrative expenses are omitted from this test; in this problem, they do not appear to relate to the operations of the segments. Interest expense and income taxes are also ignored because these costs are not viewed as operating expenses.

Allocation of Common Operating Expenses (in millions)

Industry Segments	Allocation According to Revenues
Cotton	65.1% × $900 = $585.9
Leather.	9.6% × $900 = 86.4
Synthetic fibers	5.8% × $900 = 52.2
Plastics	17.3% × $900 = 155.7
Wood	2.2% × $900 = 19.8
Total	$900.0

Operating Profit or Loss by Segments (in millions)

Industry Segments	Revenues	Traceable Expenses	Common Costs (above)	Operating Profit	Operating Loss
Cotton.	$4,004	$1,950	$585.9	$1,468.1	
Leather	593	771	86.4		$264.4
Synthetic fibers.	360	257	52.2	50.8	
Plastics	1,059	342*	155.7	561.3	
Wood	133	87	19.8	26.2	
Totals				$2,106.4	$264.4

* Includes loss on sale of equipment since it was not extraordinary.

The operating profit or loss criterion is $210.64 million (10 percent of the $2,106.4 million profit figure just derived). This total is used since it is greater, in an absolute sense, than the $264.4 million operating loss. Consequently, three of the industry segments are reportable based on this one test: cotton ($1,468.1 million profit), leather ($264.4 million loss), and plastics ($561.3 million profit).

Lastly, the identifiable assets test is performed:

Identifiable Assets Test (in millions)

Industry Segments	Total Identifiable Assets	
Cotton	$1,347	(51.0%)
Leather	662	(25.1%)
Synthetic fibers	178	(6.7%)
Plastics	377	(14.3%)
Wood	77	(2.9%)
Total.	$2,641	(100%)

Once again, cotton, leather, and plastics have qualified as reportable industry segments, this time as a result of the 10 percent identifiable assets standard.

Neither the synthetic fibers nor the wood segment has met even one of the three industry segment tests; thus, disaggregated disclosure as envisioned by *SFAS 14* is not required. However, Atwood must still verify that the FASB's 75 percent requirement has been met. As shown next, the three reportable segments have generated $5,351 million in sales to outside parties or 92 percent of the total for the entire company ($5,351/$5,810).

Sales to Unaffiliated Parties (in millions)

Reportable segments:	
Cotton.	$3,858
Leather	529
Plastics	964
Total—reportable.	$5,351
Other segments:	
Synthetic fibers.	343
Wood	116
Company total	$5,810

Thus, an adequate number of segments is being presented. Information about the synthetic fibers and wood segments will be included in the financial disclosure but under a heading such as "Other industry segments."

b. Only two tests were designed by the FASB to ascertain the geographic segments that warrant disaggregation. The first is based on revenues from outside parties and the second on identifiable assets. As shown next, Atwood's domestic (U.S.) segment as well as the company's African segment meet both of these tests. Therefore, separate disclosure of disaggregated financial information is required for each locale. Since neither the Canada/Mexico segment nor the European segment qualify as reportable, they will be aggregated for disclosure purposes.

Revenue Test (in millions)

Geographic Segments	Sales to Unaffiliated Customers	
United States	$2,823	(48.6%)
Canada and Mexico	542	(9.3%)
Europe	555	(9.6%)
Africa	1,890	(32.5%)
Consolidated total	$5,810	(100%)

Identifiable Assets Test (in millions)

Geographic Segments	Identifiable Assets	
United States	$1,834	(69.4%)
Canada and Mexico	213	(8.1%)
Europe	177	(6.7%)
Africa	417	(15.8%)
Consolidated total	$2,641	(100%)

c. According to *SFAS 14,* export sales must be reported if they amount to 10 percent or more of a company's total consolidated revenues. In the testing carried out for geographic segments, Atwood's consolidated revenues were computed to be $5,810 million. Consequently, if this company's domestic operations made at least $581 million in sales (10 percent of $5,810 million) to unaffiliated customers in foreign countries, disclosure is required.

d. The significance test for disclosure of a major customer is identical to that shown above for export sales: 10 percent of consolidated revenues. Under the guidelines of *SFAS 14,* Atwood has to report the existence of any major customer from which $581 million or more in revenues were generated during 1995.

Questions

1. Why does the consolidation process tend to disguise information that is needed to analyze the financial operations of a diversified organization?
2. What is disaggregated financial information?
3. *SFAS 14* requires many companies to present disaggregated information about several different aspects of current operations. What are the various types of segments that may necessitate disclosure?
4. What financial data must a corporation report for each of its significant industry segments?
5. What financial data must a corporation disclose for its foreign and domestic operations?
6. How did the FASB intend for disaggregated data to be used by readers of financial statements?
7. What factors should be utilized by a company in determining whether different operations fall within a single industry segment?
8. The FASB created rules that were quite flexible in connection with a company's identification of its segments. Why was that done and what problems can that create?
9. Describe the three tests that have been designed to identify industry segments that are of such magnitude to warrant disaggregated disclosure. How many of these three tests must be met before disaggregation is required for an industry segment? What disclosure is necessary for industry segments that do not qualify as significant?
10. How are the revenues of an industry segment calculated for the revenue test that was devised by the FASB? How is this data disclosed in the company's financial statements if disaggregation is necessary?
11. How is the operating profit or loss of an industry segment computed?
12. In determining the operating profit or loss of an industry segment, how are operating expenses that are not directly traceable to a single segment handled?
13. How is the operating profit and loss test devised by the FASB actually carried out?
14. What assets are included in the identifiable assets of an industry segment?

15. According to *SFAS 14,* how are the revenue test and the identifiable assets test performed in connection with industry segments?

16. What is a dominant industry segment, and how does it affect disaggregated disclosure of industry segment information?

17. *SFAS 14* states that a sufficient number of industry segments must be presented by a company. How is this rule applied?

18. What does *SFAS 14* suggest as the maximum number of industry segments that should be disclosed? What happens if a company has more than this number of reportable segments?

19. How are geographic segments determined for an international organization?

20. What tests are applied in determining significant geographic segments?

21. Under what condition should a company's export sales be disclosed?

22. Under what condition should a company disclose the amount of sales generated from a major customer?

Library Assignments

1. Locate the latest annual reports for two companies considered to be rivals such as the Coca-Cola Company and PepsiCo, Inc. or Ford Motor Company and General Motors Corporation. Based solely on the segment information, write a report describing and evaluating the two companies.

2. Read the following as well as any other published information on accounting principles for small businesses:
   "Accounting for Small Business: Bridging a Widening GAAP," *Journal of Accountancy* (Statements in Quotes section), December 1981.
   "Small Public Companies: Do They Have Different Reporting Needs?" *Financial Executive,* August 1984.
   "The World According to GAAP," *Forbes,* June 8, 1981.
   "Fitting GAAP to Smaller Businesses," *Journal of Accountancy,* February 1978.
   "The Numbers Game—Sauce for the Goose?" *Forbes,* December 15, 1977.
   "An Alternative to Little GAAP," *Journal of Accountancy* (Practitioners Forum section), November 1978.
   Write a report to either recommend the application of different accounting principles for small businesses or justify the use of a single set of accounting principles for all businesses.

3. Read the following as well as any other published information on the reporting of segment information:
   " 'An Innate Fear of Disclosure,' " *Forbes,* February 5, 1990.

"How Much Is Known?" *The Woman CPA*, October 1989.

Statement of Financial Accounting Standards No. 14, "Financial Reporting for Segments of a Business Enterprise" (especially Appendix B).

Write a report discussing whether the FASB should change the method by which segments of a business are identified to remove some of the flexibility that is currently allowed.

Problems

1. What is the purpose of requiring information about the various segments of a company?
    a. It allows a better comparison of the results of two different companies.
    b. It permits a better assessment of the enterprise's past performance and future prospects.
    c. It allows comparisons to be made between a segment of one enterprise and a similar segment of another enterprise.
    d. The FASB established reporting requirements but remained silent as to the rationale for including the data.

2. Which of the following is not a factor in identifying a company's specific industry segments?
    a. Location of the production process.
    b. Nature of the products.
    c. Nature of the production process.
    d. Markets and marketing methods.

3. Why does the FASB warn against making comparisons of the disaggregated information disclosed by two different companies?
    a. The data is not an actual part of the financial statements.
    b. The identification of specific segments may be done differently by different companies.
    c. The information is not viewed as valid in reporting trends between past and present operations.
    d. Different types of revenues are included by some companies.

4. In determining whether a particular industry segment is of significant size to warrant disclosure, which of the following statements is true?
    a. Three tests are applied and all three must be met.
    b. Four tests are applied but only one must be met.
    c. Three tests are applied but only one must be met.
    d. Four tests are applied and all four must be met.

5. Hatfield Corporation has identified one of its industry segments as being the production of computer software. Which of the following should not be included in determining this segment's revenue for disaggregation purposes?

a. Interest income on intersegment loans.
b. Interest income on intersegment trade receivables.
c. Interest income on trade receivables with outside parties.
d. Interest income on loans made to outside parties.

6. The Caso Company has three industry segments with the following information:

	Paper	Pencils	Hats
Sales to outsiders.	$8,000	$4,000	$6,000
Intersegment transfers	600	1,000	1,400
Interest income—outsiders	400	500	600
Interest income—intersegment loans	300	400	500

What is the minimum amount of revenue that each of these segments must have to be considered significant?
a. $1,950.
b. $2,100.
c. $2,250.
d. $2,370.

7. In financial reporting for the industry segments of a business enterprise, the operating profit or loss of a segment should include:
a. Federal income taxes.
b. Interest expense, even though the segment's operations are not principally of a financial nature.
c. Indirect expenses incurred at the corporate level.
d. Common operating costs allocated on a reasonable basis.
(AICPA adapted)

8. The Jarvis Corporation has six different industry segments which are reporting the following operating profit and loss figures:

K . . . . $ 80,000 loss
L . . . . 140,000 profit
M . . . . 940,000 loss
N . . . . 440,000 profit
O . . . . 90,000 profit
P . . . . 100,000 profit

Which of the following statements is not true?
a. K is not a reportable segment based on this one test.
b. L is a reportable segment based on this test.
c. O is not a reportable segment based on this one test.
d. P is a reportable segment based on this test.

9. Harstone, Inc. has a boat building industry segment. Which of the following is included in computing this segment's operating profit or loss?

a. Intersegment cost of goods sold.

b. Interest expense.

c. Income taxes.

d. Extraordinary losses.

10. In the financial reporting of a company's industry segments, the operating profit or loss of a manufacturing segment should include

	Interest Expense	Income Taxes
a.	Yes	Yes
b.	Yes	No
c.	No	Yes
d.	No	No

(AICPA adapted)

11. The Barden Company has four identifiable industry segments:

	Coffee	Cream	Sugar	Donuts
Revenues	$11,000	$9,000	$10,000	$13,000
Interest income—intersegment loans	2,000	3,000	4,000	2,000
Operating expenses	8,000	4,000	14,000	5,000
Allocation of common costs	1,000	2,000	3,000	4,000
Interest expense—outside parties.	3,000	5,000	2,000	3,000
Interest expense—intersegment loans	1,000	3,000	4,000	3,000
Income taxes (savings)	(2,000)	(1,000)	–0–	1,000

What is the minimum operating profit or loss that a segment must have to be considered significant?

a. $200.

b. $700.

c. $900.

d. $1,200.

12. The Waterson Corporation has four identifiable industry segments:

	Fruits	Bread	Milk	Eggs
Revenues	$24,000	$19,000	$22,000	$27,000
Intersegment revenues	11,000	7,000	9,000	4,000
Intersegment cost of goods sold	5,000	4,000	5,000	2,000
Operating expenses	12,000	10,000	26,000	19,000
Allocation of common costs	2,000	3,000	4,000	5,000
Interest expense—outside parties	5,000	3,000	3,000	2,000
Income taxes (savings)	2,000	1,000	(4,000)	–0–

What is the minimum operating profit or loss that a segment must have to be considered significant?

a. $1,900.

b. $2,000.

c. $2,600.

d. $3,000.

13. What is the minimum number of industry segments that must be separately reported?

   a. Ten.

   b. Segments with at least 75 percent of revenues as measured by the revenue test.

   c. At least 75 percent of the segments must be separately reported.

   d. Segments with at least 75 percent of the revenues generated from outside parties.

14. Which of the following statements is true concerning a dominant industry segment?

   a. A company has a dominant industry segment if only one segment meets any of the three tests devised by the FASB.

   b. If a company has a dominant industry segment, disclosure of extensive industry segment information is not required.

   c. A dominant industry segment must be noted by a reporting company but its presence does not have any impact on the disclosure of other industry segments.

   d. A segment that makes up 80 percent of a company's revenues, 88 percent of its identifiable assets, and 96 percent of its operating profit would be viewed as a dominant industry segment.

15. The Heartline Company is primarily a manufacturer of toys. This past year, the toy segment produced 95 percent of the company's revenues and 88 percent of operating profits. This segment held 86 percent of the identifiable assets. Three other segments were also identified, but all failed to meet even one of the three industry segment tests. Each of the company's four segments did manage to report an operating profit. Under these circumstances:

   a. The toy segment is a dominant industry segment, and segment reporting is not required.

   b. The toy segment is not a dominant industry segment; therefore, the next biggest segment must also be reported.

   c. Normal segment disclosures are required but only for the toy segment with the other segments shown as aggregated figures.

   d. Heartline should attempt to divide the toy segment into at least two identifiable segments.

16. The Medford Company has seven industry segments but only four (*G, H, I,* and *J*) are of significant size to warrant separate disclosure. Segments *K,*

L, and *M* are not large enough. As a whole, these segments have revenues generated from outside parties of $710,000 ($520,000 + $190,000). In addition, the segments had $260,000 in intersegment transfers ($220,000 + $40,000).

	Outside Sales	Intersegment Sales
G.	$120,000	$ 80,000
H.	150,000	50,000
I	160,000	20,000
J	90,000	70,000
Totals.	$520,000	$220,000

	Outside Sales	Intersegment Sales
K.	$ 60,000	–0–
L.	70,000	$20,000
M.	60,000	20,000
Totals.	$190,000	$40,000

Which of the following statements is true?

a. A sufficient number of segments is being reported because those segments have $740,000 in revenues out of a total of $970,000 for the company as a whole.

b. Not enough segments are being reported because those segments have $520,000 in outside sales out of a total of $710,000 for the company as a whole.

c. Not enough segments are being reported because those segments have $740,000 in revenues out of a total of $970,000 for the company as a whole.

d. A sufficient number of segments is being reported because those segments have $520,000 in outside sales out of a total of $710,000 for the company as a whole.

17. For geographic segments, which of the following statements is true?

a. Revenues should include intersegment transfers.

b. The operating profit or loss test is based on a 10 percent criterion.

c. To be significant, a segment must meet either the revenue or the identifiable assets test.

d. Individual countries must be included as segments.

18. How does the testing of geographic segments differ from the testing of industry segments?

a. Intersegment transactions are omitted from consideration and no operating profit or loss test is performed.

b. The revenue test is omitted and the operating profit or loss does not include intersegment transactions.

c. No identifiable assets test is made.

d. The two testing procedures are basically the same.

19. The Carson Company has four separate industry segments:

	Apples	Oranges	Pears	Peaches
Sales to outsiders	$123,000	$81,000	$95,000	$77,000
Intersegment transfers	31,000	26,000	13,000	18,000

What amount of revenues must be generated from one customer before that party must be identified as a major customer?

a. $37,600.

b. $41,200.

c. $46,400.

d. $56,400.

20. The Willes Corporation has identified three different industry segments within its operations:

	Revenues from Outsiders	Intersegment Transfers	Operating Expenses
Clothing	$1,200,000	$300,000	$900,000
Linen	900,000	500,000	200,000
Shoes	800,000	200,000	400,000

Additional operating expenses (of a general nature) incurred by the company amounted to $300,000. These costs are to be assigned to the segments based on income (before any allocation of these costs).

What is the operating profit of each of these segments?

21. A central issue in the reporting of the industry segments identified by a business enterprise is the determination of which segments are of significant size to warrant disclosure.

Required:

a. With respect to the segments of a business enterprise, explain the following terms:

- Industry segment.
- Revenue.
- Operating profit and loss.
- Identifiable assets.

b. Describe the tests used to determine whether an industry segment is of significant size to necessitate separate disclosure.

c. How does a company determine if enough industry segments have been reported within its disaggregated information? What is the guideline for the maximum number of industry segments that should be shown?
(AICPA adapted)

22. The Anton Corporation reports operating profits and losses for three industry segments in supplemental financial information. The following data is available for 1995:

	Sales	Traceable Expenses
Sporting goods	$ 900,000	$ 400,000
Furniture	2,475,000	900,000
Paper	1,125,000	1,050,000

Additional expenses not included in these figures are as follows:

General operating expenses of the segments paid by the home office	$400,000
Corporate expenses unrelated to the segments	300,000
Interest expense	200,000
Income tax expense	350,000

Common costs are allocated based on sales.
Carry out the operating profit or loss test on these industry segments.

23. The Ecru Company has identified five industry segments: plastics, metals, lumber, paper, and finance. Each of these segments has been appropriately consolidated by the company in producing its annual financial statements. Information describing each segment is presented here (in thousands):

	Plastics	Metals	Lumber	Paper	Finance
Sales	$6,319	$2,144	$636	$347	–0–
Intersegment transfers	106	131	96	108	–0–
Interest income from outside parties .	–0–	11	6	–0–	$ 27
Interest income from intersegment loans	–0–	8	–0–	–0–	159
Traceable costs	3,914	1,612	916	579	16
Interest expense	61	16	51	31	87
Tangible assets	1,291	2,986	314	561	104
Intangible assets	72	361	–0–	48	–0–
Intersegment loans	–0–	20	–0–	–0–	664

In addition, Ecru has $1,250,000 in common expenses that must be allocated to the various segments. After some discussion, management has elected to make this assignment based on segment revenues as defined by *SFAS 14.*

Required:

Perform the testing procedures designed by the FASB to determine the reportable industry segments of the Ecru Company.

24. The Graham Company has identified five geographic segments within its corporate organization. Information about these segments has been gathered by the company's accounting department:

	United States	Canada	Africa	Europe	Asia
Revenues—outsiders	$1,990,000	$722,000	$808,000	$1,432,000	$231,000
Revenues—intersegment . . .	340,000	190,000	77,000	111,000	–0–
Expenses—intersegment . . .	270,000	98,000	61,000	82,000	–0–
Operating expenses.	1,009,000	416,000	810,000	992,000	267,000
Interest expense—external . .	134,000	31,000	76,000	218,000	16,000
Income taxes (savings)	265,000	79,000	(33,000)	57,000	(14,000)
Identifiable assets—tangible . .	2,076,000	975,000	501,000	890,000	325,000
Identifiable assets—intangible .	820,000	608,000	90,000	118,000	65,000

Required:

Carry out the necessary testing to determine which of these segments are of sufficient size to warrant separate disclosure.

25. Missouri Company is reporting the following financial information for 1995:

Net income.	$ 414,000
Sales to unaffiliated customers	3,930,000
Intersegment transfers	595,000
Identifiable assets	2,391,000

The company has identified four industry segments as follows:

	Segment A	Segment B	Segment C	Segment D
Sales	$2,538,000	$354,000	$718,000	$320,000
Intersegment transfers	156,000	11,000	328,000	100,000
Identifiable assets	1,702,000	177,000	391,000	121,000
Operating expenses	1,910,000	254,000	457,000	295,000

The company also incurred $600,000 in general corporate expenses this past year. Of that amount, 60 percent is composed of costs totally unrelated to the various segments.

Required:

Each of the following questions should be viewed as an independent situation:

a. Assuming that the segments are geographic segments, which is of significant size to be reportable?

b. Assuming that the segments are industrial and that common costs are to be assigned based on revenues less operating expenses:
  • What common costs should be allocated to each segment?
  • Which of the segments is of significant size to be reportable?

c. Describe the information that should be disclosed for each reportable industry segment.

d. Assume that 60 percent of the sales of Segment C go to one unaffiliated customer. Does this information have to be disclosed in the company's financial statements?

e. Assume that the segments are geographic in nature and that Segment A is the company's domestic operation. What volume of export sales by this segment would necessitate separate disclosure?

26. Pattee Corporation has seven identifiable segments. The company is currently attempting to determine the reportable segments for disaggregation purposes. Unless otherwise stated, none of the segments has any interest expense or intersegment loans or advances, although intersegment transfers have occurred during the period.

   The following figures have been gathered from the accounting records of the various segments:

Segments	Sales to Outsiders	Sales to Affiliates (inter-segment)	Identifiable Assets	Operating Expenses	Expenses Relating to Inter-segment Revenues
A	$ 90,000	$70,000	$ 70,000	$130,000	$70,000
B	20,000	70,000	80,000	20,000	40,000
C	20,000	40,000	30,000	10,000	10,000
D	40,000	5,000	30,000	30,000	20,000
E	50,000	20,000	36,000	50,000	20,000
F	180,000	60,000	120,000	130,000	50,000
G	40,000	20,000	34,000	30,000	35,000
General corporate . .	–0–	–0–	100,000	10,000	–0–
Common costs . . .	–0–	–0–	–0–	30,000	–0–

Pattee's common costs are assigned to the seven segments based on sales made to outside parties.

Required:

a. Assume that these are industry segments. Carry out each of the tests used for determining reportable industry segments and indicate which of these segments should be disclosed by Pattee in the disaggregation process.

b. Assume that industry segments A, F, and G are the only ones considered to be reportable. Determine whether Pattee would be disclosing information on a sufficient number of industry segments.

c. Assume that segment C serves primarily as a finance operation. Assume further that Segment C's "Sales to Affiliates" is composed mostly of interest income on intersegment loans ($6,000 from each of the other six segments). All other balances in this column represent intersegment transfers of inventory. How does this information change the answer to requirement *a*?

d. Assume that these are geographic segments. Carry out each of the tests used for determining reportable geographic segments and indicate which of these segments should be disclosed by Pattee in the disaggregation process.

27. Following is financial information describing the six segments that make up Fairfield, Inc. (in thousands):

	Segments					
	Red	Blue	Green	Pink	Black	White
Sales to outside parties.	$1,811	$812	$514	$309	$121	$ 99
Intersegment revenues	16	91	109	–0–	16	302
Salary expense	614	379	402	312	317	62
Rent expense	139	166	81	91	42	31
Interest expense.	65	59	82	49	14	5
Income tax expense (savings).	141	87	61	(86)	(64)	–0–

Additional common operating expenses assignable to these segments amounts to $504,000.

The following questions should be considered independently. Unless specified, none of the six segments has primarily a financial nature.

Required:

a. If these six segments are industry segments, what minimum amount of revenue must be generated by any one segment to be of significant size to require disaggregated disclosure?

b. If these six segments are industry segments and only Red, Blue, and Green are of sufficient size to necessitate separate disclosure, is Fairfield disclosing disaggregated data for enough segments?

c. Assume that these segments are industry segments and White is a finance segment. Assume further that intersegment revenues for all six segments represent interest income derived from intersegment loans and advances. What is the minimum revenue that has to be generated by any one segment to be of significant size to require disaggregated disclosure?

d. Assume that these segments are industry segments. If common operating expenses are to be allocated based on total revenues, what is the operating profit or loss for the Blue segment?

e. If these six segments are geographic segments, what minimum amount of revenue has to be generated by any one segment to be of significant size to require disaggregated disclosure?

f. If these segments are industry segments, what volume of revenues must be generated from a single client to necessitate disclosing the existence of a major customer?

g. If these six segments are industry segments and each has an operating profit or loss (in thousands) as follows, which is of significant size to warrant separate disclosure?

Red	$1,074	Pink	$ (94)
Blue	449	Black	(222)
Green	140	White	308

28. The Simon Company has been divided into five segments. Financial information about each follows. None of these segments serves principally in a financial capacity.

	A	B	C	D	E
Sales to outsiders	$100,000	$500,000	$ 400,000	$1,000,000	$200,000
Sales—intersegment	300,000	–0–	1,800,000	1,100,000	–0–
Expenses—operating	500,000	700,000	1,100,000	900,000	300,000
Extraordinary gain	–0–	–0–	600,000	–0–	–0–
Interest expense	50,000	60,000	80,000	40,000	30,000
Income tax expense	–0–	–0–	200,000	300,000	–0–

Common operating expenses amount to $110,000 and are to be allocated to the various segments based on sales to outsiders.

Required:

a. Assume that these segments are industrial segments. Apply the revenue test.

b. Assume that the revenue test in requirement a. is the only test to be applied. Has the 75 percent rule been satisfied?

c. Assume that these segments are industrial segments. Apply the operating profit and loss test.

d. If these segments are industrial segments, what amount of revenue does a segment have to generate to be labeled a dominant industry segment?

e. How should Simon decide whether sales to a single outside party require separate disclosure?

f. Assume that these segments are geographic segments. Apply the revenue test.

g. What two major differences are found in the testing procedures for geographic segments as compared to industry segments?

29. The Mason Company has prepared consolidated financial statements for the current year and is now gathering information in connection with the following five industry segments it has identified.

   Determine the reportable segments by carrying out each of the applicable tests. Also describe the procedure utilized to ensure that a sufficient number of segments is being separately disclosed. (Figures are in thousands.)

	Company Total	Books	Computers	Maps	Travel	Finance
Sales to outside parties . . .	$1,547	$121	$ 696	$416	$314	–0–
Intersegment sales	421	24	240	39	118	–0–
Interest income— external	97	60	–0–	–0–	–0–	$ 37
Interest income— intersegment loans	177	–0–	–0–	–0–	30	147
Identifiable assets	2,408	206	1,378	248	326	250
Intersegment loans receivable (not included in identifiable assets)	1,070	–0–	–0–	–0–	80	990
Operating expenses.	1,460	115	818	304	190	33
Expenses—intersegment sales	198	70	51	31	46	–0–
Interest expense—external .	107	–0–	–0–	–0–	–0–	107
Interest expense— intersegment loans	177	21	71	38	47	–0–
Income tax expense (savings).	21	12	(41)	27	31	(8)
General corporate expenses .	55					
Common operating costs . .	80					

Common costs are allocated by Mason according to net income prior to the allocation of these common costs.

30. In the past, the Slatter Corporation has operated primarily in the United States. However, a few years ago, the company opened a plant in Spain to produce merchandise that is sold within that country. This foreign operation has been so successful that during the past 24 months, the company also started a manufacturing plant in Italy as well as another in Greece. Financial information for each of these facilities follows:

	Spain	*Italy*	*Greece*
Sales	$395,000	$272,000	$463,000
Intersegment transfers	–0–	–0–	62,000
Operating expenses.	172,000	206,000	190,000
Interest expense	16,000	29,000	19,000
Income taxes	67,000	19,000	34,000
Identifiable assets	191,000	106,000	72,000

The company's domestic (U.S.) operations reported the following information for the current year:

Sales to unaffiliated customers.	$4,610,000
Intersegment transfers	427,000
Operating expenses.	2,410,000
Interest expense	136,000
Income taxes	819,000
Identifiable assets	1,894,000

Required:

a. For disclosure purposes, Slatter is uncertain about how to group its foreign operations. The company has considered presenting them as a single European segment or as three separate segments. Another suggestion has been to report the Spanish operation as one segment while grouping the two newer plants as an additional geographic segment.

   (1) If all foreign operations are shown as a single segment, is it reportable? Why?

   (2) If the foreign operations are shown as three separate segments, which would be reportable? Why? What is done with the nonreportable segments?

   (3) If the Italian and Greek segments are combined for disaggregation purposes, what are the reportable geographic segments and why?

b. How would *SFAS 14* recommend grouping foreign operations into geographic segments?

c. Assume that 13 percent of Slatter's domestic revenues come from sales made to unaffiliated customers in France. Is disclosure of this information required?

31. Financial information for the Cummings Company follows. Cummings produces furniture, construction equipment, and chemicals. The company operates throughout the United States with additional facilities located in Mexico and Canada.

	United States	Mexico	Canada
Sales			
Furniture	$ 661*	$326	$ 18
Construction equipment	8,006†	591	75
Chemicals	673	34	281
Operating expenses			
Furniture	926	66	82
Construction equipment	6,234	476	88
Chemicals	510	71	206
Identifiable assets:			
Furniture	498	48	10
Construction equipment	4,982	308	101
Chemicals	378	42	140

* All figures in thousands.
† 20% of the construction equipment sales in the United States are intersegment.

Cummings incurred common costs during the year in the amount of $1.1 million. This balance will be assigned to the various segments based on their revenues as defined by *SFAS 14*.

During the current year, the U.S. construction equipment segment loaned $40,000 to the Canadian chemical segment. The loan is reflected in the construction equipment segment's identifiable assets, but no interest has been accrued on the loan.

Cummings also has $600,000 in general corporate assets.

Required:

Determine the segments, both industry and geographic, that Cummings must disclose. In addition, calculate whether Cummings has satisfied the 75 percent rule for industry segments.

32. Allen, Inc. is a Florida-based company operating in a variety of industries: amusement parks, car rentals, citrus fruits, motels, and restaurants. In addition, the company has a finance subsidiary used to raise funds for company expansion. For 1995, the company reported the following (in thousands):

	Amusement Parks	Car Rentals	Citrus Fruits	Motels	Restaurants
Sales	$16,019	$ 64	$ 179	$860	$612†
Operating expenses*	14,312	298	412	610	483
Income taxes	519	(116)	(161)	94	51
Loss from hurricane	(600)	–0–	(121)	–0–	–0–
Identifiable assets	6,314	89	47	591	660

* Does not include interest expense.
† 10% of restaurant sales are intersegment.

Allen has incurred an additional $390,000 in corporate expenses during 1995. The company's accountants have investigated these costs and ascertained that only $212,000 should be allocated to the various segments. Based on square footage, number of employees, and labor-hours, $140,000 of this total are to be assigned as follows:

Amusement parks	$31,000
Car rentals	11,000
Citrus fruits	10,000
Motels	31,000
Restaurants	35,000
Finance	22,000

The remaining common costs are to be distributed to the segments based on sales to unaffiliated customers.

The finance segment reports the following information for the year:

Interest income (source)	
Amusement parks	$ 52,000
Car rentals	2,000
Citrus fruits	—0—
Motels	16,000
Restaurants	24,000
Interest expense	(97,000)
Intersegment receivables	677,000

Required:

a. Which of the company's industry segments should be disclosed and why?
b. Based on the reportable segments just identified, has the company satisfied the FASB's 75 percent requirement?
c. The amusement parks segment makes up a large part of this company.
   (1) What is a dominant industry segment?
   (2) What are the disclosure requirements for a dominant industry segment?
   (3) Is the amusement parks segment a dominant industry segment?

12

ACCOUNTING FOR LEGAL REORGANIZATIONS AND LIQUIDATIONS

Questions to Consider

- What is the difference between a voluntary and an involuntary bankruptcy petition?
- What is the difference between the liquidation of an insolvent company (a Chapter 7 bankruptcy) and a reorganization (a Chapter 11 bankruptcy)?
- Why would the creditors of an insolvent company allow it to reorganize rather than attempt to force a liquidation?
- What assistance can be provided to an insolvent company by an accountant?
- What provisions are frequently found in a bankruptcy reorganization plan?
- What financial reporting is made for a company while it is going through reorganization?
- What financial reporting is made for a company that successfully leaves bankruptcy reorganization?
- If an insolvent company is liquidated, what distribution is made of the assets that result? How is a fair and equitable settlement produced?
- In bankruptcy cases, what is meant by terms such as *debtor in possession, cram down,* and *order for relief.*

One common thread that runs through a significant portion of this textbook is the accounting for an organization when viewed as a whole.[1] Chapters 2 through 7, for example, examined the consolidation of financial information generated by two or more companies that have been united in a business combination. Although the

---

[1] Intermediate accounting, in contrast, tends to examine the reporting of specific assets and liabilities such as leases, pensions, and bonds.

handling of specific accounts was included in that coverage, the primary emphasis was placed on reporting these companies as a single economic entity.

Likewise, the analysis of foreign currency translation in Chapter 9 demonstrated the procedures to be used in consolidating the financial position and operating results of a subsidiary operating anywhere in the world. Chapter 11 presented disaggregation requirements that were created as another means of disclosing complete information to describe a business. Once again, in both cases, the accounting goal was to convey data about the entire operation.

Continuing with this theme, subsequent chapters present the specialized accounting procedures utilized in reporting to the SEC as well as by partnerships, state and local government units, universities, hospitals, voluntary health and welfare organizations, estates, and trusts.

The method by which financial data is accumulated and disclosed to describe an organization is not a rigid structure. Accounting is adaptable; its development in specific circumstances is influenced by several factors: the purpose of the information, the nature of the organization, the environment in which the entity operates, and so on. Thus, to report a business combination, a foreign subsidiary, an industry segment, a partnership, a government unit, an estate, or a nonprofit organization, accountants must develop unique reporting techniques that meet particular needs and problems.

Chapter 12 extends this coverage by presenting the accounting procedures required in bankruptcy cases. Because a financially troubled company as well as its owners and creditors all face the prospect of incurring significant losses, the accountant must adapt financial reporting to meet their many and varied informational needs. The rise in the number of failed businesses in recent years has made this accounting process especially important.

Accounting for Legal Reorganizations and Liquidations

A basic assumption of accounting is that a business is considered a *going concern* unless evidence to the contrary is discovered. As a result, assets such as inventory, land, buildings, and equipment are reported based on historical cost rather than net realizable value. Unfortunately, not all companies prove to be going concerns. According to the Dun & Bradstreet Corporation, 87,226 businesses failed in the United States during 1991 alone.[2] A list of organizations beginning bankruptcy proceedings during recent years contains some of the best-known corporate names in America:

Wang Laboratories
Phar-Mor, Inc.
Savin Corporation

---

[2] "Business Failures Rose 44% in 1991 to a Record Level," *The Wall Street Journal*, February 21, 1992, p. A2.

R. H. Macy & Company

Trans World Airlines

Revco, D. S. Inc.

Colt's Manufacturing

Drexel Burnham Lambert Group

Orion Pictures

Zale Corporation

Presidential Airlines

Kaiser Steel Corporation[3]

What happens to these businesses after they fail? Who gets the assets? Are the creditors protected? How does the accountant reflect the economic plight of the company?

Virtually all businesses undergo financial difficulties at various times. Economic downturns, poor product performance, or litigation losses can create cash flow difficulties for even the best-managed organizations. Most companies take remedial actions and work to return their operations to normal profitability. However, as the preceding list indicates, not all companies are able to solve their monetary difficulties. If problems persist, a company can eventually become *insolvent*, unable to pay debts as the obligations come due. When creditors are not paid, they obviously attempt to protect their financial interests in hopes of reducing the possibility of loss. They may seek recovery from the distressed company in several ways: repossession of assets, the filing of lawsuits, foreclosure on loans, and so on. An insolvent company can literally become beseiged by its creditors.

If left unchecked, pandemonium would be the possible outcome of a company's insolvency. As a result, some of the creditors and stockholders as well as the company itself could find themselves treated unfairly. One party might be able to collect in full while another is left with a total loss. *Thus, bankruptcy laws have been established in the United States to structure this process, provide protection for all parties, and ensure fair and equitable treatment.*

Although a complete coverage of bankruptcy statutes is more appropriate for a business law textbook, significant aspects of this process directly involve accountants. "In many small business situations, the company accountant is the sole outside financial advisor and the first to recognize that the deteriorating financial picture mandates consideration of bankruptcy in one form or another. In many such situations, the accountant's role in convincing management that a timely reorganization under the bankruptcy law is the sole means of salvaging any part of the business may be critical."[4]

---

[3] The author is personally aware of the trauma associated with bankruptcy since he owned several hundred shares of both Presidential Airlines and Kaiser Steel at the time each company filed for bankruptcy. The demise of these two companies may be taken as an indication of the author's astute investment expertise.

[4] John K. Pearson, "The Role of the Accountant in Business Bankruptcies," *The National Public Accountant,* November 1982, p. 22.

Bankruptcy Reform Act of 1978

> Over the ages debtors who found themselves unable to meet obligations were dealt with harshly. Not only were all their assets taken from them, but they were given little or no relief through legal forgiveness of debts. Many of them ended up in debtors' prisons with all means of rehabilitation removed. A large number of the early settlers in this country left their homelands to escape such a fate.[5]

Based on an original provision of the U.S. Constitution, all bankruptcy laws in this country must be created by Congress. However, virtually no federal bankruptcy laws were actually passed until the Bankruptcy Act of 1898 (which was subsequently revised in 1938 by the Chandler Act). Later, following a decade of study and debate of Congress, these laws were replaced with the Bankruptcy Reform Act of 1978. Today, this legislation provides the legal structure for most bankruptcy proceedings.[6] *To this end, it strives to achieve two goals in connection with insolvency cases: (1) the fair distribution of assets to creditors and (2) the discharge of an honest debtor from debt.*

Voluntary and Involuntary Petitions. When insolvency occurs, any interested party has the right to seek protection under the Bankruptcy Reform Act.[7] Thus, the company itself can file a petition with the court to begin bankruptcy proceedings. If the company is the instigator, the process is referred to as a *voluntary* bankruptcy. In such cases, the company's petition has to be accompanied by exhibits listing all debts as well as assets (reported at fair market value). Company officials must also respond to questions concerning various aspects of the business's affairs. Such questions include:

- When did the business commence?
- In whose possession are the books of account and records?
- When was the last inventory of property taken?

Creditors also may seek to force a debtor into bankruptcy (known as an *involuntary* bankruptcy) in hopes of reducing their potential losses. To avoid nuisance actions, bankruptcy laws regulate the filing of involuntary petitions. Where a company has 12 or more unsecured creditors, at least 3 have to sign the petition. In addition, the creditors that sign must have unsecured debts of at least $5,000. If fewer than 12 unsecured creditors exist, only a single signer is required

---

[5] Homer A. Bonhiver, *The Expanded Role of the Accountant under the 1978 Bankruptcy Code* (New York: Deloitte Haskins & Sells, 1980), p. 7.

[6] The Bankruptcy Reform Act applies to corporations, partnerships, and individuals. However, certain types of companies are excluded from portions or even all of its provisions because other laws are applicable. Such organizations include insurance companies, banks, railroads, and stockbrokers.

[7] As is discussed later in this chapter, insolvency (not being able to pay debts as they come due) is not necessary for the filing of a bankruptcy petition. Such companies as the Manville Corporation, Texaco, and A. H. Robins have filed for protection under the Bankruptcy Reform Act in hopes of settling massive litigation claims.

but the $5,000 minimum debt limit remains. Zale Corporation's creditors provide an example of the former situation. ''Three Zale Corporation bondholders filed an involuntary bankruptcy law petition against the troubled jewelry chain yesterday, two days after it declared a moratorium on all payments to banks, bondholders and suppliers. Whether Zale, the nation's largest jewelry chain, will fight the petition remains to be seen.''[8]

Neither a voluntary nor an involuntary petition automatically creates a bankruptcy case. Voluntary petitions are rejected by the court if the action is considered detrimental to the creditors. Involuntary petitions can also be rejected unless evidence exists to indicate that the debtor is not actually able to meet obligations as they come due. Merely being slow to pay is not sufficient. Normally, though, the petition is accepted by the court and an *order for relief* is granted. This order halts all actions against the debtor, thus providing time for the various parties involved to develop a course of action.

In addition, the company comes under the authority of the bankruptcy court so that any distributions must be made in a fair manner. ''To prevent creditors from seizing whatever is handy once the bankruptcy is filed, the Bankruptcy Code provides for an automatic stay or injunction that prohibits actions by creditors to collect debts from the debtor or the debtor's property without the court's permission. The automatic stay bars any creditor (including governmental creditors such as the Internal Revenue Service) from taking any action against the debtor or the debtor's property.''[9]

Classification of Creditors. Following the issuance of an order for relief, each creditor's view of a bankruptcy case is obviously influenced by the possible risk of loss. However, many creditors may have already obtained some measure of security for themselves. At the time a debt is created, the parties can agree that a mortgage lien or security interest will be attached to specified assets (known as *collateral*) owned by the debtor. Such action is most likely when the amounts involved are great or the debtor is experiencing financial difficulty. In the event that the liability is not paid, the creditor has the right to force the sale (or, in some cases, the return) of the pledged property with the proceeds being used to satisfy all or part of the obligation. Thus, in bankruptcy proceedings, a secured creditor is in a much less vulnerable position than an unsecured creditor.

Because of the possible presence of liens, all loans and other liabilities are reported to the court according to their degree of protection against loss. Hence, some debts are identified as *fully secured* to indicate that the net realizable value of the collateral exceeds the amount of the obligation. Despite the debtor's insolvency, these creditors will not suffer loss; they are completely protected by the pledged property. Any money received from the asset that is in excess of the balance of the debt is used to pay unsecured creditors.

---

[8] ''Dissident Bondholders File Petition to Force Zale into Bankruptcy,'' *The Wall Street Journal,* January 2, 1992, p. A4.

[9] Pearson, ''The Role of the Accountant,'' p. 24.

Conversely, if a liability is *partially secured,* the value of the collateral covers only a portion of the obligation. The remainder is considered unsecured so that the creditor risks losing some or all of this additional amount. As an example, a bank might have a $90,000 loan due from an insolvent party protected by a lien attached to land valued at $64,000. This debt is only partially secured; $26,000 of the balance would not be satisfied by the asset and must be reported to the court as unsecured.

All other liabilities are unsecured; these creditors have no legal right to any specific assets of the debtor. They are only entitled to share in any funds that remain after all secured claims have been settled. Obviously, unsecured creditors are in a precarious position. Unless a debtor's assets greatly exceed secured liabilities (which is unlikely in most insolvency cases), significant losses can be expected if liquidation is necessary. Hence, one of the most important aspects of the bankruptcy laws is the ranking of unsecured claims. Only in this manner is a systematic distribution of any remaining assets possible.

The Bankruptcy Reform Act does identify several types of unsecured liabilities that have priority and must be paid before other unsecured debts are settled. These obligations are ranked with each level having to be satisfied in full before any payment is made to the next.

Unsecured Liabilities Having Priority

1. Claims for administrative expenses such as the costs of preserving and liquidating the estate. All trustee expenses are included in this category as well as the costs of outside attorneys, accountants, or other consultants. Without this high-priority ranking, insolvent companies would have extreme problems convincing qualified individuals to serve in these essential positions. However, in recent years, the amounts assessed for such services have come under fire from many critics: "The 26 firms involved in the Eastern Air Lines Inc. bankruptcy in 1989 charged close to $86 million in fees."[10]

2. Obligations arising between the date that a petition is filed with the bankruptcy court and the appointment of a trustee or the issuance of an order for relief. In voluntary cases, such claims are quite rare since an order for relief is usually entered at the time the petition is filed. This provision is important, however, in helping the debtor to continue operations if an involuntary petition is presented but no legal action is immediately taken. Without this ranking, suppliers would stop supplying merchandise to the debtor until the matter was resolved.

3. Employee claims for wages earned during the 90 days preceding the filing of a petition. The amount of this priority is limited, though, to $2,000 per individual. This priority ranking is designed to prevent em-

---

[10] Ronald Glover, Kathleen Kerwin, and Lisa Driscoll, "There's Plenty for All at the Bankruptcy Banquet," *Business Week,* November 4, 1991, p. 124.

ployees from being penalized by the company's problems and also encourages them to continue working until the bankruptcy issue is settled.

4. Employee claims for contributions to benefit plans earned during the 180 days preceding the filing of a petition. Once again, a limit of $2,000 per individual (reduced by certain specified payments) is enforced.

5. Claims for the return of deposits made by customers to acquire property or services which were never delivered or provided by the debtor. The priority figure, in this case, is limited to $900. These claimants did not intend to be creditors; they were merely trying to make a purchase.

6. Government claims for unpaid taxes.

All other obligations of an insolvent company are classified as general unsecured claims that can be repaid only after the creditors with priority have been satisfied. *If the funds that remain for the general unsecured debts are not sufficient to settle all claims, the available money must be divided proportionally.*

Discussion Question: What Do We Do Now?

The Toledo Shirt Company manufactures men's shirts sold to department stores and other outlets throughout Ohio, Illinois, and Indiana. For the past 14 years, one of the Toledo's major customers has been Abraham and Sons, a chain of nine stores selling men's clothing. Unfortunately, 18 months ago, Mr. Abraham retired and his two sons took complete control of the organization. Since that time, they have invested enormous sums of money in an attempt to expand each store by selling women's clothing. Success in this new market has been difficult; Abraham and Sons is not known for selling women's clothing and no one in the company has much expertise in the area.

Approximately seven months ago, James Thurber, the chief financial officer of the Toledo Shirt Company, began to notice that it was taking longer than usual to collect payments from Abraham and Sons. Instead of the normal 30 days, this retailer was taking at least 45 days—and frequently longer—to pay each invoice. Because of the amount of money involved, Thurber began to monitor the balance each day. When the age of the receivable ($71,000) hit 65 days, he placed a call to Abraham and Sons. The treasurer assured him that the company was merely having seasonal cash flow problems but that payments would soon be back on a normal schedule.

Thurber was still concerned and shortly thereafter placed Abraham and Sons on a "cash and carry" basis; no sales were to be made unless cash was collected in advance. The company's treasurer immediately called Thurber to complain bitterly. "We have been one of your best customers for well over a decade but now that we have gotten into a bit of trouble you stab us in

continued

the back. When we straighten things out here, we will remember this. We can get our shirts from someone else. Our expansions are now complete; we have hired an expert to help us market women's clothing. We can see the light at the end of the tunnel. Abraham and Sons will soon be more profitable than ever.'' In hopes of appeasing the customer while still protecting his own position, Thurber agreed to sell merchandise to Abraham and Sons on a very limited credit basis.

A few days later, Thurber received a disturbing phone call from a vice president with another clothing manufacturer. ''We've got to force Abraham and Sons into bankruptcy immediately to protect ourselves. Those guys are running the company straight into the ground. They owe me $38,000 and I can only hope to collect a small portion of it now. I need two other creditors to sign the petition and I want Toledo Shirt to be one of them. Abraham and Sons has already mortgaged all of its buildings and equipment so we can't get anything from those assets. Inventory stocks are dwindling and sales have disappeared since they've tried to change the image of their stores. We can still get some of our money but if we wait much longer nothing will be left but the bones.''

Should the Toledo Shirt Company be loyal to a good customer or start the bankruptcy process to protect itself? What actions should Thurber take?

Liquidation versus Reorganization.   The most important decision in any bankruptcy filing (either voluntary or involuntary) is the method by which the debtor will be discharged from its obligations. One obvious option is to liquidate the company's assets with the proceeds being distributed to creditors based on their secured positions and the priority ranking system just outlined. However, a very important alternative to liquidation does exist. The debtor company may survive insolvency and continue operations if a proposal for reorganization is accepted by the parties involved.

Under most reorganization plans, the creditors agree to absorb a partial loss rather than force the insolvent company to liquidate. Before accepting such an arrangement, the creditors (as well as the bankruptcy court) must be convinced that a greater return will be achieved by helping to rehabilitate the debtor. Often, as an example, payment of a specified percentage of the debt is promised to the creditors but only at some future date. One benefit associated with reorganizations is that the creditor may be able to retain the insolvent company as a customer. In many cases, continuation of this relationship is an important concern if the debtor has historically been a good client. Furthermore, the priority ranking system often leaves the general unsecured creditors with very little to lose in trying to avoid a liquidation.

Legal guidelines for the liquidation of a debtor are contained in Chapter 7 of Title I of the Bankruptcy Reform Act while Chapter 11 describes the reorganization process. Consequently, the proceedings have come to be referred to as a "Chapter 7 bankruptcy" (liquidation) or a "Chapter 11 bankruptcy" (reorganization). Accountants face two entirely different reporting situations depending on the type of bankruptcy encountered. However, in both cases, sufficient data must be obtained and reported to keep all parties adequately informed about the events as they occur.

Statement of Financial Affairs

Normally, at the start of bankruptcy proceedings, a statement of financial affairs is prepared for the debtor.[11] This schedule provides information about the current financial position of the company and helps all of the parties as they consider what actions to take. This statement is especially important in assisting the unsecured creditors as they decide whether to push for reorganization or liquidation. The debtor's assets and liabilities are reported according to the classifications relevant to a liquidation.

Consequently, assets are labeled as:

1. Pledged with fully secured creditors.
2. Pledged with partially secured creditors.
3. Available for priority liabilities and unsecured creditors (often referred to as *free assets*).

The debts of the company are then listed in a parallel fashion as:

1. Liabilities with priority.
2. Fully secured creditors.
3. Partially secured creditors.
4. Unsecured creditors.

Stockholders are included in this final group.

The statement of financial affairs is produced under the assumption that liquidation will occur. Thus, historical cost figures are not relevant. The various parties to the bankruptcy desire information that reflects (1) the net realizable value of the debtor's assets and (2) the ultimate application of these proceeds to specific liabilities. Based on this data, both creditors and stockholders are able to estimate the monetary resources that will be available after all secured claims and priority liabilities have been settled. By comparing this total with the amount of unsecured liabilities, any member of these groups can approximate the potential loss that is being faced.

---

[11] The questionnaire completed by the insolvent company at the beginning of the bankruptcy proceedings is referred to as a statement of affairs. Although the titles are similar, the schedule of assets and liabilities discussed here is quite different from the legal questionnaire.

The information found in a statement of financial affairs can affect the outcome of the bankruptcy. If, for example, the statement indicates that unsecured creditors are destined to suffer a material loss in a liquidation, this group will probably favor reorganizing the company in hopes of averting such a consequence. Conversely, if the statement shows that all creditors will be paid in full and that a distribution to the stockholders is also possible, liquidation becomes a much more viable option. Thus, all parties involved with an insolvent company should consult a statement of financial affairs before deciding on the fate of the operation.

Statement of Financial Affairs Illustrated

To demonstrate the preparation of this statement, assume that the Chaplin Company has experienced severe financial difficulties in recent times and is currently insolvent. A voluntary bankruptcy petition will soon be filed and company officials are trying to decide whether to seek liquidation or reorganization. Consequently, they have asked their accountant to produce a statement of financial affairs to assist them in formulating an appropriate strategy. A current balance sheet for Chaplin, prepared as if the company were a going concern, is presented in Exhibit 12–1.

Prior to the creation of a statement of financial affairs, additional data must be ascertained concerning the insolvent company and its assets and liabilities. Hence, in this illustration, the following information has been accumulated about the Chaplin Company:

- The investments reported on the balance sheet have appreciated in value since being acquired and are now worth $20,000. Dividends of $500 are currently due from these investments, although this revenue has not yet been recognized by Chaplin.
- Officials estimate that $12,000 of the company's accounts receivable can still be collected despite the bankruptcy proceedings.
- By spending $5,000 for repairs and marketing, the inventory currently held by Chaplin can be sold for $50,000.
- A refund of $1,000 will be received from the various prepaid expenses but the company's intangible assets have no resale value.
- The land and building are in an excellent location and can be sold for a figure 10 percent more than book value. However, the equipment was specially designed for Chaplin. Company officials anticipate having trouble even finding a buyer unless the price is reduced considerably. Hence, they expect to receive only 40 percent of current book value for these assets.
- Administrative costs of $21,500 are projected if liquidation of the company does occur.
- Accrued expenses include salaries of $13,000. Of this figure, one executive is owed a total of $3,000 but that individual is the only employee due

---

EXHIBIT 12-1   **Financial Position Prior to Bankruptcy Petition**

CHAPLIN COMPANY
Balance Sheet
June 30, 1995

Assets

Current assets:

Cash	$ 2,000	
Investment in marketable securities	15,000	
Accounts receivable (net)	23,000	
Inventory	41,000	
Prepaid expenses	3,000	$ 84,000

Land, building, equipment, and other assets:

Land	100,000	
Building (net)	110,000	
Equipment (net)	80,000	
Intangible assets	15,000	305,000
Total assets		$389,000

Liabilities and Stockholders' Equity

Current liabilities:

Notes payable (secured by inventory)	$ 75,000	
Accounts payable	60,000	
Accrued expenses	18,000	$153,000

Long-term liabilities:

Notes payable (secured by lien on land and buildings)		200,000

Stockholders' equity:

Common stock	100,000	
Retained earnings (deficit)	(64,000)	36,000
Total liabilities and stockholders' equity		$389,000

---

an amount in excess of $2,000. Payroll taxes withheld from wages but not yet paid to the government total $3,000. However, company records currently show only $1,000 portion of this liability.

- Interest of $5,000 on the company's long-term liabilities has not been accrued for 1995.

From this information, the statement of financial affairs presented in Exhibit 12–2 for the Chaplin Company can be prepared. Several aspects of this statement should be specifically noted:

1. The current and long-term distinctions usually applied to assets and liabilities are omitted. Since the company is on the verge of going out of business, such classifications are meaningless. Instead, the statement is designed to separate the secured and unsecured balances.

2. Book values are included on the left side of the schedule but only for informational purposes. These figures are not relevant in a bankruptcy. *All assets are reported at net realizable value, whereas liabilities are shown at the amount required for settlement.*

3. The dividend receivable and the interest payable are both included in Exhibit 12–2, although neither has been recorded on the balance sheet. The payroll tax liability is also reported at the amount presently owed by the company. Since these balances represent future cash flows, currently updated figures must be disclosed within the statement of financial affairs.

4. Liabilities having priority are individually identified within the liability

---

EXHIBIT 12–2

CHAPLIN COMPANY
Statement of Financial Affairs
June 30, 1995

Book Values			Available for Unsecured Creditors
	Assets		
	Pledged with fully secured creditors:		
$210,000	Land and building	$231,000	
	Less: Notes payable (long term)	(200,000)	
	Interest payable	(5,000)	$26,000
	Pledged with partially secured creditors:		
41,000	Inventory	$ 45,000	
	Less: Notes payable (current)	(75,000)	–0–
	Free assets:		
2,000	Cash		2,000
15,000	Investment in marketable securities		20,000
–0–	Dividends receivable		500
23,000	Accounts receivable		12,000
3,000	Prepaid expenses.		1,000
80,000	Equipment.		32,000
15,000	Intangible assets		–0–
	Total available to pay liabilities with priority and unsecured creditors		93,500
	Less: Liabilities with priority (listed on opposite page)		(36,500) Ⓑ
	Available for unsecured creditors		57,000 Ⓓ
	Estimated deficiency		38,000 Ⓔ
$389,000			$95,000

EXHIBIT 12–2 *(concluded)*

Book Values			Unsecured—Nonpriority Liabilities
	Liabilities and Stockholders' Equity		
	Liabilities with priority:		
–0–	Administrative expenses	$ 21,500	
$ 13,000	Salaries payable (accrued expenses) . . .	12,000	$ 1,000 Ⓒ
1,000	Payroll taxes payable (accrued expenses) .	3,000	
	Total	$ 36,500 Ⓐ	
	Fully secured creditors:		
200,000	Notes payable	200,000	
–0–	Interest payable	5,000	
	Less: Land and building	(231,000)	–0–
	Partially secured creditors:		
75,000	Notes payable	75,000	
	Less: Inventory	(45,000)	30,000
	Unsecured creditors:		
60,000	Accounts payable		60,000
4,000	Accrued expenses (other than salaries and payroll taxes)		4,000
36,000	Stockholders' equity		
$389,000			$95,000

section (point A). Because these claims will be paid before other unsecured creditors, the $36,500 total is also subtracted directly from the free assets (point B). Although not yet incurred, estimated administrative costs are included in this category since such expenses will be necessary for a liquidation. Salaries payable are also considered priority liabilities. However, the $1,000 owed to an employee in excess of the individual $2,000 limit is separated as an unsecured claim (point C).

5. According to this statement, if liquidation occurs, Chaplin expects to have only $57,000 in free assets remaining after settling all liabilities with priority (point D). Unfortunately, the liability section shows unsecured claims with a total of $95,000. These creditors, therefore, face a $38,000 loss ($95,000 − $57,000) if the company is liquidated (point E). This final distribution is often stated in a percentage form:

$$\frac{\text{Free assets}}{\text{Unsecured claims}} = \frac{\$57,000}{\$95,000} = 60\%$$

Thus, unsecured creditors can anticipate receiving only 60 percent of their claims. An individual, for example, who is owed $400 by this company should anticipate collecting only $240 ($400 × 60%) following liquidation.

6. If the statement of financial affairs had shown the company with more free assets (after subtracting liabilities with priority) than unsecured claims, all creditors could expect to be paid in full with any excess money going to Chaplin's stockholders.

Liquidation—A Chapter 7 Bankruptcy

When an insolvent company is to be liquidated, the process is regulated by the provisions found in Chapter 7 of the Bankruptcy Reform Act. This set of laws was written to provide an orderly and equitable structure for the selling of assets and payment of debts. To this end, several events occur after an order for relief has been entered by the court in either a voluntary or involuntary liquidation case.

First, an interim trustee is appointed by the court to oversee the company and its liquidation. This individual is charged with preserving the assets and preventing loss of the estate. Thus, creditors are protected from any detrimental actions that might be undertaken by the management, the ownership, or any of the other creditors. The interim trustee (as well as the permanent trustee if one is subsequently selected by the creditors) must carry out a number of tasks shortly after being appointed. These functions would include (but not be limited to) the following:

- Changing locks and moving all assets and records to locations controlled by the trustee.
- Posting notices that all assets of the business are now in the possession of the U.S. trustee and that tampering or removal of any contents is a violation of federal laws.
- Notifying the post office that all mail for the company is to be sent to the trustee.
- Opening a new bank account in the name of the trustee, and notifying banks that no withdrawals of the company's money are allowed except by the trustee.
- Compiling all financial records and placing them in the custody of the trustee's own accountant.
- Obtaining possession of any corporate records including minute books and other official documents.[12]

The court then calls for a meeting of all creditors who have appropriately filed a proof of claim against the debtor. This group may choose to elect a permanent trustee to replace the person temporarily appointed by the court. A majority (in

---

[12] Bonhiver, *The Expanded Role of the Accountant,* pp. 50–51.

number as well as in dollars due from the company) of the unsecured, nonpriority creditors must agree to this new trustee. If a decision cannot be reached by the creditors, the interim trustee is retained.

As a further action taken to ensure fairness, a committee of between 3 and 11 unsecured creditors is selected to help protect the group's interests. This committee of creditors:

- Consults with the trustee regarding the administration of the estate.
- Makes recommendations to the trustee regarding the performance of the trustee's duties.
- Submits to the court any questions affecting the administration of the estate.[13]

Role of the Trustee

In the liquidation of any company, the trustee is a central figure. This individual must recover all property belonging to the insolvent company, preserve the estate from any further deterioration, liquidate noncash assets, and make distributions to the proper claimants. Additionally, the trustee may even need to continue operating the company to complete business activities that were in progress when the order for relief was entered. To accomplish such a multitude of objectives, this individual holds wide-ranging authority in bankruptcy matters. For example, the trustee has the right to appoint attorneys, accountants, consultants, and other outside professionals as needed to provide assistance.

The trustee can also void any transfer of property (known as a *preference*) made by the debtor within 90 days *prior* to the filing of the bankruptcy petition if the company was already insolvent at the time. These payments must then be returned by the recipient and be included within the debtor's free assets.[14] For example,

> Drexel Burnham Lambert Group Inc. made more than $600 million in payments that may be recoverable under bankruptcy law because the transactions occurred during the three months immediately prior to the company's bankruptcy-court filing. The payments were disclosed in the company's statement of financial affairs, . . . such payments, with certain exceptions, can be recovered if it is shown that a company gave preference to some creditors and if the debtor was insolvent at the time.[15]

This rule is intended to prevent one party from gaining advantage over another in the sometimes hectic period just before a bankruptcy petition is filed. Return of

---

[13] Ibid., p. 26.

[14] The 90-day limit is extended to one year if the transfer is made to an inside party such as an officer or a director or an affiliated company. The one-year limit also applies to any transfer made by the debtor with the intent to defraud another party.

[15] Wade Lambert, "Drexel Payments of Over $600 Million Before Chapter 11 May Be Recoverable," *The Wall Street Journal*, May 7, 1990, p. A3.

the asset is not necessary, however, if the transfer was for no more than would have been paid to this party in a liquidation.

Not surprisingly, the trustee must make a proper recording of all activities and report them periodically to the court and other interested parties. For this purpose, the trustee can either establish a separate set of financial records or simply use the accounting system of the insolvent company. To reflect the stewardship responsibility being accepted, trustees frequently prefer to start their own independent record-keeping system, especially in cases where liquidation is to occur.

Interestingly, the actual reporting rules created by the Bankruptcy Reform Act are quite general: "Each trustee, examiner, and debtor-in-possession is required to file 'such reports as are necessary or as the court orders.' . . . In the past there have been no specific guidelines or forms used in the preparation of these reports."[16] Consequently, a wide variety of statements and reports may be encountered in liquidations. However, *a statement of realization and liquidation* is commonly used by the trustee to report the major aspects of the liquidation process. This statement is designed to convey the following information:

- The account balances reported by the company at the date on which the order for relief was filed.
- The cash receipts generated by the sale of the debtor's property.
- The cash disbursements made by the trustee to wind up the affairs of the business and to pay the secured creditors.
- Any other transactions of the company such as the write-off of assets and the recognition of unrecorded liabilities.

Any cash balances that remain after this series of events are paid to the unsecured creditors with the priority claims being settled first.

Statement of Realization and Liquidation Illustrated

To demonstrate the production of a statement of realization and liquidation, the information previously presented for the Chaplin Company is once again utilized. Assume that company officials have decided to liquidate the business, a procedure regulated by Chapter 7 of the Bankruptcy Reform Act. An interim trustee is appointed by the court and then confirmed by the creditors to oversee the liquidation of assets and distribution of cash. A creditors' committee is also formed to ensure a fair and impartial distribution.

The dollar amounts resulting from this liquidation do not necessarily agree with the balances used in creating the statement of financial affairs in Exhibit

---

[16] In a reorganization, the ownership usually remains in possession of the company. This group is allowed to continue operating the business and is referred to as a *debtor in possession*. To monitor the debtor in possession's activities, the court has the right to appoint an examiner. This individual investigates the business so that reports and recommendations can be made to the courts. (See, for example, "The CPA's Role as Bankruptcy Examiner," *The CPA Journal,* September 1991, pp. 42–50.) Quote from Bonhiver, *The Expanded Role of the Accountant,* p. 69.

12–2. The previous statement was based on projected sales and other estimations, whereas a statement of realization and liquidation reports the actual transactions and other events as they occur. Consequently, discrepancies should be expected. The following transactions occur in liquidating this company:

Liquidation of Chaplin Company

1995

July 1   The accounting records shown in Exhibit 12–1 are adjusted to correct balances as of June 30, 1995, the date on which the order for relief was entered. Hence, the dividends receivable, interest payable, and additional payroll tax liability are recognized.

July 23   The trustee expends $7,000 to dispose of the company's inventory at a negotiated price of $51,000. The net cash results are applied to the notes payable for which the inventory had served as partial security.

July 29   Collection is made of the $500 cash dividend accrued as of June 30. The related investments (originally costing $15,000) are then sold for $19,600.

Aug. 17   Accounts receivable of $16,000 are collected. The remaining balances are written off as bad debts.

Aug. 30   The trustee determines that no refund is available from any of the company's prepaid expenses. The intangible assets are also removed from the financial records because they have no cash value.

Sept. 25 The land and building are sold for $208,000 with $205,000 of this money being immediately used by the trustee to pay off the secured creditors.

Oct. 9   After an extended search for a buyer, the equipment is sold for $42,000 in cash.

Nov. 1   An invoice of $24,900 is received for various administrative expenses incurred in liquidating the company. The trustee also reclassifies the remaining partially secured liabilities as unsecured.

Nov. 9   Since the noncash assets have now been converted into cash and all secured claims settled, the trustee begins to plan for the distribution of any remaining funds. The liabilities with priority are to be paid first. The excess will then be applied to the claims of unsecured nonpriority creditors.

The actual structure used in producing a statement of realization and liquidation can vary significantly. One popular form presents the various account groups on a horizontal plane with the liquidating transactions shown vertically. In this manner, accountants are able to record the events as they occur as well as their effect on each account classification. Exhibit 12–3 has been constructed in this style to display the liquidation of the Chaplin Company.

As can be seen from this exhibit, many aspects of the statement of realization and liquidation are no more than mechanical bookkeeping procedures used to record the liquidating transactions: inventory is sold at a profit, creditors are paid, receivables and dividends are collected, and so forth. Probably the most signifi-

EXHIBIT 12–3   Final Statement

CHAPLIN COMPANY
Statement of Realization and Liquidation
June 30, 1995 to November 9, 1995

Date		Cash	Noncash Assets	Liabilities with Priority	Fully Secured Creditors	Partially Secured Creditors	Unsecured— Nonpriority Liabilities	Stockholders' Equity (Deficit)
6/30/95	Book balances.	$ 2,000	$387,000	$13,000*	$200,000	$75,000	$65,000†	$ 36,000
7/1/95	Adjustments for dividends, interest, and payroll taxes. . .		500	2,000	5,000			(6,500)
7/1/95	Adjusted book balances . . .	2,000	387,500	15,000	205,000	75,000	65,000	29,500
7/23/95	Inventory sold—recorded net of disposal costs	44,000	(41,000)					3,000
7/23/95	Proceeds from inventory paid to secured creditors.	(44,000)				(44,000)		
7/29/95	Investments sold and dividends received.	20,100	(15,500)					4,600
8/17/95	Receivables collected with remainder written off. . . .	16,000	(23,000)					(7,000)
8/30/95	Intangible assets and prepaid expenses written off		(18,000)					(18,000)
9/25/95	Land and building sold. . . .	208,000	(210,000)					(2,000)
9/25/95	Proceeds from land and building paid to secured creditors	(205,000)			(205,000)			
10/9/95	Equipment sold	42,000	(80,000)					(38,000)
11/1/95	Administrative expenses accrued			24,900				(24,900)
11/1/95	Excess of partially secured liabilities reclassified as an unsecured claim					(31,000)	31,000	
11/9/95	Final balances remaining for unsecured creditors	$ 83,100	-0-	$39,900	-0-	-0-	$96,000	$(52,800)

* Includes salary payable of $12,000 (amount due employees but limited to $2,000 per individual) and $1,000 in payroll taxes owed to the government.

† Accounts payable plus accrued expenses other than salary payable (within $2,000 per person limitation) and payroll tax liability.

cant information presented in this statement is the measurement and classification of the insolvent company's liabilities. In the same manner as the statement of financial affairs, both fully and partially secured claims are reported separately from liabilities with priority and unsecured nonpriority claims.

For the Chaplin Company, Exhibit 12–3 discloses that $135,900 in debts remain as of November 9 ($39,900 in priority claims and $96,000 in unsecured nonpriority liabilities). Unfortunately, after satisfying all of the secured liabilities, only $83,100 in cash is retained by the company. The trustee must first use this money to pay the three liabilities with priority according to the following ranking:

Administrative expenses	$24,900
Salaries payable (within the $2,000 per person limitation)	12,000
Payroll taxes payable	3,000
Total	$39,900

These disbursements leave the company with only $43,200 ($83,100 − $39,900) in cash but $96,000 in unsecured liabilities. Consequently, the remaining creditors are only able to collect 45 percent of their claims against the Chaplin Company:

$$\frac{\$43,200}{\$96,000} = 45 \text{ percent}$$

Because all liabilities have not been paid in full, the stockholders receive nothing from the liquidation process.

Interestingly, the unsecured nonpriority creditors are receiving a smaller percentage of their claims than the 60 percent figure projected in the statement of financial affairs (produced in Exhibit 12–2). Although this earlier statement plays an important role in bankruptcy proceedings, its accuracy is limited by the preparer's ability to foretell future events.

Reorganization—A Chapter 11 Bankruptcy

Reorganization under the federal Bankruptcy Code is a way to salvage a company, not liquidate it. While it's true that the original owners of a company rescued in this way are often left without anything, others whose livelihoods depend on the company's fortunes may come out with their interests intact. The company's creditors, for example, may take over as the new owners. Its suppliers still may count on the company as a customer. Its customers still may count on the company as a supplier. And perhaps most important, many of its employees may be able to keep the jobs that otherwise would have been sacrificed in a liquidation.[17]

[17] John Robbins, Al Goll, and Paul Rosenfield, "Accounting for Companies in Chapter 11 Reorganization," *Journal of Accountancy,* January 1991, p. 75.

For the year ending December 31, 1988, 15,541 petitions (both voluntary and involuntary) were filed in the United States to reorganize insolvent corporations based on Chapter 11 of the Bankruptcy Reform Act.[18] In such cases, an attempt is being made to salvage the company so that operations can continue. Although this legal procedure offers the company some hope of survival, reorganization is certainly not a guarantee of future prosperity: approximately 8 out of 10 companies that file under Chapter 11 are still eventually liquidated.[19] Many reorganizations may actually fail because the debtor struggles too long before filing a petition:

> Seeking bankruptcy because disaster looms—not after it has arrived—helps (gives the corporation time and provides equality of treatment). . . . Once a company files under the bankruptcy laws, suppliers are likely to demand cash on delivery. So management that moves before liquid assets are depleted has a better chance of making a go of reorganization.[20]

Obviously, the activities and events surrounding a reorganization differ significantly from a liquidation. One important distinction is that control over the company is normally retained by the ownership (referred to as a *debtor in possession*). However, if fraud or gross mismanagement can be proven, the court still has the authority to appoint an independent trustee to assume control. For example, a trustee was brought in to take over Eastern Airlines after the bankruptcy judge found the management of Eastern and its parent to be "unfit" to operate the airline.[21] Unless replaced, the debtor in possession continues to operate the company and has the primary responsibility for developing an acceptable plan of reorganization.

While a reorganization is in process, the owners and managers are legally required to preserve the company's estate as of the date that the order for relief is entered. In this way, the bankruptcy regulations seek to reduce the losses that may have to be absorbed by creditors and stockholders when either reorganization or liquidation eventually occurs. For this reason, a newsletter distributed by the A. H. Robins Company to employees a few days after the corporation filed for Chapter 11 protection specified that "the company cannot pay any creditor or supplier for goods delivered or services rendered before August 21, 1985. The company is prohibited from making such payments unless there is a special court order. Monthly bills will have to be prorated to assure all creditors are treated the same."[22]

---

[18] Grant W. Newton, *Bankruptcy & Insolvency Accounting, 4th ed.* (New York: John Wiley & Sons, 1989), p. 56. (This source also indicates that 38,590 petitions for Chapter 7 liquidation were filed during the same period.)

[19] Steven P. Galante, "Filing for Bankruptcy May Be Best Way to Save the Business," *The Wall Street Journal,* March 24, 1986, p. 23.

[20] Daniel B. Moskowitz and Mark Ivey, "You Don't Have to Be Broke to Need Chapter 11," *Business Week,* April 27, 1987, p. 108.

[21] Carolyn Phillips, "Marty Shugrue Has Background Needed to Save Eastern Air," *The Wall Street Journal,* April 20, 1990, p. A6.

[22] Thomas R. Morris, "Some Questions Went Unasked," *Richmond Times-Dispatch,* May 18, 1986, p. B1.

The Plan for Reorganization

> The plan is the heart of every Chapter 11 reorganization. The provisions of the plan specify the treatment of all creditors and equity holders upon its approval by the Bankruptcy Court. Moreover, the plan shapes the financial structure of the entity that emerges.[23]

The most intriguing aspect of a Chapter 11 bankruptcy is the plan developed to rescue the company from insolvency. Initially, proposals can be filed with the court only by the debtor in possession. However, if a plan for reorganization is not put forth within 120 days of the order for relief or accepted within 180 days (unless an extension is granted by the court), any interested party has the right to prepare and file a proposal. Creditors of Revco D. S. Inc. had the interesting quandry of choosing between three different reorganization plans: one backed by the company's management, one proposed by Rite Aid Corporation, and one submitted by Jack Eckerd Corporation.[24]

A reorganization plan may contain an unlimited number of provisions: proposed changes in the company, additional financing arrangements, alterations in the debt structure, and the like.[25] Regardless of the specific contents, the intent of all such plans is to provide a feasible long-term solution to the company's monetary difficulties. However, to gain acceptance by the parties involved, convincing evidence must be presented that the plan will enable the business to emerge from bankruptcy as a viable going concern. Although a definitive list of elements that could be included in a reorganization proposal is not possible, some of the most common are

1. *Plans proposing changes in the company's operations.* In hopes of improving liquidity, officials may decide to introduce new product lines or sell off unprofitable assets or even entire businesses. The closing of failing operations is especially common. A debtor in possession bears the burden or proving that the problems that led to insolvency can be eliminated and then avoided in the future. As an example, before emerging from Chapter 11 reorganization, the Wickes Company made a number of significant business changes:

> Over the past 2½ years, the new management has streamlined Wickes by closing or selling 15 divisions, reducing annual revenue to about $3 billion from $4 billion. The number of employees has been cut to about 28,000 from 40,000 with a lean corporate staff of 125, down from a peak of 400. The company also has made substantial capital improvements and installed a sophisticated electronic management-information system.[26]

---

[23] AICPA Statement of Position 90–7, *Financial Reporting by Entities in Reorganization Under the Bankruptcy Code*, November 19, 1990, par. 3.

[24] Gabriella Stern, "Timing of Revco Status Change Stays Uncertain," *The Wall Street Journal*, January 6, 1992, p. A3.

[25] See, for example, "When Will Somebody—Anybody—Rescue Battered Allegheny?" *The Wall Street Journal*, April 19, 1990, p. A1.

[26] Stephen J. Sansweet, "Wickes to Emerge from Chapter 11 Prepared to Compete in Tough Retailing Environment," *The Wall Street Journal*, January 25, 1985, p. 4.

2. *Plans for generating additional monetary resources.* Companies faced with insolvency must develop new sources of cash, often in a short time period. Loans and the sale of both common and preferred stocks are frequently negotiated during reorganization to provide funding for the continuation of the business. For example, as part of the initial reorganization plan put forth by Orion Pictures, its majority owner, Metromedia Company, agreed to invest $15 million in cash. Without the willingness of the owners to back the company, creditors would probably be hesitant about agreeing to a reorganization.

3. *Plans for changes in the management of the company.* Frequently, a financial crisis is blamed on poor management. In that situation, proposing to reorganize a company with the management team intact is probably not a practical suggestion. Therefore, many plans include the hiring of new individuals to implement the reorganization and run important aspects of the company. These changes may even affect the board of directors elected by the stockholders to oversee the company and its operations: "Manville Corporation agreed to let creditors have the final say in any board appointments, eliminating the last major obstacle in gaining approval of its 3½ year bankruptcy-law reorganization."[27]

4. *Plans to settle the debts of the company that existed when the order for relief was entered.* No element of a reorganization plan is more important than the proposal for satisfying the various creditors of the company. In most cases, their agreement is necessary before the court will confirm any plan of reorganization. The actual proposal to settle these debts may take one of several forms:

- Assets can be transferred to creditors who accept this payment in exchange for extinguishing a specified amount of debt. The book value of the liability being cancelled is usually greater than the fair market value of the assets rendered.

- An equity interest (such as common stock, preferred stock, or stock rights) can be conveyed to creditors to settle an outstanding debt.

- The terms of the outstanding liabilities can be modified: maturity dates extended, interest rates lowered, face values reduced, accrued interest forgiven, and so on.

Acceptance and Confirmation of Reorganization Plan

The creation of a plan for reorganization does not guarantee its implementation. The Bankruptcy Reform Act specifies that a plan must be voted on by both the company's creditors and stockholders before being confirmed by the court. *To be accepted, each class of creditors must vote for the plan.* Acceptance requires the approval of two thirds in dollar amount and more than one half in the number of claims that cast votes. A separate vote is also required of each class of sharehold-

---

[27] Cynthia F. Mitchell, "Manville Is Said to Have Agreed to Let Creditors Decide Board Appointments," *The Wall Street Journal,* April 25, 1986, p. 5.

ers. For approval, at least two thirds (measured by the number of shares held) of the owners who vote must agree to the proposed reorganization. Convincing all parties to support any specific plan is not an easy task since agreement often means the acceptance of a significant loss. However, any class of creditors that is not damaged by a reorganization is assumed to have accepted the plan without the necessity of a vote.

Although creditor and stockholder approval may be gained, confirmation by the court is still required. The court reviews the proposal and can reject the reorganization plan if a claimant (who did not vote for acceptance) would receive more through liquidation. The court also has the authority to confirm a reorganization plan that was not accepted by a particular class of creditors or stockholders. This provision is referred to as a *cram down*; it occurs when the court determines that the plan is fair and equitable. As an alternative, the court may convert a Chapter 11 reorganization into a Chapter 7 liquidation at any time if the development of an acceptable plan does not appear to be possible.

Financial Reporting during Reorganization

Developing and gaining approval for a reorganization plan can take years. During that period, the company continues operating under the assumption that it is eventually going to emerge from the bankruptcy proceedings. In the past, official accounting literature has provided virtually no guidance for the financial statements to be prepared by a company while in reorganization. However, the increased volume of companies (especially larger organizations) going through reorganization during the 1980s emphasized the need for some type of guidelines to be established.

Finally, in 1990, the AICPA Task Force on Financial Reporting by Entities in Reorganization Under the Bankruptcy Code issued Statement of Position 90–7 (*Financial Reporting by Entities in Reorganization Under the Bankruptcy Code*) (referred to as SOP 90–7). This pronouncement provides standards for the preparation of financial statements at two times:

1. During the period when a company is going through reorganization.
2. At the point that the company emerges from reorganization.

While going through reorganization, the company faces several specific accounting questions:

- Should the income effects resulting from operating activities be differentiated from transactions connected solely with the reorganization process?
- How should liabilities be reported? Since some of the debts may not be paid for years and then may require payment of an amount considerably less than face value, how should this information be conveyed?
- Does entering reorganization necessitate a change in the reporting basis of the company's assets?

The Income Statement during Reorganization.   According to SOP 90–7, any gains, losses, revenues, and expenses resulting from the reorganization of the business should be reported separately. Such items are placed on the income statement before any income tax expense or benefits.[28]

Reorganization items would include any gains and losses on the sale of assets necessitated by the reorganization. In addition, as mentioned previously, enormous amounts of professional fees may be incurred. Historically, these items could be handled by any one of several different methods. SOP 90–7 requires that these costs be expensed as incurred.

> What's the proper way to account for lawyers' and investment bankers' fees that can run to millions monthly for large cases like LTV? It makes sense to expense them along the way—and that's what the new rules call for. In the past, some clever companies capitalized the fees on the theory that part of the work would benefit the company as a going concern.[29]

Interest expense and interest income were also discussed in SOP 90–7. During reorganization, most interest expense does not accrue on debts owed at the date on which the order for relief is granted. Thus, recognition is only necessary if payment will be made during the proceeding (for example, on debts incurred during the bankruptcy) or if the interest will probably be an allowed claim (for example, if the amount was owed but unrecorded prior to the granting of the order for relief). However, any interest expense that must be recognized is not to be separated as a reorganization item.

In contrast, interest income tends to grow to a quite substantial amount during reorganization. Because the company is not forced to pay the debts incurred prior to the date of the order for relief, cash reserves tend to grow and the resulting interest can become a significant source of income. *Any interest income that would not have been earned except for the proceeding is reported separately as a reorganization item.*

To illustrate, assume that the Crawford Corporation files a voluntary bankruptcy petition and is granted an order for relief on January 1, 1995. Thereafter, the ownership and management of the company begins (1) to work on a reorganization plan and (2) rehabilitate the company. Several branch operations are closed and accountants, lawyers, and other professionals are hired to assist in the reorganization. At the end of 1995, the bankruptcy is still in progress. Thus, the company prepares the income statement shown in Exhibit 12–4 so that the reader can distinguish the results of the operating activities from the reorganization items.

---

[28] In a similar manner, the statement of cash flows should be constructed so that reorganization items are shown separately within the operating, investing, and financing categories.

[29] Laura Jereski, "Starting Fresh," *Forbes*, April 15, 1991, p. 105.

EXHIBIT 12-4 **Income Statement During Reorganization**

CRAWFORD CORPORATION
(Debtor-in-Possession)
Income Statement
For Year Ended December 31, 1995

Revenues:		
Sales		$650,000
Costs and expenses:		
Cost of goods sold	$346,000	
General and administrative expenses	165,000	
Selling expenses	86,000	
Interest expense	4,000	601,000
Earnings before reorganization items and tax effects		49,000
Reorganization items:		
Loss on closing of branches	(86,000)	
Professional fees	(75,000)	
Interest revenue	26,000	(135,000)
Loss before income tax benefit		(86,000)
Income tax benefit		18,800
Net loss		(67,200)
Loss per common share		$ (.56)

The Balance Sheet during Reorganization. A new entity is not created when a company moves into reorganization. Therefore, traditional generally accepted accounting principles continue to apply. Assets, for example, should still be reported at their book values. However, many of the liabilities are likely to be reduced as part of the final reorganization plan. In addition, because of the order for relief, the current/noncurrent classification system is no longer applicable; payments may be delayed for years.

Thus, in reporting the liabilities of a company being reorganized, debts subject to compromise (reduction by the court through acceptance of a reorganization plan) must be disclosed separately. Unsecured and partially secured obligations existing as of the granting of the order for relief fall into this category. Fully secured liabilities and all debts incurred since that date are not subject to compromise and must be reported in a normal manner as either a current or noncurrent liability.

According to SOP 90–7 (par. 24), liabilities subject to compromise "should be reported on the basis of the expected amount of the allowed claims . . . as opposed to the amounts for which those allowed claims may be settled." Thus, the company does not attempt to anticipate the payment required by a final plan but simply discloses the amount of these claims.

The liability section of a company during this reorganization period would appear as follows:

Liabilities Not Subject to Compromise
  Current liabilities:
    Short-term note payable . . . . $ 62,000
    Accounts payable   86,000
    Accrued expenses and other liabilities 13,000 $161,000
  Long-term liabilities: note payable   40,000

    Liabilities not subject to compromise $201,000
Liabilities Subject to Compromise
  Prior tax claims . . . . $ 77,000
  Notes payable   100,000
  Trade and other miscellaneous claims   133,000   310,000

    Total liabilities $511,000

Financial Reporting for Companies Emerging from Reorganization

Is a company that successfully leaves Chapter 11 status considered a new entity so that current values should be assigned to its accounts (referred to as fresh start reporting)? Or, is the company simply a continuation of the organization that entered bankruptcy so that historical figures are still applicable? SOP 90–7 holds that accounts should be adjusted to current value if two criteria are met (par. 36):[30]

- The reorganization (or market) value of the assets of the emerging company is less than the total of the allowed claims as of the date of the order for relief plus the liabilities incurred subsequently.
- The original owners of the voting stock are left with less than 50 percent of the voting stock of the company when it emerges from bankruptcy.

These two criteria are met in many, if not most, Chapter 11 bankruptcies. Consequently, the entity is reported as if it were a brand new business. For example, in financial staements for the year ending February 1, 1992, Carter Hawley Hale Stores, Inc. reported that "on confirmation of a plan of reorganization, the Company expects to utilize 'fresh start accounting' in accordance with the guidelines for accounting for emergence from bankruptcy. Fresh start accounting is expected to result in a restatement of Company assets to reflect current values."

In applying fresh start accounting, the reorganization value of the entity that emerges from bankruptcy must first be determined. According to paragraph 9 of SOP 90–7, "reorganization value generally approximates fair value of the entity before considering liabilities and approximates the amount a willing buyer would pay for the assets of the entity immediately after the restructuring . . . generally it is determined by discounting future cash flows for the reconstituted business that will emerge." This total value is then assigned to the specific tangible and intangible assets of the company in the same way as in a purchase combination.

---

[30] The FASB is currently looking at this same issue in its Discussion Memorandum "An Analysis of Issues Related to New Basis Accounting." If the FASB eventually acts on this issue, its pronouncement will take precedent over SOP 90–7.

If the value for the company is greater than the amounts assigned to these specific assets, an account akin to goodwill is recognized. For example, following reorganization, the balance sheet of Doskocil Companies reported an intangible asset, "reorganization value in excess of amounts allocable to identifiable assets, net of accumulated depreciation," as of December 28, 1991, of $97.5 million (out of total assets of $311.9 million). This balance can be amortized to expense over a period of up to 40 years. However, to avoid the extended write-offs that have been common with goodwill, SOP 90–7 (par. 38) does state that factors usually indicate "a useful life of substantially less than forty years."

To illustrate, assume that a company has a reorganization value of $280,000 but only two specific assets. Land (with a book value of $90,000) is worth $150,000 and a building (with a book value of $78,000) is valued at $100,000. If the criteria for fresh start accounting are met, this company would emerge from bankruptcy with these assets recorded at their market values of $150,000 and $100,000 rather than the historical book values. In addition, the excess $30,000 ($280,000 − $250,000) would be assigned to this new intangible asset account.

The reporting of liabilities following a reorganization also creates a concern since many of these balances would be reduced and the payment period extended. SOP 90–7 requires that all liabilities (except for deferred income taxes which should be accounted for according to the provisions of FASB *Statement 109*) must be reported at the present value of the future cash payments.

To make the necessary asset adjustments to fresh start accounting, additional paid-in capital is normally increased or decreased. However, any write-down of a liability creates a recognized gain. Finally, because the company is viewed as a new entity, it must leave the reorganization with a zero balance in retained earnings.

Fresh Start Accounting Illustrated

Assume that a company has the following trial balance just prior to emerging from bankruptcy:

	Debit	Credit
Current assets	$ 50,000	
Land	100,000	
Buildings	400,000	
Equipment	250,000	
Accounts payable (incurred since the order for relief was granted)		$ 100,000
Liabilities when the order for relief was granted:		
Accounts payable		60,000
Accrued expenses		50,000
Note payable (due in 3 years)		300,000
Bonds payable (due in 5 years)		600,000
Common stock (50,000 shares with a $1 par value)		50,000
Additional paid-in capital		40,000
Retained earnings (deficit)	400,000	
Totals	$1,200,000	$1,200,000

Other Information:

- *Assets.* The company's land has a market value of $120,000; the building is worth $500,000. Other assets are worth their book values. The reorganization value of the company's assets is assumed to be $1,000,000 based on discounted future cash flows.

- *Liabilities.* The $100,000 of accounts payable incurred since the order for relief was granted must be paid in full as the individual balances come due. The accounts payable and accrued expenses that were owed when the order for relief was granted will be converted into one-year notes payable of $70,000, paying interest of 10 percent. The note payable on the trial balance will be converted into a 10-year, 8 percent note of $100,000. These creditors also get 20,000 shares of stock that is to be turned in to the company by the common stockholders. Finally, the bonds payable would be converted into eight-year, 9 percent notes totaling $430,000. The bondholders also get 15,000 shares of common stock turned in by the current owners.

- *Stockholders' Equity.* The owners of the common stock will return 70 percent of their stock (35,000 shares) to the company to be issued as specified. The reorganization value of the assets is $1,000,000 and the debts of the company after the proceeding total $700,000 ($100,000 + $70,000 + $100,000 + $430,000). Thus, stockholders' equity must be the $300,000 difference. Since shares with a $50,000 par value would be outstanding, additional paid-in capital must be adjusted to $250,000.

In accounting for this reorganization, the initial question to be resolved is whether fresh start accounting is appropriate. The first criterion is met since the reorganization value of the assets ($1,000,000) is less than the sum of all postpetition liabilities ($100,000 accounts payable) and allowed claims (the $1,010,000 total of liabilities remaining from the date of the order for relief before any write-down). The second criterion is also met since the original stockholders receive less than 50 percent of the shares after the plan takes effect. At that point, they will have only 15,000 of the 50,000 outstanding shares.

Since fresh start accounting is appropriate, the assets must be adjusted to market value. In addition, an intangible asset is recognized for the $80,000 reorganization value of the company in excess of the value assigned to specific assets. The reorganization value is $1 million, but the market value of the assets is only $920,000 (current assets $50,000, land $120,000 [adjusted], buildings $500,000 [adjusted], and equipment $250,000). Since the accounts are already recorded at book value, adjustment is only necessary when market value differs from this book value:

Land	20,000	
Buildings	100,000	
Reorganization Value In Excess of Amount Allocable to Identifiable		
Assets	80,000	
Additional Paid-in Capital.		200,000
To adjust asset accounts to fresh start accounting and to recognize		
excess value as an intangible asset subject to amortization.		

Next, the 35,000 shares of common stock returned to the company by the original owners should be recorded:

```
Common Stock . . . . . . . . . . . . . . . . . . . . . . . . .    35,000
    Additional Paid-in Capital. . . . . . . . . . . . . . . . . .             35,000
    To record shares of common stock returned to the company by
    owners as part of the reorganization agreement.
```

The liability accounts on the records at the date of the order for relief must now be adjusted for the provisions of the bankruptcy reorganization plan. Because all of the new debts bear a reasonable interest rate, present value computations are not necessary. The first entry is a straight conversion with a gain recorded for the difference between the old debt and the new.

```
Accounts Payable . . . . . . . . . . . . . . . . . . . . . . .    60,000
Accrued Expenses . . . . . . . . . . . . . . . . . . . . . . .    50,000
    Notes Payable (1 year) . . . . . . . . . . . . . . . . . . .             70,000
    Gain on Debt Discharge . . . . . . . . . . . . . . . . . . .             40,000
    To convert liabilities to a one-year note as per reorganization plan.
```

The other two debt entries require a computation for the amount to be assigned to additional paid-in capital. The assumed total for the company as computed earlier is $250,000. Since the holders of the notes receive 20,000 shares of stock (or 40 percent of the 50,000 share total), this stock is assigned additional paid-in capital of $100,000 (40 percent). The holders of the bonds are to get 15,000 shares (30 percent of the company total). Hence, additional paid-in capital of $75,000 (30 percent) is recorded.

```
Note Payable (3 years) . . . . . . . . . . . . . . . . . . . .   300,000
    Note Payable (10 years) . . . . . . . . . . . . . . . . . .            100,000
    Common Stock (par value of 20,000 shares). . . . . . . . . .             20,000
    Additional Paid-in Capital (40 percent of company total) . . . . .      100,000
    Gain on Debt Discharge . . . . . . . . . . . . . . . . . . .             80,000
    To record exchange with gain recorded for difference between book
    value of old note and the amount recorded for new note and shares
    of stock.
```

```
Bonds Payable. . . . . . . . . . . . . . . . . . . . . . . . .   600,000
    Notes Payable (8 years). . . . . . . . . . . . . . . . . . .            430,000
    Common Stock (par value of 15,000 shares). . . . . . . . . .             15,000
    Additional Paid-in Capital (30 percent of company total) . . . . .       75,000
    Gain on Debt Discharge . . . . . . . . . . . . . . . . . . .             80,000
    To record exchange with gain recorded for difference between book
    value of old bonds and the amount recorded for new notes and
    shares of stock.
```

Additional Paid-in Capital now has a balance of $450,000 ($40,000 beginning balance plus $200,000 for adjusting assets plus $35,000 for shares returned by owners plus $100,000 because of shares issued for note and $75,000 because of shares issued for bonds). Therefore, this balance is $200,000 more than the amount to be reported as established through the provisions of the reorganization agreement. In addition, the Gain on Debt Discharge account has a balance of

$200,000 ($40,000 + $80,000 + $80,000), a figure that must be closed out. Adjusting and closing these accounts eliminates the deficit in retained earnings so that the emerging company has no balance in this equity account.

Additional Paid-In Capital.	200,000	
Gain on Debt Discharge	200,000	
Retained Earnings (Deficit)		400,000
To adjust Additional Paid-In Capital balance to correct amount,		
close out gain account, and eliminate deficit balance.		

After posting these entries, this company emerges from bankruptcy with

1. Its assets at fair market value.
2. Its debts equal to the present value of the future cash payments (except for deferred income taxes).
3. No deficit balance.

	Debit	Credit
Current assets	$ 50,000	
Land	120,000	
Buildings	500,000	
Equipment	250,000	
Reorganization value in excess of amounts allocable to identifiable		
assets	80,000	
Accounts payable.		$ 100,000
Note payable (due in 1 year)		70,000
Note payable (due in 10 years)		100,000
Notes payable (due in 8 years)		430,000
Common stock (50,000 shares with a $1 par value)		50,000
Additional paid-in capital		250,000
Retained earnings.	–0–	–0–
Totals	$1,000,000	$1,000,000

Discussion Question: Is This the Real Purpose of the Bankruptcy Laws?

Insolvency is not a necessary condition for bankruptcy. Moreover, a firm may petition the court for protection under Chapter 11 even though it is not insolvent. If the business can demonstrate real financial trouble, the court will generally not dismiss the petition. In recent years, Chapter 11 has been looked upon as a safe harbor for gaining time to restructure the business and to head off more serious financial problems. *For example, when Johns Manville filed a petition under Chapter 11, it was a profitable, financially sound company.* Yet. it faced numerous lawsuits

continued

for damages resulting from asbestos products it sold. Reorganization helped Johns Manville deal with its financial problems.[31] (emphasis added)

During recent years, the filing of a voluntary Chapter 11 bankruptcy petition has become a tool sometimes used by companies to settle significant financial problems. Just as Johns Manville reorganized to settle the claims of asbestos victims, A. H. Robins followed a similar path to resolve thousands of lawsuits stemming from injuries resulting from the Dalkon Shield intra-uterine device. The Wilson Foods Corporation managed to reduce union wages by filing under Chapter 11 as did Continental Airlines Corporation.

Not surprisingly, seeking protection under Chapter 11 to force a bargained resolution of a financial difficulty is a controversial legal maneuver. Creditors and claimants often argue that this procedure is used to avoid responsibility while the companies counter that bankruptcy can become the only realistic means of achieving any settlement.

Should companies be allowed to use the provisions of Chapter 11 in this manner?

Summary

1. Every year a significant number of businesses in the United States become insolvent, unable to pay debts as they come due. Since creditors as well as owners hold financial interests in each failed company, bankruptcy laws have been written to provide protection for all parties. The Bankruptcy Reform Act of 1978 currently serves as the primary structure for these legal proceedings. This act was designed to ensure a fair distribution of all remaining properties while discharging the obligations of an honest debtor.

2. Bankruptcy proceedings can be instigated voluntarily by the insolvent debtor or involuntarily by a group of creditors. In either case, an order for relief is usually granted by the court to halt all actions against the debtor. Some creditors may have already gained protection for themselves by having a mortgage lien or security interest attached to specific assets. A creditor is considered fully secured if the value of any collateral exceeds the related debt balance but is only partially secured if the obligation is larger. All other liabilities are unsecured; these creditors have legal rights but not to any specific assets of the debtor. The Bankruptcy

---

[31] Paul J. Corr and Donald D. Bourque, "Managing in a Reorganization," *Management Accounting,* January 1988, p. 34.

Reform Act does list several types of unsecured liabilities (including administrative expenses and government claims for unpaid taxes) that have priority and must be paid before other unsecured debts are settled.

3. The parties involved in a bankruptcy want, and need, to be informed of the possible outcome, especially if liquidation is being considered. Thus, a Statement of Financial Affairs is usually prepared for an insolvent company. This document lists the net realizable value of all remaining assets along with an indication of any property pledged to specific creditors. In addition, the liabilities of the business are segregated and disclosed within four classifications: fully secured, partially secured, unsecured with priority, and unsecured. Prior to the filing of a bankruptcy petition, this information can help the parties in deciding whether either liquidation or reorganization is the best course of action. However, this statement should be viewed as a projection since many of the reported values are merely estimations.

4. If the assets of the insolvent company will be liquidated to satisfy obligations (a Chapter 7 bankruptcy), a trustee is appointed to oversee the process. This individual must recover all property belonging to the company, liquidate noncash assets, possibly continue running operations to complete any business in progress, and make appropriate payments. To convey information about these events and transactions, a Statement of Realization and Liquidation is commonly prepared by the trustee. This statement provides a current report of all account balances as well as transactions to date.

5. Liquidation is not the only alternative available to an insolvent business. The company may seek to survive by developing a reorganization plan (a Chapter 11 bankruptcy). Reorganization is possible only if the plan is accepted by creditors, shareholders, and the court. While a reorganization is in process, the owners and management must preserve the company's estate as of the date on which the order of relief was entered. Although the ownership has the initial opportunity for creating a proposal for action, any interested party has the right to file a reorganization plan after a period of time.

6. Reorganization plans usually contain a number of provisions for modifying operations, generating new financing by equity or debt, and settling the liabilities existing when the order for relief was entered. To be accepted, each class of creditors and shareholders has to support the agreement. Thereafter, the reorganization plan must be confirmed by the court.

7. During reorganization, a company reports its liabilities as being subject to compromise or not subject to compromise. The first category includes all unsecured and partially secured debts that existed on the day the order for relief was granted. The balance to be reported is the expected amount of allowed claims rather than the estimated amount of settlement. Liabilities not subject to compromise are those debts fully secured or incurred following the granting of the order for relief.

8. An income statement prepared during the period of reorganization should disclose operating activities separately from reorganization items. Professional fees associated with the reorganization such as lawyers' charges are reorganization items that are expensed as incurred. Any interest income earned during this period because of an increase in the company's cash reserves should also be reported as a reorganization item.

9. Many companies that emerge from reorganization proceedings must apply fresh start accounting. Assets are recorded at fair market value and an intangible asset, "reorganization value in excess of amounts allocable to identifiable assets," might also be necessary. Liabilities (except for deferred income taxes) are reported at the present value of required cash flows. Retained earnings (or a deficit) is eliminated. Additional paid-in capital is adjusted to keep the balance sheet in equilibrium.

Comprehensive Illustration

PROBLEM

(Estimated Time: 50 to 65 Minutes)

The Roth Company is insolvent and in the process of filing for relief under the provisions of the Bankruptcy Reform Act of 1978. Roth has no cash and the company's balance sheet currently shows accounts payable of $48,000. An additional $8,000 is owed in connection with various expenses but these amounts have not yet been recorded. The company's assets with an indication of both book value and anticipated net realizable value follow:

	Book Value	Expected Net Realizable Value
Accounts receivable	$ 31,000	$ 9,000
Inventory.	48,000	36,000
Investments.	10,000	18,000
Land.	80,000	75,000
Buildings	90,000	60,000
Accumulated depreciation	(38,000)	
Equipment	110,000	20,000
Accumulated depreciation	(61,000)	
Other assets	5,000	–0–
Totals	$275,000	$218,000

Roth has three notes payable, each with a different maturity date:

• Note one due in 5 years—$120,000 secured by a mortgage lien on Roth's land and buildings.

• Note two due in 8 years—$30,000 secured by Roth's investments.

• Note three due in 10 years—$35,000 unsecured.

Of the accounts payable owed by Roth, $10,000 represents salaries to employees. However, no individual is entitled to receive more than $1,300. An additional $3,000 is included in this liability figure that is due to the U.S. government in connection with taxes.

The stockholders' equity balance reported by the company at the current date is $42,000: common stock of $140,000 and a deficit of $98,000. If the company is liquidated, administrative expenses of approximately $20,000 would be incurred.

Required:

a. Prepare a statement of financial affairs for Roth to indicate the expected availability of funds if the company is liquidated.
b. Assume that Roth owes Philip, Inc. a total of $2,000. This liability is unsecured. If Roth is liquidated, what amount of money can Philip expect to receive?
c. What amount will be paid on note 2 if Roth is liquidated?
d. Assume that Roth is immediately reorganized. The company has a reorganization value of $230,000, and the net realizable value is to be the assigned value for each asset. The accounts payable and accrued expenses are reduced to $20,000. Note one is reduced to a $30,000 note due in four years with a 7 percent annual interest rate. This creditor also receives half of the outstanding stock of the company from the owners. Note two is reduced to a $12,000 note due in five years with an 8 percent annual interest rate. This creditor also receives 10 percent of the outstanding stock of the company from the owners. Note three is reduced to $5,000 due in three years with a 9 percent annual interest rate.

Prepare a trial balance for this company after it emerges from bankruptcy.

SOLUTION

a. To develop a statement of financial affairs for this company, the following preliminary actions must be taken:

• The $8,000 in unrecorded accounts payable must be entered into the company's accounting records. Since these debts were incurred in connection with expenses, the deficit is increased by a corresponding amount.
• The unsecured liabilities that have priority are identified:

Administrative costs (estimated)	$20,000
Salary payable	10,000
Amount due to government for taxes	3,000
Total liabilities with priority	$33,000

- The secured claims should be appropriately classified:

Note one is fully secured since Roth's land and buildings can be sold for an amount in excess of the $120,000 balance.

Note two is only partially secured since Roth's investments are worth less than $30,000.

With this information, the statement of financial affairs on page 726 can be produced.

b. Based on the information provided by the statement of financial affairs, Philip, Inc., should receive 52.2 percent of its $2,000 unsecured claim or $1,044. Roth anticipates having $47,000 in free assets remaining at the end of the liquidation. This amount must be distributed to unsecured creditors with total claims of $90,000. Therefore, only 52.2 percent of each obligation can be paid:

$$\frac{\$47,000}{\$90,000} = 52.2 \text{ percent (rounded)}$$

c. The $30,000 note payable is partially secured by Roth's investments, an asset having a net realizable value of only $18,000. The remaining $12,000 is an unsecured claim which (as computed in requirement *b.*) will be paid 52.2 percent of face value. Thus, the holder of this note can expect to receive $24,264:

Net realizable value of investments	$18,000
Payment on $12,000 unsecured claim (52.2 percent)	6,264
Amount to be received.	$24,264

d. Fresh start accounting is appropriate. The reorganization value of $230,000 is less than the total amount of claims (no liabilities after the issuance of the order for relief are indicated). (See page 727.)

ROTH COMPANY
Statement of Financial Affairs

Book Values			Available for Unsecured Creditors
	Assets		
	Pledged with fully secured creditors:		
$132,000	Land and buildings	$ 135,000	
	Less: Note payable	(120,000)	$ 15,000
	Pledged with partially secured creditors:		
10,000	Investments.	18,000	
	Less: Note payable	(30,000)	–0–
	Free assets:		
31,000	Accounts receivable		9,000
48,000	Inventory.		36,000
49,000	Equipment		20,000
5,000	Intangible assets		–0–
	Total available for liabilities with priority and unsecured creditors		80,000
	Less: Liabilities with priority (listed opposite) . . .		(33,000)
	Available for unsecured creditors		47,000
	Estimated deficiency.		43,000
$275,000			$ 90,000

Book Values			Unsecured— Nonpriority Liabilities
	Liabilities and Stockholders' Equity		
	Liabilities with priority:		
–0–	Administrative expenses (estimated)	$ 20,000	
	Accounts payable:		
$ 10,000	Salaries payable	10,000	
3,000	Taxes payable.	3,000	
	Total	$ 33,000	
	Fully secured creditors:		
120,000	Note payable	120,000	
	Less: Land and buildings	(135,000)	–0–
	Partially secured creditors:		
30,000	Note payable	30,000	
	Less: Investments	(18,000)	$ 12,000
	Unsecured creditors:		
35,000	Note payable		35,000
43,000	Accounts payable (other than salaries and taxes, although unrecorded liabilities have been included).		43,000
34,000	Stockholders' equity (adjusted for unrecorded liabilities)		–0–
$275,000			$ 90,000

Accounts payable	$ 48,000
Accrued expenses	8,000
Note one	120,000
Note two	30,000
Note three	35,000
Total claims	$241,000

In addition, the original owners of the stock retain only 40 percent of the shares after the company leaves the bankruptcy proceeding.

The company's assets are assigned values equal to their net realizable value based on the information provided. Since the reorganization value of $230,000 is $12,000 in excess of the total net realizable value of $218,000, an intangible asset is recognized for that amount.

The liabilities are each adjusted to the newly agreed on amounts. Present value computations are not required since a reasonable interest rate is included in each case. These debts now total $67,000 ($20,000 + $30,000 + $12,000 + $5,000).

Because the reorganization value is $230,000, stockholders' equity must be $163,000 ($230,000 − $67,000). The number of outstanding shares of common stock has not changed so that account retains its balance of $140,000. The other $23,000 of stockholders' equity is recorded as additional paid-in capital.

	Debit	Credit
Accounts receivable	$ 9,000	
Inventory	36,000	
Investments	18,000	
Land	75,000	
Buildings	60,000	
Equipment	20,000	
Reorganization value in excess of amounts allocable to identifiable assets	12,000	
Accounts payable and accrued expenses		$ 20,000
Note payable one		30,000
Note payable two		12,000
Note payable three		5,000
Common stock		140,000
Additional paid-in capital		23,000
Totals	$230,000	$230,000

Questions

1. What is meant by the term *insolvent*?
2. At present, what federal legislation governs most bankruptcy proceedings?
3. What are the primary objectives of a bankruptcy proceeding?
4. A bankruptcy case may begin with either a voluntary or an involuntary petition. What is the difference? What are the requirements for an involuntary petition?
5. An order for relief is entered by a bankruptcy court. How does this action affect an insolvent company and its creditors?
6. What is the difference in fully secured liabilities, partially secured liabilities, and unsecured liabilities?
7. In a bankruptcy proceeding, what is the significance of a liability with priority? What are the six general categories of liabilities that have priority in a liquidation?
8. Why are the administrative expenses incurred during a liquidation classified as liabilities having priority?
9. What is the difference between a Chapter 7 bankruptcy and a Chapter 11 bankruptcy?
10. Why might unsecured creditors favor reorganizing an insolvent company rather than forcing it into liquidation?
11. What is the purpose of a statement of financial affairs? Why might this statement be prepared before a bankruptcy petition is filed?
12. In the liquidation of a company, what actions are performed by the trustee?
13. A trustee for a company that is being liquidated voids a preference transfer. What has happened, and why was this action taken by the trustee?
14. A statement of realization and liquidation is prepared for a company that is being liquidated. What information can be ascertained from this statement?
15. What is meant by the term *debtor in possession?*
16. Who can develop reorganization plans in a Chapter 11 bankruptcy?
17. What types of proposals might be found in a reorganization plan?
18. Under normal conditions, how does a reorganization plan become effective?
19. In a bankruptcy proceeding, what is a *cram down?*
20. While a company goes through reorganization, how should its liabilities be reported?
21. During reorganization, how should a company's income statement be structured?

22. What accounting is made of the professional fees incurred during a reorganization?

23. What is meant by *fresh start accounting?*

24. Under what conditions is fresh start accounting used by a company emerging from a bankruptcy reorganization?

25. When fresh start accounting is utilized, how are a company's assets reported? How are its liabilities reported?

26. How is a "reorganization value in excess of amounts allocable to identifiable assets" account computed? Where is this balance reported? What happens to the balance?

Library Assignments

1. Locate *The Wall Street Journal General Index* for a recent year. Under the heading, "Bankruptcies" identify one company that has recently completed bankruptcy proceedings (for example, the Chyron Corporation went through a bankruptcy proceeding in 1990 and 1991). Then, in *The Wall Street Journal Corporate Index,* under the name of this company, locate articles that describe the various stages of the process from beginning through resolution. Write a report to answer the following questions:

   - Was the bankruptcy voluntary or involuntary?
   - What events led up to the filing of the bankruptcy petition?
   - What actions did the company take to bring the matter to a final resolution?
   - Did the bankruptcy end in liquidation or reorganization?
   - What were the significant provisions of the liquidation or the reorganization plan?
   - What losses, if any, were the creditors forced to suffer?

2. Read the following as well as any other published articles describing the work of the accountant in bankruptcy cases:
   "Managing in a Reorganization," *Management Accounting*, January 1988.
   "What To Do When Chapter 11 Threatens," *Journal of Accountancy*, May 1993.
   "Accounting Services in Insolvency and Bankruptcy," *Connecticut CPA Quarterly*, December 1987.
   "The Role of the Accountant in Business Bankruptcies," *The National Public Accountant*, November 1982 and December 1982.
   "What a CPA Should Know Before a Business Fails," *Journal of Accountancy,* June 1991.

"The CPA's Role as Bankruptcy Examiner," *The CPA Journal*, September 1991.

"What Accountants Need to Know About the Bankruptcy Valuation Process," *The Ohio CPA Journal*, June 1992.

Write a report describing the services that can be performed by an accountant during a corporate bankruptcy. Include activities to be carried out prior to the filing of a petition as well as any functions thereafter.

3. Read the following as well as any other published articles concerning possible changes in the bankruptcy laws pertaining to Chapter 11 reorganizations:

"The Untenable Case for Chapter 11," *The Yale Law Journal*, March 1992.

"Bankruptcy Lawyers Dispute Call for Scrapping Chapter 11 Process," *The Wall Street Journal*, March 19, 1992, p. B5.

"The Bankruptcy Game," *Time*, May 18, 1992.

"Pulling a Company Through Chapter 11 Is a Risky Business as Hurdles Abound," *The Wall Street Journal*, January 16, 1990, p. A10.

"Blimey! CPAs!" *Forbes*, March 15, 1992.

Write a report describing possible problems with the current laws as they pertain to the reorganization process and changes in these laws that might be justified.

Problems

1. What are the objectives of the bankruptcy laws in the United States?
   a. Provide relief for the court system in this country and ensure that all debtors are treated the same.
   b. Distribute assets fairly and discharge honest debtors from their obligations.
   c. Protect the economy and stimulate growth.
   d. Prevent insolvency and protect shareholders.

2. In a bankruptcy, which of the following statements is true?
   a. An order for relief only results from a voluntary petition.
   b. Creditors entering an involuntary petition must have debts totaling $10,000.
   c. Secured notes payable are considered liabilities with priority on a statement of affairs.
   d. A liquidation is referred to as a Chapter 7 bankruptcy, whereas a reorganization is a Chapter 11 bankruptcy.

3. In the reporting of a liquidation, assets are shown at:
   a. Present value calculated using an appropriate effective rate.
   b. Net realizable value.

    c. Historical cost.

    d. Book value.

4. An involuntary bankruptcy petition must be filed by:

    a. The insolvent company's attorney.

    b. The holders of the insolvent company's debenture bonds.

    c. Unsecured creditors with total debts of at least $5,000.

    d. The management of the company.

5. An order for relief:

    a. Prohibits creditors from taking action to collect from an insolvent company without court approval.

    b. Calls for the immediate distribution of free assets to unsecured creditors.

    c. Can only be entered in an involuntary bankruptcy proceeding.

    d. Gives an insolvent company time to file a voluntary bankruptcy petition.

6. Which of the following is not a liability that has priority in a liquidation?

    a. Administrative expenses incurred in the liquidation.

    b. Salary payable of $800 per person owed to 26 employees.

    c. Payroll taxes due to the federal government.

    d. Advertising expense incurred before the company became insolvent.

7. Which of the following is the minimum limitation necessary for the filing of an involuntary bankruptcy petition?

    a. The signature of 12 creditors to whom the debtor owes at least $3,000 in unsecured debt.

    b. The signature of six creditors to whom the debtor owes at least $10,000 in unsecured debt.

    c. The signature of three creditors to whom the debtor owes at least $5,000 in unsecured debt.

    d. The signature of nine creditors to whom the debtor owes at least $25,000 in unsecured debt.

8. On a statement of financial affairs, how are liabilities classified?

    a. Current and noncurrent.

    b. Secured and unsecured.

    c. Monetary and nonmonetary.

    d. Historic and futuristic.

9. What is a debtor in possession?

    a. The holder of a note receivable issued by an insolvent company prior to the granting of an order for relief.

    b. A fully secured creditor.

    c. The ownership of an insolvent company that continues in control of the organization during a bankruptcy reorganization.

    d. The stockholders in a Chapter 7 bankruptcy.

10. How are anticipated administrative expenses reported on a statement of financial affairs?

    a. As a footnote until actually incurred.

    b. As a liability with priority.

    c. As a partially secured liability.

    d. As an unsecured liability.

11. Just prior to filing a voluntary Chapter 7 bankruptcy petition, Haynes Company pays a supplier $1,000 to satisfy an unsecured claim. Haynes was insolvent at the time. Subsequently, the trustee appointed to oversee this liquidation forces the return of this $1,000. Which of the following is correct?

    a. A preference transfer has been voided.

    b. All transactions prior to a voluntary bankruptcy proceeding must be nullified.

    c. The supplier should sue for the return of this money.

    d. The $1,000 claim becomes a liability with priority.

12. Which of the following is not an expected function of a bankruptcy trustee?

    a. The filing of a plan of reorganization.

    b. Recovery of all property belonging to a company.

    c. Liquidation of noncash assets.

    d. The distribution of assets to the proper claimants.

13. What is an inherent limitation of the statement of financial affairs?

    a. Many of the amounts reported are only estimations that might prove to be inaccurate.

    b. The statement is only applicable to a Chapter 11 bankruptcy.

    c. The statement covers only a short time, whereas a bankruptcy may last much longer.

    d. The figures on the statement vary between a voluntary and an involuntary bankruptcy.

14. What is a cram down?

    a. An agreement about the total amount of money to be reserved to pay creditors who have priority.

    b. The confirmation by the bankruptcy court of a reorganization even though it was not accepted by a class of creditors or stockholders.

    c. The filing of an involuntary bankruptcy petition, especially by the holders of partially secured debts.

    d. The decision made by the court as to whether a particular creditor has priority.

15. On a balance sheet prepared for a company during its reorganization, how are liabilities reported?

    a. As current and long term.

    b. As monetary and nonmonetary.

    c. As subject to compromise and not subject to compromise.

    d. As equity related and debt related.

16. On a balance sheet prepared for a company during its reorganization, at what balance are liabilities reported?

    a. At the expected amount of the allowed claims.

    b. At the present value of the expected future cash flows.

    c. At the expected amount of the settlement.

    d. At the amount of the anticipated final payment.

17. Which of the following is not a reorganization item for purposes of reporting a company's income statement during a Chapter 11 bankruptcy?

    a. Professional fees.

    b. Interest income.

    c. Interest expense.

    d. Gains and losses on closing facilities.

18. What accounting is made for professional fees incurred during a bankruptcy reorganization?

    a. They must be expensed immediately.

    b. They must be capitalized and written off over 40 years or less.

    c. They must be capitalized until the company emerges from the reorganization.

    d. They are either expensed or capitalized depending on the nature of the expenditure.

19. Which of the following is necessary for a company to use fresh start accounting?

    a. The original owners must hold at least 50 percent of the stock of the company when it emerges from bankruptcy.

    b. The reorganization value of the company must exceed the value of all assets.

    c. The reorganization value of the company must exceed the value of all liabilities.

    d. The original owners must hold less than 50 percent of the stock of the company when it emerges from bankruptcy.

20. If the reorganization value of a company emerging from bankruptcy is larger than the values that can be assigned to specific assets, what accounting is made of the difference?

    a. Because of conservatism, the difference is simply ignored.

    b. The difference is expensed immediately.

    c. The difference is capitalized as an intangible asset.

    d. The difference is recorded as a professional fee.

21. For a company emerging from bankruptcy, how are its liabilities (other than deferred income taxes) reported?

    a. At their historical value.

    b. At zero because of fresh start accounting.

    c. At the present value of the future cash flows.

    d. At the negotiated value less all professional fees incurred in the reorganization.

22. A company is to be liquidated and has the following liabilities:

Income taxes	$ 8,000
Notes payable (secured by land).	120,000
Accounts payable	83,000
Salary payable (evenly divided between two employees)	6,000
Bonds payable	70,000
Administrative expenses for liquidation	20,000

The company has the following assets:

	Book Value	Fair Market Value
Current assets	$ 80,000	$ 33,000
Land	100,000	90,000
Buildings and equipment	100,000	110,000

    How much money will the holders of the notes payable collect following the liquidation?

23. The Hamilton Corporation has the following assets and liabilities. Assets are stated at net realizable value.

Assets pledged with secured creditors	$ 82,000
Assets pledged with partially secured creditors	70,000
Other assets	120,000
Secured liabilities	60,000
Partially secured liabilities	100,000
Liabilities with priority	70,000
Unsecured creditors	150,000

    In a liquidation, how much money would be paid on the partially secured liabilities?

24. Ataway Company has had severe financial difficulties and is considering the possibility of filing a bankruptcy petition. At this time, the company has the following assets (stated at net realizable value) and liabilities.

Assets (pledged against debts of $70,000)	$116,000
Assets (pledged against debts of $130,000)	50,000
Other assets	80,000
Liabilities with priority	42,000
Unsecured creditors	200,000

In a liquidation, how much money would be paid on the partially secured debt?

25. Repetti Company has been forced into bankruptcy and all of its noncash assets will be liquidated. Unsecured claims are to be paid at the rate of 30 cents on the dollar. Hatcher, Inc. holds a $70,000 note receivable from Repetti collateralized by equipment with a liquidation value of $26,000. What is the total amount to be realized by Hatcher on this note receivable?

26. The Mondesto Company has the following:

Unsecured creditors	$230,000
Liabilities with priority	110,000
Secured liabilities:	
Debt one, $210,000; value of pledged asset	180,000
Debt two, $170,000; value of pledged asset	100,000
Debt three, $120,000; value of pledged asset	140,000

The company also has a number of other assets that are not pledged in any way. The creditors holding debt two want to receive at least $142,000. For how much do these free assets have to be sold for so that debt two would receive exactly $142,000?

27. A statement of financial affairs created for an insolvent corporation that is beginning the process of liquidation discloses the following data (assets are shown at net realizable values):

Assets pledged with fully secured creditors	$200,000
Fully secured liabilities	150,000
Assets pledged with partially secured creditors	380,000
Partially secured liabilities	490,000
Free assets	300,000
Unsecured liabilities with priority	160,000
Unsecured liabilities	500,000

Required:
a. This company owes $3,000 to an unsecured creditor (without priority). How much money can this creditor expect to collect?
b. This company owes $100,000 to a bank on a note payable that is secured by a security interest attached to property with an estimated net realizable value of $80,000. How much money can this bank expect to collect?

28. A company preparing for a Chapter 7 liquidation has the following.
   Liabilities:
   • Note payable A of $90,000 secured by land having a book value of $50,000 and a fair market value of $70,000.

- Note payable B of $120,000 secured by a building having a book value of $60,000 and a fair market value of $40,000.
- Note payable C of $60,000, unsecured.
- Administrative expenses payable of $20,000.
- Accounts payable of $120,000.
- Income taxes payable of $30,000.

Other assets:

- Cash $10,000.
- Inventory $100,000, but with fair market value of $60,000.
- Equipment $90,000, but with fair market value of $50,000.

How much will each of the company's liabilities be paid after liquidation?

29. The Addison Corporation is currently going through a Chapter 11 bankruptcy. The company has the following account balances. Prepare an income statement for this organization. The effective tax rate is 20 percent (realization of any tax benefits is anticipated).

	Debit	Credit
Advertising expense	$ 24,000	
Cost of goods sold	211,000	
Depreciation expense	22,000	
Interest expense	4,000	
Interest revenue		$ 32,000
Loss on closing of branch	109,000	
Professional fees	71,000	
Rent expense	16,000	
Revenues		467,000
Salary expense	70,000	

30. The Kansas City Corporation holds three assets when it comes out of Chapter 11 bankruptcy:

	Book Value	Market Value
Inventory	$ 86,000	$ 50,000
Land and buildings	250,000	400,000
Equipment	123,000	110,000

The company has a reorganization value of $600,000.

Required:

a. Describe the rules for applying fresh start accounting to the Kansas City Corporation.

b. If fresh start accounting is appropriate, how will the assets of this company be reported?

c. If a "reorganization value in excess of amounts allocable to identifiable assets" account is recognized, where should it be reported? What happens to this balance?

31. The Jaez Corporation is in the process of going through a reorganization. As of December 31, 1995, the company's accountant has determined the following information although the company is still several months away from emerging from the bankruptcy proceeding. Prepare a balance sheet in appropriate form.

	Book Value	*Market Value*
Assets		
Cash	$ 23,000	$ 23,000
Inventory	45,000	47,000
Land	140,000	210,000
Buildings	220,000	260,000
Equipment	154,000	157,000

	Allowed Claims	*Expected Settlement*
Liabilities as of the date of the order for relief		
Accounts payable	$123,000	$ 20,000
Accrued expenses	30,000	4,000
Income taxes payable	22,000	18,000
Note payable (due 1999, secured by land)	100,000	100,000
Note payable (due 2003)	170,000	80,000
Liabilities since the date of the order for relief		
Accounts payable	$ 60,000	
Note payable (due 1997)	100,000	
Stockholders' equity		
Common stock	$200,000	
Deficit	(223,000)	

32. The Ristoni Company is in the process of emerging from a Chapter 11 bankruptcy. The company will apply fresh start accounting as of December 31, 1995. The company currently has 30,000 shares of common stock outstanding with a $240,000 par value. As part of the reorganization, the owners will contribute 18,000 shares of this stock back to the company. A deficit balance of $330,000 is also being reported.

The company has the following asset accounts:

	Book Value	Market Value
Accounts receivable	$100,000	$ 80,000
Inventory	112,000	90,000
Land and buildings	420,000	500,000
Equipment	78,000	65,000

The company's liabilities will be settled as follows. Assume that all notes will be issued at reasonable interest rates.

- Accounts payable of $80,000 will be settled with a note for $5,000. These creditors will also get 1,000 shares of the stock contributed by the owners.
- Accrued expenses of $35,000 will be settled with a note for $4,000.
- Note payable (due 1999) of $100,000 was fully secured and has not been renegotiated.
- Note payable (due 1995) of $200,000 will be settled with a note for $50,000 and 10,000 shares of the stock contributed by the owners.
- Note payable (due 1996) of $185,000 will be settled with a note for $71,000 and 7,000 shares of the stock contributed by the owners.
- Note payable (due 1997) of $200,000 will be settled with a note for $110,000.

The company has a reorganization value of $780,000.

Required:

Prepare all of the journal entries for Ristoni so that the company can emerge from the bankruptcy proceeding.

33. The Smith Corporation has gone through bankruptcy and is ready to emerge as a reorganized entity on December 31, 1995. On this date, the company has the following assets (market value is based on the discounted future cash flows that are anticipated):

	Book Value	Market Value
Accounts receivable	$ 20,000	$ 18,000
Inventory	143,000	111,000
Land and buildings	250,000	278,000
Machinery	144,000	121,000
Patents	100,000	125,000

The company has a reorganization value of $800,000.

The company has 50,000 shares of $10 par value common stock outstanding. A deficit retained earnings balance of $670,000 is also reported. The owners will distribute 30,000 shares of this stock as part of the reorganization plan.

The company's liabilities will be settled as follows:

- Accounts payable (existing at the date on which the order for relief was granted) of $180,000 will be settled with an 8 percent, two-year note for $35,000.
- Accounts payable (incurred since the date on which the order for relief was granted) of $97,000 will be paid in the regular course of business.
- Note payable—First Metropolitan Bank of $200,000 will be settled with an 8 percent, five-year note for $50,000 and 15,000 shares of the stock contributed by the owners.
- Note payable—Northwestern Bank of Tulsa of $350,000 will be settled with a 7 percent, eight-year note for $100,000 and 15,000 shares of the stock contributed by the owners.

Required:

a. How does the accountant for Smith Corporation know that fresh start accounting must be utilized?

b. Prepare a balance sheet for the Smith Corporation upon its emergence from reorganization.

34. Ambrose Corporation reports the following information:

	Book Value	Liquidation Value
Assets pledged with fully secured creditors	$220,000	$245,000
Assets pledged with partially secured creditors	111,000	103,000
Other assets	140,000	81,000
Liabilities with priority	36,000	
Fully secured liabilities	200,000	
Partially secured liabilities	180,000	
Unsecured liabilities	283,000	

In liquidation, what amount of cash should each class of the liabilities expect to collect?

35. The following balance sheet has been prepared by the accountant for the Limestone Company as of June 3, 1995, the date on which the company is to file a voluntary petition of bankruptcy.

LIMESTONE COMPANY
Balance Sheet
June 3, 1995

Assets

Cash	$ 3,000
Accounts receivable (net)	65,000
Inventory	88,000
Land	100,000
Buildings (net)	300,000
Equipment (net)	180,000
Total assets	$736,000

Liabilities and Equities

Accounts payable	$ 98,000
Notes payable—current (secured by equipment)	250,000
Notes payable—long term (secured by land and buildings)	190,000
Common stock	120,000
Retained earnings	78,000
Total liabilities and equities	$736,000

Additional Information:

- If the company is liquidated, administrative expenses estimated at $18,000 are expected to be incurred.
- The accounts payable figure includes $10,000 in wages earned by the company's 12 employees during May. No one earned more than $1,300.
- Taxes of $14,000 owed to the U.S. government have not been included in the liabilities.
- Company officials estimate that 40 percent of the accounts receivable will be collected in a liquidation and that the inventory can be disposed of for $80,000. The land and buildings are to be sold together for approximately $310,000; the equipment should bring $130,000 at auction.

Required:

Prepare a statement of financial affairs for the Limestone Company as of June 3, 1995.

36. Creditors of Jones Corporation are considering petitioning the courts to force the company into Chapter 7 bankruptcy. The following information has been determined. Administrative expenses in connection with the liquidation are estimated to be $22,000. Indicate the amount of money that each class of creditors can anticipate receiving.

	Book Value	Net Realizable Value
Cash.	$ 6,000	$ 6,000
Accounts receivable.	32,000	18,000
Inventory	45,000	31,000
Supplies	3,000	–0–
Investments	2,000	8,000
Land	60,000	72,000
Buildings.	90,000	68,000
Equipment	50,000	35,000
Notes payable (secured by land)	65,000	
Notes payable (secured by buildings)	78,000	
Bonds payable (secured by equipment)	115,000	
Accounts payable.	70,000	
Salary payable (two weeks' salary for the 20 employees) . .	6,000	
Taxes payable	10,000	

37. The Anteium Company owes $80,000 on a note payable that is currently due. The note is held by a local bank and is secured by a mortgage lien attached to three acres of land worth $48,000. The land originally cost Anteium $31,000 when acquired several years ago. The only other account balances for this company are investments of $20,000 (but worth $25,000), accounts payable of $20,000, common stock of $40,000, and a deficit of $89,000. Anteium is insolvent and attempting to arrange a reorganization so that the business can continue to operate. The reorganization value of the company is $82,000.

   Each of the following should be viewed as independent situations:

   a. On a statement of financial affairs, how would this note be reported? How would the land be shown?

   b. Assume that Anteium develops an acceptable reorganization plan. Sixty percent of the common stock is transferred to the bank to settle that particular obligation. A 7 percent, three-year note payable for $5,000 is used to settle the accounts payable. How would Anteium record the reorganization?

   c. Assume that Anteium is liquidated. The land and investments are sold for $50,000 and $26,000, respectively. Administrative expenses amount to $11,000. How much will the various parties collect?

38. The following balance sheet has been produced for the Litz Corporation as of August 8, 1995, the date on which the company is to begin selling assets as part of a corporate liquidation.

LITZ CORPORATION
Balance Sheet
August 8, 1995

Assets

Cash	$ 16,000
Accounts receivable (net)	82,000
Investments	32,000
Inventory (net realizable value is expected	
to approximate cost)	69,000
Land	30,000
Buildings (net)	340,000
Equipment (net)	210,000
Total assets	$779,000

Liabilities and Equities

Accounts payable	$150,000
Notes payable—current (secured by inventory)	132,000
Notes payable—long term (secured by land	
and buildings [valued at $300,000])	259,000
Common stock.	135,000
Retained earnings	103,000
Total liabilities and equities	$779,000

The following events occur during the liquidation process:

- The investments are sold for $39,000.
- The inventory is sold at auction for $48,000.
- The money derived from the inventory is applied against the short-term notes payable.
- Administrative expenses of $15,000 are incurred in connection with the liquidation.
- The land and buildings are sold for $315,000. The long-term notes payable are paid.
- The accountant determines that $34,000 of the accounts payable are liabilities with priority.
- The company's equipment is sold for $84,000.
- Accounts receivable of $34,000 are collected. The remainder of the receivables are considered uncollectible.
- The administrative expenses are paid.

Required:

a. Prepare a statement of realization and liquidation for the period just described.
b. What percentage of their claims should the unsecured creditors receive?

39. The following balance sheet has been prepared by the accountant of the Becket Corporation as of November 10, 1995, the date on which the company is to release a plan for reorganizing operations under Chapter 11 of the Bankruptcy Reform Act.

BECKET CORPORATION
Balance Sheet
November 10, 1995

Assets

Cash	$ 12,000
Accounts receivable (net).	61,000
Investments.	26,000
Inventory (net realizable value is expected	
to approximate 80% of cost)	80,000
Land	57,000
Buildings (net).	248,000
Equipment (net)	117,000
Total assets	$601,000

Liabilities and Equities

Accounts payable	$129,000
Notes payable—current (secured by equipment).	220,000
Notes payable—(due in 1998)	
(secured by land and buildings)	325,000
Common stock ($10 par value)	60,000
Retained earnings (deficit)	(133,000)
Total liabilities and equities	$601,000

The company presented the following proposal:

1. The reorganization value of the company's assets just prior to emerging from bankruptcy is set at $650,000.

2. Accounts receivable of $20,000 are written off as uncollectible. Investments are worth $40,000, land is worth $80,000, the buildings are worth $300,000, and the equipment is worth $86,000.

3. An outside investor has been found who will buy 7,000 shares of common stock at $11 per share.

4. The company's investments are to be sold for $40,000 in cash with the proceeds going to the holders of the current note payable. The remainder of these short-term notes will be converted into $130,000 of notes due in 1999 and paying 10 percent annual cash interest.

5. All accounts payable will be exchanged for $40,000 in notes payable due in 1996 and paying 8 percent annual interest.

6. Title to land costing $20,000 but worth $50,000 will be transferred to the holders of the note payable due in 1998. In addition, these creditors will receive $180,000 in notes payable (paying 10 percent annual interest) coming due in 2001. These creditors are also issued 3,000 shares of previously unissued common stock.

Required:

Prepare journal entries for Becket to record the transactions as put forth in this reorganization plan.

40. The Oregon Corporation has filed a voluntary petition to reorganize the company under Chapter 11 of the Bankruptcy Reform Act. The creditors are considering an attempt to force liquidation. The company currently holds cash of $6,000 and accounts receivable of $25,000. In addition, the company owns four pieces of land. The first two (labeled A and B) cost $8,000 each. Plots C and D cost the company $20,000 and $25,000, respectively. A mortgage lien is attached to each parcel of land as security for four different notes payable of $15,000 apiece. Presently, the land can be sold for:

Plot A.	$16,000
Plot B.	$11,000
Plot C.	$14,000
Plot D.	$27,000

Another $25,000 note payable is unsecured. Accounts payable at this time total $32,000. Of this amount, $12,000 is salary owed to the company's workers. No employee is due more than $1,800.

The company expects to collect $12,000 from the accounts receivable if liquidation becomes necessary. Administrative expenses required for liquidation are anticipated to be $16,000.

Required:

a. Prepare a statement of financial affairs for the Oregon Corporation.
b. If the company is liquidated, how much cash would be paid on the note payable secured by plot B?
c. If the company is liquidated, how much cash would be paid on the note payable that is unsecured?
d. If the company is liquidated and plot D is sold for $30,000, how much cash would be paid on the note payable secured by plot B?

41. Lynch, Inc., is a hardware store operating in Boulder, Colorado. Management has recently made some poor inventory acquisitions that have loaded the store with unsalable merchandise. Because of the drop in revenues, the company is now insolvent. The entire inventory can be sold for only $33,000. Following is a trial balance as of March 14, 1995, the day the company files for a Chapter 7 liquidation.

	Debit	Credit
Accounts payable		$ 33,000
Accounts receivable	$ 25,000	
Accumulated depreciation, building		50,000
Accumulated depreciation, equipment		16,000
Additional paid-in capital		8,000
Advertising payable		4,000
Building	80,000	
Cash	1,000	
Common stock		50,000
Equipment	30,000	
Inventory	100,000	
Investments	15,000	
Land	10,000	
Note payable—Colorado Savings and Loan (secured by lien on land		
and building)		70,000
Note payable—First National Bank (secured by equipment)		150,000
Payroll taxes payable		1,000
Retained earnings (deficit)	126,000	
Salary payable		5,000
Totals	$387,000	$387,000

Company officials believe that 60 percent of the accounts receivable can be collected if the company is liquidated. The building and land have a market value of $75,000, while the equipment is worth $19,000. The investments represent shares of a nationally traded company that can be sold at the current time for $21,000. Administrative expenses necessary to carry out a liquidation would approximate $16,000.

Required:

Prepare a statement of financial affairs for Lynch, Inc. as of March 14, 1995.

42. Use the trial balance presented for Lynch, Inc., in problem 41. Assume that the company will be liquidated and the following transactions occur:

- Accounts receivable of $18,000 are collected.
- All of the company's inventory is sold for $40,000.
- Additional accounts payable of $10,000 incurred for various expenses such as utilities and maintenance are discovered.
- The land and building are sold for $71,000.
- The note payable due to the Colorado Savings and Loan is paid.
- The equipment is sold at auction for only $11,000 with the proceeds applied to the note owed to the First National Bank.
- The investments are sold for $21,000.
- Administrative expenses total $20,000 as of July 23, 1995, but no payment has yet been made.

Required:

a. Prepare a statement of realization and liquidation for the period from March 14, 1995, through July 23, 1995.

b. How much cash would be paid to an unsecured, nonpriority creditor who is owed a total of $1,000 by Lynch, Inc.?

43. The Holmes Corporation has filed a voluntary petition with the bankruptcy court in hopes of reorganizing the company. A statement of financial affairs has been prepared for Holmes showing the following debts:

Liabilities with priority:	
Salary payable	$ 18,000
Fully secured creditors:	
Notes payable (secured by land and	
buildings valued at $84,000)	70,000
Partially secured creditors:	
Notes payable (secured by inventory	
valued at $30,000)	140,000
Unsecured creditors:	
Notes payable	50,000
Accounts payable	10,000
Accrued expenses	4,000

The company has 10,000 shares of common stock outstanding with a par value of $5 per share. In addition, the company is currently reporting a deficit balance of $132,000.

Company officials have proposed the following reorganization plan:

· The company's assets have a total book value of $210,000, an amount considered to be equal to fair market value. The reorganization value of the assets as a whole, though, is set at $225,000.

· Employees will receive a one-year note in lieu of all salaries owed. Interest will be 10 percent, a normal rate for this type of liability.

· The fully secured note will have all future interest dropped from a 15 percent rate, which is now unrealistic, to a 10 percent rate.

· The partially secured note payable will be satisfied by the signing of a new six-year $30,000 note paying 10 percent annual interest. In addition, this creditor will receive 5,000 new shares of Holmes' common stock.

· An outside investor has been enlisted to buy 6,000 new shares of common stock at $6 per share.

· The unsecured creditors will be offered 20 cents on the dollar to settle the remaining liabilities.

If this plan of reorganization is accepted and becomes effective, what journal entries would be recorded by the Holmes Corporation?

PARTNERSHIPS: FORMATION AND OPERATION

Questions to Consider

- Why are some businesses legally organized as partnerships rather than as corporations?
- Why do the equity accounts of a partnership differ from those of a corporation? How do these accounts differ?
- If a partner brings an intangible attribute (such as a business expertise or an established clientele) to a partnership, how is this contribution valued and recorded?
- How is the annual net income that is earned by a partnership allocated among the individual capital accounts maintained for each partner?
- If a partner withdraws from a partnership and receives more cash than is recorded in the appropriate capital balance, what accounting does the business make of the excess payment?

A reader of college accounting textbooks might come to the conclusion that business activity in the United States is carried out exclusively by corporations. Because most large companies are legally incorporated, a vast majority of textbook references and illustrations concern corporate organizations. Contrary to the perception being relayed, partnerships (as well as sole proprietorships) make up a vital element of the American business community. Based on the filing of income tax returns, more than 1.7 million partnerships were estimated to be in existence in this country in 1986 (as compared to nearly 3.4 million corporations).

The Partnership form is found in a wide range of business activities, from small local operations to worldwide enterprises. Examples can be seen throughout the American economy:

- Individual proprietors often join together in the formation of a partnership as a means of reducing expenses, expanding services, and adding increased expertise.
- Partnerships are a common means by which friends and relatives can create and organize a business endeavor.
- Doctors, lawyers, and other professionals have historically formed partnerships because of legal prohibitions against the incorporation of their practices. Although some states now permit such organizations to become professional corporations, operating as a partnership or sole proprietorship is still necessary in many areas.

Over the years, some partnerships have grown to enormous sizes. An announcement of the merger of Deloitte Haskins & Sells and Touche Ross stated that the combined organization would have 5,470 partners. "The new international firm will have 1989 worldwide revenue in excess of $4 billion, will employ 65,000 people and will be one of the world's largest accounting and consulting firms, with a leading position in substantially all major U.S. and international markets."[1] In 1991, the investment banking partnership, Goldman Sachs, generated estimated revenues of $7 billion while the accounting firm of Ernst & Young had revenues of $6.3 billion.[2] As a means of comparison, well-known industrial giants Maytag Corporation, Dow Corning Corporation, and Polaroid Corporation had *combined* revenues at that time of $6.9 billion.

Partnerships—Advantages and Disadvantages

The popularity of the partnership format is based on several advantages inherent to this type of organization. An analysis of these attributes explains why more than 1.7 million enterprises today are maintained as partnerships rather than as corporations.

One of the most common motives is the ease of formation. Only an oral agreement is necessary to create a legally binding partnership. In contrast, depending on specific state laws, incorporation requires the filing of a formal application along with the completion of various other forms and documents. Operators of small businesses may find the convenience involved in creating a partnership to be an especially appealing characteristic.

Other justifications for structuring a business as a partnership can be discovered within the tax laws.

The partnership form of business has become increasingly popular in the United States, and it may account for a significant portion of new business formation in the future. One reason for the burgeoning of partnerships is that this form of business

---

[1] *DH & S Review,* July 17, 1989, pp. 1–2.

[2] Ronald Henkoff, "Inside America's Biggest Private Company," *Fortune,* July 13, 1992, p. 87.

offers many of the risk-sharing opportunities of the corporate form without the burden of corporate income taxation.[3]

Although a detailed investigation of taxation rules and regulations goes beyond the scope of this textbook, a few aspects are quite relevant to the current discussion. One area of the law warrants particular attention: the method by which partnerships are taxed. Although an informational tax return must be filed on an annual basis, *the partnership itself pays no income taxes.* For taxation purposes, the government does not view a partnership as an entity apart from its owners.

Partnership revenue and expense items (as defined by the tax laws) must be assigned directly to the individual partners with the income taxes being paid by them. By passing income balances through to the partners in this manner, double-taxation of profits that are earned by the business and then distributed to the owners is avoided.[4] In a corporation, income is taxed twice: when earned and again when conveyed as a dividend. A partnership's income is only taxed at the time that it is initially earned by the business.

As an illustration, assume that a business earns $100. After paying any income taxes, the remainder is immediately conveyed to its owners. A tax rate of 30 percent is assumed for both individuals and corporations. As the following table shows, if this business is a partnership rather than a corporation, the owners are left with more expendable income. This difference, though, does narrow as tax rates are lowered. Thus, the decrease in federal income tax rates during the 1980s reduced, somewhat, the tax appeal of partnerships.

	Partnership	Corporation
Income before income taxes.	$100	$100
Income taxes paid by business (30%).	–0–	(30)
Income distributed to owners	$100	$ 70
Income taxes paid by owners (30%)	(30)	(21)
Expendable income	$ 70	$ 49

The advantage of single taxation has led some larger companies in recent years to convert to the partnership form:

The next time Larry Bird drives for a layup, he'll have more than the usual Boston fans cheering him on—the shot will also be keenly watched by owners of publicly

---

[3] Harry Watson, "An Analysis of the Formation and Behavior of Partnerships," *Public Finance Quarterly,* July 1989, p. 281.

[4] Generally, the same tax advantages enjoyed by a partnership also are available to companies that qualify as S corporations. Certain restrictions, however, are placed on the usage of S corporation status by the tax laws. For example, the business can have only one class of stock and is limited to 35 stockholders. All owners must be individuals, estates, or certain types of trusts. In addition, no more than 25 percent of gross receipts can come from passive investment income (such as dividends, rents, and annuities) during any three consecutive years.

traded Boston Celtics limited partnership units. And weary travelers who stop at Motel 6 can rest easy knowing that thousands of new limited partners helped make the beds they're sleeping in. The Boston Celtics and Motel 6 are just two examples of corporations that converted to partnerships to maximize after-tax returns to investors.[5]

Another tax advantage is available to owners who invest in a partnership, although the potential benefits have been greatly reduced by recent changes in the tax laws. In the past, partnerships could be designed specifically to serve as tax shelters. The investor would acquire an interest but would not participate in the business. These investments were created, especially in certain industries, to produce immediate tax losses or write-offs in exchange for possible profits in the future. The losses were then used to offset the partner's current taxable income, thereby deferring taxes and conserving cash flows. The subsequent income that resulted from the partnership was frequently spread over a number of years so that the taxpayer was able to maintain taxable income levels within lower tax rate brackets.[6]

However, such passive activity losses (where the taxpayer does not materially participate in the actual business activities) are now only allowed for tax purposes as a reduction to offset other passive activity profits. These losses can no longer be used to reduce earned income such as salaries. Thus, unless a taxpayer has significant passive activity income (from rents, for example), little or no tax advantage comes from this type of investment.

The partnership form of business has certain significant disadvantages. Perhaps the most severe problem is the unlimited liability automatically incurred by each partner. Partnership law specifies that any partner can be held personally liable for *all* debts of the business. The potential risk is especially significant when coupled with the concept of *mutual agency*. This legal term refers to the right that each partner has to incur liabilities in the name of the partnership. Consequently, partners acting within the normal scope of the business have the power to obligate the company for any amount. If the partnership fails to pay these debts, creditors can seek satisfactory remuneration from any partner that they choose.

> Partners are jointly and severally liable for the firm's obligations. As an example, if a bank had made a $10 million loan to the partnership that it could not pay, and the bank obtained a judgment against the partnership, the bank could attempt to attach the assets of any particular partner in the firm. The bank could pick and choose the partners it wished to proceed against in order to satisfy the judgment. If a partner ended up paying more than his or her share, he or she would have a right to recover from the other partners.[7]

---

[5] Keith Wishon and Robert P. Roche, "Making the Switch: Corporation to Partnership," *Journal of Accountancy,* March 1987, p. 90.

[6] The losses of a corporation have never provided this same benefit to stockholders. Since corporations are taxed as separate entities, a loss cannot carry through as a direct reduction in the taxable income of the company's owners.

[7] An interview with Leslie D. Corwin, Esq., "What's a Partner to Do?" *The CPA Journal,* April 1991, p. 22.

Because of the potential liability, partnerships often experience difficulty in attracting large amounts of ownership capital. Possible investors frequently avoid entering into a partnership unless they are able to participate directly in the day-to-day operations of the business. Thus, absentee ownership, which is so prevalent in corporations, is not particularly common in many partnerships.

The fear engendered by unlimited liability is relieved in some cases by the creation of a *limited partnership*. In such organizations, a number of limited partners invest money as owners but are not allowed to participate in the management of the company. These partners can still incur a loss, but the amount is restricted legally to that which each has contributed. To protect the creditors of a limited partnership, one or more general partners must be designated to assume responsibility for all obligations created in the name of the business.

UDC—Development L.P. (having revenues in 1991 of approximately $345 million) and Buckeye Partners, L.P. (revenues of $151 million) are just two examples of limited partnerships that trade on the New York Stock Exchange. According to Buckeye's December 31, 1991, balance sheet, capital of $2.5 million is reported for the company's general partners whereas the same balance for the limited partners shows a total of $249.5 million.

Such legal concepts as unlimited liability and mutual agency describe partnership characteristics that have been defined and interpreted over a great number of years. To provide consistent application across state lines in regard to these terms as well as many other legal aspects of a partnership, the Uniform Partnership Act (UPA) was created. This act, which was first proposed in 1914 and has now been adopted by all states in some form, establishes uniform standards in such areas as the nature of a partnership, the relationship of the partners to outside parties, and the dissolution of the partnership. For example, the most common legal definition of a partnership is provided by Section 6 of the act: "an association of two or more persons to carry on as co-owners a business for profit."

Partnership Accounting—Capital Accounts

Despite legal distinctions, questions should be raised before proceeding as to the need for an entirely separate study of partnership accounting.

- Does an association of two or more persons require accounting procedures significantly different from those of a corporation?
- Is proper accounting dependent on the legal form of an organization?

The answer to these questions is both yes and no. Accounting procedures are normally standardized for assets, liabilities, revenues, and expenses regardless of the legal form of a business. *Partnership accounting, though, does exhibit unique aspects that warrant study, but they lie primarily in the handling of the partners' capital accounts.*

The stockholders' equity accounts of a corporation do not correspond directly with the capital balances found in a partnership's financial records. The various equity accounts reported by an incorporated enterprise display a greater degree of structuring: they are more precisely defined. These characteristics reflect the wide variety of equity transactions that can occur in a corporation as well as the influence of state and federal laws. Government regulation has certainly had an effect on the accounting for corporate equity transactions in that extensive disclosure is required to protect stockholders and other outside parties.

To provide adequate information as well as to meet legal requirements, corporate accounting must provide details about numerous possible equity transactions and account balances. For example, the amount of a corporation's paid-in capital is shown separately from earned capital; the par value of each class of stock is disclosed; treasury stock, stock options, stock dividends, and other capital transactions are reported based on prescribed accounting principles.

In comparison, partnerships provide only a limited amount of equity disclosure primarily in the form of individual capital accounts that are accumulated for every partner or every class of partners. These balances measure each partner or group's interest in the book value of the net assets of the business. Thus, the equity section of a partnership balance sheet is comprised solely of capital accounts that can be affected by many different events: contributions from partners as well as distributions to them, earnings, and any other equity transactions.

However, no differentiation is drawn in the reporting of a partnership between the various sources of ownership capital. Disclosing the composition of the capital balances has not seemed to be necessary because partnerships have historically tended to be small in size with equity transactions that were rarely complex. Additionally, absentee ownership is not common, a factor which minimizes both the need for government regulation as well as the outside interest in the receipt of detailed information about the capital balances.

Articles of Partnership

Because the demand for information about capital balances is limited, accounting principles specific to partnerships are based primarily on traditional approaches that have evolved over the years rather than on official pronouncements. These procedures attempt to mirror the relationship that exists between the partners and their business especially as defined by the partnership agreement. This legal covenant, which may be either oral or written, is often referred to as the Articles of Partnership and forms the central governance for the operation of a partnership. The financial arrangements spelled out in this contract establish guidelines for the various capital transactions. Therefore, the Articles of Partnership, rather than laws or official rules, provide much of the underlying basis for partnership accounting.

Since the Articles of Partnership is a negotiated agreement created by the partners, an unlimited number of variations can be encountered in practice. Partners' rights and responsibilities frequently differ from business to business. Consequently, accountants are often hired in an advisory capacity to participate in the creation of this document to assure the equitable treatment of all parties. Although the Articles of Partnership may contain a number of provisions, an explicit understanding should always be reached in regard to the following:

- Name and address of each partner.
- Business location.
- Description of the nature of the business.
- Rights and responsibilities of each partner.
- Initial contribution to be made by each partner along with the method to be used for valuation.
- Specific method by which profits and losses are to be allocated.
- Periodic withdrawal of assets by each partner.
- Procedure for admitting new partners.
- Method for arbitrating partnership disputes.
- Life insurance provisions enabling remaining partners to acquire the interest of any deceased partner.
- Method for settling a partner's share in the business upon withdrawal, retirement, or death.[8]

Despite the importance of the Articles of Partnership, an unusual number of partnerships fail to produce this needed document.

> "You'd be surprised at the number of American law firms that operate without partnership agreements or [use] agreements that are out of date," says Ward Bower of Altman & Weil, a consulting firm that specializes in law-firm management. "Lawyers," he adds, "will sign agreements they'd never let their clients sign."[9]

> But despite 20 years of advice on the value of partnership agreements, the reality is that, in the majority of cases, well-structured agreements are the exception, rather than the rule, in practice units.[10]

Discussion Question: What Kind of Business Is This?

After graduating from college, Shelley Williams was employed at several different jobs but found that she did not enjoy working for other people. Finally, she and Yvonne Hargrove, her college roommate, decided to start a

---

[8] A complete discussion of the provisions to be included in a partnership agreement can be found in "Partnership Agreements: Realities into Formalities," by Herman J. Lowe in the September 1986 issue of the *Journal of Accountancy*, pp. 158–66.

[9] Christi Harlan, "Lawyers Find it Difficult to Break Up Partnerships," *The Wall Street Journal*, October 6, 1988, p. B1.

[10] Herman J. Lowe, "Partnership Agreements: Realities into Formalities," *Journal of Accountancy*, September 1986, p. 158.

continued

business of their own. They rented a small building and opened a florist shop selling cut flowers such as roses and chrysanthemums that they bought from a local greenhouse.

Williams and Hargrove agreed to share profits and losses equally, although they also decided to take no money from the operation for at least four months. No other arrangements were made but the business did reasonably well and, after the first four months had passed, each began to draw out $150 in cash every week.

At year's end, they took their financial records to a local accountant so that they could get their income tax returns completed. He informed them that they had been operating as a partnership and that they should draw up an official Articles of Partnership or consider becoming an incorporated entity. They confessed that they had never really considered the issue and asked for his advice on the matter.

What advice should the accountant give to his clients?

Accounting for Capital Contributions

Several types of capital transactions occur in a partnership: allocation of profits and losses, retirement of a current partner, admission of a new partner, and so on. The initial transaction, however, is the contribution made by the partners to begin the business. In the simplest situation, the partners invest only cash amounts. For example, assume that Carter and Green form a business to be operated as a partnership. Carter contributes $50,000 in cash whereas Green invests $20,000. The initial journal entry to record the creation of this partnership is as follows:

Cash	70,000	
Carter, Capital		50,000
Green, Capital		20,000

To record cash contributed to start new partnership.

Complications have been avoided in this first illustration by the assumption that only cash was invested. Often, though, one or more of the partners transfers noncash assets such as inventory, land, equipment, or a building to the business. Although fair market value is used to record these assets, a case could be developed for initially valuing any contributed asset at the partner's current book value. According to the concept of unlimited liability (as well as present tax laws), a partnership does not exist as an entity apart from its owners. A logical extension of the idea is that the investment of an asset is not a transaction occurring between two independent parties such as would warrant revaluation. This contention holds that the semblance of an arm's-length transaction is necessary to justify a change in the book value of any account.

Although retaining the recorded value for assets contributed to a partnership may seem reasonable, this method of valuation proves to be inequitable to any partner investing appreciated property. A $50,000 capital balance always results from a cash investment of that amount but the recording of other assets would be entirely dependent on the partner's original book value.

Should a partner, for example, who contributes a building having a recorded value of $18,000 but a fair market value of $50,000 be credited with only an $18,000 interest in the partnership? Since $50,000 in cash and $50,000 in appreciated property are equivalent contributions, a $32,000 difference in the partners' capital balances cannot be justified. To prevent such inequities, each item transferred to a partnership is initially recorded for external reporting purposes at current value.[11]

Requiring revaluation of contributed assets can, however, be advocated for reasons other than just the fair treatment of all partners. Despite some evidence to the contrary, a partnership can be legitimately viewed as an entity standing apart from its owners. As an example, a partnership maintains legal ownership of its assets and (depending on state law) can instigate lawsuits. For this reason, accounting practice has traditionally held that the contribution of assets (and liabilities) to a partnership is an exchange between two separately identifiable parties that should be recorded based on fair market values.

The determination of an appropriate valuation for each capital balance is more than just an accounting exercise. Over the life of a partnership, these figures serve in a number of important capacities:

1. The totals in the individual accounts often influence the assignment of profits and losses to the partners.
2. The capital account balance is usually a factor in determining the final distribution that will be received by a partner at the time of withdrawal or retirement.
3. Ending capital balances indicate the allocation to be made of any assets that remain following the liquidation of a partnership.

To demonstrate the accounting for these capital balances, assume that Carter invests $50,000 in cash to begin the previously discussed partnership while Green contributes the following assets:

	Book Value to Green	Fair Market Value
Inventory.	$ 9,000	$10,000
Land.	14,000	11,000
Building	32,000	46,000
Totals	$55,000	$67,000

---

[11] For federal income tax purposes, the $18,000 book value is retained as the basis for this building, even after transfer to the partnership. Throughout the tax laws, no difference is seen between partners and their partnership.

As an added factor, Green's building is encumbered by a $23,600 mortgage payable that the partnership has agreed to assume.

Based on the applicable values of these accounts, Green's net investment is equal to $43,400 ($67,000 less $23,600). The following journal entry records the formation of the partnership created by these contributions:

Cash	50,000	
Inventory	10,000	
Land	11,000	
Building	46,000	
Mortgage Payable		23,600
Carter, Capital		50,000
Green, Capital		43,400

To record properties contributed to start partnership. Assets and liabilities are recorded at fair market value.

One further point should be made before leaving this illustration. Although Green has contributed inventory, land, and a building, this partner holds no further right to these individual assets; they now belong to the partnership. The $43,400 capital balance represents an ownership interest in the business as a whole but does not constitute a specific claim. Having transferred title to the partnership, Green has no more right to these assets than does Carter.

Intangible Contributions.   In forming a partnership, the contributions made by one or more of the partners may go beyond assets and liabilities. A doctor, for example, can bring a particular line of expertise to a partnership while a practicing dentist might have already developed an established clientele. These attributes, as well as many others, are frequently as valuable to a partnership as cash and fixed assets. *Hence, formal accounting recognition of such special contributions may be appropriately included as a provision of any partnership agreement.*

To illustrate, assume that James and Joyce plan to open an advertising agency and decide to organize the endeavor as a partnership. James contributes cash of $70,000 whereas Joyce invests only $10,000. Joyce, however, is an accomplished graphic artist, a skill that is considered especially valuable to this business. Therefore, in producing the Articles of Partnership, the partners agree to start the business with equal capital balances. Often such decisions result only after long, and sometimes heated, negotiations. Because the value assigned to an intangible contribution such as artistic talent is arbitrary at best, proper reporting depends on the ability of the partners to arrive at an equitable arrangement.

In recording this agreement, James and Joyce have two options available: (1) the bonus method and (2) the goodwill method. Each of these approaches achieves the desired result of establishing equal capital account balances. The recorded figures, however, can vary significantly depending on the procedure selected. Thus, the partners should reach an understanding prior to beginning business operations as to the method used. The accountant can help avoid conflicts in this area by assisting the partners in evaluating the impact created by each of these two alternatives.

The Bonus Method. This accounting option assumes that a specialization such as Joyce's artistic abilities does *not* constitute a recordable partnership asset with a measurable cost. Hence, this approach recognizes only the assets that are physically transferred to the business (such as cash, patents, inventory, etc.). Although total partnership capital is determined by these contributions, the establishment of specific capital balances is viewed as an independent process based solely on the agreement of the partners. Since the initial equity figures are the result of negotiation, they do not need to correspond directly with the individual investments.

James and Joyce have contributed a total of $80,000 in identifiable assets to their partnership and have decided on equal capital balances. According to the bonus method, this agreement is fulfilled simply by splitting the $80,000 figure evenly between the two partners. The following entry records the formation of this partnership under this assumption:

Cash	80,000	
James, Capital		40,000
Joyce, Capital.		40,000

To record cash contributions with bonus to Joyce because of artistic abilities.

Joyce received a capital bonus here of $30,000 (the recorded capital balance in excess of the $10,000 cash contribution) from James in recognition of the artistic abilities she brought into the business.

The Goodwill Method. This alternative is based on the assumption that an implied value can be mathematically calculated and recorded for any intangible contribution. In the present illustration, Joyce invested $60,000 less cash than James but receives an equal amount of capital according to the partnership agreement. Proponents of the goodwill method argue that Joyce's artistic talent has an apparent value of $60,000, a figure that should be included as part of this partner's capital investment. If not recorded, Joyce's primary contribution to the business is completely ignored within the accounting records.

Cash	80,000	
Goodwill	60,000	
James, Capital		70,000
Joyce, Capital.		70,000

To record cash contributions with goodwill attributed to Joyce in recognition of artistic abilities.

Comparison of Methods. Both of these approaches achieve the intent of the partnership agreement: equal capital balances are recorded despite a difference in the partners' cash contributions. The bonus method allocates the $80,000 invested capital according to the percentages designated by the partners, whereas the goodwill method capitalizes the implied value of Joyce's intangible contribution.

Although each of these two techniques is presently acceptable; the recognition of goodwill poses definite theoretical problems. In previous discussions of both the equity method (Chapter 1) and purchase consolidations (Chapter 2), goodwill was also recorded but only as a result of an acquisition price paid by the reporting entity. Consequently, this asset had a historical cost in the traditional accounting sense. Partnership goodwill has no such cost; the business recognizes an asset even though no funds have been spent.

The partnership of James and Joyce, for example, is able to record $60,000 in goodwill without any expenditure. Furthermore, the value attributed to this asset is based solely on a negotiated agreement between the partners; the $60,000 balance has no objectively verifiable basis. Thus, although partnership goodwill is sometimes encountered in actual practice, this ''asset'' should be viewed with a strong degree of professional skepticism.

Additional Capital Contributions and Withdrawals

Subsequent to the formation of a partnership, the owners may choose to contribute additional capital amounts. These investments can be made to stimulate expansion or to assist the business in overcoming working capital shortages or other problems. Regardless of the reason, the contribution is again recorded as an increment in the partner's capital account based on fair market value. For example, in the previous illustration, assume that James decides to invest another $5,000 cash in the partnership to help finance the purchase of new office furnishings. The partner's capital account balance is immediately increased by this amount to reflect the transfer being made to the partnership.

The partners may also reverse this process by withdrawing assets from the business for their own personal use. To protect the interests of the other partners, the amount and timing of such withdrawals should be clearly specified in the Articles of Partnership. In many instances, withdrawals are allowed on a regular periodic basis as a reward for ownership or as compensation for work done in the business. Such distributions are often recorded initially in a separate drawing account that is closed into the individual partner's capital account at year's end. Assume, for illustration purposes, that James and Joyce have agreed that they will collect $1,200 and $1,500 per month, respectively, from their business. The journal entry to record these monthly payments is as follows:

James, Drawing	1,200	
Joyce, Drawing	1,500	
Cash		2,700
To record monthly withdrawal of cash by partners.		

Larger amounts might also be withdrawn from a partnership on occasion. A partner may have a special need for money or just desire to reduce the basic investment that has been made in the business. Such transactions are usually sporadic occurrences and in amounts significantly greater than the partner's periodic drawing. Prior approval by the other partners may be required by the Articles of Partnership. Because these withdrawals can be viewed as a return of the owner's investment, they are often recorded directly to the partner's capital balance rather than to the separate drawing account.

Discussion Question: How Will the Profits Be Split?

James J. Dewars has been the sole owner of a small CPA firm for the past 20 years. Now 52 years old, Dewars is concerned about the continuation of his practice after he retires. He would like to begin taking more time off now although he wants to remain active in the firm for at least another 8 to 10 years. He has worked hard over the decades to build up the practice so that he presently makes a profit of $100,000 annually.

Lewis Huffman has been working for Dewars for the past four years. He now earns a salary of $40,000 per year. He is a very dedicated employee who generally works 52–60 hours per week. In the past, Dewars has been in charge of the bigger, more profitable audit clients whereas Huffman, with less experience, worked with the smaller clients. Both Dewars and Huffman do some tax work although that segment of the business has never been emphasized.

Sally Scriba has been working for the past seven years with another CPA firm as a tax specialist. She has no auditing experience but has a great reputation in tax planning and preparation. She currently has an annual salary of $60,000.

Dewars, Huffman, and Scriba are negotiating the creation of a new CPA firm as a partnership. Dewars plans to reduce his time in this firm although he will continue to work with many of the clients that he has served for the past two decades. Huffman will begin to take over some of the major audit jobs. Scriba will start and develop an extensive tax practice for the firm.

Because of the changes in the firm, the three potential partners anticipate earning a total net income in the first year of operations of between $130,000 and $160,000. Thereafter, they hope that profits will increase at the rate of 10 to 20 percent annually for the next five years or so.

How should this partnership allocate its future net income to the partners?

Allocation of Income

At the end of each fiscal period, partnership revenues and expenses are closed out with the resulting net income or loss being transferred to the partners' capital accounts. Since a separate equity balance is maintained for each partner, a method must be devised for this assignment of annual income. Because of the importance of the process, the procedure established by the partners should always be stipulated in the Articles of Partnership. If no arrangement has been specified, state partnership law normally holds that all partners share equally in any income or loss earned by the business. If an agreement has been set forth solely for allocating profits, any subsequent losses that occur must be divided in that same manner.

Actual procedures for allocating profits and losses can range from the simple to the elaborate.[12] Many partnerships avoid all complications by assigning net income on an equal basis among all partners. Other organizations attempt to devise plans that reward such factors as the expertise of the individuals or the amount of time that each works. Some agreements also consider the capital invested in the business as an element that should be recognized within the allocation process.

To serve as an initial illustration, assume that Tinker, Evers, and Chance form a partnership by investing cash of $120,000, $90,000, and $75,000, respectively. The Articles of Partnership are drawn up to specify that Evers will be allotted 40 percent of all profits and losses because of previous business experience while Tinker and Chance are to divide the remaining 60 percent equally. This agreement also stipulates that each partner is allowed to withdraw $10,000 in cash annually from the business. The amount of this withdrawal is not directly dependent on the method utilized for income allocation. *From an accounting perspective, the assignment of income and the setting of withdrawal limits are two separate decisions.*

At the end of the first year of operations, the partnership reports net income of $60,000. To reflect the changes made in the partners' capital balances, the closing process consists of the following two journal entries. The assumption is made here that each partner has taken the allowed amount of drawing during the year. In addition, all revenues and expenses have already been closed into an Income Summary account.

Tinker, Capital	10,000	
Evers, Capital	10,000	
Chance, Capital	10,000	
Tinker, Drawing		10,000
Evers, Drawing		10,000
Chance, Drawing		10,000

To close out drawing accounts of the three partners.

Income Summary	60,000	
Tinker, Capital (30%)		18,000
Evers, Capital (40%)		24,000
Chance, Capital (30%)		18,000

To allocate net income based on partnership agreement.

Statement of Partners' Capital.   Since retained earnings are not separately disclosed by a partnership, the statement of retained earnings reported by a corpora-

---

[12] See, for example, "Profit Allocation in CPA Firm Partnership Agreements," in the March 1986 issue of the *Journal of Accountancy*, pp. 91–95; "Paying Partners: A Challenge for the 1990s," in the June 1989 issue of the *Journal of Accountancy*, pp. 117–22; or "Selecting the Best Partner Compensation Method" in the December 1991 issue of the *Journal of Accountancy*, pp. 40–44.

tion is replaced by a statement of partners' capital. The following financial statement is based on the data presented for the partnership of Tinker, Evers, and Chance. The changes made during the year in the individual capital accounts are outlined along with totals representing the partnership as a whole.

TINKER, EVERS, AND CHANCE
Statement of Partners' Capital
For Year Ending December 31, Year 1

	Tinker, Capital	Evers, Capital	Chance, Capital	Totals
Capital balances beginning of year.	$120,000	$ 90,000	$75,000	$285,000
Allocation of net income . . .	18,000	24,000	18,000	60,000
Drawings	(10,000)	(10,000)	(10,000)	(30,000)
Capital balances end of year. .	$128,000	$104,000	$83,000	$315,000

Alternative Allocation Techniques—Example One.   Assigning net income based on a ratio may be simple, but this approach is not necessarily equitable to all partners. For example, assume that Tinker does not participate in the operations of the partnership but is the contributor of the largest amount of capital. Evers and Chance both work full time in the business, but Evers has considerably more experience in this line of work.

Under these circumstances, no single ratio would properly reflect the various contributions being made by each of the partners. Indeed, an unlimited number of alternative allocation plans could be devised in hopes of achieving fair treatment for all parties. For example, because of the different levels of capital being invested, consideration should be given to the inclusion of interest within the allocation process. A compensation allowance is also a possibility, usually in an amount corresponding to the number of hours worked or the level of a partner's business expertise.

To demonstrate one possible option, assume that Tinker, Evers, and Chance begin their partnership based on the facts presented originally except that they arrive at a more detailed method of allocating profits and losses. After considerable negotiations, an Articles of Partnership agreement is drawn up that credits each partner annually for interest in an amount equal to 10 percent of the beginning capital balance for the year. Evers and Chance will also be allotted $15,000 apiece as a compensation allowance in recognition of their participation in daily operations. Any remaining profit or loss will be split 4:3:3, with the largest share going to Evers because of the work experience that this partner brings to the business. As with any appropriate allocation, this pattern is an attempt to be fair to all three of the partners.

Under this arrangement, the $60,000 net income earned by the partnership in the first year of operation would be prorated as follows. The sequential alignment of the various provisions is irrelevant except that the ratio, which is used to divide the remaining profit or loss, must always be calculated last.

	Tinker	Evers	Chance	Totals
Interest (10% of beginning capital)	$12,000	$ 9,000	$ 7,500	$28,500
Salary	–0–	15,000	15,000	30,000
Remaining income:				
$60,000				
(28,500)				
(30,000)				
$ 1,500	450 (30%)	600 (40%)	450 (30%)	1,500
Totals	$12,450	$24,600	$22,950	$60,000

For the partnership of Tinker, Evers, and Chance, the allocations just calculated lead to the following closing entry:

Income Summary.	60,000	
Tinker, Capital.		12,450
Evers, Capital		24,600
Chance, Capital		22,950

To allocate income for the year to the individual partners based on partnership agreement.

Alternative Allocation Techniques—Example Two.   As indicated by the preceding illustration, the assignment process is no more than a series of mechanical steps reflecting the change in each partner's capital balance resulting from the provisions of the partnership agreement. The number of different allocation procedures that could be employed is limited solely by the imagination of the partners. Although interest, compensation allowances, and various ratios are the predominant factors encountered in practice, other possibilities do exist. Therefore, another approach to the allocation process is presented to further illustrate some of the variations that can be utilized. A two-person partnership is used to simplify the computations.

Assume that Tinker and Evers formed a partnership in 1983 to operate a bookstore. Tinker contributed the initial capital while Evers managed the business. With the assistance of their accountant, they wrote an Articles of Partnership agreement that contains the following provisions:

1. Each partner is allowed to draw $1,000 in cash from the business every month. Any withdrawal in excess of that figure will be accounted for as a direct reduction to the partner's capital balance.

2. Partnership profits and losses will be allocated each year according to the following plan:

a. Interest of 15 percent will be accrued by each partner based on the monthly average capital balance for the year (calculated without regard for normal drawings or current income).

b. As a reward for operating the business, Evers is to receive credit for a bonus equal to 20 percent of the year's net income. However, no bonus is earned if the partnership reports a net loss.

c. Any remaining profit or loss will be divided equally between the two partners.

Assume that Tinker and Evers subsequently begin the year of 1995 with capital balances of $150,000 and $30,000, respectively. On April 1 of that year, Tinker invests an additional $8,000 cash in the business, while on July 1, Evers withdraws $6,000 in excess of the specified drawing allowance. Assume further that the partnership reports income of $30,000 for 1995.

Because the interest factor established in this allocation plan is based on a monthly average figure, the amount to be credited to each partner has to be determined by means of a preliminary calculation:

Tinker—Interest Allocation

Beginning balance:	$150,000 × 3 months =	$ 450,000
Balance, 4/1/95:	$158,000 × 9 months =	1,422,000
		1,872,000
	×	$\frac{1}{12}$
Monthly average capital balance		156,000
Interest rate		× 15%
Interest credited to Tinker		$ 23,400

Evers—Interest Allocation

Beginning balance:	$30,000 × 6 months =	$ 180,000
Balance, 7/1/95:	$24,000 × 6 months =	144,000
		324,000
	×	$\frac{1}{12}$
Monthly average capital balance		27,000
Interest rate		× 15%
Interest credited to Evers		$ 4,050

Following this initial computation, the actual assignment of income can proceed according to the provisions specified in the partnership agreement. The stipulations drawn up by Tinker and Evers must be followed exactly, even though the business's $30,000 profit in 1995 is not sufficient to cover both the interest and the bonus. Income allocation is a mechanical process and should always be carried out as stated in the Articles of Partnership without regard for the specific level of income or loss.

Based on the plan that was created, Tinkers capital increases by $21,675 at the end of 1995 while Evers is assigned only $8,325:

	Tinker	Evers	Totals
Interest (above)	$23,400	$4,050	$27,450
Bonus (20% × $30,000)	–0–	6,000	6,000
Remaining income (loss):			
$30,000			
(27,450)			
(6,000)			
$(3,450)	(1,725) (50%)	(1,725) (50%)	(3,450)
Totals	$21,675	$8,325	$30,000

Accounting for Partnership Dissolution

In many partnerships, capital transactions are limited almost exclusively to contributions, drawings, and profit and loss allocations. Normally, though, over any extended period, changes occur in the members who make up a partnership; these events must also be monitored by the accounting function. Employees may be promoted into the partnership or new owners brought in from outside the organization to add capital or expertise to the business. Current partners eventually retire, die, or simply elect to leave the partnership. Large operations may even experience such changes on a routine basis. One international accounting firm has estimated that 50 to 70 partners leave the organization each year for a variety of reasons.

Regardless of the nature or the frequency of the event, any alteration in the specific individuals composing a partnership automatically leads to legal dissolution. In most instances, the break up is merely a prerequisite to the formation of a new partnership. For example, if Abernethy and Chapman decide to allow Miller to become a partner in their business, the legally recognized partnership of Abernethy and Chapman has to be dissolved first. The business property as well as the right to future profits can then conveyed to the newly formed partnership of Abernethy, Chapman, and Miller. The change is a legal change. Actual operations of the business would probably continue unimpeded by this change in ownership.

Conversely, should the partners so choose, dissolution can also be a preliminary step in the termination and liquidation of the business. The death of a partner, lack of sufficient profits, or management differences may lead the partners to the break up of the partnership business. Under this circumstance, partnership properties are sold, debts paid, and any remaining assets distributed to the individual partners. Thus, in liquidations (which are analyzed in detail in the next chapter), both the partnership and the business cease to exist.

Dissolution—Admission of a New Partner

One of the most prevalent changes in the makeup of a partnership is the addition of a new partner. An employee may have worked for years to gain this opportunity or a prospective partner might offer new investment capital or business experience necessary for future business success. An individual can gain admittance to a partnership in one of two ways: (1) by purchasing an ownership interest from a current partner or (2) by contributing assets directly to the business.

In recording either transaction, the accountant has the option, once again, of retaining the book value for all partnership assets and liabilities (as exemplified by the bonus method) or revaluing these accounts to their present market values (the goodwill method). Although both are acceptable, the decision as to a theoretical preference between the bonus and goodwill methods hinges on one single question: *Should the dissolved partnership and the newly formed partnership be viewed as two separate reporting entities?*

If the new partnership is merely an extension of the old, no basis for restatement exists. The transfer of ownership is only a change in a legal sense and does not directly impact on business assets and liabilities. However, if the continuation of the business represents a legitimate transfer of property from one partnership to another, revaluation of all accounts and recognition of goodwill is warranted.

Because both approaches are encountered in practice, each is presented in this textbook. However, the concerns previously discussed in connection with partnership goodwill still exist: recognition is not based on historical cost and no objective verification can be made of the amount being capitalized. As is demonstrated, one alternative revaluation approach does exist that attempts to circumvent the problems involved with partnership goodwill. This hybrid method revalues all partnership assets and liabilities to fair market value without any corresponding recognition being made of goodwill.

Admission through Purchase of a Current Interest.   As mentioned, one method of gaining admittance to a partnership is by the purchase of a current interest. One or more partners may choose to sell their portion of the business to an outside party. This type transaction is most common in operations that rely primarily on monetary capital rather than on the business expertise of the partners.

In making a transfer of ownership, a partner can actually convey only three rights:

1. *The right of co-ownership in the business property.* This right justifies the partner's periodic drawings from the business as well as the distribution settlement paid at liquidation or at the time of a partner's withdrawal.

2. *The right to share in profits and losses as specified in the Articles of Partnership.*
3. *The right to participate in the management of the business.*

Unless restricted by the Articles of Partnership, any partner has the power to sell or assign the first two of these partnership rights at any time. Their transfer poses no threat of financial harm to the remaining partners. In contrast, partnership law states that the right to participate in the management of the business can only be conveyed with the consent of all partners. This particular right is considered essential to the future earning power of the operation as well as the maintenance of business assets. Therefore, the original partners are protected from the intrusion of parties who might be considered detrimental to the management of the company.

As an illustration, assume that Scott, Thompson, and York formed a partnership several years ago. Subsequently, York decides to leave the partnership and offers to sell his interest to Morgan. Although York may transfer the right of property ownership as well as the specified share of future profits and losses, Morgan is not automatically admitted into the partnership. York legally remains a partner until such time as both Scott and Thompson agree to allow Morgan to participate in the management of the business.

To demonstrate the accounting procedures applicable to the transfer of a partnership interest, assume that the following information is available relating to the partnership of Scott, Thompson, and York:

Partner	Capital Balance	Profit and Loss Ratio
Scott.	$ 50,000	20%
Thompson	30,000	50
York.	20,000	30
Total capital . . .	$100,000	

In this example, the relationship of the capital accounts to one another does not correspond with the partners' profit and loss ratio. Capital balances are historical cost figures. They result from contributions and withdrawals made throughout the life of the business as well as from the allocation of partnership income. Therefore, any correlation between a partner's recorded capital at a particular point in time and the profit and loss percentage would probably be coincidental. Scott, for example, has 50 percent of the current partnership capital ($50,000/$100,000), although entitled to only a 20 percent allocation of income.

Instead of York selling his interest to Morgan, assume that each of these three partners elects to transfer a 20 percent interest to Morgan for a total payment of $30,000. According to the sales contract, *the money is to be paid directly to the owners.* One approach to the recording of this transaction is that, since Morgan's purchase is carried out between the individual parties, the acquisition has no impact on the assets and liabilities held by the partnership. Because the business is not involved, the transfer of ownership requires a simple reclassification without any accompanying revaluation. This approach is similar to the bonus method; only a legal change in ownership is occurring so that neither revaluation of assets or liabilities nor goodwill is appropriate.

Scott, Capital (20% of capital balance)	10,000	
Thompson, Capital (20%)	6,000	
York, Capital (20%).	4,000	
Morgan, Capital (20% of total)		20,000
Reclassification of capital to reflect Morgan's acquisition. Money paid directly to partners.		

An alternative for recording this acquisition by Morgan does exist that relies on a different perspective of the new partner's admission. Legally, the partnership of Scott, Thompson, and York is transferring all assets and liabilities to the partnership of Scott, Thompson, York, and Morgan. Therefore, according to the logic underlying the goodwill method, a transaction is occurring between two separate reporting entities, an event that necessitates the complete revaluation of all assets and liabilities.

Since Morgan is paying $30,000 for a 20 percent interest in the partnership, the implied value of the business as a whole is $150,000 ($30,000/20%). However, the current book value is only $100,000; thus, a $50,000 upward revaluation is indicated. This adjustment is reflected by restating specific partnership asset and liability accounts to market value with any remaining balance being recorded as goodwill. After the implied value of the partnership is established, the reclassification can be recorded.

Goodwill (or specific accounts).	50,000	
Scott, Capital (20% of goodwill)		10,000
Thompson, Capital (50%)		25,000
York, Capital (30%).		15,000
Recognition of goodwill based on Morgan's purchase price.		

Scott, Capital (20% of new capital balance)	12,000	
Thompson, Capital (20%)	11,000	
York, Capital (20%).	7,000	
Morgan, Capital (20% of new total).		30,000
Reclassification of capital to reflect Morgan's acquisition. Money paid directly to partners.		

As can be seen here, the $50,000 revaluation is credited to the original partners based on the profit and loss ratio rather than on their percentages of capital. Recognition of goodwill (or an increase in the book value of specific accounts) indicates that unrecorded gains have accrued to the business during the previous years of operation. Therefore, the only equitable treatment is to allocate this increment among the partners according to their profit and loss percentages.

Admission by a Contribution Made to the Partnership.   Entrance into a partnership is not obtained solely by the purchase of a current partner's interest. An outsider may be admitted to the ownership by contributing cash or other assets directly to the business rather than to the partners. For example, assume that King and Wilson maintain a partnership and presently report capital balances of $80,000 and $20,000, respectively. According to the Articles of Partnership, King is entitled to 60 percent of all profits and losses with the remaining 40 percent credited to Wilson. By agreement of the partners, Simpson is now being allowed to enter the partnership for a payment of $20,000 *with this money going into the business*. Based on negotiations that preceded the acquisition, all parties have agree that Simpson receives an initial 10 percent interest in partnership property.

Bonus Credited to Original Partners.   The bonus (or no revaluation) method maintains the same recorded value for all partnership assets and liabilities despite Simpson's admittance. The capital balance for this new partner is simply set at the appropriate 10 percent level based on the book value of the partnership taken as a whole (after the payment is recorded). Since $20,000 is currently being invested, total reported capital increases to $120,000. Thus, Simpson's 10 percent interest is computed as $12,000. *The $8,000 difference between the amount contributed and this alloted capital balance is viewed as a bonus.* Since Simpson is willing to accept a capital balance that is less than the investment being made, this bonus is attributed to the original partners (based on their profit and loss ratio). Because of the nature of the transaction, no need is perceived for recognizing goodwill or revaluing any of the assets or liabilities.

Cash	20,000	
Simpson, Capital (10% of total capital)		12,000
King, Capital (60% of bonus)		4,800
Wilson, Capital (40% of bonus)		3,200

To record Simpson's entrance into partnership with $8,000 extra payment recorded as bonus to original partners.

Goodwill Credited to Original Partners.   The goodwill method views Simpson's payment as evidence that the partnership as a whole possesses an actual value of $200,000 ($20,000/10 percent). Since, even with the new partner's investment, only $120,000 in net assets is being reported, a valuation adjustment of $80,000 is implied.[13] Over the previous years, unrecorded gains have apparently accrued to the business. This $80,000 figure might reflect the need to revalue specific accounts such as inventory or equipment, although the entire amount, or some portion, may simply be recorded as goodwill.

---

[13] Since the $20,000 is being put into the business in this example, total capital to be used in the goodwill computation has increased to $120,000. If, as in the previous illustration, payment had been made directly to the partners, the original capital of $100,000 would have been retained in determining goodwill.

Goodwill (or specific accounts) 80,000
  King, Capital (60% of goodwill)   48,000
  Wilson, Capital (40%)   32,000
 To recognize goodwill based on Simpson's purchase price.

Cash 20,000
  Simpson, Capital   20,000
 To record Simpson's admission into partnership.

Comparison of Bonus Method and Goodwill Method. Completely different capital balances (as well as asset and liability figures) result from these two approaches. In both cases, though, the new partner is properly credited with 10 percent of total partnership capital.

	Bonus Method	*Goodwill Method*
Assets less liabilities (as reported).	$100,000	$100,000
Simpson's contribution	20,000	20,000
Goodwill	–0–	80,000
Total.	$120,000	$200,000
Simpson's capital	$ 12,000	$ 20,000

Because Simpson contributed an amount greater than 10 percent of the resulting book value of the partnership, this business is perceived as being worth more than the recorded accounts presently indicate. Therefore, the bonus in the first instance and the goodwill in the second were both assumed as accruing to the two original partners. Such a presumption is not unusual in an established business, especially if profitable operations have been developed over a number of years.

Bonus or Goodwill Credited to New Partner. As previously discussed, Simpson also may be contributing some attribute other than tangible assets to this partnership. Therefore, the Articles of Partnership may be written to credit the new partner rather than the original partners, with either a bonus or goodwill. Because of an excellent professional reputation, valuable business contacts, or myriad other possible factors, Simpson might be able to negotiate a beginning capital balance in excess of the $20,000 cash contribution. This same circumstance may also result if the business is desperate for new capital and is willing to offer favorable terms as an enticement to the potential partner.

To illustrate, assume that Simpson receives a 20 percent interest in the preceding partnership (rather than the originally stated 10 percent) in exchange for the $20,000 cash investment. The specific rationale for the higher ownership percentage need not be identified.

The bonus method sets Simpson's initial capital at $24,000 (20 percent of the $120,000 book value). To achieve this balance, a capital bonus of $4,000 must be credited to Simpson by the present partners:

Cash	20,000	
King, Capital (60% of bonus)	2,400	
Wilson, Capital (40% of bonus)	1,600	
Simpson, Capital		24,000

To record Simpson's entrance into partnership with reduced payment reported as a bonus from original partners.

If goodwill rather than a bonus is attributed to the *entering partner,* a mathematical problem arises in determining the implicit value of the business as a whole. In the current illustration, Simpson paid $20,000 for a 20 percent interest. Therefore, the value of the company is calculated as only $100,000 ($20,000/20 percent), a figure that is less than the $120,000 in net assets being reported after the new contribution. Negative goodwill appears to exist. One possibility is that individual partnership assets are overvalued and require reduction. As an alternative, the cash contribution might not be an accurate representation of the new partner's investment. Simpson could be bringing an intangible contribution (goodwill) to the business along with the $20,000. This additional amount can only be determined algebraically:

$$\text{Simpson's capital} = 20 \text{ percent of partnership capital}$$

Therefore

$$\$20,000 + \text{Goodwill} = .20 \,(\$100,000 + \$20,000 + \text{Goodwill})$$
$$\$20,000 + \text{Goodwill} = \$20,000 + \$4,000 + .20 \text{ Goodwill}$$
$$.80 \text{ Goodwill} = \$4,000$$
$$\text{Goodwill} = \$5,000$$

If the partners determine that Simpson is, indeed, making an intangible contribution (a particular skill, for example, or a developed clientele), Simpson should be credited with a $25,000 capital investment: $20,000 cash and $5,000 goodwill. When added to the original $100,000 in net assets reported by the partnership, this contribution raises the total capital for the business to $125,000. As specified by the purchase agreement, Simpson's interest now represents a 20 percent share of the partnership ($25,000/$125,000).

Recognizing $5,000 in goodwill has established the proper relationship between the new partner and the partnership. Therefore, the following journal entry should be recorded to reflect this transaction:

Cash	20,000	
Goodwill	5,000	
Simpson, Capital		25,000

To record Simpson's entrance into partnership with goodwill attributed to this new partner.

Dissolution—Withdrawal by a Partner

Admission of a new partner is not the only method by which a partnership can undergo a change in composition. Over the life of the business, partners occasionally leave the organization. Death or retirement can occur, or a partner may simply elect to withdraw from the partnership. The Articles of Partnership may also allow for the expulsion of a partner under certain conditions.

Once again, any change in membership legally dissolves the partnership, although the business's operations usually continue uninterrupted under the ownership of the remaining partners. Regardless of the reason for dissolution, some method of establishing an equitable settlement of the withdrawing partner's interest in the business is necessary. Often, the partner (or the partner's estate) may simply sell the interest to an outside party, with approval, or to one or more of the remaining partners. As an alternative, cash or other assets can be removed from the business as a means of settling a partner's right of co-ownership. Consequently, life insurance policies are held by many partnerships solely to provide adequate cash to liquidate a partner's interest upon death.

Whether withdrawal is caused by death or some other reason, a final distribution does not necessarily equal the book value of the partner's capital account. A capital balance is only a recording of historical transactions and rarely represents the true value inherent in a business. Instead, payment is frequently based on the value of the partner's interest as ascertained by either negotiation or appraisal. Since the determination of a settlement can be derived in many ways, the Articles of Partnership should contain exact provisions regulating this procedure.

The withdrawal of an individual partner and the resulting distribution of partnership property can, again, be accounted for by either the bonus (no revaluation) method or the goodwill (revaluation) method. However, for partnership distributions, a hybrid option is also available.

As in earlier illustrations, if a bonus is recorded, the amount can be attributed to either of the parties involved: the withdrawing partner or the remaining partners. Conversely, any revaluation of partnership property (as well as the establishment of a goodwill balance) is allocated among all partners in recognition of possible unrecorded gains. The hybrid approach restates assets and liabilities to their fair market value but makes no recording of goodwill. In this last alternative, the legal change in ownership is reflected but the theoretical problems associated with partnership goodwill are avoided.

Accounting for the Withdrawal of a Partner—Illustration. To demonstrate the various approaches that can be taken to account for a partner's withdrawal, assume that the partnership of Duncan, Smith, and Windsor has been in existence for a number of years. At the present time, the partners have the following capital balances as well as the indicated profit and loss percentages:

Partner	Capital Balance	Profit and Loss Ratio
Duncan	$ 70,000	50%
Smith	20,000	30
Windsor	10,000	20
Total capital	$100,000	

Windsor decides to withdraw from the partnership but Duncan and Smith plan to continue operating the business. As per the original partnership agreement, a final settlement distribution for Windsor is computed based on the following specified provisions:

1. An appraisal will be made by an independent expert to determine the estimated fair market value of the business.
2. Any individual who leaves the partnership is to receive cash or other assets equal to that partner's current capital balance after recording an appropriate share of any adjustment indicated by the previous valuation. The allocation of unrecorded gains and losses is based on the normal profit and loss ratio.

Following Windsor's decision to withdraw from the partnership, an immediate appraisal is made of the business and its property. Total fair market value is estimated at $180,000, a figure $80,000 in excess of book value. According to this valuation, land held by the partnership is currently worth $50,000 more than its original cost. In addition, $30,000 in goodwill is attributed to the partnership based on the value of the business as a going concern. *Therefore, Windsor is paid $26,000 on leaving the partnership: the original $10,000 capital balance plus a 20 percent share of this $80,000 increment.* The amount of payment is not in dispute, only the method of recording the withdrawal is in question.

Bonus Method Applied. If the bonus method is used by the partnership to record this transaction, the extra $16,000 paid to Windsor is simply recorded as a decrease in the remaining partners' capital accounts. Historically, Duncan and Smith have been credited with 50 percent and 30 percent of all profits and losses, respectively. This same relative ratio is now used to allocate the reduction between these two remaining partners on a 5/8 and 3/8 basis:

Bonus Method

Windsor, Capital (to remove account balance)	10,000	
Duncan, Capital (5/8 of reduction)	10,000	
Smith, Capital (3/8 of reduction)	6,000	
Cash		26,000

To record Windsor's withdrawal with $16,000 excess distribution taken from remaining partners.

Goodwill Method Applied. This same transaction can also be accounted for by means of the goodwill (or revaluation) approach. The appraisal indicates that land is undervalued on the partnership's records by $50,000 and that goodwill of $30,000 has apparently accrued to the business over the years. The first of the following entries recognizes these valuations. This adjustment properly equates Windsor's capital balance with the $26,000 cash distribution. Windsor's equity balance is merely removed in the second entry at the time of payment.

Goodwill Method

Land	50,000	
Goodwill	30,000	
Duncan, Capital (50%)		40,000
Smith, Capital (30%).		24,000
Windsor, Capital (20%).		16,000

Recognition of land value and goodwill as a preliminary step to Windsor's withdrawal.

Windsor, Capital (to remove account balance)	26,000	
Cash		26,000

Cash distribution made to Windsor in settlement of partnership interest.

The implied value of a partnership as a whole cannot be determined directly from the amount distributed to a withdrawing partner. For example, paying Windsor $26,000 did not indicate that total capital should be $130,000 ($26,000/20%). This computation is only appropriate when (1) a new partner is admitted or (2) the percentage of capital is the same as the profit and loss ratio. Instead, the $26,000 payment here necessitates a $16,000 increase being made to Windsor's reported capital ($26,000 − $10,000). Because Windsor is entitled to 20 percent of profits and losses, a total revaluation of $80,000 is required ($16,000/20%) to arrive at this appropriate equity balance.

Hybrid Method Applied. As indicated previously, a hybrid method can also be adopted to record a partner's withdrawal. Asset and liability revaluations are still recognized but goodwill is ignored. A bonus must be recorded to reconcile the partner's adjusted capital balance with the final distribution.

In the current illustration, for example, no goodwill is recorded. However, the book value of the land is increased by $50,000 in recognition of present worth. This adjustment increases Windsor's capital balance to $20,000, a figure that is still less than the $26,000 distribution. The $6,000 difference is recorded as a bonus taken from the remaining two partners according to their relative profit and loss ratio.

Hybrid Method

Land	50,000	
Duncan, Capital (50%)		25,000
Smith, Capital (30%)		15,000
Windsor, Capital (20%)		10,000

To adjust land account to fair market value as a preliminary step in Windsor's withdrawal.

Windsor, Capital (to remove account balances)   20,000
Duncan, Capital (⅝ of bonus)   3,750
Smith, Capital (⅜ of bonus)   2,250
  Cash   26,000
Final distribution made to Windsor with $6,000 bonus taken from
remaining partners.

Summary

1. A partnership is defined as "an association of two or more persons to carry on as co-owners a business for profit." This form of business organization exists throughout the American economy ranging in size from small, part-time operations to international enterprises. The partnership format is popular for many reasons, including the ease of creation and the avoidance of the double taxation that is inherent in corporate ownership. However, the unlimited liability incurred by each general partner normally restricts the growth potential of most partnerships. Thus, although the quantity of partnerships in the United States is great, their size tends to be small.

2. The unique elements of partnership accounting are primarily found in the capital accounts that are accumulated for each partner. The basis for recording these balances is the Articles of Partnership, a document that should be established as a prerequisite to the formation of any partnership. One of the principal provisions of this agreement is the initial investment to be made by each partner. Noncash contributions such as inventory or land are entered into the partnership's accounting records at fair market value.

3. In forming a partnership, the contributions made by the partners need not be limited to tangible assets. A particular line of expertise possessed by a partner or an established clientele are attributes that can have a significant value to a partnership. Two methods of recording this type of investment are found in practice. Under the bonus method, only identifiable assets are recognized. The capital accounts are then aligned to indicate the balances negotiated by the partners. According to the goodwill approach, all contributions (even those of a nebulous nature such as an expertise) are valued and recorded, often as goodwill.

4. Another accounting issue to be resolved in forming a partnership is the allocation of annual net income. In closing out the revenue and expense accounts at the end of each period, some assignment must be made to the individual capital balances. Although an equal division can be used to allocate the profit or loss, partners frequently devise unique plans in an attempt to be equitable. Such factors as time worked, expertise, and invested capital should be considered in creating an allocation procedure.

5. Over time, changes occur in the makeup of a partnership because of the death or retirement of the individuals or the admission of new partners. Such changes dissolve the existing partnership, although the business frequently continues uninterrupted through a newly formed partnership. If, for example, a new partner is admitted by the acquisition of a present interest, the capital balances can simply be reclassified to reflect the change in ownership. As an alternative, the purchase price may be viewed as evidence of the underlying value of the organization as a whole. Based on this calculation, asset and liability balances are adjusted to market value, and any residual goodwill is recognized.

6. Admission into an existing partnership can also be achieved by a direct capital contribution to the business. Because of negotiations between the parties, the amount invested does not always agree with the beginning capital balance attributed to the new partner. The bonus method resolves this conflict by simply reclassifying the various capital accounts to align the balances with specified totals and percentages. Revaluation of assets and liabilities is never carried out under this approach. Conversely, according to the goodwill method, all accounts are first adjusted to fair market value. The price paid by the new partner is then used to compute an implied value for the partnership, and any excess over market value is recorded as goodwill.

7. The composition of a partnership can also undergo changes because of the death or retirement of a partner. Individuals may also simply decide to withdraw. Such changes legally dissolve the partnership, although business operations frequently continue under the ownership of the remaining partners. In compensating the departing partner, the final asset distribution may differ from the ending capital balance. This disparity can, once again, be accounted for by means of the bonus method, which adjusts the remaining capital accounts to absorb the bonus being paid. The goodwill approach can also be applied wherein all assets and liabilities are restated to fair market value with any goodwill being recognized. Finally, a hybrid method revalues the assets and liabilities but ignores goodwill. Under this last approach, any amount paid to the departing partner in excess of the newly adjusted capital balance is accounted for by means of the bonus method.

Comprehensive Illustration

PROBLEM   (Estimated Time: 30 to 40 Minutes)

Heyman and Mullins begin a partnership on January 1, 1995. Heyman invests $40,000 cash as well as inventory costing $15,000 but with a current appraised value of only $12,000. Mullins contributes a building with a $40,000 book value and a $48,000 fair market value. The partnership also accepts responsibility for a $10,000 note payable owed in connection with this building.

The partners agree to begin operations with equal capital balances. The Articles of Partnership also provide that profits and losses are to be allocated as follows:

1. For managing the business, Heyman is credited with a bonus of 10 percent of partnership income each year after subtracting the bonus. No bonus is accrued if the partnership records a loss.
2. Both partners accrue interest equal to 10 percent of the average monthly capital balance for the year without regard for the income or drawings of that year.
3. Any remaining profit or loss is divided 60 percent to Heyman and 40 percent to Mullins.
4. Each partner is allowed to withdraw $800 per month in cash from the business.

On October 1, 1995, Heyman invests an additional $12,000 cash in the business. For 1995, the partnership reports income of $33,000.

Lewis, an employee, is allowed to join the partnership on January 1, 1996. The new partner invests $66,000 directly into the business for a one-third interest in the partnership property. The revised partnership agreement still allows for both the bonus to Heyman as well as the 10 percent interest, but all remaining profits and losses are now split 40 percent each to Heyman and Lewis with the remaining 20 percent to Mullins. Lewis is also entitled to $800 per month in drawings.

Mullins chooses to withdraw from the partnership a few years later. After negotiations, all parties agree that Mullins should be paid a $90,000 settlement. The capital balances on that date were as follows:

Heyman, capital	$88,000
Mullins, capital	78,000
Lewis, capital	72,000

Required:

a. Assuming that the bonus method is used exclusively by this partnership, make all necessary journal entries. Entries for the monthly drawings of the partners are not required.
b. Assuming that the goodwill method is used exclusively by this partnership, make all necessary journal entries. Again, entries for the monthly drawings are not required.

SOLUTION

a. **Bonus Method**

1995

Jan. 1   Under the bonus method, all contributed property is recorded at fair market value. As specified by the Articles of Partnership, total capital is then divided evenly between the partners.

Cash	40,000	
Inventory	12,000	
Building	48,000	
Note Payable		10,000
Heyman, Capital (50%)		45,000
Mullins, Capital (50%)		45,000

To record initial contributions to partnership along with equal capital balances.

Oct. 1

Cash	12,000	
Heyman, Capital		12,000

To record additional investment by partner.

Dec. 31   Both the bonus assigned to Heyman and the interest accrual must be computed as preliminary steps in the income allocation process. Since the bonus is based on income after subtracting the bonus, the amount can only be calculated algebraically:

Bonus   = .10 ($33,000 − Bonus)
Bonus   = $3,300 − .10 Bonus
1.10 Bonus = $3,300
Bonus   = $3,000

    According to the partnership agreement, the interest allocation is based on a monthly average figure. Mullins's capital balance of $45,000 did not change during the year; therefore $4,500 (10 percent) is the appropriate interest accrual for that partner. However, because of the October 1, 1995, contribution, Heyman's interest must be determined as follows:

Beginning balance:	$45,000 × 9 months =	$405,000
New balance:	$57,000 × 3 months =	171,000
		576,000
		× 1/12
Monthly average—capital balance		48,000
Interest rate		× 10%
Interest credited to Heyman		$ 4,800

Following the bonus and interest computations, the $33,000 income earned by the business in 1995 can be allocated according to the previously specified arrangement:

	Heyman	Mullins	Totals
Bonus (above)	$ 3,000	–0–	$ 3,000
Interest (above).	4,800	$ 4,500	9,300
Remaining income:			
$33,000			
(3,000)			
(9,300)			
$20,700	12,420 (60%)	8,280 (40%)	20,700
Income allocation	$20,220	$12,780	$33,000

Thus, the partnership's closing entries for the year of 1995 would be recorded as follows:

Heyman, Capital	9,600	
Mullins, Capital	9,600	
Heyman, Drawing		9,600
Mullins, Drawing		9,600

To close out drawing accounts for the year of 1995.

Income Summary	33,000	
Heyman, Capital		20,220
Mullins, Capital		12,780

To close out profit for year to capital accounts as computed above.

At the end of this initial year of operation, the partners' capital accounts hold the following balances:

	Heyman	Mullins	Totals
Beginning balance	$45,000	$45,000	$ 90,000
Additional investment	12,000	–0–	12,000
Drawing	(9,600)	(9,600)	(19,200)
Net income	20,220	12,780	33,000
Total capital	$67,620	$48,180	$115,800

1996

Jan. 1   Lewis contributed $66,000 to the business for a one-third interest in the partnership property. Combined with the $115,800 balance computed above, the partnership now has total capital of

$181,800. Since no revaluation is recorded under the bonus approach, a one-third interest in the partnership equals $60,600 ($181,800 × ⅓). Lewis has invested $5,400 in excess of this amount, a balance viewed as a bonus accruing to the original partners:

Cash	66,000	
Lewis, Capital		60,600
Heyman, Capital (60% of bonus)		3,240
Mullins, Capital (40% of bonus)		2,160

To record Lewis's entrance into partnership with bonus
to original partners.

Several years later

The final event in this illustration is Mullins's withdrawal from the partnership. Although a capital balance of only $78,000 is reported for this partner, the final distribution is set at $90,000. The extra $12,000 payment represents a bonus assigned to Mullins, an amount that decreases the capital of the remaining two partners. Since Heyman and Lewis have previously accrued equal 40 percent shares of all profits and losses, the reduction is split evenly between the two.

Mullins, Capital	78,000	
Heyman, Capital (½ of bonus payment).	6,000	
Lewis, Capital (½ of bonus payment).	6,000	
Cash		90,000

Withdrawal of Mullins with bonus taken from remaining
partners.

b. **Goodwill Method**

1995

Jan. 1 The fair market value of Heyman's contribution is $52,000, whereas Mullins is investing only a net $38,000 (the value of the building less the accompanying debt). Because the capital accounts are initially to be equal, Mullins is presumed to be contributing goodwill of $14,000.

Cash	40,000	
Inventory	12,000	
Building	48,000	
Goodwill	14,000	
Note payable.		10,000
Heyman, Capital		52,000
Mullins, Capital		52,000

Creation of partnership with goodwill
attributed to Mullins.

Oct. 1

Cash	12,000	
Heyman, Capital		12,000

To record additional contribution by partner.

Dec. 31   Although Heyman's bonus is still $3,000 as derived in requirement *a.*, the interest accruals must be recalculated because the capital balances are different. Mullins's capital for the entire year was $52,000; thus, interest of $5,200 (10 percent) is appropriate. However, Heyman's balance changed during the year so that a monthly average must be determined as a basis for computing interest:

Beginning balance:	$52,000 × 9 months = $468,000
New balance:	$64,000 × 3 months = 192,000
	660,000
	× ¹⁄₁₂
Monthly average—capital balance	55,000
Interest rate.	× 10%
Interest credited to Heyman	$ 5,500

Consequently, the $33,000 partnership income reported for 1995 is allocated as follows:

	Heyman	*Mullins*	*Totals*
Bonus (above)	$ 3,000	–0–	$ 3,000
Interest (above)	5,500	$ 5,200	10,700
Remaining income:			
$ 33,000			
(3,000)			
(10,700)			
$ 19,300	11,580 (60%)	7,720 (40%)	19,300
Income allocation	$20,080	$12,920	$33,000

The 1995 closing entries made under the goodwill approach would be as follows:

Heyman, Capital	9,600	
Mullins, Capital	9,600	
Heyman, Drawing		9,600
Mullins, Drawing		9,600
To close out drawing accounts for the year.		
Income Summary	33,000	
Heyman, Capital		20,080
Mullins, Capital		12,920
To assign 1995 profits per allocation determined above.		

After the closing process, the capital balances are composed of the following items:

	Heyman	*Mullins*	*Totals*
Beginning balance	$52,000	$52,000	$104,000
Additional investment	12,000	–0–	12,000
Drawing	(9,600)	(9,600)	(19,200)
Net income	20,080	12,920	33,000
Total capital	$74,480	$55,320	$129,800

1996

Jan. 1 Lewis's investment of $66,000 for a one-third interest in the partnership property implies that the business as a whole is worth $198,000 ($66,000 divided by ⅓). After adding Lewis's contribution to the present capital balance of $129,800, the business reports total net assets of only $195,800. Thus, a $2,200 gain in value ($198,000 − $195,800) is indicated and will be recognized at this time. Assuming that all partnership assets and liabilities are appropriately valued, this entire balance is attributed to goodwill.

Goodwill	2,200	
Heyman, Capital (60%)		1,320
Mullins, Capital (40%)		880
To recognize goodwill based on Lewis's acquisition price.		

Cash	66,000	
Lewis, Capital		66,000
Admission of Lewis to the partnership.		

Several years later To conclude this illustration, Mullins's withdrawal must be recorded. This partner is to receive a distribution that is $12,000 greater than the corresponding capital balance of $78,000. Since Mullins is entitled to a 20 percent share of profits and losses, the additional $12,000 payment indicates that the partnership as a whole is undervalued by $60,000 ($12,000/20%). Only in that circumstance would the extra payment to Mullins be justified. Therefore, once again, goodwill is recognized with the final distribution then being made.

Goodwill	60,000	
Heyman, Capital (40%)		24,000
Mullins, Capital (20%)		12,000
Lewis, Capital (40%)		24,000
Recognition of goodwill based on withdrawal amount paid to Mullins.		

Mullins, Capital	90,000	
Cash		90,000
Money distributed to partner.		

Questions

1. What are the advantages of operating a business as a partnership rather than as a corporation? What are the disadvantages?

2. How does partnership accounting differ from corporate accounting?

3. What information is conveyed by the capital accounts found in partnership accounting?

4. What is an Articles of Partnership agreement, and what information should this document contain?

5. What valuation should be recorded for noncash assets transferred to a partnership by one of the partners?

6. If a partner is contributing attributes to a partnership such as an established clientele or a particular expertise, what two methods can be applied to record the contribution? Describe each of these methods.

7. What is the purpose of a drawing account in a partnership's financial records?

8. At what point in the accounting process does the allocation of partnership income become significant?

9. What provisions can be used in a partnership agreement to establish an equitable allocation of income among all partners?

10. If no agreement exists in a partnership as to the allocation of income, what method is appropriate?

11. What is a partnership dissolution? Does dissolution automatically necessitate the cessation of business and the liquidation of partnership assets?

12. By what methods can a new partner gain admittance into a partnership?

13. When a partner sells an ownership interest in a partnership, what rights are conveyed to the new owner?

14. A new partner enters a partnership and goodwill is calculated and credited to the original partners. How is the specific amount of goodwill assigned to these partners?

15. Under what circumstance might goodwill be allocated to a new partner entering a partnership?

16. When a partner withdraws from a partnership, why is the final distribution often based on the appraised value of the business rather than on the book value of the capital account balance?

Library Assignment

1. Read the following as well as any other published materials describing the creation of a partnership:

   "How to Choose the Right Form of Doing Business," *Management Accounting*, January 1985.

   "Helping Clients Choose the Legal Form for a Small Business," *The Practical Accountant*, October 1990.

   "Choice Not Chance," *Pennsylvania CPA Journal*, Winter 1988.

   "Making the Switch: Corporation to Partnership," *Journal of Accountancy*, March 1987.

   Write a report discussing the issues to be considered in deciding whether a partnership or corporate form is preferable.

2. Read the following as well as any other published materials discussing the legal liability faced by partners:

   "Partnership Structure Is Called in Question as Liability Risk Rises," *The Wall Street Journal*, June 10, 1992.

   "What's a Partner to Do?" *The CPA Journal*, April 1991.

   Write a report discussing whether the potential liability of partners should be limited in some manner.

Problems

1. Which of the following is not a reason for the popularity of partnerships as a legal form for businesses?
   a. Partnerships need only be formed by an oral agreement.
   b. Partnerships can more easily generate significant amounts of capital.
   c. Partnerships avoid the double-taxation of income that is found in corporations.
   d. In some cases, losses may be used to offset gains for tax purposes.

2. How does partnership accounting differ from corporate accounting?
   a. The matching principle is not considered appropriate for partnership accounting.
   b. Revenues are recognized at a different time by a partnership than is appropriate for a corporation.
   c. Individual capital accounts replace the contributed capital and retained earnings balances found in corporate accounting.
   d. All assets are reported by partnerships at fair market value as of the latest balance sheet date.

3. Pat, Jean Lou, and Diane are partners with capital balances of $50,000, $30,000, and $20,000, respectively. These three partners share profits and losses equally. For an investment of $50,000 cash (being paid to the business), MaryAnn is to be admitted as a partner with a one-fourth interest in capital and profits. Based on this information, the amount of MaryAnn's investment can best be justified by which of the following?
   a. MaryAnn will receive a bonus from the other partners upon her admission to the partnership.
   b. Assets of the partnership were overvalued immediately prior to MaryAnn's investment.
   c. The book value of the partnership's net assets was less than their fair value immediately prior to MaryAnn's investment.
   d. MaryAnn is apparently bringing goodwill into the partnership, and her capital account will be credited for the appropriate amount.
   (AICPA adapted)

4. A partnership has the following capital balances:

Albert (50% of gains and losses)	$ 80,000
Barrymore (20%)	60,000
Candroth (30%)	140,000

Danville is going to invest $70,000 into the business to acquire a 30 percent ownership interest. Goodwill is to be recorded. What will be Danville's beginning capital balance?
   a. $70,000.
   b. $90,000.
   c. $105,000.
   d. $120,000.

5. A partnership has the following capital balances:

Elgin (40% of gains and losses)	$100,000
Jethro (30%)	200,000
Foy (30%)	300,000

Oscar is going to pay a total of $200,000 to these three partners to acquire a 25 percent ownership interest from each. Goodwill is to be recorded. What will be Jethro's capital balance after the transaction?
   a. $150,000.
   b. $175,000.
   c. $195,000.
   d. $200,000.

6. Bolcar has a capital balance of $110,000 with Neary having a $40,000 balance. These two partners share profits and losses 70 percent (Bolcar) and 30 percent (Neary). Kansas invests $50,000 in cash into the partnership for a 30 percent ownership. The bonus method will be used. What is Neary's capital balance after Kansas's investment?
   a. $35,000.
   b. $37,000.
   c. $40,000.
   d. $43,000.

7. Bishop has a capital balance in a local partnership of $120,000 with Cotton having a $90,000 balance. These two partners share profits and losses by a ratio of 60 percent to Bishop and 40 percent to Cotton. Lovett invests $60,000 in cash into the partnership for a 20 percent ownership. The goodwill method will be used. What is Cotton's capital balance after this new investment?
   a. $99,600.
   b. $102,000.
   c. $112,000.
   d. $126,000.

8. Messalina has a capital balance of $210,000 with Romulus having a $140,000 balance. These two partners share profits and losses 60 percent (Messalina) and 40 percent (Romulus). Claudius invests $100,000 in cash into the partnership for a 20 percent ownership. The bonus method will be used. What are the capital balances for Messalina, Romulus, and Claudius after this investment is recorded?
   a. $216,000, $144,000, $90,000.
   b. $218,000, $142,000, $88,000.
   c. $222,000, $148,000, $80,000.
   d. $240,000, $160,000, $100,000.

9. A partnership begins 1995 with the following capital balances:

Arthur, Capital	$ 60,000
Baxter, Capital	80,000
Cartwright, Capital	100,000

The Articles of Partnership stipulate that profits and losses be assigned in the following manner:

- Each partner is allocated interest equal to 10 percent of the beginning capital balance.
- Baxter is allocated compensation of $20,000 per year.
- Any remaining profits and losses are allocated on a 3:3:4 basis, respectively.
- Each partner is allowed to withdraw up to $5,000 cash per year.

Assuming that the net income for 1995 is $50,000 and that each partner withdraws the maximum amount allowed, what is the balance in Cartwright's Capital account at the end of that year?

a. $105,800.

b. $106,200.

c. $106,900.

d. $107,400.

10. A partnership begins its first year of operations with the following capital balances:

Winston, Capital	$110,000
Durham, Capital	80,000
Salem, Capital	110,000

According to the Articles of Partnership, all profits will be assigned as follows:

- Winston will be allocated an annual salary of $20,000 with $10,000 assigned to Salem.
- The partners will be allocated interest equal to 10 percent of the capital balance as of the first day of the year.
- The remainder will be assigned on a 5:2:3 basis, respectively.
- Each partner is allowed to withdraw up to $10,000 per year.

Assume that the net loss for the first year of operations is $20,000 with net income of $40,000 in the subsequent year. Assume further that each partner withdraws the maximum amount from the business each period. What is the balance in Winston's Capital account at the end of the second year?

a. $102,600.

b. $104,400.

c. $108,600.

d. $109,200.

11. A partnership has the following capital balances:

Allen, Capital	$60,000
Burns, Capital	30,000
Costello, Capital	90,000

Profits and losses are split as follows: Allen (20%), Burns (30%), and Costello (50%). Costello wants to leave the partnership and is paid $100,000 from the business based on provisions in the Articles of Partnership. If the partnership uses the bonus method, what is the balance of Burns's Capital account after Costello withdraws?

a. $24,000.

b. $27,000.

c. $33,000.

d. $36,000.

12. As of December 31, 1995, the Cisco partnership has the following capital balances:

Montana, Capital.	$130,000
Rice, Capital.	110,000
Craig, Capital	80,000
Taylor, Capital.	70,000

Profits and losses are split on a $3:3:2:2$ basis, respectively. Craig decides to leave the partnership and is paid $90,000 from the business based on their original contractual agreement. If the goodwill method is to be applied, what is the balance of Montana's Capital account after Craig withdraws?

a. $133,000.

b. $137,500.

c. $140,000.

d. $145,000.

Problems 13 and 14 are independent problems based on the following capital account balances:

William (40% of gains and losses).	$220,000
Jennings (40%)	160,000
Bryan (20%)	110,000

13. Darrow invests $270,000 in cash for a 30 percent ownership interest. The money goes to the original partners. Goodwill is to be recorded. How much goodwill should be recognized, and what is Darrow's beginning capital balance?

a. $410,000 and $270,000.

b. $140,000 and $270,000.

c. $140,000 and $189,000.

d. $410,000 and $189,000.

14. Darrow invests $250,000 in cash for a 30 percent ownership interest. The money goes to the business. No goodwill is to be recorded. After the transaction, what is Jennings's capital balance?

a. $160,000.

b. $168,000.

c. $170,200.

d. $171,200.

15. Lear is to become a partner in the HM partnership by paying $80,000 in cash to the business. At present, Hamlet has a capital balance of $70,000 while MacBeth reports a total of only $40,000. Hamlet and MacBeth share profits on a 7:3 basis. Lear is acquiring 40 percent of the new partnership.

    a. If the goodwill method is applied, what will the three capital balances be following the payment by Lear?

    b. If the bonus method is applied, what will the three capital balances be following the payment by Lear?

16. The AKS partnership has the following capital balances at the beginning of the current year:

Arond (40% of profits and losses)	$80,000
Kant (40%)	70,000
Selvin (20%)	60,000

Required:

a. If Tronsty invests $60,000 in cash into the business for a 20 percent interest, what journal entry is recorded? Assume the bonus method is in use.

b. If Tronsty invests $50,000 in cash into the business for a 20 percent interest, what journal entry is recorded? Assume the bonus method is in use.

c. If Tronsty invests $55,000 in cash into the business for a 20 percent interest, what journal entry is recorded? Assume the goodwill method is in use.

17. A partnership has the following account balances: Cash $50,000; Other Assets $600,000; Liabilities $240,000; Nixon, Capital (50% of profits and losses) $200,000; Hoover, Capital (20%) $120,000; Polk, Capital (30%) $90,000. Each of the following questions should be viewed as an independent situation:

    a. Grant invests $80,000 into the partnership for an 18 percent capital interest. Goodwill is to be recognized. What are the capital accounts thereafter?

    b. Grant invests $100,000 into the partnership to get a 20 percent capital balance. Goodwill is not to be recorded. What are the capital accounts thereafter?

18. The C-P partnership has the following capital account balances on January 1, 1995:

Com, Capital	$150,000
Pack, Capital	110,000

Com is allocated 60 percent of all profits and losses with the remaining 40 percent assigned to Pack after interest of 10 percent is given to each partner based on beginning capital balances.

On January 1, 1995, Hal invests $76,000 cash for a 20 percent interest in the partnership. This transaction is recorded by the goodwill method. After this transaction, 10 percent interest is still to go to each partner. Profits and losses will then be split as follows: Com (50%), Pack (30%), and Hal (20%). In 1995, the partnership reports a net income of $36,000.

Required:

a. Prepare the journal entry to record Hal's entrance into the partnership on January 1, 1995.

b. Determine the allocation of income at the end of 1995.

19. The partnership agreement of Jones, King, and Lane provides for the annual allocation of the business's profit or loss in the following sequence:

- Jones, the managing partner, receives a bonus equal to 20 percent of the business's profit.
- Each partner receives 15 percent interest on average capital investment.
- Any residual profit or loss is divided equally.

The average capital investments for 1995 were:

Jones	$100,000
King	200,000
Lane	300,000

How much of the $90,000 partnership profit for 1995 should be assigned to each partner?

(AICPA adapted)

20. Purkerson, Smith, and Traynor have operated a bookstore for a number of years as a partnership. At the beginning of 1995, capital balances were as follows:

Purkerson	$60,000
Smith	40,000
Traynor	20,000

Because of a cash shortage, Purkerson invests an additional $8,000 in the business on April 1, 1995.

Each partner is allowed to withdraw $1,000 cash each month.

The partners have used the same method of allocating profits and losses since the business's inception:

- Each partner is given a compensation allowance for work done in the business: Purkerson, $18,000; Smith, $25,000; and Traynor, $8,000.
- Each partner is credited with interest equal to 10 percent of the average monthly capital balance for the year without regard for normal drawings.
- Any remaining profit or loss is allocated 4:2:4 to Purkerson, Smith, and Traynor, respectively.

The net income for 1995 is $23,600. Each partner withdraws the allotted amount each month. What are the ending capital balances for 1995?

21. On January 1, 1995, the dental partnership of Left, Center, and Right was formed when the partners contributed $20,000, $60,000, and $50,000, respectively. Over the next three years, the business reported net income and (loss) as follows:

1995	($30,000)
1996	$20,000
1997	$40,000

During this period, each partner withdrew cash of $10,000 per year. Right also invested an additional $12,000 in cash on February 9, 1996.

At the time that the partnership was created, the three partners agreed to allocate all profits and losses according to a specified plan written as follows:

- Each partner is entitled to interest computed at the rate of 12 percent per year based on the individual capital balances at the beginning of that year.
- Because of prior work experience, Left is entitled to an annual salary allowance of $12,000 while Center is credited with $8,000 per year.
- Any remaining profit will be split as follows: Left, 20 percent; Center, 40 percent; and Right, 40 percent. If a loss remains, the balance will be allocated: Left, 30 percent; Center, 50 percent; and Right, 20 percent.

Required:

Determine the ending capital balance for each partner as of the end of each of these three years.

22. The HELP partnership has the following capital balances as of December 31, 1995:

Lennon	$230,000
McCartney	190,000
Harrison	160,000
Starr	140,000
Total capital	$720,000

Answer each of the following independent questions.

a. Assume the partners share profits and losses $3:3:2:2$, respectively. Harrison retires and is paid $190,000 based on the terms of the original partnership agreement. If the goodwill method is in use, what is the capital balance of the remaining three partners?

b. Assume the partners share profits and losses $4:3:2:1$, respectively. Lennon retires and is paid $280,000 based on the terms of the original partnership agreement. If the bonus method is in use, what is the capital balance of the remaining three partners?

23. In the early part of 1996, the partners of Page, Childers, and Smith went to a local accountant seeking assistance. They had begun a new business in 1995 but had never previously used the services of an accountant.

Page and Childers began the partnership by contributing $80,000 and $30,000 in cash, respectively. Page was to work occasionally at the business whereas Childers would be employed full time. They decided that year-end profits and losses should be assigned as follows:

- Each partner was to be allocated 10 percent interest computed on the beginning capital balances for the period.
- A compensation allowance of $5,000 was to go to Page with a $20,000 amount assigned to Childers.
- Any remaining income would be split on a $4:6$ basis to Page and Childers, respectively.

In 1995, revenues totaled $90,000 with expenses reported as $64,000 (not including the compensation allowance assigned to the partners). Page withdrew cash of $8,000 during the year while Childers took out $11,000. In addition, $5,000 for repairs made to Page's home was paid by the business and charged to repair expense.

On January 1, 1996, a 20 percent interest in the partnership was sold to Smith for $43,000 cash. This money was contributed to the business with the bonus method used for accounting purposes.

Answer the following questions:

a. Why was the original profit and loss allocation, as just outlined, designed by the partners?

b. Why did the drawings for 1995 not agree with the compensation allowances provided for in the partnership agreement?

c. What journal entries should have been recorded by the partnership on December 31, 1995?

d. What journal entry should have been recorded by the partnership on January 1, 1996?

24. Following is the current balance sheet for a local partnership of doctors:

Cash and current		Liabilities	$ 40,000
assets	$ 30,000	A, capital	20,000
Land	180,000	B, capital	40,000
Building and		C, capital	90,000
equipment	100,000	D, capital	120,000
Totals	$310,000		$310,000

The following questions represent independent situations:

a. E is going to invest enough money into this partnership to receive a 25 percent interest. No goodwill or bonus is to be recorded. How much should E invest?

b. E contributes $36,000 in cash to the business to receive a 10 percent interest in the partnership. Goodwill is to be recorded. Profits and losses have previously been split according to the following percentages: A, 30%; B, 10%; C, 40%; and D, 20%. After E makes this investment, what are the individual capital balances?

c. E contributes $42,000 in cash to the business to receive a 20 percent interest in the partnership. Goodwill is to be recorded. The four original partners share all profits and losses equally. After E makes this investment, what are the individual capital balances?

d. E contributes $55,000 in cash to the business to receive a 20 percent interest in the partnership. No goodwill or other asset revaluation is to be recorded. Profits and losses have previously been split according to the following percentages: A, 10%; B, 30%; C, 20%; and D, 40%. After E makes this investment, what are the individual capital balances?

e. C retires from the partnership and, as per the original partnership agreement, is to receive cash equal to 125 percent of her final capital balance. No goodwill or other asset revaluation is to be recognized. All partners share profits and losses equally. After the withdrawal, what are the individual capital balances of the remaining partners?

25. Partnership agreements usually specify a profit and loss ratio. They may also provide such additional features as salaries, bonuses, and interest allowances on invested capital.

Required:

a. What is the objective of profit and loss sharing arrangements? Why may other features be needed in addition to a profit and loss ratio?

b. Discuss the arguments for recording salary and bonus allowances to partners as expenses of the business.

c. Discuss the arguments against treating partnership salary and bonus allowances as expenses.

d. In addition to other profit and loss sharing features, a partnership agreement might state that "interest is to be allowed on invested capital." List the additional provisions that should be included in the partnership agreement so that "interest to be allowed on invested capital" can be computed.
(AICPA adapted)

26. Boswell and Johnson form a partnership on May 1, 1995. Boswell contributes cash of $50,000; Johnson conveys title to the following properties to the partnership:

	Book Value	*Fair Market Value*
Land	$15,000	$28,000
Building and equipment	35,000	36,000

The partners agree to start their partnership with equal capital balances. No goodwill is to be recognized.

According to the Articles of Partnership written by the partners, profits and losses are allocated based on the following formula:

- Boswell receives a compensation allowance of $1,000 per month.
- All remaining profits and losses are split 60:40 to Johnson and Boswell, respectively.
- Annual cash drawings of $5,000 can be made by each partner beginning in 1996.

Net income of $11,000 is earned by the business during 1995.

Walpole is invited to join the partnership on January 1, 1996. Because of Walpole's business reputation and financial expertise, she is given a 40 percent interest for $54,000 cash. The bonus approach is used to record this investment, made directly to the business. The Articles of Partnership are amended to give Walpole a $2,000 compensation allowance per month and an annual cash drawing of $10,000. Remaining profits are now allocated:

Johnson	48%
Boswell	12%
Walpole	40%

All drawings are taken by the partners during 1996. At the end of that year, the partnership reports an earned net income of $28,000.

On January 1, 1997, Pope (previously a partnership employee) is admitted into the partnership. Each partner transfers a 10 percent to Pope. Pope makes the following payments directly to the partners:

To Johnson $5,672
To Boswell   7,880
To Pope   8,688

Once again, the Articles of Partnership must be amended to allow for the entrance of the new partner. This change entitles Pope to a compensation allowance of $800 per month and an annual drawing of $4,000. Profits and losses are now assigned:

Johnson 40.5%
Boswell 13.5%
Walpole 36.0%
Pope 10.0%

For the year of 1997, the partnership earned a profit of $46,000, and each partner withdrew the allowed amount of cash.

Required:

Determine the capital balances for the individual partners as of the end of each year: 1995 through 1997.

27. Gray, Stone, and Lawson open an accounting practice on January 1, 1995, in San Diego, California. The business is to be operated as a partnership with Gray and Stone serving as the senior partners because of their years of experience. To establish the business, Gray, Stone, and Lawson contribute cash and other properties valued at $210,000, $180,000, and $90,000, respectively. A partnership agreement is drawn up that carries the following stipulations:

    a. Personal drawings are allowed annually up to an amount equal to 10 percent of the beginning capital balance for the year.

    b. Profits and losses are allocated according to the following plan:

    (1) A salary allowance is credited to each partner in an amount equal to $8 per billable hour worked by that individual during the year.

    (2) Interest is credited to the partners' capital accounts at the rate of 12 percent of the average monthly balance for the year (computed without regard for current income or drawings).

    (3) An annual bonus is to be credited to Gray and Stone. Each bonus is to be 10 percent of net income after subtracting the bonus, the salary allowance, and the interest. The provision is also included in the agreement that the bonus cannot be a negative amount.

    (4) Any remaining partnership profit or loss is to be divided evenly among all partners.

Because of monetary problems encountered in getting the business started, Gray invests an additional $9,100 on May 1, 1995. On January 1, 1996, the partners allow Monet to buy into the partnership. Monet contributes cash directly to the business in an amount equal to a 25 percent interest in the book value of the partnership property subsequent to this contribution. The partnership agreement as to splitting profits and losses is not altered at the time of Monet's entrance into the firm; the general provisions continue to be applicable.

The billable hours for the partners during the first three years of operation are as follows:

	1995	1996	1997
Gray	1,710	1,800	1,880
Stone	1,440	1,500	1,620
Lawson	1,300	1,380	1,310
Monet	–0–	1,190	1,580

The partnership reports net income for 1995 through 1997 as follows:

1995	$ 65,000
1996	(20,400)
1997	152,800

Each partner withdraws the maximum allowable amount each year.

Required:

a. Determine the allocation of income for each of these three years (to the nearest dollar).
b. Prepare in appropriate form a statement of partners' capital for the year ending December 31, 1995.
28. A partnership of attorneys in the St. Louis, Missouri, area has the following balance sheet accounts as of January 1, 1996:

Assets	$320,000	Liabilities	$120,000
		Athos, capital	80,000
		Porthos, capital	70,000
		Aramis, capital	50,000

According to the Articles of Partnership, Athos is to receive an allocation of 50 percent of all partnership profits and losses while Porthos gets 30 percent and Aramis 20 percent. The book value of each asset and liability should be considered an accurate representation of fair market value.

Required:

For each of the following *independent* situations, prepare the journal entry or entries to be recorded by the partnership. (Round to nearest dollar.)

a. Porthos, with permission of the other partners, decides to sell half of his partnership interest to D'Artagnan for $50,000 in cash. No asset revaluation or goodwill is to be recorded by the partnership.

b. All three of the present partners agree to sell 10 percent of each partnership interest to D'Artagnan for a total cash payment of $25,000. Each partner receives a negotiated portion of this amount. Goodwill is being recorded as a result of the transaction.

c. D'Artagnan is allowed to become a partner with a 10 percent ownership interest by contributing $30,000 in cash directly into the business. The bonus method is used to record this admission.

d. Use the same facts as in requirement c. except that the entrance into the partnership is recorded by the goodwill method.

e. D'Artagnan is allowed to become a partner with a 10 percent ownership interest by contributing $12,222 in cash directly to the business. The goodwill method is used to record this transaction.

f. Aramis decides to retire and leave the partnership. An independent appraisal of the business and its assets indicates a current fair market value of $280,000. Goodwill is to be recorded. Aramis will then be given the exact amount of cash that will close out his capital account.

29. Steve Reese is a well-known interior designer in Fort Worth, Texas. He wants to start his own business and convinces Rob O'Donnell, a local merchant, to contribute the capital to form a partnership. On January 1, 1995, O'Donnell invests a building worth $52,000 and equipment valued at $16,000 as well as $12,000 in cash. Although Reese makes no tangible contribution to the partnership, he will operate the business and be an equal partner in the beginning capital balances.

To entice O'Donnell to join this partnership, Reese draws up the following agreement:

- O'Donnell will be credited annually with interest equal to 20 percent of the beginning capital balance for the year.

- O'Donnell will also have added to his capital account 15 percent of partnership income each year (without regard for the preceding interest figure) or $4,000, whichever is greater. All remaining income is credited to Reese.

- Neither partner is allowed to withdraw funds from the partnership during 1995. Thereafter, they can each draw out $5,000 annually or 20 percent of the beginning capital balance for the year, whichever is greater.

A net loss of $10,000 is reported by the partnership during the first year of its operation. On January 1, 1996, Terri Dunn becomes a third partner in this business by contributing $15,000 cash to the partnership. Dunn receives a 20 percent share of the business's capital. The profit and loss agreement is altered as follows:

- O'Donnell is still entitled to (1) interest on his beginning capital balance as well as (2) the share of partnership income just specified.
- Any remaining profit or loss will be split on a 6:4 basis between Reese and Dunn, respectively.

Partnership income for 1996 is reported as $44,000. Each partner withdraws the full amount that is allowed.

On January 1, 1997, Dunn falls ill and sells her interest in the partnership (with the consent of the other two partners) to Judy Postner. Postner pays $46,000 directly to Dunn. Net income for 1997 is $61,000 with the partners again taking their full drawing allowance.

On January 1, 1998, Postner elects to withdraw from the business for personal reasons. The Articles of Partnership contain a provision stating that any partner may leave the partnership at any time and is entitled to receive cash in an amount equal to the recorded capital balance at that time plus 10 percent.

Required:

a. Prepare journal entries to record the preceding transactions on the assumption that the bonus (or no revaluation) method is used. Drawings need not be recorded, although the balances should be included in the closing entries.

b. Prepare journal entries to record the previous transactions on the assumption that the goodwill (or revaluation) method is used. Drawings need not be recorded, although the balances should be included in the closing entries.

(Round all amounts off to the nearest dollar.)

PARTNERSHIPS: TERMINATION AND LIQUIDATION

Questions to Consider

- Under what conditions would a partnership be liquidated?
- What information should an accountant report to reflect the liquidation of a partnership?
- In a partnership liquidation, what will happen if one or more partners reports a deficit capital balance?
- How are any remaining assets distributed if a partnership or one of its partners becomes insolvent?
- What are safe capital balances and how are they determined?
- How does the accountant determine which partners receive cash during a partnership liquidation?

> I'm spending a great deal of time helping physician clients patch up partnership disputes and pull together. That is until I run up against a group where personalities, philosophies, or work styles are truly irreconcilable. In these cases, the best solution is a split. . . . Once the doctors know they want to split, they can meet to discuss their problems. While these sessions are often stormy, in the end the doctors usually find themselves agreeing for once. Their consensus? They'll each benefit more from going their separate ways than enduring a situation that's not working. Still, there's no denying that severing any partnership is emotionally wrenching.[1]

These sentiments, expressed by a financial consultant in the medical management field, indicate the potential frailty of a partnership. Although a business organized in this manner can exist indefinitely through periodic changes within the owner-

---

[1] Leif C. Beck, "When a Group Is Better Off Splitting Up," *Medical Economics*, March 5, 1984, p. 183.

ship, the actual cessation of operations is not an uncommon occurrence. Termination of business activities followed by the liquidation of partnership property can take place for a variety of reasons, both legal and personal. As indicated by the preceding quotation, the partners may simply be incompatible and choose to cease operations. The same outcome might result if profit figures fail to reach projected levels. "In the best of times, partnerships are fragile. But in the current recession, the breakup rate has worsened as cost-cutting and other pressures heighten tensions between partners."[2]

The death of a partner is another event that dissolves a partnership and frequently leads to the termination of business operations. Rather than continuing under a new partnership arrangement, the remaining owners may discover that liquidation is necessary to settle the claims of the deceased partner's estate. A similar action may be required if one or more of the partners elects to change careers or retire. Under that circumstance, liquidation is often the most convenient method for winding up the financial affairs of the business.

As a final possibility, a partnership can be legally forced into selling its non-cash assets by the bankruptcy of the business or even that of an individual partner. Laventhol & Horwath, the seventh largest public accounting firm in the United States, filed for bankruptcy protection in 1990 after the firm came under financial pressure from numerous lawsuits. "Laventhol said that at least 100 lawsuits are pending in state and federal courts. Bankruptcy court protection 'is absolutely necessary in order to protect the debtor and its creditors from the devasting results a destructive race for assets will cause' the firm said."[3]

Termination and Liquidation—Protecting the Interests of All Parties

As discussed in Chapter 12, accounting for the termination and liquidation of a business can prove to be a delicate task. Losses, especially in bankruptcy cases, are commonly incurred. Thus, both creditors and owners demand continuous accounting information that enables them to monitor and assess their financial risks. In generating this data for a partnership, the accountant records:

- The conversion of partnership assets into cash.
- The allocation of the resulting gains and losses.
- The payment of liabilities and expenses.
- The distribution of any remaining assets to the partners based on their final capital balances.

---

[2] Sue Shellenbarger, "Cutting Losses When Partners Face a Breakup," *The Wall Street Journal,* May 21, 1991, p. B1.

[3] Peter Pae, "Laventhol Bankruptcy Filing Indicates Liabilities May Be as Much as $2 Billion," *The Wall Street Journal,* November 23, 1990, p. A4.

Beyond the goal of merely reporting these transactions, the accountant must work to ensure the equitable treatment of all parties involved in the liquidation. The accounting records, for example, serve as the basis for allocating available assets to creditors as well as to the individual partners. If assets are limited, the accountant may also have to make recommendations as to the appropriate method for distributing any remaining funds. Protecting the interests of the partnership creditors is an especially significant duty since the Uniform Partnership Act specifies that they have first priority to the assets held by the business at the time of dissolution. The accountant's desire for an equitable settlement is enhanced, no doubt, in that any party to a liquidation who is not treated fairly can seek legal recovery from the responsible party.

Not only the creditors but also the partners themselves have a great interest in the financial data produced during the period of liquidation. They must be concerned, for example, about the possibility of incurring substantial monetary losses. The potential for loss is especially significant because of the unlimited liability to which the partners are exposed.

As long as a partnership can meet all obligations, a partner's risk is normally no greater than that of a corporate stockholder. However, should the partnership become insolvent, each partner faces the possibility of having to satisfy *all* remaining obligations personally. Although any partner suffering more than a proportionate share of these losses can seek legal retribution from the remaining owners, this process is not always an effective remedy. The other partners may themselves be insolvent, or anticipated legal costs might discourage the damaged party from seeking recovery. Therefore, each partner usually has a keen interest in monitoring the progress of a liquidation as it transpires.

> When a company files for bankruptcy court protection, its creditors are permitted only to make claims against the corporation, rather than against its shareholders. But when partnerships such as Laventhol file, creditors can sue individual partners in an effort to recover their money. Bankruptcy law experts say that Laventhol's creditors, which include banks, landlords, suppliers, and plaintiffs in litigation, are expected to try to recover money from partners, as well as from the partnership, if Laventhol is unable to satisfy their claims with its remaining assets."[4]

Termination and Liquidation Procedures Illustrated

The procedures involved in terminating and liquidating a partnership are basically mechanical. Partnership assets are converted into cash that is used to pay business obligations as well as liquidation expenses. *Any remaining assets are then distributed to the individual partners based on their final capital balances.* As no further ledger accounts exist, the partnership's books are permanently closed. If each partner has a large enough capital balance to absorb all liquidation losses,

---

[4] Laurie P. Cohen, "Laventhol Partners Face Long Process that Could End in Personal Bankruptcy," *The Wall Street Journal,* November 20, 1990, p. B5.

the accountant should experience little difficulty in recording this series of transactions.

To illustrate this process, assume that Morgan and Houseman have been operating an antique business as a partnership for a number of years. On May 1, 1995, the partners decide to terminate business activities, liquidate all noncash assets, and dissolve their partnership. Although a specific explanation for this action is not given, any number of reasons might exist. The partners, for example, could have come to a disagreement so that they no longer believe they can work together. As an alternative possibility, business profits may have been inadequate to warrant the continuing investment of their time and capital.

Following is a balance sheet for the partnership of Morgan and Houseman as of the termination date. The revenue, expense, and drawing accounts have been closed out as a preliminary step in terminating the business. A separate reporting will subsequently be made of the gains and losses that occur during the final winding-down process.

MORGAN AND HOUSEMAN
Balance Sheet
May 1, 1995

Assets		Liabilities and Capital	
Cash.	$ 45,000	Liabilities	$ 32,000
Accounts receivable	12,000	Morgan, capital	50,000
Inventory	22,000	Houseman, capital	38,000
Land, building, and			
equipment (net)	41,000		
		Total liabilities and	
Total assets.	$120,000	capital	$120,000

The assumption is made here that the liquidation of Morgan and Houseman proceeds in an orderly fashion through the following events:

1995

June 1 The inventory is sold at auction for $15,000. Morgan and Houseman allocate all profits and losses on a 6:4 basis, respectively.

July 15 Of the total accounts receivable, $9,000 is collected with the remainder being written off as bad debts.

Aug. 20 The fixed assets are sold for a total of $29,000.

Aug. 25 All partnership liabilities are paid.

Sept. 10 A total of $3,000 in liquidation expenses is paid to cover costs such as accounting and legal fees as well as the commissions incurred in disposing of partnership property.

Oct. 15 All remaining cash is distributed to the owners based on their final capital account balances.

As can be seen, the partnership of Morgan and Houseman incurs a number of losses in liquidating this property. Such losses are almost anticipated because the need for immediate sale is usually held as a high priority in a liquidation. Furthermore, a portion of the assets used by any business, such as equipment and buildings, may have a utility that is strictly limited to a particular type of operation. If the property is not easily adaptable, disposal at any reasonable price often proves to be a problem.

To record the liquidation of Morgan and Houseman, the following journal entries would be made. Rather than report specific income and expense balances, gains and losses are traditionally recorded directly to the partners' capital accounts. Since operations have ceased, determination of a separate net income figure for this period would provide little informational value. *Instead, a primary concern of the parties involved in any liquidation is the continuing changes in each partner's capital balance.*

6/1/95	Cash	15,000	
	Morgan, Capital (60% of loss)	4,200	
	Houseman, Capital (40% of loss)	2,800	
	Inventory		22,000
	To record sale of partnership inventory at a $7,000 loss.		
7/15/95	Cash	9,000	
	Morgan, Capital	1,800	
	Houseman, Capital	1,200	
	Accounts Receivable		12,000
	To record collection of accounts receivable with write-off of remaining $3,000 in accounts as bad debts.		
8/20/95	Cash	29,000	
	Morgan, Capital	7,200	
	Houseman, Capital	4,800	
	Land, Building, and Equipment (net)		41,000
	To record sale of fixed assets and allocation of $12,000 loss.		
8/25/95	Liabilities	32,000	
	Cash		32,000
	Payment made to settle the liabilities of the partnership.		
9/10/95	Morgan, Capital	1,800	
	Houseman, Capital	1,200	
	Cash		3,000
	To pay liquidation expenses with the amounts recorded as direct reductions to the partners' capital accounts.		

After liquidating the partnership assets and paying off all obligations, the cash that remains can be divided between Morgan and Houseman personally. The following schedule is utilized to determine the partners' ending capital account balances and, thus, the appropriate distribution for this final payment.

Cash and Capital Account Balances*

	Cash	Morgan, Capital	Houseman, Capital
Beginning balances.	$ 45,000	$50,000	$38,000
Sold inventory.	15,000	(4,200)	(2,800)
Collected accounts receivable	9,000	(1,800)	(1,200)
Sold fixed assets	29,000	(7,200)	(4,800)
Paid liabilities	(32,000)	–0–	–0–
Paid liquidation expenses	(3,000)	(1,800)	(1,200)
Final totals	$ 63,000	$35,000	$28,000

* Because of the presence of other assets as well as liabilities, the Cash and Capital accounts will not be in agreement until the end of the liquidation process.

After the ending capital balances have been calculated, the remaining cash can be distributed to the partners to close out the financial records of the partnership:

10/15/95	Morgan, Capital	35,000	
	Houseman, Capital	28,000	
	Cash		63,000
	To distribute cash to partners in accordance with final capital balances.		

Schedule of Liquidation

Liquidation may take a considerable length of time to complete. Because the various parties involved need continually updated financial information, the accountant should produce frequent reports summarizing the transactions as they occur. Consequently, a statement (often referred to as the schedule of liquidation) is prepared at periodic intervals to disclose:

- Transactions to date.
- Property still being held by the partnership.
- Liabilities remaining to be paid.
- Current cash and capital balances.

Although the preceding Morgan and Houseman example has been condensed into a few events occurring during a brief period of time, partnership liquidations can require numerous transactions that transpire over months and, perhaps, even years. By receiving frequent schedules of liquidation, both the creditors and the partners are able to stay apprised of the results of this lengthy process.

Exhibit 14–1 presents the final schedule of liquidation for the partnership of Morgan and Houseman. Previous statements would have been distributed by the

EXHIBIT 14–1

MORGAN AND HOUSEMAN
Schedule of Partnership Liquidation
Final Balances

	Cash	Noncash Assets	Liabil- ities	Morgan, Capital (60%)	Houseman, Capital (40%)
Beginning balances, 5/1/95	$ 45,000	$ 75,000	$ 32,000	$ 50,000	$ 38,000
Sold inventory, 6/1/95	15,000	(22,000)		(4,200)	(2,800)
Updated balances.	60,000	53,000	32,000	45,800	35,200
Collected receivables, 7/15/95	9,000	(12,000)		(1,800)	(1,200)
Updated balances.	69,000	41,000	32,000	44,000	34,000
Sold fixed assets, 8/20/95	29,000	(41,000)		(7,200)	(4,800)
Updated balances.	98,000	–0–	32,000	36,800	29,200
Paid liabilities, 8/25/95.	(32,000)		(32,000)		
Updated balances.	66,000	–0–	–0–	36,800	29,200
Paid liquidation expenses, 9/10/95.	(3,000)			(1,800)	(1,200)
Updated balances.	63,000	–0–	–0–	35,000	28,000
Distributed remaining cash, 10/15/95	(63,000)			(35,000)	(28,000)
Closing balances	–0–	–0–	–0–	–0–	–0–

accountant at each important juncture of this liquidation to meet the informational needs of the parties involved. The example produced here demonstrates the stair-step approach incorporated in preparing a schedule of liquidation. The effects of each transaction (or group of transactions) are outlined in a horizontal fashion so that current account balances as well as all prior transactions are immediately updated and evident. This structuring also facilitates the preparation of future statements: a new layer summarizing recent events can simply be added to the bottom each time that a new schedule is to be produced.

Deficit Capital Balance—Contribution Made by Partner

In Exhibit 14–1, the liquidation process ended with all partners continuing to report positive capital balances. Thus, Morgan and Houseman were both able to share in the $63,000 cash that remained. Unfortunately, such an outcome is not always assured. At the end of a liquidation, one or more partners may be reporting a negative capital account. Or, the partnership may not even be able to generate enough cash to satisfy all of the claims of its creditors. Such deficits are most likely to occur when the partnership is already insolvent at the start of the liquidation or when the disposal of noncash assets results in material losses. Under these circumstances, the accounting procedures to be applied depend on legal regulations as well as the individual actions of the partners.

As an example, assume that the partnership of Holland, Dozier, and Ross was dissolved at the beginning of the current year. Business activities were terminated and all noncash assets were subsequently converted into cash. During the liquidation process, the partnership incurred a number of large losses that have been allocated to the partners' capital accounts on a 4:4:2 basis, respectively. A portion of the resulting cash is then used to pay all partnership liabilities and liquidation expenses.

Following these transactions, only the following four account balances remain open within the partnership's records:

Cash $20,000	Holland, Capital	$ (6,000)
	Dozier, Capital	15,000
	Ross, Capital	11,000
	Total	$20,000

Holland is now reporting a negative capital balance of $6,000; the assigned share of partnership losses has exceeded this partner's net contribution. In such cases, the Uniform Partnership Act (Section 18[a]) stipulates that the partner "must contribute toward the losses, whether of capital or otherwise, sustained by the partnership according to his share in the profits." Therefore, Holland is legally required to convey an additional $6,000 to the partnership at this time to eliminate the deficit balance. This contribution raises the cash balance to $26,000 so that a complete distribution can be made to Dozier ($15,000) and Ross ($11,000) in line with their capital accounts. The journal entry for this final payment closes out the partnership records.

Cash	6,000	
Holland, Capital		6,000
To record contribution made by Holland to extinguish negative capital balance.		

Dozier, Capital	15,000	
Ross, Capital	11,000	
Cash		26,000
To distribute remaining cash to partners in accordance with their ending capital balances.		

Deficit Capital Balance—Loss to Remaining Partners

An alternative scenario can easily be conceived for the previous partnership liquidation. Although Holland's capital account shows a $6,000 deficit balance, this partner may resist any attempt to force an additional investment, especially since the business is in the process of being terminated. The possibility of such recalcitrance is enhanced if the individual is having personal financial difficulties. Thus, the remaining partners may eventually have to resort to formal litigation to gain

Holland's contribution. Until that legal action is concluded, the partnership records remain open, although inactive.

Distribution of Safe Payments. While awaiting the final resolution of this matter, no compelling reason exists for the partnership to continue holding $20,000 in cash. These funds will eventually be paid to Dozier and Ross regardless of any action taken by Holland. Thus, an immediate transfer should be made to these two partners to allow them the use of their money. However, since Dozier has a $15,000 capital account balance while Ross currently reports $11,000, a complete distribution is not possible. A method must be devised, therefore, to allow for a fair allocation of the available $20,000.

To ensure the equitable treatment of all parties, this initial distribution is based on the assumption that the $6,000 capital deficit will prove to be a total loss to the partnership. Holland may, for example, be completely insolvent so that no further payment will ever be forthcoming. By making this conservative presumption, the accountant is able to calculate the lowest possible amounts (or safe balances) that Dozier and Ross must retain in their capital accounts to be able to absorb all future losses.

Should Holland's $6,000 deficit (or any portion of it) prove uncollectible, the loss will be written off against the capital accounts of Dozier and Ross. Allocation of this amount is based on the *relative* profit and loss ratio specified in the Articles of Partnership. According to the information provided in this illustration, Dozier and Ross are credited with 40 percent and 20 percent of all partnership income, respectively. This 40:20 ratio equates to a 2:1 relationship (or ⅔:⅓) between the two. Thus, if no part of the $6,000 deficit balance is ever recovered from Holland, $4,000 (two thirds) of the loss will be assigned to Dozier and $2,000 (one third) to Ross.

Allocation of Potential $6,000 Loss

Dozier	⅔ of $(6,000) = $(4,000)
Ross	⅓ of $(6,000) = $(2,000)

These amounts represent the maximum potential reductions that might still be incurred by the two remaining partners. Depending on Holland's actions, Dozier could be forced to absorb an additional loss of $4,000 while Ross's capital account may decrease by as much as $2,000. These balances must, therefore, remain in the respective capital accounts until the issue is resolved. Hence, Dozier is entitled to receive $11,000 at the present time; this distribution reduces the applicable capital account from $15,000 to the minimum $4,000 level. Likewise, a $9,000 payment to Ross decreases the $11,000 capital balance to the $2,000 limit. These $11,000 and $9,000 figures represent safe payments that can be distributed to the partners without fear of new deficits being created subsequently.

Dozier, Capital 11,000
Ross, Capital 9,000
    Cash 20,000
    To distribute cash to Dozier and Ross based on safe capital balances,
    using the assumption that Holland will not contribute further to the
    partnership.

After this $20,000 in cash has been distributed, only a few other events can possibly occur during the remaining life of the partnership. Holland, either voluntarily or through legal persuasion, may contribute the entire $6,000 needed to eradicate the capital deficit. In that situation, the money should be immediately turned over to Dozier ($4,000) and Ross ($2,000) based on their remaining capital balances. The partnership records are effectively closed by this final distribution.

A second possibility is that Dozier and Ross may be unable to recover any part of the deficit from Holland. These two remaining partners must then absorb the $6,000 loss themselves. Since safe capital balances have been maintained, recording a complete default by Holland serves to close out the partnership books.

Dozier, Capital (⅔ of loss) 4,000
Ross, Capital (⅓ of loss) 2,000
    Holland, Capital 6,000
    To allocate deficit capital balance of insolvent partner.

Deficit Is Partly Collectible. One other ending to this partnership liquidation is conceivable. A portion of the $6,000 may be successfully recovered from Holland although the remainder proves to be uncollectible. This partner may become bankrupt or the other partners might simply give up trying to collect. The partners could also negotiate this settlement to avoid protracted legal actions.

To illustrate, assume that Holland manages to contribute $3,600 to the partnership but subsequently files for relief under the provisions of the bankruptcy laws. In a later legal arrangement, $1,000 additional cash goes to the partnership, but the final $1,400 will never be collected. This series of events creates the following effects within the liquidation process:

1. The initial $3,600 contribution is distributed to Dozier and Ross based on a new computation of their safe capital balances.
2. The $1,400 default is charged against the two positive capital balances in accordance with the relative profit and loss ratio.
3. The final $1,000 contribution is then paid to Dozier and Ross in amounts equal to their ending capital accounts, a transaction that closes the partnership's financial records.

The distribution of the first $3,600 depends on a recalculation of the minimum capital balances that Dozier and Ross must maintain to absorb all potential losses. Each of these computations is produced because of a basic realization: Holland's remaining deficit balance ($2,400 at this time) could prove to be a total loss. This approach guarantees that the other two partners will continue to report adequate capital until the liquidation is ultimately resolved.

	Current Capital	Allocation of Potential Loss	Safe Capital Payments
Dozier	$4,000	⅔ of $(2,400) = $(1,600)	$2,400
Ross	2,000	⅓ of $(2,400) = $ (800)	1,200

Thus, the $3,600 in cash that is now available is distributed immediately to Dozier and Ross based on their safe balances.

Cash	3,600	
Holland, Capital		3,600
Dozier, Capital	2,400	
Ross, Capital	1,200	
Cash		3,600

To record capital contribution by Holland and subsequent distribution of funds to Dozier and Ross based on safe capital balances.

After recording this $3,600 contribution from Holland and the subsequent disbursement, the capital accounts for the partnership stay open, registering the following individual balances:

Holland, Capital (deficit)	$(2,400)
Dozier, Capital (safe balance)	1,600
Ross, Capital (safe balance)	800

These accounts continue to remain on the partnership books until the final resolution of Holland's obligation.

In this illustration, the $1,000 legal settlement ultimately allows the parties to close out the records:

Cash	1,000	
Dozier, Capital (⅔ of loss)	933	
Ross, Capital (⅓ of loss)	467	
Holland, Capital		2,400

To record final $1,000 cash settlement of Holland's interest and resulting $1,400 loss.

Dozier, Capital	667	
Ross, Capital	333	
Cash		1,000

To distribute final cash balance based upon remaining capital account totals.

Marshaling of Assets

In the previous example, one partner (Holland) became insolvent during the liquidation process. Personal bankruptcy is not uncommon and raises questions as to the legal right that damaged partners have to proceed against an insolvent partner. *More specifically, is a deficit capital balance the legal equivalent of any other personal liability? Do partners who must absorb additional losses have the same rights against their partners as other creditors?*

Addressing this issue, the Uniform Partnership Act (Section 40[i]) stipulates that:

> Where a partner has become bankrupt or his estate is insolvent the claims against his separate property shall rank in the following order:
> (I) Those owing to separate creditors,
> (II) Those owing to partnership creditors,
> (III) Those owing to partners by way of contribution.

This ranking of the claims against an individual is normally referred to as the *marshaling of assets* and allows for an orderly distribution of property in bankruptcy cases.

To demonstrate the effects created by this legal doctrine, assume that Stone is a partner in a business that is undergoing final liquidation. The partnership is insolvent: all assets have been expended but liabilities of $15,000 still remain. Stone is also personally insolvent. The following assets currently held by this individual cannot satisfy all personal obligations:

Personal assets	$50,000
Personal liabilities	40,000
Deficit capital balance—partnership	19,000

Under these circumstances, the ranking established by the Uniform Partnership Act becomes extremely important. Stone does hold $50,000 in assets. However, since these assets are limited, recovery by the various parties is dependent on the pattern of distribution. According to the marshaling of assets doctrine, Stone's own creditors have first priority. After these claims have been satisfied, remaining assets should be used to remunerate any partnership creditors who have sought recovery directly from Stone. Only then, after personal creditors as well as partnership creditors are paid, can the other partners lay claim to the residual portion of Stone's assets. Obviously, because of this individual's financial condition, the chances are not good that these partners will be able to recover all or even a significant portion of the $19,000 deficit capital balance. By ranking last on this priority list, partners are forced to accept whatever assets remain.

To analyze and understand the possible effects created by the marshaling of assets concept, a variety of other situations can be considered. Assume, as an alternative to the previous example, that Stone failed to have sufficient property to satisfy even personal creditors: Stone holds $50,000 in assets but $90,000 in personal liabilities. Because of these debts, neither the partnership creditors nor the other partners are able to recoup any money from this partner. All of the personal assets must be used to pay Stone's own obligations. Even with preferential treatment, the personal creditors still face a $40,000 shortfall because of the limited quantity of available assets. This potential loss raises another legal question: can Stone's creditors seek recovery of the $40,000 directly from the partnership?

In response to this issue, the marshaling of assets doctrine specifies that personal creditors can, indeed, claim a partner's share of partnership assets. However, recovery of all, or even a portion, of the $40,000 is only possible if two specific criteria are met:

1. Payment of all partnership debts must be assured.
2. The insolvent partner has to have a positive capital balance.

Even if both of these conditions are met, personal creditors have no right to receive more than the total of that partner's capital balance nor more than the amount of the debt.

This priority ranking of claims provides legal guidance in insolvency cases. For a more complete demonstration of the marshaling of assets principle, three additional examples follow. Each is designed to present the legal and accounting responses to specific partnership liquidation problems. In the first two illustrations, one or more of the partners are personally insolvent. The third analyzes the marshaling of assets in connection with an insolvent partnership.

Insolvency—Example One.   The following balance sheet has been produced for the Able, Baker, Cannon, and Duke partnership. Profit and loss percentages are also included.

Cash.	$ 30,000	Liabilities	$ 80,000
Noncash assets	150,000	Able, capital (40%)	15,000
		Baker, capital (30%).	40,000
		Cannon, capital (20%)	30,000
		Duke, capital (10%)	15,900
		Total liabilities and	
Total assets.	$180,000	capital	$180,000

Baker is insolvent, and personal creditors have filed a $30,000 claim against this partner's share of partnership property. The litigation has forced the partnership to begin liquidation to settle Baker's interest. As shown in the balance sheet, the partnership has $30,000 in cash and Baker has a capital balance of $40,000.

Assume, in this example, that the noncash assets (with a book value of $150,000) are subsequently sold for $100,000 with the partnership's liabilities

($80,000) then being paid. These two actions increase the cash balance by $20,000 to a $50,000 figure. No other assets or liabilities exist. The adjusted capital accounts for each partner follow. Other than Baker, all partners are personally solvent.

	Able, Capital	Baker, Capital	Cannon, Capital	Duke, Capital
Beginning balances	$ 15,000	$ 40,000	$ 30,000	$15,000
$50,000 loss on liquidating of assets	(20,000) (40%)	(15,000) (30%)	(10,000) (20%)	(5,000) (10%)
Capital balances	$ (5,000)	$ 25,000	$ 20,000	$10,000

An additional contribution of $5,000 should be forthcoming from Able to eradicate the single negative capital balance. This investment raises the partnership's cash to $55,000 and permits a final distribution to Cannon ($20,000), Duke ($10,000), and *Baker's creditors* ($25,000). The liquidation losses have reduced Baker's capital account below the $30,000 level; therefore, this partner's personal creditors are unable to recover the entire amount of their claims. Despite the remaining $5,000 debt, they have no further legal recourse here; no right of recovery exists against the other partners once the capital account has been depleted.

Baker will receive nothing from this liquidation settlement because the personal obligations have not been completely satisfied. In contrast, if the final capital balance had been in excess of $30,000, Baker would have been entitled to any residual amount after all of the personal liabilities were extinguished.

Insolvency—Example Two. The following balance sheet for the partnership of Morris, Newton, Olsen, and Prince also contains the applicable profit and loss percentages. Both Morris and Prince are personally insolvent. Morris's creditors have brought an $8,000 claim against the partnership's assets while $15,000 is being sought by Prince's creditors. These claims have forced the partnership to terminate operations so that the business property can be liquidated. The question is again raised as to which partner is entitled to any cash balance that remains.

Cash	$ 10,000	Liabilities	$ 70,000
Noncash assets	140,000	Morris, capital (40%)	15,000
		Newton, capital (20%)	10,000
		Olsen, capital (20%)	23,000
		Prince, capital (20%)	32,000
		Total liabilities and	
Total assets	$150,000	capital	$150,000

The noncash assets are sold for a total of $80,000 and all liabilities paid. The partnership's accounting system records these two events as follows:

Cash	80,000	
Morris, Capital (40% of loss).	24,000	
Newton, Capital (20% of loss)	12,000	
Olsen, Capital (20% of loss)	12,000	
Prince, Capital (20% of loss).	12,000	
Noncash Assets (or specific accounts)		140,000
To record sale of noncash assets and allocation of resulting $60,000 loss.		

Liabilities	70,000	
Cash		70,000
To extinguish partnership obligations.		

Because of these two transactions, the partnership's cash has risen from $10,000 to $20,000.

After the allocation of this loss, the capital accounts for Morris and Newton report deficit balances of $9,000 ($15,000 − $24,000) and $2,000 ($10,000 − $12,000), respectively. Although Newton is solvent and would be expected to compensate the partnership, Morris's personal financial condition does not allow for any further contribution. The $9,000 deficit must, therefore, be absorbed by Newton, Olsen, and Prince. Because these three partners have historically shared profits evenly (20:20:20), they continue to do so in recording this additional capital loss.

Newton, Capital (⅓ of loss)	3,000	
Olsen, Capital (⅓ of loss)	3,000	
Prince, Capital (⅓ of loss).	3,000	
Morris, Capital.		9,000
To write off deficit capital balance of insolvent partner.		

This last allocation increases Newton's deficit to a $5,000 balance ($2,000 + $3,000), an amount which the partner should now contribute in accordance with partnership law.

Cash	5,000	
Newton, Capital		5,000
To record contribution necessitated by negative capital balance.		

Following this series of transactions, only the cash balance (now $25,000) as well as the capital accounts of Olsen and Prince remain open within the partnership records:

	Cash	Morris, Capital	Newton, Capital	Olsen, Capital	Prince, Capital
Beginning balances.	$ 10,000	$ 15,000	$ 10,000	$ 23,000	$ 32,000
Sold assets	80,000	(24,000)	(12,000)	(12,000)	(12,000)
Paid liabilities	(70,000)	–0–	–0–	–0–	–0–
Default by Morris	–0–	9,000	(3,000)	(3,000)	(3,000)
Contribution by Newton	5,000	–0–	5,000	–0–	–0–
Current balances.	$ 25,000	–0–	–0–	$ 8,000	$ 17,000

Although $8,000 of the partnership's remaining cash goes directly to Olsen, the $17,000 attributed to Prince is first subjected to the claims of the partner's personal creditors. Because of their claims, $15,000 of this amount must be used to satisfy these obligations, with only the final $2,000 being paid to Prince.

Insolvency—Example Three. The two previous illustrations have analyzed liquidations in which one or more of the partners has been personally insolvent. Another possibility is that the partnership itself may come to meet this same fate. In an active partnership, insolvency can occur if losses or drawings deplete the working capital of the operation. A bankruptcy petition may follow if debts cannot be met as they come due. Liquidation of business assets might be necessary unless additional capital is quickly generated. Even a financially sound partnership may become insolvent if material losses are incurred during a voluntary liquidation.

To serve as a basis for examining the accounting and legal ramifications of an insolvent partnership, assume that the law firm of Keller, Lewis, Monroe, and Norris is in the final stages of liquidation. All noncash assets have been sold, and available cash has been used to pay a portion of the business's liabilities. Following these transactions, the following account balances remain open within the partnership's records. The four partners in this endeavor share profits and losses equally.

Liabilities.	$ 20,000
Keller, capital.	(30,000)
Lewis, capital.	(5,000)
Monroe, capital	5,000
Norris, capital.	10,000

Note: Parentheses indicate deficit.

This partnership is insolvent; it continues to owe creditors $20,000, even after liquidation and distribution of all assets. However, additional money should be forthcoming from two of the partners. Because of their deficit capital accounts,

Keller and Lewis are legally required to contribute an additional $30,000 and $5,000, respectively, to the business. With these newly available funds, the partnership will be able to pay all $20,000 of its remaining liabilities as well as make cash distributions to Monroe ($5,000) and Norris ($10,000) in accordance with their capital account balances. The partnership books would be closed by this final payment.

Once again, the possibility exists that a partner who is reporting a negative capital balance will not step forward to make a further investment. Assume, for example, that Keller is personally insolvent and cannot contribute, whereas Lewis simply refuses to supply additional funds in hopes of avoiding the obligation. *At this point, the remaining creditors may instigate legal recovery proceedings against any or all of the partners regardless of their capital balances.* Any action, however, against the insolvent partner may prove to be a futile effort because of the marshaling of assets principle.

Predicting the exact outcome of litigation is rarely possible. Thus, the assumption is made that Norris is forced to contribute $20,000 cash to make up the entire deficit. The following journal entries would then be required for this partnership:

Cash	20,000	
Norris, Capital		20,000
Liabilities	20,000	
Cash		20,000

To record capital contribution by Norris made to pay remaining partnership creditors.

After all liabilities have been settled, the partners who still maintain positive capital accounts can demand remuneration from any partner with a negative balance. Despite this legal obligation, the chances of a significant recovery from the insolvent Keller, especially under the marshaling of assets doctrine, is not likely. Thus, the partners may choose to write off this deficit to move toward closing the partnership's financial records. Legal recovery proceedings can still continue against Keller regardless of the accounting treatment. As equal partners, the $30,000 loss is absorbed evenly by Lewis, Monroe, and Norris.

Lewis, Capital (⅓ of loss)	10,000	
Monroe, Capital (⅓ of loss)	10,000	
Norris, Capital (⅓ of loss)	10,000	
Keller, Capital		30,000

To write off deficit capital balance of insolvent partner.

The partners' capital accounts now hold the following balances:

	Keller, Capital	Lewis, Capital	Monroe, Capital	Norris, Capital
Beginning balances	$(30,000)	$ (5,000)	$ 5,000	$ 10,000
Capital contribution	–0–	–0–	–0–	20,000
Write-off of deficit balance	30,000	(10,000)	(10,000)	(10,000)
Current balances	–0–	$(15,000)	$ (5,000)	$ 20,000

Both Lewis and Monroe now have a legal obligation to reimburse the partnership to offset their deficit capital balances. Upon their payment of $15,000 and $5,000, respectively, the entire $20,000 will be distributed to Norris (the only partner with a positive balance) and the partnership's books will be closed. Should either Lewis or Monroe fail to make the appropriate contribution, the additional loss must be allocated between the two remaining partners.

Discussion Question: What Happens if a Partner Becomes Insolvent?

In 1984, three dentists—Ben Rogers, Judy Wilkinson, and Henry Walker—formed a partnership to open a practice in Toledo, Ohio. The primary purpose of the partnership was to reduce expenses since the partners could share building and equipment costs, supplies, and the services of a clerical staff. They each contributed $50,000 in cash and, with the help of a bank loan, constructed a building and acquired furniture, fixtures, and equipment. Because the partners maintained their own separate clients, annual net income has been allocated as follows: each partner receives the specific amount of revenues that he or she generated during the period less one third of all expenses. From the beginning, the partners did not anticipate expansion of the practice; consequently, they are allowed to withdraw cash each year up to 90 percent of their share of income for the period.

The partnership has been profitable for a number of years. Over the years, Rogers uses much of his income to speculate in real estate in the Toledo area. By 1995, he is spending less time with the dental practice so that he can concentrate on his investments. Unfortunately, a number of these deals prove to be bad decisions and he incurs significant losses. On November 8, 1995, while Rogers is out of town, a $97,000 claim is filed by his

continued

personal creditors against the partnership assets. Unbeknownst to Wilkinson and Walker, Rogers has become insolvent.

Wilkinson and Walker hurriedly hold a meeting to discuss the problem since Rogers cannot be located. Rogers's capital account is currently at $105,000, but the partnership has only $19,000 in cash and liquid assets. The partners estimate that Rogers's equipment has been used for a number of years and could be sold for relatively little. In contrast, the building has appreciated in value and the claim could be satisfied by selling the property. However, this action would have a tremendously adverse impact on the dental practice of the remaining two partners.

What alternatives are available to Wilkinson and Walker, and what are the advantages and disadvantages of each?

Preliminary Distribution of Partnership Assets

In all of the illustrations analyzed in this chapter, distributions have been made to the partners only after all assets were sold and all liabilities paid. As previously mentioned, a liquidation may take an extended time to complete. During this lengthy process, the partnership need not retain those assets that will eventually be disbursed to the partners. If the business is safely solvent, waiting until all affairs have been settled before transferring property to the owners is not warranted. The partners should be allowed to make use of their own funds at the earliest possible time.

The objective in making any type of preliminary distribution is to assure that enough capital is maintained by the partnership to absorb all future losses. Any capital in excess of this maximum requirement is a safe balance, an amount that can be immediately conveyed to the partner. To determine safe capital balances at any time, the accountant simply assumes that all subsequent events will result in maximum losses: no cash will be received in liquidating remaining noncash assets and each partner is personally insolvent. Any positive capital balance that would remain even after inclusion of all potential losses should be paid to the partner without delay. Although the assumption that no further funds will be generated may be unrealistic, it does ensure that negative capital balances are not created by premature payments being made to any of the partners.

Preliminary Distribution Illustrated. To demonstrate the computation of safe capital distributions, assume that a liquidating partnership reports the following balance sheet:

Cash.	$ 60,000	Liabilities	$ 40,000
Noncash assets	140,000	Mason, loan	20,000
		Mason, capital (50%)	60,000
		Lee, capital (30%).	30,000
		Dixon, capital (20%).	50,000
		Total liabilities and	
Total assets.	$200,000	capital	$200,000

Assume further that the partners estimate that $6,000 will be the maximum expense incurred in carrying out this liquidation. Consequently, the partnership needs only $46,000 to meet all obligations: $40,000 to satisfy partnership liabilities and $6,000 for these final expenses. Since $60,000 in cash is being held, the partnership can transfer the extra $14,000 to the partners immediately without fear of injuring any of the participants in the liquidation. However, the appropriate allocation of this money is not readily apparent; therefore, safe capital balances must be computed to guide the actual distribution.

Before the allocation of this $14,000 is demonstrated, the appropriate handling of a partner's loan balance should be examined. According to the prior balance sheet, Mason has contributed $20,000 to the business at some point in the past, an amount that was considered a loan rather than additional capital. Perhaps the partnership was in desperate need of funds and could only generate new financing by accepting a high interest rate loan. Regardless of the reason, the question remains as to the status of this account: is the $20,000 to be viewed as a liability to the partner or as a capital balance? The answer becomes especially significant during the liquidation process since available funds are often limited. In this regard, the Uniform Partnership Act (Section 40[b]) stipulates that loans to partners rank behind obligations to outside creditors in order of payment but ahead of the partners' capital balances.

Although this provision implies that the debt to Mason must be repaid before any distribution can be made to the other partners, this treatment is only justified if Mason has a sufficient amount of capital to absorb all possible losses. During liquidation, the overriding consideration is the maintenance of adequate partnership capital to ensure protection of all parties. Whenever a safe capital balance is projected for a partner, the immediate payment of that individual's loan (as well as the safe balance) can be made without risk. Conversely, if the partner has a negative safe balance, a portion or even all of the loan should be retained as an offset against the capital account. In this manner, future deficit balances can be minimized.

Thus, a loan is always accounted for in a liquidation as if the balance were a component of the partner's capital. Only by taking this approach can the accountant eliminate the possibility that later losses will create negative capital balances. Since the resulting pattern of distributions is unaffected, amounts owed to a partner are often transferred into the corresponding capital account at the start of the liquidation process. Similarly, any loans due from a partner should be shown as a reduction in the appropriate capital balance.

Proposed Schedule of Liquidation.   Returning to the current illustration, the accountant needs to determine an equitable distribution for the $14,000 cash presently available. To structure this computation, a proposed schedule of liquidation is developed *based on the underlying assumption that all future events will result in total losses*. In Exhibit 14–2, this statement is presented for the Mason, Lee, and Dixon partnership. To expedite coverage, the $20,000 loan has already been transferred into Mason's capital account. Thus, regardless of whether this partner arrives at a deficit or a safe capital balance, the loan figure will have already been included.

In producing Exhibit 14–2, complete losses ($140,000) are forecast in connection with the disposition of all noncash assets, and liquidation expenses are anticipated at maximum amounts ($6,000). Following the projected payment of liabilities, any partner reporting a negative capital account is assumed to be personally insolvent. These potential deficit balances are written off with the losses being assigned to the remaining solvent partners based on their relative profit and loss ratio. Lee, with a negative $13,800, is eliminated first. This allocation creates a deficit of $2,857 for Mason, an amount that must be absorbed solely by Dixon. After this series of maximum losses has been simulated, any positive capital balance that still remains is considered safe; a cash distribution of that amount can be made to the specific partners.

Exhibit 14–2 indicates that only Dixon has a large enough capital balance at the present time to absorb all possible future losses. Thus, the entire $14,000 can be distributed to this partner with no fear that the capital account will ever report a deficit. In contrast, Mason, despite having made a $20,000 loan to the partnership, is entitled to no part of this initial distribution. The loan is of insufficient size to prevent potential deficits from occurring in Mason's capital account.

One series of computations found in this proposed schedule of liquidation merits additional attention. The simulated losses initially create a $13,800 negative balance in Lee's capital account while the other two partners continue to report positive figures. Lee's projected deficit must then be absorbed by Mason and Dixon according to their relative profit and loss percentages. Previously, Mason has been allocated 50 percent of net income with 20 percent recorded to Dixon. These figures equate to a $50/70 : 20/70$ or a $5/7 : 2/7$ ratio. Based on this realigned relationship, the $13,800 deficit is allocated between Mason ($5/7$ or $9,857) and Dixon ($2/7$ or $3,943), reducing Mason's own capital account to a negative balance as shown in Exhibit 14–2.

Continuing with the assumption that maximum losses occur in all cases, Mason's $2,857 deficit is accounted for as if that partner were also personally insolvent. Therefore, the entire negative balance is assigned to Dixon, the only partner still retaining a positive capital account. Since all potential losses have been recognized at this point, the remaining $14,000 capital is a safe balance that should

EXHIBIT 14-2

MASON, LEE, AND DIXON
Proposed Schedule of Liquidation
Safe Capital Balances

	Cash	Noncash Assets	Liabilities	Mason, Capital (50%)	Lee, Capital (30%)	Dixon, Capital (20%)
Beginning balances	$ 60,000	$ 140,000	$ 40,000	$ 80,000	$ 30,000	$ 50,000
Maximum loss on noncash assets	-0-	(140,000)	-0-	(70,000)	(42,000)	(28,000)
Maximum liquidation expenses	(6,000)	-0-	-0-	(3,000)	(1,800)	(1,200)
Payment of liabilities	(40,000)	-0-	(40,000)	-0-	-0-	-0-
Potential balances	14,000	-0-	-0-	7,000	(13,800)	20,800
Assume Lee to be insolvent	-0-	-0-	-0-	(9,857) (5/7)	13,800	(3,943) (2/7)
Potential balances	14,000	-0-	-0-	(2,857)	-0-	16,857
Assume Mason to be insolvent	-0-	-0-	-0-	2,857	-0-	(2,857)
Safe balances	$ 14,000	-0-	-0-	-0-	-0-	$ 14,000

be paid to this partner. Even after the money is distributed, Dixon's capital account will still be large enough to absorb all future losses.

Liquidation in Installments. In practice, maximum liquidation losses are not likely to occur to any business. Thus, at various points during this process, additional cash amounts become available as partnership property is sold. If the assets are disposed of in a piecemeal fashion, cash may actually flow into the company on a regular basis for an extended period of time. As needed, updated safe capital schedules have to be developed to dictate the recipients of newly available funds. Because numerous capital distributions may be required, this process is often referred to as a *liquidation made in installments.*

To illustrate, assume that the partnership of Mason, Lee, and Dixon actually undergoes the following events in connection with its liquidation:

- As indicated by the schedule of liquidation in Exhibit 14–2, Dixon receives $14,000 in cash as a preliminary capital distribution.
- Noncash assets with a book value of $50,000 are sold for $20,000.
- All $40,000 in liabilities are settled.
- Liquidation expenses of $2,000 are paid; the partners now believe that only a maximum of $3,000 more will be expended in this manner. The original estimation of $6,000 was apparently too high.

As a result of these transactions, the partnership has an additional $21,000 in cash that is now available for distribution to the partners: $20,000 received from the sale of noncash assets and another $1,000 because of the reduced estimation of liquidation expenses. Once again, the accountant must assume maximum future losses as a means of determining the appropriate distribution of these funds. A second proposed schedule of liquidation is produced in Exhibit 14–3, indicating that $12,143 of this amount should go to Mason with the remaining $8,857 to Dixon. To facilitate a better visual understanding, actual transactions are recorded first on this schedule, followed by the assumed losses. *A dotted line separates the real from the potential occurrences.*

Predistribution Plan

The liquidation of a partnership can require numerous transactions occurring over a lengthy time. The continual production of proposed schedules of liquidation may become a burdensome chore. Two separate statements have already been required in the previous illustration, and the partnership still possesses $90,000 in noncash assets awaiting conversion. *Therefore, at the start of a liquidation, most accountants produce a single predistribution plan to serve as a guideline for all future payments.* Thereafter, whenever cash becomes available, this plan indicates the appropriate recipients without the necessity of drawing up ever-changing proposed schedules of liquidation.

EXHIBIT 14–3   Liquidation for Installments

MASON, LEE, AND DIXON
Proposed Schedule of Liquidation
Safe Capital Balances

	Cash	Noncash Assets	Liabilities	Mason, Capital (50%)	Lee, Capital (30%)	Dixon, Capital (20%)
Beginning balances	$ 60,000	$ 140,000	$ 40,000	$ 80,000	$ 30,000	$ 50,000
Capital distribution — safe balances .	(14,000)	–0–	–0–	–0–	–0–	(14,000)
Disposal of noncash assets	20,000	(50,000)	–0–	(15,000)	(9,000)	(6,000)
Liabilities paid	(40,000)	–0–	(40,000)	–0–	–0–	–0–
Liquidation expenses	(2,000)	–0–	–0–	(1,000)	(600)	(400)
Current balances	24,000	90,000	–0–	64,000	20,400	29,600
Maximum loss on remaining						
noncash assets	–0–	(90,000)	–0–	(45,000)	(27,000)	(18,000)
Maximum liquidation expenses . . .	(3,000)	–0–	–0–	(1,500)	(900)	(600)
Potential balances	21,000	–0–	–0–	17,500	(7,500)	11,000
Assume Lee to be insolvent	–0–	–0–	–0–	(5,357) (5⁄7)	7,500	(2,143) (2⁄7)
Safe balances—current.	$ 21,000	–0–	–0–	$ 12,143	–0–	$ 8,857

A predistribution plan is developed by simulating a series of losses that are each just large enough to eliminate, one at a time, all of the partners' claims to cash. This approach recognizes that the individual capital accounts exhibit differing degrees of sensitivity to losses. These accounts possess varying balances and may be charged with losses at different rates. Consequently, a predistribution plan is based on calculating the losses (the "maximum loss allowable") that would eliminate each of these capital balances in a sequential pattern. This series of absorbed losses then forms the basis for the predistribution plan.

To demonstrate the creation of a predistribution plan, assume that the following partnership is to be liquidated:

Cash.	–0–	Liabilities	$100,000
Noncash assets	$221,000	Rubens, capital (50%)	30,000
		Smith, capital (20%)	40,000
		Trice, capital (30%)	51,000
Total assets.	$221,000	Total liabilities and capital	$221,000

The partnership capital reported by this organization totals $121,000. However, the individual balances for the partners range from $30,000 to $51,000 while profits and losses are assigned according to three different percentages. Thus, each partner's current capital balance would be reduced to zero by differing losses. *As a prerequisite to developing a predistribution plan, the sensitivity to losses exhibited by each of these capital accounts must be measured.*

Partner	Capital Balance/ Loss Allocation	Maximum Loss that Can Be Absorbed
Rubens	$30,000/50%	$ 60,000 ✔
Smith	40,000/20%	200,000
Trice	51,000/30%	170,000

Rubens is the partner in the most vulnerable position at the present time. Based on a 50 percent share of income, a loss of only $60,000 is needed to reduce this partner's capital account to a zero balance. If the partnership does incur a loss of this amount, Rubens can no longer hope to recover any funds from the liquidation process. Thus, the potential effects of this loss (referred to as a Step 1 loss) is simulated through the following schedule:

	Rubens, Capital	Smith, Capital	Trice, Capital
Beginning balances	$ 30,000	$ 40,000	$ 51,000
Assumed $60,000 loss.	(30,000) (50%)	(12,000) (20%)	(18,000) (30%)
Step 1 balances	–0–	$ 28,000	$ 33,000

As previously discussed, the predistribution plan is based on describing the series of losses that would eliminate each partner's capital in turn and, thus, all claims to cash. In the previous Step 1 schedule, the $60,000 loss did reduce Ruben's capital account to zero. Assuming, as a precautionary step, that Rubens is personally insolvent, all further losses would have to be allocated between Smith and Trice. Since these two partners have previously shared partnership profits and losses on a 20 percent and 30 percent basis, a $20/50 : 30/50$ relationship exists between them (or 40% : 60%). Therefore, these realigned percentages must now be utilized in calculating a Step 2 loss, the amount large enough to exclude one of these two remaining partners from sharing in any future cash distributions.

Partner	Capital Balance/ Loss Allocation	Maximum Loss that Can Be Absorbed
Smith	$28,000/40%	$70,000
Trice	33,000/60%	55,000 ✔

Since Rubens's capital balance has already been eliminated, Trice is now in the most vulnerable position: only a $55,000 Step 2 loss is needed to reduce this partner's capital account to a zero balance.

	Rubens, Capital	Smith, Capital	Trice, Capital
Beginning balances	$ 30,000	$ 40,000	$ 51,000
Assumed $60,000 loss.	(30,000) (50%)	(12,000) (20%)	(18,000) (30%)
Step 1 balances	–0–	28,000	33,000
Assumed $55,000 loss.	–0–	(22,000) (40%)	(33,000) (60%)
Step 2 balances	–0–	$ 6,000	–0–

According to this second schedule, a total loss of $115,000 ($60,000 from Step 1 plus $55,000 from Step 2) would leave capital of only $6,000, a balance attributed entirely to Smith. At this final point in the simulation, an additional loss of this amount also ends Smith's right to receive any funds from the liquidation process. Having the sole positive capital account remaining, this partner would have to absorb the entire amount of the final loss.

	Rubens, Capital	Smith, Capital	Trice, Capital
Beginning balances	$ 30,000	$ 40,000	$ 51,000
Assumed $60,000 loss.	(30,000) (50%)	(12,000) (20%)	(18,000) (30%)
Step 1 balances	–0–	28,000	33,000
Assumed $55,000 loss.	–0–	(22,000) (40%)	(33,000) (60%)
Step 2 balances	–0–	6,000	–0–
Assumed $6,000 loss	–0–	(6,000) (100%)	–0–
Final balances	–0–	–0–	–0–

Once each partner's capital account has been reduced to zero through this series of simulated losses, a predistribution plan for the liquidation can be devised. *This procedure requires working backward through the final schedule above, determining the effects that will result if the assumed losses do not occur.* Without these losses, cash becomes available for the partners; therefore, a direct relationship exists between the volume of losses and the distribution pattern. The last $6,000 loss, for example, is to be absorbed entirely by Smith. Should that loss fail to materialize, Smith is left with a positive safe capital balance of this amount. Thus, as cash becomes available, the first $6,000 received (in excess of partnership obligations and anticipated liquidation expenses) should be distributed solely to Smith.

In a similar manner, the preceding $55,000 Step 2 loss was divided between Smith and Trice on a 4:6 basis. Again, if such losses do not occur, these balances need not be retained to protect the partnership against capital deficits. Therefore, after Smith has received the initial $6,000, any further cash that becomes available (up to an additional $55,000) will be split between Smith (40 percent) and Trice (60 percent). For example, if exactly $61,000 in cash is held by the partnership in excess of liabilities and possible liquidation expenses, the following distribution should be made:

	Rubens	Smith	Trice
First $6,000	–0–	$ 6,000	–0–
Next $55,000	–0–	22,000 (40%)	$33,000 (60%)
Cash distribution	–0–	$28,000	$33,000

The predistribution plan can now be completed by including the Step 1 loss, an amount that was to be absorbed by the partners on a 5:2:3 basis. Thus, all money that becomes available to the partners after the initial $61,000 is to be distributed according to the original profit and loss ratio. At this point in the liquidation, enough cash would have been generated to ensure that each partner has a safe capital balance: no possibility exists that a future deficit can occur. Any further increases in the projected capital balances will be allocated by the 5:2:3 allocation pattern. *For this reason, once all partners have begun to receive a portion of the cash disbursements, any remaining funds are divided based on the original profit and loss percentages.*

To inform all parties of the order by which available cash will be disbursed, the predistribution plan should be formally prepared in a schedule format prior to beginning liquidation. Following is the predistribution plan for the partnership of Rubens, Smith, and Trice. To complete this illustration, liquidation expenses of $12,000 have been estimated. Since these expenses have the same effect on the capital accounts as losses, they do not change the sequential pattern by which assets eventually will be distributed.

RUBENS, SMITH, AND TRICE
Predistribution Plan

Available Cash		Recipient
First	$112,000	Creditors ($100,000) and liquidation expenses (estimated at $12,000)
Next	6,000	Smith
Next	55,000	Smith (40%) and Trice (60%)
All further cash balances		Rubens (50%), Smith (20%), and Trice (30%)

Summary

1. Although a partnership can exist indefinitely through the periodic admission of new partners, termination of business activities and liquidation of property may take place for a number of reasons. A partner's death or retirement can trigger this process as well as the insolvency of a partner or even the partnership itself. Because of the risk that large losses will be incurred during liquidation, all parties usually seek frequent and timely information describing ongoing developments. The accountant is expected to furnish this data while also working to ensure the equitable treatment of all parties.

2. The liquidation process entails (*a*) converting partnership property into cash, (*b*) paying off liabilities and liquidation expenses, and (*c*) conveying any remaining property to the partners based on their final capital balances. As a means of reporting these transactions, a schedule of liquidation should be produced at periodic intervals. This statement discloses all recent transactions, the assets and liabilities still being held, and the current capital balances. Distribution of this schedule on a regular basis allows the various parties involved in the liquidation to monitor the progress being made.

3. During a liquidation, negative capital balances can arise for one or more of the partners, especially if material losses are incurred in disposing of partnership property. In such cases, the specific partner or partners should contribute enough additional assets to eliminate their deficits. If payment is slow in coming, any cash still held by the partnership can be immediately divided among the partners that have safe capital balances. A safe balance is the amount of capital that would remain even if maximum future losses occur: noncash assets are lost in total and all partners with deficits fail to fulfill their legal obligations. In making these computations, negative capital balances are absorbed by the remaining partners based on their relative profit and loss ratio.

4. To enable an orderly and fair distribution during liquidation, the Uniform Partnership Act establishes a priority listing for all claims, a ranking referred to as the *marshaling of assets*. This principle states that partners with positive capital balances can recover losses from a partner reporting a deficit but only after adequate protection has been ensured for that individual's creditors as well as the partnership's creditors. The act also specifies that a partner's personal creditors can seek recovery of losses from the partnership to the extent of that person's capital balance after protection of partnership creditors is assured.

5. The actual liquidation of a partnership can take an extended period to complete. Oftentimes, cash is generated during the early stages of this process in excess of the amount needed to cover liabilities and liquidation expenses. The accountant should propose a fair and immediate distribution of these available funds. A proposed schedule of liquidation can be created as a guide for such cash distributions. This statement is based on a *simulated* series of transactions: sale of all noncash assets, payment of liquidation expenses, and so on. At every point, maximum losses are assumed: noncash assets have no resale value, liquidation expenses are set at the maximum level, and all partners are personally insolvent. Any safe capital balance that would remain after incurring such losses represents a distribution that can be made at the present time. Even after this payment, the capital account will still be large enough to absorb all potential losses.

6. The liquidation of a partnership can require numerous transactions occurring over a lengthy time. Thus, the accountant may discover that the continual production of proposed schedules of liquidation becomes a burdensome chore. For this reason, a single predistribution plan is usually produced at the start of the liquidation process. This plan serves as a definitive guideline for all payments to be made to the partners. To create this plan, a series of losses is simulated with each one, in turn, exactly eliminating the capital balance of a partner. After all capital accounts have been reduced to zero through these assumed losses, the predistribution plan is devised by working backward through the series. In effect, the accountant is measuring the cash that will become available if such losses do not occur.

Comprehensive Illustration

PROBLEM   (Estimated Time: 30 to 40 Minutes)

For the past several years, the partnership of Andrews, Caso, Quinn, and Sheridan has operated a local department store. Based on the provisions of the original Articles of Partnership, all profits and losses have been allocated on a 4:3:2:1 ratio, respectively. Recently, both Caso and Quinn have undergone personal financial problems, and as a result, each of these individuals is now insolvent. Caso's creditors have filed a $20,000 claim against the partnership's assets while $22,000 is being sought to repay Quinn's personal debts. To satisfy these legal obligations, the partnership property must be liquidated. The partners estimate that they will incur $12,000 in expenses in disposing of all noncash assets.

At the time that active operations cease and the liquidation is begun, the following balance sheet is produced for this partnership. All measurement accounts have been closed out to arrive at the current capital balances.

Cash.	$ 20,000	Liabilities	$140,000
Noncash assets	280,000	Caso, loan	10,000
		Andrews, capital (40%)	76,000
		Caso, capital (30%)	14,000
		Quinn, capital (20%).	51,000
		Sheridan, capital (10%)	9,000
Total assets.	$300,000	Total liabilities and capital	$300,000

During the lengthy liquidation process, the following transactions take place:

- Noncash assets with a book value of $190,000 are sold for $140,000 cash.
- Liquidation expenses of $14,000 are paid.
- Safe capital distributions are made to the partners.
- Payment is made of all business liabilities.
- The remaining noncash assets are sold for $10,000.
- Deficit capital balances for any insolvent partners are deemed to be uncollectible.
- Appropriate cash contributions are received from any solvent partner who is reporting a negative capital balance.
- Final cash distributions are made.

Required:

a. Using the information that is available *prior* to the start of the liquidation process, develop a predistribution plan for this partnership.
b. Prepare journal entries to record the actual liquidation transactions.

SOLUTION

a. This partnership begins liquidation with capital amounting to $160,000. This total includes the $10,000 loan from Caso since the liability must be retained as a possible offset against any eventual deficit capital balance. Therefore, the predistribution plan is based on the assumption that $160,000 in losses will be incurred, entirely eliminating all partnership capital. As discussed in this chapter, these simulated losses are arranged in a series so that each capital account is sequentially reduced to a zero balance.

At the start of the liquidation, Caso's capital position is the most vulnerable.

Partner	Capital Balance/ Loss Allocation	Maximum Loss that Can Be Absorbed
Andrews.	$76,000/40%	$190,000
Caso	24,000/30%	80,000 ✔
Quinn	51,000/20%	255,000
Sheridan	9,000/10%	90,000

As indicated by this schedule, an $80,000 loss would eradicate both Caso's $14,000 capital balance and the $10,000 loan. Therefore, to start the development of a predistribution plan, this loss is assumed to have occurred.

	Andrews, Capital	Caso, Loan and Capital	Quinn, Capital	Sheridan, Capital
Beginning balances	$ 76,000	$ 24,000	$ 51,000	$ 9,000
Assumed $80,000 loss . . .	(32,000) (40%)	(24,000) (30%)	(16,000) (20%)	(8,000) (10%)
Step 1 balances	$ 44,000	–0–	$ 35,000	$ 1,000

With Caso's capital account eliminated, further losses are to be split among the remaining partners in the ratio of 4:2:1 (or ⁴⁄₇ : ²⁄₇ : ¹⁄₇). As only an additional $7,000 loss (the $1,000 capital divided by ¹⁄₇) is now needed to reduce Sheridan's account to zero, this partner is in the second most vulnerable position.

	Andrews	Caso	Quinn	Sheridan
Step 1 balances (above)	$44,000	–0–	$35,000	$ 1,000
Assumed $7,000 loss.	(4,000) (⁴⁄₇)	–0–	(2,000) (²⁄₇)	(1,000) (¹⁄₇)
Step 2 balances	$40,000	–0–	$33,000	–0–

Following these two simulated losses, only Andrews and Quinn continue to report positive capital balances. Thus, they divide further losses on a 4:2 basis or 66⅔%:33⅓%. Based on these realigned percentages, Andrews's position has become the most vulnerable. A further loss of only $60,000 ($40,000/66⅔%) reduces this partner's remaining capital to zero while a $99,000 loss ($33,000/33⅓%) is required to eliminate Quinn's balance.

	Andrews	Caso	Quinn	Sheridan
Step 2 balances (above)	$ 40,000	–0–	$ 33,000	–0–
Assumed $60,000 loss	(40,000) (66⅔%)	–0–	(20,000) (33⅓%)	–0–
Step 3 balances	–0–	–0–	$ 13,000	–0–

The final $13,000 capital balance belongs to Quinn; an additional loss of this amount is necessary to eradicate the last element of partnership capital.

Based on the results of this series of simulated losses, a predistribution plan can be created. However, the $140,000 in liabilities owed by the partnership still have first priority to available cash. Additionally, $12,000 must be retained to cover the anticipated liquidation expenses.

ANDREWS, CASO, QUINN, AND SHERIDAN
Predistribution Plan

Available Cash		Recipient
First	$152,000	Creditors and liquidation expenses
Next	13,000	Quinn
Next	60,000	Andrews (66⅔%) and Quinn (33⅓%)
Next	7,000	Andrews (4/7), Quinn (2/7), and Sheridan (1/7)
All further cash		Andrews (40%), Caso (30%), Quinn (20%), and Sheridan (10%)

Because of their insolvency, initial payments to Caso ($20,000) and Quinn ($22,000) may actually go to their personal creditors.

b. Journal entries for the liquidation:

Caso, Loan	10,000	
Caso, Capital		10,000
To offset loan against capital balance in anticipation of liquidation.		

Cash	140,000	
Andrews, Capital (40% of loss)	20,000	
Caso, Capital (30% of loss)	15,000	
Quinn, Capital (20% of loss)	10,000	
Sheridan, Capital (10% of loss)	5,000	
Noncash Assets		190,000
To record sale of noncash assets and allocation of $50,000 loss.		

Andrews, Capital (40%)	5,600	
Caso, Capital (30%)	4,200	
Quinn, Capital (20%)	2,800	
Sheridan, Capital (10%)	1,400	
Cash		14,000
Payment of liquidation expenses.		

- The partnership is now holding $146,000 in cash, $6,000 more than is needed to satisfy all liabilities and estimated expenses. According to the predistribution plan drawn up in requirement *a.*, this entire amount can be safely distributed to Quinn (or to Quinn's creditors).

Quinn, Capital	6,000	
Cash		6,000
To distribute available cash based on safe capital balance.		

Liabilities	140,000	
Cash		140,000
To extinguish all partnership debts.		

Cash				10,000	
Andrews, Capital (40% of loss)				32,000	
Caso, Capital (30% of loss)				24,000	
Quinn, Capital (20% of loss).				16,000	
Sheridan, Capital (10% of loss)				8,000	
Noncash Assets					90,000

To record sale of remaining noncash assets and allocation of $80,000 loss.

- At this point in the liquidation, only the cash and the capital accounts remain open on the partnership books.

	Cash	Andrews, Capital	Caso, Capital	Quinn, Capital	Sheridan, Capital
Beginning balances	$ 20,000	$ 76,000	$ 14,000	$ 51,000	$ 9,000
Loan offset	–0–	–0–	10,000	–0–	–0–
Sale of noncash assets	140,000	(20,000)	(15,000)	(10,000)	(5,000)
Liquidation expenses	(14,000)	(5,600)	(4,200)	(2,800)	(1,400)
Cash distribution	(6,000)	–0–	–0–	(6,000)	–0–
Payment of liabilities	(140,000)	–0–	–0–	–0–	–0–
Sale of noncash assets	10,000	(32,000)	(24,000)	(16,000)	(8,000)
Current balances	$ 10,000	$ 18,400	$(19,200)	$ 16,200	$(5,400)

Because Caso is personally insolvent, the $19,200 deficit balance will not be repaid and must be absorbed by the remaining three partners on a 4 : 2 : 1 basis.

Andrews, Capital (4⁄7 of loss)				10,971	
Quinn, Capital (2⁄7 of loss)				5,486	
Sheridan, Capital (1⁄7 of loss)				2,743	
Caso, Capital					19,200

To write-off deficit capital balance of insolvent partner.

- This last allocation decreases Sheridan's capital account to a $8,143 negative total. Since this partner is personally solvent, that amount should be contributed to the partnership in accordance with regulations of the Uniform Partnership Act.

Cash				8,143	
Sheridan, Capital					8,143

To record contribution made to eliminate deficit capital balance.

- Sheridan's contribution brings the final cash total for the partnership to $18,143. This amount is distributed to the two partners who continue to maintain positive capital balances: Andrews and Quinn (or Quinn's creditors).

	Andrews, Capital	Quinn, Capital
Balances above	$18,400	$16,200
Caso default	(10,971)	(5,486)
Final balances	$ 7,429	$10,714

Andrews, Capital	7,429	
Quinn, Capital	10,714	
Cash		18,143

To distribute remaining cash according to final capital balances.

Questions

1. What is the difference between the dissolution of a partnership and the liquidation of partnership property?
2. Why would the members of a partnership elect to terminate business operations and liquidate all noncash assets?
3. Why are liquidation gains and losses recorded as direct adjustments to the partners' capital accounts?
4. After liquidating all property and paying partnership obligations, how is the remaining cash allocated among the partners?
5. What is the purpose of a schedule of liquidation? What information does this statement convey to its readers?
6. According to the Uniform Partnership Act, what events should legally occur if a partner incurs a negative capital balance during the liquidation process?
7. How are safe capital balances computed when preliminary distributions of cash are to be made during a partnership liquidation?
8. What is the purpose of the marshaling of assets doctrine? What does this doctrine specifically state?
9. A partner is personally insolvent. Can this partner's creditors lay claim against partnership assets?
10. How do loans from partners affect the distribution of assets in a partnership liquidation?
11. What is the purpose of a proposed schedule of liquidation, and how is it developed?
12. How is a predistribution plan created for a partnership liquidation?

Library Assignment

1. Read the following as well as any other published articles on partnership liquidation:

    "Partnership Dissolution and Accounting," *Chicago Bar Record,* May–June 1982.

    "Breaking Up Is Hard to Do," *Nation's Business,* July 1988.

    "Reconcilable Differences," *Inc.,* April 1991.

    "Cutting Losses When Partners Face a Breakup," *The Wall Street Journal,* May 21, 1991, p. B1.

    "When a Group Is Better Off Splitting Up," *Medical Economics,* March 5, 1984.

    Write a short report describing various situations that lead to the dissolution of a partnership.

2. Read the following as well as any other published articles on the bankruptcy of the partnership of Laventhol & Horwath:

    "Laventhol Says It Plans to File for Chapter 11," *The Wall Street Journal,* November 20, 1990, p. A3.

    "Laventhol Partners Face Long Process that Could End in Personal Bankruptcy," *The Wall Street Journal,* November 20, 1990, p. B5.

    "Laventhol Bankruptcy Filing Indicates Liabilities May Be As Much As $2 Billion," *The Wall Street Journal,* November 23, 1990, p. A4.

    Write a report describing the potential liabilities incurred by the members of a partnership.

Problems

1. If a partnership is liquidated, how is the final allocation of business assets made to the partners?

    a. Equally.

    b. According to the profit and loss ratio.

    c. According to the final capital account balances.

    d. According to the initial investment made by each of the partners.

2. Which of the following statements is true concerning the accounting that is made for a partnership going through liquidation?

    a. Gains and losses are reported directly as increases and decreases in the appropriate capital account.

    b. A separate income statement is created just to measure the profit or loss generated during liquidation.

    c. Since gains and losses rarely occur during liquidation, no special accounting treatment is warranted.

    d. Within a liquidation, all gains and losses are divided equally among the partners.

3. During a liquidation, a partner's capital account balance drops below zero. What *should* happen?

    a. The other partners should file a legal suit against the partner with the deficit balance.

    b. The partner with the highest capital balance should contribute sufficient assets to eliminate the deficit.

    c. The deficit balance should be removed from the accounting records with only the remaining partners sharing in future gains and losses.

    d. The partner with a deficit should contribute enough assets to offset the deficit balance.

4. What is the marshaling of assets?

    a. A listing of all partnership assets that is prepared whenever a formal accounting is to be made.

    b. A ranking of claims to be paid when a partner has become insolvent.

    c. The method by which a retiring partner's share of partnership is determined.

    d. The gathering of partnership assets just prior to the commencement of the liquidation process.

5. A local partnership is in the process of liquidating and is currently reporting the following capital balances:

Angela, capital (50% share of all profits and losses)	$19,000
Woodrow, capital (30%)	18,000
Cassidy, capital (20%)	(12,000)

Cassidy has indicated that the $12,000 deficit will be covered by a forthcoming contribution. However, the two remaining partners have asked to receive the $25,000 in cash that is presently available. How much of this money should each partner be given?

    a. Angela, $13,000; Woodrow, $12,000.

    b. Angela, $11,500; Woodrow, $13,500.

    c. Angela, $12,000; Woodrow, $13,000.

    d. Angela, $12,500; Woodrow, $12,500.

6. A local partnership is considering the possibility of liquidation because one of the partners (Bell) is insolvent. Capital balances at the current time are as follows. Profits and losses are divided on a 4:3:2:1 basis, respectively.

Bell, capital	$50,000
Hardy, capital	56,000
Dennard, capital	14,000
Suddath, capital	80,000

Bell's creditors have filed a $21,000 claim against the partnership's assets. The partnership currently holds assets reported at $300,000 and liabilities of $100,000. If the assets can be sold for $190,000, what is the minimum amount that Bell's creditors would receive?

  a. –0–.
  b. $2,000.
  c. $2,800.
  d. $6,000.

7. What is a predistribution plan?

  a. A guideline for the cash distributions made to partners during a liquidation.
  b. A list of the procedures to be performed during a liquidation.
  c. A determination of the final cash distribution to be made to the partners on the settlement date.
  d. A detailed list of the transactions that will transpire in the reorganization of a partnership.

8. A partnership has the following balance sheet just before final liquidation is to begin:

Cash	$ 26,000	Liabilities	$ 50,000
Inventory	31,000	Art, capital (40% of	
Other assets	62,000	profits and losses)	18,000
		Raymond, capital (30%)	25,000
		Darby, capital (30%)	26,000
Total	$119,000	Total	$119,000

Liquidation expenses are estimated to be $12,000. The other assets are sold for $40,000. What distribution can be made to the partners?

  a. –0– to Art, $1,500 to Raymond, $2,500 to Darby.
  b. $1,333 to Art, $1,333 to Raymond, $1,334 to Darby.
  c. –0– to Art, $1,200 to Raymond, $2,800 to Darby.
  d. $600 to Art, $1,200 to Raymond, $2,200 to Darby.

9. A partnership has the following capital balances: A (20% of profits and losses) = $100,000; B (30% of profits and losses) = $120,000; C (50% of profits and losses) = $180,000. If the partnership is to be liquidated and $30,000 becomes immediately available, who gets that money?

  a. $6,000 to A, $9,000 to B, $15,000 to C.
  b. $22,000 to A, $3,000 to B, $5,000 to C.
  c. $22,000 to A, $8,000 to B, –0– to C.
  d. $24,000 to A, $6,000 to B, –0– to C.

10. A partnership is currently holding $400,000 in assets and $234,000 in liabilities. The partnership is to be liquidated and $20,000 is the best estimation of the expenses that will be incurred during this process. The four partners

share profits and losses on a $4:3:1:2$ basis, respectively. Capital balances at the start of the liquidation are as follows:

Kevin, capital	$59,000
Michael, capital.	39,000
Brendan, capital	34,000
Jonathan, capital	34,000

The partners realize that Brendan will be the first partner to start receiving cash. How much cash will Brendan receive before any of the other partners collect any cash?

a. $12,250.
b. $14,750.
c. $17,000.
d. $19,500.

11. Carney, Pierce, Menton, and Hoehn are partners who share profits and losses on a $4:3:2:1$ basis, respectively. They are presently beginning to liquidate the business. At the start of this process, capital balances are as follows:

Carney, capital	$60,000
Pierce, capital	27,000
Menton, capital	43,000
Hoehn, capital.	20,000

Which of the following statements is true?
a. The first available $2,000 will go to Hoehn.
b. Carney will be the last partner to receive any available cash.
c. The first available $3,000 will go to Menton.
d. Carney will collect a portion of any available cash prior to Hoehn receiving money.

12. A partnership has gone through liquidation and now reports the following account balances:

Cash	$16,000
Loan from Jones	3,000
Wayman, capital	(2,000) (deficit)
Jones, capital	(5,000) (deficit)
Fuller, capital.	13,000
Rogers, capital	7,000

Profits and losses are allocated on the following basis: Wayman, 30 percent; Jones, 20 percent; Fuller, 30 percent; and Rogers, 20 percent. Which of the following events should occur now?

a. Jones should receive $3,000 cash because of the loan balance.

b. Fuller should receive $11,800 and Rogers $6,200.

c. Fuller should receive $10,600 and Rogers $5,400.

d. Jones should receive $3,000, Fuller $8,800, and Rogers $4,200.

13. A partnership has the following account balances: Cash, $70,000; Other Assets, $540,000; Liabilities, $260,000; Nixon (50% of profits and losses), $170,000; Cleveland (30%), $110,000; Pierce (20%), $70,000. The company liquidates and $8,000 becomes available to the partners. Who gets the $8,000?

14. A local partnership has only two assets (cash of $10,000 and land with a cost of $35,000). All liabilities have been paid and the following capital balances are currently being recorded. The partners share profits and losses on a 4:3:3 basis, respectively. All partners are insolvent.

Brown, capital	$25,000
Fish, capital	15,000
Stone, capital	5,000

Required:

a. If the land is sold for $25,000, how much cash does each of the partners receive in a final settlement?

b. If the land is sold for $15,000, how much cash does each of the partners receive in a final settlement?

c. If the land is sold for $5,000, how much cash does each of the partners receive in a final settlement?

15. A local dental partnership has been liquidated and the final capital balances are as follows:

Atkinson, capital (40% of all profits and losses)	$60,000
Kaporale, capital (30%)	20,000
Dennsmore, capital (20%)	(30,000)
Rasputin, capital (10%)	(50,000)

If Rasputin contributes additional cash to partnership of $20,000, what should happen to that money?

16. A partnership currently holds three assets: cash, $10,000 book value; land, $35,000; and a building, $50,000. The partners anticipate that expenses

required to liquidate their partnership will amount to $5,000. Capital balances are as follows:

Ace, capital	$25,000
Ball, capital	28,000
Eaton, capital	20,000
Lake, capital	22,000

The partners share profits and losses as follows: Ace (30%), Ball (30%), Eaton (20%), and Lake (20%). If a preliminary distribution of cash is to be made, how much will each of these partners receive?

17. The following condensed balance sheet is for the partnership of Hardwick, Saunders, and Ferris, who share profits and losses in the ratio of 4:3:3 respectively:

Cash	$ 90,000	Accounts payable	$210,000
Other assets	820,000	Ferris, loan	40,000
Hardwick, loan	30,000	Hardwick, capital	300,000
		Saunders, capital	200,000
		Ferris, capital	190,000
		Total liabilities and	
Total assets	$940,000	capital	$940,000

The partners decide to liquidate the partnership. Forty percent of the other assets are sold for $200,000. Prepare a proposed schedule of liquidation.

18. The following condensed balance sheet is for the partnership of Miller, Tyson, and Watson, who share profits and losses in the ratio of 6:2:2 respectively:

Cash	$ 40,000	Liabilities	$ 70,000
Other assets	140,000	Miller, capital	50,000
		Tyson, capital	50,000
		Watson, capital	10,000
		Total liabilities and	
Total assets	$180,000	capital	$180,000

For how much money do the other assets have to be sold so that each partner receives some amount of cash in a liquidation?

19. A partnership's balance sheet is as follows:

Cash.	$ 60,000	Liabilities	$ 50,000
Noncash assets	120,000	Babb, capital	60,000
		Whitaker, capital	20,000
		Edwards, capital	50,000
		Total liabilities and	
Total assets.	$180,000	capital	$180,000

Babb, Whitaker, and Edwards share profits and losses in the ratio of 4 : 2 : 4, respectively. This business is to be terminated and the partners estimate that $8,000 in liquidation expenses will be incurred. How should the $2,000 in safe cash that is presently held be disbursed?

20. A partnership has liquidated all assets but still reports the following account balances:

Loan from White.	$ 6,000
Black, capital	3,000
White, capital	(9,000) (deficit)
Green, capital	(3,000) (deficit)
Brown, capital	15,000
Blue, capital	(12,000) (deficit)

The partners split profits and losses as follows: Black, 30 percent, White, 30 percent; Green, 10 percent; Brown, 20 percent; and Blue, 10 percent.

Assuming that all partners are personally insolvent except for Green and Brown, how much cash must Green now contribute to this partnership?

21. The following balance sheet is for a local partnership in which the partners have become very unhappy with each other. To avoid further conflict, they have decided to cease operations and sell all assets. Using this data, answer the following questions. Each question should be viewed as an independent situation.

Cash.	$ 40,000	Liabilities	$ 30,000
Land.	130,000	Adams, capital	80,000
Building	120,000	Baker, capital.	30,000
		Carvil, capital.	60,000
		Dobbs, capital	90,000
		Total liabilities and	
Total assets.	$290,000	capital	$290,000

Required:

a. The partnership is to be liquidated and the $10,000 cash that exceeds the partnership liabilities is to be disbursed immediately. If profits and losses are allocated on a 2:3:3:2 basis, respectively, how will the $10,000 be divided?

b. The partnership is to be liquidated and the $10,000 cash that exceeds the partnership liabilities is to be disbursed immediately. If profits and losses are allocated on a 2:2:3:3 basis, respectively, how will the $10,000 be divided?

c. The partnership is to be liquidated. The building is immediately sold for $70,000 to give total cash of $110,000. The liabilities are then paid leaving a cash balance of $80,000. This cash is to be distributed to the partners. How much of this money will each partner get if profits and losses are allocated on a 1:3:3:3 basis, respectively?

d. The partnership is to be liquidated. Assume that profits and losses are allocated on a 1:3:4:2 basis, respectively. How much money must be received from selling the land and building to assure that Carvil receives a portion?

22. The partnership of Larson, Norris, Spencer, and Harrison has decided to terminate operations and liquidate all business property. During this process, the partners expect to incur $8,000 in liquidation expenses. All of the partners are currently solvent.

     The balance sheet reported by this partnership at the time that the liquidation commenced follows. The percentages indicate the allocation of profits and losses to each of the four partners.

Cash.	$ 28,250	Liabilities	$47,000
Accounts receivable	44,000	Larson, capital (20%)	15,000
Inventory	39,000	Norris, capital (30%)	60,000
Land and buildings	23,000	Spencer, capital (20%)	75,000
Equipment	104,000	Harrison, capital (30%)	41,250
		Total liabilities and	
Total assets.	$238,250	capital	$238,250

Required:

Based on the information that has been provided, prepare a predistribution plan for the liquidation of this partnership.

23. The following partnership is being liquidated beginning on July 13, 1995:

Cash.	$ 36,000	Liabilities.	$50,000
Noncash assets	174,000	Able, loan	10,000
		Able, capital (20%)	40,000
		Moon, capital (30%)	60,000
		Yerkl, capital (50%)	50,000

Required:

a. Liquidation expenses are estimated to be $12,000. Prepare a predistribution schedule to guide the distribution of cash.

b. Assume assets costing $28,000 are sold for $40,000. How is the available cash to be divided?

24. A local partnership is to be liquidated. Commissions and other liquidation expenses are expected to total $19,000. The business's balance sheet prior to the commencement of liquidation is as follows:

Cash	$ 27,000	Liabilities	$ 40,000
Noncash assets	254,000	Simpson, capital (20%)	18,000
		Hart, capital (40%)	40,000
		Bobb, capital (20%)	48,000
		Reidl, capital (20%)	135,000
		Total liabilities and	
Total Assets	$281,000	capital	$281,000

Prepare a predistribution schedule for this partnership.

25. The following information concerns two different partnerships. These problems should be viewed as independent situations.

Part A

The partnership of Ross, Milburn, and Thomas has the following account balances:

Cash	$ 36,000	Liabilities	$17,000
Noncash assets	100,000	Ross, capital	69,000
		Milburn, capital	(8,000) (deficit)
		Thomas, capital	58,000

This partnership is in the process of being liquidated. Ross and Milburn are each entitled to 40 percent of all profits and losses with the remaining 20 percent to Thomas.

a. What is the maximum amount that Milburn might have to contribute to this partnership because of the deficit capital balance?

b. How should the $19,000 cash that is presently available in excess of liabilities be distributed?

c. If the noncash assets are sold for a total of $41,000, what is the minimum amount of cash that could be received by Thomas?

Part B

The partnership of Sampson, Klingon, Carton, and Romulan is being liquidated and currently holds cash of $9,000 but no other assets. Liabilities amount to $24,000. The capital balances are as follows:

Sampson	$ 9,000
Klingon	(17,000)
Carton	5,000
Romulan	(12,000)

Profits and losses are allocated on the following basis: Sampson, 40 percent, Klingon, 20 percent, Carton, 30 percent, and Romulan, 10 percent.

a. If both Klingon and Romulan are personally insolvent, how much money does Carton have to contribute to this partnership?

b. If only Romulan is personally insolvent, how much money does Klingon have to contribute? How will these funds be disbursed?

c. If only Klingon is personally insolvent, how much money should Sampson receive from the liquidation?

26. March, April, and May have been in partnership for a number of years. Recently, the partners have each become personally insolvent and, thus, have decided to liquidate the business in hopes of remedying their personal financial problems. The partners allocate all profits and losses on a 2:3:1 basis, respectively. As of September 1, 1995, the partnership balance sheet is as follows:

Cash	$ 11,000	Liabilities	$ 61,000
Accounts receivable	84,000	March, capital	25,000
Inventory	74,000	April, capital.	75,000
Land, building, and equipment		May, capital	46,000
(net)	38,000		
		Total liabilities and	
Total assets	$207,000	capital	$207,000

Prepare journal entries for the following transactions:

- Sold all of the inventory for $56,000 cash.
- Paid $7,500 in liquidation expenses.
- Paid $40,000 of the partnership's liabilities.
- Collected $45,000 of the accounts receivable.
- Safe cash balances are distributed; no further liquidation expenses are anticipated by the partners.

- The remaining accounts receivable are sold for 30 percent of face value.
- The land, building, and equipment are sold for $17,000.
- All remaining liabilities of the partnership are paid.
- The cash held by the business is distributed to the partners.

27. The partnership of W, X, Y, and Z has the following balance sheet:

Cash	$ 30,000	Liabilities	$42,000
Other assets	220,000	W, capital (50% of profits	
		and losses)	60,000
		X, capital (30%)	78,000
		Y, capital (10%)	40,000
		Z, capital (10%).	30,000

Z is personally insolvent and one of his creditors is considering suing the partnership for the $5,000 that is currently due. The creditor realizes that liquidation may result from this litigation and does not wish to force such an extreme action unless reasonably assured of getting the money that is due. If the other assets are sold, how much money must be received by the partnership to ensure that $5,000 would become available from Z's portion of the business? Liquidation expenses are expected to be $15,000.

28. On January 1, 1995, the partners of Van, Bakel, and Cox (who share profits and losses in the ratio of 5 : 3 : 2, respectively) decide to liquidate their partnership. The trial balance at this date is as follows:

	Debit	Credit
Cash	$ 18,000	
Accounts receivable.	66,000	
Inventory	52,000	
Machinery and equipment, net	189,000	
Van, loan	30,000	
Accounts payable.		$ 53,000
Bakel, loan.		20,000
Van, capital		118,000
Bakel, capital.		90,000
Cox, capital		74,000
Totals	$355,000	$355,000

The partners plan a program of piecemeal conversion of the business's assets to minimize liquidation losses. All available cash, less an amount retained to provide for future expenses, is to be distributed to the partners at the end of each month. A summary of the liquidation transactions is as follows:

1995

January
- $51,000 is collected on the accounts receivable; the balance is deemed uncollectible.
- $38,000 is received for the entire inventory.
- $2,000 in liquidation expenses are paid.
- $50,000 is paid to the outside creditors, after offsetting a $3,000 credit memorandum received by the partnership on January 11, 1995.
- $10,000 cash is retained in the business at the end of January to cover any unrecorded liabilities and anticipated expenses. The remainder is distributed to the partners.

February
- $3,000 in liquidation expenses are paid.
- $6,000 cash is retained in the business at the end of the month to cover unrecorded liabilities and anticipated expenses.

March
- $146,000 is received on the sale of all machinery and equipment.
- $5,000 in final liquidation expenses are paid.
- No cash is retained in the business.

Required:

Prepare a schedule to compute the safe installment payments made to the partners at the end of each of these three months.

(AICPA adapted)

29. Following are a series of independent cases. In each situation, indicate the cash distribution to be made at the end of the liquidation process. *Unless otherwise stated, assume that all solvent partners will reimburse the partnership for their deficit capital balances.*

Part A

The following accounts are presently being reported by the Simon, Haynes, and Jackson partnership:

Cash	$30,000
Liabilities.	22,000
Haynes, loan	10,000
Simon, capital (40%).	16,000
Haynes, capital (20%)	(6,000)
Jackson, capital (40%)	(12,000)

Jackson is personally insolvent and can contribute only an additional $3,000 to the partnership. Simon is also insolvent and has no available funds.

Part B

Hough, Luck, and Cummings operate a local accounting firm as a partnership. After working together for several years, they have decided to liquidate the partnership's property. The partners have prepared the following balance sheet:

Cash	$ 20,000	Liabilities	$ 40,000
Hough, loan	8,000	Luck, loan	10,000
Noncash assets	162,000	Hough, capital (50%)	90,000
		Luck, capital (40%)	30,000
		Cummings, capital (10%)	20,000
		Total liabilities and	
Total assets	$190,000	capital	$190,000

The noncash assets are sold for $80,000, with $21,000 of this amount being used to pay liquidation expenses. All three of these partners are personally insolvent.

Part C

Use the same information as in part B, except assume that the profits and losses are split 2:4:4 to Hough, Luck, and Cummings, respectively and that liquidation expenses are only $6,000.

Part D

Following the liquidation of all noncash assets, the partnership of Redmond, Ledbetter, Watson, and Sandridge has the following account balances:

Liabilities	$28,000
Redmond, loan	5,000
Redmond, capital (20%)	(21,000)
Ledbetter, capital (10%)	(30,000)
Watson, capital (30%)	3,000
Sandridge, capital (40%)	15,000

Redmond is personally insolvent.

30. The partnership of Frick, Wilson, and Clarke has elected to cease all operations and liquidate its business property. A balance sheet drawn up at this time shows the following account balances:

Cash	$ 48,000	Liabilities	$ 35,000
Noncash assets	177,000	Frick, capital (60%)	101,000
		Wilson, capital (20%)	28,000
		Clarke, capital (20%)	61,000
		Total liabilities and	
Total assets	$225,000	capital	$225,000

The following transactions occur in liquidating this business:

- Safe capital balances are immediately distributed to the partners. Liquidation expenses of $9,000 are estimated as a basis for this computation.
- Noncash assets with a book value of $80,000 are sold for $48,000.
- All liabilities are paid.
- Safe capital balances are again distributed.
- Remaining noncash assets are sold for $44,000.
- Liquidation expenses of $7,000 are paid.
- Remaining cash is distributed to the partners and the financial records of the business permanently closed.

Required:

Produce a final schedule of liquidation for this partnership.

31. **Part A**

The partnership of Wingler, Norris, Rodgers, and Guthrie was formed several years ago as a local architectural firm. Several of the partners have recently undergone personal financial problems, and decided to terminate operations and liquidate the business. The following balance sheet is drawn up as a guideline for this process:

Cash	$ 15,000	Liabilities	$ 74,000
Accounts receivable	82,000	Rodgers, loan	35,000
Inventory	101,000	Wingler, capital (30%)	120,000
Land	85,000	Norris, capital (10%)	88,000
Building and equipment (net)	168,000	Rodgers, capital (20%)	74,000
		Guthrie, capital (40%)	60,000
		Total liabilities and	
Total assets	$451,000	capital	$451,000

At the time the liquidation commences, expenses of $16,000 are anticipated as being necessary to dispose of all property.

Required:

Prepare a predistribution plan for this partnership.

Part B

The following transactions transpire during the liquidation of the Wingler, Norris, Rodgers, and Guthrie partnership:

- Of the total accounts receivable, 80 percent are collected with the rest judged as uncollectible.
- The land, building, and equipment are sold for $150,000.
- Safe capital distributions are made.
- Guthrie becomes personally insolvent. No further contributions will be forthcoming from this partner.
- All liabilities are paid.
- All inventory is sold for $71,000.
- Safe capital distributions are again made.
- Liquidation expenses of $11,000 are paid.
- Final cash disbursements are made to the partners based on the assumption that all partners other than Guthrie are personally solvent.

Required:

Prepare journal entries to record these liquidation transactions.

ACCOUNTING FOR STATE AND LOCAL GOVERNMENTS (PART ONE)

Questions to Consider

- Why is the accounting for state and local governments significantly different than that used by profit-oriented businesses?
- Who are the users of the financial data produced by state and local government units, and why is such a wide variety of informational needs encountered?
- What is fund accounting, and why is it utilized by state and local governments?
- Why is budgetary control considered so important in a government? In what ways is budgetary control established in the accounting system?
- How has the Governmental Accounting Standards Board affected the financial reporting of state and local governments?
- Why are encumbrances recorded by a government?
- When are revenues and expenditures recognized by a government?

- The June 30, 1990, balance sheet produced for the city of Albuquerque, New Mexico, disclosed a reserve for encumbrances totaling approximately $23.5 million.
- On that same date, the city of Wilmington, Delaware, reported an undesignated fund balance within the city's General Fund of more than $2.2 million.
- The city of Syracuse, New York, presented a 1990 statement of revenues, expenditures, and changes in fund balances composed of six separate columns while the accompanying balance sheet presented financial information in nine columns.

The accounting curriculum offered at many colleges is designed primarily to provide students with an understanding of the financial reporting procedures appropriate for profit-oriented enterprises. In most accounting courses, virtually every issue is analyzed in terms of the potential impact on net income and earnings per share. Textbooks contribute to this emphasis by examining numerous authoritative pronouncements that establish rigid guidelines for the recognition of revenues and expenses. Consequently, the calculation of the bottom-line figure may appear to be the ultimate objective of all accounting.

For this reason, students are frequently surprised to discover that the basic structure of financial accounting is altered dramatically when the profit motive is removed. Many accounting principles applied by the city of Syracuse, for example, vary from the principles used by Exxon Corporation. The existence of different generally accepted accounting principles is especially significant in that one third of the economic activity in the United States is conducted by nonbusiness organizations.[1] Thus, despite the apparently obscured role of governments and not-for-profit organizations within many accounting courses, coverage is no less important than that provided for profit-oriented businesses.

As indicated by the data just presented for Albuquerque, Wilmington, and Syracuse, the reporting process for state and local governments exhibits many unique characteristics. The balance sheet, as an example, usually displays numerous columns while both actual and budgetary balances are presented for many of the government's revenues and expenditures. Even the accounting terminology may appear initially to resemble a foreign language. In reporting on state and local governments, such alien terms as *fund accounting, encumbrances, nonexpendable trust funds, special revenue funds,* and *appropriations* are all quite commonplace.

Despite many special features, the accounting process applicable to state and local governments is no different in one important respect from any other type of accounting: *the overall objective is to satisfy the needs of financial statement users.* The procedures and terminology deviate from for-profit reporting primarily because the informational requirements of these users are assumed to be different. Thus, the composition of published financial statements has evolved to conform to these perceived needs.

Historically, the development of governmental accounting standards has proceeded more slowly than that of profit-oriented financial reporting. Even today, the production of authoritative accounting principles could be said to be still in its infancy. However, the recent work of the Governmental Accounting Standards Board has pushed government accounting into a highly evolutionary stage. Significant changes in both accounting and reporting have been mandated in recent years with other steps proposed. Proposals to alter the very focus of financial reporting for governments have been debated during the 1990s. The ultimate benefits that result from this current evolution may take years if not decades to judge.

---

[1] Robert N. Anthony, "Making Sense of Nonbusiness Accounting," *Harvard Business Review,* May–June 1980, p. 84.

Consequently, much discussion continues to be generated as to whether user needs are being met by current financial reporting. If not, what changes are needed? Questions are constantly raised and discussed about the propriety of many common practices found in governmental accounting as well as proposed improvements. Thus, controversy still surrounds many elements of the reporting process demonstrated herein.

Chapters 15 and 16 provide an introduction to the accounting for state and local governments (cities, towns, school districts, counties, states, and the like). However, for many aspects of this coverage, current standards as well as proposals for future financial reporting are presented.

Introduction to the Accounting for State and Local Governments

In this country, literally thousands of state and local government reporting entities exist, touching the lives of the citizenry on a daily basis. Income and sales taxes are collected, property taxes are assessed, schools are operated, fire departments are maintained, garbage is collected, and roads are paved. Actions of one or more governments affect every individual. Accounting for a government is not merely a matching of expenses with revenues so that net income can be determined. For many governments, deficit spending has become a troubling practice. The allocation of resources between such worthy causes as education, police, welfare, and the environment has created a national debate. Some services have had to be curtailed. In recent times, citizens have come to realize that additional oversight is needed so that governments are required to live within their means while still making the best use of available funding.

Over the years, a number of attempts have been made to establish generally accepted accounting principles for state and local governments. The American Institute of Certified Public Accountants (AICPA) and the National Council on Governmental Accounting (NCGA) made some significant strides during previous decades in establishing sound accounting principles.[2] More recently, in June of 1984, the Governmental Accounting Standards Board (GASB) began. The GASB has been given the primary responsibility in the United States for setting authoritative accounting standards for state and local government units.

In the same manner as the Financial Accounting Standards Board, the GASB is an independent body functioning under the oversight of the Financial Account-

---

[2] The NCGA was a quasi-independent agency of the Government Finance Officers Association. The NCGA held authority for state and local government accounting from 1973 through 1984. The National Committee on Municipal Accounting had this responsibility from 1934 until 1941 while the National Committee on Governmental Accounting established government accounting principles from 1949 through 1954 and again from 1967 until 1973. During several periods, no group held responsibility for the development of governmental accounting. An overview of the history of governmental accounting standards and the creation of the GASB can be found in "The Evolution of Governmental Accounting Standard Setting," by David R. Bean published in the December 1984 issue of *Governmental Finance*.

ing Foundation. Thus, a formal mechanism is in place to continue the appropriate development of governmental accounting. Since its creation, the GASB has produced a number of governmental accounting standards as well as technical bulletins, interpretations, and a concepts statement. In 1987, GASB produced a codification of authoritative pronouncements as a guideline for reporting purposes.

The board's most aggressive action came in 1990 with the release of its *Statement 11,* "Measurement Focus and Basis of Accounting—Governmental Fund Operating Statements." This pronouncement was designed to create a massive directional change in the emphasis of state and local government accounting to an approach more akin to that used for profit-oriented businesses. Not surprisingly, *GASB 11* generated an enormous amount of debate and considerable criticism.

> "We have gone on record twice asking the board to put off implementing *Statement No. 11* (until) issuance of broader financial reporting standards," said Bill Melton, treasurer of Dallas County, Texas, and representative of the National Association of Counties on a GASB advisory board. In seeking delay, NACO was joined by some of the public finance industry's heaviest hitters. They include the Government Finance Officers Association, the International City/County Management Association, the National Conference on State Legislatures and the U.S. Conference of Mayors. . . . The *Statement No. 11* project would have been the opening salvo in GASB's war on unclear and misleading government financial statements. It is part of the larger Financial Reporting Model, which would move governments closer to an accrual based system of accounting.[3]

GASB 11 was originally scheduled to become effective for all fiscal years beginning after June 15, 1994. Because of the controversy over both its release and the pronouncements that might have followed, that date has now been delayed indefinitely until the implementation of the reporting provisions of *GASB 11* can be determined. *GASB 11* will probably not become effective for several years and may be revised somewhat prior to that time.

GASB 11

State and local government accounting principles have been created piecemeal over the decades with no central focus (such as the determination of net income). Procedures have tended to stress the measurement of current inflows and outflows of monetary assets and liabilities. Government accounting has frequently been referred to (usually derisively) as shoe-box accounting because of its emphasis on monitoring the movement of cash and other monetary resources into and out of the government.

GASB 11 was created to provide a measurement focus that would answer three questions about the reporting of state and local government units:

- What is being expressed?
- Which resources are measured?

---

[3] Susan J. Craig, "Few Backers for Postponement of GASB Revisions," *Public Finance/Washington Watch,* January 18, 1993, p. 10.

• When are the effects of transactions recognized (what is the basis of accounting)?

In *Statement 11,* the GASB holds that governmental fund operating statements should measure and report *the flow of financial resources.* Financial resources are defined by this pronouncement as cash, claims to cash, claims to goods and services, and equity securities. The basis of accounting should be accrual accounting so that transactions and events that affect financial resources are recognized when they take place, regardless of the impact on cash. This measurement focus was established by the GASB as the best approach for reporting *interperiod equity,* "the measure of whether current-year revenues were sufficient to pay for current-year services. A measure of interperiod equity would show whether current-year citizens received services but shifted part of the payment burden to future-year citizens or used up previously accumulated resources."[4]

The provisions of *GASB 11* have been both highly praised and severely criticized. Many users of governmental financial statements have long called for improvement in the reporting process. They view *GASB 11* and its implementation as necessary conditions for generating useful and understandable financial information. However, accounting changes often tend to be resisted by those parties directly impacted. As indicated, the provisions of *GASB 11* have been delayed, perhaps permanently. At least for the time, government units continue to apply previously accepted accounting principles. Consequently, throughout sections of Chapters 15 and 16, two approaches are demonstrated: the method commonly used prior to *GASB 11* along with the requirements of this new pronouncement.

At best, the actual impact of *GASB 11* and its measurement focus and basis of accounting will not be felt for sometime. Unfortunately, achieving improvement in accounting for state and local governments may never be an easy task for the GASB. Unless a government unit is required to have an independent audit, compliance with official pronouncements is a voluntary matter. Even with an audit, a qualified opinion may be accepted by a government rather than abandoning the traditional method of reporting. In addition, the accounting systems in use by many governments might simply not be sophisticated enough to produce required data. Because of budget constraints, governments may be unwilling to pay for necessary upgrades. Thus, in its efforts to improve governmental accounting by establishing the flow of financial resources measurement focus, the GASB faces a number of problems other than just the creation of accounting principles.

Governmental Accounting—User Needs

The unique aspects of governmental accounting are a direct result of the perceived needs of financial statement users. Identification of these informational requirements is, therefore, a logical first step in the study of the accounting principles

---

[4] Governmental Accounting Standards Board *Statement No. 11,* "Measurement Focus and Basis of Accounting—Governmental Fund Operating Statements," May 1990, para. 3k.

applied by state and local governments. Specific procedures utilized in the reporting process can best be understood as an outgrowth of these needs. Often, though, user expectations are complex and even contradictory. The taxpayer, the government employee, the bondholder, and the public official may each be seeking distinctly different types of financial information about a governmental unit.

> My own reflection on the subject leads me to the conviction that appropriate and adequate accounting for state and local governmental units involves a far more complex set of interrelationships, to be reported to a more diverse set of users with a greater variety of interests and needs, than exists in business accounting and reporting.[5]

In its *Concepts Statement No. 1,* "Objectives of Financial Reporting," the GASB recognized this same problem by identifying three groups of primary users of external state and local governmental financial reports: the citizenry, legislative and oversight bodies, and creditors and investors. The needs and interests of each of these groups were then described:

> **Citizenry**—Want to evaluate the likelihood of tax or service fee increases, to determine the sources and uses of resources, to forecast revenues in order to influence spending decisions, to ensure that resources were used in accordance with appropriations, to assess financial condition, and to compare budgeted to actual results.
> **Legislative and oversight bodies**—Want to assess the overall financial condition when developing budgets and program recommendations, to monitor operating results to assure compliance with mandates, to determine the reasonableness of fees and the need for tax changes, and to ascertain the ability to finance new programs and capital needs.
> **Investors and creditors**—Want to know the amount of available and likely future financial resources, to measure the debt position and the ability to service that debt, and to review operating results and cash flow data.[6]

Thus, a significant obstacle is encountered in the quest for fair governmental reporting: user needs are so broad that no one set of financial statements or accounting principles can possibly satisfy all expectations. How can voters, bondholders, city officials, and the other users of the financial statements provided by state and local governments all receive the information that is needed? The question of satisfying a wide variety of user needs is a constant theme in discussions of state and local government accounting.

Accountability and Governmental Accounting

Despite the variety of users, one aspect of governmental reporting has remained constant over the years: the goal of making the government accountable to the public. Because of the essential role of democracy within American society, gov-

---

[5] Robert K. Mautz, "Financial Reporting: Should Government Emulate Business?" *Journal of Accountancy,* August 1981, p. 53.

[6] *GASB Concepts Statement No. 1,* "Objectives of Financial Reporting," May 1987, para. 33–37.

ernmental accounting principles have always attempted to provide a vehicle for evaluating the actions of the government. Citizens should be aware of the sources used by officials to raise money and the allocations made of these scarce resources. Voters must evaluate the wisdom, as well as the honesty, of the members of government. Since most voters are also taxpayers, they naturally exhibit special interest in the results obtained from their involuntary contributions. *Because elected and appointed officials hold authority over the public's money, governmental reporting has traditionally stressed this stewardship responsibility.*

> Accountability is the cornerstone of all financial reporting in government. . . . Accountability requires governments to answer to the citizenry—to justify the raising of public resources and the purposes for which they are used. Governmental accountability is based on the belief that the citizenry has a "right to know," a right to receive openly declared facts that may lead to public debate by the citizens and their elected representatives.[7]

For this reason, primary accounting emphasis has traditionally been directed toward measuring and identifying the public funds generated and expended by each of a government's diverse activities. To meet this objective, the financial statements attempt to answer three questions:

- Where did the financial resources come from?
- Where did the financial resources go?
- What amount of financial resources is presently held?

Obviously, stressing government accountability is an approach to accounting that is not capable of meeting all user needs; thus, many conventional reporting objectives have long been ignored. As just one example, little information has historically been required of a state or local government that would allow an assessment of projected cash flows. Not surprisingly, investors and creditors have frequently been sharp critics of governmental accounting. "When cities get into financial trouble, few citizens know about it until the day the interest can't be met or the teachers paid. . . . Had the books been kept like any decent corporation's that could never have happened."[8]

These arguments have undoubtedly provided some of the support for the work of the GASB, especially in its *Statement No. 11*. Although accountability is a central concern, other user needs must be addressed. The debate will continue for many years concerning the future evolution of accounting principles for state and local government units. However, regardless of the actions of the GASB or other bodies, accountability will undoubtedly remain a primary priority for the financial reports issued by state and local government units. The need to oversee and control elected officials simply must play a central role in the development of government accounting standards.

---

[7] *GASB Concepts Statement No. 1*, para. 56.
[8] Richard Greene, "You Can't Fight City Hall—If You Can't Understand It," *Forbes*, March 3, 1980, p. 92.

Control of Public Funds

The attempt to establish financial control over public funds goes beyond the mere monitoring of financial resources. Over the years, a complete set of procedures has been created to report the financial affairs of the vast array of functions carried out by state and local government units. This process is especially important since public officials often hold authority over sums of money that can be staggering in size. The city of Saint Paul, Minnesota, for example, reported revenues of more than $250 million for the year ending December 31, 1991. Such funds are accumulated through tolls and taxes, frequently accompanied by only a limited amount of direct public oversight. Although laws require the appropriate utilization of such monies, compliance is not always easy for the average citizen to ascertain.

Stressing accountability and the stewardship role played by government officials is in diametric contrast to a profit-oriented business where stockholders contribute capital voluntarily and then elect a board of directors to monitor operating and financial activities. Board members along with stockholders and any other interested parties have access to accounting data, such as net income, earnings per share, and return on investment, which allows an assessment to be made of management's utilization of the resources provided. In a government, though, oversight and computed measures of success are more difficult to achieve. For example, neither net income nor earnings per share can be computed for a fire department.

To compensate for the lack of business-style oversight, governmental accounting has developed its own specialized control procedures. Budgets, for example, must be legally adopted by a government's legislative body to indicate anticipated revenues and approved expenditures. To highlight these projections, many of the budget figures are physically entered into the government's accounting records and then presented as a component of the annual financial statements. In this manner, comparisons can be drawn between the expected activity for each specific function and actual revenue and expenditure figures.

Additional control over government spending is achieved by recording purchase commitments (commonly referred to as *encumbrances*). The acquisition of a typewriter, for example, is formally journalized as an encumbrance at the time the item is ordered rather than when the title transfers. By measuring both expended as well as committed funds, the entity is less likely to overspend available resources. Unfortunately, neither budgetary entries nor encumbrances have proven to be totally successful in eliminating the possibility of excessive government spending.

Reporting Diverse Governmental Activities—Fund Accounting

Beyond the goal of establishing accountability and fiscal control, the accountant also faces the challenge of reporting the diverse array of activities that exist within most government units. Because no common profit motive exists to tie all of these functions and services together, consolidated balances have traditionally been omitted. Combining the financial data from the city zoo, the fire department, the motor pool, the water system, and the like would provide a mixture of figures of questionable utility.[9] Instead, an underlying assumption of government accounting is that most statement users prefer information segregated by function so that each activity can be assessed individually. Hence, the accounting process is constructed to accumulate separate data to describe the financial affairs of every activity (library, school system, police department, road construction, etc.). The revenues, expenditures, financial resources, and the like can then be reported for each specific function.

The diversity inherent in most state or local government units mandates that a single set of accounting records is simply not sufficient to monitor all activities. Therefore, financial transactions and adjustments are recorded in quasiindependent bookkeeping systems referred to as funds. *Each fund is a self-balancing set of accounts that is used to record data generated by an identifiable government function. All of these funds taken together make up the government's financial reporting system.* Accounting for an entity as a group of funds is probably the single most unique element of governmental and not-for-profit accounting.

> The diverse nature of governmental operations and the necessity of assuring legal compliance preclude recording and summarizing all governmental financial transactions and balances in a single accounting entity. Unlike a private business, which is accounted for as a single entity, a governmental unit is accounted for through several separate fund and account group entities, each accounting for designated assets, liabilities, and equity or other balances.[10]

Although a single list of separately reportable functions of a state or local government is not possible, the following are commonly encountered:

Public safety	Judicial system
Highway maintenance	Debt repayment
Sanitation	Bridge construction
Health	Water and sewer system
Welfare	Municipal swimming pool
Culture and recreation	Data processing center
Education	Endowment funds
Parks	Employee pensions

The actual number of funds in use depends on the extent of services being offered by the government and the grouping of related activities. For example,

---

[9] Failure to consolidate the financial statements of a state or government unit has often been criticized, especially by individuals seeking statements more in line with business-oriented accounting. "When those accustomed to business financial statements try to read the financial statements of a nonbusiness organization, however, they find themselves in a different world. Instead of a report on the entity as a whole, they find fragmented data, presented in columns on a single statement, or in a succession of separate statements, each of which deals with a piece of the organization." (Robert N. Anthony, "Making Sense of Nonbusiness Accounting," *Harvard Business Review*, May–June 1980, p. 83.

[10] *Codification of Governmental Accounting and Financial Reporting Standards* (Norwalk, Conn.: Governmental Accounting Standards Board, 1992), sec. 1300.101.

separate funds may be set up for a high school and its athletic programs or all of these activities may be combined into a single fund. The National Council on Governmental Accounting (NCGA) recommended (and the GASB reaffirmed) that a "minimum number of funds consistent with legal and operating requirements should be established, however, because unnecessary funds result in inflexibility, undue complexity, and inefficient financial administration."[11]

If a government only had to account for service activities such as police and fire protection, reporting problems could be minimized. Although establishing separate funds would still be necessary for the individual functions, accounting procedures could be similar in each case, if not identical. Within these various funds, the emphasis would be placed on control and accountability through the reporting of revenues and expenditures relating to the specified service.

However, many government operations do exist (such as municipal golf courses, toll roads, convention centers, and airports) that attempt to generate revenues rather than simply serve the populace. Because this goal parallels that held by business-type enterprises, traditional government accounting procedures are not considered applicable to these functions. In effect, a municipality cannot report the activities of a police department and a golf course by using the same accounting principles; the objectives are simply too diverse.

To add to the accountant's difficulty, a third distinct type of government function (beyond service activities and revenue generating enterprises) can also be identified. State and local governments frequently serve in a trustee capacity, holding money or other assets to be used for a particular purpose. Employee pension funds, for example, are often maintained so that government workers can receive benefits after their retirement.

A similar trustee role is served if the government administers any property that has been received through donation. In some instances, the government intends to do no more than ensure an appropriate utilization of the gift. Therefore, the receipt and its ultimate use are accounted for jointly as a service activity. Money given to a city to buy school equipment falls into this category. At other times, though, the trustee capacity takes on a distinct business appearance. Assets (such as rental property, for example) can be donated to a government with the stipulation that only subsequently earned income is to be spent. To satisfy this provision, income measurement becomes a primary objective in fulfilling the government's fiduciary role.

Fund Accounting Classifications

Because of the sheer number of activities carried out by many government units, designing distinct accounting procedures for each fund is neither feasible nor even desirable. Instead, to facilitate the reporting process, a grouping system has been devised with all funds being placed into one of three broad classifications:

---

[11] GASB Cod. sec. 1100.104.

e.g. school system

- *Governmental funds*—account for "those activities of a government that are carried out primarily to provide services to citizens and that are financed primarily through taxes and intergovernmental revenues."[12] A school system would be reported within the governmental funds.

e.g. Toll road

- *Proprietary funds*—account for "a government's ongoing organizations and activities that are similar to those often found in the private sector."[13] This fund type normally encompasses operations where a user charge is assessed. A toll road would be reported within the proprietary funds.

e.g. Pensions

- *Fiduciary funds*—account for monies held by the government in a trustee capacity. A pension plan would be reported within the fiduciary funds.

A fourth category referred to as *account groups* also exists in connection with the governmental funds to provide a listing of both general fixed assets and long-term debts. These account groups provide control and accountability over these assets and liabilities. Since resources are neither received nor expended by the account groups, they are not viewed as funds in the definitional sense. However, these two groups play an integral role in the government's reporting system.

Governmental Funds. In most state or municipal accounting systems, the governmental funds tend to dominate because a service orientation usually prevails. For reporting purposes, individual records are maintained for every distinct function: public safety, education, construction of a town hall, and so on. In each of these governmental funds, financial resources are accumulated and expended to achieve one or more desired public goals.

To provide better reported information and control as well as to allow for the development of more precise accounting principles, the governmental funds are subdivided into four categories: the General Fund, Special Revenue Funds, Capital Projects Funds, and Debt Service Funds. Although the basic accounting objectives are the same for each of these fund types, actual procedures may vary depending on the nature of the service. Thus, this classification system allows specific accounting guidelines to be directed toward each fund type while providing an overall structure for financial reporting purposes.

The General Fund. The GASB's definition of the General Fund appears to be somewhat understated: "to account for all financial resources except those required to be accounted for in another fund."[14] This description seems to imply that the General Fund records only miscellaneous revenues and expenditures when, in actuality, this fund type accounts for many of a government's most important services. Whereas the other governmental funds report specific events or projects, the General Fund records a broad range of ongoing activities. For

[12] *GASB Statement No. 11,* par. 3h.

[13] GASB Cod. sec. 1300.102b.

[14] GASB Cod. sec. 1300.104

example, the financial statements for the city of Hartford, Connecticut, disclose eight major areas of current expenditures within the General Fund: general government, public safety, physical services, community development and planning, human services, education, transportation, and sundry. Expenditures recorded in the General Fund of this city made up 76.3 percent of the total for all of the governmental funds.

Special Revenue Funds.   Special revenue funds account for revenues that have been legally restricted as to expenditure. These financial resources must be spent in a specified fashion. Saint Paul, Minnesota, for example, reported approximately $60 million of revenues within special revenue funds during the 1991 fiscal year. This money was generated from more than 40 sources as diverse as cable television franchising fees, rent received from the use of Municipal Stadium, administration fees for charitable gambling, grants used for police training, and the sale of zoo animals. The Special Revenue Funds category accounts for these monies because *legal restrictions had been attached to the revenue to require that expenditure be limited to specific purposes.*[15]

Capital Projects Funds.   As the title implies, this fund type accounts for costs incurred in acquiring or constructing major government facilities such as bridges, high schools, roads, or municipal office complexes. Funding for these projects is normally derived from grants, the sale of bonds, or is transferred from general revenues. The actual asset is not recorded here but merely the money to finance the purchase or construction along with the actual expenditure. For example, at June 30, 1990, the city of Chattanooga, Tennessee, reported 17 different items within its Capital Projects Funds, including airport projects, storm sewer construction, and street projects. For the storm sewer construction, as an example, $496,000 had been expended during the previous year with $308,000 in assets currently being held for that project.

Debt Service Funds.   These funds serve to record monies accumulated to pay long-term liabilities and interest as they come due.[16] However, this fund type does not account for a government's long-term debt. Rather, debt service funds monitor the financial resources currently available to satisfy long-term liabilities and also record the eventual payment. Thus, on June 30, 1989, the city of Philadelphia, Pennsylvania, reported more than $288 million of cash and investments in its debt service funds but not one dollar of accompanying long-term debt. This same fund reported the expenditure of $320 million during the previous year to cover principal and interest payments.

---

[15] As an example, the city council of Saint Paul had specified that any money collected from the sale of zoo animals had to be spent to acquire new animals. Thus, any resources received from this source are monitored by inclusion in the special revenue funds until properly expended.

[16] Some state and local governments choose to maintain assets for debt service within the General Fund rather than in a separate category. This approach is acceptable, especially if the amounts are relatively small.

Proprietary Funds. The proprietary funds account for ongoing activities similar to those found in the business world. To facilitate financial reporting, the proprietary funds are broken down into two major divisions:

Enterprise Funds. Any government operation that is financed, at least in part, by outside user charges is classified as an Enterprise Fund. A municipality, for example, may generate revenues from the use of a public swimming pool, golf course, airport, water and sewage service, and the like. As an illustration, the city of Chicago, Illinois, reports the operation of O'Hare International Airport within its enterprise funds. In some cases, though, heavily subsidized activities such as mass transit may be viewed as either governmental funds or proprietary funds.

Because customers are assessed direct fees, enterprise fund activities resemble businesses. Not surprisingly, the accounting process parallels that found in for-profit reporting. Virtually none of the unique aspects of governmental accounting apply to this category.

Internal Service Funds. This second proprietary fund is used to account for any operation that provides services to another department or agency within the government on a cost-reimbursement basis. As with Enterprise Funds, fees are charged but the service is performed for the benefit of the government rather than for outside users. The city of Richmond, Virginia, for example, lists eight operations in its 1990 financial statements that are accounted for as separate internal service funds:

> Warehouse—provides office supplies.
> Automotive maintenance—provides for repairs and maintenance of city-owned vehicles.
> Central duplicating service—provides copying services.
> Telecommunications—provides telephone and other communication services.
> Central postage service—provides mailroom services.
> Automotive leased equipment—owns and leases vehicles to other departments and agencies.
> Public works stores—provides supplies of a bulk nature such as sand, bricks, and construction materials.
> Richmond school board warehouse—provides supplies for the public schools.

Fiduciary Funds. The final classification, the fiduciary funds (also referred to as Trust and Agency Funds), accounts for assets held in a trustee capacity. Four distinct types of fiduciary funds can exist within a government's accounting system:

Expendable Trust Funds. Used to account for resources donated to a government for a specified purpose where both the principal and any future earnings may be spent. A certificate of deposit given to a city to build a tennis court, for example, falls into this category since both the gift and subsequent income can be used for the designated project. As an illustration, the city of Amarillo, Texas, reported 11 separate expendable trust funds as of September 30, 1990, holding assets totaling nearly $1 million. These resources had been given by various groups and individuals in hopes of accomplishing a number of community goals. For example, $2,648 was held in a indigent dog bite victim trust used "to account for a private contribution made for the purpose of providing medical attention for indigent dog bite victims."

Governments are warned, however, not to overuse this designation. "Governments often classify activities as Expendable Trust Funds when they could be as easily accounted for in either the General Fund or in a Special Revenue Fund. If a formal trust agreement is not established, the trust fund classification should not be used." [17]

Nonexpendable Trust Funds.   Because they monitor resources donated to a government for a specific project where only the subsequent earnings may be expended, the principal of such funds must be left intact. This fund type would be utilized, as an example, to record a monetary gift made to a library with the provision that all income derived from this principal be spent on the purchase of books. In fact, the city of Walla Walla, Washington, has four nonexpendable trust funds including the Eyraud Endowment, a donation made with the stipulation that the income must be spent for children's books and sports reference books for the city's library.

Pension Trust Funds.   Accounts for an employee retirement system. Because of the need to provide adequate benefits for government workers, this fund type can grow to be quite large. The city of Richmond, Virginia, as an example, reported assets of more than $198 million in its pension trust fund at the end of 1990.

Agency Funds.   Used to record any resources held by a government as an agent for individuals or other government units. Taxes and tolls, for example, are occasionally collected by one body on behalf of another. To ensure safety and control, this money should be separately maintained in an Agency Fund until transferred to the proper authority.

The GASB provides specific accounting guidance for the reporting of these four fiduciary funds: "Expendable trust funds are accounted for in essentially the same manner as governmental funds. Nonexpendable trust funds and pension trust funds are accounted for in essentially the same manner as proprietary funds. Agency funds are purely custodial (assets equal liabilities) and thus do not involve measurement of results of operations." [18]

---

[17] Paul E. Glick, *Fund Structure Including Interfund Transactions* (Chicago: Government Finance Officers Association, 1987), p. 12.

[18] GASB Cod. sec. 1300.102.

The utilization here of more than one accounting approach is in recognition of the essential differences among the various Trust and Agency Funds. Determination of income is important in both Nonexpendable Trust Funds and Pension Trust Funds; therefore, financial reporting (like that of Enterprise Funds and Internal Service Funds) resembles that of for-profit businesses. In contrast, since all resources can be spent in an Expendable Trust Fund, computation of net income is not necessary. Consequently, governmental fund accounting principles are utilized. Agency Funds normally have only two transactions (the creation of a liability and its payment) so that specific accounting procedures are not required.

Coverage of Fund Accounting Procedures. The formal classification system just described is extremely useful in the financial reporting of a state or local government. However, an understanding of appropriate accounting procedures can best be achieved by labeling each fund type as either a governmental-type or a business-type:

Governmental-Type Funds	*Business-Type Funds*
Governmental funds:	Proprietary funds:
General Fund	Enterprise Funds
Special Revenue Funds	Internal Service Funds
Capital Projects Funds	
Debt Service Funds	Fiduciary funds:
Fiduciary funds:	Nonexpendable Trust Funds
Expendable Trust Funds	Pension Trust Funds

The reporting process utilized by the five government-type funds is examined in this chapter while the four business-type funds are analyzed in Chapter 16. Also presented there are accounting procedures used in the remaining fund category, the Agency Funds, although they are limited to recording an asset inflow and its subsequent disbursement.

Accounting for Governmental-Type Funds

The remainder of this chapter is designed to present many of the unique aspects of the accounting process utilized within the governmental-type funds: the General Fund, Special Revenue Funds, Capital Projects Funds, Debt Service Funds, and Expendable Trust Funds. The reporting principles for these funds have been developed without an underlying profit motive. Thus, the distinguishing features described here often fail to correspond to procedures traditionally associated with the financial accounting utilized by for-profit businesses.

For organizational purposes, coverage of governmental-type funds includes the following discussions, events, and transactions:

- The importance of budgets and the recording of budgetary entries.
- The recognition of expenditures for expenses and capital assets.
- The recognition of revenues.
- The sale of bonds: capital debt and operating debt.
- The accounting for the special assessment of citizens.
- The recording of interfund transactions.
- The purpose of, and accounting for, encumbrances.
- The reporting of fund equity.

Each of these elements is an important aspect of the accounting process for the governmental-type funds of a state or local government. Knowledge of the reporting of each of these elements is an essential first step in arriving at an understanding of governmental accounting.

The Importance of Budgets and the Recording of Budgetary Entries

"Financing is an important part of the governmental environment, particularly for governmental-type activities. For those activities, the budget is the primary method of directing and controlling the financial process."[19] In a chronological sense, the first significant accounting procedure encountered in a state or locality is the recording of budgetary entries. To enhance accountability, government officials are normally required to adopt an annual budget for each separate activity to anticipate the inflow of financial resources and establish approved expenditure levels. In its "Objectives of Financial Reporting," the GASB indicates that the budget serves these important purposes:

1. Expresses public policy. If, for example, more money is budgeted for child care and less for the environment, the citizens are made aware of the decision that has been made to allocate limited government resources.

2. Serves as an expression of financial intent for the upcoming fiscal year. The budget presents the financial plan for the government for the period.

3. Provides control because spending limitations are established.

4. Offers a means of evaluating performance by allowing a comparison between actual results and the levels of funding found in the budget.

The GASB even states that "many believe the budget is the most significant financial document produced by a government unit."[20]

Once a budget has been produced and enacted into law, formal accounting recognition is frequently required as a means of enhancing the benefits just described. In this way, the public is given the opportunity to learn of the expected

---

[19] *GASB Statement No. 11,* para. 9.

[20] *GASB Concepts Statement No. 1,* para. 19.

amounts to be received and the expenditures to be made with these financial resources. Since the General Fund and the Special Revenue Funds account for a wide range of ongoing service activities, reporting both revenue projections as well as compliance with spending limitations is considered essential for government accountability. Therefore, the approved budget figures for these two fund types are physically entered into the accounting records at the start of each fiscal year. Citizens can then draw comparisons between actual and budgeted figures at any interim point during the period.

As an illustration, assume that a city enacts a special tax levy to support high school athletic programs. Because the funding is legally restricted for this specified purpose, a separate Special Revenue Fund is established. Assume further that for the 1995 fiscal year an estimation is made that $412,000 in revenues will be generated by the tax. Based on this projection, the city council authorizes the expenditure of $400,000 (referred to as an *appropriation*) for athletics during the current year. The $12,000 difference between the anticipated inflow and this appropriation is a budgeted surplus to be accumulated by the government in case the levy proves to be too small or for use in future years. To highlight the council's action, the following journal entry is included in the accounting records of this fund:

Special Revenue Fund (beginning of year)

Estimated Revenues—Tax Levy	412,000	
Appropriations—High School Athletics		400,000
Budgetary Fund Balance		12,000

To record annual budget for tax levy to support high school athletics.

This entry indicates the source of the funding (the tax revenue) as well as the approved amount of expenditures. The Budgetary Fund Balance account indicates the presence of an anticipated surplus (or, in some cases, a shortage) projected for the period. Each of these figures remains within the records of this Special Revenue Fund for the entire year to allow for planning and control. Citizens can see how much is to be spent for these programs and the source of this funding.

As is discussed in the next chapter, one of the financial statements produced for a state or locality is the "Statement of Revenues, Expenditures, and Changes in Fund Balance—Budget and Actual." Thus, the budget figures are not simply left on the financial records for the year and then forgotten. For each of the funds that formally records a budget, the actual amounts for the period as well as the budgeted numbers are presented side by side for comparison purposes. In 1990, as an example, the financial statements for the city of Roanoke, Virginia, reported that $29,447,000 in real estate taxes were anticipated within the General Fund's budget but $29,618,363 was actually recognized. In that same statement, an appropriation of $1,422,669 was shown for police services but only $1,388,909 had actually been expended.

Because of the numerous activities encompassed by the General Fund (or any other fund), the accounting system frequently utilizes subsidiary ledgers so that each balance can be separately identified by specific function. For example, the overall budget for the General Fund could include revenue projections and approved spending limitations for scores of diverse activities such as the school system, garbage collection, and the fire department. To facilitate the recording process, control accounts can be maintained in the general ledger with balances that are explained elsewhere in the system using individual subsidiary ledgers.

As an illustration, assume that a city estimates all General Fund revenues for the current year will equal $1,640,000 while spending levels of $1,180,000 have been set by the city council. Transfers to other funds (referred to as an other financing use since the money does not leave the government) totaling $400,000 have also been approved. These budgeted totals are entered into the General Fund. Simultaneously, separate subsidiary ledgers record detailed information to list the actual source of anticipated revenues (such as property taxes, income taxes, sales taxes, tolls, licenses, and the like) and the individual appropriations and approved transfers. The accounting system is accumulating information both in total and by separate functions.

General Fund (beginning of year)

Estimated Revenues Control	1,640,000	
Appropriations Control		1,180,000
Appropriations—Other Financing Uses—		
Operating Transfers Out		400,000
Budgetary Fund Balance		60,000

To record legally adopted operating budget for the General Fund with separate subsidiary ledger accounts used by the government to explain individual revenues and appropriations.

The budget figures remain in the accounting records for informational purposes throughout the period. They are ultimately removed at the end of the fiscal year through a simple reversal of the original entry:

General Fund (closing entry)

Appropriations Control	1,180,000	
Appropriations—Other Financing Uses—		
Operating Transfers Out	400,000	
Budgetary Fund Balance	60,000	
Estimated Revenues Control		1,640,000

To remove budgetary entry.

In this manner, budgetary entries create no permanent impact on the accounting system but still serve in a control capacity throughout the year.

As mentioned previously, the reporting procedures used in each of the government-type funds are similar but not necessarily identical. Budgetary entries provide a good example of the differences in accounting for the individual fund types. *Within the General Fund, Special Revenue Funds, and Expendable Trust Funds, annual budgets are always recorded.* The volume of transactions as well as the variety of activities monitored within these three fund types can strain the government's ability to establish fiscal control. Revenues and expenditures are not necessarily subjected to reasonable oversight. Recording the annual budget within the bookkeeping system is viewed as an appropriate strategy for enhancing planning, public awareness, and accountability.

In other governmental-type funds, budgets need not be recorded if oversight can be established by alternative means. Formal budgetary entries, for example, are normally omitted from Debt Service Funds. All activities of this particular fund type (accumulation of financial resources and payment of long-term debts and interest) are governed by contractual provision. Budget entries would provide little additional control or other informational value; thus, accounting recognition is not warranted.

Conversely, the recording of a budget is optional in reporting Capital Projects Funds. This fund type accounts for the construction and acquisition of projects that in some instances consist of no more than a simple contractual arrangement. A city, as an example, might hire an independent contractor to construct a side-walk. In such cases, a contract is usually signed that legally sets the level of expenditure; thus, a budgetary entry is not necessary. However, if the government unit is building a major facility (such as a fire station) or if a number of contractors are involved in a single project, the inclusion of budgetary entries is recommended to accentuate planning and control.

Discussion Question: Is It an Asset or a Liability?

In the August 1989 issue of the *Journal of Accountancy,* R. K. Mautz discusses the unique reporting needs of governments and not-for-profit organizations (such as charities) in "Not-For-Profit Financial Reporting: Another View." As an illustration of their accounting problems, Mautz examines the method by which a city should record a newly constructed high school building. Conventional business wisdom would say that such a property represents an asset of the government. Thus, the cost should be capitalized and then depreciated over an estimated useful life. However, in paragraph 26 of FASB *Concepts Statement No. 6,* an essential characteristic of an asset is "a probable future benefit . . . to contribute directly or indirectly to future cash inflows."

Mautz reasons that the school building cannot be considered an asset since it clearly provides no net contribution to cash inflows. In truth, a high school requires the government to make significant cash outflows for maintenance, repairs, utilities, salaries, and the like. Public educational facilities (as well as most of the other properties of a government such as a fire station or municipal building) are acquired with the understanding that net cash outflows will result.

---

continued

Consequently, Mautz considers whether the construction of a high school is not actually the incurrence of a liability since the government is taking on an obligation that will necessitate future cash payments. This idea is also rejected, once again based on the guidance of *Concepts Statement No. 6* (paragraph 36), because the cash outflow is not required at a "specified or determinable date, on occurrence of a specified event, or on demand."

Is a high school building an asset or is it a liability? If it is neither, how should the cost be recorded? Can a government be accounted for in the same manner as a for-profit enterprise?

Recognition of Expenditures for Expenses and Capital Assets

Although budgetary entries are unique, their impact on the accounting process is somewhat limited because they do not directly affect a fund's financial results for the period. Conversely, the method by which a state or locality records the receipt and disbursement of resources can significantly alter the entire complexion of the reported data. For example, in the governmental-type funds, a primary emphasis is on the measurement of changes that occur in financial resources. *Therefore, neither expenses nor capital assets are recorded.*

Instead, an Expenditures account reflects any outflow or reduction of net financial resources from the acquisition of a good or service (or some other utility). A subsidiary ledger (or a system of separate accounts) normally identifies the exact reason for each change, but the actual decrease is recorded as an expenditure whether it is for rent expense, a fire truck, salary expense, or a computer. Spending $1,000 for electricity for the past three months is an expenditure of a fund's financial resources in exactly the same way that buying a $70,000 ambulance is.

Expenditures—Electricity	1,000	
Voucher (or Accounts) Payable		1,000
To record charges covering the past three months.		
Expenditures—Ambulance	70,000	
Voucher (or Accounts) Payable		70,000
To record acquisition of new ambulance.		

Although the recording of expenditures is a well-established procedure within governmental accounting, current debate involves the point in time that this recognition should be made. Historically, expenditures (and also revenues) have been reported based on an approach referred to as *modified accrual accounting*. For expenditures, modified accrual accounting required recognition to be made when a liability was created. "The measurement focus of governmental fund accounting is on *expenditures*—decreases in net financial resources—rather than expenses. Most expenditures and transfers out are measurable and should be recorded when the related liability is incurred."[21]

However, in *Statement 11* (now delayed), the GASB attempted to change that approach by requiring *accrual accounting* to be used.

> Although specific revenues and specific services of governmental-type activities bear no direct relationship to each other, they both can be related directly to specific time periods. . . . The relationship of revenues and services to a specific time period can best be expressed in financial reporting by using an accrual basis of accounting. . . . The Board believes that recognizing expenditures when the underlying transactions or events take place . . . will help accomplish the objective of measuring interperiod equity."[22]

Because the effective date for *GASB 11* has been delayed, modified accrual accounting is still appropriate, at least temporarily. For convenience in this textbook, except where noted (in inventory and prepaid expenses, for example), the underlying events that create an expenditure (a decrease in the net financial resources of a governmental-type fund) is presumed to occur simultaneously with the creation of the related liability. Under that assumption, expenditures are recorded at the same time when using either modified accrual accounting (prior to *GASB 11*) or accrual accounting (*GASB 11*).

The recording of expenditures rather than expenses and capital assets is truly one of the most distinctive characteristics of governmental accounting. A for-profit business enterprise that purchases a building or a machine capitalizes all related costs and then recognizes depreciation expense during each year of the asset's useful life. This depreciation is a factor in the computation of the organization's annual net income.

In contrast, a government-type fund records the entire cost of all buildings, machines, and other capital assets as expenditures. The same handling is used for expenses such as utilities and rent. The outflow is important. No income figure is computed for these funds; thus, the computation and recording of subsequent depreciation is not relevant to the reporting process and is omitted entirely.

Expenditures is a measurement account closed out at the end of each fiscal year. Since the financial resources have been reduced, the impact on the fund is recognized immediately. In the governmental-type funds, the amount of financial resources being utilized is the important information. This approach is clearly designed to assist the government unit in establishing accountability over current spending levels. For example, the city of Buffalo, New York, reported in its 1990 financial statements the expenditure of more than $650,000 for the acquisition of fire-fighting vehicles and another $384,000 for fire prevention services. Although

---

[21] GASB Cod. sec. 1600.117.

[22] *GASB Statement No. 11*, paragraphs 23 and 28.

one item was an asset and the other an expense, the city showed both as expenditures in the current period.

General Fixed Assets Account Group.   One interesting result of measuring and reporting expenditures is that the records of the governmental-type funds contain virtually no assets other than financial resources such as cash, receivables, and investments. All capital assets such as buildings, equipment, vehicles, and the like will have been recorded as expenditures at the time of purchase and then closed out at the end of the fiscal period. Despite the desire to focus on spending, proper control cannot be served without some recording of the government's capital assets. Thus, a separate General Fixed Assets Account Group lists the ownership of these assets as well as any capitalized leased property.

> The primary purposes for governmental fund accounting are to reflect its revenues and expenditures—the sources and uses of its financial resources—and its assets, the related liabilities, and the net financial resources available for subsequent appropriation and expenditure. These objectives can most readily be achieved by excluding general fixed assets from the governmental fund accounts and recording them in a separate General Fixed Assets Account Group.[23]

This segregation allows the governmental-type funds to focus on expendable financial resources. In addition, the issues raised in the previously presented discussion question about the true nature of a property such as a high school building are avoided somewhat by this separate listing.

The use of a separate General Fixed Assets Account Group necessitates that acquisitions actually be recorded twice. To illustrate, assume that $160,000 from a city's General Fund is used to purchase a fire truck. This expenditure is recognized in the General Fund whereas the asset itself is concurrently recorded in the General Fixed Assets Account Group. The second entry includes not only the cost and identity of the asset but also the source of funding (such as general obligation bonds, capital projects funds, gifts, and so forth). This Investment in General Fixed Assets designation is a balancing figure that reports the various sources used to acquire capital assets and appears as an *Other Credit* in the equity section of the government's balance sheet.

Although the cost of this asset is appropriately recorded here, fair market value would be used for any donated assets.

General Fund

Expenditures Control	160,000	
Vouchers Payable		160,000
To record acquisition of fire truck.		

General Fixed Assets Account Group

Machinery and Equipment	160,000	
Investment in General Fixed Assets—		
General Fund Revenues		160,000
To record acquisition of fire truck.		

---

[23] GASB Cod. sec. 1400.107.

If this fire truck is ever disposed of through trade, sale, retirement, or accident, removal from the General Fixed Assets Account Group is made by reversing this original entry.

One variation of the accounting process for capital assets is encountered in connection with construction projects. If work on any job extends into more than one fiscal period, a Construction in Progress account must be set up in the General Fixed Assets Account Group to record all costs incurred prior to completion. At the time the asset eventually becomes usable, the final balance is simply reclassified into a permanent account. The actual expenditure must also be reported. For a construction, the decrease in financial resources would normally be recorded in the Capital Projects Funds.

The very recording of some construction projects as assets within the General Fixed Asset Account Group has been questioned. A street or a sidewalk, for example, cannot be sold and has no future value apart from the services they provide. Thus, while traditional capital assets such as schools, town halls, trucks, and machinery are always recognized in the General Fixed Assets Account Group, states and localities are allowed the option of "reporting public domain or 'infrastructure' fixed assets—roads, bridges, curbs and gutters, streets and sidewalks, drainage systems, lighting systems, and similar assets that are immovable and of value only to the governmental unit."[24] Some government units meticulously record such infrastructure items whereas others do not.

Depreciation Expense.   Because of the absence of capital assets, depreciation expense is not recorded within any of the government-type funds. Although accumulated depreciation totals may be disclosed in the General Fixed Assets Account Group, recognition of an expense would belie the goal of maintaining control over expenditures that is emphasized throughout these funds. Additionally, depreciation figures are not considered relevant to the reporting process since net income is not being calculated.

> Expenditures, not expenses, are measured in governmental fund accounting. To record depreciation expense in governmental funds would inappropriately mix two fundamentally different measurements, expenses and expenditures. General fixed asset acquisitions *require* the use of governmental fund financial resources and are recorded as expenditures. General fixed asset sale proceeds *provide* governmental fund financial resources. Depreciation expense is neither a source nor a use of governmental fund financial resources, and thus is not properly recorded in the accounts of such funds. . . . Recording accumulated depreciation in the General Fixed Assets Account Group is optional. Where it is recorded, the entry should increase the Accumulated Depreciation account(s) and decrease the Investment in General Fixed Assets account(s).[25]

Supplies and Prepaid Items.   The accounting for both supplies and prepaid items demonstrates the change proposed by the GASB in *Statement 11* as it seeks to

---

[24] GASB Cod. sec. 1400.109.
[25] GASB Cod. sec. 1400.116–118.

require use of accrual accounting rather than modified accrual accounting. Traditionally, both of these items have been recorded as expenditures at the point in time that a liability is created. No asset is initially recorded because neither supplies nor prepaid items (such as rent or insurance) can be expended. For reporting purposes, though, materials or prepayments that remain at year's end must be entered into the accounting records as assets prior to production of financial statements. This adjustment is created by utilizing an equity balance with a title such as Fund Balance Reserved for Inventory of Supplies (or Prepaid Items). This account indicates an asset is present that is not available for spending purposes.

This traditional approach, referred to as the *purchases method*, is based on the modified accrual method of accounting. The expenditure is recorded when the liability is first incurred. However, when (or if) it becomes effective, *GASB 11* will require use of an alternative, the *consumption method*, so that the governmental-type funds will be in line with accrual accounting.

The consumption method parallels the process that would be applied by a for-profit business. Any supplies or prepayments are recorded as assets when acquired. Subsequently, as the items are consumed by usage or over time, the cost is reclassified into an Expenditures account. Therefore, under this approach, the expenditure is matched with the period of specific usage.

As an illustration, assume that $20,000 in supplies are purchased by a municipality for various General Fund activities. During the remainder of the period, $18,000 of this amount is used so that only $2,000 remains at year's end. These events could be recorded through either of the following sets of entries:

Consumption Method   *Accrual method*

Inventory of Supplies	20,000	
Vouchers Payable		20,000
To record purchase of supplies for various ongoing activities.		

Expenditures—Control.	18,000	
Inventory of Supplies		18,000
To record consumption of supplies during period.		

Purchases Method   *Modified accrual method*

Expenditures—Control.	20,000	
Vouchers Payable		20,000
To record purchase of supplies for various ongoing activities.		

Inventory of Supplies	2,000	
Fund Balance—Reserved for Inventory of Supplies		2,000
To record supplies remaining at year's end.		

Equity —

Recognition of Revenues

As with expenditures, revenues are currently recognized by governments based on modified accrual accounting; however *GASB 11* (when it becomes effective) will require the use of accrual accounting. Under modified accrual accounting, revenues should be reported within the governmental-type funds in the time period in which they become both *measurable and available*.

- The *measurable* criterion requires that the revenue must be subject to reasonable estimation.
- *Available* is defined as "collectible within the current period or soon enough thereafter to be used to pay liabilities of the current period."[26]

Parking fines, as an example, are not subject to reasonable estimation until received; thus, recognition is delayed until cash is physically collected. Conversely, property taxes—the largest source of revenue for many municipalities—are normally recognized under modified accrual accounting as soon as the tax is levied since the probable amount to be received during the current period can usually be anticipated at that point.

In contrast, the GASB wants to replace the measurable and available criteria of modified accrual accounting with several different sets of guidelines set out in *Statement 11* that are based on the specific nature of the revenue. Tax revenues (such as property taxes, sales taxes, and income taxes) would be recognized at the time both of these criteria are satisfied:

- The underlying transaction or event has taken place.
- The government has demanded the taxes from the taxpayer by establishing a due date on or before the end of the period. However, taxpayer-assessed taxes with a due date within two months after the end of the period for "administrative lead time" should be considered as having been demanded as of the end of the period.[27]

For fines, fees, licenses, and the like, *GASB 11* would require recognition when the underlying transaction or event takes place and the government has an enforceable legal claim. Charges for services are to be reported as revenue when earned.

Specific guidance for recognition is provided next by looking at the individual sources of government revenues.

Property Taxes.   According to modified accrual accounting, all revenues are recognized when they become measurable and available. For *GASB 11* and accrual accounting, receivables and revenue are recognized at the time of the tax levy if demand for the money has been made as of the end of the fiscal year or before. The demand date is the last day before interest and penalties begin to accrue. This distinction does cause a difference in the recording process.

For illustrative purposes, assume that Ginsburg County levies $400,000 in property taxes on May 1, 1995, that must be paid in four equal installments of $100,000 each. To avoid an interest penalty, payment must be on or before July 1, October 1, December 1, and April 15 of the following year. The government

---

[26] GASB Cod. sec. 1600.106.

[27] *GASB Statement No. 11*, paragraph 40.

estimates that $5,000 of each payment will go unpaid. An additional $3,000 that is due in 1995 ($1,000 from each of the first three dates) will not be paid until the April 15, 1996, payment.

According to modified accrual accounting, $94,000 from each of the first three payments ($100,000 − $5,000 − $1,000) is measurable and expected to be available in 1995. Another $98,000 does not become available until 1996 ($100,000 − $5,000 + $3,000) and is deferred. Although not shown here, the collection of the taxes and the write-off of any accounts would be normal entries.

Modified Accrual Accounting

May 1, 1995 Entry

Property Tax Receivable (amount levied).	400,000	
Revenue—Property Taxes ($94,000 × 3)		282,000
Deferred Revenues		98,000
Allowance for Uncollectible Taxes ($5,000 × 4).		20,000

To recognize property tax levy made in 1995.

1996 Entry

Deferred Revenues	98,000	
Revenue—Property Taxes		98,000

To recognize revenue in the fiscal period that it becomes measurable and available.

Under accrual accounting, the payments for 1996 have not yet been demanded and, thus, should not be reported. Recognition is made in the period in which the due date falls. The $3,000 in collections delayed into 1996 are still revenues when demanded in 1995.

Accrual Accounting

May 1, 1995 Entry

Property Tax Receivable (amount due in current period)	300,000	
Revenue—Property Taxes ($95,000 × 3)		285,000
Allowance for Uncollectible Taxes ($5,000 × 3).		15,000

To recognize property tax levy demanded in 1995.

1996 Entry

Property Tax Receivable (due in current period)	100,000	
Revenue—Property Taxes ($95,000 × 1)		95,000
Allowance for Uncollectible Taxes		5,000

To recognize 1995 property tax levy demanded in 1996.

These entries would probably be recorded within Ginsburg County's General Fund since property taxes provide primary support for many ongoing government activities. However, if any part of the proceeds had been restricted for a particular operating purpose, this portion of the revenues would be recorded within the Special Revenue Funds. In the same manner, any money specified for payment of long-term obligations or for construction is appropriately recorded in the Debt Service Funds or Capital Projects Funds.

Income Taxes, Sales Taxes, Fines, Fees, and Licenses. Many of the revenues anticipated by a state or locality will not meet the current criteria of being measurable and available until physically collected. For this reason, recognition of resource inflows such as income and sales taxes, parking fees, traffic court fines, and business licenses are normally delayed until cash is received. The amounts usually cannot be estimated in advance and are not available to satisfy current obligations until collected. For that reason, many individuals believe that governmental accounting is a cash-based reporting system.

GASB 11 looks at many of these revenues individually as it sets rules for the application of accrual accounting. For income taxes, as an example, revenue should be recorded in the same period as the income is earned by the taxpayer if the government has demanded the taxes by year-end (or within two months thereafter). In the same manner, sales taxes should be reported in the period in which the sale occurs. Fines should be recorded when the government has an enforceable legal claim. If a citizen is fined $1,000, recognition should be immediate unless the government does not have an enforceable claim. These changes in recognition are only required, though, when *GASB 11* becomes effective.

Many fees and licenses relate to a single event or a relatively short period. Parking meter fees, for example, or marriage licenses fall into this category. Other fees and licenses, though, cover an extended period. A business, driver's, or hunting license often conveys a privilege for a specified time such as a year or longer. Normally, no enforceable claim exists prior to payment being made (so that accrual is not required). Thus, according to *GASB 11,* unless the government has an obligation to refund the money under certain conditions, the revenue is recognized from such fees and licenses at the point of cash receipt.

After collection, the government is usually not obligated to furnish any refunds. A citizen cannot ask for money back, for example, if a hunting license is never used. Therefore, even if the privilege extends over a period of time, revenue recognition is immediate under the proposed changes. One important exception does exist: if the money must be used for a specified purpose, the inflow is usually recorded in the Special Revenue Funds and is deferred until appropriately expended.

Grants and Entitlements. A common source of revenues for many governments are grants and entitlements, monies transferred from one government to another to meet a specified purpose or because of a particular law. *Statement No. 2* of the National Council on Governmental Accounting, "Grant, Entitlement, and Shared Revenue Accounting by State and Local Governments" (March 1979), addressed recognition of these resources and was left unaffected by *GASB No. 11*. Thus, this area of governmental accounting is one that is not currently in transition.

Grants and entitlements may take many forms. A state could convey money to a city to provide financing for the acquisition of new emergency medical equipment or to assist in feeding the hungry and homeless. The federal government might transfer funds to a county for road construction. The amounts involved can be significant. In fiscal 1989, Philadelphia, Pennsylvania, reported grant revenues within its Special Revenue Funds of nearly $119 million from various federal, state, and private agencies.

When grants and entitlements are received, legal restrictions are often attached to ensure that the funds are expended for the proposed purpose. Therefore, if the money is given for an operating project, the Special Revenue Funds category is usually applicable because the money is designated for a specific purpose or expenditure. Conversely, if the funds are given for construction or acquisition of fixed assets, recording is made in the Capital Projects Funds.

Revenue recognition for such items frequently must be delayed beyond the time of receipt. In many cases, proper expenditure is required of the government to keep the funding. If the state of Kansas, for example, gives $1 million to the city of Topeka so that day-care equipment can be bought, the money may have to be returned if not utilized in this manner. *Consequently, the revenues should not be recognized until the money is appropriately spent.* Proper expenditure is necessary to earn the resources. Thus, if stipulations are included, a Deferred Revenue account is established as a liability with this balance being reclassified as a revenue at the time the required expenditure is made.

For example, at June 30, 1990, the city of Norfolk, Virginia, explains a $3 million Deferred Revenue liability found within its Special Revenue Funds as follows:

> This represents a liability incurred by the City for monies accepted from a grantor using an advancement method for payments. The liability is reduced and revenue recorded when expenditures are made in accordance with grantor's requirements. If expenditures are not made, the funds will revert back to the grantor.[28]

Assume that the city of Redlands, as an illustration, collects $300,000 on September 1, 1995, from the federal government to supplement the salaries of kindergarten teachers. The money is held for a short time and $100,000 is spent on October 1, 1995, for the designated purpose. The city should record these events through the following entries:

Special Revenue Fund
September 1, 1995

Cash	300,000	
Deferred Revenues		300,000
Receipt of grant from the federal government to supplement the salaries of kindergarten teachers.		

Special Revenue Fund
October 1, 1995

Expenditures—Teachers' Salaries	100,000	
Cash		100,000
Grant money used to supplement salaries of city's kindergarten teachers.		

---

[28] Note 20 of the city's comprehensive annual financial report.

Deferred Revenue 100,000
    Revenues—Federal Grant   100,000
    To record recognition of revenue in connection with the appropriate
expenditure of federal grant.

Issuance of Bonds

Although not a revenue, the issuance of bonds serves as a major source of funding for most state and local governments. Proceeds from such sales may be used for many purposes, including general financing and a wide variety of construction projects. In 1990, the city of Atlanta, Georgia, received $8 million from the sale of bonds; half was to be used for a municipal building and the other half for schools.

Since the proceeds of a bond have to be repaid, no revenues are recognized. However, the inflow of financial resources into a specific fund must be recorded in some manner. Assume, for example, that the town of Ruark sells $5 million in general obligation bonds to finance the construction of a new school building. Because of the purpose of this action, a Capital Projects Fund is designated to receive the cash. To emphasize that this money is not derived from a revenue, a special designation, *Other Financing Sources,* is utilized. Thus, the following entry would be appropriate to record the sale:

Capital Projects Fund

Cash 5,000,000
    Other Financing Sources—Bond Proceeds   5,000,000
    To record issuance of bond to finance construction project.

Although an inflow of cash into this fund has taken place, no revenue has been generated. However, in the same manner as a revenue, Other Financing Sources is a measurement account that is closed out at the end of the year. Furthermore, a subsidiary ledger is apparently not in use since the account title is specific: Other Financing Sources—Bond Proceeds.

General Long-Term Debt Account Group. As shown in the previous entry, the $5 million liability is completely omitted from the Capital Projects Funds. Since the governmental-type funds stress accounting for the inflows and outflows of financial resources, recognition of long-term debts in these funds has traditionally been considered inappropriate. Despite this objective, some record of these obligations is essential to the fair presentation of the government's financial position. As with general fixed assets, a separate account group (*General Long-Term Debt Account Group*) is established to perform the sole function of listing the noncurrent liabilities of the governmental-type funds. Therefore, to record the bond just issued, a second entry is needed:

General Long-Term Debt Account Group

Amount to Be Provided 5,000,000
    Bonds Payable   5,000,000
    To record issuance of bonds for new school construction.

The Amount to Be Provided account in this entry would appear as an *Other Debit* in the asset section of the combined balance sheet of the government. This balance discloses the amount of cash to be generated by the government in the future to extinguish the principal of the debt. Over time, as resources are accumulated within the Debt Service Funds for this purpose, the Amount to Be Provided figure would be reclassified into an Amount Available in Debt Service Funds account. For example, as of September 30, 1990, the city of Amarillo, Texas, reported total debt of $13,839,648 in its General Long-Term Debt Account Group. However, at that time, the city was already holding net assets of $1,785,100 in its Debt Service Fund to be used for future repayment purposes. Thus, as an Other Debit in the balance sheet of the General Long-Term Debt Account Group, the city reported two balances:

Amount available in debt service funds	$ 1,785,100
Amount to be provided for retirement of long-term debt	12,054,548
Total	$13,839,648

To illustrate further, assume that following the issuance of the $5 million bond, the town of Ruark begins to set money aside for eventual payment. Thus, $600,000 is transferred from the General Fund to the Debt Service Funds, an amount that will be used to pay the debt when due. At the time of the transfer, the government records the following adjustment in the General Long-Term Debt Account Group. No expenditure is recorded nor is the liability reduced because payment has not been made.

General Long-Term Debt Account Group

Amount Available in Debt Service Fund	600,000	
Amount to be Provided		600,000

To indicate that resources of this amount have been set aside to extinguish bonds.

***GASB 11* and Long-Term Debt.** Government accounting has traditionally recorded all long-term debt in the General Long-Term Debt Account Group. "General long-term debt is not limited to liabilities arising from debt issuances per se, but may also include noncurrent liabilities on capital leases, compensated absences, claims, judgments, pensions, special termination benefits, and other commitments that are not current liabilities properly recorded in governmental funds."[29]

---

[29] GASB Cod. sec. 1500.108.

GASB 11, when it takes effect, will distinguish between capital debt and other types of long-term obligations (referred to as *operating debt*).

> General long-term capital debt is those liabilities that are expected to be paid from the financial resources of governmental funds and that provide long-term financing (*a*) to acquire capital assets, including infrastructure, or (*b*) for certain nonrecurring projects or activities that have long-term economic benefit. (paragraph 86) Operating debt is debt that provides financial resources to and is expected to be repaid from the financial resources of governmental funds and that is not related to the acquisition of capital assets, including infrastructure, or the financing of certain nonrecurring projects or activities that have long-term economic benefit. Operating debt includes revenue and tax anticipation notes and other short- and long-term debt issued to finance operations. (para. 94)

Having divided long-term debt into two categories, *GASB 11* goes on to state that the issuance of operating debt should not be reported as an inflow of financial resources and the payment is not an outflow. Consequently, any long-term debt that does not meet the criteria established for capital debt would be reported within the fund type receiving the money. An Other Financing Source is not to be reported; the General Long-Term Debt Account Group is not utilized. If, for example, a city issues $1 million in bonds (due in 18 months) to finance ongoing government operations until taxes are collected, *GASB 11* will not record the debt in a separate account group but rather within the General Fund:

General Fund

Cash	1,000,000	
Long-Term Bonds—Operating Debt		1,000,000
To record proceeds from issuance of bonds for the purpose of financing operations until taxes are collected.		

Payment of Long-Term Liabilities.   Historically, the expenditures to recognize payment of long-term debt and related interest are recorded in the Debt Service Funds only when due. Thus, interest for an entire year that is due on January 15, 1996, is recorded in total as an expenditure on that date; no impact is recognized in 1995. This approach has been used so that the expenditure is reported in the same time period as the appropriation for the expenditure.

The following entries illustrate the current process. This example assumes that cash has previously been set aside in the Debt Service Funds to settle a bond coming due. Of the total amount, $600,000 is to satisfy the principal with $40,000 serving as the interest payment for the period. Two entries are necessary: one to record the expenditures and the other to remove the debt.

Debt Service Funds

Expenditures—Bond Principal	600,000	
Expenditures—Interest	40,000	
Cash		640,000
To pay bonds and interest that are currently due.		

General Long-Term Debt Account Group

Bonds Payable	600,000	
Amount Available in Debt Service Funds		600,000

To remove debt that is extinguished with funds held in the Debt
Service Funds.

GASB 11 will require that the interest on operating debt be accrued using the effective interest rate method in the same manner as a for-profit business. However, this pronouncement does not specifically address debt service expenditures issues relating to long-term capital debt because that topic is under separate consideration in another project. Footnote 2 of *GASB 11* does indicate that "This Statement, however, provides basic guidance to those projects; specifically, operating statement recognition and measurement criteria should be developed within the context of the flow of financial resources measurement focus and an accrual basis of accounting." Hence, whenever *GASB 11* finally becomes effective, interest accrual will be required.

Special Assessments

Governments frequently provide improvements or services that directly benefit a particular property and assess the costs (in whole or part) to the owner. In many cases, the owners actually petition the government to initiate such projects because of the enhancement of property values. Paving streets, laying water and sewage lines, and the construction of curbing and sidewalks are typical examples. To finance the work being done, the government usually issues debt while concurrently placing a lien on the property to ensure reimbursement. Payment by the owners is often made in installments, sometimes stretching over several years. If public property is also benefited or if the governing body so chooses, a portion of the cost may be absorbed by the state or locality.

Prior to 1987, these activities were accounted for within a separate governmental fund type, the Special Assessments Fund. However, the GASB now requires, in most cases, that these construction costs be recorded in the Capital Projects Fund with the debt shown in the General Long-Term Debt account group. The assessment of the owners is entered as a receivable within the Debt Service Funds. The balance sheet of Montgomery County, Maryland, as an example, shows a special assessment receivable of approximately $1.6 million within its Debt Service Funds on June 30, 1989.

To illustrate, assume that a sidewalk is to be added to a neighborhood by a city government at a cost of $15,000. Bonds are to be sold for this amount with repayment to be made over three years using money collected from the owners. Although the city will not pay this debt, the government has agreed to be secondarily liable if any defaults occur. The actual assessment is not made until after the construction is completed. The following entries reflect these various events:

Capital Projects Fund

Cash	15,000	
Other Financing Sources—Special Assessment Bonds		15,000

To record issuance of bond with proceeds to be used to construct a
sidewalk. Assessment of property owners will provide the payment for
this liability.

General Long-Term Debt Account Group

Amount to Be Provided from Special Assessments	15,000	
Special Assessment Debt with Government Commitment		15,000

To record issuance of bond with money used in construction of a
sidewalk.

Capital Projects Fund

Expenditures—Sidewalk	15,000	
Contracts Payable		15,000

To record completion of a sidewalk.

Debt Service Funds

Special Assessments Receivable.	15,000	
Deferred Revenues—Special Assessments		15,000

To record levy for construction work done in connection with a
sidewalk with costs to be paid by owners being benefited. As collections
are made, deferred revenues will be reclassified as revenues.

General Fixed Assets Account Group
(optional entry for infrastructure)

Improvements Other than Buildings	15,000	
Investment in General Fixed Assets—Special Assessments		15,000

To record construction costs of a sidewalk.

Several aspects of these entries should be noted:

- The debt is recorded by the city although the amount is anticipated to be
  paid in full by the owners rather than the government. To disclose the
  city's responsibility for possible defaults, the entire debt is included in the
  General Long-Term Debt Account Group. However, if the government
  could in no way be held liable, this obligation would be omitted. In that
  circumstance, subsequent payments by the owners are funneled through
  an Agency Fund to extinguish the debt with no other recording required.
- The asset is included at cost within the General Fixed Asset Account
  Group although no government funds were actually required. However,
  as an infrastructure item, this recording is optional.

Interfund Transactions

Interfund transactions are commonly used within most government units as a
means of directing sufficient resources to all activities and functions. Monetary
transfers made from the General Fund are especially prevalent since many

government revenues are initially accumulated in this fund. Such transactions should be recorded in both funds simultaneously at the time of authorization. However, the specific method of accounting for these transfers is based on the nature of the transfer.

Operating Transfers.   The most common intercompany transactions are *operating transfers* that are used primarily within the governmental-type funds to ensure adequate financing of budgeted expenditures. A county might transfer unrestricted funds, for example, to debt service to ensure that future obligations can be paid. A city council could vote to transfer $800,000 from the General Fund to the Capital Projects Funds to cover a portion of the cost of a new school building. In this second scenario, the following entries would be recorded:

General Fund

Other Financing Uses—Operating Transfers Out—		
Capital Projects Fund	800,000	
Due to Capital Projects Fund		800,000
Transfer is authorized for school construction.		

Capital Projects Funds

Due from General Fund	800,000	
Other Financing Source—		
Operating Transfers In—General Fund.		800,000
Transfer is to be received for school construction.		

The *Other Financing Uses/Sources* designations are appropriate here; monetary resources are being moved into and out of these funds although neither revenues nor expenditures have been earned or incurred. These balances are eventually reported by the funds in the Statement of Revenues, Expenditures, and Changes in Fund Balances. Both accounts are then closed out at the end of the current year. The *Due to/Due from* accounts are the equivalent of interfund payable and receivable balances.

When the actual transfer occurs, the following entries result:

General Fund

Due to Capital Projects Fund	800,000	
Cash		800,000
To transfer cash to Capital Projects Fund.		

Capital Projects Fund

Cash	800,000	
Due from General Fund		800,000
Receipt of transfer from General Fund.		

Residual Equity Transfers.   Not all monetary transfers are for operating purposes; nonrecurring or nonroutine transfers may also occur. In some instances, money is transferred from the General Fund to create a Proprietary Fund, either an Enterprise Fund or Internal Service Fund. For example, on July 1, 1989, the city of Wilmington, Delaware, transferred $990,877 as initial funding for the Wilmington Homeownership Fund, an enterprise fund created to offer home ownership to low-to-moderate income families.

Because of the business-type nature of proprietary funds, government financing resembles a contribution of capital more than an operating transfer. Thus, the following entries are required if a city transfers $310,000 from its General Fund for the purpose of creating a print shop to assist the rest of the government. Since the print shop provides services within the government for a fee, an Internal Service Fund is being formed. The following chapter covers accounting procedures for this type of Proprietary Fund in more detail.

General Fund

Residual Equity Transfer Out—Print Shop	310,000	
Cash		310,000

To record transfer made to begin a print shop serving all areas of the city government.

Internal Service Fund

Cash	310,000	
Contributed Capital—Government.		310,000

To record transfer providing initial funding for print shop.

As with the operating transfer, the *Residual Equity Transfer Out* account also appears within the Statement of Revenues, Expenditures, and Changes in Fund Balances. However, as can be seen in Exhibit 15–1 at the end of this chapter, this type of transfer is shown as a direct decrease in the fund balance of the General Fund rather than as an other financing use.

Quasi-External Transactions.   Some transfers made within a government actually replace revenues and expenditures. For example, a payment made by a city to its own print shop (or any other Internal Service Fund or Enterprise Fund) for services or materials is the equivalent of a transaction with an outside party. To avoid confusion in reporting, such transfers are recorded as revenues and expenditures just as if the transaction had occurred with an unrelated party. No differentiation is made.

Assuming that the print shop (or the motor pool or the data processing center) does a $20,000 project for the General Fund, the following recording is appropriate:

General Fund

Expenditures—Printing	20,000	
Cash		20,000

To pay for printing work done for the city by its print shop.

Internal Service Fund

Cash	20,000	
Revenues—Printing		20,000

To recognize revenue generated by work done for city's General Fund.

Encumbrances

Governmental accounting demonstrates many unique aspects from separate account groups to fund accounting and budgetary entries. All are basic to the reporting process used by the governmental-type funds. One additional budgetary procedure that plays a central role in this system is the recording of monetary commitments referred to as *encumbrances*. *In diametric contrast to for-profit accounting, purchase commitments and contracts are journalized in the governmental funds prior to becoming legal liabilities.* Maintaining a record of these encumbrances is designed to provide an additional means of controlling fund spending. At any point during the fiscal year, information on both expended and committed funds is available. "An encumbrance accounting system acts as an early warning device. By controlling expenditure commitments, the government significantly reduces the opportunity to overexpend an appropriation." [30]

To illustrate, assume that a city orders $18,000 in supplies for ongoing General Fund activities. A for-profit business would make no entry at this point. However, this amount of the city's financial resources is now committed even though no formal liability has yet been incurred. Therefore, the following journal entry creates a record of this order and any other orders, contracts, and commitments that are currently outstanding:

General Fund

Encumbrances Control.	18,000	
Budgetary Fund Balance—Reserved for Encumbrances		18,000
To record order placed for supplies.		

The Encumbrances account records the commitment that has been incurred while "Budgetary Fund Balance—Reserved for Encumbrances" is an equity-type balance indicating the amount of the city's assets required to fulfill future obligations.

When the preceding items are received, the commitment is replaced by a legal liability. Hence, the encumbrance is removed from the accounting records and an Inventory of Supplies account (or an Expenditure account if the purchases method rather than the consumption method is in use) is recognized. Often, because of sales taxes, freight costs, or other price adjstments, the actual invoice total differs from the estimated figure recorded at the time the order was processed. For this reason, the expenditure does not necessarily agree with the corresponding encumbrance. Assume, for illustration purposes, that the supplies received here are accompanied by an invoice for $18,160.

General Fund

Budgetary Fund Balance—Reserved for Encumbrances	18,000	
Encumbrances Control.		18,000
To remove encumbrance for supplies that have now been received.		
Inventory of Supplies (or Expenditures—Supplies)	18,160	
Vouchers Payable		18,160
To record the receipt of supplies and the accompanying liability.		

---

[30] Government Finance Officers Association, *Governmental Accounting, Auditing, and Financial Reporting* (Chicago: 1988), p. 17.

In governmental accounting, the recording of encumbrances is viewed as an additional aspect of budgetary control. Thus, recognition of purchase commitments and contracts is considered appropriate for the fund types that also record budget entries. Consequently, encumbrances are rarely found in Debt Service Funds and are optional in Capital Projects Funds. The encumbrance system, however, is always used in the General Fund, Special Revenue Funds, and Expendable Trust Funds.

Encumbrances—Outstanding at Year's End. A question arises as to the appropriate accounting for any encumbrances outstanding at the end of a fiscal period. Should a commitment be reported in a government's financial statements since no transaction has actually occurred?

Depending on governmental policy, such encumbrances may either be honored in the subsequent year or canceled. In both cases, all balances must be removed from the accounting records because no transaction occurred and financial resources were not actually affected in the initial period. If, for example, the preceding supplies had not been received by year's end, the encumbrances entry is eliminated through a simple reversal.

General Fund
(year-end)

Budgetary Fund Balances—Reserved for Encumbrances.	18,000	
Encumbrances Control.		18,000

To remove encumbrance for supplies not received by year's end.

If the commitment is to be honored by the government in the following year, this $18,000 encumbrance can be reinstated at the beginning of the new period.

Although this handling satisfies the need to remove year-end encumbrances, some method must still be devised to disclose any of these commitments that require funding in the succeeding period. Thus, if the government expects to make payment, an additional equity adjustment is prepared to alert financial statement readers of the outstanding commitment. This procedure is purely for disclosure purposes; the entry is eliminated at the beginning of the subsequent period.

General Fund
(following year)

Fund Balance—Unreserved, Undesignated.	18,000	
Fund Balance—Reserved for Encumbrances		18,000

To reclassify a portion of fund balance to indicate that an outstanding commitment will require the fund's resources in the following year.

The Fund Balance—Reserved for Encumbrances account appears as an equity on the balance sheet to indicate that financial resources currently being held are already committed. As an example, the city of Chicago, Illinois, reported the following Fund Balance—Reserved for Encumbrances figures in its December 31, 1989, balance sheet:

General Fund	$ 30,412,000
Special Revenue Funds	14,926,000
Capital Projects Funds	131,395,000

Apparently, commitments of these amounts were made by the government prior to year's end through purchase orders and contracts. However, the city did not incur the related legal liabilities before the balance sheet date. Inclusion in the financial statements of these amounts indicates that Chicago officials intend to honor these encumbrances in the following period rather than cancel them.

Fund Equity

> Fund balance is the component of fund equity that reports the excess or deficiency of a fund's current assets relative to its current liabilities. . . . Unreserved fund balance is that portion of fund balance that is appropriate for expenditures and is not legally segregated for specific future use.[31]

In a for-profit corporation, the equity section of the balance sheet is presented according to the sources of the business's net assets: paid-in capital and earned capital. Conversely, the governmental-type funds of a state or locality use equity accounts to disclose the availability of resources for future spending purposes. As an example, this chapter has examined the Fund Balance—Reserved for Inventory of Supplies, an equity balance indicating that assets are being held as supplies so expenditure is not possible. Likewise, the Fund Balance—Reserved for Encumbrances reports commitments already made for the subsequent expenditure of the fund's resources.

Fund Balance—Unreserved, Undesignated.　Governmental-type funds also possess current assets that have not been designated for a specific expenditure. For example, a General Fund holding $90,000 in cash, receivables, and investments but only $50,000 in monetary obligations (and no commitments) has $40,000 in unrestricted net assets. These resources are available for immediate expenditure. To disclose this surplus, an equity account entitled *Fund Balance—Unreserved, Undesignated* is maintained on the balance sheet. The total in this account is actually created as a result of absorbing revenues, expenditures, other financing sources and uses, and residual equity transfers within the annual closing process. In addition, as shown previously, any Fund Balance—Reserved for Encumbrances reported at year-end is created by a reclassification from Fund Balance—Unreserved, Undesignated.

---

[31] GASB, "Preliminary Views—Implementation of *GASB Statement No. 11,* 'Measurement Focus and Basis of Accounting—Governmental Fund Operating Statements,' " April 30, 1992, paragraph 27.

Long-Term Fund Equity. *GASB No. 11,* when it becomes effective, will require recognition within the governmental-type funds of certain long-term assets (notes receivable, for example) and long-term liabilities (operating debts, compensated absences, and claims and judgments) that have previously been recorded in account groups. A question currently being discussed is how the inclusion of these assets and liabilities will affect fund equity since the net amount of these accounts is not currently expendable. One proposal is that another equity account *Long-Term Fund Equity* (to be reported after Reserved Fund Balances and Fund Balance—Unreserved, Undesignated) will be included to account for the difference between long-term assets and liabilities. To date, the GASB has not resolved this issue.

Fund Balances—Illustrated. To provide a demonstration, assume that the City of Morganton had $175,000 in unrestricted net current assets (and no encumbrances) in the General Fund on July 1, 1995, the beginning of the fiscal year. During the next 12 months, the following events transpire:

Financial Resource Inflows:

Revenues (property taxes, licenses, etc.)	$600,000
Other financing sources	
Bond proceeds—capital acquisitions	200,000
Operating transfers in	100,000
	$900,000

Financial Resource Outflows:

Expenditures (trucks, salary, etc.)	$533,000
Other financing uses (transfers out)	200,000
Residual equity transfer	85,000
	$818,000

At year's end, the following closing entries are required:[32]

General Fund
(closing entries)

Revenues Control	600,000	
Other Financing Sources—Bond Proceeds	200,000	
Other Financing Sources—Operating Transfers In	100,000	
Fund Balance—Unreserved, Undesignated		900,000
To close out accounts measuring monetary inflows during period.		
Fund Balance—Unreserved, Undesignated	818,000	
Expenditures Control		533,000
Other Financing Uses—Operating Transfers Out		200,000
Residual Equity Transfer		85,000
To close out accounts measuring monetary outflows during period.		

---

[32] As illustrated previously, budgetary entries are also closed out at year-end.

The closing process indicates that resource inflows were greater than outflows by $82,000 ($900,000 − $818,000). Consequently, the Fund Balance—Unreserved, Undesignated reported for the General Fund increased during this year from $175,000 to $257,000. This balance indicates the net current asset balance at year-end that is expendable.

To carry this illustration one step further, assume that $20,000 in commitments still outstanding at year's end will be honored in the next fiscal period. The following reclassification is required, leaving only $237,000 in the unreserved category.

Fund Balance—Unreserved, Undesignated	20,000	
Fund Balance—Reserved for Encumbrances		20,000

To reclassify a portion of fund balance to indicate that outstanding commitments will require fund resources in the following year.

Based on the information provided, an illustration of a condensed statement of revenues, expenditures, and changes in fund balance can be constructed for this municipality as shown in Exhibit 15–1. In addition, a typical balance sheet (also condensed) is included. The individual current asset and current liability balances are presented for illustration purposes only and do not reflect the specific transactions indicated earlier.[33]

EXHIBIT 15–1

CITY OF MORGANTON
General Fund
Statement of Revenues, Expenditures, and
Equity Section **Changes in Fund Balance (Condensed)**
Year Ended June 30, 1996

Revenues.		$ 600,000
Expenditures		(533,000)
Excess of revenues over expenditures		$ 67,000
Other financing sources (uses):		
Bond proceeds—Capital debt.	$ 200,000	
Operating transfers in	100,000	
Operating transfers out.	(200,000)	
Total other financing sources (uses)		100,000
Excess of revenues and other financing sources over expenditures and		
other financing uses		$ 167,000
Fund balance, July 1, 1995		175,000
Residual equity transfers out		(85,000)
Fund balance, June 30, 1996		$ 257,000

---

[33] More complete governmental financial statements are examined in the following chapter. In addition, as is discussed in more detail at that time, an additional statement must also be presented for the governmental-type funds that adopt budgets, disclosing both budgeted and actual figures for revenues, expenditures, and other changes in fund balance.

EXHIBIT 15–1 *concluded*

CITY OF MORGANTON
General Fund
Balance Sheet (Condensed)
June 30, 1996

Assets

Cash	$ 61,900
Investments	105,000
Receivables (net of allowances):	
Taxes	184,000
Accounts	48,850
Due from other funds	26,000
Total assets	$ 425,750

Liabilities *[handwritten: No long term bonds payable]*

Vouchers payable	$ 125,930
Contracts payable	16,720
Due to other funds	26,100
Total liabilities	$ 168,750

Equity *[handwritten: — restricted equity]*

Fund balances: *[handwritten: nominal account commitment to pay]*

[Restricted] Reserved for encumbrances	$ 20,000 *[expenditure]*
[Unrestricted] Unreserved, undesignated	237,000
Total fund balances	257,000
Total liabilities and equity	$ 425,750

Summary

1. The accounting procedures utilized by state and local governments vary in many significant respects from the reporting process employed by profit-oriented businesses. These differences originated because the informational requirements of financial statement users are assumed to change when the profit motive is removed. Furthermore, varying needs are encountered among the users of government accounting data. The voter, the taxpayer, the city official, and the bond investor all seek specific types of information. Since 1984, the Governmental Accounting Standards Board (GASB) has been in charge of developing accounting principles to satisfy the unique needs of the users of governmental financial statements.

2. Accountability is the major emphasis found in state and local government financial reporting. The accounting principles and procedures are designed to assist in controlling financial operations as well as the government officials who serve as stewards over public funds. The reporting process must also be capable of accounting for the wide range of activities often encountered in a governmental unit (such as the police department, ambulance service, zoo, motor pool, municipal golf course, trash collection, and the like). Because income determination is not important to most of these activities, many features of governmental accounting vary significantly from the procedures traditionally associated with for-profit enterprises.

3. One of the most unique aspects of government financial reporting is the use of fund accounting. Each of the distinct functions of a state or locality is recorded in an individual, self-balancing reporting system referred to as a fund. Because of the broad range of possible activities, specific accounting procedures have been designed for the various funds. For a state or local government, ten fund types are identified that are grouped within three general categories: (1) Governmental Funds (the General Fund, Special Revenue Funds, Capital Projects Funds, and Debt Service Funds); (2) Proprietary Funds (Enterprise Funds and Internal Service Funds); and (3) Fiduciary Funds (Expendable Trust Funds, Nonexpendable Trust Funds, Pension Trust Funds, and Agency Funds). In addition, two account groups are utilized in connection with the governmental funds: General Fixed Assets Account Group and General Long-Term Debt Account Group.

4. Five of the funds (the four Governmental Funds plus the Expendable Trust Fund) are primarily service-oriented and are referred to as governmental-type funds. These funds utilize many of the unusual accounting procedures traditionally associated with governmental reporting. For example, budgetary entries are required in the General Fund, Special Revenue Funds, and Expendable Trust Funds while being optional in the Debt Service Funds and Capital Projects Funds. Annual financial budgets are adopted for each fund (to promote financial planning and control) and are entered directly into the accounting records by means of a journal entry. Comparisons can then be drawn at any time during the period between actual and budgeted figures. At year's end, both amounts are reported in the Statement of Revenues, Expenditures, and Changes in Fund Balances—Budget and Actual.

5. Another significant aspect of the accounting process found in state and local government units is the recognition of expenditures. To assist in maintaining control over spending, governmental-type funds focus on recording expenditures rather than either expenses or asset acquisitions. This approach is designed to help monitor the uses made by a government of its financial resources. Thus, spending is recorded in this manner whether it is for buildings, equipment, or traditional expenses such as rents and salaries. Historically, modified accrual accounting has been applied for recognition purposes. Under this approach, each expenditure is entered into the records at the time a liability is incurred. In 1990, the GASB issued its *Statement No. 11* which required the use of accrual accounting so that expenditures would be reported in the same period as the underlying event. Because of the controversy surrounding this pronouncement, its effective date has been postponed indefinitely.

6. Despite the emphasis on reporting expenditures, some permanent recording of fixed asset acquisitions is still considered necessary. Consequently, long-lived assets purchased by any of the governmental-type funds are listed separately in a General Fixed Assets Account Group. Since depreciation is not an expenditure, its recording is omitted entirely from these funds. *GASB 11,* when it becomes effective, will require that only fixed assets be separated into this account group.

7. Modified accrual accounting requires that revenues be recognized in the period in which they become both measurable and available. Thus, property taxes are usually accrued when assessed but many other revenues are recognized only when cash is received. *GASB 11* is designed to change revenue recognition to an accrual system so that the reporting is in the same period as the underlying transaction (or event) or when the earning process has been completed.

8. Several other aspects of the governmental accounting process that warrant special attention because of unique reporting requirements include the sale of bonds, interfund transactions, and the recording of commitments. The issuance of bonds is an especially important procedure since state and local governments often raise considerable amounts of their resources in this manner. At the time of sale, the appropriate fund records the inflow of cash as an Other Financing Source. Concurrently, the liability is listed separately in the General Long-Term Debt Account Group. *GASB 11* will continue this process for capital debt (such as for the construction of a building). However, when this standard takes effect, long-term operating bonds will be reported in the fund utilizing the money and repaying the debt.

9. Because of the need to provide sufficient monetary resources to all appropriate functions, interfund transactions are common within most government units. Three different types are identified: (1) operating transfers designed to direct money to the various governmental funds, (2) residual equity transfers made to create or finance proprietary activities, and (3) quasi-external transactions used to pay for services performed within the government for a fee.

10. An additional procedure that plays an essential budgetary role in a state or local government accounting system is the recording of monetary commitments known as encumbrances. The reporting of encumbrances is intended to help prevent the overspending of a fund's resources. An Encumbrances account balance is established at the time that a purchase order is approved or a contract signed. This account balance is eventually removed when a formal liability is incurred.

Comprehensive Illustration

PROBLEM   (Estimated Time: 30 to 55 minutes)

The town of Drexel, North Carolina, has the following financial transactions occur during the 1995 fiscal year. Prepare journal entries for these events indicating the appropriate fund(s) or group of accounts in each case. Closing entries are not required. For transactions that will be handled differently after *GASB 11* becomes effective, make two sets of entries to show the traditional approach and then the new one.

1. The town council adopts a budget estimating general revenues of $740,000 and establishing approved expenditures of $610,000 and operating transfers out of $100,000. A surplus of $30,000 is projected. The council also agrees that an additional $8,000 in anticipated parking meter receipts is to be used to send needy children to summer camp.

2. Property taxes of $700,000 are levied for 1995. Based on past experience, 3 percent of this total should be collected in subsequent fiscal periods while 2 percent are estimated as uncollectible.

3. Three new police cars are ordered at an approximate cost of $96,000.

4. A transfer of $50,000 is made from the General Fund to a Debt Service Fund. This money, along with $28,000 already in the Debt Service Fund, is used to pay a $70,000 bond payable that comes due plus accrued interest. Of the interest payment, $5,000 relates to the prior fiscal period.

5. The town council approves construction of a $850,000 town hall. Of this amount, $700,000 will be raised by a bond issue with the remainder coming from a state grant that has already been approved (although not yet received) and must be spent for this building and its furnishings.

6. The town sells the bonds mentioned in (5) for $700,000.

7. Parking meter revenues of $6,600 are collected and immediately used to send deserving children to camp.

8. Property tax collections amount to $660,000.

9. A contract to build the new town hall at a cost of $828,000 is signed and the commitment is recorded.

10. The town agrees to put curbing on several local streets at a cost of $80,000. Ten percent of this money will come from the General Fund with the remainder to be charged to the property owners being benefited. The town will be secondarily liable for the entire amount.

11. The three new police cars arrive at an actual cost of $95,000.

12. An invoice for the work to date of $120,000 is received from the contractor in connection with the new town hall. Five percent is retained to ensure completion of the contract with the remainder to be paid by the town in 60 days.

13. Bonds of $72,000 are sold to finance the curbing project.

14. Licenses and fees of $18,000 are collected by the town. No previous recording had been made.

15. The state pays the $150,000 grant described in (5) in connection with the town hall. Of this total, $20,000 is spent immediately to acquire furniture for the facility.

16. The town issues an $80,000 two-year bond to finance ongoing operating activities.

SOLUTION

The following entries should be recorded within the accounting system of the town of Drexel. In some cases, the entries are optional and are so identified. Changes created by the eventual impact of *GASB 11* are also noted.

1.   *General Fund*

Estimated Revenues Control	740,000	
Appropriations Control		610,000
Estimated Other Financing		
Uses—Operating Transfers Out		100,000
Budgetary Fund Balance		30,000
To record 1995 budget.		

Special Revenue Fund

Estimated Revenues—Parking Meter Receipts	8,000	
Appropriations—Summer Camp		8,000
To record 1995 budget for parking meter revenues and related expenditures.		

2.   *General Fund*

Taxes Receivable—Current	700,000	
Allowance for Uncollectible Taxes (2%)		14,000
Deferred Revenues (3%)		21,000
Revenues Control (95%)		665,000
To record property tax levy. Of the total, 3% will not be available until 1996.		

GASB 11 Entry

Taxes Receivable—Current	700,000	
Allowance for Uncollectable Taxes (2%)		14,000
Revenues Control (98%)		686,000
To record property tax levy for the year of 1996.		

3.   *General Fund*

Encumbrances Control	96,000	
Budgetary Fund Balance—Reserved for Encumbrances		96,000
Police cars ordered.		

4.   *General Fund*

Other Financing Uses—Operating Transfer Out	50,000	
Cash		50,000
Transfer made to Debt Service Fund.		

Debt Service Fund

Cash	50,000	
Other Financing Sources—Operating		
Transfer In		50,000
Transfer received from General Fund.		
Expenditures Control	78,000	
Cash		78,000
Payment of bond principal ($70,000) and interest ($8,000).		

General Long-Term Debt Account Group

Bonds Payable	70,000	
Amount Available in Debt Service Funds		28,000
Amount to Be Provided		42,000
To remove extinguished debt.		

GASB 11 Entry (Only the third entry must be changed.)

Expenditures Control	73,000	
Accrued Interest Payable.	5,000	
Cash		78,000
Payment of principal and interest with $5,000 of interest relating to prior year.		

5.   *Capital Projects Fund*

Estimated Revenues—State Grant	150,000	
Estimated Other Financing		
Sources—Bond Proceeds	700,000	
Appropriations—Construction of Town Hall		850,000
Optional entry to record construction budget.		
Due from State	150,000	
Deferred Revenues—State Grant		150,000
To accrue approved grant from state. Revenue will be earned by making appropriate expenditure.		

6.   *Capital Projects Fund*

Cash	700,000	
Other Financing Sources—Bond Proceeds		700,000
To record receipt from bond issue.		

General Long-Term Debt Account Group

Amount to Be Provided	700,000	
Bonds Payable		700,000
To record receipt from bond issue.		

7.   *Special Revenue Fund*

Cash	6,600	
Revenues—Parking Meter Receipts		6,600
To record parking meter revenues.		
Expenditures—Children to Camp	6,600	
Cash		6,600
Money is spent to send children to camp.		

8. *General Fund*

Cash. 660,000
    Taxes Receivable—Current.   660,000
Property tax collections.

9. *Capital Projects Fund*

Encumbrances—Town Hall Construction 828,000
    Budgetary Fund Balance—Reserved for
      Encumbrances   828,000
Contract signed to construct town hall.

10. *Capital Projects Fund*

Estimated Revenues—Special Assessments 72,000
Estimated Other Financing Sources—
    Operating Transfers In. 8,000
      Appropriations—Curbing.   80,000
Optional entry to record budget for curbing project with 10 percent
payable from General Fund.

Due from General Fund 8,000
    Other Financing Sources—Operating Transfer In   8,000
To accrue interfund transfer that has been authorized.

General Fund

Other Financing Uses—Operating Transfers Out 8,000
    Due to Capital Projects Fund.   8,000
To record authorized transfer.

11. *General Fund*

Budgetary Fund Balance—Reserved for
    Encumbrances 96,000
      Encumbrances Control.   96,000
To remove encumbrance on police cars.

Expenditures Control 95,000
    Vouchers Payable.   95,000
To record actual invoice price for police cars.

General Fixed Assets Account Group

Machinery and Equipment 95,000
    Investment in General Fixed Assets—
      General Fund.   95,000
To record acquisition of police cars.

12. *Capital Projects Fund*

Budgetary Fund Balance—Reserved for
    Encumbrances 120,000
      Encumbrances—Town Hall Construction   120,000
To cancel portion of encumbrance.

Expenditures—Town Hall Construction   120,000
   Contracts Payable   114,000
   Contracts Payable—Retained
     Percentage (5%)   6,000
   To establish liability for town hall construction.

General Fixed Assets Account Group

Construction in Progress   120,000
   Investments in General Fixed Assets—
     Capital Projects Funds   120,000
   To record cost to date of construction of town hall.

13.   *Capital Projects Fund*

Cash   72,000
   Other Financing Sources—
     Special Assessment Bonds   72,000
   To record cash received from issuance of special assessments
   bonds.

General Long-Term Debt Account Group

Amount to Be Provided from Special Assessments   72,000
   Special Assessment Bond with
     Government Commitment   72,000
   To record outstanding bonds.

14.   *General Fund*

Cash   18,000
   Revenue Control   18,000
Collection of licenses and fees.

15.   *Capital Projects Fund*

Cash   150,000
   Due from State   150,000
Grant is collected from state government for town hall and
furnishings.

Expenditures—Furniture   20,000
   Cash   20,000
Part of state grant is spent to furnish new town hall.

Deferred Revenues—State Grant   20,000
   Revenues—State Grant   20,000
To recognize revenue in connection with state grant properly spent.

General Fixed Asset Account Group

Furniture   20,000
   Investment in General Fixed Assets—State Grant   20,000
To record cost of furniture for town hall.

16.   *General Fund*

Cash   80,000
   Other Financing Sources—Bond Proceeds   80,000
Sold bond to finance ongoing activities.

General Long-Term Debt Account Group

Amount to Be Provided 80,000

    Bond Payable 80,000

To record two-year bond that was issued to finance ongoing activities.

GASB 11 Entry

General Fund

Cash 80,000

    Long-Term Bond Payable—Operating Debt 80,000

To record inflow of cash from sale of bond for operating purposes.

Questions

1. Identify the different users of the financial statements of state and local governments. How do their informational requirements vary?
2. What is the primary reporting emphasis in governmental accounting? Why has this emphasis been adopted?
3. Why are consolidated financial statements not considered appropriate for a government reporting unit?
4. What is a fund? Why are governmental accounting records broken down into individual funds?
5. Why are differing accounting methods used by the various funds of a state or local government?
6. What are the three broad classifications into which all funds can be categorized? What are the identifying characteristics of each of these fund types?
7. What is an account group? Why is an account group not considered a fund?
8. What are the four fund types that fall within the governmental funds? What activities are accounted for by each of these funds?
9. Which two major fund types are within proprietary funds? What activities are accounted for by each?
10. What is the difference between an Expendable Trust Fund and a Nonexpendable Trust Fund?
11. All of the funds of a state or local government (except for the Agency Funds) can be viewed as either governmental-type or business-type. What is the difference in accounting emphasis between these two groups?
12. What are some of the changes in government accounting called for by *GASB Statement No. 11?* Why is the future of this pronouncement currently in doubt?
13. Why are budgets formally recorded in the accounting records of some governmental funds? Which of the fund types record budgetary entries?

14. What is an appropriation?

15. Why does the accounting process that is utilized by governmental-type funds emphasize expenditures rather than expenses?

16. Under modified accrual accounting, when should expenditures be recorded? Under accrual accounting, when should expenditures be recorded?

17. Since the governmental-type funds record expenditures, how are fixed assets reported?

18. Why is depreciation expense not recognized in the governmental-type funds?

19. Under modified accrual accounting, when should revenues be recognized? Under accrual accounting, when should revenues be recognized?

20. How does the recognition of property tax revenues differ between traditional government accounting and the rules established by *GASB Statement No. 11?*

21. When is the Other Financing Sources designation considered to be appropriate? When is the Other Financing Uses designation used?

22. What is the traditional method of recording the long-term liabilities issued by the governmental-type funds? How will this process be affected by *GASB Statement No. 11?*

23. Describe the revenue recognition process in connection with grants.

24. What are the three types of interfund transactions? How should each be recorded?

25. What is the purpose of an encumbrance? When is an encumbrance recorded?

26. What accounting is made for encumbrances that remain outstanding at the end of a fiscal year?

27. What is a special assessment, and how are special assessments accounted for by a state or local government?

28. What are the two ways to account for the supplies bought and used by governmental-type funds? Which approach is required by *GASB Statement No. 11?*

29. What account balances are closed out annually in a governmental-type fund? Into what account are these balances closed?

Library Assignments

1. Read the following articles and any other published information discussing the unique features of not-for-profit accounting:
   "Making Sense of Nonbusiness Accounting," *Harvard Business Review,* May–June 1980.

"Advantages of Fund Accounting in 'Nonprofits,'" *Harvard Business Review*, May–June 1980.

"Financial Reporting: Should Government Emulate Business?" *Journal of Accountancy*, August 1981.

"Monuments, Mistakes, and Opportunities," *Accounting Horizons*, June 1988.

"The Nature of Public Assets: A Response to Mautz," *Accounting Horizons*, June 1990.

"Not-for-Profit Financial Reporting: Another View," *Journal of Accountancy*, August 1989.

In this last article, the following question is raised: Are not-for-profit organizations truly so different from for-profit entities that an entirely different reporting system is necessary? Write a short report to address this issue.

2. Obtain a copy of the latest comprehensive annual financial report of a state or local government. If one is not available in the library, request a copy, either by telephone or mail, from the Director of Finance of the governmental unit. Write a report to answer the following questions:

- How many separate fund types are presented in the balance sheet?
- What types of assets are found in the General Fund?
- For the General Fund, what amount is shown as the Fund Balance—Unreserved, Undesignated?
- What is the total reported balance of assets in the General Fixed Asset Account Group?
- What types of activities are reported within the Special Revenue Funds?
- What is the total amount of debt reported in the General Long-Term Debt Account Group?
- Does the General Fund show a year-end total for Fund Balance—Reserved for Encumbrances? If so, what is this balance?
- What amount of total revenues and expenditures are reported for the General Fund?
- Were General Fund revenues greater or less than the budgeted figure?
- What other financing sources and uses are listed for the General Fund?
- Are any residual equity transfers listed?
- If the government has Expendable Trust Funds, what specific funds are included under this category?

Problems

1. What is the underlying reason a governmental unit uses separate funds to account for various transactions?

    a. Governmental units are so large that accounting for all transactions as a single unit would be unduly cumbersome.

    b. Because of the diverse nature of the services offered and legal provisions regarding activities of a governmental unit, activities must be segregated by functional nature.

    c. Generally accepted accounting principles require that all not-for-profit entities report on a funds basis.

    d. Many activities carried on by governmental units are short-lived so that inclusion in a general set of accounts could cause undue probability of error or omission.

  (AICPA adapted)

2. Which of the following is not a Governmental Fund?

    a. Special Revenue Fund.

    b. Internal Service Fund.

    c. Capital Projects Fund.

    d. Debt Service Fund.

3. What is the purpose of a Special Revenue Fund?

    a. To account for revenues legally restricted as to expenditure.

    b. To account for ongoing activities.

    c. To account for gifts where only subsequently earned income can be expended.

    d. To account for the cost of long-lived assets bought with designated funds.

4. What is the purpose of Enterprise Funds?

    a. To account for operations that provide services to other departments within a government.

    b. To account for asset transfers.

    c. To account for ongoing activities such as the police and fire departments.

    d. To account for operations financed in whole or in part by outside user charges.

5. How do Expendable Trust Funds differ from Nonexpendable Trust Funds?

    a. Expendable Trust Funds account for monies that have already been spent whereas Nonexpendable Trust Funds account for monies to be spent.

    b. Expendable Trust Funds account for gifts where the entire amount can be spent whereas Nonexpendable Trust Funds account for gifts where only subsequently earned income can be spent.

    c. Expendable Trust Funds account for monies that can be spent at any time whereas Nonexpendable Trust Funds account for monies that can only be spent after the passage of a specified time.

    d. Expendable Trust Funds account for monies that must be spent for operating activities whereas Nonexpendable Trust Funds account for monies that must be spent for fixed assets.

6. Which of the following statements is true concerning the recording of a budget?
   a. At the beginning of the year, Appropriations is debited.
   b. A debit to the Budgetary Fund Balance account indicates an expected surplus.
   c. At the beginning of the year, Estimated Revenues is debited.
   d. At the end of the year, Appropriations is credited.

7. Which of the following funds does not always record a budgetary entry?
   a. Debt Service Funds.
   b. Expendable Trust Funds.
   c. Special Revenue Funds.
   d. General Fund.

8. When fixed assets purchased from General Fund revenues were received, the appropriate journal entry was made in the General Fixed Assets Account Group. What account, if any, should have been debited in the General Fund?
   a. No journal entry should have been made in the General Fund.
   b. Expenditures.
   c. Fixed assets.
   d. Encumbrances.
   (AICPA adapted)

9. How will *GASB Statement No. 11* impact the recording of expenditures?
   a. *GASB 11* requires expenses and capital assets to be reported rather than expenditures.
   b. *GASB 11* requires expenditures to be recorded in the same period as the underlying event or transaction rather than when the liability becomes due.
   c. *GASB 11* requires that expenses be recorded as expenditures but capital assets are recorded as assets.
   d. *GASB 11* requires that capital assets be recorded as expenditures but expenses are recorded as expenses.

10. A police department is acquiring a new car that is being accounted for within the General Fund. What recording should be made?
    a. As a vehicle within the General Fund.
    b. As an expenditure within the General Fixed Assets Account Group.
    c. As a vehicle within the General Fund and as an expenditure within the General Fixed Assets Account Group.
    d. As an expenditure within the General Fund and as a vehicle within the General Fixed Assets Account Group.

11. Machinery is acquired for the fire department using monies from the General Fund. Which of the following is true?
    a. Depreciation expense is not recognized although the reporting of accumulated depreciation within the General Fixed Assets Account Group is allowed.

b. Depreciation is recorded but only if the machinery is recorded within the General Fund.

c. The machinery's reported balance is adjusted each year to its market value.

d. Depreciation expense is allowed but only if no Expenditure has been recorded.

12. A city acquires supplies and is using the consumption method of recording. Which of the following statements is true?

a. An Expenditures account was debited at the time of receipt.

b. An expense is recorded as the supplies are consumed.

c. An Inventory account is debited at the time of the acquisition.

d. The supplies are recorded within the General Fixed Assets Account Group.

13. According to modified accrual accounting, when should revenues be recognized?

a. When earned and collected.

b. When earned and collection is reasonably assured.

c. When measurable and available.

d. When the underlying transaction has taken place and a demand for the money has been made.

14. According to *GASB 11,* when should tax revenues be recognized?

a. When earned and collected.

b. When earned and collection is reasonably assured.

c. When measurable and available.

d. When the underlying transaction has taken place and demand for the money has been made.

15. A county mails out property tax assessments. Of the total, $22,000 are not expected to be collected for several years. How should this amount be recorded at the time of the assessment?

a. As a revenue under modified accrual accounting but as a deferred revenue under *GASB 11.*

b. As a revenue under all circumstances.

c. As a deferred revenue under modified accrual accounting but as a revenue under *GASB 11.*

d. As a deferred revenue under all circumstances.

16. During the year ending December 31, 1995, Leyland City received a state grant of $500,000 to finance the purchase of buses, and an additional grant of $100,000 to aid in the financing of bus operations. Only $300,000 of the capital grant was used in 1995 for the purchase of buses although the entire operating grant of $100,000 was spent during the year.

If Leyland's bus transportation system is accounted for as part of the General Fund, how much should Leyland report as revenues for this year?

a. $100,000.

b. $300,000.

    c. $400,000.

    d. $500,000.

    (AICPA adapted)

17. A city receives a state grant that must be spent to remove litter. When is the revenue recognized?

    a. When received.

    b. When appropriately spent.

    c. When measurable and available.

    d. When earned.

18. A city issues a five-year bond to finance the construction of a new government building. Which of the following statements is not true?

    a. An Amount to be Provided account appears in the General Long-Term Debt Account Group.

    b. The bond appears in a Debt Service Fund.

    c. The cash is recorded in a Capital Projects Fund.

    d. An Other Financing Source account appears in the Capital Projects Fund.

19. Money is transferred from the General Fund to the Capital Projects Funds to provide financing for a new construction project. This transaction is an example of

    a. An operating transfer.

    b. A residual equity transfer.

    c. A capital contribution.

    d. A quasi-external transaction.

20. When is the Other Financing Source designation used?

    a. For revenues other than property taxes.

    b. For bond proceeds and transfers-in.

    c. For interest and other investment income.

    d. For quasi-external transactions.

21. What is a residual equity transfer?

    a. A transfer by a government of money to provide permanent financing for a Proprietary Fund.

    b. A transfer that increases the Fund Balance of the General Fund.

    c. A transfer of the remaining book value of a fixed asset.

    d. A transfer of any funds remaining after a project has been entirely completed.

22. Which of the following is an example of a quasi-external transaction of a city?

    a. Money is transferred from the General Fund to the Capital Projects Fund.

    b. A transfer is made to start an Enterprise Fund.

    c. The General Fund pays the city print shop for work done.

    d. A building is acquired with the proceeds of a bond.

23. A city constructs a special assessment project (a sidewalk) for which it is secondarily liable. Bonds of $90,000 are issued. Another $10,000 is authorized and transferred out of the General Fund. The sidewalk is built for $100,000. The citizens are billed for $90,000. They pay this amount and the debt is paid off. Where is the $100,000 expenditure recorded?

   a. No recording is made by the city.

   b. Agency Fund.

   c. General Fund.

   d. Capital Projects Fund.

24. Work is done by a city as a special assessment. Curbing is constructed in a new neighborhood. Under what condition should this activity be recorded in an Agency Fund?

   a. Never; the work is reported in the Capital Projects Funds.

   b. Only if the city is secondarily liable for any debt incurred to finance construction costs.

   c. Only if the city is in no way liable for the costs of the construction.

   d. In all cases.

25. When is an encumbrance first recorded?

   a. At the time the budget is passed.

   b. When the appropriation is made.

   c. When a purchase commitment is made.

   d. When an acquired asset is received.

26. An encumbrance is outstanding at the end of a city's fiscal year. The encumbrance will still be honored in the next period. How is this information reported in the first year?

   a. All encumbrance balances are removed but a fund balance amount is reclassified to disclose the commitment.

   b. If the encumbrance is to be honored, nothing is done at the end of the first period.

   c. Since the encumbrance is to be honored, the amount is reclassified as a liability.

   d. Since the financial impact will be in the following period, no disclosure is necessary.

27. When supplies ordered by a governmental unit are received at an actual price less than the estimated price on the purchase order, the Encumbrance account is:

   a. Credited for the estimated price on the purchase order.

   b. Credited for the actual price for the supplies received.

   c. Debited for the estimated price on the purchase order.

   d. Debited for the actual price for the supplies received.

(AICPA)

28. Which of the following account balances found in the General Fund is not closed out at the end of the fiscal period?
    a. Due to Capital Projects Fund.
    b. Other Financing Sources—Bond Proceeds.
    c. Expenditures Control.
    d. Residual Equity Transfer.

29. The board of commissioners of the city of Hartmoore adopted a General Fund budget for the year ending June 30, 1996, which indicated revenues of $1,000,000, bond proceeds of $400,000, appropriations of $900,000, and operating transfers out of $300,000. If this budget is formally integrated into the accounting records, what is the required journal entry at the beginning of the year? What later entry is required?

30. A city orders a new computer at an anticipated cost of $88,000. It is received with an actual cost of $89,400. Payment is subsequently made. Give all of the required journal entries and identify the type of fund or account group in which each entry is recorded.

31. Cash of $90,000 is transferred from a city's general fund to start construction on a police station. A bond of $830,000 is issued at face value. The police station is built for $920,000. Prepare all necessary journal entries for these transactions and identify the type of fund or account group in which each entry is recorded. Assume that the commitment is not recorded by the city.

32. On December 31, 1995, the city of Crawford paid $3.8 million for the total cost of a new fire station built during the year. To finance the project, $3 million in bonds were issued at face value with the remaining $800,000 transferred from the General Fund. What journal entries should be recorded by the Capital Projects Fund? What other journal entries should be made within Crawford's accounting system?

33. The following balances are found in the accounting system for Burwood Village's parks and recreation department at March 31, 1995:

Appropriations—supplies	$7,500
Expenditures—supplies	4,500
Encumbrances—supplies ordered	750

A request has been made for additional baseball bats. How much does the department have available for this purchase?
(AICPA adapted)

34. The following data relates to Lely Township:

Cost of printing and binding equipment used for servicing all of Lely's departments on a cost-reimbursement basis	$100,000
Cost of equipment used for supplying water to Lely's residents	900,000
Receivables for completed sidewalks to be paid in installments by affected property owners (the town is secondarily liable)	950,000
Cash received from federal government which must be used for highway maintenance . . .	995,000

How much of these assets should be reported in a Special Revenue Fund? How much of these assets should be accounted for in an Internal Service Fund? How much of these assets should be accounted for in an Enterprise Fund?

(AICPA adapted)

35. A local government incurs the following transactions during the current fiscal period. Prepare journal entries without dollar amounts. Indicate the fund type or account group in which each entry is being recorded.

   a. Budget is passed for the police department, ambulance service, and other ongoing activities. Funding is from property taxes, transfers, and bond proceeds. All monetary outflows will be for expenses and fixed assets. A deficit is projected.

   b. A bond is issued at face value to fund the construction of a new municipal building.

   c. A computer is ordered to be used by the tax department.

   d. The computer is received.

   e. The invoice for the computer is paid.

   f. City council agrees to transfer money from General Fund as partial payment for a special assessments project. This money has not yet been transferred. The city will be secondarily liable for any money borrowed for this work.

   g. City council creates a motor pool to service all government vehicles. Money is transferred from General Fund to provide permanent financing for this facility.

   h. Property taxes are levied. Although officials believe that most of these taxes should be collected during the current period, a portion will be received during the subsequent year with a small percentage estimated to be uncollectible. Modified accrual accounting is being used.

    i. Grant money is collected from the state to be spent as a supplement to the salaries of the police force. No entry has previously been recorded.

    j. A portion of the grant money in (*i*) is properly spent.

36. Make journal entries for the governmental funds of the city of Pudding to record the following transactions. Indicate the fund or account group in which each entry is being made.

    a. Ordered a new truck for the sanitation department at a cost of $94,000.

    b. The city print shop did work for the school system (but has not yet been paid). The printing was charged out at $1,200.

    c. A $700,000 bond was issued to build a new road.

    d. Cash of $20,000 is transferred from the General Fund to provide permanent financing for a municipal swimming pool that will be viewed as an Enterprise Fund.

    e. The truck ordered in (*a*) is received at an actual cost of $96,000. Payment is not made at this time.

    f. Cash of $32,000 is transferred from the General Fund to a Capital Projects Fund.

    g. A state grant of $30,000 is received that must be spent to promote recycling.

    h. The first $5,000 of the state grant received in (*g*) is appropriately expended.

37. Prepare journal entries for a state or local government to record the following transactions. Indicate the funds or account groups involved. Only entries in the governmental-type funds need be recorded.

    a. A $300,000 bond is sold at face value by the government to finance construction of a warehouse.

    b. A $400,000 contract is signed for construction of the warehouse.

    c. A $20,000 transfer of unrestricted funds was made for the eventual payment of the debt in (*a*).

    d. Equipment for the fire department is received with a cost of $12,000. When ordered, an anticipated cost of $11,800 had been recorded.

    e. Supplies to be used in the schools are bought for $2,000 cash. The consumption method is being used.

    f. A state grant of $5,000 is received to supplement police salaries.

    g. Property tax assessments are mailed to citizens of the government. The total assessment is $600,000 although officials anticipate that 4 percent will never be collected and another 5 percent will not be received for several years. Modified accrual accounting is to be used.

38. The following trial balances are for the governmental funds of the city of Copeland prepared from the current accounting records:

General Fund

	Debit	Credit
Cash	$ 19,000	
Taxes receivable	112,000	
Allowance for uncollectible taxes		$ 2,000
Vouchers payable		24,000
Due to debt service fund		10,000
Deferred revenues		16,000
Budgetary fund balance—Reserved for encumbrances		9,000
Fund balance—Unreserved, undesignated		103,000
Revenues control		176,000
Expenditures control	110,000	
Other financing uses control	90,000	
Encumbrances control	9,000	
Estimated revenues control	190,000	
Appropriations control		171,000
Budgetary fund balance		19,000
Totals	$530,000	$530,000

Debt Service Fund

	Debit	Credit
Cash	$ 8,000	
Investments	51,000	
Taxes receivable	11,000	
Due from general fund	10,000	
Fund balance—Designated for debt service		45,000
Revenues control		20,000
Other financing sources—Operating transfers in		90,000
Expenditures control	75,000	
Totals	$155,000	$155,000

Capital Projects Fund

	Debit	Credit
Cash	$ 70,000	
Special assessments receivable	90,000	
Contracts payable		$ 50,000
Deferred revenues		90,000
Budgetary fund balance—Reserved for encumbrances		16,000
Fund balance—Unreserved, undesignated		–0–
Other financing sources		150,000
Expenditures control	130,000	
Encumbrances	16,000	
Estimated other financing sources	150,000	
Appropriations		150,000
Totals	$456,000	$456,000

Special Revenue Fund

	Debit	Credit
Cash	$ 14,000	
Taxes receivable	41,000	
Inventory of supplies	4,000	
Vouchers payablè		$ 25,000
Deferred revenues		3,000
Fund balance—Reserved for inventory of supplies		4,000
Budgetary fund balance—Reserved for encumbrances		3,000
Fund balance—Unreserved, undesignated		19,000
Revenues control		56,000
Expenditures control.	48,000	
Encumbrances	3,000	
Estimated revenues	75,000	
Appropriations		60,000
Budgetary fund balance		15,000
Totals	$185,000	$185,000

Required:

Based on the information presented for each of these governmental funds, answer the following questions:

a. How much more money can be expended or committed by the General Fund during the remainder of the current year?

b. Which closing entries would be necessary for the General Fund?

c. Deferred revenues appear in three of these trial balances. What possible explanations exist for these balances?

d. Why does the Capital Projects Fund have no construction or fixed asset accounts?

e. What does the $150,000 Appropriations balance found in the Capital Projects Fund represent?

f. Several of the funds have balances for Encumbrances and Budgetary Fund Balance—Reserved for Encumbrance. How will these amounts be accounted for at the end of the fiscal year?

g. Why does the Fund Balance—Unreserved, Undesignated account in the Capital Projects Fund have a zero balance?

h. What are possible explanations for the $150,000 Other Financing Sources balance found in the Capital Projects Fund?

i. What does the $75,000 balance in the Expenditures Control account of the Debt Service Fund represent?

j. What is the purpose of the Special Assessments Receivable found in the Capital Projects Fund?

k. In the Special Revenue Fund, what is the purpose of the Fund Balance—Reserved for Inventory of Supplies account?

l. Why does the Debt Service Fund not have budgetary account balances?

39. Following are descriptions of transactions and other financial events for the city of Tetris for the year ending December 31, 1995. Not all transactions have been included here. Only the General Fund formally records a budget. No encumbrances were carried over from 1994.

Paid salary for police officers	$ 21,000
Government grant is received to pay ambulance drivers	40,000
Estimated revenues	232,000
Invoices were received for rent on equipment used by fire department during last four months of the year.	3,000
Paid for newly constructed city hall	1,044,000
Commitment made to acquire new ambulance.	111,000
Cash received from bonds sold for construction purposes	300,000
Order placed for new sanitation truck	69,000
Paid salary of ambulance drivers—money derived from state government grant given for that purpose	24,000
Paid for supplies for school system	16,000
Transfer made by General Fund to eventually pay off a long-term debt	33,000
Received but did not pay for a new ambulance	120,000
Property tax receivables were levied. City anticipates that 95 percent will be collected and 5 percent will be bad.	200,000
Acquired and paid for new school bus	40,000
Cash received from business taxes and parking meters (not previously accrued)	14,000
Appropriations	225,000

The following questions are independent although each is based on the preceding information. When making journal entries, indicate the fund.

 a. What is the balance in the Budgetary Fund Balance account for the year and is it a debit or credit?

 b. Assume that 60 percent of the school supplies are used during the year so that 40 percent remain. If the consumption method is being applied, how is the recording handled?

 c. The sanitation truck that was ordered was not received prior to the end of the year. The commitment will be honored in the subsequent year when the truck arrives. What journal entries are needed at the end of 1995?

 d. Assume the ambulance was received on December 31, 1995. Provide all necessary journal entries on that date.

 e. Give all journal entries that should have been made when the $33,000 transfer was made to eventually pay off a long-term debt.

 f. What amount of revenue would be recognized for the period? Explain the makeup of this total.

   g. What deferred revenue figures would appear in this city's balance sheet?

   h. What are the total expenditures? Explain the makeup of this total.

   i. What journal entries were prepared when the bonds were issued?

40. Zuraw County is located in the western part of the state. At the beginning of the current fiscal year, the county's accountant retired. Government officials of Zuraw County were unable to fill this accounting vacancy for a number of months. When a qualified individual was finally hired for the job, a current trial balance for the General Fund was prepared:

	Debit	Credit
Cash	$ 56,000	
Due from capital projects fund	50,000	
Vouchers payable		$ 31,000
Deferred revenues		18,000
Budgetary fund balance—Reserved for encumbrances		9,000
Fund balance—Unreserved, undesignated		17,000
Revenues control		330,000
Expenditures control.	264,000	
Truck	16,000	
Encumbrances control	9,000	
Estimated revenues	390,000	
Appropriations		350,000
Budgetary fund balance		30,000
Totals	$785,000	$785,000

Upon investigation, the new accountant discovered that the following events had occurred during the time that Zuraw County was without an accountant:

- The property tax levy for the current year was never entered into the financial records. Instead, the county recorded all cash collections as revenues when received. The original assessment was $400,000. Of that amount, $300,000 has been received to date with $90,000 more expected by the end of the year with the remaining $10,000 judged to be uncollectible. Receivables of $18,000 carried over from the previous year were also collected during the period and credited to taxes receivable. Modified accrual accounting is used.
- A new truck was acquired for $16,000 in cash during the year. The only entry relating to this acquisition was made in the General Fund.
- During the year, the county followed the policy of recording encumbrances for all purchase commitments. At the time a legal liability was incurred, the original encumbrance was eliminated based on the final invoice price. For the current period, $175,000 in encumbrances have been

recorded. Subsequently, related expenditures of $166,000 were journalized, although the original encumbrances for these acquisitions totaled to only $162,400.

- A transfer of $50,000 was made to the Capital Projects Fund during the year as permanent financing for a new city hall. This amount was recorded in the Capital Projects Fund as a credit to the Fund Balance—Unreserved, Undesignated account.
- County officials had estimated that $10,000 would be collected from parking meters and other miscellaneous revenues. This figure was debited to Estimated Revenues at the beginning of the period and credited to the Fund Balance—Unreserved, Undesignated account.
- The General Fund owes $5,000 to the Capital Projects Fund as the county's portion of the cost of a sidewalk construction project.

Required:

Prepare the correcting entries for Zuraw County needed to adjust the records of the General Fund as well as any other fund.

41. Chesterfield County incurred the following list of transactions. Record these transactions indicating, in each case, the fund type or account group in which the entry is recorded.

    a. A budget is passed for all ongoing activities. Revenue is anticipated to be $834,000 with approved spending of $540,000 and operating transfers out of $242,000.

    b. A contract is signed with a construction company to build a new central office building for the government at a cost of $8 million. A budget for this project has previously been recorded.

    c. Bonds are sold for $8 million (face value) to finance construction of the new office building.

    d. The new building is completed. An invoice is received and paid.

    e. Previously unrestricted cash of $1 million is set aside to begin paying the bonds issued in (*c*).

    f. A portion of the bonds come due and $1 million is paid. Of this total, $100,000 represents interest. The interest had not been previously accrued.

    g. Property tax levies are assessed to the citizens. Total billing for this tax is $800,000. Ninety percent is assumed to be collectible in this period with receipt of an additional 6 percent during subsequent periods. The remainder is expected to be uncollectible. (Make this entry twice: once using modified accrual accounting and then using accrual accounting.)

    h. Cash of $120,000 is received from a toll road. Legally, 80 percent of this money has to be spent on highway maintenance. The remainder is held until the end of the year and then transferred to the state.

    i. Investments valued at $300,000 are received by the county as a donation from a grateful citizen. Income from these investments must be used to beautify local parks.

42. The following trial balance is taken from the General Fund of the city of Jennings for the year ending December 31, 1995. Prepare a condensed statement of revenues, expenditures, and changes in fund balance and also prepare a condensed balance sheet.

	Debit	Credit
Budgetary fund balance—Reserved for encumbrances		$ 90,000
Cash	$ 30,000	
Contracts payable		90,000
Deferred revenues		40,000
Due from capital projects funds	60,000	
Due to debt service funds.		40,000
Encumbrances.	90,000	
Expenditures	420,000	
Fund balance—Unreserved, undesignated.		170,000
Investments	410,000	
Residual equity transfer.	70,000	
Revenues		740,000
Other financing sources—Bond proceeds		300,000
Other financing sources—Transfers in		50,000
Other financing uses—Transfers out	400,000	
Taxes receivable.	220,000	
Vouchers payable		180,000
Totals.	$1,700,000	$1,700,000

43. In a special election held on May 1, 1995, the citizens of the city of Nicknar voted to approve a $10 million issue of 6 percent bonds maturing in 2015. The proceeds of this sale will help finance the construction of a new civic center. The total cost of the project was estimated at $15 million. The remaining $5 million will be funded by a state grant that has been approved but not yet received. The grant can only be used for this specific construction.

A Capital Projects Fund was established to account for the project. The budget authorization has previously been recorded in a memorandum entry. The following transactions occurred during the fiscal year beginning July 1, 1995, and ending June 30, 1996:

- On July 1, the General Fund loaned $500,000 to this project to defray engineering costs and other initial expenses.
- Preliminary engineering and planning costs of $320,000 were paid to Akron Engineering Company. No encumbrance had been recorded for this cost.
- On December 1, the bonds were sold at 101. The premium on these bonds was transferred to the Debt Service Funds to be used for eventual repayment purposes.

- On March 15, a contract for $12 million was entered into with Candu Construction Company for the major part of the building project.
- Orders were placed for materials estimated to cost $55,000.
- On April 1, a partial payment of $2.5 million was received from the state. This money can only be spent after the city has expended $7 million of its own funds.
- The previously ordered materials were received at a cost of $51,000 and paid. (Use the purchases method.)
- On June 15, an invoice for $2 million was received from Candu Construction for work done to date on the project. As per the terms of the contract, the city will withhold 6 percent of any billing until the building is completed and pay the remainder at the end of 30 days.
- The General Fund was repaid the $500,000 previously loaned.

Required:

Based on the preceding transactions:

a. Prepare journal entries to record the transactions for this capital projects fund for the period July 1, 1995, through June 30, 1996. Include the appropriate closing entries at June 30, 1996.
b. Prepare a balance sheet for this fund as of June 30, 1996.
   (AICPA adapted)

44. Following are a series of events undergone by Dawn Village. Prepare the appropriate journal entries for these transactions indicating the specific fund type or account group within which each entry is being recorded.

- A formal budget is adopted for the village. Revenues of $385,000 are predicted. Of this total, $360,000 has been assigned to the General Fund and $25,000 to Special Revenues Funds. Approved expenditures are set at $370,000: General Fund—$345,000 and Special Revenues Funds—$25,000.
- A new police car is received at an invoice cost of $41,900. A $42,500 encumbrance had been recorded previously by the village.
- A $100,000 grant is received by the village to be used for trash removal.
- Property taxes of $350,000 are levied by the village. Of this amount, 85 percent collection is expected during the current year with 10 percent anticipated during subsequent periods. The remainder will probably be uncollectible. The first $25,000 portion of this levy that is collected is for the Special Revenues Fund. (Make this entry twice, using modified accrual accounting and then using accrual accounting.)
- $69,000 of the grant money is spent for trash removal.
- A special assessments project costing $90,000 is approved; a section of a local road is to be repaved. The village provides the initial support by putting up 10 percent of this cost (from the General Fund). Residents

who will benefit from this project will contribute the remaining 90 percent at the time of completion. The county issues a $80,000 bond payable at face value to help finance the work. The transfer is also made at this time.

- The village collects cash of $112,000. Of this amount, $100,000 is from property taxes while the remainder comes from fines, licenses, and the like that had not previously been accrued. Property tax receivables of $5,000 were judged to be uncollectible.

- The village orders a new computer at an estimated cost of $46,250.

- A total of $70,000 is transferred from the General Fund to the Capital Projects Fund as the initial funding in anticipation of building a new fire station.

- The village pays $60,000 from the General Fund. Salaries for government employees accounted for $13,000 of this total with the rest being paid for the computer which arrived two weeks before.

- A bond payable of $900,000 was issued for $893,000 to finance construction of a new fire station. A contract for $839,000 is then signed with the contractor who will build the new facility.

- A first payment of $87,000 is made on the new fire station based on the current degree of completion.

45. The following trial balance is for the General Fund of the city of Torndup at December 31, 1995. The city plans to honor all remaining commitments during 1996. Prepare a condensed statement of revenues, expenditures, and changes in fund balance as well as a condensed balance sheet.

	Debit	Credit
Accounts payable		$ 4,000
Accounts receivable	$ 32,000	
Allowance for doubtful accounts—Taxes.		6,000
Budgetary fund balance—Reserved for encumbrances		30,000
Cash	18,000	
Deferred revenues.		8,000
Encumbrances control	30,000	
Expenditures control.	370,000	
Fund balance—Unreserved, undesignated (1/1/95).		170,000
Investments.	117,000	
Other financing sources—Bond proceeds.		72,000
Other financing sources—Operating transfers in.		5,000
Other financing uses—Operating transfers out	80,000	
Residual equity transfers	20,000	
Revenues control		440,000
Taxes receivable	91,000	
Vouchers payable		23,000
Totals	$758,000	$758,000

16

ACCOUNTING FOR STATE AND LOCAL GOVERNMENTS (PART TWO)

Questions to Consider

- In what ways does the accounting process used by the business-type activities of a state or local government differ from the procedures applied to governmental-type funds?
- How are proprietary and fiduciary funds reported within the financial statements of a government?
- What controversies surround the reporting of Internal Service Funds?
- How is the reporting unit defined for a state or local government? What activities are included within the financial reporting of most governments?
- What is the difference in the primary government and its component units? How has *GASB Statement No. 14* affected the composition of governmental financial statements?
- What financial statements and other information are presented in the comprehensive annual financial report of a state or locality?

Chapter 15 introduced the accounting procedures utilized by state and local government organizations. To initiate this coverage, the reporting process applied to governmental-type funds (such as the General Fund and Special Revenue Funds) was analyzed in detail. Budgetary entries, the possible impact of *GASB Statement No. 11*, expenditures, encumbrances, transfers, fund balances, and other unique aspects of governmental reporting were examined at that time. However, governmental accounting is not limited to the procedures previously illustrated. Consequently, the current chapter expands on this introductory material.

Chapter 16 analyzes three additional aspects of state and local government reporting:

- The first section presents appropriate financial accounting for the various business-type activities of state and local government units. Included are overviews of both the functioning and the reporting of funds such as the Enterprise Funds, Internal Service Funds, and Nonexpendable Trust Funds.
- The second section describes the identification of the specific reporting unit encompassed by the financial statements of a government. The GASB has recently looked at this issue and set forth guidelines for the activities that should be included within the financial statements of a state or local government.
- The third section completes coverage of governmental accounting with a discussion of the comprehensive annual financial report utilized by these entities for external reporting purposes.

Business-Type Funds

The 1990 financial statements published by the city of Richmond, Virginia, indicate the ownership and operation of a convention center, a river port, a coliseum, a parking garage, a gas utility, an electric utility, and a water utility. According to the financial statements for Wichita, Kansas, that city maintains a motor pool to service city-owned vehicles as well as a stationery store and a data processing center, both of which assist various government operations. Although these activities are not unusual for a government, their functions are markedly different from those of a police or fire department. A coliseum, parking garage, and water utility do serve the public but only for a specified charge. A motor pool or data processing center also offers services but to the government itself; even then, monetary fees are still assessed.

As previously discussed, the operations of most state and local governments include a broad range of activities accounted for in governmental funds, proprietary funds, and fiduciary funds. Such internal diversity has always complicated the accounting and reporting process. While service-oriented activities utilize one approach to financial reporting, the proprietary funds and certain of the fiduciary funds are fundamentally different in nature and require alternative means of accounting.

The previous chapter examined the governmental-type funds. Coverage of the reporting procedures employed in the five remaining fund categories (Enterprise Funds, Internal Service Funds, Pension Trust Funds, Nonexpendable Trust Funds, and Agency Funds) has been deferred until the current chapter to avoid possible confusion. The dissimilarities between these two accounting approaches are more easily understood when introduced separately.

Exhibit 16–1 presents an overview of several of the major differences between governmental-type and business-type funds.

EXHIBIT 16–1   Fund Accounting—State and Local Governments

	Governmental-Type Funds*	*Business-Type Funds***
Accounting emphasis	Accountability; flow of financial resources.	Measurement of net income.
Budgets	Recorded in most funds.	Adopted but not recorded in the accounting system.
Encumbrances	Recorded in most funds at the time a purchase commitment or contract is made.	Not recorded.
Basis of accounting	Modified accrual accounting (*GASB 11* would require accrual accounting).	Accrual accounting.
Outflow of financial resources	Recorded as expenditures.	Recorded as assets or expenses.
Depreciation	Not reported.	Reported as an expense each period.
Recognition of revenues	When measurable and available (*GASB 11* would require accrual accounting based on the type of revenue, but usually when measurable and demanded).	When earning process is substantially completed.
Fixed assets and long-term debt	Recorded in separate account groups (*GASB 11* would require long-term operating debt and certain noncurrent assets to be reported within individual funds).	Recorded within the individual funds.
Equity accounts	Fund balances.	Most funds report contributed capital and retained capital.

---

* The governmental-type funds are the General Fund, Special Revenue Funds, Debt Service Funds, Capital Projects Funds, and Expendable Trust Funds.

** The business-type funds are the Enterprise Funds, Internal Service Funds, Nonexpendable Trust Funds, and Pension Trust Funds. The Agency Funds record only the creation and settlement of liabilities.

Objective—Income Determination

The primary emphasis underlying the accounting for business-type funds (except for Agency Funds) stresses income determination rather than the flow of financial resources. In the proprietary fund types (Enterprise Funds and Internal Service Funds), operating costs are recovered, at least partially, through user charges rather than from property taxes or other government revenues. Because of the functional similarity with commercial endeavors, the operational efficiency of these activities is reflected by the computation of an earned income figure. "The generally accepted accounting principles here are those applicable to similar businesses in the private sector; and the measurement focus is on determination of net income, financial position, and changes in financial position."[1]

The two remaining funds (Pension Trust Funds and Nonexpendable Trust Funds) are fiduciary in nature; assets are held by the government to be used for stipulated purposes. Income is also calculated for these funds as a means of measuring the effective utilization of the resources on hand. For the Nonexpendable Trust Funds, this computation also indicates the amount of resources that can be expended for the designated purpose.

Because profitability determination, rather than accountability, is underscored in these four fund categories, the following characteristics are applicable:

- Budgetary entries are never recorded. Although budgets should always be adopted by the business-type funds, physically entering the amounts into the financial records provides little benefit. Expenditure levels for the fiduciary funds, as an example, are regulated by contract or agreement; the inclusion of budgetary entries neither reinforces nor changes those stipulations. In the proprietary funds, "the demand for the goods and services provided largely determines the appropriate level of revenues and expenses. . . . Thus, as in commercial accounting, flexible budgets—prepared for several levels of possible activity—typically are better for proprietary fund planning, control, and evaluation purposes than are fixed budgets. . . . Thus, integration of fixed dollar budgetary accounts usually is neither necessary nor appropriate in proprietary fund accounting systems."[2]

- Accrual accounting—and not modified accrual accounting—has historically served as the basis for recognizing revenues and expenses. Since income calculation rather than accountability for financial resources is being stressed in these funds, all revenue and expense figures are recorded in the same manner and time period as in for-profit accounting. Depreciation expense, as an example, is recognized annually to allocate the cost of fixed assets over their useful lives. By the same rationale, revenues are only recognized when the earning process is substantially complete. Because of this change in emphasis, encumbrances are never recorded by the business-type funds and acquisitions are either capitalized or expensed instead of being reported as expenditures.

- Fixed assets and long-term debts are entered directly into the individual funds rather than being maintained in separate account groups. *Consequently, these business-type funds stand by themselves in presenting the financial activities of specific government activities.* In addition, since the presence of these assets and liabilities permits the recognition of depreciation expense and interest accruals, net income calculation is possible.

[1] *Codification of Governmental Accounting and Financial Reporting Standards* (Norwalk, Conn.: Governmental Accounting Standards Board, 1992), sec. 1300.102b.

[2] GASB Cod. sec. 1700.120–122.

Once again, as with most aspects of these funds, a parallel to commercial accounting is evident.

Enterprise Funds

As previously indicated, state and local governments use Enterprise Funds to account for operations financed at least partially through outside user charges. Swimming pools, water utilities, municipal airports, amusement parks, and the like all fall under this heading. One survey found that 80 percent of local governmental units report at least one Enterprise Fund.[3] The city of Clearwater, Florida, operates a yacht basin; the city of Hartford, Connecticut, has a civic center; the city of Roanoke, Virginia, owns a bus service; the city of Walla Walla, Washington, maintains a cemetery.

Deciding whether an operation is an Enterprise Fund or part of the General Fund as an ongoing activity is not always easy. Should a municipal swimming pool that is 80 percent funded by the government and only 20 percent by users be considered an Enterprise Fund? No exact answer exists. The GASB permits subjectivity by allowing governments to use this fund type whenever income determination is considered appropriate:

> Enterprise funds—to account for operations *(a)* that are financed and operated in a manner similar to private business enterprises—where the intent of the governing body is that the costs (expenses, including depreciation) of providing goods or services to the general public on a continuing basis be financed or recovered primarily through user charges; or *(b)* where the governing body has decided that periodic determination of revenues earned, expenses incurred, and/or net income is appropriate for capital maintenance, public policy, management control, accountability, or other purposes.[4]

In the past, 50 percent of the costs of an activity had to be recovered from user charges before the Enterprise Funds designation was considered applicable. Now this fund type is appropriate either when user charges are the primary means of recovery or at the discretion of the governing body. Consequently, one state or locality might account for an ongoing function (such as a bus service operating at a significant loss) within the General Fund whereas another government could classify this same activity as an Enterprise Fund.

The accounting process for an Enterprise Fund parallels that of a profit-oriented company; thus, a complete overview here is unwarranted. In Exhibit 16–2, the financial statements for Chicago–O'Hare International Airport (operated by the city of Chicago, Illinois) disclose information similar to that of a corporation. Little resemblance can be found to the governmental accounting procedures introduced in Chapter 15. (The statement of cash flows has been omitted here.)

---

[3] *Local Governmental Accounting Trends & Techniques,* 4th ed. (New York: American Institute of Certified Public Accountants, 1991), p. 3–1.

[4] GASB Cod. sec. 1300.104.

The financial statements for O'Hare Airport could pass for those of a for-profit business operation. Both revenues and expenses are reported for this fund, including nearly $34 million in depreciation and amortization. A net income figure of approximately $38 million is reported. The asset section of the balance sheet shows more than $1.1 billion in structures, equipment, and improvements. Liabilities disclose both current and noncurrent balances. Contributed capital and retained earnings figures are also reported.

A few of the accounting procedures utilized in Enterprise Funds, however, are unique. For example, normally capital stock is not issued by an Enterprise Fund for financing purposes. Contributed capital (more than $150 million for O'Hare Airport) comes from residual equity transfers made within the government itself or from outside grants or other sources. To illustrate this aspect of Enterprise Fund accounting, assume a city makes a residual equity transfer of $400,000 from the General Fund to begin a local bus system. Assume further that this amount is matched with a $200,000 grant for the same purpose from the state government.

EXHIBIT 16–2   Financial Statements for an Enterprise Fund

CITY OF CHICAGO, ILLINOIS
Chicago–O'Hare International Airport
Statement of Revenues, Expenses, and Changes in Fund Equity
Year Ended December 31, 1989
(in thousands)

Operating Revenues:	
Charges for services	$ 93,556
Rents	197,383
Total operating revenues	290,939
Operating Expenses:	
Personal services	77,633
Repairs and maintenance	24,878
Depreciation and amortization	33,937
Other	61,872
Total operating expenses	$198,320
Operating Income	92,619
Nonoperating revenues (expenses):	
Interest income	17,832
Interest expense	(72,492)
Total nonoperating revenues (expenses)	(54,660)
Net income (loss)	37,959
Fund equity (deficit)—Beginning of year	276,442
Contributed capital	16,323
Fund equity (deficit)—End of year	$330,724

EXHIBIT 16–2   *(concluded)*

CITY OF CHICAGO, ILLINOIS
Chicago–O'Hare International Airport
Balance Sheet
December 31, 1989
(in thousands)

Assets

Current Assets:

Cash and cash equivalents	$ 16,918
Investments	2,587
Accounts receivable (Net of allowance for estimated uncollectibles)	35,448
Due from other funds	716
Due from other governments	1,284
Other	14,826
Total current assets	71,779

Restricted Assets:

Cash and cash equivalents	241,680
Investments	186,843
Total restricted assets	428,523

Property, Plant and Equipment:

Land	55,295
Structures, equipment and improvements	1,145,571
Allowance for depreciation	(292,095)
Construction work in progress	397,151
Total fixed assets	1,305,922
Total assets	$1,806,224

Liabilities and Fund Equity

Current Liabilities:

Voucher warrants payable	$ 13,213
Revenue bonds payable in one year	11,770
Due to other funds	18,511
Accrued and other liabilities	20,792
Deferred revenue	1,377
Total current liabilities	65,663
Current liabilities payable from restricted assets	121,487

Noncurrent Liabilities:

Revenue bonds payable	1,288,350
Total liabilities	1,475,500

Fund Equity:

Contributed capital	150,658
Retained earnings:	
Reserve for debt service on bonds	84,464
Reserve for emergencies	6,693
Reserve for maintenance	44,590
Unreserved	44,319
Total fund equity	330,724
Total liabilities and fund equity	$1,806,224

Because charges are assessed to those individuals who ride the buses, the city creates an Enterprise Fund to account for this operation. Within this fund, these two initial contributions are recorded as follows:

Enterprise Fund

Cash.	600,000	
Contributed Capital—Governmental.		400,000
Contributed Capital—Intergovernmental		200,000

    To record residual equity transfer from the General Fund and state grant received to start a local bus system.

These equity accounts represent the source of the beginning capital for this particular operation in the same way that the capital stock accounts of Ford Motor Company indicate the amounts invested by the company's stockholders.

Another reporting complexity encountered in connection with some Enterprise Funds is the legal restriction of cash or other assets. As can be seen from its statements, O'Hare Airport reported more than $428 million in restricted assets. Many reasons might exist for holding these amounts. Public utilities, as an example, often collect deposits from customers that must be returned when service is discontinued. Local laws may require that these monetary amounts be formally segregated in the accounting records to assure safekeeping.

Similar restrictions often result from contractual provisions included in bond agreements. Bond indentures frequently stipulate that monies collected from issuing debt be separated and spent only for the intended purposes. Money raised, for example, to build a new hangar must be used to build the new hangar and not diverted to other projects. Furthermore, the indenture may require that specified amounts of cash must be set aside each year to ensure the availability of funds to extinguish the debt when due.

Regardless of the reason for the restriction, the asset balances are identified and usually invested until time for disbursement. The restriction of such assets is recorded directly within the Enterprise Fund. A typical entry for this purpose would be as follows:

Enterprise Fund

Restricted Cash (or Investments)—Bond Debt Service.	90,000	
Restricted Cash (or Investments)—Customer Deposits.	10,000	
Restricted Cash (or Investments)—Bond Proceeds	200,000	
Cash		300,000

    To classify various cash balances into restricted asset accounts as required by bond indenture and by local laws.

Internal Service Funds

Not surprisingly, Internal Service Funds and Enterprise Funds utilize very similar accounting procedures. The functions of these two proprietary fund types are analogous; therefore, significant variations in reporting techniques are not justified. In both cases, charges are assessed for services being rendered. However, for Internal Service Funds, the users are internal departments or agencies within the government, rather than the public in general. A central print shop that provides services for an entire city government and a county's data processing center would both fall under this heading. Typical Internal Service Funds are as follows:

New Haven, Connecticut   Printing and duplicating
Atlanta, Georgia   Automotive services
Norfolk, Virginia   Storehouse for materials
St. Paul, Minnesota   Manufacturing plant for asphalt

The use of Internal Service Funds appears to have become especially popular during recent years. One report found that only 16 percent of local governments reported Internal Service Funds in 1986 whereas 42 percent did just three years later in 1989.[5] In many areas, the range of government activities has increased in hopes of offering better services while reducing costs. Creating a motor pool, for example, may be cheaper than using outside mechanics. The city of St. Paul,

---

EXHIBIT 16-3   **Financial Statements for Computer Services, City of Portsmouth, Virginia**

CITY OF PORTSMOUTH, VIRGINIA
Computer Services
Statement of Revenues, Expenses, and Changes in Retained Earnings
Year Ended June 30, 1990

Operating Revenues:	
Charges for services	$2,485,889
Other	77,940
Total operating revenues	2,563,829
Operating Expenses:	
Personal services	1,174,479
Contractual services	396,269
Materials	124,380
Telephone	20,021
Rent	245,054
Depreciation and amortization	393,206
Other	1,966
Total operating expenses	2,355,375
Operating Income	208,454
Nonoperating revenues (expenses):	
Interest income	6,865
Interest expense and fiscal charges	(136,159)
Net nonoperating revenues (expenses)	(129,294)
Net income	79,160
Retained earnings at beginning of year	701,058
Retained earnings at end of year	$ 780,218

---

[5] *Local Governmental Accounting Trends & Techniques*, p. 3–1.

EXHIBIT 16–3   *(concluded)*

CITY OF PORTSMOUTH, VIRGINIA
Computer Services
Balance Sheet
June 30, 1990
Assets

Current Assets:	
Cash and temporary investments	$ 22,316
Receivables	6,057
Due from other funds	744,622
Total current assets	772,995
Property, Plant and Equipment:	
Machinery and equipment	5,519,483
Less accumulated depreciation	(3,316,690)
Net property, plant and equipment	2,202,793
Total assets	$2,975,788

Liabilities and Fund Equity

Current Liabilities:	
Vouchers payable	$ 110,818
Accrued vacation and compensatory pay	113,997
Due to other funds	155,771
Current installments of long-term debt	347,817
Total current liabilities	728,403
Long-Term Debt:	
Obligations under capital leases	1,675,481
Less current installments	(347,817)
Long-term debt, excluding current installments	1,327,664
Total liabilities	2,056,067
Fund Equity:	
Contributed capital	139,503
Retained earnings	780,218
Total fund equity	919,721
Total liabilities and fund equity	$2,975,788

Minnesota, lists 13 different Internal Service Funds in its 1991 annual report. Separate Internal Service Funds are formed for these individual functions for several reasons; they

- Provide the ability to account for each activity.
- Assist in costing and pricing decisions.
- Allow for the allocation of government overhead.[6]

---

[6] *Governmental Accounting, Auditing and Financial Reporting* (Chicago: Government Finance Officers Association, 1988), p. 73.

Exhibit 16–3 contains the 1990 financial statements for computer services (an Internal Service Fund) of the city of Portsmouth, Virginia. As with Enterprise Funds, the statements are similar to those of a for-profit operation; property, plant, and equipment are reported as well as long-term debt, contributed capital, retained earnings, and depreciation expense. (Once again, the statement of cash flows has been omitted since it is based on information provided by these remaining statements.)

Although these financial statements resemble those of an Enterprise Fund, no restricted assets are indicated. Internal Service Funds do not offer services directly to the public; thus, the presence of customer deposits would not be anticipated. Furthermore, contractual restrictions resulting from bond obligations are not nearly as common. The capital outlays required to support Internal Service Fund activities are normally less costly than those needed by many Enterprise Funds. A subway system or water utility costs many times more than a motor pool or print shop. Therefore, a significant portion of the funding of Internal Service Funds is often provided by transfers from within the government. Sinking funds or restricted assets are rarely necessary to service the debts of these operations.

As shown in the balance sheet figures in Exhibit 16–3, Internal Service Funds frequently report "Due from . . ." and, to a lesser extent, "Due to . . ." accounts to indicate receivables and payables within the government. Since these operations utilize accrual accounting, such balances are established as a result of revenue and expense recognition. If work is done for another unit of the government, a "Due from . . ." account records and reports the intragovernmental receivable.

To illustrate, assume that a government print shop prepares $3,000 in materials for one of the ongoing activities (for example, the police or fire department) accounted for within the General Fund. Because of the nature of the work performed, the print shop is accounted for as an Internal Service Fund. As discussed in the previous chapter, this transfer of funds is known as a quasi-external transaction because the interaction is the same as that between two unrelated parties. Thus, the charge for the service being carried out is not recorded as a transfer but as a regular business transaction.

The following journal entries would be appropriate at the time this work is completed:

Internal Service Fund

Due from Other Funds—General Fund	3,000	
Operating Revenues—Charges for Services.		3,000

To record completion of printing work for a General Fund activity.

General Fund

Expenditures Control	3,000	
Due to Other Funds—Internal Service Funds.		3,000

To record work done by the print shop.

Both the receivable and the payable remain in the financial accounts of these fund types until the money is actually transferred. At that time, the $3,000 "Due from . . ." and "Due to . . ." balances are eliminated.

Discussion Question: Should Internal Service Funds Be Abolished?

If a city's school system decides to open a garage to service its buses, the activity is recorded as a part of this system. Acquisition of the building and equipment would be reported as expenditures within the General Fund or Special Revenue Funds (depending on the method used to monitor the school system). The assets themselves are listed in the General Fixed Assets Account Group. No depreciation is recorded. Cash inflows from issuing any long-term debt used to purchase the building and equipment are reported as Other Financing Sources in the appropriate governmental-type fund. This debt is then included in the General Long-Term Debt Account Group.

However, if the city created this same garage to service vehicles for several different activities (the school system, the police force, the ambulance service, and the like), it probably would report the garage as an Internal Service Fund. Thus, the garage maintains its own building and equipment as well as the long-term debt needed for financing. No expenditures are recorded by the fund but depreciation and other expenses are now appropriately reported.

Some question the validity of making such a radical change in accounting principles to account for activities providing services solely for governmental-type funds. For instance, David L. Falk and Michael H. Granof assert:

> The weakest component of the accounting system that is generally accepted for state and local governments is the internal service fund—a fund used to account for the financing of goods or services provided by one department or agency to other departments, agencies or units. So flawed is this, that allowed to stand, it weakens the persuasiveness of arguments that government should be accounted for by a model separate from business.[7]

Although Falk and Granof acknowledge that Internal Service Funds should be maintained for internal reporting purposes to promote efficiency and facilitate sharing of costs, they hold that the individual transactions and accounts should be returned to the appropriate governmental-type funds for external reporting.

Several faults have been attributed to the current reporting of Internal Service Funds:

- No consistency exists between reporting units. Some governments make wide use of Internal Service Funds; others do not utilize them— the same activities are recorded within the governmental-type funds.

---

[7] David L. Falk and Michael H. Granof, "Internal Service Funds Are beyond Salvation," *Accounting Horizons*, June 1990, p. 58.

continued

- Fixed assets that should be reported as expenditures by the governmental-type funds are capitalized. Thus, the expenditures of the reporting unit may be understated.
- The government is able to remove some of its general obligation debts from the General Long-Term Debt Account Group.
- Governments can create surpluses or deficits within Internal Service Funds to manipulate fund balances. For example, price increases for intragovernmental services could be used to reduce the financial resources available in the General Fund to justify a tax increase.

In Madison, Wisconsin, a suit brought by taxpayers underscores the policy dilemma which results from the accumulation of assets which are legally unrestricted in restricted funds. The suit charged that the city's "Nonlapsing Building Reserve Fund" was being used as a vehicle to maintain an illicit surplus which should instead be used to reduce taxes. Although the taxpayers were unsuccessful in their action, the litigation nevertheless pointed to the potential use of Internal Service Funds to undermine policy as understood by a community's citizens.[8]

- Depreciation becomes an expenditure through transfer pricing. If a garage, for example, has depreciation of $100 as its only expense, a charge of that amount to a General Fund for a repair would be recorded as an expenditure. Depreciation has effectively become an expenditure to the governmental-type fund.

Should internal service funds continue to be included by state and local governments for external reporting purposes?

Pension Trust Funds

Pension Trust Funds are fiduciary in nature rather than proprietary; money is held by the government to provide employees with retirement benefits. The major activities of such funds include collecting and investing monetary amounts as well as paying out benefits to appropriate recipients. Such trusts are common and can become huge. The city of Chicago, Illinois, for example, maintains pension trusts with total assets of more than $4.3 billion for four different groups: municipal employees, laborers, police officers, and firefighters.

Three of the four largest pension funds in the United States as of 1989 were created by state or local governments:

---

[8] Ibid., p. 63.

California Public Employees	$54.0 billion in assets
New York City Employees	$45.4 billion
New York State and Local Employees	$44.2 billion[9]

Funding for such pension trusts comes primarily from the government (as the employer) although employees themselves may add extra amounts if the plan is contributory. All cash balances are then invested by the trust with subsequently earned income added to the retirement benefits accruing to each employee. Because of the importance of maximizing the earnings produced by the assets being held, the accounting emphasis is again placed on income determination rather than on resource control. However, a significant degree of control is inherent in Pension Trust Funds because both contribution and expenditure levels are established by contractual agreement or actuarial estimation.

Assets can come into a Pension Trust Fund from (1) contributions or (2) earned income. The major expense is the pension benefits that are distributed. For example, in the municipal pension fund of the city of Philadelphia, Pennsylvania, for the year ending June 30, 1989, 95 percent of operating revenues were derived from just four sources:

Employer's contributions	$152.3 million
Employees' contributions	40.7 million
Interest and dividends	90.6 million
Gain from sale of investments	34.6 million

At the same time, 93 percent of the operating expenses for this fund were made up of $250 million in pension benefits.

To illustrate the accounting procedures, assume that the city of Jung maintains a pension plan for its government employees. Typical transactions for this fund include:

- The city contributes $44,000 in cash to the pension trust fund based on a contractual agreement with its employees.
- Employees voluntarily contribute $9,000 to their pensions.
- Investments acquired in previous years earn interest of $7,000.

To record these three increases in cash, the following entry is appropriate:

Pension Trust Fund

Cash	60,000	
Operating Revenues—Employer Contribution		44,000
Operating Revenues—Employee Contribution		9,000
Operating Revenues—Interest		7,000

To record revenue for the period by the pension trust fund.

---

[9] James A. White, "Giant Pension Funds' Explosive Growth Concentrates Economic Assets and Power," *The Wall Street Journal,* June 28, 1990, p. C1.

As indicated, the number of different expenses incurred by a Pension Trust Fund is also rather limited. Some administrative and other miscellaneous expenses are periodically incurred in connection with maintaining the trust. However, the major cost is the normal benefits paid out to retired or other qualified individuals based on their pension agreement. Assuming that the city's pension pays $2,000 in expenses and distributes $14,000 to members, the following journal entry is required:

Pension Trust Fund

Operating Expenses—Administrative	2,000	
Operating Expenses—Employee Benefits	14,000	
Cash		16,000

Payments made by the pension trust fund during the current period.

Nonexpendable Trust Funds

The final fund category requiring income determination is the Nonexpendable Trust Funds. As discussed in the previous chapter, these trust funds account for assets donated to a government with the stipulation that all subsequently derived income be used for a designated purpose. The principal itself, however, must be kept intact to continue generating earnings. The city of Richmond, Virginia, for example, currently maintains four Nonexpendable Trust Funds to account for donations made to support:

Cemetery maintenance.

Scholarships and prizes for local students.

Public library.

Specific memorial purposes.

Although most gifts to a government are relatively small, some can be of significant size. The city and county of San Francisco, California, reported at June 30, 1990, more than $30 million in assets in its Nonexpendable Trust Funds.

To ensure that the legal provisions attached to each gift are followed, determination of net income is essential. This figure sets the amount to be spent for the specified purpose. In practice, the government unit may actually opt to establish two separate accounting funds: one to maintain a record of the original gift with a second to monitor net income and its ultimate disposition. Although not required, protection of the principal is more easily assured when two funds are utilized.

As an illustration of the procedures to account for Nonexpendable Trust Funds, assume that two pieces of rental property are given to a city by a citizen with the provision that all future income be used for maintenance of the local cemetery. These donated assets are appraised at a value of $140,000 and the following journal entry is made:

Nonexpendable Trust Fund

Buildings	140,000	
Fund Balance—Reserved for Cemetery Maintenance		140,000

To record fair market value of rental property given with the
specification that all income is to be used for cemetery maintenance.

During the remainder of the current fiscal year, these properties are rented to various tenants and revenues of $16,000 are earned and subsequently collected. As with all of the business-type funds, accrual accounting is utilized in the recording process.

Nonexpendable Trust Fund

Rent Receivable	16,000	
Operating Revenues Control		16,000

To accrue rental income for current period.

Cash	16,000	
Rent Receivable		16,000

Collection of rents (following earlier accrual).

To maintain this property, the city incurs and pays a variety of maintenance expenses totaling $4,400. In addition, $7,000 in depreciation is computed for the period.

Nonexpendable Trust Fund

Operating Expenses—Maintenance	4,400	
Operating Expenses—Depreciation	7,000	
Cash		4,400
Accumulated Depreciation—Buildings		7,000

To recognize expenses associated with rental property including depreciation.

At the end of this year, net income of $4,600 is indicated ($16,000 in revenues less total expenses of $11,400). According to the terms of the gift, this balance should now be spent for the designated objective: cemetery maintenance. Frequently, the city will transfer the money to an Expendable Trust Fund to be used for the appropriate purpose. Overspending can be prevented in this manner:

Nonexpendable Trust Fund

Operating Transfer-Out—Income Earned	4,600	
Cash		4,600

To record transfer of net income balance to separate Expendable Trust Fund to be used for specified purpose.

Expendable Trust Fund

Cash	4,600	
Other Financing Sources—Trust Income (Transferred)		4,600

To record income on gifts donated to the city with the stipulation that all earnings will be used for cemetery maintenance.

Agency Funds

State and local governments use one additional fund category; however, this fund records neither a governmental-type service activity nor a business-type operation. Agency Funds account solely for monies held by a government that it must eventually convey to an outside party. The city of Saint Paul, Minnesota, for example, maintains 21 different Agency Funds that monitor assets received from a variety of sources including payroll taxes, social security taxes, money withheld from employees for U.S. savings bonds, and birth certificate surcharges that must be remitted to the state of Minnesota.

Periodically, the city transfers each of these amounts to the proper authorities. Until remitted, the balances are maintained within an Agency Fund for control purposes. Classified as a fiduciary fund, the reporting procedures are primarily designed to establish a formal record of the amounts being held at any point in time. Agency Funds have no equity, revenues, or expenses. They report only assets (usually cash or investments) and the related liabilities.

To illustrate, assume that Keith County collects a toll from each car that uses one of the local highways. Because the original cost of constructing this road was financed in part by the adjacent city of Simmons, a portion of all toll receipts are separated and shared with this city government. The following two entries would be made by the county in connection with the receipt and conveyance of this money. Assume that the county has collected $108,000 from this toll that must be given to the city of Simmons.

Agency Fund (Keith County)
Time of Collection

Cash	108,000	
Due to City of Simmons		108,000
To record portion of toll receipts that must be paid to the city.		

Time of Payment

Due to City of Simmons	108,000	
Cash		108,000
To transfer tolls (accumulated by county) to the city of Simmons.		

Defining the Reporting Entity

Although gathering and maintaining financial information is a vital step in governmental accounting, the reporting of this data to the public is equally important.

> Governmental accountability is based on the belief that the citizenry has a "right to know," a right to receive openly declared facts that may lead to public debate by the citizens and their elected representatives. Financial reporting plays a major role in fulfilling government's duty to be publicly accountable in a democratic society.[10]

In producing financial statements, a state or locality often encounters a unique problem: the determination of the specific functions to be included. Except in rare cases, a business enterprise such as Xerox or IBM simply consolidates all corporations over which control has been achieved. A state or locality, however, may interact with a number of departments, agencies, boards, institutes, commissions, and the like that have only a moderate relationship with the government. Should all of these activities be included as separate funds within the comprehensive annual financial report of the government? If not, what reporting is required?

---

[10] GASB Cod. sec. 100.156.

An almost unlimited number of examples could be presented of the types of functions that create problems for government officials who are attempting to define the entity to be reported. Separate organizations such as turnpike commissions, port authorities, public housing authorities, and downtown development boards have become commonplace in recent years. Creating separate organizations allows such groups to focus on specified issues or problems and sometimes provides better efficiency because of their corporate-style structure. In addition, capital markets may be more receptive to debt issued by these groups. Examples of separate organizations include the following:

- A museum is built on city land but operates as a nonprofit corporation funded by citizen contributions. Half of the board of directors are appointed by these donors with the remainder named by the city. The property is leased from the city for $1 per year. A special tax is levied and collected by the city to help maintain the grounds and building. Should the museum be reported within the city's financial statements?
- The state establishes a school system within a city. The school board is elected by the public and, thus, is not under the control of city officials. Property taxes are levied by the city and then distributed to the school for funding purposes. For this reason, the school budget must be approved by city officials. Should the school system be reported as part of the city?

Because of the extremely wide variety of possible activities and functions, determining the components that make up a state or locality is not always an easy task. Thus, in June 1991, the GASB issued its *Statement No. 14,* "The Financial Reporting Entity." This pronouncement provides guidance to assist governments in identifying the reporting entity. According to the Board, the major criterion for inclusion in a government's comprehensive annual financial report is financial accountability:

> Financial reporting based on accountability should enable the financial statement reader to focus on the body of organizations that are related by a common thread of accountability to the constituent citizenry. . . . Elected officials are accountable to those citizens for their public policy decisions, regardless of whether these decisions are carried out directly by the elected officials through the operations of the primary government or by their designees through the operations of specially created organizations.[11]

The Primary Government

In defining the overall reporting entity, *GASB Statement No. 14* indicates that the primary government must first be identified. According to this official pronouncement, the primary government is any government (and all of its funds, organizations, agencies, offices, and departments that are not legally separate) meeting the following three criteria:

---

[11] GASB, *Statement No. 14,* "The Financial Reporting Entity," June 1991, par. 2 and 8.

- Has a separately elected governing body.
- Is legally separate.
- Is fiscally independent of other state and local governments.

The GASB provides additional guidance for judging the last two of these criteria, legal separation and fiscal independence. The legal separation of a government is demonstrated by having corporate powers such as the right to sue and be sued in its own name and the right to buy, sell, and lease property in its own name.

A city has such powers; its police department does not. The fiscal independence of a government is indicated by having the authority to do all three of the following:

- Determine its own budget without having to present the figures to any other government for approval or modification.
- Levy taxes or set rate fees without having to seek approval by another government.
- Issue bonded debt without the need for approval by another government.

A city is fiscally independent because it meets these criteria; a fire department normally is not.

Consequently, any organization that has an elected governing body, is legally separate, and is fiscally independent is a primary government. Any activity that is not legally separate from this government must be included within its financial statements.

Component Units

Many activities are legally separate from a primary government but are so closely connected that complete omission from the statements of the primary government cannot be justified. The elected officials of the primary government are still financially accountable for these separate organizations. Such entities are referred to as *component units* of the primary government.

GASB Statement No. 14 specifies two methods for identifying a separate organization as a component unit of a primary government. In the first set of criteria, officials of the primary government must appoint a voting majority of the governing board of the separate organization. Additionally, either the primary government must be able to impose its will on this board, or the separate organization must provide a financial benefit to or impose a financial burden on the primary government. For example, a commission to oversee off-track betting might well be a separate legal entity. However, if the state (the primary government) appoints a voting majority of the membership and benefits from the revenues generated, the commission is considered a component unit of the state for financial reporting purposes.

The second method established by *Statement No. 14* for identifying component units is more general: "the primary government may be financially accountable if an organization is *fiscally dependent* on the primary government regardless of whether the organization has (1) a separately governing board, (2) a governing board appointed by a higher level of government, or (3) a jointly appointed board.'' (paragraph 21b; emphasis added)

To apply the criteria of either method to the determination of a component unit, several terms need to be clarified:

A Voting Majority of the Governing Board.   The authority to elect a voting majority must be substantive. If, for example, the primary government simply confirms the choices of another party, financial accountability is not created. Furthermore, *GASB Statement No. 14* states that this criterion is not met if the primary government selects the governing body from a limited slate of candidates (such as three individuals from an approved list of five). Thus, the primary government must actually appoint a voting majority of the board before the organization can be viewed as a component unit.

Imposition of the Primary Government's Will on the Governing Board.   Such power is indicated if the government can significantly influence the programs, projects, activities, or the level of services provided by the organization. This degree of influence is present if the primary government can remove an appointed board member at will, modify or approve budgets, override decisions of the board, and hire or dismiss the individuals responsible for day-to-day operations.

Financial Benefit or Financial Burden on the Primary Government.   According to *GASB Statement No. 14,* a financial connection between the organization and the government exists if any of the following are met:

- The government is entitled to the organization's resources.
- The government is legally obligated to finance any deficits or provide financial support.
- The government is responsible in some manner for the debts of the organization.

Fiscal Dependence on the Primary Government.   As indicated previously, financial dependency is produced if the organization cannot do any one of the following three actions:

- Adopt its own budget.
- Levy taxes or set rates or charges for its services.
- Issue bonded debt without approval.

The Financial Reporting of a Primary Government and Its Component Units

As demonstrated in the appendix at the end of this chapter, the various funds of the primary government (the General Revenue, Special Revenue Funds, etc.) are all reported within the general purpose financial statements. However, any component units must also be included in these same statements. The financial figures must be clearly separated so that the operations and financial position of the primary government can be distinguished from these other activities. Therefore, figures for component units are presented to the right of those presented for the primary government. The component units may be combined into a single column or presented according to the specific activities. As another alternative, separate columns may be created for governmental and proprietary organizations.

GASB Statement No. 14 does allow the primary government to include certain component units as if they were part of the government (a process referred to as *blending*). Although these organizations are legally separate, they are so intertwined with the primary government that their inclusion is necessary for the appropriate presentation of the primary government's financial information.

> This provision was written with organizations like the Municipal Assistance Corporation of New York (MAC) in mind. MAC was created in 1975 as a financing mechanism for the city. Under the previously mentioned *GASB Statement 14* definition of financial accountability, the MAC would not qualify for inclusion in New York City's entity because the state appoints the MAC's board. But the MAC is so inextricably linked to New York City's finances that its exclusion would render the city's financial statements misleading.[12]

One other aspect of the reporting process to be noted: *GASB Statement No. 14* also identifies the possible existence of *related organizations*. In such cases, the primary government is accountable because it appoints a voting majority of the governing board. However, financial accountability does not exist. Fiscal dependency is not present and the primary government cannot impose its will on the board or gather financial benefits or burdens from the relationship. Without financial accountability, the organization does not qualify as a component unit to be included in the financial reporting. Instead, because of the ability to appoint a voting majority of the governing board, the primary government must disclose in notes to its financial statements the nature of the accountability for such related organizations.

Discussion Question: Is It Part of the County?

Harland County is in a financially distressed portion of Missouri. In hopes of enticing business to this area, the state legislature appropriated $3 million to start an industrial development commission. The federal government provided an additional $1 million. The state appointed 15 individuals to a board to oversee the operations of this commission while county officials named 5 members. The commission began operations by raising funds from local

---

[12] Barbara A. Chaney, "The Governmental Financial Reporting Entity: Inclusion and Display," *The CPA Journal,* January 1993, p. 42.

(continued)

citizens and businesses. It received an extra $700,000 in donations and pledges. The county provided clerical assistance and allowed the commission to use one floor of the county office building for its headquarters. The commission's budget must be approved by the county government.

During the current period, the commission spent $2.4 million and produced financial statements. Notable success was achieved as several large manufacturing companies have begun to explore the possibility of opening plants in the county.

Harland County is presently beginning the process of producing a comprehensive annual financial report. Should the revenues, expenditures, assets, and liabilities of the industrial development commission be included? Is it part of the county's primary government, a component unit, or a related organization?

Is the industrial development commission a component unit of the state of Missouri? How should its activities be presented in the state's comprehensive annual financial report?

Accounting for State and Local Governments—External Reporting Process

The final aspect of governmental accounting examined here is the financial reporting process. Because so many diverse fund types exist within state and local governments, the amount and variety of data to be presented could become overwhelming to readers. To alleviate this problem, governments present information about a state or locality to the public in the form of a comprehensive annual financial report, frequently referred to as CAFR. The CAFR provides both a general perspective of every fund type and additional detailed data concerning individual funds. Readers can learn as much or as little as they desire. The structure of the CAFR includes:

- *General purpose financial statements*—to provide an overview of the financial position and operations of all fund types and account groups.
- *Combining statements by fund type*—to present financial data generated by the individual funds making up a fund type. For example, if four separate funds compose the Special Revenue Funds, financial statements for each would be included in this section of the CAFR. The city and county of San Francisco, California, as an illustration, presents financial information in this section about each of its 17 Special Revenue Funds.
- *Individual fund and account group statements*—to disclose more detailed information where needed about specific funds and account groups. If,

for example, one of the Special Revenue Funds requires additional reporting, this information is presented here.

- *Schedules and statistical tables*—to demonstrate legal and contractual compliance and present other useful information.

The inclusion of schedules allows a government considerable latitude in the types of additional information that can be disclosed. For example, the 1990 comprehensive annual financial report for the county of Henrico, Virginia, included numerous supplemental statements and schedules, such as:

General governmental expenditures by function.

Assessed and estimated value of all taxable property.

Property tax levies and collections.

Property values, construction, and bank deposits.

Ratio of bonded debt to assessed value and bonded debt per capita.

Principal taxpayers.

Property tax rates.

Because of the layered construction of the CAFR, readers have the option of either reviewing the entire financial picture of the government unit or getting very specific information about a particular activity. The CAFR is often compared to a pyramid with the general purpose financial statements at the top.

Obviously, unless a government unit is quite small, the comprehensive annual financial report just outlined frequently contains a massive amount of material. As an example, the 1991 comprehensive annual financial report for the city of Saint Paul, Minnesota, contains 251 pages of statements, schedules, notes, and statistics. The CAFR for the city of Philadelphia, Pennsylvania, had 172 pages, while the report for the city of Clearwater, Florida, was 182 pages in length.

Realizing that not all financial report users are interested in this extended volume of information, governments are allowed to issue just the general purpose financial statements by themselves "for inclusion in official statements for bond offerings and for widespread distribution to users requiring less detailed information about the government unit's finances than is contained in the CAFR."[13] In this way, adequate data is provided to these users without overburdening them with excessive amounts of material. Financial information concerning individual funds and fund types is not viewed as particularly relevant in such cases and is, therefore, omitted.

General Purpose Financial Statements

Five separate statements (as well as their accompanying notes and supplemental information) make up the general purpose financial statements produced by a government unit. Since these statements are not only included in the comprehen-

---

[13] GASB Cod. sec. 2200.102.

sive annual financial report but also may be presented alone, they are central to the entire reporting process. To assist in visualizing their construction, the appendix to this chapter contains complete illustrations. These five general purpose financial statements are as follows:

1. *Combined balance sheet—all fund types and account groups.* Balance sheets for each fund type (General Fund, Capital Projects Funds, Enterprise Funds, etc.) as well as the two account groups are presented together in a columnar format. Summation figures for the governmental unit as a whole are optional but, if included, must be labeled as "memorandum only" because no actual consolidation of the financial information takes place. Based on the requirements of *GASB Statement No. 14,* the balance sheets for any component units should also be included, normally to the right of the primary government information. These additional activities may be combined into a single column, divided into governmental and proprietary figures, or presented by specific function.

2. *Combined statement of revenues, expenditures, and changes in fund balances—all governmental fund types.* The statement provides a detailed listing of all revenues and expenditures of the governmental-type funds (the four governmental funds as well as any Expendable Trust Funds). "Other financing sources and uses" (such as bond proceeds and interfund transfers) are also disclosed in this statement as are residual equity transfers. Based on the changes created by these monetary inflows and outflows, a final fund balance total is computed for each of these fund types. Information describing any component units similar in nature to the governmental-type funds is also included.

3. *Combined statement of revenues, expenditures, and changes in fund balances—budget and actual.* Once again, revenues, expenditures, other financing sources/uses, and changes in fund balances are disclosed. However, in this instance, both actual and budgetary figures are reported with the data structured in columns for comparison purposes. This statement is appropriate for any fund type (such as the General Fund and the Special Revenue Funds) that records budgetary entries. As an example, in 1989, the city of Darien, Connecticut, reported within this statement that appropriations of $3,354,982 had been budgeted for public safety from the General Fund but only $3,309,077 of this amount was actually expended.

4. *Combined statement of revenues, expenses, and changes in retained earnings (or equity)—all proprietary fund types.* As the equivalent of the income statement found in for-profit accounting, this statement is developed solely for the business-type activities: Enterprise Funds, Internal Service Funds, Pension Trust Funds, and Nonexpendable Trust Funds. Net income is calculated and disclosed for each of these fund types along with the revenues and expenses that constitute this figure. Any

component unit that is the equivalent of a business-type organization is also reported in this manner.

5. *Combined statement of cash flows—all proprietary fund types.* Because of the recent renewed emphasis on monitoring changes in cash, a statement of cash flows is now required for the business-type funds (as well as similar component units). However, this statement's format varies somewhat from that utilized by for-business enterprises. Cash flows are disclosed for four activities rather than just three: operating, noncapital financing, capital financing, and investing.[14]

Summary

1. The previous chapter examined the procedures that state and local governments use in accounting for governmental-type activities. However, the operations of many governments often extend beyond providing services to the public. Business-type functions require a different approach to financial reporting. More specifically, accounting for four government funds (Enterprise Funds, Internal Service Funds, Pension Trust Funds, and Nonexpendable Trust Funds) emphasizes income determination. The procedures utilized by these funds parallel the methods found in for-profit accounting. In these specific funds, neither budgetary entries nor encumbrances are recorded. Accrual accounting is appropriate. Fixed assets and long-term debts are entered directly into the specific funds. Depreciation is calculated and recognized each period.

2. Enterprise Funds and Internal Service Funds are both proprietary in nature. The various activities recorded in these fund types are financed, at least in part, by user charges. More specifically, Enterprise Funds account for activities where public customers pay for the use of such facilities as municipal swimming pools, toll roads, bus services, and golf courses. Internal Service Funds provide services (data processing or printing, for example) for the benefit of departments and agencies within the government. Other than the absence of capital stock accounts, these two fund types are basically accounted for in the same manner as a commercial activity.

3. Pension Trust Funds and Nonexpendable Trust Funds are fiduciary rather than proprietary; cash or other assets are conveyed to the government to be held for a particular purpose. In Pension Trust Funds, the money provides retirement benefits for public employees. Computation of net income is necessary as a means of measuring the effective utilization of the available resources. Nonexpendable Trust Funds maintain control over donations made to the government with the

---

[14] GASB, *Statement No. 9,* "Reporting Cash Flows of Proprietary and Nonexpendable Trust Funds and Governmental Entities that Use Proprietary Fund Accounting" (Norwalk, Conn.: GASB, 1989).

stipulation that only the resulting income can be expended (usually for a specified purpose). Once again, the computation of annual net income is considered to be the primary accounting objective to determine the amount available for spending purposes.

4. In preparing financial statements, a state or locality must identify all agencies, commissions, and other activities that should be included. The main consideration for inclusion is financial accountability. The primary government is first determined: an entity that is legally separate, has an elected governing board, and is fiscally independent. Once identified, any activity that is not legally separate should be included in the financial reporting process of the primary government.

5. A primary government must also report any component units that are legally separate but so closely connected that omission cannot be justified. A component unit has a voting majority of its governing board appointed by the primary government. In addition, the primary government must be able to impose its will on the board or the component unit must provide a financial benefit or impose a financial burden on the primary government. As an alternative, the outside organization is considered to be a component unit if it is fiscally dependent on the primary government. Component units are reported to the right of the primary government in the entity's financial statements.

6. The external financial reporting of a state or locality takes the form of a comprehensive annual financial report (CAFR). This document includes general purpose financial statements for the government as a whole supplemented by individual statements for each fund type and account group. Schedules and statistics may also be included to demonstrate compliance with legal regulations or to provide more detailed information about a specific function.

Comprehensive Illustration

PROBLEM   (Estimated Time: 20 to 25 Minutes)

The city of Edison created a water utility to provide services to local residents. The following transactions occurred in connection with the project. Record the appropriate journal entries for this utility. Entries for other funds may be omitted.

1. Cash of $300,000 was transferred from the city's General Fund as initial financing for the utility. This balance was regarded as permanent funding. An additional $225,000 was loaned by the General Fund to the utility.
2. A $560,000 bond payable was issued at face value to provide the additional capital needed for the operations of this utility.
3. A $790,000 building was constructed and payment was made. The facility houses the water utility, both the administrative offices and the operations.

4. As a preliminary step in acquiring services from the city, customers pay a total of $110,000 to the utility in refundable deposits. For control purposes, this amount will be segregated in the utility's accounting records.

5. The first series of invoices was mailed to customers with charges totaling $225,000.

6. The utility pays the following expenses:

Salaries	$48,000
Utilities	12,000
Maintenance	31,000

An additional $21,000 in salaries was owed at the end of the fiscal period. Depreciation expense of $13,000 has been calculated.

7. A total of $40,000 was paid on the bonds payable with $21,000 of this amount representing interest for the period.

8. Closing entries were recorded by the utility.

SOLUTION

Since this utility should be accounted for as an Enterprise Fund, the following journal entries are appropriate:

1. Cash 525,000
       Contributed Capital—Governmental   300,000
       Due to General Fund   225,000
       To record initial transfers made to start water utility project.

2. Cash 560,000
       Bonds Payable   560,000
       Proceeds received from bonds issued to finance water utility.

3. Building 790,000
       Cash   790,000
       Building construction costs incurred by water utility.

4. Restricted Cash—Customers' Deposits 110,000
       Customers' Deposits Payable.   110,000
       To record refundable deposits received from utility customers.

5. Accounts Receivable 225,000
       Utility Revenues   225,000
       To accrue income for period.

6. Salary Expense.   69,000
   Utilities Expense   12,000
   Maintenance Expense   31,000
   Depreciation Expense   13,000
      Cash   91,000
      Salary Payable   21,000
      Accumulated Depreciation   13,000
    To record expenses for current fiscal period.

7. Bonds Payable   19,000
   Interest Expense   21,000
      Cash   40,000
    Payment made on bond interest and principal.

8. Utility Revenues 225,000
      Retained Earnings   225,000
    To close out revenues for the period.

   Retained Earnings 146,000
      Salary Expense.   69,000
      Utilities Expense   12,000
      Maintenance Expense   31,000
      Depreciation Expense   13,000
      Interest Expense   21,000
    To close out water utility's expenses.

APPENDIX
GENERAL-PURPOSE FINANCIAL STATEMENTS—STATE OR LOCAL GOVERNMENT

The next several pages contain examples of the general-purpose financial statements prepared by a state or local government unit. In reading these statements, assume that the primary government has several component units. Some of these components are similar to governmental funds whereas the others are proprietary in nature.

For adequate disclosure and fair presentation, a Summary of Significant Accounting Policies and other appropriate notes to the financial statements must also be included. This information has been omitted here. Note that the total columns presented in these statements are optional.

EXHIBIT 16–4

CITY OF RAPHAEL
Combined Balance Sheet—All Fund Types and Account Groups
December 31, 19X5

	Governmental Fund Types				Proprietary Fund Types	
	General	Special Revenue	Debt Service	Capital Projects	Enterprises	Internal Service
Assets and Other Debits						
Assets:						
Cash	$255,029	$101,385	$ 10,889	$ 666,285	$ 279,296	$ 29,700
Investments	65,000	37,200	197,638	—	—	—
Receivables (net of allowances for uncollectibles):						
Taxes, including interest, penalties, and liens	61,821	2,525	3,528	—	—	—
Accounts	8,300	3,300	—	100	26,480	—
Special assessments	—	—	—	646,385	—	—
Due from other funds	12,000	—	—	—	2,000	12,000
Due from other governments	85,000	75,260	—	640,000	—	—
Inventory, at cost	7,200	5,190	—	—	23,030	40,000
Prepaid expenses	—	—	—	—	1,200	—
Restricted assets—cash	—	—	—	—	306,753	—
Fixed assets (net, where applicable, of accumulated depreciation)	—	—	—	—	5,769,759	103,100
Other Debits:						
Amount available in debt service funds	—	—	—	—	—	—
Amount to be provided for retirement of general long-term debt	—	—	—	—	—	—
Total assets	$494,350	$224,860	$212,055	$1,952,770	$6,408,518	$184,800
Liabilities, Equity, and Other Credits						
Liabilities:						
Vouchers and accounts payable	$118,261	$ 32,454	$ —	$ 49,600	$ 116,471	$ 15,000
Contracts payable	46,900	20,300	—	166,000	26,107	—
Accrued general obligation interest	—	—	—	—	14,000	—
Other accrued expenses including compensated absences	10,700	—	—	—	2,870	—
Payable from restricted assets:						
Deposits	—	—	—	—	176,948	—
Due to:						
Other taxing units	—	—	—	—	—	55,000
Other funds	24,189	2,000	—	1,000	—	10,000
Deferred revenues	15,000	1,396	1,845	—	—	—
General obligation bonds payable	—	—	—	—	700,000	—
Revenue bonds payable	—	—	—	—	1,798,000	—
Special assessment bonds payable, with government commitment	—	—	—	—	—	—
Total liabilities	215,050	56,150	1,845	216,600	2,834,396	80,000
Equity and Other Credits:						
Contributed capital	—	—	—	—	1,406,766	95,000
Investment in general fixed assets	—	—	—	—	—	—
Retained earnings	—	—	—	—	2,167,356	9,800
Fund balance:						
Reserved for encumbrances	38,000	46,500	—	1,725,070	—	—
Reserved for inventory	7,200	5,190	—	—	—	—
Reserved for loans	—	—	—	—	—	—
Reserved for endowments	—	—	—	—	—	—
Reserved for employees' retirement system	—	—	—	—	—	—
Reserved for debt service	46,070	—	210,210	—	—	—
Unreserved, undesignated	188,030	117,020	—	11,100	—	—
Total equity and other credits	279,300	168,710	210,210	1,736,170	3,574,122	104,800
Total liabilities, equity, and other credits	$494,350	$224,860	$212,055	$1,952,770	$6,408,518	$184,800

The notes to the financial statements are an integral part of this statement.

Fiduciary Fund Type — Trust and Agency	General Fixed Assets	General Long-Term Debt	Total Primary Government (memorandum only)	Component Units — Governmental	Component Units — Proprietary	Total Reporting Entity (memorandum only)
$ 216,701	$ —	$ —	$ 1,559,285	$ 36,497	$185,044	$ 1,780,826
1,239,260	—	—	1,539,098	27,312	99,609	1,666,019
617,666	—	—	685,540	—	—	685,540
—	—	—	38,180	—	—	38,180
—	—	—	646,385	—	—	646,385
11,189	—	—	37,189	—	—	37,189
—	—	—	800,260	55,000	38,765	894,025
—	—	—	75,420	6,245	116,740	198,405
—	—	—	1,200	—	8,200	9,400
—	—	—	306,753	—	—	306,753
—	6,913,250	—	12,786,109	—	344,520	13,130,629
—	—	210,210	210,210	—	—	210,210
—	—	1,489,790	1,489,790	—	—	1,489,790
$2,084,816	$6,913,250	$1,700,000	$20,175,419	$125,054	$792,878	$21,093,351
$ 5,200	$ —	$ —	$ 336,986	$ 17,441	$114,494	$ 468,921
—	—	—	259,307	—	56,000	315,307
—	—	—	14,000	—	13,111	27,111
4,700	—	—	18,270	4,400	21,475	44,145
—	—	—	176,948	—	—	176,948
680,800	—	—	735,800	—	—	735,800
—	—	—	37,189	24,500	66,575	128,264
—	—	—	18,241	3,112	—	21,353
—	—	1,145,000	1,845,000	—	375,000	2,220,000
—	—	—	1,798,000	—	—	1,798,000
—	—	555,000	555,000	—	—	555,000
690,700	—	1,700,000	5,794,741	49,453	646,655	6,490,849
—	—	—	1,501,766	—	80,000	1,581,766
—	6,913,250	—	6,913,250	—	—	6,913,250
—	—	—	2,177,156	—	66,223	2,243,379
—	—	—	1,809,570	6,900	—	1,816,470
—	—	—	12,390	6,245	—	18,635
50,050	—	—	50,050	—	—	50,050
160,865	—	—	160,865	—	—	160,865
1,183,201	—	—	1,183,201	—	—	1,183,201
—	—	—	256,280	—	—	256,280
—	—	—	316,150	62,456	—	378,606
1,394,116	6,913,250	—	14,380,678	75,601	146,223	14,602,502
$2,084,816	$6,913,250	$1,700,000	$20,175,419	$125,054	$792,878	$21,093,351

EXHIBIT 16–5

CITY OF RAPHAEL
Combined Statement of Revenues, Expenditures, and Changes in Fund Balances—
All Governmental Fund Types and Expendable Trust Funds
For the Fiscal Year Ended December 31, 19X5

| | Governmental Fund Types | | | | Fiduciary Fund Type | Total Primary Government | Component Units | Total Reporting Entity |
	General	Special Revenue	Debt Service	Capital Projects	Expendable Trust	(memorandum only)	Governmental	(memorandum only)
Revenues:								
Taxes.	$ 881,300	$ 189,300	$ 79,177	$ —	$ —	$1,149,777	$ —	$1,149,777
Special assessments levied . . .	—	—	240,000	—	—	240,000	—	240,000
Licenses and permits. . . .	103,000	—	—	—	—	103,000	39,000	142,000
Intergovernmental revenues. . .	186,500	831,100	41,500	1,250,000	—	2,309,100	200,000	2,509,100
Charges for services . . .	91,000	79,100	—	—	—	170,100	17,400	187,500
Fines and forfeits . . .	33,200	—	—	—	—	33,200	—	33,200
Miscellaneous revenues. . . .	19,500	71,625	36,235	3,750	200	131,310	26,045	157,355
Total revenues.	1,314,500	1,171,125	396,912	1,253,750	200	4,136,487	282,445	4,418,932
Expenditures:								
Current:								
General government	121,805	—	—	—	—	121,805	—	121,805
Public safety	258,395	480,000	—	—	—	738,395	21,490	759,885
Highways and streets. . . .	85,400	417,000	—	—	—	502,400	—	502,400
Sanitation.	56,250	—	—	—	—	56,250	—	56,250

Health	44,500				44,500	54,908	99,408
Welfare	46,800				46,800	46,361	93,161
Culture and recreation . .	40,900	256,450			297,350	119,440	416,790
Education	509,150			2,420	511,570	22,500	534,070
Capital outlay	—		1,625,500		1,625,500		1,625,500
Debt service:							
Principal retirement . . .	—	373,100			373,100	—	373,100
Interest and fiscal charges . .	—	68,420			68,420	—	68,420
Total expenditures . . .	1,163,200	1,153,450	1,625,500		4,386,090	264,699	4,650,789
Excess (deficiency) of revenues over (under) expenditures . . .	151,300	17,675	(371,750)	(2,220)	(249,603)	17,746	(231,857)
Other financing sources (uses):							
Proceeds of general obligation bonds	—	—	900,000	—	900,000	—	900,000
Operating transfers in . .	—	10,000	64,500	2,530	77,030	—	77,030
Operating transfers out . .	(74,500)	—	—	—	(74,500)	—	(74,500)
Total other financing sources (uses)	(74,500)	10,000	964,500	2,530	902,530	—	902,530
Excess of revenues and other sources over (under) expenditures and other uses.	76,800	(34,608)	592,750	310	652,927	17,746	670,673
Fund balances—January 1 . . .	242,500	151,035	1,143,420	26,555	1,808,328	57,855	1,866,183
Residual equity transfer out . . .	(40,000)	—	—	—	(40,000)	—	(40,000)
Fund balances—December 31	$ 279,300	$ 168,710	$1,736,170	$26,865	$2,421,255	$ 75,601	$2,496,856

The notes to the financial statements are an integral part of this statement.

EXHIBIT 16–6

CITY OF RAPHAEL
**Combined Statement of Revenues, Expenditures, and
Changes in Fund Balances—Budget and Actual—
General and Special Revenue Fund Types
For the Fiscal Year Ended December 31, 19X5**

	General Fund		
	Budget	*Actual*	*Variance— Favorable (Unfavorable)*
Revenues:			
Taxes	$ 882,500	$ 881,300	$ (1,200)
Licenses and permits	125,500	103,000	(22,500)
Intergovernmental revenues	200,000	186,500	(13,500)
Charges for services	90,000	91,000	1,000
Fines and forfeits.	32,500	33,200	700
Miscellaneous revenues	19,500	19,500	—
Total revenues	1,350,000	1,314,500	(35,500)
Expenditures:			
Current:			
General government	129,000	121,805	7,195
Public safety	277,300	258,395	18,905
Highways and streets	84,500	85,400	(900)
Sanitation	50,000	56,250	(6,250)
Health.	47,750	44,500	3,250
Welfare	51,000	46,800	4,200
Culture and recreation	44,500	40,900	3,600
Education	541,450	509,150	32,300
Total expenditures	1,225,500	1,163,200	62,300
Excess (deficiency) of revenues over (under) expenditures	124,500	151,300	26,800
Other financing sources (uses):			
Operating transfers out	(74,500)	(74,500)	—
Excess (deficiency) of revenues over (under) expenditures and other uses	50,000	76,800	26,800
Fund balances—January 1.	242,500	242,500	—
Residual equity transfer out	(40,000)	(40,000)	—
Fund balances—December 31	$ 252,500	$ 279,300	$ 26,800

The notes to the financial statements are an integral part of this statement.

Special Revenue Funds			Totals (Memorandum Only)		
Budget	Actual	Variance— Favorable (Unfavorable)	Budget	Actual	Variance— Favorable (Unfavorable)
$ 189,500	$ 189,300	$ (200)	$1,072,000	$1,070,600	$ (1,400)
—	—	—	125,500	103,000	(22,500)
837,600	831,100	(6,500)	1,037,600	1,017,600	(20,000)
78,000	79,100	1,100	168,000	170,100	2,100
—	—	—	32,500	33,200	700
81,475	71,625	(9,850)	100,975	91,125	(9,850)
1,186,575	1,171,125	(15,450)	2,536,575	2,485,625	(50,950)
—	—	—	129,000	121,805	7,195
494,500	480,000	14,500	771,800	738,395	33,405
436,000	417,000	19,000	520,500	502,400	18,100
—	—	—	50,000	56,250	(6,250)
—	—	—	47,750	44,500	3,250
—	—	—	51,000	46,800	4,200
272,000	256,450	15,550	316,500	297,350	19,150
—	—	—	541,450	509,150	32,300
1,202,500	1,153,450	49,050	2,428,000	2,316,650	111,350
(15,925)	17,675	33,600	108,575	168,975	60,400
—	—	—	(74,500)	(74,500)	—
(15,925)	17,675	33,600	34,075	94,475	60,400
151,035	151,035	—	393,535	393,535	—
—	—	—	(40,000)	(40,000)	—
$ 135,110	$ 168,710	$ 33,600	$ 387,610	$ 448,010	$ 60,400

EXHIBIT 16–7

CITY OF RAPHAEL
Combined Statement of Revenues, Expenses, and Changes in Retained Earnings/Fund Balances—All Proprietary Fund Types and Similar Trust Funds
For the Fiscal Year Ended December 31, 19X5

	Proprietary Fund Types		Fiduciary Fund Types		Totals Primary (memorandum only)	Component Units Proprietary	Total Reporting Entity (memorandum only)
	Enterprise	Internal Service	Nonexpendable Trust	Pension Trust			
Operating revenues:							
Charges for services	$ 672,150	$88,000	$ —	$ —	$ 760,150	$186,315	$ 946,465
Interest	—	—	2,480	28,460	30,940	16,010	46,950
Contributions	—	—	—	160,686	160,686	—	160,686
Total operating revenues	672,150	88,000	2,480	189,146	951,776	202,325	1,154,101
Operating expenses:							
Cost of sales and services	247,450	32,500	—	—	279,950	149,633	429,583
Contractual services	75,330	400	—	—	75,730	—	75,730
Supplies	20,310	1,900	—	—	22,210	11,442	33,652
Materials	50,940	44,000	—	—	94,940	1,088	96,028
Heat, light, and power	26,050	1,500	—	—	27,550	990	28,540
Depreciation	144,100	4,450	—	—	148,550	6,496	155,046
Benefit payments	—	—	—	21,000	21,000	—	21,000
Refunds	—	—	—	25,745	25,745	—	25,745
Total operating expenses	564,180	84,750	—	46,745	695,675	169,649	865,324
Operating income	107,970	3,250	2,480	142,401	256,101	32,676	288,777
Nonoperating revenues (expenses):							
Grants and gifts	55,000	—	45,000	—	100,000	—	100,000
Interest revenue	3,830	—	—	—	3,830	—	3,830
Other	5,000	—	—	—	5,000	—	5,000
Interest expense and fiscal charges	(92,988)	—	—	—	(92,988)	(15,410)	(108,398)
Total nonoperating revenues (expenses)	(29,158)	—	45,000	—	15,842	(15,410)	432
Income before operating transfers	78,812	3,250	47,480	142,401	271,943	17,266	289,209
Operating transfers in (out)	—	—	(2,530)	—	(2,530)	—	(2,530)
Net income	78,812	3,250	44,950	142,401	269,413	17,266	286,679
Retained earnings/fund balances—January 1	2,088,544	6,550	139,100	1,040,800	3,274,994	48,957	3,323,951
Retained earnings/fund balances—December 31	$2,167,356	$ 9,800	$184,050	$1,183,201	$3,544,407	$ 66,223	$3,610,630

The notes to the financial statements are an integral part of this statement.

EXHIBIT 16-8

CITY OF RAPHAEL
Combined Statement of Cash Flows
All Proprietary Fund Types and Nonexpendable Trust Fund
For the Fiscal Year Ended December 31, 19X5

	Proprietary Fund Types		Nonexpendable Trust Fund	Total Primary Government (memorandum only)	Component Units Proprietary	Total Reporting Entity (memorandum only)
	Enterprise	Internal Service				
Cash flows from operating activities:*						
Cash from customers	$ 661,440	$ 89,160	$ —	$ 750,600	$183,405	$ 934,005
Interest received	—	—	2,480	2,480	15,310	17,790
Cash paid to suppliers	(86,100)	(62,970)	—	(149,070)	(140,945)	(290,015)
Cash paid to employees	(310,380)	(13,760)	—	(324,140)	(12,866)	(337,006)
Cash paid for other operating expenses	(39,640)	(5,494)	—	(45,134)	(9,451)	(54,585)
Net cash provided (used) by operating activities	225,320	6,936	2,480	234,736	35,453	270,189
Cash flows from noncapital financing activities:						
Grants and gifts	—	—	45,000	45,000	—	45,000
Operating transfers out	—	—	(2,530)	(2,530)	—	(2,530)
Net cash provided (used) by noncapital financing activities	—	—	42,470	42,470	—	42,470
Cash flows from capital and related financing activities:						
Proceeds from issuance of long-term debt	443,449	—	—	443,449	121,000	564,449
Principal payments—long-term debt	(325,000)	—	—	(325,000)	(25,000)	(350,000)
Proceeds from sale of fixed assets	11,400	—	—	11,400	11,400	11,400
Purchase of fixed assets	(306,921)	(22,000)	—	(328,921)	(98,450)	(427,371)
Net cash provided (used) by capital and related financing activities	(177,072)	(22,000)	—	(199,072)	(2,450)	(201,522)
Cash flows from investing activities:						
Proceeds from sale of investments	26,100	—	11,000	37,100	—	37,100
Purchase of investments	—	—	(48,800)	(48,800)	(10,000)	(58,800)
Net cash provided (used) by investing activities	26,100	—	(37,800)	(11,700)	(10,000)	(21,700)
Net increase (decrease) in cash	74,348	(15,064)	7,150	66,434	23,003	89,437
Cash, January 1	204,948	44,764	9,290	259,002	162,041	421,043
Cash, December 31	$ 279,296	$ 29,700	$ 16,440	$ 325,436	$185,044	$ 510,480

The notes to the financial statements are an integral part of this statement.

* Since the direct approach of deriving cash from operating activities is being used here, a reconciliation of net cash flows from operating activities to net income should also be included.

Questions

1. What is the primary emphasis in accounting for the business-type funds of a state or local government?
2. What characteristics of accounting for business-type funds are unique from the reporting procedures identified in the previous chapter for the governmental-type funds?
3. Why is accrual accounting rather than modified accrual accounting considered appropriate for the business-type funds of a state or local government unit?
4. How are commitments accounted for in an Enterprise Fund? Why?
5. Give examples of government operations appropriately classified as Enterprise Funds. Give examples of government operations appropriately classified as Internal Service Funds.
6. Describe the controversies that surround the recording of Internal Service Funds for external reporting purposes.
7. What are "Due to" and "Due from" accounts and how are they reported?
8. Why do some Enterprise Funds have restricted asset accounts?
9. Why is income determination emphasized in a Pension Trust Fund?
10. What is the accounting objective for a Nonexpendable Trust Fund? Why?
11. What is the difference between a Nonexpendable Trust Fund and an Expendable Trust Fund?
12. What is the purpose of Agency Funds? What transactions are recorded in Agency Funds?
13. How is the presence of a primary government identified?
14. How can a government demonstrate its fiscal independence?
15. How does a primary government determine its component units?
16. How does a primary government report the financial positions and operations of its component units?
17. What is meant by blended component units?
18. In government reporting, what is a related organization and how is a related organization reported by a primary government?
19. What items are included in the comprehensive annual financial report produced for a state or local government?
20. When may a government unit issue only general purpose financial statements rather than a comprehensive annual financial report?
21. What specific financial statements make up the general purpose financial statements of a state or local government?

Library Assignments

1. Read the following articles and any other published information discussing the history of governmental accounting:

    "Capital Accounts of a Municipality," *The Journal of Accountancy,* October 1918.

    "Governmental Sinking Funds, Serial Bonds and Depreciation Reserves," *The Journal of Accountancy,* October 1918.

    "25 Years of State and Local Governmental Financial Reporting—An Accounting Standards Perspective," *Government Accountants Journal,* Fall 1992.

    Write a short paper discussing the changes in governmental accounting during the 20th century.

2. Read the following article:

    "Internal Service Funds Are beyond Salvation," *Accounting Horizons,* June 1990.

    Write a short paper discussing whether Internal Service Funds should be eliminated from the external reporting of a state or local government unit.

3. Read the following:

    "Statement No. 14 of the Governmental Accounting Standards Board— The Financial Reporting Entity," *Journal of Accountancy,* November 1991.

    "The Governmental Financial Reporting Entity: Inclusion and Display," *The CPA Journal,* January 1993.

    Write a report describing the changes made by the GASB in defining the reporting entity of a government unit. Discuss the identification of component units and their reporting.

Problems

1. Which of the following statements is not true of the business-type funds of a state or local government unit?

    a. The basis of accounting is accrual accounting.

    b. Depreciation expense is recorded each period.

    c. Budgetary entries are recorded by most but not all of these funds.

    d. Fixed assets are recorded within the individual funds.

2. Which of the following accounts would not be recorded by an Enterprise Fund?

    a. Encumbrances.

    b. Buildings.

    c. Notes payable.

    d. Contributed capital.

3. What is the purpose of Nonexpendable Trust Fund?

    a. To account for monetary gifts that must be used for fixed assets.

    b. To account for monetary gifts that cannot be spent until the end of a specified period of time.

    c. To account for a gift where only the subsequently earned income can be spent.

    d. To account for a gift where the money must be used to reduce a government's debts rather than to buy assets.

4. A city's municipal airport charges a customer for rental space. When is the revenue recognized?

    a. When received.

    b. When appropriately spent.

    c. When measurable and available.

    d. When the earning process is substantially completed.

5. Fixed assets owned by a city-owned utility are accounted for in which of the following?

	Enterprise Fund	General Fixed Assets Account Group
a.	No	No
b.	No	Yes
c.	Yes	No
d.	Yes	Yes

(AICPA adapted)

6. If a pension trust fund pays out benefits to a retired city employee, what account balance is directly affected?

    a. Operating expenses.

    b. Fund balance.

    c. Pension liability.

    d. Membership contribution.

7. Money that must be turned over to the state government is collected by a city periodically. While the money is being held by the city, within which fund should it be recorded?

    a. General Fund.

    b. Agency Fund.

    c. Special Revenue Fund.

    d. Expendable Trust Fund.

8. Lake City operates a centralized data processing center through an Internal Service Fund, to provide data processing services to Lake's other govern-

mental units. In 1995, this Internal Service fund billed Lake's police department $100,000 for data processing services. How should the Internal Service Fund record this billing?

	Debit	Credit
a. Memorandum entry only	—	—
b. Due from police department	100,000	
Data processing expenses		100,000
c. Intragovernmental transfers	100,000	
Interfund exchanges		100,000
d. Due from police department	100,000	
Operating revenue		100,000

(AICPA adapted)

9. Which of the following is not a criterion for identifying a primary government?
   a. A separately elected governing board.
   b. Identifiable geographical boundaries.
   c. Legal separation such as being able to sue and be sued.
   d. Fiscal independence.

10. Which of the following is not a criterion for determining the fiscal independence of a government entity?
    a. The right to buy, sell, or lease property in the entity's name without the approval of another government.
    b. Determining the budget for the entity without the approval of any other body.
    c. Being able to levy taxes without having to seek approval of another government unit.
    d. Issuing bonds without the need for approval by another government.

11. What is a component unit?
    a. An Internal Service Fund.
    b. An activity that is legally separate from a primary government but must still be reported within the government's financial statements.
    c. Any fund type included in a primary government's financial statements.
    d. An account group of a governmental fund.

12. Which of the following would not indicate that a primary government has the ability to impose its will on a component unit?
    a. Being able to modify the component unit's budgets.
    b. Being able to appoint more than 21 percent of the members of the component unit's governing board.
    c. Hiring the individuals who operate the component unit on a daily basis.
    d. Overriding decisions of the governing board of the component unit.

13. Which of the following is not a general purpose financial statement of a state or local government?
    a. Combined balance sheet—all fund types and account groups.
    b. Combined income statement—all fund types and account groups.

   c. Combined statement of revenues, expenditures, and changes in fund balance—budget and actual.

   d. Combined statement of revenues, expenses, and changes in retained earnings—all proprietary fund types.

14. In the comprehensive annual financial report (CAFR) of a governmental unit, the account groups are included in

   a. Both the combined balance sheet and the combined statement of revenues, expenditures, and changes in fund balances.

   b. The combined statement of revenues, expenditures, and changes in fund balances, but not the combined balance sheet.

   c. The combined balance sheet but not the combined statement of revenues, expenditures, and changes in fund balances.

   d. Neither the combined balance sheet nor the combined statement of revenues, expenditures, and changes in fund balances.

(AICPA)

15. Which of the following would be included in the Combined Statement of Revenues, Expenditures, and Changes in Fund Balances—Budget and Actual in the comprehensive annual financial report (CAFR) of a governmental unit?

	Enterprise Fund	*General Fixed Asset Account Group*
a.	Yes	Yes
b.	Yes	No
c.	No	Yes
d.	No	No

(AICPA)

16. Which of the following accounts would be included in the fund equity section of the combined balance sheet of a governmental unit for the general fixed asset account group?

	Investment in General Fixed Assets	*Fund Balance Reserved for Encumbrances*
a.	Yes	Yes
b.	Yes	No
c.	No	No
d.	No	Yes

(AICPA)

17. The comprehensive annual financial report (CAFR) of a governmental unit should contain a Combined Statement of Revenues, Expenses, and Changes in Retained Earnings for

	Account Groups	Governmental Funds
a.	Yes	Yes
b.	Yes	No
c.	No	No
d.	No	Yes

(AICPA)

18. A city received the following: a state government grant of $100,000 to be used for a specific project, a gift from a citizen of $20,000 cash where only the subsequent income can be spent, property tax revenues of $530,000, bond proceeds of $240,000 for construction of a building for the data processing operation that services the entire city government. In which funds should each of these cash receipts be recorded?

	Grant	Gift	Tax	Bond
a.	Expendable Trust	Nonexpendable Trust	General Fund	General Fund
b.	Special Revenue	General Fund	Capital Projects	Debt Service
c.	Special Revenue	Nonexpendable Trust	General Fund	Internal Service
d.	General Fund	Expendable Trust	Special Revenue	Debt Service

19. The city of Francois, Texas, has begun the process of producing its comprehensive annual financial report (CAFR). Within the city, several organizations exist that are related to the government. The city's accountant is trying to decide how these organizations should be included in the reporting process.

   a. What is the major criterion for inclusion in a government's CAFR?

   b. How is a primary government unit identified?

   c. How is the legal separation of a government unit evaluated?

   d. How is the fiscal independence of a government unit evaluated?

   e. What is a component unit and how are the financial position and operations of a component unit reported by a primary government?

   f. How does a primary government prove that it can impose its will on a component unit?

   g. What is meant by the blending of a component unit?

   h. What is a related organization and how does a primary government report its related organizations?

20. The city of Walkup incurred the following debts at face value on July 1, 1995:

   • Bonds totaling $600,000 were issued to construct locker rooms for the city's swimming pool. The interest rate was 8 percent per year. Repayment was to be made from admission charged to the swimmers.

   • A $50,000 note was signed with a bank to buy equipment for the city's print shop. The interest rate was 9 percent per year. Repayment was to be made from surplus amounts generated by the charges assessed by the print shop.

In both cases, the money was received and appropriately expended. On July 1, 1996, a $70,000 payment was made on the bonds that included the interest to date. An $8,000 payment made on the note on April 1, 1996, also included the interest to date.

Make all necessary journal entries for 1995 and 1996 and indicate the appropriate fund types. The city has a calendar year.

21. The city of Mexvell operated a motor pool serving all city-owned vehicles. The motor pool bought a new garage by paying $22,000 cash and signing a note with the local bank for $215,000. Subsequently, the motor pool did work for the police department at a cost of $13,000, which has not yet been paid. Depreciation on the garage amounted to $15,000. The first $9,000 payment made on the note included $3,700 in interest.

    Give all of the entries for these transactions including the fund type or account group in which each entry would be recorded.

22. Hawkins County decided to create a sanitation service and offer it to the public for a fee. As a result, county officials planned to account for this activity within an Enterprise Fund. To begin the operations, $55,000 of previously unrestricted funds were transferred on February 1, 1995, as permanent financing. An additional $158,000 was borrowed from a local bank on March 1, 1995. The debt had a 10 percent annual interest rate. A truck was ordered from a local dealer on June 1, 1995, at an anticipated cost of $98,000. The truck was received on July 1, 1995, with an actual cost of $102,000. The truck had a $12,000 salvage value and an expected life of 10 years (assume straight-line depreciation was used). Rental space to house the truck was located at a charge of $100 per month. Rent for the first 15 months of operation was paid on June 30, 1995. During the last six months of the year, citizens were charged $15,000 for services rendered and actually paid $13,000. The remaining accounts were assumed to be collectible.

Required:

a. Make all journal entries for this activity including any adjuting entries needed at December 31, 1995. Only entries within the Enterprise Fund are required.

b. Prepare financial statements for this operation.

23. The following transactions are for the city of Jamin. For each, prepare all needed journal entries including an identification of the fund types.

    a. The city collected $13,000 from parking meters that must be transferred to the county government.

    b. The city transferred $21,000 into a Pension Trust Fund. Of this amount, $15,000 was contributed by the city with the remainder coming from the employees.

    c. Investments valued at $55,000 were donated to the city with the stipulation that subsequent dividend income be used to plant trees in the downtown area.

    d. Unrestricted funds totaling $23,000 were transferred to begin a print shop to service the entire city government.

    e. The city motor pool did work for the fire department at a cost of $13,000. This money has not yet been paid.

    f. The money collected in (*a*) was paid to the county.

    g. The investments received in (*c*) generated $8,000 in dividends. The agent holding these investments charged a commission of $1,000 and mailed the remaining $7,000 to the city.

    h. The $7,000 profit in (*g*) was reclassified into an Expendable Trust Fund.

    i. The print shop in (*d*) bought a building at a cost of $130,000, paid $21,000 immediately and signed a note for the remainder.

24. The following transactions are for the city of Lights. For each, prepare all necessary journal entries including an identification of the funds or account groups involved.

    a. The city council transferred $44,000 from the General Fund as permanent financing to create a print shop to service the needs of the various agencies and branches of the government.

    b. The print shop ordered printing equipment for an estimated cost of $22,000 along with approximately $4,000 in supplies.

    c. The city's golf course issued $500,000 in bonds at a price of $512,000 to finance the construction of a new club house.

    d. The printing equipment and supplies ordered in (*b*) were received by the government with an actual cost of $23,500 and $3,800, respectively. Payment will be made in 30 days.

    e. The city collected $14,600 in tolls from the roads in the area. Of this total, 90 percent must be spent by the city for highway maintenance. The remaining 10 percent will be held until the end of the year and then turned over to the state government.

    f. The print shop did work for the school system for a price of $930. This amount has not, as of yet, been collected.

    g. The city's golf course made a first payment of $25,000 on the bond issued in (*c*). Of this balance, $5,000 covered current interest charges with the remainder applied to the principal.

    h. By the end of the year, the print shop consumed $2,600 of supplies.

    i. The club house for the golf course was completed and the contractor paid $477,000.

    j. Depreciation on the printing equipment was calculated as $4,700.

    k. The appropriate portion of the money collected from the toll roads was conveyed to the state government.

25. The city of Merlot operated a central garage to provide repairs and maintenance for all city-owned vehicles. The Central Garage Fund was established by a contribution of $200,000 from the General Fund on July 1, 1994, at which time the building was acquired. The after-closing trial balance at June 30, 1996, was as follows:

	Debit	Credit
Cash	$150,000	
Due from General Fund	20,000	
Inventory of materials and supplies	80,000	
Land	60,000	
Building	200,000	
Accumulated depreciation—Building		$ 10,000
Machinery and equipment	56,000	
Accumulated depreciation—Machinery and equipment		12,000
Vouchers payable		38,000
Contribution from General Fund		200,000
Retained earnings		306,000
Totals	$566,000	$566,000

The following information applies to the fiscal year ended June 30, 1997:

a. Materials and supplies were purchased on account for $74,000.

b. The inventory of materials and supplies at June 30, 1997, was $58,000, based on the physical count taken.

c. Salaries and wages paid to employees totaled $230,000.

d. An invoice from the city's water and electrical utility totaling $30,000 was paid.

e. Depreciation for the period was computed as follows: building—$5,000 and machinery and equipment—$8,000.

f. Billings to other departments for services rendered to them were as follows:

General Fund	$262,000
Water and Sewer Fund	84,000
Special Revenue Fund	32,000

g. Unpaid interfund receivable balances at June 30, 1997, were as follows:

| General Fund . . . . | $ 6,000 |
| Special Revenue Fund . . . . | 16,000 |

h. Vouchers payable at June 30, 1997, were $14,000.

Required:

a. For the period July 1, 1996, through June 30, 1997, prepare journal entries to record all of the transactions in the Central Garage Fund accounts.

b. Prepare closing entries for the Central Garage Fund at June 30, 1997.

(AICPA adapted)

26. The following transactions were incurred by the city of Metropolis. Prepare all appropriate journal entries for the following fund categories:

> Enterprise Funds
>
> Internal Service Funds
>
> Pension Trust Funds
>
> Nonexpendable Trust Funds
>
> Agency Funds

a. A transfer of $360,000 was made from the city's General Fund to finance a data processing center being established to provide services for all government operations.

b. A gift of $88,000 in cash was received by the city from a local school teacher with the provision that all earnings be used to provide scholarships for local students.

c. The municipal airport reported revenues of $460,000 ($320,000 from assessments made to the airline companies and $140,000 from rental charges). Only $97,000 of the rents have been collected. The airport has also incurred the following expenses:

Salaries	$160,000
Depreciation	80,000
Advertising	9,000
Maintenance	79,000

Although the advertising has already appeared in the newspaper, the cost has not yet been paid.

d. A contract was signed to acquire an $154,000 building for the data processing center. This facility is presently under construction.

e. The city collected $160,000 in general sales taxes. Of this amount, 20 percent will eventually be transferred to the state.

f. The building was completed for the data processing center and payment was made.

g. The municipal airport signed an $800,000 note payable and immediately used these funds to acquire a new hangar.

h. The appropriate amount of sales taxes collected in (*e*) was conveyed to the state.

i. Cash of $27,000 was transferred from the city's General Fund to the Pension Trust Fund representing the government's current year contribution.

j. The data processing center did the following work; as of yet, no amounts have been collected:

General Fund.	$4,000
Special Revenue Fund.	900
Municipal Airport	1,400

k. The municipal airport paid the first $8,000 interest installment on the note signed in (*g*).

l. Income of $12,000 was received on the gift donated in (*b*). This money was transferred to an Expendable Trust Fund to be used in the stipulated manner.

m. Retired city employees were paid benefits of $44,000 in cash.

27. An examination of the accounts of the city of Delmas, as of June 30, 1995, revealed the following:

a. On December 31, 1994, the city paid $315,000 out of General Fund revenues to acquire a central garage to service its vehicles, with $167,500 of this amount being paid for a building with an estimated life of 25 years, $44,500 for land, and $103,000 for machinery with an estimated life of 15 years. An additional $12,200 cash contribution was received by the garage from the General Fund to finance daily operations.

b. The garage maintained no formal accounting records, but a review of deposit slips and canceled checks for the period revealed the following:

Collections for services to city departments	
financed from the General Fund	$30,000
Office salaries paid	6,000
Utilities	700
Mechanics' wages	11,000
Materials and supplies	9,000

c. At June 30, 1995, the garage also had uncollected billings of $2,000, accounts payable for materials and supplies of $500, and an inventory of materials and supplies of $1,500.

d. On June 30, 1995, the city issued $200,000 in special assessment bonds at par to finance a street improvement project estimated to cost $225,000. The project was to be paid by a $15,000 contribution from the city and a $210,000 levy against property owners (payable in five equal annual installments beginning on October 1, 1995). The levy was made on June 30. A $215,000 contract was signed on July 2, 1995, but work has not yet begun. The city has agreed to guarantee payment on the bonds in case any forfeitures occur.

e. On July 1, 1993, the city issued $400,000 in 30-year, 6 percent general obligation term bonds at par to finance the construction of a public health center. Construction was completed and the contractors fully paid a total of $397,500 on May 9, 1995.

f. For the health center bonds, the city set aside General Fund revenues of $20,000 on each October 1 to cover future interest and principal payments.

Required:

The preceding information was recorded only in the General Fund. Prepare the formal entries as of June 30, 1995, to adjust all funds other than the General Fund. (AICPA adapted)

28. Gotham City was incorporated on July 1, 1995. The following transactions occurred during its first fiscal year, July 1, 1995, to June 30, 1996:

a. The city council adopted a budget for general operations during the fiscal year ending June 30, 1996. Revenues were estimated at $900,000. Legal authorizations for expenditures were $724,000 along with transfers out of $170,000.

b. Property taxes were levied in the amount of $790,000; 2 percent of this amount was estimated to be uncollectible. These taxes were considered available as of the date of levy to finance current expenditures.

c. During the year, a resident of the city donated marketable securities valued at $50,000 to the city. The terms of the trust agreement stipulated that the principal amount be kept intact; use of revenue generated by the securities was restricted to financing college scholarships for needy students. Dividends earned and received on these marketable securities amounted to $5,500 through June 30, 1996. This money was transferred to an Expendable Trust Fund for expenditure in the following period.

d. A General Fund transfer of $5,000 was made to establish an Internal Service Fund to provide for a permanent supply of materials and other items to be used by other funds.

e. The city decided to install lighting on several local streets. A special assessment project was authorized with a budgeted cost of $175,000. Budgetary entries were not formally recorded. A bond was issued for $175,000, with the city guaranteeing payment. The lights were installed. Residents were then assessed $165,000, with the remainder to come from the General Fund. No payments have yet been received.

f. During the year, the Internal Service Fund purchased supplies at various times at a total cost of $4,900.

g. Cash collections recorded by the General Fund during the year were as follows:

Property taxes.	$779,000
Licenses and permits.	33,000

h. The city council decided to build a municipal swimming pool at an estimated cost of $500,000. Bonds bearing an annual interest rate of 8 percent were issued for financing purposes. On June 30, 1996, a contract was signed for this project but no expenditures have been made.

i. Revenues of $66,000 were earned by a local parking garage used by the citizens of Gotham City. Maintenance expenses were $12,000 and depreciation, $53,000.

j. A fire truck was purchased for $85,000, and the voucher approved and paid by the General Fund. This expenditure was previously encumbered for $82,700.

Required:

Prepare journal entries to properly record each of the previous transactions in the appropriate fund(s) or group of accounts of Gotham City for the fiscal year ended June 30, 1996.

17

ACCOUNTING FOR NOT-FOR-PROFIT ORGANIZATIONS: COLLEGES AND UNIVERSITIES

Questions to Consider

- Why does a college or university utilize fund accounting and what fund types are employed by these not-for-profit organizations?
- What accounting is made of the pledges of support received by a college or university?
- Why do the expenditures recorded in a college or university's Restricted Current Funds equal the total amount of revenues recognized in that same fund?
- What changes are being made in the financial statements of private colleges and universities and other not-for-profit organizations?
- Why do the 1992 financial statements for Southern Methodist University indicate depreciation expense of nearly $9 million, while the statements for the University of Virginia for the same year state that "consistent with current generally accepted accounting principles for public colleges and universities, depreciation on plant assets is not recorded"?
- What hierarchy has been developed of the authoritative pronouncements produced to guide the financial reporting of for-profit businesses and not-for-profit organizations?

In its 1990 financial statements, Yale University reported holding investments in its endowment valued at more than $2.5 billion. At the same time, Princeton University disclosed that $89 million of its revenues came from tuition and fees, while $162 million resulted from government grants and contracts. Statements for the Pennsylvania State University indicated that $286 million had been expended during that year on instruction, $201 million on research, and $38 million on student services. Figures reported by the University of New Mexico showed revenues of $33.7 million from private gifts and contracts (up from $23.8 million in the previous year): $3.4 million in unrestricted funds and $30.3 million that had been restricted in some fashion by the donor.

Students, parents, alumni, donors, and any other interested parties can discover a wealth of information in the financial statements of a college or university. Although these organizations are not-for-profit by nature, they differ considerably from the state and local governments discussed in Chapter 16. Such schools do not have the ability to tax their citizens to gain financial support. Rather, they must compete for students and other types of funding. Their existence is guaranteed only if they make wise use of their resources. Therefore, although some similarities do exist, the accounting that is appropriate for a college or university varies significantly from that of a state or local government. Although these educational institutions employ fund accounting, they have developed a distinctly different approach to the gathering and reporting of financial information.

Accounting for Colleges and Universities

Quite obviously, many different types of not-for-profit organizations exist within this country: churches, charities, hospitals, foundations, and the like. Among the most obvious examples, though, are colleges and universities. Thousands of these schools are in operation throughout the United States. These educational institutions range from gigantic state universities with tens of thousands of students to small, private colleges serving only a few hundred.

This chapter examines the financial accounting and reporting process appropriately utilized by these schools. Historically, a predominant characteristic of not-for-profit accounting has been that each type of organization utilizes the process particularly suited to its own needs. Although distinctive accounting aspects still exist, in recent years, some elements of that diversity have begun to break down. Thus, a number of the procedures discussed here parallel the reporting techniques found in other not-for-profit organizations, while some remain unique to colleges and universities.

To guide the accounting for for-profit enterprises, volumes of official standards have been created to ensure the fair presentation of all financial information. State and local governmental accounting has also become well defined over the years through the efforts of the National Council on Governmental Accounting, the Government Finance Officers Association, the AICPA, and now the GASB.

In comparison, a scarcity of authoritative literature exists in college and university accounting. At present, generally accepted accounting principles for these educational institutions are best described in two sources:

- *Audits of Colleges and Universities,* the AICPA's industry audit guide.
- *College and University Business Administration (CUBA),* a guidebook

produced by the National Association of College and University Business Officers (sometimes referred to as the *Manual*).

These two sources are not radically different. As the AICPA's audit guide admits, "much of the material in this guide is presented as it appears in the Manual."[1]

These two documents, however, concentrate primarily on describing current practices rather than prescribing theoretically preferable approaches. Consequently, a great degree of flexibility exists in the financial reporting practices of the colleges and universities across the country. As just a single example, investments (other than plant assets) are usually recorded at cost if purchased by the school or at fair market value at date of gift if received by donation. The AICPA industry audit guide notes, however, that "as a permissible alternative, investments, exclusive of physical plant, may be reported in the financial statements at current market value or fair value, provided this basis is used for investments of all funds."[2] In effect, each institution is allowed to choose between two theoretically different accounting techniques.

Unfortunately, no practical guidance is provided to assist schools in selecting an appropriate valuation principle for their investments. Not surprisingly, one survey found both methods in wide use: 78 percent of the colleges and universities that responded use the prescribed method but a significant minority (22 percent or 195 schools) have adopted current market value or some other valuation approach to account for investments.[3] James Madison University, for example, reports its investments at historical cost whereas the University of Vermont uses market value.

As is discussed subsequently, in recent years both the FASB and the GASB have become actively involved in setting accounting standards for colleges and universities and other not-for-profit organizations. Some impact on the financial reporting process has already been seen that will almost certainly expand in the coming years. Certain procedures might eventually become standardized while others are eliminated as inappropriate. The flexibility that has been a characteristic of college and university accounting will probably be narrowed as these bodies issue additional pronouncements.

Despite the limited quantity of authoritative literature created to date, a number of standard (and unique) procedures have evolved over the years in connection with college and university accounting. The present reporting process resembles that utilized by state and local governments in two important aspects: first, determination of the school's profitability is not an accounting emphasis. Educational institutions are primarily involved with furnishing services rather than with generating income. The most visible goals of a college or university are to provide an education for enrolled students while also encouraging scholarly research. Neither of these goals can be measured accurately in pure profits. Thus, as in

---

[1] AICPA, *Audits of Colleges and Universities* (New York: AICPA, 1992), par. 1.02.

[2] Ibid., par. 2.16.

[3] Peat, Marwick, Mitchell & Co., *Principles & Presentation: Higher Education* (New York: Peat, Marwick, Mitchell, 1985), p. 25.

governmental accounting, income determination does not serve as a basic financial reporting objective.

Second, fund accounting is utilized by these schools. Like a city or county, the operation of any college or university necessarily encompasses a broad range of dissimilar activities. Library operations, research grants, cafeterias, athletic teams, bookstores, computer centers, and the like, all fall under the financial control of most colleges and universities. The number as well as the diversity of these functions mandate some degree of separation within the accounting process. Hence, once again, the use of fund accounting becomes appropriate.

> Service, rather than profits, is the objective of an educational institution; thus, the primary obligation of accounting and reporting is one of accounting for resources received and used rather than for determination of net income. . . . In order to account properly for a diversity of resources and their use, there has developed, over a period of years, the principles and practices of "fund accounting."[4]

Fund accounting is considered especially important to colleges and universities because of the significant amount of restricted donations that are received. To ensure that each gift is expended as stipulated, individual funds are established and monitored. If a donation, for example, is made to finance the study of Shakespeare, the school must take the necessary precautions to ensure that the money is used as specified. Fund accounting is one aspect of that control structure. As stated in a note to the 1990 financial statements of the University of Maryland, "in order to ensure observance of limitations and restrictions placed on the use of resources available to the College Park campus, the accounts are maintained in accordance with the principles of fund accounting."

Fund Accounting for Colleges and Universities

Understanding the accounting procedures utilized by colleges and universities requires a familiarity with the various fund categories. Six general fund groups exist within the accounting records of most colleges and universities:

Current Funds	Annuity and Life Income Funds
Loan Funds	Plant Funds
Endowment and Similar Funds	Agency Funds

As in governmental accounting, several of these fund headings are further divided into subgroups to enable schools to account for specific activities or monetary amounts. The Current Funds category, for example, is actually comprised of two distinct fund types: Unrestricted Current Funds and Restricted Current Funds. To provide a basis for the subsequent discussion of college and university accounting, a brief synopsis of each individual fund type follows:

---

[4] AICPA, *Audits of Colleges and Universities* (New York: AICPA, 1992), par. 2.01.

1. *Current Funds*
   a. *Unrestricted Current Funds.* Unrestricted Current Funds account for all currently expendable resources to be used in accomplishing the primary objectives of the institution, such as education and research. Because of the general operating nature of this category, a majority of the financial transactions of any college or university is normally recorded in the Unrestricted Current Funds. The University of Hawaii, as an example, reported unrestricted revenues and other additions of $381 million for the year ending June 30, 1990, along with expenditures and other deductions of nearly $366 million. These figures represented 73 percent of the university's total revenues and additions and 79 percent of all expenditures and deductions.

   Revenues to be recognized in the Unrestricted Current Funds include general student tuition and fees, unrestricted grants and gifts, and amounts generated by a school's auxiliary operations such as the cafeteria and bookstore. Likewise, expenditures cover a broad spectrum of payments made in connection with ongoing activities including professors' salaries, student services, general maintenance, library acquisitions, and other similar costs. For the University of Hawaii, the largest revenue was state appropriations of $308 million and the largest expenditure was $146 million for instruction.

   b. *Restricted Current Funds.* Restricted Current Funds are utilized by colleges and universities to account for resources to be spent for current operating purposes. *However, as the title implies, external restrictions have been placed on the ultimate usage of the money.* Such stipulations are common in connection with gifts as well as with many government grants. A donation made to a university under the provision that the money must be used to buy library books would be accounted for within restricted current funds.

   As an example, for the fiscal year ending June 30, 1991, the University of Virginia reported revenues of approximately $172 million within restricted current funds. According to the university's financial statements, this balance was generated from six specific sources:

   > State appropriations.
   > Federal grants and contracts.
   > State grants and contracts.
   > Local grants and contracts.
   > Private gifts, grants, and contracts.
   > Endowment income.

   The eventual use of this entire $172 million in revenues was designated by outside parties for specified operating purposes. In 1991, the largest portion ($68 million) went to fund research with another

$28 million for instruction. To ensure the appropriate handling of these gifts and grants, the assets were recorded separately within the Restricted Current Funds.

2. *Loan Funds*. Loan Funds account for loans made by the institution. Such money is granted primarily to students to assist them in financing their educations although loans to the school's faculty and staff are also possible. This category maintains a record of the monetary resources available as well as the outstanding loan balances currently owed to the university. The University of Georgia Loan Funds balance sheet, for example, showed the following assets as of June 30, 1988:

Cash.	$ 87,637
Temporary investment—at cost	3,455,000
Notes receivable—student loans	9,384,329
Investments	67,101

3. *Endowment and Similar Funds*. This third general category is extremely important because endowment gifts are significant to the financing of most schools. A number of universities, including Harvard, Texas, Princeton, and Yale have managed to accumulate endowments of more than $1 billion.[5] To ensure adequate safeguards, these monies are separated and accounted for within several individual classifications:

a. *Endowment Funds*. College and university Endowment Funds parallel the Nonexpendable Trust Funds found in state and local governments. More specifically, Endowment Funds account for gifts or grants awarded to a school with the stipulation that the principal must be kept intact. Future earnings derived from the gift may be expended, usually for a purpose specified by the original donor. These assets are considered to be permanently restricted because the principal can never be expended.

b. *Term Endowment Funds*. This classifiction is identical to Endowment Funds except that the principal may also be spent after an established time or following the occurrence of a specific event. Consequently, these assets are referred to as temporarily restricted.

c. *Quasi-Endowment Funds*. Historically, one of the more unusual aspects of college and university accounting has been the use of Quasi-Endowment Funds. This category records unrestricted monetary balances voluntarily set aside by the school rather than being applied to current operations. In other types of not-for-profit accounting, the

---

[5] Christopher Knowlton, "How the Richest Colleges Handle Their Billions," *Fortune*, October 26, 1987, p. 106.

use of Endowment (or Nonexpendable Trust) Funds is normally restricted to amounts given with donor-restrictions. However, colleges and universities can reclassify money into Endowment Funds based solely on the decision of the governing board. The University of Virginia, for example, reported on June 30, 1991, a total endowment of $508 million with $297 million of this amount being labeled as Quasi-Endowment Funds. Although maintained in the Endowment Funds, those $297 million in assets have no external restriction.

The use of Quasi-Endowment Funds has been questioned at times because transfers between Unrestricted Current Funds and Quasi-Endowment Funds are discretionary. Therefore, a college or university has the ability to alter the reported size of its Unrestricted Current Funds by moving money into or out of these Quasi-Endowment Funds.[6] In 1990, as an illustration, Princeton University transferred approximately $19 million from Unrestricted Current Funds to its Endowment Funds.

However, the possible impact of this practice has been limited in recent years. The AICPA audit guide mandates (in paragraph 2.08) that "a clear distinction between the balances of funds which are externally restricted and those which are internally designated within each fund group should be maintained in the accounts and disclosed in the financial reports." Thus, readers can distinguish restricted from unrestricted amounts.

The FASB has also shown interest in ensuring that adequate disclosure differentiates restricted from unrestricted funds. In *Statement of Financial Accounting Concepts No. 6,* the Board stated: "Net assets of not-for-profit organizations is divided into three mutually exclusive classes, permanently restricted net assets, temporarily restricted net assets, and unrestricted net assets. . . . The three classes of net assets reflect differences in, or absence of, donor-imposed restrictions on a not-for-profit organization's use of its assets."[7]

The FASB went one step further in 1993 by requiring not-for-profit organizations to report the financial position for the entity as a whole rather than by fund type and identify net assets as permanently restricted, temporarily restricted, and unrestricted.[8] Quasi-Endowment Funds can still be maintained by private schools for internal reporting purposes but they would not affect externally reported figures. Public schools will not be directly affected by the FASB's actions.

---

[6] For example, see Kavasseri V. Ramanathan and William L. Weis, "How to Succeed in Nonbusiness without Really Trying: A University Case Study," *Journal of Accountancy,* October 1980.

[7] *SFAC No. 6,* "Elements of Financial Statements," December 1985, par. 91 and 95.

[8] See *FASB Statement No. 117,* "Financial Statements of Not-for-Profit Organizations." This statement takes effect for fiscal years beginning after December 15, 1994.

4. *Annuity and Life Income Funds*

   a. *Annuity Funds.* "The annuity funds group consists of funds acquired by an institution subject to agreements whereby assets are made available to the institution on the condition that the institution bind itself to pay stipulated amounts periodically to designated individuals. Payments of such amounts terminate at a time specified in the agreements."[9] Obviously, such arrangements are designed to allow a donor (or the donor's family or friends) to continue receiving specified cash inflows for a time from property or other assets that have been legally conveyed to a college or university. Giving to a school is encouraged in this manner because an individual can make a donation without jeopardizing future income levels.

   b. *Life Income Funds.* Similar in nature to Annuity Funds, the major difference is that all income earned on the principal of a gift is distributed to the designated individual(s) rather than just a set amount. Once again, a time limitation is normally imposed on the payments; oftentimes they must continue until the death of the recipient.

5. *Plant Funds*

   a. *Unexpended Plant Funds.* As the title implies, this fund accounts for a school's monetary balances that have been designated for the future acquisition of physical properties such as a library addition or a science laboratory. For example, the 1990 financial statements for Yale University disclosed that $38.9 million was spent during the period for property acquisition, construction, and renovation using the resources held in that school's Unexpended Plant Funds. The monetary amounts maintained in this fund may be derived from numerous sources including gifts, the income earned on earlier donations, or discretionary transfers made from the university's Unrestricted Current Funds.

   b. *Funds for Renewals and Replacements.* A fund that accounts for all money eventually used to update or replace assets presently in service. As an alternative, these assets may be maintained in the Unexpended Plant Funds.

   c. *Funds for Retirement of Indebtedness.* In a manner similar to that of a government's Debt Service Fund, this category records "funds set aside for debt service charges and for the retirement of indebtedness on institutional properties."[10]

   d. *Investment in Plant.* This final Plant Fund subgroup reports the cost of all long-lived assets owned by the college or university. In addition, any debts incurred in connection with the procurement of these properties are also accounted for here. The George Washington University, as an example, reported more than $386 million in land,

---

[9] AICPA, *Audits,* par. 10.01.

[10] Ibid., par 9.01.

buildings, and equipment within its Investment in Plant Fund as of June 30, 1990. This fund also reported approximately $167 million in notes and bonds payable relating to the acquisition of these properties.

6. *Agency Funds.* As in governmental accounting, the Agency Funds category maintains a record of all monies held by a school as a fiduciary for other parties. Often, for example, a college or university serves as a financial caretaker for various student organizations. The College of William and Mary held more than $1.2 million in its Agency Funds on June 30, 1990. Although such monetary balances are frequently accounted for within a separate Agency Fund, an alternative is simply to report them as liabilities in the Unrestricted Current Funds.

Application of Accrual Accounting

Several aspects of the reporting process utilized by colleges and universities resemble that of state and local governments. For example, numerous funds are set up (each with its own Fund Balance account) to record the various resources and expenditures. However, significant accounting differences do exist. Probably the most important variation is that these educational institutions employ accrual accounting rather than modified accrual accounting. "Revenues should be reported when earned and expenditures when materials or services are received. Expenses incurred at the balance sheet date should be accrued and expenses applicable to future periods should be deferred." [11]

Depreciation Expense

Traditionally, colleges and universities have been permitted but not required to report depreciation expense. Not surprisingly, because of the impact on current balances (and the work necessary to compute amounts), few institutions chose to include annual depreciation figures. Instead, as in state and local government accounting, the cost of long-lived assets was recognized immediately (usually in the Unexpended Plant Funds) as an expenditure. The properties themselves were then listed in the school's Investment in Plant Fund in much the same fashion as a government records its long-lived assets in a General Fixed Assets Account Group.

In discussing depreciation, the argument was frequently made that profitability is not a goal of these organizations so that the calculation and recording of this expense is inappropriate. College officials have usually contended that the recording of expenditures is applicable for a not-for-profit organization. Furthermore, new acquisitions are commonly financed by fund-raising projects (rather than from operations) so that ensuring the availability of adequate resources through the recognition of depreciation is not considered necessary.

---

[11] Ibid., par. 2.09.

However, in August 1987, the FASB issued *Statement No. 93,* ''Recognition of Depreciation by Not-for-Profit Organizations.'' This pronouncement required the recognition of depreciation by all not-for-profit organizations (other than state and local governments). The rule pertained to both purchased assets and properties acquired by donation and was aimed at colleges and universities as well as religious institutions and other not-for-profit organizations. The FASB justified this action by stating in paragraph 20:

> Using up assets acquired involves a cost to the organization because the economic benefits (or service potential) used up are no longer available to the organization. That is as true for assets acquired without cost as it is for assets acquired at a cost.

At that time, several types of not-for-profit organizations (governmental colleges and universities, public benefit corporations and authorities, public employee retirement systems, governmental utilities, and governmental hospitals and other health care providers) had been directed to follow the pronouncements of the GASB. However, if the accounting treatment of a transaction or event was not explicitly specified by a GASB pronouncement, applicable FASB pronouncements had to be utilized. Thus, the GASB found itself in the position of having to respond to each statement of the FASB unless it wanted the provisions to apply automatically to this list of governmental not-for-profit organizations.

Consequently, in January of 1988, the GASB countered with a pronouncement of its own, *Statement 8,* ''Applicability of FASB Statement No. 93, *Recognition of Depreciation by Not-for-Profit Organizations,* to Certain State and Local Governmental Entities.'' This standard exempted public colleges and universities (as well as other governmental not-for-profit institutions) from the necessity of recording depreciation. According to paragraph 4,

> Some governmental entities that engage in activities similar to private, not-for-profit organizations covered by *FASB Statement 93* follow governmental fund accounting and reporting principles. Those governmental entities follow GASB standards for depreciation and are therefore not affected by *FASB Statement 93.*

Suddenly, colleges and universities found themselves being guided by two different bodies. Public schools, such as Ohio State University and the University of Texas, were to follow GASB so that the recording of depreciation was voluntary. In contrast, private institutions such as Harvard and Duke came under the auspices of the FASB and had to report depreciation expense. A power struggle quickly resulted with colleges and universities caught in the middle. ''I see the two groups as somewhat entrenched in their positions,'' said Carl Hanes, the vice president for administration at the State University of New York at Stonybrook. ''I see it as a real mess. We have two credible, professional organizations with different voices, and the imposition of their views on the different types of institutions could generate financial information that's not comparable.'' [12]

---

[12] John B. Thomas, ''Higher Education Is the Victim in FASB-GASB Dispute,'' *Business Officer,* January 1988, p. 20.

College and university officials reacted with dismay at the dual set of rules that had been established. Debates arose as to whether depreciation was truly applicable to these types of not-for-profit organizations. Many school administrators (but certainly not all) seemed to prefer the traditional view that the cost of generating depreciation data would outweigh any possible benefits.

> "Depreciating the university's 160 buildings and equipment worth over $1 billion could cost us up to $200,000 for new computer software to do the figuring each year," estimates William J. Hogan, comptroller of the University of Chicago, a private institution. "It really isn't worth it." [13]

versus

> Depreciation accounting not only ought to be adopted, but it should be adopted in the operating statement and funded by mandatory transfer to the plant funds. Only in this way will financial statements show the true impact and cost of depreciation, providing users of such statements with more accurate information. [14]

Just before *Statement No. 93* was scheduled to take effect, the FASB postponed the effective date to allow time for a compromise to be developed. No one appeared to want the establishment of two sets of rules. The Financial Accounting Foundation (FAF), which oversees and funds both the FASB and the GASB, stepped in to help mediate a solution to the territorial argument. Numerous compromises were proposed. On October 30, 1989, the FAF voted to give the FASB jurisdiction over both public and private not-for-profit organizations. Thus, only one set of accounting standards would apply to such entities.

However, that ruling did not stop the controversy. Ten different government groups immediately threatened to stop supporting the GASB unless all public entities (such as state universities) remained under its jurisdiction. [15] Faced with a problem having no end in sight, the FAF reversed itself and gave the GASB authority over governmental not-for-profit organizations. Thus, the FASB now requires the reporting of depreciation expense by private colleges and universities (and other private not-for-profit organizations) whereas public schools (and other public not-for-profit organizations) follow the GASB and show depreciation on a voluntary basis. For this reason, the University of Richmond (a private school) reported depreciation expense of approximately $6 million in its 1992 financial statements while Virginia Commonwealth University (a public school just five miles away) indicated that "no provision for depreciation is made."

The GAAP Hierarchy

At some point, the relationship between governmental not-for-profit organizations and FASB pronouncements almost had to be redefined. The GASB could not stop

---

[13] Lee Berton, "Several Private Colleges May Ignore New Accounting Rule on Depreciation," *The Wall Street Journal*, February 4, 1988.

[14] Phillip Jones, Sr.; Clarence Jung, Jr.; and Herbert Peterson, "Why Not Depreciate and Why Not in Operations?" *Business Officer*, April 1989, p. 33.

[15] See, for more information, "The Great GASB," *Forbes*, December 11, 1989, p. 60.

its ongoing work every time a FASB statement was issued to evaluate whether the new standard should be voided for governmental not-for-profit organizations. Apparently, an adequate resolution has been crafted by the AICPA Auditing Standards Board in its *Statement on Auditing Standards 69,* ''The Meaning of 'Presents Fairly in Conformity with Generally Accepted Accounting Principles' in the Independent Auditor's Report'' issued in 1991. This standard creates a hierarchy for determining whether an accounting treatment should be judged as being in compliance with generally accepted accounting principles (GAAP). For both nongovernmental entities as well as state and local governments, accounting pronouncements and other potential guidelines are grouped into five layers. The higher levels are more authoritative than the lower levels.

The GAAP hierarchy created by *SAS 69* is presented in Exhibit 17–1. For state and local governments, GASB statements and interpretations are placed at the highest level. This same ranking is appropriate for AICPA and FASB pronouncements *but only if they are made applicable to state and local governments by a GASB Statement or Interpretation.* Thus, even though a GASB statement may not provide specific guidance in a particular area of financial reporting, FASB statements no longer become automatically appropriate for governmental not-for-profit organizations. Instead, the GASB can study and evaluate each new pronouncement and act if it believes that the guidelines should be followed.

Traditional Financial Statements for Colleges and Universities

Historically, most colleges and universities have produced financial statements in conformity with examples found in *Statement of Position 74–8,* ''Financial Accounting and Reporting by Colleges and Universities,'' issued on August 31, 1974, by the Accounting Standards Division of the AICPA. That pronouncement indicated that three basic financial statements are normally prepared by colleges and universities (often referred to as the AICPA college guide model):[16]

- A statement of changes in fund balances.
- A statement of current funds revenues, expenditures, and other changes.
- A balance sheet.

Each of these statements is presented in a columnar format to provide financial information about the various fund types. Financial statements produced for the University of Minnesota using this format are included in Appendix A of this chapter.

Statement of Changes in Fund Balances.   In broad categories, the first statement reports:

---

[16] A second model (known as the governmental model because it was established by the *National Council of Governmental Accounting Statement 1*) is also available but it is much less frequently encountered.

- Revenues and other fund balance additions.
- Expenditures and other deductions.
- Interfund transfers.

As can be seen in Appendix A, this information is included for each of the various fund types. Readers learn the underlying cause of all changes occurring during the year in the Fund Balance account for Unrestricted Current Funds,

---

EXHIBIT 17-1   GAAP Hierarchy Summary

Nongovernmental Entities	*State and Local Governments*
Established Accounting Principles	
FASB Statements and Interpretations, APB Opinions, and AICPA Accounting Research Bulletins	GASB Statements and Interpretations, plus AICPA and FASB pronouncements if made applicable to state and local governments by a GASB Statement or Interpretation
FASB Technical Bulletins, AICPA Industry Audit and Accounting Guides, and AICPA Statements of Position	GASB Technical Bulletins, and the following pronouncements if specifically made applicable to state and local governments by the AICPA: AICPA Industry Audit and Accounting Guides and AICPA Statements of Position
Consensus positions of the FASB Emerging Issues Task Force and AICPA Practice Bulletins	Consensus positions of the GASB Emerging Issues Task Force† and AICPA Practice Bulletins if specifically made applicable to state and local governments by the AICPA
AICPA accounting interpretations, "Qs and As" published by the FASB staff, as well as industry practices widely recognized and prevalent	"Qs and As" published by the GASB staff, as well as industry practices widely recognized and prevalent
Other Accounting Literature*	
Other accounting literature, including FASB Concepts Statements; APB Statements; AICPA Issues Papers; International Accounting Standards Committee Statements; GASB Statements, Interpretations, and Technical Bulletins; pronouncements of other professional associations or regulatory agencies; AICPA *Technical Practice Aids;* and accounting textbooks, handbooks, and articles	Other accounting literature, including GASB Concepts Statements; pronouncements in the first four categories of the hierarchy for nongovernmental entities when not specifically made applicable to state and local governments; APB Statements; FASB Concepts Statements; AICPA Issues Papers; International Accounting Standards Committee Statements; pronouncements of other professional associations or regulatory agencies; AICPA *Technical Practice Aids;* and accounting textbooks, handbooks, and articles

* In the absence of established accounting principles, the auditor may consider other accounting literature, depending on its relevance in the circumstances.

† As of the date of this Statement, the GASB had not organized such a group.

Restricted Current Funds, Loan Funds, and so forth. As an example, this statement reports that the University of Minnesota recognized $992 million in unrestricted revenues in its Unrestricted Current Funds during the year ended June 30, 1990, whereas $593 million was expended for education and general purposes in this same period. These total figures are explained in more detail in the next financial statement.

Statement of Current Funds Revenues, Expenditures, and Other Changes.   The second statement provides information for just the two current funds. Since these fund types record all of the ongoing activities of a college or university, this statement presents more detailed information about the operating transactions of the fiscal period. The revenue totals for both the Unrestricted Current Funds and the Restricted Current Funds are broken down to disclose specific figures for sources such as student tuition and fees, federal grants, endowment income, sales made by auxiliary operations, and so on.

Expenditures made from these two funds are then individually identified including amounts paid for instructional costs, research, academic support, and student services. Explanatory figures also indicate any transfers made to or from other funds as well as any other changes in the fund balances. For example, the statement presented in Appendix A for the University of Minnesota explains the makeup of the $992 million in unrestricted revenues recognized by the Unrestricted Current Funds ($140 million came from tuition and fees, $367 million from state appropriations, and so on). The $593 million expenditures for education and general purposes found in the previous statement include $289 million for instruction, $17 million for research, and so on.

Balance Sheet.   The final financial statement prepared by a college or university indicates assets, liabilities, and the final fund balance for each of the separate fund categories (or major fund subgroups). As presented in Appendix A, the columnar presentation that conveys data about all of the funds resembles the state and local government accounting format. Although total figures for the educational institution as a whole are not required on either the balance sheet or the statement of changes in fund balances, most schools do provide them.

The FASB and Changes in the Financial Statements for Not-for-Profit Organizations

As indicated previously in the discussion of quasi-endowment funds, the FASB has opted to set standards for the financial statements of not-for-profit organizations. Because of the GAAP hierarchy that has been developed, these statements will apply only to private colleges and universities—such as Stanford and Villanova—unless also adopted by the GASB.

The major emphasis of the FASB is to provide financial statements for the entity as a whole rather than segmented by fund type (although that information can still be presented). Three statements are now required: a statement of financial position, a statement of activities, and a statement of cash flows. The purpose of such financial statements is to provide information about:

a. The amount and nature of an organization's assets, liabilities, and net assets.

b. The effects of transactions and other events and circumstances that change the amount and nature of net assets.

c. The amount and kinds of inflows and outflows of economic resources during a period and the relation between the inflows and outflows.

d. How an organization obtains and spends cash, its borrowing and repayment of borrowing, and other factors that may affect its liquidity.

e. The service efforts of an organization.

As discussed earlier in this chapter, these statements would distinguish between permanently restricted net assets, temporarily restricted net assets, and unrestricted net assets. In addition, the statement of activities (or the notes) must report the organization's expenses according to functional classifications. Expenses for individual program services (student instruction and research, for example) should be presented separately from supporting activities (such as management and general expenses and fund-raising costs). As seen in Chapter 18, this information is already provided by voluntary health and welfare organizations but has not yet been widely used in the statements of other types of not-for-profit organizations.

Examples of the statements recommended by the FASB are presented in Appendix B of this chapter. Note the difference in format to the statements produced by the University of Minnesota in Appendix A using the AICPA college guide model. If the new model is not adopted by the GASB, an interesting split will surely exist between the financial statements of governmental colleges and universities (Appendix A) and the financial statements of private colleges and universities (Appendix B).

Discussion Question: Are Two Sets of GAAP Really Needed for Colleges and Universities?

A public college or university normally does not report depreciation on its buildings and equipment. A private college or university must calculate depreciation on each of these long-lived assets and recognize that figure in its financial statements.

A public college or university reports a balance sheet and a statement of changes in fund balance for each of its fund types. A statement of revenues, expenditures, and other changes is produced for the Unrestricted Current Funds and the Restricted Current Funds. A private college or university

---

continued

should report a statement of financial position, a statement of activities, and a statement of cash flows. These statements are designed to reflect the school as a whole rather than focusing on any of the individual fund types.

Many readers of college and university financial statements make comparisons between the data presented by various institutions. The use of this information is especially important to potential donors attempting to evaluate each school's effectiveness and efficiency in utilizing the funding that it receives. Are these readers well served by the division that appears to be growing between the financial reporting that is appropriate for public colleges and universities and that utilized by private colleges and universities?

Accounting for Current Funds

Since most college and university financial transactions are recorded within the Current Funds, the primary emphasis in the remainder of this chapter is on analyzing the accounting and reporting of the Unrestricted Current Funds and the Restricted Current Funds. At times, these funds interface with every other fund category through transfers and other interactions. Thus, the following coverage must necessarily involve some introduction to virtually all fund classifications. To assist in explaining applicable accounting procedures in more depth, several additional transactions relating primarily to the noncurrent funds are included at the end of the chapter.

Unrestricted Current Funds

As mentioned previously, the transactions recorded within the Unrestricted Current Funds cover the entire range of ongoing university activities: instruction, research, student services, administration, and the like. Since the accrual basis is in use, timely recognition of all transactions is essential. Student tuition and fees of $5 million, for example, are entered into the financial records as follows. This entry assumes that 5 percent of this balance will prove to be uncollectible.

Unrestricted Current Funds

Accounts Receivable	5,000,000	
Expenditures—Bad Debts	250,000	
Revenues—Student Tuition and Fees		5,000,000
Allowance for Doubtful Accounts		250,000
To record billings for tuition and fees with 5 percent estimated as being uncollectible.		

Just as in governmental accounting, expenditures are recorded by colleges and universities. However, the preceding recognition of bad debts indicates that the Expenditure classification is used here for more than just the recording of financial resource outflows. The reporting by private colleges and universities of depreciation is another example of this same flexibility.

A variation of the previous entry may be necessary for summer school tuition and fees. The fiscal year for many colleges and universities ends each June 30, a date that may well fall during the middle of a summer school session. Revenues generated by any courses that operate in both fiscal periods are to be recognized *in the year in which most of the instruction occurs*. For example, a course that begins on June 20 but does not end until August 1 should have all of its revenues recorded in the year beginning July 1. Consequently, a deferred revenue account must be recorded in the first period which is then reclassified as revenue in the second.

Contributions. Other revenues recognized within the Unrestricted Current Funds include gifts, endowment income, and government appropriations. In each case, *inclusion in this category is only appropriate if expenditure of the money has not been restricted by the donor*. To illustrate the mechanics of the recording process, assume that an individual gives $250,000 in cash to a local university. Of this amount, $50,000 is completely unrestricted but another $120,000 is earmarked for a specific research project. The remaining $80,000 must be used for renovation of present physical facilities. Because the donation is designated for such diverse activities, several separate fund subgroups are involved:

Unrestricted Current Funds

Cash	50,000	
Revenues—Contribution		50,000
To record unrestricted portion of gift from private donor.		

Restricted Current Funds

Cash	120,000	
Fund Balance—Temporarily Restricted for Research Project		120,000
Gift received to finance specified research project.		

Funds for Renewals and Replacements

Cash	80,000	
Fund Balance—Temporarily Restricted for Facilities Renovation		80,000
Gift to be used for renovation of physical facilities.		

The recording here of an increase in the Fund Balance account for the Restricted Current Funds and the Funds for Renewal and Replacements may seem perplexing since the specific source of the change is not noted. However, within the financial statements, a college or university must disclose the identity of the increases and decreases that occur in its net assets. Therefore, for reporting purposes, the $120,000 and $80,000 asset inflows are identified as contributions.

Traditionally, in the internal recording of a school's noncurrent funds, net asset inflows and outflows have been made directly to the Fund Balance account as shown here. Subsidiary ledgers are usually maintained to record the actual nature of each change.

These three entries demonstrate one of the primary objectives of fund accounting for colleges and universities: to monitor the institution's stewardship and ultimate employment of resources restricted for diverse activities. Educational institutions can receive enormous amounts of money with numerous stipulations attached. The accounting system must be able to ensure that all such funding is expended for the appropriate purposes. Although the foregoing donation was received as a single amount, the balances have been segregated within the financial records to ensure proper utilization.

Donated Assets Other than Cash.   One of the major reporting problems of all not-for-profit organizations in the handling of donated assets other than cash. The AICPA audit guide states (in paragraph 2.11):

> Gifts, bequests, grants, and other receipts restricted as to use by outside grantors or agencies are recorded as additions directly in the fund group appropriate to the restricted nature of the receipt. Unrestricted gifts, bequests, and grants are recorded as unrestricted current funds revenues.

To illustrate, assume that a donor gives the following to a college or university:

Item	Use	Fair Market Value
Note receivable	Unrestricted	$ 21,000
Investments	Income to be used for student scholarships	40,000
Building (near campus)	Administrative offices	150,000
Art work	Addition to school's permanent collection	700,000

Following the guidelines of the AICPA audit guide, the following journal entries would have been recorded by this college or university. Receipt of the note is recorded immediately as revenue since its use is unrestricted. Because of the external restrictions included, donation of both the investments and the building increase fund balance accounts (the Investment in Plant account is used for the building rather than a fund balance since no monetary resources are maintained in that fund).

A problem arises, though, in connection with the art work being donated to the school's permanent collection. This item will be held for research or public exhibit and should create little or no direct increase in future cash flows. Thus, it is not an asset in the traditional sense. Until recently, very little authoritative guidance could be found as to the appropriate recording of such additions to permanent collections. Historically, not-for-profit organizations have disclosed these contributions in their financial statements but have made no formal recording. This illustration shows that handling.

Unrestricted Current Funds

Note Receivable	21,000	
Revenues—Contribution		21,000
To record unrestricted gift of note.		

Endowment Funds

Investments	40,000	
Fund Balance—Permanently Restricted for Student Scholarships .		40,000
To record investments given to university with stipulation that subsequent income is to be used for student scholarships.		

Investment in Plant

Building.	150,000	
Investment in Plant		150,000
To record gift of building that will be used by the school for administrative offices.		

Memorandum: Received gift of art work to be included in permanent collection. Fair market value of this item is $700,000.

In 1990, the FASB proposed to create consistent generally accepted accounting principles for contributions. The Board issued an exposure draft at that time that would have required all contributions to be recorded as assets with a corresponding increase in revenues. This accounting also was to include collection items (such as art works or museum pieces) if the not-for-profit organization planned to sell the work or if a market existed in which the work could be sold or exchanged. Perhaps no accounting proposal ever put forth created such adverse public reaction. The FASB was deluged with more than 1,000 letters, virtually all of them in opposition.

To illustrate, assume that a university receives a gift of a painting by Picasso (valued at $10 million) to be exhibited in its permanent collection. Under the 1990 proposal, an asset of that amount would have to be recorded along with the recognition of revenue. Many not-for-profit organizations argued that additions to a permanent collection should never be classified as a revenue since the gift did not provide the same kinds of future benefits as contributions of cash or investments. Officials for these groups contended that recognizing such donations as revenues would mislead potential donors who were evaluating the operating results of the organization. Not surprisingly, considering the extreme opposition generated, the FASB rescinded this proposal.

In 1993, the FASB issued a revised *Statement No. 116,* "Accounting for Contributions Received and Collections Made," to establish accounting guidance for private not-for-profit organizations. The new pronouncement held that all gifts *except additions to collections* should be recognized as either revenue or restricted support based on their fair values.

The restricted support designation would be used for gifts that had been restricted by the donor in some way. If these provisions were only for a time or only for a specified action or activity, the gift would create an increase in the temporarily restricted net assets being reported by the organization. The contribution of a building, for example, is considered temporarily restricted support since this asset will eventually wear out and no longer be usable by the school. Conversely, if a gift was made with a stipulation that would never be lifted, an increase is made in permanently restricted net assets.

The FASB did make an important exception for gifts of art works, historical treasures, and the like. Recognition is not required if (1) they are added to a collection for public exhibition, education, or research; (2) they are protected and preserved; and (3) they are ever sold any receipts will be used to acquire other collection items.

Pledges.   Before leaving the reporting procedures that are applied to donations, one additional accounting consideration should be mentioned. Often, a college or university receives a definite pledge of support prior to the actual conveyance of any money or other assets. Fund-raising campaigns seeking hundreds of millions of dollars are now relatively common. Most large gifts begin with a pledge followed by periodic payments made over a specified number of years. The AICPA's audit guide states that such pledges should either be disclosed in the financial statement footnotes or actually recognized as an asset.

> Pledges of gifts, including uncollected subscriptions, subscription notes, and estate notes, should be disclosed in the notes unless they are reported in the financial statements. . . . If the pledges are reported in the financial statements, they should be accounted for at their estimated net realizable value in the same manner as gifts received (except as to asset classification, for which pledges would be reported as a receivable), and credited to unrestricted revenues, deferred income, current restricted funds, plant funds, etc., as appropriate.[17]

The 1990 financial statements of the Ohio State University indicate one approach to the reporting of pledges. This university discloses the amount of outstanding pledges in a note to its statements: "The University does not report pledges in the financial statements until the gifts are received. The University's gift records indicate that approximately $138,058,000 in pledges are outstanding at June 30, 1990. Since those pledges are often payable either at the discretion of the donors or through their estates, neither the realizable value nor the period of collection can be estimated."

Unfortunately, in accounting for pledges, many schools apparently have chosen to ignore the need for either recording or disclosure:

> In reporting on a review of financial statements of colleges and universities, the author of the report made this striking statement: "Hundreds of colleges found violating

---

[17] AICPA, *Audits*, par. 2.12–2.13.

accounting rules in finance reports." Leading to this statement was a finding that "415 of 598 responding institutions did not record or disclose donors' pledges, either on their balance sheets or in notes to their financial statements." [18]

Consequently, the FASB has created authoritative guidelines for the accounting and recognition of pledges by private not-for-profit organizations. *The board now requires that an unconditional promise to make a contribution should be viewed as an asset by the recipient.* The receipt of any such pledges where the payments are to be made in future years normally should be recorded as temporarily restricted support.

Accounting for Expenditures. The Unrestricted Current Funds must also record the great variety of operating expenditures incurred by any college or university. Faculty salaries, research support, student service costs, and operations of the physical plant are just a few examples of the necessary costs that fall under this heading. Although numerous entries would be made each day in connection with operating expenditures, the following single example demonstrates the impact of these recordings. This entry assumes that all but $85,000 of the current year expenditures have been paid.

Unrestricted Current Funds

Expenditures—Instruction	1,900,000	
Expenditures—Research	325,000	
Expenditures—Student Services	61,000	
Expenditures—Operation and Maintenance of Plant	56,000	
Cash		2,257,000
Accrued Liabilities		85,000

To record current operating expenditures. Payment is made for all but $85,000.

One further cost incurred by most colleges and universities is the loss of revenue stemming from scholarship grants and other tuition reductions. Often schools decrease or eliminate their fees entirely based on a student's financial needs, academic excellence, or athletic abilities. In addition, faculty and staff members (as well as their families) may be granted similar reductions because of past service to the institution. To provide a measure of the financial impact of such reductions, "tuition and fees should be recorded as revenue even though there is no intention of collection from the student. The amounts of such remissions or waivers should be recorded as expenditures and classified as Scholarships and Fellowships or as staff benefits associated with the appropriate expenditure functional category to which the personnel relate." [19]

Assume, as an illustration, that the normal tuition to be charged a group of students by a college is $1,900,000. However, this amount is reduced during the

---

[18] Arthur R. Kagle and William P. Dukes, "Financial Reporting for Pledges at Educational Institutions," *The CPA Journal*, January 1988, p. 40. The article being discussed within this quotation is by Robert L. Jacobson, "Hundreds of Colleges Found Violating Accounting Rules in Finance Reports," *The Chronicle of Higher Education 32*, no. 6 (April 9, 1986).

[19] AICPA, *Audits*, Appendix A, pp. 53–54.

year by $300,000 because academic scholarships have been granted to several of these individuals. An additional $200,000 will not be assessed because the students have relatives who are faculty or staff members employed by the school. Thus, only $1,400,000 of the tuition is actually subject to collection; that information is recorded through the following journal entry. *By recording both the revenue in total along with separate expenditures for the reductions, the school is better able to mirror the events that have occurred as well as the impact of the various reductions.*

Unrestricted Current Funds

Accounts Receivable	1,400,000	
Expenditures—Student Aid	300,000	
Expenditures—Staff Benefits	200,000	
Revenues—Student Tuition and Fees		1,900,000

    To accrue revenues along with reductions for students receiving financial aid and tuition remissions.

Auxiliary Enterprises.   A final group of ongoing activities reported within the Unrestricted Current Funds are the auxiliary enterprises operated by a school: food services, athletic programs, bookstores, and the like. Memphis State University, for example, reported that $17.4 million of the revenues reported in 1988 by the Unrestricted Current Funds were generated by such auxiliary endeavors. The two largest sources were intercollegiate athletics ($6.7 million) and the university store ($4.3 million). Auxiliary enterprise expenditures at this school for the same period totaled only $14.3 million (including $5.6 for intercollegiate athletics and $4.2 million for the university store).

    Although detailed subsidiary ledgers are necessary to monitor the many specific transactional activities, general journal entries record the total revenues and expenditures of these enterprises. Thus, entries such as the following would be prepared periodically by a college or university:

Unrestricted Current Funds

Cash	2,860,000	
Revenues—Auxiliary Enterprises Control		2,860,000

    Revenues generated during the period by the various auxiliary operations of the school.

Expenditures—Auxiliary Enterprises Control	2,018,000	
Cash		2,018,000

    Payments made in connection with operating expenditures of auxiliary activities.

Interfund Transfers.   Revenues and expenditures do not provide the only means by which the net assets of the Unrestricted Current Funds can be affected. As in governments, transfers to and from other fund categories are commonly encountered in colleges and universities. Such interfund transactions may be discretionary in nature, made voluntarily to reflect the allocation of unrestricted financial resources. In 1990, for example, the administration of James Madison University decided to transfer approximately $2.3 million from Unrestricted Current Funds to Unexpended Plant Funds for future acquisitions and construction.

However, in many instances, transfers are contractually mandated. A bond indenture might, as an example, require that specific cash amounts be physically set aside each year to ensure eventual payment. For this reason, James Madison University also made more than $300,000 in mandatory transfers into its Fund for Retirement of Indebtedness during 1990. As shown in Appendix A, all such inter-fund transfers are reported in the statement of changes in fund balances after the revenues and expenditures. However, such internal transfers would not be applicable to financial statements for the entity as a whole as shown in Appendix B.

To illustrate, assume that a college is required by a bond contract to transfer $50,000 in cash each year to its Fund for Retirement of Indebtedness. In addition, the school's board of trustees votes to set aside $80,000 in unrestricted cash to finance student loans and an additional $150,000 for future building construction. The board also decides to transfer $90,000 to a Quasi-Endowment Fund with subsequent earnings to supplement faculty salaries. These four interfund transfers appear in the following Unrestricted Current Funds entry. In each case, a corresponding entry is made in the fund receiving the money (Fund for Retirement of Indebtedness, Loan Fund, etc.) increasing the specific Fund Balance account.

This journal entry draws a clear distinction between mandatory and discretionary (or nonmandatory) transfers. For disclosure purposes, this same identification is made within the published financial statements.

Unrestricted Current Funds

Mandatory Transfer for Bond Principal and Interest Repayment. . . .	50,000	
Discretionary Transfer for Student Loans.	80,000	
Discretionary Transfer for Future Building Construction	150,000	
Discretionary Transfer to Quasi-Endowment Fund for Faculty Salaries	90,000	
Cash		370,000

To record mandatory and discretionary transfers made by college's board of trustees.

Restricted Current Funds

In a manner identical to that of the Unrestricted Current Funds, the Restricted Current Funds category of a college or university operates on an accrual basis. Therefore, a natural presumption would be that these two current fund subgroups utilize the same accounting principles. One significant difference, however, does exist. All financial resources of the Restricted Current Funds are provided by outside parties who have stipulated the operational usage to be made of the gift or grant. If the school does not follow these provisons, the money might well have to be returned. *Hence, these restricted funds are considered to be earned only at the time that the specified expenditure is made.*

For this reason, the actual spending of the money (rather than the original receipt) secures the contribution. Thus, donations, grants, and any other similar inflows that are restricted for current operating purposes are initially recorded as increases in the Fund Balance account of the Restricted Current Funds and not as revenues. Subsequently, when the expenditure is eventually made to achieve the stated goal, the revenue is recognized by means of a reclassification entry. The earnings process is said to be completed by spending the money for the appropriate purpose.

Under this approach, revenues and expenditures must always be equal within the Restricted Current Funds. For example, in the statement of current funds revenues, expenditures, and other changes found in Appendix A, the University of Minnesota reports $378,770,000 in total revenues for the Restricted Current Funds as well as $378,770,000 in total expenditures and mandatory transfers.

To demonstrate the recording process that provides such precise equilibrium, assume that $120,000 in cash is donated to a university with the provision that this money must be spent to acquire new library books. Several weeks after receiving the gift, the first $50,000 is used for this specified purpose. The journal entries necessary to record these transactions would be as follows. The revenue is recognized at the point of appropriate expenditure.

Restricted Current Funds
Initial Entry

Cash	120,000	
Fund Balance—Temporarily Restricted for Acquisition of Library Books		120,000
Gift received by school to be used in purchasing library books.		

Subsequent Entries

Expenditures—Libraries	50,000	
Cash		50,000
Library books acquired with money received as a restricted gift.		

Fund Balance—Temporarily Restricted for Acquisition of Library Books	50,000	
Revenues—Gifts and Private Grants		50,000
To recognize as revenue money received and appropriately expended for library books.		

In reporting on the entity as a whole, as required by the FASB, unrestricted net assets would be increased at the point of spending and temporarily restricted net assets would be decreased.

Accounting for Noncurrent Funds

A detailed discussion of all possible transactions that could occur within the noncurrent fund categories and subgroups of a college or university would require several chapters. However, an overview of common transactions can be used to provide coverage of the basic reporting techniques incorporated by this type of not-for-profit organization. Hence, descriptions of three transactional situations frequently encountered by educational institutions, with the journal entries that would result, follow:

1. A university receives a cash grant of $100,000 from an individual donor to finance student loans. Of this amount, $80,000 is immediately distributed to students who have temporary financial needs while the remainder is invested in stocks and bonds. The school estimates that 2 percent of the loan balances will eventually prove to be uncollectible. By year's end, cash of $75,000 is received with $1,000 of the remaining receivables being formally written off as bad accounts. During the period, $3,000 in interest is earned on the investments.

   The appropriate entries to record this series of events are as follows. As indicated previously, subsidiary ledger entries would be necessary to monitor the individual changes in the Fund Balance account.

Loan Funds

Cash	100,000	
Fund Balance—Permanently Restricted for Student		
Loans		100,000
Private grant received.		
Notes Receivable—Students	80,000	
Investments	20,000	
Cash		100,000
Loans and investments made.		
Fund Balance—Permanently Restricted for Student Loans . .	1,600	
Allowance for Uncollectible Loans.		1,600
Bad accounts are estimated (2%).		
Cash	75,000	
Allowance for Uncollectible Loans.	1,000	
Notes Receivable—Students		76,000
Loans are collected with $1,000 written off as uncollectible.		
Cash	3,000	
Fund Balance—Permanently Restricted for Student		
Loans		3,000
Earnings received on investments.		

2. A cash contribution of $400,000 is made to a university with the provision that all income derived from this money be distributed as supplements to faculty salaries. This gift is immediately invested, and $50,000 in income is earned during the year. Because expenditure of this money has been restricted, the income is transferred to the Restricted Current Funds and subsequently paid to the appropriate faculty members. For these transactions, the following journal entries are appropriate:

Endowment Funds

Cash	400,000	
Fund Balance—Permanently Restricted		400,000
Donation received; income to be used for faculty salaries.		
Investments	400,000	
Cash		400,000
Investments are acquired.		

Restricted Current Funds

Cash	50,000	
Fund Balance—Temporarily Restricted for Faculty		
Salaries		50,000
Endowment income received.		
Expenditures—Instruction	50,000	
Cash		50,000
Expenditures made to faculty members as stipulated.		
Fund Balance—Temporarily Restricted for Faculty		
Salaries	50,000	
Revenues—Endowment Income		50,000
Revenue recognized at time of appropriate expenditure.		

3. Cash of $100,000 that had been previously transferred from a college's Unrestricted Current Funds to its Unexpended Plant Funds is spent for new science laboratory equipment. At the same time, the school pays $60,000 held in its Funds for Retirement of Indebtedness to extinguish a bond payable. While the laboratory equipment was purchased with funds that were not subject to external restriction, the debt was retired with money that had been specifically designated by a donor for that purpose.

    As mentioned previously, the Investment in Plant account shown in the final entry is the equivalent of a fund balance for this particular subgroup. The reported figure represents the fixed assets of the school in excess of the related liabilities. Thus, both the acquisition of land, buildings, and equipment and the payment of long-term debt relating to such acquisitions increases this balance.

Unexpended Plant Funds

Fund Balance—Unrestricted	100,000	
Cash		100,000
Payment made to purchase lab equipment.		

Investment in Plant

Equipment	100,000	
Investment in Plant		100,000
To record acquired lab equipment.		

Funds for Retirement of Indebtedness

Fund Balance—Temporarily Restricted.	60,000	
Cash		60,000

Payment made to retire debt.

Investment in Plant

Bonds Payable.	60,000	
Investment in Plant		60,000

To record retirement of debt.

Summary

1. State and local governments are not the only organizations in this country that operate without a profit motive. Thousands of colleges and universities across the United States also fall into this category. Although these schools are not-for-profit in nature, many aspects of the reporting process differ from that used by state and local governments. Accrual accounting, as just one example, is utilized rather than modified accrual accounting.

2. Fund accounting is appropriate for colleges and universities because of their diverse activities and the many restricted gifts that are received. Funds are grouped into six general classifications: Current Funds, Loan Funds, Endowment and Similar Funds, Annuity and Life Income Funds, Plant Funds, and Agency Funds. Subgroups exist for many of these fund types.

3. The Current Funds category of a college or university is divided into Unrestricted and Restricted Current Funds. Unrestricted Current Funds account for presently expendable resources used in accomplishing the primary operating objectives of the school. A majority of the institution's transactions are normally reported within this fund including recognition of tuition, unrestricted grants, cafeteria services, maintenance expense, and faculty salaries. Transfers, which are common in college and university acounting, are classified as either mandatory or discretionary to reveal the underlying nature of the transaction.

4. One unique aspect of the accounting process for colleges and universities is the method by which tuition reductions are reported. Financial aid and scholarships frequently decrease the amount to be collected from students. Schools report the tuition at the gross figure charged to reflect the amount earned. Any corresponding reduction is then recorded as an expenditure. Maintaining separate balances presents a better view of the financial events that have occurred.

5. Historically, the recording of depreciation expense has been allowed but not required of colleges and universities. However, in 1987, the FASB's *Statement 93* mandated the reporting of depreciation by not-for-profit organizations. Shortly thereafter, the GASB exempted public institutions from this requirement.

Since that time, a hierarchy has been created of generally accepted accounting principles to provide guidance for the production of financial statements. Based on this hierarchy, FASB statements only apply to governmental not-for-profit organizations if accepted by the GASB. Consequently, private colleges and universities must report depreciation whereas public schools are not required to do so.

6. The Restricted Current Funds account for operating resources that have been designated by the donor or grantor for a specified purpose. Only the restricted nature of these assets separates this category from the Unrestricted Current Funds. Because the monetary resource is ultimately earned by making the stipulated expenditure, the gift or grant is initially recorded as an increase in the Fund Balance account. When an appropriate expenditure is subsequently made, an equal dollar amount is reclassified from the Temporarily Restricted Fund Balance into a Revenue account. Thus, for Restricted Current Funds, revenues always equal expenditures.

7. The remainder of the funds utilized by a college or university are designated to maintain a record of assets being held for specific, nonoperational purposes. Loan Funds, for example, report the financial assistance provided to students. Unexpended Plant Funds monitor the monetary balances held by the school for future acquisitions of physical properties. The Investment in Plant Fund maintains a record of all long-lived assets as well as liabilities incurred in acquiring these properties.

8. Three financial statements have traditionally been produced by a college or university. Each of these is segmented to provide information about each fund type. A statement of changes in fund balances is presented for each fund category and major fund subgroup. Using broad categories, this statement reports revenues and other fund additions, expenditures and other deductions, and transfers. A statement of current fund revenues, expenditures, and other changes then follows to reflect current operations in much more specific detail. Finally, a balance sheet is prepared which includes information describing the financial position of each fund category. The FASB now requires that three new financial statements be prepared for a private not-for-profit organization as a whole: a statement of financial position, a statement of activities, and a statement of cash flows.

9. In the past, contributions have been recorded as increases in a fund balance account if restricted and as revenue if not. Additions (such as art works) to permanent collections have usually been omitted from the reporting process. For private not-for-profit organizations, the FASB now requires reporting all contributions as either unrestricted revenues or restricted support based on the presence of any donor-imposed restrictions. Additions to collections would not need to be capitalized if they met certain specified conditions.

10. Most colleges and universities do not report pledges although they are allowed to do so. The FASB has required that unconditional promises should be reported as assets.

Comprehensive Illustration

PROBLEM   (Estimated Time: 25 to 30 Minutes)

The College of Lincoln incurs the following financial transactions during the current fiscal period. Prepare all journal entries including an indication of the fund category or subgroup in which the recording should be made.

1. Students were charged $1 million in tuition for the academic year but the college anticipated receiving only $890,000 of this amount. Uncollectible balances were expected to equal 5 percent of the total (or $50,000). In addition, fees of $60,000 related to faculty members and their families. Because of school policy, these individuals were not actually assessed tuition charges.

2. A gift of $900,000 was conveyed to the school by a private donor. Of this total, $100,000 was restricted for replacement of classroom facilities. The remaining $800,000 was split evenly between a Life Income Fund and an Endowment Fund. Earnings from the Life Income Fund will be paid to the donor's sister until her death with the money then to be used by the school for athletics. All income generated by the Endowment Fund was restricted to the acquisition of equipment for the college's engineering department.

3. Loans of $100,000 were awarded by the school's Loan Funds. When making these payments, the school estimated that 8 percent would eventually prove to be uncollectible.

4. A government grant of $200,000 for biological research was received by the college. The school immediately distributed $160,000 to qualifying projects.

5. Faculty salaries of $400,000 were paid from Unrestricted Current Funds. Additionally, a transfer of $300,000 was made into Unexpended Plant Funds. Another $600,000 of unrestricted funds was set aside with the subsequent income to be used for scientific research. These transfers reflected decisions made by the college's board of trustees.

6. Income of $50,000 was generated by the Life Income Fund created in (2) with the money being immediately distributed to the appropriate recipient.

7. The school paid $1.5 million for a new wing for its art school building. This money had been set aside several years earlier from unrestricted funds.

SOLUTION

1.   *Unrestricted Current Funds*
Accounts Receivable.   940,000
Expenditures—Staff Benefits   60,000
Expenditures—Bad Debts   50,000
    Revenues—Student Tuition and Fees   1,000,000
    Allowance for Uncollectible Accounts   50,000
    To recognize current revenues, remissions, and estimated bad
accounts.

2.   *Funds for Renewals and Replacements*
Cash   100,000
    Fund Balance—Temporarily Restricted for Replacement of
      Classroom Facilities   100,000
    To record restricted gift made to college.

                            Life Income Funds
Cash   400,000
    Fund Balance—Temporarily Restricted   400,000
    To record gift made to college with income being paid to the
donor's sister until death.

                            Endowment Funds
Cash   400,000
    Fund Balance—Permanently Restricted   400,000
    To record endowment gift—income to be used to buy
equipment for engineering department.

3.   *Loan Funds*
Notes Receivable—Students   100,000
Fund Balance—Permanently Restricted for Student Loans   8,000
    Cash   100,000
    Allowance for Uncollectible Accounts   8,000
    To record granting of student loans and estimation of bad
accounts.

4.   *Restricted Current Funds*
Cash   200,000
    Fund Balance—Temporarily Restricted for Research   200,000
    Government grant received—must be used for biological
research.

Expenditures—Research   160,000
    Cash   160,000
    Partial distribution is made of government grant.

Fund Balance—Temporarily Restricted for Research   160,000
    Revenues—Government Grants   160,000
    To recognize revenue in connection with appropriate
expenditure of government biological research grant.

5.
                      Unrestricted Current Funds

Expenditures—Instruction   400,000
Discretionary Transfer to Quasi-Endowment Fund for Scientific
    Research   600,000
Discretionary Transfer to Unexpended Plant Funds   300,000
    Cash   1,300,000
    To record faculty salaries and transfers made of unrestricted
    cash balances.

                      Quasi-Endowment Funds

Cash   600,000
    Fund Balance—Unrestricted   600,000
    To record receipt of funds set aside for scientific research by
    board of trustees.

                      Unexpended Plant Funds

Cash   300,000
    Fund Balance—Unrestricted   300,000
    To record receipt of funds transferred from Unrestricted
    Current Funds by board of trustees.

6.   *Life Income Funds*

Cash   50,000
    Due to Stated Recipient   50,000
    To recognize income generated from investments held in Life
    Income Funds.

Due to Stated Recipient   50,000
    Cash   50,000
    To distribute entire income of Life Income Funds to recipient
    as specified by donor.

7.   *Unexpended Plant Funds*

Fund Balance—Unrestricted   1,500,000
    Cash   1,500,000
    To pay for newly constructed addition to art school.

                      Investment in Plant

Buildings   1,500,000
    Investment in Plant   1,500,000
    To record cost of art school addition.

APPENDIX A
FINANCIAL STATEMENTS FOR A UNIVERSITY

Following are the financial statements for the University of Minnesota for June 30, 1990, and the year then ended. These statements have been produced using the AICPA college guide model. The notes to these financial statements have not been included.

EXHIBIT 17–2

UNIVERSITY OF MINNESOTA
Statement of Changes in Fund Balances (in thousands)
For the Year Ended June 30, 1990

	Current Funds	
	Unrestricted	*Restricted*
Revenues and other additions:		
Unrestricted revenues	$992,877	$ —
Federal appropriations	—	14,643
State appropriations	—	74,119
Federal grants and contracts	—	175,496
State grants and contracts	—	19,106
Local grants and contracts	—	2,314
Private gifts, grants, and contracts	—	121,959
Endowment income	—	9,865
Investment income	—	3,458
Realized gains (losses) and adjustments to market value, net	—	(240)
Student loan interest	—	—
Expended for plant facilities (including $64,341 charged to current funds expenditures)	—	—
Retirement of indebtedness	—	—
Other additions	—	—
Total revenues and other additions	992,877	420,720
Expenditures and other deductions:		
Education and general	593,136	378,032
Auxiliary enterprises	101,358	111
University hospitals	250,057	613
Indirect costs recovered	—	37,118
Loan cancellation	—	—
Administrative and collection costs	—	—
Expended for plant facilities, including $8,090 not capitalized	—	—
Retirement of indebtedness	—	—
Interest on indebtedness	—	—
Disposal of plant facilities	—	—
Other deductions	—	388
Total expenditures and other deductions	944,551	416,262
Interfund transfers, additions (deductions):		
Mandatory:		
Principal and interest	(2,043)	(14)
Renewals and replacements	(317)	—
Loan fund matching grant	(70)	—
Nonmandatory	(32,791)	(3,513)
Total transfers	(35,221)	(3,527)
Net increase (decrease) for the year	13,105	931
Fund balances, beginning of year, as restated	261,425	102,904
Fund balances, end of year	$274,530	$103,835

The notes are an integral part of the financial statements.

EXHIBIT 17-2 (*concluded*)

Loan Funds	Endowment Funds		Plant Funds			Totals
	True	*Quasi*	*Unrestricted*	*Restricted*	*Net Investment in Plant*	
—	—	—	—	—	—	$ 992,877
—	—	—	—	—	—	14,643
—	—	—	—	$ 74,880	—	148,999
$ 627	—	—	—	—	—	176,123
—	—	—	—	—	—	19,106
—	—	—	—	2,281	—	4,595
66	$ 535	—	$ 300	1,008	—	123,868
—	—	—	—	—	—	9,865
217	982	$ 338	17,619	2,045	—	24,659
—	8,452	8,859	581	(259)	—	17,393
1,467	—	—	—	—	—	1,467
—	—	—	—	—	$ 112,503	112,503
—	—	—	—	—	6,172	6,172
99	—	—	548	4,185	—	4,832
2,476	9,969	9,197	19,048	84,140	118,675	1,657,102
—	—	—	—	—	—	971,168
—	—	—	—	—	—	101,469
—	—	—	—	—	—	250,670
—	—	—	—	—	—	37,118
530	—	—	—	—	—	530
519	—	—	—	—	—	519
—	—	—	43,374	12,878	—	56,252
—	—	—	—	6,172	—	6,172
—	—	—	—	18,364	—	18,364
—	—	—	—	—	19,318	19,318
—	—	—	—	—	—	388
1,049	—	—	43,374	37,414	19,318	1,461,968
—	—	—	(14,871)	24,898	(7,970)	—
—	—	—	419	(102)	—	—
70	—	—	—	—	—	—
(313)	(1,350)	8,494	41,530	(16,495)	4,438	—
(243)	(1,350)	8,494	27,078	8,301	(3,532)	—
1,184	8,619	17,691	2,752	55,027	95,825	195,134
47,036	142,765	104,712	196,578	53,993	1,450,906	2,360,319
$48,220	$151,384	$122,403	$199,330	$109,020	$1,546,731	$2,555,453

EXHIBIT 17–3

UNIVERSITY OF MINNESOTA
Statement of Current Funds Revenues, Expenditures, and Other Changes (in thousands)
For the Year Ended June 30, 1990

	Unrestricted	Restricted	Total
Revenues:			
Tuition and fees	$140,427	—	$ 140,427
Federal appropriations	—	$ 14,473	14,473
State appropriations	367,566	71,859	439,425
Federal grants and contracts	33,536	149,294	182,830
State grants and contracts	169	18,256	18,425
Local grants and contracts	19	1,993	2,012
Private gifts, grants, and contracts	5,530	113,782	119,312
Endowment income	276	7,958	8,234
Investment income	26,899	1,155	28,054
Realized gains (losses) and adjustments to market value, net	(578)	—	(578)
Equity in earnings (losses) of unconsolidated subsidiary	(1,837)	—	(1,837)
Sales and services of educational activities	65,181	—	65,181
Sales and services of auxiliary enterprises	106,205	—	106,205
Sales and services of hospitals	249,484	—	249,484
Total revenues	992,877	378,770	1,371,647
Expenditures and mandatory transfers:			
Education and general:			
Instruction	289,168	57,621	346,789
Research	17,466	211,370	228,836
Public service	17,474	56,804	74,278
Academic support	84,683	16,120	100,803
Student services	36,928	3,330	40,258
Institutional support	57,694	733	58,427
Operation and maintenance of plant	74,132	1,409	75,541
Scholarships and fellowships	15,591	30,645	46,236
Education and general expenditures	593,136	378,032	971,168
Mandatory transfers for:			
Principal and interest	712	14	726
Loan fund matching grant	70	—	70
Total education and general	593,918	378,046	971,964
Auxiliary enterprises:			
Expenditures	101,358	111	101,469
Mandatory transfers for:			
Principal and interest	1,137	—	1,137
Renewals and replacements	317	—	317
Total auxiliary enterprises	102,812	111	102,923
University hospitals:			
Expenditures	250,057	613	250,670
Mandatory principal and interest transfers	194	—	194
Total university hospitals	250,251	613	250,864
Total current expenditures and mandatory transfers	946,981	378,770	1,325,751
Other transfers, additions (deductions):			
Excess of restricted additions over expenditures	—	4,832	4,832
Refunded to grantors	—	(388)	(388)
Nonmandatory transfers	(32,791)	(3,513)	(36,304)
Total other transfers, additions (deductions)	(32,791)	931	(31,860)
Net increase in fund balances	$ 13,105	$ 931	$ 14,036

The notes are an integral part of the financial statements.

EXHIBIT 17–4

UNIVERSITY OF MINNESOTA
Balance Sheet (in thousands)
June 30, 1990

	Current Funds		Loan Funds	Endowment and Similar Funds	Plant Funds	Total All Funds
	Unrestricted	*Restricted*				
Assets:						
Cash and temporary investments . . .	$210,731	$ 54,064	$ 1,786	$ 5,844	$ 179,469	$ 451,894
Receivables	106,825	41,825	46,287	—	103,149	298,086
Inventories.	27,441	36	—	—	—	27,477
Prepaid expenses and deferred charges	11,038	—	—	—	5,226	16,264
Investments	55,216	25,192	361	267,978	61,594	410,341
Investment in unconsolidated subsidiary	6,525	—	—	—	—	6,525
Investment in plant	—	—	—	—	1,806,180	1,806,180
Other assets	8,137	—	—	—	—	8,137
Total assets	$425,913	$121,117	$48,434	$273,822	$2,155,618	$3,024,904
Liabilities and Fund Balances:						
Liabilities:						
Accounts payable.	53,603	11,674	37	—	4,972	70,286
Accrued liabilities and other	81,699	5,405	—	35	9,429	96,568
Unearned income.	13,738	—	—	—	—	13,738
Bonds payable and capital lease obligations	—	—	—	—	288,859	288,859
Interfund borrowing.	2,343	203	177	—	(2,723)	—
Total liabilities	151,383	17,282	214	35	300,537	469,451
Fund balances:						
Unrestricted:						
Undesignated.	139,209	—	—	—	—	139,209
Designated	135,321	—	136	—	213,367	348,824
Restricted	—	103,835	11,495	—	94,983	210,313
U.S. government grants and other refundables	—	—	36,589	—	—	36,589
Endowment	—	—	—	144,631	—	144,631
Term endowment	—	—	—	6,666	—	6,666
Quasi-endowment, restricted	—	—	—	74,713	—	74,713
Quasi-endowment, unrestricted. . .	—	—	—	47,690	—	47,690
Life income	—	—	—	87	—	87
Net investment in plant	—	—	—	—	1,546,731	1,546,731
Total fund balances	274,530	103,835	48,220	273,787	1,855,081	2,555,453
Total liabilities and fund balances. . .	$425,913	$121,117	$48,434	$273,822	$2,155,618	$3,024,904

The notes are an integral part of the financial statements.

APPENDIX B
FINANCIAL STATEMENTS FOR PRIVATE NOT-FOR-PROFIT COLLEGES OR UNIVERSITIES

Following are examples of the financial statements for private colleges and universities (and other private not-for-profit organizations) required by the FASB in its *Statement No. 117* "Financial Statements of Not-for-Profit Organizations." The notes to these financial statements have not been included. These statements represent the entity as a whole rather than as a group of funds as is demonstrated in the financial statements in Appendix A.

The FASB offered several formats for the statement of activities but only one has been included here. In addition, both the direct method and the indirect method were demonstrated for the statement of cash flows. The direct method is shown in Exhibit 17–7.

EXHIBIT 17–5

PRIVATE NOT-FOR-PROFIT COLLEGE OR UNIVERSITY
Statement of Financial Position
June 30, 19X1 and 19X0
(in thousands)

	19X1	19X0
Assets:		
Cash and cash equivalents.	$ 75	$ 460
Accounts and interest receivable.	2,130	1,670
Inventories and prepaid expenses	610	1,000
Contributions receivable.	3,025	2,700
Short-term investments	1,400	1,000
Assets restricted to investment in land, buildings, and equipment.	5,210	4,560
Land, buildings, and equipment	61,700	63,590
Long-term investments	218,070	203,500
Total assets	$292,220	$278,480
Liabilities and net assets:		
Accounts payable.	$ 2,570	$ 1,050
Refundable advance	—	650
Grants payable.	875	1,300
Notes payable	—	1,140
Annuity obligations.	1,685	1,700
Long-term debt.	5,500	6,500
Total liabilities	10,630	12,340
Net assets:		
Unrestricted.	115,228	103,670
Temporarily restricted	24,342	25,470
Permanently restricted	142,020	137,000
Total net assets	281,590	266,140
Total liabilities and net assets	$292,220	$278,480

EXHIBIT 17–6

PRIVATE NOT-FOR-PROFIT COLLEGE OR UNIVERSITY
Statement of Activities
Year Ended June 30, 19X1
(in thousands)

	Unrestricted	Temporarily Restricted	Permanently Restricted	Total
Revenues, gains, and other support:				
Contributions	$ 8,640	$ 8,110	$ 280	$ 17,030
Tuition and fees	5,400	—	—	5,400
Investment income on long-term investments	5,600	2,580	120	8,300
Other investment income	850	—	—	850
Net unrealized and realized gains on long-term investments. . .	8,228	2,952	14,620	25,800
Other	150	—	—	150
	28,868	13,642	15,020	57,530
Net assets released from restrictions	14,740	(14,740)	—	—
Total revenues, gains, and other support	43,608	(1,098)	15,020	57,530
Expenses and losses:				
Program services:				
Instruction	13,100	—	—	13,100
Research	8,540	—	—	8,540
Public service	5,760	—	—	5,760
Management and general	2,420	—	—	2,420
Fund raising.	2,150	—	—	2,150
Total expenses.	31,970	—	—	31,970
Fire loss	80	—	—	80
Actuarial loss on annuity obligations	—	30	—	30
Total expenses and losses.	32,050	30	—	32,080
Change in net assets:				
Before changes related to collection items not capitalized. . . .	11,558	(1,128)	15,020	25,450
Paintings purchased for art collection but not capitalized	—	—	(10,000)	(10,000)
Change in net assets	11,558	(1,128)	5,020	15,450
Net assets at beginning of year	103,670	25,470	137,000	266,140
Net assets at end of year	$115,228	$24,342	$142,020	$281,590

EXHIBIT 17–7

PRIVATE NOT-FOR-PROFIT COLLEGES AND UNIVERSITIES
Statement of Cash Flows
Year Ended June 30, 19X1
(in thousands)

Cash flows from operating activities:	
Cash received from tuition.	$ 5,220
Cash received from contributors	8,030
Cash collected on contributions receivable.	2,615
Interest and dividends received.	8,570
Miscellaneous receipts.	150
Interest paid	(382)
Cash paid to employees and suppliers.	(23,808)
Grants paid	(425)
Net cash used by operating activities	(30)
Cash flows from investing activities:	
Insurance proceeds from fire loss on building	250
Purchase of equipment	(1,500)
Proceeds from sale of investments	86,100
Purchase of paintings	(10,000)
Purchase of investments.	(74,900)
Net cash used by investing activities	(50)
Cash flows from financing activities:	
Proceeds from contributions restricted for:	
Investment in endowment	200
Investment in term endowment.	70
Investment in plant	1,210
Investment subject to annuity agreements	200
	1,680
Other financing activities:	
Interest and dividends restricted for reinvestment	300
Payments of annuity obligations	(145)
Payments on notes payable	(1,140)
Payments on long-term debt	(1,000)
	(1,985)
Net cash used by financing activities	(305)
Net decrease in cash and cash equivalents.	(385)
Cash and cash equivalents at beginning of year.	460
Cash and cash equivalents at end of year	$ 75

EXHIBIT 17–7   *(concluded)*

Reconciliation of change in net assets to net cash used by operating activities:	
Change in net assets	$ 15,450
Adjustments to reconcile change in net assets to net cash used by operating activities:	
Depreciation	3,200
Fire loss	80
Actuarial loss on annuity obligations	30
Increase in accounts and interest receivable	(460)
Decrease in inventories and prepaid expenses	390
Increase in contributions receivable	(325)
Increase in accounts payable	1,520
Decrease in refundable advance	(650)
Decrease in grants payable	(425)
Contributions restricted for long-term investment	(2,740)
Interest and dividends restricted for long-term investment	(300)
Unrealized gains on investments	(14,300)
Realized gain on sale of investments	(1,500)
Net cash used by operating activities	$ (30)

Questions

1. Why have colleges and universities traditionally exhibited a significant degree of flexibility in their financial reporting practices?

2. From what sources are the generally accepted accounting principles of colleges and universities derived?

3. In what ways does the reporting process for a college or university resemble that of a state or local governmental unit?

4. What six general fund groups can be encountered in a college or university?

5. What transactions or events are normally accounted for within the Unrestricted Current Funds? Within the Restricted Current Funds?

6. What are the various types of Endowment and Similar Funds utilized within college and university accounting?

7. Describe the individual Plant Funds in a college or university's accounting records.

8. Which funds or subgroups of a college or university most resemble the General Fixed Assets Account Group and General Long-Term Debt Account group of a state or local government?

9. How are revenues and expenditures recorded by the various funds in a college or university?

10. Describe the controversy that has arisen concerning the recognition of depreciation expense by colleges and universities. How has that issue been resolved?

11. What is the GAAP hierarchy? Where was it developed? How has it affected colleges and universities in selecting appropriate accounting principles?

12. A school receives a pledge for a large sum of money. How should this pledge be accounted for prior to the actual receipt of cash? How has the FASB changed the handling of this pledge?

13. A museum operated by the University of Hopewell receives a contribution of a Egyptian bowl thought to be more than 3,000 years old and worth millions of dollars. The bowl will be the center piece of a new exhibition area in the museum. How will the university probably record this gift? What suggestion was originally made by the FASB concerning the recording of this gift? How does the FASB now believe that this contribution should be recorded?

14. A college awards a number of scholarship grants while also reducing tuition for the children of its employees. How are these transactions reflected within the school's financial records?

15. Why must revenues and expenditures always be equal in the Restricted Current Funds?

16. A gift of $1 million is given to a university with the stipulation that it be used to build a new dormitory. The money is ultimately spent for that purpose. How are these events recorded by the school?

Library Assignments

1. Read the following articles and any other published information discussing the recording of depreciation expense by colleges and universities:

   "Accounting-Standards Boards' Rift Irks Many Colleges, May Hurt Private Ones," *The Wall Street Journal*, August 31, 1987.

   "The Impact of SFAS 93 on Colleges and Universities," *The CPA Journal*, July 1991.

   "Several Private Colleges May Ignore New Accounting Rule on Depreciation," *The Wall Street Journal*, February 4, 1987.

   "High Dudgeon in the Ivory Tower," *Forbes*, April 4, 1988.

   "Depreciation for Colleges and Universities: Is It Useful Information?" *Government Accountants Journal*, Winter 1987–1988.

   "How College and University Business Officers View Depreciation," *Government Accountants Journal*, Spring 1988.

Write a short report recommending whether depreciation should be reported by a college or university and give the justification for this opinion.

2. Write to the vice president of financial affairs at one or more colleges and universities and request a copy of the most recent financial statements. Using these statements, answer the following questions:
   - How large is the school's endowment?
   - Is the school a public or private institution?
   - What was the largest source of revenues in the Unrestricted Current Funds?
   - What was the largest source of revenues in the Restricted Current Funds?
   - What was the largest expenditure in the Unrestricted Current Funds?
   - What was the largest expenditure in the Restricted Current Funds?
   - What was the cost of the school's land, buildings, and equipment?
   - Does the school record depreciation expense?
   - Does the school record its pledges? Is the amount of pledges currently outstanding disclosed?
   - Were any interfund transfers made during the period? If so, were they mandatory or discretionary?

Problems

1. Which of the following should be used in accounting for colleges and universities?
   a. Fund accounting and accrual accounting.
   b. Fund accounting but not accrual accounting.
   c. Accrual accounting but not fund accounting.
   d. Neither accrual accounting nor fund accounting.
   (AICPA adapted)

2. A large cash gift was made to Johnstone University with the following specific instructions: the income earned on this money is to be used to buy library books for five years. Thereafter, all of the principal can be spent to improve facilities in the dining hall. Within which of the school's fund types is this money initially recorded?
   a. Nonexpendable Trust Funds.
   b. Life Income Funds.
   c. Annuity Funds.
   d. Term Endowment Funds.

3. Money is given to a college or university with the stipulation that it be used solely for the acquisition of new equipment for the physics laboratory. Within which fund is this money recorded?
   a. Capital Projects Funds.
   b. Investment in Plant Fund.

    c. Unexpended Plant Funds.

    d. Endowment Funds.

4. The current funds group of a university includes which of the following subgroups?

	Term Endowment Funds	Life Income Funds
a.	No	No
b.	No	Yes
c.	Yes	Yes
d.	Yes	No

    (AICPA adapted)

5. Why are Quasi-Endowment Funds somewhat unique to college and university accounting?

    a. Money held within the school's endowment is classified according to the source of the gift.

    b. Internally restricted amounts are classified separately from unrestricted funds.

    c. Assets other than cash are held within the school's endowment.

    d. Several types of gifts are merged together to form a single endowment fund.

6. Which of the following fund types is most similar?

    a. General Fund of a state or local government and the Unrestricted Current Funds of a college or university.

    b. Capital Projects Funds of a state or local government and the Endowment Funds of a college or university.

    c. Debt Service Funds of a state or local government and the Loan Funds of a college or university.

    d. Nonexpendable Trust Funds of a state or local government and the Restricted Current Funds of a college or university.

7. Which of the following fund types is most similar?

    a. Capital Projects Funds of a state or local government and the Investment in Plant of a college or university.

    b. Special Revenue Funds of a state or local government and the Restricted Current Funds of a college or university.

    c. Enterprise Funds of a state or local government and the Quasi-Endowment Funds of a college or university.

    d. Internal Service Funds of a state or local government and the Unrestricted Current Funds of a college or university.

8. Apteck University computes normal tuition charges of $480,000. However, of this amount, $140,000 is to be covered by scholarships. How does the school report this information?

    a. As revenues of $340,000.

    b. As revenues of $480,000 less an allowance balance of $140,000.

    c. As revenues of $340,000 and expenditures of $140,000.

    d. As revenues of $480,000 and expenditures of $140,000.

9. A college receives a cash gift of $300,000 that must be used to assist in building a new dormitory in several years. How is this amount recorded?
   a. Traditionally, it would be recorded as revenue in the Unrestricted Current Funds but the FASB has required it be shown as an increase in temporarily restricted net assets.
   b. Traditionally, it would be recorded as an increase in the fund balance of the Unexpended Plant Funds but the FASB has required it be shown as restricted support increasing the temporarily restricted net assets.
   c. Traditionally, it would be recorded as a deferred revenue in the Restricted Current Funds but the FASB has required that it be recognized immediately as a revenue increasing the temporarily restricted net assets.
   d. Traditionally, it would be recorded as an increase in the Investment in Plant of the school but the FASB has required that it be recognized as an increase in permanently restricted net assets.

10. The following information was available from Forest College's accounting records for its current funds for the year ended March 31, 1995 (it is a public school):

Restricted gifts received	
Expended	$100,000
Not expended	300,000
Unrestricted gifts received	
Expended	600,000
Not expended	75,000

   What amount should be included in current funds revenues (restricted and unrestricted) for the year ended March 31, 1995?
   a. $600,000.
   b. $700,000.
   c. $775,000.
   d. $1,000,000.
   (AICPA adapted)

11. For 1995, Hawkeye University charges its students $1.7 million, covering tuition and fees for educational and general purposes. However, only $1.5 million was expected to be realized because scholarships totaling $150,000 were granted to these students, and tuition remissions of $50,000 were allowed to faculty members' children attending the school. What amount should be included in the Unrestricted Current Funds as revenues from student tuition and fees?
   a. $1,500,000.
   b. $1,550,000.
   c. $1,650,000.
   d. $1,700,000.
   (AICPA adapted)

12. An endowment gift is donated to a public college with the stipulation that the subsequent income is to be spent on medical research. During 1995, endowment revenue is $60,000 but only $47,000 is spent for the research. Which of the following is correct?
    a. Revenues of $47,000 are reported in Restricted Current Funds.
    b. Expenditures of $47,000 are reported in the Endowment Funds.
    c. Revenues of $60,000 are reported in Restricted Current Funds.
    d. Revenues of $47,000 are reported in the Endowment Funds.

13. A $100,000 cash gift is made to a public university at the beginning of 1995. The money is designated to be spent to enhance salaries of valued professors who write textbooks. During 1995, $42,000 of the money is spent for this purpose. What reporting is made at the end of the year in the Restricted Current Funds?
    a. Fund Balance—0; Revenues—$100,000; Expenditures—$42,000
    b. Fund Balance—$58,000; Revenues—$42,000; Expenditures —$42,000
    c. Fund Balance—$100,000; Revenues—$58,000; Expenditures—0
    d. Fund Balance—$58,000; Revenues—$100,000; Expenditures—$42,000

14. In college and university accounting, where are the operations of auxiliary activities (such as the campus bookstore) normally reported?
    a. Restricted Current Funds.
    b. Endowment Funds.
    c. Quasi-Endowment Funds.
    d. Unrestricted Current Funds.

15. A college holds money in its Unexpended Plant Fund that is to be used to buy new laboratory equipment. During 1995, a total of $650,000 is spent in this way. What internal recording is made of this $650,000?
    a. A $650,000 reduction is recorded to the Fund Balance of the Unexpended Plant Fund, and Equipment of $650,000 is recorded in the Investment in Plant.
    b. Equipment of $650,000 is recorded in the Unexpended Plant Fund.
    c. An Expenditure of $650,000 is recorded in the Unexpended Plant Fund, and Equipment of $650,000 is recorded in the Unrestricted Current Funds.
    d. A Discretionary Transfer of $650,000 is recorded in the Unexpended Plant Fund, and both an Expenditure and Equipment of $650,000 are reported in the Investment in Plant.

16. The following receipts were among those recorded by Allied College (a public school) during 1995:

Unrestricted gifts	$500,000
Restricted current funds (expended for current operating purposes)	200,000
Restricted current funds (not yet expended)	100,000

The total amount that should be included in current funds revenues is
a. $800,000.
b. $700,000.
c. $600,000.
d. $500,000.
(AICPA adapted)

17. According to the GAAP hierarchy, which of the following is correct?
    a. Pronouncements of the FASB apply to governmental not-for-profit organizations unless the GASB specifically overrules the FASB.
    b. Pronouncements of the FASB only apply to governmental not-for-profit organizations if specifically accepted by the GASB.
    c. FASB pronouncements always take precedence over GASB pronouncements.
    d. Governmental not-for-profit organizations now fall under the jurisdiction of the FASB.

18. For the spring semester of 1995, Manning University assessed its students a total of $4.4 million, covering tuition and fees for educational and general purposes. However, scholarships of $600,000 were granted to selected students. Tuition reductions of $100,000 were also allowed to faculty members' children attending the school. An additional $75,000 in bad debt expenses are expected.

    How much should Manning recognize as current funds revenues from student tuition and fees?

    What journal entry should be recorded at the time the assessment is made?

    Assume that some of the classes are in summer school and start in one fiscal year and end in the next. How is the revenue to be recognized?

19. A university transferred cash of $100,000 from unrestricted funds to be held as eventual financing for the construction of a dormitory. A bond of $830,000 was issued at face value. A contract was signed for $908,000. The dorm was built with the final cost being $898,000. That amount was paid.

    Prepare all necessary journal entries for these transactions. Identify the fund type for each entry.

20. An outside donor gave cash of $140,000 to a university to study frogs. The first $97,000 was spent in that manner. Make the proper journal entries. Identify the fund type for each entry.

21. The following assets were being held in various funds by Wilkenson Tech at July 1, 1995:

Funds to be used for acquisition of additional properties for
university purposes $1,450,000
Funds set aside for debt service charges and for retirement of indebtedness
on university properties 2,657,000

In what funds will these two amounts be maintained? Assume that $500,000 was expended from the first fund to buy new equipment for the science laboratories. Assume that $700,000 was expended from the second fund to pay off a bond payable ($650,000) and interest ($50,000). What journal entries are required?

22. The following transactions were incurred by Garrison Tech, a public university in the southeastern section of the United States. Prepare all necessary journal entries. Include the fund types in which each entry would be recorded. Amounts are not to be presented.

- Students were assessed tuition charges for the current year. A percentage of this amount was expected to be uncollectible. Another portion was to be covered by academic scholarships.
- A cash gift was awarded to the school with the stipulation that all future income generated from this money should be used to finance genetic research.
- A pledge was received from a donor who specified that the amount would be paid in two years for use in that period.
- A patron of the school donated a collection of paintings by Gris to be added to the permanent collection of the art museum on campus.
- A cash transfer was made from unrestricted funds to finance student loans. Another amount of unrestricted cash was set aside by school officials. This money will be invested with future income to be used for library acquisitions.
- Student loans were awarded for the current year. A portion of this money will never be collected.
- Income was generated from the preceding gift that was restricted for genetic research. This money has not yet been expended.
- A portion of the income just earned was appropriately expended for genetic research.
- An addition was built to the school of business. Money previously set aside by school officials was used to pay a portion of the costs of the construction. A long-term liability was signed to cover the remainder.

23. During the year ended June 30, 1995, Central State College began to conduct a cancer research project financed by a $10 million donation from an alumnus. This entire amount was pledged by the donor on August 1, 1994. The first payment of $3 million was made at that time. The remaining money was given exactly one year later. The gift was restricted to the financing of this particular research project. Central State spent $2 million per year on this project for five consecutive years beginning with the year ended June 30, 1995. Central State follows a policy of recording all pledges.

    How much revenue should Central State report in 1995 and in what fund should it be recognized?

    What journal entry was recorded when the pledge was received?

    What entries are required for the first year's expenditures?

24. The following series of issues concern the accounting procedures utilized by colleges and universities. Prepare answers to each question.
    a. A cash donation is made to a university with the stipulation that the money must be used for biology research. Discuss the accounting procedures necessitated by this gift.
    b. One of the subgroups found within the Plant Funds of a college accounting system is the Investment in Plant. What is the purpose of this subgroup?
    c. The recording of depreciation expense by colleges and universities has become the subject of controversy. What are the positions and what are the justifications for each?
    d. The current funds category of a university has two subgroups. Identify these subgroups and explain their differences.
    e. How are student scholarships recorded in college and university accounting?
    f. Debt Service Funds and Capital Projects Funds are found in the accounting for state and local government units. Which fund types found in college accounting parallel these two funds?
    g. For colleges and universities, what is the significance of the GAAP hierarchy that has been created?
    h. The governing body of a college transfers previously unrestricted money into the Loan Funds. How is this transfer recorded?
    i. What is a Quasi-Endowment Fund? What makes the use of this fund somewhat controversial from an accounting perspective?
    j. What method of recording should be used for pledges of money received by a college or university?
    k. What accounting should be made of contributions made to the permanent collection of a not-for-profit organization?

25. The following series of transactions is for Orlando University. For each, prepare all needed journal entries including an identification of the fund types.
    a. An unrestricted cash donation of $44,000 was given to the school by a former student.
    b. A cash gift of $78,000 was presented to the school with the specification that the money be used to study political processes in Eastern Europe.
    c. An investment portfolio valued at $50,000 was given to the school with the stipulation that all income generated from these assets must be used to research computer applications in education.
    d. A cash gift of $231,000 was conveyed to the school with the stipulation that the money eventually be used to help pay for the construction of a new chemistry building.
    e. The money from (a) was used to pay faculty salaries.
    f. The money from (b) was used for the specified purpose.
    g. Cash dividends of $7,000 are received from the investments in (c). This money will be spent for the intended purpose but not until next year.

h. The chemistry building mentioned in (*d*) was built at a cost of $1,950,000. The $231,000 was used as a first payment and a note was signed for the remaining $1,719,000.

26. Jurgeson State College incurred the following transactions during its 1995 fiscal year. Prepare all necessary journal entries indicating the fund category or fund subgroup within which the entry is recorded.

    • An Annuity Fund reported income of $30,000. By the provisions of the original gift, 80 percent of all income goes to the donor's mother with the remainder to be used by the college for a cancer research project. Both amounts were appropriately expended during the current year.

    • The college borrowed $900,000 during the year to begin construction of a new gymnasium. The building is completed before the end of the year and the $900,000, plus a previously received gift of $340,000, were used to pay for the construction. The first $25,000 installment on the loan was paid; this amount included $11,000 in interest expense.

    • A government grant of $70,000 (received during the previous year to investigate health disorders) was spent for that purpose.

    • The college's athletic teams reported a $200,000 loss for the year based on revenues of $1,400,000 and expenditures of $1,600,000.

    • Student tuition of $600,000 was assessed. Of this total, 4 percent was assumed to be uncollectible and an additional 10 percent was covered by financial aid scholarships.

    • The college's board of trustees transferred $100,000 at the beginning of the year to a Quasi-Endowment Fund. All future income derived from this principal was to be used for law student scholarships. Earnings of $8,000 were reported during the current year and granted to two students.

    • Depreciation of $620,000 was recorded on the long-lived assets being reported in the Investment in Plant Fund.

    • Student loans of $90,000 were made with the anticipation that only 92 percent would actually be repaid. Interest of $3,000 accrued on these loans during the current year.

27. The following journal entries have been taken from the financial records of the University of Jonesville. In each case, the fund category or fund subgroup in which each entry has been recorded is identified. For each transaction, indicate the correcting entry or entries that should be prepared by the university. If no correction is needed, indicate this fact.

a.

	Endowment Fund		
Cash		13,000	
Revenues Control.			13,000
Expenditures Control		13,000	
Cash			13,000

To record revenue earned on endowment gift and subsequent
expenditure as per original specifications attached to gift.

b.

Unrestricted Current Funds

Expenditures—Student Loans	50,000	
Cash		50,000

Money transferred to loan fund to finance future student loans.

Loan Funds

Cash	50,000	
Revenues—Transfer from Unrestricted Funds		50,000

Money transferred by administration to finance student loans.

c.

Unrestricted Current Funds

Depreciation Expense	73,000	
Accumulated Depreciation		73,000

Depreciation of university property recorded for the current year.

d.

Restricted Current Funds

Cash	100,000	
Revenues—Government Grant		100,000
Expenditures—Research Project	33,000	
Cash		33,000

To record grant made by federal government to finance a project to study molecular structures as well as the initial expenditures made to start this project.

e.

Unexpended Plant Funds

Cash	125,000	
Revenues—Philanthropic Gift		125,000

To record gift made to university with the stipulation that the money be used in construction of a new library.

f.

Unrestricted Current Funds

Pledges Receivable	50,000	
Deferred Revenues		50,000

Pledge made by university supporter for an unrestricted cash gift to be made in five years.

g.

Unexpended Plant Funds

Building	600,000	
Cash		200,000
Bonds Payable		400,000

To record construction of new dormitory—part of cost paid through an earlier gift with the rest covered by the issuance of long-term bonds payable.

h.

Unrestricted Current Funds

Accounts Receivable	480,000	
Revenues—Student Tuition and Fees		480,000

To record billings for current tuition—5 percent of above total is considered uncollectible while an additional $60,000 has not been recorded because that amount relates to student scholarships.

28. The following transactions were incurred by the University of South Central. For each, prepare all needed journal entries including an identification of the fund types.

a. Students were charged $378,000 for tuition. Of this amount, $22,000 is anticipated as being uncollectible.

b. A cash gift of $85,000 was made to the school with the stipulation that this money be used to finance fine arts performances at the school.

c. The university paid its faculty $54,000 in cash for normal salaries.

d. A building was acquired for $800,000. Of the total, previously designated funds of $300,000 were used with the remainder covered by the signing of a note payable.

e. From the receivables in (a), $210,000 in cash was collected. An additional $43,000 was covered by scholarships.

f. A discretionary transfer of $40,000 was made from unrestricted funds into a quasi-endowment fund.

g. Of the $85,000 received in (b), 40 percent was spent for the intended purpose.

h. A loan of $110,000 was made to students.

29. Following is the current funds balance sheet of Burnsville University (a public school) as of June 30, 1995, the end of the school's fiscal year.

BURNSVILLE UNIVERSITY
Current Funds Balance Sheet
June 30, 1995

Assets

Current funds:		
Unrestricted:		
Cash	$210,000	
Accounts receivable—student tuition and fees, less allowance for doubtful accounts of $9,000.	341,000	
State appropriations receivable	75,000	$626,000
Restricted:		
Cash	7,000	
Investments	60,000	67,000
Total current funds		$693,000

Liabilities and Fund Balances

Current funds:		
Unrestricted:		
Accounts payable.	$ 45,000	
Deferred revenues	66,000	
Fund balances	515,000	$626,000
Restricted:		
Fund balances		67,000
Total current funds		$693,000

The following transactions occurred during the fiscal year ended June 30, 1996:

- On July 7, 1995, a gift of $100,000 in cash was received from an alumnus with the request that one half be used for the purchase of books for the university library with the remainder used for the establishment of a scholarship fund. The alumnus further specified that the income generated by the scholarship fund be awarded annually to a qualified disadvantaged student. On July 20, 1995, the board of trustees resolved that the funds of the newly established scholarship fund be invested in high-grade bonds. On July 21, 1995, these bonds were purchased.
- Revenue from student tuition and fees applicable to the year ended June 30, 1996, amounted to $1,900,000. Of this amount, $66,000 had been collected in the prior year and $1,686,000 was received during the current year ended June 30, 1996. In addition, by June 30, 1996, the university had received cash of $158,000 representing fees for the session beginning in September 1996.
- During the year ended June 30, 1996, the university collected $349,000 of the outstanding accounts receivable at the beginning of the year. The balance was deemed to be uncollectible and was written off against the allowance account. At June 30, 1996, the allowance account was increased by $3,000.
- Interest charges of $6,000 were earned and collected during the year on late student fee payments.
- During the year, the state appropriation was received. An additional unrestricted appropriation of $50,000 was made by the state but had not been paid to the university as of June 30, 1996.
- An unrestricted gift of $25,000 cash was received from alumni of the university.
- During the year, investments of $21,000 were sold for $26,000. Dividend and interest income amounting to $1,900 was also received.
- Unrestricted operating expenses of $1,777,000 were accrued during the period. At June 30, 1996, $59,000 of these expenses remained unpaid.
- Restricted current funds of $13,000 were spent for authorized purposes during the year.
- The accounts payable at June 30, 1995, were paid during July 1995.
- During the current year, $7,000 interest was earned and received on the bonds purchased in accordance with the board of trustees resolution, as discussed above.

Required:

a. Prepare journal entries to record these transactions for the year ended June 30, 1996. Label each entry to indicate which funds would be involved.
b. Prepare a statement of changes in fund balances for the year ended June 30, 1996, for the Unrestricted Current Funds and the Restricted Current Funds. (AICPA adapted)

30. Following are descriptions of balances found in the various accounts of the University of Northwest Wichita as of December 31, 1995:

Inflow of Net Assets

Revenue generated by bookstore	$ 85,000
Gifts received from graduates designated to buy a new dormitory	100,000
Note is signed to buy new dormitory	300,000
Research grants made to fund cancer research	120,000
Income earned on an endowment where money must be spent on researching fog	30,000
Charges for tuition (does not include reductions of $50,000 because of scholarships and $10,000 because of class cancellations)	545,000

Outflow of Net Assets

Spent for new dormitory	400,000
Spent for faculty salaries	300,000
Spent for research on fog (money was earned in endowment)	30,000
Loaned to students	65,000
Spent for cancer research	75,000

Other

Money restricted by board of trustees for future studies of endangered animals	100,000

Answer each of the following questions:

   a. What is the total revenue recorded in the Unrestricted Current Funds and what are the components?
   b. What is the total revenue recorded in the Restricted Current Funds and what are the components?
   c. Identify the journal entry or entries recorded in the Investment in Plant fund.
   d. How is the money recorded that is being set aside to study endangered animals?
   e. What is the total Expenditures balance to be shown in the Unrestricted Current Funds?
   f. Identify the journal entry or entries recorded when the gift is received for the new dormitory.

31. Record each of the following transactions as if it were incurred by a state or local government. Then, record each transaction as if it were incurred by a college or university. In each case, indicate the fund or fund type in which the entry would be being recorded. Optional entries should be made.

   a. A budget was passed for normal operating activities. Income was anticipated as $760,000 with approved spending amounting to $740,000.
   b. A contract was signed with a construction company for a new building at a cost of $8 million.
   c. Bonds were sold for $8 million (face value) to finance construction of the new building.
   d. The new building was completed and payment of $8 million immediately made.

    e. Cash of $1 million was transferred from unrestricted funds to be set aside to pay off the bonds sold in (*b*).

    f. The $1 million was paid to retire this portion of the bonds before maturity.

    g. Annual assessments were sent out; they are to be collected with the money to be used in this period. The receivables are for $800,000 and the cash collected will be unrestricted. Only 94 percent of the assessment will actually be collected.

    h. Cash of $70,000 was received as a gift which must be spent for a designated operating purpose.

    i. Of the cash in (*h*), $40,000 was spent for the specified purpose.

    j. Investments of $300,000 were received as a gift. Future income that is received from this donation will be used for a stipulated operating purpose.

18

ACCOUNTING FOR NOT-FOR-PROFIT ORGANIZATIONS

Health Care Entities and Voluntary Health and Welfare Organizations

---

Questions to Consider

- How are hospitals and other health care entities able to account for all of their revenues and expenses within a single fund?
- What are third-party payors and what influence have they had on the financial reporting of health care services?
- How do health care entities report the diverse types of revenues usually earned by these organizations?
- Both health care entities and voluntary health and welfare organizations receive significant amounts of donated services and materials. How are these contributions reported?
- Why does a voluntary health and welfare organization report public support separately from its revenues?
- How can a contributor to a voluntary health and welfare organization determine the utilization being made of monetary resources?
- What controversy has arisen in the accounting for voluntary health and welfare organizations concerning the allocation of joint costs?

Chapter 17 examined one approach utilized in accounting for not-for-profit organizations. That chapter examined the reporting process for colleges and universities. As shown, fund accounting formed the basic structure for accumulating financial information for these schools. However, actual fund categories as well as the individual reporting procedures were shown to vary significantly from previously described state and local government accounting. Although neither possesses a profit motive, government units and educational institutions exhibit many fundamental differences. In each case, the accounting process currently in use has had to evolve in a distinct fashion to meet specific reporting needs. Consequently, unique approaches to fund accounting have been developed.

This chapter analyzes the reporting procedures appropriate for two other types of not-for-profit enterprises, *health care entities* and *voluntary health and welfare organizations*. For both, fund accounting continues to be applicable but, once again, the specific techniques commonly utilized depend on the nature of the operations as well as the accounting objectives of the entity. Thus, this chapter describes the environment these organizations face as well as their unique reporting problems. This approach should help explain the accounting procedures that have been developed over the years.

Accounting for Health Care Entities

From a quantitative perspective, the providers of health care services are quite prevalent throughout the United States with many thousands of institutions in operation; virtually every city and town has hospitals, nursing homes, and medical clinics. The large number of enterprises is not surprising; health care expenditures now make up more than 12 percent of the gross national product in this country.[1]

A number of these health care entities are proprietary in nature and, therefore, attempt to generate income for their owners. However, a great many are not-for-profit organizations. This latter category is composed largely of entities operated by the federal or state governments, local communities, educational institutions, religious groups, and other charitable organizations.[2] Currently, not-for-profit hospitals make up approximately 85 percent of the hospital market in the United States.[3]

Accounting for health care entities is a somewhat unique blend of recording procedures that combine elements of for-profit and not-for-profit reporting. From 1972 until 1990, the primary authoritative guidance for this process was provided by the AICPA's *Hospital Audit Guide* which was revised on several occasions during that period.[4] However, in 1990, a new audit and accounting guide issued by the AICPA, *Audits of Providers of Health Care Services* replaced the old guide.

---

[1] Leon E. Hay and John Engstrom, *Essentials of Accounting for Governmental and Not-for-Profit Organizations* (Homewood, Ill.: Richard D. Irwin, 1993), p. 277.

[2] As discussed in the previous chapter, organizations operated by a state or local government come under the jurisdiction of the GASB, whereas other not-for-profit entities (such as those operated by charities or religious groups) must follow the regulations of the FASB.

[3] Leslie Spencer, "College Education without the Frills," *Forbes,* May 27, 1991, p. 294.

[4] Although not authoritative, two professional associations have historically had a significant influence on the financial reporting of hospitals: the American Hospital Association and the Healthcare Financial Management Association.

This new pronouncement broadened the list of organizations that was covered and updated much of the accounting guidance.

One of the most significant aspects of these audit guides is the requirement that health care entities must apply generally accepted accounting principles (GAAP) to their financial reporting.[5] Hence, these organizations utilize accrual accounting in recording both revenues and expenses. In addition, depreciation expense is calculated and recognized each year for all buildings, equipment, and other long-lived assets (other than land). Because of these procedures, the reporting process used by a not-for-profit health care entity resembles that of a commercial enterprise in many respects.

Influence of Third-Party Payors

One of the major factors influencing the application of GAAP in accounting for health care entities is the presence of third-party payors such as insurance companies, Medicare, Medicaid, and Blue Cross/Blue Shield. Third-party payors presently bear approximately 90 percent of hospital fees in this country.[6] With the constantly escalating cost of health care, patient charges are rarely paid in full by the individual receiving the services. Because of the significant monetary amounts involved, third-party payors are constantly seeking reliable financial data, especially concerning the costs of patient care. In an attempt to satisfy this demand for accurate financial information, health care entities have come to rely on accrual accounting as well as the recognition of depreciation expense.

Fund Accounting for Health Care Entities

Despite a basic similarity to commercial reporting, the accounting process used for health care entities still separates all financial resources into fund types. The funds are divided into two categories: General Funds and Donor-Restricted Funds. *The General Funds accounts for the operating activities of the organization whereas the various Donor-Restricted Funds maintain a record of resources given by outside parties for stipulated purposes.* As the name implies, Donor-Restricted Funds are strictly limited to externally restricted contributions. Thus, land, buildings, equipment, and long-term debts—which are not restricted by outside parties—are all reported by a health care entity within its General Funds. Likewise, any unrestricted assets designated for a particular purpose by the entity's administration continues to be recorded in this same category. Consequently,

---

[5] AICPA, *Audit and Accounting Guide—Audits of Providers of Health Care Services* (New York: AICPA, 1990), par. 3.01.

[6] AICPA, *Audits,* par. 1.06.

the interfund transfer of unrestricted assets that is common in both governmental and university accounting is virtually nonexistent in the financial records of a health care entity.

The following overview of the various fund types provides a foundation for subsequent analysis of specific accounting procedures for a health care entity. To assist in this coverage, Appendix A at the end of this chapter presents examples of the financial statements prepared for a governmental not-for-profit hospital.[7] These illustrations can be helpful in discerning the accounts reported within each of the fund types.

General Funds.   The extensive use of the General Funds is an especially significant aspect of the reporting of health care entities. This fund type accounts for all financial resources of the organization that have not been restricted by an outside donor or other party. Patient service revenues, interest revenues, and unrestricted gifts and grants would, thus, be recorded here. Restricted gifts are also recognized in the General Funds but only when earned. In addition, this category accounts for all of the expenditures of a health care entity, including amounts that were originally designated by an external donor for a specific purpose. Although such restricted assets are maintained in a separate fund, the eventual expenditure is reported in the General Funds.

By funneling restricted resources into the General Funds as they are spent, all revenues, expenses, and expenditures of a health care provider are reported together. *Consequently, in contrast to governmental or university accounting, this single fund type effectively records all operating transactions of the reporting entity.* Because this information is not being spread across several funds, readers of the financial statements have been better able to evaluate the operational efficiency of the enterprise.[8]

As can be seen in Exhibit 18–1, the balance sheet that appears in Appendix A, the assets recorded within the General Funds of a health care entity has normally been divided into three separate classifications for reporting purposes:

- Current assets.
- Assets whose use is limited.
- Property and equipment.

---

[7] Examples of financial statements for a nursing home, a continuing care retirement community, a home health agency, a health maintenance organization, and an ambulatory care facility are found in Appendix A of the AICPA's *Audits of Providers of Health Care Services.* Examples of financial statements for private not-for-profit organizations are presented in the previous chapter of this textbook.

[8] As discussed in the previous chapter, the FASB now requires that the financial statements of private not-for-profit organizations represent the entity as a whole rather than as a group of funds. Because of the broad use made of the General Funds, such a change would have less impact on health care entities than on other not-for-profits.

The first category encompasses cash, receivables, supplies, prepayments, and the like arising from the day-to-day operations of the organization.

"Assets whose use is limited" often includes *board-designated funds:* cash and investments set aside by the administration of the organization for a specified purpose. These assets are not separated into a different fund because "the board retains control over them and may, at its discretion, subsequently use them for other purposes."[9] Thus, in contrast to college and university accounting, a distinct Quasi-Endowment Fund is not created when health care officials decide to restrict the use of certain assets. The amounts are separately identified but left within General Funds.

However, this assets whose use is limited category is not restricted to such board-designated funds. For example, bond indentures often state that a specific application is to be made of the proceeds received upon issuance. Until expended in the appropriate manner, the cash received from the bond is reported on the balance sheet in this same fashion. Third-party payors may also specify that amounts be held by the entity for a particular purpose; this money is also included as an asset whose use is limited.

For example, the June 30, 1990, balance sheet of the General Funds of the Medical College of Virginia Hospitals indicates that more than $67 million of its assets have a limited use:

Assets whose use is limited—board designated	$33,102,162
Assets whose use is limited under bond agreements	34,268,187

A footnote to these financial statements discloses: "At June 30, 1990, cash totaling $33,102,162 has been designated by the Board of Visitors for plant replacement, expansion, improvement and capital equipment purchases."

Finally, the land, buildings, and equipment owned by the health care provider as well as accumulated depreciation and long-term debt are also reported within General Funds. This placement is unique; other not-for-profit organizations separate these balances into a General Fixed Asset Account Group/General Long-Term Debt Account Group or an Investment in Plant subgroup. The rationale for leaving these accounts in General Funds is quite simply that no donor restrictions exist on such assets and liabilities. "Property and equipment of health care entities that use fund accounting for external financial reporting purposes is reported in general funds, because segregation in a separate fund implies the existence of restrictions on those assets."[10] However, any land, buildings, or equipment given to generate profits for an endowment are recorded in the Endowment Funds.

---

[9] AICPA, *Audits,* par. 3.05.

[10] Ibid., par. 8.06.

Health Care Entities and Voluntary Health and Welfare Organizations

Donor-Restricted Funds.   Donor-Restricted Funds are broken down into several subgroups based on the type of restriction placed on an asset when it was conveyed. The three most common are:

Specific Purpose Funds. Specific Purpose Funds account for any donation or grant made to a health care entity for a stipulated operating purpose. As an example, money given to buy medicine or to finance a hospital's research project would be maintained in this fund category. At December 31, 1990, the Presbyterian Hospital in the City of New York held more than $39 million in its Specific Purpose Funds.

Receipt of such gifts and grants is recorded initially as an increase in the Temporarily Restricted Fund Balance account. At the time an appropriate expenditure is made, this same fund balance is decreased. However, this amount is simultaneously reported in the General Funds as both an expense and a revenue. In this manner, the gift is monitored in a separate fund until spent. At that point, the effect of the donation as well as its actual utilization are reported along with all of the other operating figures of the organization.

Plant Replacement and Expansion Funds. Plant Replacement and Expansion Funds record any monetary resource given to a health care entity with the provision that the asset must be spent on land, buildings, equipment, or capital debt retirement. Once again, though, when the money is eventually expended for the stated purpose, the actual transaction is recorded within the General Funds. Each of the Donor-Restricted Funds is used solely for monitoring balances that have an external restriction attached.

Endowment Funds. As in other types of not-for-profit accounting, Endowment Funds record donated assets given with the stipulation that only subsequently earned income may be spent. These funds are divided further based on whether restrictions are temporary or permanent.

If income use is unrestricted, it is actually recorded when earned in the General Funds. However, in many cases, the exact utilization of these amounts is specified by the donor. In that circumstance, any assets generated as income should be maintained in either Specific Purpose Funds or Plant Replacement and Expansion Funds until expended. At that time, the final recording is made in the General Funds.

Accounting for Patient Service Revenues

The revenues of a health care facility are traditionally separated within the General Funds into three broad classifications:

1. Patient (or resident) service revenues.
2. Other revenues.
3. Nonoperating gains and losses.

The largest source of revenues normally comes from the first of these categories: charges assessed for services provided to patients and/or residents. This balance includes fees for surgery, nursing services, medicine, laboratory work, X rays, blood, housing, food, and so forth.

Patient (or Resident) Service Revenues and Reductions.   For a variety of reasons, health care entities (especially hospitals) often receive less than the total payment normally charged for patient services. Bad debts as well as other fee reductions can be significant. One survey indicated that the median in the state of Virginia is the collection of only 68 percent of hospital charges because of bad debts, charity care, and discounts.[11] *However, to provide complete financial data about the operations of the organization, revenues are still recorded at standard rates if the intention of full collection is present.*

Assume, for example, that patient charges for the current month at a local hospital total $750,000. Of this amount, $170,000 is due from patients with the remaining $580,000 billed to third-party payors: Medicare, Medicaid, Blue Cross/Blue Shield, and various insurance companies. Regardless of expected receipts, the hospital should record revenues through the following journal entry:

General Funds

Accounts Receivable—Third-Party Payors	580,000	
Accounts Receivable—Patients	170,000	
Patient Service Revenues		750,000
To accrue patient charges for current month.		

The entire $750,000 is initially reported as patient service revenue by this hospital although complete collection is doubtful. This approach is considered the best method of allowing the hospital to monitor activities during the period.

To continue with this illustration, assume that $20,000 of patient receivables are estimated to be uncollectible. Furthermore, not-for-profit hospitals and other similar entities often make no serious attempt to collect amounts owed by indigent patients. In many cases, these facilities were originally created to serve the poor. Assume, therefore, that $18,000 of the accounts receivable will never be collected because several patients earn incomes at or below the poverty level. Thus, to mirror these anticipated revenue reductions, the hospital records two additional entries. Of the $170,000 due from patients, collection of $38,000 is not expected.

As shown here, the handling of the two reductions is not the same. The bad debts create an expense but the revenue and receivable for the charity care are removed entirely. The AICPA audit and accounting guide holds that no reporting should be made if the entity has no intention of making the collection.

---

[11] Beverly Orndorff, ''Report Shows Case Mix Affects Hospital Costs,'' *Richmond Times-Dispatch,* October 20, 1990, p. C1.

General Funds

Bad Debt Expense. 20,000
    Allowance for Uncollectible and Reduced Accounts   20,000
    To record estimation of receivables that will prove to be uncollectible.

Patient Service Revenues. 18,000
    Accounts Receivable—Third-Party Payors   18,000
    To remove accounts that will not be collected because patients' earned
    income is at the poverty level.

Contractual Agreements with Third-Party Payors. The adjustments just recorded reflect amounts that will not be collected from patients. An additional reduction is usually encountered but only in connection with receivables due from third-party payors. Organizations such as Medicare and Blue Cross/Blue Shield often establish contractual arrangements with health care providers stipulating that set rates are to be paid for specific services. The entity agrees, in effect, to accept *as payment in full* an amount computed by the third-party payor as reasonable (based frequently on the average cost within the locality for the service rendered). Thus, although a patient is charged $3,000, for example, the health care entity might collect only $2,700 (or some other total) from a third-party payor if the lower figure is determined to be an appropriate cost. The remaining $300 must be written off by the hospital and is commonly referred to as a *contractual adjustment*.

Some third-party payors have switched in recent years to an alternative method of determining the amount to be paid: prospective payment plans. Under this system, reimbursement is not based on the cost of the health services being provided but on the diagnosis of the patient's illness or injury. Thus, if a patient has a broken leg, as an example, the hospital would be entitled to a set reimbursement regardless of the actual expense incurred. "Payment rates vary according to a classification system based on patient diagnostic, clinical, and other factors called diagnosis-related groups (DRGs)." [12]

Such plans were developed in an attempt to encourage a reduction in medical costs since no additional charge is collected if a patient remains in a hospital longer than necessary. "Intent on controlling rampant increases in Medicare spending, [the federal government] implemented a prospective payment system (PPS) in 1983. Under this plan hospitals are paid a predetermined amount per case. Since that time, more and more third-party payors have followed suit, limiting in advance what they'll pay for healthcare services." [13]

---

[12] AICPA *Audits*, par. 1.25.

[13] Richard G. Kleiner, Martha Garner, and Robin G. Colbert, "A Preview of the New Healthcare Audit Guide," *Journal of Accountancy*, September 1989, p. 33.

In many cases, the health care entity is not certain of the amount to be collected under these reimbursement plans. The AICPA audit and accounting guide (paragraph 7.04) requires that this amount be estimated and any reductions recognized in the same period as the patient service revenue. "Estimates of contractual adjustments, other adjustments, and the allowance for uncollectibles are reported in the period during which the services are provided even though the actual amounts may become known at a later date."

Consequently, in the example just presented, the hospital probably does not anticipate collecting the entire $580,000 billed to third-party payors. Assume, for illustration purposes, that this hospital projects only $520,000 of the $580,000 charge will actually be received. To establish a proper value for the hospital's revenues, another $60,000 adjustment must be recorded.

General Funds

Contractual Adjustments 60,000
　　Allowance for Uncollectible and Reduced Accounts . . . .　　60,000
　To recognize estimated reduction in patient billings because of
　contractual arrangements made with third-party payors.

To determine the exact amount to be paid (especially under cost-reimbursement plans), the health care entity's costs are usually subject to audit by the third-party payors. Although payment is normally made currently, adjustments may be made later based on this examination. Thus, a facility might receive additional payments at a later date or be required to make reimbursements based on subsequent cost calculations made by the third-party payor. In 1990, St. Mary's Hospital of Richmond explained this arrangement through the following financial statement footnote (number 8):

> The Hospital participates in the Medicare and Medicaid Programs. . . . Payment rates for inpatient services provided to program beneficiaries are governed by the applicable regulations and implementation provisions thereunder, based generally on prospectively determined rates using clinical, diagnostic and other factors. However, services such as skilled nursing and certain outpatient services and capital costs are subject to cost-based reimbursement principles, subject to certain limitations. . . . *Programs utilizing cost based reimbursement principles are subject to review and final determination by appropriate program representatives.* (emphasis added)

Thus, some amounts to be collected are based on cost figures developed by the hospital and subject to audit by the payor at a later time. Consequently, current payments may either be increased or decreased in a subsequent year. Under that circumstance, a question must be addressed: should any differences that arise between the expected collection and the final total be carried back to the period of accrual to correct the originally recorded contractual adjustment? If the hospital in the previous example recognizes a $60,000 contractual adjustment because it expects to collect $520,000, what accounting is made if the correct amount is ultimately determined to be only $509,000?

As no error has occurred in an accounting sense, GAAP is followed; any change needed to alter the initial estimation is recorded in the subsequent year. A prior period adjustment would not be considered appropriate.

> Although final settlements are not made until a subsequent period, they are usually subject to reasonable estimates and are reported in the financial statements in the period in which services are rendered. Differences between the estimates originally reported in the financial statements and final settlements are included in the statement of revenue and expenses in the period the settlements are made.[14]

Assume that in the previous illustration $520,000 is collected as anticipated. However, in the subsequent year, an audit of the hospital's costs by a third-party payor indicates that only $509,000 was appropriate. Thus, an $11,000 reimbursement from the hospital would now be required. Although this change relates to the first time period, no retroactive restatement is permitted.

General Funds
Initial Period

Cash	520,000	
Allowance for Uncollectible and Reduced Accounts	60,000	
Accounts Receivable—Third-Party Payor		580,000

To record collection from third party based on initial analysis of costs.

Subsequent Period

Allowance for Uncollectible and Reduced Accounts (or Contractual		
Adjustments)	11,000	
Cash		11,000

To record reimbursement paid to third-party payor based on audit indicating that costs were too high.

Reductions—Financial Statement Presentation. Historically, reductions such as bad debts, charity care, and contractual adjustments were shown by health care entities as decreases to the patient service revenues being reported. For example, the statement of revenues and expenses for Thomas Jefferson University Hospital for the year ended June 30, 1990, presented the following information:

Patient service revenue	$580,298,000
Less contractual allowances and provision	
for uncollectible amounts	(269,255,400)
Net patient service revenue	$311,042,600

---

[14] AICPA *Audits,* par. 7.09.

As indicated previously, the new audit and accounting guide requires that bad debts now be shown as expenses rather than as reductions to patient service revenues. Furthermore, charity care deductions are no longer recorded at all if the health care entity has no intention of collecting. Finally, contractual adjustments still reduce patient service revenues but are not shown explicitly on the financial statements. Rather, patient service revenues are now shown as a net figure after removing all such reductions. Since the entity has little chance of collecting the entire balance, reporting total revenues could mislead readers. "Increasing amounts of hospital revenue no longer bear any relationship to established charges. Consequently, gross patient service revenue (that is, the hospitals' charges) has come to have little meaning for financial statement users."[15] Thus, if an organization charges $10 million but anticipates contractual adjustments of $3 million, the statement of revenues and expenses would report net patient service revenues of $7 million.

Accounting for Other Revenues

As previously noted, patient service revenues is just one of the revenue categories utilized by a health care entity. *An other revenues classification is also reported to present the amounts generated from activities that are major and central to ongoing operations other than patient services.* The proceeds from gift shops, cafeterias, educational programs, snack bars, newsstands, and parking lots, are all recorded under this heading. Also included in other revenues would be the fair market value of any donated medicines, linen, office supplies, or other materials if used in the major and central activities of the hospital.[16]

To illustrate the accounting for such contributions, assume that a gift of medicine (with a value of $10,000) is made to a nursing home by an outside party. The first of the following journal entries records the receipt of this donation while the second presents the eventual usage of this asset.

General Funds
Initial Entry

Drugs and Medicine	10,000	
Other Revenues—Donations		10,000
To record gift of medicines.		

Subsequent Entry

Supplies and Other Expenses	10,000	
Drugs and Medicines		10,000

    To record use of medicines that had been donated to the nursing home.

Additional sources of other revenues are the designated grants and gifts often received by hospitals and other health care entities. The expenditure of these

---

[15] "Preview," p. 41.

[16] As discussed in the previous chapter, the FASB has recently established rules for the recognition of donated assets and services by private not-for-profit organizations.

contributions is restricted by the donor for a specific operating purpose such as nursing salaries, charity care, use in research projects, and the acquisition of medicines. As with the Restricted Current Funds of a college or university, revenue recognition is delayed until the appropriate utilization is made.

For illustration purposes, assume that a hospital receives a $100,000 grant to finance a study to determine the proper medical treatment for burn victims. Because of this stipulation, the money is donor restricted and must be maintained in the Specific Purpose Funds until expended. When appropriately spent, the General Funds records both the expense and an other revenue. Although somewhat cumbersome from a mechanical perspective, this method of accounting enables the entity to monitor restricted gifts while still reporting all revenues, expenses, and other expenditures within the General Funds category.

Assuming in this example that the hospital spends the first $67,000 of the grant for the specified research project, the following entries are appropriate:

Specific Purpose Funds
Initial Entry

Cash	100,000	
Fund Balance—Temporarily Restricted—Research Grant		100,000

To record research grant received by hospital to finance study of treatment for burn victims.

Subsequent Entries

Fund Balance—Temporarily Restricted—Research Grant	67,000	
Cash		67,000

To transfer recording of funds that have now been expended for designated research project.

General Funds

Research Expense	67,000	
Cash		67,000

To record expense incurred in connection with research project.

Cash	67,000	
Other Revenues—Grants		67,000

To recognize as revenue the portion of a restricted grant that has now been appropriately expended.

Because of this method of reporting, the Specific Purpose Funds of the Medical College of Virginia Hospitals reported a reduction in its fund balance for the year ended June 30, 1990, due to a transfer of $117,922 "to general funds for expense reimbursement and patient care." At the same time, the General Funds reported a $117,922 other revenue.

Accounting for Nonoperating Gains and Losses

A third income category reported by health care entities is nonoperating gains and losses. As shown in Appendix A, these items have traditionally been reported at the bottom of the statement of revenues and expenses (Exhibit 18–2). This classification primarily includes asset inflows peripheral and incidental to the operating activities of the entity, such as investment income and

- Unrestricted gifts or grants.
- Donated services.
- Unrestricted endowment income.
- Income of board-designated funds.

As an illustration, assume that a hospital receives a $700,000 grant. If no donor-imposed restrictions are specified in connection with this money, the following entry would be appropriate:

General Funds

Cash 700,000
    Nonoperating Gain—Unrestricted Grant 700,000
    To record unrestricted grant made to hospital with no stated provision
    as to expenditure.

Donated Services.   Health care entities have traditionally reported the value of services voluntarily provided as nonoperating gains. However, because guidelines in this area were vague, accounting procedures have tended to vary among organizations. A consistent method of reporting is an important issue because the volume of such contributions can be quite significant. In one study, approximately 90 percent of the not-for-profit hospitals surveyed indicated the utilization of contributed services. Of this group, 88 percent estimated that *more than 10,000 hours of such services were received each year.*[17]

The AICPA audit and accounting guide issued in 1990 limits recognition of contributed services except in well-defined situations. Three conditions were established as a prerequisite for recording such donations (par. 2.07):

- The services performed are significant and form an integral part of the efforts of the entity as it is presently constituted; the services would be performed by salaried personnel if donated services were not available; and the entity would continue this program or activity.
- The entity controls the employment and duties of the donors and is able to influence their activities in a way comparable to the control it would exercise over employees with similar responsibilities.
- The entity has a clearly measurable basis for the amount to be recorded.

Thus, for example, if an outside accountant prepares financial statements for a health care entity for free rather than charging the normal rate of $2,500, the following journal entry would be necessary assuming that each of these three

---

[17] Jane B. Adams, Ronald J. Bossio, and Paul Rohan, *Accounting for Contributed Services: Survey of Preparers and Users of Financial Statements of Not-for-Profit Organizations* (New York: FASB, 1989), pp. 7–8.

criteria have been met. By recording the donated services as both a gain and an offsetting expense, the resulting financial statements more accurately reflect the actual cost of operating the health care entity as well as the benefit of the gift.

General Funds

Salary Expense—Accounting	2,500	
Nonoperating Gains—Donated Services		2,500

To record accountant's fees donated to hospital.

Although donated services are potentially a very significant figure, the study just mentioned also discovered that 97 percent of the not-for-profit hospitals surveyed did not assign a dollar amount to contributed services in preparing their external financial statements. Most stated that the number of volunteers caused the information to be too difficult to maintain or that the the volunteers did not replace salaried personnel.[18]

As discussed in the previous chapter, the FASB now requires the recognition of contributions by *private* not-for-profit organizations. The FASB has stated that donated services should be recognized if the services received either create or enhance nonfinancial assets or require specialized skills, are provided by individuals possessing those skills, and would need to be purchased if not provided by donation.[19]

Unrestricted Endowment Income.   The nonoperating gain category also includes any unrestricted endowment income. If expenditure of endowment earnings has not been stipulated by the donor, all income should be transferred immediately into the General Funds when earned and accounted for, at that point, as a nonoperating gain. No expenditure is required as a prerequisite for this recognition. Conversely, if spending of the income has been restricted, the transfer would have initially been made to the Specific Purpose Funds. Only at the time of expenditure is the recording made in the General Funds as an other revenue.

Income from Board-Designated Funds.   Also classified under the heading of nonoperating gains and losses are earnings derived from board-designated funds, money set aside by the governing body of a health care entity for a particular purpose. As discussed previously, these assets must remain within the General Funds because no donor restriction exists. Segregation within the balance sheet is used for informational purposes; the balance is included in the Assets Whose Use is Limited section as shown in Appendix A (Exhibit 18–1).

To demonstrate the accounting procedures applied to such funds, assume that the administration of a not-for-profit entity decides to invest $75,000 of unrestricted cash with the intention of eventually utilizing this money for the acquisition of equipment. Since the restriction is internal in nature, the assets are separated in the accounting records although remaining within the General Funds.

---

[18] Adams et al., *Survey of Preparers and Users,* pp. 10–12.

[19] FASB, Statement of Financial Accounting Standards No. 116, "Accounting for Contributions Received and Contributions Made," par. 9.

General Funds

Investments—Internally Restricted 75,000
    Cash 75,000
    To record acquisition of investments to establish board-designated fund
    in connection with future purchase of equipment.

To complete this illustration, assume that the following events occur subsequently in connection with these board-designated funds:

- Interest of $6,000 was earned on the investments.
- The investments were sold for $84,000 (increasing the amount of restricted cash from $6,000 to $90,000).
- Equipment of $150,000 was acquired. The $90,000 in internally restricted cash was applied to this purchase, and a note for $60,000 was signed for the remainder.

The following journal entries would record these transactions within the General Funds. Since no externally restricted assets were involved, no other entries are needed.

General Funds

Cash—Internally Restricted 6,000
    Nonoperating Gain—Income from Board-Designated Funds 6,000
    To recognize income earned on investments.

Cash—Internally Restricted 84,000
    Investments—Internally Restricted 75,000
    Nonoperating Gain—Gain on Board-Designated Funds 9,000
    To record sale of investments.

Equipment 150,000
    Cash—Internally Restricted 90,000
    Note Payable 60,000
    To record acquisition of equipment with board-designated funds and
    the signing of a note payable.

Accounting for Pledges

As with a college or university, a health care entity frequently receives a verbal commitment or pledge from the donor of a gift or grant prior to the physical transfer of assets. Although most of these pledges are not legally enforceable, the AICPA audit and accounting guide requires that a receivable be immediately recorded to reflect the contribution.[20] Because of the inherent uncertainty involved in collecting such receivables, an adequate provision for doubtful accounts must also be established. If the pledge is to be applied during a future period, the amount should be recorded as a deferred revenue.

---

[20] The FASB now requires that unconditional promises to give should be reported by private not-for-profit organizations.

In recording a pledge where the eventual use of the money is specified by the donor, the receivable should be presented in the appropriate restricted fund category (such as the Specific Purpose Funds) along with an increase to the temporarily or permanently restricted fund balance. Conversely, unrestricted pledges (less an allowance for uncollectibles) are reported in the financial statements of the General Funds in the period in which the pledge is made as a nonoperating gain.

Discussion Question: Is This Really an Asset?

Mercy Hospital is located near Springfield, Missouri. The hospital was created over 70 years ago by a religious organization to meet the needs of area residents who could not otherwise afford adequate health care. Although the hospital is open to the public in general, its primary mission has always been to provide medical services for the poor.

On December 23, 1995, a gentleman told the hospital's chief administrative officer the following story: "My mother has been in your hospital since October 30. The doctors have just told me that she will soon be well and can go home. I cannot tell you how relieved I am. The doctors, the nurses, and your entire staff have been just wonderful; my mother could not have gotten better care. She owes her life to your hospital.

"I am from Idaho. Now that my mother is on the road to recovery, I must return immediately to my business. I am in the process of attempting to sell an enormous tract of land in Idaho. When this acreage is sold, I will receive $15 million in cash. Because of the services that Mercy Hospital has provided for my mother, I want to make a donation of $5 million of this money." The gentlemen proceeded to write this promise on a piece of stationery that he dated and signed.

Obviously, all of the hospital's officials were overwhelmed by the gentleman's generosity. This $5 million gift was 50 times larger than the biggest gift ever received. However, the controller was a bit concerned about preparing the financial statements for 1995. "I have a lot of problems with recording this type of donation as an asset. At present, we are having serious cash flow problems; but if we show $5 million in this manner, our normal donors are going to think we have become rich and don't need their support."

What problems are involved in accounting for the $5 million pledge and how should the amount be reported by Mercy Hospital?

Financial Statements for a Health Care Entity

In concluding this coverage of the accounting for health care entities, the financial statements prepared for these institutions should be examined. Traditionally, the external reporting process has been comprised of four basic statements (as well as the accompanying footnotes):[21]

- Balance sheet (for all funds, although the separate identification of donor-restricted funds is not necessary for external reporting purposes). See Exhibit 18–1.
- Statement of revenues and expenses of general funds. See Exhibit 18–2.
- Statement of changes in fund balances (all funds). See Exhibit 18–3.
- Statement of cash flows. See Exhibit 18–4.

These statements have been designed to provide readers with complete information concerning the financial position and operations of a not-for-profit health care entity. For illustration purposes, Appendix A presents a traditional set of financial statements for a public not-for-profit hospital.

Accounting for Voluntary Health and Welfare Organizations

The final area of not-for-profit accounting concerns the reporting process used by voluntary health and welfare organizations (sometimes referred to as a VHWO). This classification includes such well-known groups as the American Heart Association, the Boy Scouts and Girl Scouts, Greenpeace, the National Multiple Sclerosis Society, the United Way, and the March of Dimes.

> Voluntary health and welfare organizations take many forms and have been developed under many and varied auspices. Basically, they are organizations formed for the purpose of performing voluntary services for various segments of society. . . . Most voluntary health and welfare organizations concentrate their efforts and expend their resources in an attempt to solve health and welfare problems of our society and, in many cases, those of specific individuals.[22]

Guidance for the accounting procedures applicable to this particular type of not-for-profit enterprise is presently provided by the AICPA's *Audits of Voluntary Health and Welfare Organizations* and the *Standards of Accounting and Financial Reporting for Voluntary Health and Welfare Organizations* published by the National Health Council, National Assembly for Social Policy and Development, and the United Way of America. Practical accounting advice is also available in *What a Difference Nonprofits Make: A Guide to Accounting Procedures* published by the Accountants for the Public Interest.

---

[21] As described in Chapter 17, the FASB now requires (for years beginning after December 15, 1994) that private not-for-profit organizations prepare the following statements for the entity as a whole: statement of financial position, statement of activities, and statement of cash flows. See Appendix B in Chapter 17. Public health care entities are not subject to the requirement.

[22] AICPA, *Audits of Voluntary Health and Welfare Organizations* (New York: AICPA, 1992), p. v.

These documents are designed primarily to describe current reporting practices rather than create numerous accounting policies. For this reason, the reporting process in use by these entities is not as precisely defined as that of hospitals and universities. A significant degree of variation exists in the financial reporting procedures utilized by voluntary health and welfare organizations operating across the country. Future pronouncements of the FASB may begin to limit the flexibility that is currently available.

Application of Generally Accepted Accounting Principles

A primary objective in accounting for voluntary health and welfare organizations is to provide contributors with a means of evaluating the utilization of resources. *What did the organization do with the money collected?* In describing this reporting process, the audit guide states that "a fundamental purpose of the financial statements, therefore, should be to disclose how the entity's resources have been acquired and used to accomplish the objectives of the organization."[23]

To satisfy this reporting goal, the audit guide concludes that the financial statements should be prepared based on the application of generally accepted accounting principles (GAAP). Thus, accrual accounting is appropriately utilized by voluntary health and welfare organizations. A note to the 1990 financial statements of the National Easter Seal Foundation confirms that "the financial statements of the National Society are prepared in accordance with generally accounted standards of accounting and financial reporting for voluntary health and welfare organizations. The accrual basis method of accounting is used."

Furthermore, as with health care entities, depreciation expense is calculated and recorded for each fiscal period. Prior to the advent of the AICPA audit guide, depreciation expense was often omitted or only recorded for those assets to be replaced from unrestricted funds. Discussing the rationale for recognizing depreciation, the audit guide stresses that outside readers of the financial statements need to be able to assess and compare the efficiency of one voluntary health and welfare organization against another:

> The relative effort being expended by one organization compared with other organizations and the allocation of such efforts to the various programs of the organization are indicated in part by cost determinations. Whenever it is relevant to measure and report the cost of rendering current services, depreciation of assets used in providing such services is relevant as an element of such measurement and reporting process. . . . Where depreciation is omitted, the cost of performing the organization's services is understated.[24]

---

[23] Ibid., par. 1.01.

[24] Ibid., par. 3.10–3.11

Comparison of Not-for-Profit Accounting—Recording of Depreciation Expense

- Colleges and universities
  The FASB requires the recognition of depreciation by private schools; the GASB holds that recognition of depreciation is optional for public schools.

- Health care entities
  Normally recognize depreciation expense although GASB holds that recognition is only optional for public entities.

- Voluntary health and welfare organizations
  Recognize depreciation expense.

Fund Accounting by Voluntary Health and Welfare Organizations

In the same manner as other not-for-profit groups, voluntary health and welfare organizations record financial transactions through the use of fund accounting. According to the 1990 financial statements for Habitat for Humanity International,

> to insure the observation of limitations and restrictions placed on the use of resources available to the organization, the accounts of the organization are maintained in accordance with the principles of fund accounting. This is the procedure by which resources for various purposes are classified for accounting and reporting purposes into funds established according to their nature and purposes.

As an introduction to this process, the following brief overview presents the typical fund categories. The structuring of these funds exhibits a strong similarity to the system found in college and university accounting. This parallel is especially evident in the current funds that are divided in both cases to segregate restricted from unrestricted assets.

1. *Current Unrestricted Fund.* The Current Unrestricted Fund classification maintains a record of all assets that are not donor restricted. However, in contrast to the accounting for health care entities, the land, buildings, and equipment of a voluntary health and welfare organization are usually maintained in a separate fund category. "The current unrestricted fund accounts for all resources over which the governing board has discretionary control to use in carrying on the operations of the organization in accordance with the limitation of its charter and by-laws except for unrestricted amounts invested in land, buildings and equipment that may be accounted for in a separate fund." [25]

   Any assets that have been internally designated by the organization's administrative board for a specific purpose remain within the Current Unrestricted Funds. Such restrictions have historically been disclosed on the organization's balance sheet by the use of separately identified fund balance accounts. For example, as of September 30, 1988, the National Multiple Sclerosis Society reported holding unrestricted net assets of $26.7 million. Two fund balance accounts were presented for this fund:

---

[25] Ibid., par. 1.03.

Fund balances:

Funds designated and committed by board for research and research fellowship grants	$15,571,416
Undesignated general fund	11,096,692

2. *Current Restricted Funds*. Current Restricted Funds account for all gifts and grants conveyed to a VHWO for a specific *operating* purpose. As an example, money given to the American Cancer Society and designated by the donor for research purposes is recorded in this particular fund. Although colleges and universities as well as health care entities defer the recognition of restricted gifts until they are appropriately spent, a different pattern is applied here. A VHWO recognizes the support immediately (at the receipt of either an asset or a pledge) unless the donor has restricted the usage until a future time period. Apparently, the proper application of the donation can be assumed in most cases.

   To illustrate, a footnote to the 1992 financial statements for the Christian Children's Fund indicates that "current restricted funds are used to account for funds restricted by donors to specific operating purposes. Such funds are recognized as revenue when received, except for gifts for children which are recognized as revenue when authorized for payment." In this case, the charity must believe that gifts for children have been restricted until actually paid.

3. *Land, Building, and Equipment Fund (or Plant Fund)*. The third fund category maintains a record of several account balances, each relating to the charity's long-lived assets:

   a. The land, buildings, and equipment possessed by the reporting entity as well as the accumulated depreciation recognized on these assets.

   b. Mortgages and other liabilities incurred by the organization in obtaining its land, buildings, and equipment.

   c. Cash, investments, pledges receivable, and other assets contributed to the organization with the restriction that the donation must be used to acquire or replace long-lived assets.

Comparison of Not-for-Profit Accounting—Reporting of Land, Buildings, and Equipment and Related Debts

• Colleges and universities	Long-lived assets are reported in a separate Investment in Plant subgroup of the Plant Funds. The Investment in Plant also reports long-term liabilities. Money to acquire fixed assets and pay debts is recorded in a separate subgroup.
• Health care entities	Long-lived assets as well as long-term liabilities are reported within the General Funds.
• Voluntary health and welfare organizations	Long-lived assets and long-term liabilities are reported in a separate Land, Building, and Equipment Fund. This fund also monitors amounts given specifically to acquire long-lived assets.

---

4. *Endowment Funds.* Once again, as in the accounting for colleges and universities as well as health care entities, Endowment Funds record grants or gifts restricted by the donor (either permanently or temporarily) so that only the income can be expended (frequently for a specified purpose).

   One of the important questions in reporting Endowment Funds is the definition of income (since that is the appropriate amount to be spent). Dividends and interest are obviously included in this computation. However, gains and losses from the sales of investments are considered as adjustments to the principal of an endowment fund unless the donor has specified that such amounts be included in the determination of income.

The funds of a voluntary health and welfare organization are not necessarily limited to the preceding four categories. For example, Custodian Funds parallel the Agency Funds found in governmental accounting. However, since other fund types are not prevalent in these organizations, no direct examination is undertaken here.

Overview of Accounting Process

Many aspects of the financial reporting used by voluntary health and welfare organizations are virtually identical to the procedures incorporated by other not-for-profit groups. The accrual of pledges, for example, as well as the recording of depreciation, has been demonstrated previously in examining the accounting for health care entities. The very use of fund accounting is the most distinctive characteristic associated with not-for-profit entities and, although voluntary health and welfare organizations have some unique funds, the process of recording transactions is similar to that of colleges and universities.

Voluntary health and welfare organizations do, however, have certain features that are not necessarily encountered in colleges, health care entities, or government units, such as:

- Donations of cash, materials, and services are normally much more significant to these organizations than to other not-for-profit groups. For most VHWOs, contributions (referred to as public support in accounting for these groups) greatly exceed any earned revenues. VHWOs rely very heavily on the generosity of individuals, foundations, and corporations. Gifts to all charities totaled $122.57 billion in the United States during 1990 alone.[26] Although not all charities are VHWOs, a large portion of this money would have been collected by such organizations.[27]

---

[26] Lourdes Lee Valeriano, "Charitable Giving Grew Only 5.75% in U.S. Last Year," *The Wall Street Journal*, September 9, 1991, p. A9.

[27] Museums, civic organizations, religious organizations, and performing arts organizations are examples of charities that do not qualify as voluntary health and welfare organizations.

- The expenses incurred by VHWOs fall naturally into two broad classifications: (1) *program service expenses* directed toward the stated objectives of the organization and (2) *supporting service expenses* for fund raising and administrative (or management and general) costs. The readers of the financial statements are interested in the amount attributed to each category as a measure of the organization's efficiency and effectiveness.

Because of such characteristics, the accounting process cannot be a mirror image of that utilized by any of the other not-for-profit groups. Rather, procedures have been developed over the years to meet the specific reporting needs of these charitable organizations.

Accounting for Public Support. As mentioned, the financial resources of a voluntary health and welfare organization are largely provided by contributions rather than from earned revenues. Because of this dependence on nonrevenue sources, public support is reported as a resource classification separate from revenues (such as membership dues, interest income, dividends, etc.). As an example, for the year ending December 31, 1990, the March of Dimes Birth Defects Foundation reported public support of more than $113 million but revenues of only $11 million. Readers of the financial statements are, thus, better able to assess a VHWO's success at generating resources. The public support category includes donations from direct mailings, door-to-door campaigns, legacies and bequests, auctions, dinners, and the like.

Whenever resources are received by a voluntary health and welfare organization, the amounts must be recorded in the appropriate fund categories. To demonstrate this process, assume that a VHWO receives the following contributions and revenues:

1. Door-to-door solicitations for the charity raise $623,000 in cash. These funds are in no way restricted by the donors.
2. At the death of a wealthy patron, a bequest of $400,000 in cash is left to the organization with the stipulation that half of the money be used to acquire a building to serve as new headquarters. The remaining funds must be invested with the earnings to be expended to feed the homeless and poor.
3. A grant of $100,000 is received from a philanthropic foundation with the provision that the money be spent on a research project that the VHWO has already started. Although this money cannot be received or expended until the next fiscal year, the organization believes that the foundation will fulfill the commitment.
4. The charity collects $90,000 in cash from its members as payment of their annual dues entitling them to belong to the organization.

To record these transactions, a voluntary health and welfare organization prepares the following journal entries. Because restrictions have been placed on several of these donations, the resources have been separated where appropriate into restricted fund categories.

1.   *Current Unrestricted Funds*

Cash 623,000
    Public Support—Contributions   623,000
    To record money received from door-to-door solicitations.

2.   *Land, Building, and Equipment Fund*

Cash 200,000
    Fund Balance—Temporarily Restricted.   200,000
    Bequest made to organization with the stipulation that the money be
    used to acquire a new headquarters building.

                             Endowment Fund

Cash 200,000
    Fund Balance—Permanently Restricted   200,000
    Bequest made to organization with the stipulation that all earnings
    on this principal to be used to feed the poor and homeless.

3.   *Current Restricted Funds*

Contributions Receivable 100,000
    Fund Balance—Temporarily Restricted   100,000
    Pledges made by foundation to support research project. Because
    this money cannot be spent until future years, contribution is
    restricted support.

4.   *Current Unrestricted Funds*

Cash 90,000
    Revenue—Membership Dues   90,000
    Annual dues received from members.

Accounting for Donated Materials.   Cash is not the only type of support relied on by VHWOs. Many organizations receive donations of materials intended either to be used by the charity itself (such as vehicles, office furniture, and typewriters) or distributed to needy groups or individuals (food, clothing, and toys). For organizations such as the Salvation Army and Goodwill Industries, these donations provide a central resource essential to the charity's ongoing operations.

Since donated supplies and other materials are given to provide support for the voluntary health and welfare organization, these contributions should be reported. If significant, donated materials are recorded as support at current fair value. The dilemma, of course, is in establishing the worth of the items being received. Although a value is sometimes apparent (for example, if a new truck is given), donations such as used clothing, furniture, and toys can be difficult to assess. For this reason, organizations that receive and distribute materials for which a market value is not easily determined may opt to record neither the contribution nor the ultimate use. However, even in these cases, information is usually retained and conveyed in the form of a memo record. Thus, although no formal journal entry was prepared, a report might disclose that a VHWO "collected 20,000 toys distributed to 7,000 families."

Assume, as an illustration, that a local voluntary health and welfare organization begins a drive to gather furniture and clothing for needy families living in the geographic area. The following items are received:

Bed	$200 fair market value
Tables and chairs	130 fair market value
New clothing	500 fair market value
Used clothing	75 estimated resale value
Total	$905

In addition, one merchant donates a new desk (with an established sales price of $400) for use in the organization's headquarters.

Since the value of these gifts has been determined, the amounts should be recorded by the VHWO through the following journal entries. Assume that the furniture and clothing are distributed to needy individuals as soon as they are received.

Current Unrestricted Funds

Inventory of Donated Materials	905	
Public Support—Contributions		905
Gifts made to organization to be distributed to needy individuals.		

Community Service Expense—Assistance		
to Needy	905	
Inventory of Donated Materials		905
Distribution of furniture and clothing is made to needy individuals.		

Land, Building, and Equipment Fund

Furniture	400	
Fund Balance—Temporarily Restricted		400
Organization receives gift of desk for its own use. Public support will be recognized over life of assets.		

Accounting for Donated Services.　　Donated services are also an especially significant means of support for most VHWOs.[28] The number of volunteers working in some organizations can reach into the thousands. Charities often rely heavily on these individuals to fill administrative positions as well as to serve in massive fund-raising efforts. As with donated materials, an appropriate method for reporting such services is not readily apparent. Merely arriving at a monetary value for the work being done can prove to be a difficult task. To provide a consistent

---

[28] The guidelines described here for donated materials and donated services are based on the AICPA industry audit guide, *Audits of Voluntary Health and Welfare Organizations.* As mentioned in the section on health care entities, FASB rules will take effect for private not-for-profit organizations for years beginning after December 15, 1994.

accounting treatment, formal recognition is structured according to set guidelines consistent with those shown previously for health care entities. To be recognized, three specific criteria must be met:

1. The services performed are a normal part of either the VHWO's program or supporting services and would otherwise be performed by salaried personnel.
2. The organization exercises control over the employment and duties of the individual.
3. The VHWO has a clearly measurable basis for the amount being recognized as a donation.[29]

Because of these guidelines, a significant amount of donated services go unrecorded. For example, entries are not usually made to reflect services provided by volunteer fund-raisers who participate in door-to-door solicitations. Determining a fair value for such activities is virtually impossible and these workers rarely replace salaried personnel. The 1990 financial statements of the American Cancer Society includes a disclosure common to many VHWOs:

> A substantial number of volunteers have donated significant amounts of their time in the Society's program services and in its fund-raising campaigns. However, since no objective basis exists for recording and assigning values to their services, they are not reflected in the accompanying combined financial statements. Similarly, the value of space and time contributed by various media for Society educational and fund-raising messages is not subject to control or measurement and has not been recorded.

Despite common practice, the preceding criteria would require a voluntary health and welfare organization to record, for example, the value of accounting services donated to it by a Certified Public Accountant. If not for the assistance supplied by this volunteer, the charity would have to pay an individual to do the job. The work is most likely under the control of the organization, and the value of the services being performed can be determined based on standard billing rates. Thus, assuming that a $2,000 value is assigned to this person's efforts, the following journal entry is appropriate:

Current Unrestricted Funds

Expenses—Professional Fees 2,000
    Public Support—Contributions.   2,000
    To record value of services donated by accountant.

Recording Expenses and Expenditures

Another aspect of the accounting process for voluntary health and welfare organizations differs from that used by health care entities: the handling of expenses and expenditures. In VHWOs, these transactions are not funneled exclusively into a

---

[29] AICPA, *Audits of Voluntary Health and Welfare Organizations,* par. 5.05.

single fund. Most voluntary health and welfare organizations receive a majority of their financing through freely given contributions often restricted by the donors for stipulated purposes. The proper use of this money is more likely to be ensured by the maintenance of separate funds.

Consequently, the recording of a VHWO's expenses and expenditures (as well as its public support and revenues) is spread across several fund categories. The acquisition of a building, as an example, is accounted for in the Land, Building, and Equipment Fund, whereas the cost of a designated research project is monitored in the Current Restricted Funds.

To demonstrate these procedures, assume that $200,000 is spent by a voluntary health and welfare organization to purchase an office building. Of this amount, $80,000 had been received at an earlier date as a gift restricted by the donor for this acquisition. The remaining cost is covered by the signing of a long-term note. This transaction is recorded by means of the following entry:

Land, Building, and Equipment Fund

Building.	200,000	
Cash		80,000
Note Payable		120,000

Acquisition of building using restricted resources and the signing of a note.

In the same manner, the spending of resources restricted by an outside donor for a specific operating purpose is accounted for entirely within the Current Restricted Funds. This handling is the same as in a college or university but different from a health care entity where the General Funds category records all expenditures. As an illustration of VHWO accounting, assume that $140,000 is contributed to one of these organizations with the stipulation that specific research is to be performed. The receipt of this donation as well as the eventual expenditure are entered into the financial records of the VHWO as follows:

Current Restricted Funds
Initial Entry

Cash	140,000	
Public Support—Contributions*		140,000

To record receipt of donation restricted for research project.

Subsequent Entry

Program Service Expense—Research	140,000	
Cash		140,000

To record expenditure of restricted resources as stipulated by donor.

* As previously indicated, this voluntary health and welfare organization will record temporarily restricted net assets of $140,000 if expenditure is restricted to a future fiscal period.

Reporting the Expenses of a Voluntary Health and Welfare Organization

A large number of voluntary health and welfare organizations operate throughout the world. The purpose of each is to achieve one or more stated objectives such as the cure of a particular disease or the cleanup of the environment. Many individuals (especially current and potential contributors) are interested in assessing the utilization of the money a VHWO receives. They want to know:

- Which of these organizations should receive money and how much?
- Is contributing to a particular charity a wise allocation of resources?
- Will donated funds be used effectively by an organization to accomplish its specified purpose or will the money be wasted?

Such questions are faced by every voluntary health and welfare organization. Future gifts and grants are based, at least in part, on the organization's ability to convince donors that resources are being used wisely to accomplish stated goals.

Financial statements certainly reflect a VHWO's attempt to reach its objectives by reporting the resources generated and the spending decisions that have been made. To this end, a voluntary health and welfare organization has traditionally produced a *balance sheet* (Exhibit 18–5) as well as a *statement of support, revenue, and expenses and changes in fund balances* (Exhibit 18–6). However, because expenses are recorded within several fund categories, readers analyzing this second statement might have considerable difficulty in evaluating the actual use made of donated and other monetary resources. For this reason, a separate *statement of functional expenses* (Exhibit 18–7) is also prepared by voluntary health and welfare organizations.[30] As shown in Appendix B of this chapter, this statement discloses the charity's expenses without regard for funds or fund types. Complete data is made available to assist readers in evaluating the organization's efforts to achieve its stated purposes.

The statement of functional expenses initially divides all expenses incurred by a voluntary health and welfare organization into two broad categories:

- Program services expenses.
- Supporting service expenses.

The program service classification includes expenses of the VHWO that relate to the organization's basic objectives. Within this category, organizations may report several programs or only one. In this manner, an interested party can easily ascertain the charity's goals and the monetary amounts allocated to meet each. As an example, the Richmond (Virginia) Goodwill Industries indicated three different program services in its 1990 statement of functional expenses:

---

[30] As described in Chapter 17, the FASB has required that private not-for-profit organizations prepare the following statements for the entity as a whole: statement of financial position, statement of activities, and statement of cash flows. However, the FASB has stated that VHWOs should continue to produce a statement of functional expenses. See Appendix B in Chapter 17.

Industrial Workshops—Donated Goods

Industrial Workshops—Contracts and Customs

Vocational Rehabilitation Services

Each voluntary health and welfare organization must also report (within this same statement of functional expenses) all expenses that relate to supporting services, those costs of running the charity that are not directly related to one of its stated goals. These expenses are normally split into two subgroups: (1) management and general expenses and (2) fund-raising expenses. Thus, readers of the statements are better able to assess the use made of the organization's resources for purposes other than its objectives.

The informational content of this statement can be demonstrated by looking at the 1990 financial statements for the American Red Cross. The statement of functional expenses for this VHWO discloses the following allocation of resources between program services and supporting services:

Program Services	*Total Expenses*
Services to members of the armed forces, veterans, and their families	$ 74,949,000
Disaster services	224,159,000
Biomedical services	741,175,000
Health services	115,970,000
Community volunteers	60,768,000
International services	7,484,000
Total program services	$1,224,505,000
Supporting Services	
Membership and fund-raising	$ 35,291,000
Management and general	69,120,000
Total supporting services	$ 104,411,000

Thus, a potential donor for the American Red Cross can see that approximately 92 percent of this VHWO's total expenses (approximately $1.225 million out of total expenses of $1.329 million) were spent in connection with the various program services supported by the organization.

Interestingly, one aspect of the statement of functional expenses has become quite controversial in the last few years. Until 1987, the costs of direct mailings and other solicitations made to potential donors that provided information about the charity and its purposes as well as a request for funds were allocated solely to fund-raising. Thus, when producing the statement of functional expenses, fund-raising costs tended to be quite high for many organizations. This approach

was originally adopted in 1964 by the voluntary health and welfare industry in the industry's Standards as a practical solution to a credibility problem that existed then.

The industry responded to public criticism by not permitting the reported costs of fund-raising to be less than they would otherwise be solely because public education efforts were structured in a way that would absorb fund-raising costs.[31]

In 1987, the Accounting Standards Division of the AICPA changed this requirement stating that joint costs could be allocated between fund-raising and program service expenses if "it can be demonstrated that a bona fide program or management and general function has been conducted in conjunction with the appeal for funds."[32] Apparently, this group believed that proper accounting should not be subjugated simply because VHWOs wanted to avoid public criticism. If a cost was expended for both a program service and a supporting service, an allocation in some manner was deemed to be appropriate. Unfortunately, no specific guidance for making this allocation was proposed.

Almost immediately, a great many charities started reporting an additional program service usually with a title such as professional or public education. Direct mailings and other solicitations could now be charged partially to program services as long as educational materials were included with the request for funds. Costs that had been previously recorded as fund-raising were now shown as program services. The methods of allocation have varied significantly; some have been considered dubious. Criticism of this practice has been harsh:

> As so often happens with solicitations for charities, a great deal of the money raised is spent to raise the money. Now, because of changes in accounting rules, charities can pass many of those expenses off as "public education." Such practices are legal but might come as a surprise to millions of Americans who reply to solicitations with personal checks.[33]

> There is a growing concern on the part of states' attorneys general that some charitable organizations have been "too liberal" in allocating costs to program expenses (instead of to administration or fund-raising), particularly costs to educate the public. Without objective guidelines, auditors have difficulty determining the reasonableness of nonprofit organizations' joint cost allocations.[34]

From an accounting perspective, the rationale for allocating joint costs is easy to understand. If both a program service and a supporting service are being carried out by a single cost, it should be divided between them in some manner. Unfortunately, the use of this rule by some charities to reduce the amount that appears as fund-raising costs is probably not surprising. However, the outcome of this change does indicate that all accounting rules can be used by many organizations to place themselves in the best possible light.

---

[31] AICPA, *Statement of Position 87–2*, "Accounting for Joint Costs of Informational Materials and Activities of Not-for-Profit Organizations that Include a Fund-Raising Appeal," issued August 21, 1987, par. 8.

[32] Ibid., par. 15.

[33] Cynthia Crossen, "Organized Charities Pass Off Mailing Costs as 'Public Education'," *The Wall Street Journal,* October 29, 1990, p. A1.

[34] Dennis P. Tishlias, "Reasonable Joint Cost Allocations in Nonprofits," *Journal of Accountancy,* November 1992, p. 65.

Summary

1. A major influence on the current development of accounting for health care entities is the presence of third-party payors such as insurance companies and Medicare, groups that bear a significant portion of the health care costs in this country. To satisfy the informational needs of these as well as other interested parties, the financial statements produced by not-for-profit health care entities are prepared according to generally accepted accounting principles. Although fund accounting is still utilized, revenues and expenses are recorded based on accrual accounting. In addition, depreciation expense is calculated and recognized for each time period.

2. The funds of a health care provider are divided into two general categories: General Funds that account for normal operating activities and Donor-Restricted Funds that monitor the financial resources given to an entity for specified uses. Health care accounting is unique in that Donor-Restricted Funds merely serve to maintain the assets being held for each stipulated purpose. All revenues, expenditures, and expenses as well as all assets (except those specially restricted) and all liabilities are reported within the General Funds.

3. The revenues of a health care entity are traditionally separated into three broad classifications: (1) patient service revenues, (2) other revenues, and (3) nonoperating gains and losses. Patient service revenues include fees charged for surgery, nursing services, X rays, and the like. For financial reporting purposes, the patient service revenues are reported net of reductions for contractual adjustments. Contractual adjustments arise as a result of agreements with third-party payors whereby the entity accepts (as payment in full) a reduced amount if a lesser figure is assessed to be reasonable for either the diagnosis or the services rendered. Bad debts are now reported as separate expenses rather than as a reduction in patient service revenues. Amounts for charity care that were never intended to be collected are no longer recognized as either revenues or reductions.

4. Other revenues are generated by activities that are major and central to ongoing operations but do not relate directly to patient care. Sources would include educational programs, gift shops, cafeterias, and parking garages. In addition, the fair market value of donated items such as medicine or supplies are reported as other revenues. Grants or gifts awarded to a hospital for a specific operating purpose are also included in this category. However, these contributed resources are maintained in one of the Donor-Restricted Funds until appropriate disbursement is made. At that time, both the revenue and expenditure are recorded in the General Funds. The Donor-Restricted Funds only show increases and decreases in their fund balances.

5. The nonoperating gains and losses category is used by a health care entity to report all unrestricted grants and gifts as well as any donated services. However, donated services can only be recognized by private organizations if certain criteria now specified by the FASB are met. Also classified as nonoperating gains are investment income and earnings derived from board-designated funds. These resources are identified by the governing board for a particular purpose and are separated within General Funds as "assets whose use is limited."

6. This chapter concludes with coverage of the accounting procedures utilized by voluntary health and welfare organizations (VHWOs). Each of these groups is created in hopes of resolving specific health and welfare problems of our society. Although these organizations use fund accounting, they apply generally accepted accounting principles including accrual accounting and the recognition of depreciation expense.

7. At least four different types of funds are normally maintained by a voluntary health and welfare organization. Current Unrestricted Funds account for operating resources over which the charity has discretionary control. The Current Restricted Funds also record operating resources but these assets have been conveyed by an outside donor for a specified purpose. A third category—the Land, Building, and Equipment Fund—reports the costs and accumulated depreciation of all long-lived assets as well as any liabilities incurred to acquire these properties. This fund also maintains a record of monetary amounts donated to the organization with the stipulation that expenditure must be for acquisition or replacement of plant assets. The Endowment Funds record gifts or grants awarded with the restriction that only subsequent income can be spent.

8. A significant portion of the resources generated by most voluntary health and welfare organizations is derived from contributions. Because of the nature of the inflows, these amounts are disclosed within the financial statements as public support rather than revenues. The revenue designation is only appropriate when an earning process is present such as in the collection of interest income, dividends, or dues. Often, public support is conveyed to VHWOs in the form of contributed materials that should be recorded at fair market value. Donated services can also be furnished to a voluntary health and welfare organization and should be recorded if the FASB's criteria are met. To reflect the impact of donated services, both the public support and the normal expense are recorded simultaneously.

9. Many individuals (donors, trustees, administrators, etc.) are interested in evaluating the utilization made of the resources raised by a voluntary health and welfare organization. For this reason, a statement of functional expenses is normally prepared to accompany the balance sheet and the statement of support, revenue, and expenses and changes in fund balance. This statement divides all expenses into two broad classifications: program service expenses (incurred in connection with the stated purposes of the VHWO) and supporting service expenses (incurred in running the organization). By reporting these two categories separately, the application of an enterprise's assets can be more easily ascertained. In recent years, a controversy has grown up surrounding this statement. VHWOs are now allowed to allocate a portion of the costs of fund-raising appeals to program services if educational or informational material is included. Critics hold that this practice allows the organization to label fund-raising costs as program services.

Comprehensive Illustration 1

PROBLEM   (Estimated Time: 30 to 35 Minutes)

Bethlehem Hospital, located in the southern part of Indiana, is operated by a group of counties. The hospital was started a number of years ago with the primary objective of offering medical care to the underprivileged. In addition, the hospital serves the needs of the local area and, in recent years, it has undertaken research into the cure of several normally fatal children's diseases.

During 1995, the hospital has the following financial transactions. Prepare all necessary journal entries and indicate the fund category in which each entry is being recorded.

1. A local business donated $3,000 in sheets, towels, and other linens to the hospital.
2. A $600,000 pledge was made to the hospital to support general operating costs. Of this total, $100,000 in cash was received immediately with the remainder to be paid over the next 10 years for use in those future periods.
3. The hospital rendered $900,000 in services to patients. The administration estimated that 60 percent will never be collected because many patients lack the financial resources to pay. Of the remainder, $300,000 was due from third-party payors. Because of contractual arrangements, officials anticipate that only 90 percent of this balance will be received.
4. A gift of $800,000 in cash was received by the hospital. Half of this amount was restricted to research with the remainder to be applied to the cost of a new wing being added to the hospital.
5. The hospital administration invested $200,000 of unrestricted cash. According to these officials, future earnings will be used to help pay for the new hospital wing.
6. Payment of $245,000 was received from 1994 charges made to third-party payors. Originally, these groups had been billed $270,000, but subsequent audits indicated that the lower amount constituted reasonable costs for the services rendered. The hospital originally estimated in 1994 that collection would be $252,000.
7. Citizens of the counties that operate the hospital volunteered their services in various maintenance capacities normally performed by salaried employees. The value of the work being done was set at $18,000.
8. The new hospital wing was completed at a cost of $1 million. The $400,000 gift in (4) was used as a partial payment. Additionally, the

hospital sold the investments in (5) for $250,000 with the proceeds also being applied to the cost of the wing. A note payable was signed for the remainder.

Comprehensive Illustration 1

SOLUTION 1

1.   *General Funds*

Inventory of Supplies	3,000	
Other Revenues—Donations		3,000

To recognize fair market value of donated linens.

2.   *General Funds*

Cash.	100,000	
Contributions Receivable	500,000	
Nonoperating Gain—Unrestricted Grant.		100,000
Fund Balance—Temporarily Restricted		500,000

To record $100,000 donation along with pledge for $500,000 in additional funding.

3.   *General Funds*

Accounts Receivable—Patients.	600,000	
Accounts Receivable—Third Party Payors	300,000	
Patient Service Revenues		900,000

To accrue billings for current period at standard rates.

Contractual Adjustments.	30,000	
Allowance for Uncollectible and Reduced Accounts		30,000

To recognize estimation of accounts that will not be collected from third-party payors.

Patient Service Revenues	540,000	
Accounts Receivable—Patients.		540,000

To remove amount for charity care where no intention exists to collect.

4.   *Specific-Purpose Funds*

Cash.	400,000	
Fund Balance—Temporarily Restricted for Research Grants		400,000

Gift made to hospital with provision that it be spent for research.

Plant Replacement and Expansion Funds

Cash.	400,000	
Fund Balance—Temporarily Restricted for Hospital Addition		400,000

To record donation restricted for payment on new hospital wing.

5.   *General Funds*

Investments—Internally Restricted 200,000

    Cash. 200,000

To record collection board-designated fund is established to finance wing being added to hospital.

6.   *General Funds*

Cash. 245,000

Allowance for Uncollectible and

    Reduced Accounts 25,000

        Accounts Receivable—Third-Party Payors. 270,000

To record collection of prior year receivables from third-party payors after reduction for contractual adjustments.

7.   *General Funds*

Salary Expenses—Maintenance 18,000

    Nonoperating Gain—Donated Services 18,000

Volunteer work performed by citizens.

8.   *Plant Replacement and Expansion Funds*

Fund Balance—Temporarily Restricted for Hospital Addition 400,000

    Cash. 400,000

To transfer recording of funds expended for new hospital wing.

General Funds

Cash. 400,000

    Fund Balance—Temporarily Restricted for Plant 400,000

To record restricted funds now to be applied to new hospital wing.

Cash. 250,000

    Investments—Internally Restricted 200,000

    Nonoperating Gain on Board-Designated Funds 50,000

Investments are sold so that proceeds can be applied to cost of new hospital wing.

Buildings. 1,000,000

    Cash. 650,000

    Note Payable. 350,000

To record acquisition of new hospital wing.

Comprehensive Illustration 2

PROBLEM   (Estimated Time: 20 to 30 Minutes)

At the beginning of 1995, the residents of Duling, Georgia, created a voluntary health and welfare organization to minister to the needs of the town's elderly citizens. A volunteer bookkeeper maintained the accounting records and produced the following trial balance at the end of the first year of operation. All journal entries have been recorded solely within the Current Unrestricted Funds.

	Debit	Credit
Cash	$ 15,000	
Investments.	32,000	
Furniture and fixtures	18,000	
Accounts payable		$ 17,000
Notes payable—Long term		18,000
Revenues.		65,000
Program service expenses	25,000	
Supporting service expenses	10,000	
Totals	$100,000	$100,000

The following information concerns the financial activities of this VHWO during the period:

1. Investment income of $3,000 was earned and recorded. In addition, a $5,000 donation was given with the stipulation that the money had to be used to pay for feeding the elderly. Although this money is still being held, the organization has definite plans to spend the gift for the designated purpose. The remaining revenues reported in the trial balance represent unrestricted contributions made by the public.

2. The furniture and fixtures were acquired at the beginning of the current period by the signing of the note payable. These assets have a five-year life and no salvage value. Depreciation (which is considered a supporting service expense) has not been recorded.

3. A pledge of $10,000 was given to the charity by a wealthy resident. The money is unrestricted but will not be received and cannot be used until 1997. No record has yet been prepared for this future contribution.

4. New clothing with a fair market value of $5,000 was donated by a local department store and immediately disbursed to needy individuals. Again, no journal entry was recorded.

5. Local citizens contribute their time each week to answer the telephone for the charity and perform other routine clerical tasks. No fair market value could be established for these services.

6. A total of $2,000 was paid for heating oil which was distributed to several elderly residents. The bookkeeper charged this entire amount to supporting service expenses.

Required:

Prepare adjusting entries to correct the accounting records of this voluntary health and welfare organization. Indicate the fund category in which each entry is recorded.

SOLUTION 2

1.   *Current Unrestricted Funds*

Revenues 5,000
    Cash   5,000
To remove the recording of a donation restricted for feeding the
elderly.

Revenues 57,000
    Public Support—Contributions   57,000
To reclassify amounts received as donations ($60,000 adjusted
amount less $3,000 investment income).

Current Restricted Funds

Cash 5,000
    Fund Balance—Temporarily Restricted   5,000
To record contribution restricted for feeding elderly citizens.

2.   *Current Unrestricted Funds*

Notes Payable—Long Term 18,000
    Furniture and Fixtures   18,000
To remove fixed assets and long-term liabilities from the Current
Unrestricted Funds.

Land, Building, and Equipment Fund

Furniture and Fixtures 18,000
    Notes Payable—Long Term   18,000
To record acquisition of furniture and fixtures through the signing of
a note.

Supporting Services Expenses—Depreciation 3,600
    Accumulated Depreciation   3,600
Depreciation expense is recorded for the year of 1995. The $18,000
cost of furniture and fixtures is being allocated over a five-year
period.

3.   *Current Unrestricted Funds*

Contributions Receivable 10,000
    Fund Balance—Temporarily Restricted   10,000
Gift is promised to charity to be received in 1997.

4.   *Current Unrestricted Funds*

Program Service Expenses—Clothing 5,000
    Public Support   5,000
To record donation of new clothing already distributed.

5. No entry is recorded here since the fair market value of the donated services cannot be
determined.

6.   *Current Unrestricted Funds*

Program Service Expenses—Heating Oil 2,000
    Supporting Service Expenses.   2,000
To reclassify the cost of heating oil given to needy individuals.

APPENDIX A
FINANCIAL STATEMENTS FOR A GOVERNMENTAL NOT-FOR-PROFIT HOSPITAL

Following is an illustrative set of financial statements as might be produced by a governmental not-for-profit hospital. This example is based on the illustrations provided in the AICPA audit and accounting guide, *Audits of Providers of Health Care Services*. Notes that accompany such financial statements are not being presented here. In 1993, statements for private not-for-profit were established by the FASB. Examples are shown in Appendix B of the previous chapter.

EXHIBIT 18–1

MIDLOTHIAN HOSPITAL
Balance Sheet
December 31, 1995, with Comparative Figures for December 31, 1994

	December 31, 1995	December 31, 1994		December 31, 1995	December 31, 1994
Assets			**Liabilities and Fund Balances**		
		General Funds			
Current assets:			Current liabilities:		
Cash	$ 104,000	$ 72,000	Notes payable	$ 190,000	$ 170,000
Receivables (less $106,000 and			Accounts payable	309,000	323,000
$84,000 estimated uncollectible			Accrued expenses	84,000	16,000
and other allowances)	991,000	946,000	Total current liabilities	583,000	509,000
Inventories	89,000	114,000	Deferred liabilities:		
Total current assets	1,184,000	1,132,000	Third-party reimbursement	118,000	69,000
Assets whose use is limited:			Long-term debt:		
By board for capital			Bonds payable	600,000	600,000
improvements	312,000	211,000	Notes payable	3,060,000	2,980,000
Under indenture agreement	510,000	460,000	Total long-term liabilities	3,660,000	3,580,000
Total assets whose use is			Fund balance	6,374,000	5,943,000
limited	822,000	671,000		$10,735,000	$10,101,000
Net property, plant, and equipment:	8,729,000	8,298,000			
	$10,735,000	$10,101,000			
		Donor-Restricted Funds			
Specific-purpose funds:			*Specific-purpose funds:*		
Cash	$ 12,600	$ 1,090	Fund balances:		
Investments	174,600	169,800	Research grants	$ 60,000	$ 50,000
			Other	127,200	120,890
	$ 187,200	$ 170,890		$ 187,200	$ 170,890
Plant Replacement and Expansion funds:			*Plant replacement and expansion funds:*		
Cash	$ 22,000	$ 190,000	Fund balance	$ 757,000	$ 681,000
Investments	640,000	491,000			
Pledges receivable, net of					
estimated uncollectibles of					
$10,000 in 1995	95,000	–0–		$ 757,000	$ 681,000
	$ 757,000	$ 681,000			
Endowment funds:			*Endowment funds:*		
Cash	$ 10,000	–0–	Fund balances:		
Investments	978,000	880,000	Permanently restricted	$ 908,000	$ 810,000
			Temporarily restricted	80,000	70,000
Total endowment funds	$ 988,000	$ 880,000	Total endowment funds	$ 988,000	$ 880,000

EXHIBIT 18–2

MIDLOTHIAN HOSPITAL
Statement of Revenues and Expenses of General Funds
For Year Ended December 31, 1995 and 1994

	1995	1994
Net patient service revenue*	$ 5,480,000	$5,117,000
Other revenue	190,000	118,000
Total revenue	5,670,000	5,235,000
Expenses:		
Professional care of patients	3,675,000	3,666,000
Dietary services	757,000	498,000
Administrative services	791,000	854,000
Medical malpractice costs	410,000	266,000
Depreciation	626,000	488,000
Interest	170,000	160,000
Provision for bad debts	300,000	200,000
Total operating expenses	6,729,000	6,132,000
Loss from operations	(1,059,000)	(897,000)
Nonoperating Gains:		
Unrestricted gifts and bequests	960,000	912,000
Income on investments:		
Whose use is limited by board for capital improvements	93,000	76,000
Whose use is limited under indenture agreement	84,000	79,000
Total nonoperating gains	1,137,000	1,067,000
Revenue and gains in excess of expenses	$ 78,000	$ 170,000

* Patient service revenue less contractual adjustments.

EXHIBIT 18-3

MIDLOTHIAN HOSPITAL
Statement of Changes in Fund Balances
Years Ended December 31, 1995 and 1994

| | 1995 | | | | 1994 | | | |
| | | Donor-Restricted Funds | | | | Donor-Restricted Funds | | |
	General Funds	Specific-Purpose Funds	Plant Replacement and Expansion Funds	Endowment Funds	General Funds	Specific-Purpose Funds	Plant Replacement and Expansion Funds	Endowment Funds
Balances at beginning of year	$5,943,000	$170,890	$ 681,000	$ 880,000	$5,609,000	$121,390	$ 613,000	$748,000
Additions:								
Excess of revenues over expenses	78,000	—	—	—	170,000	—	—	—
Restricted gifts and bequests	—	29,910	373,000	46,000	—	40,600	198,000	81,000
Research grants	—	10,000	—	—	—	15,000	—	—
Income from investments	—	16,400	56,000	77,000	—	11,900	34,000	63,000
Transferred to finance property, plant, and equipment expenditures	353,000	—	(353,000)	—	164,000	—	(164,000)	—
	6,374,000	227,200	757,000	1,003,000	5,943,000	188,890	681,000	892,000
Deductions:								
Transferred to General Funds as other revenue	—	(40,000)	—	(15,000)	—	(18,000)	—	(12,000)
Balances at end of year	$6,374,000	$187,200	$ 757,000	$ 988,000	$5,943,000	$170,890	$ 681,000	$880,000

EXHIBIT 18–4

MIDLOTHIAN HOSPITAL
Statements of Cash Flows (Indirect Method)
For Years Ended December 31, 1995 and 1994

	1995	1994
Cash flow from operating activities and gains and losses:		
Revenue and gains in excess of expenses and losses	$ 78,000	$ 170,000
Adjustments to reconcile revenue and gains in excess of expenses to net cash provided by operating activities and gains and losses:		
Depreciation	626,000	488,000
Deferred third-party reimbursement—Increase	49,000	11,000
Increase in receivables.	(45,000)	(22,000)
Decrease in inventories	25,000	56,000
Decrease in accounts payable.	(14,000)	(23,000)
Increase in accrued expenses.	68,000	16,000
Net cash provided by operating activities and gains and losses . .	787,000	696,000
Cash flows from investing activities:		
Acquisition of property and equipment	(1,057,000)	(719,000)
Less: Property and equipment financed by donor-restricted assets . .	353,000	164,000
Cash outflows for property and equipment	(704,000)	(555,000)
Increase in assets whose use is limited	(151,000)	(66,000)
Net cash used by investing activities	(855,000)	(621,000)
Cash flows from financing activities:		
Repayment of long-term debt.	(200,000)	(320,000)
Issuance of long-term debt	300,000	175,000
Net cash generated (used) by financing activities:	100,000	(145,000)
Change in cash	32,000	(70,000)
Beginning cash	72,000	142,000
Ending cash	$ 104,000	$ 72,000

APPENDIX B
FINANCIAL STATEMENTS FOR A NOT-FOR-PROFIT VOLUNTARY HEALTH AND WELFARE ORGANIZATION

Following are the financial statements for the Christian Children's Fund for June 26, 1992, and the year then ended. These statements are provided as examples of the financial reporting appropriate for a not-for-profit voluntary health and welfare organization. The notes that accompanied these statements have not been included here. In 1993, statements for private not-for-profit organizations were established by the FASB. Examples are shown in Appendix B of the previous chapter. The FASB has indicated that voluntary health and welfare organizations should continue to produce a statement of functional expenses.

EXHIBIT 18–5

CHRISTIAN CHILDREN'S FUND, INC.
Balance Sheet
June 26, 1992

	Current Funds		Land, Buildings, and Equipment Funds	Endowment Funds	Total All Funds
	Unrestricted	*Restricted*			
Assets					
Cash and short-term investments	$ 5,996,939	$4,739,871	—	$ 390,262	$11,127,072
Investments, at cost	9,362,255	—	—	1,166,884	10,529,139
Accrued interest and other receivables	1,016,313	—	—	—	1,016,313
Prepaid expenses and other assets	1,636,952	—	—	—	1,636,952
Advances to affiliates	16,107	—	—	—	16,107
Land, buildings, and equipment, at cost, less accumulated depreciation	—	—	$16,506,112	—	16,506,112
Total assets	$18,028,566	$4,739,871	$16,506,112	$1,557,146	$40,831,695
Liabilities and Fund Balances					
Liabilities					
Accounts payable	537,697	—	—	—	537,697
Accrued salaries and related expenses	521,549	—	—	—	521,549
Accrued severance pay—Overseas employees	387,861	—	—	—	387,861
Accrued subsidy and program grants.	—	93,615	—	—	93,615
Accrued interest.	—	—	66,178	—	66,178
Deferred sponsorship contributions	7,648,471	—	—	—	7,648,471
Deferred revenue—Gifts for children	—	700,056	—	—	700,056
Deferred revenue—Other.	262,648	—	—	—	262,648
Bonds payable	—	—	5,560,000	—	5,560,000
Total liabilities and deferred revenue.	9,358,226	793,671	5,626,178	—	15,778,075
Fund Balances					
Designated by board of directors	239,993	—	—	—	239,993
Undesignated	8,430,347	—	—	—	8,430,347
Restricted.	—	3,946,200	—	—	3,946,200
Endowment—Term	—	—	—	44,948	44,948
Endowment—Perpetual	—	—	—	1,512,198	1,512,198
Land, buildings, and equipment	—	—	10,879,934	—	10,879,934
Total fund balances	8,670,340	3,946,200	10,879,934	1,557,146	25,053,620
Total fund balances and liabilities	$18,028,566	$4,739,871	$16,506,112	$1,557,146	$40,831,695

Accompanying notes have not been included.

EXHIBIT 18–6

CHRISTIAN CHILDREN'S FUND, INC.
Statement of Support, Revenue, and Expenses and Changes in Fund Balances
Period from July 1, 1991 to June 26, 1992

	Current Funds		Land, Buildings, and Equipment Funds	Endowment Funds	Total All Funds
	Unrestricted	*Restricted*			
Public Support and Revenue					
Public support					
Sponsorship contributions	$75,683,573	—	—	—	$ 75,683,573
Other contributions	4,512,753	$8,773,377	—	$ 160,875	13,447,005
Gifts-in-kind	3,489,475	—	—	—	3,489,475
Bequests	730,601	88,328	—	—	818,929
Total public support	84,416,402	8,861,705	—	160,875	93,438,982
Payments from foreign affiliates	7,101,295	842,842	—	—	7,944,137
Other revenue:					
Interest and dividends	1,661,487	—	—	—	1,661,487
Gain on sales of property, net	—	—	230,048	—	230,048
Gain on investment transactions	447,743	—	—	—	447,743
Gain on foreign exchange transactions, net	1,975,898	—	—	—	1,975,898
Recovery of supporting services costs (1991, $856,842)	423,923	(423,923)	—	—	—
Other	396,293	—	—	—	396,293
Total other revenue	4,905,344	(423,923)	230,048	—	4,711,469
Total public support and revenue	96,423,041	9,280,624	230,048	160,875	106,094,588
Expenses					
Program services for:					
Children's support in the family	66,227,710	8,077,720	600,543	—	74,905,973
Children's education	7,920,260	816,644	70,613	—	8,807,517
Homeless children	428,522	55,933	3,915	—	488,370
Total program expenses	74,576,492	8,950,297	675,071	—	84,201,860
Supporting services:					
Fund-raising	10,721,940	—	95,727	—	10,817,667
Management and general	9,031,350	—	982,175	—	10,013,525
Total supporting services	19,753,290	—	1,077,902	—	20,831,192
Total expenses	94,329,782	8,950,297	1,752,973	—	105,033,052
Excess (deficiency) of public support and revenue over expenses	2,093,259	330,327	(1,522,925)	160,875	
Other changes in fund balances:					
Mandatory transfer for debt service	(851,367)	—	851,367	—	
Transfer of proceeds from sale of property and equipment	1,476,904	—	(1,476,904)	—	
Property and equipment acquistions, net . .	(1,010,321)	—	1,010,321	—	
Fund balances at June 30, 1991	6,961,865	3,615,873	12,018,075	1,396,271	
Fund balances at June 30, 1992	$ 8,670,340	$3,946,200	$10,879,934	$1,557,146	

Accompanying notes have not been included.

EXHIBIT 18–7

CHRISTIAN CHILDREN'S FUND, INC.
Statement of Functional Expenses
Period from July 1, 1991 to June 26, 1992

	Program Services				Supporting Services			Total Program and Supporting Services
	Children's Support in the Family	Children's Education	Homeless Children	Total	Fund-Raising	Management and General	Total	
Subsidy for children	$61,820,147	$7,268,871	$403,054	$69,492,072	—	—	—	$69,492,072
Program grants	2,511,298	295,281	16,373	2,822,952	—	—	—	2,822,952
Supplies	170,365	20,032	1,111	191,508	$200,846	$238,643	$439,489	630,997
Occupancy	392,544	46,156	2,559	441,259	81,191	634,797	715,988	1,157,247
Professional services	52,335	6,154	341	58,830	51,260	88,056	139,316	198,146
Contract services	479,890	56,426	3,129	539,445	470,038	807,441	1,277,479	1,816,924
Travel	597,691	70,277	3,897	671,865	60,123	81,468	141,591	813,456
Conferences and meetings	126,030	14,819	822	141,671	16,340	22,141	38,481	180,152
Automobile and truck expense	259,994	30,570	1,695	292,259	7,275	3,577	10,852	303,111
Advertising	418,354	49,190	2,728	470,272	7,591,825	748,844	8,340,669	8,810,941
Equipment rentals	174,899	20,565	1,140	196,604	21,776	470,735	492,511	689,115
Telephone and cables	105,380	12,391	687	118,458	124,234	147,613	271,847	390,305
Postage and freight	735,158	86,441	4,793	826,392	866,690	1,029,790	1,896,480	2,722,872
Staff training	157,579	18,528	1,027	177,134	10,566	40,898	51,464	228,598
Other	412,726	48,529	2,691	463,946	147,578	571,255	718,833	1,182,779
Total expenses before personnel cost and depreciation	68,414,390	8,044,230	446,047	76,904,667	9,649,742	4,885,258	14,535,000	91,439,667
Salaries	4,886,626	574,574	31,860	5,493,060	915,676	3,544,263	4,459,939	9,952,999
Employee benefits	602,351	70,825	3,927	677,103	81,182	310,214	391,396	1,068,499
Payroll taxes	402,063	47,275	2,621	451,959	75,340	291,615	366,955	818,914
Total personnel costs	5,891,040	692,674	38,408	6,622,122	1,072,198	4,146,092	5,218,290	11,840,412
Total expenses before interest and depreciation	74,305,430	8,736,904	484,455	83,526,789	10,721,940	9,031,350	19,753,290	103,280,079
Interest	18,085	2,127	118	20,330	20,330	365,940	386,270	406,600
Depreciation	582,458	68,486	3,797	654,741	75,397	616,235	691,632	1,346,373
Total functional expenses	$74,905,973	$8,807,517	$488,370	$84,201,860	$10,817,667	$10,013,525	$20,831,192	$105,033,052

Accompanying notes have not been included.

Questions

1. Why are generally accepted accounting principles (GAAP) utilized in the financial reporting of a health care entity?

2. What is a third-party payor, and how does the presence of third-party payors affect the financial accounting of a health care entity?

3. What are the two types of funds in the financial reporting of health care entities?

4. What is the purpose of the Donor-Restricted Funds category in health care accounting?

5. Monetary resources are given to a not-for-profit hospital by an outside donor who has set specific provisions as to the ultimate expenditure. At the time these funds are actually spent for the designated purpose, how is the transaction recorded?

6. How are the land, buildings, and equipment acquired by a health care entity reported in its financial statements?

7. What separate fund subgroups exist within the Donor-Restricted Funds classification of a health care entity?

8. What is the purpose of the Specific Purpose Funds in a health care entity's financial records?

9. What are the three types of income reported by a health care entity? Give examples of each.

10. What reductions are frequently encountered in connection with the patient service revenues of a health care entity? Why does a health care entity only report net patient service revenues within its statement of revenue and expenses?

11. How are the reductions made for charity care reported by a health care entity?

12. What is a contractual adjustment? How is a contractual adjustment accounted for by a health care entity? Why do contractual adjustments often necessitate changes being recorded in subsequent years?

13. A local not-for-profit hospital has many services performed for it at no charge by local citizens. Under what condition would these services be reported? How are donated services recorded by a health care entity?

14. How should a health care entity account for pledges received in connection with future gifts?

15. Why is depreciation expense recognized in the accounting records of a voluntary health and welfare organization?

16. What fund categories are found in a voluntary health and welfare organization?

17. Cash is given to a voluntary health and welfare organization for a specified operating purpose. When is this contribution recognized as public support? What revenues are reported by a VHWO?

18. What general types of account balances are maintained in the Land, Building, and Equipment Fund of a voluntary health and welfare organization?

19. How are donated materials recorded in the financial records of a voluntary health and welfare organization? How are donated services recorded?

20. Why is a statement of functional expenses prepared for a voluntary health and welfare organization?

21. What distinction is drawn in a voluntary health and welfare organization between program service expenses and supporting service expenses?

22. In a statement of functional expenses, how many separate program services should be identified and reported? How many supporting services are usually identified?

23. What is the current controversy surrounding the allocation of joint costs between program service expenses and supporting service expenses?

24. What are the basic financial statements traditionally prepared by a health care entity? What are the basic financial statements prepared for a voluntary health and welfare organization?

Library Assignments

1. Locate an annual report for a voluntary health and welfare organization. If one cannot be found in the school library, obtain a copy by calling the local office of an organization such as the American Lung Association, American Cancer Society, or National Multiple Sclerosis Society.

   Using the annual report obtained, answer the following questions about the voluntary health and welfare organization:

   How many different program services are being offered?

   What percentage of total expenses went to supporting services?

   Did the organization have a program service entitled public or professional education?

   Do the notes to the financial statements indicate that any contributed services are recognized within the financial statements?

   What dollar amount was spent on fund-raising?

   How much public support was received and how much revenue was earned?

   How many different fund types are reported within the balance sheet?

   In which fund is the organization's land, buildings, and equipment presented?

   What is the largest expense category?

   What amount of depreciation was recognized for the period?

2. Read the following concerning the allocation of joint costs by not-for-profit organizations:

"Organized Charities Pass Off Mailing Costs as 'Public Education'," *The Wall Street Journal,* October 29, 1990, p. A1.

"Reasonable Joint Cost Allocations in Nonprofits," *Journal of Accountancy,* November 1992.

AICPA, *Statement of Position 87–2,* "Accounting for Joint Costs of Information Materials and Activities of Not-for-Profit Organizations that Include a Fund-Raising Appeal," paragraphs 14–22.

Write a short report indicating whether the costs of direct solicitations made by voluntary health and welfare organizations that also contain informational material should be allocated between program service expenses and supporting service expenses. If allocation is considered appropriate, indicate how that allocation should be made.

Problems

1. A gift to a not-for-profit health care entity that is not restricted by the donor should be credited directly to:
   a. Fund balance.
   b. Deferred revenue.
   c. Other revenue.
   d. Nonoperating gain.
   (AICPA adapted)

2. A hospital has the following account balances:

Revenue from newsstand	$ 50,000
Amounts charged to patients	800,000
Interest income	30,000
Salary expense—nurses	100,000
Bad debts	10,000
Undesignated gifts	80,000
Contractual adjustments	110,000

What is the hospital's net patient service revenue?
a. $880,000.
b. $800,000.
c. $690,000.
d. $680,000.

3. The property, plant, and equipment of a not-for-profit continuing care retirement community should be accounted for as part of
   a. General Funds.
   b. Donor-Restricted Funds.

    c. Specific Purpose Funds.

    d. Other Nonoperating Funds.

    (AICPA adapted)

4. In the accounting for health care providers, what are third-party payors?

    a. Doctors who reduce fees for indigent patients.

    b. Charities who supply medicines to hospitals and other health care providers.

    c. Friends and relatives who pay the medical costs of a patient.

    d. Insurance companies and other groups who pay a significant portion of the medical fees in the United States.

5. Inazu Hospital's accounting records disclosed the following information:

Cost of property and equipment net of accumulated depreciation	$19,000,000
Board designated funds	6,000,000

    What amount should be included as part of the General Funds?

    a. $25 million.

    b. $19 million.

    c. $6 million.

    d. $0.

    (AICPA adapted)

6. A local not-for-profit health care entity has the following account balances:

Donated materials	$18,000
Donated services.	11,000
Investment income	6,000
Income of cafeteria.	13,000

    How should they be accounted for in its General Funds?

    a. Nonoperating gains = $17,000; other revenues = $31,000.

    b. Nonoperating gains = $11,000; other revenues = $37,000.

    c. Nonoperating gains = $24,000; other revenues = $24,000.

    d. Nonoperating gains = $29,000; other revenues = $19,000.

7. Which of the following is not a nonoperating gain for a not-for-profit health care entity?

    a. An unrestricted gift.

    b. Dividend income.

    c. The value of donated services.

    d. The value of donated materials.

8. Mercy for America, a not-for-profit health care facility located in Durham, North Carolina, charged a patient $8,600 for services. This amount was

actually billed to a third-party payor. The third-party payor submitted a check for $7,900 with a note stating that "the reasonable amount is paid in full." Which of the following statements is true?

   a. The patient was responsible for paying the remaining $700.

   b. The health care facility will rebill the third-party payor for the remaining $700.

   c. The health care facility recorded the $700 as a contractual adjustment that will not be collected.

   d. The $700 was retained by the third-party payor and will be conveyed to the health care facility at the start of the next fiscal period.

9. During 1995, Ruark Hospital in Peoria, Illinois, purchased medicines totaling $538,000 from various vendors and other suppliers. One shipment costing $18,000 was received from a local business. However, the charge for this supply of medicine was canceled because the owner of the company wished to donate the medicine to Ruark. This donation should be recorded as

   a. An $18,000 increase in the Restricted Funds fund balance.

   b. An $18,000 increase in other revenue.

   c. An $18,000 reduction of medicine expense.

   d. A direct $18,000 increase in the General Funds fund balance.

10. What is a contractual adjustment?

   a. An increase in a patient's charges caused by revisions in the billing process utilized by a health care entity.

   b. A year-end journal entry to recognize all of a health care entity's remaining receivables.

   c. A reduction in patient service revenues caused by agreements with third-party payors that allows them to pay a health care entity based on their determination of reasonable costs.

   d. The results of a cost allocation system that allows a health care entity to determine a patient's cost by department.

11. A not-for-profit hospital provides its patients with services that would normally be charged at $1 million. However, a $200,000 reduction is estimated because of contractual adjustments. Another $100,000 reduction is expected because of bad debts. Finally, $400,000 will not be collected because the amounts are deemed to be charity care. Which of the following is correct?

   a. Patient service revenues = $1 million; net patient service revenues = $300,000.

   b. Patient service revenues = $1 million; net patient service revenues = $400,000.

   c. Patient service revenues = $600,000; net patient service revenues = $300,000.

   d. Patient service revenues = $600,000; net patient service revenues = $400,000.

12. On July 1, 1995, the governing board of Saint Anne's Mercy Hospital near Toledo, Ohio, set aside $600,000 in investments for future expansion of hospital facilities. This $600,000 is expected to be expended in the fiscal year ending June 30, 1999. In the hospital's balance sheet at June 30, 1995, this investment should be classified as an:
    a. Asset whose use is limited in the Specific Purpose Funds.
    b. Restricted noncurrent asset in Restricted Funds.
    c. Asset whose use is limited in the General Funds.
    d. Investment in the Specific Purpose Funds.

13. A local citizen gives a hospital a donation that is restricted for research activities. The money has not yet been expended. In what fund should it be recorded?
    a. Specific Purpose Funds.
    b. Special Revenue Funds.
    c. Restricted Research Funds.
    d. Expendable Trust Funds.

14. How are board-designated funds reported in the accounting for health care entities?
    a. As one of the Donor-Restricted Funds.
    b. Under the heading "assets whose use is limited" in the General Funds.
    c. Within the Specific Purpose Funds.
    d. The reporting depends on the reason for the restriction.

15. Late in 1995, a not-for-profit nursing home accepts a $75,000 cash gift with the stipulation that this money must be expended for operating supplies. The money is spent for that purpose but not until the early part of 1996. In which year should the entity recognize this revenue?
    a. The donation would not be recorded as revenue of any kind.
    b. 1995.
    c. 1996.
    d. May be recognized in either 1995 or 1996.

16. The Hospital of South Boston (a not-for-profit organization) receives a $50,000 cash donation for research into preventing lung cancer. Subsequently, $18,000 of this amount is appropriately expended. What should be recorded in General Funds?
    a. –0–.
    b. $18,000 as an other revenue.
    c. $18,000 as a nonoperating gain.
    d. $50,000 as an other revenue.

17. Theresa Johnson does voluntary work for a local hospital as a community service. She replaces without charge an administrator who would have otherwise been paid $31,000. Which of the following statements is true?
    a. A nonoperating gain of $31,000 should be recognized?
    b. Public support of $31,000 should be recognized.
    c. An expense reduction of $31,000 should be recognized.
    d. No entry should be made.

18. In 1995, Wells Hospital received an unrestricted bequest of common stock with a fair market value of $50,000. The testator had paid $20,000 for the stock in 1988. Wells should record the bequest as a:

   a. Nonoperating gain of $50,000.

   b. Nonoperating gain of $30,000.

   c. Nonoperating gain of $20,000.

   d. A memorandum entry only.

   (AICPA adapted)

19. An organization of high school seniors performs services for the patients at a nearby nursing home. These students are volunteers and perform services that the nursing home would not otherwise provide, such as wheeling patients in the park and reading to them. The nursing home has no employer-employee relationship with these volunteers, who donated more than 5,000 hours of service to the nursing home in 1995. At the minimum wage rate, these services would amount to $21,320, while the actual market value of these services is estimated to be $27,400. In the nursing home's 1995 statement of revenues and expenses, what amount should be reported as nonoperating gain?

   a. $27,400.

   b. $21,320.

   c. $6,080.

   d. $0.

   (AICPA adapted)

20. How does the accounting for a health care entity differ from college and university accounting?

   a. In accounting for a health care entity, depreciation is never recorded.

   b. In accounting for a health care entity, long-term debts are reported in a fund separate from unrestricted funds.

   c. In accounting for a health care entity, all revenues are reported in a single fund.

   d. In accounting for a health care entity, internally restricted assets are reclassified in a fund that is separate from unrestricted funds.

21. Pons Nursing Home (a not-for-profit health care entity) was given a cash gift of $600,000. The money was to be invested with income to be used to provide care for elderly residents. No stipulation was made by the donor as to the computation of income. In 1995, the following occurred:

   $40,000 in dividends were earned.
   $16,000 in interest were earned.
   $11,000 in gains on sales of investments were reported.
   $2,000 in losses on sales of investments were reported.

What income does the nursing home have to spend for the designated purpose?

a. $40,000.

b. $56,000.

c. $65,000.

d. $67,000.

22. Which of the following is not a fund type used by a voluntary health and welfare organization?

    a. Current Unrestricted Funds.

    b. Current Restricted Funds.

    c. Land, Building, and Equipment Fund.

    d. Special Revenue Funds.

23. A voluntary health and welfare organization has the following asset in-flows:

Membership dues	$3,000
Donated supplies	1,000
Interest income	4,000
Dividend income	2,000
Cash gifts	8,000

How should these items be reported?

a. Revenues of –0– and public support of $18,000.

b. Revenues of $10,000 and public support of $8,000.

c. Revenues of $9,000 and public support of $9,000.

d. Revenues of $6,000 and public support of $12,000.

24. In a voluntary health and welfare organization, donated services are

    a. Always recorded if fair market value can be determined.

    b. Recorded only if fair market value can be determined, control is present, and the person is doing the work of a salaried employee.

    c. Never recorded since it is too subjective.

    d. Recorded but only if the person is required to do specified tasks.

25. A voluntary health and welfare organization receives a gift of new furniture having a fair market value of $2,100. The group gives the furniture to needy families following a flood. How should the receipt and distribution of this donation be recorded by the organization?

    a. No entry should be made.

    b. Public support of $2,100 should be recorded along with community assistance of $2,100.

    c. Recognize revenue of $2,100.

    d. Recognize revenue of $2,100 and community expenditures of $2,100.

26. George H. Ruth takes a leave of absence from his job to work full-time for a voluntary health and welfare organization for six months. Ruth fills the position of finance director, a position that normally pays $38,000 per year. Ruth accepts no remuneration for his work. How should these donated services be recorded?
    a. As public support of $19,000 and an expense of $19,000.
    b. As public support of $19,000.
    c. As revenue of $19,000.
    d. No entry should be recorded.

27. A voluntary health and welfare organization produces a statement of functional expenses. What is the purpose of this statement?
    a. Separates current unrestricted and current restricted funds.
    b. Separates program service expenses from supporting service expenses.
    c. Separates cash expenses from noncash expenses.
    d. Separates fixed expenses from variable expenses.

28. A voluntary health and welfare organization has the following expenditures:

Research to cure disease	$60,000
Fund-raising costs	70,000
Work to help disabled	40,000
Administrative salaries	90,000

    How should these be reported by the organization?
    a. Program service expenses of $100,000 and supporting service expenses of $160,000.
    b. Program service expenses of $160,000 and supporting service expenses of $100,000.
    c. Program service expenses of $170,000 and supporting service expenses of $90,0000.
    d. Program service expenses of $190,000 and supporting service expenses of $70,000.

29. A voluntary health and welfare organization accumulates the earnings from an endowment and acquires a truck to be used in transporting donated materials. Within what fund should the truck be recorded?
    a. Endowment Fund.
    b. General Fixed Asset Account Group.
    c. Current Restricted Funds.
    d. Land, Building, and Equipment Fund.

30. Why do voluntary health and welfare organizations record and recognize depreciation of fixed assets?
    a. Fixed assets are more likely to be material in amount in a voluntary health and welfare organization than in other types of not-for-profit organizations.

    b. Voluntary health and welfare organizations purchase their fixed assets, and therefore have a historical cost basis from which to determine amounts to be depreciated.

    c. A fixed asset used by a voluntary health and welfare organization has alternative uses in private industry, and this opportunity cost should be reflected in the organization's financial statements.

    d. Contributors look for the most efficient use of funds, and since depreciation represents a cost of employing fixed assets, a voluntary health and welfare organization should reflect this expense as a cost of providing services.

(AICPA adapted)

31. A voluntary health and welfare organization receives $32,000 in cash from solicitations made in the local community. The organization receives an additional $1,500 from members in payment of annual dues. How should this money be recorded?

    a. Revenues of $33,500.

    b. Public support of $33,500.

    c. Public support of $32,000 and a $1,500 increase in the fund balance.

    d. Public support of $32,000 and revenue of $1,500.

32. A voluntary health and welfare organization received a pledge in 1995 from a donor specifying that the amount pledged be used in 1997. The donor paid the pledge in cash in 1996. The pledge should be accounted for as:

    a. Deferred support in the balance sheet at the end of 1995, and as support in 1996.

    b. Deferred support in the balance sheet at the end of 1995 and 1996, and as support in 1997.

    c. Support in 1997.

    d. Support in 1996, and with no deferred credit in the balance sheet at the end of 1997.

(AICPA adapted)

33. How are donated land and a building reported by a voluntary health and welfare organization?

    a. As assets within the General Funds.

    b. By reclassifying an amount of the fund balance account within the Current Plant Funds.

    c. By separating the assets into a Quasi-Endowment Fund.

    d. By placing the assets within the Endowment Funds.

34. Baker Hospital (a not-for-profit facility) has land costing $1.4 million, buildings costing $2.9 million, equipment costing $870,000, inventory of supplies costing $33,000, and investments set aside by the board of directors costing $45,000. How are these assets reported by the entity?

35. What are three types of revenues included by a health care entity within nonoperating gains and losses? What are three types of revenues included within other revenues?

36. During the year ended December 31, 1995, the Anderson Hospital (operated by a not-for-profit organization) received and incurred the following:

Fair market value of donated medicines	$ 54,000
Fair market value of donated services (replaced salaried workers)	38,000
Fair market value of additional donated services (did not replace salaried workers)	11,000
Interest income on board-designated funds	23,000
Regular charges to patients	176,000
Charity care	210,000
Bad debts	66,000

How should this hospital report these various items?

37. The following questions concern the appropriate accounting for a not-for-profit health care entity. Write complete answers for each question.
    a. What is a third-party payor and how have third-party payors affected the development of accounting principles for health care entities?
    b. What function does the General Funds category play in accounting for health care entities?
    c. What is a contractual adjustment and how is this figure recorded in accounting for a health care entity?
    d. What are the three types of revenues and gains recognized by a health care entity? Give examples of each.
    e. What are board-designated funds and where are these amounts reported?
    f. How are donated materials and services accounted for by a not-for-profit health care entity?

38. For each of the following items recorded by a not-for-profit hospital or other health care provider, indicate the specific classification to be used for reporting purposes (patient service revenues, other revenues, or nonoperating gains and losses):
    · Donated materials.
    · Cafeteria revenues.
    · Revenues earned on board-designated funds.
    · Charges for educational classes.
    · Charges for X rays.
    · Unrestricted gifts.
    · Grant received from state for research costs that have been incurred.
    · Donated services.
    · Dividend income.

39. Under Lennon Hospital's rate structure, the hospital earned patient service revenue of $9 million for the year ended December 31, 1995. However, Lennon did not expect to collect this amount because $1.4 million was deemed to be charity care and contractual adjustments were estimated to be $800,000.

During 1995, Lennon purchased bandages and other supplies from Harrison Medical Supply Company at a cost of $4,000. Harrison notified Lennon that the supplies were being donated to the hospital.

At the end of 1995, Lennon had board-designated assets consisting of cash of $60,000 and investments of $800,000.

How much should Lennon record as patient service revenue and how much as net patient service revenue? How should Lennon record the donation of the bandages? How much of Lennon's board-designated assets should be included in General Funds? How are these board-designated assets shown on the balance sheet?

40. The Wilson Center is a voluntary health and welfare organization. During 1995, unrestricted pledges of $600,000 were received by the center, 60 percent of which were payable in 1995, with the remainder payable in 1996 (for use in 1996). Officials estimate that 15 percent of these pledges will be uncollectible.

    In addition, a local social worker, earning $9 per hour working for the state government, contributed 600 hours of time to the Wilson Center at no charge. Except for these donated services, an additional staff person would have been hired by the organization.

    How much should the Wilson Center report as net public support for 1995? How should the Wilson Center record the contributed service?

41. Cura Foundation, a voluntary health and welfare organization supported by contributions from the general public, included the following costs in its statement of functional expenses for the year ended December 31, 1995:

Fund-raising	$500,000
Administrative (including $70,000 for data processing)	300,000
Research	100,000

What should Cura report as program service expenses? What should be reported as supporting service expenses?
(AICPA adapted)

42. Make the following journal entries for the transactions of St. John's Hospital (a not-for-profit health care provider). Indicate the fund in which each entry is being recorded.
    a. Patients were charged $500,000 for medical services. The hospital estimates that 10 percent of these fees will never be paid by the patients and another 15 percent reduction will be made by third-party payors based on the diagnosis of patients' illnesses and injuries.
    b. Cash of $40,000 was donated to the hospital to be used for paying a portion of the salary of a newly hired medical specialist.
    c. Cash of $10,000 was donated without restriction.
    d. Hospital officials decided to set aside $112,000 in cash to pay for new X-ray equipment that will eventually be acquired.

    e. The specialist in (*b*) was paid the $40,000 salary supplement.

    f. The X-ray equipment was acquired for $152,000 using the cash in (*d*) and a note for $40,000.

    g. Medicine with a value of $2,000 was donated to the hospital.

    h. Services valued at $11,000 were donated to the hospital. The volunteer workers do replace salaried workers.

43. A local health care entity incurred the following transactions during 1995. Record each of these transactions in appropriate journal entry form indicating the fund in which the entry is being made.

    a. The governing board of the organization announced that $160,000 in previously unrestricted cash will be used in the future for the acquisition of equipment. The funds are invested until the purchase eventually occurs.

    b. A donation of $80,000 was made to the entity with the stipulation that all income derived from this money be used to supplement nursing salaries.

    c. The health care entity expended $25,000 for medicines. The money was received the previous year as a restricted gift for this purpose.

    d. The organization charged its patients $600,000. Of this amount, 80 percent is expected to be covered by third-party payors.

    e. The health care entity collected $78,000 from third-party payors who were billed during the preceding year for $84,000. Administrative officials had only anticipated collecting $75,000 of this amount.

    f. Interest income of $15,000 was received on the investments acquired by the board in the first transaction.

    h. The health care entity estimated that $20,000 of current accounts receivable from patients will not be collected and amounts owed by third-party payors will be reduced by $30,000 because of contractual adjustments.

    i. The medicines acquired in (*c*) were consumed.

    j. The investments acquired in (*a*) were sold for $172,000. All restricted cash and $25,000 that had been previously given to the organization (with the stipulation that the money be used to acquire plant assets) are spent for new equipment.

    k. This health care entity receives pledges for $126,000 in unrestricted donations. Ten percent of the pledges are paid immediately with the remainder to be received and used in future years. Officials estimate that $9,000 of this money will never be collected.

44. Prepare the following journal entries for Ames Hospital indicating the funds or account groups involved:

    a. Patients were charged $300,000 for work done. Of this amount, $50,000 was actually charged to the patients although hospital officials anticipate that $12,000 will be bad accounts. The remaining $250,000 was billed to insurance companies and other third-party payors. Officials believe that these companies will only pay $220,000 after determining reasonable costs for the procedures performed.

    b. Insurance companies and other third-party payors paid $187,000 to cover 80 percent of the charges in (*a*). The remaining invoices are under investigation.

    c. An unrestricted pledge for $40,000 was received from a wealthy individual but the money cannot be spent for several years.

    d. Interest income of $1,000 was received.

    e. The administration decided to set aside $100,000. Investments were acquired for that amount with this money to be held to cover part of the cost of building a new wing to the hospital.

    f. A local volunteer contributes services to the hospital to replace a retired worker. The value of these services is $9,000.

45. The following account balances were taken from the General Funds accounts of the St. Warren's Hospital for the year ending December 31, 1995. All of the accounts of the General Funds have not been included here. After making any necessary corrections and adjustments, prepare in proper form a statement of revenues and expenses for the General Funds.

	Debits	Credits
Cash	$ 50,000	
Salary expenses—Professional care	120,000	
Depreciation expense	30,000	
Revenues from vending machines		$ 22,000
Supplies expense	11,000	
Contractual adjustments	60,000	
Buildings	200,000	
Revenues—Undesignated gifts		90,000
Revenues—Charged to patients		500,000
Charity care	70,000	
Donated salaries (fair market value):		
Replaced salaried worker		20,000
Did not replace salaried worker		45,000
Accounts receivable—third parties	200,000	
Insurance expenses	90,000	
Interest income		10,000

In addition, a $60,000 gift was received to be used to pay salaries. Salaries of $40,000 were paid this period but no journal entry was made to record the impact of this donation or payment.

46. The following transactions are from the financial records of a local not-for-profit hospital. In each case, the journal entry recorded by the hospital is reproduced. Develop formal adjusting entries (where necessary) for the hospital in anticipation of the preparation of year-end financial statements.

    a. All patients were billed for services rendered. A large percentage of these invoices was actually sent to third-party payors. The following patient receivables were recorded net of $25,000 estimated to become bad and $40,000 anticipated to be charged off by the hospital as charity allowances. The balance due from third-party payors has been recorded net of $50,000 estimated as contractual adjustments for the period.

General Funds

Accounts Receivable—Third Party Payors	610,000	
Accounts Receivable—Patients	193,000	
Patient Service Revenues		803,000

b. An unrestricted grant of $10,000 was received by the hospital.

General Funds

Cash	10,000	
Operating Revenues		10,000

c. Donated services (maintenance work) valued at $12,000 were contributed to the hospital by members of a local church organization. These individuals were under the control of the hospital and replaced salaried employees. No entry was recorded by the hospital.

d. The hospital acquired new equipment with cash from the Plant Replacement and Expansion Funds. Additional funding came from a note payable.

Plant Replacement and Expansion

Equipment.	110,000	
Cash		80,000
Note Payable		30,000

e. Depreciation expense for the current year was recorded.

General Funds

Depreciation Expense.	102,000	
Accumulated Depreciation.		102,000

f. A pledge of $100,000 was received by the hospital to finance a particular research project. The initial $20,000 will be collected within the next few months with annual installments of $20,000 to be paid in each of the four years thereafter. Expenditure is restricted to the period of time in which the money is received.

Specific-Purpose Funds

Contributions Receivable	100,000	
Operating Revenues		20,000
Deferred Revenues		80,000

g. Materials valued at $40,000 have been donated to the hospital by local merchants. By year-end, 60 percent of these items have been consumed in the operations of the hospital. No journal entry was recorded when the gift was received but the following adjustment was made at the end of the year:

General Funds

Inventory of Supplies.	16,000	
Donated Revenues		16,000

h. The administration of the hospital decided to set aside $325,000 in cash to be used eventually to replace certain hospital equipment.

General Funds

Other Financing Uses.	325,000	
Cash		325,000

Plant Replacement and Expansion

Cash	325,000	
Other Financing Sources		325,000

i. The hospital received a $90,000 cash gift to be expended in a specific project. Of this total, $65,000 was immediately spent for this purpose.

Specific-Purpose Funds

Cash	90,000	
Revenues—Contributions		90,000
Expenditures—Control	65,000	
Cash		65,000

47. The following questions concern the accounting principles and procedures applicable to a voluntary health and welfare organization. Write out answers to each of these questions.
    a. What is the difference in revenue and public support?
    b. What is the significance of the statement of functional expenses?
    c. What accounting process is used in connection with donated materials?
    d. What is the difference in the two current funds found in the financial records of a voluntary health and welfare organization?
    e. Under what conditions should donated services be recorded?
    f. What accounts would be recorded within the Land, Building, and Equipment Fund?
    g. What controversy has arisen as to the handling of costs associated with direct mail and other solicitations for money that also contain educational materials?

48. The following four transactions or events are independent.
    · Unrestricted cash of $25,000 was disbursed for the purchase of new equipment.
    · An unrestricted cash gift of $100,000 was received from a donor.
    · Investments in stocks with a book value of $50,000 were sold by an endowment fund for $55,000. No restrictions exist on this gain.
    · Bonds payable with a face value of $1 million were sold at par. The proceeds had to be used solely for the construction of a new building. The structure was eventually completed at a cost of $1 million and payment is made with the funds generated by the bond issuance.

Required:

a. Prepare journal entries for the previous four transactions (including the fund in which each entry is being made) for a state or local government.

b. Prepare journal entries for these transactions (including the fund in which each entry is being made) for a voluntary health and welfare organization. (AICPA adapted)

49. Prepare journal entries for a voluntary health and welfare organization that has the following transactions:

   a. A cash dividend of $4,000 was received on investments being held to serve as funding for the acquisition of new equipment.

   b. A cash gift of $21,000 was received that must be used for research into the cure for several diseases.

   c. A cash gift of $120,000 was received that must be used to acquire new equipment.

   d. A cash gift of $65,000 was received that is completely unrestricted.

   e. The money in (b) was used for research.

   f. The money in (a) and (c) was used to buy equipment.

   g. Salary expense of $18,000 was paid to the administrative officers of the charity.

   h. Donated services having a value of $15,000 were rendered. These services replaced a salaried administrative employee.

50. The adjusted trial balances of the Community Association for Handicapped Children, a voluntary health and welfare organization, at June 30, 1995, are presented on the following page.

Required:

a. Prepare a statement of support, revenue, and expenses and changes in fund balances, separately presenting each current fund, for the year ended June 30, 1995.

b. Prepare a balance sheet separately presenting each current fund as of June 30, 1995.

   (AICPA adapted)

51. A voluntary health and welfare organization was started by community leaders in Edwards, Texas. The organization's goal was to provide child care services for indigent families in the area. Local citizens canvassed the town and raised $120,000 in cash and $75,000 more in pledges to be collected and used in subsequent years. The group estimated that only 80 percent of this amount will actually be received.

   A resident of the community assumed the role of executive director for the organization. The person accepted no compensation for this work, although an outsider would have been paid $10,000 per year to accept the responsibility. A local merchant provided office space to the organization to serve as its headquarters. This space would normally rent for $2,000 per year but was occupied without charge. Another merchant donated $4,000 in furniture to be used by the charity.

   The organization acquired a building at a cost of $90,000. Of that amount, $50,000 in cash was paid immediately with the rest provided by a

COMMUNITY ASSOCIATION FOR HANDICAPPED CHILDREN
Adjusted Current Funds Trial Balances
June 30, 1995

	Unrestricted		Restricted	
	Dr.	Cr.	Dr.	Cr.
Cash	$ 40,000		$ 9,000	
Bequest receivable			5,000	
Contributions receivable	12,000			
Accrued interest receivable	1,000			
Investments (at cost, which approximate market value)	100,000			
Accounts payable and accrued expense.		$ 50,000		$ 1,000
Deferred revenue.		2,000		
Allowances for uncollectible pledges		3,000		
Fund balances, July 1, 1994:				
Temporarily restricted		12,000		
Unrestricted		26,000		
Permanently restricted				3,000
Transfers of endowment fund income.		20,000		
Contributions		300,000		15,000
Membership dues		25,000		
Program service fees		30,000		
Investment income.		10,000		
Deaf children's program	120,000			
Blind children's program	150,000			
Management and general services	45,000		4,000	
Fund-raising services	8,000		1,000	
Provision for uncollectible pledges	2,000			
	$478,000	$478,000	$19,000	$19,000

loan from the local bank. A resident contributed $10,000 to the organization with the stipulation that the money be used solely to pay the workers who care for the children. An employee was hired for this purpose and the first $1,400 of this donation was expended. Membership dues of $600 were collected and this money was used to buy toys to entertain the children.

The trustees of the child care center elected to set aside $40,000 in cash as an investment to provide future working capital for the organization.

Depreciation expense on the building was calculated for the year at $6,000.

Required:

Prepare all necessary journal entries for this voluntary health and welfare organization. For each entry, indicate the fund category in which the entry would be recorded.

52. Children's Agency, a voluntary health and welfare organization, conducts two programs: a medical services program and a community information services program. This charity had the following transactions during the year ended June 30, 1995:

    a. Received the following contributions:

Unrestricted pledges	$800,000
Restricted cash	95,000
Building fund pledges	50,000
Endowment fund cash	1,000

    b. Collected the following pledges:

Unrestricted	450,000
Building fund	20,000

    c. Received the following unrestricted cash revenues:

From theater party (net of direct costs)	12,000
Bequests	10,000
Membership dues	8,000
Interest and dividends	5,000

    d. Program expenses incurred (vouchers created for these amounts):

Medical services	60,000
Community information services	15,000

    e. Service expenses incurred (vouchers created for these amounts):

General administration	150,000
Fund raising	200,000

    f. Fixed assets purchased with unrestricted cash . . . . | 18,000

    g. Depreciation of all buildings and equipment in the Land, Buildings, and Equipment Fund was allocated as follows:

Medical services program	4,000
Community information services program	3,000
General administration	6,000
Fund raising	2,000

    h. Paid vouchers payable . . . . | 330,000

Required:

Prepare journal entries for the following funds:
- Current Unrestricted Funds
- Current Restricted Funds
- Land, Buildings, and Equipment Funds
- Endowment Funds

(AICPA adapted)

53. This textbook has examined the accounting procedures utilized by four different types of not-for-profit organizations:
    - State and local government units.
    - Colleges and universities.
    - Health care entities.
    - Voluntary health and welfare organizations.

    For the following individual transactions describe the accounting procedures appropriate for each of these four types of organizations. Indicate the method by which the entry would be recorded as well as the proper fund category.

    a. A commitment was made to acquire a new truck.

    b. Employee salaries were paid.

    c. Depreciation expense for the current year was computed.

    d. A billing for normal revenues was made.

    e. A building was acquired through the use of unrestricted funds.

    f. Money was set aside by the entity's officials for a specified future use.

    g. A note payable was signed to finance construction of a new building.

    h. A cash gift was received with the stipulation that the money be used for a specific operating purpose. The appropriate expenditure was immediately made with these available funds.

19

ACCOUNTING FOR ESTATES AND TRUSTS

Questions to Consider

- If a person dies without having written a will, how are the estate's assets managed and distributed?
- If the assets held by an estate are insufficient to satisfy all claims against the estate as well as all bequests made by the decedent, what reductions are made?
- How can an individual or a couple limit the federal estate taxes that must be paid so that the amount of assets being conveyed to beneficiaries is maximized?
- In accounting for an estate or trust, why is the distinction between principal and income often considered to be especially significant?
- What are the most common types of trust funds? What is each type of trust designed to accomplish?

Individuals labor throughout their lives in part to accumulate property that eventually can be conveyed for the benefit of spouses, children, relatives, friends, charities, and the like. After amassing such funds, human nature usually seeks to achieve two goals:

- To minimize the amount of these assets that must be surrendered to the government.
- To ensure that the ultimate disposition of all property is consistent with the person's own wishes.

Therefore, accountants (as well as attorneys and financial planners) often assist individuals who are developing estate plans or creating trusts. At a later date, the accountant may serve in the actual administration of the estate or trust.

In either estate or trust planning, the person's intentions must be spelled out in clear detail so that no misunderstanding can ever arise. All available techniques should also be considered to limit the impact of taxes. To carry out all of these varied responsibilities properly, a knowledge of the legal and reporting aspects of estates and trusts is of paramount importance.

Although many of the complex legal rules and regulations in these areas are beyond the scope of an accounting textbook, an overview of both estates and trusts can serve as an introduction to the issues frequently encountered by members of the accounting profession.

Accounting for an Estate

You may work hard all your life and accumulate a substantial fortune, but if you don't have an estate plan Uncle Sam may be your largest heir. With estate tax rates beginning at 37 percent and topping out at 55 percent, the failure to develop an estate plan can cancel out a lifetime of brilliant investing.[1]

The term *estate* simply refers to the property owned by an individual. However, in this chapter, an estate is more specifically defined as a separate legal entity holding title to the assets of a deceased person. *Thus, estate accounting refers to the recording and reporting of financial events from the time of a person's death until the ultimate distribution of all property.* To ensure that this disposition is as intended and to avoid disputes, each individual should prepare a will, "a legal declaration of a person's wishes as to the disposition of his or her property after death."[2] If an individual dies *testate* (having written a valid will), this document serves as the blueprint for settling the estate and disbursing all remaining assets.

In cases where a person dies *intestate* (without a legal will), state inheritance laws must be followed. Although these legal rules will vary from state to state, they are normally designed to correspond with the most common patterns of distribution. When inheritance laws rather than a will are applicable, real property is conveyed based on the *laws of descent* whereas personal property transfers are made according to the *laws of distribution*.

Laws governing wills and estates are established by each individual state and are known as *probate laws*. A *Uniform Probate Code* has been developed by the National Conference of Commissioners on Uniform State Laws in hopes of creating consistent treatment in this area. To date, a number of states have officially adopted the Uniform Probate Code. In many of the other states, the rules and regulations applied are somewhat similar to the Uniform Probate Code. In practice, though, an accountant should always become familiar with the specific laws of the state having jurisdiction over an estate.

---

[1] Mark Wallace, "Investor's Corner," *Investor's Daily,* March 21, 1990, p. 1.

[2] Stuart Berg Flexner, Editor-in-Chief, *The Random House Dictionary of the English Language,* 2nd ed. (New York: Random House, 1987), p. 2175.

Administration of the Estate

Regardless of the locale, probate laws generally are designed to achieve three goals:

1. Gather and preserve all of the decedent's property.
2. Carry out an orderly and fair settlement of all debts.
3. Discover the decedent's intent for the remaining property held at death and then follow those wishes.

This process usually begins with the filing of a will with the probate court or an indication that no will has been discovered. If a will is presented, the probate court must rule on the document's validity. A will must meet specific legal requirements to be accepted. For example, would the following signed and dated statement constitute a valid will?

"I want my children to have my money."

Since the writer is dead, the intention of this statement cannot be verified. Was this an idle wish made without thought or did the decedent truly intend this one sentence to constitute a will conveying all money to these specified individuals upon death? Did the decedent mean for all noncash assets to be liquidated with the proceeds being split among the children? Or, did the writer strictly mean that just the cash on hand at the time of death should be transferred to these individuals? Obviously, in some cases, the validity (and the intention) of a will are not easily proven.

If deemed to be both authentic and valid, the will is admitted to probate and the decedent's specific intentions will be carried to conclusion. Whether a will is present or not, an estate administrator must be chosen to serve in a stewardship capacity. All property of the decedent must be located, debts paid, and distributions appropriately conveyed. This individual serves in a fiduciary position and is responsible for (1) satisfying all applicable laws and (2) making certain that the decedent's wishes are achieved (if known and if possible).

If a specific person is named in the will for this position, the individual is referred to as the *executor of the estate*. If the will does not designate an executor or if the named person is unwilling to serve in this capacity (or if the decedent dies without a will), the courts must select a personal representative. A court-appointed individual is known legally as the *administrator of the estate*. An executor/administrator is not forced to serve in this role for free; that person is legally entitled to reasonable compensation for all services rendered.[3]

The executor is normally responsible for fulfilling several tasks:

• Taking possession of all the decedent's assets and completing an inventory of this property.

---

[3] To avoid having to use convoluted terminology, the term *executor* is generally used throughout this textbook to indicate both executors and administrators.

- Discovering all of the claims against the decedent and settling these obligations.
- Filing estate income tax returns, federal estate tax returns, and state inheritance or estate tax returns.
- Distributing property according to the provisions of the will, or according to state laws if a valid will is not available.
- Making a full accounting to the probate court to demonstrate that the executor has properly fulfilled the fiduciary responsibility.

Property Included in the Estate

The basis for all estate accounting is the property held by the decedent at death. These assets are used to settle claims and pay taxes. Any property that remains is distributed according to the decedent's will (or applicable state laws). For reporting purposes, all items are shown at fair market value; the historical cost originally paid by the deceased individual is no longer relevant. Fair market value is especially important since the sale of some or all properties may be required to obtain enough cash to satisfy claims against the estate. If valuation problems arise, hiring an appraiser might become necessary.

Normally, an estate includes assets such as

- Cash.
- Investments in stocks and bonds.
- Interest accrued to the date of death.
- Dividends declared prior to death.
- Investments in businesses.
- Unpaid wages.
- Accrued rents and royalties.
- Valuables such as paintings and jewelry.

At the time of death, certain assets were legally owned by the decedent. The executor is merely trying to locate and value each item belonging to the estate as of that date.

Some states specify that real property such as land and buildings (and possibly certain types of personal property) are conveyed directly to the beneficiary at the time of death. Therefore, in these states, these assets are not included in the inventory of estate property that is developed by the executor for probate purposes. However, in the filing of estate and inheritance tax returns, such items must still be listed because a legal transfer has occurred.

Discovery of Claims against the Decedent

An adequate opportunity should be given to the decedent's creditors to allow them to file claims against the estate. Usually, the printing of a public notice in an appropriate newspaper is required one time per week for three weeks. In many states, all claims have to be presented within four months of the first of these notices. The validity of these claims must be verified by the executor and placed in order of priority. If insufficient funds are available, this ordering becomes quite important in establishing which parties receive payment. Consequently, claims in category 4 of the following list have the greatest chance of going unpaid.

Order of Priority

1. Expenses of administering the estate. Without this preferential treatment, the appointment of an acceptable executor and the hiring of lawyers, accountants, and/or appraisers could become a difficult task in estates with limited funds.
2. Funeral expenses and the medical expenses of any last illness.
3. Debts and taxes given preference under federal and state laws.
4. All other claims.

To ensure that some amount of protection is available for a surviving spouse and/or the decedent's minor and dependent children, relatively small allowances are conveyed to these parties prior to the payment of claims. The Uniform Probate Code specifies that a $5,000 homestead allowance is provided to a surviving spouse and/or minor and dependent children. Thus, even an estate heavily in debt would still furnish some financial relief for the members of the decedent's immediate family. In addition, a family allowance of $500 per month (up to a total of $6,000) is given to these same individuals during the period of estate administration.

These family members are also entitled to exempt property such as automobiles, furniture, and jewelry having a value not to exceed $3,500 in total. *All other property is included in the estate to pay claims and be distributed as per the decedent's will or state inheritance laws.* Consequently, a surviving spouse along with minor and dependent children are entitled to receive the following from an estate, regardless of the claims made against the assets:

Homestead allowance	$5,000
Family allowance	6,000 (if the estate administration lasts a full year)
Exempt property.	3,500 (fair market value)

Estate Distributions

If a will has been located and probated, property remaining after all claims are settled is conveyed according to that document's specifications.[4] A gift of real

---

[4] Property legally held in joint tenancy with one or more individuals passes to the surviving joint tenants at death and is not subject to the provisions of a will or intestate distribution.

property such as land or a building is referred to as a *devise* whereas a gift of personal property such as stocks or furniture is a *legacy* or a *bequest*. A devise is frequently specific: "I leave three acres of land in Henrico County to my son," or "I leave the apartment building on Monument Avenue to my niece." Unless the estate is unable to pay all claims, a devise is simply conveyed to the intended party. However, if claims cannot be otherwise satisfied, the executor may be forced to sell the property despite the will's intention.

In contrast, a legacy may take one of several forms. The identification of the type of legacy becomes especially important if the estate has insufficient resources to meet the specifications of the will.

A *specific legacy* is a gift of personal property that is directly identified. "I leave my collection of pocket watches to my son" is an example of a specific legacy since the property is named.

A *demonstrative legacy* is a cash gift made from a particular source. As an illustration, the statement "I leave $10,000 from my savings account in the First National Bank to my sister" is a demonstrative legacy since the source is identified. If the savings account does not hold $10,000 at the time of death, the beneficiary will receive the amount available. In addition, the decedent may specify alternative sources if sufficient funds are not available. Ultimately, any shortfall is usually considered a general legacy.

A *general legacy* is a cash gift with the source being undesignated. "I leave $8,000 in cash to my nephew" is a gift viewed as a general legacy.

A *residual legacy* is a gift of any remaining estate property. Thus, assets left after all claims, taxes, and other distributions are conveyed according to the residual provisions of the will. ("The balance of my estate is to be divided evenly between my two brothers.")

An obvious problem arises if an estate does not have enough funds to satisfy all of the legacies specified in the will. The necessary reduction of the various gifts is referred to as the *process of abatement*. For illustration purposes, assume that a will lists the following provisions:

I leave 1,000 shares of AT&T to my brother. (a specific legacy)

I leave my savings account of $20,000 to my sister. (a demonstrative legacy)

I leave $40,000 cash to my son. (a general legacy)

I leave all remaining property to my daughter. (a residual legacy)

Example One. *Assume that the estate holds the shares of AT&T stock, the savings account, and $46,000 in other cash.* The first three parties (the brother, sister, and son) get the assets stated in the will, while the residual legacy (to the daughter) would be the $6,000 cash balance left after the $40,000 general legacy is paid.

Example Two.   *Assume that the estate holds the shares of AT&T stock, the savings account, but only $35,000 in other cash.* The first two individuals (the brother and sister) get the specified assets but the son is only able to claim the remaining $35,000 cash rather than the promised $40,000. Based on the process of abatement, the daughter receives nothing; no amount is left after the other legacies have been distributed.

Example Three.   *Assume that the estate holds the shares of AT&T stock but the savings account has a balance of only $12,000 rather than the promised $20,000. Other cash held by the estate totals $51,000.* The stock is distributed to the brother, but the sister gets just the $12,000 cash in the savings account. In most cases, the courts would hold that the remaining $8,000 is a general legacy. Consequently, the sister gets the additional $8,000 in this manner and the son receives the specified $40,000. The daughter is then left with only the remaining $3,000 in cash.

Example Four.   *Assume that the shares of AT&T stock were sold by the decedent before death and that the savings account holds $22,000. Other cash amounts to $30,000.* The brother receives nothing from the estate since the specific legacy did not exist at death.[5] The sister collects the promised $20,000 from the savings account with the remaining $2,000 being added to the general legacy. Therefore, the son receives a total of $32,000 from the two cash sources. Since the general legacy was not fulfilled, no remainder exists as a residual legacy; thus, the daughter collects nothing from the estate.

Insufficient Funds.   The debts and expenses of the administration are paid first in settling an estate. If the estate has insufficient available resources to satisfy these claims, the process of abatement is again utilized. Each of the following categories is exhausted completely to pay all debts and expenses before money is taken from the next:

> Residual legacies.
> General legacies.
> Demonstrative legacies.
> Specific legacies and devises.

Estate and Inheritance Taxes

Taxes incurred after death can be quite costly. For example, Helen Walton received $5.1 billion in stock at the death of her husband Sam Walton (founder of

---

[5] The legal term *ademption* refers to a situation where a specific bequest or devise fails because the property is not available for distribution. As a different possibility, a bequest or devise is said to lapse if the beneficiary cannot be located or dies before the decedent. This property then becomes part of the residuary estate.

Wal-Mart Stores). At this value, these shares could eventually cost her heirs as much as *$2.8 billion* in taxes at her death: $2.2 billion to the United States government and $640 million to the state of Arkansas.[6]

Federal estate tax rates are as high as 55 percent with an additional 5 percent charged on extremely large estates (from $10 million to approximately $21 million). Every state also imposes a separate inheritance or estate tax (commonly known as a "death tax").[7] The federal government allows a limited credit for such taxes assessed by the state. The effect of this credit is to reduce the federal estate tax by exactly the amount paid to the state so that the estate is not double-taxed. However, the amount of this credit (commonly referred to as the "pickup" or "sponge" tax) is limited. As an illustration, the allowable credit is $99,600 on an estate with a value for federal tax purposes of $2 million. Any amount charged by a state above this ceiling may reduce the size of the estate but is not a direct credit against the federal estate tax.

Currently, 28 states simply charge the pickup tax so that the estate is not penalized whereas the other 22 states impose an excess tax. For example, on an estate of $2 million, Massachusetts imposes an additional tax bill of $145,900; New York, $42,900; Kentucky, $85,000; and South Dakota, $46,650.[8] Because many elderly citizens choose to move from states that have this extra tax, a number of states have recently eliminated the assessment in hopes of actually increasing revenues.

Federal Estate Taxes.   The federal estate tax is an excise tax assessed on the right to convey property. The computation begins by determining the fair market value of all property held at death. Therefore, even if real property is transferred immediately to the beneficiary and is not subject to probate, the value must still be included for federal estate tax purposes.[9] In establishing fair market value, the executor may choose an alternative valuation date if that decision will reduce estate taxes. This date is six months after death (or the date of disposition for any property disposed of within six months after death). Thus, the federal estate tax process starts by determining all asset values at death or this alternative date. However, a piecemeal valuation cannot be made; one of these two must be used for all properties.

The gross estate figure is then reduced by several items to arrive at the taxable value of the estate:

- Funeral expenses.
- Estate administration expenses.

---

[6] Warren Midgett, "Mrs. Walton's Options," *Forbes*, October 19, 1992, pp. 22–23.

[7] Coverage of the many and varied state inheritance and estate tax laws is beyond the scope of this textbook. An overview is provided by "How to Minimize State Death Tax Liabilities," by Paul J. Lochray in the July 1990 issue of the *Journal of Financial Planning*, pp. 120–23.

[8] Laura Sanders, "Wising up," *Forbes*, June 22, 1992, pp. 138–39.

[9] Life insurance policies with named beneficiaries are also included in the value of the estate as long as the decedent had the right to change the beneficiary.

- Liabilities.
- Casualties and thefts during the administration of estate.
- Charitable bequests.
- Marital deduction for property conveyed to spouse.

The remaining figure is taxed at graduated rates that, as indicated before, rise to a maximum of 55 percent. Individuals are then allowed to deduct a unified transfer credit of $192,800. *The credit was set at this figure so that (based on current tax rates) estates of $600,000 and less may avoid any taxation.* For example, if an estate tax of $210,000 is computed, the required payment is only $17,200 after deducting the $192,800 credit. Also, as mentioned earlier, state inheritance or estate taxes serve as another credit (to the upper limitation allowed) in arriving at the final amount to be paid to the federal government.

The impact of the unified transfer credit is reduced, though, if the decedent made any taxable gifts while alive. Although annual gifts not in excess of $10,000 per person may be made tax free (the amount is $20,000 per year if conveyed by a married couple), gifts above this level are taxed by the federal government in the same manner as an estate tax since they are both transfers to beneficiaries. To avoid or reduce this gift tax, the donor is allowed to apply the unified transfer credit. *However, any portion of this credit used to shelter gifts from taxation reduces the $192,800 credit available to the estate after death.*

Federal Estate Taxes—Example One.   The determination of the taxable estate is obviously an important step in determining estate taxes. Assume for illustration purposes that a person dies holding assets valued at $3 million. Assume further that no taxable gifts were made during the individual's lifetime. Total debts of $400,000 were owed at death. Funeral expenses had a cost of $20,000, and estate administration expenses amounted to $10,000. In this person's will, $300,000 has been left to charitable organizations, with the remaining $2,270,000 (after debts and expenses) given to the surviving spouse.[10] Under this set of circumstances, no taxable estate exists:

Gross estate (fair market value)		$3,000,000
Funeral expenses	$ 20,000	
Administration expenses.	10,000	
Debts	400,000	
Charity bequests	300,000	
Marital deduction	2,270,000	(3,000,000)
Taxable estate		–0–
Estate tax		–0–

---

[10] Although not applicable in this case, surviving spouses do have the right in most states to denounce the provisions of a will and take an established percentage (normally 1/3) of the decedent's estate. Such laws protect surviving spouses from being disinherited.

Federal Estate Taxes—Example Two.   For estate planning purposes, having a taxable estate of exactly $600,000 is often considered wise since that amount can be conveyed tax free. In the preceding example, if the couple has already identified the recipient of the estate at the eventual death of the second spouse (their children, for example), a conveyance at the time of the first death may be advantageous. The second estate will then be $600,000 smaller for subsequent taxation purpose. Frequently, a trust fund is established for this purpose as a means of protecting the money and ensuring its proper distribution.

To illustrate, assume that the previous will is identical except that only $1,670,000 is conveyed to the surviving spouse with $600,000 being placed in a trust for the couple's children (a nondeductible amount for estate tax purposes). The estate tax return must now be adjusted to appear as follows:

Gross estate.		$3,000,000
Funeral expenses	$ 20,000	
Administration expenses	10,000	
Debts.	400,000	
Charity bequests.	300,000	
Marital deduction	1,670,000	(2,400,000)
Taxable estate (conveyed to trust)		$ 600,000
Estate tax on $600,000 value		$ 192,800
Unified transfer credit		(192,800)
Taxes to be paid		–0–

Once again, no taxes are paid by the estate, but the surviving spouse has only $1,670,000 added to his or her own taxable estate rather than $2,270,000. Thus, an eventual decrease in the couple's *total* estate taxes has been established.

Other Approaches to Reducing Estate Taxes.   Until recently, one technique used by families with large fortunes to reduce estate taxes was the transfer of assets to grandchildren or even great-grandchildren. In this manner, the number of separate conveyances (each of which would be subject to taxation at a top rate of 55 percent) from parent to child to grandchild was reduced. However, the government effectively eliminated the appeal of this option by establishing a generation-skipping transfer tax. This flat-rate tax of 55 percent is assessed on any transfers by gift, bequest, or trust distribution to individuals who are two or more generations younger than the donors or decedents.

However, estate taxes may still be reduced by making tax-free gifts prior to death. As just stated, gifts of $10,000 (or $20,000 for a married couple) can be made to an unlimited number of individuals each year without incurring any tax. The size of the donor's taxable estate is gradually reduced over time. ''If properly planned, shifting assets can accomplish your objectives and ensure that the rewards of a lifetime of work pass to your heirs and not to the IRS."[11]

State Inheritance Taxes.   State inheritance taxes are assessed on the right to receive property with the levy and all other regulations varying, as discussed earlier, based on state laws. However, the actual impact on the individual beneficiaries is determined by the specifications of the will. Many wills dictate that all inheritance tax payments are to be made out of any residual amounts held by the estate. Consequently, any individuals receiving residual legacies are forced to bear the entire burden of this tax.

If the will makes no provisions for state inheritance taxes (or if the decedent dies intestate), the amounts conveyed to each party must be reduced proportionately based on the fair market value received. Thus, the recipient of land valued at $200,000 would have to contribute twice the inheritance tax of a beneficiary collecting cash of $100,000. Decreasing a cash legacy to cover the cost of inheritance taxes creates little problem for the executor. However, a direct reduction of an estate asset such as land, buildings, or corporate stocks might be virtually impossible. Normally, the beneficiary in such cases is required to pay enough cash to satisfy the applicable inheritance tax.

Estate Income Taxes.   Although all estates require time to be settled, the period can become quite lengthy if complex matters arise. From the date of death until ultimate resolution, the estate is viewed legally as a taxable entity and must file and pay income taxes to the federal government if gross income is $600 or more. The return is due by the 15th day of the fourth month following the close of the estate's taxable year. The calendar year may be adopted for this purpose or any other fiscal year may be chosen as the taxable year.

Applicable income tax rules are generally the same as those utilized by individual taxpayers. Therefore, dividend, rental, interest, and other income earned by the estate in the period following death are taxable to the estate unless of a type that is specifically nontaxable (such as municipal bond interest).

A personal exemption of $600 is provided as a decrease to the taxable balance. In addition, a reduction is allowed for (1) any taxable income donated to charity as well as (2) any taxable income for the year distributed to a beneficiary. Federal tax rates are 15 percent on the first $3,600 of taxable income per year with a 28 percent levy on any excess income earned up to $10,900. At a taxable income level more than $10,900, a 31 percent rate is incurred.

As an illustration, assume that an estate earns net rental income during the current year of $30,000 and dividend income of $8,000. The dividend income is distributed immediately to a beneficiary, while $6,000 of the rental income is given to charity. Estate income taxes for the year would be computed as follows:

---

[11] *Strategies for Individual Planning 1990–1991* (New York: KPMG Peat Marwick, 1990), p. 64.

Rental income	$30,000
Dividend income	8,000
Total revenue	$38,000
Personal exemption	(600)
Gift to charity	(6,000)
Distributed to beneficiary	(8,000)
Taxable income	$23,400

Income tax:

15% of first $3,600	$ 540
28% of next $7,300 ($10,900 − $3,600)	2,044
31% of remaining $12,500 ($23,400 − $10,900)	3,875
Income tax payable	$ 6,459

The Distinction between Income and Principal

In many estates, the executor is faced with the problem of differentiating between income and principal transactions. For example, a will might state "all income earned on my estate for five years after death is to go to my sister, with the estate then being conveyed to my children." The recipient of the income is known as an *income beneficiary* whereas the party that ultimately receives the principal (also known as the *corpus*) is called a *remainderman*. As the fiduciary for the estate, the executor must ensure that all parties are treated fairly. Thus, if amounts are distributed incorrectly, the executor can be held legally liable by the court.

The definitional difference between principal and income appears to pose little problem. The estate principal encompasses all assets of the decedent at death; income is the earnings on these assets after death. However, many transactions are not easily categorized as either principal or income. As examples,

- Are funeral expenses charged to principal or income?
- Is the executor's fee charged to principal or income?
- Are dividends that are declared before death but received after death viewed as principal or income?
- If stocks are sold for a gain, is this gain viewed as income or an increase in principal?
- Are repairs to rental property considered a reduction of principal or of income?

Clearly, the distinction between principal and interest is not always obvious. For this reason, in writing a will, an individual may choose to spell out the procedure by which principal and income are to be calculated. If defined in this manner, the executor merely has to follow these instructions.

However, in many cases, no guidance is provided by the decedent as to the method by which transactions are to be classified. State laws must then be applied by the executor to determine these two figures. The *Revised Uniform Principal and Income Act* has been adopted as a standard by many states for this purpose. However, some states have created their own distinct laws while still others have adopted modified versions of the *Revised Uniform Principal and Income Act*. Generally accepted accounting principles are not applicable; the distinction between principal and income is defined solely by the decedent's intentions or by state laws.

Although differences exist because of unique state laws or the provisions of a will, the following transactions are normally viewed as adjustments (either increases or decreases) to the *principal of the estate:*

- Life insurance proceeds if the estate is named as the beneficiary.
- Dividends declared prior to death and any other income earned prior to death.
- Liquidating dividends declared after death.
- Debts incurred prior to death.
- Gains and losses on the sale of corporate securities or rental property.
- Major repairs (improvements) to rental property.
- Investment commissions and other costs.
- Funeral expenses.
- Homestead and family allowances.

The *income of the estate* includes all revenues and expenses recognized after the date of death. Within this calculation, the following items are included as reductions to income:

- Recurring taxes such as property taxes.
- Ordinary repair expenses.
- Water and other utility expenses.
- Insurance expenses.
- Other ordinary expenses necessary for the management and preservation of the estate.

Several costs such as the executor's fee, court costs, and attorney's and accountant's charges must be apportioned between principal and interest in some fair manner.

Recording the Transactions of an Estate

The accounting process used by the executor of an estate is quite unique. *Since this individual has been given responsibility by the probate court over the assets of the estate, the accounting system is designed to demonstrate the proper distribution of these properties.* Thus, several features of estate accounting should be noted:

- All estate assets are recorded at fair market value to indicate the amount of the executor's accountability. Any assets that are subsequently discovered are disclosed separately so that these adjustments to the original estate value can be noted when reporting to the probate court. The ultimate disposition of all properties must then be recorded to provide evidence that the fiduciary responsibility has been fulfilled.

- Debts, taxes, or other obligations are only recorded at the date of payment. In effect, the system is designed to monitor the disposition of assets. Thus, claims are only relevant to the accounting process at the time that the assets are disbursed. Likewise, distributions of legacies are not entered into the records until actually conveyed. As mentioned earlier, devises of real property are often transferred at death so that no accounting is necessary.

- Because of the importance in many estates of separately identifying income and principal transactions, the accounting system must always note whether income or principal is being affected. Quite frequently, two cash balances are maintained to assist in this process.

To illustrate, assume that James T. Wilson dies on April 1, 1995. The following valid will has been discovered:

I name Bob King as executor of my estate.

I leave my house, furnishings, and artwork to my aunt, Ann Wilson.

I leave my investments in stocks to my uncle, Jack E. Wilson.

I leave my automobile and personal effects to my grandmother, Nancy Wilson.

I leave $38,000 in cash to my brother, Brian Wilson.

I leave any income earned on my estate to my niece, Karen Wilson.

All remaining property is to be placed in trust for my children.

The executor will have to (1) make a search to discover all estate assets and (2) allow an adequate opportunity for every possible claim to be filed. The assets should be recorded immediately at fair market value along with the creation of an Estate Principal account. This total represents the amount of assets for which the executor is accountable. The following journal entry establishes the values for the assets owned by James T. Wilson at his death that have been found to date:

Cash—Principal	11,000	
Interest Receivable on Bonds	3,000	
Dividends Receivable on Stocks	4,000	
Life Insurance—Payable to Estate	40,000	
Residence	90,000	
Household Furnishings and Art Work	24,000	
Automobile	4,000	
Personal Effects	2,000	
Investment in Bonds	240,000	
Investment in Stocks	50,000	
Estate Principal		468,000

Following is a list of subsequent transactions incurred by this estate along with each appropriate journal entry. Since estate income is to be conveyed to one party but the remaining principal is to be placed in trust, careful distinction between these two elements is necessary.

Transaction 1.   Funeral expenses of $4,000 are paid by the executor.

Funeral and Administrative Expenses	4,000	
Cash—Principal		4,000

Transaction 2.   The life insurance policy payable to the estate (shown in the initial entry) is collected.

Cash—Principal	40,000	
Life insurance—Payable to Estate		40,000

Transaction 3.   The title to four acres of land is discovered in a safe deposit box. This asset was not included in the original inventory of estate property. An appraiser sets the value of the land at $22,000.

Land	22,000	
Assets Subsequently Discovered		22,000

Transaction 4.   The executor receives claims totaling $24,000 for debts incurred by the decedent prior to death. This figure includes medical expenses covering the decedent's last illness ($11,000), property taxes ($4,000), utilities ($1,000), personal income taxes ($5,000), and other miscellaneous expenses ($3,000). The executor pays all of these claims.

Debts of the Decedent	24,000	
Cash—Principal		24,000

Transaction 5.   Interest of $8,000 is collected on the bonds held by the estate. Of this amount, $3,000 was earned prior to the decedent's death.

Cash—Principal	3,000	
Cash—Income	5,000	
Interest Receivable on Bonds		3,000
Estate Income		5,000

Transaction 6.   Dividends of $6,000 are collected from the stocks held by the estate. Of this amount, $4,000 was declared prior to the decedent's death.

Cash—Principal	4,000	
Cash—Income	2,000	
Dividends Receivable on Stocks		4,000
Estate Income		2,000

Transaction 7. The executor now has a problem. The Cash—Principal balance is currently $30,000:

Beginning balance	$11,000
Funeral expenses	(4,000)
Life insurance	40,000
Payment of debts	(24,000)
Interest income	3,000
Dividends	4,000
Current balance	$30,000

However, the decedent's brother has been bequeathed $38,000 in cash. This general legacy cannot be fulfilled without the sale of some property. Most of the assets have been promised as specific legacies and cannot, therefore, be used to satisfy a general legacy. Two assets, though, are residual: the investment in bonds and the land that was discovered. The executor must sell enough of these properties to generate the remaining funding needed for the $38,000 conveyance. In this illustration, assume that the executor chooses to dispose of the land and negotiates a price of $24,000. Because a principal asset is being sold, the extra $2,000 received above the recorded value is considered an adjustment to principal rather than an increase in income.

Cash—Principal	24,000	
Land		22,000
Gain on Realization		2,000

Transaction 8. Fees of $1,000 charged for administering the affairs of the estate are paid. Of this amount, $200 is considered to be applicable to estate income.

Funeral and Administrative Expenses	800	
Expenses—Income	200	
Cash—Principal		800
Cash—Income		200

Transaction 9. On October 13, 1995, the house, furnishings, and artwork are given to the decedent's aunt (Ann), the stocks are transferred to the uncle (Jack), and the grandmother (Nancy) receives the decedent's automobile and personal effects.

Legacy—Ann Wilson (residence, furnishings,		
and artwork)	114,000	
Legacy—Jack E. Wilson (stocks)	50,000	
Legacy—Nancy Wilson (automobile and		
personal effects)	6,000	
Residence		90,000

Household Furnishings and Artwork	24,000
Investment in Stocks	50,000
Automobile	4,000
Personal Effects	2,000

Charge and Discharge Statement

As necessary, the executor will file periodic reports with the probate court to disclose the progress being made in settling the estate. This report is referred to as a *charge and discharge statement*. If income and principal must be accounted for separately, the statement is prepared in two parts. For both principal and income, the statement should indicate:

1. The assets under the control of the executor.
2. Disbursements made to date.
3. Any property still remaining.

Thus, the statement on page 1097 could be produced by the executor of James T. Wilson's estate immediately after Transaction 9. (Transaction numbers are included in parenthesis for clarification purposes.)

At this point in the illustration, only three transactions remain: distribution to the decedent's brother of the $38,000 cash, conveyance to the niece of the $6,800 cash generated as income since death, and establishment of the trust fund with the remaining principal. The trust fund will receive the $240,000 in bonds and the $15,200 in cash that is now left in principal ($53,200 total less $38,000 paid to the brother).

Legacy—Brian Wilson	38,000	
Cash—Principal		38,000
Distribution to Income Beneficiary—Karen Wilson	6,800	
Cash—Income		6,800
Principal Assets Transferred to Trustee	255,200	
Cash—Principal		15,200
Investment in Bonds		240,000

A final charge and discharge statement would then be prepared by the executor followed by closing entries to signal the conclusion of the estate as a reporting entity.

Discussion Question: Is This Really an Asset?

Robert Sweingart died during December 1994 at the age of 96. Sweingart had outlived many of his relatives including the person named in his will as executor of his estate. Thus, the decedent's nephew Timothy J. Lee was

ESTATE OF JAMES T. WILSON
Charge and Discharge Statement
April 1, 1995–October 13, 1995
Bob King, Executor

As to Principal

I charge myself with:

Assets per original inventory			$468,000
Assets subsequently discovered: land (Trans. 3)			22,000
Gain on sale of land (Trans. 7)			2,000
Total charges			$492,000

I credit myself with:

Debts of decedent (Trans. 4):			
Medical expenses	$ 11,000		
Property taxes	4,000		
Utilities	1,000		
Personal income taxes	5,000		
Others	3,000	$ 24,000	
Funeral and administrative expenses (Trans. 1 and 8)		4,800	
Legacies distributed (Trans. 9):			
Ann Wilson (house, furnishings, and artwork)	114,000		
Jack E. Wilson (stocks)	50,000		
Nancy Wilson (automobile and personal effects)	6,000	170,000	
Total credits			198,800
Estate principal			$293,200

Estate principal:

Cash			$ 53,200
Investment in bonds			240,000
Estate principal			$293,200

As to Income

I charge myself with:

Interest income (Trans. 5)		$ 5,000
Dividend income (Trans. 6)		2,000
Total charges		7,000

I credit myself with:

Administrative expenses charged to income (Trans. 8)		200
Balance as to income		$ 6,800

Balance as to income:

Cash		$ 6,800

---

continued

selected by the probate court as administrator. Lee promptly began his duties including the reading of the will and the taking of an inventory of Sweingart's properties. Although the will had been written in 1959, Lee could see that most of the provisions would be easy to follow. Sweingart had made a number of specific and demonstrative legacies that could simply be conveyed to the beneficiaries. Also included in the will was a $20,000 general legacy to a local church with a residual legacy to a well-known charity. Unfortunately, after all other legacies were distributed, the estate would only have about $14,000 cash.

One item in the will concerned the administrator. Sweingart had made the following specific legacy: "I leave my collection of my grandfather's letters which are priceless to me to my cousin, William." Lee discovered the letters in a wall safe in Sweingart's home. About 40 letters existed, all in excellent condition. They were written by Sweingart's grandfather during the Civil War and described in vivid detail the Second Battle of Bull Run and the Battle of Gettysburg. Unfortunately, Lee could find no trace of a cousin named William. He apparently had died or vanished during the period since the will was written.

Lee took the letters to two different antique dealers. One stated: "A museum that maintains a Civil War collection would love to have these. They do a wonderful job of explaining history. But a museum would not pay for them. They have no real value since many letters written during this period still exist. I would recommend donating them to a museum."

The second dealer took a different position: "I think if you can find individuals who specialize in collecting Civil War memorabilia they might be willing to pay a handsome price especially if these letters help to fill out their collections. A lot of people in this country are fascinated by the Civil War. The number seems to grow each day. The letters are in great condition. It would take some investigation on your part but they could be worth a small fortune."

Lee now has to prepare an inventory of his uncle's property for probate purposes. How should these letters be reported? What should Lee do next with the letters?

Accounting for a Trust

A trust is created by the conveyance of assets to a fiduciary (or trustee) who manages the assets and ultimately disposes of them to one or more beneficiaries. The trustee may be an individual or an organization such as a bank. Over the years, trust funds have become quite popular in this country for a number of reasons. They are often established to reduce the size of a person's estate and, thus, the amount of estate taxes that must eventually be paid. As one financial advisor has stated: "Who needs to establish a trust? You do, and so does your spouse. There may be several good reasons, but start with this: if you don't set up trusts, your heirs may pay hundreds of thousands of dollars in unnecessary estate taxes." [12]

Estate taxes are not the only reason for establishing a trust. Trust funds are often formed by a person as a means of protecting assets and ensuring that their eventual use is as intended. Trusts can also result from the provisions of a will, specified by the decedent as a means of guiding the distribution of estate property. In legal terms, an *inter vivos trust* is one started by a living individual, whereas a *testamentary trust* is created by a will.

Frequently, the *trustor* (the person who funds the trust) will believe that a chosen trustee is simply better suited to manage complicated investments than is the beneficiary. A young child, for example, would not be capable of directing the use of a large sum of money. The trustor may have the same opinion of an individual who possesses little business expertise. Likewise, the creation of a trust for the benefit of a person with a mental or severe physical handicap might be considered a wise decision.

During recent years, one specific type of trust fund, a revocable living trust, has become especially popular as well as controversial. The trustor usually manages the fund and receives most, if not all, of the income until death. After that time, future income and possibly principal payments are made to one or more previously named beneficiaries. Because the trust is revocable, the trustor can change these beneficiaries or other terms of the fund at any time.

> You want to leave knowing your loved ones have the best financial breaks possible. That's why the idea of a revocable living trust may sound so promising. During your lifetime, you turn over all assets to a trust. But you act as your own trustee, so you determine how the assets will be managed and distributed. Then, happy in the knowledge that you can change the trust at any time, you have the joy of knowing you're setting up a financial plan for your life and after death. [13]

Revocable living trusts offer several advantages that appeal to certain individuals. First, this type trust avoids the delay and expense of probate. At the death of the trustor, the trust continues with future payments being made as defined in the trust agreement. In some states, this advantage can be quite important, but in others the cost of establishing the trust may be more expensive than the potential probate costs.

Second, conveyance of assets through a trust can be made without publicity whereas a will is a public document. Thus, anyone who values privacy may want to consider the revocable living trust. The entertainer Bing Crosby, for example,

---

[12] Jeff Burger, "Which Trust Is Best for Your Family?" *Medical Economics*, August 1, 1988, p. 141.

[13] Estelle Jackson, "Living Trust May Sound Promising," *Richmond Times-Dispatch*, October 13, 1991, p. C1.

set up such a trust so that no outsider would know how his estate was distributed.[14] However, certain disadvantages also exist with this type fund including the possible difficulty of establishing financing and insurance arrangements. For a complete discussion of revocable living trusts, see "Revocable Trusts: Appealing But Beware," in the October 1991 issue of the *Journal of Accountancy,* pages 91–96.

Although the number of other types of trust funds is quite large, several of the more common include:

- *Qualified Terminable Interest Property Trust* (known as a Q-TIP Trust). The income, and possibly a portion of the principal, of this type trust are paid to a surviving spouse with the remainder going to the spouse or another party after a specified period of time (or at the death of the spouse). Such trusts are popular because the spouse is provided with a steady income, but the principal can be guarded by the trustee and then conveyed at a later date to the individual's children or other designated parties.
- *Charitable Remainder Trust.* All income is paid to one or more beneficiaries identified by the trustor. After a period of time (or at the death of the beneficiaries), the principal is given to a stated charity. Thus, the trustor is guaranteeing a steady income to the intended parties while still making an eventual gift to a charitable organization.
- *Charitable Lead Trust.* This trust is the reverse of a charitable remainder trust. Income from the trust fund goes to benefit of a charity for a specified time with the remaining principal then being given to a different beneficiary. For example, a charity might receive the income from trust assets until the donor's children reach their 21st birthdays.
- *Credit Shelter Trust.* This trust is designed for couples. Each spouse agrees to transfer at death an amount of up to $600,000 to a trust fund for the benefit of the other. Thus, the income generated by these funds goes to the surviving spouse, but at the time of this individual's subsequent death, the principal is conveyed to a different beneficiary. As discussed in the previous section, this arrangement can be used to reduce the estate of the surviving spouse and, therefore, the amount of estate taxes paid by the couple.
- *Grantor Retained Annuity Trusts* (known as GRANTs). The trustor maintains the right to collect fixed payments from the trust fund with the principal being given to a beneficiary after a stated time or at the death of the trustor. For example, the trustor might retain the right to receive an amount equal to 7 percent of the initial investment annually with any remaining balance of the trust fund to go to his or her children at death.
- *Minor's Section 2503(c) Trust.* This trust fund is established for a minor and is usually designed to receive a tax-free gift of up to $10,000 each

---

[14] Ibid., p. C5.

year ($20,000 if the transfer is made by a couple). Over a period of time, especially if enough beneficiaries are available, a significant amount of assets can be removed from a person's estate. In this particular trust, though, principal and income must be conveyed to the minor prior to the 21st birthday.

- *Spendthrift Trust.* A trust that is established so that the beneficiary cannot transfer or assign any unreceived payments. Such trusts are usually established in hopes of preventing the beneficiary from squandering the assets being held by the fund.

As can be seen from these examples, many trust funds generate income for one or more beneficiaries (known as *life tenants* if the income is to be conveyed until the person dies). At death or at the end of a specified period, the remaining principal is then transferred to a different beneficiary (a *remainderman*). Therefore, as with estates, differentiating between principal and income is ultimately important in accounting for trust funds. This distinction is especially significant since trusts frequently exist for decades and can control and generate enormous amounts of assets.

The reporting function is also important because of the legal responsibilities of the trustee. This fiduciary is charged with carrying out the wise use of all funds and may be sued by the beneficiaries if actions are considered to be unnecessarily risky or in contradiction to the terms of the trust arrangement. To avoid potential legal problems, the trustee is normally called on to exercise reasonable and prudent care in managing the assets of the fund.

Record-Keeping for a Trust Fund

Trust accounting is quite similar to the procedures that were demonstrated previously for an estate. However, because of the many different types of trusts that can be created as well as the extended time period that might be involved, the accounting process may become more complex than for an estate. As an example, an apartment house or a significant portion of a business could be placed in a trust for 20 years or longer. Thus, the possible range of transactions to be recorded becomes quite broad. In such cases, the fiduciary might choose to establish two separate sets of accounts: one for principal and one for income. As an alternative, a single set of records could also be utilized with the individual accounts identified as to income or principal.

In the same manner as an estate, the trust agreement should specify the distinction between transactions to be recorded as income and those to be recorded as principal. If the agreement is silent or if a transaction is incurred that is not covered by the agreement, state laws are applicable. Generally accepted accounting principles are usually not considered appropriate. For example, the cash method rather than accrual accounting is utilized by trusts in recording most transactions. Although a definitive set of rules is not possible, the following list indicates the normal division of principal and income transactions.

Adjustments to the trust's principal:

Investing costs and commissions.

Income taxes on gains added to the principal.

Costs of preparing property for rent or sale.

Extraordinary repairs (improvements).

Adjustments to the trust's income:

Rent expense.

Lease cancellation fees.

Interest expense.

Insurance expense.

Income taxes on trust income.

Property taxes.

Trustee fees and the cost of periodic reporting must be allocated evenly between trust income and principal.

Accounting for the Activities of a Trust

For an inter vivos trust, reporting on an annual basis (or perhaps more frequently) is made to all of the income and principal beneficiaries. However, testamentary trusts come under the jurisdiction of the courts so that additional reporting becomes necessary. Normally, a statement resembling the charge and discharge statement of an estate is adequate for these purposes. Two accounts, Trust Principal and Trust Income, are established to monitor changes that occur. For a testamentary trust, the opening principal balance is the fair market value used by the executor for estate tax purposes.

To illustrate, assume that the following events occur in connection with the creation of a charitable remainder trust. In the will of Samuel Statler, a trust is created with the income earned each year to go to his niece for 10 years with the principal then being conveyed to a local university.

1. Cash of $80,000 and stocks (that originally cost $39,000 but are now worth $47,000) are transferred from the estate to the First National Bank of Michigan because this organization has agreed to serve as trustee for these funds.

2. Cash of $76,000 is invested by the trustee in bonds paying 11 percent annual cash interest.

3. Dividends of $6,000 are collected on the stocks, and interest of $7,000 is received on the bonds. No receivables had been included in the estate for these amounts.

4. At the end of the year, an additional $3,000 in interest is due on the bonds.

5. As trustee, the bank charges $2,000 for services rendered for the year.

6. The niece is paid the appropriate amount of money from the trust fund.

As the trustee, the bank should record these transactions as follows:

1. Cash—Principal 80,000
   Investment in Stocks 47,000
      Trust Principal 127,000
      To record trust assets at the fair market value figure used for estate
   tax purposes.

2. Investment in Bonds 76,000
      Cash—Principal 76,000
      To record acquisition of bonds using cash in trust fund.

3. Cash—Income 13,000
      Trust—Income 13,000
      To record dividends and interest collected.

4. No entry is recorded. These earnings cannot be paid to the income beneficiary until collected so that accrual provides no benefit. Therefore, a cash system rather than accrual accounting is used by the trustee.

5. Expenses—Income 1,000
   Expenses—Principal 1,000
      Cash—Income 1,000
      Cash—Principal 1,000
      To allocate the trustee's fees evenly between principal and income.

6. Equity in Income: Beneficiary 12,000
      Cash—Income 12,000
      To record yearly payment made to income beneficiary. Amount is
   computed as the dividends and interest of $13,000 less expenses of
   $1,000.

Summary

1. An estate is the legal entity that holds title to a decedent's property until a final settlement and distribution can be made. State laws, known as probate laws, govern this process. These laws become particularly significant if the decedent died intestate (without a will).

2. An executor to oversee the estate should be named in the decedent's will. If not, the probate court selects an administrator. The executor takes possession of all properties, settles valid claims, files tax returns, pays taxes due, and distributes any remaining assets according to the provisions of the decedent's will or state inheritance laws. The executor must issue a public notice so that all creditors have adequate opportunity to file a claim against the estate. Prior to paying these claims, a homestead allowance and a family allowance are provided to the members of the decedent's immediate family. Claims are then ranked in order of priority to indicate the payment schedule if existing funds prove to be insufficient. For example, administrative expenses and funeral expenses are at the top of this priority listing.

3. Devises are gifts of real property; legacies (or bequests) are gifts of personal property. Legacies can be classified legally as specific, demonstrative, general, or residual depending on the type of property and the identity of the source. If insufficient funds are available to fulfill all legacies, the process of abatement is applied to determine the loss allocations. Residual legacies are reduced to zero first, and then, if necessary, general legacies are decreased. Demonstrative legacies are reduced next followed by specific legacies.

4. Federal estate taxes are assessed on the value of estate property. Reductions in the total value of an estate are allowed for funeral and administrative expenses as well as for liabilities, charitable gifts, and all property conveyed to a spouse. In addition, a unified transfer credit is available so that estates worth less than $600,000 are not taxed. A portion (or all) of the decedent's unified transfer credit could have already been used prior to death to reduce or avoid the payment of taxes on gifts of more than $10,000 per person per year (or $20,000 per couple). Federal estate taxes are reduced by amounts paid, within defined limits, to the states for inheritance or estate taxes.

5. In both estates and trusts, the distinction between income and principal is frequently an important issue. Income may be assigned to one party with the principal eventually going to a different beneficiary. Such arrangements are especially common in trust funds such as charitable remainder trusts. The decedent (for an estate) or the trustor (for a trust) should have identified the method of classification to be used for complicated transactions. If no guidance is provided, state laws become applicable. For example, major repairs and investment costs are usually considered reductions in principal, whereas expenses such as property taxes and ordinary repairs are charged to income. The bookkeeping procedures for estates and trusts are designed to separate and then reflect the transactions affecting principal and income.

6. To provide evidence of the fiduciary's proper handling of an estate or trust, a charge and discharge statement is produced. This statement reports the assets over which the individual has been given responsibility. The statement also indicates all disbursements of assets as well as the property remaining at the current time. Separate reports are prepared for income and principal.

Comprehensive Illustration

PROBLEM   (Estimated Time: 30 to 40 minutes)

Part A

The will of James Daily contains the following provisions:

I leave my house, my personal effects, and my investments in corporate stocks to my wife, Nora.

I leave the balance in my savings account up to a total of $26,000 to my son, George.

I leave $6,000 in cash to my niece, Susan.

I direct that all remaining assets, including my rental properties, be placed in trust. The income from this trust will go to my wife. At her death, the principal of this trust fund will be conveyed to the First United Church of Burlington, Alabama.

The executor of this estate has now paid all claims and the following properties remain (fair market value is indicated):

House and personal effects.	$320,000
Savings account.	23,000
Cash.	9,000
Investment in bonds	35,000

All rental property as well as corporate stocks were sold by Daily prior to his death.

Required:

a. Identify the following:

- Trustor.
- Life tenant.
- Remainderman.
- General legacy.
- Demonstrative legacy.

b. Answer the following questions:

- Is this trust an inter vivos trust or a testamentary trust?
- What specific type of trust has been created?
- To whom will the properties be distributed?

Part B

The will of Susan York contains the following provisions:

I leave my house and personal effects to James J. York.

I leave $9,000 in cash to M. J. York.

I leave all my investments to Bishop University.

Any income earned on my investments prior to distribution I leave to the Freedom Church of Lubbock, Texas.

I leave the remainder of my estate to Cindy Ruark.

The executor, Brendan Jaminson, takes an inventory and discovers the following assets. An appraisal is made of every item to determine their fair market values at the time of death.

Cash	$ 46,000
House and personal effects	310,000
Investments:	
Stocks	21,000
Bonds	44,000
Land (rental property)	65,000
Collection of antiques	19,000
Dividends receivable	1,000
Interest receivable	2,000
Rent receivable	4,000
Total	$512,000

The following valid claims are made against the estate and paid by the executor:

Funeral expenses	$17,000
Executor charges	9,000
Medical expenses	11,000
Debts	5,000

The following cash collections are received by the estate:

Dividends	$ 2,000 (half declared prior to death)
Interest	3,000
Rent	7,000
Sold antique collection	21,000

Prior to June 25, 1995, the current date, the executor made complete distributions to both James J. York and M. J. York.

Required:
Prepare a charge and discharge statement for this estate. The date of death was January 23, 1995.

SOLUTION

Part A

   a.

- James Daily established the trust fund and would, therefore, be legally referred to as the trustor.

- James Daily's wife, Nora, will receive the benefits of the trust fund until her death. She is a life tenant.
- The First United Church of Burlington, Alabama, has been designated to receive the principal of the trust fund after the death of Nora Daily. Thus, the church is termed the remainderman of the fund.
- Since the $6,000 gift to Daily's niece Susan does not come from a designated source, it is known as a general legacy.
- The cash gift to Daily's son is to be taken from a savings account. A conveyance that is to be derived from a specified source is known as a demonstrative legacy.

b.

- This trust fund is a testamentary trust because it was created by the provisions of the decedent's will.
- This trust is an example of a charitable remainder trust. For a stated time, the earnings generated by the trust are to be conveyed to an income beneficiary. After that date (the death of Nora Daily, in this case), the principal is transferred to a charitable organization.
- The following distributions should be made by the executor of this estate:

House and personal effects are given to Nora Daily. Since investments in corporate stocks are no longer held by the estate, this portion of the will cannot be fulfilled.

The $23,000 cash found in the savings account is conveyed to George Daily. Although a maximum of $26,000 was promised, the account is not large enough to reach the upper limit specified by the will. However, because the provisions as written have been fulfilled, the remaining $3,000 is not a general legacy.

Cash of $6,000 is given to Daily's niece.

The remaining property (the investment in bonds and the $3,000 cash) is placed in the trust.

ESTATE OF SUSAN YORK
Charge and Discharge Statement
January 23, 1995–June 25, 1995
Brendan Jaminson, Executor

As to Principal

I charge myself with:

Assets per original inventory		$512,000
Gain on sale of antiques		2,000
Total charges		$514,000

I credit myself with:

Debts of decedent:

Medical expenses	$ 11,000		
Other debts	5,000	$ 16,000	
Funeral and administrative expenses ($17,000 + $9,000)		26,000	
Legacies distributed:			
James J. York (house and personal effects)	$310,000		
M. J. York (cash)	9,000	319,000	
Total credits		$361,000	
Estate principal		$153,000	

Estate principal:

Cash (see below)	$ 23,000
Investments:	
Stocks	21,000
Bonds	44,000
Land	65,000
Estate principal	$153,000

Cash balance:

Beginning balance	$ 46,000
Sale of antique collection	21,000
Collection of receivables (dividends $1,000, interest $2,000, and rent $4,000)	7,000
Payment of debts and expenses (funeral expenses $17,000, executor charges $9,000, medical expenses $11,000, and debts $5,000)	(42,000)
Legacy distribution (M. J. York)	(9,000)
Cash balance	$ 23,000

As to Income

I charge myself with:

Dividend income ($2,000 collection less $1,000 receivable at death)	$ 1,000
Interest income ($3,000 less $2,000)	1,000
Rent income ($7,000 less $4,000)	3,000
Balance as to income	$ 5,000

Balance as to income:

Cash	$ 5,000

Questions

1. What is the meaning of the terms *testate* and *intestate*?
2. If a person dies without having written a will, how is the distribution of property regulated?
3. What are probate laws? What are their objectives?
4. What responsibilities are given to the executor of an estate?
5. At what value are the assets within an estate reported?
6. How are the claims against an estate discovered by an executor?
7. What claims against an estate have priority?
8. What are homestead and family allowances?
9. What is the difference between a devise and a legacy?
10. Describe and give examples of the four types of legacies.
11. What is the purpose of the process of abatement? How is this process utilized by the executor of an estate?
12. How is the federal estate tax computed?
13. What is the unified transfer credit and how is this credit applied?
14. What is a taxable gift?
15. For couples, why is the establishment of a $600,000 trust fund considered a good estate planning technique?
16. What deductions are allowed in computing estate income taxes?
17. In accounting for an estate or trust, how is the distinction between principal and income determined?
18. What transactions are normally viewed as changes in the principal of an estate? What transactions are normally viewed as changes in the income of an estate?
19. What is the alternative date for valuing the assets of an estate? When should this alternative date be used?
20. In the initial accounting for an estate, why does the executor only record the assets?
21. What is the purpose of the charge and discharge statement that is issued by the executor of an estate?
22. What is a trust fund? Why have trust funds become especially popular in recent years?
23. What is an inter vivos trust? What is a testamentary trust?
24. What are Q-TIP trusts, GRANTs, and charitable remainder trusts?
25. Why is the distinction between principal and income so important in accounting for most trusts?

Library Assignment

Read the following and any other published materials on estate planning:

"Advantages of Planned Giving," *The CPA Journal,* September 1992.

"Special Needs Trusts: Financial and Estate Planning for the Disabled," *Journal of Accountancy,* July 1991.

"Charitable Remainder and Wealth Replacement Trusts: Too Good to Be True?" *Journal of Accountancy* (Personal Financial Planning Section), April 1992.

"Keeping Down Estate Taxes," *Fortune: 1990 Investor's Guide* (Special Issue), Fall 1989.

"The Bad News about Estate Taxes," *Forbes,* June 26, 1989.

"A Primer on Trusts," *Journal of Accountancy,* May 1993.

"How to Pass on Your Nest Egg without Probate," *Business Week* (Personal Business Section), July 11, 1988.

"Revocable Trusts: Appealing, But Beware," *Journal of Accountancy,* October 1991.

"Death and . . . ," *The Wall Street Journal,* December 2, 1988, p. R33.

Write a report describing the various techniques used in estate planning to both reduce estate taxes and ensure that a decedent's assets are utilized as intended.

Problems

1. Which of the following is not a true statement?
   a. *Testate* refers to a person having a valid will.
   b. Personal property is conveyed by the laws of descent if an individual dies without a valid will.
   c. *Intestate* refers to a person having no valid will.
   d. A specific legacy is a gift of personal property that is specifically identified.

2. Why might real estate be omitted from an inventory of estate property?
   a. Real estate is subject to a separate inheritance tax.
   b. State laws prohibit real property from being conveyed by an estate.
   c. State laws require a separate listing of all real estate.
   d. In some states, real estate is considered to be conveyed directly to a beneficiary at the time of death.

3. What is the purpose of the laws of distribution?
   a. They guide the distribution of personal property when an individual dies without a will.

     b. They are used to verify the legality of a will, especially an oral will.

     c. They guide the distribution of real property when an individual dies without a will.

     d. They outline the functions of the executor of an estate.

4. A bond was owned by a deceased individual. Which of the following amounts is included in the estate principal?

     a. All interest collected prior to distributing the bonds to a beneficiary is considered part of the estate principal.

     b. Only the first cash payment after death is included in the estate principal.

     c. Interest that was not collected prior to death is excluded from the estate principal.

     d. Interest earned prior to death is considered part of the estate principal even if received after death.

5. Which of the following is not a goal of probate laws?

     a. To gather and preserve all of the decendent's property.

     b. To ensure that each individual produces a valid will.

     c. To discover the decedent's intent for property held at death and then to follow those wishes.

     d. To carry out an orderly and fair settlement of all debts and distribution of property.

6. How are claims against a decedent's estate discovered by an executor?

     a. Public notice must be printed in an appropriate newspaper to alert all possible claimants.

     b. The executor waits for nine months until all possible bills have been received.

     c. All companies that the decedent did business with are contacted directly by the executor.

     d. Claims to be paid by the estate are limited to all of the bills received, but not paid, prior to the date of death.

7. Why are claims against an estate put into an order of priority?

     a. To help the executor determine the due date for each claim.

     b. To determine which claims are to be paid if funds are insufficient to pay all claims.

     c. To assist in determining which specific assets are to be used to satisfy these claims.

     d. To list the claims in order of age so that the oldest can be paid first.

8. Which of the following claims against an estate does not have priority?

     a. Funeral expenses, since the amounts incurred are usually at the discretion of family members.

     b. Medical expenses associated with the decedent's last illness.

     c. The costs of administering the estate.

     d. Unpaid rent on the decedent's home if not paid for the three months immediately prior to death.

9. How does a devise differ from a legacy?
   a. A devise is a gift of money and a legacy is a nonmonetary gift.
   b. A devise is a gift to an individual and a legacy is a gift to a charity or other organization.
   c. A devise is a gift of real property and a legacy is a gift of personal property.
   d. A devise is a gift made prior to death and a legacy is a gift made at death.

10. What is the homestead allowance?
    a. A reduction of $20,000 that is made in estate assets prior to computing the amount of federal estate taxes.
    b. The amount of property conveyed in a will to a surviving spouse.
    c. An allotment of $5,000 cash made from an estate to a surviving spouse and/or minor and dependent children before any claims are paid.
    d. A decrease made in the value of property on which state inheritance taxes are assessed. The reduction is equal to the value of property conveyed to a surviving spouse.

11. Which of the following is a specific legacy?
    a. The gift of all remaining estate property to a charity.
    b. The gift of $44,000 cash from a specified source.
    c. The gift of $44,000 cash.
    d. The gift of 1,000 shares of stock in IBM.

12. A will has the following statement: ''I leave $20,000 cash from my savings account in the Central Fidelity Bank to my sister, Angela.'' This gift is an example of:
    a. A residual legacy.
    b. A general legacy.
    c. A demonstrative legacy.
    d. A specific legacy.

13. What is the objective of the process of abatement?
    a. To give legal structure to the reductions that must be made if an estate has insufficient assets to satisfy all legacies.
    b. To ensure that all property distributions take place in a timely manner.
    c. To provide adequate compensation for the estate executor and any appraisers or other experts that must be hired.
    d. To ensure that all legacies are distributed to the appropriate party as specified by the decedent's will or state laws.

14. For estate tax purposes, what date is used for valuation purposes?
    a. Property is always valued at the date of death.
    b. Property is always valued at the date of distribution.
    c. Property is valued at the date of death unless the alternative date is selected which is the date of distribution or six months after death whichever comes first.

    d. Property is valued at the date of death although a reduction is allowed if the value declines within one year of death.

15. Which of the following statements is true concerning the unified transfer credit?

    a. It is reduced by any charity bequests made by the decedent during the three years just prior to death.

    b. It only applies to decedents who produced valid wills.

    c. It is reduced by nontaxed gifts to individuals made during the decedent's lifetime if over $10,000 per person per year.

    d. It enables estates valued at $900,000 or less to avoid federal estate taxes.

16. In computing federal estate taxes, deductions from the value of the estate are allowed for all of the following except

    a. Charitable bequests.

    b. Losses on the disposal of investments.

    c. Funeral expenses.

    d. Debts of the decedent.

17. The estate of John Lexington has a taxable value of $550,000. The estate of Dorothye Alexander has a taxable value of $650,000. The estate of Scotty Fitzgerald has a taxable value of $750,000. None of these individuals made any taxable gifts during their lifetimes. Which of the following statements is true?

    a. Only Fitzgerald's estate will have to pay federal estate taxes.

    b. All three of the estates will have to pay federal estate taxes.

    c. None of these estates is large enough to necessitate the payment of estate taxes.

    d. Only the estates of Alexander and Fitzgerald are large enough to necessitate the payment of estate taxes.

18. Sally Anne Williams dies on January 1, 1995. All of her property is conveyed to several relatives on April 1, 1995. For federal estate tax purposes, the executor chooses the alternative valuation date. On what date is the value of the property determined?

    a. January 1, 1995.

    b. April 1, 1995.

    c. July 1, 1995.

    d. December 31, 1995.

19. M. Wilson Waltman dies on January 1, 1995. All of his property is conveyed to beneficiaries on October 1, 1995. For federal estate tax purposes, the executor chooses the alternative valuation date. On what date is the value of the property determined?

    a. January 1, 1995.

    b. July 1, 1995.

    c. October 1, 1995.

    d. December 31, 1995.

20. Which of the following is true concerning gift taxes?
    a. A couple may make gifts of $25,000 each year to a person without having to pay a gift tax.
    b. A gift tax can be avoided by applying the unified transfer credit but this use reduces the amount of the credit that can be applied by the donor's estate after death.
    c. Gift tax computations and estate tax computations are unrelated.
    d. Gift taxes can be avoided by making all gifts to blood relatives.

21. A couple has written a will that leaves part of their money to a trust fund. The income from this trust will benefit the surviving spouse until death with the principal then going to their children. Why was the trust fund created?
    a. To reduce the estate of the surviving spouse and, thus, decrease the total amount of estate taxes to be paid by the couple.
    b. To make certain that the surviving spouse is protected from lawsuits filed by the children of the couple.
    c. To give the surviving spouse discretion over the ultimate use of these funds.
    d. Trust funds generate more income than other investments so that the earning potential of the money is maximized.

22. The executor of an estate is filing an income tax return for the current period. Revenues of $12,000 have been earned. Which of the following is not a deduction allowed in computing taxable income?
    a. Income distributed to a beneficiary.
    b. Funeral expenses.
    c. A personal exemption.
    d. Charitable donations.

23. What is a remainderman?
    a. A beneficiary that receives the principal left in an estate or trust after a specified time.
    b. The beneficiary of the decedent's life insurance policy.
    c. An executor or administrator after an estate has been completely settled.
    d. If a legacy is given to a group of people, the remainderman is the last of the individuals to die.

24. In an estate, which of the following is charged to income rather than to principal?
    a. Funeral expenses.
    b. Investment costs.
    c. Property taxes.
    d. Losses on the sale of investments.

25. In recording the transactions of an estate, when are liabilities recorded?
    a. When incurred.
    b. At the date of death.

    c. When the executor takes responsibility for the estate.

    d. When paid.

26. What is the difference between an inter vivos trust and a testamentary trust?

    a. A testamentary trust conveys money to a charity, while an inter vivos trust conveys money to individuals.

    b. A testamentary trust is created by a will, while an inter vivos trust is created by a living individual.

    c. A testamentary trust conveys income to one party and the principal to another, while an inter vivos trust conveys all monies to the same party.

    d. A testamentary trust ceases after a specified period of time, while an inter vivos trust is assumed to be permanent.

27. Which of the following is a charitable lead trust?

    a. The income of the trust fund goes to an individual until death with the principal then being conveyed to a charitable organization.

    b. Charitable gifts are placed into the trust until a certain dollar amount is achieved that is then transferred to a specified charitable organization.

    c. The income of a trust fund goes to a charitable organization for a specified time with the principal then being conveyed to a different beneficiary.

    d. A charity conveys money to a trust that generates income for use by the charity in its various projects.

28. The estate of Nancy Hanks reports the following information:

Value of estate assets	$1,400,000
Conveyed to spouse	700,000
Conveyed to children	100,000
Conveyed to charities	420,000
Funeral expenses	50,000
Administrative expenses	20,000
Debts	110,000

What is the taxable estate value?

    a. $70,000.

    b. $100,000.

    c. $180,000.

    d. $420,000.

29. An estate has the following income:

Rental income	$5,000
Interest income	3,000
Dividend income	1,000

The interest income was immediately conveyed to the appropriate beneficiary. The dividends were given to charity as per the decedent's will. What is the taxable income of the estate?

a. $4,400.

b. $5,000.

c. $8,000.

d. $8,400.

30. Define each of the following terms:
   - Will.
   - Estate.
   - Intestate.
   - Probate laws.
   - Trust.
   - Inter vivos trust.
   - Charitable remainder trust.
   - Remainderman.
   - Unified transfer credit.
   - Executor.
   - Homestead allowance.

31. Answer each of the following questions:
   - What are the objectives of probate laws?
   - What tasks are performed by the executor of an estate?
   - What assets are normally included as estate properties?
   - What claims have priority to the distributions made by an estate?

32. The will of Victor Laslo has the following stipulations:

Antique collection goes to Ilsa Lunn.

All money in the First Savings Bank goes to Richard Blaine.

Cash of $9,000 goes to Nelson Tucker.

All remaining assets are put into a trust fund with the income going to Lucy Van Jones. At her death, the principal is to be conveyed to Howard Amadeus.

Identify the following:

a. Remainderman.

b. Trustor.

c. Demonstrative legacy.

d. General legacy.

e. Specific legacy.

f. Life tenant.

33. The will of Carson M. Newman has the following provisions:

"I leave the cash balance deposited in the First National Bank (up to a total of $50,000) to Jack Abrams. I leave $18,000 cash to Suzanne Benton. I leave 1,000 shares of Coca-Cola Company stock to Cindy Cheng. I leave my house to Dennis Davis. I leave all of my other assets and properties to Wilbur N. Ed.''

    a. Assume that the estate has the following assets: $41,000 cash in the First National Bank, $16,000 cash in the New Hampshire Savings and Loan, 800 shares of Coca-Cola stock, 1,100 shares of Xerox stock, a house, and other property valued at $13,000. What distributions will be made from this estate?

    b. Assume that the estate has the following assets: $55,000 cash in the First National Bank, $6,000 cash in the New Hampshire Savings and Loan, 1,200 shares of Coca-Cola stock, 600 shares of Xerox stock, and other property valued at $22,000. What distributions will be made from this estate?

34. The estate of Jeb Stewart reports the following information:

Value of estate assets	$2,300,000
Conveyed to spouse	1,000,000
Conveyed to children	230,000
Conveyed to trust fund for benefit of spouse	500,000
Conveyed to charities	260,000
Funeral expenses	23,000
Administrative expense	41,000
Debts	246,000

What is the taxable estate value?

35. An estate has the following assets (all figures are valued at values approximating market value):

Investments in stocks and bonds	$900,000
House	260,000
Cash	70,000
Investment land	60,000
Automobiles (three)	51,000
Other assets	100,000

    The house, cash, and other assets are left to the decedent's spouse. The investment land is contributed to a charitable organization. The automobiles are to be given to the decedent's brother. The investments in stocks and bonds are to be put into a trust fund. The income generated by this trust will go annually to the decedent's spouse until all of the couple's children have reached the age of 25. At that time, the trust will be divided evenly among the children.

The following amounts are paid prior to distribution and settlement of the estate: funeral expenses of $20,000 and estate administration expenses of $10,000.

a. What is the value to be reported as the taxable estate for federal estate tax purposes?

b. How does the Unified Transfer Credit affect the computation of federal estate taxes? How is this credit used in computing gift taxes during the decedent's lifetime?

36. During the current year, an estate generates income of $20,000:

Rental income	$9,000
Interest income	6,000
Dividend income	5,000

The interest income is conveyed immediately to the beneficiary stated in the decedent's will. Dividends of $1,200 are given to the decedent's church.

What amount of federal income tax must be paid by this estate?

37. The executor of the estate of Wilbur Stone has listed the following properties (at fair market value):

Cash	$300,000
Life insurance receivable	200,000
Investments in stocks and bonds	100,000
Rental property	90,000
Personal property	130,000

The following transactions occur in the months following the decedent's death:

• Claims of $80,000 are made against the estate for various debts incurred before the decedent's death.
• Interest of $12,000 is received from bonds held by the estate. Of this amount, $5,000 had been earned prior to death.
• Ordinary repairs costing $6,000 are made to the rental property.
• All debts ($80,000) are paid.
• Stocks recorded in the estate at $16,000 are sold for $19,000 cash.
• Rental income of $14,000 is collected. Of this amount, $2,000 had been earned prior to the decedent's death.
• Cash of $6,000 is distributed to Jim Arness, an income beneficiary.

- The proceeds from the life insurance policy are collected with the money being immediately distributed to Amanda Blake as specified in the decedent's will.
- Funeral expenses of $10,000 are paid.

Required:

a. Prepare journal entries to record each of the preceding transactions.

b. Prepare in proper form a charge and discharge statement.

38. The executor of the estate of James Cooper has recorded the following information:

Assets discovered at death (at fair market value):	
Cash	$600,000
Life insurance receivable	200,000
Investments:	
Walt Disney Company	11,000
Polaroid Corporation	27,000
Ford Motor Company	34,000
Compaq Computer Corporation	32,000
Rental property	300,000
Cash outflows:	
Funeral expenses	$ 21,000
Executor fees	12,000
Ordinary repairs of rental property.	2,000
Debts.	81,000
Distribution of income to income beneficiary	4,000
Distribution to charitable remainder trust	300,000
Cash inflows:	
Sale of Polaroid stock	$ 30,000
Rental income ($4,000 earned prior to death)	11,000
Dividend income ($2,000 declared prior to death)	12,000
Life insurance proceeds	200,000

Debts of $17,000 still remain to be paid. The shares of Compaq have been conveyed to the appropriate beneficiary.

Required:

Prepare a charge and discharge statement for this estate.

39. The will of Jane T. Simmons has the following provisions:

- $150,000 in cash goes to Thomas Thorne.
- All shares of Coca-Cola go to Cindy Phillips.
- Residence goes to Kevin Simmons.
- All other estate assets are to be liquidated with the resulting cash going to the First Church of Freedom, Missouri.

Prepare journal entries for the following transactions:

a. The executor of this estate has discovered the following assets (at fair market value):

Cash	$ 80,000
Interest receivable	6,000
Life insurance policy	300,000
Residence	200,000
Shares of Coca-Cola Company	50,000
Shares of Polaroid Corporation	110,000
Shares of James River	140,000

b. Interest of $7,000 is collected.

c. Funeral expenses of $20,000 are paid.

d. Debts of $40,000 are discovered.

e. An additional savings account of $12,000 is located by the executor.

f. Title to the residence is conveyed to Kevin Simmons.

g. Life insurance policy is collected.

h. Additional debts of $60,000 are discovered. Debts totaling $100,000 are paid.

i. Cash of $150,000 is conveyed to appropriate beneficiary.

j. The shares of Polaroid are sold for $112,000.

k. Administrative expenses of $10,000 are paid.

40. After the death of Lawrence Pope, his will was read. It contained the following provisions:

- $110,000 in cash goes to decedent's brother, Ned Pope.
- Residence and other personal property goes to his sister, Sue Pope.
- Proceeds from the sale of Ford stock goes to uncle, Harwood Pope.
- $300,000 goes into a charitable remainder trust.
- All other estate assets are to be liquidated with the cash going to Victoria Jones.

The following transactions subsequently occur:

a. The executor of this estate discovers the following assets (at fair market value):

Cash	$ 19,000
Certificates of deposit	90,000
Dividend receivable	3,000
Life insurance policy	450,000
Residence and personal effects	470,000
Shares of Ford Motor Company	72,000
Shares of Xerox Corporation	97,000

b. Life insurance policy is collected.

c. Dividends of $4,000 are collected.

d. Debts of $71,000 are discovered.

e. Title to the residence is conveyed to Sue Pope along with the decedent's personal effects.

f. Title to land valued at $15,000 is discovered by the executor.

g. Additional debts of $37,000 are discovered. All of the debts, totaling $108,000, are paid.

h. Funeral expenses of $31,000 are paid.

i. Cash of $110,000 is conveyed to Ned Pope.

j. The shares of Ford are sold for $81,000.

k. Administrative expenses of $16,000 are paid.

l. The appropriate payment is made to Harwood Pope.

Required:

a. Prepare journal entries for the preceding transactions.

b. Prepare a charge and discharge statement.

41. James Albemarle creates a trust fund at the beginning of 1995. The income from this fund will go to his son, Edward. When Edward reaches the age of 25, the principal of the fund will be conveyed to United Charities of Cleveland.

    Prepare all necessary journal entries for the trust to record the following transactions:

    a. Cash of $300,000, stocks worth $200,000, and rental property valued at $150,000 are transferred by James Albemarle to the trustee of this fund.

    b. Cash of $260,000 is immediately invested in bonds issued by the U.S. government. Commissions of $3,000 are paid on this transaction.

    c. Permanent repairs of $7,000 are incurred so that the property can be rented. Payment is made immediately.

    d. Dividends of $4,000 are received. Of this amount, $1,000 had been declared prior to the creation of the trust fund.

    e. Insurance expense of $2,000 is paid on the rental property.

    f. Rental income of $8,000 is received.

    g. The trustee collects $4,000 from the fund for services rendered.

    h. Cash of $5,000 is conveyed to Edward Albemarle.

42. An inter vivos trust fund is created by Henry O'Donnell. O'Donnell owns a large department store in Higgins, Utah. Adjacent to the store, he also owns a tract of land used as an extra parking lot, especially when the store is having a sale or during the Christmas season. O'Donnell expects the land to appreciate in value and eventually be sold for an office complex or additional stores.

    O'Donnell places this land into a charitable remainder trust which will hold the land for 10 years until O'Donnell's son is 21. At that time, title will be transferred to the son. The store will pay rent to use the land during the interim. The income generated each year from this usage will be given to a local church. The land is currently valued at $320,000.

During the first year of this arrangement, the trustee records the following cash transactions:

Cash inflows:	
Rental income	$60,000
Cash outflows:	
Insurance	$ 4,000
Property taxes	6,000
Paving (considered an extraordinary repair)	4,000
Maintenance	8,000
Distribution to income beneficiary	30,000

Prepare all journal entries for this trust fund including the entry to create the trust.

20 FINANCIAL REPORTING AND THE SECURITIES AND EXCHANGE COMMISSION

Questions to Consider

- How does the U.S. government ensure that adequate reliable information is available to encourage investors to buy and sell securities so that sufficient capital can be raised by businesses for financing purposes?
- What companies are subject to the rules and regulations of the Securities and Exchange Commission?
- How does the SEC influence the development of accounting principles in the United States?
- What is the purpose of the registration statements filed with the SEC? What various periodic filings must also be made?
- What steps usually occur in the registration process?
- Which types of securities are exempt from registration with the SEC?

> The Securities and Exchange Commission was born on June 6, 1934—a time of despair in the markets. Americans were still suffering from the 1929 market crash after a roaring 1920s when they bought about $50 billion in new securities—half of which turned out to be worthless. Their confidence also was eroded by the 1932 indictment (later acquittal) of Samuel Insull for alleged wrongs in the collapse of his utility "empire," and by the 1933–34 Senate hearings on improper market activity.[1]

The financing of the American industrial complex is very much dependent on raising vast amounts of monetary capital. During every business day in the United States, billions of dollars of stocks and bonds are sold to thousands of individuals, corporations, trust funds, pension plans, mutual funds, and other institutions. Such investors cannot be expected to venture their money without forethought.

---

[1] "D-Day for the Securities Industry, 1934," *The Wall Street Journal*, May 9, 1989, p. B1.

They have to be able to assess the risks involved: the possibility of either profit or loss being returned to them as well as the expected amount.

Consequently, disclosure of sufficient, accurate information is absolutely necessary to stimulate the inflow of large quantities of capital. Enough data must be available to encourage investors to consider buying and selling securities in hopes of generating profits. *Without adequate information on which to base these decisions, investing becomes no more than gambling.*

The Work of the Securities and Exchange Commission

In the United States, the responsibility for ensuring that complete and reliable information is available to investors lies with the Securities and Exchange Commission (SEC), an agency of the federal government created by the Securities Exchange Act of 1934. Although the SEC's authority applies mainly to publicly held companies, the commission's guidelines and requirements surely have been a major influence in the United States on the development of all generally accepted accounting principles.

> The Securities and Exchange Commission was established in 1934 in an effort to foster honest and open securities markets. Congress, in establishing the SEC, gave broad powers to the Commission to regulate securities and to ensure proper financial reporting and disclosure by American businesses.[2]

The SEC is headed by five commissioners appointed by the president of the United States (with the consent of the Senate) to serve five-year staggered terms. To ensure the bipartisan nature of this group, no more than three of these individuals can belong to the same political party. The chairman is from the same political party as the president. The commissioners provide leadership for an agency that has grown over the years into a large organization composed of more than a dozen divisions and major offices including:

- The *Division of Corporation Finance* helps to establish standards of reporting and disclosure for the companies filing with the SEC.
- The *Division of Market Regulation* assists the commission in regulating national securities exchanges and investment brokers and dealers.
- The *Division of Enforcement* reviews and directs all enforcement activities and supervises investigations.
- The *Office of the Chief Accountant* is responsible for all accounting and auditing matters that arise in connection with the securities laws.

The SEC's budget for 1991 was $192.4 million. A breakdown of this appropriation gives some indication of the work of the organization:

---

[2] K. Fred Skousen, *An Introduction to the SEC,* (Cincinnati: South-Western Publishing, 1991), p. v.

Major Programs

Prevention and suppression of fraud	33 percent
Full disclosure programs	22 percent
Regulation of securities markets.	13 percent
Program direction	13 percent
Investment management regulation	12 percent

This chapter provides an overview of the workings of the Securities and Exchange Commission along with the agency's relationship to the accounting profession. Unfortunately, a complete examination of the organization is beyond the scope of this textbook. Therefore, only a portion of the SEC's functions are discussed here. This coverage provides an introduction to the role the agency currently plays in the world of American business.

Purpose of the Federal Securities Laws

Before examining the SEC and its various functions in more detail, a historical perspective needs to be established. The development of laws regulating companies involved in interstate commerce were discussed as early as 1885. In fact, the Industrial Commission created by Congress suggested in 1902 that all publicly held companies should be required to disclose material information including annual financial reports. However, only the crisis following the stock market crash of 1929 and the subsequently discovered fraud prompted Congress to act in hopes of reestablishing the trust and stability needed for capital markets.

> The securities market activities of the 1920s are legend. While trading and investment were brisk, the underlying strength of the market was eroding as a result of certain common practices. The first was price manipulation. It was not uncommon for brokers or dealers to indulge in "wash sales" or "matched orders," in which successive buy and sell orders created a false impression of activity and forced prices up. This maneuver allowed those involved to reap huge profits before the price fell back to its true market level.[3]

Eventually, Congress enacted two primary pieces of securities legislation:

- The Securities Act of 1933 regulates the initial offering of securities by a company or underwriter.
- The Securities Exchange Act of 1934 regulates the subsequent trading of securities through brokers and exchanges.

These laws put an end to the legality of many abuses that had previously been common practices such as the manipulation of stock market prices and the misuse

---

[3] Skousen, *An Introduction to the SEC*, p. 4.

of corporate information by officials and directors (often referred to as *inside parties*) for their own personal gain. Just as important, these two legislative actions were designed to help rebuild public confidence in the capital market system. Because of the large losses suffered during the market crash and subsequent depression, many investors had begun to avoid buying stocks and bonds. This reduction in the pool of available capital simply compounded the economic problems of the day.

The creation of federal securities laws did not end with the 1933 Act and the 1934 Act. During the decades since the first commissioners were appointed, the SEC has administered rules and regulations created by a number of different congressional actions. Despite the passage of subsequent legislation, the major objectives of this organization have remained relatively constant. Over the years, the SEC has attempted to achieve several interconnected goals that include:

- Ensuring that full and fair information is disclosed to all investors before the securities of a company are allowed to be bought and sold.
- Prohibiting the dissemination of materially misstated information.
- Preventing the misuse of information especially by inside parties.
- Regulating the operation of securities markets such as the New York Stock Exchange and American Stock Exchange.

As judged by the dollar amounts exchanged each day in the trading of securities, the capital market system in the United States is flourishing. At least part of the responsibility for this success lies with the SEC and the agency's ability to attain the preceding goals. Today, most investors apparently believe in the overall integrity of the market system as well as the sufficiency and fair presentation of the data that they receive. Even the insider trading indictments during recent years and the stock market plunges of October 19, 1987, and October 13, 1989, have not appeared to shake investor faith appreciably. Thus, any introduction to the SEC must examine the methods used to maintain public confidence as it regulates the honest distribution of both financial and nonfinancial information.

Full and Fair Disclosure

Probably no responsibility of the SEC is more vital than the task of ensuring that sufficient, reliable information is disclosed by a company before its stocks, bonds, or other securities can be publicly traded. Unless specifically exempted, all publicly held companies (frequently referred to as *registrants*) must file detailed reports with the SEC periodically. These filings are required and regulated by the Securities and Exchange Commission as a result of a number of laws passed by Congress over the years:

1. Securities Act of 1933: Requires the registration of new securities offered for public sale so that potential investors can have adequate infor-

mation. The act is also intended to prevent deceit and misrepresentation in connection with the sale of securities.[4]

2. Securities Exchange Act of 1934: Requires continuous reporting by publicly owned companies and registration of securities, security exchanges, and certain brokers and dealers.

3. Public Utility Holding Company Act of 1935: Requires registration of interstate holding companies of public utilities covered by this law. This act was passed because of abuses in the 1920s where huge, complex utility empires were created to minimize the need for equity financing.

4. Trust Indenture Act of 1939: Requires registration of trust indenture documents and supporting data in connection with the public sale of bonds, debentures, notes, and other debt securities.

5. Investment Company Act of 1940: Requires registration of investment companies that engage in investing and trading in securities.

6. Investment Advisers Act of 1940 and Securities Investor Protection Act of 1970: Requires registration of investment advisers. Also requires them to follow certain standards created to protect investors.

7. Foreign Corrupt Practices Act of 1977: Affects registration only indirectly through amendment to the Securities Exchange Act of 1934. This act requires the maintenance of accounting records and adequate internal accounting controls.

8. Insider Trading Sanctions Act of 1984 and Insider Trading and Securities Fraud Enforcement Act of 1988: Also affects registration only indirectly. Increases the penalties against persons who profit from illegal use of inside information and who are associated with market manipulation and securities fraud.

Because of these laws, a large number of registrants are required to periodically disclose a wide variety of financial and other relevant information to the public. Tens of thousands of filings are now processed each year; in the late 1980s, securities registered for sale with the SEC totaled nearly $500 billion per year.

SEC Requirements. As is obvious from the previous list, the filing requirements administered by the SEC are extensive. Thus, accountants who specialize in working with the federal securities laws must develop a broad knowledge of a great many reporting rules and regulations. The SEC specifies most of these

---

[4] Interestingly, one of the provisions originally suggested for this act would have created a federal corps of auditors. The defeat of this proposal (after some debate) has allowed for the rise of the independent auditing profession as it is currently structured in the United States. For more information, see "The SEC and the Profession, 1934–1984: The Realities of Self-Regulation," by Mark Moran and Gary John Previts, *Journal of Accountancy,* July 1984.

disclosure requirements in two basic documents, *Regulation S–K* and *Regulation S–X,* which are supplemented by periodic releases and staff bulletins.

Regulation S–K establishes requirements for all nonfinancial information contained in filings with the SEC. A description of the registrant's business as well as its securities are just two items covered by these regulations. A partial list of other nonfinancial data to be disclosed includes specified data about the company's directors and management, a discussion and analysis by the management of the current financial condition and the results of operations, and descriptions of both legal proceedings and the company's properties.

Regulation S–X prescribes the form and content of the financial statements (as well as the accompanying notes and related schedules) included in the various reports filed with the SEC. Thus, before being accepted, all financial information must meet a number of clearly specified requirements.

Integrated Disclosure System. The SEC's disclosure and accounting requirements are not limited to the filings made directly with that body. At the current time, *Rule 14c–3* of the 1934 Act states that the annual reports of publicly held companies furnished to stockholders in connection with the company's yearly meeting should include financial statements that have been audited. This information (referred to as *proxy information* because it accompanies the management's request to cast votes for the stockholders at the annual meeting) must present balance sheets as of the end of the two most recent fiscal years along with income statements and cash flow statements for the three most recent years. *Rule 14c–3* also states that additional information, as specified in *Regulation S–K,* should be included in this annual report.

In recent years, the SEC has moved toward an *integrated disclosure system.* Under this approach, much of the same reported information that is required by the SEC must also go to the shareholders. Thus, the reporting process is simplified because only a single set of information must be generated in most cases. The integrated disclosure system is also intended as a way of improving the quality of the disclosures received by the shareholders.

Information required in proxy statements includes the following:

1. Five-year summary of operations including sales, total assets, income from continuing operations, and cash dividends per share.
2. Description of the business activities including principal products and sources and availability of raw materials.
3. Three-year summary of industry segments, export sales, and foreign and domestic operations.
4. Listing of company directors and executive officers.
5. Market price of the company's common stock for each quarterly period within the two most recent fiscal years.
6. Any restrictions on the company's ability to continue paying dividends.

7. Management's discussion and analysis of financial condition, changes in financial condition, and results of operations. Discussion should include liquidity, trends and significant events, causes of material changes in the financial statements, and the impact on the company of inflation.

In addition, the SEC has required certain disclosures in proxy statements describing the services provided by the registrant's independent external auditor. This information is intended as a means of helping to ensure that true independence is not endangered. Such disclosure must include:

1. All nonaudit services provided by the independent auditing firm.
2. A statement as to whether the board of directors (or its audit committee) approved all nonaudit services after considering the possibility that such services might impair the external auditor's independence.
3. The percentage of nonaudit fees to the total annual audit fee. This disclosure helps indicate the importance of the audit work to the firm versus the reward provided by any other services provided to the registrant.
4. Individual nonaudit fees that are larger than 3 percent of the annual audit fee.

The SEC's Authority over Generally Accepted Accounting Principles

Since financial reporting standards can be changed merely by amending *Regulation S–X,* the SEC holds the ultimate legal authority for establishing accounting principles for most publicly held companies in this country. In the past, the SEC has usually restricted the application of this power to disclosure issues while looking to the private sector (with the SEC's oversight) to formulate accounting principles. For this reason, the Financial Accounting Standards Board rather than the SEC is generally viewed today as the main standards-setting body for financial accounting in the United States. "Under federal law, the SEC has the mandate to determine accounting principles for publicly traded companies. But it has generally ceded that authority to private-sector accounting bodies such as the Financial Accounting Standards Board."[5]

However, the Securities and Exchange Commission does retain the ability to exercise its power with regard to the continuing evolution of accounting principles. The chief accountant of the SEC is responsible for providing the commissioners and the commission staff with advice on all current accounting and auditing matters and also helps to draft rules for the form and content of financial statement disclosure and other reporting requirements. "Perhaps the most powerful accounting position in the United States is that of Chief Accountant of the

---

[5] Kevin G. Salwen and Robin Goldwyn Blumenthal, "Tackling Accounting, SEC Pushes Changes with Broad Impact," *The Wall Street Journal,* September 27, 1990, p. A1.

SEC.''[6] The work of the chief accountant can lead to amendments being passed by the SEC to alter various aspects of *Regulation S–X*.

Financial Reporting Releases (FRR) are also issued by the SEC as needed to supplement *Regulation S–X* and *Regulation S–K*. They explain desired changes in the reporting requirements. In addition, the staff of the SEC publishes a series of *Staff Accounting Bulletins* (SAB) as a means of informing the financial community of its views on current matters relating to accounting and disclosure practices.[7] For example, SAB 90 was issued in January 1991 to indicate disclosures that became necessary for some companies because of the bankruptcy of their CPA firm, Laventhol & Horwath, in November 1990.[8]

Additional Disclosure Requirements. *Historically, the SEC had tended to restrict the use of its authority to the gray areas of accounting where official guidance is not available.* New reporting problems arise each year while many other accounting issues, even after years of discussion, have never been completely addressed by any authoritative body. In such cases, the commission may require the disclosure of additional data if current rules are viewed as insufficient. For example, the SEC took the lead in the reporting of segment information. Although the FASB eventually passed *Statement 14* in 1976 to mandate disaggregation, such data had already been required for some time of registants making appropriate filings with the SEC.

Moratorium on Specific Accounting Practices. The commission can also exert its power by declaring a moratorium on the use of specified accounting practices. When authoritative guidance is not present, the SEC can simply prohibit a particular method from being applied. As an example, in the early 1980s, companies were utilizing a variety of procedures to account for computer software costs because no official pronouncement had yet been issued. Hence, during the summer of 1983, the SEC

> imposed a moratorium that will prohibit companies that plan to go public from capitalizing the internal costs of developing computer software for sale or lease or marketed to customers in other ways. . . . The decision doesn't prevent companies currently capitalizing internal software expenses from continuing, but the companies must dis-

---

[6] Skousen, *An Introduction to the SEC,* p. 16.

[7] As of the end of 1991, 38 FRRs had been issued and 91 SABs. From 1937 until 1982, more than 300 *Accounting Series Releases* (ASRs) were issued by the SEC to (1) amend *Regulation S–X,* (2) express interpretations regarding specific accounting and auditing issues, and (3) report disciplinary actions against public accountants. The ASRs that dealt with financial reporting matters of continuing interest were codified by the SEC in 1982 and issued as *Financial Reporting Release No. 1.*

[8] The SEC also releases *Accounting and Auditing Enforcement Releases (AAER)* when SEC enforcement activities are involved.

close the effect of not expensing such costs as incurred. The moratorium continues until the Financial Accounting Standards Board issues a standard on the issue.[9]

When the FASB eventually arrived at a resolution of this question in August 1985 by issuing *Statement 86,* "Accounting for the Costs of Computer Software to Be Sold, Leased, or Otherwise Marketed," the SEC dropped the moratorium. Hence, the FASB was allowed to set the accounting rule, but the SEC ensured appropriate reporting until that time.

Challenging Individual Statements.　As described above, officially requiring additional disclosure and prohibiting the application of certain accounting practices are two methods commonly used by the SEC to control the financial reporting process. Forcing a specific registant to change its filed statements is another, less formal approach that can create the same effect. For example:

> The Securities and Exchange Commission charged B. F. Goodrich Company with failing to disclose that it paid $41 million in "greenmail" to buy back its stock from Carl Icahn in 1984. The SEC alleged in administrative proceedings that the company's failure to disclose the repurchase of Mr. Icahn's Goodrich stake at a 25 percent premium above the market price resulted in "materially misleading statements" in its 1984 annual report and its 1985 proxy statement. Without admitting or denying the allegations, the company settled the charges yesterday, promising to comply hereafter with the SEC's reporting and proxy rules."[10]

No authoritative literature existed that specifically required the reporting of excess payments such as were made by B. F. Goodrich. However, following the action taken by the SEC, any company involved in a similar transaction would certainly be well advised to provide appropriate disclosure. Through this single enforcement, a reporting precedent was established by the SEC.

Overruling the FASB.　The SEC's actions are not necessarily limited, however, to the gray areas of accounting. Although the commission has allowed the FASB (and previous authoritative groups) to establish accounting principles, the SEC retains the authority to override or negate any pronouncements produced in the private sector. This power was dramatically demonstrated in 1977 when the FASB issued *SFAS 19* "Financial Accounting and Reporting by Oil and Gas Producing Companies." After an extended debate over the merits of alternative methods, this statement was issued requiring oil and gas producing companies to apply the successful-efforts method when accounting for unsuccessful exploration and drilling costs.

---

[9] "SEC Imposes 'Software Costs' Moratorium," *Journal of Accountancy,* September 1983, p. 3.

[10] Bruce Ingersoll, "Goodrich Paid $41 Million 'Greenmail' in Buyback from Carl Icahn, SEC Says," *The Wall Street Journal,* January 16, 1986, p. 6.

In response, the SEC almost immediately invoked a moratorium on the use of this practice until an alternative approach could be evaluated. Thus, companies filing with the SEC were not allowed to follow the method established by the FASB (after years of formal study and deliberation). Although the commission's reaction toward the accounting profession was a unique instance, the handling of this one issue clearly demonstrates the veto power that the SEC maintains over the work of the FASB.[11]

Filings with the SEC

Because of legal regulations, registrants may be required to make a number of different filings with the SEC. The SEC actually receives approximately 700,000 filings per year.[12] However, for the overview being presented here, the reporting process is divided into two broad categories:

- Registration statements.
- Periodic filings.

Registration statements ensure the disclosure of sufficient, relevant financial data before a security can be *initially offered* to the public by either a company or its underwriters. The dissemination of such information is mandated by the Securities Act of 1933. Registration is necessary except in certain situations described at a later point in this chapter. The SEC charges a registration fee which was increased in 1992 to an amount equal to 1/32th of 1 percent of the value of the securities offered. Such revenues were estimated to be $244 million for 1991, an amount 27 percent larger than the SEC's proposed expenditures.[13] Thus, the SEC actually is able to generate a profit.

Thereafter, periodic filings with the SEC are required of registrants by a number of federal laws, the most important of which is the Securities Exchange Act of 1934. This legislation has resulted in the *continual reporting of specified data* by all companies that have securities publicly traded on either a national securities exchange or an over-the-counter market.[14]

For registration statements as well as periodic filings, the SEC has established forms that provide the format and content to be followed in providing required information. "These forms contain no blanks to be filled in as do tax forms. Instead, they are narrative in character, giving general instructions about the items of information to be furnished. Detailed information must be assembled by

---

[11] For a detailed account of the activities surrounding the SEC's rejection of *SFAS 19*, see "The SEC Decision Not to Support SFAS 19: A Case Study of the Effect of Lobbying on Standard Setting," by Donald Gorton in *Accounting Horizons*, March 1991.

[12] Sandra Block, "SEC Gets Closer to Electronic Filing," *The Wall Street Journal*, August 30, 1991, p. C1.

[13] "SEC Budget for 1991," *Deloitte & Touche Review*, February 2, 1990, p. 2.

[14] A company that has securities traded on an over-the-counter market does not have to file under the 1934 act unless it has at least $5 million in assets and 500 shareholders.

the companies using the form designed for the type of security being offered as well as the type of company making the offer.''[15]

Registration Statements. As indicated, a registration statement must be filed with and made effective by the Securities and Exchange Commission before a company can publicly offer a security. A security is broadly identified to include items such as a note, stock, treasury stock, bond, debenture, investment contract, evidence of indebtedness, or transferable share.

The SEC's role is not to evaluate the quality of the investment. Rather, the SEC seeks to ensure that the content and disclosure of the filing complies with all applicable regulations. The responsibility for the information always rests with corporate officials. The SEC is charged with ensuring full and fair disclosure of relevant financial information. The registrant has the responsibility to provide such data, and the decision to invest must remain with the public.

A number of different forms are available for this purpose, depending on the specific circumstances. Some of the most commonly encountered registration statement forms are:

- S–1   Used by new registrants or by companies that have been filing reports with the SEC for less than 36 months.
- S–2   Used by companies that have filed with the SEC for 36 months or longer but are not large enough to file a Form S–3.
- S–3   Used by companies that are large in size and already have a significant following in the stock market (at least $150 million of its voting stock is held by nonaffiliates). Disclosure is reduced for these organizations because the public is assumed to already have access to a considerable amount of information.
- S–4   Used for securities issued in connection with business combination transactions.
- SB–2 Used by small business issuers with annual revenues of less than $25 million and less than $25 million voting securities held by non-affiliates.

The use of Form S–3 offers a distinct advantage to established companies that are issuing securities. Rather than duplicate voluminous information that has already been disclosed in other filings with the SEC, the registrant can simply indicate the location of the data in these other documents, a process referred to as *incorporation by reference*.

Registration Procedures. The actual registration process is comprised of a series of events leading up to the permission to "go effective" by the SEC. Since the registrant is seeking to obtain significant financial resources through

---

[15] Skousen, *An Introduction to the SEC*, p. 47.

the issuance of new securities in public markets, each of these procedures is of vital importance.

After selecting the appropriate form, information is accumulated by the company according to the requirements of *Regulation S–K* and *Regulation S–X*. If problems or questions are anticipated, a prefiling conference with the SEC staff may be requested by the company to seek guidance prior to beginning the registration. For example, if uncertainty exists concerning the handling or disclosure of an unusual transaction, a prefiling conference can save all parties considerable time and effort.

> The Commission has a long-established policy of holding its staff available for conferences with prospective registrants or their representatives in advance of filing a registration statement. These conferences may be held for the purpose of discussing generally the problems confronting a registrant in effecting registration or to resolve specific problems of an unusual nature which are sometimes presented by involved or complicated financial transactions.[16]

When received by the SEC, the registration statement is reviewed by the Division of Corporation Finance.[17] An analyst makes a determination as to whether all nonfinancial information complies with the SEC's disclosure requirements in *Regulation S–K*. At the same time, an accountant verifies that the financial statement data included in the filing meet the standards of *Regulation S–X* and have been prepared according to generally accepted accounting principles. *Since a formal audit is not conducted by the SEC, the report of the company's independent CPA is essential to this particular evaluation.* In addition, an SEC lawyer also reviews the registration statement to verify the legal aspects of the document.

The Division of Corporation Finance almost invariably requests clarifications, changes, or additional information, especially for those filings involving an initial registration. A *letter of comments* (also known as a *deficiency letter*) is issued to the company to communicate these findings. In most cases, the registrant attempts to provide the necessary data or changes to expedite the process. However, in controversial areas, the issuer may begin discussions directly with the SEC staff in hopes of resolving the problem without making the requested adjustments or disclosure or, at least, with limited inconvenience.

When the Division of Corporate Finance is eventually satisfied that all SEC regulations have been fulfilled, the registration statement is made effective and the securities can be sold. *Effectiveness does not, however, indicate an endorsement*

---

[16] *SEC Compliance* (Englewood Cliffs, N.J.: Prentice Hall), par. 30,641, November 11, 1983.

[17] All registration statements filed by issuers offering securities to the public for the first time are carefully reviewed. Subsequent registration statements and periodic filings are only reviewed on a selective basis. Because of the enormous increase in filings over the past decade, concern has been raised as to whether the SEC continues to have adequate staffing capabilities to review a sufficient number of these filings. See, for example, "Busy SEC Must Let Many Cases, Filings Go Uninvestigated," by Bruce Ingersoll in the December 16, 1985, issue of *The Wall Street Journal*, p. A1.

of the securities by the SEC. With most offerings, the stock is actually sold by the company to one or more underwriters (stock brokerage firms) that market the shares to their clients to earn commissions.

For convenience and to save time and money, large companies are allowed to use a process known as *shelf registration*. They file once with the SEC and are then allowed to offer those securities at any time over the subsequent two years without having to go back to the SEC.

The registration statement is physically composed of two parts. Part I, referred to as a *prospectus*, contains extensive information that includes:

1. Financial statements for the issuing company along with appropriate supplementary data.
2. An explanation of the intended use of the proceeds to be generated by the sale of the new securities.
3. A description of the capital structure of the company.
4. A description of the business and the properties owned by the company.

The registrant must furnish every potential buyer of the securities with a copy of this prospectus, thus ensuring the adequate availability of information for their investment analysis.

Part II of the registration statement is primarily for the informational needs of the SEC staff. Additional data is disclosed about the company and the securities being issued such as marketing arrangements, expenses of issuance, sales to special parties, and the like. The registrant is not required to provide this information to prospective buyers, although the entire registration statement is available to the public through the SEC.

Securities Exempt from Registration. According to the 1933 Act, not all securities issued by companies and their underwriters require registration. For example, securities sold strictly to the residents of the state in which the issuing company is chartered and principally doing business are exempted. However, these offerings are still regulated by the securities laws of the individual states (commonly known as *blue sky laws*) which vary significantly across the country.[18]

Other exempt offerings include but are not limited to the following:

- Securities issued by governments, banks, and savings and loan associations.
- Securities issued that are restricted to a company's own existing shareholders where no commission is paid to solicit the exchange.
- Securities issued by nonprofit organizations such as religious, educational, or charitable groups.

---

[18] "These early laws became known as 'blue sky' laws after a judicial decision characterized some transactions as 'speculative schemes which have no more basis than so many feet of "blue sky".' " (Skousen, *An Introduction to the SEC*, p. 3.)

- Small offerings of no more than $5 million. In most cases, though, a Regulation A offering circular must still be filed with the SEC and given to prospective buyers. However, much less information is required of a company in an offering circular than in a registration statement.

- Offerings of no more than $5 million made to 35 or fewer purchasers. No general solicitation is allowed for securities issued in this manner. Accredited investors (such as banks, insurance companies, and individuals with net worth of more than $1 million) are not included in the restriction on the number of buyers. Unaccredited investors must still be furnished with audited financial statements and other specified information. Parties making purchases have to hold the securities for at least two years or the filing exemption is lost.

- The private placement of securities to no more than 35 sophisticated investors (having knowledge and experience in financial matters) who already have sufficient information available to them about the issuing company. Again, the number of accredited investors is unlimited and general solicitation is not permitted. These private placement rules have become quite important in recent years. Private placements in the United States rose from $16 billion in 1980 to more than $170 billion in 1989. The SEC estimated that private placements in 1989 represented 35 percent of all corporate financings.

Periodic Filings with the SEC.   Once a company has issued securities that are then publicly traded on a securities exchange or an over-the-counter market, information must be continually filed with the SEC so that adequate disclosure is available. As with registration statements, several different forms are utilized for this purpose. However, for most companies with actively traded securities, three of these are common: Form 10–K (an annual report), Form 10–Q (a quarterly report), and Form 8–K (disclosure of significant events). Smaller businesses use Form 10–KSB for annual reports and Form 10–QSB for quarterly reports.

In addition, as mentioned previously, proxy statements must also be filed with the SEC. These statements are issued to a company's owners by the management or other interested party in hopes of securing voting rights to be used at stockholders' meetings.

Form 10–K.   A 10–K form is an annual report filed with the SEC within 90 days of the end of a registrant's fiscal year to provide information and disclosures required by *Regulation S–K* and *Regulation S–X*. Fortunately, because of the integrated disclosure system, the annual report that is distributed by companies to their stockholders includes most of the basic financial disclosures required by the SEC in Form 10–K. Thus, a company can simply attach the stockholders' annual report to the Form 10–K each year and use the incorporation by reference procedure to meet most of the SEC's filing requirements. This process is sometimes known as a *wrap around* filing.

Form 10–K, as with the various other SEC filings, is constantly undergoing assessment to determine if investor needs are being met. Thus, the SEC's reporting requirements are evolutionary and change over time.

> The Securities and Exchange Commission issued guidelines aimed at making public companies provide a more detailed look at the trends and business changes that management expects in the future. . . . In the main part of yesterday's interpretation, the commissioners said that in the 10–K reports, companies must discuss "trends, demands, commitments or events" that it knows are "reasonably likely" to occur and have a material effect on financial condition or results.[19]

As indicated by this quote, the SEC has become especially interested during recent years in the quality of the information provided by the Management's Discussion and Analysis (MD&A) section of a registrant's filings. Basically, the management should describe verbally the company's past, present, and future. This information can give a nonquantified feel for the prospects of the company; it is a candid narrative to provide statement readers with a sense of management's priorities, accomplishments, and concerns. The MD&A is a feature carefully reviewed by the SEC staff.[20] "If the management of a company knows something that could have a material impact on earnings in the future, officials have an obligation to share that information with shareholders."[21]

Form 10–Q. A 10–Q form contains condensed interim financial statements for the registrant and must be filed with the SEC within 45 days of the end of each quarter. However, no Form 10–Q is required following the fourth quarter of the year since a Form 10–K is forthcoming shortly thereafter. A Form 10–Q does not have to be audited by an independent CPA.

Information to be contained in each Form 10–Q includes the following:

- Income statements must be included for the most recent quarter and for the year to date as well as for the comparative periods in the previous year.
- A statement of cash flows is also necessary, but only for the year to date as well as for the corresponding period in the preceding year.
- Two balance sheets are reported: one as of the end of the most recent quarter with the second showing the company's financial position at the end of the previous fiscal year.
- Each Form 10–Q should also include any needed disclosures pertaining to the current period including the management's discussion and analysis of the financial condition of the company and results of operations.

---

[19] Paul Duke, Jr., "SEC Issues Guidelines for 10–K Filings Seeking More Details on Trends, Changes," *The Wall Street Journal,* May 19, 1989, p. A2.

[20] See, for example, "Annual Reports: The SEC Cracks the Whip," by Tim Smart in *Business Week,* April 10, 1989.

[21] Kevin G. Salwen, "SEC Charges Caterpillar Failed to Warn Holders of Earnings Risk Posed by Unit," *The Wall Street Journal,* April 2, 1992, p. A3.

Form 8–K. An 8–K form is used only to disclose a unique or significant happening. Consequently, the 8–K is not filed at regular time intervals but rather within 15 calendar days of the event (or within 5 business days in certain specified instances). According to the SEC's guidelines, Form 8–K may be filed to report any action that company officials believe is of importance to security holders. However, several events are designated for required disclosure in this manner; this list includes the following:

- Resignation of a director.
- Changes in control of the registrant.
- Acquisitions or dispositions of assets.
- Changes in the registrant's certified accountants.
- Bankruptcy or receivership.

Proxy Statements. As was mentioned in a previous section, most of the significant actions undertaken by a company must first be approved at stockholders' meetings. For example, the members of the board of directors are elected in this manner to oversee the operations of the company. Although such votes are essential to the operations of a business, few (if any) major companies could possibly assemble enough shareholders at any one time and place for a voting quorum. The geographic distances are simply too great. Hence, before each of the periodic meetings, the management (or any other interested party) usually requests signed proxies from shareholders granting the legal authority to cast votes for the owners in connection with the various actions to be taken.[22]

Because of the power conveyed by a proxy, any such solicitation sent to shareholders (by any party) must include specific information as required by the SEC in its *Regulation 14A*. This proxy statement has to be filed with the SEC at least 10 days before being distributed. A number of the disclosed items were described previously. Other data that must be reported to the owners includes:

- The proxy statement needs to indicate on whose behalf the solicitation is being made.
- The proxy statement must disclose fully all matters that are to be voted on at the meeting.
- In most cases, the proxy statement has to be accompanied (or preceded) by an annual report to the shareholders.

As with all areas of disclosure, the SEC's regulation of proxy statements has greatly enhanced the information available to investors.

Thus was the president of one company able to respond cavalierly to a shareholder's request for information, ''I can assure you that the company is in a good financial

---

[22] Any person who owns at least 5 percent of the company's stock or has been an owner for six months or longer has the right to look at a list of shareholders to make a proxy solicitation.

position. I trust that you will sign and mail your proxy at an early date.'' Quaint. But that was nothing. One unlisted company printed its proxy on the back of the dividend check—so when you endorsed the check you voted for management.[23]

From a 1902 annual report to shareholders: "The settled plan has been to withhold all information from stockholders and others that is not called for by the stockholders in a body. So far no request for information has been made in the manner prescribed by the directors.''[24]

Electronic Data Gathering, Analysis, and Retrieval System (Edgar)

During recent years, the SEC has become almost overwhelmed by the sheer mountain of documents that it receives, reviews, and makes available to the public. Filings with the SEC are estimated to contain 5 million pieces of paper each year.

For a number of years, the SEC has been attempting to develop an electronic data gathering, analysis, and retrieval system (nicknamed Edgar). As envisioned, all filings would arrive at the SEC on disks or through some other electronic transmission. Each filing could be reviewed, analyzed, and stored by SEC personnel on a computer so they would no longer constantly have to shift through stacks of paper. Perhaps more importantly, investors would have the ability to access this data through on-line computer systems. Thus, investors throughout the world could have information available for their decisions literally minutes after the documents are made effective by the SEC.

This system is designed to benefit the registrant as well as the investor. The SEC hopes to make the entire filing system simpler for all parties.

General Motors Acceptance Corporation, which has been filing on the Edgar pilot program for several years, reports that Edgar has substantially reduced the amount of time it takes to get SEC approval for GMAC deals. . . . Mr. Folbigg, of GMAC, agrees that small companies should be able to convert from paper to electronic filing without much trouble. "The key to the Edgar system is a good secretary who can follow instructions," he says. GMAC does its filings via a personal computer.[25]

Unfortunately, establishing the Edgar system has been a much more difficult project than was originally expected. Costs have skyrocketed and the work has been hampered by both political and technical problems.[26] However, the SEC now hopes to add more and more companies to the system until most filings are done electronically by the middle 1990s.

---

[23] Laura Jereski, "You've Come A Long Way, Shareholder," *Forbes*, July 13, 1987, p. 282.

[24] Skousen, *An Introduction to the SEC*, p. 75.

[25] Block, "SEC Gets Closer to Electronic Filing," pp. C1 and C5.

[26] "In the mid-1980s, Edgar had become so unpopular on Capitol Hill that one member of the House Energy and Commerce Committee suggested renaming the project Mr. Ed, 'since the SEC has a much better chance of finding a talking horse than it does of achieving an efficient computer filing system.' " (*Ibid.*, p. C1.)

Discussion Question: Is the Disclosure Worth the Cost?

Filing with the SEC requires a very significant amount of time and effort on the part of the registrant. Companies frequently resist every attempt by the commission to increase the levels of disclosure. Usually, the argument is made that additional information will not necessarily be useful to a great majority of investors. Regardless of the issue, the cost of the extra data is said to far outweigh any benefits that might be derived from this disclosure.

Such contentions are not necessarily made just to avoid disclosing information. One survey estimated the cost of SEC disclosures to be more than $400 million in 1975 alone. "The table reports an estimated $213,500,000 for the fully variable costs of 10–K, 10–Q and 8–K disclosures in 1975. To this should be added the separate estimate (not shown) of $191,900,000 for disclosure related to new issues in 1975, for a total estimate of about $400,000,000 for SEC disclosure costs in 1975. These estimates are biased downward because they do not include various fixed costs."[27] Such costs are either passed along to the consumer in the form of higher prices or serve to retard the growth of the reporting company.

The author of one survey (that has been widely discussed and debated over the years) held that federal securities laws are not actually helpful to investors.

> I found that there was little evidence of fraud related to financial statements in the period prior to the enactment of the Securities Acts. Nor was there a widespread lack of disclosure. . . . Hence, I conclude that there was little justification for the accounting disclosure required by the Acts. . . . These findings indicate that the data required by the SEC do not seem to be useful to investors.[28]

The SEC was created, in part, to ensure that the public has fair and full disclosure about companies that have their securities publicly traded. However, the commission must be mindful of the cost of such disclosures. How can the SEC determine whether the cost of a proposed disclosure is more or less than the benefits that will be derived by the public?

---

[27] J. Richard Zecher, "An Economic Perspective of SEC Corporate Disclosure," *The SEC and Accounting: The First 50 Years,* ed. Robert H. Mundheim and Noyes E. Leech (Amsterdam: North-Holland, 1985), pp. 75–76.

[28] George J. Benston, "The Value of the SEC's Accounting Disclosure Requirements," *The Accounting Review,* July 1969, p. 351.

Summary

1. In the United States, the Securities and Exchange Commission (SEC) has been entrusted with the responsibility for ensuring that complete and reliable information is available to investors who buy and sell securities in public capital markets. Since being created in 1934, this agency has administered numerous reporting rules and regulations created by congressional actions starting with the Securities Act of 1933 and the Securities Exchange Act of 1934.

2. Before a company's securities (either equity or debt) can be publicly traded, appropriate filings must be made with the SEC to ensure that sufficient data is made available to potential investors. Disclosure requirements for this process are outlined in two documents: *Regulation S–K* (for nonfinancial information) and *Regulation S–X* (describing the form and content of all included financial statements).

3. The ability to require the reporting of specified information gives the SEC enormous legal power over the accounting profession in the United States. Traditionally, this authority has only been wielded to increase disclosure requirements and to provide guidance where none was otherwise available. However, in a significant demonstration of its authority, the SEC overruled the FASB's decision in 1977 as to the appropriate method to account for unsuccessful exploration and drilling costs incurred by oil and gas producing companies.

4. Filings with the SEC are divided generally into two broad categories: registration statements and periodic filings. Registration statements are designed to provide information about a company prior to its issuance of a security to the public. Depending on the circumstances, several different registration forms are available for this purpose. After the statement is produced by the registrant and initially reviewed by the SEC, a letter of comments is furnished describing desired explanations or changes. These concerns must be resolved before the security can be sold.

5. Not all securities issued in the United States require registration with the SEC. As an example, formal registration is not necessary for securities sold by either government units or banks. Certain issues for relatively small amounts are also exempt although some amount of disclosure is normally required. Securities sold solely within the state in which the business operates are not subject to federal securities laws but must comply with state laws frequently referred to as *blue sky laws*.

6. Companies that have their stocks or bonds publicly traded on a securities exchange must also submit periodic filings to the SEC to ensure that adequate disclosure is constantly maintained. Among the most common of these filings are Form 10–K (an annual report) and Form 10–Q (condensed interim financial information). Form 8–K is also required to report any significant events that occur. In addition, proxy statements (documents that are used to solicit votes at stockholders' meetings) also come under the filing requirements monitored by the SEC.

Because no computations were presented in this chapter, a Comprehensive Illustration is not included.

Questions

1. Why were federal securities laws originally passed by Congress?
2. What is covered by *Regulation S–K?*
3. What is covered by *Regulation S–X?*
4. What are some of the major divisions within the SEC?
5. What is covered by the Securities Act of 1933?
6. What is covered by the Securities Exchange Act of 1934?
7. What are the goals of the SEC?
8. What information is required in a proxy statement?
9. Why is the content of a proxy statement considered to be so important?
10. How does the SEC affect the development of generally accepted accounting principles in the United States?
11. What is the purpose of Financial Reporting Releases and Staff Accounting Bulletins?
12. What was the SEC's response to the FASB's handling of accounting for oil and gas producing companies, and why was this action considered so significant?
13. What is the purpose of a registration statement? Under what law is a registration statement filed?
14. What are the two parts of a registration statement? What is contained in each part?
15. How does the SEC generate revenues?
16. Three forms commonly used in the registration process are Form S–1, Form S–3, and Form SB–2. Which registrants should use each of these forms?
17. What is incorporation by reference?
18. What is a prefiling conference, and why might it be helpful to a registrant?
19. What is a letter of comments? By what other name is a letter of comments often referred?
20. What is a prospectus? What is contained in a prospectus?

21. What is a shelf registration?
22. Under what circumstances is a company exempt from filing a registration statement with the SEC prior to the issuance of securities?
23. What is a private placement of securities?
24. What are blue sky laws?
25. What is a wrap around filing?
26. When is a Form 8–K issued by a company? What specific information does a Form 8–K convey?
27. What is the purpose of the Management's Discussion and Analysis?
28. What is the difference in a Form 10–K and a Form 10–Q?
29. What is the purpose of creating the Edgar system?

Library Assignments

1. Locate a recent annual report of a publicly traded company such as Ford Motor Company or IBM. Read the Management's Discussion and Analysis for the most recent years. Write a report to answer the following questions:
   • What information is provided in the MD&A that is not found in the financial statements?
   • What were the most important pieces of information in the MD&A?
   • Was anything included in the MD&A that was purely speculation on the part of the management?
   • Was anything omitted from the MD&A that would have been helpful information?
2. Read the following as well as any other published information on the work of the SEC:
   "Tackling Accounting, SEC Pushes Changes with Broad Impact," *The Wall Street Journal,* September 27, 1990, p. A1.
   "Annual Reports: The SEC Cracks the Whip," *Business Week,* April 10, 1989.
   "The SEC and the Profession, 1934–84: The Realities of Self-Regulation," *Journal of Accountancy,* July 1984.
   "Arthur Young Professors' Roundtable: The SEC—Past, Present, Future," *Journal of Accountancy* (News Feature Section), March 1985.
   "If Life Is Volatile, Account for It," *Forbes,* November 12, 1990.
   Write a report discussing the work of the SEC. Give a historical perspective as well as information on its current activities.

Problems

1. Which of the following statements is true?
   a. The Securities Exchange Act of 1934 regulates intrastate stock offerings made by a company.
   b. The Securities Act of 1933 regulates the subsequent public trading of securities through brokers and markets.
   c. The Securities Exchange Act of 1934 is commonly referred to as blue sky legislation.
   d. The Securities Act of 1933 regulates the initial offering of securities by a company.

2. What is the purpose of *Regulation S–K?*
   a. Defines generally accepted accounting principles in the United States.
   b. Establishes required disclosure of nonfinancial information with the SEC.
   c. Outlines enforcement procedures carried out by the SEC.
   d. Indicates which companies must file with the SEC on an annual basis.

3. What is the difference between *Regulation S–K* and *Regulation S–X?*
   a. *Regulation S–K* establishes reporting requirements for companies in their initial issuance of securities whereas *Regulation S–X* is directed toward the subsequent issuance of securities.
   b. *Regulation S–K* establishes reporting requirements for companies smaller than a certain size whereas *Regulation S–X* is directed toward companies larger than that size.
   c. *Regulation S–K* establishes regulations for nonfinancial information filed with the SEC whereas *Regulation S–X* prescribes the form and content of financial statements included in SEC filings.
   d. *Regulation S–K* establishes reporting requirements for publicly held companies whereas *Regulation S–X* is directed toward private companies.

4. The Securities Exchange Act of 1934:
   a. Regulates the public trading of previously issued securities through brokers and exchanges.
   b. Prohibits blue sky laws.
   c. Regulates the initial offering of securities by a company.
   d. Requires the registration of investment advisors.

5. What is a registration statement?
   a. A statement that must be filed with the SEC before a company can begin an initial offering of securities to the public.
   b. A required filing with the SEC before a large quantity of stock can be obtained by an inside party.
   c. An annual filing made with the New York Stock Exchange.

    d. A filing made by a company with the SEC to indicate that a significant change has occurred.

6. Which of the following is a registration statement used by large companies that already have a significant following in the stock market?

    a. Form 8–K.

    b. Form 10–K.

    c. Form S–1.

    d. Form S–3.

7. What was the significance of the controversy in 1977 over the appropriate accounting principles to be used by oil and gas producing companies?

    a. Several major lawsuits resulted.

    b. Companies refused to follow the dictates of the SEC.

    c. Partners of a major accounting firm were indicted on criminal charges.

    d. The SEC overruled the FASB on the handling of this matter.

8. Which of the following must be provided to every potential buyer of a new security?

    a. A letter of comments.

    b. A deficiency letter.

    c. A prospectus.

    d. Form S–16.

9. What is meant by the term *incorporation by reference?*

    a. The legal incorporation of a company in more than one state.

    b. Filing information with the SEC by indicating that the information is already available in another document.

    c. A reference guide indicating informational requirements specified in *Regulation S–X.*

    d. Incorporating a company in a state outside of its base of operations.

10. What is a letter of comments?

    a. A letter sent to a company by the SEC indicating needed changes or clarifications in a registration statement.

    b. A questionnaire supplied to the SEC by a company suggesting changes in *Regulation S–X.*

    c. A letter included in a Form 10–K to indicate the management's assessment of the company's financial position.

    d. A letter composed by a company asking for information or clarification prior to the filing of a registration statement.

11. What is a prospectus?

    a. A document attached to a Form 8–K.

    b. A potential stockholder as defined by *Regulation S–K.*

    c. A document filed with the SEC prior to the filing of a registration statement.

    d. The first part of a registration statement that must be furnished by a company to all potential buyers of a new security.

12. Which of the following is not exempt from registration with the SEC under the Securities Act of 1933?

    a. Securities issued by a nonprofit religious organization.

    b. Securities issued by a government unit.

    c. A public offering of no more than $5.9 million.

    d. An offering made to only 26 sophisticated investors.

13. Which of the following is usually not filed with the SEC on a regular periodic basis?

    a. Form 10–Q.

    b. A prospectus.

    c. A proxy statement.

    d. Form 10–K.

14. What is a shelf registration?

    a. A registration statement that is formally rejected by the SEC.

    b. A registration statement that is rejected by the SEC due to the lapse of a specified period of time.

    c. A registration process for large companies that allows them to offer securities over a period of time without seeking additional approval by the SEC.

    d. A registration form that is withdrawn by the registrant without any action having been taken.

15. What is Edgar?

    a. A system used by the SEC to reject registration statements that do not contain adequate information.

    b. The enforcement arm of the SEC.

    c. A system being designed for the SEC to allow electronic filings.

    d. A branch of the government that oversees the work of the SEC.

16. Identify each of the following as they pertain to the SEC:

    · Blue sky laws.

    · S–1 Statement.

    · Letter of deficiencies.

    · Prospectus.

17. Discuss the objectives of the Securities Act of 1933 and the Securities Exchange Act of 1934. How are these objectives accomplished?

18. What are the steps involved in filing a registration statement with the SEC?

19. Discuss the methods by which the SEC can influence the development of generally accepted accounting principles in the United States.

20. Which forms do most companies file with the SEC on a periodic basis? Explain the purpose of each form and its primary contents.

21. Which forms do most companies file with the SEC in connection with the offering of securities to the public?

22. What is the importance of a Form 8–K? What is the importance of a proxy statement?

23. Discuss each of the following terms:
    - Financial reporting releases.
    - Wrap around incorporation.
    - Incorporation by reference.
    - Division of corporation finance.
    - Integrated disclosure system.
    - Management's discussion and analysis.
    - Chief accountant of the SEC.

24. Which organizations are normally exempted from the registration requirements imposed by the SEC?

INDEX